D0151329

Martin Luther

And the Reformation

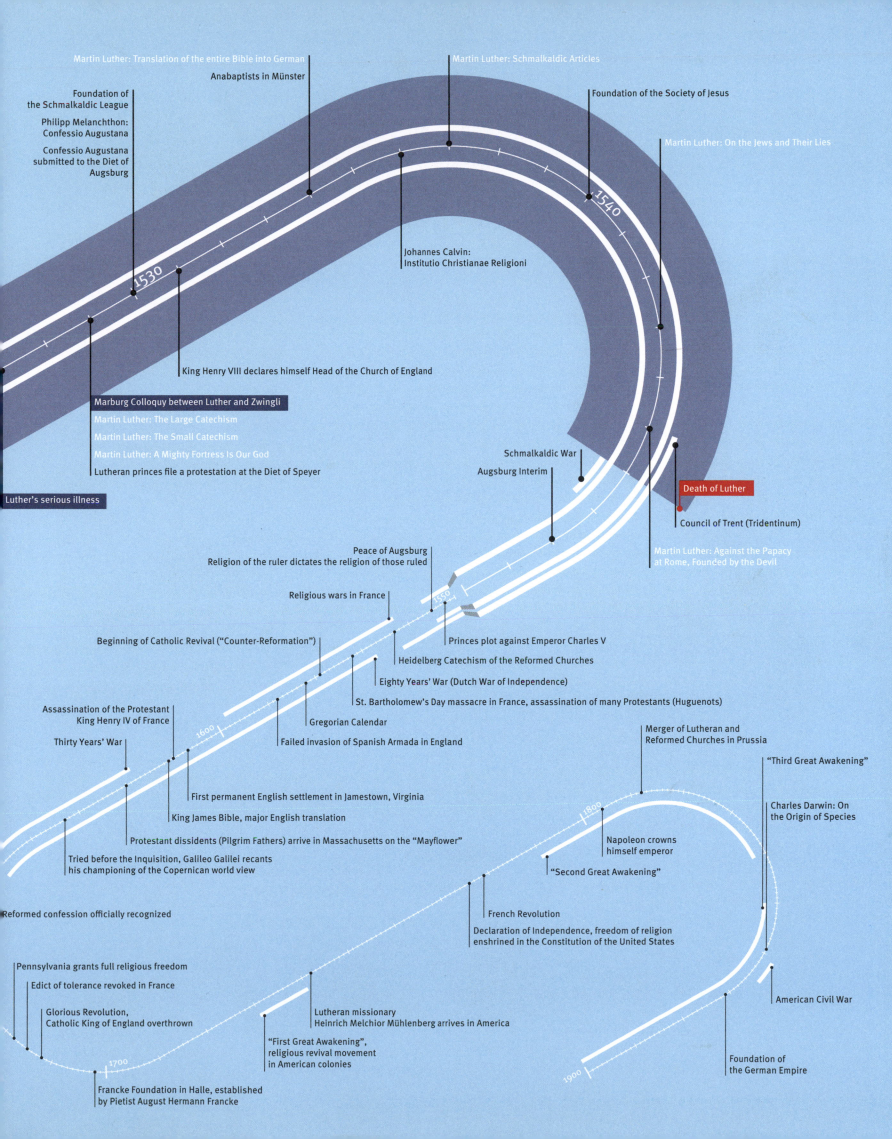

Martin Luther: Translation of the entire Bible into German

Anabaptists in Münster

Martin Luther: Schmalkaldic Articles

Foundation of the Schmalkaldic League

Foundation of the Society of Jesus

Philipp Melanchthon: Confessio Augustana

Martin Luther: On the Jews and Their Lies

Confessio Augustana submitted to the Diet of Augsburg

1530

1540

Johannes Calvin: Institutio Christianae Religioni

King Henry VIII declares himself Head of the Church of England

Marburg Colloquy between Luther and Zwingli
Martin Luther: The Large Catechism
Martin Luther: The Small Catechism
Martin Luther: A Mighty Fortress Is Our God
Lutheran princes file a protestation at the Diet of Speyer

Schmalkaldic War

Augsburg Interim

Death of Luther

Council of Trent (Tridentinum)

Luther's serious illness

Martin Luther: Against the Papacy at Rome, Founded by the Devil

Peace of Augsburg
Religion of the ruler dictates the religion of those ruled

Religious wars in France

1550

Princes plot against Emperor Charles V

Beginning of Catholic Revival ("Counter-Reformation")

Heidelberg Catechism of the Reformed Churches

Eighty Years' War (Dutch War of Independence)

St. Bartholomew's Day massacre in France, assassination of many Protestants (Huguenots)

Merger of Lutheran and Reformed Churches in Prussia

Assassination of the Protestant King Henry IV of France

Gregorian Calendar

"Third Great Awakening"

Thirty Years' War

1600

Failed invasion of Spanish Armada in England

Charles Darwin: On the Origin of Species

First permanent English settlement in Jamestown, Virginia

1800

King James Bible, major English translation

Napoleon crowns himself emperor

Protestant dissidents (Pilgrim Fathers) arrive in Massachusetts on the "Mayflower"

"Second Great Awakening"

Tried before the Inquisition, Galileo Galilei recants his championing of the Copernican world view

French Revolution

Reformed confession officially recognized

Declaration of Independence, freedom of religion enshrined in the Constitution of the United States

Pennsylvania grants full religious freedom

Edict of tolerance revoked in France

American Civil War

Glorious Revolution, Catholic King of England overthrown

Lutheran missionary Heinrich Melchior Mühlenberg arrives in America

"First Great Awakening", religious revival movement in American colonies

1700

Foundation of the German Empire

1900

Francke Foundation in Halle, established by Pietist August Hermann Francke

State Office for Heritage Management
and Archaeology Saxony-Anhalt –
State Museum of Prehistory
Luther Memorials Foundation of Saxony-Anhalt
Stiftung Deutsches Historisches Museum
Foundation Schloss Friedenstein Gotha
Minneapolis Institute of Art
The Morgan Library & Museum

Martin Luther

AND THE REFORMATION

CONCORDIA UNIVERSITY LIBRARY
PORTLAND, OR 97211

Sandstein Verlag

**We wish to thank
our supporters and sponsors**

The patron of the exhibition project
"Here I Stand" is the German Federal
Minister for Foreign Affairs,
Dr. Frank-Walter Steinmeier.
The realization of the project has been
made possible due to the support of the
Foreign Office of the Federal Republic
of Germany within the framework
of the Luther Decade

 Federal Foreign Office

**The exhibition project
has been supported by**

SACHSEN-ANHALT

SACHSEN-ANHALT
Investitions- und
Marketinggesellschaft

Verein zur Förderung
des Landesmuseums für
Vorgeschichte Halle (Saale) e.V.

**The restoration of the Gotha Altar
has been enabled by**

 Federal Foreign Office

RAO
RUDOLF-AUGUST OETKER-
STIFTUNG

K U L T U R
S T I F T U N G · D E R
L Ä N D E R

BÜNDNIS ZUR ERSCHLIESSUNG
UND SICHERUNG VON MUSEUMSDEPOTS

The restoration of the Luther Pulpit
from St. Andrew's Church in Eisleben
has been enabled by

Minneapolis Institute of Art

The exhibition **"Martin Luther:
Art and the Reformation"** at the Minneapolis
Institute of Art is presented by

Lead Sponsors:

John and Nancy Lindahl

The Hognander Foundation

K.A.H.R. Foundation

The Bradbury and Janet Anderson
Family Foundation

Jim and Carmen Campbell

 **THOMSON REUTERS**

Major Sponsors:

 DELTA

**National
Endowment
for the Arts**
arts.gov
ART WORKS.

The exhibition **"Word and Image:
Martin Luther's Reformation"** at
The Morgan Library & Museum, New York

was also generously supported by

the **Johansson Family Foundation**

and **Kurt F. Viermetz, Munich**

with assistance by

the **Arnhold Foundation** and

the **Foreign Office**
of the Federal Republic of Germany.

The exhibition **"Law and Grace:
Martin Luther, Lucas Cranach and
the Promise of Salvation"** at the
Pitts Theology Library of Candler School
of Theology at Emory University, Atlanta

has been supported by:

THE HALLE FOUNDATION
www.hallefoundation.org

Contents

Greeting

Legend has it that Martin Luther declared "Here I stand; I can do no other" when ordered to recant his earlier writings before the emperor in Worms. For reasons of conscience and because he was convinced of the word of God in the Holy Scripture, he stood up to the pressure exerted by the authorities. By criticising the Roman Catholic Church, the sale of indulgences, and the lavish lifestyle of the Pope, he challenged both clerical and secular power. Today, 500 years later, we remember this courageous man who lived on the cusp of the modern era and played such an important role in the development of a modern society.

We owe the crucial impetus for how we understand freedom, education, and social coexistence today to Luther and other reformers. This includes the right to be wrong—also as regards Luther himself. Some of his statements on the Jews, the peasants, or women cannot serve as examples to us. We now distance ourselves in particular from Luther's anti-Semitic views, which were exploited under National Socialism to foster anti-Semitism by the state.

The movement triggered by the reformers, with Martin Luther leading the way, did not only have a lasting impact on societies in Germany and Europe – we also associate the Enlightenment and the notion of freedom with the United States in particular. This was one of the reasons for showing the exhibition, "Here I stand," in different forms at the same time in Minneapolis, New York and Atlanta. The history of the foundation of the United States, and the way the country defines itself, are based on Reformation ideas. These include the separation of church and state, religious tolerance, freedom of religion, and the Mayflower Compact by the Pilgrim Fathers (and Mothers)—the first democratic set of rules on American soil.

This volume of essays provides background information and different viewpoints, and thus serves as a supplement to the catalogue for the exhibitions "Here I stand." It contains some 50 essays by German- and English-speaking academics on Martin Luther's life and teachings and on the history of the Reformation. A key chapter is devoted to Protestantism in the United States. The volume is thus an outstanding supplement to the exhibitions.

I hope it makes interesting and inspiring reading.

Federal Minister for Foreign Affairs

Foreword

In 2017, we commemorate the 500th anniversary of the publishing of Martin Luther's Ninety-Five Theses condemning the sale of indulgences. This momentous event is now generally considered to mark the start of the Reformation and the birth of a movement that has had a profound influence on the course of world history to this day. In Germany, the birthplace of the Reformation, many of the authentic sites of Luther's life and work have been preserved to welcome a constant flow of visitors from all over the world. In addition, Germany will host nationwide festivities in 2017, which include three national special exhibitions in Wittenberg, Berlin, and Wartburg Castle, as well as numerous other exhibitions and events. These activities not only commemorate the birth of the Reformation, but also take a deeper look at its subsequent and enduring history and worldwide influence.

The prospect of the upcoming anniversary clearly demanded an exhibition project of extraordinary dimensions—and we are very happy that we have been able to conceptualize, plan, and realize this vision with the support of the German Federal Foreign Office. The result of these ambitions is the project called "Here I stand", which is set to commemorate the Reformation Anniversary from October 2016 to January 2017 in three separate locations in the USA—a nation that has been strongly shaped by Lutheran and Protestant traditions. This huge undertaking encompasses no less than three exhibitions on Martin Luther, his life, and his achievements. While these events are roughly simultaneous, they each aim at a different target audience and focus on a particular subject selection. We count ourselves lucky that the institutions with which we cooperate in this endeavor—The Morgan Library & Museum, New York, the Minneapolis Institute of Art, Minneapolis (Minnesota) and the Pitts Theology Library of Emory University, Atlanta (Georgia)—were undoubtedly predestined to host exhibitions of this scope and particular subject.

Apart from our shared overall ambition to realize these three exhibitions, we agreed with our American colleagues from the very beginning that the scholarly harvest of the joint exhibitions and our fruitful collaboration should be presented to a wider public through a comprehensive printed publication. The first result is a catalog that not only presents all those fascinating objects from the birthplace of the Reformation displayed in Minneapolis, New York and Atlanta, but also captures the special and singular atmosphere of these events. Expanding upon this, we were also able to compile this present volume, which contains insightful scholarly articles on the various aspects of the subject. Mirroring the rich diversity of the exhibitions that make up our project, it assembles the research of renowned representatives in the fields of general and ecclesiastical history, the history of art, cultural history, mentality studies, archaeology, and economic and social history. The articles cover an amazing range of subjects, and they display the present state of our knowledge in a comprehensive manner. The scope of the articles extends from the geographic and intellectual background of Luther himself to the main events and aspects of the history of the Reformation, seen in their cultural and artistic context, and includes the captivating story of the Lutheran faith in the North American continent. We are extremely grateful to the authors who contributed their work and insights to this substantial volume.

The project and the exhibitions that form the background to these publications were supported by the Foreign Office of the Federal Republic of Germany with generous financial backing, without which the realization of "Here I stand" could never have been accomplished. For this unstinting support, we owe a particular debt of gratitude both to the Federal Foreign Office and to the Federal Minister for Foreign Affairs, Dr. Frank-Walter Steinmeier, who graciously consented to become the patron of the project.

We would also like to thank the many colleagues in our American partner institutions for the fruitful and close collaboration that has led to the extraordinary results documented in this volume. Of this dedicated host, we can only name the directors Dr. Kaywin Feldman (Minneapolis Institute of Art) and Dr. Colin B. Bailey (The Morgan Library & Museum). Side by side with their teams, they exhibited a maximum of commitment both in the joint production of the exhibitions and in their share of the editorship of the accompanying publications. Prof. Dr. M. Patrick Graham, the director of the Pitts Theology Library and his colleagues backed the idea of a Luther-themed exhibition in Atlanta from the very beginning, and like their colleagues in Minneapolis and New York, they never wavered in their professional cooperation. The exhibition at the Pitts Theology Library, Atlanta, was made possible by the generous support of the Halle Foundation, Atlanta, and we would like to express our sincerest gratitude to the chairman of the board, Dr. Eike Jordan, and the administrator of the Halle Foundation, W. Marshall Sanders.

The unique range of Luther-related subjects that is covered by the three exhibitions in the USA could not have been achieved without the support of the lending institutions that obligingly opened the doors of their treasure vaults for this unique occasion. We are deeply indebted to these partners for their open-handed generosity.

Finally, we would like to offer our thanks to the many colleagues who toiled, both in the foreground and in the wings, to make the various parts of the project become reality. Among these, we would like to single out the project team behind "Here I stand", ably led by Dr. Tomoko Emmerling and including Dr. Ingrid Dettmann, Susanne Kimmig-Völkner M. A., Robert Kluth M. A., Franziska Kuschel M.A. and Prof. Dr. Louis D. Nebelsick. Throughout the process, they took on their various responsibilities with supreme dedication and a great deal of personal commitment. As if organizing the exhibitions was not enough, they also invested considerable energy into the production of this publication, the catalog volume, and the accompanying website www.here-i-stand.com, which provides a digital and downloadable exhibition, #HereIstand, to visitors. Particular mention must be made of the outstanding work of the editors of the accompanying publications, Dr. Katrin Herbst, Dr. Ralf Kluttig-Altmann, Robert Noack M.A. and Dr. habil. Anne-Simone Rous. With all of these efforts, the diverse parts and elements of the project could not have been completed without the countless contributions of a great number of colleagues belonging to the various departments of our own institutions. To all of these unnamed contributors, we extend our warmest thanks for their invaluable work.

Harald Meller
Director
State Office for Heritage Management
and Archaeology Saxony-Anhalt
State Museum of Prehistory

Martin Eberle
Director
Foundation Schloss Friedenstein
Gotha

Ulrike Kretzschmar
President a.i.
Stiftung Deutsches Historisches
Museum

Stefan Rhein
Chairman and Director
Luther Memorials Foundation
of Saxony-Anhalt

Foreword

The Minneapolis Institute of Art is honored to present "Martin Luther: Art and the Reformation," an unprecedented exhibition marking the 500th anniversary of the Ninety-Five Theses that shook Europe to its core and gave rise to religious beliefs now shared by millions of Minnesotans and 800 million Protestants throughout the world. Luther's thoughts and actions brought radical changes that redrew the spiritual and political map of Europe. Five centuries later scholars of Luther and his era continue to make fresh discoveries and achieve a new understanding of known events, many of which strike contemporary chords because many of the questions of Luther's age are still with us today.

We live in a time of media revolution, economic, political, and military conflict, religious strife, and questioning of gender roles. This weighty volume of essays explores these themes and more. Contributors include leading scholars in the field as well as new voices, and we thank all of them for their research and insights. Catalyzed by the anniversary and the triumvirate of exhibitions presented in Minneapolis, New York, and Atlanta, this outpouring of scholarship allows us to sharpen our understanding of the remarkable objects so generously lent by nearly twenty-five German institutions and will have enduring benefit as a resource for years to come.

We are deeply grateful to our brilliant and generous partners working directly with the Minneapolis Institute of Art in this endeavor, beginning with project organizer, the State Museum of Prehistory, Halle (Saale), also working with the Luther Memorials Foundation of Saxony-Anhalt, Wittenberg; the Deutsches Historisches Museum, Berlin; and the Foundation Schloss Friedenstein Gotha. I am especially pleased to recognize the visionary leadership of the Director of the State Museum of Prehistory Halle [Saale], Prof. Dr. Harald Meller, who first offered us the opportunity to bring so many artistic, cultural, and religious treasures to Minneapolis. I am also grateful for the work of Dr. Tomoko Emmerling, whose curatorial and organizational excellence has kept this complex project on track. I appreciate the work of the entire team based in Halle, who helped to execute the exhibition and related publications. In Minneapolis, special recognition goes to Tom Rassieur, John E. Andrus III Curator of Prints and Drawings, for his dedicated work on this important project over a number of years.

I am grateful to chief editor Anne-Simone Rous and her team for overseeing the intricacies of recruiting the authors, editing their texts and translating them to and from English and German. Without the support of the Foreign Office of the Federal Republic of Germany within the framework of the Luther Decade, the project would have never gotten off the ground. We are particularly grateful for the support of Thrivent Financial, our Minneapolis Presenting Sponsor of "Martin Luther: Art and the Reformation." We also extend our appreciation to John and Nancy Lindahl, Joe Hognander/ The Hognander Foundation, Jeannine Rivet and Warren Herreid/K.A.H.R. Foundation, The Bradbury and Janet Anderson Family Foundation, Jim and Carmen Campbell/ Campbell Foundation, Thomson Reuters, Delta Air Lines, and the National Endowment for the Arts for their additional support in helping bring this once-in-a-lifetime exhibition to Minnesota. On behalf of everyone at the Minneapolis Institute of Art, I extend our warmest thanks to everyone who made this important project possible.

Kaywin Feldman
Duncan and Nivin MacMillan Director and President
of the Minneapolis Institute of Art

Foreword

The Morgan Library & Museum is proud to participate in a major German-American exhibition project in 2016 featuring Martin Luther and the birth of the Reformation. Located in the heart of Manhattan, our founder had once crossed the path of the Reformation and German history.

John Pierpont Morgan (1837–1913) was an international financier and art collector. Born in Hartford, Connecticut, he was educated in Switzerland and at Göttingen University in Germany, where he spent his summers as few Americans at that time could: visiting historical sites and art collections. These experiences had a profound impact upon his appreciation of history and desire to form his own collection of artistic and literary masterworks. One such opportunity arose when the extraordinary letter that Martin Luther wrote to Emperor Charles V asserting his religious convictions came up for auction in Leipzig in May 1911. The bidding quickly soared to 20-times the estimated price, and ultimately, Morgan walked away with this gem of German heritage. Two months later, Morgan presented the famous letter to his friend and sailing companion Kaiser Wilhelm II as a gift for the nation that Morgan held in such high esteem.

Although he had collected some autographs in his youth, it was not until the 1890s that Morgan started acquiring art and books. For his personal collection he sought out the high points of western culture, including an exceptional collection of Germanic works such as the 9th-century Lindau Gospels, with its gold and jewel-encrusted binding, three copies of the Gutenberg Bible, the works of Martin Luther, and the drawings and prints of Albrecht Dürer. The leading American architects McKim, Mead & White designed a building to house and to match Morgan's collection: a grand Renaissance palazzo in the heart of New York City. Today, the Morgan collection encompasses over 6,000 years of literary and artistic creation, from the 4th millennium B.C. to the present. The Morgan Library & Museum thus incorporates the same symbiosis of word and image exemplified by the powerful use of textual and visual media during the Reformation. The essays in this volume represent a similar multi-faceted perspective on the complex issues regarding Martin Luther and the Reformation, with the added emphasis of the Lutheran impact on modern society through the contemporary relevance of historical materials and events.

We are grateful for support from the Foreign Office of the Federal Republic of Germany within the framework of the Luther Decade in cooperation with the Luther Memorials Foundation in Saxony-Anhalt, the Deutsches Historisches Museum, Berlin, and the Foundation Schloss Friedenstein, Gotha, under the leadership of the State Museum of Prehistory, Halle (Saale) for helping to bring this historic exhibition to American audiences. Our gratitude as well goes to the Metropolitan Museum of Art, New York, for their assistance providing material for the exhibition.

The exhibition in New York was also generously supported by the Johansson Family Foundation and Kurt F. Viermetz, Munich, and assistance from the Arnhold Foundation and the Federal Foreign Office.

Colin B. Bailey
Director
The Morgan Library & Museum

I

The Eve of the

Reformation

LUISE SCHORN-SCHÜTTE

Europe and the World around 1500

The year 1500 saw the birth of Emperor Charles V. According to his contemporaries who were much in awe of his powers he was a ruler in whose realm the sun never set. Charles V stood for the continuity of the *monarchia universalis*, the medieval concept of power that included the whole of Europe. This was also the reason why he adhered so closely to the unity of Christianity and displayed such strict opposition to the reform movement of Martin Luther in the Holy Roman Empire of the German Nation. He was opposed on the one hand by the reformers of the empire: four secular and three spiritual Electors (the Count Palatine of the Rhine, the Duke of Saxony, the Margrave of Brandenburg, the King of Bohemia, and the archbishops of Mainz, Cologne, and Trier) and on the other by the reformers of the church (Martin Luther, Huldrych Zwingli, and Jean Calvin). Were these figures the forerunners of the "new era" so frequently referred to in literature and historiographies that deal with the beginning of the sixteenth century? Unlike the reformers of the twentieth and twenty-first centuries, contemporary politicians and theologians of the time did not invoke a vague future but rather the force of tradition. All that lay in the past was good, and the re-creation of the past involved reformist and even reformatory power. This idea was a highly explosive concept as the restoration of the ancient order that was deemed so good had the potential to shake the very foundations of contemporary life.

The majority of educated persons saw the turn of the sixteenth century as a time of radical change. This was, on the one hand, due to economic and social transformations of the time: the economic decay of the late fifteenth century was coming to an end, and the new century would bring modest wealth to all social levels over several generations. On the other hand, the transformation also had its origins in the sense of impending religious change which, triggered by the spread of humanism throughout Europe, received strong impetus from Luther's reformatory movement, even though this did not reach all regions of Europe.

What were the precise economic, judicial, social, and religious foundations of European life at the beginning of the sixteenth century? What did Europe signify for its contemporaries, and what was important from a geographical perspective? And finally, has the perception of an era of change withstood the judgment of historians?

Time and Space

At the beginning of the sixteenth century, although the earth revolved around the sun at the same speed as today, humans had a different concept of time. The great majority was oriented toward a natural daily routine framed by sunrise and sunset—and the presence or lack of daylight. All other sources of light (oil or candles) were expensive and thus employed sparingly. It was equally natural for humans to orient themselves to the rhythms of the seasons in a largely agricultural society. This rhythm determined the length of the working day in both towns and rural communities. In summer the days were long, as were the working days, hence there was more work to perform. During winter when days were shorter, the working day was likewise truncated. The rural population used simple sundials as a rough temporal orientation, with bells as an additional "acoustic timepiece."[1] Bells called people to meetings, acted as emergency sirens and pealed during the final journey to the cemetery. Moreover, bells also helped to keep urban order; many towns (especially larger ones) had alarm or town bells which rang the loudest.[2]

Time

In towns and cities, these imprecise measurements of time were augmented by the mechanical clock, which had been invented around 1300. In view of the growing necessity for differentiated and more precise indications of time within the trades and skilled handcrafts, this had been a considerable improvement; ever since the end of the fifteenth century, a public municipal clock was considered compulsory in all smaller towns.[3] Scholars of historical technology have equated the significance of this invention with book printing. Ever since the beginning of the sixteenth century, clocks had displayed both hours and minutes with two clock hands. As these instruments could only be manufactured with great technical effort and at a substantial cost, they were initially only owned by members of the aristocracy or municipal authorities serving as clocks on town halls, towers, castles, or in the inventory of prestigious buildings. It was not until technical progress enabled the construction of smaller portable clocks that they became private possessions; in Germany, these types of spring-mounted clocks were produced by the Nuremberg clockmaker Peter Henlein during the first half of the sixteenth century (fig. 1).

Fig. 1 Necklace- or pocket-watch (also known as "Nürnberger Eierlein," i. e. Nuremberg Small Egg),
        Germany or Switzerland, probably sixteenth century

The existence of these precise timekeepers altered the temporal rhythms of societies throughout Europe during the early modern period. The rhythm set by the new mechanical clocks slowly but steadily displaced the earlier orientation towards the pace set by nature, which had prevailed up to the beginning of the sixteenth century. The hourly divisions dictated by clocks gradually became discernable in all spheres of life, such as the rules governing schools, churches, and law courts, and the enactment of public security, which all adhered to precise temporal rules. Since the sixteenth century, clocks have served as a symbol for the regulated order of heaven and earth and a characteristic representation of the order of creation. As a consequence, clocks became models for smaller-scale social units and for the home and the family; the Protestant theologian Johann Heinrich Alsted even compared the "entire house" of Europe in the sixteenth and seventeenth centuries to a clockwork mechanism.[4]

One characteristic of the early modern period was the management of shortages. This not only applied to the challenges of feeding a growing population but also to the limitations of time. Time was a rare commodity for the people of the early modern period, as the average life expectancy was forty years shorter than in today's Europe. This explains why up to the mid-seventeenth century time was

integrated into the concept of transcendence, part of the growing realization of the dangers threatening life itself.[5]

The high probability that one's own life could end abruptly at any time sensitized the contemporary population to the worthlessness and transience of earthly values. These were compared to the swift passing of the day or the cycle of the seasons. Besides this the concept of a staircase of life, in which life progressed gender specifically in ten steps each a decade long, was particularly widespread among the urban bourgeoisie of the early modern period. This reflected temporal schemes of ten times ten or seven times seven which dated back to antiquity. All reflections on the chronological progress of human life had religious foundations. Transcendency was an integral part of all these considerations. The time on earth allotted to humans was oriented toward specific objectives that could only be realized in a better afterlife.[6]

1 Münch, *Lebensformen*, p. 180. 2 Ibid., p. 182. 3 On the following, see ibid., pp. 184 f.; also Pettegree, *Europe*, pp. 7 f. 4 See Münch, *Lebensformen*. 5 On the topic of non-European orders, see Reinhard, *Lebensformen*, pp. 582–585. 6 See Münch, *Lebensformen*, p. 169.

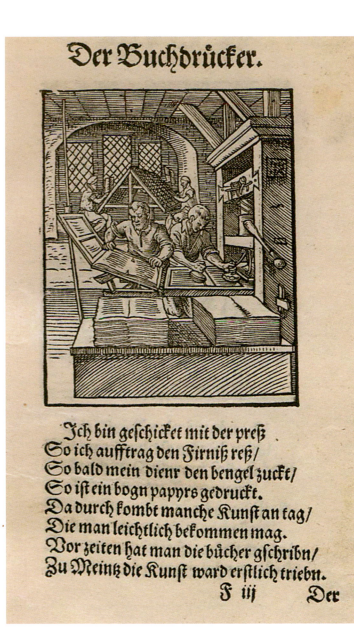

Der Buchdrucker.

Ich bin geschicket mit der preß
So ich aufftrag den Firniß reß/
So bald mein dienr den bengel zuckt/
So ist ein bogn papyrs gedruckt.
Da durch kombt manche Kunst an tag/
Die man leichtlich bekommen mag.
Vor zeiten hat man die bücher gschribn/
Zu Meintz die Kunst ward erstlich triebn.

                 F iij   Der

Fig. 2 Jost Ammann, The Book Printer, illustration from: Hans Sachs,
Eygentliche Beschreibung Aller Stände auff Erden,
Frankfurt am Main 1568

Space

At the beginning of the sixteenth century, the European horizon expanded to include new geographical regions, augmenting and extending the concept of the world. For the majority of the population, however, the world was ordered on a very much smaller scale. Its scope was limited to family and the village or town and its immediate vicinity. Everyday information and news were exchanged within a relatively limited geographical area, and contacts beyond this were normally only made on pilgrimages and by traveling journeymen or vagrants.

In contrast, the upper classes of Europe had far more extensive possibilities of communication at their disposal, largely due to their literacy. Technical innovation, particularly the invention of printing,

opened up new possibilities for the dissemination of news and different media (fig. 2). Changing political and geographical terminology reflected the spatial experiences of the early modern period. This is perfectly illustrated by the term *patria* (homeland), which around 1500 delineated not only the immediate vicinity but also larger spatial units. There was no consistent organization of territory in Europe during the early modern period, as each territorial area—the manorial system and church parishes or the military and tax administrations—had its own borders, which remained virtually unchanged up to the end of the eighteenth century.[7]

Territories were defined by geographical and/or political criteria. The majority of the European population during the early modern period was embedded in these contained living areas, but there were always migrations, population movements and travels. There was, however, a completely new form of mobility, confessional migration (i.e. religious groups fleeing persecution) that originated around the middle of the sixteenth century: traveling had been necessary for trade and the exertion of power since medieval times, but from the beginning of the sixteenth century, wealthy merchants in major European trading cities began to decrease their traveling activities. Instead they began building up a network of foreign commercial relationships. During subsequent decades, this form of economic expansion was also extended into politically definable areas. The physical presence of a ruler was superseded by the presence of his representatives, the public officials.

Did the elite of Europe actually possess a concept of their own continent at the beginning of the sixteenth century? Is it possible to determine a geographically identifiable image of Europe, or was the continent more an idea or a myth?

Within its geographic contours Europe was described precisely. Characteristic features included the preeminence of its mainland, the existence of numerous islands, and the highly variable coastal areas. Europe was allotted a more prominent role in comparison with other parts of the world. In the second edition of the *Cosmographia universalis* compiled by the cartographer Sebastian Münster and printed in Basel in 1588, for instance, the European continent is represented as the queen of the world, with Africa and Asia as much smaller territories squeezed into the corners (fig. 3).

This traditional image of a female Europe as ruler and center of the world remained unchanged throughout the entire early modern period.[8] In territorial maps, the borders of regional units gradually became more prominent and precisely defined, but whether this can be interpreted as the origin of national territories remains a controversial issue among historians.[9] Equally disputed is whether one can speak of "national" prejudices at the beginning of the sixteenth century. For historians, the political unity of this geographic territory

7 For more details on this topic see Reinhard, *Lebensformen*, p. 417. In this essay, forms of rule are considered: rule on local, regional, and central "state" levels. These forms of rule only developed during the early modern period and it is therefore not correct to speak of the "state" in the sense of the nineteenth century in reference to the sixteenth to eighteenth centuries. 8 See Vogler, *Aufbruch*, p. 20. 9 See ibid.

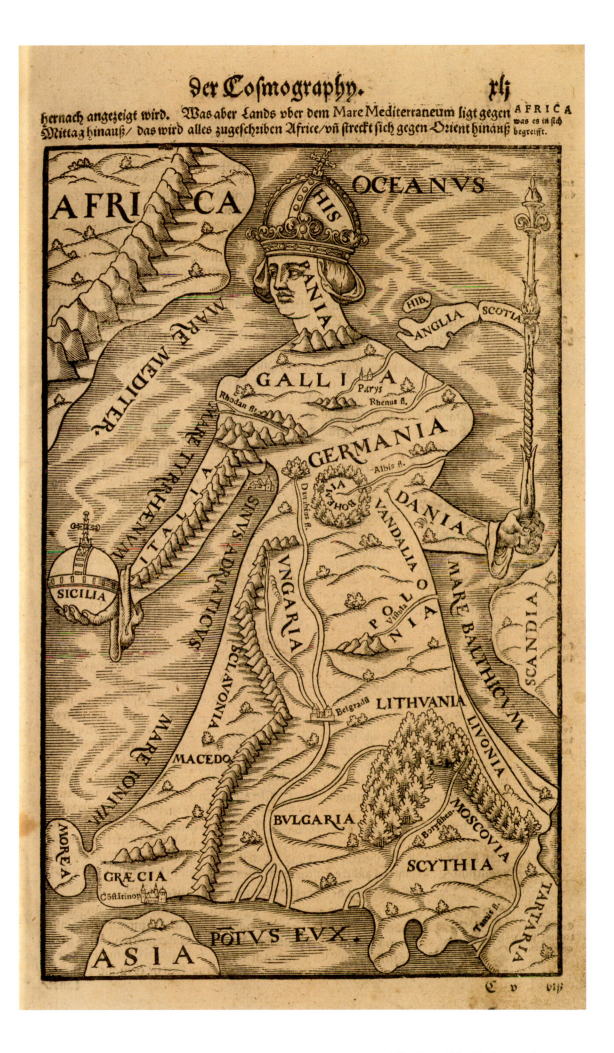

Fig. 3
Europa Regina,
from: Sebastian Münster,
Cosmographia, Basel 1588

Fig. 4 Martin Waldseemüller, Universalis cosmographia secundum Ptholomaei traditionem et Americi Vespucii
alioru[m]que lustrationes, Saint-Dié-des-Vosges 1507. The first map that refers to the land mass of the newly discovered
western continent as "America"—after Amerigo Vespucci.

can be defined according to specific historical and political factors that have been visible since antiquity and medieval times,[10] and with greater clarity since the beginning of the sixteenth century. The foremost factor is Christianity, which has emphatically and distinctly molded European culture. This also happened and indeed took place particularly because of the denominational schism triggered by the Reformation in 1517. While this did indeed lead to the establishment of new borders based on regional factors, reciprocal dependencies made denominational agglomerations possible.

The Roman Catholic Church's claim of universal validity with the Pope at its head nevertheless prevailed. It justified the legitimacy of European expansion with reference to the validity of the biblical missionary mandate. Despite the growing schism ever since the middle of the sixteenth century, most contemporaries saw the unity of Christianity maintained with the terms *christianitas* and *res publica christiana*. These terms were used to describe the political territory of Europe. According to Machiavelli, the Christian rulers and republics of Europe came together by distinguishing themselves from "despotic great empires" such as Turkey, and claimed the notion of political freedom without tyranny for themselves. Denominationally divided Europe still saw itself in this politicized sense of the word as building a single unit against the outside world. Around the middle of the sixteenth century, the term "Europe" was used by all denominations parallel to the concept of *christianitas*, within the fields

of journalism and literature and in the colloquial language of mercantilism, and had become fully established by the end of the sixteenth century.[11]

The second factor that must be named is the existence of relationships of power based on the division of property and land and the reciprocal duties and privileges which bonded the rulers and the ruled. The system of feudal tenure was a distinctive element of historical and political Europe at this time. For this reason the contrast between freedom and bondage which was based on the diferring property rights was codified as the basic standard of all models of sovereignty. Economics and ethical norms became interconnected in their support of sovereign order. The ruling individual had a duty to protect his subjects, while his subjects had to agree to provide advice and assistance. This arrangement reinforced the concept of obedience toward a just master.

This standard regulating the relationship between the social groups of rulers and the ruled remained a permanent subject of debate. A competition between two differing legal concepts was characteristic of Europe at the dawn of the sixteenth century. On the one hand aristocrats, clerics, burghers, and in certain areas even farming classes (e.g., Tyrol, East Friesland, and the Swiss Confederation) had the right to participate in sovereignty, and on the other there was the tendency to concentrate power in the hands of the families of the high nobility and to repress the right of the others to participate.

Since the 1530s, the conflict about the nature of sovereignty received a new impetus because of the religious schism. Now denominational affiliation was used to reinforce the legitimating of the relevant political arguments. This development did not, however, result in the separation of religion and politics, but instead forged new denominationally specific interconnections.

It is hard to establish to what extent contemporaries recognized these political-historical elements of European unity at the beginning of the sixteenth century. Historians at the end of the twentieth century attempted to characterize these elements as a "European ideology."[12] While current research uses different terms it does not dispute such a sense of community.

Economics, Law, and Religion

Europe at the dawn of the sixteenth century was strongly formed by economic, social, legal, and religious commonalities. This appraisal holds true despite, and indeed because of, the recognition of a multiplicity of regional differences throughout the continent. Nowadays, historians underscore the connecting lines running through East, Central, and Western Europe, and the concept of a uniquely European path has gradually fallen out of favor.

Economics

As in medieval times, the European economy around 1500 was largely based on agriculture; only 10 percent of the population at most lived in towns and cities. In rural areas, a highly differentiated peasant population lived alongside the gentry and nobility, the latter frequently resided in the courts of the high aristocracy or in their own manor houses. The townspeople, who were in possession of civil rights (which entailed both duties and privileges), belonged to the bourgeoisie or middle class, a group whose situation was strongly variable across the whole of Europe. In contrast to the aristocracy and the rural population, townspeople did not derive their livelihood from agriculture, instead they worked within the fields of skilled handcrafts or trade. Craftsmen and merchants organized themselves in guilds, trade unions, and similar associations. These bodies were far more than mere professional organizations; they controlled all aspects of life, determining the structure of everyday life, controlling production, and providing social security.

Around the beginning of the sixteenth century, the European economy was in the process of a sustained upswing. This can be seen not only on the basis of the demographic changes but also by the growth of European trade, which had already begun its transformation into a global trading network. Because economic success had its roots in the last decades of the fifteenth century and continued into the first years of the seventeenth century, the sixteenth century is also known by historians as the "long century." The population decline in the wake of the plague toward the end of the fifteenth century had gradually been offset by a new period of growth. This growth was built on the foundations of demographic mechanisms that, for societies characterized by shortages, were shaped by the oscillation between population growth and famines. There were limited sources of nourishment and only little opportunity to increase food production. Rising population levels since the beginning of the sixteenth century increased demand, forcing up the prices of essential foodstuffs such as meat and cereals. Since the population increased again, the demand for labor was low within a certain time span and wages dropped. These factors led irrevocably to the next shortage crisis of the recent modern period, and is recorded as having taken place around the middle of the seventeenth century.

At the beginning of the sixteenth century, agriculture initially experienced an upswing. Moreover craft manufacturing in the towns increased, and long-range trade expanded. The Mediterranean dominated as a center of trade. It was at the intersection of major European trade routes, linking the larger commercial centers as well as the northern and southern parts of the continent. Transport routes ran from Venice and Florence via Augsburg and Nuremberg in the south of Germany, continuing through Cologne to cities in the Northeast such as Hamburg, Lübeck, and Danzig. These transport routes enabled trade and exchange between the agriculturally oriented Northeast and the commercial Southwest of Germany. At this time, the Baltic Sea represented a second significant trading area dominated by the Hanseatic League which flourished up to the first decades of the sixteenth century, made up of merchants from the North and the Baltic Sea.

Law

The great majority of the European population—90 percent—was integrated into rural population groups, social structures shaped by the aristocracy and farmers. For this reason, the manorial system became the dominant institution, shaping economic, social, political, and, ultimately, religious interactions among the majority of the population.

What is the manorial system? It originated in early medieval times as an economic, political, and social relationship between ecclesiastical or aristocratic landowners on the one hand and farmers who worked the land (dependent peasants, in German: *Grundholde* and *Hintersassen*) on the other. The manorial system was based on hierarchical power structures, it was not a free association. The lord was responsible for the protection and defense of the peasants, who in turn paid for this protection by giving him dues from the yield of their land. Peasants were additionally exempt from military service. A depersonalization of the manorial relationships regarding loyalty and production can be observed from the end of the fifteenth century onward, resulting in an apparent increase in the political and economic freedom of the farming population. This process, however, came to a swift end at the beginning of the sixteenth century due to the upswing in agricultural activity and increase in popula-

---

10 More on this topic cf. ibid., pp. 22–24, and Blickle, *Europa*, pp. 15–17. **11** On this topic with references see Schulze, *Europa*, pp. 64 f. **12** Barraclough, *Einheit*, p. 26.

tion, discussed above. It marked the beginning of the division of Europe along the Elbe: while the manorial system in Western Europe allowed farmers a certain degree of freedom despite economic change, the system in Eastern Europe became much stricter, and peasants became increasingly dependent. In historical-research terms, this development is known as "re-feudalization." It must, however, be emphasized that this process was not simply history repeating itself but represented a new form of the division of labor: Eastern Europe supplied Western Europe with cattle and cereals (in particular the Netherlands and urban areas along the Rhine). Alongside the Margraviate of Brandenburg and Poland, other supplying regions of this type also included Lithuania, Russia, the Ukraine, and Hungary. This era saw the beginning of Danzig's economic upswing as a major export port. In return, Western Europe supplied luxury articles and finished goods to the spheres of agriculture and trade.

The social stratification of the European population had also been legally formalized ever since the early Middle Ages. Each individual belonged by right of birth to a certain social group that he or she was generally not able to leave. All social structures were thought to be tripartite. The one group prayed, the second group fought, and the others worked.[13] By late-medieval times, this structure had developed a characteristic allocation of status: aristocrats were considered *status politicus/bellatores*, the clergy, *status ecclesiasticus/oratores*, and farmers (and, from the end of the fifteenth century on, the middle class), *status oeconomicus/laboratores*. Each status group had its own indispensable task to guarantee the functioning of society. The concept remained predominant from the eleventh to the seventeenth century, providing continuity throughout Europe. At the beginning of the sixteenth century, however, first changes were noticeable without, however, challenging the fundaments of social hierarchy. These involved on the one hand mobility between social classes and on the other the demarcation between these social classes.

The rank structure around 1500 was social and political differentiation. The ancient European social groups were the basis of political representations at regional councils, thereby documenting the specifically European participation of regional powers in governance. At the beginning of the sixteenth century, ecclesiastical, aristocratic, and bourgeois groups were represented in these types of councils; in some regions (Tyrol, Switzerland, and East Friesland) farmers also participated.

Religion

In the wake of the reformatory movement, the composition of these councils had been changing radically since the middle of the sixteenth century. This was due to the separation of religion and politics which the reformers saw as a crucial issue. Initially it manifested itself in the barring of curiae from the councils within Protestant regions.

The reform movement had been sparked in 1517 by Martin Luther, professor of theology and Augustinian monk, with the publication of his Ninety-Five Theses. The reform in turn had ignited the long-smoldering criticism of the political function of the church and the secularization of clerics, bringing the issue out into the open. There had been many previous reform movements during the fifteenth century, including the *devotio moderna*, a new late-medieval religious movement in which the future Emperor Charles V had felt obliged to participate during the years of his youth. The momentum gained by the Lutheran Reformation movement brought the end of the unity of Christianity already within the two decades following 1520, the publication year of Luther's three major reformist treatises, creating a genuine epochal break. Research undertaken during the past few years has, however, established that the crisis of the church around 1500 was not a devotional crisis; on the contrary, there was an intensification of religious practice, rituals, and processions and an increase in the establishment of religious foundations. Europeans at the end of the Middle Ages were deeply embedded in the Christian faith as a theology of redemption that promised a better world following the misery of human existence.

It was critique of this piety that, at the turn of the century, was largely expressed in good deeds, generous charitable donations, and a self-interest in individual redemption, that was the focal point of Martin Luther's reformist theology which also criticized its secularization. It was not the intensity of piety that needed to change, but its direction: according to one of Luther's central theses, God's divine promise of salvation for every single believer made, and this is one of Luther's main theses, buying away your sins ("indulgences") and justification by good works redundant.

The "Europeanization" of the World: The Beginnings of Establishing European Colonies

The early modern period is the era marked by the emergence of Europe from its own shadow and the spread of its influence across the world. This process which had begun during the sixteenth century, would have global repercussions. The European elite were quick to use the expansion of their trading possibilities as an extension of their economic radius, simultaneously extending their political horizons.

It is understandable that Europeans focused on themselves. The opening up of Europe to the wider world also resulted in the Europeanization of that wider world. This perspective was vital and self-evident during the centuries of the early modern period and pointed European politics in an entirely new direction. The often-repeated accusation is that the academic view of this expansion solely as a movement within European history is Eurocentric, but it underestimates history's complexity and ignores the interaction between European and non-European reality.[14]

European expansion was neither unified and focused nor unavoidable and without alternatives.[15] Between 1500 and 1650, large portions of territories and peoples across the world were brought under the control of Europeans, a phenomenon known as colonialism. On the one hand, there was "overseas-settlement colonization," with the English and French settlements in North America being classic examples. On the other hand, there were "empire-building wars of conquest," that were characterized by the fact that an imperial center is maintained as a source of prowess and legitimacy, and which is the source also of military expansion. This type of empire-building was customarily created through the conquering and subordination of existing institutions, a pertinent example being the colonies established by Portugal and Spain.

These forms of expansion generally create two characteristic types of colonies: settler and exploitation colonies. European expansion had begun with the voyages of exploration undertaken by the Spanish and Portuguese around the middle of the fifteenth century. Developments during the early modern period were therefore built upon structures created during the late Middle Ages and were not linked with revolutionary new beginnings.

The motives for these highly risky expeditions were primarily economic. Since 1453, the search had been on for a new passage to India by sea to replace the overland commercial route for trade in spices, cotton, silk, dyes, and other goods, which had largely been obstructed by the Turkish conquest of Constantinople in 1453. Other factors included the expansion of the slave trade and the intensification of the sugar trade, but a further goal was to gain strategic allies in the struggle against the Ottomans. In the fifteenth century, these hopes could best be fulfilled in Asia. Europe's experienced sailors and its advanced technical knowledge, which enabled reliable orientation on the high seas, provided decisive advantages on these expeditions. The caravel, for example, was a highly maneuverable ship, and nautical instruments including the compass, Jacob's staff, quadrant, sundial, and sea charts, which had been known as such for a long time previously, became indispensable aids on expeditions.

The competition between Portugal and Spain in the exploitation of the west coast of Africa on the passage to Asia significantly accelerated the exploration process. In order to define economic spheres of interest, contracts, such as the contracts of Alcáçovas in 1479 and Tordesillas in 1494, were drawn up with the aid of the Pope. Spain was allocated the western areas and Portugal the territories in the East. The contracts stipulated that each of the two parties to the agreement would have the monopoly of sea voyages, trading, and conquests in his territory.

Christopher Columbus had been exploring the sea route to India on behalf of the King of Spain since August 1492 but, as is well known, reached the Caribbean islands, which he mistook for India, on October 12, 1492 (fig. 4). Columbus never accepted this "most original error in the entire history of exploration"[16]; for the rest of his life, he remained convinced that he had discovered the sea route to the east coast of Asia.

Vasco da Gama sailed around the Cape of Good Hope in 1497 under Portuguese mandate and reached the coast of India north of Calicut in May 1498, thereby discovering the trade route for Indian spices for Portugal. At the beginning of the sixteenth century, the Portuguese Fernando Magellan sailed under the Spanish crown toward America to achieve Columbus's objective of discovering the western sea route to Asia. He reached the Philippines in 1521, but was killed there. Juan Sebastián Elcano continued the circumnavigation of the world. The sale of the spices brought back on his return journey in 1522 fetched such a high sum that it more than covered the costs of the expedition. The Spanish, however subsequently renounced a part of their sphere of influence (with the Treaty of Zaragoza in 1529 which drew a new dividing line between the colonial powers), believing that the costs of trade with Asia would be too high. It was more worthwhile, they believed, to exploit the treasures of America. Since the beginning of the sixteenth century, they had been exploring the Caribbean and its islands and the south and west coasts of the American mainland. At the same time, a number of expeditions set off from locations in Panama and Mexico to explore the interior of the continent. One of these expeditions was undertaken in 1521 under the leadership of Hernán Cortés, who set himself up as the successor of the Aztec rulers.

The starting point for the conquest of South America was Panama: Francisco Pizarro embarked from here on a journey to Peru and succeeded in destroying the Inca Empire between 1531 and 1534. In 1571, the Spanish declared Manila as the capital city of their East Asian colonial empire in the hopes of setting up a base for trading spices and thereby securing entry into China. The two Iberian nations had additionally committed themselves to spreading Christianity in the contract of Tordesillas, and this commitment continued to be a significant motive for Spanish-Portuguese colonial politics. The desire to explore beyond the confines of Europe was a result not only of economic factors, but also of social, scientific, and religious motives. This is why the expansion, which had led to the discovery of completely new worlds and soon took on the characteristics of power politics, placed the new continent firmly in the foreground. These circumstances are all the more astounding in view of the fact that the technical accomplishments that made the Europeanization of the world at all possible had already long been mastered in non-European regions such as China and Egypt well before the sixteenth century.

The realization of contemporaries that they were living through a period of fundamental transformation was only shared by the elites. Later-born historians have confirmed this impression. The critical fact remains, however, that this perception was never described by contemporaries as being revolutionary, a term alien to that historical period. Instead, this time of change was perceived as *reformatio*, a return to circumstances that had previously been judged favorable.

---

13 Thus the earliest formulation by Adalbert of Laon in 1025; on this topic see Münch, *Lebensformen*. **14** See Wendt, *Kolonialismus*, p. 18. **15** See ibid., p. 19. **16** Cited in: Vogler, *Aufbruch*, p. 280, fn. 11.

BIBILOGRAPHY

Barraclough, Geoffrey (1967), *Die Einheit Europas als Gedanke und Tat*. Göttingen. **Blickle,** Peter (2008), *Das Alte Europa. Vom Hochmittelalter zur Moderne*. München. **Münch,** Paul (1992), *Lebensformen in der Frühen Neuzeit 1500–1800*. Frankfurt am Main. **Pettegree,** Andrew (2005), *Europe in the Sixteenth Century*. 2nd ed. Oxford. **Reinhard,** Wolfgang (2006), *Lebensformen Europas. Eine historische Kulturanthropologie*. 2nd ed. München. **Schulze,** Winfried (1997), Europa in der Frühen Neuzeit—Begriffsgeschichtliche Befunde. In: Duchhardt, Heinz et al. (eds.), *"Europäische Geschichte" als historiographisches Problem*. Mainz. **Vogler,** Günter (2003), *Europas Aufbruch in die Neuzeit. 1500–1650* (= Handbuch der Geschichte Europas. 5). Stuttgart. **Wendt,** Reinhard (2007), *Vom Kolonialismus zur Globalisierung. Europa und die Welt seit 1500*. Paderborn.

THE WORLD AROUND 1500

Around the beginning of the early modern period, the largest metropolises were not found in Europe, nor was Europe the center of the world.

Great empires existed in Asia, Africa, as well as in Central and South America. They boasted well-organized social and administrative structures, rich cultures and sometimes very advanced technology.

China was a pioneer in the sciences and led expeditions with huge treasure ships. The Great Wall was built against the Mongols. Different raw materials in the various regions of the world provided the basis for close economic relations and even for offshore trade.

The traces of the architecture of that time still bear witness to cultural diversity.

Cities

uninhabited

Hunter-gatherers

Pastoral nomads

Simple societies of farmers

Advanced societies of farmers / chiefdoms

Societies with administrative structures

Empires, comprising several societies

PUEBLO FARMERS

INCA EMPIRE
Capital: Cusco
Inhabitants: 70,000

AZTEC EMPIRE
Capital: Tenochtitlan
Inhabitants: 200,000

MAYA CITY-STATES
Capital: Iximché
Inhabitants: 10,000

Why did Europe become the leading power?

Around 1500, there were a number of empires which were on a similar or even higher level than Europe in various fields (such as technology, science, culture, or economics). The main reason why Europe became a global player in the long term was its highly diverse geography, which unlike Asia lacks the vast plains that can be controlled by equestrian peoples. Conversely, Europe has many navigable rivers and is structured by mountain ranges and large forests with different climates.

It is surrounded by seas, and is therefore difficult to conquer. It is due to these geographical conditions that no central government could develop here. Instead, the European continent was shaped by the rivalry of several sovereigns. The various goods stimulated a flourishing trade; technical and scientific progress was triggered by competition. It is because of these factors that Europe became the leading power of the world.

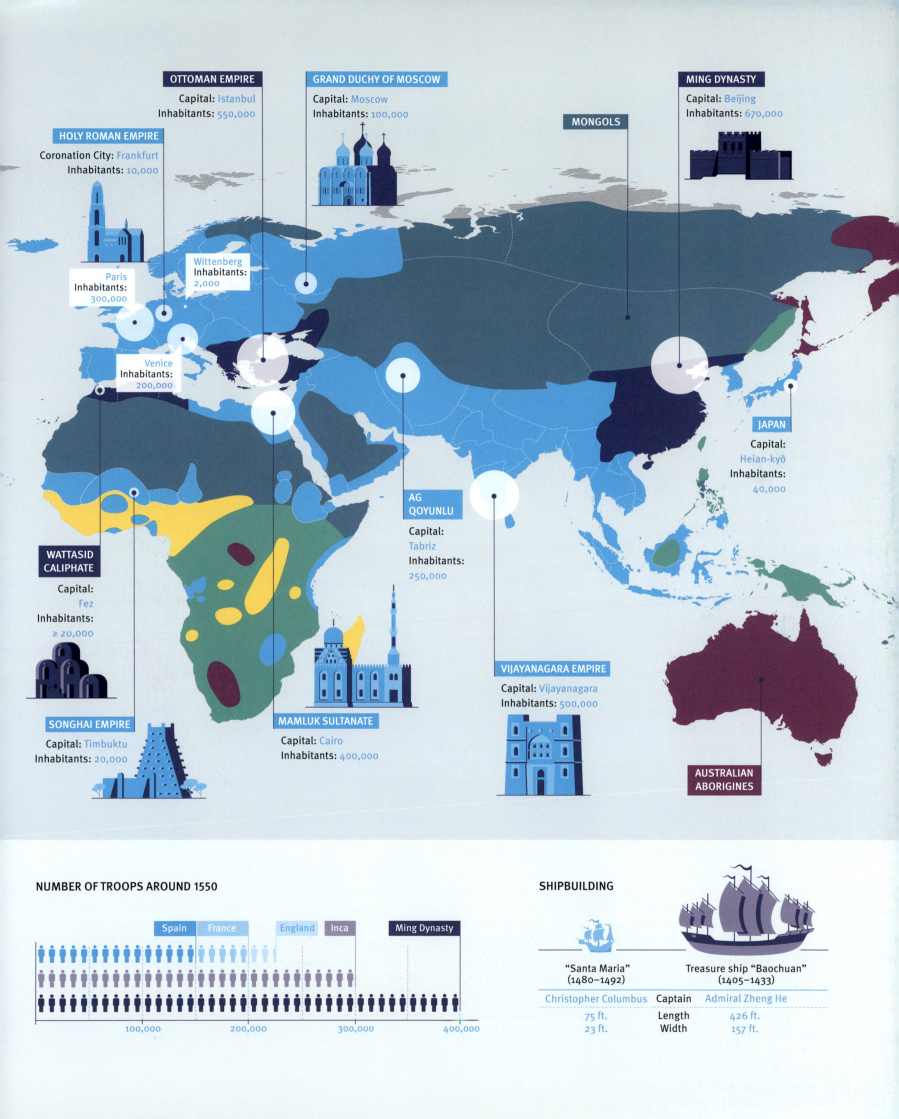

OTTOMAN EMPIRE
Capital: Istanbul
Inhabitants: 550,000

GRAND DUCHY OF MOSCOW
Capital: Moscow
Inhabitants: 100,000

MING DYNASTY
Capital: Beijing
Inhabitants: 670,000

HOLY ROMAN EMPIRE
Coronation City: Frankfurt
Inhabitants: 10,000

MONGOLS

Wittenberg
Inhabitants: 2,000

Paris
Inhabitants: 300,000

Venice
Inhabitants: 200,000

JAPAN
Capital: Heian-kyō
Inhabitants: 40,000

AG QOYUNLU
Capital: Tabriz
Inhabitants: 250,000

WATTASID CALIPHATE
Capital: Fez
Inhabitants: ≥ 20,000

VIJAYANAGARA EMPIRE
Capital: Vijayanagara
Inhabitants: 500,000

SONGHAI EMPIRE
Capital: Timbuktu
Inhabitants: 20,000

MAMLUK SULTANATE
Capital: Cairo
Inhabitants: 400,000

AUSTRALIAN ABORIGINES

NUMBER OF TROOPS AROUND 1550

Spain France England Inca Ming Dynasty

100,000   200,000   300,000   400,000

SHIPBUILDING

"Santa Maria"
(1480–1492)

Treasure ship "Baochuan"
(1405–1433)

Christopher Columbus		Admiral Zheng He
	Captain	
75 ft.	Length	426 ft.
23 ft.	Width	157 ft.

PHILIPP ROBINSON RÖSSNER

Economics and Religion
in the Late Middle Ages
and Reformation Period

Devotional Practice in the Middle Ages

Throughout the religious reform and renewal movement that is now known as the Reformation, Luther created a separation of secular and sacred worlds.[1] The Reformation demystified the all-encompassing ceremonial and devotional religious practices, with their primary focus on visual and ritual elements, as well as the simultaneously physical and primordial experience of religion and spirituality. In the emerging Protestant and Reformed churches after 1517, Luther's Reformation stripped the new ecclesiastical ritual of excessive materiality and haptic elements that the church had nurtured and congregations had gladly accepted for centuries. Despite the fact that economic origins, circumstances, and consequences of Martin Luther's Reformation have repeatedly evaded the attention of scholarly research over the last three decades, it is nevertheless possible to delineate significant parallels and connections between the fields of religion and economics. These play a crucial role in understanding not only the origins, progress, and effectiveness of Martin Luther's Reformation but also of other subsequent reform movements, including the Counter-Reformation and diverse reformatory movements within the Catholic Church, ever since the sixteenth century.

The Reformation had significant economic origins and consequences.[2] What is more, the current general tendency to isolate religion and economics not only as subjects of academic interest but in everyday matters is not because the two have nothing to do with each other, but more because of the tendency to consider them less important than one's spiritual life, emotional life, or daily life. It is, however, impossible to sufficiently comprehend Martin Luther or the developments of his Reformation and appreciate them within their historical context without devoting due attention to the prevalent economic circumstances on the eve of the sixteenth century. It is equally impossible to comprehend economic processes without understanding the prevailing religious and cultural indicators. The division of different aspects and spheres of individuals and their actions and values (mentality, spirituality, political outlook, world view) is also virtually inconceivable. This is vividly illustrated by the example of Martin Luther himself.

The devotional practices during medieval times (i.e., the centuries prior to the Reformation) had not made a clear distinction between sacred and secular issues. The divine-mystical aspects of religion constantly spilled over into secular life. The separation between church and state and between secular life on the one hand and religious practice and emotion on the other, as subsequently emphasized by Luther's followers and various forms of Protestant doctrine, was largely unfamiliar to the medieval church. With slight exaggeration, it could be said that after 1517, Protestant theologians by calling for a return to introspection and constant self-reflection had genuinely destroyed people's pleasure in believing in miracles, the veneration of saints, and other forms of enchantment. Certain variants of the Protestant doctrine, such as the Scottish Presbyterianism of the seventeenth century and the Calvinism prevalent in Swiss towns, were in many respects far more unworldly and pleasure-denying than the traditional Catholic forms of religious practice ever had been. The world of the ancient church had been full of miracles as an expression of divine will and work. Images of saints and the mortal remains of martyrs were venerated, the latter giving rise to a remarkable commercialization of these practices through the exorbitant trading value which holy relics enjoyed. High prices were paid to obtain these objects, since the sites of venerated relics customarily also attracted great flocks of pilgrims. The greater the prominence of the saint, the greater would be the attraction of the respective places of pilgrimage. The fact that these customs also gave rise to improper business practices and that more physical relics were circulating in Europe during the late Medieval Ages than the sheer bodily mass of saints that were known to exist would permit, provides evidence not only of the criminal energy of counterfeiters and dealers in stolen goods, but also of the intensity of demand for this type of divine relic: the market was virtually insatiable.

People were united in their fear of eternal damnation; many, therefore, undertook pilgrimages and venerated these icons. Magnificent crucifixes and monstrances in cathedrals and monastery churches were as much a part of everyday life and experience within the Christian faith as the purchase of indulgences (fig. 1). The latter took the form of small written notes or indulgence cards promising the believer a form of redemption in the reduction of the time spent in purgatory.[3] It was even possible to purchase indulgences for already deceased individuals—those who had not been able to obtain their own reduction of suffering in purgatory in time or in sufficient

Fig. 1 Indulgence chest, beginning of the sixteenth century. Tradition has it that it was used by the Dominican monk and
        indulgence preacher Johann Tetzel to secure the money from his sale of indulgences.

quantity or through carelessness. Great benefits were seen in the collection of these relics and their public manifestation, displayed in a pilgrim chapel for arriving believers to see and admire, for example. These benefits were not purely religious: pilgrimages were one of the most substantial sources of economic surplus of their time and an important source of income for cities and rulers, that is, the owners and providers of the relevant holy images and relics. Today we might call it religious tourism. Payment for food, board, and lodging by arriving and departing pilgrims from all corners of Germany financed the surrounding regional economies, generating a not insignificant demand for everyday goods far exceeding the normal quantities produced for the relevant region. Elector Frederick the Wise, contemporary and protector of Luther, who during his life never actually relinquished his confessions of faith for the old church nonetheless held a high opinion of his churchman from Wittenberg—the town where one of the newest and upcoming universities in the empire was situated—and remained utterly convinced of his political and religious clout, was himself the owner of one of the greatest collections of treasures of his time (fig. 2). The

collection, held in the Castle Church of his electoral residence in Wittenberg, consisted of thousands of precisely documented relics as well as objects necessary for the maintenance of these resources, such as wax candles, which were expensive but indispensable for church rituals and liturgy. The large mining towns of this period, in the Saxon Erzgebirge region, where the silver mines were bountiful, employed large numbers of nonlocal cutters and mineworkers who also had to be supervised in prayer and church services. The location and scope of a pilgrimage, or even the veneration of relics taking place within the Saxon electoral principalities, had a substantial influence on princely and regional politics of development and, in addition, shaped the economic activity and wealth of emerging states and regional temporal authorities.

1 On the Reformation, its origins, development, and consequences, see the standard works: Cameron, *European Reformation*; MacCulloch, *Reformation*; Rublack, *Reformation Europe*; Kaufmann, *Geschichte*; Ehrenpreis/Lotz-Heumann, *Reformation*. **2** Most recently: Rössner, *Martin Luther*; id., *Burying Money*; id., *Ökonom*. **3** Id., *Martin Luther*.

Fig. 2 Georg Spalatin/Lucas Cranach the Elder (woodcuts),
Dye zaigung des hochlobwirdigen hailigthums der Stifftkirchen
aller hailigen zu wittenburg (Wittenberger Heiltumsbuch / Wittenberg
Book of Relics), Wittenberg 1509. The Wittenberg Book of Relics
was commissioned by Prince Elector Frederick the Wise.
It illustrates the mass of reliquaries in his relic collection.

The Critique of Indulgences and Church Life

Historians dispute whether the cut-off date of the years around 1500 separating the Middle Ages from the early modern period is possible or sensible at all—whether the lack of significant upheavals or change questions the labeling of this period as the dawn of a "new era." It is dubious to search for periods of transformation and upheaval in eras when humans and their everyday lives have continued virtually unchanged for many years and even centuries. Nevertheless, with his Reformation, Luther did actually create something radically different, particularly through his theses of 1517 regarding indulgences. He reformed the practice of medieval piety, but thereby simultaneously created new long-term structures and tendencies within the field of economics that had never been seen before in these forms and that

at the same time decisively benefitted education and the growth of modern states and market economy.[4] This transformation was particularly embedded within the separation of church and state and the desacralization of everyday life.

The reformers chiefly focused their repudiation on the overloading of contemporary ritual with materialism. Incense, precious chalices, chandeliers and monstrances, crucifixes encrusted with jewels, and magnificent altar cloths were all virtually banned in Protestant Churches after 1517 (fig. 3). Pilgrimages became rare in reformed areas as they were not seen as beneficial for salvation and were occasionally even regarded as the work of the devil. The Word formed the core of Lutheran-Protestant doctrine and religious practice.[5] The exclusive path to the Word of God—and therefore also to salvation—was the Bible (sola scriptura) and the purely personal relationship between the individual and God (sola fide). All individuals stood equal before God. Luther particularly directed his criticism at the practice of indulgences. Purgatory was an innovation developed by the papal curia dating back to the thirteenth century as an intermediate world between heaven and hell, where the poor souls of sinners arrived after death.[6] According to contemporaneous belief, human souls traveled either up to heaven or down to hell after this cleansing fire, depending on their conduct during their lives on earth. It was possible to shorten the time in purgatory through certain pious deeds and the resulting indulgences awarded. The letters of indulgence were distributed by the local monastery, church, or abbey. The indulgence privilege or certificate normally issued by the Pope stipulated that the individual's time to be spent in purgatory was to be reduced by the number of days or years stated on the indulgence bill. Such indulgences were tied to a specific location, usually a church or chapel. A sort of administrative fee was charged to the receiver of the indulgence note for the grace of indulgence, customarily a small sum that would not financially overtax believers.[7]

It was this practice that provided the impetus for the Reformation. The majority of theologians during the late-medieval period were able to make a clear distinction between indulgences and the individual temporal punishment of sin. Only God could forgive sins, but indulgences could reduce the additional repentance practices imposed alongside penitence. Moreover, the "price" of indulgences was not monetarily quantified but graded according to "social tariffs,"[8] meaning that theoretically anyone could afford an indulgence—the richer you were the more you had to pay (but this could also mean, by the same token, that the richer you were the more days off purgatory you were able to afford). This could explain the popularity of indulgences, which reached unprecedented heights around 1500.

A new interpretation had, however, emerged by 1475 at the latest with the pontifical public announcement of the jubilee plenary indulgence, which clearly ran counter to academic theological interpretation. This was, however, countenanced by the church, as an increased need for financial resources also played a role here; the church was the greatest multinational corporation of its time. The announcement of the indulgence campaign in 1475 covered not only living persons but also the deceased. Flocks of legates and papal agents made their way across Europe to praise the new source of sal-

Fig. 3 Sacrament monstrance from the Halberstadt Cathedral Treasury, Germany, 2nd quarter of the fifteenth century

vation in this jubilee indulgence.[9] In 1516, Johann Tetzel, the famous "indulgence seller" of the archbishop of Mainz and bishop of Magdeburg and Halberstadt, Cardinal Albert, advertised in Central Germany with the rhyming couplet: "As soon as a coin in the coffer rings, the soul from purgatory springs."[10] This constituted a perilous extension of the original theological concept of indulgences, as Tetzel was hereby clearly implying that salvation could be directly purchased, making redundant the good deeds of repentance that were the actual focal point. Huge sums of money consequently poured into the monasteries, churches, and abbeys. Fired up and inspired by the gigantic pan-European indulgence campaigns, large swaths of the population came to believe that salvation of the soul was for sale. The parties profiting from indulgences did nothing to dispel this skewed interpretation of indulgence theory. Cardinal Albert, who had purchased his electorship as the Archbishop of Mainz with the aid of the indulgence money collected under his auspices, saw no reason to act, as he himself was ultimately one of the profiteers. In contrast, the overwhelming majority of the population in villages and towns already neglected the practice of prayer and penitence and were not well-versed in the Bible and complex church doctrine. A widespread belief in witches, magicians, and magic was still prevalent, along with a general lack of interest in the Christian way of life and religious practice. There is substantial evidence that a large proportion of the population were what we would today call functional atheists; the borders between superstition and atheism and between ecclesiastical practice and Christian belief were at this time perhaps as fluid and indeterminate as today. Since there was, however, a residual insecurity regarding what would happen after one's death, the church of that time occupied a much more significant and central role in the life of society than is imaginable in the Northwestern Europe of today.[11] Human beings have at all times been receptive to an adherence to the essential precepts of a Christian ecclesiastical life and the simplification of the uncomfortable practice of self-reflection.

Luther was offended by these practices but not fundamentally so, at first, by the principle of indulgences, which he only completely abandoned around 1530. His doctrine was based on the conviction that the form of indulgence practiced in his time was false. His initial issue focused on the perversion of paying for the salvation of the soul—the amalgamation of religion and economics.

4 Recently: Gregory, *Unintended Reformation*. 5 Barth, *Theologie*; Beutel, *Luther-Handbuch*. 6 Le Goff, *Wucherzins*. 7 Moeller, *Ablaßkampagnen*. 8 See ibid. 9 Tewes, *Kurie*. 10 This paragraph partly follows the text in Rössner, *Ökonom*. 11 In this respect, central and northwest Europe represent a special region; there is no other part of the world after 1950 where atheist values have been displayed on such a wide scale, fundamentally affecting everyday life, the political world, and the actions of the population—for example religious freedom within the public sphere guaranteed by many nations under basic law or the constitution. Several researchers—such as Gregory, *Unintended Reformation*—identify the origins of this desacralization in Martin Luther's Reformation. Through the separation of church and state and the two kingdoms doctrine, Luther paved the intellectual and academic way for these developments— an irony of history? This is clearly a direction that was surely never intended by the great Reformer.

The Economic Background of Luther's Thought

Luther was not born into a farming household as suggested in his later self-stylization. His father had amassed wealth as a copper-mining entrepreneur in the county of Mansfeld (one of the smaller territories in the early sixteenth-century Holy Roman Empire or "Germany"), leaving a considerable fortune that consisted of goods worth at least 1,250 Rhenish guilders. Luther's key experience of a lightning strike prompted his entry into a monastery in 1505 and subsequently his work as a theologian. In the Augustinian monastery in Erfurt, Luther not only experienced the harsh everyday life of a monk, but also the financial purchasing power of a monastic treasure the volume of which had greatly increased through the sale of indulgences, endowments, requiems, and other donations. As a mendicant, he was presumably familiar with the subsequent practice of collecting money. His journey to Rome in 1510/11 alerted his attention to the wealth flowing into the Holy City from central Europe. Luther considered the almost mechanical rhythm of the constant, virtually obsessive repetition of devotional prayers to be cold, soulless, and not conducive to the salvation of the soul.[12] In Wittenberg, Luther's sphere of activity from 1512 on, where Elector Frederick the Wise had amassed one of the most substantial collections of relics of the time in his Castle Church, consisting of almost 19,000 individual pieces, almost 41,000 candles had been used for liturgical purposes alone in the year 1512. The corresponding volume of sixty-six tons of wax valued at 1,112 Rhenish florins would have been sufficient to purchase four or five typical rural homesteads. This was where Luther became familiar with the material excess of contemporary ritual, which he would subsequently oppose with great vehemence.

Luther spent his childhood and youth in the county of Mansfeld, a mining region in Saxon Thuringia.[13] He would later become an active reformer in Wittenberg. The town was like most other regions in the principality situated in a thoroughly agrarian landscape. Luther was therefore familiar with both sides of economic life in his time: the dominant rural economy as well as the processes of structural transformation and commercialization that had been prevalent in the Saxon-Thuringian mining region since 1470. An above-average proportion of the population in mining regions was dependent on the supply of foodstuffs. Places such as Falkenstein in Tyrol and Annaberg in the Saxon Erzgebirge mountains expanded virtually overnight from villages to large towns during the silver boom of the 1470s and 1480s. The population of Annaberg literally exploded between 1470 and 1490 from a population of a few hundred to, at its height, nine thousand, thereby developing into the largest Saxon town. It was far ahead of the former commercial center of Leipzig or the princely centers of residence with magnificent castles such as Dresden, Torgau, and Wittenberg. At the toll post of Borna (near Leipzig), around 3,500 wagons loaded with around 8,000 kilos of cereals pulled by approximately 14,000 horses were registered as having passed through in 1525 alone.[14] These deliveries were intended for the miners and their families working in the ore-mining sector in the Erzgebirge. The cereals chiefly originated from localities in the agrarian regions of Saxony, such as Wittenberg. This vol-ume of cereals would have been sufficient to feed a non-farming population of at least forty thousand persons, in other words, the population of four or five large towns in Saxony of this period. Due to peasants' revolts and the silver-mining depression, 1525 was a year of crisis; during times of greatest productivity in silver mining, the quantities mentioned above would have been substantially greater.

The volume of mined silver was, however, subject to dramatic annual fluctuation. Figures document an increase from almost seven to nearly nineteen tons of raw silver between 1470 and 1475 alone (an increase of 170 percent). Production fell again in 1480 to twelve tons and during the decade of the 1490s dropped to the paltry annual figure of one ton.

Measured in five-year averages, the volume of silver mined between 1470 and 1500 decreased by over half. The former peaks in production were not achieved again until 1535, with a figure of almost nineteen tons. Temporary compensation was provided by the numerous *saiger* huts (i.e. refineries or smelting huts for the separating of copper and silver using lead) established in the Thuringian Forest during the beginning of the crisis around 1480. This refining process transformed the mined silver-bearing copper ore into pure copper or anode copper and silver through the addition of lead, a vital ingredient that was largely imported from England and Poland. The production potential of these mining works soared during the highest growth period of 1525/30 to around five annual tons, thereby falling far short of the previous peak values achieved in mining operations in the Erzgebirge.[15]

The *saiger* industry was therefore not in a position to compensate for the drop in production volume in the silver-mining sector (Erzgebirge and Tyrol) during the crisis between around 1490 to 1530. In the course of normal mining work, individual miners entered the mines equipped with their own relatively primitive tools, whereas the *saiger* industry was based on far larger operational entities. More capital was required to finance the workers' pay, the fuel, and the refineries themselves in addition to the maintenance of the individual *saiger* furnaces. The copper and silver produced could be sold profitably in African markets (copper) and markets in the Indian Ocean (silver for the purchase of spices). The necessary volume of investment exceeded the reserves of the local entrepreneurs. Borrowed capital came from Nuremberg or Augsburg and later increasingly from Central Germany itself. In China, silver as measured in gold units (a customary comparative figure used by economic historians to calculate global price differentials for silver) was double the value compared with prices in central and Northwestern Europe.[16] The shipment of silver to Asia alone brought the mercantile companies a minimum arbitrage profit of 100 percent! This was augmented by profits from the sale of spices on the European market, which had been acquired in an exchange of goods. Discourses that focused on the Upper German wholesalers and their profit margins and practices, which were considered unlawful, subsequently dominated the debates at the Diets in the early 1520s—parallel to the *causa Lutheri*. The central German mining region was firmly integrated into the structures of the beginning world economy or early globalization in the sixteenth century.

Luther was involved in these structural transformation processes in mining areas and greatly familiar with contemporary attempts to form cartels or monopolies within this "industry." Since the middle of the 1530s, the smelting works and mines in Mansfeld had increasingly been taken over and managed in-house by the counts of Mansfeld. These noble men already owned most of the copper shale mines and neighboring smelting works. They cooperated with the larger *saiger*/trade consortiums to accelerate the concentration of economic processes on the copper market. Since the late 1520s, this had been accompanied by attempts to form cartels, which can be understood as a reaction to the deteriorating situation of the *saiger* industry on the global copper and silver market. There was an increasing influx of American silver, which progressively weakened the profitability of the central European silver industry. In the 1530s and 1540s, Martin Luther was personally involved as a consultant within these restructuring processes on repeated occasions. His expertise was based on his reputation as a public figure who enjoyed a certain degree of prominence, his being well-versed in legal and economic issues, and the fact that he was intimately familiar with the economic structures of the Mansfeld mining industry due to his origins and family background.[17]

On the strength of his studies in Law and, since 1505 Theology, he was thoroughly conversant with all contemporary major economic authors, since economic treatises were during this period almost exclusively written by theologians and lawyers. He possessed additional knowledge of mining in the Mansfeld region and the restructuring processes of the 1530s. One can therefore be certain that the assumption that Luther lacked knowledge and interest in economic issues which is frequently presented within the field of traditional research belongs to the realms of myth. On the contrary, Luther concerned himself directly with economic matters.[18] As demonstrated below, it is also possible to provide evidence of certain connections between the field of economics and Luther's new interpretation of the Holy Scripture, which were of great significance for the shaping and dissemination of the Reformation.

Economic and Social History of the Reformation

Initially, the Reformation was slow in altering the religious opinions of the faithful. People after 1517 were most likely to have been hardly less pious or superstitious than their ancestors. In addition, the late-medieval church was not in the middle of a crisis, as is frequently asserted in older research literature and especially emphasized in Protestant historiography. On the contrary, an intense increase in popular piety could be observed around 1500. The traditional church and its opportunities for salvation were seen as more attractive than ever before. Luther's criticism of indulgences was in a certain sense a minority opinion. There are numerous conceivable connectors between his "new" concepts (which were actually not really new, as the criticism of indulgences had been expressed as far back as the fourteenth century) and the contemporary economic situation, which would explain particularly well why his doctrine regarding biblical scripture found increasing resonance in the population after 1517.

Fig. 4 Double Guldengroschen struck in commemoration of Frederick the Wise's entitlement to general vice-regent, Nuremberg, 1512

It is possible that the surge of popular and indulgence piety was fueled by the growth in importance of central European silver mining between 1470 and 1490/1500. Toward the end of the fifteenth century, silver mines in Tyrol, the Erzgebirge in Saxony, and Bohemia and Upper Hungary (now Slovakia) were producing more than ever before. This resulted in the circulation of money on the market in the form of silver coins (fig. 4). The new coins, called thaler, ultimately gave the dollar its name.[19] After 1490/1500, there was a slump in the silver-mining industry. Coins in general deteriorated in value and in particular the small pfennig and groschen of the "man in the street." A large proportion of mined silver and coins was exported overseas from Central Germany, frequently to the distant lands of India and China. The growing German population was faced with progressively less money for additional expenditure. There is copious evidence of diverse complaints on the shortage of silver and ready cash, particularly as a large proportion of the population suffered the economic consequences of the devalued coins.[20] Even Luther wrote about the subject of the large trade fairs in Frankfurt, the supreme financial, monetary, and trading hub of his time, calling them the "silver and gold sink" from which everything

12 Brecht, *Martin Luther*, pp. 71f. **13** Specifically on Luther's social and economic context: Westermann, *Konzentrationsprozeß*. **14** Straube, *Nahrungsmittelbedarf*; id., *Notwendigkeiten*. **15** The latest figures can be found in Blanchard, *Economy*, Ch. 1, and extensive tables in Munro, *Monetary Origins*. **16** Flynn/Giráldez, *Global Economic History*. **17** See Rössner, *Commerce*, introduction. **18** See literature listed in footnote 2. **19** On monetary dimensions of the Reformation: Rössner, *Deflation*. **20** Ibid., Ch. IV.

"creeps and flies."[21] The topic of usurers who charged interest of up to 40 percent and more cropped up in a number of his texts. In a passage from his major economic volume *On Commerce and Usury (Von Kauffshandlung vnd Wucher,* 1524), he reports on the nationwide shortage of money and that "there are debts everywhere and no money, that all lands and cities are burdened with *interest* payments and milked dry by usury."[22] In correspondence to his wife, Katharina, around 1540, he wrote: "We were unable to get one penny in change at court, just as you cannot get any in Wittenberg."[23] The scarcity of cash with full value was a familiar social and economic problem during this period. Coin conflicts, that is, disputes over the correct exchange rate of small coins, were a frequent topic in debates and the cause of late-medieval riots in both urban and rural areas. This culminated in the Great Peasants' War of 1524/25—and the value of small change was still a sensitive subject right up to the beginning of the nineteenth century. Economic affairs in Central Germany during the decades before and after 1517 were far from good in numerous aspects, although one cannot talk of economic contexts to the extent that is customary today.

The last large-scale indulgence campaigns (1503–14) were an even greater burden on the purses of citizens and farmers and must be viewed as a critical economic factor. This despite the fact that they have, in the meantime, been described by historians as an "insurance against purgatory," which helped to ease people's consciences in an age of anxiety and possibly serving an important and reassuring psychological function. Within this context, Luther with his new doctrine certainly had his finger firmly on the pulse of the time.

Economic Results of the Reformation

It would be presumptuous to imply that the shortage situation had a direct influence on Luther's religious doctrine. His new interpretation of the Holy Scripture and Christian practice was surely not, or at least not exclusively, driven by economics. In fact economics probably remained firmly in the background of Luther's deliberations. What is significant, however, is that these economic problems did exist, and many people had personal experiences of economic shortages. Importantly this situation was the ground in which Luther's doctrine was sown. Luther and his contemporary reformers were dependent on gaining the maximum number of followers for their new theories and doctrines. Contemporary circumstances ensured that a progressively increasing number of individuals viewed his teachings to be rightful and correct, and felt that these were better adapted to the current situation than traditional practices.[24] Luther's doctrine of Christian freedom for example, was eagerly heard by bonded peasants. The doctrine concerning the falsity and corruption of the papacy fell on fertile ground in larger free imperial towns such as Nuremberg, which were characterized by an emerging class of citizens and a large sector of market-oriented skilled craftsmen. In these towns, goods were produced for and also consumed via the "market." These social classes were also the most receptive to the idea of dissolving monasteries and secularizing ancient sacred treasures. This would result in the transfer of these properties and collections

Fig. 5 The coin hoard from Naumburg: 498 coins, struck between 1470/71 and 1562, Naumburg excavation, Kleine Jakobgasse

to higher authorities and their subsequent transformation into "state property." Certain authorities including the council in the city of Constance took advantage of the introduction of reformed structures during the 1520s and 1530s to consolidate their municipal finances with the treasure from the dissolved monasteries and convents within the city walls. The local lords used the income from the sale of chalices and monstrances for the salaries of pastors, financing soldiers and other public expenditures in their newly acquired role defined by Luther and the other reformers as the protectors of public and consequently divine order.[25]

The separation of religious capital (redemption through indulgences, for example) and economic and/or financial capital by Luther and other reformers created greater and more extensive economic latitudes. In areas where the Reformation had already been introduced, monasteries, churches, and abbeys no longer had use for their chalices of gold and silver, crucifixes, and monstrances. The fact that the common man no longer had to pay extortionate sums for indulgences and other forms of ritual within the framework of his active Christian life alongside all his other everyday expenses had the effect of releasing additional money into the economic cycle. Even if each person's savings were fairly modest, the huge number of individuals involved did make a difference. This is above all a quantitative law. In a world with low wages, a lower life expectancy, almost no existing opportunities for growth, and a depressingly low level of investment that in good times would be sufficient for the retrieval of scarce resources but not for sustainable investment (i.e., that would exceed the amortization of the depreciating asset), even small sums of money that suddenly become available will be noticeable in the long term. In places where the majority of people are frequently threatened by poverty, hunger, and destitution and are only just able to cover the costs of everyday life, often from their own paltry resources, the effects of newly available, albeit small, amounts of money should not be underestimated.

Luther's new doctrine forbidding indulgences, the discontinuation of pilgrimages and of the veneration of saints made small sums of money available that, in the long term, assumed an unprecedented magnitude in scale. According to Luther's and other reformers' teachings, people no longer had to pay for the salvation of their souls with money. All that they had been scrimping and saving for could now be employed for economic purposes (fig. 5). Luther would perhaps have taken great pleasure in the concepts of the renowned British economist John Maynard Keynes, whose teachings still retain a certain degree of relevance for modern economic activities, particularly in times of crisis. The struggle against indulgences is certainly one of the most attractive sections of Luther's new doctrine, and this was where he found a wide and responsive audience, even in the "old" or "Catholic" church, which ultimately forbade the sale of indulgences in 1570.

Luther's opinions were therefore not new; reformers had existed long before his time with similar views of the papacy and sale of indulgences (such as Jan Hus, who had been active around 1400). His opinions were however imbedded in the contemporary climate of economic and monetary shortage. The results engendered a religious and cultural transformation of manifest consequences, which could be directly traced back to Luther's Reformation. What is more, although substantial parts of the Holy Roman Empire and the rest of Europe remained loyal to the old faith, even Catholic areas absorbed several significant elements of Luther's new doctrine after 1517. The Catholic Church also underwent a later Reformation process, chiefly toward the end of the sixteenth century and over the course of the seventeenth century. It would also relinquish the practice of indulgences after 1560. Religion as a denominational and cultural practice and the field of economics have a lot in common. Seen from this aspect, Luther made a significant contribution to the development of modern worlds and modern capitalism. This was without doubt not his intent nor would he have been able to anticipate this. But the economic origins and consequences of his Reformation cannot be dismissed nor overlooked.

21 Rössner, *Commerce.* **22** Ibid. **23** *LW* 50, 212–217, esp. 214. **24** This is not uncommon. Nowadays, Protestant or Lutheran Christians would surely no longer associate themselves with forms of confession such as that of the German Christians' movement with National Socialism (1933–45). Practices and declarations of faith on the one hand and religious belief on the other hand must be distinguished from one another. And even if religion and economics display *per se* few common factors or reciprocal influential areas (*pro forma* and *prima facie*, the former and the latter have nothing whatsoever to do with each other), this is a completely different case in the specific forms and practices of religious conviction: these can indeed be motivated by "daily politics" or economic factors or connected in some form with "everyday" circumstances, i.e., be reciprocally influenced. **25** For Constance see e.g., Heuschen, *Reformation*, pp. 55–59.

BIBLIOGRAPHY

Barth, Hans-Martin (2009), *Die Theologie Martin Luthers. Eine kritische Würdigung.* Gütersloh. **Beutel**, Albrecht (ed.) (2010), *Luther-Handbuch.* 2nd ed. Tübingen. **Blanchard**, Ian (2009), *The International Economy in the "Age of the Discoveries," 1470–1570. Antwerp and the English Merchants' World.* Stuttgart. **Brecht**, Martin (2013), *Martin Luther. Vol. 1: Sein Weg zur Reformation: 1483–1521.* 3rd ed. Stuttgart. **Cameron**, Euan (2012), *The European Reformation.* 2nd ed. Oxford/New York. **Ehrenpreis**, Stefan/**Lotz-Heumann**, Ute (2008), *Reformation und konfessionelles Zeitalter.* 2nd ed. Darmstadt. **Flynn**, Dennis O./**Giráldez**, Arturo (2002), Conceptualizing Global Economic History: The Role of Silver. In: Gömmel, Rainer/Denzel, Markus A. (eds.), *Weltwirtschaft und Wirtschaftsordnung. Festschrift für Jürgen Schneider zum 65. Geburtstag.* Stuttgart, pp. 101–114. **Gregory**, Brad S. (2012), *The Unintended Reformation: How a Religious Revolution Secularized Society.* Cambridge/Mass. **Heuschen**, Diethelm (1969), *Reformation, Schmalkaldischer Bund und Österreich in ihrer Bedeutung für die Finanzen der Stadt Konstanz 1499–1648.* Tübingen/Basel. **Kaufmann**, Thomas (2009), *Geschichte der Reformation.* Frankfurt am Main/Leipzig. **Knape**, Rosemarie (ed.) (2000), *Martin Luther und der Bergbau im Mansfelder Land. Aufsätze.* Lutherstadt Eisleben. **Le Goff**, Jacques (1988), *Wucherzins und Höllenqualen. Ökonomie und Religion im Mittelalter.* Stuttgart. **MacCulloch**, Diarmaid (2003), *Reformation. Europe's House Divided 1490–1700.* London et al. **Moeller**, Bernd (1989), Die letzten Ablaßkampagnen: Der Widerspruch Luthers gegen den Ablaß in seinem geschichtlichen Zusammenhang. In: Boockmann, Hartmut (ed.), *Lebenslehren und Weltentwürfe im Übergang vom Mittelalter zur Neuzeit: Politik–Bildung–Naturkunde–Theologie. Bericht über Kolloquien der Kommission zur Erforschung der Kultur des Spätmittelalters* 1983 bis 1987. Göttingen, pp. 539–567. **Munro**, John (2003), The Monetary Origins of the 'Price Revolution.' In: Flynn, Dennis O./Giráldez, Arturo/Glahn, Richard von (eds.), *Global Connections and Monetary History, 1470–1800.* Aldershot/Burlington, pp. 1–34. **Rössner**, Philipp Robinson (2012), *Deflation—Devaluation—Rebellion. Geld im Zeitalter der Reformation.* Stuttgart. **Rössner**, Philipp Robinson (2015), Luther—Ein tüchtiger Ökonom? Über die monetären Ursprünge der Deutschen Reformation. In: *Zeitschrift für Historische Forschung*, vol. 42, no. 1, pp. 37–74. **Rössner**, Philipp Robinson (2015), *Martin Luther on Commerce and Usury.* London/New York. **Rössner**, Philipp Robinson (2016), Burying Money? The Monetary Origins of Luther's Reformation, History of Political Economy. In: *History of Political Economy* (in print). **Rublack**, Ulinka (2004), *Reformation Europe.* London et al. **Straube**, Manfred (1997), Notwendigkeiten, Umfang und Herkunft von Nahrungsmittellieferungen in das sächsische Erzgebirge zu Beginn des 16. Jahrhunderts. In: Westermann, Ekkehard (ed.), *Bergbaureviere als Verbrauchszentren im vorindustriellen Europa. Fallstudien zu Beschaffung und Verbrauch von Lebensmitteln sowie Roh- und Hilfsstoffen (13.–18. Jahrhundert).* Stuttgart, pp. 203–221. **Straube**, Manfred (1987), Nahrungsmittelbedarf, Nahrungsmittelproduktion und Nahrungsmittelhandel im thüringisch-sächsischen Raum zu Beginn des 16. Jahrhunderts. In: Ebner, Herwig (ed.), *Festschrift Othmar Pickl zum 60. Geburtstag.* Graz/Wien, pp. 579–588. **Tewes**, Götz-Rüdiger (2001), *Die römische Kurie und die deutschen Länder am Vorabend der Reformation.* Tübingen. **Westermann**, Ekkehard (2000), Der wirtschaftliche Konzentrationsprozess im Mansfelder Revier und seine Auswirkungen auf Martin Luther, seine Verwandte und Freunde. In: Knape, Rosemarie (ed.): *Martin Luther und der Bergbau im Mansfelder Land. Aufsätze.* Lutherstadt Eisleben, pp. 63–92.

MONEY STORIES

After the discovery of America, trade was spurred by precious metal imports from the territories conquered by the Spanish. Around 1500, there were about 500 mints in the Holy Roman Empire. Stock exchanges and lending banks began to form. The Fuggers, with their fortune of five million thalers, organized the papal cash flow from the European dioceses to Rome, lending money and sponsoring the Swiss Guard.

Crop failures, inflation and price increases led to social unrest. The hardship heightened apocalyptic expectations among the population; the sale of indulgences flourished. Part of the money obtained by indulgences was used for the construction of the Basilica of Saint Peter in Rome. Indulgences used for the construction of buildings were nothing new; hospitals and churches had been financed this way before.

THE SALE OF INDULGENCES UNDER CARDINAL ALBERT OF BRANDENBURG

LIABILITIES

I. Lending business
Albert of Brandenburg borrows several ten thousand guilders from the Fuggers' banking business.

II. Agreement
Against payment, the Pope made Albert of Brandenburg the ruler of several dioceses. The Pope authorized Albert to organize the sale of indulgences in his territories.

III. Debt settlement
With the revenue from indulgences Albert pays off his debts to the Fuggers.

BANK → CARDINAL ALBERT OF BRANDENBURG

CARDINAL ALBERT OF BRANDENBURG → POPE

CARDINAL ALBERT OF BRANDENBURG → BANK

TRADE

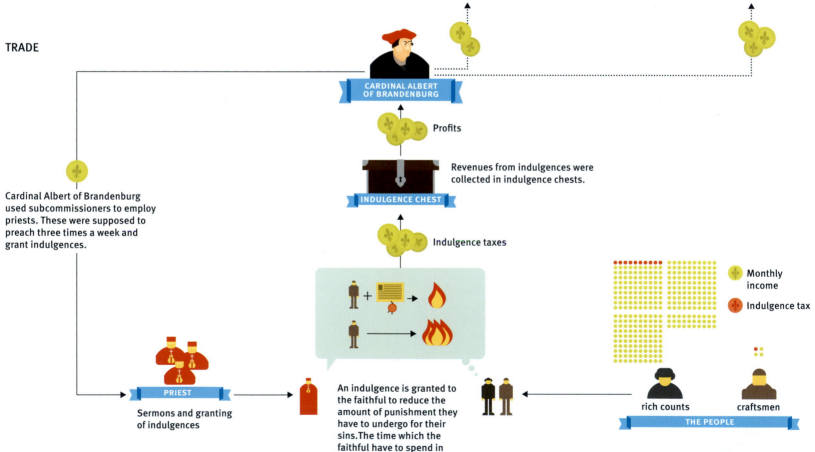

CARDINAL ALBERT OF BRANDENBURG

Profits

Revenues from indulgences were collected in indulgence chests.

INDULGENCE CHEST

Indulgence taxes

Cardinal Albert of Brandenburg used subcommissioners to employ priests. These were supposed to preach three times a week and grant indulgences.

PRIEST

Sermons and granting of indulgences

An indulgence is granted to the faithful to reduce the amount of punishment they have to undergo for their sins. The time which the faithful have to spend in Purgatory is thus shortened.

rich counts   craftsmen

THE PEOPLE

○ Monthly income
● Indulgence tax

HANSJÖRG KÜSTER

Landscape Usage in Mansfeld Land

Mansfeld Land: A Geographical Orientation

Mansfeld Land, the region where Martin Luther was born in 1483 (figs. 1 and 2), lies on the margins of the Harz Mountains—an extensive low mountain range in Germany. The summit of the Harz—the Brocken—is the tallest peak in Northern Germany, with a height of 1,141 meters (3,743 ft.). The Harz range is composed mainly of old basement rock interspersed with numerous veins of ore. Mining has been carried out here for centuries, and in some places for millennia. In times past and along with the Erzgebirge (meaning "ore mountains"), the Harz was among the most important mining regions on earth.

On the periphery of the Harz range, the landscape is characterized by considerable contrasts. In the west and north, the mountain range rises several hundred meters above the surrounding area, which is a low-lying, rolling countryside ranging from nearly flat to slightly hilly. In the east and south, the Harz recedes more gradually into the surrounding landscape, though the boundary of the range can be readily discerned here too. The upper Harz is one of the regions with the highest precipitation in Central Europe, while the area directly to the east is one of the driest far and wide. This "central-German dry zone," which includes Mansfeld Land, lies in the rain shadow of the Harz Mountains.

The soil in the Harz region is generally rocky and of low fertility; agriculture is only possible in a few locations. In contrast, the bordering regions are some of the most fertile of Central Europe, since a large quantity of loess was deposited there during the last ice age. This fine dust was blown out of the glacial forefields, to be deposited again at the edge of or between the mountain ranges. The loess regions at the northern edge of the range are referred to as *Börde* (fertile plain) landscapes: the Hildesheim and Magdeburg Börden border the Harz Mountains. Particularly in Southern Germany, loess zones between mountain ranges are referred to as "Gäu" or "Gau." This designation, however, is sometimes also found in Northern Germany, one example being the "Ambergau" around the town of Bockenem on the western edge of the Harz region. Loess deposits in the depressions between mountain ranges are referred to as "intermontane loess." Actually, the fine dust was also deposited on the higher areas of the mountains but was gradually eroded by rain and brought down the valleys by streams in the subsequent millennia. This so-called alluvial loess would then be deposited downstream at a point where the current was no longer strong enough to transport it further. In many places the loess on sloping valley sides and hills was also eroded as the streams dug deeper into the bedrock, deepening the valleys over the course of the last several thousand years.

Mansfeld Land is one of the loess regions skirting the Harz Mountains and borders the Magdeburg Börde to the north. The loess, which is the basis for several areas of rich black topsoil in this district, contains a large array of minerals necessary for plant growth. Loess topsoil can be readily cultivated with hoes, plows, and other farm implements, as it contains no stones. The requisite conditions for agriculture have thus been present, and indeed optimal, in Mansfeld Land and other regions bordering the Harz for millennia. Due to intensive agricultural use, however, the loess regions have been largely deforested, while the Harz itself and several other low mountain ranges in the vicinity remain covered in forests. This has the effect of further accentuating the contrast in landscape between the Harz Mountains and the surrounding area.

History of Cultivation and Land Use

As far back as the early Neolithic period, in the sixth millenium B.C.E., the loess-rich soils around the Harz Mountains were being used for farming, but not permanently. Time and again forests would be cleared—the wood was required for constructing houses, making implements, and as a source of energy. The deforested areas could be cultivated with crops. In the summer the farmers kept watch over their fields, while in the other seasons they watched their provisions. For this reason it was necessary to have enduring settlements in the vicinity of the fields. As a rule these settlements arose on the perimeter of areas upon which the loess deposits had formed: on the so-called loess plateaus between the river valleys. The settlements can be alternatively described as being located on the edges of valleys. Above the settlements the fields extended out across the stone-free, loess-rich clearings. Beneath the farmsteads the animals could graze, as they had free access to the water in the streams and could easily be herded.[1]

1 Küster, *Landschaft*.

Again and again archaeologists studying the remains of such settlements have determined that they were abandoned (and presumably relocated) after a period of decades or, at most, centuries. Thus, these settlements can always be associated with one or a few consecutive eras in prehistory. It is not easy to identify the reason for the abandonment and relocation of the settlements, but it seems certain that the fulfillment of some prerequisite for their continued existence must have been no longer available. The agricultural yields may have begun to wane, though this is unlikely due to the great fertility of the loess topsoil. It is possible that, after a number of decades, the vicinity of the settlement had been stripped of the wood necessary for the construction and repair of huts. Since open fires were made in the wooden huts, it was not uncommon for these structures to burn down. When fresh wood was needed, it could either be transported from ever-greater distances, or a new settlement could be founded at a spot where wood was more plentiful.[2] Upon abandonment, new forests grew on the areas previously occupied by the settlements and agricultural holdings.

This mode of settlement and land use was the dominant system across broad tracts of Europe for thousands of years. It was not until the early Middle Ages that the settlements achieved greater stability, which also meant that at any appropriate location various different forms of land use were pursued: agriculture, animal husbandry, and forest exploitation. Areas where wood was harvested and where animals grazed were not clearly separated from each other. The wooded areas enclosed the core tracts of fields and served as common lands that could be used by anyone. This was where the herdsmen herded their livestock, and where wood could be harvested for construction, the manufacture of implements, and as firewood. The different modes of land use contradicted each other, however. Although many plants and trees naturally tended to regenerate after harvesting, the young shoots were often eaten by the grazing animals, so much so that the woods regenerated very slowly—if at all.

The system of land use whereby settlements were repeatedly relocated was not compatible with the system of continual, stable residence that arose in the Middle Ages. Only one system of land use could be applied in a given region. Both state and church administrations pushed for the establishment of permanent settlements, with both bodies helping to secure a completely new land-use strategy. If there was a deficit of timber, grain, or other essential goods, an economic safety net now had to be available so that goods lacking at a given location could be supplied. Roadways, therefore, had to be upgraded, and they had to be protected by castles. Furthermore, it became more and more important to produce a surplus of goods that could be fed into systems of trade. Only then would people stand a chance of attaining essential goods in times of shortage.

Official documents mentioned increasing numbers of permanent settlements in individual regions, which were thus recorded for history, although they had presumably already existed for some time. A typical process of the establishment and initial documentation of settlements is noticeable, and it can easily be traced in Mansfeld Land as well as in other regions.[3] Most of the early settlements were rural and were settled by farmers for agriculture. Larger villages followed

Fig. 1 Historic entrance to Luther's Birth House
in Lutherstadt (Luther town) Eisleben, Mansfeld Land

that were perhaps formed by the consolidation of smaller settlements, and towns developed into focal points for trade and administration. Eventually, the subsequent settlements were extended or enlarged, and in Mansfeld Land these were mainly mining settlements.

Rural and Municipal Settlements

Some of the oldest settlements in Mansfeld Land—that is, those that were established and first mentioned in historical documents in the early Middle Ages—have remained small to this day. For example, there are references to Osterhausen from the seventh century and to Greifenhagen and Polleben from the eighth century. Also from this period, there are references to the existence of the first castles: Seeburg Castle at Lake Süßer See, to the east of Eisleben, was first mentioned in documents from 743. The first documentary evidence of the towns and villages of Volkstedt, Hornburg, Aseleben, Röblingen, Amsdorf, and Wansleben are from the ninth century. Beesenstedt was also mentioned for the first time in the ninth century, though it is considerably older. Wormsleben can be found in a document from 948; Helfta has been known as a royal estate since 969; a document from 973 names Klostermansfeld as the predecessor to the settlement of Mansfeld, while Vatterode preceded Thondorf. First mentioned in

985, Gerbstedt was initially a purely agricultural settlement, which would not develop in size until mining activity later began. Aside from numerous other places that have been documented since the tenth century, the so-called Alte Dorf (old village) of Eisleben is interesting, in that it was located before the walls of the town that developed later. For the most part, all of these (originally) purely rural settlements could exist in a largely self-sufficient manner. Furthermore, only a small number of people in the neighboring towns or castles of the region had to be supplied with foodstuffs, due to the complete absence of larger municipal settlements in Mansfeld Land in the early Middle Ages. Indeed, almost all of the people in the area had access to their own parcel of land from which they could feed themselves.

There were also long-distance paths and roads in the early Middle Ages. The roads ran mostly along the heights of the hill country and mountain regions and did not pass through the settlements directly. Transporting goods was safer on these higher elevations as the traveler had a clear view from his wagon and could not be attacked from above as he could be in a valley. The roads could also be constructed to run approximately along watersheds, thus minimizing inclines. Since the Carolingian period, if not earlier, such roadways would lead over the Harz Mountains.

Perhaps formed by the consolidation of smaller settlements, larger villages from later times include Höhnstedt (established in 1121) and the clustered village of Rothenschirmbach (known since 1140). Such villages (i.e., those formed by consolidation) were often particularly successful in an economic sense. In 1734, for example, the Mansfeld chronicler Johann Albert Biering declared Höhnstedt to be one of the best and largest villages in the county of Mansfeld: "Around here are the richest farmers and the best wheat fields," he noted.[4] More villages of this kind arose in later times, such as Holdenstedt (also a large clustered village), which was first documented in 1271. The deserted settlement of Barwelle lies in the immediate vicinity—quite possibly, the establishment of Holdenstedt is connected with the desertion of Barwelle.

At approximately the same time, the foundation of towns began. Towns had a markedly different topography than rural settlements and were typically founded along streams or rivers that powered water mills. For this reason there are several cases where older settlements located at the edges of valleys were given up and replaced with towns at the bottoms of the valleys. In this way Mansfeld arose from the partial relocation of Klostermansfeld. Known since the eleventh century, the town was situated immediately on the banks of the Wipper river. The town of Hettstedt was founded on the same river and was first mentioned around the same time (in 1046).

In its current location, Eisleben emerged at the end of the twelfth century as a successive settlement of the "Altes Dorf" along a large stream referred to as the "Böse Sieben" (The Evil Seven)—a bizarre name whose origin has yet to be identified. Around 1500, the Petriviertel *trans aquam* (meaning the Petri quarter, or neighborhood, on the other side of the "Böse Sieben"), the sites of the "Altes Dorf" and "Neues Dorf", as well as the Friesian settlement around St. Nicolai's, were enclosed by a town wall. Mills developed into central service providers, in which grain from numerous surrounding villages could be ground into flour. This was done in exchange for either a

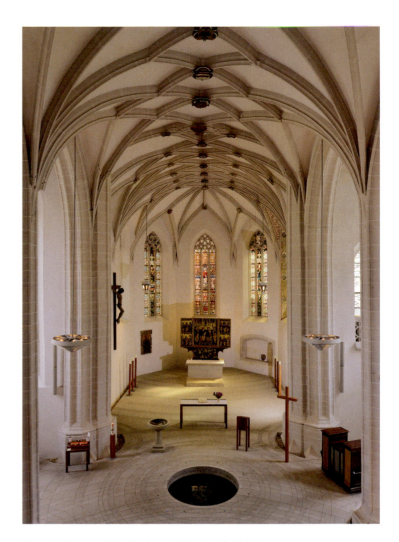

Fig. 2 St. Peter and Paul's church, Eisleben, built between 1446 and 1513, the church where Martin Luther was baptized

monetary fee or for payment in kind. A portion of the flour was often withheld to contribute to the nourishment of the town's population. With the mill situated inside the town walls, flour could be produced at all times—even if the town was under siege.

Many monasteries were not founded at the beginning of the Middle Ages but at later dates. In Mansfeld Land, Sittichenbach Abbey was founded in 1141, and the Premonstratensian Klosterrode Abbey near Blankenheim shortly after 1150.

Economic Relations between Town and Countryside

As the Middle Ages wore on, there were more and more people who required food but that were not themselves directly involved in agriculture. They lived in towns and monasteries. Their material existence was provided for by the taxation system, which was continually refined. With ever-greater consistency, it was ensured that farmers should use a three-field crop-rotation system. The entire

2 Küster, *Geschichte des Waldes*. **3** The representation of the history of settlements in Mansfeld Land follows the compilations in Neuß/ Zühlke, *Mansfelder Land*. **4** Ibid., p. 151.

Fig. 3
View of *Pingen* fields,
scarred by ancient mining,
in the surroundings of
Wimmelburg in Mansfeld Land

area of arable land in a settlement was divided into three fields, each of which was subdivided into long, narrow parcels of tillage. The individual parcels belonged to different farmers, and each farmer was obliged to own parcels in each of the three fields, with each field sown with a single, uniform crop. This strict arrangement of ownership and crop rotation was referred to as *Flurzwang*. For example, rye was planted on the first field in the fall, growing as a winter cereal to be harvested the following summer. There was no room for pathways between the long, narrow parcels of land, thus requiring them to be tilled and harvested sequentially, with the harvest wagon often having to be parked upon the already harvested neighboring parcel. This was the reason for enforcing the *Flurzwang*. In the following year, the crops were rotated. On the field where rye had been harvested, a spring cereal would be planted—for example, barley—which would be sown in spring and harvested that summer. In the third year, the field would lie fallow, or would perhaps be used as pastureland. In the fallow year, the soil could recover, and livestock would restore mineral nutrients to the earth through their waste. Apart from this field, two others were cultivated upon which the crops would be similarly rotated each year. Thus, each village had one field with a winter cereal, another with a spring cereal, and one fallow at any given time, with the three-field system serving to organize the crop rotation.

Because the transportation of foodstuffs from rural settlements into the burgeoning towns increased, new connecting roads became necessary to link urban and rural settlements. Furthermore, roads were constructed between the towns, replacing the older ones that led along the hilltops. The roads were not paved, so the wheels of goods wagons dug deep into the roadway after a rain, or when snow thawed to slush. Water would gather in the wheel ruts. The drivers of subsequent goods carriages were forced to find new tracks next to the rutted ones, where the going was perhaps better. As the amount of traffic increased, the roads became wider, with more and more new tracks being formed. In their attempts to find firmer tracks, car-

riage drivers didn't often consider the plight of the farmer, recklessly driving over fields where crops were growing. If a section of a field was driven over even once, the entire yield of that section would be lost for that year.[5] However, more grain was urgently needed since the population was growing, and the villages had to feed more and more townspeople (who did not possess fields of their own). The dependence of rural settlements and their residents on the municipal centers increased. Clearly, however, rural settlements could exist in a self-sufficient manner, even when they might be relocated due to their lack of a certain resource. In contrast, municipal settlements were never self-sufficient—they always required supplies from their surrounding rural areas. As such, when the old chronicles and historical works emphasize the dominance of towns, castles, and monasteries, the true living conditions are actually presented in a somewhat upside-down manner.

Mining and the Overuse of Land

This precarious land-use situation came to a head—particularly around the Harz region and at the perimeter of the Erzgebirge. In Mansfeld Land, the western Harz region, and the Erzgebirge, there was an enormous increase in mining activity toward the end of the Middle Ages, whereas previously mining had played a much smaller role. From 1199, a chapel was located on the Kupferberg (meaning "copper mountain") near Hettstedt to serve the copper miners who worked there. Around the turn of the twelfth to the thirteenth century, the importance of Hettstedt grew dramatically; more miners were finding work in the copper mines and settling there. In the fourteenth and fifteenth centuries, further mining locations proliferated: Wolferode was described as a "Berg- und Hüttenleutedorf" (miners and smelters village) in official documents from 1336. Starting in 1432, a smelting works could be found on the Schlenze, a river in the northeast of Mansfeld Land. Water power was exploited there (presumably) to drive the bellows, forcing air into the smelting

Fig. 4
Pingen seen in an aerial
photograph taken between
Benndorf and
Klostermannsfeld

ovens. From 1450 to 1470 in particular—and only a few years before Martin Luther's birth—copper production increased significantly. Many people settled in these areas, particularly in the towns, so that these required expansion. Around 1500 in Eisleben, a new district for miners took shape, the *Neustadt* (new town). In many places and particularly in towns, not only were new houses built, but new churches were constructed in the late-gothic style, and grandly furnished. Additionally, many townhouses were built, and the castle in Mansfeld was renovated. New town halls were also required. In particular, the cities of Eisleben, Mansfeld, and Hettstedt were gripped by the construction boom. The prosperity of these settlements came from the mining operations: in 1536 there were 110 smelters in the vicinity of these three towns. In the first half of the sixteenth century, up to forty thousand hundredweights of copper were extracted per year in the Mansfeld fields, an incredible amount. Prior to the onset of the extensive exploitation of copper mines in the New World, Mansfeld Land could be counted as one of the most important copper-mining regions in the world. In addition, salt and lignite were also extracted.

Among the many people who were drawn by the mining boom were Martin Luther's parents. His father, Hans, originally came from the village of Möhra in Thuringia, south of Eisenach.[6] He was the eldest of four sons who grew up on a farm. Only the youngest was entitled to inherit the farm so that the property remained undivided and undiminished from generation to generation. Martin Luther's father could have chosen to labor as a farmhand on his brother's estate, or try his luck in another trade. He chose the latter and, together with his wife, Margarethe, moved to Eisleben shortly before the birth of his son Martin (fig. 1 and 2). Together with a business partner, Luther's father leased the necessary rights to operate a mine, and from that point on he became a successful businessman.

With mining, it was primarily the landowners who earned the lion's share of the profits, that is, the counts of Mansfeld, and later the princes of Saxony. The Saxons continually increased their influence over Mansfeld Land. Businessmen involved in mining, however, also became quite wealthy. Around the turn of the sixteenth century, a very well-functioning trade network was in place between the states of Northern Italy, family enterprises from the south of Germany (in particular the Fugger family from Augsburg), the mining regions in the Harz and Erzgebirge, and the coastal regions along the Baltic and North Seas.

Many others also sought to earn a living in the mining regions but ended up profiting from the boom to a much lesser degree, since they were so poorly paid. There arose a veritable army of the poor that labored simply to survive. For a multitude of reasons, the social problems of the day intensified in their severity, and there were considerably more crises—such as the Peasants' War of 1525. During Martin Luther's lifetime, many mine shafts had been driven down to the water table. As the necessary technology had not yet been invented, it was not known at that time how to pump water out of the mines, and so mining activity came to a halt once a mine began to fill with water. Soon after the discovery of the New World, metals from the Americas became available on the European markets. The American ore was often cheaper, so much so that many European mines were no longer economically viable. This caused many miners to lose their source of income, though they did not have any alternative means of earning a living.

Ecological problems arose as well, though it is perhaps more fitting not to regard it as direct environmental damage as such. Around the mines, mining waste dumps grew that were laden with poisonous heavy metals. These heavy metals would then leach into and poison neighboring waterways. Most plants grew poorly on soil that had been tainted with heavy metals like copper, lead, or zinc, and livestock could be poisoned by eating any plants that did manage to grow on the waste heaps.

5 Küster, *Landschaft*. **6** Biographical information according to Schilling, *Rebell*.

Fig. 5 Lucas Cranach the Younger, The Vineyard of the Lord (Epitaph for Paul Eber),
1573–74, Town and Parish Church of St. Mary's, Wittenberg

More ominously, however, it became clear that the resources available were not sufficient to provide for the people operating the mines and smelters. Foodstuffs were needed for an ever-increasing population, yet the land available for agriculture could not be further expanded, nor did the yields increase. In fact, the area available for agriculture even shrank due to the land appropriated for mines, smelters, and residential areas. Above all, the increasing amount of traffic put pressure on farmlands: thousands of hundredweights of copper were being transported overland, and the wagon drivers could only arrive at their destinations by continually forging new paths—often straight across croplands. However fertile the soil was, it didn't matter: once torn up by horse hooves and wagon wheels, the seeds could no longer grow, mature, and bear fruit.

Forests were also under immense stress. They had already been suffering through the entire Middle Ages, since forestry land had not been separated from pastureland. The possibilities for keeping livestock in woodlands were limited, and where the livestock grazed, saplings could not mature, meaning forests could not regenerate. Furthermore, the industrial demand for wood was ever increasing: mine shafts and tunnels required pit props for stabilization. Above all, however, wood and charcoal were the only energy sources available for smelting the large quantities of ore. In the smelters, the varying melt-

ing points of different metals were exploited to separate one from the other. In Mansfeld Land, the wood supply was soon exhausted, so charcoal was imported over the Via Regia, which had been in use since the early Middle Ages, from the Harz Mountains. Charcoal was produced in the cleared forests of the Harz Mountains and would be transported instead of fresh wood—charcoal is much lighter than wood. Mansfeld Land, however, was not the only mining area near the Harz range: other regions also required charcoal for the smelting of ore, so charcoal was similarly in short supply.

The Reformation and Other Reforms as Solutions to the Crisis

It was becoming more and more apparent that, since the end of the Middle Ages, many places were being damaged by excessive utilization and human activity (figs. 3 and 4). In particular, the poor among the population were experiencing hunger with ever-greater regularity, and not only as the result of bad harvests. Even in normal years, the yield of foodstuffs frequently did not suffice to satisfy the hunger of the populace. There was also a deficit of raw materials, especially wood. It also seemed that no one had any idea how these shortages could be effectively combated. This situation served to prime the societal climate for reform: the people yearned for change.

One such reform was the Reformation. Indeed, the people were hoping for a renewal not just of religious institutions but of their general living conditions. This is one important message to be taken from the painting *The Vineyard of the Lord: Epitaph for Paul Eber* (1569) by Lucas Cranach the Younger, in the Town and Parish Church of St. Mary's in Wittenberg (fig. 5). On the left-hand side, Catholics are overusing and destroying the land; they can be equated with those who were plundering the land in the manner typical of that era. On the right-hand side, the reformers are cultivating the land and replanting. Of course, the theological meaning of this painting is of primary importance, but it can also be interpreted ecologically: it acknowledges the possibility of an alternative to improper land use and its unsustainable consumption of resources.

The development of a more considerate form of land utilization would become a greatly important topic of societal dialogue for the next several centuries. Initially, this dialogue was held within the *paterfamilias* literature (household handbooks), the beginnings of which can be traced to Martin Luther and the Reformation.[7]

Luther's contemporaries recognized excessive use of the forests as another pressing topic. Tacitus and his *Germania* had been rediscovered as the first written text on Germany, and scholars went on to interpret it in various ways.[8] One of the most recognizable themes therein was the expansive forestland that Tacitus had described as being typically German. Thus, their restoration and reestablishment were held to be worthy goals. In this context, Heinz Schilling's statement on Hans Holbein the Younger's woodcut *Luther as Hercules Germanicus* is interesting. He considers the piece as an expression of the "… struggle for freedom of the Germans against Roman infiltration and exploitation by the curia." Luther is depicted in the woodcut as "dispatching the Cologne Dominican and papal inquisitor Jacob van Hoogstraten with a wooden club carved in the Germanic forests" (fig. 6).[9]

Some may regard this as overinterpretation, including perhaps the reference to the lengthy debates on the proper treatment of forests in Germany. However, it is quite clear that since the time of the Reformation, further reforms have been sought in order to improve the conditions in the country, the nourishment of the populace, and the supply of resources. These reforms were largely achieved through concepts and phenomena from the eighteenth century, such as the introduction of new crops like the potato; new concepts for field division in conjunction with enclosure and the *Flurbereinigung* (land consolidation) land reforms; the associated phasing out of shared commons; the clear separation of forest and pastureland; the introduction of sustainable forestry, whereby the amount of wood harvested over a certain period should not exceed the amount that could regrow in that period, and so on. These ideas concerned not only Protestants but Catholics too. Ultimately, the landscapes of the nineteenth century took shape—landscapes that many people today would picture when they think about the "good old days." The ideas that led to the creation of these landscapes have numerous roots in Reformation-era thought, and particularly in the problematic environmental situation in Mansfeld Land as well as in other mining regions of the Central Europe of the late Middle Ages and the early modern period.

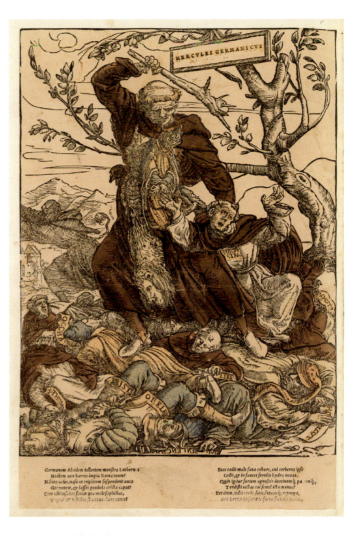

Fig. 6 Hans Holbein the Younger, Luther as Hercules Germanicus, 1522

7 Frühsorge, *Luthers Kleiner Katechismus*, pp. 380–393; Van Haag, *Hausväterliteratur*. 8 Küster, *Tacitus*, pp. 10–16. 9 Schilling, *Rebell*, p. 47.

BIBLIOGRAPHY

Frühsorge, Gotthardt (1984), Luthers Kleiner Katechismus und die "Hausväterliteratur." In: *Pastoraltheologie*, vol. 73, pp. 380–393. **Küster**, Hansjörg (2013), *Geschichte der Landschaft in Mitteleuropa. Von der Eiszeit bis zur Gegenwart.* 6th ed. München. **Küster**, Hansjörg (2013), *Geschichte des Waldes. Von der Urzeit bis zur Gegenwart.* 4th ed. München. **Küster**, Hansjörg (2001), Das folgenreiche Missverständnis des Tacitus: Auch der Wald hat seine Geschichte. Natürliche und kulturelle Bedingungen der Bewaldung Mitteleuropas. In: *Der Bürger im Staat*, vol. 51, no. 1: special issue, "Der deutsche Wald." Stuttgart, pp. 10–16. **Neuß**, Erich/**Zühlke**, Dietrich (eds.) (1982), *Mansfelder Land. Ergebnisse der heimatkundlichen Bestandsaufnahme im Gebiet um Leimbach, Hettstedt, Dederstedt, Holdenstedt, Hornburg und Seeburg* (= Werte unserer Heimat. 38). Berlin. **Schilling**, Heinz (2012), *Martin Luther. Rebell in einer Zeit des Umbruchs.* München. **Van Haag**, Maike-Franziska (2014), *Hausväterliteratur. Der "Oeconomus Prudens et Legalis" von Franz Philipp Florin im Kontext seiner Zeit.* Berlin.

Luther Places, Famous and Unknown

In Luther's days, the House of Wettin ruled in Saxony. From 1485 on, there were two lines: the Ernestines and the Albertines. As we can see from the locations of Luther Places, he moved around in an area covering mainly Central German territory. After Luther's death, myths arose connecting his person even to places he had never been to.

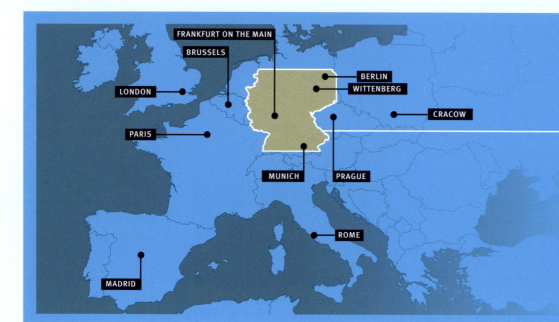

FRANKFURT ON THE MAIN
BRUSSELS
LONDON
BERLIN
WITTENBERG
PARIS
CRACOW
MUNICH
PRAGUE
ROME
MADRID

Luther Places

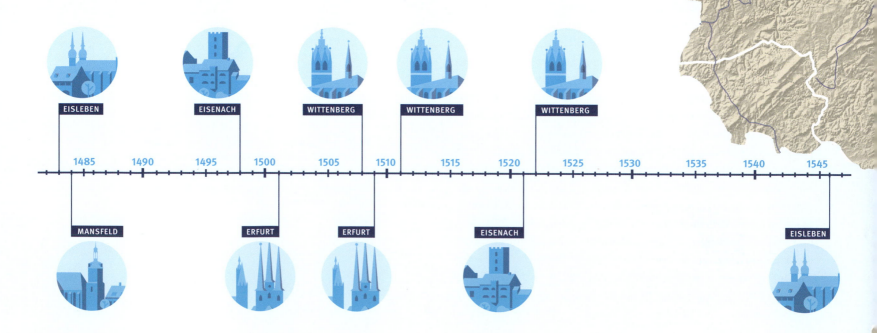

| EISLEBEN | EISENACH | WITTENBERG | WITTENBERG | WITTENBERG |

| 1485 | 1490 | 1495 | 1500 | 1505 | 1510 | 1515 | 1520 | 1525 | 1530 | 1535 | 1540 | 1545 |

MANSFELD   ERFURT   ERFURT   EISENACH   EISLEBEN

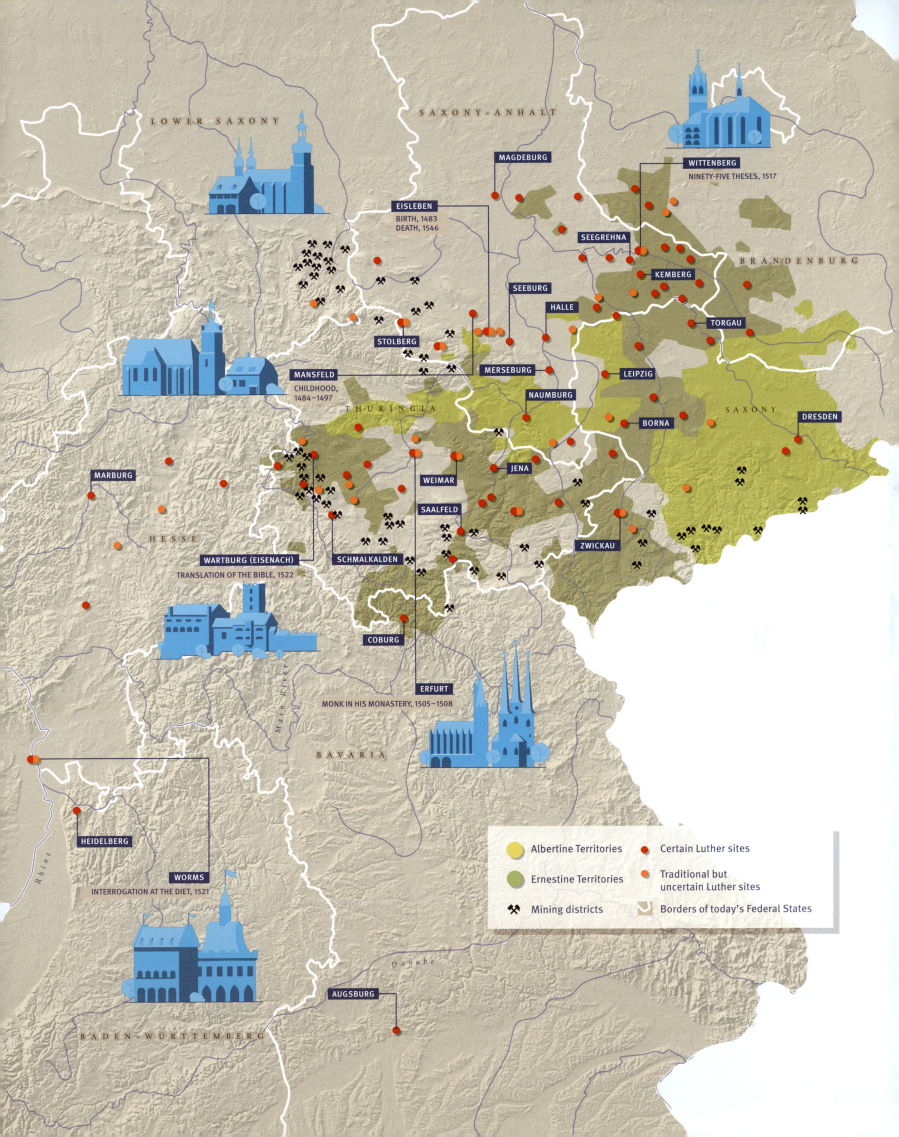

LOWER SAXONY

SAXONY-ANHALT

MAGDEBURG

WITTENBERG
NINETY-FIVE THESES, 1517

BRANDENBURG

EISLEBEN
BIRTH, 1483
DEATH, 1546

SEEGREHNA

SEEBURG

KEMBERG

STOLBERG

HALLE

TORGAU

MANSFELD
CHILDHOOD,
1484–1497

MERSEBURG

LEIPZIG

THURINGIA

NAUMBURG

SAXONY

BORNA

DRESDEN

MARBURG

WEIMAR

JENA

HESSE

SAALFELD

WARTBURG (EISENACH)
TRANSLATION OF THE BIBLE, 1522

SCHMALKALDEN

ZWICKAU

COBURG

ERFURT

MONK IN HIS MONASTERY, 1505–1508

BAVARIA

Main River

HEIDELBERG

Rhine

WORMS
INTERROGATION AT THE DIET, 1521

Danube

AUGSBURG

BADEN-WÜRTTEMBERG

🟡	Albertine Territories	🔴	Certain Luther sites
🟢	Ernestine Territories	🟠	Traditional but uncertain Luther sites
⚒	Mining districts		Borders of today's Federal States

MICHAEL FESSNER

Mining and Metallurgy in Mansfeld Land in the Time of Martin Luther

Next to Banská Bystrica in Lower Hungary and Schwaz in Tyrol, Mansfeld Land was the most important black-copper mining area in continental Europe after 1470. At the end of the fifteenth century, around 80 to 90 percent of European copper was produced in these three districts. Historians Ian Blanchard and Karl-Heinrich Kaufhold have referred to this late-medieval and early modern mining and metallurgy boom as the "age of the *saiger* process" (*Zeitalter des Saigerprozesses*). According to them, the proliferation of the *saiger* procedure was the driving force behind the increase in European silver, copper, and lead production between 1460 and 1560. In the *saiger* process, lead was used to extract silver from copper in several smelting stages.

Saiger works were founded, in rapid succession, in Nuremberg (1453), Schleusingen (1461), Gräfenthal and Hohenkirchen (1462), Steinach (1464), Enzendorf (1466), Arnstedt (1467), Brixlegg near Rattenberg (1467/68), Kraków (1468), Chemnitz (1471), Schwarza (1472), Mansfeld (1472), Eisfeld (1479), Fuggerau near Arnoldstein in Carinthia (1494), Banská Bystrica (1495), and Moštenicá in Lower Hungary/Slovakia (1497). In these *saiger* works argentiferous black copper produced in the copper districts was further processed into tough-pitch copper and silver. The *saiger* works commonly formed the nucleus of enterprises with vertical production chains. When it was finally completed, the Fuggers' *saiger* works in Arnoldstein, for instance, included a hammer mill, a brass foundry, and a cannon and rifle factory next to the smelting hut proper.[1]

The Origins of Copper Shale Mining in Mansfeld Land

The origins of copper shale mining in Mansfeld Land can be traced to the turn of the twelfth to the thirteenth century. After Henry the Lion, in his confrontation with Emperor Frederick Barbarossa, had destroyed the Rammelsberg smelting works and mines in Goslar in 1180/1181, numerous miners and smelting workers moved to the Erzgebirge (Ore Mountains), where substantial deposits of silver had been discovered in the area around Freiberg in 1168. According to the Mansfeld chronicler Cyriacus Spangenberg, two miners from Goslar, Nappian and Neucke, are said to have discovered the local copper shale deposits at the Kupferberg (Copper Mountain) near Hettstedt around 1200 on their way to the Erzgebirge.

Spangenberg also reports that many foreign miners were attracted by the discovery of ore so that Hettstedt, heretofore a desolate village, became a considerable market town that was subsequently awarded quite a number of privileges by the counts of Arnstein. A deed issued by Count Albert of Arnstein in 1223 offers the as yet earliest written mention of the copper shale deposits at the Kupferberg near Hettstedt. There are no documents, however, to precisely date the beginning of copper mining in and around Eisleben. An award certificate for the Cistercian monastery of Neu-Helfta in Eisleben from 1376 mentions smelting works in the context of the description of local mill locations. Copper shale mining was taken up around the city of Mansfeld on a large scale only after the invention of *saiger* technology had triggered the so-called copper boom.[2]

The Legal Requirements of Mining

The mining and metallurgy sector in Mansfeld Land had its legal basis in the count's license for operating copper smelting works—a license that, at the same time, provided the authorization to open copper shale mines. Apart from a few exceptions, mines in the Mansfeld area were not operated independently of smelting works.

The counts of the House of Mansfeld did not take long to react to the rapid economic upturn that had started in the 1470s. In the following decades (viz., in 1477, 1484, 1487, 1497, 1504, and 1508), they adopted six regulations for mining and smelting that laid down the legal framework for the three mining districts of Hettstedt, Eisleben, and Mansfeld. These regulations can be seen as the sovereign's response to the conditions already prevailing in his territory. Their rapid modification is evidence that the dynamic development of mining and metallurgy made the continuous adaptation of existing regulations necessary. At the same time, the legal standards laid down here determined the further development of the mining and metallurgy sector. In particular, these regulations governed the mutual relationship between the operators of the different smelting works, who, as a result of the enormous upturn, poached miners, smelting workers, and carters from one another, sometimes by dishonest methods, and mutually outbid each other in the purchase of coal. The regulations for mining and smelting had a controlling effect on this conflict-ridden sector. In 1521, the House of Mansfeld

Acervus lapidum ærosorum A. Pyra accensa B.
Lapides inuehens in fasces uirgultorum C.

Atuenæ

Fig. 1
Basilius Weffringer, Mining and
roasting copper shale.
Illustration from: Georg Agricola,
De re metallica libri XII, Basel 1556

eventually adopted a comprehensive mining reform for the county, which encapsulated previous legal experience. This regulation marked both the endpoint of the development and a paradigm shift. The legal relationship of the smelting works operators on the one hand, and the *saiger* companies on the other, came more and more into the foreground. As a result of the increasing tasks to be performed by a growing number of mining and smelting officials, the regulations—especially those adopted after 1521—gave the count an ever-stronger influence over the organization and management of mining and metallurgy, also providing him with an opportunity to secure his fiscal claims.[3]

The Smelter Masters

In the 1470s, the rapid economic growth of copper shale mining in the mining districts of Hettstedt, Eisleben, and Mansfeld began to change the social fabric of Mansfeld Land. The smelter masters, who held the key position in the production of crude copper, emerged as a new social class. This class fell into two categories: smelter masters who owned the so-called *Erbfeuer* ("hereditary" smelting furnaces)

and those who owned the so-called *Herrenfeuer* (smelting furnaces belonging to the count). The *Erbfeuer* were owned by long-established smelter-master families from Hettstedt, Mansfeld, and Eisleben, and they were bequeathed to the next generation. The heirs had to ask the count of Mansfeld for a formal confirmation of their rights, which was usually granted to them. The count of Mansfeld kept one-tenth of the *Erbfeuer*-produced crude copper as a tax levied on mining and smelting (fig. 1).

Herrenfeuer, smelting works in the possession of the count and managed by his appointed smelting officials, are likely to have been operated well into the 1480s. Toward the end of the fifteenth century, however, the counts of Mansfeld ceased operating their own mines and smelting furnaces when they found them to have become uneconomical, and instead introduced the so-called *Herrenfeuer*. From today's point of view, this process could be described as the privatization of unprofitable state-owned enterprises. The counts probably

1 See Fessner, *Voraussetzung*, pp. 317 f. 2 See id., *Kupferschieferbergbau*, pp. 15 – 19. 3 See id., *Montanwesen*, pp. 295 – 301.

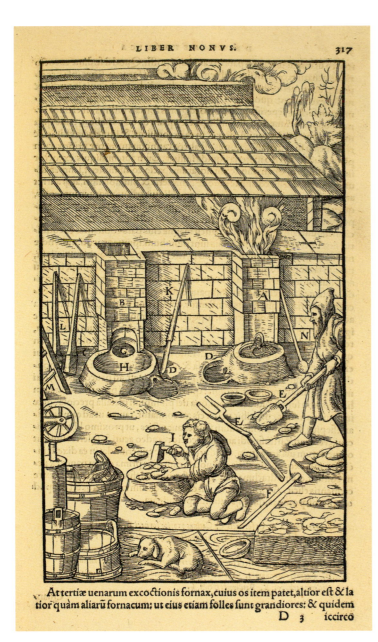

At tertiæ uenarum excoctionis fornax, cuius os item patet, altior eſt & la
tior quàm aliarū fornacum: ut eius etiam folles ſunt grandiores: & quidem
D 3   iccircō

Fig. 2 Basilius Weffringer, Smelting the roasted copper shale.
Illustration from: Georg Agricola, De re metallica libri XII,
Basel 1556

offered their smelting officials permission to operate the smelting
works and existing furnaces. In this way the smelting officials became private operators who ran the smelting works under their own
management and at their own entrepreneurial risk, while the counts
of Mansfeld secured the reliable revenues from the leasing contracts
for themselves. For the payment of an annual fee, the counts would
also lease the smelting works and their furnaces for a specified period to experienced smelter masters.

As a consequence of this development, all of the furnaces in
Hettstedt, the oldest copper-mining district, were *Erbfeuer*. Initially,
this was also the case in the mines which were later established in
the Eisleben mining district, where *Herrenfeuer* were only introduced
around the 1470s or 1480s. In contrast, in the mines which were in
operation up to the 1470s in the Mansfeld district, all the operating

furnaces were *Herrenfeuer*. Thus in the 1470s, the counts of Mansfeld
clearly favored the *Herrenfeuer* operators over the *Erbfeuer* propri-
etors. While the former only paid a fixed annual lease that was
linked to the amount of crude copper produced, the latter traditionally had to pay one-tenth of their crude-copper production to the
count. The amount of the lease and the duration of the lease contract for the *Herrenfeuer*, however, were not subject to standard regulations but mostly negotiated individually between the operators
and the count. Also, the count tended to grant new smelter masters
temporary exemption from, or reduction of, the mining taxes due
to him. This privileged treatment of *Herrenfeuer* operators can be
understood as an economic measure to stimulate the mining and
smelting sector and to offer investors—especially newcomers such
as Hans Luder—an economic incentive for opening new mines and
smelters. This economic support program came to an end in 1515 or
1516, however, after the market situation for copper had reached its
peak. The counts of Mansfeld now also requested *Herrenfeuer* operators to pay one-tenth of the crude copper produced instead of the
rent, thereby putting them on an equal footing with the *Erbfeuer*
operators (fig. 2).

When, around the turn of the fifteenth to the sixteenth century,
the mining sector grew more and more rapidly thanks to the operation of water-drainage systems and the digging of deeper shafts, the
smelter masters engaged so-called *Dinghauer* (hewers), to whom they
assigned the direct management of the mines. They then confined
themselves to the technically more complex operation of the smelting works. Within the companies in the Mansfeld mining district,
the *Dinghauer* acted as intermediaries, as it were, between exploited
simple wage earners and the smelter masters. They were working as
subcontractors on behalf of the latter to organize the mining of copper shale by the former.

Since the capital-intensive *saiger* process usually exceeded their
financial capabilities, the smelter masters would sell the crude copper produced to *saiger* companies in Nuremberg and Leipzig. Only
very few Mansfeld smelter masters or masters' families, such as the
Drachstedts or Reinickes,[4] had the necessary capital to hold equities
in the *saiger* companies. Experienced smelter masters would quickly
achieve economic prosperity. Some of the smelter masters, however,
were less successful and had to shut down their mines and smelters
or, as in the case of Hans Luder, sell them to other smelter masters
or to the *saiger* companies (fig. 3).[5]

Hans Luder in Mansfeld Land

Martin Luther's father, Hans Luder, hailed from a wealthy farming
family that belonged to the rural upper class in and around the village
of Möhra, Thuringia. He had been active in the Möhra area as an entrepreneur in mining and metallurgy. His wife, Margarethe, was born
into the Lindemann family, a prestigious bourgeois family in Eisenach, whose descendants rose to important academic positions. The
marriage between a son from an upper-class farming family and the
daughter of a townsman perfectly fitted in with the medieval and early
modern social structure, with its combined rural-urban character.

Fig. 3
Basilius Weffringer, Smelting
the copper stone (ore).
Illustration from: Georg Agricola,
De re metallica libri XII,
Basel 1556

An atmosphere of economic growth prevailed in Mansfeld Land when Hans and Margarethe Luder moved there in 1483. The mining and smelting of argentiferous copper shale deposits in Hettstedt, Eisleben, and Mansfeld offered a wide field for profitable commercial operations, particularly for nonlocal investors. Since experienced miners and smelting workers were sought-after specialists in the late Middle Ages, Hans Luder's professional experience is likely to have been much in demand. Certainly, his move to Mansfeld Land was prompted by the suggestion of his wife's uncle, Antonius Lindemann, who was not only Mansfeld Land's chief mining administrator but also operated his own smelting works in the Teufelstal. With his outstanding knowledge of the economic situation, he provided Hans Luder with the necessary business contacts to smelter-master families from Eisleben and Mansfeld. Hans Lüttich, scion of a long-established smelter-master family from Eisleben, first assigned Hans Luder the management of his smelting works.

In spring 1485, Hans Luder settled in the Mansfeld district, where he leased and successfully operated several *Herrenfeuer*. Having become part of the community leadership of Mansfeld, he quickly achieved economic prosperity and social status. One of the few extant documents from the city of Mansfeld's early period records him as being one of the "four (mayors) of the municipality" of Mansfeld in 1491. In 1502, he again became a member of the city's council, if he had not been so all along. In Mansfeld, the smelter-master families formed the middle and upper classes of the town and occupied its administrative positions. At the beginning of the sixteenth century, Hans Luder was one of the most prestigious

4 See Bullerjahn, *Familiendynastien*, pp. 26, 33. 5 See Fessner, *Mansfelder Revier*, pp. 345–348.

smelter masters in Mansfeld Land. Starting in 1508, if not earlier, he carried out the duties of a higher comital mining official (*Schauherr*) in the districts of Lerchenfeld, Steudenberg, Rödichen, and Pfaffental—a considerable position that he would occupy until his death in 1530. The marriage of his children into other smelter-master families strengthened his strong role in the upper social circles of Mansfeld and Eisleben. One of his daughters, for instance, married into the long-established Mackenrodt family. The Mackenrodts owned an *Erbfeuer* and its members, as part of the urban middle class of Eisleben, were eligible to run for city council, which is what Hans Mackenrodt did in 1512.[6]

The *Saiger* Companies and the Smelter Masters

The beginning of the sixteenth century was a time when the smelter masters were still capable of making substantial profits. The mining and smelting of copper shale required sufficient financial resources, however, which, as was the case in almost all mining districts, involved progressively higher investments with the continued operation of the mining and smelting works. In the 1480s and early 1490s, near-surface mining was the mining method still practiced in Eisleben and especially in Mansfeld. However, toward the end of the 1490s, if not earlier, the near-surface copper shale deposits had been exhausted and mines were being dug deeper and deeper; the water table stood at a depth of around thirty meters. Sinking deeper shafts and draining the mines with pump systems incurred a considerable increase of expenditure.

In October 1508, for instance, the mining authorities urged the smelter masters operating a mine at the Sandtberg (mountain) to continue work on a water-drainage shaft, had them drill a shaft for a pump system (sump shaft) and then install a pump system. This combination of drainage passageway and pumping installations is clear evidence that early sixteenth-century mining in Eisleben and Mansfeld had already penetrated to great depths below the water table over a large area and that mining, as a consequence of the installation and maintenance of the drainage systems (dewatering), had become quite costly. Most of all, the high expenditures were caused by the use of horses to drive the pump systems. In the districts of Mansfeld and Eisleben, more than three hundred horses were employed in the 1520s (a number that had grown to more than four hundred in the 1540s), and the cost for their maintenance totaled approximately 13,900 guilders a year. As the operators of the mines, the smelter masters had to pay these operating costs jointly in an allocation procedure. Those failing to meet their payment obligations faced penalties from the mining authorities.

The rise in wood and charcoal prices and additional operating materials was another factor in the steady cost increase of smelting the copper shale. The mining regulations of 1477, 1487, and 1497 and other sources offer sufficient evidence of the price increases of the indispensable charcoal. Although the nominal price of one Rhenish guilder for a cartload of coal remained the same in all three mining regulations, the size of one cartload decreased over time. In the district of Eisleben, one cartload of coal measured twelve buckets in 1477, ten buckets in 1487, and only nine, in 1497. This reduction of the cartload by three buckets between 1477 and 1497 implied a hidden price increase of 25 percent: for one Rhenish guilder, the smelter masters in 1497 only received 75 percent of the coal quantity they had received in 1477.

The price increase was less dramatic in the district of Mansfeld. Here, one cartload of coal also measured twelve buckets in 1477, and still ten, in 1497. This reduction in the size of one cartload of coal by 18 percent meant that, for one Rhenish guilder, the smelter masters received 18 percent less coal than in 1477. The price of charcoal continued to rise. In 1508, smelter masters, for one Rhenish guilder, received a cartload of eight buckets of coal in Eisleben and nine buckets in Mansfeld. Compared to 1477, the price of coal had increased by 33 percent in Eisleben, and by 25 percent in Mansfeld (fig. 4).

The fixing of prices for charcoal, as specified in the mining regulations, represented a significant encroachment on the economic principle of supply and demand on the part of the count, whose maximum price-fixing aimed to steer the smelter masters' ruinous competition for this necessary aggregate into orderly channels. One can assume, however, that, in practice, charcoal would be traded at prices far above this specified maximum and that the mining administration's attempts were merely directed at mitigating the price expansion.

Since the funds available in Mansfeld Land were becoming less and less sufficient to cover the steadily rising operating costs, the smelter masters, as early as in the 1510s (and possibly earlier), had to rely on the inflow of foreign capital. Merchants and *saiger* companies from Nuremberg and Leipzig, in particular, advanced the necessary capital (putting-out system) and in return received the crude copper produced (black copper). The amount of money advanced in this way clearly reflects the increase of production costs in the mining and metallurgy sector: before 1500, the *saiger* companies usually advanced 500 guilders per furnace and year; this figure rose to 700 guilders by around 1510, and to 1,000 guilders by the beginning of the 1520s; toward the end of the 1520s or at the beginning of the 1530s, it had reached the amount of 1,500 guilders, in some cases even 2,000 guilders. According to these figures, the production costs for a hundredweight of crude copper (black copper) must have increased threefold within a little over twenty-five years.

The increased operating expenses, however, were not compensated by an adequate increase in the purchase prices of crude copper. As a result, the smelter masters grew more and more dependent on, and increasingly ran up debts with, the *saiger* companies. Quite a number of them were forced to give up both their smelting works and their private assets to cover their debts with the trading companies. As a result, sixteen out of the eighty-eight furnaces operating in 1536 belonged entirely to *saiger* companies.

In their *saiger* works in Thuringia, the companies further processed the crude copper into silver and tough-pitch copper, whose worldwide marketing generated high profits. The copper would be

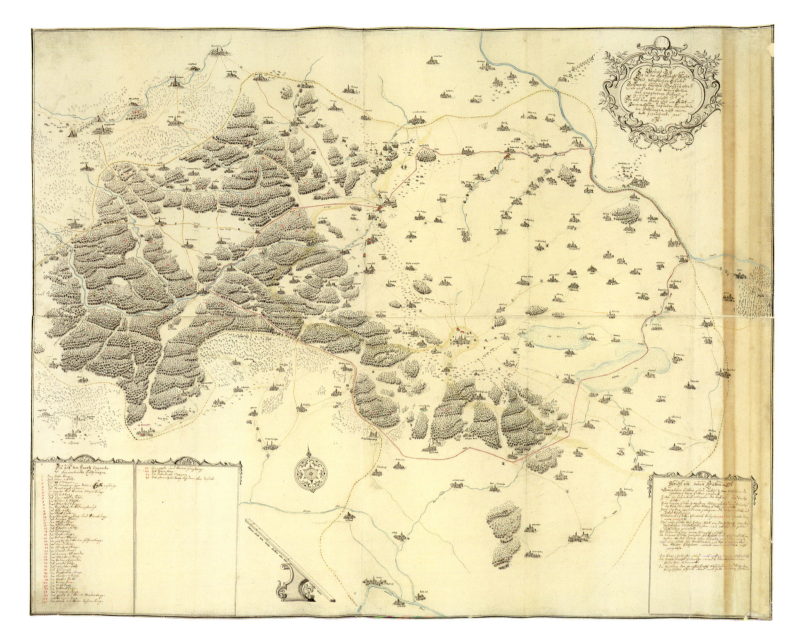

Fig. 4 Detail of the map of the copper shale mines in Mansfeld County, the accessible smelting works, the sequestered woods (red numbers) in the Harz mountains as well as the "Kohlenstraße" ("Coal Street") that linked the Harz to Mansfeld Land

exported, via Antwerp and Lisbon, to Southeast Asia; in return, spices such as pepper and cloves, which were highly sought after in Europe, were shipped to Portugal. Dutch merchants acted as intermediaries for the European spice trade. They bought Asian spices in Portugal and distributed them farther to the north of Europe, using the Dutch harbors as trading hubs between Northern and Southern Europe. In this way, Mansfeld Land became the financial playing field for the foreign *saiger* companies. The fluctuating business cycles in international tough-pitch copper markets fully impacted the overall economic situation of Mansfeld Land, eventually affecting each individual *Erbfeuer* or *Herrenfeuer* operator as the final link in a worldwide exploitation chain.[7]

Hans Luder and the Schwarza *Saiger* and Merchant Company

Hans Luder was also caught up in this vicious circle. After a profitable period that lasted until the beginning of the sixteenth century and during which he would operate up to seven *Herrenfeuer*, he became increasingly dependent financially on the *saiger* companies from the 1520s onward—a fate that was shared by many other smelter masters. As security for his debts, he was forced to pledge his mines and smelting works to the Schwarza company. The origi-

6 See Fessner, *Grafschaft*, pp. 17–21. **7** Id., *Kupferschieferbergbau*, pp. 32–35.

Fig. 5 Paul Pfinzing, Saiger works at Ludwigsstadt 1588, c. 1594,
colored pen and ink drawing from the Pfinzing Atlas.
The refinery passed into the hands of count Hans-Georg I
of Mansfeld-Vorderort in 1559.

nal bond has apparently survived neither in its original form nor as a copy. Similar bonds from other smelter masters, however, provide sufficient information about this business practice on the part of the *saiger* companies. By 1531, smelter masters Facius Bethem and Titzel Müller had run up debts in the amount of 5,835 guilders with the Ludwigsstadt company. They were forced to transfer the profits they made with their furnaces in Mansfeld to the *saiger* company and were paid an annual salary in the amount of only 60 guilders each. The Schwarza *saiger* company appointed a works manager (factor) to administer Hans Luder's total revenue from his smelting and mining operations. Thus, in the last years of his life, Hans Luder only worked as a kind of employee in his own smelting works—a position for which he received an annual wage of 50 guilders (fig. 5).

Despite his debts to the Schwarza company, he died as a relatively wealthy man, since, unlike the majority of smelter masters, he had managed to separate operating capital from private property. In addition, his economic situation was based on three aspects other than his mining and smelting works: his land, his money-lending business, and his income as the count's mining official. This additional income secured the Luder family a source of revenue independent of mining and metallurgy. At his death, Hans Luder left behind goods valued at 1,250 guilders. His property in mines and smelting works, on the other hand, was transferred to the *saiger* company to repay his debts—his son Jacob Luder did not take over his father's mines and smelting works, confining himself to operating his own business.[8]

Outlook

Jacob Luder, who after the death of his father, Hans, continued the smelter-master tradition, ultimately fell victim to the changed economic policy implemented by the early modern sovereigns. With the emergence of the modern territorial state, these sovereigns strove to strengthen their power by consolidating public finances. Due to its favorable revenue prospects, the mining and metallurgy sector became more and more important for their economic and financial policy. The ones who suffered most were the private entrepreneurs; the sovereigns ousted them from the market, taking control of the mines and smelting works—and the marketing of the product—for their own benefit.

Having lost his *Herrenfeuer* in Mansfeld Land to the local count in the 1550s, Jacob Luder in 1563/64 had to give up the smelting works on the Rammelsberg in Goslar, which he had jointly operated with his son Fabian, to the reigning Duke of Braunschweig-Wolfenbüttel. Later descendants of the formerly independent smelter-master family of Luder failed to maintain their social status. In the third and fourth generations after Hans Luder, they would work as hired laborers in the Mansfeld mining business.[9]

8 See Fessner, *Grafschaft*, pp. 23 f. **9** See Fessner, *Familie Luder*, p. 241.

BIBLIOGRAPHY

Bullerjahn, Kerstin (2015), Zwei Familiendynastien des Mansfelder Kupferschieferbergbaus in Abhängigkeit zum Grafenhaus im 16. Jahrhundert. In: Meller, Harald (ed.), *Mansfeld—Luther(s)stadt. Interdisziplinäre Forschungen zur Heimat Martin Luthers* (= *Forschungsberichte des Landesmuseums für Vorgeschichte Halle*. 8). Halle (Saale), pp. 9–37. **Fessner**, Michael (2007), Die Familie Luder und das Bergwerks- und Hüttenwesen in der Grafschaft Mansfeld. In: Knape, Rosemarie (ed.), *Martin Luther und Eisleben* (= *Schriften der Luthergedenkstätten in Sachsen-Anhalt*. 8). Leipzig, pp. 11–31. **Fessner**, Michael (2008), Die Familie Luder und das Berg- und Hüttenwesen. In: Meller, Harald/Rhein, Stefan/Stephan, Hans-Georg (eds.), *Luthers Lebenswelten* (= *Tagungen des Landesmuseums für Vorgeschichte Halle*. 1). Halle (Saale), pp. 235–243. **Fessner**, Michael (2012), Die Voraussetzung für eine neue Hochphase. In: Bartels, Christoph/Slotta, Rainer (eds.), *Der alteuropäische Bergbau. Von den Anfängen bis zur Mitte des 18. Jahrhunderts* (= *Geschichte des deutschen Bergbaus*. 1). Münster, pp. 317–330. **Fessner**, Michael (2012), Das Mansfelder Revier. In: Bartels, Christoph/Slotta, Rainer (eds.), *Der alteuropäische Bergbau. Von den Anfängen bis zur Mitte des 18. Jahrhunderts* (= *Geschichte des deutschen Bergbaus*. 1). Münster, pp. 340–352. **Fessner**, Michael (2015), Der Kupferschieferbergbau in der Grafschaft Mansfeld bis zum Dreißigjährigen Krieg. In: Jankowski, Günther, *Mansfelder Schächte und Stollen* (= *Forschungsberichte des Landesamtes für Vorgeschichte*. 6). Halle (Saale), pp. 11–43. **Fessner**, Michael (2012), Das Montanwesen in der Grafschaft Mansfeld vom ausgehenden 15. bis zur zweiten Hälfte des 16. Jahrhunderts. In: Westermann, Angelika (ed.), *Montanregion als Sozialregion*. Husum, pp. 293–320.

HARALD MELLER

Why Luther Archaeology?

Archaeology is unquestionably a crucial discipline for research on preliterate epochs. As soon as written sources become available, however, one often tends to think that they can better represent historical events. Indeed, this impression can sometimes be misleading, since in many cases written sources can be biased or even purposely distorted by the approach and intentions of the author. Furthermore, text sources are largely silent about aspects of daily life, as contemporary witnesses did not consider them to be relevant.

It is exactly at this point where archaeological research can achieve great significance because it relies on sources that end up in the ground without anticipation of their future impact. Moreover, they are especially suitable to illuminate daily living conditions. When professionally interpreted, these fragments of a former living environment supply us with hard evidence that, when compared with written sources, may contribute to revise earlier assumptions. For a long time, one believed that almost everything relevant about the reformer Martin Luther could be found in his writings and those of his associates.

By a great stroke of luck, in 2003 a large trash pit was uncovered during the excavation at his parents' home in Mansfeld which contained a substantial collection of personal belongings. Moreover, these finds are material evidence directly connected to Martin Luther's childhood and youth. Through these investigations it was ultimately possible to correct Martin Luther's own account of his somewhat poor family conditions drastically in favor of a childhood in a well-to-do household. Based on this, further archaeological and architectural investigations in his parents' home in Mansfeld, the house in which he was born in Eisleben, and his residence as professor in Wittenberg yielded numerous insights into Luther's daily living conditions. Lodging, food, clothing, work, and recreation were undoubtedly essential and formative aspects in the life even of an eminent theologian. These newly acquired material sources make it possible to expand earlier perceptions and come to a more realistic assessment of a historically significant personality like Luther. At the same time they can lead on to new questions. These wide-ranging results, which also serve to calibrate the written sources, impressively demonstrate why an archaeology of the early modern period, including Luther archaeology makes such extraordinary sense.

ANDREAS STAHL / BJÖRN SCHLENKER

Luther in Mansfeld:
Excavations and Accompanying Architectural Research on Martin Luther's Parents' Home

Historical Sources

With the help of historical topography and archival research, the location of Luther's family's residence in Mansfeld can be conclusively pinpointed at the modern-day sites at Lutherstraße 24, 25, and 26.[1] From which point in time the Reformer's family actually lived and dwelled here, however, can no longer be verified. Both the circumstances and duration of their residence in Eisleben with the birth of Martin Luther in 1483 and their standing as subtenants in the Stufenberg street in Mansfeld have been shown to be historical constructs of nineteenth-century Luther scholarship. Having grown up in his family home in the village of Möhra in Thuringia, Luther's father, Hans Luder, migrated to Mansfeld as a "Metallicus" (an ore miner or metallurgist). In order to enter the mining industry in Mansfeld's mining region, Hans Luder would have had to lease a smelting work and to invest a high sum for both its lease and operational maintenance. Thanks to the parish records of the church of St. George's in Mansfeld, it is known that on June 24, 1491 (on which date he witnessed the donation of an altar), he occupied the position of *Vierherr*.[2] It is not mentioned which quarter of Mansfeld he represented, but the fact that his name is written at the top of the list makes it probable that he lived in the town's inner district, and that he was among the dignitaries of the municipality.

There is a significant piece of evidence to support both this and the actual location of the Luthers' home. Martin Luther was nostalgically evoking his childhood home in 1544, when he dedicated a copy of the Bible to his childhood friend Nikolaus Oemler, observing that he had often carried Martin Luther "ynn vnd aus der schulen" (in and out of school). The school, which Martin Luther attended from 1488 on, was located across and to the north of St. George's, while the house of the wealthy smelter master Oemler lay three lots uphill from the modern-day house at Lutherstraße 26. There is every reason to believe that by 1491, when Hans Luder appeared in the parish records as *Vierherr*, the Luther family had long been settled in the place where they can be irrefutably confirmed to have lived in the sixteenth century. It is also probable that Hans Luder already belonged to the influential circle of the local smelter-master

Fig. 1 Mansfeld, Lutherstraße 24–26 (Luther street) seen from the east. In the foreground the extant part of Luther's parents' home (Lutherstraße 26), 2007

1 As a basis for the entire chapter, see Stahl, *Historische Bauforschung*.
2 A *Vierherr* was an elected provost of a town quarter, with some degree of executive power (police, defence, etc.).

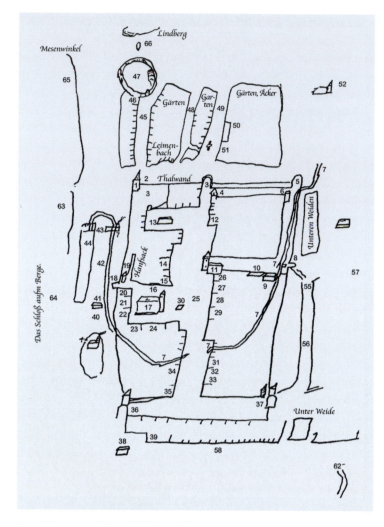

Fig. 2 Town map of Mansfeld from Cyriacus Spangenberg's
Mansfeldisch Chronica. Among other things it shows
the smelter masters' houses 26 (Kaufmann), 28 (Reinicke)
and 33 (Luther). Prior to 1561 (reproduction)

1507 was the one that the family had moved into in 1484 (at the latest) than that the source is related to a later purchase.

How does this fit in with the thesis postulated as early as the nineteenth century, of "zweien ins eins gebrachte Haus" (two houses turned into one)? After 1510, this house was structurally expanded. On St. Martin's Day in 1510, Hans Luder paid the parish of Vatterode an annual land tribute of two chickens for his house. In 1542, however, the tribute for his son and heir, Jacob, was three old pence and three chickens, which was to be paid explicitly for two houses. Even if the written records of the annual fees contain omissions, it can still be said that the second house was not acquired by Jacob, but by his father, Hans. It was then reconstructed in such a manner that it could be combined with the older house to form one property. This information appears again in a rent register from 1570. Indeed, this feud did not lapse until 1885. It can therefore be demonstrably confirmed that the Reformer's parents, Hans and Margarethe, lived there—along with his brother Jacob, who inherited the property in 1534. Jacob's son Veit kept it in the family until 1578.

Results of the Architectural Research

Along with the farmyard buildings that have since disappeared, the property originally consisted of a four-sided courtyard construction with a garden at the rear. Parts of a stable building that flanked the courtyard along the eastern side still exist and serve as a garage today. A common vaulted cellar that still connects the buildings of Lutherstraße 24 and 26 proves that this house—which is still in private hands—represents the western third of the former front house of the Luther family. It is certain that the missing portion had a gateway. To the east the town wall and its inner *Rabentor* (literally "raven's gate," now Lutherstraße 27), is still visible. An old tavern opposite and to the south of the Luther property is also shown on Spangenberg's sketch. It was once a vacant lot and is now the site of a museum (Museum Luthers Elternhaus Mansfeld). Similarly, structural finds from "des Canzlers Georgen Lauterbecks Behausung" (the residence of the provost Georg Lauterbeck) on the neighboring property to the west (number 22) can be detected. This is where the property of the Luther family is apparent today, with the above-mentioned stable wing. Beside the Luthers' site at the northeastern edge of the town center, older archeological investigations found traces of the old road to the town gates along the town walls. At the same time, the bent back course of the town wall which is still clearly discernible marks the boundary of the courtyard area to the north and east. The distinctive southern street front was closed with a single front building, now two separate buildings, Lutherstraße 24 and 26, which are separated from each other by an empty space (see fig. 1).

The one-story house number 26, whose eaves face the main street, is roughly square, measuring 9.65 by 10.38 meters. Despite sources that maintain the contrary, upstanding walls from Luther's lifetime can be seen very clearly. The cellar of the house which was constructed later is made up of two barrel vaults running parallel to the street. Because the site slopes downward to the east, the cellar has an entrance from the street that is accessed through a portal framed in the form of a round arch, above which the inscription "Luther-

community by this time. Thus Martin Luther spent his childhood in this social environment until 1498, later he and his children would come back for visits (fig. 1).

An extremely rare and detailed town map of Mansfeld provides decisive graphic evidence for the veracity of the traditional localization of Luther's childhood home. This well-known sketch of the town was produced by Cyriacus Spangenberg, a contemporary witness, before 1571 (fig. 2). In the enclosed caption, the original sketch in Vienna states for house number 33: "Jacob Luthern Schultheißen, Doctor Martin Luthers Brudern Behausung so von ihrer beider Vatern Hans Luthern enfenglich erbauet." (The house of Jacob Luther, the *Schultheiss* [mayor], Doctor Martin Luther's brother, and originally built by the father of both, Hans Luther.) The first written record of this family house is an entry in the town of Mansfeld's book of accounts, made in 1507 when the beneficiaries of the estate of Andres Kelner demanded and received the sum of 100 guilders. This transaction involved the remaining installment of an unknown purchase price, which Hans Luder had paid Kelner (during Kelner's lifetime) for the house in which the Luthers dwelled. It is more likely that the house that was fully paid for in

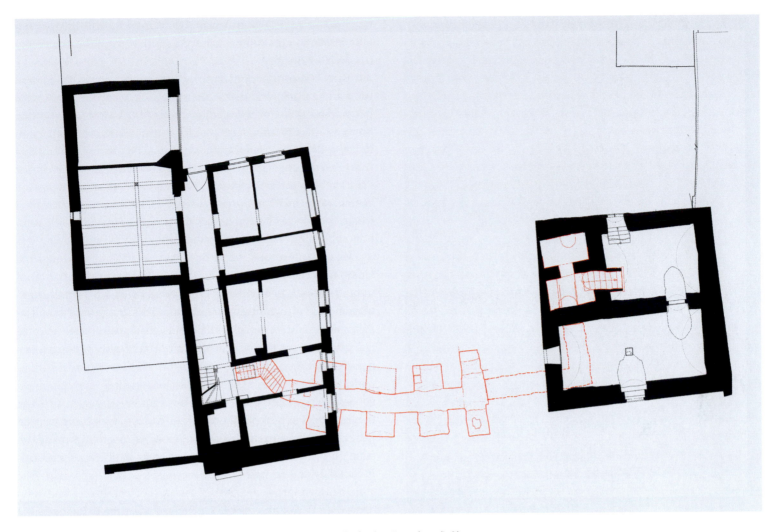

Fig. 3 Deformation-true longitudinal plan of the buildings at Lutherstraße (Luther Street) 24 (left)
and 26 (right: Luther's parents' home) with the cellar-like vaulted passage (red in the middle)
that connects them

haus" (Luther's House) has been applied. The cellar on the courtyard side was later fitted with a separate entrance. Beside it is the current main portal and entrance to the house, which is flanked by seating alcoves and framed with tracery, i.e., with stone components as in the tracery windows. Upon closer examination, one can discern a narrow round-arched door opening from the previous structure in the northeast corner of the courtyard façade, adjoining the inner town wall. During the period from 1885 to 1887 when it was being reconstructed as a memorial site, the structures from Luther's time were gravely impacted, especially during the installation of new windows. These square windows have horizontal windowsills and jambs with channels cut into them, into which the mullions are laid. There are two such windows on each freestanding side. The ground floor masonry consists of quarried stones that are mainly laid horizontally. The windows and doors are framed with cut stone, with the lintels flashed with a built-in segmented arch. Later adjustments can be clearly seen in the unplastered masonry. This building was reduced by one story in 1807 at the latest, and now has a freely-accessible gable to the west and a tiled saddleback roof[3] with a short hip. Two pitched dormer windows project from the side of each eave.[4]

The reconstruction of the construction-phase chronology of the Middle Ages and early modern times was helped significantly by the discovery and surveying of a cellar-type vault, the largest part of which lies, starting at Lutherstraße 24, in the vacant lot at Lutherstraße 26 (fig. 3). This form of cellar has also been found under contemporary buildings in Eisleben (e.g., at Petrikirchplatz). The existing lateral entrance ramps are secondary features, as the original access route was through the courtyard. The position of the cellar and the inclusion of the town wall as the eastern gable wall indicate that the modern-day structure at Lutherstraße 26 is an extension. According to more recent archaeological investigations, a vacant site was left between the courtyard and the inner town wall for fortification reasons.

House number 24 could not be mapped precisely as it is still inhabited today and covered with a thick layer of plaster. However it

3 A saddleback roof has two sloping surfaces that meet at a ridge. On the short side, the roof is enclosed by a gable, while on the long side lie the eaves. **4** The eaves are the lower horizontal borders of a roof, running parallel to the roof ridge (and normally along the longest side of a house).

Fig. 4 Mansfeld, Lutherstraße (Luther Street) 26 with entrance facing the courtyard, before it was enclosed in 1983

is likely that analogous to the western gable on the neighboring site, Luther period masonry lies under the plaster facing. In 1807, during the Napoleonic Kingdom of Westphalia, this wing of the building was also changed drastically. Thermal imaging has revealed that, among other details, a round-arched portal is concealed in the façade facing the street.

The originally smaller courtyard of the property was flanked by stables and farmyard buildings. To the north, it was closed off by a half-timbered shed, behind which a large garden extended to and along the slope to the town wall. The shed itself was demolished in 1807 and/or partially overbuilt with an early neoclassical *mairie* (French mayor's residence and office). The former kitchen garden behind it was then reconstructed as a formal garden in the late Baroque style. All of this belonged to the significant site of number 25. In order to access the building, which stood back from the street, the center of the late-medieval Luther house where the entrance gate was located, was demolished along the length of the vacant lot visible today. The remaining house segments served as terminal pavilions of a *cour d'honneur* (forecourt). Its open flanks were closed, in the case of the Luther house, by a quarry-stone wall with a large window for the parlor and quoins, as well as by a half-timbered gable abutting a hip roof. In 1811, the incumbent mayor, Rosen-

treter, acquired the eastern part of the complex, while the present Lutherstraße 24 probably remained the property of the town magistrate, Honigmann.

Only house number 26 received local recognition as a memorial site commemorating Luther. After the masonry opening of 1807, the party responsible for the maintenance of the eastern third of the house was the building inspector for the Mansfeld region and son-in-law of Rosentreter, Georg Franke. He had his office in the building from 1816 until 1853, and in 1840 ensured that it was entered in the Prussian Monuments Register. The establishment of a deaconess's center and a small memorial dedicated to Luther on the attic level can be traced to a citizens' association established in 1883, the four-hundredth anniversary of Luther's birth.

Up until now, house number 26 has been examined through the lens of the generally accepted life story of Luther's father, the "poor miner." It is not, as would appear from the courtyard portal, an extension from 1530, nor was it a farmyard building, as this is contradicted by several arguments. The architectural studies have revealed clues that indicate the existence of a previous building with a number of construction phases. In addition, it was a practical and originally two-story house with cellars, kitchen, parlors, and chambers, as well as a separate entrance. With an adjacent gateway to the west, it was originally part of the front house under one common roof. In light of the Spangenberg map and a reliable record from the eighteenth century regarding a house sign with initials from 1530, this part of the house was most likely reserved for Hans and Margarethe Luder in their old age.

Up until now, the current portal in the northern façade facing the courtyard was considered to have dated the completion of the construction work on house number 26 (fig. 4). This, however, must be critically assessed and questioned. According to archival records from the nineteenth century, the portal originally framed the entrance of the front-facing house that was demolished in 1807. It was secured at that time and only inserted into its current location by the Prussian district construction supervisor Franke in 1836. Above the round-arched finish, the broad keystone was shifted upwards from its original position in order to make room for a carved banderole bearing the date "1530." At the apex of the arch, an *à bouche* coat of arms covers the circumferential profiling. It is divided vertically, with a rose, crossbow and the initials J. L. for Jacob Luder. A house sign that is located above the keystone is decorated with two crossed miners' hammers. There is a clear contradiction in the heraldry of these two sculptures. On the one hand the coat of arms with the rose, crossbow, Jacob Luder's initials, and the year 1530, and on the other the stylistically older house sign of his father above it. Because of what we know from the restoration, and with the support of the written sources, the following is certain: the only stones that originally belonged to this entrance are the two arch stones at the sides. During the 1886 restoration of the Luthers' house, old cut stones were used to produce a new keystone with a coat of arms and inscription, as well as a mining-related house sign. These stones were then built into the structure. The reason for this was that both the original house sign and the initials, part of the 1530 inscription, had decayed. An erroneous reinterpretation from the late nineteenth

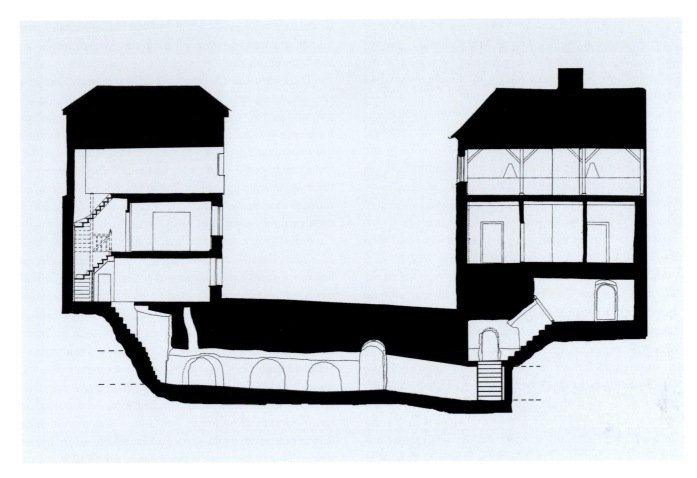

Fig. 5 Deformation-true longitudinal section of Lutherstraße
(Luther Street) 24 (left) and 26 (right) with measurements
of the storys' heights and of the cellar tract

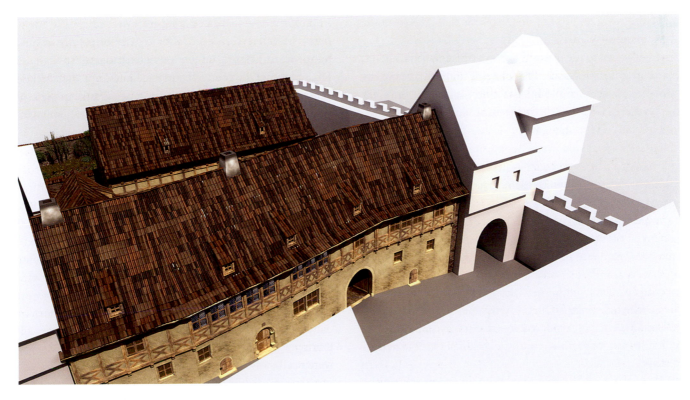

Fig. 6 Reconstruction of the Luthers' residence near the
Inner Raven's Gate, c. 1530. Digitale Archäologie/Freiburg Brsg.

century was in this way "cemented," as it were, into the equation, as the house was remade into an architectural facsimile of the life of Hans Luder. This portal, therefore, is a significantly modified *spolium* introduced much later, and therefore cannot be drawn upon when dating Martin Luther's familial home.

The evaluation of a survey which accounts for structural deformation, first made in 2007, produced spectacular results. The plans and sections revealed unknown structural relationships between the two buildings on the street front, which up until that point had been regarded as isolated entities (fig. 5). A horizontal alignment above the ground floor and approximately equal gable widths strongly imply a common first floor and attic. The surprising issue, however, was the discovery of a vault under houses 24 and 26 that had been previously unknown. The survey located two large, deep cellars from two separate earlier structures on the street front. In their footprints, they range a considerable distance beyond the enclosing walls that lie above them. However, the cellars were incorporated into the houses that were later newly constructed above them.

Ultimately, these finds serve as clear confirmation of the thesis of "zweien ins eins gebrachte Haus" (two houses brought into one). They also affirm the street side extension of the Luthers' property. At the same time, the finds account for several construction phases. It is likely that both houses were acquired and merged together by Hans Luder, and this, as we now know, occurred not only under one (top story and) roof, but also in the cellar area. The front house was not only remodeled and/or expanded shortly before the death of Hans Luder in 1530, but also during the lifetime of Jacob. For obvious reasons, this is verified in the uninhabited house (number 26) by subsequently constructed barrel vaults and sandstone jambs in the cellars. As we shall see, recently excavated filling material from the cellar included remarkable archaeological finds that date from the second third of the sixteenth century.

The merger of two previous buildings into one side-gabled building with a large courtyard ensemble was not unusual among the wealthy smelter masters around Mansfeld. In Eisleben, a representative house is that of Dr. Philipp Drachstedt at "am Markt 56," which was combined into one building by his father-in-law, Thile Rinck, as early as 1517.[5] Rinck was also a smelter master. Philipp Drachstedt, however, was not only Hans Luder's business partner and a role model for his son's judicial career path; it was in his house on the market square that Martin Luther died in 1546. The neighboring building toward Eisleben's Andreaskirchplatz is quite long and was also constructed of a number of houses—including the house of smelter master Hans Lüttich. Hans Luder administered the inheritances of Lüttich's children. It was not by chance that several of the counts of Mansfeld later set up their city palaces and chambers in such houses, which distinguish their townscapes to this day. In the town center of Mansfeld, the side-gabled smelter-master houses of Reinicke, Kaufmann, or Oemler continue to form a visible part of the streetscape.

In terms of space and appearance, the Luthers' property was similar to the guest house that was then situated across the street, the Goldener Ring (Golden Ring). The structure was adapted to the slope of the street with a *souterrain* and a deep cellar, its side-facing

gable had a high-pitched roof and was almost certainly two stories high with a timber-framed upper floor. Asynchronously-arranged windows are evidence of multiple reconstructions, as can also be shown in the case of the round-arched portals. The most richly decorated portals always led to the most impressive rooms of the house. These *Bohlenstuben* (wooden parlors) were probably found in the present low-ceilinged timber-framed first floor. *Bohlenstuben* were comfortable, wood-lined, and heated living spaces for families. The perhaps partially open kitchen, which was appropriate for both the size and reputation of the Luther household, faced the courtyard. It is certain that the front house also possessed a gateway into the courtyard (fig. 6).

In has been verified that there were at least three phases of construction of Martin Luther's father's house during Luther's lifetime. These measures ultimately served to functionally and visually unite two separate houses. After the death of Hans Luder, Jacob Luther occupied the house until his passing in 1571. Jacob was also a respected smelter master in addition to his position as *Schultheiss*, a position akin to a modern-day mayor. Even when his descendents lost the property in the course of debt repayments in 1578/79, the house was still prestigious enough to accommodate respected persons such as the Eisleben alderman Tobias Stossnack or the mayor Heinrich von Bülow, before gradually falling into disrepair in the eighteenth century. Measures that have left their mark to this day are the demolition of the central axis in 1807, and the development of number 26 into a monument to Luther from 1885 to 1897.

Applying methods of historical architectural research on Martin Luther's parents' home has brought previously unknown facts to light. The new assessment of his father's social status, that has been corrected by local and mining history research, is reflected in this impressive courtyard complex from which significant structural fabric still survives. Indeed, after Wittenberg, the house(s) in Mansfeld provide the most authentic evidence for the Luther family's daily life. The discovery of archaeological finds from Mansfeld that will be presented below were a particular stroke of luck as they help to impress the circumstances of Luther's childhood in our consciousness.

Archaeological Excavations

The architectural investigations of Luther's parents' home were triggered by excavations carried out on the above-mentioned site in the fall of 2003. The archaeological features will not be discussed here. Suffice it to say that the finds discussed in this essay were found in a stairwell driven into the loess subsoil, which led into the excavation pit of the previously mentioned vaulted cellar corridor.[6] After the cellar was completed, the staircase was filled with domestic waste, which must have originated from a central household waste heap on the site.

It was a particular stroke of luck that circumstances allowed for a further excavation to be conducted in 2008. It took place in the upper cellar of the building traditionally referred to as "Luther's parents' home." This previously unknown brick-lined cellar room, like the stairwell that was opened up in 2003, had been filled with household waste over time. The comparison of these two finds is quite compelling. As will be shown, its findings are of great historical

Fig. 7 Goose-bone bird calls and refuse from their manufacture, around 1500, from the excavation at Martin Luther's parents' home

most part, do not allow for the differentiation of the species) take second place with 30 percent. The lowest number of bones comes from cattle (10 percent). In addition, the consumption of domestic fowl was of vital importance to the Luther household, as illustrated by some two thousand bones.

The Luthers' appreciation of high-quality food is shown in the choice of domestic foul with utmost clarity. The goose was the most common meat by a considerable measure, while young chickens were often consumed along with the occasional duck or pigeon. The thorough sieving of the excavated material in Mansfeld further enabled the discovery of countless fish bones. At that time freshwater fish was considered to be of the highest quality, and the species confirmed at the site included carp, bream, roach, asp, pike, pike-perch, perch, and eel. In addition, imported fish such as herring, cod, and plaice could also be identified. These saltwater fish reached Mansfeld as salted herring and in a dried form (i.e., as stockfish). The confirmed fish species are of interest not only because they were considered a delicacy, but also because they simultaneously represented a considerable proportion of the Lenten diet. The church ban on the consumption of meat applied to well over one hundred days in the Catholic Church Year, which serves to illustrate the importance of fish, which was exempt from the ban.

One extremely rare discovery was proof that songbirds were on the menu. Remains of song thrush, whitethroat warbler, and yellowhammer were documented, while robins and chaffinches were even more common. Eating small birds was a matter of course in Germany until well into the nineteenth century and is certainly no cause for surprise in the years around 1500. There is even evidence that these birds were caught by members of the Luther household themselves: among the finds were small pipes fashioned out of goose bones (fig. 7).[8] These pipes which were designed as bird calls for attracting songbirds were made in exactly the same manner into the twentieth century. A further spectacular discovery is that these pipes were manufactured on-site. Among the many goose bones, several longer bones were strategically severed at the joint end so that the medullary cavity could be used in pipe production.

Botanical analyses were also highly informative. Alongside documented finds of cereals such as rye, wheat, and barley, a wide range of gathered wild plants (elderberries, plums, sloes, hazelnuts, raspberries) and medicinal plants (opium poppy, St. John's wort, henbane) were also documented. The Luther household also consumed grapes and figs.

The evaluation of the pottery assemblage is particularly interesting, as German earthenware of the early modern period has not been dealt with in a comprehensive manner to date. It was thus scarcely possible to date the finds in a remotely satisfactory manner during the excavation itself. According to the analysis of the material to date,[9] the kitchen ceramics were found to be of a simple and functional form and originated in the period immediately before and after

interest. It illustrates in a remarkably effective way how the careful evaluation of comprehensive archaeological finds can yield extensive information. They allow unimagined insights into the private life of Martin Luther's family.

The Finds of the 2003 Excavation

The verification and analysis of more than seven thousand animal bones[7]—skeletal fragments of cattle, pigs, and sheep or goats—revealed the spectrum of species considered typical for the Middle Ages and the early modern period. Of considerable interest, however, is the percentage represented by each species. At 60 percent, it is clear that the domestic pig was the favorite source of meat in the Luther household. The bones were mainly from young, fully grown animals. These animals had, on the one hand, reached an economically acceptable weight at slaughter while, on the other hand, they would have provided meat of the highest quality in terms of flavor. It is known that even in his later years Martin Luther deeply appreciated such culinary delights. Sheep and goats (whose bones, for the

5 See Stahl, *Lutherstadt Eisleben*. **6** Schlenker, *Archäologie*, pp. 22–31.
7 Döhle, *Schwein, Geflügel und Fisch*. **8** Schlenker, *Archäologie*, pp. 79 f. The entire find material is described in detail in this publication which can also be consulted for further literature. **9** Stephan, *Keramische Funde*.

Fig. 8   Decorated dinner knives, around 1500, from the
excavation at Martin Luther's parents' home

1500. The *Grapen*—three-legged pots that could be placed directly into the coals of the open fire—were by far the most common vessel. A large number of unglazed lids for such pots were also found.

Two fragments confirmed that the Luthers were also in possession of metal *Grapen* pots. Such pots were so valuable that they were regularly mentioned in wills and testaments of the time. However, there are only items of pottery tableware. There is reason to suspect, therefore, that household waste was also disposed of elsewhere. Despite this some sherds of Waldenburg stoneware—Waldenburg was an important center of pottery in Saxony—were found that prove the existence of a variety of tableware shapes. Fragments of a so-called *Igelgefäß* (hedgehog vessel) deserve special mention. Such pieces were highly rare representation or trick vessels that were used to decorate the table during festive occasions. Two large, yellow-glazed serving plates can also be counted among the tableware. A green-glazed rim-sherd belongs to a chalice-shaped vessel that is commonly interpreted as a salt cellar. A very small number of glass vessels were found which can hardly be seen as representative. Close inspection identified the sherds as the remains of stemmed glasses, knobbed glasses, and ribbed beakers.[10] Stemmed glasses served as vessels for beer, while the others were more typically used to consume wine.

Along with animal bones, botanical macro-remains, and kitchen pottery, other—initially often inconspicuous—finds provide information about events that happened in the Luther family's kitchen. Among the finds, iron objects play a special role. Remarkable finds include especially the nails of which 1,600 examples were recovered from the feature. Not surprisingly, the analysis and interpretation of such a large assemblage is difficult, but it is likely, however, that the nails were disposed of because of the need for wood. As many sources report, firewood in Mansfeld, as in all mining districts, was a valuable commodity. It is therefore quite conceivable that households were happy to use rejected construction wood that in some cases may have been virtually peppered with nails. For example, window shutters studded with nails can often be identified in contemporary paintings. If such shutters were then burned, several hundred nails could rapidly be deposited on the waste heap together with the ashes.[11]

Large quantities of copper-slag fragments were found associated with the ash that came from the hearths.[12] Glowing copper slag still served as a heating agent for the smelter workers of the Mansfeld Land as late as the 1920s. In Hettstedt, in the current district of Mansfeld-Südharz, spa and bathing activity became popular for a number of years during the mid-nineteenth century, and water heated with glowing copper slag was thought to alleviate gout, rheumatism, and similar complaints. The oldest source for this again dates to around 1500. A special slag-bath is mentioned, without the slightest hint of astonishment, in a report with regard to an event in 1484. It seems almost obvious therefore that the household of smelter master Hans Luder resorted to using the roughly 1,000-degree-Celsius-hot slag as a cheap source for heating the rooms or boiling the water.

The variety of the fragments of knives that were recovered from this cellar is quite remarkable.[13] In the majority of cases, the fragments come from fairly small table knives that were often richly

Fig. 9 Clay marbles, around 1500, from the excavation at Martin Luther's parents' home

decorated (fig. 8). Several knife handles were decorated with hilts made of bone, while others had wooden handle mounts. Decorative elements made of brass which are found on several examples are particularly charming. These elaborate and often delicate examples alone show that the Luther household possessed a certain degree of wealth, which was appropriately expressed at the table. A number of finds were related to handicrafts and may thus be related in particular to the female members of the household.[14] Along with a perfectly preserved thimble, these include a spindle whorl (the gyrating weight at the lower end of a spindle), a pair of scissors, a knitting pin, and a sewing needle. In this assemblage of finds, the spindle whorl seems somewhat out of place, as it can hardly be assumed that the production of yarn was carried out in the house on any significant scale. The other objects, however, represent the normal set of tools that would be required to carry out repairs or to tailor textiles and garments.

The evidence for toys is particularly alluring. A *Pfeifvogel* (bird whistle) is particularly interesting as it could be filled with water to produce a warbling song.[15] In addition, seven clay marbles were found (fig. 9). Their differing sizes and irregular shapes give one the impression that the children of the house had perhaps made them themselves and had fired them in their mother's hearth.[16] Two further toy components are particularly difficult to interpret. One of them is the phalanx bone of a cow, which has a drilled hole in the surface of its broader/distal end.[17] Bones processed in this manner were commonly used as simple bowling pins. Liquid lead was poured into the hole, which gave the bone a degree of stability. Several such pins would be placed standing in a row, to be then aimed

10 Schlenker, *Archäologie*, pp. 81–85. **11** Ibid., p. 94. **12** Ibid., pp. 92 f.
13 Ibid., pp. 85–92. **14** Ibid., pp. 70–72. **15** Ibid., pp. 74 f. **16** Ibid., pp. 72.
17 Ibid., pp. 72–74.

Fig. 10 Pilgrim's horn from Aachen (Aachhorn), a typical souvenir from the pilgrimage
        to Aachen/Aix-la-Chapelle and evidence for the pious life in the Luthers' household,
        from the excavation at Martin Luther's parents' home

at and knocked over by throwing another bone. A scene of this kind is accurately portrayed in the well-known painting *Children's Games* by Pieter Bruegel the Elder. Although the scene mentioned is located in the background of the picture, the shape of the bone-pins can still be discerned exactly.

Measuring no more than seventeen millimeters along its longest axis, another small object made of bone possesses two holes, each of which was drilled in the opposite direction to the other, which characterizes it as a technical object.[18] Under close examination, the find turned out to be a miniature version of the nut of a crossbow. The nut was the essential component of the trigger mechanism of a crossbow from the Middle Ages. In those days, the nut of a hunting or combat crossbow was fashioned from antler horn. It was fixed in the stock of the crossbow by means of a metal axle. On its top there was a groove to accommodate the string, while the trigger guard was located at the bottom of the nut to allow the shot to be released. Due to the small size of our find, it is obvious that it is a fragment from a toy crossbow. Corresponding pieces of evidence are very rare indeed; only occasionally paintings or tapestry would depict children playing with crossbows.

Some finds afford an insight into the security requirements of the wealthier members of society at this time. Due to a range of written sources from this period, researchers are exceptionally well informed about events in Mansfeld.[19] Contemporary court records from the town provide information about crimes. As miners were

not prohibited to carry weapons, such weapons came to use in the most trivial of circumstances—and often with lethal consequences. In addition these sources tell us that break-ins, theft, and robberies were practically everyday occurrences. It is therefore not surprising that a number of objects that can be attributed—in the broadest sense—to this topic were found among the artifacts from the Luthers' property. This connection becomes particularly conspicuous with the examination of a find that, at first glance, would appear to be the handle of a heavy knife with a remarkable pommel.[20] Yet wholly intact examples in various collections as well as pictorial representations from the first half of the sixteenth century show that the fragment recovered in Mansfeld is, in fact, the handle of a *Hauswehr* (house weapon), which is the name for a single-edged melee weapon of the period. It can therefore be assumed that not only miners but also smelter masters possessed weapons. Furthermore, it was particularly the wealthier citizens of the town that would have felt the need to adequately secure their possessions. Two keys—of which the larger may be viewed as a front-door or house key—bear further testament to this assumption. In terms of archaeological finds, iron padlocks represent an absolute rarity;[21] two such locks with square cases show that the Luther household also strove to protect its property against unauthorized access.

Alongside the iron articles mentioned above, numerous other iron objects, which are extremely important in terms of cultural history, were identified among the finds.[22] Of particular interest here is a completely preserved spade iron as well as several curious-looking objects with cleats or studs. The latter have been interpreted as heel-plates, though there is no documentation of corresponding pieces in the literature. It can well be imagined that miners wore safety shoes made of wood, with such metal plates fitted to the bottoms to prevent them slipping on unstable ground.

A find of extraordinary interest, which was initially completely inconspicuous, was made of unglazed fired clay. Due to its faceted surface as well as the base of a broken-off lug , this fragment can be accurately interpreted as a broken piece of a Pilgrim's Horn or *Aachhorn* (fig. 10).[23] Such horns are regarded by scholars as souvenirs of a pilgrimage to Aachen (hence their name). In addition, evidence increasingly points to their use in superstitious activities. This is illustrated tellingly in a seventeenth-century quotation from the sermons of Konrad Dietrich of Ulm: "In many places there were *Wetterhorner (weather horns)*, which were consecrated in Ach (Aachen) in Brabant and, therefore, were referred to as *Achhörns.*" On the one hand, this establishes a reference to the pilgrimages to Aachen, while on the other, however, the term "Wetterhorn" (weather horn) provides a link to the realm of superstition, as weather horns were used to guard against thunder and lightning. In the Middle Ages and early modern period, Aachen was one of the most prominent centers of Christianity in central Europe. Thus, in 1515, Pope Leo X granted the same indulgence for a pilgrimage to Aachen as for one to Rome or Jerusalem. Four important relics stood at the center of the veneration, which had been shown to the faithful in a seven-year cycle since 1349 (for example, in 1496, 1503, and 1510). The description of one such exhibition from 1510 is extraordinarily vivid: "When they [the relics] are displayed to the pilgrims, the people begin to blow their horns, so that you could not have heard even the thunder of the good Lord himself […] and there is no one there whose hair does not stand on end, nor whose eyes are not filled with tears. This is accompanied by the sound of trumpets and many horns. In Aachen's environs, little horns of clay are baked." According to this account, such pilgrim's horns were actually produced in the area around Aachen, which is confirmed by corresponding archaeological analyses. The find from the Luther house therefore opens up a completely new perspective on the religiosity of the family of Martin Luther, who—as is well known—declared himself in later years to be a vehement opponent of the institution of pilgrimage.

While the objects described thus far can be quite easily viewed as ordinary household waste, the items yet to be mentioned—costume accessories and coins—were of considerable value at the time of their disposal. Moreover, the fact that both groups are present in quite impressive numbers raises the question of how and, above all, why these items were disposed of. The find of over three hundred brass objects was particularly spectacular.[24] The vast majority of them are elements that are directly connected with a woman's festive costume. In particular, decorated mounts stand out among the finds. Floral, blossom-shaped mounts are the most common, although cross and shield-shaped appliqués were also recovered. Elongated and abstract-shaped appliqués are more unusual. Many of these mounts have rivets, which are as a rule three millimeters long. Thus

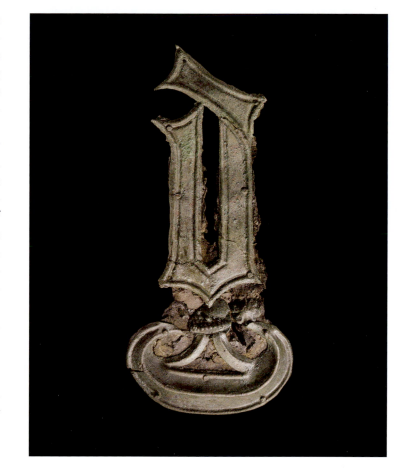

Fig. 11 Terminal mount of a belt in the shape of the letter "D," around 1500, from the excavation at Martin Luther's parents' home

it is highly likely that they were attached to a material of this thickness, making their use on leather goods (e.g., belt straps or bags) logical candidates.

Of great significance and rarity is an almost eighteen-centimeter-long brass-plate fitting, the leather substrate of which is still well preserved.[25] It decorated the end of a broad strap and is composed of several elements. The main part forms a letter of the alphabet punched from brass plate, a lowercase "d." It is augmented by a single preserved rosette and a half-moon-shaped final. This find is clearly the strap-end mount of a sumptuous belt (fig. 11). Of course the question is raised what the significance of the letter "D," which is most likely an initial letter, is likely to be. As it happens, it was a popular custom in the period around 1500 to complement traditional clothing with pieces of jewelry or embroidery with initials. This practice was especially common in wedding portraits of the time. One famous example is Dürer's portrait of Elsbeth Tucher, in which she wears a brooch with the initials of her bridegroom, Niklas Tucher, on her fichu. It is, in fact, easy to indentify the person in the

18 Ibid., pp. 75–78. **19** Particular mention must be made of the Chronicles of Cyriacus Spangenberg, who was the local priest in Mansfeld at the close of the sixteenth century and who recorded happenings from his past and present environs. **20** Schlenker, *Archäologie*, pp. 94–96. **21** Ibid., pp. 101f. **22** Ibid., pp. 103–109. **23** Ibid., pp. 96–99. **24** Ibid., pp. 34–47. **25** Ibid., pp. 62–67.

Luther household for whom the initial "D" comes into question: the core family according to what is known to date consisted of the parents, Hans and Margarethe Luther (actually, Luder), their two sons (Martin and Jacob) and three daughters, one of whom was named Dorothea. It is therefore conceivable that the end fitting and at least some portion of the other brass fittings came from a belt that belonged to one of Martin Luther's sisters.

Strap buckles of widely varying designs were found.[26] Along with a number of brass pieces, six iron specimens were also recovered. One outstanding example is a more than four-centimeter-long buckle, the strap fitting of which is decorated with depictions of flowers. While blossoms and flowers are used relatively often as ornamental designs, the representation of entire flowers—that is, with stems and leaves—is exceedingly rare.

Sixty pins including twenty-six complete pieces make up a representative group of finds.[27] These are mostly pins that are several centimeters long and decorated with spherical heads. In the truest sense of the word, they served as dressmaker pins and were used to help position bonnets and other clothing for stitching. In many cases the folds of the clothing were gathered by laboriously laying them together by hand before fixing them with such a needle. Such effort was not made for day-to-day clothing, of course, but was reserved exclusively for feast-day apparel.

The number of aglets—seventy-five complete examples and over seventy fragments—is even more impressive.[28] The function of these objects is quite difficult to determine at first glance. Aglets are reinforcements that are applied to the ends of straps and laces to help (among other things) prevent fraying, much like the plastic sleeves on the ends of modern-day shoelaces. Strictly speaking, they are simply tiny pipes manufactured from thin brass plate, with an average length of two centimeters. They were properly identified only after plant fibers had been discovered in several pieces. Once they were on the right track, researchers discovered that similar objects could be found in many paintings from that era—and in particular those of Pieter Bruegel the Elder. In the traditional clothing of the time, around 1500, laces and drawstrings played a part that should not be underestimated. As buttons were used very rarely, pieces of clothing were commonly closed by means of straps. Hook-and-eye fasteners, also present in the archeological assemblage, also served this function.

If the metal clothing components proved to be a great surprise, this was by far exceeded by a total of more than 250 silver coins. The first pieces were already recovered from the very top layers of the find. All in all, the coins were scattered throughout the entire fill of the stair pit, with the last piece being recovered at the deepest point.

After scholarly examination, it could be determined that, with a small number of exceptions, the specimens consisted of Eisleben bracteates, small-change mintage made of thin sheet metal.[29] The counts of Mansfeld ordered the one-sided minting of the coins from silver sheet as early as the first half of the fifteenth century. As the counts had illegally reduced the silver content of this legal tender on repeated occasions, their production of these coins was forbidden in 1526 by the souvereign. The coins, therefore, are not suitable for precisely dating the find. Bracteates represented the smallest unit of coinage in circulation. They were still manufactured from silver, however, making them surely too valuable to simply dispose of in the household waste.

The composition of the find material in Mansfeld is highly unusual, and, from an archaeological point of view, quite difficult to comprehend. As can be shown, the find is obviously composed of kitchen and household waste, as well as the animal bones and pottery and the majority of the iron nails and copper slag found on the site. The numerous silver coins and metal clothing clearly fall outside of this normal framework. These last-mentioned finds—coins and clothing appliqués—are of particular interest, since such specimens are rarely found during excavations in towns of the Middle Ages. Furthermore, outside of hoard finds they almost always come to light as individual pieces. Why did coins and decorative elements get mixed into the rubbish? The archaeological evidence itself does not yield any other clues. Sources do exist, however, that could help in the further interpretation of the find:[30] "As I had just become a monk, my father almost went berserk, was deeply unhappy, and didn't want to allow me, but I wanted to do it with both his knowledge and his blessing nonetheless. When I wrote to him to inform him, he replied to me in writing, theeing and thouing me. Previously, as I held a master's degree, he had addressd me with the formal 'you'. He revoked all fatherly favor and disinherited me. But there came a pestilence, so that two of his sons died, and he was informed that I must have died too, although I was still alive, and for as long as God wills it."

The quotation recorded and handed down in this form by Valentinus Bavarus in 1548 is claimed to be an excerpt from Luther's sermon from January 20, 1544. In spite of extensive research it has remained unclear who this Bavarus ("a citizen of Naumburg") actually was. It is, however, likely that he was a student and boarder of Luther who—as was also common during his *table talks*—recorded this quote.[31] This quotation, which only differs from Bavarus's in formal terms, is published in the WA (see footnote). However, Georg Rörer, an actual student and confidant of Luther, here abbreviates the quotation after the passage "und hies mich ' 'Du,' prius ' 'vos,' Et sagt mir veterlich trewe ab" (theeing and thouing me, whereas previously he had addressed me with the formal 'you,' and revoked all his paternal fidelity) with the words "et ab aliis admonitus etc." The rest of the quote did not seem to him to be worthy of reproduction, the motif of the furious father obviously being far more interesting.

As it turns out, however, at least two people recorded Luther's remarks in their own words. The authenticity of this quotation thus seems to lie in the realm of the probable. For this reason the death of two of Martin Luther's brothers is also accepted unequivocally and as a matter of course by Martin Brecht, author of a foremost biography of Luther. This quotation is also illuminating in that it describes how Hans Luder was informed that his son Martin—a recent resident in the monastery in Erfurt—had also died of the plague. As it happens, it is on record that in 1505, the year in which Luther entered the order of the Augustinians, the plague was rampant in Erfurt, claiming many victims. A last link in the "chain of evidence" is provided by Cyriacus Spangenberg in his first book of the *Chronicle of Mansfeld*, published in 1572 in Eisleben: "1505 was a wet summer / what is more, there came the plague / and lasted for many years / even worse among the livestock." The plague, then, had soon reached Mansfeld too. At that time, the town lay on one of the most important transport routes between the Hanseatic cities to the north and the trading centers of the south. The Luther property in Mansfeld was located close to the lower town gate on the main traffic artery and across the street from a highly-frequented guest house. It is little wonder, then, that the Luthers were not spared from the disease either.

In light of these arguments, it appears reasonable to consider the death of two of Luther's brothers in their parents' house in Mansfeld a historical fact. Such a catastrophic scenario, however, raises the question of whether the plague could perhaps have been the trigger for the disposal of the exceptional finds. The causes of the plague—that is to say, the illnesses subsumed under this term—were not known to the people at that time. Nevertheless, it was absolutely customary that the clothing, underwear, bedclothes, and bedding straw used by infected persons was burned.

The rooms where Luther's brothers had died would have been cleared out, and all of the objects stored there, been disposed of. In the midst of this calamity, the richly decorated pieces of clothing and leather goods would have been committed to the fire. This assumption is supported by the discovery of a small, charred fragment of textile with a simply woven pattern, which was also found in the waste material. Even a purse fixed to a belt was paid no heed to and was burned with the rest. The remaining ashes and the smaller objects ruined by the fire were then thrown onto the waste pile in the courtyard, where the kitchen waste was normally disposed of.

The Finds from the 2008 Excavation

This section describes very briefly the finds recovered from another excavation in 2008 in the cellar of the Luthers' house.[32] They originate from a vault 1.30 meters deep and about four cubic meters in volume, which was discovered to have been sunk into the clay earth. Its walls were made of flat, block-shaped stones, while the floor was of clay.

When the cellar was no longer needed, it was filled in much the same way as the cellar shaft already described. Both ashes from the fire and copper slag that had been used to heat water play a major role here too. The finds are, without exception, more modest, but are of considerable importance in that they are approximately thirty to forty years younger than the finds recovered in 2003.

In this case, the ceramic material originated mainly in the kitchen area,[33] in particular the finds related to three-legged *Grapen*/cooking pots, which at this time were predominantly yellow glazed. In this find, too, very few of the fragments could be attributed to tableware. The sherds from drinking glasses correspond approximately to the older finds. It is remarkable, however, that here the fragments exclusively belong to beer glasses, while the classic wine glasses are completely absent.[34] Particularly exciting is the fact that marbles were discovered in this find as well.[35] Once again, the marbles were homemade with noticeably irregular shapes. In addition, several pieces were also found to have come from tradesmen, that is, there

were some professionally produced examples. Similarly, a semi-finished dice made of bone deserves mention. As it is not completely finished, it may be assumed that it was produced by a family member or one of the family's servants.[36]

Two fragments of clay-pipe figures were recovered from the Luthers' cellar. In terms of their connection to the Luther family, one of them is possibly of some importance.[37] This figurine has a female form with a full-length dress, both the head and shoulders are missing. The fragment is preserved up to a height of 6.2 centimeters. The hands at rest before the abdomen hold rosary beads, on which an apparently reddish-brown paint can be discerned. The pose and presentation, meanwhile, suggest that the figurine could have depicted a saint. In contemporary art, only two female saints are represented with a rosary as their attribute. One is Mary, the mother of God, while the other is Saint Monica, the mother of Saint Augustine, the patron saint of the Augustinian order to which Martin Luther had dedicated himself. The mother of Saint Augustine was afforded particular veneration by the community of brothers, so it is pertinent to ask whether this figurine might have come from the monastery in Erfurt. In a pamphlet from the sixteenth century, "baked saints of Erffurdt" are mentioned, making this idea seem much less far-fetched. The interpretation of the fragment as constituting a figurine of Mary, however, would be quite reconcilable with the sources on the Luther family. It is known, for example, that Hans Luder was a member of the *Mansfelder Marienbruderschaft* (Mansfeld Brotherhood of Mary) as early as before 1505. It is therefore quite possible that the recovered figurine once served private devotion in the Luther household.

Coins and decorative items made of brass were again recovered, though this time in much lower quantities. In this case, they were likely to have been lost items that were then disposed of. One remarkable find, however, is a large and richly decorated fragment of a belt.[38] This belt consists of several individual parts, which, put together, are approximately fifty centimeters long. The entire surface of the belt is decorated with metal fittings. These include small brass rivets, but it is the realistic acorn-shaped decorations that deserve to be mentioned in particular. These seem to hang on little twigs, but it is only upon closer examination that these twigs can be recognized as bones!

As acorns are normally a symbol of fertility and life, while bones often stand for death and the transience of life, these two elements may have been combined into a motif in the sense of a *memento mori* (a reminder of mortality). The shape clearly indicates that it was a woman's belt, though it must be asked whether the owner was even aware of the deep symbolism of the valuable piece she wore. It is also worth mentioning that, among the numerous finds recovered from the cellar, a fragment of a man's shoe was also found.

26 Ibid., pp. 54–61. **27** Ibid., pp. 53 f. **28** Ibid., pp. 49–53. **29** Dräger, *Münzen*. **30** Stahl/Schlenker, *Lutherarchäologie*, pp. 129 f. **31** The reason why this quote was apparently not deemed worthy of inclusion in the *Kritische Gesamtausgabe der Werke Martin Luthers* was only determined by inquiring with Gerhard Hammer, one of its editors. **32** Schlenker, *Kellerbefund* with follow-up literature. **33** Ibid., pp. 270–277. **34** Ibid., pp. 282–284. **35** Ibid., p. 284. **36** Ibid., p. 286. **37** Ibid., pp. 287–289. **38** Ibid., p. 289.

Fig. 12
Bones of salted fish (salted herrings), around 1500, from the excavation at Martin Luther's parents' home

Results of the Archaeological Excavations

Two archaeological features can, with convincing arguments, be attributed to a certain family, and they cover a time frame of about forty years. These finds offer the opportunity to follow the habits, practices, and diet of this family over this period of time. In determining familial preferences, nothing is as reliable as the kitchen. As can be shown based on the confirmed animal species and an extremely painstaking evaluation of the finds, the Luther household placed great emphasis on a rich and high-quality diet around 1500—a diet in which meat was obviously of great importance. The trapping of birds seems to have played a less important role in this diet and served as a form of pastime.

What was the situation in the kitchen of the Luther family some decades later? Among the domesticated mammals, the pig far outweighed all others. Oxen came in second, followed closely by sheep or goats. Poultry continued to feature regularly on the table, though chickens were evidently consumed more often than geese. This could have been due to a wide range of reasons, although it may simply have been because of deteriorating conditions for keeping geese. Geese, after all, require grassland and a plentiful water supply to thrive. Perhaps the family simply consumed more ducks, which were more commonly identified in the cellar than pigeons. The trapping of birds also continued in this period. Along with a bird-call pipe, the bones of thrushes, song thrushes, fieldfares, passerine birds and, from time to time, robins could be verified. An impressive list of mainly quite tasty varieties of fish illustrates that the consumption of fish was not necessarily associated with their importance as Lenten fare. In terms of freshwater fish (which likely came from local bodies of water), pike and carp, bream, eel, perch, and roach were all discovered. Saltwater fish, too, continued to be popular in the form of herring (salted herrings), flatfish, and cod (stockfish) (fig. 12).

As the highly informative analyses of the two animal-bone collections show, the kitchen of the Luther family seems to have maintained certain preferences. They preferred to eat pork and bacon, perhaps from their own livestock, though from 1540 onward more beef was served at the table. The consumption of mutton seems to have remained both stable and high over this period. Poultry played an important role in both finds, and over time chicken was preferred to goose, though the family also indulged in duck more often. Similarly, the Luther family enjoyed fish regularly. The fact that evidence for bird snaring was confirmed in both features suggests a passion for hunting that was handed down through generations but that also served as a supplementary source of food. Altogether, it can be assumed that the Luther family cultivated certain preferences in terms of their diet. Even a certain tendency toward opulence can be discerned here, which can be reconstructed satisfactorily over a period of perhaps thirty to fifty years.

Conclusion

Until the present day, Martin Luther has remained a historic figure whose facets we have come to understand primarily through written sources. His own works fill bookshelves, while the variety of writings about him is almost beyond belief. It seems all the more surprising, therefore, how scanty the information is that we have on Luther's own family, his childhood, or on the social origins of the Reformer. As the most famous of his personal testimonials, two quotes from his *table talks* are of importance. According to these quotes, his father, Hans Luder, came from a farming family and moved to Mansfeld as a poor quarryman, that is, a simple miner.

There are now accessible studies of the family's archaeological legacies, the architectural heritage of Luther's parents' house, and the written heritage gleaned from the archives. When these are put together, Luther's statements do not correspond to the actual circumstances. It is not known whether Martin Luther himself sought to make an enduring, if overly modest, understatement when it came to matters related to his youth and origins. Perhaps the transcripts of his table companions did not exactly correspond to his statements—though this, similarly, cannot be confirmed with certainty today. The fact is that the core family in Thuringia was already wealthy, and that Hans Luder had to have already possessed previous knowledge when he took up his position in the mining and smelting industries in the county of Mansfeld. This elevated social position in Mansfeld was derived from different economic footholds that, seemingly independent, were actually linked to each other. The archaeological finds from the house of Martin Luther's parents were verified by the insights from the subsequent research into both the archives and the architectural heritage of the site. Martin Luther came from a home that was perhaps not excessively rich, but that can nevertheless quite reasonably be described as wealthy. As a smelter master, *Vierherr* (mayor of a town quarter), and *Schauherr* (i.e., as a mining official appointed by the count), Hans Luder was closely associated with the administration of the town of Mansfeld and the county.

Only time will tell to what extent these new insights will be taken into account by future research on the Reformation. All the same, statements from Martin Luther that seem completely exaggerated when compared with the currently accepted evaluation and estimation of his social origins have been known of for some time. In particular, this applies to his taking sides in the Peasants' War (*Bauernkrieg*). In the text *Against the Robbing and Murdering Hordes of Peasants* (1525), the leaders of the imperial army were called upon to oppose the peasants with the utmost severity and with God's blessing: "Therefore, dear lords, here is a place where you can release, rescue, help. Have mercy on these poor people! Let whoever can stab, smite, slay. If you die in doing it, good for you! A more blessed death can never be yours, for you die while obeying the divine word and commandment in Romans 13, and in loving service of your neighbor, whom you are rescuing from the bonds of hell and of the devil."[39]

On the basis of the results now available from the archaeological and architectural research, a contradiction arises that has never before been discussed: up to this day one has assumed that the son of a poor farmer—who had worked his way up from miner to smelter master—had written these words. Now we really know that Martin Luther had very little in common with the rebels of the Peasants' War. He came from a social class that could only have lost had the radical philosophy of Thomas Müntzer (a radical cleric and leader of the peasants) had been victorious.

39 LW 46, 54.

BIBLIOGRAPHY

Döhle, Hans-Jürgen (2007), Schwein, Geflügel und Fisch—bei Luthers zu Tisch. Tierreste aus einer Abfallgrube der Familie Hans Luther. In: Meller, Harald (ed.), *Luther in Mansfeld. Forschungen am Elternhaus des Reformators (= Archäologie in Sachsen-Anhalt. Sonderband 6).* Halle (Saale), pp. 169–186. **Dräger**, Ulf (2007), Die Münzen—Eine verlorene Haushaltskasse? In: Meller, Harald (ed.), *Luther in Mansfeld. Forschungen am Elternhaus des Reformators (= Archäologie in Sachsen-Anhalt. Sonderband 6).* Halle (Saale), pp. 159–168. **Schlenker**, Björn (2007), Archäologie am Elternhaus Luthers. In: Meller, Harald (ed.), *Luther in Mansfeld. Forschungen am Elternhaus des Reformators (= Archäologie in Sachsen-Anhalt. Sonderband 6).* Halle (Saale), pp. 17–112. **Schlenker**, Björn (2015), Ein bemerkenswerter Kellerbefund im Elternhaus Martin Luthers. Befunde und Funde der Frühen Neuzeit aus Mansfeld. In: Meller, Harald (ed.), *Mansfeld—Luther(s)stadt. Interdisziplinäre Forschungen zur Heimat Martin Luthers (= Forschungsberichte des Landesmuseums für Vorgeschichte Halle. 8).* Halle (Saale), pp. 263–320. **Stahl**, Andreas/**Schlenker**, Björn (2008), Lutherarchäologie in Mansfeld. Ausgrabungen und begleitende Bauforschungen am Elternhaus Martin Luthers. In: Meller, Harald (ed.), *Fundsache Luther—Archäologen auf den Spuren des Reformators.* Stuttgart, pp. 120–131. **Stahl**, Andreas (2007), Historische Bauforschung an Luthers Elternhaus. Archivalische Voruntersuchungen und erste Baubeobachtungen. In: Meller, Harald (ed.), *Luther in Mansfeld. Forschungen am Elternhaus des Reformators (= Archäologie in Sachsen-Anhalt. Sonderband 6).* Halle (Saale), pp. 113–138. **Stahl**, Andreas (2015), Die Lutherstadt Eisleben als Residenzstadt der Mansfelder Grafen. In: *Burgen und Schlösser in Sachsen-Anhalt,* vol. 24, pp. 316–347. **Stephan**, Hans-Georg (2007): Keramische Funde aus Luthers Elternhaus. In: Meller, Harald (ed.), *Luther in Mansfeld. Forschungen am Elternhaus des Reformators (= Archäologie in Sachsen-Anhalt. Sonderband 6).* Halle (Saale), pp. 139–158.

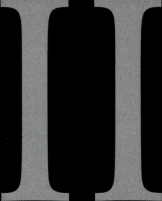

The Birth of the Reformation

NATALIE KRENTZ

The Wide-Ranging Impact of the Reformation

The Reformation was initially a rather dry, academic affair. Complex theological questions, which were probably difficult to grasp for the majority of the population, were debated in Latin texts, university colloquies, and long series of academic theses. But very quickly it became clear that the issues raised by the Reformation were extremely relevant to politics, the church, and many other aspects of religious and everyday life. Martin Luther's theses, initially written in Latin in 1517, were soon printed and disseminated in German. In 1520 there followed his three great Reformation tracts, and at the Imperial Diet of Worms of 1521, his teaching received an audience at the highest political level of the empire.

The Reformation also quickly reached a wider audience: around 1520, pastors began to include its ideas in their sermons and monks started leaving their monasteries to become itinerant preachers of the new faith. Pamphlets and illustrated handbills with theological tracts, as well as more easily digestible writings such as printed sermons, caricatures, and poems, quickly spread the ideas of the Reformation. They also mocked the dignitaries and customs of the old church through humor, satire, and irony. Since many people could not read the pamphlets themselves, they were often read aloud and discussed in taverns, presented in theatrical performances held on the market-places, and set to music by ballad makers.[1] Thus the teachings of the Reformation spread rapidly using a broad assortment of media. A "Reformation public" [reformatorische Öffentlichkeit] emerged with a lively and varied debating culture, in which, especially in this early period, the laity and women were particularly active.[2]

But people did not merely want to debate; they soon demanded that the reform of the church be implemented in practice and set about doing so themselves. Thus in the early 1520s, especially in the towns, numerous "Reformation movements" arose.[3] In a wide range of symbolic actions, which included pageants and satirical processions, disruptions of the Mass and other traditional ecclesiastical rituals, attacks on priests and monks, the singing and reciting of satirical songs and poems, and finally the removal and destruction of religious works of art ("iconoclasm"), people expressed their discontent with the current condition of the church and demanded change.

Recent research has convincingly shown that this was not a one-way "top-down" process, flowing from learned theologians to "the common man."[4] The actions of people in the streets and marketplaces might well have reflected what they had learned from Reformation sermons and handbills, but beyond this people also made their own demands and put forward their own creative interpretations of the Reformation's message—which in turn found their way into theological writings and sermons. And it was by no means only "the mob," composed of the lower orders, that participated in such actions but, as research has shown, very often master craftsmen and other members of the urban elites.[5] In many towns and estates of the empire, the demands of the "Reformation movements" were subsequently put into practice in church and city ordinances. The Reformation was especially successful in the cities, in particular imperial cities such as Nuremberg, Basel, Strasbourg, Constance, and Ulm, which is the reason why historians speak of the Reformation as an "urban event" (A. G. Dickens). However, in the 1520s the ideas of the Reformation spread rapidly in small towns as well as in the countryside, initiating debates which had a wide range of consequences varying greatly from region to region. Events sparked by these ideas include the Peasants' War as well as the Münster Rebellion. In this process, the ideas of the Reformation came into contact with already existing disputes and conflicts, which varied greatly depending on the town or region and the political, social, or ecclesiastical situation.

This was also true of the city of Wittenberg, which was and is considered the birthplace and center of the Reformation (fig. 1). As the electoral residency of the Elector of Saxony, a supporter of Luther, and with a young university and a bishop who was already largely powerless, Wittenberg offered particularly favorable conditions for the nascent Reformation. At the beginning of the sixteenth century and within a short span of years, Wittenberg was transformed from a center of late-medieval religiosity, famous for Elector Frederick the Wise's collection of relics, to the hub of the Reformation. A tight net of personal relations and close connections between university and town allowed the new theology to spread quickly beyond the walls of the university; several professors, including Luther himself, preached regularly in the castle and parish churches and were also often consulted on theological matters by the town council and the Elector's court.[6] Melchior Lotter's printing press allowed for rapid dissemination of Reformation ideas beyond Wittenberg itself.[7] Through the printing press, the leaders of the Reformation in Wittenberg were able to report and comment on their own activities, often leading to myth-building that still influences our perception of the Reformation today.[8] Wittenberg was the first city, as early as 1521–22, to experience a "Reformation movement." At the beginning of 1522 it passed the first Reformation ordinance, which, though modest in nature, introduced the Reformation into the city, completing the process one step at a time by 1525. As Luther's own city, Wittenberg quickly became a model for reformers in other cities and soon a symbol of the entire Reformation. In the following, the example of Wittenberg will be used to illustrate the "wide-ranging impact of the Reformation" as the city progressed from late-medieval piety to introducing the Reformation. As will be shown, the many and varied public expressions of late-medieval piety at the start of the sixteenth century underwent changes with the building of the electoral residence in the city. How did religion and the church manifest themselves to the people of Wittenberg at the beginning of the sixteenth century, and how did people react to the changes brought about by the nascent Reformation? Finally, the beginnings of the Reformation that rose from this foundation will be described.

From Plurality to Standardization:
Piety in Wittenberg before the Reformation

Religious life in Wittenberg at the beginning of the sixteenth century was colorful and multifaceted. In the Parish and the Castle Church, endowed Masses were read and sung day and night. Numerous church services and religious festivals were simultaneously celebrated by monasteries and churches, often in a spirit of rivalry. Three different religious orders were active in the city: the Franciscans, the Augustinian Eremites, and the Antonites. Monks and priests in the black and brown cowls of their orders were a prominent sight in the city. Many students were also members of religious orders.

In the day-to-day life of the city, this social constellation was the cause of many conflicts. Both, ecclesiastics and students enjoyed specific privileges. University and bishop maintained their own jurisdiction, so much so that their members were exempt from appearing before the city court. Indeed, jurisdiction in religious questions was far from clear even before the Reformation: the bishop of Brandenburg, who was responsible for Wittenberg, sought to demonstrate his ecclesiastical power several times before the Reformation by putting the city under a ban of excommunication, which impressed the citizens of Wittenberg to only a limited degree.[9] Bishop, monasteries, parish, and Castle Church vied with each other as spiritual institutions. This provided the citizenry with many choices, but at the same time it tended to fragment the community, weakening its sense of common identity and possibly caused excessive social strain, a situation which was typical for cities of the late Middle Ages.[10]

But shortly before—and initially completely independent of—the Reformation, significant ecclesiastical and religious changes had already taken place in Wittenberg. In 1492, the Elector of Saxony,

Frederick the Wise, had begun to build himself a castle in Wittenberg and thus to transform the city into one of his two permanent residences. Wittenberg grew in size and gained in reputation and importance. In addition, in 1502 the Elector founded a university that quickly attracted teachers and students from beyond the boundaries of Saxony. The newly constructed Castle Church was transformed through its enormous collection of new relics and indulgences —the so-called *Wittenberg Heiltum*—into a place of pilgrimage which was famous within and beyond the borders of Saxony. Together with the city council, the Elector strove to unify religious life within the city and focus it on his Castle Church. Thus, for instance, in 1508 a new church service ordinance stipulated that only one church or monastery should be responsible for celebrating each holy day in the year—whereby the castle and parish churches clearly claimed the lion's share of holy days between them.[11]

From the Marketplace to the Church:
Changes in the Ritual of Holy Week

The celebration of Holy Week in Wittenberg offers a vivid example of both the variety of religious expression in the city and of the trend to unify such expression and focus it on the Elector and his Castle Church. This important pre-Easter festival was also celebrated in the streets and marketplace of the city with religious services and popular Passion plays. We know, for instance, that in Wittenberg around 1500, every year so-called "descents into hell" were enacted in the marketplace.[12] Such performances of the *descensus ad inferos* were a well-loved popular extension of the Easter liturgy, based on Jesus's descent into hell before his Resurrection as described in the apocryphal Gospel of Nicodemus.[13] At the performances, representatives of the city's different social groups were charged with their various sins before being led off into "hell" by actors dressed as devils. Such performances were very popular in medieval cities and served as both entertainment and admonition. They also functioned to bond the citizenry together, for all social groups were represented as being equally sinful and in need of re-

1 See Scribner, *Flugblatt*. **2** Wohlfeil, *Reformatorische Öffentlichkeit*. **3** Scribner, *Reformation*, pp. 53–55. **4** Id., *Flugblatt*. **5** Id., *Reformation*, pp. 63–79. **6** On this background, see in greater detail Rublack, *Reformation*, pp. 32–40; Krentz, *Ritualwandel und Deutungshoheit*, pp. 25–33. **7** Pettegree, *Brand Luther*. **8** See in greater detail on this theory Krentz, *Roots*. **9** See Krentz, *Ritualwandel und Deutungshoheit*, pp. 23–65. **10** See on a typical "late-medieval complexity crisis," using the Imperial City of Nuremberg as an example, Hamm, *Zentrierung*. **11** Ordnung der Stifftkyrchenn zw Wittenbergk, Thüringisches Hauptstaatsarchiv Weimar (ThHStA Weimar), Ernestinisches Gesamtarchiv (EGA), Reg. O 159, fol. 105r–115v, reproduced in Barge, *Andreas Bodenstein*, pp. 525–529. **12** The performances are recorded only in the account books of Wittenberg city council (Stadtarchiv Wittenberg (StAW), Kämmereirechnungen (KR)). There is a detailed description of expenditures for the performances under "Ausgaben uff die passio und ander spile" in the accounts for 1502, fol. 246v; in the accounts for the following years too may be found similar entries under "general expenditures," e.g. StAW, KR 1503/04, fol. 443v–444r; see also Krentz, *Ritualwandel und Deutungshoheit*, pp. 86–88. **13** A more recent account is provided in Henkel, *Descensus ad inferos*.

pentance. In Wittenberg, these performances were very elaborately staged. Every year the city council had scenery representing several palaces constructed and costumes made for the actors. The devils Lucifer and Satan, together with their followers, appeared onstage; mention of other figures such as Judas and a peasant suggest a large variety of scenes and performances.[14]

While at the beginning of the sixteenth century a multitude of liturgical, ecclesiastical, and popular urban rituals coexisted side by side, in the years that followed a significant process of standardization may be observed. Rituals were transferred from the streets to the parish and the Castle Church. In the second decade of the century, the "descents into hell" ceased to be performed.[15] Instead, starting in 1517, so-called "Descent from the Cross" plays were introduced during Holy Week. These had also enjoyed great popularity in the late Middle Ages,[16] and here too the entire city participated. Yet the focus of these activities was clearly the electoral court: representatives of the city, the university, and the court chose fourteen men in need to play the principal roles. On the Tuesday before Easter, all needy people in the city received a herring, a loaf of bread, and a penny in the Elector's castle. On Maundy Thursday, the fourteen men received new clothing and visited the city bathhouse. Afterward they went to confession and prayed in the church. On the evening of Maundy Thursday, together they set up a large wooden cross bearing the figure of Christ before the Holy Cross altar in the Castle Church.

On Good Friday, the figure was taken down from the cross in a solemn ceremony, wrapped in linen, and carried on a bier through the church. Afterward it was laid in a grave together with a consecrated host. The fourteen poor men remained praying by candlelight in the church until Easter Sunday. Compared with similar ceremonies at other locations, the one in Wittenberg was relatively unpretentious; elsewhere, for instance, cloths were torn down from the cross and the altar washed with water and wine. In Wittenberg, the emphasis was on the events of Good Friday and the pious reenactment of the Passion. The Good Friday ceremonies were thus transferred from the street into the Castle Church and more strictly regimented. The loud, colorful, and popular "descents into hell" plays, in which all groups in the city could participate, were replaced by something more earnest and more closely in line with the orthodox liturgy of the Descent from the Cross. The egalitarian character of the plays and self-mocking representation of the sinful nature of all social groups in the city disappeared. The focus was now much more on the Elector as dispenser of charity and benefactor of the city.

Relics and Indulgences: The *Wittenberg Heiltum*

Just as Elector Frederick the Wise standardized religious life in Wittenberg, focusing it on the Castle Church, so he also made the city through his collection of relics and indulgences a center of pre-Reformation piety within his territory. In assembling his collection, the Elector spared neither expense nor effort, increasing its size at the beginning of the sixteenth century many times over. The first inventory of the collection in 1506 recorded only 80 relics. The last one in 1520 listed no less than 18,970 relics and fragments, amount-

ing to indulgences for 1,902,202 years, 270 days and 1,915,983 *quadragenes* (an indulgence of forty days).[17]

The relics' high sacral value was derived from papal indulgence privileges, which granted pilgrims plenary indulgence on two special days in the year, namely the third Monday after Easter and All Saints' Day, November 1. Both days were celebrated with much pomp and ceremony, attracting many pilgrims to the city. Papal bulls of indulgence were paraded round the city to the sound of music and read aloud. The indulgence for attending the presentation of the relics was announced to the multitudes. Then the highest-ranking priests carefully carried the individual relics, contained in elaborate caskets, out of the Castle Church and ceremoniously showed them to the people, enunciating both their origin and significance. Thus the citizens of Wittenberg were constantly being reminded of the significance of relics and indulgences.

But this intense veneration of relics and indulgences was not, as might at first seem, the remnants of a medieval piety that had somehow survived the turn of the century. To the contrary, they were an innovation introduced after that date.[18] In fact, a castle chapel with its own indulgence privileges had existed earlier in Wittenberg under the Ascanian dynasty in the fourteenth century. But the Ascanians soon lost interest in the castle and its collection of relics, with the result that not a single pilgrim came to Wittenberg during the entire fifteenth century. Thus Frederick the Wise built up not only his collection of relics but also his treasure of grace in the form of indulgences entirely from scratch at the beginning of the sixteenth century. He had the old, long-forgotten indulgence privileges reconfirmed by the Pope and acquired new ones in addition. The Elector also vigorously promoted the presentation of the relics—a new religious mega-event. In 1510 he commanded his civil servants and nobles to broadcast news of the event throughout his lands. And with the help of neighboring bishops he also saw to it that the presentation was announced from the pulpits of the surrounding territories.[19] A pamphlet designed to attract new students to Wittenberg University extolled not only its famous teachers and excellent resources for study but in particular the collection of relics, the *Wittenberg Heiltum*, for, so the pamphlet declared, even a student should "focus his gaze first and foremost on the Kingdom of God."[20] Clearly this advertising campaign was successful, for three years later the Castle Church recorded that its presentation of relics enjoyed great popularity among visitors from outside the kingdom. The roads to Wittenberg were guarded during the presentation in order to guarantee the safe arrival and departure of visitors. In 1517, so many people obviously made the pilgrimage to Wittenberg that the local bishop complained that other locations offering similar instruments of salvation were being disadvantaged.[21] Visitors from outside the kingdom who came to Wittenberg at this time, such as the Bavarian nobleman Hans Herzheimer in February 1519, were extremely impressed by the opulence and significance of the collection of relics.[22]

Thus even before the Reformation, Wittenberg had a reputation for religiosity and piety well beyond the frontiers of Saxony. And the city maintained this reputation into the Reformation era; whereas previously it had been relics that had attracted people to the city

Fig. 1 The town of Wittenberg as seen from the Elbe. Drawing from the travel album of Count Ottheinrich (Otto Henry), Elector of the Palatinate, 1536

in large numbers, now it was sermons and university lectures—in short "the Word" of the reformers—that attracted scholars and non-scholars alike, also in large numbers. Wittenberg thus remained a city of spiritual healing, if in a completely different sense.

Carnivals and Plays as Precursors of the Reformation

The veneration of indulgences and relics before the Castle Church reached a climax as late as in 1520, and only recently, in 1517, the elector had added to religious ceremony in the city by endowing the Descent from the Cross plays. But these practices were already being vehemently discussed and criticized in the university. Luther and his colleagues had attacked indulgences in particular but also other pious works such as sponsored Masses, endless prayers, and meaningless rituals. They considered these as the "good works" of a misdirected piety that relied on the individual's own deeds and merits instead of on faith and the grace of God, thus lulling people into a deceptive sense of having been saved.[23] In the city itself, Luther's criticism remained largely unheard. Other problems were occupying people's attention: around 1520 riots broke out between students and citizens over the right to bear arms, as well as over lesser problems such as high rents and disturbing the peace at night. The riots were so severe that the Elector had to send in his troops in order to restore order.[24]

Since we must now assume that Luther did not in fact nail his Ninety-Five Theses to the door of the Castle Church but simply sent them by letter to his bishops,[25] the burning of the papal bull threat-ening excommunication before the Elster Gate in Wittenberg on December 10, 1520, may be seen as the first public event of the Refor-mation (fig. 2). The break with the Church of Rome and its regime was being made manifest here to the people of Wittenberg for the first time. Finally the Reformation was leaving the confines of the university and going out into the city streets. There people welcomed

14 StAW, Kämmereirechnung 1502, fol. 246v, see also Krentz, *Ritualwandel und Deutungshoheit*, p. 87. 15 Expenditures for these Passion plays, which at the beginning of the sixteenth century were only irregularly recorded, ceased to appear in the account books after 1509. 16 These plays were introduced thanks to an endowment of the Elector: "Die Stifftung der abnemung des bildnus unsers liebn hern und Seligmachers vom Creutz und wie die besuchung des grabs von den viertzehn mansspersonen ztu wittenberg in aller heyligen kirchen bescheen soll 1517," ThHStA Weimar, EGA, Reg. O 158, fol. 24r–31v. 17 Kalkoff, *Ablass*, pp. 64–66. A *quadragene* was a period of 40 days and, besides days and years, was a common unit for measuring indulgences. The origin is Christ's 40-day fast. 18 See too for the following Krentz, *Ritualwandel und Deutungshoheit*, pp. 69–83. 19 "Ausschreiben Friedrichs des Weisen an Adelige und Amtsleute," ThHStA Weimar, EGA, Reg. Q 126a. 20 See Andreas Meinhardi, *Dialogus illus-trate ac augustissime urbis Albiorene vulgo Wittenberg dicte* […] [1508]. Trans. Treu, *Andreas Meinhard*, p. 142. 21 See Krentz, *Ritualwandel und Deutungs-hoheit*, p. 80. 22 The account of this journey is part of a chronicle of 300 folio pages written by Hans Herzheimer between 1514 and 1519. It is displayed in man-uscript form in the Works on Paper Collection of the Museum of Applied Art in Vienna (no ref.), fol. 271r–292v. 23 See for instance Martin Luther, Ein Sermon von den guten Werken [1520]. In: *WA* 6, 206–276; Martin Luther, Ein Sermon von dem Neuen Testament, das ist von der heiligen Messe [1520], pp. 353–378. 24 Krentz, *Ritualwandel und Deutungshoheit*, pp. 103–124. 25 See Ott/Treu, *Thesenanschlag*. See also the contribution of Martin Treu to this volume.

its message and creatively elaborated it themselves. The papal bull delivered on September 10, 1520, in Wittenberg gave Luther and his supporters three months to recant their writings. Otherwise they would be excommunicated from the church, together with all those who gave them protection. As is well known, Luther refused to recant. Instead, on the morning of December 10, 1520, the Wittenberg professors and students were summoned by a public notice posted on the parish church to go to the Elster Gate where magister Johann Agricola burned several books of canon law and other works by opponents of the Wittenberg theologians.[26] Afterward, Luther himself threw a copy of the papal bull into the fire, speaking some words in Latin, to which those present answered "Amen." The decision of the Wittenberg professors not to submit to the bull but, on the contrary, to burn it in public is considered a decisive turning point of the early Reformation, for it represents Luther's final and public break with the Pope and the entire Church of Rome. Nevertheless, this event took place in the early hours of the morning at a somewhat secluded spot outside the city walls. As such it might well have escaped attention. Probably Luther himself did not attach much significance to it until later.[27]

But whereas the professors quickly left the scene, the students marched in procession through the city behind a farm cart bearing a long pole, to which was attached a papal bull, flapping like a sail in the wind.[28] The townspeople were attracted by the sound of a student playing the trumpet and followed the procession through the city back to the Elster Gate. There, more books by unloved theologians were burned and numerous satirical rituals enacted: the students conducted a requiem Mass for the burned books and sang ironic funerary songs as well as other popular satirical ballads.[29] It was only through these student antics that the incident of the burning of the papal bull, and possibly the existence of the bull itself with its threat of excommunication, was made known at all throughout the city. Citizens and students joined together in this symbolic act against the papacy and thus made common cause against the Church of Rome. By rejecting the Pope and mocking his symbols and jurisdiction, they effected a radical break with the traditional church hierarchy. Yet critique of the church and ritual protests by the students and citizens of Wittenberg were nothing new: urban unrest and opposition to the ecclesiastical authority of bishop and monasteries had happened before in Wittenberg. This opposition to the Pope was simply another instance—although a decisive one. The students lampooned traditional ecclesiastical rituals, thus depriving them of legitimacy. Such ritualistic parodies are typical of "Reformation movements" and may be observed in many other cities.[30] The inclusion of carnival elements is likewise typical: dressing up in costumes and parading to the sound of music and song. The same kind of jester's license claimed at carnival time was used here to turn social norms on their head.[31] Like the Wittenberg "descents into hell," such customs served to articulate conflicts with the city and church establishment while offering a legitimate framework within which to express criticism.

Thus it was no coincidence that a few weeks later, during the pre-Lenten carnival season of 1521, another theatrical performance was staged in the city criticizing the old church. The students first led an actor dressed as the Pope, accompanied by cardinals, bishops, and attendants, around the city "with great pomp." Then they chased him through the streets and tried to throw him into the town sewer.[32] Like the bull threatening excommunication, this ritual played out by townspeople and students helped to symbolically complete the break with the old ecclesiastical order by holding its dignitaries up to ridicule.

Interruptions of the Mass and Iconoclasm Seal the Breach with the Old Church

In the following months, similar actions were repeatedly carried out by students in the streets, while the debate continued in the university. At this time, Luther was not in Wittenberg; since the beginning of May, he had been in hiding in the Wartburg. In particular, the traditional Masses that were read and sung without intermission in all Wittenberg churches, were increasingly becoming subject to severe critique.[33] Sermons quickly spread this criticism throughout the city—several professors of theology also preached in churches. The incidents that followed in the fall of 1521 were to a degree influenced by this new theological criticism. They were nevertheless also manifestations of older urban conflicts that had come into being independently of the Reformation. The first incident after the carnival season occurred at the beginning of October 1521 when two Antonite monks, as was their custom, entered the city to solicit alms for their order.[34] As soon as they arrived, their servants were assaulted with dung and stones. The following morning, the Antonite preceptor's Mass was so badly interrupted that he had to shorten it. When he wanted to consecrate water at the university's collegiate hall, students knocked over his bucket. On December 3, 1521, early-morning Mass in the parish church was interrupted by students who crowded before the altar and snatched the Mass books from the priests, thus preventing them from reading the Mass.[35] Two days later, a group gathered in front of the Franciscan monastery, threatening and abusing the monks. At the request of the Franciscans, the city council had the monastery guarded overnight, and indeed, forty students and "nobles" were alleged to have paraded through the city at night to the sound of drums and trumpets.[36] Masses were once again interrupted on Christmas Eve, first in the parish church, in whose churchyard the perpetrators afterward "howled like wolves," and later in the Castle Church, from whose gallery they poured scorn down on the priests.[37]

On the one hand, these actions were in line with the new theological debate at the university attacking the Mass. Then again, student disturbances were nothing new. Ever since the founding of the university, the town had complained about disturbances of the peace in the streets at night and unseemly behavior in the churchyard. "Nobles"—that is aristocratic students who were allowed to bear arms—had frequently been involved in brawls in the past. The Antonite monks had likewise long been a source of annoyance, for they took money out of the city and competed for alms with local clerics.[38] For this reason, as early as 1508 a church ordinance had

Fig. 2 Paul Thumann, Martin Luther burns the papal bull *Exsurge Domine*,
in front of Wittenberg's Elster Gate in 1520, 1872–73

26 For two different interpretations of what happened, see Schubert, *Lachen*; Krentz, *Ritualwandel und Deutungshoheit*, pp. 128–140. **27** This thesis is developed in more detail in Krentz, *Roots*. **28** This action by the students is recorded only in a pamphlet by an anonymous student: Exustionis Antichristianorum decretalium acta. In: *WA* 7, 184–186, here 185. See also on the students' antics Kruse, *Universitätstheologie*, p. 269; Rublack, *Reformation*, p. 26. **29** See the report of the anonymous student, Exustionis Antichristianorum decretalium acta. In: *WA* 7, 184–186, here 186. **30** Scribner, *Reformation*. **31** See Ridder, *Fastnachtstheater*. **32** As Luther reported to Spalatin, February 17, 1521, in *WA.B* 2, 265 f.; see Krentz, *Ritualwandel und Deutungshoheit*, p. 138. **33** See Simon, *Messopfertheologie*, pp. 419–472. **34** Two letters provide sources for this incident: "Brief des kurfürstlichen Kanzlers Gregor Brück an Kurfürst Friedrich von Sachsen," (October 8, 1521), in Müller, *Wittenberger Bewegung*, pp. 19–21; "Wolfgang Reißenbusch an Friedrich den Weisen," (October 7, 1521), ThHStA Weimar, EGA, Reg. Kk 781, fol. 7r+v. See also on the following Krentz, *Ritualwandel und Deutungshoheit*, pp. 144–150. **35** Letter of the Wittenberg city council to Frederick the Wise, December 5, 1521. In: Müller, *Wittenberger Bewegung*, pp. 77 f. **36** The source here is a letter from a student named Hermann Mühlpfort to the mayor of Zwickau of the same name. In: *Mitteilungen des Altertumsvereins für Zwickau und Umgebung* 11 (1914), pp. 26–28, here p. 27. **37** See letter from the collegiate canon of the Castle Church to Frederick the Wise of December 29, 1521. In: Müller, *Wittenberger Bewegung*, pp. 133 f. **38** See Ocker, *Rechte Armut*.

limited their right to solicit alms to two holy days a year.[39] Thus already existing conflicts had simply found new objects for dispute in the Reformation's demands to abolish the Mass and in its critique of the monastic life.

In contrast to previous years, the disturbances of 1521, mostly involving students, were actually quite moderate in nature, and the Elector, who in 1520 had sent in his troops to restore order, hardly paid them any attention. Even the so-called Wittenberg iconoclasts, who still receive a lot of attention in contemporary literature on this period, and who in February 1522 are alleged to have destroyed numerous works of art, appear on closer examination of the sources hardly worth mentioning (fig. 3).[40] The only evidence of iconoclasm we have is a note in the town records concerning the punishment of a single perpetrator who had damaged pictures in the parish church.[41] But in the theological debate, the question of tolerating images in churches played an increasingly important role from January 1522 onward. Andreas Karlstadt published a pamphlet entitled *On the Removal of Images*, in which he put forward theological arguments against images in churches, and at the end of January, the city council had all images removed from churches. An explicit act of iconoclasm took place on January 10, 1522, in the Augustinian monastery: the monks lit a fire in the courtyard and burned inventory from the monastery church such as wooden altars, carved pictures, banners, candles, and candlesticks.[42] They also knocked the heads off the stone statues of saints and destroyed paintings in the monastery church. But all this happened *in camera*, within the monastery walls. The Augustinians were ritually drawing a line under their own past.

The Introduction of the Reformation

The reckoning with the old order was soon followed by the first attempts to set up a new one. The first public act in this sense was Andreas Karlstadt's celebration of an "evangelical Mass" in Wittenberg Castle Church on Christmas Day of 1521.[43] Karlstadt wore secular clothing and made the sermon the main focus of the service. At the celebration of the Eucharist, he spoke the words of institution out loud in German, omitted the elevation of the host, and placed both host and chalice in the hands of the communicants. The chalice had previously been reserved for the priest alone. In so doing, Karlstadt enhanced the role of the laity and reinterpreted the Mass and the sacrament of the Eucharist. He entirely omitted those aspects of the traditional Mass liturgy that focused on the "Sacrifice of the Mass"—aspects that had been much criticized in recent theological discussions. Whereas the citizens of Wittenberg had hitherto not participated in large numbers in the students' actions, they attended this church service in droves. According to contemporary sources, almost the entire city attended.[44] Eyewitness reports also described a regular stampede as the laity rushed to take the sacrament. Karlstadt himself would later write about the "fervent ardor and overwhelming desire" of the citizens of Wittenberg. In the following years, the introduction of the "lay chalice" became in many places a symbol of the Reformation itself. In Wittenberg, starting with Christmas 1521, the Eucharist was henceforth celebrated under both kinds in the Parish and the Castle Church.

In January 1522, the city council passed an ordinance giving official sanction to the changes that had already partly been introduced. Masses without participation of the congregation were abolished; and yet, the existing liturgical form of the Mass was by and large preserved. Celebrating the Eucharist under both kinds, however, was explicitly allowed, and those elements of the liturgy that highlighted the sacrificial nature of the Mass were abolished. Correspondingly the council resolved to remove images from the parish church. But by far the largest portion of the new ordinance concerned sociopolitical measures. Begging was forbidden in the city; on the other hand the "common chest" for the welfare of the poor was stocked up, in part by redirecting donations originally intended for the reading of Masses. Widows, orphans, and artisans who had fallen on hard times were to receive support. While these sociopolitical measures were not controversial, the article concerning the Mass generated some debate: the collegiate chapter of the Castle Church in particular clung to the old beliefs and resisted the changes. In February 1522, through the mediation of officials from the Elector's court, a compromise was negotiated: sponsored Masses without the participation of the congregation were once again allowed to a limited degree, thus for the time being assuring the priests of a livelihood. In March 1522, after his return from the Wartburg, Martin Luther effected further minor changes to the liturgy, and in his *invocavit sermons* [beginning on the first Sunday in Lent] he criticized the hasty manner in which the Reformation had been introduced as harmful to those of weaker faith.[45] But on the whole, the reforms were initially moderate in nature: the Mass was still read in Latin with, apart from the Eucharist, only a few alterations scarcely noticed by the congregation.

Even the collection of relics was still being presented to visitors in 1522, to the accompaniment of the usual Masses and ceremonies. Further reforms were introduced little by little in the following years until, at the end of 1525, a "German Mass" was introduced, and sponsored Masses and other ceremonies—and likewise the collection of relics itself—were finally abolished. This process was facilitated by the fact that the Elector had already largely standardized church practices in Wittenberg before the Reformation, thereby reducing the influence of both monasteries and bishop. The founding of the university, however, had initiated a period of close collaboration between city council, university, and electoral court, allowing them, starting in 1522, to introduce the Reformation as a joint venture.

39 Ordnung der Stifftkyrchenn zw Wittenbergk (note 11, above). **40** On the traditional view of the "Wittenberg disturbances" and "Wittenberg iconoclasts" see Schnitzler, *Ikonoklasmus*, p. 73; Eire, *War*, p. 64; Ullmann, *Unruhen*, p. 120; Bubenheimer, *Scandalum*, p. 217. **41** See Krentz, *Ritualwandel und Deutungshoheit*, p. 204. **42** Bubenheimer, *Scandalum*; see also in general Schnitzler, *Ikonoklasmus*. **43** See Barge, *Andreas Bodenstein*, pp. 358–360; Simon, *Messopfertheologie*, pp. 496–500; Kaufmann, *Abendmahl*; Krentz, *Ritualwandel und Deutungshoheit*, pp. 145–168. **44** Thus wrote the Collegiate Provost Justus Jonas to Johann Lang, January 8, 1522. In: Müller, *Wittenberger Bewegung*, p. 165. **45** Acht Sermone D. M. Luthers von ym geprediget zu Wittenberg in der Fasten. In: *WA* 10, 3, 1–64, see Krentz, *Ritualwandel und Deutungshoheit*, pp. 220–242.

Fig. 3 Martin Luther halts the iconoclastic fury in Wittenberg, 1847.
From: Gustav König, Dr. Martin Luther, der deutsche Reformator.
In bildlichen Darstellungen von Gustav König, Stuttgart 1857

BIBLIOGRAPHY

Barge, Hermann (1905), *Andreas Bodenstein von Karlstadt*. Vol. II: Karlstadt als Vorkämpfer des laienchristlichen Puritanismus. Leipzig. **Bubenheimer**, Ulrich (1973), Scandalum et ius divinum. Theologische und rechtstheologische Probleme der ersten reformatorischen Innovationen in Wittenberg 1521–1522. In: *Zeitschrift der Savigny-Stiftung für Rechtsgeschichte, Kanonistische Abteilung*, vol. 90, pp. 263–342. **Eire**, Carlos (1986), *War Against the Idols. The Reformation of Worship from Erasmus to Calvin*. New York. **Hamm**, Berndt (2005), Normative Zentrierung städtischer Religiosität zwischen 1450 und 1550. In: Safely, Max (ed.), *Ad historiam humanam. Aufsätze für Hans Christoph Rublack*. Epfendorf, pp. 63–80. **Henkel**, Nikolaus (2006), Der 'Descensus ad inferos' im geistlichen 'Drama' des Mittelalters. In: Herzog, Markwart (ed.), *Höllen-Fahrten. Geschichte und Aktualität eines Mythos*. Stuttgart, pp. 87–108. **Kalkoff**, Paul (1907), *Ablass und Reliquienverehrung in der Schlosskirche zu Wittenberg*. Gotha. **Kaufmann**, Thomas (2007), Abendmahl und Gruppenidentität in der frühen Reformation. In: Ebner, Martin (ed.), *Herrenmahl und Gruppenidentität*. Freiburg/Basel/Wien, pp. 194–210. **Krentz**, Natalie (2014), *Ritualwandel und Deutungshoheit. Die frühe Reformation in der Residenzstadt Wittenberg*. Tübingen. **Krentz**, Natalie (2016), The Early Roots of Confessional Memory. Martin Luther Burns the Papal Bull on 10 December 1520. In: Luebke, David/Plummer, Elizabeth/Johnson, Carina (eds.), *Reformations Lost and Found: Confessional Histories after the Reformation*. Oxford [in press]. **Kruse**, Jens-Martin (2002), *Universitätstheologie und Kirchenreform. Die Anfänge der Reformation in Wittenberg 1516–1522*. Mainz. **Müller**, Nikolaus (ed.) (1911), *Die Wittenberger Bewegung 1521 und 1522. Die Vorgänge in und um Wittenberg während Luthers Wartburgaufenthalt. Briefe, Akten und dgl. u. Personalien*. 2nd ed. Leipzig. **Ocker**, Christoph (1999), 'Rechte Armut' und 'Bettler Orden.' Eine neue Sicht der Armut und die Delegitimierung der Bettelmönche. In: Jussen, Bernhard/Koslofsky, Craig (eds.), *Kulturelle Reformation. Sinnformationen im Umbruch 1400–1600*. Göttingen, pp. 129–157. **Ott**, Joachim/**Treu**, Martin (eds.) (2008), *Luthers Thesenanschlag—Faktum oder Fiktion*. Leipzig. **Pettegree**, Andrew (2015), *Brand Luther. How an Unheralded Monk Turned His Small Town into a Center of Publishing, Made Himself the Most Famous Man in Europe—and Started the Protestant Reformation*. New York. **Ridder**, Klaus (2009), Fastnachtstheater. Städtische Ordnung und fastnächtliche Verkehrung. In: id. (ed.), *Fastnachtspiele. Weltliches Schauspiel in literarischen und kulturellen Kontexten*. Tübingen, pp. 65–82. **Rublack**, Ulinka (2014), *Die Reformation in Europa*. 2nd ed. Frankfurt am Main. **Schnitzler**, Norbert (1996), *Ikonoklasmus—Bildersturm. Theologischer Bilderstreit und ikonoklastisches Handeln während des 15. und 16. Jahrhunderts*. München. **Schnitzler**, Norbert (2002), Wittenberg 1522—Reformation am Scheideweg? In: Dupeux, Cecile/Jetzler, Peter/Wirth, Jean (eds.), *Bildersturm: Wahnsinn oder Gottes Wille?* 2nd ed. Zürich, pp. 68–74. **Schubert**, Anselm (2011), Das Lachen der Ketzer. Zur Selbstinszenierung der frühen Reformation. In: *Zeitschrift für Theologie und Kirche*, vol. 108, no. 4, pp. 405–430. **Scribner**, Robert W. (1979), The Reformation as a Social Movement. In: Mommsen, Wolfgang J./Alter, Peter/Scribner, Robert W. (eds.), *Stadtbürgertum und Adel in der Reformation. Studien zur Sozialgeschichte der Reformation in England und Deutschland*. Stuttgart, pp. 49–79. **Scribner**, Robert W. (1981), "Flugblatt und Analphabetentum. Wie kam der gemeine Mann zu reformatorischen Ideen? In: Köhler, Hans-Joachim (ed.), *Flugschriften als Massenmedium der Reformationszeit*. Stuttgart, pp. 65–76. **Scribner**, Robert W. (1984), Reformation, Karneval und 'verkehrte Welt'. In: Dülmen, Richard van/Schindler, Norbert (eds.), *Volkskultur. Zur Wiederentdeckung des vergessenen Alltags (16.–20. Jahrhundert)*. Frankfurt am Main, pp. 117–152. **Simon**, Wolfgang (2003), *Die Messopfertheologie Martin Luthers. Voraussetzungen, Genese, Gestalt und Rezeption*. Tübingen. **Treu**, Martin (1986), *Andreas Meinhard: Über die Lage, die Schönheit und den Ruhm der hochberühmten Stadt Alboris, gemeinhin Wittenberg genannt*. Leipzig. **Ullmann**, Ernst (1992), Die Wittenberger Unruhen. Andreas Bodenstein von Karlstadt und die Bilderstürme in Deutschland. In: International Committee on the History of Art (ed.), *L'Art et les révolutions*, vol. 4: Les iconoclasmes. Straßburg. **Wohlfeil**, Rainer (1984), Reformatorische Öffentlichkeit. In: Grenzmann, Lutger/Stackmann, Karl (eds.), *Literatur und Laienbildung im Spätmittelalter und der Reformationszeit*. Stuttgart, pp. 41–52.

MARTIN EBERLE

The Saxon Dynasty and Ernestine Wittenberg

The House of Wettin, from which originated some of the political players of the Reformation, is among the oldest lineages of European high nobility. Since 1089, the dynasty has produced the margraves of Meissen and the landgraves of Thuringia, as well as the dukes and princes of Saxony. In the modern era even monarchs in Saxony, Poland, Belgium, Portugal, Bulgaria, and Great Britain originated from the Wettin dynasty which is still thriving and qualifies as a dynasty of European stature. The name of the house is derived from Wettin Castle, located near Halle (on the Saale River). As is common among German dynastic houses, there has been continual subdivision of territorial rule within the family. The Partition of Leipzig of 1485 was a special turning point in the history of the Wettins, since it resulted in a permanent division within the dynasty.

The founder of the Ernestine line, Prince Ernest, obtained the landgraviate of Thuringia, which included the Duchy of Saxe-Wittenberg. His younger brother, Duke Albert, received the margraviate of Meissen and became the founding father of the Albertine line. Despite this division, there were initially unifying factors, which were particularly manifested on an economic level, such as the shared use of the Saxon silver mines and the joint minting of coins. The Albertines chose Dresden as their primary residence with access to the university in Leipzig. The Ernestines, by virtue of their electorship, were able to develop a dazzling courtly lifestyle in their Torgau and Wittenberg residences which was unparalleled in the empire and attracted artistic personalities such as Lucas Cranach the Elder. Because of his great influence, Frederick the Wise was under consideration as candidate for king of the Holy Roman Empire in 1519, but he chose to give his support to the Habsburg who later became Charles V.

Unlike his brother Frederick the Wise, John the Steadfast publicly committed himself to the goals of the Reformation. With the foundation of the Evangelical Lutheran State Church in 1527, the prince became its first regional bishop. Subsequently, John the Steadfast went to great lengths to avoid political conflict with Emperor Charles V. This was not the case with his son and successor, John Frederick the Magnanimous, under whose rule tensions arose with Charles V. The main cause was the prince's presiding over the Schmalkaldic League, an alliance of Protestant princes and states who were against the religious politics of Emperor Charles V. After the emperor had crushed the league in the Schmalkaldic War, the subdued and imprisoned prince had to give up his electorship to his Albertine cousin, Maurice, who had fought on the emperor's side. Now only allowed the title of "born Elector," John Frederick chose to present himself and his successors as "defenders of the true faith."

Reinforced by the principle of primogeniture, the Albertines continued to rise inexorably, and even ruled the kingdom of Poland from 1697 to 1763 in a personal union. Meanwhile, the Ernestine branch in Thuringia was fractured by a number of divided inheritances. Thanks to some skillful political marriages, the line finally reached world-class status again in the nineteenth century. The many resulting residences and court households in Thuringia and the scintillating courtly life in Saxony still characterize Thuringia's rich and varied cultural landscape, which remains unsurpassed in all of Europe.

Most of the aristocratic dynasties in Europe were very closely related. The ruling families in Saxony and Hesse, in particular, spurred the Reformation by their intense marriage politics which, for generations, was a token of their mutual solidarity. In the families, which often had many children, partners were chosen from suitable other families of European nobility—suitability depending on the same denomination and political considerations. Situations of either excessive or insufficient supply of marriageable offspring, male or female, had to be taken into account too. Last but not least, financial aspects mattered when it came to dowries and potential inheritances. Unsuitable marriages were not frowned upon as much as in later times.

The Reformation princes had clear preferences, entering into relationships with families that were also stalwarts of the Reformation. A Protestant and a Catholic marriage market thus evolved in the course of the Reformation, denominational intermarriage being a rare exception. A noble line would only manage to stand its ground on a different marriage market if it permanently converted to the other faith.

The Saxon-Hessian Family Network

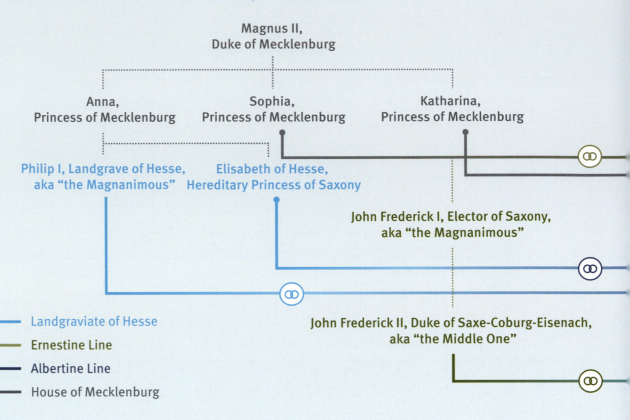

Magnus II,
Duke of Mecklenburg

Anna,
Princess of Mecklenburg

Sophia,
Princess of Mecklenburg

Katharina,
Princess of Mecklenburg

Philip I, Landgrave of Hesse,
aka "the Magnanimous"

Elisabeth of Hesse,
Hereditary Princess of Saxony

John Frederick I, Elector of Saxony,
aka "the Magnanimous"

John Frederick II, Duke of Saxe-Coburg-Eisenach,
aka "the Middle One"

— Landgraviate of Hesse
— Ernestine Line
— Albertine Line
— House of Mecklenburg

The Top Ten Marriage Partners
among the princes of Saxony and Hesse in the sixteenth century

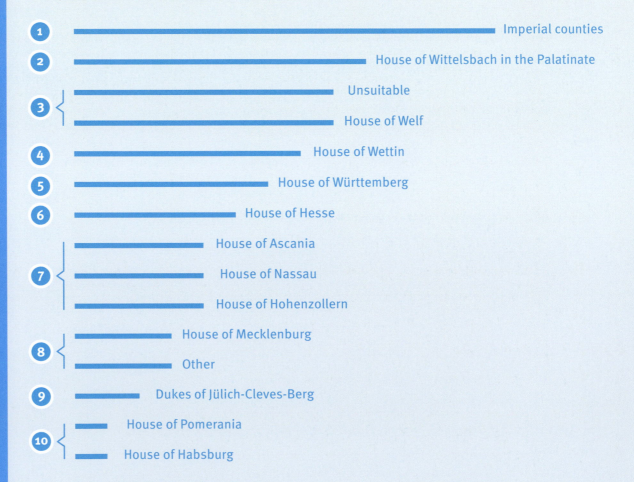

1. Imperial counties
2. House of Wittelsbach in the Palatinate
3. Unsuitable
   House of Welf
4. House of Wettin
5. House of Württemberg
6. House of Hesse
7. House of Ascania
   House of Nassau
   House of Hohenzollern
8. House of Mecklenburg
   Other
9. Dukes of Jülich-Cleves-Berg
10. House of Pomerania
    House of Habsburg

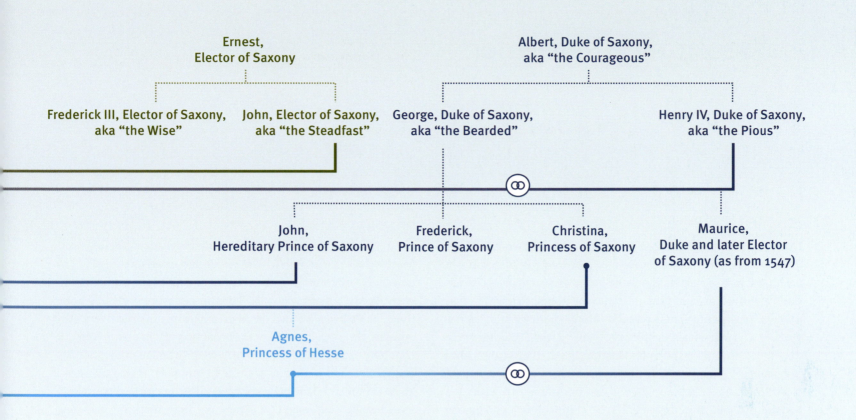

Ernest,
Elector of Saxony

Albert, Duke of Saxony,
aka "the Courageous"

Frederick III, Elector of Saxony,
aka "the Wise"

John, Elector of Saxony,
aka "the Steadfast"

George, Duke of Saxony,
aka "the Bearded"

Henry IV, Duke of Saxony,
aka "the Pious"

John,
Hereditary Prince of Saxony

Frederick,
Prince of Saxony

Christina,
Princess of Saxony

Maurice,
Duke and later Elector
of Saxony (as from 1547)

Agnes,
Princess of Hesse

The Family Ties of the Reformation Princes

Number of marriages in the respective house

Total number of marriages
in the sixteenth century

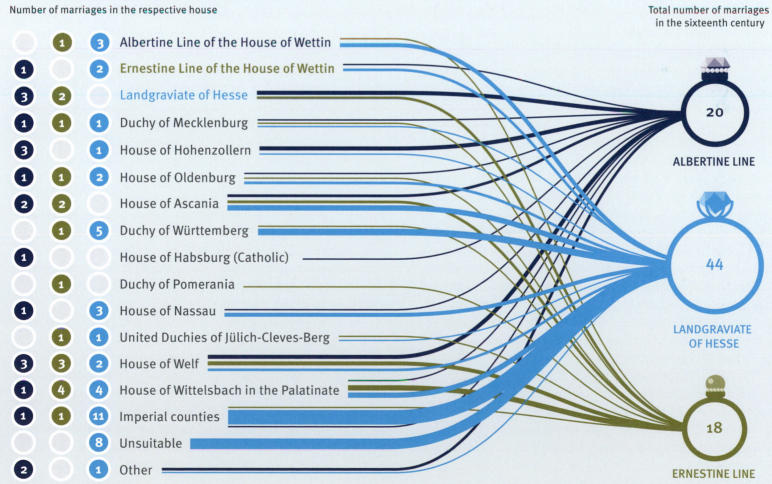

	1	3	Albertine Line of the House of Wettin
1		2	Ernestine Line of the House of Wettin
3	2		Landgraviate of Hesse
1	1	1	Duchy of Mecklenburg
3		1	House of Hohenzollern
1	1	2	House of Oldenburg
2	2		House of Ascania
	1	5	Duchy of Württemberg
1			House of Habsburg (Catholic)
	1		Duchy of Pomerania
1		3	House of Nassau
	1	1	United Duchies of Jülich-Cleves-Berg
3	3	2	House of Welf
1	4	4	House of Wittelsbach in the Palatinate
1	1	11	Imperial counties
		8	Unsuitable
2		1	Other

20

ALBERTINE LINE

44

LANDGRAVIATE
OF HESSE

18

ERNESTINE LINE

VOLKER LEPPIN

Becoming a Reformer

Martin Luther did not become a reformer overnight—even though his own stories sometimes convey this impression. Relatively late in life, in the year 1545, he tells how he had been struggling to understand a passage in Saint Paul's Letter to the Romans (1:17): "For in it the righteousness of God is revealed through faith for faith; as it is written, 'The one who is righteous will live by faith'."[1] Luther wrote that he had previously always understood righteousness as so-called distributive righteousness. By this he meant that righteousness provided the basis for rewarding good and punishing evil—and as a consequence one must make efforts to be righteous enough to earn the reward. As he grew older, Luther's move away from this understanding became the core of his insights as a reformer. He had, he said, left behind the idea of distributive, active righteousness and had recognized that, ultimately, God's righteousness is in giving his righteousness to humanity without the persons themselves being able or obliged to do anything about it: this he called passive righteousness.

The fact that, according to his own account, Luther as a scholar had this sudden insight while engaging in a thorough study of scripture evoked a familiar image in the minds of Luther researchers of the nineteenth and twentieth centuries. There he was—the bookworm, the quintessential professor, whose insights were based on meticulous intellectual work. With great effort they tried to find these insights Luther described in his early lectures. They tried to reconstruct his exegetical progress and searched his work to find the turning point from the Middle Ages to the Reformation, from the old idea of righteousness to the new reformatory doctrine of justification. And while doing so, they envisioned Luther in his study, whose location they also quite precisely imagined. In Luther's famous *table talks*, he repeatedly mentions a tower as the site where his inspiration supposedly struck. What a stunning idea: one moment, one man, one place—and it was in this way that one believed it was possible to describe the exact moment when the Middle Ages disappeared and the Reformation began.

This great narration, however, has become unreliable, and the tower is a case in point. How firmly the "tower experience" is rooted in cultural memory becomes obvious by the fact that a few years ago the discovery of an ancient toilet on the property of the Luther House in Wittenberg caused quite a sensation (fig. 1). Luther's interest was focused not on the toilet's role as a hygienic fixture but rather as a spiritual place. For Luther had "auff dieser cloaca auff dem thurm" (on this cloaca in the tower)[2] come to his new understanding of righteousness—according to the records of one of the authors who wrote down Luther's *table talks*. Thus, in discovering the toilet one thought one had identified the place of reformatory discovery. Admittedly, the exact location of the event was still in doubt: modern research puzzled over the question whether, by mentioning the "cloaca," Luther had wanted to say that he had been sitting one story above the toilet, as Martin Brecht believed[3]—or if, as Heiko Augustinus Oberman gaily imagined, there was a deeper meaning involving the reformer having had his insight while literally sitting on the toilet, reflecting on the long-standing connection between the devil and filth. Thus, egesting the devil along with his excrements[4] might definitely make reasonable sense.

Reformation historians could have easily avoided this disgusting debate, however, for the location is less clear than they believed it to be. This is because of the difficulties in transcribing the *table talks*. They alone make up six volumes in the extended edition of Luther's works, and do not even include all the talks that have been recorded. Individual *table talks* have been preserved in different versions. Moreover, they show traces of reworking, which not only include attempts at scrupulously recording the original talks but also of editing them in a way that could be connected to an appropriate memory of this honorable man. If we take a closer look at the tradition of the *table talks*, it becomes obvious that the oldest versions of the story of the Reformation's breakthrough did not mention a tower at all. In 1532, Johann Schlaginhaufen, who was recording the talks, noted that Luther had said: "Diese kunst hat mir der Spiritus Sanctus auf diss Cloaca eingeben." (It was on this cloaca (toilet pit) where I was inspired with this art by the Holy Spirit.)[5]

Just how tenuous the conviction of an event in the tower at Wittenberg was, is demonstrated by the fact that Georg Rörer, one of Luther's closest confidants, when copying Schlaginhaufen's notes just a few years after the death of the Reformer, completed the passage in question with "in horto" (in the garden).[6] This was, in fact, an extraordinarily subtle theological addition. Educated people were aware that the garden was a proven place for theological breakthroughs: the church father Augustine, the patron saint of Luther's order, had described the famous garden scene in *his Confessions*. In a garden, he wrote, he had heard a voice but could not say where it was coming from. It called out to him with the now proverbial "Take up and read!"[7] and Augustine took up the letters of Saint Paul and felt immediately inspired and changed by the Bible passage he read. Thus, it would definitely have been in line with this tradition if Luther had also come to his new way of understanding righteousness in a garden. However the fact that Rörer added the garden to this account also demonstrates above all that at about the year 1550 he had no knowledge at all of any event taking place in a tower. This, however, allows for only one reasonable conclusion: if Luther spoke of his reformatory insight, perhaps he localized it: "auff diser cloaca" (on this cloaca) but not "auff dem thrum" (on/in the tower). The mention of such a tower was recorded by his faithful followers, who probably knew of the existence of a tower with a toilet inside. It may well be that they had that toilet, which has been excavated in Wittenberg, in mind when they added this information. But still it must be made clear that it is not Luther himself who speaks of a tower, but rather his successors and adherents.

Once we have abandoned the idea of a clearly defined place, be it in the garden or the tower, the "cloaca" itself acquires a completely different and simultaneously a more harmless but also much weightier meaning than one believed it to have before the above-mentioned debate between Brecht and Oberman. The solution is much more obvious than once thought possible. In another *table talk*, on the praise of music, Luther explained: "If the Lord in this life has provided the shithouse with such noble gifts, what will happen in that eternal life [where everything will be perfect and delightful]?"[8] Obviously, in this particular case the vulgar German word "scheißhaus" (shithouse), which is the equivalent of the Latin "cloaca," does not mean anything else but the misery of the sinful world. It is nothing but a metaphor, indeed a vulgar one, but a metaphor nonetheless. This place is neither in a tower nor in a garden. What the Reformer wants to give expression to is the mighty miracle that in the midst of his sinful life God gave him the gift of a new insight. It is not always, as in this case, Luther's epigones, however, who are responsible for distorting the narratives; precisely when crucial moments of his development are involved it was Luther himself who left us differing accounts. After all, such mistakes or distortions are not due to ill will but are an integral part of our memory as such.

Whoever has once tried to compare his or her own memory of something that happened thirty years ago with the memories of friends and siblings will soon make the experience that memory is malleable. And that it is usually formed into a version that exactly suits the rememberer. Memory can expand or contract; it changes the colors of clothes and the words of the participants. A wedding day may become sunnier than it actually was, and one or the other is absolutely sure, at least in retrospect, to have known beforehand what would happen. What is possible today, in a world where so much is documented in print, by photographs, or videos, must have certainly been the case in the world of the sixteenth century. And this can be reconstructed in Luther's case as well.

We can even reconstruct, in detail, the way his memory worked, because the above-mentioned memory of the reformatory break-

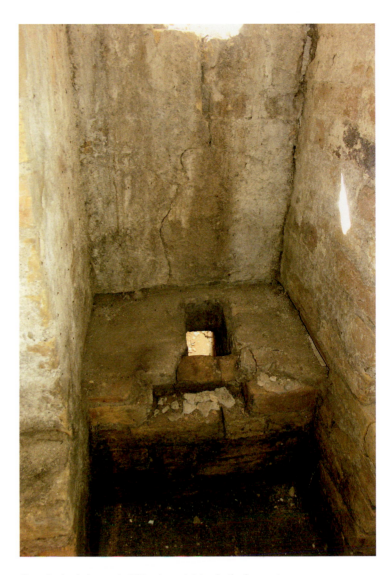

Fig. 1 Luther's house in Wittenberg, latrine in the lower story of the southern annex (tower), 2006

through of 1545 does not stand alone. There is a quite similar recollection that was recorded much closer in time to when the event happened. In 1518 the Reformer told his confessor, Johann von Staupitz, about a struggle, similar to that of 1545, about the meaning of a word (fig. 2).[9] In both narratives he laments his earlier suffering on account of this one word—and he is jubilant that now it has become "sweet." In both cases he fixes the event in great, almost cosmic dimensions: in 1518 he hears his confessor speak to him "as if from heaven"; in 1545 he feels like he had been transferred to the open doors of paradise.

1 *WA* 54, 185f. 2 *WA*.TR 3, 228 (no. 3232b). 3 Brecht, *Martin Luther*, p. 220. 4 Oberman, *Luther*, pp. 163–166. 5 *WA*.TR 2, 177 (no. 1681). 6 Ibid., ann. 1. 7 Augustinus, *Confessiones*, ed. by Luc Verheijen (= Corpus Christianorum. Series Latina 27, 131), Tournhout 1981, VIII, 12, 29: "Nimm und lies!" 8 *WA*.TR 4, 191, 31–33 (no. 4192). "So unser Her Gott in diesem leben in das scheißhaus solche edle gaben gegeben hat, was wird in jhenem ewigen leben geschehen, ubi omnia erunt perfectissima et iucundissima." 9 *WA* 1, 525–527.

Fig. 2 Unknown artist, Johann von Staupitz, c. 1520.
Staupitz was the Vicar General of the German Observant-
Congregation of the Augustinian Order up to 1520.

but from the readiness to be completely shaped by God. This is how it stands in the aforementioned thesis against indulgences.

According to the account Luther gave about this insight, the beginning of this theological reorientation regarding penitence was triggered by Staupitz's own words. Chronologically, his remarks indicate the time frame to be about 1515/16. Thus, on the one hand these ideas are connected to the time in which he was interpreting the Letter to the Romans, but on the other hand it is also linked to that period in his life when he was intensively studying the writings of the late-medieval mystic Johannes Tauler. The fact that Luther had recommended the *Theologia Deutsch*, which also dates to the fourteenth century, to a friend with the words: "Now taste it and see how sweet the Lord is,"[11] makes us prick up our ears, given what we have explained above. "Sweet" is a word that is linked to a terminology that has broad currency in the context of mysticism, something that obviously connected Luther closely with Tauler.

Thus, there is every indication that what is commonly considered a "reformatory" discovery was initially a mystic one. Luther studied Johannes Tauler's sermons intensively. When he found the hint among them that the sinner should at first present his repentance to God and that while doing so he was even allowed to forget about going to the confessor, he made the marginal note: "Mark this well!"[12] At a different passage from his reading of the mystic, he drew the conclusion: "Thus entire salvation, as he teaches here, consists of giving up on one's own will concerning all things, may they be spiritual or worldly. And of the naked belief in God."[13] What takes shape here is the insight that man depends completely on God and passively receives total salvation from God. Later Luther grasped this by the terminology of the doctrine of justification. In this way he developed the idea of passive justice. Topically, the notion shows up already now, when reading Tauler—and that is what makes this observation remarkable: not in contradiction to the Middle Ages but as a continuation of a certain kind of medieval piousness.

In this context, reading Tauler was a most important stimulus from which the young monk and professor of theology absorbed further ideas (fig. 3). As has already become apparent by his reminiscence of 1518, his conversations with his confessor, Johann von Staupitz, were of particular significance. It was Staupitz who not only made Luther aware of a new way of understanding penitence—and possibly of the writings of Tauler—but also, and most of all, of Jesus Christ. It was probably in 1516 that the event must have happened, which Luther describes as follows: "Once I complained to my Staupitz of the fact that predestination is so sublime. He answered me: predestination is understood and found in the wounds of Christ, nowhere else, because it is written: You must listen to this! The Father is too high. But the Father said: 'I will show you a way to me, and that is Christ'. Go, believe, hang on to Christ, and you will find out who I am, when the time has come. We are not doing so, thus God is incomprehensible to us, unimaginable; He is not understood, He wants to be incomprehensible outside Christ."[14]

The problem that Luther presented to his confessor was the corollary of an essential doctrine of their order's patron saint, Augustine. While interpreting Saint Paul, he had developed the idea that, ultimately, the whole of humankind was doomed because of

And in both cases this new understanding of one specific word results either in an improved insight into the entire Holy Scripture or as being confirmed by Scripture. One might even believe that in both cases Luther actually is referring to the same event, if it were not for one crucial difference: the word that troubled him in 1518 was not "justice," as in 1545, but "penitence."

This difference is easily explained: the topic that—necessarily—troubled Luther in 1518 was indeed penitence, for he had to defend his Ninety-Five Theses against Indulgences, which had been exactly focused on this one single topic, starting with the momentous sentence: "Our Lord and Master Jesus Christ, when saying: 'Repent' [...], wanted the whole lives of the believers to be penitence," in the first thesis.[10] Yet when writing in 1545, his theology had developed further and gained more shape. Now it was clear that the focus was on the doctrine of justification.

If one describes the situation in this way, it is obvious that, at any rate, the retrospection of 1545 is a massive retrojection. Historically, it is implausible compared to the memories recorded in 1518, which are chronologically much closer to the event. If one accepts this assessment, which has been long overlooked by research, one really gains a new insight into Luther's early development. Then, according to the description he gave, his focus was placed on the insight that penitence comes from the love of God as well as from righteousness, which is not derived from a negative, fearful, or tormented attitude

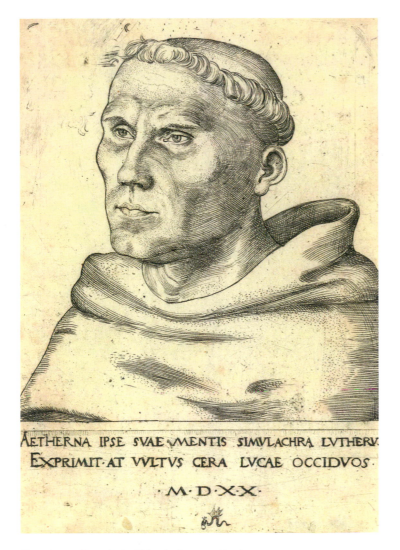

AETHERNA IPSE SVAE MENTIS SIMVLACHRA LVTHERV
EXPRIMIT AT VVLTVS CERA LVCAE OCCIDVOS
· M · D · X · X ·

Fig. 3 Lucas Cranach the Elder, Luther as a Monk, 1520

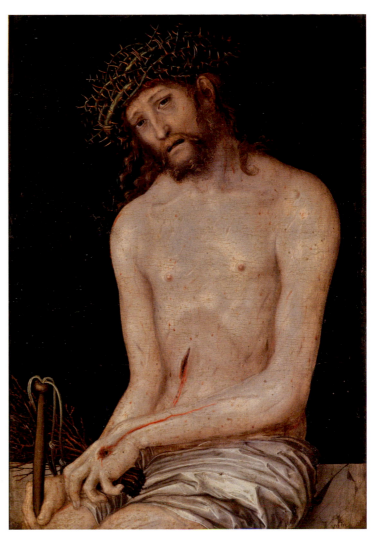

Fig. 4 Lucas Cranach the Elder, Man of Sorrows, after 1515

the sins of their forefathers, but that God had nevertheless marked, that is, predestined, some humans for salvation. He emphasized that God's mercy alone was at work by referring to the fact that there was no comprehensible reason for this within the chosen humans but by God alone. While this made God's mercy wonderful, it also had the potential to make it seem frightening. Obviously young Luther was struggling precisely with this dark side of the issue. It was Staupitz who showed him a way out of these cogitations and toward the suffering Savior depicted by Lucas Cranach as the Man of Sorrows with his wounds (fig. 4). Trust was thought to be fostered by completely relying on Christ. Thus, in the conversation between confessant and confessor there developed what later Reformation theology understood to be the formula of *solus Christus*, "Christ Alone." This doctrine is a genuine legacy of medieval theology, like the concept *sola gratia*, "By Grace Alone," which Luther himself had already developed in the years 1515/16. This is the idea that Augustine had formulated in his doctrine of predestination, and which Luther found again in his studies of Saint Paul—that is, that all salvation for human beings comes from God's grace alone and not from any achievement of man of any kind whatsoever. Such a claim was a conceivable position within medi-

eval theology, if a debated one. As such Luther presented it to university audiences in the context of academic disputations. A first careful step in this direction was his disputation on the powers of a human being without grace in 1516.[15]

This rather calm approach escalated into a fundamental opposition that Luther based on theological arguments. For him the emphasis on grace, and most of all on the interconnected, deep skepticism of human capabilities, was in contradiction to the anthropology he perceived inherent to Scholasticism. Strictly speaking, his knowledge of this kind of medieval theology was very limited. In the course of his studies in Erfurt he had come to consider Gabriel Biel, who had written an important textbook in the late fifteenth century, the very representative of Scholasticism. In Biel he now actually found an idea he had still shared in his first lecture on Psalms but had then sharply rejected in his lecture on the Letter to the Romans. That is, that God would not deny his grace to those who do what they are able to do. In the course of his progressive

10 *WA* 1, 233, 10 f. **11** *WA.B* 1, 79, 63 (no. 30). **12** *WA* 9, 104, 11: "Merk dir das!" **13** *WA* 9, 102, 24 – 26. **14** *WA.TR* 2, 112, 9 – 16 (no. 1490). **15** *WA* 1, 142 – 151.

Fig. 5 Eyn Deutsch Theologia (A German theology),
Wittenberg 1518. Luther had this manuscript from the
fourteenth century published.

ogy that showed every sign of the above-described theological re-
ductionism and was directed predominantly against Gabriel Biel.
The main objective, however, was to defend the honor of the most
important church father: "Saying that Augustine's accusations of the
heretics had been excessive would amount to saying that he tells lies
almost everywhere. This is contrary to common knowledge."[17] That
was the first thesis of the disputation.

Just as the confrontation between the ancient authorities of
Aristotle and Augustine lead to this disputation, the theses against
indulgences, that were presented less than two months later, summarized Luther's theological development regarding penitence: if
penance must actually be understood in a comprehensive way, as he
had learned in the course of discussing Tauler, then the system of
indulgences, as it had adhered to the sacrament of penance in the
late Middle Ages, could not continue in its given form. This was a
far-reaching attack, yet still one Luther himself would comment on
just a few weeks later: "Of course I followed the theology of Tauler
and that booklet [i.e., *Theologia Deutsch*], which you recently sent to
our Christian Goldschmied for printing" (fig. 5).[18] As astonishing as
it seems in the run-up to the great anniversary of the Reformation,
in Luther's view, what happened on October 31, 1517, was nothing
more than the consequence of late-medieval mystic theology.

It was only gradually that things developed into a fundamental
confrontation, partly of Luther's own volition, and partly in the
course of the controversy with his opponents. During the spring of
1518, Luther became aware that the Augustinian idea, according to
which human salvation is exclusively due to God's grace, must inevitably conclude that nothing else was required of human beings than
faith alone. At this point the thoughts he had once expressed as marginal notes on Tauler became programmatic. It is by faith alone, *sola
fide*, that human beings find salvation. The Reformer would now
declare in his *Sermo de triplici iustitia* (*Sermon on Three Kinds of Righteousness*) that those who believe will not perish—even if they sin.[19] This
was inevitably provocative and frightening. It led to the question
about how, within this cognitive framework, human beings could
be instructed to do the right thing if, in the end, their fate in the afterlife was quite unrelated to their behavior.

Even more striking, however, was the shift occurring somewhere else: in Christendom's structure of authority. Early on, Luther's
opponents noticed that his ideas might endanger the status of the
Pope. The latter's court theologian, Sylvester Prierias, who had been
given the task of writing an expert's assessment of Luther's positions, accused him, writing: "Whoever does not accept the doctrine
of the Roman Church and of the Roman pontiff as the infallible rule
of faith from which sacred Scripture derives strength and authority
is a heretic."[20] This was by no means the official, generally binding
doctrine—but it was a position, powerfully supported, that flew in
the face of Luther. Against his own will, he was now forced to discuss
the issue of the Pope, and he soon came to the realization that there
very well had been and might yet be a church without a Pope, and
that the latter's status was justified in human but not in divine law.
In issuing these statements he entered dangerous territory, and it
was one of his most astute opponents who made him aware of this:
Johannes Eck, who challenged Luther and his colleague Karlstadt to

reading of Saint Paul, he came to the conclusion that relying in this
way on human achievements was biblically inappropriate. Moreover, he could identify the person who was responsible for what he
believed to be this misconception. It was Aristotle, who in academic
theology had become the most important authority on matters
philosophical and had thus also greatly influenced Scholasticism.
Consequently, Luther's first attempts at reform were aimed at a renewed theology. By this time, in May 1517, he was able to write tri-
umphantly to a friend: "With God's help, our theology and Saint
Augustine make good progress and are predominant at our university. By and by, Aristotle is on the decline and is close to eternal fall.
To an astonishing degree the lectures on the maxims of Aristotle
are rejected, so that nobody may hope for listeners who does not
want to read about this theology, i.e., on the Bible, on Saint Augustine, or any other teacher of church authority."[16]

Augustine versus Aristotle, that was the alternative, not the Reformation versus the Middle Ages. This struggle was a struggle about
authorities within the medieval framework—even when Luther, on
September 4, 1517, organized a disputation against Scholastic theol-

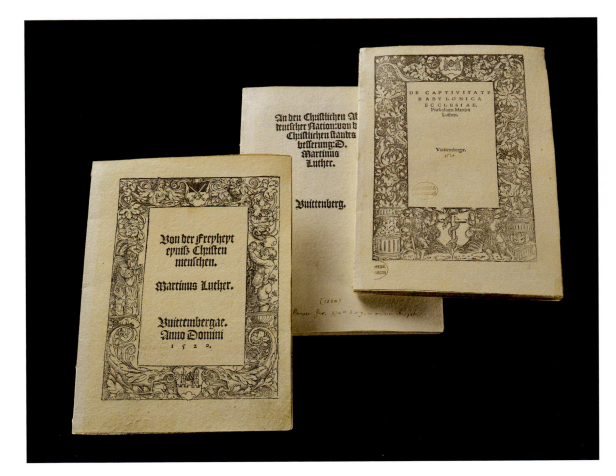

Fig. 6
The main publications
of the Reformation, Martin
Luther (Wittenberg 1520):
De captivitate Babylonica
ecclesiae praeludium
(On the Babylonian Captivity
of the Church), An den christ-
lichen Adel deutscher Nation
(To the Christian Nobility of the
German nation), Von der Frei-
heit eines Christenmenschen
(On the Freedom of a Christian)

a disputation. This battle of words was waged in Leipzig in 1519—and Eck's strategy was successful: Luther was under pressure from his opponent and had been made to look like a fool. He had no choice but to make statements about the office of the Pope, which had been condemned at the Council of Constance more than a hundred years earlier. Thus it was clear to Eck that Luther was a habitual heretic. Luther had made another important development in the course of the disputation: it was obvious that not only the Pope could be fallible, as he had been claiming for a long time referring to medieval church law, but a church council as well. Consequently, this meant: there was no earthly church authority that could guarantee Christian truth (fig. 6). The only thing that remained was scripture alone, *sola scriptura*. The Reformer, however, was neither the only one nor the first to reach this conclusion. It was Philipp Melanchthon who, in the context of an examination he had to pass in theology, formulated: "It is not necessary for a Catholic to believe any articles of faith than those to which scripture is a witness."[21] This pleased Luther, who stated that Melanchthon's theses were "quite fresh, but absolutely correct."[22]

Conclusion

Thus, in September 1519, the arsenal of reformatory theology, which later became formalized as the exclusive principles of Lutheran theology—*solus Christus, sola gratia, sola fide,* and *sola scriptura*—was complete. They had not been developed by one man alone—he had had advisers and friends who guided him, supported him, and even pushed him further. Consequently, we will not be able to name just one place on this sinful earth where his insight made its breakthrough. The intellectual developments and leaps that were part of this whole process took place here and there. These thoughts did not emerge at a single moment. Rather, we can identify a years-long development process, in the course of which the theology of the Reformation gained ever clearer and sharper contours, without being able to identify the exact moment when a sudden break with the Middle Ages took place. In any case, the idea of a break hardly applies. Rather, we are dealing with gradual and often very cautious transformations in the theology and piety Luther had grown up with. Reformatory theology did not break with the theology of the Middle Ages but grew out of it.

16 *WA*.B 1, 99 (no. 41, 8–13). **17** *WA* 1, 224, 7 f. **18** *WA*.B 1, 160, 8 f. **19** *WA* 2, 45, 5–10. **20** Fabisch/Iserloh, *Dokumente,* p. 55. **21** Stupperich, *Melanchthons Werke,* pp. 24, 29 f. **22** *WA*.B 1, 514, 33 f. (no. 202).

BIBLIOGRAPHY

Brecht, Martin (1981), *Martin Luther*. Vol. 1. Stuttgart. **Fabisch**, Peter/**Iserloh**, Erwin (ed.) (1988), *Dokumente zur Causa Lutheri (1517–1521)*. Vol. 1. Münster. **Leppin**, Volker (2010), Martin Luther. 2nd edition. Darmstadt. **Oberman**, Heiko Augustinus (1981), *Luther. Mensch zwischen Gott und Teufel*. Berlin. **Stupperich**, Robert (ed.) (1951), *Melanchthons Werke*. Vol. 1: Reformatorische Schriften. Gütersloh.

Luther's Posting of His Theses: Much Ado about Nothing?

Any great historical narrative requires a distinct starting point: what would the French Revolution be without the storming of the Bastille? How could the American War of Independence be part of public memory without the Boston Tea Party? As a matter of fact, there is historic evidence that the Bastille was not stormed but surrendered and that material damage in Boston was limited. All this does not change the fact that certain historical events were and are remembered as the beginning of world-historical developments.

The situation is similar when it comes to the posting of the Ninety-Five Theses against the misuse of indulgences in Wittenberg on October 31, 1517.[1] It is Luther himself who, in a letter to his friend Nikolaus von Amsdorf of November 1, 1527, refers to this date as the beginning of his public impact; in a postscript he refers to the tenth anniversary of the fight against indulgences to date his letter.[2] However, both here and in all other preserved works by Luther, there is no mention of any posting of theses. The version of the event that is still alive in public memory comes from Philipp Melanchthon in his preface to the second volume of Luther's Latin works published in 1546: "And he [Luther] posted them [the theses] publicly at the church next to the castle, on the eve of All Souls' in the year 1517."[3] Melanchthon had not been an eyewitness to the event. He came to Wittenberg as late as August 1518. When he wrote the text, Luther was already dead.

On these two facts, Roman Catholic Church historian Erwin Iserloh based his hypothesis that the posting of the theses never happened.[4] This claim has troubled the academic community until most recently.[5] Iserloh based his opinion on two letters by Luther from the year 1518. Luther explained to Pope Leo X in May that same year and to Elector Frederick the Wise on November 21 that he had originally intended to make his theses public only after receiving a response from Albert of Mainz, the archbishop in charge.[6] It is inarguable that the Wittenberg professor sent his theses to the archbishop on October 31. If we stick to a posting of the theses, Iserloh states, we must assume that Luther made a false statement to his superior. According to historian Konrad Repgen, professor emeritus at the University of Bonn, it was he himself who gave Iserloh the idea that the posting of the theses might not have happened.[7] Iserloh's thesis has been reiterated several times and triggered a fierce debate among German researchers which, unlike most controversies among historians, also found its way to the public.[8] In this context

it was largely immaterial that Iserloh's arguments were consistently negative. In one of his most recent studies, Helmar Junghans, professor at the University of Leipzig, has refuted Iserloh's argument that Luther may have deceived Archbishop Albert and shown that there is still scope allowing for the posting of the theses.[9]

The task of this essay is to make the fact of the posting of the theses plausible with the help of a source that has been ignored by previous research, while at the same time asking about the physical shape of the original theses. In addition, the event shall be assessed in terms of its historical development. The rediscovery of the source in question resembles a winding road. In 1746, the librarian Johann Christian Mylius published the first catalogue of the University Library of Jena,[10] which gives a detailed description of the existing manuscripts in Jena. It also mentions one of the most important authors, Georg Rörer. One of the showpieces of the collection is a copy of Luther's translation of the New Testament of 1540,[11] which contains some notes in Luther's own hand. According to Mylius, the following little note is counted among them: "On the eve of All Souls' Anno Domini 1517, Doctor Martin Luther posted theses concerning indulgence at the doors of the churches in Wittenberg."[12]

If Mylius's opinion that the note is in Luther's own hand, were correct, the debate on the posting of the theses would be over. The note was widely neglected by research in Germany, but not by the much-read American Luther researcher Ernest G. Schwiebert. Schwiebert brought back a copy of the catalogue from a research trip in Jena in 1936, but did not evaluate his find until 1995. In his book *The Reformation*, published at that time, he boasts, "This remarkable discovery by Mylius is no longer known to scholars today. Mylius's findings should remove all doubts about Luther's nailing the Ninety-Five Theses on the door of the Castle Church on October 31, 1517."[13]

A physical investigation of the original New Testament at the Thuringian University and State Library in Jena has shown that indeed many marginal notes can be attributed to Luther, and also that some were written by Melanchthon. The most important contributor, however, and indeed the author of the debated marginal note is Georg Rörer (fig. 1).[14] Although at first glance the handwritings of Luther and Rörer are similar, they cannot be confused when directly compared to each other. This also answers the question of why Luther should have written about himself in the third person. That these treasures can be found in Jena today is due to the Schmalkaldic War, one of the well-known results of which was that the Ernestine John Frederick lost his electorate and his residence in Wittenberg. As he considered the library of the University of Wittenberg his private property, the books were first taken to Weimar and were subsequently sent from there to form the basis of the newly founded University of Jena.

This New Testament is well known to researchers. It is the revision exemplar that in 1545 was to result in the definitive edition. The reformers met at regular intervals to discuss improvements to the text, which was assessed word by word. Each mutually achieved agreement was written down as a marginal note. Luther and Rörer took turns writing these marginal notes, the latter acting as a kind of scholar-secretary of the team, although the notes don't reveal any particular systematic approach. Thus, when it comes to the creation of the *Luther Bible*, this volume is of outstanding significance, which is why these marginal notes were edited by Otto Reichert as early as 1923.[15] Reichert, however, did not include Rörer's note in the edition, as it is outside the actual corpus on the last page of the register. It was the historian Hans Volz, who played an influential role in the debate on the posting of the theses, who actually printed the note.[16] Volz suggested fixing November 1 as the date of the posting of the theses.[17] If Konrad Repgen's memories are correct, this book was the immediate cause of Iserloh's hypotheses.[18] Inexplicably, however, Volz declared Rörer's note worthless, as it depended on Melanchthon's story.

There is both chronological and topical evidence that this is not the case. The revision of the translation of the New Testament, as it is documented by the Jena copy, lasted from 1541 to December 19, 1544.[19] As Rörer owned the volume until his death, it cannot be completely ruled out that he made the entry even later. It is much more probable, however, that the note on the last page of the volume, scribbled among the colophon, dates from shortly before December 19, 1544. This is also suggested by the fact that it is immediately followed by a second remark: "Anno 1518/Postri die Bartholomei circa hora 10//Phil. Mel.//Primum venit Wittebergae" ("On the morning of August 25, 1518, at about ten o'clock, Philipp Melanchthon came to Wittenberg for the first time")[20] (fig. 2). This is the only exact information on his arrival time that is available, and it may be assumed to be based on information from Melanchthon himself. Both notes deal with the same topic, the starting of the Reformation by the two most important university professors in Wittenberg. Indeed, it is the altogether irrelevant detail of the exact time of Melanchthon's arrival that gives evidence to Rörer's interest in meticulous historiography. Moreover, the physical shape of the source increases the probability that it is an adequate depiction of reality. Had Volz seen a reproduction of it, his judgment probably would have been more prudent.

If this is true, Rörer's note is the oldest evidence for Luther posting his theses on October 31, 1517, in the context of which it must be noted that Rörer, who at this point had not yet arrived in Wittenberg, was no eyewitness. Also thematically, Rörer's story is different from Melanchthon's later one. As proven by its appearance, it is a carelessly and informally written note, whereas Melanchthon in the preface to the second volume of the Luther edition presents a per-

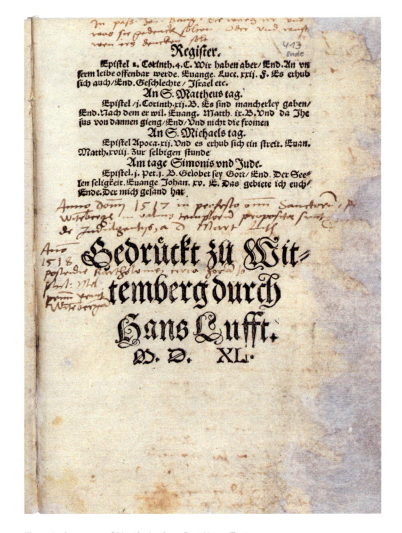

Fig. 1 Index page of Martin Luther, *Das Newe Testament* (The New Testament), Wittenberg 1540, with an apostil by Georg Rörer

1 This text is found in *WA* 1, 228, 233–238. **2** *WA.B* 4, 275, 25–27. **3** Philipp Melanchthon, Opera quae super sunt Omnia. In: Brettschneider, *Corpus Reformatorum*, p. 156: "Et has (sc. Propostiones) publice Templo, quod arci Witebergensi contiguum est affixit pridie festi omnium Sanctorum anno 1517." **4** Iserloh, *Thesenanschlag*. **5** Recently Wolf/Iserloh/Hallensleben, *Thesenanschlag*. **6** *WA* 1, 528f. on the Pope, *WA.B* 1, 236–246, here 245, 358–365 on the elector. **7** Repgen, *Rückblick*, p. 101. **8** For example in the news magazine *Der Spiegel* 20, no.1–2 of January 3, 1966, pp. 32–34. **9** Junghans, *Martin Luther*. **10** Memorabilia Bibliotheca Academiae Jenensis Sive Designation Manuscriptorum in illa Bibliotheca et Librorum Impressorum Plerumque Roriorum Concinnata POTISSIMUM ad USUS Suorum in Collegiiis Litteraturus Auditorum, a Joh. Christoph Mylio. Venundatantur Jenae et Weissenfelsae apud Joh. Christoph Crocerum. MDCC XXXXVI. **11** Printed by Hans Lufft in Wittenberg, VD 16 B 4429, Jena Shelfmark Ms App. 24. **12** Memorabilia, (see note 10), p. 289: "... haec leguntur b. Lutheri manuscripta." **13** Schwiebert, *Reformation*, pp. 360f. On Schwiebert and his interesting biography, see Kolb, *Nachruf*. **14** On Rörer's life and works, see Stefan/Speer, *Georg Rörer*. **15** *WA.DB* 4, 279–418. **16** Revisionary addendum to *WA* 48, 1972, 116 and note 3. **17** Volz, *Thesenanschlag*. **18** See Repgen, *Rückblick*, p. 101. **19** Buchwald, *Luther-Kalendarium*, p. 153. **20** Ms. App. 24 (see note 11), fol. 413r.

Fig. 2
Detail of the index page of
Martin Luther, Das Newe
Testament (The New Testament),
Wittenberg 1540, with an apostil
by Georg Rörer

fectly styled treatise according to the rules of ancient historiography. There is one small, extremely significant thematic difference, however. Whereas Melanchthon explicitly gives the door of the Schlosskirche (Castle Church) as the sole place of the event, Rörer speaks sweepingly of the churches in Wittenberg, using the plural. In fact, this is in line with the regulations of the first statutes of the University of Wittenberg of 1508, according to which it was the caretakers' task to "announce the dates of academic celebrations, disputations, awards of doctorates at the university at the doors of the churches."[21] This regulation does not rule out that Luther posted the theses personally, for there is no indication that this task was the monopoly of the caretakers. It is more probable, however, that the monk and professor left this work to those who were in charge of it. The practice of using all the church doors in Wittenberg as a bulletin board was so common that exceptions were explicitly stated, such as on December 30, 1509, when the principal, by way of a notice only at the doors of the Town Church, told a criminal student to turn himself in.[22]

Here we must pause for an assessment. Otto Reichert, in his introduction to the edition of Luther's and Rörer's marginal notes, in the context of preparing the new edition of the New Testament, had already remarked that the "document must always be stronger than the reflection."[23] This means that sources that seem to contradict one's own pattern of interpretation must be dealt with particularly intensively, but also critically. After all, the posting of the theses presents a problem of historical events that evades any clear conclusion according to the *sic et non* (yes and no) principle.[24] An eyewitness report or an official document that mentions the event is unlikely to materialize in the future. There are two reasons for this. Firstly, the publishing of theses as the basis for a disputation was routine, even if in this special case the expected disputation did not happen. Secondly, none of the participants was aware that this posting would be the start of a world-historical development. It took some time even for Luther to understand it this way. It hardly seems responsible to presume, however, based on the silence of the sources, that the event as such was invalid. Indeed, Rörer's seemingly unmotivated note contradicts this idea.

If Luther upheld the statutes of the university, and this we must assume, he needed several copies of the theses for the various churches. Exactly how many must remain unresolved, as it is not clear if, apart from the Stadtkirche (parish church) and the Schlosskirche (Castle Church), the two cloister chapels of the Franciscans and Augustinians were also included, and perhaps even the chapel of the Brothers of St. Anthony and the Corpus Christi Chapel at the cemetery of Wittenberg near the Stadtkirche.[25] It is at any rate certain that the theses must have existed in print on October 31, 1517, as Luther needed at least two more copies as appendices to a letter to Archbishop Albert, which has been preserved, as well as to a lost letter to the Archbishop of Brandenburg, Hieronymus Scultetus.[26]

However, no printed copy of the theses in Wittenberg has ever been discovered. This does not necessarily come as a surprise, as printed posters do not always find their way into libraries. Still, a unique copy of Franz Günther's disputation theses for his graduation to *Baccalaureus biblicus* of September 4, 1517, also authored by Luther and known to researchers by the title *Contra scholasticam theologiam*, was discovered at the Herzog August Bibliothek in Wolfenbüttel as late as 1983.[27] Such discoveries cannot be ruled out in the future.

At the time, the only printer in Wittenberg would have been Johann Rhau-Grunenberg, who, after some itinerant humanist printers had briefly provided their services, had served the university as printer since 1508.[28] Some of his early printings were labeled *Apud Augustinos*, which indicates that his first workshop might have been located on the property of the Schwarzes Kloster (Black/Augustinian Monastery). Its operation, however, was most likely limited.[29] Even in 1513 the *Schösser* (tax collector) Anton Niemegk complained to the Elector about insufficient printing services, and there is knowledge of a similar complaint in the spring of 1516.[30] Thus Martin Pollich von Mellerstadt, the founding principal of the University of Wittenberg, had, for the purpose of his lectures, a Thomasian logic textbook and a physics textbook printed in Leipzig in 1512 and 1514 respectively. In both cases the printer was Jacob Thanner, who served as a university printer there. Between 1501 and 1519, 82 percent of the capacity of his office was absorbed by the needs of the university.[31]

For Rhau-Grunenberg, on the other hand, there is evidence of only five printings in the year 1517, the second-lowest number for the period in question.

Thus there is the question of whether the first edition of the theses might have been printed outside Wittenberg. Research identifies three prints of the Theses that date as early as 1517: the Basel print by Adam Petri cannot be considered because of the format he uses, the Nuremberg example by Hieronymus Höltzel may also be assumed to be ineligible due to the distance from Wittenberg. There are no such concerns with the Leipzig print by Jacob Thanner.[32] As already mentioned above, Thanner had printed for Wittenberg several times. On one of the few preserved copies of his printing of the theses there is a brief note by Luther: "Anno 1517 ultimo Octobris vigilie Omnium sanctorum indulgentie primum impugnante." (On October 31, 1517, the eve of All Souls', the indulgences were fought for the first time) (fig. 3).[33] As in Luther's letter to Amsdorf, there is no mention of a posting of the theses but of fixing the beginning of the Reformation at a certain date. Now, however, it must be asked why Luther had this note printed in Leipzig. There is no conclusive answer, but it is another substantial indication pointing to Thanner as the originator of the first printing of the theses.

In conclusion, let us consider how the posting of the theses is to be understood as the beginning of the Reformation. We can quickly agree how *not* to speak about the posting of the theses: "There is no more brilliant day in German history than October 31, 1517. Light, sun, a new spring had been given to the German people: light from above, to seek and recognize truth; to find a way and grasp the freedom of faith! Poets have praised this day, researchers and scholars have celebrated it as the day of the salvation of Germany's development. Let us thus hold fast to this day. Let us come before our God on this day once more, on this day when once he granted us our rebirth, the Reformation of the German Church and of German faith."[34] Apart from its feverish schoolmaster's poetry, which has spring starting in October, this is a perfect example, one of countless others, of how not to speak of the posting of the theses, since, in fact, the original reaction to Luther's theses was rather moderate. "Astonishingly, at first everything seemed to remain calm."[35] This expression can only be made by someone, one could say in retrospect, who considers the posting of the theses an extraordinary event. Even in his own lifetime Luther contributed to this kind of reinterpretation when speaking of his theses having spread quickly, "as if the angels had been messengers."[36] In reality, the Reformer had missed the appropriate platform of communication with this message. The issue of indulgences was no mere academic issue but in fact concerned the piousness of the laypeople in a radical fashion. In sum, scholars did not usually buy letters of indulgence, and laypeople were not capable of understanding Luther's deliberations.

Luther's breakthrough to the broad German-speaking public happened only subsequently with his *Sermon on Indulgences and Grace* in March 1518. This was no translation of the Ninety-Five Theses, which even in a German version would have overtaxed a nonexpert audience, but an independent script on the same topic, which was adapted to the interests of laypeople. In this printed version of a spoken format (particularly suitable for reading aloud), Luther stated his

criticism of indulgences in just four sheets, providing what was a clearly weaker yet more effective argument than in the theses.[37] Its small size made it cheap to produce; a list format provided a clear structure of the arguments.

This was to be his breakthrough with the German-speaking reading public, which was in the process of being created by his influence. In contrast to the three printings of the Ninety-Five Theses which probably only involved a few hundred copies, twenty-three editions of the sermon were published until 1530.[38] In addition translations were made into Dutch, Czech, and Danish, as well as a retranslation into Latin. Compared to the normal edition sizes of pamphlets, Luther's sermon, with more than 25,000 copies virtually flooded the market. This was the first step on a path at the end of which Luther was called "the most successful publicist in history," which can be proven numerically at least for the years between 1518 and 1525.[39]

Thus the foundation was laid for the success of the Lutheran version of the Reformation. However important his acceptance among academic circles was for Luther, his public support in Germany was crucial. Even the Saxon Elector Frederick III's policy of protecting Luther may have been influenced by this fact. At the Diet of Worms in 1521, the fear of an uprising by the "common man" if something happened to Luther was ever-present.

Finally we must come back to our initial question: why did the "belittling of a historic legend"[40] trigger such a broad reaction by the public, at least as it was perceived in German-speaking countries? In 2003, director Eric Till in his film *Luther* had his protagonist hammer away without hesitation. If one considers the visualized perception of the event, it is conspicuous that the posting of the theses does not belong to the original canon of visualizations of Luther's life, as shown, for instance, in Ludwig Rabus's *Martyr book* of 1557. The subjects depicted in the book are the interrogation by Cardinal Cajetan, the Leipzig disputation, Luther's appearance in Worms, the Marburg Colloquy, and his burial. An image of the posting of the theses is

21 Friedensburg, *Urkunden*, p. 30: "festa, dispucationes, promotiones in scholis publicare et ecclesiarum valvis intimare ..." **22** Ibid., p. 61: "... per edictum publicum in valvis parochialis ecclesie Wittenbergensis ..." The reason for the exception could not be investigated. **23** *WA.DB* 4, XLVI. **24** See also Repgen, *Thesenanschlag*, p. 100. **25** On the two monasteries, see Bünger/Wentz, *Germania Sacra*, pp. 372–397 and pp. 440–499. **26** The both ingenious and fruitless speculations in Honselmann, *Urfassung* may easily be ignored. **27** The text is found in *WA* 1, 224–228. See Moeller, *Thesenanschläge*, p. 13. **28** On the significance of the early Wittenberg printing, see Treu, *Klima*, p. 83. **29** Still fundamental: Grossmann, *Wittenberger Drucke*. On criticism of Grossmann's judgements, see Treu, *Klima*. **30** Friedensburg, *Urkundenbuch*, p. 71, no. 49 and p. 80, no. 49. **31** Döring, *Buchdruck*, p. 92. **32** Benzing/Claus, *Lutherbibliographie*, p. 16, no. 87–89. **33** The copy is found at the Geheimes Staatsarchiv Preußischer Kulturbesitz, Geheimer Rat Rep. 13, no. 4–5. **34** Schulze, *Doktor*, p. 43. **35** Brecht, *Martin Luther*, p. 198. **36** *WA* 51, 540, 19–24. **37** *WA* 1, 239, 243–246. **38** Benzing/Claus, *Lutherbibliographie*, no. 90–114. **39** Burkhardt, *Reformationsjahrhundert*, p. 53. It remains inexplicable, however, why Burkhardt concludes that because of this success, the posting of the theses cannot have happened (p. 32). **40** Brandt, *Reformator*, p. 139, with the explicit reservation that using the term *legend* does not say anything about the facticity of the posting of the theses.

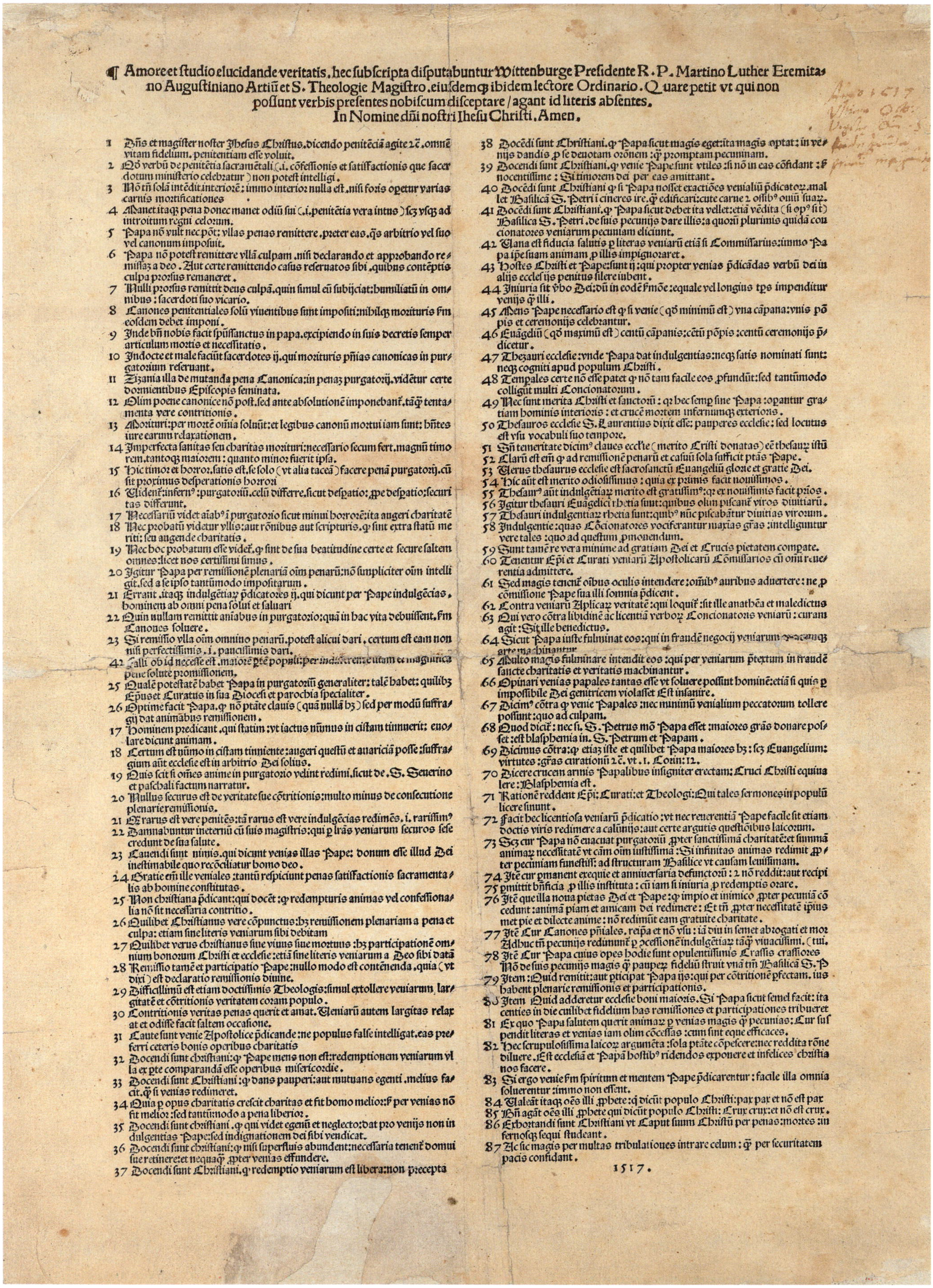

¶ Amore et studio elucidande veritatis, hec subscripta disputabuntur Wittenburge Presidente R. P. Martino Luther Eremitano Augustiniano Artiū et S. Theologie Magistro, eiusdemq; ibidem lectore Ordinario. Quare petit vt qui non possunt verbis presentes nobiscum disceptare / agant id literis absentes. In Nomine dñi nostri Ihesu Christi. Amen.

1517.

Fig. 3 Broadside of the Ninety-Five Theses on Indulgence from Leipzig printer Jacob Thanner with a hand written annotation by Martin Luther, 1517

missing. This image can be found for the first time on a copperplate print shortly before 1700.[41] The posting of the theses as part of to-day's collective memory is a product of the *long nineteenth century*. An analysis of the impact of this nineteenth-century iconography on the current image of Luther would go beyond the scope of this essay. But there is reason to assume that it is still stronger than one is generally aware of.

That is not to say, however, that we may simply ignore the existence of sources such as the note by Rörer discussed here. In 2005 an academic catalogue claimed that in the sixteenth century nobody except Melanchthon spoke of a posting of theses. No matter how valid it is to emphasize the significance of pamphlets for the spread of the Reformation, this cannot justify ignoring existing sources that describe a posting of theses.[42] After all, Shakespeare, in the play to which this essay owes its title, long ago addressed this same problem: "If you dare not trust that you see, confess not that you know."[43]

---

41 See Holsing, *Thesenanschlag*, p. 142. **42** E.g. Burkhardt, *Reformation*, p. 41. **43** William Shakespeare, *Much Ado About Nothing*, Act III, Scene 2.

BIBLIOGRAPHY

Benzing, Josef/**Claus**, Helmut (eds.) (1989), *Lutherbibliographie: Verzeichnis der gedruckten Schriften Martin Luthers bis zu dessen Tod*. Vols. 1 and 2. Baden-Baden. **Brandt**, Reinhard (2008), Reformator ohne Hammer. Zur öffentlichen Aufmerksamkeit für die Bestreitung des Thesenanschlags. In: Ott, Joachim/Treu, Martin (eds.), *Luthers Thesenanschlag—Faktum oder Fiktion*. Leipzig, p. 127–140. **Brecht**, Martin (1986), *Martin Luther. Sein Weg zur Reformation*. Berlin. **Brettschneider**, Karl Gottlieb/**Bindseil**, Heinrich Ernst (eds.) (1834 f.), *Corpus Reformatorum*. Halle (Saale). **Buchwald**, Georg (1929), *Luther-Kalendarium*. Leipzig. **Bünger**, Fritz/**Wentz**, Gottfried (eds.) (1941), *Germania Sacra, Section 1*. Vol. 3: Das Bistum Brandenburg. Berlin. **Burkhardt**, Johannes (2002), *Das Reformationsjahrhundert. Deutsche Geschichte zwischen Medienrevolution und Institutionenbildung. 1517–1617*. Stuttgart. **Burkhardt**, Johannes (2015), *Reformation und Konfessionsbildung. Von oben oder von unten?* Dresden. **Döring**, Thomas (2006), Der Leipziger Buchdruck vor der Reformation. In: Bünz, Enno (ed.), *Bücher, Drucker, Bibliotheken in Mitteldeutschland. Neue Forschungen zur Kommunikations und Mediengeschichte um 1500*. Leipzig, pp. 87–98. **Friedensburg**, Walter (ed.) (1926), *Urkunden der Universität Wittenberg*. Vol. 1. Magdeburg. **Grossmann**, Maria (1971), *Wittenberger Drucke. 1502 bis 1517. Ein bibliographischer Beitrag zur Geschichte des Humanismus in Deutschland*. Wien. **Holsing**, Henrike (2008), Luthers Thesenanschlag im Bild. In: Ott, Joachim/Treu, Martin (eds.), *Luthers Thesenanschlag—Faktum oder Fiktion*. Leipzig, p. 141–172. **Honselmann**, Klemens (1966), *Urfassung und Drucke der Ablassthesen Martin Luthers und ihre Veröffentlichung*. Paderborn. **Iserloh**, Erwin (1961), Luthers Thesenanschlag—Tatsache oder Legende. In: *Trierer Theologische Zeitschrift*, vol. 70, pp. 303–312. **Junghans**, Helmar (2008): Martin Luther, kirchliche Magnaten und Thesenanschlag. Zur Vorgeschichte von Luthers Widmungsbrief zu den "Resolutiones disputationum de indulgentiarum virtute" an Papst Leo X. In: Ott, Joachim/Treu, Martin (eds.), *Luthers Thesenanschlag—Faktum oder Fiktion*. Leipzig, pp. 33–46. **Kolb**, Robert (2000), Nachruf. In: *Lutherjahrbuch*, vol. 67, pp. 19–21. **Moeller**, Bernd (2008), Thesenanschläge. In: Ott, Joachim/Treu, Martin (eds.), *Luthers Thesenanschlag—Faktum oder Fiktion*. Leipzig, pp. 9–31. **Repgen**, Konrad (2008), Ein profangeschichtlicher Rückblick auf die Iserloh-Debatte. In: Ott, Joachim/Treu, Martin (eds.), *Luthers Thesenanschlag—Faktum oder Fiktion*. Leipzig, pp. 99–110. **Schulze**, Otto, (1917), *Doktor Martinus. Ein Buch für das deutsche Volk zum Reformationsjubelfest 1917*. Gotha. **Schwiebert**, Ernest G. (1995), *The Reformation*. Minneapolis. **Stefan**, Michel/**Speer**, Christian (eds.) (2012), *Georg Rörer (1492–1557). Der Chronist der Wittenberger Reformation*. Leipzig. **Treu**, Martin (2015), Das geistige Klima an der Universität Wittenberg vor der Ankunft Melanchthons. In: Asche, Matthias et al. (eds.), *Die Leucorea zur Zeit des späten Melanchthons. Institutionen und Formen gelehrter Bildung um 1550*. Leipzig, pp. 77–92. **Volz**, Hans (1959), *Martin Luthers Thesenanschlag und dessen Vorgeschichte*, Weimar. **Wolf**, Uwe/**Iserloh**, Erwin/**Hallensleben**, Beate (eds.) (2014). *Der Thesenanschlag fand nicht statt* (= Studia oecumenica friburgensia. 61). With a foreword by Friedrich Weber and a research report by Volker Leppin. Basel.

MARTIN TREU

Disputations and the Main Writings of the Reformation

During the late Middle Ages, academic arguments, called disputations, were held on a regular basis. They were conducted in universities along with lectures like those held to this day. Disputations involved controversial questions, debated according to formal propositional logic, for or against, in order to find a solution. Student participation was mandatory, and senior students were required to actively engage as respondents or defenders of the theses. These orderly disputations, whose objectives were comparable to today's seminars, can be clearly distinguished from the extraordinary disputations that were to become something of a specialty of the University of Wittenberg. In 1516, Luther was already treading uncharted territory by having theses involving questions of Christian anthropology discussed in a disputation. When he realized that there was no binding regulation in canon law for the concept of indulgences (this was not issued by Rome until the summer of 1518), he once again chose the disputation as a vehicle with which to present what he felt to be appropriate theses. It is well known that the actual debate never took place, but it was the publication of those theses that triggered the Reformation.

The year 1520 was especially productive for Martin Luther. Many of his texts appeared within a short period, four of which later came to be considered "main writings," not just for their fundamental content but also for their broad distribution. The first one, *Sermon on Good Works*, became available in June of 1520. It dealt with the relationship between faith and works and consequently offered a comprehensive ethic within a brief text. *To the Christian Nobility of the German Nation* followed shortly after. The title is misleading because Luther was appealing to the political ruling class in the broadest sense, demanding far-reaching reforms from it because of the church's failings. These were certainly not new proposals, and they applied to society as a whole. In October of that year, Luther addressed the European public with a Latin treatise, *De captivitate Babylonica (On the Babylonian Captivity of the Church)*, which he also published in German shortly thereafter. In this text, Luther, using biblical arguments, challenged the pre-eminence of the Pope, the intrinsic difference between the clergy and the laity, and the doctrine of the seven sacraments. This was Luther's most radical criticism of the church so far, and would alienate some of his reform-minded supporters. This was because this treatise made it clear that Luther was not in fact seeking changes to the existing church; he wanted a completely different one instead. He concluded with his treatise *On the Freedom of a Christian*, which was an unpolemical portrayal of the Christian as master in his faith and as a servant to his neighbor. Ironically, Luther had prefaced this text with an open letter to Pope Leo X to prove his loyalty as a member of the church. In fact, however, these four main texts could only be regarded as signalizing an inevitable break with Rome.

HEINZ SCHILLING

The Tied Majesty. The Emperor's (Version of) "Here I stand, I can do no other…"

The way to Worms was not an easy one for the Augustinian monk Martin Luther. For even though the journey eventually turned out to be a triumph, it was accompanied by mental and physical distress. An excruciating indigestion, which had troubled Luther for some time, now plagued him, the closer he approached Worms, "in a way which previously has been unknown to me."[1] The 1521 Diet of Worms was convened to negotiate imperial politics. All members of the empire were assembled: first, the Electors, who were entitled to elect the emperor and had their say in imperial matters, even after the election; second, the secular and ecclesiastical princes (i.e., dukes, imperial counts, imperial bishops, imperial abbots, etc.); and, third, the representatives of the free and imperial towns and cities. Diets were both symbolic representations of the empire and its highest decision-making body. Because of the public attention that Luther's criticism of the church had excited in Germany and beyond, the *causa Lutheri* (the case of Luther) was the most important issue on the Diet's agenda—important not only for the emperor and the imperial estates, as well as for the church hierarchy in Germany and in Rome, but also for the many Christians in Germany and Europe, whom Luther's Reformation message had relieved from anguish and anxiety and who hoped that empire and church would adopt his Protestant teaching. Cardinal Aleander, as Pope Leo X's *legatus a latere* (i.e., his special nuncio), had been instructed to prevail on emperor and imperial estates to condemn Luther as a heretic and to impose the imperial ban on him. If the Protestant movement had to be gotten under control, the Pope thought, this was the last chance to do so—particularly as the horrified Aleander had reported to Rome: "The whole of Germany is in an uproar. Nine persons out of ten are for Luther, and even the tenth does not trouble himself about the edict that condemns him; but all wish for the destruction of the Roman Church."[2]

Germany was at a turning point when the Diet of Worms was convened in 1521. Not only was it Charles V's first diet—at age twenty-one, the emperor was very much a youth compared to then twenty-seven-year-old Martin Luther—but due to the *causa Lutheri*, it was also a diet of world-historical significance. Momentous decisions needed to be made mainly on the constitutional question and the closely related church question. Criticism of the church, to be sure, had long existed; what made Luther's so explosive was the unprecedented new concept of faith Luther had formulated in Witten-

berg, a town far beyond the sphere of traditional Roman and Romanized culture.[3] After a long and exhausting wait in the hostel, Luther was eventually called to appear before the Diet on April 17, 1521. His writings were placed before him by the orator speaking on behalf of the emperor, a high-level imperial prince. Among these were the three major reform writings of 1520, which had so upset Christendom and the German nation: *On the Babylonian Captivity of the Church*, *On the Freedom of a Christian*, and *To the Christian Nobility of the German Nation*. When asked whether he was the author of these writings, Luther, "with subdued voice,"[4] answered in the affirmative. When called to retract his theses, he demanded that he be given more time for deliberation, arguing that the retraction concerned "the Word of God, the greatest and most precious treasure of heaven or earth."[5] The emperor granted the plea by act of grace—procedurally, he would not have been required to accommodate the accused's wish. In contrast to the heroic gesture Protestant myth-making was soon to proclaim to the world, Luther's first appearance before the diet utterly failed to make a convincing impression. Even his sovereign and protector, Frederick III (the Wise), the Elector of Saxony, was disappointed.

It must have been a hard night for Luther, who in that period produced a kind of crib on which he tried to clarify his position (fig. 1), reminding himself not to talk "imprudently" about matters concerning the holy Word of God and faith.[6] The text breaks off in the middle of the sentence. On the next day, Luther delivered his statement in a firm and determined voice. All his doubts were cast aside—and so were his inhibitions in front of the great men of the world. When he was again called upon to retract his writings, he replied with the words soon to become famous, saying that, since popes and councils had demonstrably been in error, it was impossi-

---

1 *WA*.B 2, 396, 298; *LW* 48, 198. For a more detailed account of his illness, see Schilling, *Rebell*, pp. 212–215. **2** Stoughton, *Homes and Haunts*, p. 128. **3** For a detailed account, see Schilling, *Rebell*; for a "global historical" perspective, see Schilling, *Epochejahr*. This essay elaborates ideas presented in a speech given at the Cathedral of Toledo, during the official commemoration ceremony of the Spanish Court on October 5, 2000. **4** Wrede, *Deutsche Reichstagsakten*, no. 194. **5** Ibid., p. 582. **6** Beginning of a speech manuscript before the second hearing at the Diet of Worms on April 17 and 18, 1521, Thüringisches Hauptstaatsarchiv Weimar (ThHStA Weimar), Ernestinisches Gesamtarchiv, Reg. E 81, fol. 1.

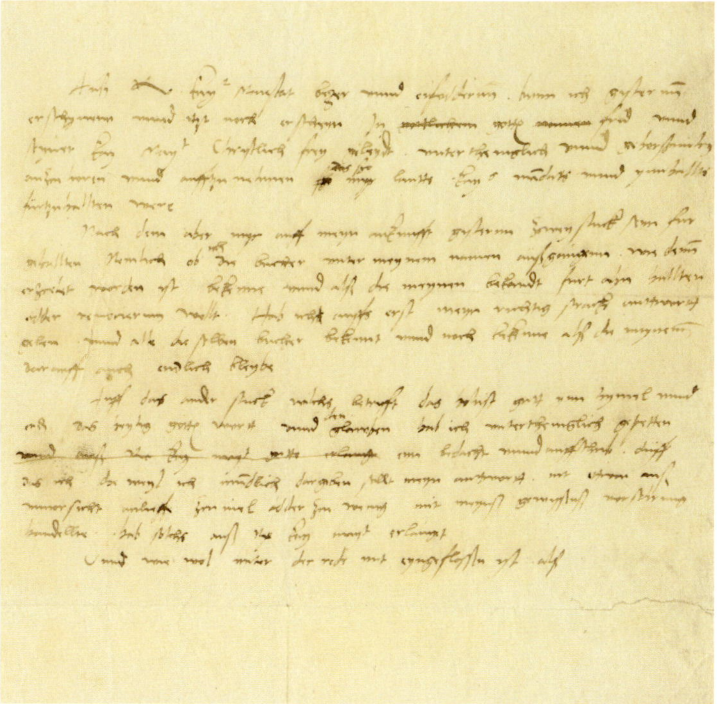

Fig. 1 Beginning of the notes for a speech prepared by Martin Luther before the second hearing at the Diet of Worms, April 17/18, 1521. This document was registered as part of the UNESCO world documentary heritage "Memory of the World" in 2015.

ble for him to recant unless he was proven to be wrong by the testimony of scripture. He argued that he was "bound by the scriptures I have quoted, and my conscience is captive to the Word of God. I cannot and will not recant anything, since it is neither safe nor right to go against conscience … May God help me. Amen."[7] Thus, the essence of Luther's revolutionary position of 1521 is not the enlightened freedom of conscience, which would be formulated in late eighteenth-century Europe, but rather the religious freedom in Christ as the source of both man's freedom and his commitment to the Word of God.

The still-lingering Protestant myth of "Here I stand, I can do no other" was only put into Luther's mouth when his apologia was published. It does, however, serve as a brilliant intensification of his position. Luther argues that he is captive in his statement both to his conscience and to God, and thus cannot do other than persist in his theological belief. For Emperor Charles V, the multiply interrelated question of church and constitution was one of the key problems of his government.[8] He was not the "noble German blood"[9] initially celebrated by the followers of the Reformation in the empire but had been raised in the culture of Dutch Burgundy. He had his greatest success as King of Spain, and his power was anchored in Castile both militarily and fiscally. His life's achievements, however, were to be judged in Germany. For here lay the key to the success of his universal concepts of Empire and Christianity, and thus to the success of his "European Politics."[10] The constitutional question arose from the fact that, if the empire was to survive in the then emerging world of modern states, its feudal association and medieval organization were in need of reform. The question was whether this reorganiza-

tion should generate a federation of more or less sovereign territorial states, as desired by the princes, or an imperial state under the sovereign government of the German king, as desired by the House of Habsburg. It was clear to Charles in 1521 that his empire, stretching from the New World to Spain and Burgundy and well into the Balkans, would only continue to exist on the foundation of the Roman Universal Church. With this in mind, that is to say, to strengthen both his position as emperor and the empire itself, he sought to reform the church, aiming to restore the original unity that had been shaken by the rise of the early modern nations.

Luther's words, "Here I stand, I can do no other," could just as well have been pronounced by the emperor himself. Similarly to the Protestant Reformer, Charles, in the night following the second day of hearing, wrote a "confession slip," from which it becomes clear that he, too, followed his conscience. His personal confession of faith, formulated by himself, was read out to the imperial estates on the next morning. In it, Charles invoked the noble line of his ancestors as the foundation of his faith: "You know that I am descended from the most Christian emperors of the noble German nation, the Catholic kings of Spain, the archdukes of Austria, and the dukes of Burgundy, who all were, until death, faithful sons of the Holy Roman Church, and they have always defended the Catholic faith, the sacred ceremonies, decretals, ordinances, and laudable customs, for the honor of God, the propagation of the faith, and the salvation of souls. After their deaths they left, by natural law and heritage, these holy Catholic rites, for us to live and to die following their example […] What is true and a great shame and offense to us is that a single monk, going against God, [is] mistaken in his opinion, which is against what all of Christendom has held for over a thousand years to the present. I am therefore determined to use all my kingdoms and possessions, my friends, my body, my blood, my life, and my soul. For it would be a great disgrace for you and me, the noble and greatly renowned German nation, appointed by privilege and singular preeminence to be the defenders and protectors of the Catholic faith […] I declare that I now regret having delayed so long the proceedings against him and his false doctrines. I am resolved that I will never again hear him talk […] and [to] act and proceed against him as against a notorious heretic."[11]

Luther had invoked his subjective conscience as a conscience that was justified by God, opposing the young emperor's self-confident reasoning by establishing "eternal salvation" and religious self-assurance as ideas never to be questioned again. The emperor, on the other hand, invoked the objective level, referring to the institutions and the tradition of his dynasty, which he equated with the history of Christianity and its self-assertion in the face of internal and external dangers. Both Luther and Charles, however, were firmly convinced that God was on their side. The emperor fully trusted in God—also, and above all, in his struggle against the German heresy or *pestis Germaniae*, as it would soon be called in his Spanish environment.[12] Luther's speech is rightly regarded as a "key text of Protestantism" (Bernd Moeller); still today, it opens up the collective identity of the Protestants. The emperor's confession is largely forgotten today; the Habsburg dynasty did not establish a denomination of its own. The emperor's confession therefore cannot be used to constitute a collective identity. What can be gleaned from Charles's words, though, is an inside view of his personality and policy. His personal *majestas*, his rootedness in his position as emperor, and his dynastic tradition were the three cornerstones of a personal piety that did not have any impact on the inner reform of the Roman Church. It is on account of this difference that, while Luther's words conquered the world, the emperor's were forgotten—his speech was hardly ever mentioned in the numerous pamphlets disseminated after Luther's interrogation.[13] And if historians do so, then in the most cases it is only as proof of the alleged superficial traditionalism of Charles and his court in matters of religion and church policy.

An impartial look at the 1521 events in Worms shows that Charles, no less than Luther, followed his conscience, both as emperor and as a Christian. Again, Luther's "Here I stand, I can do no other. May God help me. Amen," might just as well have been pronounced by Charles—with the difference that the emperor's conscience, as opposed to Luther's, was not centered on his own subjectivity and God but collectively related to his ancestors and all Christians living before and simultaneously with him. Charles's personal religiosity was rooted less in the study of the Bible than in the works of Erasmus and the Dutch *devotio moderna*, a late-medieval piety movement promoting personal lay piety in the sense of "following Christ."[14] Another important factor was the aristocratic piety and its idea of the *miles Christianus*, the chivalrous soldier battling for the triumph of Christianity and for a doctrine purified of heresy. This idea was cultivated by the late-medieval orders of knights, such as the chapter of the Order of the Golden Fleece in the Duchy of Burgundy and the Spanish Order of Sant Jordi d'Alfama i.e. Knights of Saint George (fig. 2).

Charles had been raised in Burgundy, the successor state to a lost era. He lived at the court of his aunt and godmother, Margaret of Austria, in Mechelen. As becomes clear from the many religious artworks in her collection, which testify to an intense Marian devotion, Margaret was a deeply religious woman. Items especially dear to her were even stored in her bedroom cupboard.[15] The above-mentioned *devotio moderna* played a major role in Charles's education at the Burgundian court, where he was tutored by cleric Adriaan of Utrecht who would later become unsuccessful reformist Pope Adrian VI. It was probably he who taught Charles the moderate use of temporal goods and the quest for personal piety.

Fig. 2 Charles V. in prayer, wearing the chain of the Order of the Golden Fleece and accompanied by an angel.
Miniature from Emperor Charles V's book of prayer, 1516

7 *LW* 32, 112 – 123. **8** For a more detailed account of the following, and extensive references to sources and research literature, see Schilling, *Charles V and Religion*. **9** This was the key concept in the Habsburg party's nationally oriented propaganda prior to the 1519 imperial election. **10** Charles V's 500th anniversary in 2000 prompted numerous publications. See in particular Soly, *Charles V*, an international collection of essays by leading experts, published in numerous languages, as well as Kohler, *Karl V*. Both publications provide extensive references to sources and research literature. **11** Quoted from Cowans, *Early Modern Spain*, pp. 49 f. **12** A key concept in the Spanish Habsburg party's anti-Protestant pamphlet propaganda. **13** A short summary of the emperor's speech can be found in a recently rediscovered pamphlet published in 1521 in the remote ore-mining area of Tyrol, see Möncke, *Editionsnachtrag*, pp. 273 – 280. **14** See Thomas à Kempis, *Imitatio Christi*, Köln, about 1486. **15** Eichberger, *Leben mit Kunst*, p. 191.

Fig. 3 Titian, The Adoration of the Holy Trinity ("La Gloria"), 1551–54

Charles was not meant to win the conflicts about the Empire's constitutional order. After various struggles and gaining temporary predominance in the Schmalkaldic War in 1547/48, the final decision fell in 1555 in favor of the princes and territorial states. However, the emperor was not altogether unsuccessful. The Peace of Augsburg—that is, the basic constitutional law adopted toward the end of Charles's reign at the Diet of Augsburg in 1555—far from spelling the end of the empire, opened the way for its partial modernization.

This was the foundation on which the empire survived maintaining central European political order until 1806. Just under a century after 1555, the political compromise was reconsolidated in the Peace of Westphalia. Though not a state in the proper sense of the word, the early modern political system then emerging in Western and Northern Europe fulfilled its functions as a legal, cultural, and defensive entity. In addition, it was an institution that promoted, albeit not always successfully, a peaceful balance of interests in Germany and Europe.[16] In this respect, the empire newly created under Charles was a pre- and supranational system creating order and balance and protecting the rights and peace between its member states. It was a far cry from the nineteenth- and twentieth-century German myth of the *Reich* that sometimes causes confusion in discussions about Europe today. From the point of view of historical research, Charles V's involvement in creating a complex constitutional balanced system makes him one of the founding fathers of a united Europe.

What was much harder for the emperor to bear than his defeat in the constitutional question was his realization toward the end of his life that the unity of Christendom was lost. Several princes sided with Maurice, Elector of Saxony, in his 1552 rebellion against Charles, which forced Charles to leave Innsbruck and flee to Villach. The bitter truth, conveyed to him in in this remote exile by his brother Ferdinand, was that the empire and Europe would only get its much-needed rest if the Protestants were granted unlimited tolerance. The emperor was too frail to oppose but refused to lay the burden of this solution on his conscience. Thus, Ferdinand I had to negotiate the Peace of Augsburg in 1555 by himself. Although the treaty granted religious freedom not to individuals but only to territories, it paved the way to a legally regulated coexistence of the denominations.[17]

Because of his intransigence and severity in opposing the Reformation, Charles was berated by his Protestant opponents as the "Butcher of Flanders" and "Bloodhound of the Pope."[18] Governed by a Protestant mindset, nineteenth-century historians would stylize Luther into a German hero of faith and the emperor into an antihero and sinister power seeker. The five-hundredth anniversary of his birthday on February 24, 2000, provided sufficient grounds to radically revise this image.

In spite of all his readiness to fight for the Catholic faith of his ancestors, Charles was neither a medieval hunter of heretics nor an early modern confessionalist. This becomes evident in the large-scale painting Charles commissioned from Titian in 1550, and which, having sent it from Brussels to St. Yuste (Spain), he bequeathed in his testament as the backdrop to the high altar of that monastery's church. The painting is known both as *Gloria* and *The Last Judgment*, and its iconographic hierarchy was certainly determined in close

consultation with, if not inspired by, Charles. It shows the emperor, clad in sackcloth or a shroud, kneeling before the throne of the Trinity (fig. 3) and, at his side, the two already deceased women closest to him, Empress Isabella, his wife, and Margaret of Austria, his aunt and guardian. Even this last vision, which Charles, after he had gone to Spain, had before his eyes every day until his death, conveys the transitional character of his piety and religious self-assurance. It is not a picture for a "man of the deepest medieval piety," as his great biographer Karl Brandi almost self-evidently puts it;[19] nor is it a forerunner of those huge baroque apotheoses, in which the Catholic princes of the late sixteenth and the seventeenth century would glorify themselves. Rather, it is a dialogue between Charles, the human being, and his God—a dialogue in which is expressed the ultimate examination of conscience, in the rigorous form characteristic of the laws of the Catholic Church of his ancestors. But this form takes nothing away from the highly personal spirituality of Charles's religious feeling as a Christian, which the painting radiates. And even though Charles was neither a humanist in the strict sense of the word, nor a humble and devout believer,[20] one cannot help feeling that the religious education he had received as a young man at his aunt Margaret's Mechelen court from Adriaan of Utrecht comes full circle in Titian's *Gloria*. The piety here embraced by Charles is, of course, not the devout piety that emerged as a hallmark of civil modesty in the large and small towns of Lower Burgundy (the Netherlands) during the fifteenth century, but a piety that aims at the innermost individual soul of every Christian. This is clear from the fact that Charles is shown without crown and scepter and vestments of earthly power, clad in the plain shroud in which he is to face his judge.

The intermediate position of Charles and Titian's heavenly vision between the Middle Ages and the Baroque is further highlighted by an iconographic feature of the *Gloria* emphasized only recently: "Unlike dozens of similar preceding representations and many following it, Titian's heaven is empty of martyrs and saints, virgins and saintly founders; nor are there popes and emperors—except for Charles, his wife, and his aunt. The scene looks like an anticipation of a temporal and personal Last Judgment. The only figures represented are the patriarchs and prophets of the Old Covenant, and they are united with the imperial family. In line with what had always been assured to him by his court panegyrists and the age-old and ever-new imperial prophecies they invoked, Charles is being ranked with the foremost characters of the chosen people—Moses and Abraham, Noah, David, and Saul—as part of a congregation similar to that which Saint Augustine had in mind around 400 C.E., when the medieval tradition was still a far cry. Hence, the heaven into

16 For the assessment of the Holy Roman Empire in research discussions, see Schnettger, *Imperium Romanum*. **17** See Schiling/Smolinsky, *Religionsfrieden*; Gotthard, *Religionsfrieden*. **18** Thus the epithets given to Charles in anti-imperial pamphlets during the Schmalkaldic War, reproduced in Kohler, *Quellen*, pp. 337–343. In the Netherlands, too, opposition circles of the time referred to the blood judgments passed by the Inquisition as "butchery." For propaganda during the Schmalkaldic War, see Vogler, *Kurfürst Johann Friedrich*, pp. 178–206. **19** Brandi, *Karl V.*, p. 537. **20** See Seibt, *Karl*, pp. 29, 219.

Fig. 4 Bernard van Orley, Window in the northern transept of the Cathedral of St. Michael and
St. Gudula in Brussels with portraits of Queen Isabella of Portugal and Emperor Charles V,
accompanied by their titular patrons St. Elizabeth of Hungary and Charlemagne, 1537

which the shroud-clad Charles enters is not the heaven of the Catholic Church. Charles and his family kneel in a post-Reformation heaven, as it were, which is void of the Roman Catholic glorification of saints. It is a heaven in which both Luther and Calvin would have been able to join Charles in singing hosanna."[21]

Much the same can be said about the actual scene of the emperor's death on September 21, 1558, in Yuste, provided one does not look at it from the perspective of confessionalism, that is to say, with Protestant or Catholic eyes. For although confessionalism occurred in the emperor's immediate vicinity during precisely those years, it had no significant influence on his pre-confessionalist religiosity— a religiosity that helped him prepare for the transition to the other world that he had had before his eyes in Titian's *Gloria*. Charles found refuge in a plain crucifix that had already consoled his beloved wife, Isabella, in the hour of her death (fig. 4). For the confessionalist guardians of doctrine and morals at the Spanish court, it was a move that came so close to Luther's *solus Christus* theology that they immediately suspected the archbishop of Toledo, Don Bartolomé Carranza, who had handed the crucifix to the emperor, of heresy. For a brief moment, even Charles's corpse was in danger of being put on trial for heresy. Today, we can grasp that which even the dying man's attendants failed to understand, for we look at this scene in terms of the pre-confessionalist *devotio moderna*, which had been propagated in the vicinity of the Mechelen court at the beginning of the century and had become an important formative factor, not only in the pious education of the adolescent Charles but also in the spirituality of the student and monk Martin Luther. When seen in the right light, Charles V, in his church politics, was anything but a servant of the Pope. On the contrary, the emperor literally wrested his reform policy from the reluctant Popes. Consequently, he has, not unduly, been called the "real father of the Council of Trent."[22] Modern, confessionalized Catholicism owes a lot to the emperor. So much so that one could say that Max Weber wrongly traced the emergence of the modern world to Luther and Protestantism alone. Impetus for the modern era, and for modernity, also came from Charles V and the renewed confessionalized Catholicism originating at the Council of Trent. This should be kept in mind when commemorating Luther and the Reformation in 2017—not only for the sake of historical accuracy, but also when it comes to giving new momentum to the ecumenical commitment on both sides.

21 Ibid., p. 212. 22 See Schulin, *Kaiser Karl V.*

BIBLIOGRAPHY

Brandi, Karl (1964), *Karl V*. 7th ed. München. **Brieger**, Theodor (1884), *Aleander und Luther. Die vervollständigten Aleander-Depeschen über den Wormser Reichstag*. Vol. 1. Gotha. **Cowans**, Jon (ed.) (2003), *Early Modern Spain: A Documentary History*. Philadelphia. **Eichberger**, Dagmar (2002), *Leben mit Kunst—Wirken durch Kunst. Sammelwesen und Hofkunst unter Margarethe von Österreich, Regentin der Niederlande*. Turnhout. **Gotthard**, Axel (2004), *Der Augsburger Religionsfrieden*. Münster. **Kohler**, Alfred (1999), *Karl V. Eine Biographie*. München. **Kohler**, Alfred (1999), *Quellen zur Geschichte Karls V*. Darmstadt. **Merle d'Aubigné**, Jean Henri (1842), *History of the Great Reformation of the Sixteenth Century in Germany, Switzerland, etc*. Vol. 2. Trans. Henry Beveridge. New York. **Möncke**, Gisela (2012), Editionsnachtrag zu einer Flugschrift über Luther in Worms. In: *Archiv für Reformationsgeschichte*, vol. 103, pp. 273–280. **Schilling**, Heinz (1999), Charles V and Religion: The Struggle for the Integrity and Unity of Christendom. Trans. Suzanne Walters. In: Soly, Hugo (ed.) (1999), *Charles V, 1500–1558, and His Time*. Antwerp, pp. 285–364. **Schilling**, Heinz (2014), *Martin Luther. Rebell in einer Zeit des Umbruchs*. 3rd ed. München. **Schilling**, Heinz, *1517. Ein weltgeschichtliches Epochejahr wird besichtigt*. München (in press). **Schilling**, Heinz/**Smolinsky**, Heribert (eds.) (2007), *Der Augsburger Religionsfrieden 1555*. Gütersloh. **Schnettger**, Matthias (ed.) (2002), *Imperium Romanum—Irregulare Corpus—Teutscher Reichs-Staat*. Mainz. **Schulin**, Ernst (1999), *Kaiser Karl V. Geschichte eines übergroßen Wirkungsbereiches*. Stuttgart. **Seibt**, Ferdinand (1990), *Karl V. Der Kaiser und die Reformation*. Berlin. **Soly**, Hugo (ed.) (1999), *Charles V, 1500–1558, and His Time*. Antwerpen. **Stoughton**, John (1883), *Homes and Haunts of Luther*. 2nd ed. London. **Vogler**, Günter (1998), Kurfürst Johann Friedrich und Herzog Moritz. Polemik in Liedern und Flugschriften während des Schmalkaldischen Krieges 1546/47. In: *Archiv für Reformationsgeschichte*, vol. 89, pp. 178–206. **Wrede**, Adolf (ed.) (1962), *Deutsche Reichstagsakten. Jüngere Reihe: Deutsche Reichstagsakten unter Kaiser Karl V*. Vol. 2. Göttingen.

MONK AGAINST EMPEROR

In his Ninety-Five Theses of 1517, the Augustinian monk Martin Luther criticized the Church's practice of indulgences. During his conflict with the Church, Luther radicalized his views. In 1520, he publicized his break with the Church. He burned the bull threatening him with excommunication and writings of canon law. Luther was thereupon excommunicated in 1521. Elector Frederick the Wise was Luther's sovereign. He obtained the guarantee that Luther was not extradited to Rome. Luther was therefore interrogated on German soil at the 1521 Diet of Worms. In front of the emperor and imperial estates, the monk defended his theses and refused to revoke.

The famous words, "Here I stand, I can do no other," were disseminated in pamphlets after the interrogation. However, there is no evidence that Luther really pronounced these words.

✉ Correspondence
💬 Speech
📖 Publications
👥 Meetings
🔥 Burning

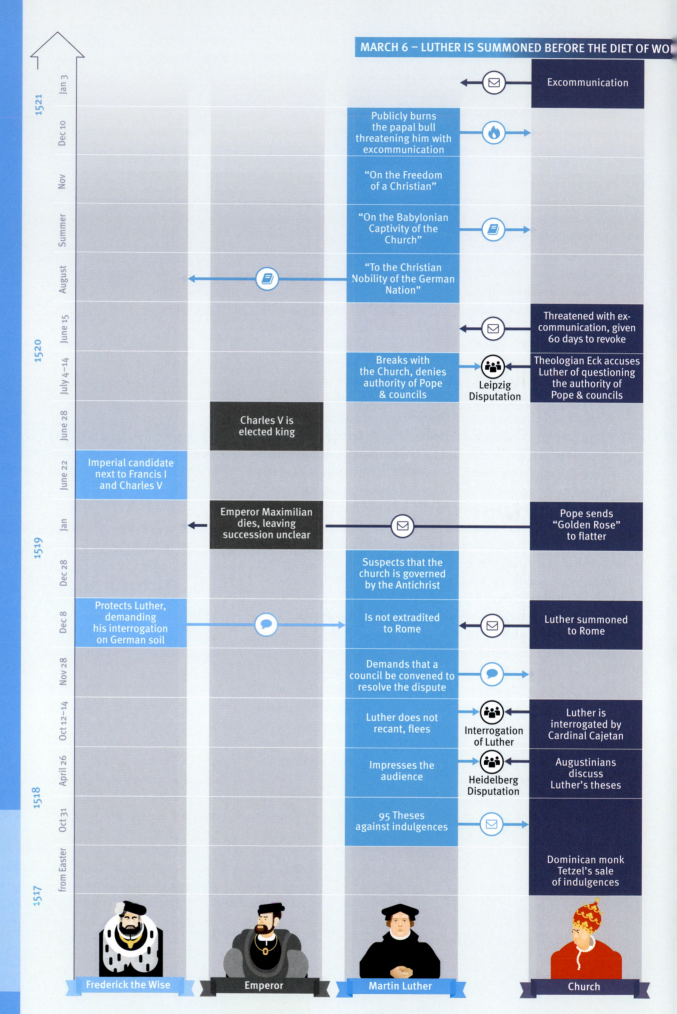

MARCH 6 – LUTHER IS SUMMONED BEFORE THE DIET OF WO[RMS]

1521
Jan 3 — Excommunication
Dec 10 — Publicly burns the papal bull threatening him with excommunication
Nov — "On the Freedom of a Christian"
Summer — "On the Babylonian Captivity of the Church"
August — "To the Christian Nobility of the German Nation"

1520
June 15 — Threatened with excommunication, given 60 days to revoke
July 4–14 — Breaks with the Church, denies authority of Pope & councils / Leipzig Disputation / Theologian Eck accuses Luther of questioning the authority of Pope & councils
June 28 — Charles V is elected king
June 22 — Imperial candidate next to Francis I and Charles V
Jan — Emperor Maximilian dies, leaving succession unclear / Pope sends "Golden Rose" to flatter

1519
Dec 28 — Suspects that the church is governed by the Antichrist
Dec 8 — Protects Luther, demanding his interrogation on German soil / Is not extradited to Rome / Luther summoned to Rome
Nov 28 — Demands that a council be convened to resolve the dispute
Oct 12–14 — Luther does not recant, flees / Interrogation of Luther / Luther is interrogated by Cardinal Cajetan
April 26 — Impresses the audience / Heidelberg Disputation / Augustinians discuss Luther's theses

1518
Oct 31 — 95 Theses against indulgences
from Easter — Dominican monk Tetzel's sale of indulgences

1517

Frederick the Wise | Emperor | Martin Luther | Church

JOHN T. MCQUILLEN

Pierpont Morgan and
Martin Luther's 1521 Letter to Emperor Charles V

Sold! The news rang through the C. G. Boerner auction house in Leipzig on May 3, 1911, like a thunderbolt: the most important letter ever written by Martin Luther had just broken a record for a manuscript letter sold at auction (fig. 1).[1] Not only did it achieve the unheard of price of 102,000 German marks (or $ 25,500; approximately $ 680,000 today), but also this extraordinary artifact of German history went to an American: Pierpont Morgan, the international financier and one of the wealthiest men in the world. The Luther letter was significant for its historical content. After leaving the Diet of Worms, where he purportedly made his "Here I stand" statement, Luther wrote to Emperor Charles V, thanking him for the safe conduct that allowed him to attend the diet without fear of arrest and reiterating his stance that he could not recant anything he had written unless shown how he had specifically erred through scripture.[2] Directly after writing the letter, and another, similar one, to the congress of German Electors, Luther was abducted by his supporters and taken into hiding at Wartburg Castle.[3] The letter, however, never reached its intended audience but instead was printed at a press in Hagenau.[4] The manuscript letter eventually entered the collection of Dr. Carl Geibel, a Leipzig book publisher, whose heirs put the manuscript collection up for auction.[5]

Pierpont Morgan had been acquiring a considerable collection of artwork, medieval and literary manuscripts, and printed books that were destined to reside in his grand Italianate library next to his house on Madison Avenue in New York City.[6] Among his vast and quickly growing art and book collection, Morgan, an ardent Anglican, already had a significant collection of manuscript and printed material related to the German and English Reformations, including a letter dated October 30, 1520, from Luther thanking Duke John Frederick of Saxony for his support,[7] dozens of printed pamphlets and books by Luther, his supporters and papal detractors, and the so-called *Golden Gospels* of Henry VIII, a tenth-century Ottonian manuscript that Pope Leo X purportedly gave to King Henry VIII of England in 1521 when he conferred on him the title *Fidei Defensor*, "Defender of the Faith."[8] There was immediately strong opposition in Germany that such an important piece of German cultural patrimony had been purchased by a foreigner and would soon set sail for New York. This, however, was not to be, for within two months of the purchase Morgan presented the historic letter to Kaiser Wilhelm II for the German people, and since then it has resided in the Luther House (the "Lutherhalle" at that

time) in Wittenberg. This essay will discuss two distinct aspects in the history of Luther's 1521 letter to Charles V: first, the historical position of the letter in relation to the public political struggles of the early Reformation and Luther's specific use of the printing press to publicize his ideas in that struggle, and, second, the narrative of Morgan's acquisition and donation of the letter in 1911.

The Reformation scholar Bernd Moeller has made the unequivocal statement "No books, no Reformation" to describe the incontrovertible influence that the printing press had in the spread of the Reformation, and while it is inherently true that Luther's critiques and reforming ideas spread orally, the printing press was the tool par excellence for the Reformation.[9] Luther's university lectures on the Bible were printed; Luther's sermons were printed; Luther's image circulated in autonomous woodcuts and engraved prints; even his Ninety-Five Theses, a list of points against the efficacy of indulgences intended for a university debate, were printed in both a small pamphlet (quarto) format and at least two different single sheet broadsides.[10] The quick and widespread distribution of printed material was a basic tenet of the print industry.[11] No single town or region could absorb the entire number of printed books produced by an individual press, so printers had to sell their products over a large area in order to make a financial success of the endeavor.[12] Luther referred to printing as "God's highest act of grace," and perhaps no one before made use of the technology quite so well as he.[13] The printing press brought a distribution and dissemination to Luther's words and ideas that no sermon could match. Thus, we should consider the slightly refined notion of "no *printing*, no Reformation" to include the full variety of print media utilized through the Lutheran movement, and which plays a considerable part in the events surrounding the Diet of Worms.

On March 6, 1521, Emperor Charles V summoned Luther to the imperial diet to stand before the assembled court of German Electors, nobles, and Church magnates to answer the charge of heresy.[14] Aside from the initial rallying point questioning the spiritual validity of indulgences in 1517 and numerable publications refuting orthodox Church doctrine in the following years, in 1520 Luther had published three important tracts detailing his position against the abuses of the Church: *An den christlichen Adel deutscher Nation (To the Nobility of the German Nation)*,[15] *De captivitate babylonica ecclesiae (On the Babylonian Captivity of the Church)*,[16] and *Von der Freiheit eines Christenmenschen (On*

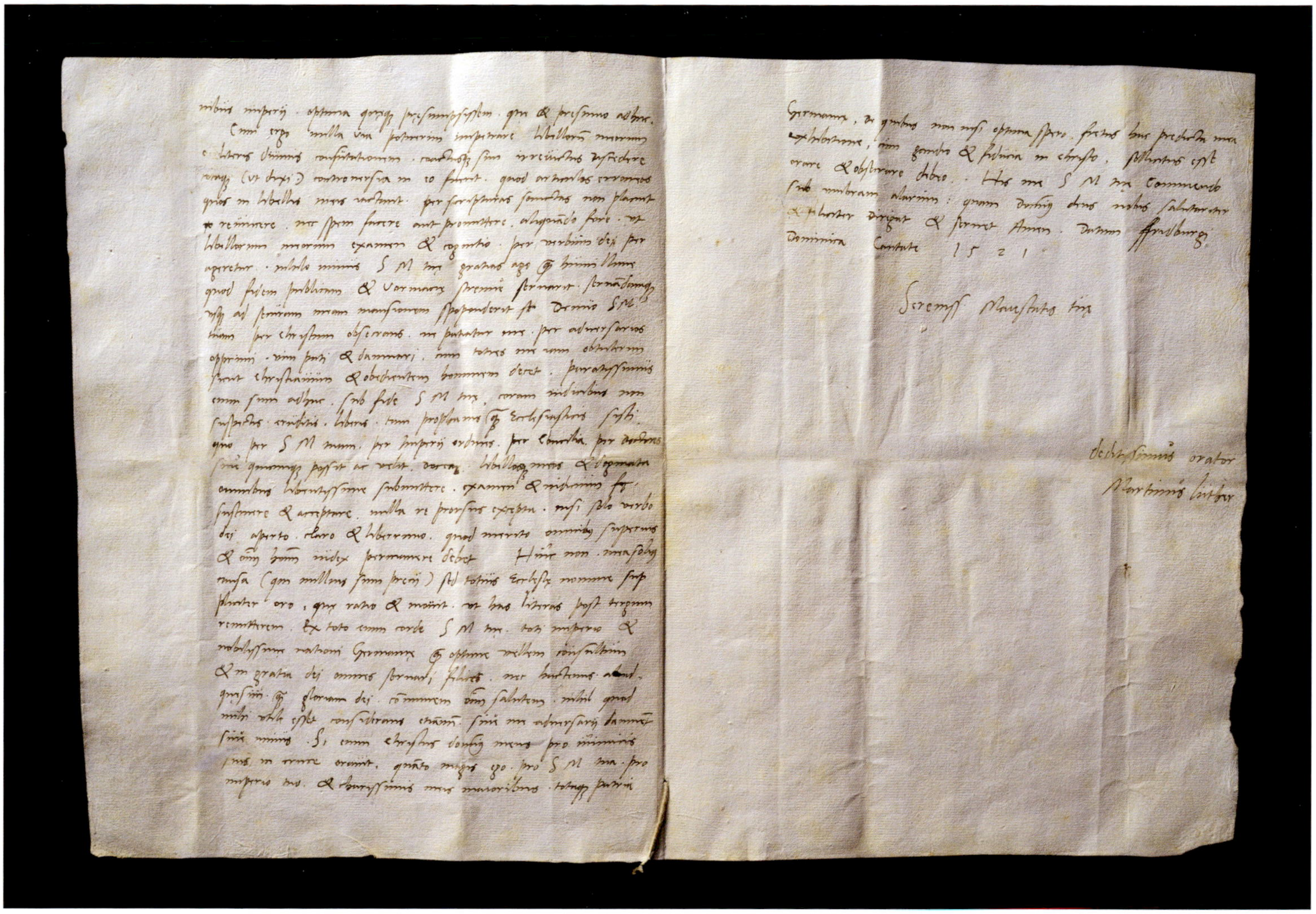

Fig. 1 Martin Luther, Letter to Emperor Charles V, April 28, 1521. The document has been registered as part of the UNESCO world documentary heritage "Memory of the World" in 2015.

the *Freedom of a Christian*).[17] These three books provide a clear exposition of many of Luther's reforming ideas wherein he criticized some current Church practices as lacking any basis in scripture.

As an example of the sheer dissemination of Lutheran ideas in print, in 1520 alone *An den christlichen Adel deutscher Nation* was printed in approximately ten editions at printing presses in six different German cities; *De captivitate babylonica ecclesiae* came out in five editions from four cities with a German version in four editions from two different printing cities; and *Von der Freiheit eines Christenmenschen* was printed in twenty-one editions from eight cities but in only ten editions from six cities for the Latin version. Thus, these three "little books," as Luther referred to them, were printed in sixty editions in a single year.[18] The first edition of *An den christlichen Adel deutscher Nation* was printed in four thousand copies, which was a remarkable number for the print

1 Boerner, *Autographen Sammlungen*, lot 109. **2** *WA* 4, 2, 306–310/*LW* 48, 203–209; see also Laube, *Lutherbrief*, pp. 265 f.; Rhein, *Feder*, pp. 153–155. **3** News of Luther's kidnapping spread, but few immediately knew of its true nature. The artist Albrecht Dürer recorded the event in his diary while traveling through the Netherlands and his fear that Luther was indeed dead, see Albrecht Dürer, Diary of the journeys to Venice and the Low Countries [1505–07/1520/21] In: Fry, *Record*, pp. 83 f. **4** Benzing, *Lutherbibliographie*, no. 1027. **5** On the provenance of the letter, see Rhein, *Feder*, p. 154. **6** Pierpont Morgan Library, *In August Company*, pp. 13–22; Strouse, *American Financier*, pp. 485–508; for his art collection and its later donations and dispersals, see id., *Financier and Collector*. **7** Morgan Library, MA 376.24. *WA* 4, 2, 204–206; *LW* 48, 181–183. **8** Morgan Library, MS M.23. James Carley suggests that the manuscript did not enter Henry VIII's collection until after 1541 and was in England well before the sixteenth century, see Carley, *Provenance*. **9** Moeller, *Stadt und Buch*; Schmitz, *Reformation und Gegenreformation*. **10** Honselmann, *Urfassung*, pp. 11–17.

See also Moeller, *Thesenanschläge*. **11** On the idea of print dissemination, see Eisenstein, *Printing Press*, pp. 71–80; Flood, *Book*, pp. 25–27; Pettegree, *Reformation*, pp. 156–170. **12** Flood, *Volentes*. **13** *WA* 2, 2, 650. On Luther's use of printed media, see the recent overviews by Heijting, *Media*; Creasman, *Censorship*, pp. 4–9. **14** *WA* 4, 2, 278–281. **15** *WA* 4, 6, 381–469; *LW* 44, 115–217. **16** *WA* 1, 6, 484–573; *LW* 36, 3–126. The German translation was produced by Thomas Murner, a Franciscan monk and vehement opponent of Luther, who believed that Luther's vitriolic attack would turn many against him; however, the translation only helped to spread Luther's antipapal message to non-Latinate audiences; see also Edwards, *Printing*, pp. 72–76. **17** *WA* 1, 7, 12–73; *LW* 31, 327–377. **18** 1520 was one of the more prolific years for Luther printing with over 300 works printed, see Edwards, *Printing*, pp. 17–28. Literacy rates among the general populace were still rather low in the early sixteenth century, and most information would have been spread orally, see Scribner, *Oral Culture*.

run of an edition in the early sixteenth century. The edition sold out in only five days and was reprinted in an even larger run.[19] Luther's effect on the book market and reading public was unmistakable, and it is surely no surprise that both the emperor and Pope were alarmed not only at his ideas but also the very rapid spread of them.

These three little books were among those that Luther stood before at Worms on April 17, 1521, when he was interrogated regarding the authorship and content of his publications.[20] The assembly was ready for Luther to recant and retract his writings, yet Luther stridently defended his publications. Speaking both in Latin and then German, he stated that he would recant only if he could be shown by scripture or through reason how he had erred. He had come to a complete impasse with Charles V, and even a delegation of Electors could not convince him *through reason* to return to orthodox teaching. With imperial approval Luther left Worms on April 26, still under the imperial safe conduct, but he was forbidden from preaching or writing anything for the next twenty-one days. Perhaps the imperial factions hoped to forestall any Lutheran publications before they could produce their own account of the proceedings, and Charles was already pushing ahead with the official imperial edict against Luther and his supporters.

Luther and his party had reached Friedberg (just north of Frankfurt am Main) on April 28 when Luther penned the letter to Charles V. After thanking the emperor for the safe conduct that allowed him to come to Worms without fear of arrest,[21] Luther summarizes the events of the diet and his willingness to recant only if he were shown his error "on the basis of divine, that is, evangelical and prophetical, scripture." Since he had supported his writings with "clear and intelligible scripture passages," he could not revoke anything lest he deny the Word of God. Luther surely felt that he was standing on very firm ground by basing his defense solely on scripture rather than falling in line with Church teaching, the work of men rather than God as he saw it. The letter repeatedly invokes scripture in the defense of his writings, a condition never fulfilled at the diet: "The whole controversy, as I have mentioned, rests upon the fact that no one was willing to refute on the basis of Holy Scripture any erroneous articles that are supposed to be in my little books." If the emperor ever had any doubts as to Luther's willingness to face a critical examination or his conditions of that examination, the letter surely would have answered them.

Caspar Sturm, the imperial herald traveling with the party (as the guarantee of safe conduct) was given the letter, included with one to be given to Georg Spalatin, the secretary of Duke Frederick of Saxony who was still in Worms, and was dismissed.[22] A note in Spalatin's handwriting on the letter to Charles V states that it was never given to the emperor, since no one was brave enough to deliver it.[23] Whether for this reason or more likely according to Luther's intentions, both the imperial letter and one to the imperial Electors were soon available in print (fig. 2).[24] Even though the *Edict of Worms* was issued on May 25, 1521, which officially proclaimed Luther a heretic, these two letters and numerable other publications summarizing the events at Worms were circulating in support of Luther's cause and showing the failure of the imperial and church delegations to adequately refute his works.[25] The letter to Charles V was printed in only a single Latin edition, while the letter in German to the German Electors appeared in fifteen editions all in 1521. Both letters are extremely significant for Luther's explanation of his position at Worms[26], but his defense in German for the German audience proved the significantly more marketable text.

This was not the first letter that Luther wrote to the emperor that ended up in print circulation, and, in fact, it might have been the plan from the beginning to have the letter published.[27] Luther frequently wrote letters specifically for publication, both those that were specific defenses aimed at his detractors as well as open letters to superiors, such as his attempted peacemaking letter to Pope Leo X from 1520, *Ein Sendbrief an den Papst Leo X (An Open Letter to Pope Leo X)*.[28] Luther also had previously written to Charles V at the end of August 1520 defending himself against the attacks of his enemies and suggesting a fair hearing; this letter was printed in a single edition.[29] These 1520 letters to Leo X and Charles V came out in the midst of the growing tensions that resulted from *An den christlichen Adel deutscher Nation* and *De captivitate babylonica ecclesiae* as Luther hoped to assuage their anxiety. Luther successfully used the open letter publication to defend himself from public/printed and private attacks and effectively to keep the debate on the abuses of the Church and the relationship between man and God in the public realm rather than sequestered in personal correspondence to Church elite. The letter to Charles V represents a crucial moment in the development of the Reformation when Luther turned against centuries of Church traditions to rest solely on the authority of scripture, *sola scriptura*. The publication of Luther's letters to Charles V and the German Electors made his defense at Worms a public event and simultaneously empowered that public to take the same *sola scriptura* stance.

19 Luther mentioned Melchior Lotter's "unspeakable profit" from printing such excessively large print runs of Luther's works, see *WA* 2, 2, 58; *LW* 54, 141. **20** *WA* 1, 7, 840; *LW* 32, 106 and 131, and *WA* 2, 5, 65–74. Brecht, *Martin Luther*, pp. 452–460. **21** Luther surely feared sharing in the same fate of Jan Hus, the Bohemian reformer who was tried and executed as a heretic at the Council of Constance in 1414–15 after attending the council on the promise of an imperial safe conduct. **22** Luther possibly also wrote a similar letter to the German Electors, or Spalatin himself translated the imperial letter from Latin into German for the Electors, see *WA* 4, 2, 310–318; on the letter to Spalatin, see *WA* 4, 2, 318 f. The dismissal of the herald suggests that Luther either felt safe enough in friendly territory that he considered the safe conduct now unnecessary, or he took the opportunity of sending the letters as a way to remove any witnesses from the upcoming kidnapping. **23** "Hae literae Caesari non sunt redditae, quod in tanta vi procerum ne unus quidem esset, qui redderet." Brecht, *Martin Luther*, p. 471. **24** Benzing, *Lutherbibliographie*, nos. 1027 and 1028–1042. There are five extant copies of the printed Charles V letter; the Morgan Library's copy was acquired in 1958 as a gift of Lathrop C. Harper (PML 49060). **25** See *WA* 1, 7, 814–824 on the published Lutheran accounts of events at Worms. **26** The letter to Charles V was integrated into the UNESCO "Memory of the World" register in 2015. **27** Roper, *Reading*, pp. 284 f. **28** *WA* 1, 7, 1–11; *LW* 31, 334–343; Benzing, *Lutherbibliographie*, nos. 731–733. The Latin version of the letter to Leo X, *Epistola ad Leonem Decimum summum pontificem*, was printed as the prologue to the Latin *Tractatus de libertate christiana* (see above, note 17), but the German publications were separate. **29** *WA* 4, 2, 172–178; *LW* 48, 175–179; Benzing, *Lutherbibliographie*, no. 818.

Ratiam & pacem/cum omni subiecti
one sui in Christo Iesu domio nostro
Sereniss.& Inuictiss.imperator,idem
domine clementiss.cum sacra tua ma
iestas me publica fide, liberoq con
ductu euocasset Vormatiam, explo
ratura animum meum super libellis nomine meo edi
tis,& ego cum omi humilitate coram S,M.tua, uniuer
soq ordine imperii comparuissem/obediens per om
nia,proponi mihi mandauit S.Maiestas tua in primis,
an libellos praedictos agnoscerem tanquam meos,
& an reuocare eos,uel in eis perseuerare paratus essem
nec ne.Ego uero ubi meos esse agnouissem(modo nul
lius uel aduersarii uel scioli ingenio & arte quicquam
in eis inuersum aut mutatum esset)indicaui cum reue
rentia & submissione multa, eum mihi esse animum,
quod cum libellos meos claris & apertis sacris scriptu
ris muniissem,mihi non esse integrum, neq aequum,
neq ullo modo comittendum,ut uerbum Dei negarē,
et libellos meos eo pacto reuocarem,rogans humiliter
ne S.M,tua,me ad huiusmodi reuocationem adigi pa
teretur ullo modo,sed hoc potius curaret,vt libelli mei
siue per seipsam,siue per alios, etiam cuiuscuq ordinis
ut minimos(si quis posset)perlustrare,& errores quos
inesse causant,litteris diuinis scilicet Euangelicis & Pro
pheticis redarguere dignaretur, offerens me Christia
na promptitudine,si redargutus & reuictus de errore
fuissem,omnia me reuocaturum,& primum futurum,
qui libellos meos igni traderem, & pedibus conculca

a ii

Fig. 2 Martin Luther, Ad DN. Carolum V. Austrium Imp. Cęs. Aug. doctoris Martini Lutheri Augustiniani
epistola post abitionem ex conventa Imperiali Wormaciæ, Hagenau 1521

Fig. 3 Order of the Red Eagle, First Class. Pendant cross and breast star, Prussia.
Awarded to Pierpont Morgan in 1911

Pierpont Morgan met Kaiser Wilhelm II on July 2, 1902, when the coronation of Edward VII of England had been postponed due to his emergency appendectomy.[30] Morgan sailed his yacht *Corsair* to Kiel, where he was invited aboard the imperial yacht *Hohenzollern*.[31] After a childhood spent at boarding school in Switzerland and then attending Göttingen University, Morgan spoke German fairly well, an advantage that no doubt helped put the Kaiser at ease. A mutual love of sailing and ships also helped to join the two in a seemingly cordial friendship, and most of their business relationship centered on mercantile shipping. Through several transactions Morgan already had acquired interests in several lucrative British-American shipping lines, followed by the 1901 acquisition of the British luxury line White Star, but he sought the cooperation of the German Hamburg-Amerika line (HAPAG), the largest shipping company at the time, to make his new shipping trust, the International Mercantile Marine, truly successful.[32] Ultimately Morgan's business acumen was no match for the entrenched politics of international commerce, and even his iron will could not prevent the trust from failing—as the *Wall Street Journal* quipped, "The ocean was too big for the old man."[33] What did develop out of the abortive shipping venture, though, was a friendship between Morgan and the Kaiser that lasted for the remainder of Morgan's life.[34]

It was perhaps with thoughts toward his friend that Morgan acquired Luther's 1521 letter to Charles V. The extraordinarily important letter to the Holy Roman Emperor was the perfect acquisition for the emperor of finance. As the letter came up for auction, few could have known what would transpire. The Florentine book dealer Tammaro De Marinis was acting as Morgan's agent at the auction. The letter was estimated at 5,000 to 6,000 marks and bidding started at 3,000 marks. Both the Royal Library in Berlin and the Lutherhalle in Wittenberg were attempting to acquire the letter, but they were both out at their maximum bids of 10,000 and 25,000 marks, respectively; then only Marinis and Carl Marfels, a collector from Berlin, were left. The bidding war continued up to 100,000 marks, when Marfels declined and Marinis won the letter for 102,000 marks. Morgan was infamously silent on his personal thoughts regarding any of the artworks, books, or manuscripts he purchased—"money talks but Morgan does not"—so we have no idea what he actually thought about paying such an exorbitant sum for the Luther letter, and yet it might have been Morgan's plan to orchestrate an elevated price for the trophy letter. Morgan was already acquainted with the collector Carl Marfels. In March of 1910 Morgan purchased an outstanding collection of decorated pocket watches from him for

$ 25,000 (which many considered to be a steal) and a further group the following year, just prior to the Luther auction. Marinis recounted that after the auction he discovered that, unknown to each other, both he and Marfels were bidding for Morgan. Marfels had been instructed not to bid above 100,000 marks, while Marinis was allowed to go as high as 125,000 marks.[35] This style of acquisition was an entirely uncharacteristic practice for Morgan, who was typically rather shrewd in his purchases and liked to get a good deal on acquisitions and rarely so flagrantly flaunted a purchase.[36]

It is unclear, however, if Morgan purchased the letter with the intention of presenting it to Wilhelm. The letter was sent to Morgan's London residence, where he had wanted it to be bound by the London binders Riviere & Son.[37] In June Morgan once again visited the Kaiser at Kiel, where they both participated in a German-American yacht race. It was during this visit on June 26 that Morgan offered Kaiser Wilhelm his recent acquisition, and the Kaiser bestowed on him the Imperial Order of the Red Eagle, First Class (fig. 3).[38] The donation of the costly Luther letter was heralded in newspapers around the world, while some, like Joseph Pulitzer's *New York World*, well known for its sensationalism rather than fact checking, claimed that Morgan had to be cajoled into offering up the letter as appropriate reciprocation for the medal (fig. 4). In fact, the letter was not with Morgan but still in London when he offered it to the Kaiser; it was not until July that Morgan sent the letter to the Kaiser, along with a seven-volume set of Luther's printed works from 1558.[39] The Kaiser presented the letter to the Lutherhalle in Wittenberg, where it was monumentalized in a shrine-like alcove and ornate reliquary frame for public display.[40] In July the *Outlook*, a weekly magazine in New York City, wrote Morgan asking him for information on the letter's donation, since there were so many conflicting stories then circulating. Morgan responded that he would furnish them with the details, but he did not wish anything under his own name to be written.[41] Morgan's clarification was never published.

Even though Morgan did not leave personal thoughts on the artworks, manuscripts, and books that he purchased, his acquisitions, donations, and foundations show that he was inherently conscientious of history and the preservation of artistic and cultural artifacts for future generations. Morgan's purchase and presentation of the Luther letter should be understood in relation to the other cultural and artistic donations he made throughout his lifetime. Aside from his major support of such institutions as the Metropolitan Museum of Art, the American Museum of Natural History, the Wadsworth Atheneum (America's oldest art museum), the Ameri-

30 Strouse, *American Financier*, pp. 470 f. **31** Kaiser Wilhelm II gave Morgan a photograph of himself, signed July 2, 1902, in Kiel (Morgan Library, MA Unassigned). **32** Chernow, *House*, pp. 101–103; Röhl, *Wilhelm II*, pp. 216–223. **33** Chernow, *House*, p. 103. **34** At another visit to Germany in 1912, the Kaiser gave Morgan a life-size marble bust of himself in full military regalia, which, after Morgan's death and with the outbreak of World War I in 1914, disappeared from the Morgan collections, see Strouse, *American Financier*, p. 648. The Kaiser was also one of the few European heads of state to respond immediately with condolences to the family upon Morgan's death. **35** Breslauer, *Tammaro*, p. 263. There is no evidence in the Morgan Library archives surrounding this acquisition. In spite of the fact that Morgan purchased nearly 30 medieval man-

uscripts from Marinis, there are no invoices or correspondence extant between him and Morgan. The correspondence with Marfels makes no mention of the Luther letter, and there is no extant invoice from Boerner's auction house. **36** See Strouse, *Financier and Collector*, p. 25. **37** See correspondence from J. Pearson & Co. to Morgan, May 16, 1911, Morgan Library, ARC 1310. Riviere & Son also bound the majority of Morgan's existing collection of printed and manuscript material related to the German Reformation, the majority of which he had purchased in 1906 from J. Pearson & Co. **38** Strouse, *American Financier*, p. 636. **39** VD16 L3428. **40** Laube, *Lutherbrief*, pp. 275–283; Rhein, *Feder*, pp. 154 f. **41** Morgan Library, ARC 1310.

can Academy in Rome, and St. George's Church (his local church in New York City), he donated to hundreds of cultural and social organizations and individuals every year, many anonymously. Among German institutions also gaining his favor, Morgan donated a pulpit to the Protestantische Gedächtniskirche (Protestant Memorial Church) in Speyer, to which Wilhelm II was also a major donor, and in 1912 he gave the library of Göttingen University $ 50,000 for book acquisitions and a copy of Edward Curtis's *The North American Indian*, a project Morgan underwrote. By returning the Luther letter to the German people, Morgan's gift stands out as perhaps the most historically significant donation that Morgan ever made. Three hundred and ninety years after being written, Luther's letter was finally given to the emperor, and yet now on display in the Luther House (the former Lutherhalle) in Wittenberg, the letter is still for public consumption, just as Luther intended.

BIBLIOGRAPHY

Benzing, Josef (1965), *Lutherbibliographie. Verzeichnis der gedruckten Schriften Martin Luthers bis zu dessen Tod*. Baden-Baden. **Boerner**, Carl Gustav (1911), *Autographen Sammlungen Dr. Carl Geibel, Leipzig und Carl Herz von Hertenried, Wien, 3.–6. Mai 1911, Erste Abteilung*. Leipzig. **Brecht**, Martin (1985), Martin Luther. Vol. 1: His Road to Reformation, *1483–1521*. Trans. J. L. Schaff. Philadelphia. **Breslauer**, Bernhard H. (1997), Tammaro De Marinis Rememberd. In: Jung, Joseph (ed.), "… *am literarischen Webstuhl …" Ulrico Hoepli, 1847–1935: Buchhändler, Verleger, Antiquar, Mäzen*. Zürich, pp. 259–277. **Carley**, James (2013), The Provenance of the Morgan Golden Gospels (Morgan Library, MS M.23): A New Hypothesis. In: Doyle, Kathleen/McKendrick, Scot (eds.), *1000 Years of Royal Books and Manuscripts*. London, pp. 53–68. **Chernow**, Ron (1990), *The House of Morgan: An American Banking Dynasty and the Rise of Modern Finance*. New York. **Creasman**, Allyson F. (2012), *Censorship and Civic Order in Reformation Germany, 1517–1648, 'Printed Poison & Evil Talk'*. Farnham, U.K. **Edwards**, Mark U. Jr. (1994), *Printing, Propaganda, and Martin Luther*. Minneapolis. **Eisenstein**, Elizabeth L. (1979), *The Printing Press as an Agent of Change: Communications and Cultural Transformations in Early-Modern Europe*. Cambridge. **Flood**, John L. (1998), The Book in Reformation Germany. In: Gilmont, Jean François (ed.), *The Reformation and the Book*. Trans. Karin Maag. Aldershot, pp. 21–103. **Flood**, John L. (2003), Volentes sibi comparare infrascriptos libros impressos … Printed Books as a Commercial Commodity in the Fifteenth Century. In: Jensen, Kristian (ed.), *Incunabula and their Readers: Printing, Selling, and Using Books in the Fifteenth Century*. London, pp. 139–151. **Fry**, Roger Eliot (ed.) (1995), *Dürer's Record of Journeys to Venice and the Low Countries*. Dover. **Heijting**, Willem (2010), The Media in Reformation Historiography. In: Hascher-Burger, Ulrike/Den Hollander, August/Janse, Wim (eds.), *Between Lay Piety and Academic Theology: Studies Presented to Christoph Burger on the Occasion of his 65th Birthday*. Leiden, pp. 421–425. **Honselmann**, Klemens (1966), *Urfassung und Drucke der Ablaßthesen Martin Luthers und ihre Veröffentlichung*. Paderborn. **Laube**, Stefan, Lutherbrief an den Kaiser, Kaiserbrief an die Lutherhalle. In: id./Fix, Karl-Heinz (eds.) (2002), *Lutherinszenierung und Reformationserinnerung* (= Schriften der Stiftung Luthergedenkstätten in Sachsen-Anhalt. 2). Leipzig, pp. 265 f. **Moeller**, Bernd (1979), Stadt und Buch. Bemerkungen zur Struktur der reformierten Bewegung in Deutschland. In: Mommsen, Wolfgang J. (ed.), *Stadtbürgertum und Adel in der Reformation. Studien zur Sozialgeschichte der Reformation in England und Deutschland*. Stuttgart, pp. 25–39. **Moeller**, Bernd (2008), Thesenanschläge. In: Ott, Joachim/Treu, Martin (eds.), *Luthers Thesenanschlag—Faktum oder Fiktion* (= Schriften der Stiftung Luthergedenkstätten in Sachsen-Anhalt. 9). Leipzig, pp. 16–22. **Pettegree**, Andrew (2005), *Reformation and the Culture of Persuasion*. Cambridge. **Pierpont Morgan Library** (1993), *In August Company: The Collections of the Pierpont Morgan Library*. New York. **Rhein**, Stefan (2014), "… das entscheidenste und inhaltsschwerste, was des Reformators Feder je geschieben." Luthers Brief an

Fig. 4 Caricature "Here's How Morgan Got the Red Eagle," The New York World, 1911

Kaiser Karl V. (28. April 1521). In: Dingel, Irene/Jürgens, Henning P. (eds.), *Meilensteine der Reformation: Schlüsseldokumente der frühen Wirksamkeit Martin Luthers*. Gütersloh, pp. 145–158. **Röhl**, John C. G. (2014), *Wilhelm II: Into the Abyss of War and Exile, 1900–1941*. Cambridge. **Roper**, Lyndal (2010), 'To his Most Learned and Dearest Friend': Reading Luther's Letters. In: *German History*, vol. 28, no. 3, pp. 283–295. **Schmitz**, Wolfgang (1999), Reformation und Gegenreformation in der Entwicklung von Druck und Buchhandel. In: Tiemann, Barbara (ed.), *Die Buchkultur im 15. und 16. Jahrhundert*. Vol. 2. Hamburg, pp. 253–338. **Scribner**, Robert W. (1989), Oral Culture and the Transmission of Reformation Ideas. In: Robinson-Hamerstein, Helga (ed.), *The Transmission of Ideas in the Lutheran Reformation*. Dublin, pp. 83–104. **Strouse**, Jean (1999), *Morgan: American Financier*. New York. **Strouse**, Jean (2000), J. Pierpont Morgan: Financier and Collector. In: *Metropolitan Museum of Art Bulletin*, Winter 2000.

ANDREW PETTEGREE

A Media Event

The media explosion of the Reformation period was sudden, unexpected, and totally unprecedented. To many of Germany's citizens, it was an opportunity to be relished. Through print they were invited to deliberate over questions that went to the heart of their Christian life and the society of which they were part. This was flattering and, to some, intoxicating. To others who never warmed to the heretic friar from Wittenberg, the pamphlet wars surrounding Luther were a calamity—a spur to disorder and rebellion, and a sign of social dissolution.

To understand the tenor of the times, we can do no better than to listen to the voice of a contemporary witness like Hieronymus Aleander, who in 1521 attended the Diet of Worms as a representative of the Roman Church—he was papal legate to the German lands. Aleander was no admirer of Luther, and his reports back to Rome were intended to make clear the danger of what was unfolding.[1] Aleander saw that something quite extraordinary was going on, and nothing he observed on the streets of Worms boded well for the Catholic cause. When he first arrived he found that the accommodation reserved for him was mysteriously unavailable; he could secure only a single unheated room. When he walked the streets, citizens muttered as he passed; some tapped their swords in an obvious gesture of warning. Contrast this with the welcome that Worms afforded Luther. The leading citizens formed a procession to greet their celebrity guest. As he alighted from his wagon, a monk pressed forward to touch his hem. There was little doubt where public sympathy lay.

It was now barely four years since Luther had announced himself to the German people with his criticism of indulgences. Aleander was well aware that print had played a leading role in stoking the flames of controversy and making Luther a public hero. "A shower of Lutheran writings in German and Latin comes out daily. There is even a press maintained here, where hitherto this art has been unknown. Nothing else is bought here except Luther's books." The effect on public opinion was all too obvious. "Now the whole of Germany is in full revolt; nine-tenths raise the war cry 'Luther', while the watchword of the other tenth is 'Death to the Curia.'" People bought not only Luther's writings but his image as well. "A little while ago at Augsburg they were selling Luther's picture with a halo; it was offered without the halo for sale here, and all the copies were disposed of in a trice."[2]

How had it come to this? That the Reformation had already come so far was the result of sequential improbabilities. Why had the Elector of Saxony, a devout Catholic and owner of one of Europe's greatest collections of relics, protected his heretic professor? No one, least of all Luther, could quite understand Frederick's refusal to turn Martin over to the authorities and let the process against him take its course. If he had done so, the Reformation would have been over before it had begun. How had Luther emerged as a writer of such extraordinary power? Before 1517 Luther had published virtually nothing. By the end of 1521 he was the most published author in the history of print. And this popularity would prove remarkably enduring. Luther was by far the most popular published author of the whole sixteenth century.[3]

Flugschriften

How, finally, could such a transforming event emerge from a place like Wittenberg? Before 1517 Wittenberg was a small town of around 2,000 inhabitants, perched on Europe's northeastern extremity, distant from Europe's main centers of culture, trade, and intellectual life.[4] Visitors to Wittenberg on the whole were not impressed; one famously described it as "a miserable poor, dirty village ... not worthy to be called a town of Germany."[5] Luther's own first impressions were not much different. Arriving from sophisticated Erfurt in 1511, he felt himself almost on the edge of civilization. Indeed, one of the reasons early opponents may have underestimated the significance of Luther's challenge was that they could not conceive of anything of importance emerging from such a place. George, Duke of Albertine Saxony and a dogged opponent of Luther, put the matter most succinctly: "That a single monk, out of such a hole, could undertake a Reformation, is not to be tolerated."[6]

Wittenberg had no printing press at all until 1502; the first age of print, the incunabula period of the fifteenth century, had passed

1 Kalkoff, *Depeschen*. Useful English translations of crucial letters can be found in Smith/Jacobs, *Correspondence*, I, pp. 422, 429, 521 f. **2** Ibid., pp. 455 f. **3** Data available from the Universal Short Title Catalogue: http://ustc.ac.uk/ [04/07/2016]. **4** Junghans, *Wittenberg als Lutherstadt*; Krentz, *Ritualwandel*. **5** Schwiebert, *Electoral Town*, p. 108. **6** Ibid., pp. 108 f.

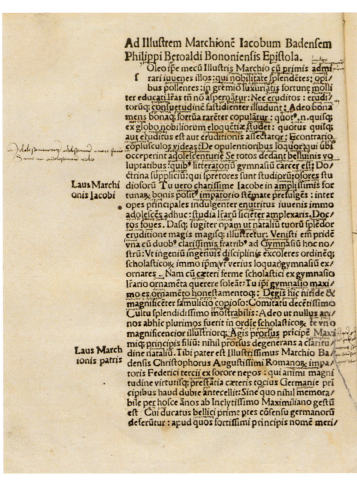

Fig. 1 Filippo Beroaldo, *Oratio Philippi Beroaldi Bononiensis
de Summo Bono*, Wittenberg 1508.
An early work of the printer Johann Rhau-Grunenberg

it by altogether. Even when, on the insistence of the Elector, a press was established in Wittenberg, printing hardly flourished. The routine work of the university, publishing dissertation theses and the like, was hardly enough to sustain a viable business. The professors could not be said to be supportive, continuing to send their more ambitious compositions for printing to Leipzig, home to several established print shops.[7] Leipzig's booksellers also provided most of the more substantial texts required by Wittenberg's professors and students.

It required a real effort of will to imagine Wittenberg as a major center of the book trade or, as it indeed became, one of the largest publishing centers of Germany. This transformation was certainly not immediate. In the first years of the Reformation, the movement spread through reprints of Luther's works published in the established print capitals: Leipzig, Augsburg, and Nuremberg, and Basel and Strasbourg on the Rhine. It was through these reprints that Luther first entered the bloodstream of German society. In 1518 Johann Froben, a suave and venturesome publisher in Basel (and Erasmus's favored printer), published a collected volume of Luther's early Latin works, a book that sold so well that a second edition was soon required. But this spoke to an intellectual, clerical audience. In

many ways the critical moment came when Luther took up his pen to address a popular audience, writing in German. The success of his *Sermon on Indulgence and Grace*, published in the spring of 1518, was what lit the fire of a popular movement.

This was in many respects a remarkable work, not least as a publishing phenomenon, since it was reprinted around Germany in no fewer than thirteen editions in the first year alone.[8] Remarkable too was the manner in which Luther, a relatively inexperienced author, had intuitively developed a method to articulate complex theological ideas to a lay audience. The *Sermon* was divided into twenty propositions, each a paragraph of no more than one or two sentences. Its 1,500 words could be read, or read aloud, in less than ten minutes.[9] It was an ideal work for a pamphlet, the new genre that became known as *Flugschriften* (pamphlets): it fitted neatly into eight pages of text. This was the sort of work that even the novice printer or print shop could undertake, since it required little in the way of investment beyond securing the necessary paper.

Before Luther the mainstay of the print industry was the traditional market for scholarly works, largely in Latin. Many such texts were long and sometimes took many months to complete. This meant that a considerable amount of capital had to be raised, or borrowed, to pay for paper, wages, and type before the edition was ready for sale. Even then the market for such books was often widely dispersed throughout Europe; extra expense was required to move the stock to the point of sale, and booksellers demanded their cut. Under-estimate demand and the whole text would have to be laboriously reset, but printing too many copies risked calamity, with unsold stock rotting expensively in storage, and no income with which to repay loans. The economics of this part of the market were daunting. Few publishers made money in the first age of print; for the overambitious, bankruptcy was a frequent fate.[10]

A Reformation pamphlet, in contrast, was a far more attractive proposition from the publisher's point of view. Eight or sixteen pages could be set up in type and printed off in a day or two. Often the entire edition sold out locally, negating the complex and expensive problems of distribution and storage. Luther, and the controversies that engulfed him, provided wonderful business for the print industry. Encouraged by the success of the *Sermon on Indulgence*, and goaded by the response of his Catholic critics, Luther wrote and wrote—a total of forty-five original writings in the two years to the end of 1519. Of these, half were eight pages or shorter.[11] The flow of words continued through 1520 with the milestone statements of Luther's emerging theology and defiant protests against his condemnation. By the time he journeyed to Worms to defend the impressive pile of publications stacked on a table before the congregated princes of the empire, he was a household name. By this time his publications had gone through an accumulated six hundred editions, probably around half a million copies, for some of these books were published in notably larger editions than the established norm of around seven hundred copies.

At this point only a very modest proportion would have been published in Wittenberg itself. In 1517 Wittenberg had only a single press, run by the stolid and unadventurous Johann Rhau-Grunenberg (fig. 1).[12] This man had many virtues, and he was a firm admirer of Luther, but used as he was to the gentle rhythms of work turning out student dissertations, he was swiftly overwhelmed by the hectic pace of Reformation controversy. It was soon obvious to Luther that Rhau-Grunenberg could not cope. It was equally obvious that his workmanship, relying on a limited range of type and little visual adornment, could not stand comparison with the reprints being published in major commercial cities such as Augsburg and Basel (fig. 2).

By the end of 1518 Luther had decided that something must be done. He put out feelers to one of the leading Leipzig publishers, Melchior Lotter the Elder.[13] Until this moment Lotter had been a satisfied servant of the Catholic Church. Like many who later published Luther, he had been heavily involved in promoting the indulgence for the building of St. Peter's in Rome, to which Luther had taken such violent exception.[14] But Lotter was a businessman; he saw the profits to be made from publishing Luther. In 1519 he agreed to open a branch office in Wittenberg, furnished with a full range of his typefaces and managed by his son, Melchior Junior. The new press found space in the huge workshop residence of Wittenberg's court painter (and leading businessman) Lucas Cranach the Elder (fig. 3).[15]

This partnership, of Luther, Lotter, and Cranach, would transform the look of the Wittenberg book. Cranach supplied the new print shop not only with space but with a series of exquisite title-page illustrations: frames in a renaissance style into which the text of the title could be dropped.[16] These gave the Wittenberg imprints a distinctive look, for the first time the equal of or superior to Luther editions published elsewhere in Germany. This was important, because it dressed the new works of the Reformation in a distinctive livery, easily picked out in the bookseller's stall. The printers enhanced the effect by separating Luther's name into a line of its own, often in a larger typeface, rather than burying it in the body of the title. With Cranach's help, Luther became not only a best-selling author but a recognizable brand (fig. 4).

The Power of Print

Of course the Reformation was not wholly reliant on Luther. Luther was a commanding, dominant presence, not least because he wrote such a wide variety of different sorts of work. There were works of theological exposition, fiery polemic, expositions of the scripture, sermons, and biblical commentaries. Among the most popular were short devotional tracts written explicitly for the German laity; the Luther they came to know was a gentler, more sympathetic figure than the turbulent and sometimes wild controversialist of the early exchanges with his Catholic critics. But for all the power and ubiquity of Luther's extraordinary writings, the Reformation could not have succeeded as a movement of one. Luther was ably supported by the band of admirers that had gathered around him in Wittenberg: Philipp Melanchthon, Johannes Bugenhagen, Nikolaus von Amsdorf and, before his fall from grace, Andreas von Karlstadt. Although most dutifully defended Luther during the polemical exchanges of the first years, each also brought his own special gifts.

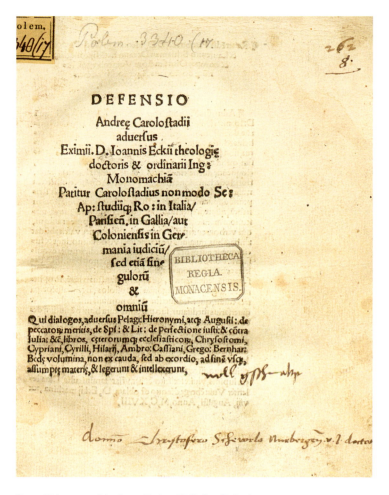

Fig. 2 Title page of Andreas Karlstadt, Defensio Andreae Carolostadii adversus Eximii. D. Ioannis Eckii theologiae doctoris, printed by Rhau-Grunenberg, Wittenberg 1518

7 On early Wittenberg printing, see Grossmann, *Humanism in Wittenberg*; Grossmann, *Wittenberger Drucke*. On Leipzig, see Döring, *Buchdruck*. 8 Benzing/Claus, *Lutherbibliographie*, pp. 90–103 with a further nine editions in 1519 and 1520. 9 *WA* 1, 243–246. The *Sermon* is available in an accessible English translation in Alard, *95 Theses*, pp. 63–67. 10 Pettegree, *Book in the Renaissance*. 11 Moeller, *Berühmtwerden*. 12 Reske, *Buchdrucker*. 13 The story is told in Pettegree, *Brand Luther*. 14 Volz, *St. Peters-Ablass*. 15 Lück, *Wittenberg*. 16 Falk, *Cranach-Buchgraphik*, vol. I, pp. 307–412. See also Strehle, *Cranach im Detail*. A selection of the book title-pages are also illustrated in Hollstein, *German Engravings*, vol. VI, pp. 163–175.

Fig. 3 Martin Luther, Evangelium Von den tzehen außsetzigen vorteutscht und außgelegt, Wittenberg 1521. It shows the powerful combination of the expertise of the printer Melchior Lotter with the woodcuts of the Cranach Workshop.

Melanchthon was the finest forensic theological mind of the movement, someone who even Luther treated with a certain awed fascination. Johannes Bugenhagen would be the leading writer of the first church orders. Their efforts were supported by a new circle of acolytes working not only in Wittenberg but in other cities: Strasbourg, Augsburg, Nuremberg, and a host of secondary towns.[17]

For all the importance of print, the first that many citizens would have known of the Reformation was when a respected local priest mounted his own pulpit and pledged his support for the new teachings. Soon these dramatic words were also spread in print. This was a crucial endorsement of the Wittenberg movement, and an implicit repudiation of the charge that Luther was a rogue individual—in the lyrical words of the papal bull of excommunication, *Exsurge Domine*, a "wild boar running amok in the Lord's Vineyard." In the German imperial cities many would give Luther's words a hearing not just because his criticisms of the church rang true, but because they were supported by respected local preachers whom they knew and trusted. Such endorsements provided a crucial point of orientation through the welter of charge and counter-charge that soon filled the air, and the booksellers' stalls.[18]

Between 1520 and 1525 German presses turned out over seven thousand editions, more than doubling output since the previous decade. Almost all of this new capacity could be accounted for by the works of Luther and his supporters. Luther's Catholic critics, however, were far from idle; they were fully aware of the need to challenge Luther's appeal to the German public. Many of those who took up their pens against him were able and persistent: Johannes Eck, Johannes Cochlaeus, Hieronymus Emser.[19] All these men showed courage and resolution in defending the church, and they landed some shrewd blows. But they struggled to get a hearing in the one place they were not used to conducting theological business: in the court of public opinion to which Luther had so maddeningly appealed.

This mattered, because it was in precisely these years, after the Diet of Worms, that Germany's free cities and princely states faced the critical decision: whether they would enforce the edict of condemnation against Luther and close down the evangelical movement. For the best part of a year after the Diet of Worms, Luther was invisible, having been removed to Wartburg Castle for his own protection. City councils, for their part, were reluctant to defy the emperor, traditionally their protector against the predatory princes. A few evangelical preachers were removed from their places and banished from town. What saved the Reformation was clear evidence that a sizeable proportion of the population in these places would not accept an end to reform. The councils could control the pulpits, but they could not control the flow of pamphlets. Here the overwhelming and continuing evangelical supremacy acted as a sort of surrogate for the public voice. Gradually it became clear that for local harmony to be restored, the evangelical cause would have to be found a place in the local church.[20]

These conflicts were fought over in a host of urban communities across Germany, and books played an important role, not just as instruments of persuasion but as a barometer of the balance of the contending forces. In terms of published numbers, evangelicals enjoyed an overwhelming advantage, and this sense of overwhelming force was brutally reinforced by defiant appropriation of the symbolic world of justice and social order. Attempts to burn Luther's books in obedience to papal and imperial condemnation often met with active opposition—and sometimes had to be abandoned altogether. The bull and copies of the *Edict of Worms* were torn down and defaced, sometimes replaced by pamphlets and broadsheets supporting Luther. Similar indignities were visited on the works of Luther's Catholic opponents, which were subjected to symbolic acts of desecration at places of public indignity like the town privy or customary place of execution. In some instances Catholic works were forcibly removed from booksellers' stalls, or even the printer's shop.[21]

Not surprisingly in this hostile climate, printers were increasingly reluctant to take on works by Luther's Catholic opponents. Conservative theologians angrily denounced the printers as Lutheran sympathizers, but the decision was most likely wholly pragmatic;

Fig. 4a/b The success of the Cranach design can be judged by the high number of unauthorized copies.
left: Martin Luther, *Eyn brieff an die Fürsten zu Sachsen von dem auffrurischen geyst*, Wittenberg 1524
right: Reprint by the Augsburg printer Heinrich Steine, Augsburg 1524

why risk danger to one's shop or reputation to publish books that were simply not selling very well? Whereas Luther's works and those of his supporters frequently went through multiple editions, works by Catholic opponents scarcely ever did. Cochlaeus and Emser were both driven to the humiliating expedient of underwriting the costs of publishing their own works. The works of Luther and his friends, in contrast, were a gold mine, in Wittenberg and elsewhere, transforming the face of the industry.

In the end, the most significant print challenge to Luther would come from a wholly different direction, from men who would certainly have regarded themselves as friends of his Gospel teaching. In 1525 much of Germany was convulsed by a series of peasant revolts. Far better organized than heretofore, the peasant bands also took to print to publish their manifestos, cogently argued documents that blended traditional grievances against oppressive conditions of life with the new language of the Gospel. The best of these manifestos were soon reprinted across all of Germany.[22] For a time it seemed as if Luther had lost control of his movement. His eventual repudiation of the peasant cause in a notorious tract, *Against the Robbing and Murdering Hordes of Peasants*, was brutal in tone and language.[23] When the German princes annihilated the peasant bands at the Battle of Frankenhausen, it appeared as if Luther had given his sanction to the slaughter. It marked a definitive break with the springtime of evangelism, the first exultant years when it had seemed that the Reformation might fulfil the aspirations of all of Germany's Christian folk.

17 Chrisman, *Conflicting Visions*; Strauss, *Nuremberg*. **18** Pettegree, *Reformation*, pp. 166 – 168. **19** Baghi, *Opponents*. **20** Moeller, *Reichstadt*. For an indicative local study, see Postel, *Reformation*. **21** Pettegree, *Brand Luther*, pp. 211 – 220. **22** Claus, *Bauernkrieg*. **23** WA 18, 344 – 361.

Building the Church

With his attack on the rebellious peasants, Luther threw in his lot with the forces of order. The Reformation survived; indeed in the decade after 1525 it made considerable strides, as cities and a number of key princely states opted decisively for the Reformation. Others, including alienated former supporters in the towns and countryside, turned their backs on Luther and definitively repudiated his leadership. This brought clarity but posed new questions. It was clear that the new evangelical lands had rejected the old church, but what had taken its place? How was Luther's vision of an active, informed Christian people to be achieved? Who was to staff the new churches— who was to preach, and what was to be preached?

These were the questions that would essentially be answered in the two decades between the Peasants' War and Luther's death in 1546. Once again, print would play a critical role. The need to teach the essentials of faith to the entire Christian congregation stimulated the development of a range of new pedagogic tools in a new genre, the catechism. Along with this went a wholesale renovation of school provision in the new evangelical territories, a development that over the next century would bring about a revolution of both male and female literacy. Luther again led the way, with exhortation to both city fathers and parents to embrace the opportunity to send their children to school. He also provided the most widely published of the new catechisms (the *Large Catechism* and the *Small Catechism* of 1529), though in this he was by no means prescriptive. Rather, Luther positively encouraged variety, and his ministerial colleagues responded with literally hundreds of their own compositions.[24] The evangelical stress on congregational participation brought a further major innovation with the vogue for hymn singing.[25] Luther again led the way, with a number of original compositions that remain classics of the repertoire to this day. All of this activity and the new form of worship were codified in a formal church order for each evangelical territory. Then there was the Bible, to many Luther's most enduring gift to the Christian people, published in a new German translation in successive parts between 1522 and 1534, and throughout Germany thereafter.[26]

All of this brought a new bonanza for Germany's printers. In Wittenberg the old duopoly of Rhau-Grunenberg and Lotter was refreshed with the arrival of new men: men like Hans Lufft, who built a large business publishing the works of Luther and his colleagues. His milestone creation was the complete Wittenberg Bible, a book of a size and complexity that would have defeated the much smaller businesses of the early Reformation.[27] Luther had a close relationship with Lufft, but he was careful not to allow one print shop to develop a monopoly. His own original works were spread around the newly established shops, those of Lufft, Georg Rhau, Joseph Klug, and Nickel Schirlentz. In addition each was allowed his own specialty: Lufft the Bible and the postils, Klug the German songbook, Schirlentz a monopoly on publication of Luther's *Small Catechism*, and Klug the *Large Catechism* and the *Augsburg Confession*.[28] The avoidance of harmful competition ensured a living for all.

The extent of Luther's personal and deeply practical involvement in the day-to-day work of the Wittenberg print shops is not always acknowledged. He took great care to put work their way and kept a close eye on the quality of the work emerging from the workshops. The full extent of this involvement only really emerges when Luther left Wittenberg for a time and had to organize by letter what previously he would have done in person: his year at Wartburg Castle, for instance, or the frustrating months holed up at Coburg Castle during the Diet of Augsburg in 1530 (due to his condemnation by the Imperial Diet of Worms, Luther could not attend in person).[29] On both occasions his letters home contained a stream of instructions for the printers, often testy and insistent, for Luther never lost his suspicions that without his commanding presence printers would consider their own profit ahead of his wishes.[30]

This was of course true; printers were first and foremost businessmen rather than ideologues. Overwhelmingly they chose Luther because his works offered the best return. The real foundation of the media phenomenon that was the Reformation was that its publications provided such secure and enduring profit for Germany's publishing industry. Until the end of the century and beyond, the diverse print needs of Protestantism provided the backbone of new businesses that sprang up all over Germany, seeding the establishment of a printing press in places where the industry would not previously have been viable. Over the course of two generations the geography of print was transformed. Many German cities where printing had fizzled or died altogether experienced a revival of activity in the first decade of the Reformation; in a large number of other places (among them Berlin, Bonn, Düsseldorf, Dortmund, and Jena) up to Luther's death a press was established for the very first time.[31] Even when the polemical fires receded, publishers looked to retain the new readers lured into buying books by the Reformation controversies by devising new sorts of cheap small books: news pamphlets, for instance.[32] These new pamphlet genres followed the successful format of the Reformation *Flugschriften*. They were short, cheap, and written in an accessible language. In this way the media transformation of the Reformation was instrumental not only in spreading access to Luther's teachings but as a fundamental step in the building of a mass audience for the printed word. This was a transformative moment indeed in the history of European culture.

24 Wengert, *Earliest Catechism*. **25** Brown, *Singing the Gospel*; Wagner-Oettinger, *Music*. **26** Reinitzer, *Biblia deutsch*. **27** Ibid., pp. 116–127; Schmidt, *Illustration*. **28** Pettegree, *Brand Luther*, pp. 267–270. **29** The evidence, largely from Luther's correspondence, is explored ibid., pp. 137–142, 271–273. **30** Ibid., pp. 140, 196, 271 f. **31** Reske, *Buchdrucker*. **32** Pettegree, *Invention*.

BIBLIOGRAPHY

Alard, Kurt (1967), *Martin Luther's 95 Theses*. Saint Louis. **Baghi**, David V.N. (1991), *Luther's Earliest Opponents. Catholic Controversials, 1518–1525*. Minneapolis. **Benzing**, Josef/**Claus**, Helmut (eds.) (1966–94), *Lutherbibliographie. Verzeichnis der gedruckten Schriften Martin Luthers bis zu dessen Tod*. 2 vols. Baden-Baden. **Brown**, Christopher Boyd (2005), *Singing the Gospel. Lutheran Hymns and the Success of the Reformation*. Cambridge, MA. **Chrisman**, Miriam Usher (1996), *Conflicting Visions of Reform*. Boston. **Claus**, Helmut (1975), *Der deutsche Bauernkrieg im Druckschaffen der Jahre 1524–1526*. Gotha. **Döring**, Thomas (2006), Der Leipziger Buchdruck vor der Reformation. In: Bünz, Enno (ed.), *Bücher, Drucker, Bibliotheken in Mitteldeutschland*. Leipzig, pp. 87–98. **Falk**, Tilman (1976), Cranach-Buchgraphik der Reformationszeit. In: Koepplin, Dieter/Falk, Tilman (eds.) (1974/76), *Lukas Cranach. Gemälde, Zeichnungen, Druckgraphik*. Stuttgart/Basel, pp. 307–412. **Grossmann**, Maria (1971), *Wittenberger Drucke 1502–1517: Ein bibliographischer Beitrag zur Geschichte des Humanismus in Deutschland*. Wien. **Grossmann**, Maria (1975), *Humanism in Wittenberg, 1485–1517*. Nieuwkoop. **Hollstein**, F. W. H. (1954), *German Engravings, Etchings and Woodcuts, c. 1400–1700*. Amsterdam. **Junghans**, Helmar (1979), *Wittenberg als Lutherstadt*. Berlin. **Kalkoff**, Paul (ed.) (1897), *Die Depeschen des Nuntius Aleander vom Wormser Reichstage 1521*. Halle (Saale). **Krentz**, Natalie (2014), *Ritualwandel und Deutungshoheit. Die frühe Reformation in der Residenzstadt Wittenberg (1500–1533)*. Tübingen. **Lück**, Heiner (ed.) (2015), *Das Ernestinische Wittenberg: Spuren Cranachs in Schloss und Stadt*. Petersberg. **Moeller**, Bernd (1962/2011), *Reichstadt und Reformation*. Tübingen. **Moeller**, Bernd (1988), Das Berühmtwerden Luthers. In: *Zeitschrift für Historische Forschung,* vol. 15, pp. 65–92. **Pettegree**, Andrew (2005), *Reformation. The Culture of Persuasion*. Cambridge. **Pettegree**, Andrew (2010), *The Book in the Renaissance*. London. **Pettegree**, Andrew (2013), *The Invention of News*. London. **Pettegree**, Andrew (2015), *Brand Luther. 1517, Printing and the Making of the Reformation*. New York. **Postel**, Rainer (1986), *Die Reformation in Hamburg, 1517–1528*. Gütersloh. **Reinitzer**, Heimo (1983), *Biblia deutsch. Luthers Bibelübersetzung und ihre Tradition*. Wolfenbüttel. **Reske**, Christoph (2007), *Die Buchdrucker des 16. und 17. Jahrhunderts im deutschen Sprachgebiet. Auf der Grundlage des gleichnamigen Werkes von Josef Benzing*. Wiesbaden. **Schmidt**, Philipp (1977), *Die Illustration der Lutherbibel, 1522–1700*. Basel. **Schwiebert**, Ernest G. (1945), The Electoral Town of Wittenberg. In: *Medievalia et Humanistica*, pp. 99–116. **Smith**, Preserved/**Jacobs**, Charles M. (eds.) (1913–18), *Luther's Correspondence and other Contemporary Letters*. 2 vols. Philadelphia. **Strauss**, Gerald (1966/1976), *Nuremberg in the Sixteenth Century*. Bloomington. **Strehle**, Jutta (ed.) (1994), *Cranach im Detail. Buchschmuck Lucas Cranachs des Älteres und seiner Werkstatt*. Wittenberg. **Volz**, Hans (1966), Der St. Peters-Ablass und das Deutsche Druckgewerbe. In: *Gutenberg-Jahrbuch*, vol. 41, pp. 156–172. **Wagner-Oettinger**, Rebecca (2001), *Music as Propaganda in the German Reformation*. Aldershot. **Wengert**, Timothy J. (1993), Wittenberg's Earliest Catechism. In: *Lutheran Quarterly*, vol. 7, pp. 247–260.

GÜNTER SCHUCHARDT

Luther at Wartburg Castle

Wartburg Castle was formerly the main fortress of the Thuringian landgraves; it is enthroned atop the rocky "Wartberg" promontory on the southwest fringe of Eisenach. Because of the location on the western edge of the principality of Saxony—only 250 kilometers from Worms—Frederick the Wise ordered that Martin Luther be sheltered in the castle after the announcement of the *Edict of Worms*, an imperial ban by Emperor Charles V. Luther was brought to the Wartburg late on the evening of May 4, 1521, after a mock raid near Altenstein Castle that was staged by the bailiff of Gotha, Sir Burkhard Hund von Wenckheim. Martin Luther was in on the "kidnapping." Bailiff Hans von Berlepsch had created a cavalier's prison within the castle bailiwick that served as Luther's haven for ten months. The first letters that were sent to his comrades Melanchthon, Amsdorf, Agricola, and Spalatin were given deceptive return addresses such as "in the region of the birds," "on the island of Patmos," and, frequently, "from my wilderness." They reflect the fear for his person and his movement; and at the same time, Luther was grappling with the themes of celibacy and the justification for baptizing children.

After a short illness, Luther began his most productive period of creativity. "I'm constantly writing," he noted in a letter to Spalatin, who kept the Elector informed about Luther's health. His favorite book, The *Wartburg Postil* containing sixteen sermons for the Christmas season, was among the most important texts written during his stay. In December of 1521, driven by apparent riots, he left his hideout for a few days and hurried to Wittenberg. There he learned of the high level of support for and popularity of his ideas, which had begun to change the world of central Europe. His friends pressured him into writing his own critical translation of the Bible. On his return from the imperial diet, there had been a Hebrew Old Testament and a Greek New Testament in his baggage. He needed only ten weeks for the first part of the Holy Scripture—a masterpiece still unparalleled today. He sent the four books of the Gospel to Wittenberg in late January of 1522. Everything else—from the stories of the apostles to the revelation of John—was translated by the end of February. Luther translated analogously and vividly into the Upper Saxon or Thuringian idiom, thereby contributing significantly to the founding of a uniform new High German standard language. Legend has it that he threw his inkwell at the devil while working. On March 1, 1522, he began his journey home to Wittenberg. Luther would never see the Wartburg again.

It was during the three-hundredth anniversary of the Reformation in 1817, that the German student leagues made the first public demand for German unity during the Wartburg festival. In 1999 the Wartburg was added to the list of UNESCO's world heritage sites.

TRANSLATION OF THE BIBLE

The European Reformation strengthened the vernacular languages: the Bible was translated in a number of countries. These were analogous translations of the original Greek and Hebrew texts which, instead of slavishly following the sources word for word, rendered their intention. The national languages became fixed due to these vernacular translations, which, since appropriate words were often missing, also led to new word creations.

One of the most important Bible translations of the sixteenth century is William Tyndale's (c. 1494–1536). His 1525 English translation of the New Testament enjoyed widespread renown and influenced the further development of English. In analogy to Luther's Bible translation, Tyndale coined the phrase: "The spirit is willing, but the flesh is weak" (Matthew 26:41). Also the English quote from Matthew 10:29-30 in the picture below is taken from his translation.

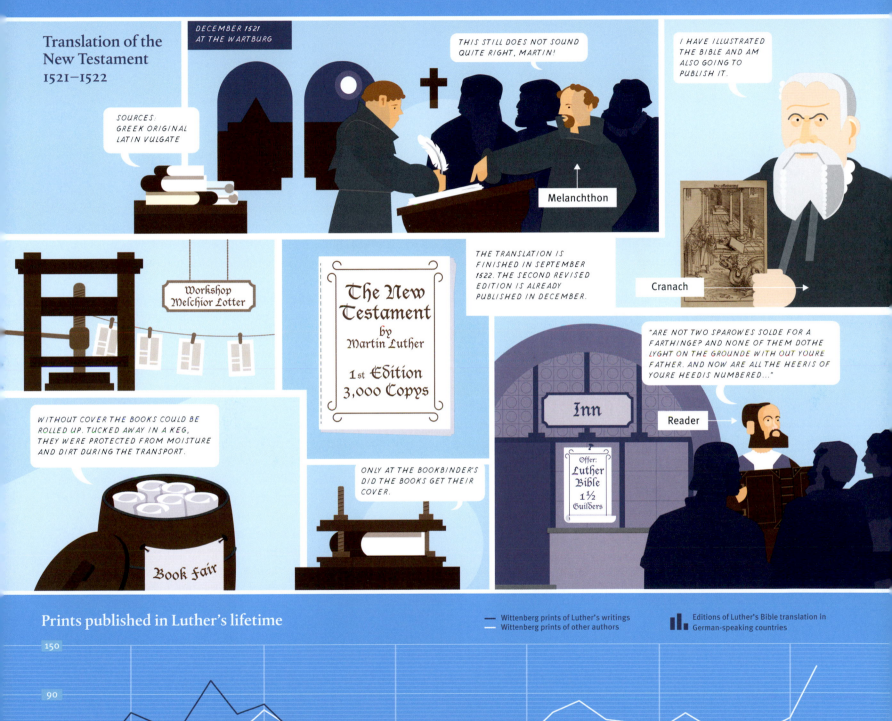

HANS-JOACHIM SOLMS

Luther and the German Language

Still a Topical Issue: Power of Luther's Language

It seems quite impossible to consider Martin Luther and Protestantism without immediately taking into account, and indeed highlighting, Luther's language, which is one of the reasons for his momentous and inestimable influence. In this vein, German orientalist Navid Kermani, 2015 recipient of the Peace Prize of the German Book Trade, speculated in a recent interview that "Protestantism [...] would never have spread without the poetic force of the Luther Bible."[1] Thus, the focus is the poetic force, the linguistic form and its immediate appeal to the senses—a form that was both the prerequisite and the guarantor of the tremendous reception of its content. Navid Kermani's statement also shows that the popular assessments of Luther and his language are interested less in the details of its grammatical-syntactic structure or lexical makeup than in its style, that is to say, in the question of how Luther so exceptionally implemented the poetic function of language[2]—a function that is, after all, relevant to every language. Next to this implementation, this essay also looks at the grammatical-syntactic structure and the lexical material of Luther's language, questioning the still-popular belief that the German language in its current form can be essentially attributed to Luther. A recent radio feature, for example, argued that by virtue of his Bible translation Luther had become "a father (sic!) of the German language."[3]

The Language of Luther's Time: Early New High German

In terms of language history, Martin Luther's works in vernacular German—preceded and accompanied, all his life long, by works in Latin—can be placed right at the heart of the linguistic period designated as Early New High German (about 1350–1700).[4] As becomes clear from its name, this period is defined and evaluated from the perspective of today's New High German. The German spoken and written today (largely consistent, with the exception of some national variants in Austria, Switzerland, Luxembourg, and parts of Belgium) essentially evolved around this time. Geographically bound to smaller or larger regions with their own dialectal forms, vernacular written German was far from acquiring supra-regional uniformity until the late Middle Ages. Moreover vernacular writing was not used universally, Latin being the predominant language of the sciences, administration, and theology.

Only in the course of the Early New High German period does the written vernacular in its basic aspects attain an irreversible supraregional "linguistic unity"—namely by overcoming both "this foreign [i.e., Latin] language in the German territories" and the regional/dialectal forms of written German existing until then.[5] This historical process of language development is accompanied by communication, social, and societal processes, which are in turn followed by a political-historical process important for the further development of German history, especially during the nineteenth century, as well as playing a role in the formation of the idea of a "cultural nation."

Due to, among other things, its use in the commercial and academic sectors, vernacular written German during the Early New High German period made its way into many areas of life. In this way, a "scripturalization of life"[6] set in that has since become indispensable and until today has shaped the organization of society as a whole. Almost all areas of life are now informed via and by the culture of writing. Socio-historically, this development has its counterpart in the comprehensive participation of the population in written communication, that is, the radical social universalization of the practice of writing in the everyday lives of the broad majority of the population ("demoticization").[7] Extending beyond these communication and socio-historical developments, a societal process can be observed, particularly from the sixteenth century onward, in which a German "people" was formed independently of its respective regions. While until the fifteenth century, this people did not yet exist as a communication community,[8] a major change was taking place from the sixteenth century onward. A community formed around a common language and evolved well into the eighteenth century. Slowly, German became a "historical and autonomous language"[9] alongside the other cultural languages of Europe. The indirect result of these linguistic-historical changes is a political process extending beyond the communication, social, and societal processes that came into effect particularly since the nineteenth century. Inasmuch as language also contributes to shaping the social-cultural identities of individuals,[10] thus shaping the identify of society as a whole, such a "historical and autonomous language" may become the main element and signum/sign of a nation defining itself via its society and its society-forming symbols. In fact, as becomes clear from the historical development, the uniform German language that evolved in the nineteenth century played a special role in defining the German nation, this latecomer in the "rise of the early modern nations."[11] All of these communication, social, societal, and political processes are related to the language development that was part of the Early New High German period—a period that saw "the gradual emergence and acceptance of a specific, authoritative type of language for literature and written communication. For this type of language, expressions such as 'standard,' 'common,' 'high-level,' 'national,' or 'written' are being used."[12] If, as current research agrees, Martin Luther's language "in the course of time [contributed] to the linguistic unity of Germany,"[13] then his significance not only for the development of German itself, but also and especially for all further language-informed historical contexts can hardly be overestimated. Luther's momentous importance in the history of German was already realized by the scholars of the early modern period. Justus Georg Schottelius, for instance, in his *Comprehensive Work on the German Language* (*Ausführliche Arbeit Von der Teutschen HaubtSprache*)[14] dates the fourth era in the history of the German language as beginning with Luther.

Luther's Linguistic Creativity and His Impact on the Development of a Common Written German Language

Luther's significance for the development of German mainly derives from getting the written German language "off the ground" with his Bible translation, which succeeded in overcoming regional language barriers.[15] From a linguistic point of view, then, regionality and transcending it are the primary foci of Luther's creativity, his most important texts, next to the German Bible, being his catechism and his hymns. The written German used in these texts achieved that kind of supraregional validity that is the criterion here. The supraregional uniformity of spoken German that is taken for granted today was modeled on the written language, and thus only followed much later; it was characterized by regional dialects much after Luther's time. Luther helped establish a national German language because he left behind the regionalisms of his mother tongue ("Thuringian-Eastern Central German-Lower German")[16] by writing in a way that would be intelligible beyond the limits of regional dialects. He was fully aware that the spoken dialects, of which the German language of his time exclusively consisted, were only intelligible within a very limited sphere—so much so that people "living at a distance of thirty miles could not understand each

other."[17] At the same time, he was aware of the state of the written and printed language as practiced in contemporary manuscripts, documents, and the increasing number of prints. Beyond the fragmentation of German into spoken dialects, a number of different regional writing customs existed, some of them already widely distributed. With regard to the German used in late fifteenth- and early sixteenth-century prints, current research distinguishes seven different "types of printed languages":[18] South-East, Swabian, Upper Rhine-Alemannic, Inner Swiss, East Franconian West Central German, and Eastern Central German.

In the context of such regional spelling variants, Luther considered the form of language he used as conforming to a very special kind of officialese, to which he attributed general validity and that he thought would ensure his being understood in both upper and lower Germany: "Nullam certam linguam Germanice habeo, sed commune,[19] ut me intellegere possint ex superiori et inferiori Germania.[20] I use the language of the Saxon Chancery [...]; all imperial cities, princes, and courts write according to the Saxon chancery of our electoral princes."[21] The electoral Saxon chancery language of those days had, indeed, limited to a considerable extent the use of dialectal-regional spelling variants of (Eastern) Central German,[22] giving it a leading position in the evolution of the standardized New High German written language.[23] Luther followed this usage and with the support of printer Hans Lufft and proofreaders Caspar Cruciger and Georg Rörer[24] (to name but his most important collaborators) created a form of language consistent enough in terms of graphics and inflections as to avoid variants.[25] In "ongoing linguistic revisions," which he continued up to the end of his life, Luther abandoned competitive northern, local, or southern variants with the aim of eliminating regionally limited forms. For the purpose of supra-regionality, either the southern (e.g., *kelch* instead of *kilch*, "chalice") or northern variant (*brennen* instead of *brinnen*, "to burn") was chosen, and sometimes also a local variant (e.g., *teuffen* instead of *tauffen*, "to baptize"); occasionally, older phonetic forms were retained in spite of already emerging developments (e.g., *helle* instead of *hölle*, "hell").[26]

In all of this, however, Luther introduced hardly any individual linguistic innovations. If one compares the graphic-phonetic form, especially of his printed language, with contemporary usage in the Wittenberg area, it becomes obvious in most cases that Luther, "as one might expect, was quite naturally embedded in the circumstances of his time. There is no evidence of him playing a spe-

1 Kermani, *Religion*, p. 38. **2** In addition to the poetic function of language, Roman Jakobson (see Lewandowski, *Linguistisches Wörterbuch*, art. "Sprachfunktionen") analytically differentiates its symptomatic/expressive, appellative, referential, phatic, and metalinguistic functions. **3** Müller, *Asche*. **4** For a temporal delimitation, see Solms, *Soziokulturelle Voraussetzungen*, pp. 1515 f. **5** Tschirch, *Entwicklung*, pp. 95–97. **6** Erben, *Frühneuhochdeutsch*, p. 393. **7** See Maas, *Lesen—Schreiben—Schrift*. **8** Giesecke, *'Volkssprache,'* p. 75. **9** Coseriu, *Historische Sprache*, p. 109. **10** See Dressler, *Spracherhaltung—Sprachverfall—Sprachtod*, p. 1558. **11** Schilling, *Rebell*, p. 217. **12** Penzl, *Frühneuhochdeutsch*, p. 19. **13** Besch, *Die Rolle Luthers*, p. 1715. **14** Justus Georg Schottelius: Ausführliche Arbeit Von der Teutschen HaubtSprache, Braunschweig 1663, p. 49; for a compilation of contemporary judgments on Luther, see Josten,

Sprachvorbild, p. 152. **15** Besch, *Rolle*, p. 1717. **16** Erben, *Luther*, pp. 445 f. **17** *WA* 2, 5, 512 (no. 6146) (dating from 1538/39, see p. LX). **18** Hartweg/Wegera, *Frühneuhochdeutsch*, p. 97. **19** "I have no special German language of my own but use the general German language so that I can be understood by Lowlanders and Uplanders." (English tr. Ana Deumert, quoted after Mattheier, *German*, p. 217). **20** See "Hochdeutsch," "Niederdeutsch," "Oberdeutsch," Grimm, *Deutsches Wörterbuch*, vol. 10, col. 1609–1612; vol. 13, col. 752–755; vol. 13, col. 1083 f., resp. **21** *WA* 2, 2, 639 (no. 2758b) (dated 1532, see p. XXIV) (English tr. Ana Deumert, quoted after Mattheier, *German*, p. 217; different spelling of "chancery" here). **22** Besch, *Rolle* , p. 1722. **23** See Kettmann, *Kanzleisprache*, p. 309, quoted after Besch, *Rolle*, p. 1722. **24** See Kettmann, *Überlieferung*, p. 44. **25** Wells, *Deutsch*, p. 206. **26** Besch, *Rolle*, p. 1719.

cial role."[27] Morphologically, too, "only a few [...] changes within Luther's printed language point straightly in the direction of Early Modern German"[28] (e.g., imperatives such as *stehe* instead of *stand*, "stand," or *sey* instead *biß*, "be"). One exception in this context is the grammatically motivated capitalization of nouns, subsequently to become a characteristic feature of German. True, individual words had already been capitalized in the preceding centuries. Until the early sixteenth century, however, capitalization particularly served as a graphic marker of terms considered important, such as *Gott*, *Christus*, or *Herr* (i.e., "Lord," as a designation of God, in contrast to *herr* in the sense of "man"). This use, which was still customary in his early prints, is changed in Luther's later works: as from 1532, approximately 70 percent of nouns are capitalized,[29] majuscules being used for semantic as well as the grammatical reasons still in use today. Since nouns are much less frequently capitalized in contemporary texts from the Wittenberg and, more generally, the Eastern German area (approximately 15.7 percent around 1530, and approximately 61.2 percent, only around 1560),[30] Luther can undoubtedly be considered an innovator in this respect.

Indisputably, the linguistic changes in terms of spelling and inflection, to be observed in all of Luther's texts (and increasing with the chronology of his work), can be attributed to his aim to achieve greater uniformity and to reduce variants. Within the context of the overall language work of Luther and his Wittenberg collaborators, such purely formal changes seem only logical. In his early language work leading to the 1522 translation of the New Testament, on the other hand, Luther first sought to accomplish the divine task of making Christ's truth in its scriptural form accessible to everybody. In this, he was aware of the function of language as the "sheath, in which the sword of the Spirit is contained. [...] And let us be sure of this: we will not long preserve the gospel without the languages. The languages are the sheath in which this sword of the Spirit is contained; they are the casket in which this jewel is enshrined; they are the vessel in which this wine is held, they are the larder in which the food is stored; and, as the gospel itself points out, they are the baskets in which are kept these loaves and fishes and fragments."[31]

To keep a knife sharp and functioning, a corresponding sheath is necessary, or else it will be damaged. With respect to his language work this meant that Luther had to find a form in which the biblical content would be preserved unharmed and from which it could, time and again, be drawn forth undamaged. This, precisely, was the task Luther had set himself in translating the New Testament. The so-called *September Testament* was published in Wittenberg, without the translator's name, in September 1522 (fig. 1). It soon went out of print in spite of its high price ("a journeyman's weekly wage"[32]), the edition, which had totaled three thousand to five thousand copies, was reprinted with revisions (Luther corrected "almost every line"[33]) by December (the so-called *December Testament*). The translation was to ensure that all people who could not immediately grasp the revealed Word of God (because they were incapable of reading the foreign languages of the Bible), would now receive it in the specific form of language Luther had given it. This form was achieved by a "simple style of translation in accordance with the *stilus mediocris* of

Latin rhetoric," which, instead of preceding from the Bible's own level of style, was oriented to the recipient. Earlier vernacular translations of biblical texts, such as Matthias von Behaim's 1343 *Gospel*,[34] had already aspired to such a style without, for that matter, coming even close to Luther's achievement.

Luther wanted all people, regardless of social or other distinctions, to understand what the biblical text said—not only in terms of single words but as a whole. The postulate of intelligibility is concerned with the vocabulary and, thus, with the choice of concrete words; the intended "comprehensibility," on the other hand, goes further and strives for a language whose syntactic and stylistic figures facilitate the immediate perception, understanding, and experience of what is being conveyed. Conscious work with language was required to achieve intelligibility and be sensually comprehensible. Accordingly, Luther, in his preface to the Book of Job, writes: "We have done our best to use language that is clear and that everybody can understand, providing the genuine sense and meaning" (1524).[35] For Luther, this was a theological task in the first place, and a philological one, only in the second. With respect to his Reformation theology and its doctrines of *sola fide* (i.e., man's justification through faith alone) and *sola scriptura* (i.e., scripture as the only source from which man learns of this justification, being assured of his salvation through faith), he had a twofold task to fulfill. Not only did the existing (Hebrew, Aramaic, or Greek) text need to be intelligibly rendered in the vernacular, it also had to be implemented so that Luther's theology—conveyed and established via his translation of the original text—was comprehensible to everyone. Consequently, the guiding principle of the translation was not the faithful reproduction of the source text, but the production of a target text.[36]

And since this work involved, next to the work of translation, also an exegesis of the biblical text, it became a central issue of the theological controversy of his time, Luther being publicly accused of being a "heretic who uses his language to mislead and deceive the 'common people.'"[37] The fear that his translation might reach this so-called common people was more than justified, for Luther had indeed succeeded in making the biblical text intelligible and sensually comprehensible with his language. He achieved this through an attitude to translation that "appears to us almost trivial (today)"[38] and thanks to the example and achievement of Luther can be found in every introduction to the science of translation. In his day, however, it needed to be explained, which is what Luther did in his *September Testament* of 1522: what mattered first was understanding form and content of the source text ("Auffs erst mussen wyr [...] wissen / was sanct Paulus meynet durch dise wort [...] sonst ist keyn lesen nutz daran"[39]), in order to then provide an analogous translation which, instead of slavishly following the original word for word, rendered its intention. To translate the source text in accordance with "the nature of the German language" and to ensure that "we have a full, clear, German sentence," Luther writes in his 1530 *Sendbrief vom Dolmetschen* (*Open Letter on Translation*) (fig. 2), "one need not ask the letters of the Latin language [...], rather one should ask the mother in her house, the children in the streets, the common man in the marketplace, about it and see by their mouths how they speak,

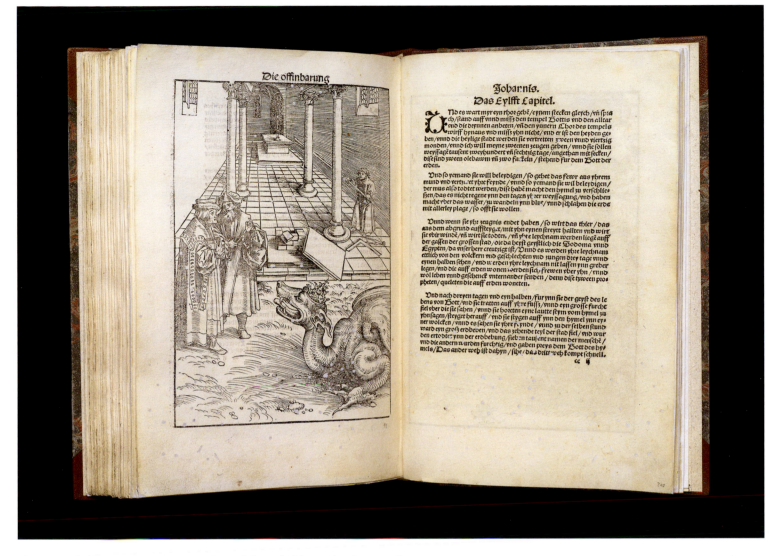

Fig. 1 Martin Luther, Das Neue Testament Deutsch (so-called September Testament),
Wittenberg 1522. With woodcuts from Lucas Cranach the Elder printed by
Melchior Lotter the Younger

and translate accordingly: then they understand it well and recognize that one is speaking German to them."[40]

Luther drew on expressions people used in everyday life, and also on their experience; he knew that it was possible to "learn from proverbs how to write German books."[41] Nevertheless, the phrase used in the *Sendbrief*, "that one is speaking German to them," expressed something more than the obvious use of vernacular German and connotes comprehensibility, clarity, and outspokenness.[42] It made clear that Luther intended to speak in a language that the people not only read, heard, and recognized as, but also felt to be,

their own. At the same time, they learned from Luther that their language was capable of expressing the holiest of the holy, which did them honor and enhanced their dignity.

His *Address To the Christian Nobility of the German Nation*, published in 1520, for instance, places man, regardless of social standing or class, at the center; it is considered to be awarding "a 'patent of nobility' to the hitherto despised and oppressed 'common' man,"[43] whom Luther wanted to introduce to the revelation of God. If he sought to reach these common people, he therefore had to be familiar with their conceptual world, needing to be in command of the

27 Ibid., p.1723. **28** Ibid., p. 1721. **29** Ibid., p. 1720. **30** See Bergmann et al., *Entwicklung*, p. 848. **31** *WA* 1, 15, 38 (English translation quoted from: Luther, To the Councilmen of All Cities in Germany, p. 360). **32** Von Polenz, *Deutsche Sprachgeschichte*, p. 134. **33** Besch, *Rolle*, p. 1719. **34** Sonderegger, *Geschichte*, p. 244. **35** *WA* 3, 10.1, 1956, 6, 11 – 13 (English translation quoted from: Luther, Preface to the book of Job. In: *LW* 384). **36** Gardt, *Übersetzungstheorie*, p. 94. **37** Besch, *Rolle*, p. 1714, see also p. 1715. **38** Albrecht, *Übersetzung*, p. lxxviii. **39** Luther, Das Newe Testament Deutzsch, p. 223. **40** *WA* 30/II, 637 (English translation by Jennifer Tanner quoted from: Weissbort/Eysteinsson, *Translation*, p. 61). **41** Thiele/Brenner, *Sprichwörtersammlung*, p. 639. **42** "deutsch," in: Grimm, *Wörterbuch*. **43** Besch, *Rolle*, p. 1718.

way in which they used their natural language in order to have access to their inner and outer worlds. It is to the credit of his personal attitude and talent (his *ingenium bonum*[44]) that Luther, who never thought of language merely as the abstract medium of a detached, analytical mind, in each individual case discovered the language appropriate for this aim. Naturally, there was also always an emotive trait in Luther's language, and he uses it as the expression of humans as thinking and feeling beings. "For Luther, as for the Bible, the heart is the organ of man's spiritual perception."[45] So, to safeguard the intelligibility and sensual comprehensibility of the divine message, Luther needed to clothe this message in a vernacular form capable of reaching the people's hearts—all the more so since "no one can properly receive scripture unless his feelings are addressed in such a way that he inwardly feels what is heard and spoken externally."[46]

Luther himself, however, never prided himself on having found the right form and the right words. In his profound and humble piety, in which he felt wholly secure, he did not consider his language his own achievement, but attributed it to the works and words of Christ himself: "I am convinced that my word is not my own word but the Word of Christ" (Jch bynn yhe gewisz, das meyn wort nitt meyn, sondernn Christus wort sey).[47] In reality, the form he had found was also the result of a rigorous and life-long work with language, carried out in cooperation with his editorial team: "I have taken pains in translating in order to render a pure and clear German. And it often happened that we sought and questioned a single word for fourteen days, three, four weeks, and at times still could not find it. In Job we worked this way, Master Philips, Aurogallus, and I, so that in four days we could hardly finish three lines" (1530).[48] This "pure and clear German" had to be accurate if it was to convey the intended intelligibility and sensual comprehensibility. For this purpose, "Luther [...] not only had acquired an extensive and diverse set of linguistic instruments; he was also the first to grind these instruments for his particular tasks. And there is another factor: the multiplication of his [...] tools [...] by the formation of new words [...] which designate the referred-to facts more accurately or descriptively than the available words."[49] Neologisms of this type include *Blutgeld* ("blood money," Matt 27:6), *erndten* ("to harvest," Matt. 6:26), *Fewreyffers* ("fiery indignation," Heb. 10:27), *Fewrofen* ("furnace of fire," Matt. 13:42), *die Fridfertigen* ("the peacemakers," Matt. 5:9), *gottselig* ("devout," Acts 10:2), *Hertzenlust* ("heart's content," 1 Thess. 2:8), *jr Kleingleubigen* ("O ye of little faith," Matt. 6:30), *Menschenfischer* ("fishers of men," Matt. 4:19), *plappern* ("to prattle," Matt. 6:7), *Linsengericht* ("dish of lentils," Gen. 25:34), *nacheifern* ("to emulate," Prov. 3:31).[50] In these neologisms, Luther showed a strong tendency to the formation of compounds, which subsequently became such a characteristic feature of German.[51] Where he found that an existing word was lacking in specificity or profile for the statement it was to convey, he would change the content of hitherto common terms, also beyond the field of such religious concepts as *Glaube* ("faith") and *Gnade* ("grace"): *Abend* ("direction of the sunset/west or evening"), *sich begeben* ("to happen"), *entrüstet* ("indignant"), *fassen* ("to grasp"), *Memme* ("coward"), *Richtschnur* ("rule"), *rüstig* ("thoroughgoing"), *verfassen* ("put into words").[52]

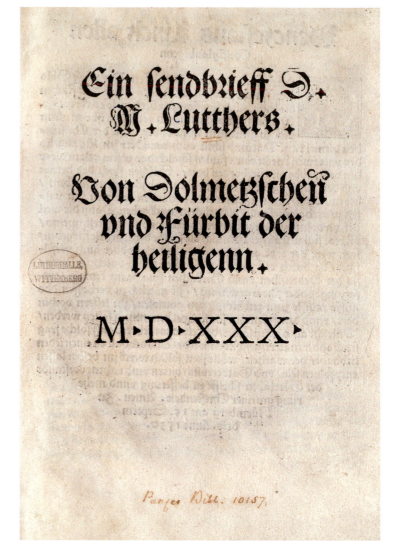

Fig. 2 Martin Luther, Ein sendbrieff D. M. Luthers. Von Dolmetzschen vnd Fürbit der heiligenn, Nürnberg 1530

For Luther, the use of a vocabulary that would be understood across different regions was the prerequisite for the cross-regional comprehensibility of his works, which is why he chose very accurate and the most widely disseminated words in each case. At the same time, and beyond his mother-tongue vocabulary, Luther had increasingly "become acquainted with the vocabulary of other linguistic landscapes."[53] He was familiar with geographical variants and selected among them but also drew on his native vocabulary (*freien*, "to court, marry"; *hain*, "grove"; *heucheln*, "to feign"; *trödeln*, "to trade"; *Vogelbauer* "bird cage"), and that of Low German (*Lippe* instead of *Lefze*, "lip"; *fett* instead of *feist*, "fat"; *Hälfte* instead of *Halbteil*, "half").[54] Not infrequently, he would step "out of the narrow confines of his native region," using words of the East Central and East Upper German area,[55] such as *offt* versus *dicke* ("often"),[56] *gebrechen* versus *gebrestehain(n)* ("affliction"),[57] *ob* (conjunction) versus *ab*, ("if")[58] *gespenst* versus *spugniß* ("ghost"). Also, Luther drew on the vocabulary of late-medieval mysticism in using words like *geistreich* ("rich in spirit/smart") , *(gott) wohlgefällig* ("pleasing (to god)").[59]

Luther's impact on the further development of the New High German written language is more obvious from his vocabulary than from his spellings and inflections. In terms of lexis, the situation of written German at the beginning of the sixteenth century was marked by a geographical diversity similar to that of spelling and inflection. A contemporary author from the Breisgau region, for instance, remarked that people there used the word "grossuatter" (for "grandfather"), whereas in the nearby Black Forest they said "eny." "Here, we say "dochterman"; in many countries they say "ayden" [for "son-in-law"]."[60] It is mainly to Luther's credit that a largely uniform word usage was already being practiced across different regions by the seventeenth century: "The Bible becomes the vehicle of the great movement for the unification of written-language vocabulary. In tandem with hymns and the catechism, it is established in the hearts and mouths of the congregations, helping the impact of Luther's language transcend all regional boundaries."[61] Initially, however, Luther's words were not understood everywhere, needing explanations and translations in some regions. The 1522 *September Testament* was in high demand and soon out of print, which made a new edition necessary. In other parts of the empire, too, people immediately asked for the unprecedented vernacular translation of the New Testament by Luther, even though its vocabulary gave rise to considerable problems of comprehensibility. Since no one dared change "the Reformer's wording [. . .], it was thought preferable to enlighten readers by introducing a short glossary explaining the incomprehensible words Luther had used. The first example was invented by the Basel printer Adam Petri,"[62] who added such a glossary to his second reprint of 1523 and informed readers on the title page: "Die außlendigen wörtter, auff unser teutsch angezeygt" (*Foreign words are being shown in our German language*) (fig. 3).[63] Petri's list, which includes 197 words, suggests that many words commonly used in present-day German entered the general vocabulary through Luther,[64] for example, *ähnlich* (Petri: *gleich*, "similar"), *Aufschub* (*verzug*, "delay"), *bang* (*engstich*, "anxious"), *beteuben* (*kraftlos machen*, "to numb"), *darben* (*nott leiden*, "to suffer"), *Gefäß* (*Geschir*, "tableware").

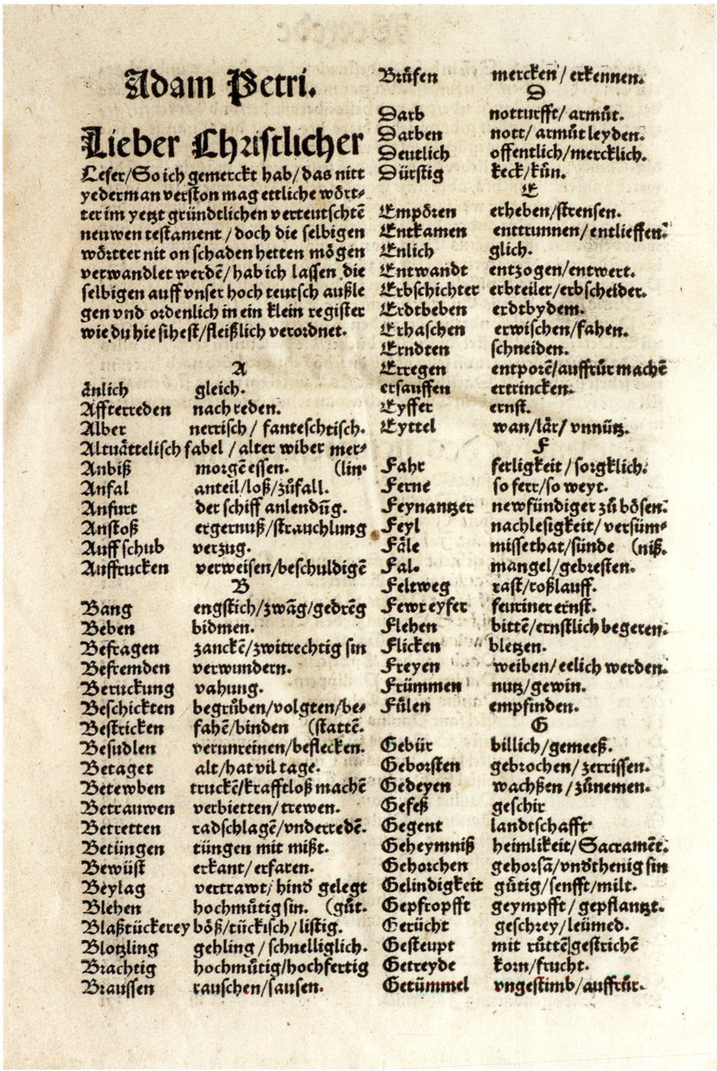
Adam Petri.
Lieber Christlicher
Leser/So ich gemerckt hab/das nitt yederman verston mag ettliche wörtter im yetzt gründtlichen verteutschtẽ neuwen testament/doch die selbigen wörtter nit on schaden hetten mögen verwandlet werdẽ/hab ich lassen die selbigen auff vnser hoch teutsch außlegen vnd ordenlich in ein klein register wie du hie sihest/fleißlich verordnet.
A
änlich gleich.
Afftterreden nach reden.
Alber nerrisch/ fanteschtisch.
Altuättelisch fabel / alter wiber mer/(lin
Anbiß morgẽ essen.
Anfal anteil/loß/zůfall.
Anfurt der schiff anlendũg.
Anstoß ergernuß/strauchlung
Auff schub verzug.
Auffrucken verweisen/beschuldigẽ
B
Bang engstich/zwãg/gedrẽg
Beben bidmen.
Befragen zanckẽ/zwitrechtig sin
Befremden verwundern.
Berückung vahung.
Beschickten begrůben/volgten/be/(stattẽ.
Bestricken fahẽ/binden
Besudlen verunreinen/beflecken.
Betaget alt/hat vil tage.
Betewben truckẽ/krafftloß machẽ
Betrauwen verbietten/trewen.
Betretten radschlagẽ/vnderredẽ.
Betüngen tüngen mit mißt.
Bewüst erkant/erfaren.
Beylag vertrawt/ hind gelegt (gůt.
Blehen hochmůtig sin.
Blaßtückerey böß/tückisch/listig.
Blotzling gehling / schnelliglich.
Brachtig hochmůtig/hochfertig
Braussen rauschen/sausen.
Brüfen mercken / erkennen.
D
Darb notturfft/ armůt.
Darben nott/ armůt leyden.
Deutlich offentlich/mercklich.
Dürstig keck/kün.
E
Empören erheben/strensen.
Entkamen enttrunnen/entlieffen.
Enlich glich.
Entwandt entzogen/entwert.
Erbschichter erbteiler/erbscheider.
Erdtbeben erdtbydem.
Erhaschen erwischen/fahen.
Erndten schneiden.
Erregen entporẽ/auffrůr machẽ
ersauffen ertrincken.
Eyffer ernst.
Eyttel wan/lär/ vnnütz.
F
Fahr ferligkeit / sorgklich.
Ferne so ferr/so weyt.
Feynantzer newfündiger zů bösen.
Feyl nachlesigkeit/ versüm/(niß.
Fäle missethat/sünde
Fal. mangel/gebresten.
Feltweg rast/roßlauff.
Fewr eyfer feuriner ernst.
Flehen bittẽ/ernstlich begeren.
Flicken bletzen.
Freyen weiben/ eelich werden.
Frümmen nutz/gewin.
Fülen empfinden.
G
Gebür billich/gemeeß.
Geborsten gebrochen/ zerrissen.
Gedeyen wachßen / zůnemen.
Gefeß geschir
Gegent landtschafft
Geheymniß heimlikeit/Sacramẽt.
Gehorchen gehorsã/vndthenig sin
Gelindigkeit gůtig/senfft/milt.
Gepfropfft geympfft / gepflantzt.
Gerücht geschrey/leümed.
Gesteupt mit růttẽ gestrichẽ
Getreyde korn/frucht.
Getümmel vngestimb/auffrůr.

Fig. 3 Glossary in the reprint of the New Testament by Adam Petri, Basel 1513

After Luther: The Delay of Language Unification due to Confessional Strife

In spite of their wide dissemination during his lifetime, the language of Luther's writings had not yet become common currency. On the contrary, the continuous historical development of the German language was interrupted soon after Luther's death by the political and, particularly, the confessional division of Germany—and at times even seemed to be suspended in favor of a two-culture solution. The "confessional dispute significantly delayed the formation of a national German written language."[65] The 1555 Peace of Augsburg, in fact, triggered off a far-reaching process sweeping through all German-speaking countries and resulted in a religiously informed use of language. With its final clause of *cuius regio, eius religio*, (whose realm, his religion) it led to the territorialization of the confessions and their respective linguistic forms, and resulted in a situation that has been described as "cuius re(li)gio, eius scriptio (whose religion, his writing)."[67] Language forms were used as so-called shibboleths (linguistic distinguishing marks) so as to stigmatize the respective text or even the speaker without further examination.[68] Catholics of

44 Ibid., p. 1730. **45** Stolt, *Lieblichkeit*, p. 333. **46** Ibid., p. 335, reference to *WA* 1, 3, 559, 33–35. **47** *WA* 8, 683, 15–17. **48** *WA* 30/II, 635 (English translation by Jennifer Tanner quoted from: Weissbort/Eysteinsson, *Translation*, p. 60). **49** Erben, *Luther*, p. 455. **50** Ibid., p. 460–464. **51** Solms, *Substantivkomposition*. **52** Erben, *Luther*, p. 450. **53** Ibid., p. 447. **54** Ibid., pp. 445 and 487. **55** See Besch, *Rolle*, p. 1724. **56** See id., *Sprachlandschaften*, p. 341. **57** See ibid., p. 344. **58** See ibid., p. 346. **59** See Erben, *Luther*, pp. 447 and 487.

60 Riederer, Spiegel der waren Rhetoric, Straßburg 1509, Xa, quoted after: Erben, *Rolle*, p. 439. **61** Besch, *Rolle*, p. 1724. **62** Kluge, *Luther*, p. 83. **63** URL: www.deutsche-bibeln.de/bis%201599/bis%201529/1523k.html [08/31/2015]. **64** See Kluge, *Luther*, pp. 85–90. **65** Besch, *Standardisierungsprozesse*, p. 266. **66** Ibid., p. 265. **67** Rössler, *Schreibvariation*, p. 365. **68** See Besch, *Standardisierungsprozesse*, p. 267.

Fig. 4
Martin Luther, Geistliche Lieder
aufs Neue gebessert zu Wittenberg
(so-called Klug Hymnal),
Wittenberg 1533. It includes
the first printing of the hymn:
Ein feste Burg ist unser Gott
(A Mighty Fortress is Our God)

the time, for instance, would identify the use of a morpheme as innocuous as the final letter *e* (in the dative singular of masculine and neutral nouns) as Lutheran, and impose a ban on it. Well into the eighteenth century, Catholics in Upper Germany said and wrote *Höll*, *Sünd*, and *Seel* ("hell," "sin," and "soul"), in contradistinction to the Protestant written forms of *Hölle*, *Sünde*, and *Seele*.[69]

The eventual prevalence of the language Luther had used in several hundred thousand copies of the Bible, catechism, and hymnal was due not only to their wide dissemination and the fact that many people had learned to read and write from them, as well as the great popularity of hymns such as *Ein feste Burg ist unser Gott* (*A Mighty Fortress Is Our God*) (fig. 4); it was also due to the social and political development, which had been gaining momentum since the end of the Thirty Years' War, toward the formation, determination, and affirmation of a German people above its territorial fragmentation—a people whose culture, albeit not its political reality, was defined mainly in terms of language. Jacob Grimm in 1822 succinctly put it like this: "Only by virtue of the written language do we Germans feel the bond of our descent and community to be alive, and no tribe can believe to have paid too high a price for such an advantage."[70] Grimm considered Luther as the creator of this written language and further characterized written German as a "Protestant dialect." Placed within the political context of his own time, Grimm emphasized the "freedom-breathing nature"[71] as the outstanding feature of the German language—a feature as important and essential to his own generation and its political struggle as it had been for Luther's theology and the language advancing this theology.

Outside Germany: Luther as a Catalyst of Nationwide Language Processes

Luther's idea of placing the vernacular language at the center of his theological work of mediation inspired the vernacular language work of many other European nations. His translation of the Bible into German was followed by similar translations into English (Tyndale, 1525), Dutch (Doen Pieterson, 1523), Danish (Christian den Trejdes, 1550), Swedish (Gustav Wasa, 1541), and Icelandic (1540),[72] his example as a teacher providing the impetus for vernacularizing the Bible, and thus for the formation of vernacular written languages in, for example, Finland and the Baltic countries. Luther and, in particular, his linguistic achievements thus helped shape European reality and can be credited with an importance that stretches far beyond the German-speaking world.

69 See Raab, "*Lutherisch-Deutsch*," p. 21. **70** Grimm, *Vorrede zur Deutschen Grammatik*, p. XIII (English translation quoted after Benes, *In Babel's Shadow*, p. 128). **71** Ibid., p. XI. **72** Erben, Luther, pp. 485 f.

BIBLIOGRAPHY

Albrecht, Otto (1929), Luthers Übersetzung des Neuen Testaments. Historisch-theologische Einleitung. In: *D. Martin Luthers Werke. Kritische Gesamtausgabe. Die deutsche Bibel*. Vol. 6, pp. xxix–xcvi. **Bergmann**, Rolf et al (eds.) (1998), *Die Entwicklung der Großschreibung im Deutschen von 1500 bis 1700*. Vol. 2. Heidelberg. **Benes**, Tuska (2008), *In Babel's Shadow: Language, Philology, and the Nation in Nineteenth-Century Germany*. Detroit. **Besch**, Werner (1967), *Sprachlandschaften und Sprachausgleich im 15. Jahrhundert. Studien zur Erforschung der spätmittelalterlichen Schreibdialekte und zur Entstehung der neuhochdeutschen Schriftsprache* (= Bibliotheca Germanica. 11). München. **Besch**, Werner (1988), Standardisierungsprozesse im deutschen Sprachraum. *Sociolinguistica. Internationales Jahrbuch für Europäische Soziolinguistik* 2, pp. 186–203; reprinted in: id. (2003), *Deutsche Sprache im Wandel. Kleine Schriften zur Sprachgeschichte*. Frankfurt am Main, pp. 257–284. **Besch**, Werner (2000), Die Rolle Luthers für die deutsche Sprachgeschichte. In: id. et al. (eds.), *Sprachgeschichte. Ein Handbuch zur Geschichte der deutschen Sprache und ihrer Erforschung*. Vol. 2 (= Handbücher zur Sprach- und Kommunikationswissenschaft. 2/2). 2nd ed. Berlin/New York, pp. 1713–1745. **Coseriu**, Eugenio (1980), Historische Sprache und Dialekt. In: Göschel, Joachim (ed.), *Dialekt und Dialektologie. Ergebnisse des Internationalen Symposions 'Zur Theorie des Dialekts'. Marburg 5.–10. September 1977* (= Zeitschrift für Dialektologie und Linguistik, Beiheft NF 26). Wiesbaden, pp. 106–122. **Dressler**, Wolfgang (1988), Spracherhaltung—Sprachverfall—Sprachtod. In: Ammon, Ulrich et al. (eds.), *Soziolinguistik. Ein internationales Handbuch zur Wissenschaft von Sprache und Gesellschaft*. Vol. 2 (= Handbücher zur Sprach- und Kommunikationswissenschaft. 3.2). Berlin/New York, pp. 1551–1563. **Erben**, Johannes (1959), Luther und die neuhochdeutsche Schriftsprache. In: Maurer, Friedrich/Stroh, Friedrich (eds.), *Deutsche Wortgeschichte*. Vol. 1 (= Grundriß der germanischen Philologie. 17/1). Berlin, pp. 439–492. **Erben**, Johannes (1970), Frühneuhochdeutsch. In: Schmidt, Ludwig Erich (ed.), *Kurzer Grundriß der germanischen Philologie bis 1500*. Vol. 1: *Sprachgeschichte*. Berlin, pp. 386–440. **Gardt**, Andreas (1992), Die Übersetzungstheorie Martin Luthers. In: *Zeitschrift für Deutsche Philologie*, vol. 111, p. 87–111. **Giesecke**, Michael (1992), 'Volkssprache' und 'Verschriftlichung des Lebens' in der frühen Neuzeit. Kulturgeschichte als Informationsgeschichte. In: id., *Sinnenwandel—Sprachwandel—Kulturwandel. Studien zur Vorgeschichte der Informationsgesellschaft*. Frankfurt am Main, pp. 73–121. **Grimm**, Jacob (1822), Vorrede. In: id., *Deutsche Grammatik*. Erster Theil. 2nd ed. Göttingen, pp. III–XIX. **Grimm**, Jacob/**Grimm**, Wilhelm (eds.) (1854–1961), *Deutsches Wörterbuch*. Leipzig. **Hartweg**, Fréderic/**Wegera**, Klaus-Peter (2005), *Frühneuhochdeutsch. Eine Einführung in die deutsche Sprache des Spätmittelalters und der frühen Neuzeit* (= Germanistische Arbeitshefte. 33). 2nd rev. ed. Tübingen. **Josten**, Dirk (1976), *Sprachvorbild und Sprachnorm im Urteil des 16. und 17. Jahrhunderts. Sprachlandschaftliche Prioritäten. Sprachautoritäten. Sprachimmanente Argumentation* (= Europäische Hochschulschriften. 1). Frankfurt am Main. **Kermani**, Navid (2015), Religion ist eine sinnliche Erfahrung. In: *DIE ZEIT*, August 20, p. 38. **Kettmann**, Gerhard (1967), *Die kursächsische Kanzleisprache zwischen 1486 und 1546. Studien zum Aufbau und zur Entwicklung* (= Bausteine zur Sprachgeschichte des Neuhochdeutschen. 34). Berlin. **Kettmann**, Gerhard (2008), Zur schreibsprachlichen Überlieferung Wittenbergs in der Lutherzeit. In: id., *Wittenberg—Sprache und Kultur in der Reformationszeit* (= Leipziger Arbeiten zur Sprach- und Kommunikationsgeschichte. 16). Frankfurt am Main, pp. 17–54. **Kluge**, Friedrich (1888), *Von Luther bis Lessing. Sprachgeschichtliche Aufsätze*. Straßburg. **Lewandowski**, Theodor (1994), *Linguistisches Wörterbuch*. 6th ed. Heidelberg. **Luther**, Martin (1962), To the Councilmen of All Cities in Germany That They Establish and Maintain Christian Schools. In: Brandt, Walther I. (ed.), The Christian in Society II (= Luther's Works. 45). Trans. Albert T. W. Steinhaeuser. Philadelphia, pp. 347–378. **Maas**, Utz (1985), Lesen—Schreiben—Schrift. Die Demotisierung eines professionellen Arkanums in der frühen Neuzeit. In: *Zeitschrift für Literaturwissenschaft und Linguistik*, vol. 59, pp. 55–81. **Mattheier**, Klaus J. (2003), German. In: Deumert, Ana/Vandenbussche, Wim (eds.), *Germanic Standardizations. Past to Present*. Amsterdam/Philadelphia, p. 211–244. **Müller**, Burkhard (2015), "Aus der Asche wird ein Schwan entstehen." Zur Verbrennung von Jan Hus als Ketzer vor 600 Jahren. Radio feature. Available from: http://rundfunk.evangelisch.de/kirche-im-radio/feiertag/aus-der-asche-wird-ein-schwan-entstehen-7480 [08/22/2015]. **Penzl**,

Herbert (1984), *Frühneuhochdeutsch* (= Langs Germanistische Lehrbuchsammlung. 9). Bern. **Raab**, Heribert (1984), "Lutherisch-Deutsch." Ein Kapitel Sprach- und Kulturkampf in den katholischen Territorien des Reiches. In: Breuer, Dieter et al. (eds.), *Oberdeutsche Literatur im Zeitalter des Barock*. München, pp. 15–41. **Rössler**, Paul (2005), *Schreibvariation—Sprachregion—Konfession. Graphematik und Morphologie in österreichischen und bayrischen Drucken vom 16. bis ins 18. Jahrhundert* (= Schriften zur deutschen Sprache in Österreich. 35), Frankfurt am Main. **Schilling**, Heinz (2012), *Martin Luther. Rebell in einer Zeit des Umbruchs*. München. **Solms**, Hans-Joachim (2000), Soziokulturelle Voraussetzungen und Sprachraum des Frühneuhochdeutschen. In: Besch, Werner et al. (eds.), *Sprachgeschichte. Ein Handbuch zur Geschichte der deutschen Sprache und ihrer Erforschung*. Vol. 2 (= Handbücher zur Sprach- und Kommunikationswissenschaft. 2/2). 2nd ed. Berlin/New York, pp. 1513–1527. **Solms**, Hans-Joachim (2016), Substantivkomposition und nominale Attribuierung im Frühneuhochdeutschen. Zur Wortschatzerweiterung und Monosemierung. In: Quekkeboom, Sarah/Waldenberger, Sandra (eds.), *Perspektivwechsel. Festschrift für Klaus-Peter Wegera*. Berlin. **Sonderegger**, Stefan (1998), Geschichte deutschsprachiger Bibelübersetzungen in Grundzügen. In: Besch, Werner et al. (eds.): *Sprachgeschichte. Ein Handbuch zur Geschichte der deutschen Sprache und ihrer Erforschung*. Vol. 1 (= Handbücher zur Sprach- und Kommunikationswissenschaft. 2.1). Rev. and amended 2nd ed. Berlin/New York, pp. 229–284. **Stolt**, Birgit (1989), Lieblichkeit und Zier, Ungestüm und Donner. In: *Zeitschrift für Theologie und Kirche*, vol. 86, pp. 282–305; reprinted in: Wolf, Herbert (ed.), *Luthers Deutsch: Sprachliche Leistung und Wirkung* (= Dokumente germanistischer Forschung. 2). Frankfurt am Main, pp. 317–339. **Thiele**, Ernst/**Brenner**, Oskar (1914), Luthers Sprichwörtersammlung. In: *D. Martin Luthers Werke. Kritische Gesamtausgabe*. Vol. 51, pp. 634–733. **Tschirch**, Fritz (1989), *Entwicklung und Wandlungen der deutschen Sprachgestalt vom Hochmittelalter bis zur Gegenwart. Geschichte der deutschen Sprache* (= Grundlagen der Germanistik. 9). Vol. 2/3. Rev. and ext. Werner Besch. Berlin. **Von Polenz**, Peter (2000), *Deutsche Sprachgeschichte vom Spätmittelalter bis zur Gegenwart*. Vol. 1: Einführung—Grundbegriffe—14. bis 16. Jahrhundert. 2nd ed. Berlin. **Weissbort**, Daniel/**Eysteinsson**, Ástráður (2006), *Translation—Theory and Practice: a Historical Reader*. Oxford. **Wells**, Christopher J. (1990), *Deutsch: Eine Sprachgeschichte bis 1945* (= Reihe Germanistische Linguistik. 93). Tübingen.

The Reformation Movement

STEFAN MICHEL

Why Wittenberg?
How a Small Electoral City in Saxony Was Transformed into the Hub of the Reformation

Were conditions in Wittenberg especially well suited for it to become a center of religious reform that left its mark on an entire generation? The question is justified, for in other places in the Holy Roman Empire of the German Nation shortly before 1517 critical voices were also being raised against the lamentable state of the church. Secular lords tried to reduce or curtail the privileges of the bishops responsible for directing ecclesiastical affairs in their territories. At imperial diets, long lists of grievances against Pope and church—the so-called *Gravamina*—were presented, denouncing the power of the curia. The "common man" openly derided the clergy's extravagant lifestyle or railed against the extortionate tithes required. A variety of devotional practices, both private and public—reading the Bible and devotional texts, going on pilgrimages, buying indulgences—competed for the attention of the faithful and bore witness to their search for salvation in the late Middle Ages. So why in Wittenberg, of all places, did these phenomena proliferate and then undergo such a radical transformation? To find an (admittedly speculative) answer to this question, it is worth taking a look at the situation in this flourishing university city and electoral seat during the years 1517 and 1518.

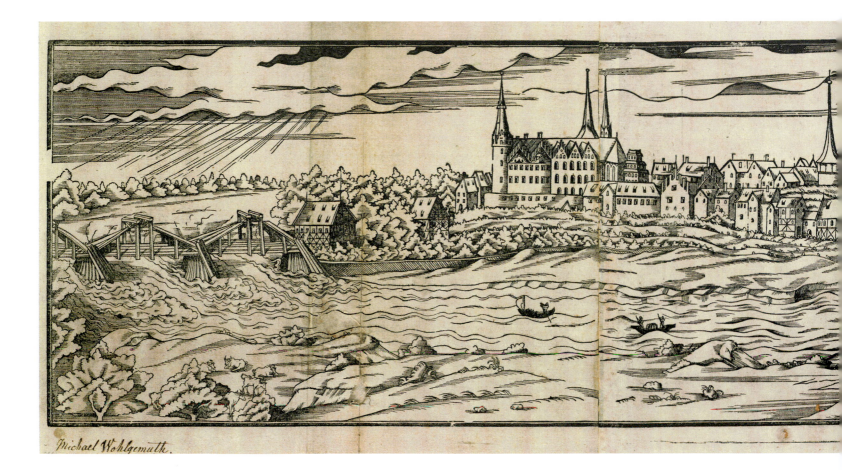

The City and University of Wittenberg

Wittenberg lay at the northern extremity of the Electorate of Saxony (fig. 1). The Partition of Leipzig of 1485 gave the city and its electoral district to Ernest of Saxony, father of Frederick the Wise and John the Steadfast. The House of Wettin had only possessed the city, situated at a crossing point on the Elbe River and expanded by the Ascanian dynasty, since 1483. The rise of Wittenberg began during the reign of Frederick the Wise. In 1486, the year he ascended the throne, Wittenberg had a population of about 2,000.

With the founding of its university, the *Leucorea* (fig. 2), Wittenberg began to surpass the other electoral seats, Torgau and Weimar, in importance. On October 18, 1502, accompanied by his co-regent and brother John, Frederick ceremoniously opened the university. By founding a university in Wittenberg, Frederick was able to compensate for the fact that, since the Partition of Leipzig of 1485, the Wettin University of Leipzig was no longer under his immediate authority. The newly founded University of Wittenberg, or the *Leucorea* (the Greek equivalent of "Wittenberg"— both names refer to "white mountains"), also provided him with a training center for future civil servants in his territories, making him independent of "foreign" institutions. In 1502, as many as 416 students registered. However, this high enrollment could not be maintained; thus, until 1509, students were enticed to the university with the promise of not having to pay a fee for graduation.

According to the university statutes, periodic reforms—for instance, of the curriculum—were to be encouraged to sharpen the profile of the *Leucorea* and secure its reputation. Such comprehensive reforms took place in 1518.[1] The Faculty of Arts was endowed with five new chairs, designed principally to strengthen classical studies and occupied for the most part by young teachers,[2] such as Augustin Schurff, with whom students could now read Aristotle's *Logic* in the original language instead of having to rely on medieval Scholastic texts. A Hellenist, Philipp Melanchthon, and a Hebraist, Johann Böschenstein, were appointed to teach language. Whereas the latter stayed in Wittenberg for only a matter of months, Melanchthon pursued a distinguished teaching career at the *Leucorea* for the remainder of his life (fig. 3). The two other chairs were for zoology and physics, occupied respectively by Johann Eisermann, latinized to Ferrarius Montanus, and Bartholomäus Bernhardi. The already existing scholastic curriculum remained untouched because the professors teaching it could not simply be dismissed.

---

1 See Treu, *Leucorea*; id., *Klima*. **2** All sources on the history of the University of Wittenberg at this time are easily accessible in Friedensburg, *Urkundenbuch*, especially pp. 82 – 93.

Fig. 1
Unknown Artist, View of Wittenberg from the South, 1536 – 46.
In the foreground the river Elbe, the palace to the left,
in the middle the Town and Parish Church of St. Mary's,
from right to left: Luther's house, Melanchthon's house and the
Collegium (University)

Fig. 2
Emperor Maximilian I's founding charter for the University of Wittenberg, Ulm, July 6, 1502

In 1517 and 1518, the *Leucorea* had a large intake of students—242 were matriculated in 1517 and 273 in 1518. Considering the proximity of rival universities in Erfurt, Leipzig, and Frankfurt on the Oder, this was a tremendous success. Most of the students attracted to the young university were from Central Germany, though other parts of the empire and Europe were also represented. Considering there were constant complaints about the Faculties of Medicine and Law, the high matriculation figures are quite remarkable. The Faculty of Medicine was chronically understaffed, and in the Faculty of Law hardly any teaching took place because the lawyers were constantly busy producing expert reports or judging cases in the courts of law.

The University of Wittenberg was probably attractive since, as a young institution, its teaching faculty was not yet set in its ways. In addition, care had been taken to see that all intellectual schools of thought were represented equally, thus avoiding any ideological bias. Indeed, students could attend courses offering a wide range of intellectual methodologies. The theologians, for instance, gave courses representing a variety of scholastic approaches. In addition, Frederick the Wise did all he could to ensure that his new university, modeled on the one in Tübingen, built up a good reputation. Thus, in 1514 he founded a chair for mathematics. Renowned university teachers were recruited, and these in turn attracted large numbers of students. The teachers included the first rector of the university, the physician Martin Pollich from Mellrichstadt, known as Mellerstadt; the professor of rhetoric and poetics Hermann von dem Busche; and the lawyers Christoph Scheurl and Hieronymus Schurff. Frederick also had new university buildings erected, including lecture rooms and student accommodations (fig. 4).

Shortly before Melanchthon, the renowned Hellenist Johannes Rak, known as Aesticampianus, was appointed in Wittenberg. He lectured on the Latin author Pliny and the church fathers Hieronymus and Augustine. These appointments strengthened the Humanist faction in Wittenberg, whose members included Balthasar Fabricius—called Vacha Phacchus after his birthplace—a professor of grammar at the *Leucorea*. It was probably no coincidence that when Fabricius was rector in 1517, humanist studies began to expand in Wittenberg.[3]

The enthusiasm with which Luther greeted Melanchthon's inaugural lecture is proof that these developments were felt beyond the Faculty of Arts. The humanists' philological endeavors, which amounted to a reform of the curriculum, corresponded with Luther's own interests. To study the Bible in depth, one needed knowledge of

Hebrew and Greek. Thus, it is no wonder that in 1519, together with his colleagues Bartholomäus Bernhardi, Andreas von Bodenstein, Peter Burchard, and Nikolaus von Amsdorf, Luther proposed that Thomist philosophy no longer be taught at the university. The money thus saved could be used to augment Melanchthon's salary. The proposal was only later agreed to.

Martin Luther, the Committed Professor of Theology

Martin Luther, who had been teaching theology at Wittenberg University since 1512, participated enthusiastically in the radical changes taking place there.[4] In his lectures on the books of the Bible, he explored the meaning of Holy Scripture. From 1513 to 1515 he lectured on the book of Psalms, in 1515–16 on the Epistle to the Romans, in 1516–17 on the Epistle to the Galatians, and in 1517–18 on the Epistle to the Hebrews, returning in 1521 to the book of Psalms. He also intensively studied the writings of the church father Augustine, and the sermons of the mystic Johannes Tauler. A major influence in this respect was probably the pietistic theology of his teacher Johann von Staupitz, Vicar General of the Augustinian Eremites. In inspiring tracts, von Staupitz stressed God's grace as manifested in the incarnation and passion of Christ.

Whether Luther was himself a humanist has often been the subject of debate. He was certainly open to many of the Humanists' ideas but probably cannot be counted among their numbers. Nevertheless, his exhaustive research led him to insights that coincided with a number of Humanist concerns. Those who did not attend his lectures were first confronted with Luther's radical exposé of theological questions in a disputation held in 1516, at which Bartholomäus Bernhardi, who had listened to Luther's lectures, represented Luther's position. In doing so, he put forward anthropological theses touching on questions of divine grace. Was the individual, relying on his own natural powers alone, capable of keeping God's laws and of doing good, thus meriting grace and recognizing that he did so? Bernhardi answered the question in the negative since the individual is hampered by sin. Here it may be seen how the debate was to develop: divine grace was to become a central tenet of Luther's theology. Through his studies, Luther also prompted those around him to reflection: his colleague and comrade-in-arms Andreas Bodenstein, known as Karlstadt, began, at Luther's prompting, to study the writings of Augustine and Tauler. Luther similarly influenced Nikolaus von Amsdorf, to whom he above all recommended Augustine's writings against the heretic Pelagius. Thus Luther, so to speak, converted his friend from Scholasticism.

Luther's new theology was even more obviously apparent in a disputation on September 4, 1517, in which Franz Günther of Nordhausen was examined for the degree of *Baccalaureus biblicus*. For the disputation, Luther had drafted theses that made clear his rejection of the late-medieval theology curriculum: *Disputatio contra scholasticam theologiam*, according to which the study of Aristotle should be removed from the curriculum. Luther also addressed anthropological questions in these theses, though such issues were more radically foregrounded in his renowned Ninety-Five Theses published

Fig. 3 Lucas Cranach the Elder (workshop),
Portrait of Philipp Melanchthon, 1540

on October 31, 1517.[5] According to Luther, at least, divine grace could not be obtained simply by buying indulgences.

His Ninety-Five Theses consequently attacked the common late-medieval practice of buying and selling indulgences. As a letter from Luther to Georg Spalatin indicates, at the time his critics assumed that he was representing the interests of his sovereign, the Elector Frederick.[6] To be sure, this was not Luther's intention. Rather, he merely wanted to start a discussion on his insights gained from reading the Bible and Augustine, insights that led him to a new understanding of divine grace.

As he affirmed in a letter from the spring of 1518, Luther was nevertheless soon assured that his sovereign would protect him: "Our Prince, who is extraordinarily devoted to this noble study of theology, has, without our requesting, eagerly taken Karlstadt and

3 See Rudersdorf/Töpfer, *Fürstenhof*. **4** See the contribution of Volker Leppin in this volume, and Hamm, *Luther*; Kohnle, *Reichstag und Reformation*, pp. 22–44; Leppin, *Martin Luther*, pp. 62–143. **5** See Kaufmann, *Ausgangsszenario*. **6** See WA.B 1, 118, 50.

Fig. 4
Jacob Johann Marchand, Disputation lectern in
the Luther House in Wittenberg, after 1685.
The lectern is a memorial to the significance
of the University of Wittenberg for the early Reformation.
This is shown by the portrait of Martin Luther and
the Crucifixion with the caption "Sola Fide" (faith alone).

myself into his protection and will by no means allow them to drag
me off to Rome. This they know very well and are mortally vexed."[7]
He urgently needed such protection when, in August 1518, the sum-
mons to appear in Rome arrived in Wittenberg. Frederick the Wise
was able to arrange for Luther to be interrogated in Germany. But at
his interrogation in Augsburg, it became clear that this Augustine
monk was not to be fobbed off with doctrinal injunctions. He was
prepared to be beaten only by arguments. He was a seeker after truth
and was not satisfied with prefabricated answers.

Frederick the Wise,
the Ambitious Sovereign

Frederick the Wise became Elector of Saxony in 1486 at the age of
twenty-three (fig. 5).[8] As is evident, he systematically proceeded to
develop Wittenberg into his electoral seat. First of all, he had a stone
bridge built over the Elbe and the old castle constructed by the Ascanians torn down. Between 1490 and 1496, he had a three-wing
castle erected, later extended to four wings through the addition of

utility buildings on the east side. The north wing consisted of the Castle Church, which was completed only in 1506. It housed the *Allerheiligenstift* (All Saints Seminary) and Frederick's collection of religious relics, the so-called *Heiltum*. He thus, as it were, made the Castle Church the religious center of his electorate. Here, at annual presentations of the relics, indulgences could be obtained in quantities unknown elsewhere in Central Germany. Other endowments— for instance, for masses or anniversaries, and especially endowments to All Saints Seminary—further emphasized the Castle Church's prominence. The elector's subjects no longer had to make expensive pilgrimages to distant lands but could find in their own electorate a location where their spiritual thirst could be quenched. At the same time, Frederick thus boosted the local economy.

In answering the question as to why Wittenberg, of all places, became such an important center of the Reformation, one has to consider Frederick's pre-Reformation church policy. From the beginning of his reign, the Elector of Saxony pursued a well thought-out ecclesiastical policy designed to strengthen his own privileges. Thus, for instance, he explicitly promoted the Observance Movement in the religious orders, with its insistence on strict observance of monastic rules, in order to raise the status of monastic life once more. One aspect of the Wettins' overall church policy was directed at the neighboring bishoprics: the ruling family strove constantly to ensure that bishoprics in surrounding territories—for instance, Magdeburg, Halberstadt, Meißen, Merseburg, and Naumburg—were occupied by individuals who did not pose a threat to its own ambitions. In 1476, the family achieved a major success in this respect when Frederick's younger brother Ernest was elected to the archbishopric of Magdeburg at the tender age of eleven. His episcopal ordination only took place in 1489, but thus, a suitable family member could be placed on a bishop's throne, strengthening the influence of the Wettins in Central Germany and in the empire as a whole. Ernest's sudden death in 1513 constituted a severe loss for Frederick—he was no longer able to influence the policy of this neighboring territory. Henceforth, he strove remorselessly to extend and consolidate his privileges vis-à-vis the surrounding bishoprics.

In line with these endeavors, on the death of John III of Schönberg, Bishop of Naumburg, in 1517, Frederick campaigned to have Philip of the Palatinate, who was already Bishop of Freising, elected to the vacant bishopric. Since 1512, Philip had been coadjutator in Naumburg, an ancillary post that carried with it the right of succession. Philip's election resulted in the administration of Naumburg being taken over by an ecclesiastical council, in whom Frederick found a compliant negotiating partner—with significant results for the course of the Reformation in the 1520s.

In light of his ecclesiastical policy, it must have come as a shock to Frederick when, in 1518, one of his theology professors was summoned before a papal commission of inquiry. He therefore campaigned vigorously for the proceedings to take place in Germany before impartial judges. Frederick finally managed to have Luther interrogated in Augsburg by Cardinal Cajetan, also known as Thomas de Vio, from Gaeta. Additionally, he did not leave Luther to his fate, but provided him with the support and advice of experienced lawyers. The most prominent of these was the knight Philip of Feilitzsch,

Fig. 5 Lucas Cranach the Elder, Portrait of Frederick the Wise, Elector of Saxony, 1525–27

who was bailiff in Weida and frequently employed by the Ernestine line in imperial affairs. He helped Luther to draft his first appeal, presented on October 22, 1518, in which he invoked the arbitration of a church council. Feilitzsch had already been present at the debate between Luther and Cajetan on October 14. Here in Augsburg, the strategy was developed that Frederick would henceforth work to protect Luther. The elector declared he was not competent to decide a theological dispute, and so far, he argued, Luther had not been tried by due process of law, the right of every subject. Consequently, Frederick concluded he was powerless to undertake anything against the monk—especially as Frederick refused to get involved in Luther's dispute with the church. In this way, Frederick skillfully protected his subject as well as his university.

7 See *WA.B* 1, 155, 20–22. **8** See Kirn, *Friedrich der Weise*; Ludolphy, *Friedrich der Weise*; Stephan, *Werck*.

The Network of Discussion

Without a doubt, Luther was certainly the most important Reformation theologian in Wittenberg. Nevertheless, it must be borne in mind that until he published his Ninety-Five Theses against indulgences, he was just one university professor among many. Andreas Bodenstein, for instance, enjoyed an equally high reputation. Luther's significance was to grow only as his theology developed. Nevertheless, far into the 1520s, there were those in Wittenberg who hesitated to follow Luther or even opposed him. In particular, many members of All Saints Seminary did not see why masses should no longer be read. Thus it is important to take a look at the environment in which Luther developed his ideas.

Without a doubt, the Reformation would never have succeeded in Wittenberg had Luther not had so many friends and allies. He continually discussed his ideas with a wide range of teachers and administrative officials, among whom were Andreas Karlstadt and Nikolaus von Amsdorf. From 1517 onward, Luther's most important contact and patron at the electoral court was Georg Spalatin (fig. 6).[9] Spalatin saw to it that his sovereign was thoroughly informed on all that was going on. In addition, Frederick authorized Spalatin to liaise with the university on reform issues. One reason for Spalatin's support of Luther was that Spalatin's humanist sympathies made him open to Luther's ideas. Spalatin had studied in Erfurt and Wittenberg, completing a bachelor's degree in the Faculty of Arts and going on to study law and theology. His teacher was Nikolaus Marschalk, who had been called from Erfurt to an appointment in Wittenberg in 1502. Spalatin returned to Erfurt in 1504 and, thanks to the intercession of the humanist Mutianus Rufus, was appointed preceptor at the monastery at Georgenthal. In 1508, he became tutor of the Prince-Elector John Frederick and rose in the court of Frederick the Wise to the rank of custodian of the library and the elector's personal secretary. He was also at various times his confessor, court preacher, and traveling companion. Spalatin was instrumental in formulating and executing Frederick's strategy for protecting Luther. Luther appreciated Spalatin's support and often turned to him in confidence when he needed the backing of the court. The importance of Spalatin's position as castle and university librarian should also not be underestimated, for in this capacity he strove assiduously to bring the latest academic publications to Wittenberg. These included Johannes Reuchlin's books and editions of classical authors published by Aldus Manutius of Venice. Spalatin thus provided important intellectual nourishment for the knowledge-hungry theologians of Wittenberg.

With the appointment of Philipp Melanchthon to the university in 1518, Luther found an intellectual sparring partner who was receptive to his ideas and with whom he could discuss his concerns openly. Thenceforth, they took up the common cause in campaigning on university issues. Melanchthon placed his linguistic skills, above all his knowledge of Greek, at the service of Luther's nascent theology, such that Luther exclaimed, "This little Greek even beats me at theology!" Besides Plutarch, Melanchthon studied Paul's Epistles to Titus, James, the Galatians, and the Romans. As early as 1519, he published a textbook on rhetoric.[10]

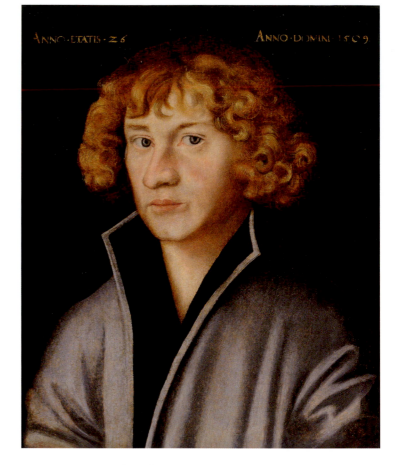

Fig. 6 Lucas Cranach the Elder,
Portrait of Georg Spalatin, 1509

Next to Karlstadt and Amsdorf, Spalatin and Melanchthon were Luther's most important intellectual discussion partners in Wittenberg at this time. Nevertheless, we may assume that he also discussed his ideas with other monks, such as Johannes Lang, as well as with members of the court and with lawyers. He thus deepened his theological insights not only in the great public disputations in Heidelberg (1518) and Leipzig (1519) but also in private conversations in Wittenberg.[11]

Politics as a Promoter of Reform

In the preceding discussion, reference has often been made to Humanism, said to have prepared the soil from which the Reformation in Wittenberg grew. There is certainly some truth in this. Nevertheless, though a number of humanists were active in Wittenberg under Fredrick's patronage, no distinct humanist circle as such was active at the university. Rather, the Wittenberg humanists were individual scholars who prospered there but who each worked independently. Frederick himself was no humanist, although he had an ear for many of their concerns and corresponded with a number of them.

Frederick the Wise supported the university he had founded with all the resources at his disposal. In many areas of university life, especially in finances and personnel matters, he made sure his voice was heard. He encouraged specific appointments and kept an eye on the curriculum and teaching activities. Frederick could more directly intervene in university affairs through his control over All Saints Seminary because the canons were also professors at the university. He thus found the prospect of one of his professors being hauled in front of an external court, and very possibly taken away from Wittenberg, unacceptable.

There were certainly many reasons why Wittenberg was a suitable breeding ground for Reformation theology. First of all, the university was open to new ideas—thanks largely to the humanists. Secondly, the church policy pursued by Frederick the Wise ensured that his privileges as sovereign were strengthened. In addition, he had a strong sense of justice. Condemning Luther without due process of law was for him simply unthinkable and contradicted his other views of church politics. For him such a course would have been an arrogant misuse of ecclesiastical authority, that he could not agree to. He was also concerned about protecting the reputation of his university. Finally, an important factor in the growth of a strong reform movement in Wittenberg was certainly Luther's charismatic leadership qualities: he was skilled at integrating other opinions into his own and at winning people over to his point of view. But the fact remains that the Reformation was able to survive only thanks to the political protection of Frederick the Wise and his successor, John the Steadfast. A brief comparison with Zurich, an important center of the Reformation in Switzerland, shows that there, too, a prominent reformer succeeded only with the support of the city authorities. In Zurich, Huldrych Zwingli was able gradually to convince both the Great and the Little City Councils to support his theological position. His methods differed from Luther's, as he used disputations to put forward his ideas. The city fathers were open to Zwingli's theological teaching, among other reasons because it strengthened the political position of the city within the Swiss Confederacy and vis-à-vis the Bishop of Constance.[12]

Let us return to our original question as to why Wittenberg, of all places, became such an important center of the Reformation. Certainly there is no simple answer to this question. Rather, a fortuitous synergy of a number of forces was at work. But one thing is certain: without the political will of Frederick the Wise and, in the 1520s, his successor, John the Steadfast, the Reformation would never have taken place (fig. 7).

Fig. 7 Lucas Cranach the Elder, Portrait of John the Steadfast, Elector of Saxony, after 1532

9 See Höss, *Georg Spalatin*. **10** See Scheible, *Melanchthon*, especially pp. 31–33. **11** See Kruse, *Universitätstheologie*. **12** See Gäbler, *Huldrych Zwingli*, pp. 61–101.

BIBLIOGRAPHY

Friedensburg, Walter (ed.) (1926), *Urkundenbuch der Universität Wittenberg. Teil 1: 1502–1611 (= Geschichtsquellen der Provinz Sachsen und des Freistaates Anhalt. 2).* Magdeburg. **Gäbler**, Ulrich (2004), *Huldrych Zwingli. Eine Einführung in sein Leben und sein Werk.* Zürich. **Hamm**, Berndt (2010), *Der frühe Luther. Etappen reformatorischer Neuorientierung.* Tübingen. **Höss**, Irmgard (1989), *Georg Spalatin (1484–1545). Ein Leben in der Zeit des Humanismus und der Reformation.* Weimar. **Kaufmann**, Thomas (2012), Ausgangsszenario. Luthers 95 Thesen in ihrem historischen Zusammenhang. In: id., *Der Anfang der Reformation. Studien zur Kontextualität der Theologie, Publizistik und Inszenierung Luthers und der reformatorischen Bewegung.* Tübingen, pp. 166–184.

Kirn, Paul (1926), *Friedrich der Weise und die Kirche.* Leipzig, reprinted Hildesheim, 1972. **Kohnle**, Armin (2001), *Reichstag und Reformation. Kaiserliche und ständische Religionspolitik von den Anfängen der Causa Lutheri bis zum Nürnberger Religionsfrieden.* Gütersloh. **Kruse**, Jens-Martin (2002), *Universitätstheologie und Kirchenreform. Die Anfänge der Reformation in Wittenberg 1516–1522.* Mainz. **Leppin**, Volker (2006), *Martin Luther.* Darmstadt. **Ludolphy**, Ingetraut (1984), *Friedrich der Weise, Kurfürst von Sachsen (1463–1525).* Göttingen. **Rudersdorf**, Manfred/**Töpfer**, Thomas (2006), Fürstenhof, Universität und Territorialstaat. Der Wittenberger Humanismus, seine Wirkungsräume und Funktionsfelder im Zeichen der Reformation. In: Maissen, Thomas/Walther, Gerrit (eds.), *Funktionen des Humanismus. Studien zum Nutzen des Neuen in der humanistischen Kultur.* Göttingen, pp. 214–261. **Scheible**, Heinz (1997), *Melanchthon. Eine Biographie.* München. **Stephan**, Bernd (2014), *Ein itzlichs Werck lobt seinen Meister. Friedrich der Weise, Bildung und Künste.* Leipzig. **Treu**, Martin (1998), Die Leucorea zwischen Tradition und Erneuerung. Erwägungen zur frühen Geschichte der Universität Wittenberg. In: Lück, Heiner (ed.), *Martin Luther und seine Universität. Vorträge anläßlich des 450. Todestages des Reformators.* Köln/Weimar/Wien, pp. 31–51. **Treu**, Martin (2015), Das geistige Klima an der Universität Wittenberg vor der Ankunft Melanchthons. In: Asche, Matthias/Lück, Heiner/Rudersdorf, Manfred/Wriedt, Markus (eds.), *Die Leucorea zur Zeit des späten Melanchthon. Institutionen und Formen gelehrter Bildung um 1550.* Leipzig, pp. 77–92.

1 Electoral Castle

In Luther's time, Saxony was ruled by Elector Frederick the Wise. On the site of an ancient castle, he built an early modern castle with a castle church.

2 Castle Church

In exceptional cases, the castle church was also used as the auditorium of the Leucorea University. Legend has it that Martin Luther nailed his Ninety-Five Theses to its portal.

3 Cranach's House

Lucas Cranach the Elder was a Wittenberg painter and entrepreneur. He operated a printing shop, worked as a publisher and pharmacist, and was appointed court painter in 1505.

4 Cranach's Printing Shop

Among the works printed in Cranach's printing shop is Luther's first translation of the New Testament.

5 Town Hall and Market Square

The construction of the town hall lasted 20 years and was finished in 1541. It was the meeting place of the City Council of Wittenberg.

6 Bugenhagen's House

This is the location of the house in which Bugenhagen lived with his family. It was the oldest Protestant parsonage in the world.

7 The Town and Parish Church of St. Mary's

The medieval church has a magnificent altar-piece by Lucas Cranach the Elder. Reformer Johannes Bugenhagen was elected parish pastor of St. Mary's. He and Martin Luther regularly preached here.

8 The New College

To further increase the university's capacity, the construction of the New College, located opposite the Old College, was begun in 1509. The major part of the academic events took place here.

9 The Old College

The Leucorea University was founded in 1502. The name is derived from the Greek word for "white mountain", i.e., Wittenberg. As from 1503, the Old College was built according to plans by Konrad Pflüger to manage the growing number of students.

Bugenhagen's House 6

The Town and Parish Church of St. Mary's 7

Town Hall and Market Square 5

Cranach's Printing Shop 4

Cranach's House 3

2 Castle Church

Moat

Electoral Castle 1

10 Melanchthon's House

This is the place where reformer Philipp Melanchthon lived. On the elector's initiative, the house was built in 1536 to keep the humanist in the town.

11 Luther's House

The "Black Monastery" of the Augustinian monks was begun to be built in 1503/04. When the monastery was dissolved in the wake of the Reformation, Martin Luther lived here with his family. The square annex on the southern side of the house facing the city wall seems to have served Luther as a study.

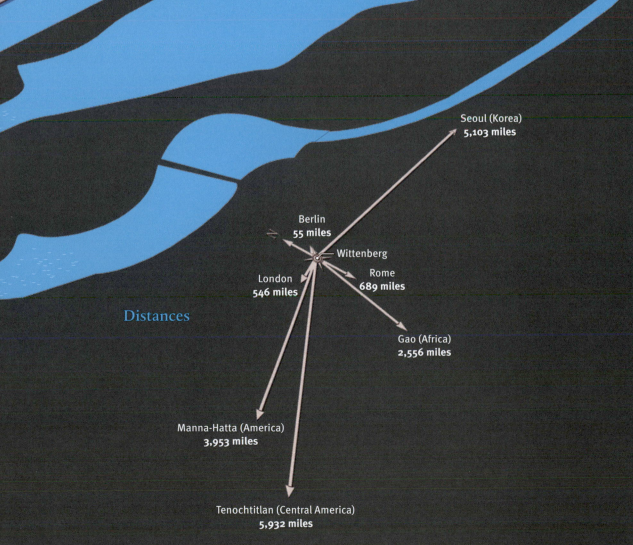

10 Melanchthon's House

11 Luther's House

New College 8

9 Old College

Distances

Seoul (Korea)
5,103 miles

Berlin
55 miles

Wittenberg

London
546 miles

Rome
689 miles

Gao (Africa)
2,556 miles

Manna-Hatta (America)
3,953 miles

Tenochtitlan (Central America)
5,932 miles

WITTENBERG

The model shows the residential town of the Electors of Saxony on the Elbe River. In 1487, the construction of the Renaissance Castle had begun. It was created as a three-wing complex, the Castle Church being integrated into the construction; Luther is alleged to have nailed his 95 theses to its doors. Lucas Cranach the Elder was active as a painter for the Electoral court as from 1505; in his houses, he had a workshop and a printing shop. To the east of the market square, the Town and Parish Church of St. Mary towers above the other buildings of the town. The eastern part of the town houses the building complex of the Leucorea University, founded in 1502. As early as 1503, the Old College was structurally completed. Complemented by the New College and the use of the Castle Church as University Church, the Elector's educational institution continued to grow. Martin Luther's house is located on the eastern edge of the town. The residential house of Melanchthon, located halfway between Luther's house and the university, is easily recognizable by its arched gables.

JOHANNA REETZ / HOLGER RODE

Early Modern Domestic and Dining Culture in Wittenberg Reflected by Prestigious Archaeological Finds

The numerous archaeological excavations which have been carried out in Wittenberg in the last few years augment the town's unique historical position as the center of the Reformation by offering outstanding research possibilities. This includes the remarkable opportunity to compare material remains from Martin Luther's household with other contemporary discoveries from properties of Wittenberg's burghers. Moreover it offers the opportunity to describe the town's social fabric and to develop categories in order to assess household remains from the Reformation period.

The material discussed below was discovered primarily in excavations at Arsenalplatz (Arsenal Square), the grounds of the prince elector's castle, and in Luther's house in Wittenberg. In this essay certain outstanding finds that can be labeled as status or luxury objects will be localized in the city in order to establish their social context. A particularly interesting aspect of such studies is that they provide an excellent opportunity to compare inventories from town houses to those of the electoral palace. The wide scale excavations at Arsenalplatz permit a comprehensive comparison of archaeological finds contextualized in specific property locations. Property boundaries were discovered that had remained unchanged from their establishment around 1200 until the buildings were destroyed in October 1760. During the town's golden age, numerous new houses were constructed that were inhabited primarily by university staff, printers, bookbinders, and other higher-ranking citizens.[1]

When seen as a whole, exclusive finds in a particular location or overlapping areas within the town have a particular relevance.[2] These archaeological discoveries can be viewed as elements of nonverbal communication, that can contribute to social- and status-oriented differentiation. During the past few years, the authors of this paper have supervised almost all the archaeological excavations in Wittenberg. In this short article certain exceptional finds will be introduced which have been excavated recently. Up until now only a small number of comparable artifacts within the region or beyond have been published.[3]

Representation and Comfort

Polychrome glazed tiles represent a very special find group pertaining to residential culture that can be undoubtedly categorized as luxury goods (fig. 1). It is possible to see a significant distribution of these tiles within the old town of Wittenberg. Only two fragments of these tiles were discovered in middle-class areas. One piece originates from a plot on the corner of Bürgermeister-Scharrenstraße (fig. 1, below left). The other fragment was found on the property Markt 4 (fig. 1, below right), which, during the sixteenth century, was owned by Lucas Cranach the Elder and his son-in-law Caspar Pfreundt.[4] In addition to polychrome tile fragments, monochrome glazed tiles in shades of honey yellow and green also were discovered in both plots. This type of floor covering is also extremely rare. Beyond the limits of the elector's residence, it has been discovered additionally only on the property plot Schlossstraße 10.

During excavations in the former south wing of Wittenberg Castle between 2010 and 2011, six additional fragments of polychrome glazed tiles were discovered alongside monochrome tiles, some of which have an etched decoration. In a small-scale excavation in the summer of 2015, more fragments of polychrome glazed tiles were excavated from a levelling layer at the west side of Wittenberg Castle. Two types of tiles can be reconstructed from these fragments, and an almost complete tile of each type has survived. The first is square, with a lateral length of 15 cm (fig. 1, top left). The stamped tile pattern consists of one-quarter of a double garland and a circular band—a décor known from earlier excavations. The second type (fig. 1, center), which is completely new, is a pentagonal tile with a triangular point on one side, making it reminiscent of a flat roof tile. A quarter of the garland appears on each pointed edge, followed by two rhombuses and a triangle with a circular band.

Both types of tiles can be combined to form a floor mosaic with alternating patterns and colors (fig. 2). The assembled pentagonal tiles produce an octagonal star framed by a circle with a disk with a stylized flower in its center. The square tiles form a flower made up of two concentric petal sprays. The reconstruction shows that the two tile variations can produce a coherent pattern only in combination with each other. It is possible that these very rare polychrome tiles were used only in a small part of a room, with the rest of the floor decorated with monochrome glazed tiles, possibly in a checkerboard pattern. The polychrome tiles were undoubtedly part of the initial decoration of the newly renovated electoral castle and therefore date to the first quarter of the sixteenth century. The recently discovered fragments had already been discarded by the middle of the sixteenth century, which may be related to the glaze's low resistance to abrasion. The tiles were certainly manufactured at the neighboring potter's center at Bad Schmiedeberg, where an identical fragment was discovered as a biscuit firing in the waste pit of a potter's workshop. A single identical find was made in Schloss Freudenstein (Freudenstein Castle) in Freiberg (Saxony), where polychrome glazed tiles with the same motif were excavated in 2006.[5]

This evidence of such a high-quality polychrome tiled floor documents a form of luxurious interior design that was apparently reserved for a small élite. In Wittenberg, this meant that only the castle of the prince elector and the Cranach household had them.

The distribution of polychrome glazed stove tiles in Wittenberg is similar to the distribution pattern of glazed floor tiles, but the proportion of excavated stove tiles is generally much higher. What is most striking is that late Gothic polychrome glazed cornice and recess tiles were also found in the Augustinian monastery which was later to become Luther's house, and in the castle, some of which bore the representation of saints (see the article by Mirko Gutjahr in this volume). The same type of tile but with a monochrome green glaze has been found in civic residential quarters in Wittenberg's oldtown. This differentiation continues in the case of polychrome glazed stove tiles originating from the Renaissance period. In middle-class contexts, polychrome glazed stove tiles have been discovered in Luther's house, on the property of Cranach's house at Markt 4, in the area of the town hall, and a plot to the south of the Arsenalplatz. Individual fragments have also been excavated in other parts of the old town (fig. 3). After around the year 1540, polychrome stove tiles went out of fashion in Wittenberg; only monochrome, predominantly green glazed tiles have been found dating from the subsequent period. Prior to 1540, polychrome tiles were a clear indication of luxurious interior architecture, and apparently limited to the court and upper-class residents of the town. The new town hall also appears to have had an ostentatious and correspondingly valuable polychrome stove. The majority of the stoves dating from this period found within Wittenberg's urban area were monochrome and, therefore, probably also more affordable. The decorative motifs on monochrome and polychrome tiles are identical.

Fig. 1 Fragments of polychrome glazed floor tiles, from excavations at the Wittenberg sites of the prince elector's palace (top and middle) as well as from the properties Jüdenstraße 1 (lower left) and Markt 4 (lower right)

Fig. 2 Reconstruction of a floor made of polychrome tiles like those found in Wittenberg on a 90 × 90 cm surface

1 Hennen, *Reformation und Stadtentwicklung*. 2 Kottmann, *Materielle Kultur*, p. 84. 3 For individual floor tile fragments, see Kluttig-Altmann, *Baukeramik*, esp. pp. 158 f. and 224, fig. 9, and Kluttig-Altmann, *Archäologische Funde*, p. 365, fig. 2. 4 See Hennen, *Reformation und Stadtentwicklung*, pp. 60 f. 5 These tiles do not have the same model as the motif is slightly altered. Schmiedeberg was evidently not the production location for these tiles due to the extremely atypical glazed coloring. See Gräf, *Buntes*; Kluttig-Altmann, *Auf breiter Basis*, pp. 187–189, figs. 16 f.

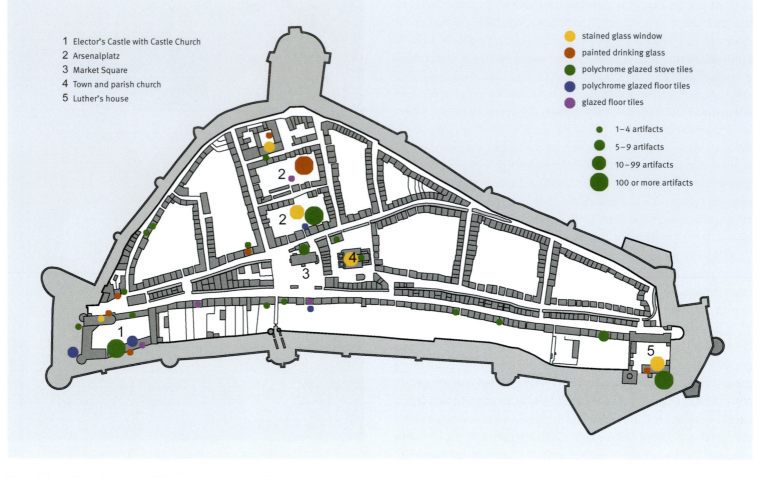

1 Elector's Castle with Castle Church
2 Arsenalplatz
3 Market Square
4 Town and parish church
5 Luther's house

● stained glass window
● painted drinking glass
● polychrome glazed stove tiles
● polychrome glazed floor tiles
● glazed floor tiles

● 1–4 artifacts
● 5–9 artifacts
● 10–99 artifacts
● 100 or more artifacts

Fig. 3 Schematic tracing of the Wittenberg town map of 1623
with the quantitative distribution of certain find categories

A further group of finds that can be categorized as part of residential sumptuary is polychrome painted window glass. Examples are extremely rare, both in Wittenberg and elsewhere. Until now, painted window glass has been excavated from Luther's house, the Arsenalplatz area, the Castle Church, the Town Church, and the Augustinian monastery.

Six shards of painted window glass from Luther's house have survived among the archaeological finds.[6] These originate from the remains of a round pane painted with letters in *Schwarzlot* (lead based grisaille) and colored with silver/yellow stain. It most likely originally belonged to the monastery, as suggested by the Gothic lettering on the glass and its excavated context. The shards were found near the monastery refectory, or dining room, which conceivably could have been decorated with stain glass windows. Other finds containing painted window glass in Wittenberg were made near the three major churches and also suggest the use of this special material to augment sacred space (i.e. as stain glass windows).

To date, the only pieces of painted window glass that conclusively originated from a middle-class context were found in several Arsenalplatz properties. These include several round glass panes (fig. 4) manufactured from white molded glass, with a fine painted decoration in black lead and silver yellow. From the late fifteenth century onward, it was popular to use these so-called cabinet panes to decorate windows in town houses. The decorative motifs included coats of arms, house signs, and inscriptions, but also figured scenes from the Old and New Testaments as well as moral, mythological, and allegorical themes.[7]

The best preserved painted window glass finds were excavated on the grounds of Jüdenstraße 1, which is situated in the town center directly adjacent to both the town hall and Town Church. On the first pane of glass, which is almost fully preserved, an escutcheon is represented with a house identification mark and the initials of the owner, "VO." The banner below is inscribed "Valten O … in anno domini 1537."[8] A second very similar object from the same plot, of which about half the pane has been preserved, also displays an escutcheon with a patterned background of fine coils and a house sign. Similar objects have been excavated in Lüneburg and Osnabrück, both in Lower Saxony.[9]

A round window pane was discovered alongside many drinking glasses, some of which were also painted, in a large latrine complex on the north edge of Arsenalplatz. On this site, three latrine pits had been linked to form a single disposal facility. The painting on the window pane was not completely preserved, but an escutcheon and a banner below it are decipherable. From the same latrine, further sections of a banner surrounding this type of round pane were found. The letter sequence "PATRI—HVC—BONI—" is legible on one fragment, and the numeral 78 is below it, suggesting the year 1578. On another piece, the letters "AVFFEMRVI" can be deciphered. A painted glass fragment originating from Arsenalplatz was found in the residential area on Klostergasse. It displays a portrait that cannot be more closely identified in any specific context.

These painted window panes which date back to an extremely early period in Wittenberg, in comparison with archaeological finds in other locations—particularly in the federal state of Lower Saxony—are evidence of the opulence and individuality of interior decoration in some of Wittenberg's town houses.

Delights of the Table

Table culture represents another "focal point of social representation."[10] Objects in this category primarily include glass and clay drinking and serving vessels. The differing distribution of finds provides clear clues about patterns of social representation.

In the fifteenth- and sixteenth-century objects excavated in Wittenberg, stoneware—the classical material for drinking and pouring vessels at this time—plays a relatively minor role. The stoneware objects discovered at various sites in town show significant differences in their individual distribution. A large number of stoneware beakers were found around the castle area, which was in use during the second half of the fifteenth and beginning of the sixteenth centuries. These beakers are between 20 and 25 cm tall and are mostly cylindrical, and rarely have wider or even rounded bases (fig. 5). The characteristic feature of these beakers is roulette decoration across their entire central section. The patterns are widely varied and have been applied meticulously. These vessels were most likely manufactured at the nearby Bad Schmiedeberg. Conclusive proof hasn't yet been made, but the great similarity in material and surface decoration and the large volume of the finds suggests a production location close to Wittenberg.

Another group of beakers, found in smaller quantities but significantly limited to the castle and castle grounds, also appears to have originated during the second half of the fifteenth century. All fragments of cylindrical beakers found so far are completely undecorated and made of reddish-brown fired, relatively coarse and loose clay. The presumably untreated surface of the beakers ranges from brown to a slightly lilac color. This type of pottery is completely atypical for Wittenberg and the surrounding region, but similar tableware was manufactured in the Neustadt quarter of Dresden.[11] The Dresden material, however, is normally characterized by an individually stamped decoration.[12] The undecorated Wittenberg finds

Fig. 4 Fragments of round window glass discs decorated with Schwarzlot/grisaille glass painting and silver/yellow stain, from excavations at the site of the Arsenalplatz, Wittenberg

are dated a few decades later than the Dresden beakers but they could well have been imported from Dresden or its environs to Wittenberg and the elector's residence. These beakers appear to be one of the rare products that didn't find their way into the inventories of Wittenberg's middle-class town houses.

The distribution pattern of the stoneware beakers in Wittenberg is unambiguous: with the exception of the castle, little evidence of this characteristic ware is found across the entire town. Particularly after the comprehensive excavation of Arsenalplatz, it has become clear that this is not a research gap but that these vessels were indeed rarely used in the town. The situation is completely different within the area of the castle and the later palace complex, where large quantities of these fragments were found. We do not wish to insinuate that every type of beaker possessed a status above all other types of material culture, as is the case with the polychrome stove tiles. On the contrary, the massive presence of these beakers (in the environs of the castle) suggests that large quantities of drink, probably of an al-

6 Meller, *Fundsache* Luther, p. 282. **7** Witzleben, *Bemalte Glasscheiben*, p. 13. **8** If it is assumed that Valten O is the name of the property owner, the attribution by Insa Christiane Hennen is not correct. No owner of the property Jüdenstraße 1 named Valten O. is known for around the year 1537. See Hennen, *Reformation und Stadtentwicklung*, p. 65. The name is also completely non-existent in the whole of Wittenberg. This represents a further discrepancy between written sources and archaeological finds. **9** Steppuhn, *Blick*, p. 186. **10** Kottmann, *Materielle Kultur*, p. 89. **11** Mechelk, *Stadtkernforschung*, p. 106. Colored illustrations of the Dresden beakers can be found in Krabath, *Entwicklung*, p. 52, fig. 16. **12** An extremely close connection between the Dresden ware and the ceramics of the so-called Falke group suggests itself. See Rode, *Untersuchungen*.

Fig. 5 Fragments of a roulette decorated stoneware beaker which was probably used during the prince elector's feasts. From excavations at the site of the palace courtyard in Wittenberg

Fig. 6 Fragments of a trick vessel made of stoneware, from excavations at the site of Markt 4, Wittenberg

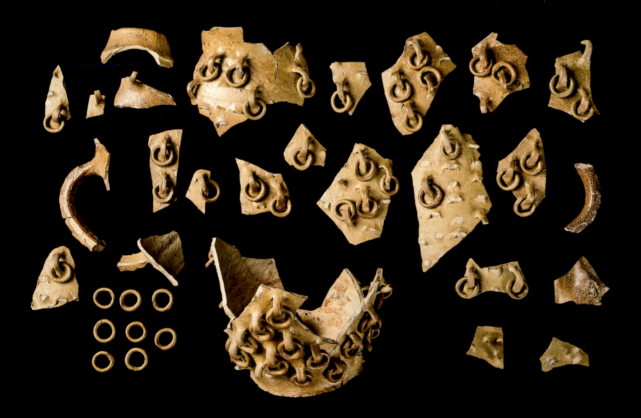

Fig. 7 Fragments of stoneware ring-beakers or ring-jugs covered with applied lugs and rings, from excavations at the site of Arsenalplatz, Wittenberg

coholic nature, were consumed here by large groups of people. The significant amount of beaker fragments therefore points toward an archaeologically measurable unique feature of the castle. The large number of these beakers perhaps even indicates they were used as "disposable drinking ware," as has already been established for a group of closely related beakers made of hard gray ware.[13] It seems reasonable to consider the drinking sessions and feasts suggested by the beaker fragments as a direct indication for the representative ambitions of their organizers.[14]

Naturally stoneware drinking vessels were also found in middle-class town households. Among them, a few vessels and/or fragments were found that would have caused merriment at the table. One fragment of this type of joke or trick vessel was found in the Cranach house at Markt 4 (fig. 6). It was made of salt-glazed stoneware with more strongly tempered clay material used for the separately modeled handle. This design is typical for stoneware production in Waldenburg, Saxony, and the surrounding area. The humorous trick effect when drinking was produced by several pipes positioned on the vessel's upper edge, through which the drink would spill in a relatively uncontrolled manner over the hapless drinker. This effect was further enhanced by blubbering noises produced while drinking from it. A very similar vessel originates from Luther's household.[15] Three smaller fragments from the upper edge of the vessel were discovered in the courtyard south of Luther's house. It appears that a pipe ran around its rim interconnecting several nozzles. This vessel, which was also most probably manufactured in West Saxony, would have contributed to the drinker's merriment in a similar way as the Cranach vessel did.

The ring jugs or beakers which were documented by three finds had a completely different function (fig. 7). The numerous rings hung on small loops on the exterior of the vessel's body and created a rattling noise with the vessel's every movement. It can be clearly imagined that the aim when drinking in a convivial gathering was to avoid creating too much noise when drinking from the vessel.

The scant evidence of these beakers in Wittenberg suggests that their production was extremely complicated and their purchase price expensive. Interestingly enough, they were also found in two very small plots in the south of Klostergasse, an area that otherwise displays little evidence of further luxury goods. The fact that two beakers were found on neighboring plots could provide evidence for a certain imitation effect. A third ring beaker found on the plot Jüdenstraße 1 was excavated together with the above-mentioned glass pane, which is dated to 1537.

Despite the extremely high degree of fragmentation, it is possible to make fairly accurate reconstructions of the ring beakers. They have a slightly bulging form and an accentuated, vertical rim. With the exception of the rim, the entire exterior surface of the vessels is covered by loops in which free-moving rings were inserted. These vessels appear to have regularly had three or four handles attached to their shoulders. The handles found to date are all decorated on the upper side with finger-pinching. The ring beakers were manufactured from stoneware with a relatively regular light brown, salt-glazed surface. The surface treatment of these objects, in particular the pinched handles, possibly indicates that the ring beakers were made in nearby Bad Schmiedeberg. Finds excavated in Penig, Saxony, and, above all, a note in the *Meißnische Bergchronik* (Chronicle of the Meissen Mountains) by Petrus Albinus indicate that Penig in west Saxony is the likely manufacturing location of these ring beakers.[16] It is not yet possible to establish an exact date for the Wittenberg ring beakers. All three objects were found in waste pits during excavations of Arsenalplatz. The dates of associated finds are relatively wide ranging, meaning that it is possible to narrow down the date of their manufacture and use to the second half of the sixteenth century.

In addition to the trick vessels, other highly rare vessels were also discovered in the plots of town houses in Wittenberg, namely anthropomorphic polychrome glazed ware. Two fragments of this type of vessel were discovered in a pit alongside the afore-mentioned fragment of a polychrome glazed floor tile. The two fragments originate from the upper end of a vessel in the shape of a woman (fig. 8). Only the head and the right side of her upper body have been preserved. An additional fragment is decorated with colored stripes and short, separately attached legs (fig. 9 top right). Fragments of a lid and a lower section of this type (fig. 9 bottom) were additionally discovered during excavations in Luther's house in Wittenberg. These fragments were also decorated with polychrome glazed stripes divided by incised lines. Quite possibly, the vessel from Luther's house may also have had a mask-like decoration as documented at the pottery at Schmiedeberg (fig. 9, top middle). Up to now, the presence of polychrome glazed vessels in anthropomorphic form or with added masks in archaeological finds in Wittenberg has been extremely rare. These vessels would certainly have been very expensive to acquire, due to the high manufacturing costs. For this reason, they would most likely have been prized by their owners not only for their decorative function but also as prestigious possessions.

For the first time in Wittenberg, a larger number of drinking glasses was discovered during the excavations of Arsenalplatz, alongside the stoneware drinking and pouring vessels discussed above. The glass forms displayed great variety and, include club-shaped glasses, octagonal glasses with filament decoration, beakers, Roemers and Berkemeier glasses with bud decoration, glasses with engraved decoration and diamond cuts, as well as winged and snake-

13 The find distribution is similar for hard gray ware beakers in Wittenberg. 633 rim sherds, 238 body sherds and 355 base sherds were excavated which can unambiguously be attributed to beakers from a single pit within the area of the former castle. This is not the only waste pit which has its origins in drinking feasts in which the material discovered is composed to between 80 and 90 percent of beaker fragments. The remaining finds within the area of the old town are in comparison extremely modest. See Reetz, *Untersuchungen*, p. 18. A detailed article by the author on beakers from this area of the castle in relation to the utilization of this stoneware within the framework of life at court is in preparation. A presentation of the small number of beakers from the remainder of the old town: Kluttig-Altmann, *Grau*. **14** See Fouquet, *Festmahl*; Verblen, *Theorie*. **15** Meller, *Fundsache Luther*, p. 254, fig. p. 256. **16** Thoma, *Ausgrabungen*.

shaped glasses. A particularly outstanding highlight of the painted glass finds is an almost completely preserved large cylindrical beaker (*Humpen*) decorated with a coat of arms (fig. 10). It was discovered in a deep waste pit at the lower end of a plot in Bürgermeisterstraße. One side of the tankard displays the Electoral Saxon coat of arms, and the opposite side the coat of arms of the Margraviate of Brandenburg topped with a prince's hat, painted meticulously in very high quality.[17] The year 1585 is painted above the Saxon coat of arms and topped by the letters "F C V." The letters "H D (…) D" are written above the Brandenburg coat of arms. This type of large enamel-painted beakers decorated with coats of arms came into fashion during the second half of the sixteenth century. The early glasses were produced in Venice for the Northern Alpine market and imitated in Southern Germany a short time later.[18] The manufacture of enamel-painted tankards began in Bohemia in the early 1570s and at a slightly later point in Saxony.

This beaker found in Wittenberg is a particularly early specimen, and the painting's quality is excellent.[19] It was produced in glassworks either in Bohemia or Saxony. Other glasses of this type, for example in the Saxon group of so-called *Hofkellerei* beakers (court wine cellar beakers), were also decorated with the initials of the princes or their wives. The letters on the Wittenberg tankard, however, do not correspond to any initials of members of the families ruling in Saxony or Brandenburg whose coats of arms are presented on the glass; therefore, the meaning of these letter sequences remains unsolved. It is nevertheless possible to suggest an occasion for the combination of both coats of arms on this vessel: the marriage of the Saxon Prince Christian I to Sophie of Brandenburg on April 25, 1582. How the glass became incorporated into the town house inventory, however, remains unknown. The accompanying finds from the latrine pit include simple household pottery objects like those found in all the excavated properties in Wittenberg.

No further glass objects were discovered here. One possibility is that the homeowner purchased the valuable glass at a later point as an antique from a third party. Several other fragments of enamel-painted drinking glasses were discovered in a walled latrine in the northeast of Arsenalplatz. The decoration displays a wide variety of motifs. They include a blue goblet with representations of cherubs and lily of the valley blossoms. The cherubs' heads are painted and have been applied in raised form. Until now, only a very few examples of this type of glass have been found; the vessels were probably manufactured in Bohemia.[20] Another glass features geese traveling

in a boat with a fox. A glass jug with a similar motif is found in the collection of London's Victoria and Albert Museum.[21] The London jug was made in Bohemia in 1592. The "geese in a boat" motif, an illustration of a contemporary animal fable, was a favorite, long-lived pattern that still appeared on a glass as late as 1723.[22]

Christian motifs featured on enamel-painted glasses found in Wittenberg include the baptism of Christ, the sacrifice of Isaac,[23] and representations of the Apostle Paul and the evangelists Saint Matthew and probably also Saint Luke, from which only his symbol, the winged ox has been preserved. The glasses frequently have an inscribed banner with a more detailed description of the image and, on occasion, also the manufacture date.

Additional glasses excavated from other latrines and waste pits in Arsenalplatz display representations of couples arm in arm or standing opposite each other, with the man raising his glass in a toast to his wife.[24] Other motifs include a stag with a bridle, two rearing horses, and coats of arms. Up to now, the glasses found in Wittenberg seem to have been largely manufactured between the end of the sixteenth or beginning of the seventeenth centuries in Bohemia. Lilies of the valley are almost always shown framing these scenes.[25] This motif is described in *Lilium Convallium* (Lily of the Valley) by Protestant theologian Stephan Praetorius, published in 1578 as the symbol for the church cleansed by the blood of Christ. After drops of Jesus' blood had fallen onto the lily of the valley, they are said to have bloomed with new purity and clarity.[26] The lily of the valley symbol assumes even greater potency when paired with scenes of the crucifixion. Parallels to the glasses painted with lilies of the valley occur in archaeological finds in Annaburg[27] (Saxony-Anhalt) and Lüneburg[28] (Lower Saxony). In Wittenberg, hardly any glass objects have been discovered beyond the confines of Arsenalplatz.[29] This also holds true for the castle but is surely due only to missing evidence. Despite extensive searches, hardly any latrines or waste pits dating from the sixteenth century have been discovered at the castle. The absence of glass finds in other town plots can be explained by the particular preservation conditions and also the possibility that old pieces of glass were recycled.

The glass finds at Arsenalplatz, particularly the painted glass objects, provide an impressive illustration of the possibilities that several households had of displaying prestigious tableware toward the end of the sixteenth century. As indicated by a number of finds, a clear differentiation existed between preference and acquisition of these objects within the middle class. Painted glass was encountered

17 Quartered coat of arms, the heart shield bearing the Hohenzollern family coat of arms: Field 1 a gold-reinforced red eagle with golden bunches of clover against a silver/white background (Markgraviate Brandenburg), Field 2 a gold-reinforced red griffin against a silver/white background (Duchy of Pomerania); Field 3 a red-reinforced black lion against a golden background, surrounded by a twelve-lined border in silver red (Burggraviate of Nuremberg), and Field 4 the Zollern shield, quartered in silver and black (Hohenzollern family coat of arms). **18** Von Saldern, *German Enameled Glass*, pp. 37–39; Haase, *Sächsisches Glas*. **19** The earliest imperial eagle beaker manufactured in Bohemia dates from 1571 and is housed in the British Museum. See Hess, *Timothy Husband*, p. 214. **20** Steppuhn, *Die elegante Art*, pp. 134 f. **21** Von Saldern, *German Enameled Glass*, p. 109, fig. 161. **22** Ibid., p. 119, fig. 162. Similar glasses with representations of

the goose sermon originate from latrines in Lüneburg and Höxter, see Steppuhn, *Die elegante Art*, p. 91. **23** A glass from Bohemia (dated 1591) with the identical illustration is housed in the Kunstmuseum Düsseldorf. See Von Saldern, *German Enameled Glass*, p. 89, fig. 101. **24** A comparative glass was found in Lüneburg. See Steppuhn, *Die elegante Art*, p. 87. **25** A cylindrical painted glass featuring this type of lily of the valley motif was found in Annaburg, and a goblet in Lüneburg. On the former, see Eichhorn, *Frühneuzeitliche Glasfunde*, pp. 228 f. On the latter, see Steppuhn, *Die elegante Art*, pp. 132 f. **26** Düker, *Freudenchristentum*, p. 92. **27** Eichhorn, *Glasfunde*, pp. 228 f., fig. 11. Full version, see id., *Glasfunde aus Wittenberg*, pp. 49 and 126, color plate 4. **28** Steppuhn, *Die elegante Art*, pp. 132 f. **29** A small assemblage was found in the Luther House's garden. See the essay of Mirko Gutjahr in this volume.

Fig. 8
Fragment of a polychrome glazed vessel
in the shape of a woman's bust,
from the excavations at the site of the
Arsenalplatz, Wittenberg

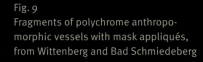

Fig. 9
Fragments of polychrome anthropomorphic vessels with mask appliqués,
from Wittenberg and Bad Schmiedeberg

Fig. 10 Large *Humpen* (tall cylindrical beaker) painted with
enamel with an image of the coat of arms of the Electorate
of Saxony and the Mark Brandenburg (on the reverse),
1585, from the excavations at the site of the Arsenalplatz,
Wittenberg

30 On this topic, see current research on the interior decoration of the electoral palace as reflected by written, visual and building sources: Neugebauer,
Wohnen.

in only a very small number of plots, particularly those in the vicinity
of the marketplace. By contrast, stem glasses and beakers made from
forest glass are present in almost all Arsenalplatz plots. Personal taste
on the part of homeowners began to play an ever-increasing role in
the choice of prestigious objects. This is documented in an exemplary
plot directly on Bürgermeisterstraße, in which a relatively high standard of living appears to have been possible. Nevertheless, hardly any
glass was excavated from the latrines and waste pits, even though
copious material was found in the neighboring plots.

Conclusion: Wealth and Representation at Court and in Town Houses

The objects presented here provide only a small insight into the material culture of Wittenberg in the sixteenth century. The finds
within the areas of domestic and table culture at the end of the medieval period document a clear prosperity gap between the citizens
and the court. At the beginning of the sixteenth century, the standard of prosperity increased in a few town houses, indicated by the
polychrome glazed floor tiles and polychrome stove tiles. Cranach's
household and, subsequently, Luther's house appear to have possessed an exceptional status. Cranach in particular achieved a comparable quality of household objects on Markt 4 to those of the electoral castle. This standard has not yet been substantiated for any
other properties, even those in the town's central areas.

Presumably, the development was predominantly triggered by
the establishment of Wittenberg University in 1502 and the increasing importance and extension of the electoral residence, which was
inseparable from the activities of Frederick the Wise. Between 1520
and about 1550, the middle-class standard of living increased further.
Among other aspects, this is documented by the painted glass windows in the town houses and the general substantial "building
boom" during this period that is clearly visible from an archaeological perspective. After the middle of the sixteenth century, the gap
in cultural prosperity between the aristocracy and middle classes
continued to shrink. Increasing numbers of Wittenberg citizens
could afford prestigious glasses and other luxury goods. These tendencies are naturally valid only for objects of everyday culture. Significant differences in comparison to the court would presumably
have been expressed in other types of possessions, such as valuable
paintings, furniture, and other forms of interior decoration.[30]

Surprisingly, the numerous finds within the categories of prestigious objects and table culture from the middle of the fifteenth
century onward—in particular during the earlier period under investigation—demonstrate that the intended result i.e. status display
was not always achieved with the help of imports. The decorated
stoneware beakers, polychrome floor tiles, and the majority of the
Wittenberg ceramic stove tiles were manufactured nearby in the
potters' settlement at Bad Schmiedeberg. Evidently, the representative function of these objects was created not through extended
trading routes but through high quality standards and the relatively
complex manufacturing process. On the other hand, in the case of
the decorated and undecorated beakers, their function as status indicators was probably communicated solely by their quantity.

BIBLIOGRAPHY

Düker, Eckhard (2013), *Freudenchristentum: Der Erbauungsschriftsteller Stephan Praetorius*. Göttingen. **Eichhorn**, Nicole (2014), Frühneuzeitliche Glasfunde aus Grabungen in Wittenberg, Naumburg und Annaburg. In: Meller, Harald (ed.), *Mitteldeutschland im Zeitalter der Reformation* (= Forschungsberichte des Landesmuseums für Vorgeschichte Halle. 4). Halle (Saale), pp. 223–231. **Eichhorn**, Nicole (2014), Glasfunde aus Wittenberg. Frühneuzeitliche Hohl- und Flachglasfunde aus Mitteldeutschland, dargestellt an ausgewählten Fundkomplexen aus Wittenberg, Naumburg und Annaburg. In: Meller, Harald (ed.), *Glas, Steinzeug und Bleilettern aus Wittenberg* (= Forschungsberichte des Landesmuseums für Vorgeschichte Halle. 5). Halle (Saale), pp. 9–148. **Fouquet**, Gerhard (1992), Das Festmahl in den oberdeutschen Städten des Spätmittelalters. Zu Form, Funktion und Bedeutung öffentlichen Konsums. In: *Archiv für Kulturgeschichte*, vol. 74, pp. 83–123. **Gräf**, Daniela (2008), Buntes aus Schloss Freudenstein. Glasierte Bodenfliesen als Zeugnis einer wechselhaften Baugeschichte. In: *Archaeo, Archäologie in Sachsen*, vol. 5, pp. 35–39. **Haase**, Gisela (1988), *Sächsisches Glas. Geschichte—Zentren—Dekorationen*. München. **Hennen**, Insa Christiane (2013), Reformation und Stadtentwicklung—Einwohner und Nachbarschaften. In: Lück, Heiner/Bünz, Enno/Helten, Leonhard/Kohnle, Armin/Sack, Dorothée/Stephan, Hans-Georg (eds.), *Das ernestinische Wittenberg: Stadt und Bewohner* (= Wittenberg-Forschungen. 2.1). Petersberg, pp. 33–76. **Hess**, Cathrine (1997), *Timothy Husband, European Glass in the J. Paul Getty Museum: Catalogue of the Collections*. The J. Paul Getty Museum. Los Angeles. **Kluttig-Altmann**, Ralf (2011), Baukeramik aus Wittenberger Grabungen: Archäologisches Fundmaterial als interdisziplinärer Gegenstand. In: Lück, Heiner/ Bünz, Enno/ Helten, Leonhard et al. (eds.), Das ernestinische Wittenberg: Universität und Stadt (1486–1547) (= Wittenberg-Forschungen. 1). Petersberg, pp. 154–163 and 223–225. **Kluttig-Altmann**, Ralf (2014), Auf breiter Basis – Fundanalysen aus Wittenberg. In: Meller, Harald (ed.), *Mitteldeutschland im Zeitalter der Reformation* (= Forschungsberichte des Landesmuseums für Vorgeschichte Halle. 4). Halle (Saale), pp. 179–194. **Kluttig-Altmann**, Ralf (2015), Archäologische Funde von Grundstücken der Familie Cranach in Wittenberg. In: Lück, Heiner/Bünz, Enno/Helten, Leonhard/Kohnle, Armin/Sack, Dorothée/Stephan, Hans-Georg (eds.), *Das ernestinische Wittenberg: Spuren Cranachs in Schloss und Stadt* (= Wittenberg-Forschungen. 3). Petersberg, pp. 363–399. **Kluttig-Altmann**, Ralf (2015), Grau, aber interessant. Ein gehobenes Wittenberger Geschirr des Spätmittelalters im "used look". In: Meller, Harald (ed.), *Fokus: Wittenberg. Die Stadt und ihr Lutherhaus* (= Forschungsberichte des Landesmusems für Vorgeschichte Halle. 7). Halle (Saale), pp. 19–40. **Kottmann**, Aline (2007), Materielle Kultur und soziale Affiliation. Erkenntnismöglichkeiten hinsichtlich einer sozialen Grenzziehung aus archäologischer Perspektive. In: Knefelkamp, Ulrich/Bosselmann-Cyran, Kristian (eds.), *Grenze und Grenzüberschreitungen im Mittelalter*. Berlin, pp. 81–92. **Krabath**, Stefan (2012), Die Entwicklung der Keramik im Freistaat Sachsen vom späten Mittelalter bis in das 19. Jahrhundert. Ein Überblick. In: Smolnik, Regina (ed.), *Keramik in Mitteldeutschland—Stand der Forschung und Perspektiven* (= Veröffentlichungen des Landesamtes für Archäologie. 57). Dresden, pp. 35–172. **Mechelk**, Harald W. (1970), *Stadtkernforschung in Dresden* (= Forschungen zur ältesten Entwicklung Dresdens. 4). Berlin. **Meller**, Harald (ed.) (2008), *Fundsache Luther. Archäologen auf den Spuren des Reformators*. Halle (Saale). **Neuge-**

bauer, Anke (2015), Wohnen im Wittenberger Schloss—Zur Nutzung und Ausstattung der fürstlichen Gemächer, Stuben und Kammern. In: Lück, Heiner/Bünz, Enno/Helten, Leonhard et. al. (eds.), *Das ernestinische Wittenberg: Spuren Cranachs in Schloss und Stadt* (= Wittenberg-Forschungen. 3). Petersberg, pp. 315–333. **Reetz**, Johanna (2014), Die Untersuchungen auf dem Hof des Wittenberger Schlosses. In: Meller, Harald (ed.), *Archäologie in Wittenberg I. Das Schloss der Kurfürsten und der Beginn der frühneuzeitlichen Stadtbefestigung von Wittenberg* (= Archäologie in Sachsen-Anhalt. Sonderband 22). Halle (Saale), pp. 9–18. **Rode**, Holger (2000), Neue Untersuchungen zur Keramik der "Falke-Gruppe". Ein Beitrag zur Erforschung der spätmittelalterlichen Steinzeugproduktion in Sachsen und der Oberlausitz. In: *Keramos*, vol. 169, pp. 27–56. **Saldern**, Axel von (1965), *German Enameled Glass. The Edwin J. Beinecke Collection and Related Pieces*. New York. **Steppuhn**, Peter (2003), Die elegante Art, Getränke zu genießen. In: Ring, Edgar (ed.), *Glaskultur in Niedersachsen. Tafelgeschirr und Haushaltglas vom Mittelalter bis zur frühen Neuzeit*. Husum, pp. 110–137. **Steppuhn**, Peter (2003), Der (un)getrübte Blick nach draußen. In: Ring, Edgar (ed.), *Glaskultur in Niedersachsen. Tafelgeschirr und Haushaltglas vom Mittelalter bis zur frühen Neuzeit*. Husum. **Thoma**, Winfried (2001), Die archäologischen Ausgrabungen im Umfeld des Rathauses von Penig. In: *Arbeits- und Forschungsberichte zur sächsischen Bodendenkmalpflege*, vol. 43, pp. 213–267. **Verblen**, Thorstein (2007), *Theorie der feinen Leute. Eine ökonomische Untersuchung der Institutionen*. Frankfurt am Main. **Witzleben**, Elisabeth von (1977), *Bemalte Glasscheiben. Volkstümliches Leben auf Kabinett- und Bierscheiben*. München.

THE REFORMATION MOVEMENT

The Reformation, in its initial phase, was an urban event. Cities were places of humanism, and inhabitants were usually capable of reading. Also, the Protestant ideas often corresponded to the bourgeois mindset. Rulers often embraced Reformation doctrine as a political opportunity. Many of the imperial cities were surrounded by foreign dominations. By changing their faith, the imperial cities marked their independence, proving their autonomy vis-à-vis other powers.

After the 1525 Peasants' War, the princes made the Reformation their own concern. Their commitment made it clear that they were no longer ready to tolerate the encroachment of the Roman Catholic Church on their territories. The decision in favor of the Reformation was not always a tumultuous and turbulent one. Frequently, the transition was a lengthy and bureaucratic process.

Introduction of
the Reformation
in cities and territories

● 1520–1525
● 1526–1531
● 1532–1537
● 1538–1542
● 1543–1548
● 1549–1554

■ Archbishoprics in 1500
■ University towns in 1500
— Border of the Holy
Roman Empire

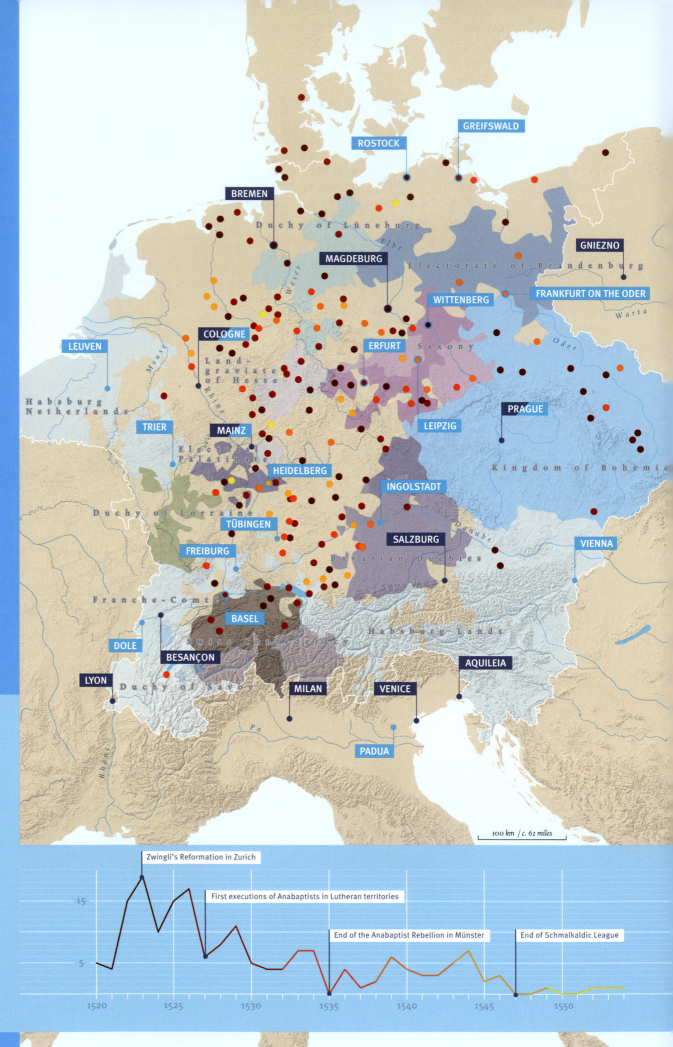

Zwingli's Reformation in Zurich

First executions of Anabaptists in Lutheran territories

End of the Anabaptist Rebellion in Münster

End of Schmalkaldic League

100 km / c. 62 miles

CHRISTOPHER SPEHR

Martin Luther and the Protestant Church Service

The pivotal issue of the Reformation in the sixteenth century was the worship service, and it was through changes to services that the Reformation received its true shape. That which had been discussed and asserted theologically became concrete and visible for the Christian congregation in the space of the church. The development of the liturgical pattern, therefore, became a central concern of the Reformation movement. Their main demands were the introduction of a Protestant sermon, the celebration of the Eucharist with both bread and wine, services in the vernacular, and the abolition of the Roman Mass. Only once these demands had been fulfilled in the local community would one consider the Reformation as introduced. This process was dependent upon spontaneous, often stormy beginnings and tough debates mainly among the civic or territorial rulers. The implementation usually proceeded over the course of a longer process and took place with various intensities from place to place. This led to a number of different, and at times competing, liturgical orders of service that would become the basis of Reformation church law.[1]

Martin Luther and his theology of Reformation were the impulses for this process of revolutionizing the whole church system of cultic mediation of salvation and representation. But what did this process look like in practice? What contribution did Luther make? And how were his ideas implemented in theological and liturgical practice? In what follows, an orienting definition of the term *Gottesdienst* (service of God) is contextualized biographically in Luther's liturgical horizon of experience, in order to analyze his theological critique of the Mass. Then an overview of the first Protestant initiatives in church services is given. These flow into Luther's order of service. A short summary brings the investigation to a close.[2]

The Term *Gottesdienst*

The German word *Gottesdienst* (service of God) became widespread from the thirteenth century on as a translation of the Latin word *cultus* in the form of the Old High German genitive connection, "gods dienst" (God's service). Luther and the Reformation then remodeled the meaning of this word in a significant way. In Protestantism it developed into a central liturgical term signifying the communal and ritual celebration and prevailed over the term *Mass*. Since the Second Vatican Council, the word previously limited to Protestant churches is also beeing used in the Catholic church.[3]

For Luther and his contemporaries, the *Gottesdienst* was never limited to the specifically liturgical actions of the congregation, but was rather a synonym for the worship of God in general. Since Luther understood the whole of a Christian's life as in service of God, *Gottesdienst* became the key term for expressing Christian faith and life in general. The Reformer characterized *Gottesdienst* as worship and fear of God and identified in it the shortest description of the relationship between God and humanity. This relationship is expressed in terms of fundamental theology as faith. In terms of ethics, the relationship is expressed in Luther's doctrine of the three estates, and its liturgical expression is the worshiping process of the celebrating congregation.

Coming from this general identification, Luther paid attention to the specific terms *Gottesdienst* or "cultus," which he used synonymously with the terms "Mass," "missa," and "communion." These were also sometimes interpreted with terms like "gathering," "office of the servant and pastor," or "the word of God."[4] He described the liturgical order of service through the phrase "Ordnung Gottesdienst," which he used in the two German titles of his three writings on church services: *Concerning the Order of Public Worship*[5] (German, 1523), *An Order of Mass and Communion for the Church at Wittenberg*[6] (Latin, 1523), and *German Mass and Order of Service*[7] (German, 1526). But before the main thoughts of these writings can be expounded, we must remember the horizon of the church in the late Middle Ages, the church which formed Luther.

---

1 See Smend, *Messen*; *Die evangelischen Kirchenordnungen*; as well as more generally Cornehl, *Gottesdienst*; Leaver, *Gottesdienst*. **2** For more detail, see Spehr, *Gottesdienst bei Martin Luther*. **3** See Bieritz, *Liturgik*, pp. 5 f.; Dondelinger, *Gottesdienst*. **4** See Kalb, *Liturgie*, p. 363. **5** *LW* 53, 11–14. Original: "Von Ordnung Gottesdiensts in der Gemeinde" *WA* 12, 35–37. **6** *LW* 53, 19–40. Original: "Formula missae et communionis pro Ecclesia Wittembergensi" *WA* 12, 205–220. **7** *LW* 53, 61–90. Original: "Deutsche Messe und Ordnung Gottesdiensts" *WA* 19, 70–113.

The Late Middle Ages as the Horizon of Luther's Experience

Everyday life in the late Middle Ages was religious through and through. Churches and chapels dominated every village and townscape. One would meet priests, monks, nuns, and other religious people in large numbers on the streets and not just in the churches. Bells rang for times of prayer and called people to the church services. Church attendance on Sundays and other holy days was compulsory. The center of liturgical life was the Eucharist (Mass, from the Latin *missa*, "sending"). In the Eucharist, the death and resurrection of Jesus Christ were understood to be sacramentally realized. The priest would quietly read the Latin text of the Mass and consecrate the bread and wine into the body and blood of Christ. The lay believers, distinguished from the celebrating clerics by lack of ordination, received in the distribution (the communion) the body, while the blood of Christ remained the privilege of the priests. Often, the laity would only observe the communion as bystanders, or indeed miss it entirely.[8]

In the Middle Ages, the Mass was understood as a sacrifice. The priest, through the authority given in his consecration, became a mediator between God and humanity. He mediated by bringing the sacrificial gift of the body and blood of Christ to God at the altar. The Mass was, therefore, a priestly cultic action whose aim was to make God gracious and forgiving. In order to effectively carry out this action, the priest had to be free from sin and was not allowed to make a mistake in the Eucharistic prayer. If the priest made a mistake in the liturgy of the Mass, this was deemed a terrible sin. If he celebrated the Mass in sin, this counted as a deadly sin.[9] In the imagination of believers of the Middle Ages, the Mass was more effective than every prayer. Thus, numerous Mass stipends were created. These could range from ensuring the regular holding of Mass for a departed soul up to the donation of an altar and priest's stipend for the dead members of a whole family. Through this practice of Mass, going far beyond the main Mass on Sundays, the larger churches were full of altars and crouded with priests.

Luther grew up in this religious world with its numerous liturgical traditions and spiritual exercises. The young Martin Luther experienced his first masses in the Church of St. George in his hometown of Mansfeld, where he lived from 1484 to 1497. There he saw the priests celebrating Mass in colorful vestments. Luther's father, Hans Luder, was a "Vierherr," (town quarter's mayor) one of the four representatives of the town folk, and was actively involved in church matters. For instance, in 1491 Martin Luther experienced his father making the donation of an altar for the Church of St. George, which had been damaged by fire in 1489. As a pupil in the neighboring town's school, Martin became familiar with liturgical antiphonal singing. Together with his fellow pupils, he performed in the choir, singing pieces such as the *Introit* (sung opening of the liturgy), the *Kyrie eleison* (Lord, have mercy), and the *Gloria in excelsis Deo* (Glory to God in the highest) in regular and exceptional services.[10]

Upon switching to a school in Magdeburg in 1497, Luther encountered church life in a large town for the first time. The center of that life was the rich liturgy of the cathedral church. Luther was

Fig. 1 Martin Luther, *Ein Sermon von dem newen Testament. das ist von der heyligen Messe* (Sermon on the New Testament, that is, the Holy Mass), Wittenberg 1520

probably educated at the cathedral school next door. Living in a kind of dormatory for pupils, he learned various forms of prayer and devotion from the "Brethren of the Common Life," tradition of spirituality in the *devotio moderna* movement which emanated from the Netherlands. Further experiences of church services were gathered as a pupil of the St. George School in Eisenach, where he moved in 1498. Alongside the services in the town church, he encountered the Daily Offices and similar forms of prayer in the nearby Franciscan monastery. From 1501, he participated in the riches of church life in the important city of Erfurt, while a student at the university. He lived in the Georgenburse (a student residence), which had monastic characteristics.

When he entered the monastery of the Erfurt Augustinian Hermits in 1505, Luther left the secular estate of a layperson behind him and entered the religious estate. From then on, Masses and prayer times structured Luther's daily life. His experience of liturgy spanned a breadth of forms, from the monastic Daily Offices to the daily conventual Mass, the Monday requiem Mass, and private, or votive, masses, as well as celebratory services such as the Benediction of the Blessed Sacrament and processions.[11] In 1507, Luther the monk was consecrated as a priest in the Erfurt Cathedral. Now he himself participated in the monastery's Service of the Altar, which was regarded as the highest service of all. Luther had become a mediator between God and humanity. From then on, he had a duty to offer God the sacrifice of the Mass. Luther celebrated his first Mass shortly after his consecration as priest in the Erfurt Black Monastery in early 1507. His father and relatives from Mansfeld traveled to attend. Looking back at the first Mass, Luther reports that on reading the Eucharistic prayer, the heart of the liturgy, he faltered. Suddenly, he saw himself before God without a mediator, and doubts arose within him about his own worthiness. Full of fear, he interrupted the prayer, and his assisting superior admonished him to continue the Mass. Luther's reverence for the sacrifice and prayer and his fear of not being worthy of the Service of the Altar as a priest can be heard in this narrative many years later.[12]

It was not necessary to study theology to become a priest. However, his monastery superior determined he should undertake some academic study. Luther, therefore, undertook such studies, which he completed in 1512 with a theological doctorate. Part of the degree was training in how to preach, which led to him preaching in the monastery. From 1514 onwards, he was preaching in the Wittenberg town church, so he had practical experience of Sunday Mass, the main service, and additional daily services.[13] It is, therefore, no surprise that it was the church service—or, more precisely, the Mass with its practice of sacrifice—where Luther's theological insights into the doctrine of justification were concretized.

Luther's Criticism of the Roman Mass

In the framework of the development of Luther's reformed understanding of God and humanity, the Mass experienced a fundamentally new interpretation. He first addressed the theme at length in *A Treatise on the New Testament, that is, the Holy Mass,*[14] which was printed at the beginning of August 1520 (fig. 1). The fourteen surviving prints show the wide reach of this foundational pamphlet. Luther dealt here with the core of the Mass, the Eucharist, and reformulated its biblical basis using Jesus' Words of Institution in the New Testament. Luther argued that because Jesus' words at his last meal were his testament and, thus, God's binding promise to the people, they should, as God's gift, precede all human activity. For God's Word is before all other words. Since for Luther the Word is God's ultimate medium and object of revelation, the Words of Institution become foundationally significant as legacy and testament of Christ.[15] As a "gospel in a nutshell," these words are assurance, promise, and the word of forgiveness that God in Jesus Christ gives as a blessing to his church by faith. From this theological center of the Mass, Luther develops his theo-

logical critique of the contemporary Mass: "If we desire to observe mass properly and to understand it, then we must surrender everything that the eyes behold and that the senses suggest—be it vestments, bells, songs, ornaments, prayers, processions, elevations, prostrations, or whatever happens in the mass—until we first grasp and thoroughly ponder the words of Christ, by which he performed and instituted the mass and commanded us to perform it."[16]

In his *Treatise on the New Testament,* Luther radically identifies three abuses of the Roman Mass that together, he stated, had destroyed the essence of the Mass. First, the Words of Institution were spoken by the priest in a low voice and, therefore, kept from the laity. Thus, the most important goods—testament and faith—were lost to them. Second, the Mass had become a good work through which people desired to do God service, but this is in fact impossible because of the gift-character of the testament. Third, the Mass had been made a sacrifice brought to God, which completely contradicts the use of the sacrament for the salvation of the believers. In an inversion of the understanding of the Mass in the late Middle Ages, Luther was not concerned with a service of humanity to God. The Mass was not about the humans achieving rightousness through good works and the sacrifice of the Mass, but about the consoling promise of the forgiveness of all sins, of grace, and of eternal life, and thus about God's service toward us: "in the mass we give nothing to Christ, but only receive from him."[17] On the basis of this christological and soteriological insight, Luther could no longer see the Mass as an active sacrifice or work of the human, or of the church.

Thus, for Luther it was the Roman doctrine of the sacrifice of the Mass, and the corresponding practice of the Mass, which was perhaps *the* central point of disagreement with the Catholic Church. For example, he still emphasized in 1537, in the *Smalcald Articles,*[18] a Lutheran confessional text, that the Mass under the papacy was the greatest and most terrible abhorrence which to strive against the doctrine of justification because it turned the relations on their head. Luther formulated his disagreement with the Roman understanding of the Mass in a sharp and uncompromising tone: "Thus we are and remain eternally separated and opposed to one another."[19]

However, if the divine gift-event is put at the center of the Mass, then the Mass is true service of God in the Protestant sense. In 1520, Luther had already emphasized in his *Treatise on the New Testament* that "henceforth, therefore, there is to be no other external order for the service of God except the mass. And where the mass is used, there is true worship; even though there be no other form, with singing, organ playing, bell ringing, vestments, ornaments, and gestures. For everything of this sort is an addition invented by men."[20]

8 See for example Bünz/Kühne, *Alltag und Frömmigkeit.* **9** See Simon, *Messopfertheologie,* pp. 131–164; Angenendt, *Offertorium.* **10** On Luther's time at school and as a student, see Brecht, *Martin Luther,* pp. 21–32. **11** On the monastery and prayer service of the young Luther, see ibid., pp. 70–77; Odenthal: *Liturgie,* pp. 208–250. **12** See Brecht, *Martin Luther,* pp. 78–82. For Luther's religious perfection, see Hamm, *Naher Zorn.* **13** Luther began preaching in 1510 in the monastery. See Brecht, *Martin Luther,* pp. 150–154; Spehr, *Predigten*

Luthers. **14** *LW* 35, 79–111; "Sermon von dem Neuen Testament, das ist von der heiligen Messe," *WA* 6, 353–378. **15** See Beutel, *Anfang,* pp. 87–130. **16** *LW* 35, 82; *WA* 6, 355, 21–25. **17** *LW* 35, 93; *WA* 6, 364, 22 f. See also Wendebourg, *Essen zum Gedächtnis,* p. 47. **18** *The Smalcald Articles.* In: Triglot Concordia: The Symbolical Books of the Evangelical Lutheran Church: German-Latin-English, St. Louis, 1921. Available: http://bocl.org?SA; *WA* 50, 192–254. **19** Ibid., Part II, Article II, 10; *WA* 50, 204, 15 f. **20** *LW* 35, 81; *WA* 6, 354, 24–28.

In 1520 Luther devised the coordinates for his evangelical understanding of the church service. He himself, however, did not introduce any liturgical changes. In the *Treatise on the New Testament*, he argued that the Words of Institution in the Eucharistic prayers should be spoken aloud and intelligibly for the communicant church. He also expressed the wish that the Mass be celebrated in German.[21] And already in the fall of 1519, he suggested in *The Blessed Sacrament of the Holy and True Body of Christ, and the Brotherhoods* that the chalice should be given to the laity in the Eucharist, thus practicing the communion of the Eucharist in both forms, which was previously limited to priests.[22] Nevertheless, Luther avoided implementing the liturgical suggestions and hoped for changes wrought through the bishops or a general council.[23]

With the conclusion of the Diet of Worms in 1521, and proclamation of the *Edict of Worms* against Luther and his followers, these hopes were dashed. Luther, now hidden away at Wartburg Castle, developed a plan to celebrate the Eucharist in both forms and to celebrate private masses only with the church, once he had returned to Wittenberg from exile. While Luther expressed his concerns for theological enlightenment through the written word, in Wittenberg there were debates and sermons against the Mass in its previous form. In the end, the Augustinian hermit Gabriel Zwilling and the theology professor Andreas Bodenstein von Karlstadt took practical steps to change the services. The Eucharist was distributed in house masses in both forms from the end of September 1521 onward. In the Wittenberg Augustinian monastery, private masses were abolished, and in the town church the Mass services were either disturbed or even completely obstructed.[24]

Luther reacted to these changes in the late fall of 1521 with the Latin writing *De abroganda Missa privata sententia*[25] ("The Abrogation of the Private Mass") and the German version, *Vom Missbrauch der Messe*[26] ("The Misuse of the Mass"). Here he criticized the church's understanding of the office of priest and admonished priests to either proclaim the gospel as preachers or to end their career. Apart from this, Luther emphasized again the gift-character of the Mass and exhorted priests to hold the Mass according to the example of Christ and limit the celebration of the Mass to Sundays. In addition, he advised that the Roman canon of the Mass, with its sacrificial understanding resting on human laws, and its private masses and masses for the dead, should be opposed. However, in view of the weak in the church, he recommended proceeding carefully. The court secretary, Georg Spalatin, first held these and other manuscripts of Luther's back until December 1521, so they appeared in print in January 1522. They, therefore, had no influence on the accelerating development in Wittenberg and the surrounding area.[27]

The culmination of that development was the first Evangelical service that Karlstadt celebrated on Christmas 1521 in the Wittenberg chapter church. He held the Mass in his street clothes and, reading the Words of Institution in German, distributed the Eucharist in both forms to all believers. For the host and the chalice to be placed in the hands of the communicants was not only unheard of for the congregation and an expression of Protestant freedom, but also

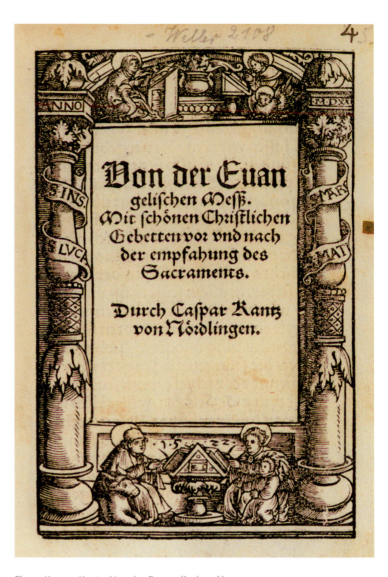

Fig. 2 Kaspar Kantz, *Von der Evangelischen Messz.*
Mit schönen Christlichen Gebetten von und nach der empfahung des Sacraments (On the Evangelical Mass, with beautiful Christian prayers before and after partaking the sacrament), Tübingen 1524

an obvious scandal for those of Catholic persuasion.[28] The preacher Martin Reinhart of Jena also distributed the Eucharist in both forms at Christmas 1521. Additional places, such as Eilenburg, Lochau, Hirschfeld, and Schmiedeberg, followed by the time of the feast of Epiphany in 1522.[29] On January 24, 1522, the Wittenberg council finally passed "a praiseworthy ordinance," the pioneering Protestant town ordinance.[30] On the one hand, this ordinance put up some opposition to the radical demands for the reform of the Mass put forward by Zwilling and Karlstadt. On the other hand, it demanded the abolition of pictures and altars in the churches and allowed the celebration of the Eucharist in both forms. Article 14 of this ordinance named the liturgical pieces of the Mass that should be kept or omitted. Those omitted were the spiritual songs, or *sequens*; the *canon maior*; the *canon minor*; and the concluding formula, *ite missa est* ("Go, you are sent"). Thus, here for the first time, a liturgy reform was commissioned by the secular rulers, who in this case mandated according to Luther's demands.[31]

Concerned about the radical developments in Wittenberg, Luther returned quickly from Wartburg Castle in order to intervene in the situation by holding eight sermons in March 1522, the so-called *invocavit sermons*.[32] He condemned the radical changes because they took place without the permission of the elector and without consideration of the weak in spirit. It was not the external form of the liturgical ceremony that was decisive for him, but the inner preparedness of the congregation. On the basis of Christian freedom, the liturgical ordinances seemed to Luther a human invention that should only be changed when they darkened God's Word.

Luther, therefore, repealed various liturgical changes, as he emphasized in the writing from April 1522, *Receiving Both Kinds in the Sacrament*.[33] The Mass should again be held in Latin by a priest wearing traditional vestments and with the elevation of the host. Furthermore, the Words of Institution should again be spoken in a soft voice and the laity should only be given the sacrament in one form. Outside of the Sunday Mass, however, Luther allowed the distribution of the Eucharist in both forms, disallowed private masses (that is, when communicants were not present), and recommended that priests leave out all statements concerning the sacrifice of the Mass in the liturgy, in accordance with the Wittenberg town liturgical ordinances.[34]

Luther himself aimed to make a broad impact, raising consciousness of the gospel in the ordinary people of the church. Therefore, he concentrated his efforts on the preaching of the Word of God and implemented that which he demanded: the true and right *Gottesdienst* accomplished through the office of preaching appointed by Christ. In the time that followed, two groups debated against the Reformer: on the one side were the opponents from the old faith who wanted to hold onto the Roman teaching about the sacrifice of the Mass and its corresponding traditional practice. On the other side were radical reformers who increasingly taught and demanded an uncompromising understanding of the church service, based on early Christianity. Luther saw himself as needing to develop and practically implement his theology in distinction from both these positions.[35]

The Creation of Protestant Orders of Service

While Luther was carefully allowing changes in Wittenberg in 1522, the experimentation with and change to the liturgy was more forthright in other places, such as Basel, Breslau, and Augsburg. Probably the oldest surviving Protestant formulation of a Mass was drafted by Kaspar Kantz in 1522. He was Prior of the Carmelite monastery in Nördlingen and changed his conventual Mass into a Protestant

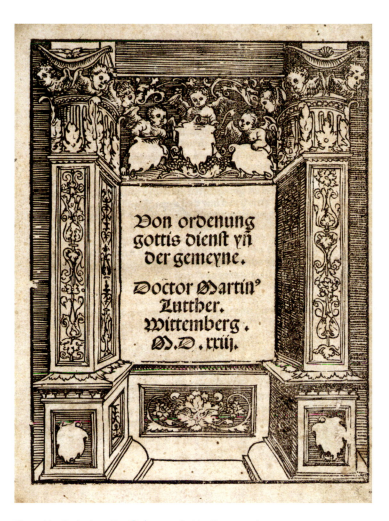

Fig. 3 Martin Luther, *Von Ordenung Gottis dienst yn der gemeyne* (On the Order of Divine Service in the Congregation), Wittenberg 1523

celebration of the Eucharist. In 1522—1524 at the latest—Kantz's order was printed with the title *Von der Evangelisch Messz* ("On the Evangelical Mass") (fig. 2).[36]

In Allstedt in Thuringia, Thomas Müntzer introduced a German Mass at Easter in 1523. It was focused on the praise and thanks of the church and oriented strongly toward the traditional liturgy. However, from the canon of the Mass only the Words of Institution were retained. The truly new element was the use of German all the way through. In his widely circulated writing of 1523, *Deutsches Kirchenamt* ("German Church Office"), Müntzer developed the services of Matins, Lauds, and Vespers, but concentrated on the main festivals of the church year, abolishing all celebrations of the saints and

21 See *LW* 35, 90 f.; *WA* 6, 362, 13–35. Until the Second Vatican Council, the "canon missae," in which the words of consecration or institution were spoken, were spoken quietly and in Latin. **22** *LW* 35, 49–74, here: 50 f.; *WA* 2, 742–758, here: 742, 24–743, 1. **23** See Spehr, *Luther und das Konzil*, pp. 184–194. **24** See Bubenheimer, *Luthers Stellung*, pp. 161–169; Kaufmann, *Anfang*, pp. 217–221; on contextualization, see Spehr, *Entstehung des evangelischen Kirchenwesens*. **25** *WA* 8, 413–476. **26** *LW* 36, 133–230; *WA* 8, 482–563. For more detail, see Simon, *Messopfertheologie*, pp. 327–385. **27** See *LW* 36, 130; *WA* 8, 407 f. **28** See Krentz, *Ritualwandel*, pp. 154–169. **29** See among others the letter of Justus Jonas to Johann Lang, [Wittenberg] January 8, 1522. In: Müller:

Wittenberger Bewegung, pp. 164–167, here: p. 165. **30** Critical edition in: Delius, *Martin Luther*, pp. 525–529. **31** Delius, *Martin Luther*, pp. 527, 22–528, 5. On the changes to the Mass and the Wittenberg movement in general, see Brecht, *Martin Luther*, vol. 2, pp. 34–53; Kaufmann, *Geschichte der Reformation*, pp. 380–392; Krentz, *Ritualwandel*, pp. 143–214. **32** On the *invocavit sermons*, see *LW* 51, 70–100; *WA* 10/III, 1–64 and Spehr, *Invokavitpredigten*. **33** *LW* 36, 237–267; "Von beider Gestalt des Sakraments zu nehmen," *WA* 10/II, 1, 11–41. **34** See Schwarz, *Luther*, pp. 123 f.; Krentz, *Ritualwandel*, pp. 215–242. **35** On the debate in Wittenberg, see Krentz, *Ritualwandel*, pp. 243–324. **36** *Die evangelischen Kirchenordnungen*, vol. 12, pp. 285–288.

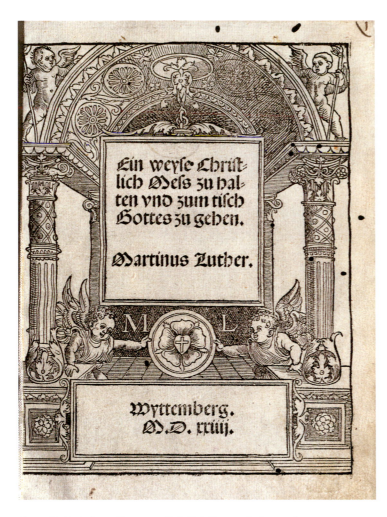

Fig. 4 Martin Luther, Ein weyse Christlich Mess zu halten und zu tisch Gottes zu gehen (A way to hold Christian Mass and to go to God's table), Wittenberg 1524

a formulated liturgy. The basic structure of the morning and evening services should be the Old or New Testament reading, an exposition of the text read, and intercession. The thanks and praise of the church should be expressed in the singing of psalms and responses (*responsorien*). As participants in the daily gathering, Luther imagined priests and pupils who would voluntarily take part. Finally, Luther offered suggestions for the Scripture readings in the Sunday services of the church, underlining the concentration of liturgical practice on the read and preached Word. Structural changes in the service could emerge, said Luther, in time. Christian freedom should not be endangered by human rules. However, one thing he deemed immovable: "We can spare everything except the Word. Again, we profit by nothing as much as by the Word."[41] In early 1523, Luther also published a German baptismal liturgy: *The Order of Baptism*.[42]

Because the emerging Protestant churches were pressuring Luther for concrete suggestions for how services should be held, in the fall of 1523, he drafted a Mass in Latin, the *Formula Missae et Communionis pro Ecclesia Wittembergensi* ("An Order of Mass and Communion for the Church in Wittenberg") (German: fig. 4). In this first liturgical order of service, Luther emphasized programmatically that "in all these matters we will want to beware lest we make binding what should be free … For these rites are supposed to be for Christians, i.e., children of the 'free woman' [Gal. 4:31], who observe them voluntarily and from the heart, but are free to change them how and whenever they may wish. Therefore, it is not in these matters that anyone should either seek or establish as law some indispensable form by which he might ensnare or harass consciences."[43]

In the *Formula Missae*, Luther nevertheless did offer concrete suggestions for the form of services: from the introit to the readings, sermon and celebration of the Eucharist, and the closing blessing. When he did this, he did it in order to show how one could hold Mass and go to Communion in a God-fearing way. He wanted to continue to celebrate the liturgy in Latin and only have the sermon in German. Yet, he expressly recommended the singing of spiritual songs in German and, since there were hardly any church songs in German in 1523, composed his own.[44] He thought liturgical garments and the form of the space in which services were celebrated to be negligible. Instead, he emphasized that, since the Holy Scriptures did not prescribe anything in external matters, the freedom of the Spirit should reign according to the character of the place, time, and people.

A consequence of the free approach to the liturgy was the creation of numerous new orders of service. Luther himself held back for a long time and first tried holding the Sunday Town Church Mass in German on October 29, 1525.[45] The German Mass was finally introduced in Wittenberg at Christmas 1525, four years after Karlstadt's first attempt.[46] Luther's writing *German Mass and Order of Service*,

demanding Gregorian chorales sung in unison, in German.[37] His writing from 1524, *Deutsche Evangelische Messe* ("German Evangelical Mass") finally contained an order for Mass.[38] In Worms, Strasbourg, Nuremberg, and other places, orders of service were also created from 1523 on.[39]

Luther himself announced in March 1523 that he would introduce Protestant changes. The daily masses, abolished by Karlstadt in the town church, would be replaced by services with sermons. He laid out the reasons behind his suggestions for the form of daily church services in *Von Ordnung Gottesdienst in der Gemeinde* ("On the Order of Service in the Church") (fig. 3).[40] Here Luther developed his thinking according to the principle that nothing should be done in the service other than furthering the Word of God. Using this principle, he made suggestions for the weekly church services, albeit without proposing

37 Franz, *Thomas Müntzer*, pp. 30–155. **38** Ibid., pp. 161–206. **39** On the historical development in the 1520s, see Smend, *Messen*; Niebergall, *Agende*; Pahl, *Coena Domini*. **40** LW 53, 11–14; WA 12, 35–37. **41** LW 53, 14; WA 12, 37, 29 f. **42** LW 53, 96–103; WA 12, 42–48. **43** LW 53, 30 f.; WA 12, 214, 14–20. **44** On Luther as hymn writer and on the first *Wittenberg hymnbook* of 1525,

see Jenny, *Luthers geistliche Lieder*. On the significance of music for Luther, see Schilling, *Musik*. See also the essay by Johannes Schilling in this volume. **45** See WA 17 1, 459, 15–33 (sermon delivered October 29, 1525). **46** See Brecht, *Martin Luther*, vol. 2, pp. 246–253.

Fig. 5 Martin Luther, Deudsche Messe und ordnung Gottisdiensts (German Mass and Order of Service), 1526, frontispiece.
Registered as part of the UNESCO world documentary heritage "Memory of the World" in 2015

Fig. 6 Martin Luther, Deudsche Messe und ordnung Gottisdiensts (The German Mass and Order of Divine Service), 1526, beginning of the communion formula. Registered as part of the UNESCO world documentary heritage "Memory of the World" in 2015

liturgical structure was innovative and, briefly, as follows: a song or psalm, *Kyrie eleison*, offertory prayer, reading of the Epistle, song, reading of the Gospel, hymn of faith, sermon, paraphrase of the Lord's Prayer, exhortation to communicants, Word of Institution and distribution of the bread, Word of Institution and distribution of the chalice, final collect, and Aaronite blessing.

More effective than the liturgical order itself was the foreword in which Luther repeated his basic theological position concerning the church service, emphasizing regional uniformity and placing the notion of freedom in the service of one's neighbor.[49] The liturgical freedom ends where the conscience of the members of the church is troubled. Based on his practice in Wittenberg, Luther presented three forms of the church service: He thought the Latin Mass according to the pattern of his *Formula Missae* was a linguistically universal form of service appropriate for the school and university context. The German Mass according to the pattern which Luther explained in his writing was for "simple laypersons" and should contribute to the church's practice of faith. Both forms should be accessible publicly in the churches and promote faith in Christ. A "third way" of gathering for a service is valid for "those who want to be Christians in earnest and who profess the gospel with hand and mouth."[50] The house-church form of fellowship, oriented upon the original Christian church structures where everything was focused on the Word, on prayer, and on love, remained a vision for Luther. He simply did not have enough people for this type of church service.[51]

Even with his *German Mass*, Luther did not try to establish a new norm, but remained faithful to his understanding of the service, which was critical of any legalism, as he noted at the end of the tract: "In short, this or any other order shall be so used that whenever it becomes an abuse, it shall be straightway abolished and replaced by another."[52]

Conclusion

Luther's *German Mass* was introduced officially in Electoral Saxony in 1526 on the instruction of Elector John. It was also implemented beyond the region, but did not remain the only order of service.[53] In Southern Germany and Switzerland, these orders of service followed the preaching service rather than the Mass, not least because of the dispute over the Eucharist between Luther and Huldrych Zwingli. But also in Northern and Central Germany, Luther's suggestions were not closely implemented. Yet, the Brunswick Church Ordinance of 1528, written by Johannes Bugenhagen, and the Brandenburg-Nuremberg Church Ordinance of 1533 included revised versions of Luther's

which appeared in print at the beginning of 1526, was the accompanying publicity of this far-reaching change (figs. 5 and 6).[47] The occasion of this most significant of Luther's writings on the church service was the elector's efforts to acchieve regional uniformity, the churches' desire for authoritative orientation, problems with the musical aspects of a German-language service, and the keen reforming attitude of the new Elector of Saxony, John, who reigned from 1525. The *German Mass* was enriched by examples of musical notation and designed for use on Sundays in the churches. It was for Luther the end of the process of introducing the Evangelical Mass.[48] The

47 See Ott, *Luthers Deutsche Messe*. 48 Later writings in which Luther expresses his position on church services are concerned with individual aspects and were written on account of particular circumstances: LW 38, 97–137; WA 30/2, 595–626 and 691–693 (Admonition Concerning the Sacrament of the Body and Blood of Our Lord, 1530); LW 38, 147–214; WA 38, 195–256 (The Private Mass and the Consecration of Priests, 1533); LW 38, 287–319; WA 54, 141–167 (Brief Confession Concerning the Holy Sacrament, 1544); WA 50, 192–254 (The Smalcald Articles, 1537/38; for the English translation, see note 18). Significant contributions to research into the liturgy and church history in addi-

tion to those already mentioned include: Meyer, *Luther und die Messe*; Schultz, *Luthers liturgische Reformen*; Messner, *Messreform*; Schultz, *Reformen des Gottesdienstes*; Schwarz, *Angelpunkt*. 49 See LW 53, 61–67; WA 19, 72–78. 50 LW 53, 64; WA 19, 75, 5 f. 51 See LW 53, 64; WA 19, 75, 18–21. 52 LW 53, 90; WA 19, 113, 4–18. 53 See Krentz, *Ritualwandel*, pp. 340–353. 54 See Pahl, *Coena Domini* I, pp. 29–104; Bieritz, *Liturgik*, pp. 467–474. 55 LW 51, 333–354; WA 49, 588–615. See also Zschoch, *Predigten*, p. 320. 56 LW 51, 333; WA 49, 588, 12–18.

Mass formula. Sometimes, especially for the Eucharist, mixed forms were chosen, using both the *Formula Missae* and the *German Mass*. Despite these variations, the order of the Words of Institution and subsequent distribution of bread and wine was the important constant which has remained stable up to this day. Additionally, the use of the people's language in the Mass service would become characteristic for Lutheranism.[54]

Luther himself was concerned with that which occurs between God and humanity. He understood this relationship as a dialogical language-event of Word and answer. He formulated this pointedly in his sermon for the consecration of the Torgau Castle Church on October 5, 1544:[55] "My dear friends, we are now to bless and consecrate this new house to our Lord Jesus Christ. This devolves not only upon me; you, too, should take hold of the aspergillum [brush] and the censer, in order that the purpose of this new house may be such that nothing else may ever happen in it except that our dear Lord himself may speak to us through his holy Word and we respond to him through prayer and praise."[56]

BIBLIOGRAPHY

Angenendt, Arnold (2013), *Offertorium. Das mittelalterliche Messopfer* (= Liturgiewissenschaftliche Quellen und Forschungen. 101). Münster. **Beutel**, Albrecht (1991), *In dem Anfang war das Wort. Studien zu Luthers Sprachverständnis* (= Hermeneutische Untersuchungen zur Theologie. 27). Tübingen. **Bieritz**, Karl-Heinrich (2004), *Liturgik*, Berlin/New York. **Brecht**, Martin (1981), *Martin Luther. Vol. 1: Sein Weg zur Reformation 1483–1521*. Stuttgart. **Brecht**, Martin (1986), *Martin Luther. Vol. 2: Ordnung und Abgrenzung der Reformation 1521–1532*. Stuttgart. **Bubenheimer**, Ulrich (1985), Luthers Stellung zum Aufruhr in Wittenberg 1520–1522 und die frühreformatorischen Wurzeln des landesherrlichen Kirchenregiments. In: *Zeitschrift der Savigny-Stiftung für Rechtsgeschichte. Kanonistische Abteilung*. Vol. 102, pp. 147–214. **Bünz**, Enno/**Kühne**, Hartmut (eds.), *Alltag und Frömmigkeit am Vorabend der Reformation in Mitteldeutschland. Wissenschaftlicher Begleitband zur Ausstellung "Umsonst ist der Tod"* (= Schriften zur sächsischen Geschichte und Volkskunde. 50). Leipzig. **Cornehl**, Peter (1985), Gottesdienst VIII. Evangelischer Gottesdienst von der Reformation bis zur Gegenwart. In: *Theologische Realenzyklopädie*. Vol. 14, pp. 54–85. **Delius**, Hans-Ulrich (1992), *Martin Luther: Studienausgabe*. Vol. 2. 2nd ed. Leipzig. **Die evangelischen Kirchenordnungen** *des XVI. Jahrhunderts*. Vols. 1–5, Leipzig 1902–1913. Vols. 6 ff., Tübingen 1955 ff. **Dondelinger**, Patrick (2000), Gottesdienst I. Zum Begriff. In: *Religion in Geschichte und Gegenwart*. Vol. 3, 4th ed., column 1173. **Franz**, Günther (ed.) (1968), *Thomas Müntzer: Schriften und Briefe. Kritische Gesamtausgabe* (= Quellen und Forschungen zur Reformationsgeschichte. 33). Gütersloh. **Hamm**, Berndt (2010). Naher Zorn und nahe Gnade: Luthers frühe Klosterjahre als Beginn seiner reformatorischen Neuorientierung. In: id., *Der frühe Luther. Etappen reformatorischer Neuorientierung*. Tübingen, pp. 25–64. **Jenny**, Markus (ed.) (1985), *Luthers geistliche Lieder und Kirchengesänge. Vollständige Neuedition in Ergänzung zu Bd. 35 der Weimarer Ausgabe* (= Archiv zur Weimarer Ausgabe. 4). Köln/Wien. **Kalb**, Friedrich (1991), Liturgie I. Christliche Liturgie. In: *Theologische Realenzyklopädie*. Vol. 21, pp. 358–377. **Kaufmann**, Thomas (2009), *Geschichte der Reformation*, Frankfurt am Main/Leipzig. **Kaufmann**, Thomas (2012), *Der Anfang der Reformation. Studien zur Kontextualisierung der Theologie, Publizistik und Inszenierung Luthers und der reformatorischen Bewegung* (= Spätmittelalter, Humanismus, Reformation. 67). Tübingen. **Krentz**, Natalie (2014), *Ritualwandel und Deutungshoheit. Die frühe Reformation in der Residenzstadt Wittenberg (1500–1533)* (= Spätmittelalter, Humanismus, Reformation. 74). Tübingen. **Leaver**, Robin A. (2000), Gottesdienst II. Historisch 6. Westen b) Reformation. In: *Religion in Geschichte und Gegenwart*. Vol. 3. 4th ed., columns 1187–1190. **Messner**, Reinhard (1989), *Die Messreform Martin Luthers und die Eucharistie der Alten Kirche. Ein Beitrag zu einer systematischen Liturgiewissenschaft* (= Innsbrucker theologische Stu-

dien. 25). Innsbruck/Wien. **Meyer**, Hans-Bernhard (1965), *Luther und die Messe. Eine liturgiewissenschaftliche Untersuchung über das Verhältnis zum Messwesen des späten Mittelalters* (= Konfessionskundliche und kontroverstheologische Studien. 11). Paderborn. **Müller**, Nikolaus (1911), *Die Wittenberger Bewegung 1521 und 1522. Die Vorgänge in und um Wittenberg während Luthers Wartburgaufenthalt. Briefe, Akten und dergleichen und Personalien*. 2nd ed. Leipzig. **Niebergall**, Alfred (1978), Agende. In: *Theologische Realenzyklopädie*. Vol. 1, pp. 1–15. **Odenthal**, Andreas (2011), *Liturgie vom Frühen Mittelalter zum Zeitalter der Konfessionalisierung. Studien zur Geschichte des Gottesdienstes* (= Spätmittelalter, Humanismus, Reformation. 61). Tübingen. **Ott**, Joachim (2014), Luthers Deutsche Messe und Ordnung Gottesdiensts (1526). Historische, theologische und buchgeschichtliche Aspekte. In: Dingel, Irene/Jürgens, Hennig P. (eds.), *Meilensteine der Reformation. Schlüsseldokumente der frühen Wirksamkeit Martin Luthers*. Gütersloh, pp. 218–234. **Pahl**, Irmgard (ed.) (1983), *Coena Domini I. Die Abendmahlsliturgie der Reformationskirchen im 16./17. Jahrhundert* (= Spicilegium Friburgense. 29). Freiburg. **Schilling**, Johannes (2005), Musik. In: Beutel, Albrecht (ed.), *Luther Handbuch*. Tübingen, pp. 236–244. **Schultz**, Frieder (1983), Luthers liturgische Reformen. Kontinuität und Innovation. In: *Archiv für Liturgiewissenschaft*, vol. 25, pp. 249–275. **Schultz**, Frieder (2002), Reformen des Gottesdienstes in der Wittenberger Reformation. In: Klöckener, Martin/Kranemann, Benedikt (eds.), *Liturgiereformen. Historische Studien zu einem bleibenden Grundzug des christlichen Gottesdienstes. Teil 1: Biblische Modelle und Liturgiereformen von der Frühzeit bis zur Aufklärung* (Liturgiewissenschaftliche Quellen und Forschungen. 88). Münster, pp. 381–416. **Schwarz**, Reinhard (1986), *Luther* (= Die Kirche in ihrer Geschichte. 3,I). Göttingen. **Schwarz**, Reinhard (1992), Der hermeneutische Angelpunkt in Luthers Meßreform. In: *Zeitschrift für Theologie und Kirche*, vol. 89, pp. 340–364. **Simon**, Wolfgang (2003), *Die Messopfertheologie Martin Luthers. Voraussetzungen, Genese, Gestalt und Rezeption* (= Spätmittelalter und Reformation. Neue Reihe. 22). Tübingen. **Smend**, Julius (1896), *Die evangelischen deutschen Messen bis zu Luthers Deutscher Messe*, Göttingen. **Spehr**, Christopher (2010), *Luther und das Konzil. Zur Entwicklung eines zentralen Themas in der Reformationszeit* (= Beiträge zur historischen Theologie. 153). Tübingen. **Spehr**, Christopher (2012), Der Gottesdienst bei Martin Luther. Facetten eines theologischen Grundbegriffs. In: *Lutherjahrbuch*, vol. 79, pp. 9–37. **Spehr**, Christopher (2014), Invokavitpredigten. In: Leppin, Volker/Schneider-Ludorff, Gury (eds.), *Das Luther-Lexikon*. Regensburg, pp. 313 f. **Spehr**, Christopher (2014), Predigten Luthers. In: Leppin, Volker/Schneider-Ludorff, Gury (eds.), *Das Luther-Lexikon*. Regensburg, pp. 560–569. **Spehr**, Christopher (2016), Martin Luther und die Entstehung des evangelischen Kirchenwesens. In: Blaha, Dagmar/Spehr, Christopher (ed.), *Reformation vor Ort. Zum Quellenwert von Visitationsprotokollen*. Beiträge der Tagung des Projektes "Digitales Archiv der Reformation" und des Lehrstuhls für Kirchengeschichte der Friedrich-Schiller-Universität Jena am 26. und 27. November 2014 in Jena (= Veröffentlichungen der staatlichen Archivverwaltung des Landes Sachsen-Anhalt, Reihe A: Quellen zur Geschichte Sachsen-Anhalts. 21; Schriften des Hessischen Staatsarchivs Marburg. 29; Schriften des Thüringischen Hauptstaatsarchivs Weimar. 7). Leipzig, pp. 9–30. **Wendebourg**, Dorothea (2009), *Essen zum Gedächtnis. Der Gedächtnisbefehl in den Abendmahlstheologien der Reformation* (= Beiträge zur historischen Theologie. 148). Tübingen. **Zschoch**, Hellmut (2005), Predigten. In: Beutel, Albrecht (ed.), *Luther Handbuch*. Tübingen, pp. 315–321.

SUSANNE KIMMIG-VÖLKNER

Fleeing Nuns and Declining Pastoral Care: The Reformation and Monasteries

On June 13, 1525, the former monk Martin Luther married the former nun Katharina von Bora. The young woman moved in with her husband at the former Augustinian monastery that Frederick the Wise had given Luther as a residence. After the Reformation, Luther had continued to live in the monastery until only he and the prior remained. Katharina had fled from the Nimbschen convent near Grimma with eight other nuns in 1523. Legend has it that Luther freed them by hiring a wagon in which they hid among barrels of herring.

The events of the Reformation did indeed lead to many monks and nuns abandoning their monasteries. They left to become devotees of Luther's teachings or because the redistribution of monastery assets caused them to lose their religious and secular livelihoods. For example, the mendicant monasteries lost their main source of income when their members were forbidden to beg for alms in nearby towns and their right to earn incomes from the celebration of Masses was rescinded. In most monasteries, once the assets were inventoried by secular authorities, the result was a gradual secularization. Subsequently, the territorial rulers now had to provide financial support for clerics, such as severance pay. The abbots and abbesses transferred the title of their convents over to the princes, which was not quite legal according to canon law. Certainly, the decline of the monastery was exacerbated by regulations that banned both holding the traditional Mass and financing prayers for the spiritual welfare of the deceased by donors. The result was on the one hand a loss of subsistence income, and the fact that the rites of monastic life could no longer be exercised without penalties.

While monks often found alternative employment opportunities in the ecclesiastical sector, whether preacher, deacon, or teacher, most former nuns became destitute and homeless. Therefore, it was crucial to have them marry. Because this wasn't always achieved, severance payments or pensions were arranged, and in some cases, evangelical convents were established.

The specific way each monastery was dealt with varied according to local circumstances. Some were occupied by their monastic residents until the last one died. Their empty structures were used in a variety of ways. Some became schools and libraries, others hospitals and orphanages, others fell into ruin and were used as "quarries" for their stones.

MIRKO GUTJAHR

The First Protestant Parsonage?
Luther's House and Household According
to Archaeological Evidence

The investigation of everyday past realities is particularly fascinating if one succeeds in linking architectural, archeological and historical observations to historic figures such as Martin Luther, interlinking them and using this new synthesis to reach new results. On the one hand the comparison of material evidence and surviving written sources enables one to juxtapose and critically evaluate differing sources. On the other hand the material evidence offers an insight into historical processes which have either been omitted from surviving written documents or have been seen through the subjective perspective of the authors and reproduced in falsified form. The excavations in towns with close ties to Luther such as Mansfeld and Wittenberg are therefore a special stroke of luck, particularly for the relatively recent discipline archaeology of the early modern period, as the copious written evidence relating to the person of the Reformer Martin Luther can be linked to a mass of material finds. This revealed an intense and immediate image of the real everyday life of Luther and his family.

From an Augustinian Monastery to the Luther Family Home:
the Architectural Development of the Luther House[1]

Unlike the field of architectural history, which had already begun to take interest in the Luther House in Wittenberg during the nineteenth century, archaeological research was relatively slow to focus on the potential of the site (fig. 1). Although excavations had taken place there during the first half of the nineteenth century accompanying the construction of the so-called director's house in an attempt to search for the location of Luther's "tower experience," these efforts remained undocumented. Systematically planned archaeological excavations in and around Luther's house were not initiated until 1998, around the same time as the implementation of extensive historical-architectural and restoration measures. In the years 2000 and 2002, a stone foundation of a tower of the former town wall was revealed next to the south-east corner of the Luther House. It was initially considered to be the long anticipated tower which had housed Luther's study. In the Luther House itself, original paving from Luther's lifetime was discovered during the process of lowering the floor. The most extensive excavation, however, was undertaken in 2004/05 within the framework of the redesign of the garden area

and the construction of a new access to the basement in the courtyard lying directly to the south of the Luther House. Surprisingly well-preserved foundations of a tower-like extension to the house were discovered only a few centimeters below the modern surface (fig. 2). Moreover, the area was backfilled with large amounts of finds mainly dating from the sixteenth century. They offered a unique insight into the use of the former monastery and the conversions undertaken by its most prominent inhabitant, Martin Luther. As is not untypical for the then recently founded order of the Augustine Hermits who were thus rather late in establishing themselves in medieval towns, their monastery in Wittenberg was built on the town's edge and incorporated the town walls as well as pre-existing structures into its fabric. It is obvious that this monastery, which was founded in 1502 at the instigation of Frederick the Wise, was planned as a traditional quadrangular cloister. A stone church was planned as the main building in the north replacing a late-medieval wooden church of the preexisting Holy Ghost Hospital. The only part of this projected building to be completed were the foundations of the apse which were subsequently razed, probably in order to make room for the construction of fortifications in 1526. Only the south wing of the originally planned four-wing construction was actually completed by 1508. This building initially housed the most important living and working spaces in the monastery: the chapter house, the dining room (*refectorium*), the kitchen and the dormitory (*dormitorium*). Parts of the old town wall were incorporated into the southern front of the new construction and two of its towers on the east and south-west were also included in the monastery building, both serving as stair wells. The reuse of still existent parts of the former Hospice of the Holy Spirit is shown by the existence of a vaulted room in the north-west of the ground floor. It appears that work had already commenced on the east and west wings of the cloister quadrangle as remains of abutting walls were revealed during excavations on the north side of the extant south wing.

In the years 1515/16, a rectangular tower shaped annex with a lateral length of c. 8 meters was constructed on the south side of the

---

1 On this topic, see Laube, *Lutherhaus*; Neser, *Luthers Wohnhaus*; Schmitt, *Baugeschichte*.

Fig. 1
Wittenberg, Luther House
(former Augustinian monastery)

monastery building in the former town moat (figs. 2 and 3). The basement of this tower contained a latrine and a furnace for heating the upper rooms. The surface of the south façade of the tower, whose masonry was structured through the addition of a cornice and three pilasters, was originally coated with plaster. It is now universally accepted that this extension housed Luther's former study which must have been located on the upper floor of the building's original three stories. Luther makes several references to this chamber in his correspondence and *table talks*, especially as the location for his reformatory breakthrough which he claims to have experienced here: "The Holy Spirit gave me this knowledge on this tower."[2] Unfortunately, only the lower floor and the surface of the ground floor of the annex survived, which was still designated as a "laundry house" in, amongst others, a town map dating from 1757 (fig. 3). The upper stories were demolished in 1850. Thus nothing further is known about the specific form of Luther's study. It is however probable that a door led from the first floor directly into the main building and that the basement and ground floors were connected by a stone staircase. This tower-like bow construction was probably originally conceived as a sort of interim solution until the priory (separate living quarters for the abbot) had been built, even though this was in fact a rare feature for an Augustinian monastery. This building would have provided space for comfortable and prestigious studies for the prior of the monastery as well as the district or provincial vicar of this

order in Central Germany. This post, whose competences far exceeded those of the prior, was occupied by Martin Luther between May 1515 and April 1518. Two years after the monastery had been dissolved in 1522, the building was assigned to Martin Luther and he was given it for permanent use in 1532. He and his family resided in a series of rooms in the west part of the south wing, and he gradually had them renovated accordingly up until his death in 1546. Just as had been the case during their use as the Augustine monastery the buildings and rooms now used as Luther's living quarters were never completed. The Reformer complained in 1542 that a third of his house was not usable. Extensive refurbishment was not begun until after the sale of Luther's house by Luther's heirs to the University of Wittenberg in 1564 and this measure has decisively shaped the character of the Luther House up to the present day.

2 *WA*.TR 3, 228 (no. 3232a). Original: "Diesse kunst hatt mir der Heilige Geist auff diesem thurm geben."

Fig. 2
Archaeological excavations in the
Luther House's garden. View of the
foundations of the southern annex.
It was built into the former town moat
and adjacent to a well tower that
had been erected shortly before.

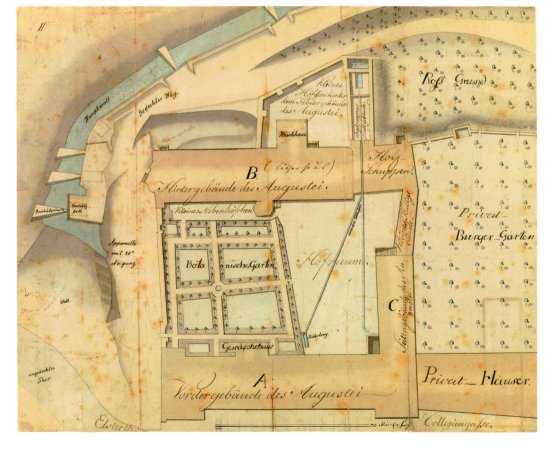

Fig. 3
Historical map of Wittenberg.
Detail with the Luther House, 1757.
The annex rediscovered in 2004/05
is visible and labeled as "Waschhaus"
("laundry house").

Fig. 4 a Neck of a polychrome faience jug manufactured in Turkish Iznik (enhanced), first half of the sixteenth century, from the excavation in the Luther House's Garden in Wittenberg

Fig. 4 b Polychrome faience jug from Iznik, mid-sixteenth century. The entire vessel (handle as well as parts of the neck and base restored) allows to gain an impression of how the faience jug in Luther's possession once looked like.

The Reformer's Living Environment

When the university acquired the residence 18 years after Luther's death from his heavily indebted sons in 1564 this evidently resulted in the disposal of the Reformer's remaining household effects which accompanied the wide ranging rebuilding measures. According to a contemporary witness, there was not a lot left in a usable condition. The court master Christian Küssow described the desolate state of the property one year prior to its sale: "When my gentlemen came here, there was nothing left in the house: no wardrobes, only broken benches and tables."[3] It appears that the remains of the scholar's household that still existed had been thrown out of the windows of Luther's house onto the adjacent southern courtyard.

This material appears to have first been placed to the east of the "Luther tower" before being evenly distributed across the entire area of the courtyard. The courtyard was surrounded by the so-called garden wall, actually a supporting wall that buttressed the town rampart which had been built around 1540 and had drastically reduced the size and thus the usefulness of the yard. Evidently, large quantities of kitchen waste had already been disposed of there before the renovation of the house.

The extensive finds shed a detailed light on the living conditions in Luther's house during the second third of the sixteenth century and serve as identification of the various functional areas of the property:[4] alongside the estimated thirty-five to fifty members of the household, the building was chiefly used for the formal reception of illustrious guests (the famous table talks) and the accommodation of students. The economic activities which were overseen by Luther's wife Katharina such as gardening and farming, beer brewing, fishing and the care of productive livestock alongside her household tasks are in part reflected by the archaeological finds, for example a spade iron[5] and a spindle whorl.[6]

The largest proportion of the finds consists of fragments of domestic pottery, most of which were made of yellow-brown and green glazed ware. The range of shapes ranges from typical kitchenware such as flat bottomed pots, glazed three-legged pots (*Grapen*) and pans to large serving plates and bowls as tableware. Small bowls and basins display evidence of the preparation of everyday foodstuffs such as cottage cheese. These vessel types are augmented by large and small glazed jugs for storing and serving beverages. Surprisingly, stoneware which originates almost exclusively from Saxon production plays a very small role in the assemblage and is mainly

Fig. 5 Polychrome stove tile with an image of Eve, first half of the sixteenth century, from the excavation in the Luther House's garden in Wittenberg

Fig. 6 Wall fountain decorated with an image of Law and Grace, first half of the sixteenth century, from the excavation in the Luther House's garden in Wittenberg

made up of simple undecorated shapes. A number of small so-called ointment pots used by pharmacists for the dispensing of medication, which were probably disposed of after a single use, were also made of stoneware.

The second-largest group of finds, animal bones, provides an insight into the diet of the inhabitants in Luther's house. Besides beef, pork, and mutton or goat meat, various kinds of poultry and fish were also part of the menu. Although Luther's aversion to game is clearly documented in his correspondence and *table talks*, the bones of hares and red deer show that game was in fact consumed in the house. Venison from stags was most likely to have been delivered to Luther's larder as gifts from noble patrons and was probably only served on festive occasions. The fact that pigs were kept close to the house is verified by the skeletons of two animals which may have died from an epidemic and were subsequently buried directly in the courtyard.[7]

Excavated fragments of exotic faience vessels underline the special status of Luther's residence. They include fragments of a faience jug decorated with white glaze and blue-violet décor originating from the west Turkish region of Iznik (ancient Nicaea) which must have been a very special gift presented to honor the Reformer (fig. 4a

and 4b). A small faience bowl with blue and white décor appears to have been manufactured in Venice. Parallels in design and decor are found on Nuremberg patrician plates showing allied coats of arms that were certainly commissioned in the city of the Doges. This type of ceramic ware reminiscent of porcelain was, however, probably originally derived from the blue and white Ming porcelain from distant China which had influenced upper Italian ceramic via the Ottoman Empire.[8]

Fragments of lavish polychrome stove tiles serve to illustrate the prestigious character of Luther's living quarters. Dated tiles show that this ostentatious stove was installed in 1536 most likely in the present Luther Room. The decorated front-faces of these tiles show a number of biblical personalities whose images are based on wood carvings by the minor master Erhard Schön from Nuremberg as well as coats of arms and scenes from biblical stories (fig. 5). The large

3 Medem, *Universitätsjahre*, p. 28. **4** On the following topic, also see Schmitt/ Gutjahr, *Kloster;* Stephan, *Archäologie.* **5** Stephan, *Lutherarchäologie*, pp. 20– 22 and p. 26, fig. 16; Schlenker, *Spatenschuhe.* **6** Schlenker, *Spinnwirtel.* **7** Döhle, *Tierreste.* **8** Stephan, *Lutherarchäologie*, pp. 24 f. and pp. 27–29, figs. 19 and 21; Gutjahr, *Fayence-Schälchen*; Gutjahr, *Fragmente.*

Fig. 7 Pottery writing set, first half of the sixteenth century,
from the excavation in the Luther House's garden in Wittenberg

quantity of simple green-glazed bowl-shaped vessel tiles and flat tiles decorated with figures and heraldic images indicates the existence of several possibly contemporaneous stoves in other rooms in Luther's house. These stoves were presumably replacements for tiled stoves installed in the building when it was used as a monastery. Only a few finds can be related to these earlier stoves including a well-preserved bi-chromed glazed tile from an ornate stove showing an image of St. Dorothy.[9] Further distinctive features of this domestic assemblage are numerous fragments of box-shaped water containers green glazed inside and out. The fronts of these so-called water fountains were decorated with religious images in a similar manner to the stove tiles. The best preserved example displays a version of the Law and Grace allegory, which was repeatedly painted by Lucas Cranach the Elder. The use of this motif is a clear affirmation of the new faith (fig. 6). These wall fountains also featured covers in the form of small gabled roofs and bronze taps.[10] The function of these containers is not clear, most likely they were used for washing one's hands with water that had been heated by the stove.

The *Alte und Neue Curiosa Saxonica* (Old and New Curiosities in Saxony) dating from 1737 reports: "The papists mock that D. Luther's household possessed so many beakers and glasses that it appears as though he must have been a good drinking companion."[11]

It is indeed true that the proportion of hollow glasses, admittedly very much fragmented, among the total collection of finds appears relatively high with a total of c. 1,600 shards (corresponding to approximately 100 vessels). This assemblage displays a typical spectrum of vessels used in the first half of the sixteenth century ranging from pear-shaped bottles, tall club-shaped and stemmed glasses for drinking beer to prunted beakers which were primarily used as wine glasses. Rarer glasses which are, however, not atypical for the era include a pouch-shaped vessel made of sealing-wax red glass only preserved in small fragments and ribbed bowls colored in vivid shades of blue and green. In contrast to these more mundane shapes, few small fragments of high-quality Reticello glass must have belonged to the special objects in Luther's cupboard. Either imported from or inspired by Venice their impressive decoration with alternating broad white bands and rhombus network patterns are reminiscent of the Venetian lace which was also in great demand at this time.[12]

What would be a surprisingly high number of brass book clasps and corner fittings for a private household provides evidence not only for the academic activity taking place in Luther's household but also for Luther's extensive library which has for the most part not survived. Three bone penknife handles and green glazed pottery writing sets on which small bowls and inkwells were attached bear witness to the vast amount of writing undertaken in Luther's house (fig. 7). Pottery and bronze candle sticks, oil lamps and fragments of clear window panes underline Luther's need for natural and artificial light for his prodigious literary output as documented in written sources.[13]

There are few finds which indicate a direct personal relationship to other persons resident in the house. A bird-call pipe corresponding to similar objects from Luther's parents' house in Mansfeld[14] points towards Wolfgang Sieberger who was reprimanded by Luther due to his passion for bird hunting. A golden ring with the stone missing[15] (fig. 8) and a double-sided ivory comb (fig. 9)[16] must have belonged to a lady of high standing in Luther's house, possibly even Katharina von Bora, whereas a knife with a silver handle is reminiscent of the Bohemian knifes sent to Luther as gifts.[17] Miniature cooking utensils among the finds which display similarities in form and construction to the full-size examples in Luther's house in Wittenberg must have belonged to the resident children.[18]

Fig. 8 Golden ring, first half of the sixteenth century, from the excavation in the Luther House's Garden in Wittenberg

Summary[19]

From a current culture historical perspective, the Reformation is seen as the culminating point of a processual transformation of late Middle Age to the Early Modern Period society accelerated by numerous factors. The significance of archaeological sources from the Luther sites Eisleben, Mansfeld and Wittenberg lies among other factors in the opportunity to illuminate this process specifically in the locations from which one of its chief impulses emanated. Seen under this aspect it is at first astounding that there are so few finds with an unequivocal Protestant context. Apart from a few individual exceptions such as the Protestant parable of Law and Grace on the fronts of wall fountains and the absence of catholic images of saints, there is no clear indication of the theological convictions held by the owner of the house between 1525 and 1546. Even the series of images on the tiled stove featuring a sequence of biblical role models and negative examples in place of the earlier ubiquitous representations of saints can also be found cast from identical models[20] in the residence of Cardinal Albert of Brandenburg in Halle. The absence of

Fig. 9 Ivory comb, first half of the sixteenth century, from the excavation in the Luther House's Garden in Wittenberg

9 Stephan, *Lutherarchäologie*, pp. 47–62. **10** König, *Wandbrunnen—Wasserblasen—Wasserkasten*. **11** Von des seeligen D. Martini Lutheri Reliquiis [1737]. In: *Alte und Neue Curiosa Saxonica*, Maius, pp. 174–180. **12** Eichhorn, *Glasfunde*. **13** Stephan, *Lutherarchäologie*, pp. 20–22. **14** Also see the article by Björn Schlenker und Andreas Stahl in this volume. **15** Gutjahr, *Goldener Ring*. **16** Schlenker, *Kamm*. **17** Id., *Beschlag eines Messergriffs*. **18** Id., *Fragmente von Miniaturgefäßen*. **19** On the following topic, also see Scholkmann, *Fragestellungen*; Gutjahr, *Lutherarchäologie*. **20** Dräger, *Drei polychrome Blattkacheln*.

objects with a specifically denominational connotation—if this is not due to a merely coincidental lack of appropriate finds—can be explained by the relatively early date of the find complex within the history of the Reformation. The disassociation between the denominational parties only became intensified during the course of the sixteenth century. What is more, Luther possessed other means of distancing himself from other denominational groups which cannot be verified by archaeological excavations: such as his countless letters, sermons and writings.

Even though subsequent generations would have it so, the Luther House in Wittenberg was not the first Protestant parsonage. Not only had other pastors gotten married years before Luther, but also Luther himself, despite his intensive preaching activities, was not a parish minister in the proper sense of the word. In Wittenberg this position had in fact been undertaken since 1523 by Luther's long-standing friend and co-reformer Johannes Bugenhagen.[21] Luther's house was not so much a parsonage but rather a multifunctional residence. This is also reflected in the copious mount of finds: objects such as the pottery writing sets—of which several examples had been found among the archaeological discoveries—numerous metal fittings for books and penknife handles define Luther's house as a professorial scholar's household. Precious imported goods such as the Reticello glass which was either imported from Venice or based on Venetian models, the Venetian faience bowls and the faience jug from Iznik were probably brought into the household as gifts by Luther's supporters. These precious gifts reflect the social status of the prominent householder Martin Luther as a respected member of the social and academic upper class in Wittenberg whose residence also served as a meeting place for its most important members. The extensive finds containing kitchen utensils and tableware bear witness to the economic function of the house as a large self-sufficient household and student hostel.

It is interesting to note that Katharina von Bora, who in her capacity as lady of the house controlled the economic destinies of the family, is only sporadically highlighted by the archaeological finds. If the former monastery was not a parsonage in the proper sense of the term and its most prominent inhabitant Martin Luther was not a pastor, both were seen as such by posterity. In the case of Luther's household, this does not alter the fact that the abundant written evidence in both personal and third person's testimonies enters into a significant, unorthodox and informative dialogue with the relevant archaeological discoveries. The archaeological finds as a quasi impartial and newly discovered source material make it possible to directly and tangibly grasp the living environment of the Reformer and his family and add further important facets to the facts that have already been gleaned from written records.

21 Schilling, *Leitbild Luther*.

BIBLIOGRAPHY

Döhle, Hans-Jürgen (2008), Tierreste aus den Küchenabfällen der Familien Hans Luder in Mansfeld und Martin Luther in Wittenberg. In: Meller, Harald/Rhein, Stefan/Stephan, Hans-Georg (eds.), *Luthers Lebenswelten* (= Tagungen des Landesmuseums für Vorgeschichte Halle. 1). Halle (Saale), pp. 329–335. **Dräger**, Ulf (2008), Drei polychrome Blattkacheln. In: Meller, Harald (ed.), *Fundsache Luther—Archäologen auf den Spuren des Reformators*. Halle (Saale), p. 282, E 109. **Eichhorn**, Nicole (2014), Glasfunde aus Wittenberg. Frühneuzeitliche Hohl- und Flachglasfunde aus Mitteldeutschland, dargestellt an ausgewählten Fundkomplexen aus Wittenberg, Naumburg und Annaburg. In: Meller, Harald (ed.), *Glas, Steinzeug und Bleilettern aus Wittenberg* (= Forschungsberichte des Landesmuseums für Vorgeschichte Halle. 5). Halle (Saale), pp. 9–148. **Gutjahr**, Mirko (2014), Lutherarchäologie. In: Meller, Harald (ed.), *Mitteldeutschland im Zeitalter der Reformation* (= Forschungsberichte des Landesmuseums für Vorgeschichte Halle. 4). Halle (Saale), pp. 19–28. **Gutjahr**, Mirko (2008), Fayence-Schälchen. In: Meller, Harald (ed.), *Fundsache Luther—Archäologen auf den Spuren des Reformators*. Halle (Saale), pp. 258–260, E 67. **Gutjahr**, Mirko (2008), Fragmente eines Fayencekruges aus Iznik. In: Meller, Harald (ed.), *Fundsache Luther—Archäologen auf den Spuren des Reformators*. Halle (Saale), p. 260, E 69. **Gutjahr**, Mirko (2008), Goldener Ring. In: Meller, Harald (ed.), *Fundsache Luther— Archäologen auf den Spuren des Reformators*. Halle (Saale), p. 238, E 10. **König**, Sonja (2008), Wandbrunnen-Wasserblasen-Wasserkasten. In: Meller, Harald/Rhein, Stefan/Stephan, Hans-Georg (eds.), *Luthers Lebenswelten* (= Tagungen des Landesmuseums für Vorgeschichte Halle. 1). Halle (Saale), pp. 101–112. **Laube**, Stefan (2003), *Das Lutherhaus in Wittenberg. Eine Museumsgeschichte*. Leipzig. **Medem**, Friedrich Ludwig Karl Freiherr von (1867), *Die Universitätsjahre der Herzöge Ernst Ludwig und Barnim von Pommern*. Anklam. **Neser**, Annemarie (2005), *Luthers Wohnhaus in Wittenberg. Denkmalpolitik im Spiegel der Quellen* (= Stiftung Luthergedenkstätten in Sachsen-Anhalt. Catalogue 10). Leipzig. **Schilling**, Johannes (2013), Leitbild Luther? Martin Luther, das deutsche Pfarrhaus und der evangelische Pfarrerstand. In: Deutsches Historisches Museum Berlin (ed.): *Leben nach Luther. Eine Kulturgeschichte des evangelischen Pfarrhauses*. Bönen, pp. 33–43. **Schlenker**, Björn (2008), Beschlag eines Messergriffs. In: Meller, Harald (ed.), *Fundsache Luther—Archäologen auf den Spuren des Reformators*. Halle (Saale), Sp. 234, E 4. **Schlenker**, Björn (2008), Fragmente von Miniaturgefäßen. In: Meller, Harald (ed.), *Fundsache Luther—Archäologen auf den Spuren des Reformators*. Halle (Saale), p. 292, E 131. **Schlenker**, Björn (2008), Kamm. In: Meller, Harald (ed.), *Fundsache Luther—Archäologen auf den Spuren des Reformators*. Halle (Saale), pp. 291 f., E 129. **Schlenker**, Björn (2008), Spatenschuhe. In: Meller, Harald (ed.), *Fundsache Luther—Archäologen auf den Spuren des Reformators*. Halle (Saale), p. 240, E 15. **Schlenker**, Björn (2008), Spinnwirtel. In: Meller, Harald (ed.), *Fundsache Luther—Archäologen auf den Spuren des Reformators*. Halle (Saale), p. 240, E 13. **Schmitt**, Reinhard (2008), Zur Baugeschichte des Augustiner-Eremitenklosters in Wittenberg. In: Meller, Harald/Rhein, Stefan/Stephan, Hans-Georg (eds.), *Luthers Lebenswelten* (= Tagungen des Landesmuseums für Vorgeschichte Halle. 1). Halle (Saale), pp. 177–191. **Schmitt**, Reinhard/**Gutjahr**, Mirko (2008), Das "schwarze Kloster" in Wittenberg. In: Meller, Harald (ed.), *Fundsache Luther—Archäologen auf den Spuren des Reformators*. Halle (Saale), pp. 132–139. **Scholkmann**, Barbara (2007), Fragestellungen, Möglichkeiten und Grenzen einer Archäologie der Reformation in Mitteleuropa. In: Jäggi, Carola/Staecker, Jörn (eds.), *Archäologie der Reformation. Studien zur Auswirkung des Konfessionswechsels auf die materielle Kultur* (= Arbeiten zur Kirchengeschichte. 104). Berlin/New York, pp. 3–25. **Stephan**, Hans-Georg (2008), Archäologie der Reformationszeit. Aufgaben und Perspektiven der Lutherarchäologie in Sachsen-Anhalt. In: Meller, Harald (ed.), *Fundsache Luther—Archäologen auf den Spuren des Reformators*. Halle (Saale), pp. 108–113. **Stephan**, Hans-Georg (2008), Lutherarchäologie. Funde und Befunde aus Mansfeld und Wittenberg. In: Meller, Harald/Rhein, Stefan/Stephan, Hans-Georg (eds.), *Luthers Lebenswelten* (= Tagungen des Landesmuseums für Vorgeschichte Halle. 1). Halle (Saale), pp. 14–77.

TOMOKO EMMERLING

Luther Archaeology.
Results and Promise

Because of the Reformer's great popularity one might suppose otherwise, but until recently there was little known that was verifiable about Martin Luther's family background and childhood. Likewise, characteristics of his daily life as a theology professor and family man in Wittenberg remained obscure until just a short while ago. Credit goes to archaeology for shedding light in the darkness in order to detect and highlight these aspects of Luther's life.

The surprising artifacts uncovered in Luther's parents' house in Mansfeld make it possible to reconstruct the immediate environment of the young man and his family from day-to-day objects, including food remnants, high-quality metal clothing decorations that were originally sewn onto a woman's festive garments, children's toys, and much more. Did the vestiges of holiday apparel belong to his mother Margarethe? Might Luther himself have fashioned the clay marbles that landed in the trash pit on his parents' property around 1500? Thanks to the current research that has been initiated by these remarkable finds, we now have an image of a well-to-do family from the town's upper class. They lived in an imposing structure at a prime location. The head of the family, Luther's father, Hans, had already arrived in Mansfeld as an investor and soon belonged to the town's elite. He was not, as earlier believed, a poor miner and smelter who had to work his way up.

The archaeological discoveries in Luther's house in Wittenberg were also of special significance. They make his living environment literally palpable, and also make it possible to enrich or correct important facets of his image as conveyed by historical sources. They reflect the everyday activities in the farmyard that supported the Luther household, thanks to the resourcefulness of Katharina von Bora. Many writing implements are tangible witnesses to Luther's scholarly life as professor of theology, the protagonist of the Reformation, and author of innumerable texts. His position as a member of the highest social class in Wittenberg can also be archaeologically verified. Thus, the remains of imported luxury goods from the upper social classes can be traced back—likely gifts from patrons or students. Other discoveries, including a golden ring, are associated with the female sphere and thus bring Luther's wife, Katharina, and her immediate environment to light. Together, these artifacts make it possible to contextualize the Luther household within early modern Wittenberg.

SUSAN C. KARANT-NUNN

Martin Luther, Women, and Womankind

At Home among Women and Girls

Martin Luther liked and respected women.[1] Despite his mother's having beaten him for stealing a nut, as he later recalled, he had a loving relationship with her. He movingly reveals this in his letter of consolation to her as she lay dying in 1531, quoting Jesus: "'Be of good cheer; I have overcome the world!'"[2] Besides his pastoral attention to Christ's atonement for the sins of humankind, he expresses genuine affection and the sincere desire that his mother find reassurance in the Gospel message. In closing, he signs "Your loving son." This is no mere epistolary formula. Luther had at least three sisters, but we know almost nothing about them. As a male child on whom the rise of the family depended, he was sent away to school as a young boy. We cannot reconstruct Luther's youthful circle of friends, but we do hear of his benefiting from the care of Frau Ursula Cotta in Eisenach, his mother's hometown, when he attended grammar school there. He called upon a woman, Saint Anne, when he was frightened in a summer storm and altered the direction of his life. As a member of the Order of Hermits of Saint Augustine, he took a vow of celibacy (refraining from marriage), which assumed an accompanying sexual abstinence. He did not hear the confession of any female.

Luther appears not to have absorbed the more hateful forms of clerical misogyny that were intended to aid monks and priests in their fleshly renunciations. He was capable of committed intimacy with his wife Katharina von Bora and of caring deeply for his daughters (Elisabeth, Magdalena, and Margarethe) as well as his sons (Hans, Martin, and Paul). Women, too, were frequent guests at the Luther table—though they were mainly relatives and the wives of colleagues and friends, and certainly not intellectuals and authors in their own right.[3] They played a subordinate role in the dining room, and yet their voices are occasionally heard if what they said or what Luther responded chanced to attract the young scribes' attention, as when Katharina's paternal aunt Magdalena ("Muhme Lena") stated categorically that she did not wish to return to the monastic life.[4] Elisabeth Cruciger, wife of Caspar Cruciger, asked Luther one day what the attitude of a Christian should be who finds him- or herself in a Catholic church during high Mass. Luther urged "liebe Els" ("dear Els") to treat it as a genuine sacrament within the consensus of the church, albeit from a perspective different from that of the presiding

priest.[5] Katharina herself, supervisor of meal preparation and service, was an audible presence, for which her husband occasionally criticized her. As a former nun, she could probably understand some of what was said in Latin.

Heir to a Hierarchical World-view

Despite his friendly acknowledgment of females' humanity and their equal standing before God, Martin Luther was in fact heir to and perpetrator of a pervasive view that, on earth, women were inferior to men. In his sermons and lectures on the book of Genesis, he emphasized that God created Eve as Adam's helpmeet and subordinate (fig. 1).[6] She was intellectually weaker than her husband and more vulnerable to emotion. This was why Satan, in the guise of a serpent, approached her instead of Adam and was easily able to convince her that there would be no harm in violating God's directive concerning the avoidance of the Tree of the Knowledge of Good and Evil. Eve was, in Luther's estimation, chiefly responsible for the disaster called the Fall and all its consequences.[7] Her subjection to her husband was now deepened. She was to obey her spouse in all matters except orders that were manifestly opposed to the divine will. The husband even governed the household, though he might delegate its administration to his wife.[8] The Reformer strongly disapproved of husbands' use of violence against their wives. He quoted the maxim, "A wife unbeaten is the best wife."[9] Yet many wives were subject to physical discipline and the victims of spousal abuse in the sixteenth century. Battering one's wife was not a punishable offense unless it drew blood (was *blutrünstig*).

---

1 On the broader subject of "Women and the Reformation," the essays by Merry E. Wiesner-Hanks are the standard by which other treatments are measured: Wiesner-Hanks, *Gender*; id., *Studies*; id., *Response*. **2** *WA*.B VI, 103–106. **3** Elisabeth Cruciger (d. 1535) wrote a hymn, *Herr Christ, der einig Gottes sohn*, that was long attributed to her husband Caspar Cruciger. Haemig, *Elisabeth Cruciger*; Schneider-Böklen, *Elisabeth Cruciger*. **4** *WA*.TR II, 2589, 534. **5** *WA*.TR I, 803, 382 f. **6** For the range of opinion in the Reformation era about the original parents, see Crowther, *Adam and Eve*. **7** Genesisvorlesung [1535–45]. In: *WA Schriften* 42, 114. **8** *WA*.TR III, 2847b, 26. **9** "Ungeschlagen ist am besten." In: Eine predigt vom Ehestand [1525]. In: *WA Schriften* XVII/1, 27; also 24.

Fig. 1 Lucas Cranach the Younger, *Eve Being Created from Adam's Rib*, 1542

This household ranking by no means ruled out a loving, solicitous bond between the two, and Luther and his clerical followers all strove to foster this marital affinity by means of school curricula and wedding sermons.[10] Luther was persuaded that every single woman ought to marry, and nearly every man should. He departed from one of the basic aspects of Catholic teaching: that suppression of sexual impulses was superior to expression of them. God, he said, had ordained the sex-drive for the perpetuation of the human species. Nevertheless, even spouses should avoid erotic excesses in order to keep the marriage bed pure and undefiled.

He also innovated by pulling away from the late-medieval clerical insistence, most starkly drawn by the Dominican author of *The Hammer of Witches* (*Malleus maleficarum*), that women's carnality could never be sated. Luther lifted the onus of blame for concupiscence from women. His arguments equalized the sex drive of men and women; they desired one another. Marriage was the remedy for sin (*remedium ad peccatum*) for both men and women, who, in light of their teenage urgings, should seek wedded partners before their mid-twenties, which was the preferred practice by Northern Europeans in that era.[11]

Martin Luther reconciled the clerical estate with women. He brought the pastorate into regular and intimate familiarity with the so-called distaff sex. Clergymen's sexual relations with their wives were encouraged, and they were now honorable. Their offspring were no longer tainted by illegitimacy. Changing entrenched popular attitudes took generations, nevertheless.[12]

Martin Luther regarded the universe as binary in structure—half masculine and half feminine. Late-medieval scientists may have taken note of ambiguities between the sexes, anatomical and otherwise, but if the Wittenberg Reformer knew of such theories, he was untroubled by them.[13] For Luther, even trees, rocks, and gemstones were divided between male and female; male trees bent over female ones in an effort to shelter them.[14] Other signs in nature seemed to support the Reformer's perspective. The shape of women's bodies (broad hips and, as Luther saw it, their small shoulders and heads) manifested their appointment to the role of mother. Women were meant to stay close to home, to tend to housekeeping and childrearing, and to teach those skills to their daughters and young maids. They were also to carry out the moral and elementary religious instruction of both sexes, and for this they needed to be literate.

Luther and Female Literacy

When in 1524 Luther published his call to the mayors and council members of all German cities to establish schools, he devoted nearly all his attention to the grammar school education of boys.[15] They alone needed to learn the biblical languages and scriptural and classical literature so that they could serve in the future as pious clergymen, teachers, and members of the bureaucracies that were expanding at every level of government.[16] Girls could benefit from vernacular literacy in order to read devotional materials and raise their children to be pious Christians. Girls, Luther said, should learn to "keep house and train children and servants aright."[17] Many parents were reluctant to send either their sons or their daughters to school.

Luther's promotion of basic education had an encouraging effect, nonetheless, although the realization of universal literacy was very long in coming, even to Saxony. Only in the 1570s did Elector August of Saxony order the establishment of boys' schools throughout his territories and provided that the sextons should take on the instruction in the countryside. Yet many sextons themselves could not read and write. Families often did not want their daughters taught by men, in any case, and women teachers were a very scarce commodity. Pastors' families had a higher rate of feminine literacy than society at large and may have practiced in-house instruction. Sometimes pastors' and deacons' wives presided over village schools for little girls.

Martin Luther did not specialize in devising curricula for girls' schools. We can deduce from his remarks on childhood education that he wanted all young children to learn the fundamental tenets of their faith, as contained in key texts such as the Lord's Prayer, the Decalogue, and the Creed—and from 1529 the simple explanations of these and his other teachings contained in his *Small Catechism*. Beyond these, he wanted girls to be able to read Bible verses conducive to daily piety and such other items as the lyrics of hymns. They sang core Evangelical hymns in class. Proverbs and Psalms, the Apocryphal Book of *Ecclesiasticus*, also called Jesus Sirach, contained passages pertaining to girls' and women's lives—some of them, indeed, admonitory verses about *bad* women.

More advanced pupils might learn elementary arithmetic, if their parents approved. The purpose, again, was practical: to avoid being cheated in the market square and to keep basic household accounts. Luther's motives for advocating childhood literacy and his inclusion of girls in the earliest phase cannot be seen as either modernizing or liberating. The Reformer was a man of his day. He desired, above all, to promote an understanding of the Christian faith and implant within readers' hearts, including women's hearts, the further love of God.

Saints and Patriarchs

On the eve of the Reformation, the painted and sculpted countenances of women, along with those of men, were a presence in all church interiors. When women entered the sanctuaries of Germany, they encountered images of the Virgin Mary everywhere, and in addition those of the myriad other female saints, for many of whom days in the church calendar were named. The Reformation incited a major cultural shift away from the display of female figures in places of worship. Within Catholicism, such "holy" women were seen to provide incentives to their admirers to imitate them and thus find favor with God. Such figures were also believed to possess intercessory powers with the Divine. Now Luther demoted all saints, both female and male: none had supernatural powers, their shrines should not be visited, and they should not be appealed to in prayer. Instead, they should be regarded as recipients from God of gifts of faith that produced self-restraint and compassion—good fruits growing on good trees. All that one saw as unusual in them came from God and should be attributed exclusively to the Godhead. Not even Mary had special powers, even though God had, Luther affirmed, honored this simple maiden by making her the vessel of His

Son's incarnation. Mary was *Theotokos*, the bearer of God. On the days assigned by custom to events in Mary's life, Luther preached against the non-scriptural legends that had grown up around her across the ages.

Martin Luther honored Mary, but he lowered her station among believers.[18] After initial hesitation, he removed the *Hail Mary* from the prayers that his followers should recite. In place of the panoply of popular saints, Luther elevated the patriarchs and also their wives.[19] In his commentaries on Genesis, he showed his regard of Sarah in her barrenness and Rachel in the face of polygamy. These wives, pious though they were, did not presume to mediate between people and God nor to incur the special veneration of people beyond their family members. They dealt with complicated earthly affairs, which Luther saw as proper in that age and in his own. These women were better models. He assigned polygamy to the ancient, pre-Christian past.[20] The net result of the Reformer's theological shift was to downplay, through rhetorics and semiotics, the role of women in the churches. Attention was now concentrated on Christ's atoning act and on other salient events of the Gospels. Sixteenth-century people did not conceive of such changes in our terms. Nonetheless, we ourselves note that nearly all that remained of feminine models in the sanctuaries were a few paintings and statues of scripturally attested personages and scenes. In Luther's homeland, the Wettin electors strictly banned iconoclasm and discreetly, peaceably removed unsuitable imagery over perhaps two generations. Some pieces survived owing to their storage in sacristies and balconies, until, at a much later date, they could be regarded as admirable relics of a distant past.

Within Lutheranism, the market for new religious art did not collapse. Lucas Cranach the Elder's altarpiece in the Wittenberg Town Church may be taken as exemplary.[21] A woman appears as a godmother in the depiction of Philipp Melanchthon carrying out a baptism, while other matrons are in attendance; in the panel devoted to Johannes Bugenhagen hearing confessions, women, assigned as in the Middle Ages to his lefthand side, are among those waiting to be heard; and in the predella at the bottom, women and girls sit and stand as Luther, from his preacher's niche, points to the body of the crucified Christ. These women are solidly in and of the world, adhering to biblical prescriptions.

We should recall, too, that throughout Germany the practice predominated of allocating to females the northern, less favorable, side of the sanctuary, whether for standing or—after pews were built for the general laity—for sitting. Luther, however, did not retain a different liturgy for the baptism of female infants.

Katharina von Bora and Martin Luther

Luther was rather late in taking a wife; numerous colleagues had hearkened earlier to his insistence that celibacy was misguided. As he became famous, Luther was an extraordinarily busy scholar, teacher, and preacher. His advice was increasingly sought. At the same time, he imagined that he would experience the same fate as the Bohemian reformer Jan Hus a century earlier: being burned as a heretic. This made him an unreliable groom. When he finally did respond favorably to the virtual proposal of Katharina von Bora, a former nun (fig. 2), of

the lower and impoverished nobility, he defensively declared in writing to Nikolaus von Amsdorf, after their nuptials, "I do not love my wife!"[22] He meant that he had not married out of lust, but that he had freely chosen to enter what for him was a new estate.

By December 1525, he clearly was in love with his wife. In his correspondence with friends, he included brief news of her and relays her greetings. He sent salutations to their wives and other family members. He was enmeshed in a social milieu that accorded significant standing to women even as the cultural prejudice against them stood firm. By means of the labors of the busy scribes at the dinner table, we know about Käthe's nausea during pregnancy and her illness as she prepared for and recovered from childbirth. At least once, Martin expressed his fear that she would die. On another occasion, she rubbed salve into his sore legs. Especially by means of the dozen extant letters from Martin to Käthe—none of her letters to him have survived—we see into the heart of their marriage. Hierarchically conditioned as he was, he was aware that her rank was higher than his, and he played on this fact by calling her "My Lord," and "Mistress of the Sow Market." These epithets simultaneously acknowledged his dependence upon her for running their huge household on very little money, one solution to which lay in the couple's purchase of farming land and her careful production of plant-based food and also, clearly, pigs. He punned and joked with her in his missives, drawing this practice from having observed his father Hans joking with his mother, called Hannah. Jesting lay at the root of familial happiness. I have suggested that Martin and Käthe had what anthropologists call an "asymmetrical joking relationship"; Martin poked fun at her, and she bore it in good humor.[23] Some of his misogynistic remarks at the dinner table that we find distasteful were, in fact, designed to assure her of his love. He declared on one occasion that he would have preferred to marry another of the nuns from the Nimbschen convent, Ave von Schönefeld, for he had found Käthe to be arrogant. But, he concluded, God had had mercy on her, and he had chosen her instead! On another occasion, he opined that it was most inappropriate to have a significant age difference between husbands and wives—knowing as he made this pronouncement that a full 15 years lay between him and his bride.

Katharina von Bora "die Lutherin" and Martin Luther were partners in a gigantic enterprise. Although he explicitly reserved for himself the supervision of even her domestic chores, he freely delegated

10 Schools for girls and the ministerial duty to preach wedding sermons were hardly in place before the second half of the sixteenth century, however. **11** The foundational essay on this subject is Hajnal, *European Marriage*. **12** Plummer, *Whore*. **13** Cadden, *Meaning*. **14** *WA*.TR 1, 1133, 560 f. **15** An die Ratsherren aller Städte deutsches Lands, daβ sie christliche Schulen aufrichten und erhalten sollen [1524]. In: *WA Schriften* XV, 27–53. **16** Ibid., esp. 37 f. **17** Ibid., 44. **18** Kreitzer, *Reforming Mary*; Heal, *The Cult*, which suggest that Lutherans in practice did not completely resign their honor of the Virgin. **19** See Jordon, *Patriarchs and Matriarchs*; McGuire, *The Mature Luther's Revision*; Mattox, *Defender*. **20** With the notable exception of his approval of the bigamy of Philip, Landgrave of Hesse. See also the contribution of Franziska Kuschel in this volume. **21** Cranach continued to paint the Virgin and female saints for the Catholic art market. **22** "Ego enim nec amo nec aestuo, sed deligo uxorem." In: *WA*.B III, 900, 541. **23** Karant-Nunn, *Masculinity*.

JO. FRID. MAYERI,

S. S. Th. Doct. P. P. Augustiss. Svec. Regis Consiliarii
in Sacris Primar. & ad D. Jac. Pastoris Hamb.

de

CATHARINA LUTHERI CONJUGE,

Dissertatio.

J. W. Michaeli fecit.

Respondente

MICHAELE RICHEY, Hamburgensi.

Solenniter habenda

Die 17. Febr. A. 1698.

HAMBURGI, Typis NICOLAI SPIRINGI, 1698.
Et Lipsiæ apud THOMAM FRITSCH.

Fig. 2 Johann F. Mayer, Catharina Lutheri Conjuge. Dissertatio (Dissertation on Luther's wife Katharina),
Hamburg 1698. Frontispiece with a portrait of Katharina von Bora

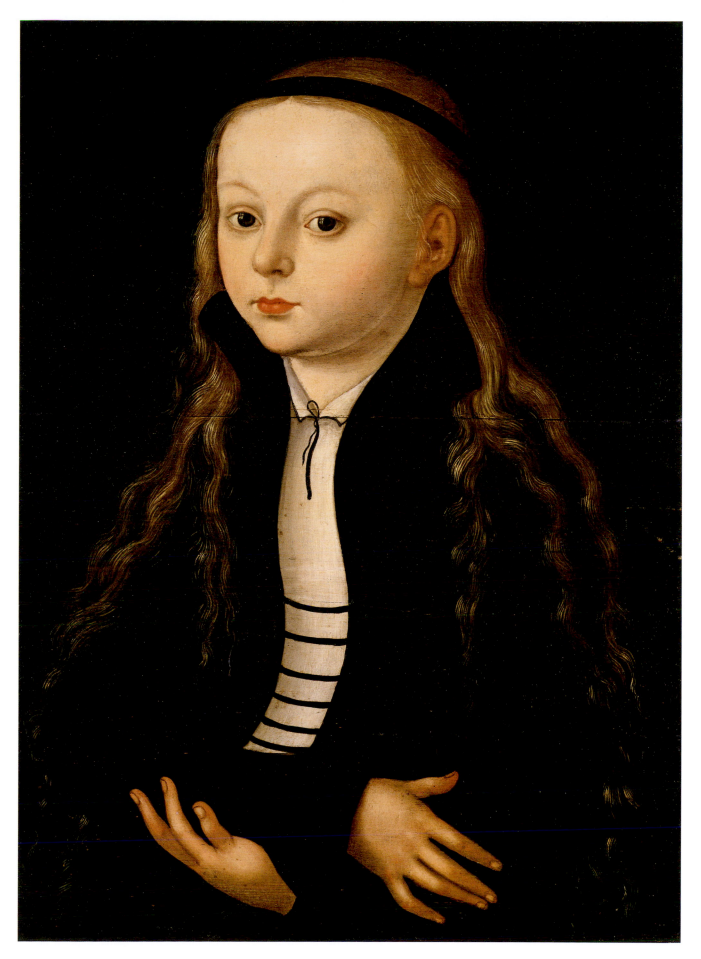

Fig. 3 Lucas Cranach the Elder, Portrait of a girl, c. 1520. This painting was long thought
to be a portrait of Martin Luther's daughter Magdalena.

actual decision-making to her. He recognized that without her energetic participation, he could not manage the herculean tasks of lecturing, preaching, and especially writing. He appreciated, too, that she took upon herself his own definition of the appropriate role and demeanor of women. Insofar as possible, she complied with his every wish, becoming irritated mainly when he was too generous with their slender resources. They ran an expansive, expensive household with up to forty people at dinner. Luther offered the following prayer at the table: "Dear heavenly Father . . . grant me the grace and bless me so that I may govern and nourish my dear wife, children, and servants in a godly and Christian manner. Give me the wisdom and strength to govern and raise them well, and give them a good heart and the will to follow your teaching and to be obedient. Amen."[24]

Like the patriarchs of old—and certainly in contrast with the Catholic idea that couples should cease their sexual relationship as soon as they were able—Martin and Käthe made love long after they hoped to produce additional offspring. When, shortly before his death in his early sixties, Martin became impotent, he wrote to his wife, "I would gladly love you if I could."[25] She evidently feared that he no longer desired her. He joked with her that he was no longer tempted by beautiful women.[26] In all seriousness, he advised her to consult Melanchthon, who would surely be able to counsel her, based on his experience with his own wife.[27] He is nevertheless still her "little love." Luther did not intend to publicize his domestic happiness. It simply spilled out in his personal correspondence and doubtless also in his conversation with close friends. He asked after their families and they after his. His contentment as the *Hausvater* (housefather) in a new model of life within the parsonage spread outward in Lutheran circles. Other leading reformers who married, such as Huldrych Zwingli and Jean Calvin, left no record similar to Luther's of their intimate existence.

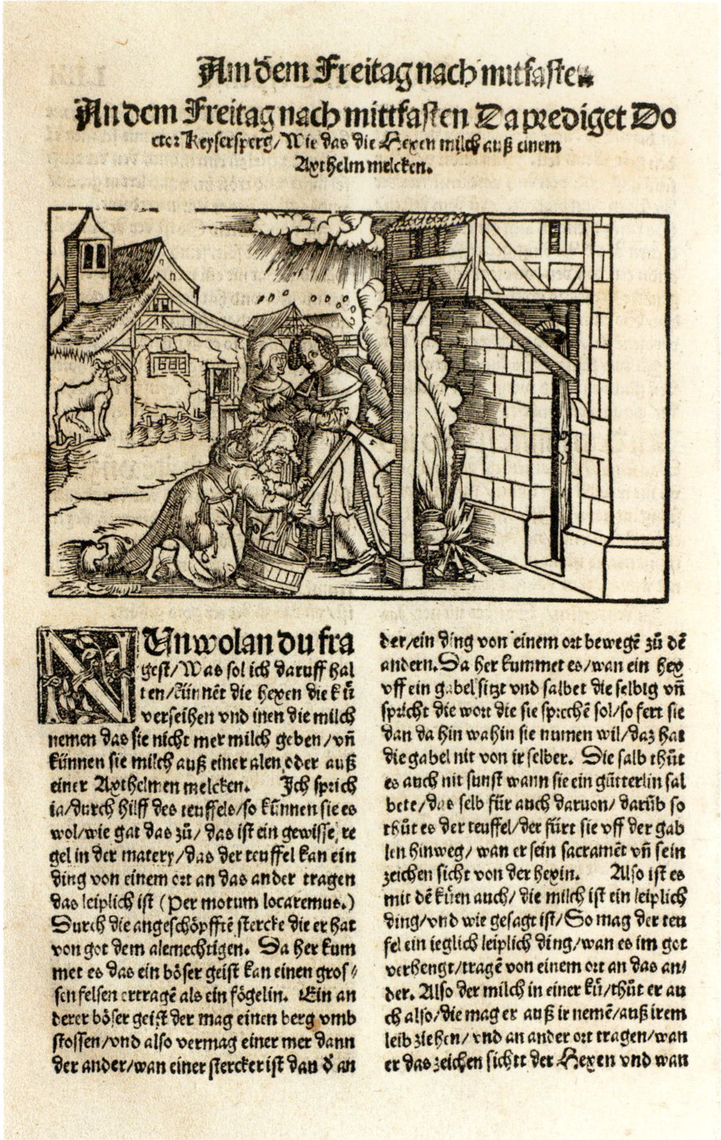
Am dem Freitag nach mitfasten.
An dem Freitag nach mittfasten Da prediget Do ctor Keysersperg/ Wie das die Hexen milch auß einem Axthelm melcken.

Nun wolan du fragest/ Was sol ich daruff halten/ künnen die hexen die kü verseihen vnd inen die milch nemen das sie nicht mer milch geben/ vñ künnen sie milch auß einer alen oder auß einer Axthelmen melcken. Jch sprich ia/ durch hilff des teuffels/ so künnen sie es wol/ wie gat das zü/ das ist ein gewisse regel in der matery/ das der teuffel kan ein ding von einem ort an das ander tragen das leiplich ist (Per motum locaremus.) Durch die angeschöpfftē stercke die er hat von got dem alemechtigen. Da her kummet es das ein böser geist kan einen grossen felsen ertragē als ein fögelin. Ein anderer böser geist der mag einen berg vmb stossen/ vnd also vermag einer mer dann der ander/ wan einer stercker ist dan d' ander/ ein ding von einem ort bewegē zü dē andern. Da her kummet es/ wan ein hex vff ein gabel sitzt vnd salbet die selbig vñ spricht die wort die sie sprechē sol/ so fert sie dan da hin wahin sie numen wil/ daz hat die gabel nit von ir selber. Die salb thüt es auch nit sunst wann sie ein gütterlin salbete/ das selb für auch daruon/ darūb so thüt es der teuffel/ der fürt sie vff der gablen hinweg/ wan er sein sacramēt vñ sein zeichen sicht von der hexin. Also ist es mit dē küen auch/ die milch ist ein leiplich ding/ vnd wie gesagt ist/ So mag der teufel ein ieglich leiplich ding/ wan es im got verhengt/ tragē von einem ort an das ander. Also der milch in einer kü/ thüt er auch also/ die mag er auß ir nemē/ auß irem leib ziehen/ vnd an ander ort tragen/ wan er das zeichen sicht der Hexen vnd wan

Fig. 4 Woodcut with foolish women, from: Johannes Geiler von Kaysersberg, Die Emeis [. . .], Straßburg 1516.
The image of a woman milking an axe in front of a fire is evidence for the widespread obsessive belief in witches to which mainly women fell victim.

The Paternal Luther

Luther was called "Father" as soon as he was ordained a priest. Before he went to Wittenberg and began to preach, those in his spiritual care were mainly men. Now, when he looked down from the pulpit in Saint Mary's Church, he saw as many citizens who stereotypically held the distaff as those who guided the plow. When he married and became the progenitor by Katharina of sons and daughters, fatherhood took on new meaning for him. The emergence of a person from the womb deeply touched him. He agreed with Saint Cyprian that kissing a brand-new baby before it was baptized was like witnessing God in the act of creation. He cared for all his children but consigned their early nurturing, by the standard of his times, to their mother and the women attendants under her direction. Nonetheless, he said that a father might wash diapers if he did so in faith.[28]

The prospect of giving birth was fearful, for survival was not assured for either mother or child. Pregnant women throughout Germany sought to receive the Eucharist as their delivery approached, for they clung superstitiously to the hope that the bread, and now the wine too, would improve their chances of safe parturition. Even before Luther entered marriage, his enduring vision of women's signal function was to bring forth and rear the next generation of Christians. This was women's vocation, a concept that Luther would develop further. Already in 1522, he considered childbirth to be the primary calling of the female sex, and this calling carried with it all discomfort and every risk to life and health. Luther wrote that women in labor should say to themselves: "Think, dear Greta, that you are a woman and that this work of yours is pleasing to God. Console yourself happily by [thinking of] His will, and let Him do with you what is His right. Bring that child forth, and do it with all your might! If you die in the process, so pass on over, good for you! For you actually die in a noble work and in obedience to God."[29] Modern readers are sometimes shocked by Luther's seemingly callous indifference to women's death in childbed; this passage must be understood within the context of his theology and his personal welcoming of death as a transition to a better life. A few years later, Katharina's pregnancies and their children's illnesses and deaths surely deepened his perspective. When their eight-month-old daughter Elisabeth died in 1528, Luther wrote that the event had rendered him "womanish." He meant that the intensity of his emotion was greater than he felt proper for a man. When the thirteen-year-old Magdalena lay on her deathbed in 1542 and finally passed away, both parents were simply overcome. Luther composed an epigraph for her (fig. 3).[30] He wept bitterly in private, all the while consoling the little girl with the assurance that she would soon be with her heavenly Father. In public, at the funeral, Luther put on the mask of acceding to God's will and at least in part rebuffed the expressions of sympathy from his fellow Wittenbergers. He felt compelled to set a good example.

We know very little about Magdalena and Margarethe's education—not even whether they joined other girls in attending an elementary school in Wittenberg. Katharina could have taught them herself. Martin did attempt to bring the regional noblewoman Else von Kanitz to Wittenberg as a girls' schoolteacher in 1527, and told her that she could board at his own home. She did not consent. At the same time, we know that Luther had high expectations for his eldest son, engaged tutors for him, and kept himself apprised of young Hans's progress. The sons of an international celebrity surely had to achieve something in their own right, but the Reformer's daughters chiefly needed to model to the public the pious propriety that was sought in women. Luther's expectations of his children were differentiated by gender. When he was protectively confined in the fortress at Coburg in 1530, during the Diet of Augsburg, he wrote back to Käthe and conversationally, affectionately referred to his small daughter Magdalena as "the little whore" (das Hürlin).[31] This was not a malicious slur in his mouth but indicated once again that society judged females chiefly by their sexual behavior. In this same letter, Martin advises his wife on weaning.

Luther as Pastoral Advisor and Friend to Women

Luther wrote in a natural and genuine way to women as well as men who sought his advice or warranted his reproach. He admired Argula von Grumbach for her intrepidity in confronting the faculty of the University of Ingolstadt for its persecution of a Lutheran student, Arsacius Seehofer, in 1523.[32] He congratulated friends on the birth of a child, consoled them on a death, and gave them spiritual counsel. His tone was that of one who had gained the same lessons that he dispensed, based on significant personal experience.

He explicitly cited his own suffering in his moving epistle to Barbara Lyßkirchen of Freiberg in 1531, who was tormented by fears that God had not elected her to salvation: "I know this sickness well and have lain in the sickroom [Spital] with it up to the point of eternal death."[33] He was utterly sympathetic. He told her that her fears, like his own, were the devil's work. She must set aside what God did not desire people to inquire into, just as if she were spitting out a piece of excrement that had fallen into her mouth. "This is the way God helped me." The Reformer responded humbly and gratefully

when the Electress Sibylle of Saxony, wife of the territorial ruler, inquired into his and Katharina's well-being and expressed her loneliness in the absence of the elector in 1544. The exchange is candid and warm.[34] Luther could be critical as well. In 1539, when the widowed mother of Johannes Schneidewein, one of the Luthers' long-term student boarders, would not permit her son to marry the upstanding young Wittenberger with whom he had fallen in love, Luther wrote a series of three entreaties to her. Each was less complimentary than the last; Ursula Schneidewein did not reply. In the end, the Reformer harshly criticized her effort to control her son, especially because the object of his affection was entirely appropriate. He threatened, "When parents are unwilling, the pastor must be willing." When silence nevertheless ensued, he married the couple.[35]

Luther even involved himself in the controversy over the adultery of one Katharina Hornung, wife of Wolf Hornung, with Elector Joachim of Brandenburg. He poured condemnation upon her: "You know that you are perpetrating upon your poor husband such a great vice and outrage by withholding yourself, his child, his house and yard, his goods and honor, and in addition have hounded him into misery …" He gave her a deadline of March 27, 1530, after which, Luther threatened, he himself would declare the pair to be divorced.[36] Although Luther had redefined marriage as a civil transaction rather than a sacrament, divorce was virtually as difficult to come by as in the Catholic past. The sole grounds for it, adultery or abandonment, he saw as part of the Gospel message (Matthew 19). Nevertheless, he evidently did not declare this couple to be divorced.

Suspicions of Evil

As much as we might like to think that we can depart radically from the values and structures of our cultural milieu, it is extremely difficult to do so. Luther shared the pervasive anti-Semitism of his day; and he believed that witches, as agents of Satan, not only existed but conformed to the image that ordinary people had of them. They were mainly female, they allied themselves with Satan and thus abandoned the oaths of their baptism, they disrupted the normal functioning of nature in both human and beast, and they could bring about disaster. Luther articulated the late-medieval belief that a witch could, calling upon Satan, wring milk from a towel or any sort of handle (fig. 4)![37] Witches and warlocks were heretics. The Reformer took as seriously as any of his contemporaries the biblical injunction, "Thou shalt not suffer a witch to live" (Exodus 22: 18). Lucas Cranach the Younger depicted the execution by burning of four witches in Wittenberg in 1540.

24 *WA*.TR VI, 6927, 274. **25** *WA*.B XI, 4201, 286 f. **26** *WA*.B XI, 4195, 275 f. **27** *WA*.B XI, 4201, 782 f. **28** Vom ehelichen Leben [1522]. In: *WA Schriften*, X/2, 297. **29** Ibid., 296. **30** *WA*.TR V, 5490, 185–187. **31** *WA*.B V, 1582, June 5, 1530, 347. **32** *WA*.B III, 787, Luther to Spalatin, 364 f., for example. **33** *WA*.B XII, 4244a, 135. **34** *WA*.B X, 3977, 546–548; 3978, 548 f. **35** *WA*.B VIII, 3344, 454 f.; 3357, 492 f. **36** *WA*.B V, 1526, 230 f.; see *WA*.B IV, 1206, 346. **37** Dominica Oculi Ex C. XXII" [sermon preached March 4, 1526]. In: *WA Schriften* XVI, 551.

If Martin Luther was not the gender-relations revolutionary in that some have liked to posit, he nonetheless planted seeds that had the potential to germinate and to foster an environment within which women and girls of later generations might be able to flourish. Luther reconciled the clergy with women. Pastors were now honorably wedded, sexually active men. As such they were acquainted with and generally on good terms with their wives, and also with their daughters. Together, husbands and wives fostered a veritable culture of literate piety located in the parsonage. This, at least, was the ideal, and it was partly realized within a period that extended well beyond Luther's lifetime. The Luthers' own marriage proved to be an implement in this process. Martin and Katharina loved one another deeply. The Reformer spontaneously reflected their mutual affection in his correspondence and unwittingly contributed to the creation of a familial model that spread far beyond the walls of his hometown. It had validity well into the twentieth century.

Luther theoretically equalized the sex drive between the genders. Women were no longer carnally insatiable, in his view, nor were they mainly culpable for the seduction of their erotic partners. He was nevertheless shaped by and adhered to a binary definition of the characters and the proper roles of women and men. Men engaged in public matters even as they governed the household. Women kept house, gave birth, and raised young children while submitting in all things to their husbands. Despite his fundamentally positive attitude toward the women around him, Luther perpetuated the view, bolstered by the book of Genesis, that women were invariably weaker intellectually than men and more inclined to give in to their feelings. Women needed to be under men's dominion.

The demotion of the Virgin Mary and the saints meant that women's images all but disappeared from church sanctuaries. This process symbolized to women that their functions within the official church were close to nonexistent. They were to minister to their own children and young servants within the domestic setting, ideally a "domestic church." At the same time, the penetration into convents and monasteries of Luther's teachings against salvation by works of self-abnegation brought some women (along with men) of high social rank, like Katharina von Bora, back into the secular world. Some nuns, however, refused to repudiate their vows and had to be accommodated. Luther's advocacy of universal literacy, including for girls, had a limited devotional intention and marginal success in the sixteenth century. The era of elementary education's chief expansion lay in the eighteenth and nineteenth century, but Luther laid the ideological foundation for its acceptance by both nobles and peasants, and reinforced the already existing convictions of societal levels in between. Literacy had the potential to expand the horizons of all who acquired it.

BIBLIOGRAPHY

Cadden, Joan (1995), *The Meaning of Sex Difference in the Middle Ages: Medicine, Science, and Culture*. New York/Cambridge. **Crowther**, Kathleen M. (2010), *Adam and Eve in the Protestant Reformation*. Cambridge/New York. **Haemig**, Mary Jane (2001), Elisabeth Cruciger (1500?–1535): The Case of the Disappearing Hymn Writer. In: *The Sixteenth Century Journal*, vol. 32, no. 1, pp. 21–44. **Hajnal**, John (1965), European Marriage Patterns in Perspective. In: Glass, David Victor/Eversley, David. E. (eds.), *Population in History*. London, pp. 101–143. **Heal**, Bridget (2007), *The Cult of the Virgin Mary in Early Modern Germany: Protestant and Catholic Piety, 1500–1648*. Cambridge/New York. **Jordon**, Sherry Elaine (1995), *Patriarchs and Matriarchs as Saints in Luther's Lectures on Genesis*, PhD thesis, Yale University. **Karant-Nunn**, Susan C. (2008), Martin Luther's Masculinity: Theory, Practicality, and Humor. In: id./Hendrix, Scott H. (eds.) (2008), *Masculinity in the Reformation Era* (= Sixteenth Century Essays and Studies). Kirksville/MO, pp. 167–189. **Kreitzer**, Beth (2004), *Reforming Mary: Changing Images of the Virgin Mary in Lutheran Sermons of the Sixteenth Century*. Oxford/New York. **Levack**, Brian P. (2006), *The Witch-Hunt in Early Modern Europe*. 3rd ed. New York. **Mattox**, Mickey Leland (2003), *"Defender of the most holy matriarchs": Martin Luther's Interpretation of the Women of Genesis in the "Enarrationes in Genesin," 1535–1545*. Leiden. **McGuire**, Marilyn M. (1999), *The Mature Luther's Revision of Marriage Theology: Preference for Patriarchs over Saints in His Commentary on Genesis*. PhD thesis, Saint Louis University. **Plummer**, Marjorie Elizabeth (2012), *From Priest's Whore to Pastor's Wife: Clerical Marriage and the Process of Reform in the Early German Reformation*. Farnham/Burlington/VT. **Schneider-Böklen**, Elisabeth (1994), Elisabeth Cruciger, die erste Dichterin des Protestantismus. In: *Gottesdienst und Kirchenmusik*, vol. 2, pp. 32–40. **Wiesner**, Merry E. (1988), Women's Response to the Reformation. In: Po-Chia Hsia, Ronnie (ed.), *The German People and the Reformation*. Ithaca, pp. 148–172. **Wiesner-Hanks**, Merry E. (1992), Studies of Women, the Family, and Gender. In: Maltby, William S. (ed.), *Reformation Europe, a Guide to Research II*. St. Louis/MO, pp. 159–187. **Wiesner-Hanks**, Merry E. (2009), Gender and the Reformation. In: *Archive for Reformation History*, vol. 100, no. 1, pp. 350–365. **Zika**, Charles (2007), *The Appearance of Witchcraft: Print and Visual Culture in Sixteenth-Century Europe*. London/New York.

FRANZISKA KUSCHEL

Marriage: A Constant Work in Progress. An Examination of the Lutheran Understanding of Marriage and Family

Landgrave Philip of Hesse, a protector and one of the most import-ant political supporters of the Reformation, wrote to Martin Luther in December 1539 describing a heartsickness that threatened his sal-vation.[1] Philip was already married to Christine of Saxony and blessed with seven children from the marriage but he was never-theless fervently in love with young Margarethe von der Saale. He wanted to marry her in a God-fearing manner—that is, without divorcing his wife. Philip wrote to Luther seeking the theological absolution for bigamy, and he employed a cunning trick to achieve these ends. Philip's argument was based on the case of the married Count of Gleichen, who returned from the Crusades in 1240 with a Saracen concubine. The count asked for and received the blessing for a second (bigamous) marriage from Pope Gregory IX. The land-grave put pressure on Luther with this fully fictional tale.[2] If Luther were not to sanction his theologically untenable "polygyny," Philip threatened to return to old beliefs. Backed into a corner, Luther and Philipp Melanchthon granted the landgrave the desired dispensa-tion; they feared they would otherwise lose one of the Reformation's most important advocates.

In his reflections about the cohabitation of men and women Luther was always conscious of the complexity of this social con-struct. Traditions associated with the initiation and consummation of Christian marriage that had been valid up to the Reformation needed to be adjusted to fit a humanistic and pragmatic understanding, in accordance with the times. Thus, Luther succumbed relatively often to the temptation to pass judgments and/or give advice. Against his own principles, he became involved in "secular matters," even though he was a clergyman.[3] He requested Philip's discretion in the matter so the case would not set a precedent.[4] This was unsuccessful, however.

The affair became public—and a problematic counterpoint in the development of the Reformation's concept of marriage.[5]

In June 1525, at age 42, Luther married Katharina von Bora, a former nun who had fled from the convent at Nimbschen. Luther was acting contrary to every paradigm of the celibate clergyman's life but was fully conscious that he was doing it in order to further theological and social reform. He would raise six children with Katharina in the Black Monastery in Wittenberg. Luther claimed he would have rather married a different woman: Ave of Schönfeld. Nevertheless, he reported experiencing true love over time through his wife and children. Luther regarded marriage as a gift from God. In his view, a marriage usually developed into a happy partnership; often, however, not until some time had passed. The fact that some marriage covenants "go awry" was surely apparent to the Reformer; such thoughts led him to utter the aphorism "then it is hell."[6]

Until the turn of the sixteenth century, marriage was the public ratification of a private contractual agreement between two fami-lies.[7] The conditions and arrangements for the cohabitation of husband and wife were established entirely secularly and without church interference. Marriage did not require a uniform procedure. A man and woman simply exchanged wedding vows and then con-summated the marriage, thus rendering the vow indissoluble.

The medieval church was slow to intervene in the marriage cer-emony and justified its declaration that only its consent made matri-mony valid through the sacramental significance of the wedding vow. In order to marry, a couple had to perform "the act of speaking together" in front of the church door, followed by a proclamation of marriage in the church itself. This was followed by a wedding mass. After these steps had been taken a final benediction prayer sealed the

1 See Hessisches Staatsarchiv Marburg (HStAM), Sign. Best. 3 no. 2842, fol. 132r–133v. 2 In the sixteenth century, this story was generally held to be true; it originated from a gravestone in the Erfurt's St. Marien cathedral, which depicts a knight with two wives. See Rockwell, *Doppelehe*, pp. 210–212, note 6. 3 Marriage is a divine institution, which serves the purpose of creating order in Paradise (see *WA* 17, 1, 12 f.). Additionally marriage was regulated by public authority; the priest was supposed to enlist its assistance in order to solve problematic legal questions. See *WA* 26, 225, 29 f. As Martin Luther wrote in his *Traubüchlein* (Marriage Booklet) from 1529, marriage is a law, a "secular matter"

within the divine order, and therefore it concerns the lay authorities and not a judging religious authority (See *WA* 30, 3, 75; Brecht, *Ehe*). 4 See the letter from Martin Luther to the Landgrave Philip of Hesse from April 10, 1540, HStAM, Sign. Best. 3 no. 2687, fol. 140r. 5 According to Martin Brecht, Luther's decision to grant Philip of Hesse a carte blanche for his bigamy reflects a "practicing of Protestant freedom," which was permitted to "the pastor in contrast to the judge." See Schilling, *Rebell*, p. 505. 6 *WA*.TR 4, 504, 26, (no. 4786). 7 See van Dülmen, *Kultur und Alltag*, p. 141.

covenant between the wedding pair.[8] The obligation to celibacy and the prohibition of incest had been introduced "for the sake of the kingdom of heaven" (Matthew 19:12). The indissolubility of marriage was another addition by the church. The canons declared marriage to be a "reflection of the covenant between Christ and his church" (Ephesians 5:32). Through their joint promise, the couple received God's help for their common future. In conjunction with the rise in the church's importance with relation to the family and the community, the influence of the church on married couples' private lives grew through the sacred marriage ceremony. The result was the increasing formalization and institutionalization of marriage.[9]

With Johannes Gutenberg's invention of the printing press in the mid-fifteenth century, writers with humanistic views who challenged existing traditions began to gain currency in German-speaking countries. With his frequently republished work *The Little Book of Marriage: Whether a Man Can Take a Wife or Not* (1472), Albrecht von Eyb raised misogynous arguments against the existing concept of marriage. Nevertheless, he invoked a statement fundamental to creation theology, namely that "marriage was created in Paradise in order to fill the world with people, to immortalize mankind, to grow families and their lineage, and to avoid the sin of unchastity."[10] In humanist circles, objections to obligatory celibacy grew. In the view of humanists, chastity and purity, as related to spiritual perfection, were idealistic and rarely practiced concepts. Marriage, however, was a fundamentally unavoidable matter for the "regeneration of mankind."[11] In his book *About Married Life* (1522),[12] Luther condemned the view "that a woman is a necessary evil, and no house should be without such an evil" strongly as the conviction of a blind pagan who mocks God's creatures.[13] The Reformer divested marriage of its status as a sacrament. For him, marriage was not an integral component of redemption. As opposed to baptism, for example, he believed marriage was not a sign of the receipt of divine grace or the purification of man from original sin.[14] Luther did not find any proof in the Bible that marriage was a sign received from God. From time immemorial, marriage had, according to him, been independent of faith.[15] Luther argued that marriage is "a completely secular thing"[16] and therefore part of human nature, which itself is subject to the divine order of creation. Man and woman should respect each other; and God's blessing serves to protect and honor this respect. According to Luther, therefore, marriage is a holy element of order pursuant to creation, which serves the purpose of fulfilling God's work; "be fruitful and multiply; populate the earth abundantly and increase upon it" (Genesis 9:7).

In his own theological training, Luther criticized what he considered to be the overemphasis of monasticism.[17] In the Roman Catholic Church the much lauded celibacy and virginity was reserved for the clergy. They were considered as the highest and most perfect state. In contrast, marriage was imperfect and therefore "second-rate," following the advice of the apostle Paul: "He who marries the virgin does right, but he who does not marry her does better" (1 Corinthians 7:38). Matrimony was nothing more than a vent for fornication and sexual desire.[18] Following church father Augustine, whose "confessions" concerning marriage in the year 401 had determined the direction of moral-theological and

Fig. 1   Johann Eberlin von Günzburg, Wie gar gfarlich sey. So Ain Priester kain Eeweyb hat […] (How very dangerous, that a priest does not have a wife), Augsburg, 1522. The author criticizes celibacy and the fornication that results from it.

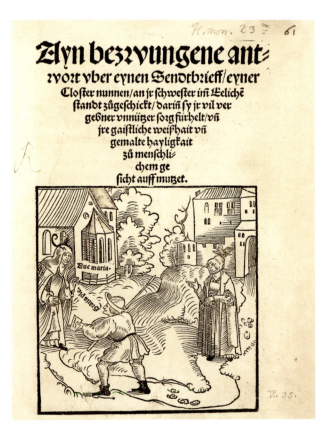

Fig. 2   Ayn bezwungene antwort vber einen Sendtbrief (A compelled answer to an open letter), Nuremberg 1524. This frontispiece of a pamphlet illustrates the positive evaluation of marriage and criticizes celibate monastery life.

philosophical interpretations of marriage for centuries,[19] Luther granted natural urges and desires a legitimate framework, the institution of marriage. He saw it as a way of life for all those who did not wish to follow the chaste life of a monk or nun. Fornication was reclassified through marriage and raised to a "standard that pleases the Lord."[20]

Nevertheless, it is important to point out Luther's earlier understanding of marriage, from before his own union with Katharina von Bora. In the first version of his *Sermon About Marriage* (1519), presumably published in Leipzig without his authorization by a follower, Luther expressed views that followed the established sacramental teachings of the Roman Catholic Church.[21] At this point, Luther regarded marriage as, in the words of Thomas Kaufmann, merely a "protective layer that covered the depravity of the flesh."[22] At this point, there is absolutely no mention of the transformation of man's animal instincts into a state of purity simply through the act of matrimony. Virginity was the highest possible form of life.[23] Luther responded quickly, publishing a corrected version of the *Sermon* in May 1519.[24] In this new, authorized version, virginity played a secondary role. Nevertheless, in his marriage theology Luther remained true to the Augustinian original sin theory. Even though Luther denounced marriage as a "hospital of the sickly,"[25] he ostensibly saw it primarily as a means to have children; "that it bears progeny, since that is the purpose and principal duty of marriage."[26]

Marriage is therefore an instrument of the actual purpose of Christian society. The wedded couple has the task of producing children, training them in the Christian way of life, and raising them with a responsible fear of God.[27] Luther recommended corporal punishment as an educational measure and a way to save a child's soul. In his mind, the soul was of more worth than the flesh; "following Solomon: if you beat your children with rods, then you will save their souls from hell."[28] Luther's elevation of marriage to a fundamental component of Christian belief needed to be protected from all forms of disparagement and hostility. In the course of his theological development, but above all during his pastoral work, Luther recognized more and more that the "Papist church's" dogma, which valued chastity more than marriage, endangered the social order. For Luther and his comrades-in-arms, the fact that marriage was given a lower standing put the social order at risk.[29] Ultimately, this vilification resulted in increased adultery and excessive fornication. Catholicism's "false doctrine" regarding marriage became a declared point of contention of the Reformation movement.

Against the backdrop of heavy criticism of celibacy, the endorsement for the marriage of priests became a fundamental tenant of the reform program, even until the Diet of Augsburg.[30] The question of whether clergy were allowed to marry moved the Christian community. Criticism of celibacy quickly left the narrow circle of theological debate to become a journalistic topic. Broadsheets were distributed and found their way behind the walls of countless convents and monasteries (fig. 1). Nuns and monks fled their cells and followed the new Lutheran marriage ideal. In propagating clerical marriage as a new social model, the reformers developed a propaganda topic, clearly rejecting the Roman Catholic Church and its understanding of marriage (fig. 2).[31] The social order began to falter. Seemingly precarious constellations gave way to new possibilities—and not only in the marital life of husband and wife. Older protagonists also chose the new marriage construct; priests who married their concubines became Protestant figureheads with virtuous wives.

During the following centuries, Luther and Katharina von Bora were elevated to the level of declared archetype for the Protestant rectory.[32] Protestants purposely used the double portrait of Luther and Katharina as a popular propaganda image. Up to the nineteenth century, wedding portraits of Luther and his wife, which were all based on the portraits so zealously brought to market by Lucas Cranach the Elder and his workshop, became the template for innumerable illustrations. They served to elevate Katharina as the ideal minister's wife to a "Lutheran icon" (fig. 3 and 4).[33] Meanwhile, a controversial marriage discourse began. New forms of confession and role assignments were discussed, with the tone ranging from polemic to outright misogynistic. In 1537, Cranach completed two pen drawings in which apparently middle-class women are depicted beating clerics, who are lying on the ground and lamenting, with farming tools such as flails and pitchforks. These illustration titled *Women Attack Clergy* show supposed concubines with children using violence against ostensibly celibate clergymen (fig. 5). Are these the potential wives and husbands of a new, reformed status? The polemic in this image is not only satirical about marriage but, to a much greater extent, also shows women, the allegedly weaker sex, spurning the Catholic Church and, in doing so, voicing scandalous derision.[34]

The individual role assignments of husband, wife, and child are critical for the Lutheran understanding of marital and familial coexistence. The father was the family's provider, breadwinner, and "regimental commander."[35] The wife, as the husband's helper, was the conscientious housekeeper and responsible for childcare. Respective

8 See Nave-Herz, *Hochzeit*, p. 11. 9 See Schröter, *Ehe*, pp. 379–398. 10 See Kaufmann, *Ehetheologie*, p. 285. For more about Albrecht von Eyb's connection between humanist and Christian ideologies about marriage and the relationship between man and wife, see Eib, *Humanismus*. 11 Ibid., p. 288. 12 *WA* 10/II, 267–304. 13 See *WA* 10/II, 293, 6 f. 14 Jordahn, *Trauung*. 15 See *WA* 6, 550, 33–37. 16 *WA* 30/III, 205, 12. 17 See *WA* 8, 573–669. In *De votis monasticis M. Lutheri iudicium*, from 1521, Luther questioned the healing properties and fairness of the monastic life and vows. 18 See Cor. I 7, 2–9. 19 In the scholasticism of the Middle Ages, Augustine was the starting point for every discussion about marriage, sexuality and original sin. In this process, Augustine's work was not called into question, but rather further refined. See Margraf, *Hochzeitspredigt*, pp. 52–75. 20 See Beintker, *Ehe und Ehelosigkeit*, p. 165. 21 See Beyer, *Luthers Ehelehre*, p. 62. 22 Kaufmann, *Ehetheologie*, p. 289. 23 Ibid. 24 *WA* 2, 166–171. 25 *WA* 2, 168, 3. 26 *WA* 2, 169, 30 f. 27 See Gause/Scholz, *Ehe und Familie*, pp. 13 f. 28 *WA* 2, 170, 23–25. 29 See also Tiller, *Frau im Spiegel*, p. 271. 30 Thomas Kaufmann follows Stephen E. Buckwalter in his analysis. The Reformation's concept of marriage was dynamized by the clamerous demand to allow priests to marry which was championed in February 1520 through Luther's publication *Ad schedulam inhibitionis sub nomine episcopi Miscensis*. See Kaufmann, *Ehetheologie*, p. 290. 31 See ibid., p. 291. 32 See Schilling, *Leitbild Luther*. 33 See Schilling, *Rebell*, pp. 528–530; quoted from Jancke, *Katharina von Bora*, p. 105. 34 See Ulbich, *Unartige Weiber*. 35 See Tiller, *Frau im Spiegel*, p. 276.

Fig. 3 Lucas Cranach the Elder, Martin Luther, 1529

Fig. 4 Lucas Cranach the Elder, Katharina von Bora, 1529

Fig. 5
Lucas Cranach the Elder, Women Attack Clergy, c. 1537. The putatively weaker and more lustful sex spurns the Catholic Church and its dignitaries.

to their divine mandate, the parents were responsible for the provision, upbringing, and care of their child or children. The child, balanced between the counteracting maternal leniency and care and paternal earnestness and strictness, was expected to show unlimited obedience and respect.[36] Furthermore, Luther's patriarchal concept of marriage meant that married men, through their new sexual self-confidence, were permitted to express and pursue their natural sexual desires in the interest of divinely ordained procreation.[37]

As a father, a man won the right to love and protect wife and children. The consciousness of the Reformation propagated a Christ like image of a loving, educative father. Subjects such as Lucas Cranach the Elder's *Christ Blessing the Children* were intended to arouse empathy and sensitivity (fig. 6). These images depicting the new ideals of coexistence, charity and family were intended to evoke a parallel to God and his close relationship to his believers.[38] Due to his own paternal experiences, which were rarely characterized by love, support, or confidence, Luther had difficulties with the "loving father role."[39] These images also helped solidify obligations to the Protestant religious community, emphasizing one fundamental aspect of the Reformation's philosophy, namely the enormous value accorded to the family.[40]

Statements that seem outlandish by today's standards, such as Luther's proclamation that "men have broad chests and narrow hips, which is why they have more sense than women, who have narrow

chests and broad hips and bottom, so that they should stay home, sit quietly in the house, keep the household, and bear and raise children,"[41] begging the question to what extent Luther and the reformers really produced a new concept of marriage and, pursuant, a new understanding of the family. A new, controversial image of women underwent a form of suitability test during the Reformation. In her roles as economical manager and housekeeper, the wife was implicitly elevated to the status of equal partner. Even in the course of Luther's lifetime, his wife Katharina was celebrated as a perfect example and glorified for centuries to come.[42] The chaste nun or the damned prostitute were both elevated in the marital state; "integrated" into the family, they were then released from their previous identification.[43] Lyndal Roper identified this as the "domestication" of the woman. The Protestant ideal image of a woman was the central focus of Christian family-planning and leading a life pleasing to God. Motherhood, as related to the duty to procreate, was upgraded to a "joyful punishment." In the self-contained universe of house and home, wives and mothers assumed responsibilities to which they weren't entitled outside their domestic framework.[44] New marriage laws and regulations dealing with marital disputes, divorce, and remarriage set the stage for marriages based on partnership within the patriarchal construct.[45]

With marriage partners capable of action—common practice in the families of craftsmen and workers in the late Middle Ages,

36 See Lemmer, *Haushalt und Familie*. 37 Ute Gause writes about the "valorization of male sexuality." See Gause, *Durchsetzung*, p. 334. 38 See also Schellenberger, *Solus Christus*. 39 See also Schilling, *Rebell*, p. 349. 40 At the same time, the image *Christ Blessing the Children*, which was the subject of numerous paintings by Cranach's workshop from the mid-1530s onwards, was clearly a statement supporting the baptism of children, a practice which had been called into question by the Anabaptists. See Brinkmann, *Cranach der Ältere*, p. 50. 41 *WA*.TR 1, 19, 15–18 (no. 55). 42 See Jancke, *Katharina von Bora*, p. 107. 43 See Roper, *Haus*, p. 9. 44 See Tiller, *Frau im Spiegel*, pp. 279 f. 45 See Ozment, *Fathers*, pp. 48 f. 46 See Burghartz, *Umordnung*, p. 172. 47 See ibid., pp. 172–185. 48 Hans Sachs wrote "pro-reformatory propaganda" in the form of numerous short poems. Among these were such treatises as *The Bittersweet Wedded Life*, which repeatedly presented Luther's views in new ways, from traditional to scholarly-satirical. See Stuplich, *Werk des Hans Sachs*, pp. 111, 122. 49 On July 29, 2008, American author Paul Auster wrote J. M. Coetzee, winner of the Nobel Prize in literature, "Marriage is above all a conversation, and if husband and wife do not figure out a way to become friends, the marriage has little chance of surviving. Friendship is a component of marriage, but marriage is an ever-evolving free-for-all, a continual work in progress, a constant demand to reach down into one's depths and reinvent oneself in relation to one another [...]" (Auster/Coetzee, *Briefe*). 50 Margraf, *Hochzeitspredigt*, p. 87.

Fig. 6
Lucas Cranach the Elder,
Christ Blessing the Children, 1545.
The picture identifies the blessing
Christ as child-loving model father.

according to Susanna Burghartz—a regulative instrument was created that intended to appear more effective and useful than other social constructs such as chaste religious life. Burghartz describes this as the "familiarization of work and life."[46] The focus was not on the gender roles of husband and wife but rather on the cultivation and maintenance of exemplary roles for an ideal basic structure of human coexistence.[47]

Numerous publications from the same time as the Lutheran exegeses show how difficult *The Bittersweet Wedded Life*[48] could be. The search for a good, fair coexistence parallel to the duties of marriage, whether as a holy sign or sacrament, was a challenge in the sixteenth century. Nevertheless, the re-evaluation of marriage during the Reformation initiated a structural process that has been continually redefined and stylized throughout the following centuries. Marriage was and is a "work in progress" that needs to be adjusted to the circumstances and requirements of the current time.[49] For Luther, marriage was the one and only God-given nucleus of Christian society, in which the partners take "the troubles of day-to-day life with pleasure and optimism" upon themselves.[50]

BIBLIOGRAPHY

Auster, Paul/**Coetzee**, John M. (2014), *Von hier nach da: Briefe 2008–2011.* n. p. **Beintker**, Horst (1983), Über Ehe und Ehelosigkeit im Anschluß an Paulus in 1. Kor. 7. In: id. (ed.), *Martin Luther: Taschenausgabe. Vol. 4: Evangelium und Leben.* Berlin, p. 165. **Beyer**, Michael (1999), Luthers Ehelehre bis 1525. In: Treu, Martin/Stiftung Luthergedenkstätten in Sachsen-Anhalt (eds.), *Katharina von Bora, die Lutherin.* Wittenberg, pp. 59–82. **Brecht**, Martin (2013), *Inwiefern ist die Ehe ein weltlich Ding?* Zur Orientierungshilfe des Rats der EKD über die Familie, August 8, 2013. Available: http://www.kblw.de/ekd-orientierungshilfe/ [03/03/2016]. **Brinkmann**, Bodo (ed.) (2007), *Cranach der Ältere.* Frankfurt am Main. **Burghartz**, Susanna (2003), Umordnung statt Unordnung? Ehe, Geschlecht und Reformationsgeschichte. In: Puff, Helmut/Wild, Christopher (eds.), *Zwischen den Disziplinen. Perspektiven der Frühneuzeitforschung.* Göttingen, pp. 165–186. **Eib**, Maja (2001), *Der Humanismus und sein Einfluss auf das Eheverständnis im 15. Jahrhundert: eine philosophisch-moraltheologische Untersuchung unter besonderer Berücksichtigung des frühhumanistischen Gedank-enguts Albrechts von Eyb.* Münster. **Gause**, Ute (2013), Durchsetzung neuer Männlichkeit? Ehe und Reformation. In: *Evangelische Theologie,* vol. 73, no. 5, pp. 326–338. **Gause**, Ute/**Scholz**, Stephanie (eds.) (2012), *Ehe und Familie im Geist des Luthertums. Die Oeconomia Christiana (1529) des Justus Jonas.* Leipzig. **Jancke**, Gabriele (2014), Katharina von Bora—Rezeptionen machen Geschichte. In: Schellenberger, Simona/Thieme, André/Welich, Dirk (eds.), *Eine STARKE FRAUENgeschichte. 500 Jahre Reformation.* Beucha, pp. 103–110. **Jordahn**, Bruno (1953), Die Trauung bei Luther. In: *Luther. Mitteilungen der Luthergesellschaft,* vol. 24, pp. 13–15. **Kaufmann**, Thomas (2008), Ehetheologie im Kontext der frühen Wittenberger Reformation. In: Holzem, Andreas/Weber, Ines (eds.), *Ehe—Familie—Verwandtschaft. Vergesellschaftung in Religion und sozialer Lebenswelt.* Paderborn et al., pp. 285–299. **Lemmer**, Manfred (1991), Haushalt und Familie aus der Sicht der Hausväterliteratur. In: Ehlert, Trude (ed.), *Haushalt und Familie in Mittelalter und früher Neuzeit.* Sigmaringen, pp. 186–189. **Margraf**, Erik (2007), Die Hochzeitspredigt der frühen Neuzeit. München, pp. 52–75. **Nave-Herz**, Rosemarie (1997), *Die Hochzeit. Ihre heutige Sinnzuschreibung seitens der Eheschließenden: eine empirisch-soziologische Studie.* Würzburg. **Ozment**, Steven (1983), *When Fathers Ruled. Family Life in Reformation Europe.* Cambridge. **Rockwell**, William Walker (1904), *Die Doppelehe des Landgrafen Philipp von Hessen.* Marburg. **Roper**, Lyndal (1999), *Das fromme Haus. Frauen und Moral in der Reformation.* Frankfurt am Main/New York. **Schellenberger**, Simona (2014), Solus Christus—oder Vater-Mutter-Kind—ein Spiel für Jeder(mann). In: id./Thieme, André/Welich, Dirk (eds.), *Eine STARKE FRAUENgeschichte. 500 Jahre Reformation.* Beucha, pp. 53–56. **Schilling**, Heinz (2012), *Martin Luther. Rebell in einer Zeit des Umbruchs.* München. **Schilling**, Johannes (2013), Leitbild Luther? Martin Luther, das deutsche Pfarrhaus und der evangelische Pfarrstand. In: Baumunk, Bodo-Michael/Koschnik, Leonore/Deutsches Historisches Museum (eds.), *Leben nach Luther: eine Kulturgeschichte des evangelischen Pfarrhauses.* Bönen, pp. 33–43. **Schröter**, Michael (1985), *"Wo zwei zusammenkommen in rechter Ehe…"—Sozio- und psychogenetische Studien über die Eheschließungsvorgänge vom 12. bis 15. Jahrhundert.* Frankfurt am Main. **Stuplich**, Brigitte (2006), Die "unordentlich lieb" im Werk des Hans Sachs. In: Tacke, Andreas (ed.): *"… wir wollen der Liebe Raum geben:" Konkubinate geistlicher und weltlicher Fürsten um 1500.* Göttingen, pp. 111–126. **Tiller**, Elisabeth (1996), *Frau im Spiegel: die Selben und die Anderen zwischen Welt und Text: von Herren, Fremden und Frauen, ein 16. Jahrhundert.* Vol. 1. Frankfurt am Main et al. **Ulbich**, Claudia (1990), Unartige Weiber. Präsenz und Renitenz von Frauen im frühneuzeitlichen Deutschland. In: Van Dülmen, Richard (ed.), *Studien zur historischen Kulturforschung. Vol. 2: Arbeit, Frömmigkeit und Eigensinn.* Frankfurt am Main, pp. 13–42. **Van Dülmen**, Richard (1990), *Kultur und Alltag in der Frühen Neuzeit. Vol. 1: Das Haus und seine Menschen, 16.–18. Jahrhundert.* München.

REFORMATION NETWORKS

To the extent to which existing data permit, the diagram shows all correspondents of the pictured major protagonists of the Reformation. Although many letters have been lost, it is clear that both of the main reformers were prolific correspondents. Around 4,300 letters by Luther, and around 7,500 by Philipp Melanchthon have been preserved. Each of the two had his own circle of correspondents, with only about 30 joint addressees, including, as important branch points, Johannes Bugenhagen, Justus Jonas, and also the emperor. Melanchthon had a significantly greater number of correspondents than Luther.

Ulrich von Hutten was well-integrated into the Reformation network—unlike Thomas Müntzer, who appears an outsider.

They had hardly any contact with representatives of the Catholic Church (Pope, cardinals), who had their own (Catholic) correspondents. The artists were networked with imperial politicians and reformers alike, but wrote comparatively few letters. Only seven letters by Lucas Cranach the Elder have survived.

Further research will be necessary to build a more complete image of the Reformation networks.

THE CORRESPONDENCE OF THE REFORMATION'S PROTAGONISTS
according to edited sources

- ● Reformers
- ● Princes
- ● Humanists
- ● Artists
- · Correspondents

INTENSITY OF CORRESPONDENCE COUNTED BY LETTERS

- 1–10 letters
- 10–100 letters
- > 100 letters

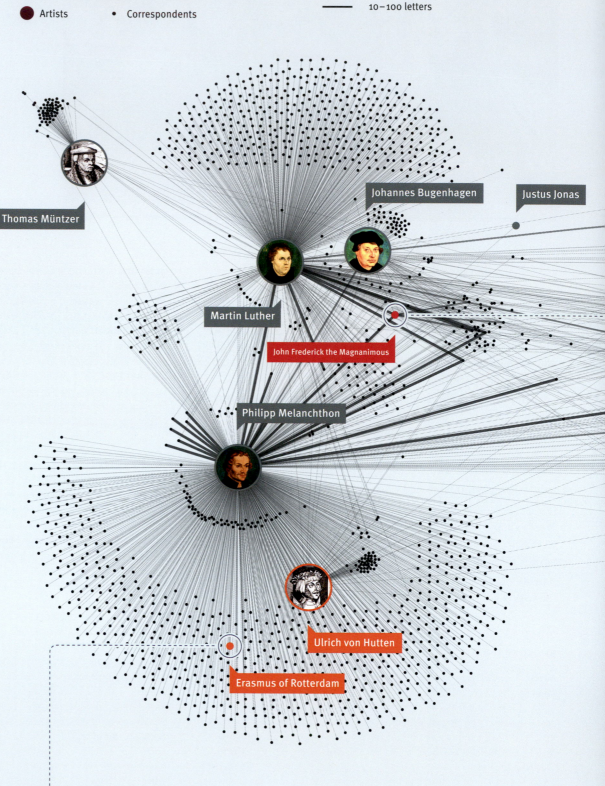

Thomas Müntzer

Johannes Bugenhagen

Justus Jonas

Martin Luther

John Frederick the Magnanimous

Philipp Melanchthon

Ulrich von Hutten

Erasmus of Rotterdam

✉ ERASMUS OF ROTTERDAM

Erasmus of Rotterdam, the most important humanist of his time, left 150 books and over 2,000 letters when he died. There seems to have had been little contact with the reformers: Erasmus only wrote four letters to Melanchthon, and eleven to Luther, receiving from them in response seven and two letters, respectively.

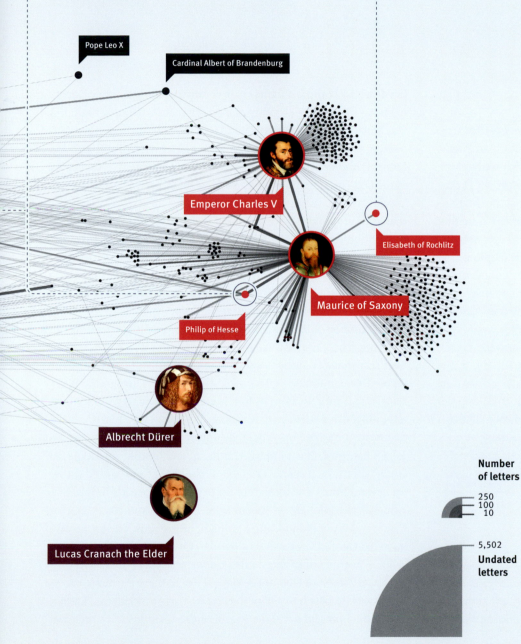

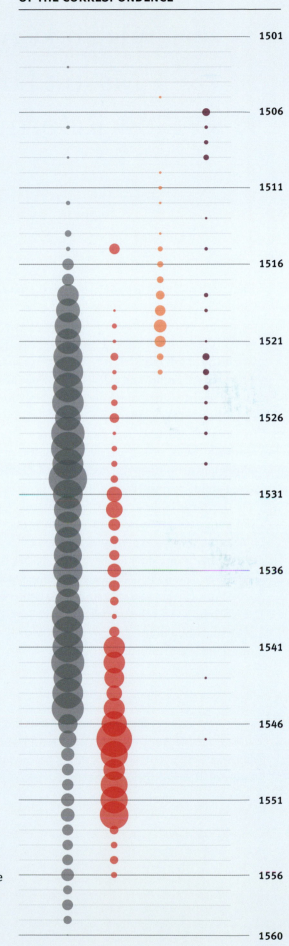

ELISABETH OF ROCHLITZ

Elisabeth of Rochlitz (actually, Elisabeth of Hesse), the sister of Philip of Hesse, appears as an inconspicuous correspondent of Maurice of Saxony. However, she had a lively correspondence with many princes not pictured here.

THE KEY PEOPLE OF THE SCHMALKALDIC LEAGUE

John Frederick the Magnanimous and Philip of Hesse, the leaders of the Protestant imperial princes, served as a bridge between the reformers and imperial politicians.

Pope Leo X

Cardinal Albert of Brandenburg

Emperor Charles V

Elisabeth of Rochlitz

Maurice of Saxony

Philip of Hesse

Albrecht Dürer

Lucas Cranach the Elder

Number of letters

250
100
10

5,502
Undated letters

1501

1506

1511

1516

1521

1526

1531

1536

1541

1546

1551

1556

1560

CHRONOLOGICAL DISTRIBUTION

Many of the letters were not dated by the senders. Despite this lack of clarity, an interesting picture emerges from the dated letters. The reformers' correspondences have been preserved evenly, with a significant decline after Luther's death (1546). Most of the preserved letters from politicians date from the time of the Schmalkaldic War between Emperor Charles V and the Protestant princes (1546/47).

STEFAN RHEIN

Friends and Colleagues: Martin Luther and His Fellow Reformers in Wittenberg

The Solitary Reformer

There are two scenes in particular from the life and works of Martin Luther that have become landmarks of collective cultural memory: the nailing up of his theses on October 31, 1517, which marked the birth of the Reformation, and Luther's appearance before the Diet of Worms, on April 17 and 18, 1521, where he pronounced the momentous words, "I cannot and will not recant anything, since it is neither safe nor right to go against conscience. May God help me. Amen."[1] With these words Luther emerged as the unwavering epitome of freedom of conscience and moral courage. Over the course of the centuries, these two scenes have, in the form of text and image, solidified into national myths; in them, Luther is presented as a solitary hero fighting against his enemies.[2]

The image of the lonely reformer was all but engraved in stone and immortalized in public. So much so that Wittenberg, in the nineteenth century, experienced an intense debate as to whether the 1821 Luther monument in the market square ought to be supplemented by a monument dedicated to Philipp Melanchthon. Did this not—literally—amount to "a sin against Luther's greatness?" A walk across today's Wittenberg market square shows that the proponents of Melanchthon prevailed: in 1865, the two reformers were peacefully united on their pedestals.[3]

The Circle of Wittenberg Reformers

In contrast to the public focus on Luther as individual and personality, academic research has dealt intensely with the Wittenberg Reformation in general, increasingly perceiving the collaborative nature of the Reformation. The same is true for the Bible translation.

Contrary to common belief, it was not merely the single consequence of a solitary eleven-week sojourn at Wartburg. Rather, it was Melanchthon's brainchild, and it occupied him and other Wittenberg scholars well into the 1540s.[4] In a letter written at Wartburg, Luther had already considered the translation of the Bible, especially of the Old Testament, a work to be distributed among several translators: "For I hope we will give a better translation to our Germany than the Latins have. It is a great and worthy undertaking on which we all should work."[5] The German Bible thus became a joint effort in the best sense, and numerous Wittenberg scholars, in many lengthy meetings, contributed to it. The professors at Wittenberg University—*Alma Mater Leucorea*, as it was then called—joined their expertise in linguistic, theological, and other matters, particularly for the revision of the translation. Johannes Matthesius provides an arresting description of these meetings in the thirteenth of his seventeen sermons on Luther's life: "After the first publication of the whole German Bible […] Doctor Luther would return to the Bible, reviewing it entirely, from its first book onward, with great seriousness, diligence, and prayers. And since the Son of God had promised that he would be present where several are gathered in his name and ask for his Spirit, Doctor Martin Luther quickly summoned a special council of the best people available at the time. These would gather for several hours a week before dinner in the doctor's monastery, namely Doctor Johannes Bugenhagen, Doctor Justus Jonas, Doctor Cruciger, Master Philipp, and Matthäus Aurogallus. The group also included Georg Rörer, the proofreader. Often, foreign doctors and scholars would contribute to this important work, such as Doctor Bernhard Ziegler or Doctor Forster … Prior to these meetings, everyone would prepare himself for the text … This president (i.e., Luther) would then present a text, letting all of the assembly have their say,

1 For the Diet of Worms, Luther's various interrogations and his statements, see Leppin, *Martin Luther*, p. 177; Schilling, *Rebell*, p. 222. **2** For myth-making around Luther, see Joestel, *Luthermythen*; see also Münkler, *Die Deutschen*, pp. 181–196. **3** For the monuments of the two Wittenberg reformers, see Kammer, *Reformationsdenkmäler*, pp. 172 f. For the dispute about the site of the Melanchthon monument, see Kammer, *Melanchthondenkmal*. **4** See Zur Mühlen, *Luthers Bibelübersetzung*. **5** Letter to Amsdorf of January 13, 1522. In: *LW* 48, 363. **6** Johannes Matthesius, *Historien von des Ehrwirdigen inn Gott seli-*

gen thewren Manns Gottes, Doctoris Martini Luthers anfang, Lehr, leben unnd sterben [1570]. Nürnberg, fol. 151a – 152a. **7** Luther's biographer, Martin Brecht, shows his understanding for the attempt to consider Luther and his fellow reformers as a team ("There is some truth to the notion of the Wittenberg team"), but eventually treats the idea with skepticism: "Nevertheless, the notion of the Wittenberg team is not altogether adequate. In the majority of fields, Luther's creativity and charisma and, hence, his competence and authority simply outshone the others." See Brecht, *Geist*, p. 72. The notion of the "Wit-

and listen to their discussion … Splendid and instructive statements are said to have been made in the course of this work."[6] Ultimately, however, decisions on the translation were made by Luther, which highlights his prominent role on the Wittenberg team.[7]

The Group of Reformers, Presented in a Picture

The collaboration of the Wittenberg reformers is most strikingly presented on Lucas Cranach the Younger's epitaph for Paul Eber at the Wittenberg Town Church (fig. 1).[8] It was occasioned by Paul Eber's role as Bugenhagen's successor as Wittenberg parish priest and general superintendent, as well as his previous positions as teacher at the Wittenberg *Pädagogium* and professor of physics and Hebrew. In the last eleven years of his life, Eber served as professor of theology and priest of the Town Church, where he was also buried after his death. The epitaph polemically contrasts Protestant collaboration with Catholic chaos. While the vineyard on the left is laid waste by the destructive deeds of the Pope, bishops, priests, and monks, the vineyard of the Lord, on the right-hand side of the painting, thrives and prospers. Each worker here has a task of his own; all of them are working hand in hand. In the foreground, Luther, Melanchthon, and Bugenhagen form a prominent triangle, which is extended by the vine-pruning Eber in front of them. Luther's portrayal as a gardener—he is smoothing the soil with a rake—is closely related to reality, inasmuch as the Reformer enjoyed gardening as his favorite pastime when recovering from his work as professor of theology. "In my next life, I want to be a gardener," he wrote in a letter.[9] Melanchthon is drawing water from a well to irrigate the soil, that is to say, he goes ad *fontes*, to the sources, the three holy languages of Hebrew, Greek, and Latin; knowledge of these is the prerequisite for an authentic understanding of the Bible. Bugenhagen, finally, is hoeing the soil, thus establishing order in a way similar to his church orders, which regulated ecclesial and political life in Protestant countries and cities. The captions are German verses explaining the polemical intention of the antithetically arranged painting; they draw a parallel between the work in the vineyard and the reformers' joint development work in rediscovering the Word and the Grace of God. Other historical figures can be recognized next to those mentioned: Johannes Forster, who is watering the soil; Georg Major, who is tying the vines; Paul Krell, who is carrying the grapes away in a tub; Caspar Cruciger, who is driving a rod into the ground; Justus Jonas, who is digging the soil with a spade; Georg Spalatin, with a muck shovel; Georg Rörer, who is picking up stones; and Sebastian Fröschel, who empties the stones from a trough.

The painting merges different temporal levels in showing the reformers next to their early disciples; that is to say, it presents two generations of reformers, all of whom, as professors of theology at Wittenberg University and as ministers, are part of the institutions of university and church, thus sharing the same professional background as Martin Luther. Describing his personal development over the years, Luther remarked that, at the beginning of the Reformation task, he had been all alone; it was only over the course of years that a "Schola Witebergensis," as he called it, in the service of the revealed and purified Word of God, had emerged which, as a critical authority, would promote the welfare of the Church of the Gospel after his death.[10] The term "Schola Witebergensis" denotes a circle of colleagues serving a common cause in an atmosphere of intense cooperation and, obviously, in mutual affection. Why, otherwise, would Melanchthon have compared heaven with an academy, a university of colleagues?[11]

Looking back on the group's gradual emergence and, as a result, treating it, Lucas Cranach the Younger translated the motif of the Wittenberg team into a painting—not only in the *Vineyard of the Lord* but also in the epitaph for Nordhausen mayor Michael Meyenburg (preserved as a copy in the Church of St. Blasius at Nordhausen after World War II). He staged the Wittenberg reformers as a group authority, thus emphasizing that Luther was not the only repository and witness of the truth of faith that had been established by the Reformation.[12] The earliest representation of the group is, however, not a spectacular painting but a hidden collection of coats of arms, which dates from 1533. The coats of arms of Luther, Melanchthon, Jonas, Bugenhagen, and Cruciger—quite obviously, the inner circle of the Wittenberg group—can be found both in the matriculation book of Wittenberg University and on the title border of the print of *Luther's Sermon on the Lost Sheep*, published by Wittenberg printer Hans Lufft in 1533.[13]

The Joint Work of Reformation Theology

Even though the group of reformers only took shape in the arts after the deaths of Luther and Melanchthon, it had become a reality much earlier, as has been made clear by recent research. As early as 1516, Luther had been part—most certainly the part with the greatest say—of a group of Wittenberg theologians who opposed scholastic theology and Aristotelian philosophy and aimed to replace them with the study of the Bible and the church fathers. This can be seen from the development of central Reformation axioms, such as the principle of scripture, that is, the emphasis placed on the Bible as the only source of faith. This scriptural principle was first advocated

tenberg team" is emphatically stressed by Kolb, *Theology*, pp. 103 f.: "Without teams, no Reformation … The Wittenberg Reformation certainly revolved around the professor, who sparked it, Martin Luther, but Luther would not have been able to change the face and heart of the church in Germany and beyond without his team … They were not called to be—and were not—Luther clones; they were members of his team." **8** For the Eber epitaph, see Albrecht Steinwach, *Der Weinberg des Herrn. Epitaph für Paul Eber von Lucas Cranach d. J.* [1569]. Spröda 2001; Harasimovicz/Seyderhelm, *Cranachs Kirche*, pp. 101–112; for Paul Eber, see Rhein, *Paul Eber*; and Gerth/Leppin, *Paul Eber*. **9** *WA.B* 4, 310, 13 (no. 1189). For Luther's gardening activities, see Heling, *Zu Haus bei Luther*, pp. 33–44. **10** See Leder, *Beziehungen*, p. 420. **11** Thus Melanchthon in a letter to Sigismund Gelous, May 20, 1559, see Scheible/Mundhenk, *Melanchthons Briefwechsel* (hereinafter MBW), Letter No. 8961. **12** See the comprehensive and knowledgeable study by Hasse, *Luther und seine Freunde*, pp. 84–119. **13** See ibid., pp. 86 f.; for representations of the Wittenberg group, see also Zerbe, *Reformation*, especially pp. 417 f.

with indubitable clarity by Melanchthon, in the presentation and defense of his bachelor's theses in theology on September 9, 1519. Having studied and taught the liberal arts at Heidelberg and Tübingen, the twenty-two-year-old Melanchthon had only come to Wittenberg slightly more than a year before and taken up theological studies at Luther's instigation. Luther found Melanchthon's theses "a little audacious but most true," and was deeply impressed: "He (i.e., Melanchthon) so replied as to appear a wonder to us all. If Christ pleases, he will go beyond many Martins, a most strenuous foe to the devil and scholastic theology."[14] Among his twenty-four theses, the ones to cause a stir were theses sixteen and eighteen, in particular; their explosive nature was noticed also by the Catholic opponents and prompted Johannes Eck to complain to Elector Frederick of Saxony. What caused the stir was that Melanchthon asserted scripture, against the authority of councils, as the only norm, as well as the resulting conclusion that both the sacrament of Holy Orders and the transubstantiation of bread and wine into the body and blood of Christ lacked a biblical basis and were therefore no truths of faith.[15] Melanchthon's bachelor's theses are an early but strong example of the joint work of the Wittenberg Reformation. Against their background, Luther's self-understanding as a "solitary prophet" is a fiction rather than historical reality—a fiction, however, reinforced by the intense literary and visual stylization of Luther as a hero.[16]

The solidarity of the group did not only show in the appearance of its individual members but also in their respective writings: they contributed forewords to each other's publications, published together in anthologies, or translated each other's works. Among them, the "triumvirate" of Luther, Melanchthon, and Bugenhagen was particularly prominent. The authority of the Wittenberg Reformation was concentrated in these three figures and their numerous advice and expert opinions on ecclesial and political questions. As they also answered questions addressed to them, their joint authority soon met with recognition, both internally and externally.[17] The one to hold a special position in Luther's life was Bugenhagen. While all of his other colleagues were Luther's juniors by at least ten years —Jonas was born in 1493; Melanchthon, in 1497; Cruciger, in 1504— the 1485-born Bugenhagen was almost of the same age, and, like Luther, he had been a priest who had gradually broken his vows. As the first Protestant parish priest, Bugenhagen was Luther's theological colleague at the university from October 1523 onward, and also his spiritual director and confessor. When Luther, in the second half of 1527, was stricken with disease and deep sadness, Bugenhagen and

his family even moved into Luther's house to see him through his affliction. He thus spent more than six months in the company of Luther, who compared Bugenhagen's encouragement with an *angeli vox*, an angel's voice.[18]

In the course of the 1530s, the Wittenberg triad developed into a five-man committee; it was extended to include Justus Jonas and Caspar Cruciger, who together with Luther, Melanchthon, and Bugenhagen thenceforth represented the collective authority's inner circle.[19] Cruciger, the youngest of them, served as professor of theology and preacher at the Castle Church from 1533 onward; he was particularly appreciated by Luther, who loved him like a son and chose him as his theological heir. Cruciger thus became the publisher of Luther's *Summer Postil* and the main person responsible for the Wittenberg Luther edition. When he died at age forty-four, Melanchthon wrote an impressive memorial address that bears eloquent testimony to the two men's amicable relationship and their mutual humanistic, scientific, and theological interests.[20]

Ranking second after Luther in the spiritual hierarchy of the Wittenberg theologians was Jonas, who served as provost at the All Saints' congregation. Jonas stood out for his numerous translations of Luther's and Melanchthon's Latin texts, which helped popularize the Reformation ideas—two of these works were his German translations of Luther's reply to Erasmus, *On the Bondage of the Will* (Wittenberg, 1526), and Melanchthon's *Against the Pope's Unclean Celibacy and the Prohibition of Clerical Marriage* (Wittenberg, 1541). His translation of Luther's *On the Bondage of the Will*—the Latin version was published in December 1525—was ready for printing at the beginning of January 1526. Obviously, the two men worked hand in hand with each other—often, Jonas would render the German version in greater detail and added commentaries so as to make Luther's statements clearer and more easily graspable for nontheological readers.[21]

The five most prominent reformers made themselves a name with collectively formulated expert opinions on theological, religiopolitical, church organizational, and matrimonial matters, which, written for the most part at the sovereign's request, serve as early examples of political advice. The authors of these opinions were primarily Melanchthon, Luther, and Bugenhagen, and, considerably less so, Jonas and Cruciger.[22] Melanchthon, although lowest in academic rank (he had only earned a master's degree), is most commonly mentioned as a coauthor. This does not come as a surprise, for the jointly published texts in which the Wittenberg theologians' group authority expressed itself benefited much from his structured

---

14 *WA*.B 1, 514, 33–36 (no. 202). Quoted after Edwards, *Life of Philip Melanchthon*, p. 337. In those years, Wittenberg professor of theology Andreas Karlstadt also considered Melanchthon as "primus dux ecclesiae Wittenbergensis," see Kruse, *Anfänge*, p. 282. **15** For an English translation of Melanchthon's theses, see Hill, *Some Theses*, pp. 245–248. **16** See, by way of introduction, Kruse, *Universitätstheologie*. In his doctoral thesis, Kruse explains in detail the themes and figures of the Wittenberg "reform group," a "community of discussion" advocating the new theological notion of scripture as a basis, and sharing positions aiming at the supersession of scholastic theology, with different emphasis in each case, see Kruse, *Universitätstheologie*. For early attempts to stylize and heroize Luther, see Kaufmann, *Anfang*, pp. 266–333. **17** See Seidel, *Frankreich*, pp. 115 f. A letter from Paracelsus, written in 1525, to the "Christian broth-

ers" Luther, Bugenhagen, and Melanchthon has been preserved, see Rhein, *Melanchthon und Paracelsus*, p. 63. Elector John Frederick on December 13, 1543, addressed an inquiry to the three Wittenberg reformers regarding the deployment of a court preacher to Grimmenstein Castle, see *MBW*, no. 3397. **18** See Gummelt, *Pomeranus*, p. 96. **19** For the extension of the trias into a five-man body, see Wolgast, *Luther*, pp. 91 f. **20** The address has been reprinted in Corpus Reformatorum (1842). Halle, pp. 833–841; for Cruciger, see Leder, *Beziehungen*, pp. 436–438; Wolgast, *Luther*, p. 93. **21** Thus Mennecke, *Justus Jonas*. **22** See Kohnle, *Gemeinschaftsgutachten*. **23** Junghans, *Melanchthon*, p. 152, with note 155. **24** *WA*.B 1, 269, 33–35 (no. 120), quoted after Edwards, *Life of Philip Melanchthon*, p. 337. **25** *MBW* T 1, p. 196, 97 f. (no. 84), quoted after Manschreck, *Melanchthon*, p. 54. **26** *WA* 30/II, 68, 9–11.

Fig. 1 Lucas Cranach the Younger, The Vineyard of the Lord (Epitaph for Paul Eber),
1573–74, Town and Parish Church of St. Mary's, Wittenberg

thinking, rhetorical style, and precise formulations. Thanks to these gifts, Melanchthon became the "theological secretary of the Wittenberg Reformation;" in terms of conceptual responsibility, he is even something of a "theological state secretary," as Helmar Junghans anachronistically paraphrases Melanchthon's important task in the reformers' text production.[23]

Martin Luther and Philipp Melanchthon

The Wittenberg reformers were partners in a closely related team, and some of them also shared intense personal relations. The relationship most discussed in Reformation research is that between Luther and Melanchthon, who first met in August 1518, when twenty-one-year-old Melanchthon—Luther's junior by more than

thirteen years—came to Wittenberg as a professor of Greek. The two men were deeply impressed with one another; Luther was even prompted to make a euphoric profession of sympathy: "Our Philipp Melanchthon is a wonderful man; yea hardly anything can be found in him which is not more than human,"[24] he wrote in a letter four months after Melanchthon's arrival. Melanchthon, on the other hand, wrote the following lines in 1520, when Luther was at Wartburg: "I would rather die than be separated from this man."[25] The shared feelings of euphoria gradually transformed into mutual respect for the other's intellectual achievements. In his foreword to Melanchthon's interpretation of the Letter to the Colossians, translated into German by Justus Jonas, Luther in 1529 wrote: "Master Philipp's books are more agreeable to me than my own, and I rather see them in Latin and in German at their place than my own."[26]

The differences of temperament, however, became more and more obvious. In the preface quoted above, Luther described them with illuminating, yet serene and respectful, words: "For this I was born: to fight and take the field against mobs and devils. Therefore many of my books are stormy and warlike. I must pull out the stumps and roots, hack away at thorns and thistles, drain the swamps. I am the coarse woodsman who must blaze a new trail. But Master Philipp comes neatly and quietly behind me; cultivates and plants, sows and waters with joy, according to the gifts that God has richly given him."[27] But the differences in character also show in Melanchthon's lack of understanding for, and irritation about, Luther, whose often unbridled "contentiousness" he considers a "humiliating servitude;" Luther, on the other hand, is annoyed at Melanchthon's timidity during the 1530 Diet of Augsburg, denouncing his worries as a lack of faith.[28]

In spite of their various dissonances in character and content and their controversial debates about good works, the right understanding of the Lord's Supper, and the way of dealing with the Catholic Church, there are situations that seem to be far more relevant for the personal relationship between Luther and Melanchthon—situations in which one of the two is sick and in need of help. In 1540, Melanchthon, while on a journey, suffered a physical and psychological breakdown near Weimar that was so severe that his companions thought he was going to die. Luther, upon hearing the disturbing news, immediately left Wittenberg and hurried to Melanchthon's bedside, praying for hours and trying to uplift the seriously ill man who had already lost all hope of life. Luther snapped at his colleague—who imagined himself on the brink of death—and told him that he had to continue to serve God: "Do you hear, Philipp, in a word, either you eat or I will excommunicate you!" Melanchthon recovered, and during dinner conversations Luther would repeatedly tell the story of how his prayers were answered.[29]

A little-known story deals with the care returned by Melanchthon when successfully treating the sick Luther in 1544. Melanchthon tells the story in a lecture taken down by an attentive student: "Doctor Martin Luther, a year before his death, called me at two o'clock in the morning. Coincidentally, I had already gotten up. I went to him and asked him what was wrong. O, he said, I suffer great and dangerous pain. I asked him if it was the stone. He replied: No, it's larger than a stone. I felt his pulse, which was regular. I said: The heart is intact, it's not a stroke. He replied: Something is tightening around my heart, but I don't feel my heart contracting, nor do I feel any pulse complaints. I thought it was nothing other than liquids rising at the cardia. Hence the heavy pressure; the name of the disease is breast stinging. I then tried to determine where the illness

came from. He had gone to the toilet (he was that well-behaved), when a serious cold prevailed. Immediately, he felt that the cold and, withal, the illness took hold of him. In fact, the cold was so severe that it stimulated his humors and made them rise. I immediately ordered his chest and back to be rubbed with warm towels, and a soup or a broth to be prepared for him. I forbade him to drink new wine, which he had been drinking. I sent my servant to fetch some wine from my cellar, where I had good Rhine wine. Soon after he'd eaten the soup, the humor settled, and I told him to rest and to keep the heated towels. Later, when he was dead, people said he had died from a stroke. But it wasn't a stroke; he died of the illness I have described. For shortly before his death, he wrote to me that he was again stricken by this illness."[30] Melanchthon's services as personal physician at Luther's sickbed illustrate the two men's relationship of trust in an unexpected way. Melanchthon's deep bond to Luther, on the other hand, shows most strikingly in his lament over Luther's death: "Gone is the Chariot of Israel which ruled the church in this last age of the world!" On another occasion he confesses his heartfelt gratitude: "I have learned the Gospel from him."[31]

Luther's Friendships, or Fighting the Devil

Although the Wittenberg theologians primarily knew each other as collaborators who worked for the same cause, they had also formed close and confidential friendships and helped each other in case of physical and mental conditions. Jonas and Bugenhagen, for instance, would support Luther when he was tormented by fits of self-doubt and depression. In one of his letters, Jonas relates how Luther, at the beginning of July 1527, suffers a collapse that is accompanied by tinnitus and tachycardia; the arresting account includes a verbatim quote of Luther's utterances: "O Doctor, Jona, I am sick; give me water or whatever you have at hand, or I'll die … Lord, my very dear God, I would fain have shed my blood for your Word, you know, but perhaps I am unworthy … My very dear God, you have led me into this, you know that your Truth and Word exist."[32] Luther even bade last farewells to his wife and to Hans, his small son, but then recovered and in hindsight found the temptations of the spirit far more irksome than his physical disease. Bugenhagen was also present; he heard Luther's confession and fortified him in a confessional conversation that lasted several hours.[33]

The need for friendship grows with increasing individualization—that is, when a person's life is characterized by the liberation of individuality as a result of social differentiation, a release from traditional and local structures of order, increased mobility, vocational differentiation, and the growing heterogeneity of social con-

27 *WA* 30/II, 68, 12 – 69, 1; quoted after Hendrix, *Martin Luther*, p. 215. **28** For Melanchthon's suffering under Luther, see, by way of example, his letter of April 28, 1548, to Carlowitz. In: Scheible, *Melanchthon*, pp. 304 – 332; for the relationship of the two reformers, see ibid., pp. 139 – 152; for Luther's criticism of Melanchthon's timidity, see Kobler, *Protestantische Melanchthonkritik*, pp. 257 – 260. **29** See Mülhaupt, *Luther*, p. 133; English translation of Luther's dictum quoted in Hendrix, *Martin Luther*, p. 259. **30** For a detailed account, see

Rhein, *Melanchthon als Hausarzt*, pp. 363 f. **31** For Melanchthon's relationship to Luther—from "infatuation" to "posthumous appreciation"—see Scheible, *Biographie*, pp. 143 – 169. **32** See Kawerau, *Briefwechsel*, p. 105. **33** See Vogt, *Briefwechsel*, pp. 64 – 73; see also *WA.TR* 3, 81 – 90 (no. 2922 b); see also Gummelt, *Pomeranus*. **34** See Tenbruck, *Freundschaft*, p. 439. **35** See Imhof, *Verlorene Welten*, p. 158. **36** See Treml, *Humanistische Gemeinschaftsbildung*. **37** It may be no accident, therefore, that Wittenberg became the birthplace of

tacts. Friendship compensates for the uncertainty that arises as a result of these processes of social differentiation.[34] While the early modern era was marked, among other things, by a structurally stable and well-ordered world of everyday life, where most people's horizons rarely stretched beyond a distance of twenty-five miles,[35] the reformers were exposed to a situation that was far more complex and confusing. By this time the humanistic scholars of the fifteenth and sixteenth centuries had already entertained a high ideal of friendship, establishing close communication networks with numerous correspondences and sodalities, that is, scholarly networks.[36] Here, individuals would encounter other individuals and become friends because they shared common intellectual interests, wanted to experience their own personalities, and were looking for communication as a means of self-development. These friendships were personal relationships that individuals had freely entered into, and they would go beyond the narrow confines of neighborhood or family. The painful experience of loneliness also led (and still leads) to the complementary experience of friendship. The reformers are part of this learned set. Hailing from very different regions when they encountered each other in Wittenberg—Luther was from Mansfeld County, Melanchthon from the Palatinate, Bugenhagen from Pomerania, Jonas from Thuringia, Cruciger from Saxony—they were particularly dependent on friendships in their new environment.[37]

As becomes clear from his *table talks*, Luther himself sought and enjoyed the conviviality and conversation with friends and guests. In letters of consolation, he would repeatedly invite his correspondents to overcome their sorrows by joining the cheerful company of others. Not least through his own experiences, Luther was sure that depressions were the devil's work: "I know him (i.e., Satan) well and am aware that he likes to involve me in the situation. He is a doleful, disagreeable spirit who cannot bear to see anyone happy or at peace, especially with God."[38] The aid of friends in spiritual temptations is also one of the themes in Luther's *Lectures on Genesis* (1535–45), in which he expresses his commitment to the value of friendship when dealing with Lot's separation from Abraham: "A faithful friend is a great boon and a precious treasure in any situation of life, not only because of common dangers in which he can be both an aid and a comfort but also because of spiritual trials. Even if one's heart is well grounded by the Holy Spirit, it remains a great advantage to have a brother with whom one can converse about religion and from whom one can hear words of comfort … I for my part consider the loss of all my possessions less important than a faithful friend … Loneliness distresses a person who is solitary and deprived of his intimate friends. He can exert himself and struggle against it, but he does not overcome it without great difficulty. Everything is less

burdensome if you have a brother with you, for then the promise applies (Matt. 18:20): 'Where two or three are gathered in My name, there am I in the midst of them.' Therefore solitude should be shunned and the companionship of familiar people be sought, especially in spiritual perils."[39]

Next to his university colleagues, Luther's friends also included Lucas Cranach the Elder, who in 1525 was witness to Luther's wedding with Katharina von Bora and, in the following year, godfather to Luther's first-born son, Johannes. In 1520, Luther, for his part, had acted as godfather to Cranach's daughter Anna, and in 1521 Cranach had been the only Wittenberg friend whom Luther made privy to his impending "imprisonment" in Wartburg. A moving document of their close relationship is Luther's visit to Cranach on December 1, 1537. Cranach was in total despair over his son Hans's death in Bologna, and was comforted by Luther who told him that he, too, had recommended Hans go to Italy, thus mitigating the father's self-reproach. Their friendship is the personal aspect of a close professional cooperation that was dedicated to jointly communicating the Reformation in text and image. As Steven Ozment has shown, Cranach with his workshop became a central player in the "Making of the Reformation," particularly through the public iconic presence of Luther starting with his first portraits of 1520.[40]

Luther was also in close contact with some Wittenberg citizens, such as master clothier Bartholomäus Schadewald, whom he visited at his sickbed after Schadewald had fallen deathly ill with the plague in 1535,[41] or Blasius Matthäus, another master clothier who, in a university announcement published on the occasion of his death, was praised as a close confidant of Luther.[42] Obviously, Luther also entertained a particularly close relationship with his barber Peter Beskendorf, who was the only person he allowed to shave him. Beskendorf's occupation extended beyond shaving and hair-cutting and included wound medicine, or the treatment of external injuries. Luther supported Beskendorf when the latter was indicted for stabbing his son-in-law after a dispute about money, defending his friend before the court and averting the death penalty imposed on him by submitting a request to Elector John Frederick. What is interesting about Luther's friendship with Beskendorf is the writing that was triggered by it, Luther's *Simple Method How to Pray, written for Master Peter, the Barber*, a generally comprehensible introduction to praying, with explanations of the Lord's Prayer, the Creed and the Ten Commandments. First published in Wittenberg in 1535, it impressively illustrates that Luther's reformatory work had its roots in pastoral care; addressee-centered and dialogically structured, it always makes human existence its direct concern.[43]

the *Alba Amicorum*, i.e., the albums of friendship: the university attracted students and guests from all over Europe who wanted to take home a lasting reminder of the encounters they had made there. The owners of these friendship books were people for whom the written entries were personal reminders and a testimony of their scholarly company. See Schnabel, *Stammbuch*. **38** Oberman, *Luther*, pp. 320 f.; for Luther as a spiritual guide and comforter, see Mennecke-Haustein, *Luthers Trostbriefe*. **39** Luther, *Lectures on Genesis*. In: *LW* 2,

335. **40** See Ozment, *Serpent*, particularly pp. 119–147; for Luther's consolatory visit, see Rhein, *Caspar Khummer*. **41** See *WA*.TR 5, 195, 14–16 (no. 5503). **42** See *Scriptorum publice propositorum a professoribus in Academia Witebergensi*, vol. 4 [1561]. Wittenberg, fol. h5r: "Familiaris Luthero fuit et valde carus" (announcement of March 9, 1561). **43** See Köpf/Zimmerling, *Martin Luther, Wie man beten soll*; for Beskendorf, see Müller, *Peter Beskendorf*.

Not Just Luther

The Reformation is not the work of a single individual; it sprang from the ideas and actions of a group of scholars, assembled at one place by the *kairos* (the opportune moment) of the Reformation. It thus cannot be grasped as the work of a solitary mind. In its vital diversity, it is the result of a productive cooperation to which many talents contributed and which was driven by personal friendships.

BIBLIOGRAPHY

Brecht, Martin (1998), "Dein Geist ist's, den ich rühme." Johannes Brenz—Luthers Mann in Süddeutschland. In: Freybe, Peter (ed.), *Luther und seine Freunde. "… damit ich nicht allein wäre."* Wittenberg, pp. 72 – 88. **Edwards**, B. B. (1846), *Life of Philip Melanchthon. Bibliotheca Sacra and Theological Review 3.* New York/London/Andover, pp. 301 – 346. **Gerth**, Daniel/**Leppin**, Volker (eds.) (2014), *Paul Eber (1511 – 1569). Humanist und Theologe der zweiten Generation der Wittenberger Reformation.* Leipzig. **Gummelt**, Volker (1998), "Pomeranus hat mich oft getröstet." Johannes Bugenhagen—Freund und Seelsorger Luthers. In: Freybe, Peter (ed.), *Luther und seine Freunde. "… damit ich nicht allein wäre."* Wittenberg, pp. 89 – 104. **Harasimovicz**, Jan/**Seyderhelm**, Bettina (eds.) (2015), *Cranachs Kirche. Begleitbuch zur Landesausstellung Sachsen-Anhalt Cranach der Jüngere.* Markkleeberg. **Hasse**, Hans-Peter (1996), *Luther und seine Freunde. Zum Erscheinungsbild einer Gruppe in der Kunst und Publizistik des 16. Jahrhunderts* (= Wartburg-Jahrbuch. Sonderband). Eisenach. **Heling**, Antje (2003), *Zu Haus bei Martin Luther. Ein alltagsgeschichtlicher Rundgang.* Wittenberg. **Hendrix**, Scott H. (2015), *Martin Luther: Visionary Reformer.* New Haven/London. **Hill**, Charles Leander (1954), Some Theses of Philip Melanchthon. In: *The Lutheran Quarterly*, vol. 6, pp. 245 – 248. **Imhof**, Arthur E. (1984), *Die verlorenen Welten. Alltagsbewältigung durch unsere Vorfahren—und weshalb wir uns heute so schwer damit tun.* München. **Joestel**, Volkmar (2013), *"Hier stehe ich!" Luthermythen und ihre Schauplätze.* Wettin-Löbejün. **Junghans**, Helmar (2000), Philipp Melanchthon als theologischer Sekretär. In: Günter Frank (ed.), *Der Theologe Melanchthon.* Stuttgart, pp. 129 – 152. **Kammer**, Otto (1999), *Das Melanchthondenkmal in Wittenberg. Planung und Errichtung, Geschichte und Gegenwart.* Wittenberg. **Kammer**, Otto (2004), *Reformationsdenkmäler des 19. und 20. Jahrhunderts.* Leipzig. **Kaufmann**, Thomas (2012), *Der Anfang der Reformation. Studien zur Kontextualität der Theologie, Publizistik und Inszenierung Luthers und der reformatorischen Bewegung.* Tübingen. **Kawerau**, Gustav (1884), *Der Briefwechsel des Justus Jonas.* Vol. 1. Halle (Saale). **Kobler**, Beate (2014), *Die Entstehung des negativen Melanchthonbildes. Protestantische Melanchthonkritik bis 1560.* Tübingen. **Kohnle**, Armin (2002), Wittenberger Autorität. Die Gemeinschaftsgutachten der Wittenberger Theologen als Typus. In: Dingel, Irene/Wartenberg, Günther (eds.), *Die theologische Fakultät Wittenberg 1502 bis 1602.* Leipzig, pp. 189 – 200. **Kolb**, Robert (2009), The Theology of Justus Jonas. In: Dingel, Irene (ed.), *Justus Jonas (1493 – 1555) und seine Bedeutung für die Wittenberger Reformation.* Leipzig, pp. 103 – 120. **Köpf**, Ulrich/**Zimmerling**, Peter (eds.) (2011), *Martin Luther: Wie man beten soll, für Meister Peter den Barbier.* Göttingen. **Kruse**, Jens-Martin (2002), *Universitätstheologie und Kirchenreform. Die Anfänge der Reformation in Wittenberg 1516 – 1522.* Mainz. **Kruse**, Jens-Martin (2002), Universitätstheologie und Kirchenreform. Die Bedeutung der Wittenberger Universitätsprofessoren für die Anfänge der Reformation. In: Luther: *Zeitschrift der Luther-Gesellschaft*, vol. 73, no. 1, pp. 10 – 31. **Leder**, Hans-Günther (1983), Luthers Beziehungen zu seinen Wittenberger Freunden. In: Junghans, Helmar (ed.), *Leben und Werk Martin Luthers von 1526 bis 1546. Festgabe zu seinem 500. Geburtstag.* Vol. 1. Berlin, pp. 419 – 440. **Leppin**, Volker (2010), *Martin Luther.* 2nd ed. Darmstadt. **Manschreck**, Clyde Leonard (1958), *Melanchthon: The Quiet Reformer.* Eugene. **Mennecke**, Ute (2009), Justus Jonas als Übersetzer—Sprache und Theologie. Dargestellt am Beispiel seiner Übersetzung von Luthers Schrift "De servo arbitrio"—"Das der freie wille nichts sey" (1526). In: Dingel, Irene (ed.), *Justus Jonas (1493 – 1555) und seine Bedeutung für die Wittenberger Reformation.* Leipzig, pp. 131 – 144. **Mennecke-Haustein**, Ute (1988), *Luthers Trostbriefe.* Gütersloh. **Mülhaupt**, Erwin (1982), *Luther im 20. Jahrhundert.* Göttingen. **Müller**, Nikolaus (1912), Peter Beskendorf: Luthers Barbier und Freund. In: Clemen, Otto/Eger, Rudolf (eds.), *Aus Deutschlands kirchlicher Vergangenheit. Festschrift zum 70. Geburtstage von Theodor Brieger.* Leipzig, pp. 37 – 92. **Münkler**, Herfried (2009), *Die Deutschen und ihre Mythen.* Berlin. **Oberman**, Heiko A. (1986), *Luther. Mensch zwischen Gott und Teufel.* München. **Ozment**, Steven (2012), *The Serpent and the Lamb. Cranach, Luther and the Making of the Reformation.* New Haven. **Rhein**, Stefan (1991), Melanchthon und Paracelsus. In: Telle, Joachim (ed.), *Parerga Paracelsica. Paracelsus in Vergangenheit und Gegenwart.* Stuttgart, pp. 57 – 73. **Rhein**, Stefan (2009), Philipp Melanchthon als Hausarzt. In: Friedrich, Christoph/Telle, Joachim (eds.), *Pharmazie in Geschichte und Gegenwart. Festgabe für Wolf-Dieter Müller-Jahncke.* Stuttgart, pp. 363 – 376. **Rhein**, Stefan (2011), Paul Eber aus Kitzingen—Schüler und Kollege Philipp Melanchthons. In: *Zeitschrift für Bayerische Kirchengeschichte*, vol. 80, pp. 239 – 259. **Rhein**, Stefan (2015), Caspar Khummer (gest. vor 1575). Sammlung der Tischreden Martin Luthers. In: Enke, Roland/Schneider, Katja/Strehle, Jutta (eds.), *Lucas Cranach der Jüngere. Entdeckung eines Meisters.* München, pp. 158 – 193. **Scheible**, Heinz (1996), *Melanchthon und die Reformation. Forschungsbeiträge* (= Veröffentlichungen des Instituts für Europäische Geschichte. 41). Mainz. **Scheible**, Heinz (1997), *Melanchthon. Eine Biographie.* München. **Scheible**, Heinz/**Mundhenk**, Christine (eds.) (1977 seq.), *Melanchthons Briefwechsel. Kritische und kommentierte Gesamtausgabe.* Stuttgart/Bad Cannstatt. **Schilling**, Heinz (2014), *Martin Luther. Rebell in einer Zeit des Umbruchs.* 3rd ed. München. **Schnabel**, Werner Wilhelm (2003), *Das Stammbuch. Konstitution und Geschichte einer textsortenbezogenen Sammelform bis ins erste Drittel des 18. Jahrhunderts.* Tübingen. **Seidel**, Karl Josef (1970), *Frankreich und die Protestanten. Die Bemühungen um eine religiöse Konkordie und die französische Bündnispolitik in den Jahren 1534/35.* Münster. **Tenbruck**, Friedrich H. (1964), Freundschaft. Ein Beitrag zu einer Soziologie der persönlichen Beziehungen. In: *Kölner Zeitschrift für Soziologie und Sozialpsychologie*, vol. 18, pp. 431 – 456. **Treml**, Christine (1989), *Humanistische Gemeinschaftsbildung. Sozio-kulturelle Untersuchung zur Entstehung eines neuen Gelehrtenstandes in der frühen Neuzeit.* Hildesheim. **Vogt**, Otto (ed.) (1888), *Dr. Johannes Bugenhagens Briefwechsel.* Stettin. **Wolgast**, Eike (2009), Luther, Jonas und die Wittenberger Kollektivautorität. In: Dingel, Irene (ed.), *Justus Jonas (1493 – 1555) und seine Bedeutung für die Wittenberger Reformation.* Leipzig, pp. 87 – 100. **Zerbe**, Doreen (2013), *Reformation der Memoria. Denkmale in der Stadtkirche Wittenberg als Zeugnisse lutherischer Memorialkultur im 16. Jahrhundert.* Leipzig. **Zur Mühlen**, Karl Heinz (1978), Luthers Bibelübersetzung als Gemeinschaftswerk. In: Meurer, Siegfried (ed.), *Eine Bibel—viele Übersetzungen. Not oder Notwendigkeit?* Stuttgart, pp. 90 – 97.

PETER BLICKLE

The Republic of Reformers:
Huldrych Zwingli, Christoph Schappeler, and Jean Calvin

The Parish Church Saint Maurice sits high above the vineyards of the village Hallau in Klettgau, looking out toward the Rhine, the Black Forest, and Switzerland. In 1491, the community received permission to build its own church. In 1508, it separated from its mother parish, Neunkirch. The community had thus fought for and won the right to choose its own pastor. Hallau is not typical of church affairs of the time before the Reformation; it is, however, also not an isolated incident. In neighboring Thurgau, one-fifth of all priests were financed by village community funds; there were similar numbers in Grisons, the borderlands between the Palatinate region and Alsace, and the area around Lake Lucerne. The goal of these rural foundations was to always be able to celebrate Mass but also to be able to baptize children on site and inter the dead in the village. The congregation obligated its priest to live in the village, to settle legal disputes not at the episcopal court but in the local one, to accompany believers on pilgrimages, and to preach; this was the case in Urseren near the Gotthard pass in 1481.

To improve pastoral care, even in the cities people donated generously. The highest amount of donations were made to sponsor masses. The funding of pastoral positions through citizens or corporations in the city was also characteristic during the decades before the Reformation. The funded preacher gave catechetical lessons and preached on Sundays. The practice was obviously about acquiring belief in a new, more intellectual way, as the job profiles for preachers verify; they should be able to prove they have a doctorate in theology. Around 1500, nearly all larger cities in the southwest German region had a funded preacher.

The peasantry, town citizenry, and other communal groups all strove for an improvement of pastoral care. This can be linked with a second observance: "Reformatory ideas had their earliest effects in the German empire and in the Swiss confederation, two polycentric entities with weak central power and many essentially independent communities."[1] Such independent communities were concentrated in the southern part of the Holy Roman Empire and in Switzerland. Interestingly, this area also developed its own form of the Reformation that diverged from the Reform movement in central and Northern German.[2] Early Reformation propaganda seems to imply that this distinction indeed occurred to a great extent because of the concentration of aforementioned independent communities in this region.

In 1521, a pamphlet appeared in Zurich titled *The Description of the Holy Mill* (fig. 1). In the woodcut on the frontispiece, the common man, shown as the figure of the "Karsthans," takes a central role; to some degree, he also represents a personification of the community. He threatens monks, bishops, and cardinals with his flail, thereby protecting a second group, in which Erasmus of Rotterdam, Luther, and Zwingli (standing behind Luther) are depicted. Christ is pouring the Gospels into the mill. Erasmus is gathering the pure flour of God's word with a shovel. Luther then processes the flour into bread dough, while Zwingli unsuccessfully attempts to serve the bread in the form of the Holy Scripture to representatives of the old church. The group in the middle conveys the message: the humanist Erasmus from Basel, Zwingli from Zurich, and the common man (Karsthans) are standing up for the Reformation. Naturally, Luther can't be omitted, even in Southern Germany.

Huldrych Zwingli:
Theology as an Ethical Rehabilitation of Politics

As Huldrych Zwingli took up his pastoral duties in the Grossmuenster (large minster/main church) in Zurich in 1519, he did so in a congregation that was identical with the citizenry. Twice a year, the people performed the citizens' oath in the Grossmuenster. Even before his time at Grossmuenster, Zwingli had had an effect in regions and towns with a strong communal character. His home of Toggenburg had developed a considerable representation (*Landschaft*) that was more or less in constant conflict with its landlord, the abbot of Saint Gallen. His move to Glarus (1506–16) led Zwingli to a canton of the Swiss Federation that was administrated democratically by the cantonal assembly (*Landsgemeinde*) and its designated bodies. In Zurich, the power ("der Gewalt"), as contemporaries called the sovereignty, was held by the Great Council, a committee of more than two hundred members, who were representatives of the guilds. It was responsible for enacting laws, collecting taxes, making military decisions, and filling administrative positions. This municipal environment made more than one impression in Zwingli's theology.

---

1 Schnyder, *Reformation*, p. 96. **2** Most recent overview: Blickle, *Reformation*.

Zwingli revered Erasmus of Rotterdam. Through Erasmus and the study of the Holy Scripture, Zwingli was brought to theological positions not far removed from general reformed positions and therefore also close to Martin Luther's. Luther's *sola fide, sola gratia, sola scriptura* were also Zwingli's axioms for justification before God; however, he differed from Luther in two central points: the relationship between Law and Gospel and his understanding of Holy Communion. The way that "Law" (the Old Testament) and "Gospel" (the New Testament) were brought into relationship with each other also decided the extent of the lawful authorities' power. In general—here all reformers were unanimous—every person is subject to the lawfull authorities, because authority is given by God. Zwingli worked through this issue in his 1523 work *Interpretation and Justification of the Final Word.* How is the relationship between here and the beyond constituted, from obedient to God and obedient to the authorities? Zwingli stated, "If the ruler's law goes against God, then the Christians would say that one must be more obedient to God than to men."[3] Luther had interpreted this sentence as meaning that obedience to God requires passive resistance in matters relating to belief, and not more.

Zwingli, on the other hand, drew a different conclusion from the same passage in the Acts of the Apostles, as seen in the next statement in his argument: "For this reason, Christian rulers must have laws that do not go against God; otherwise their citizens will go against them, which will lead to unrest." Zwingli thus required the authorities to be Christian authorities. Luther, however, left secular organization the way it had been historically. "All old existing laws"—for Zwingli, the existing positive legal norms—must therefore be reviewed, "whether they conform to or violate the divine laws of nature and one's fellow man, which are one."

From this, Zwingli also derived the right to resist, although he didn't develop it in a detailed way. The king selected "by the common hand" can be dethroned. If the monarchy is based on an estate-based constitution, then the nobles are required to reject the "vexing life" of the king. Even a king who accedes to the throne in dynastic succession and without being voted into office can be removed if "the vast majority of the people are unified in their desire for it." Zwingli viewed both the monarchy and democracy with suspicion—monarchy because it tended to degenerate into tyranny, and democracy because of its proximity to anarchy. He favored republics (whose public officials were patricians who were elected democratically) such as those in Zurich, Basel, Saint Gallen, and in many cities in Southern Germany that had guild constitutions. Zwingli, as well as the Humanists aimed at a renaissance of the republic. But the authorities of antiquity on which republics should be based weren't Aristotle and Cicero but rather the evangelists.

Zwingli first addressed the topic of how the political order should be newly conceived in the sense of the Reformation in an oral presentation in the course of the First Zurich Disputation of 1523. The disputation was sensational in several ways. The venue wasn't one of the universities but rather the city hall; it was the Great Council of Zurich as a representation of the Zurich community, not theologians, who decided what were the best arguments (fig. 2). In church history, one speaks of the discovery that happened

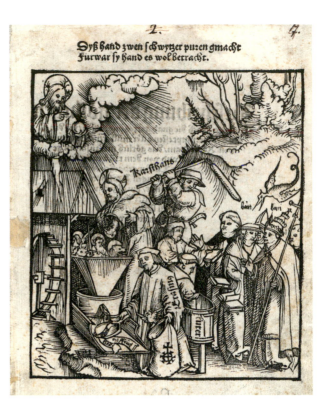

Fig. 1 Martin Seger/Hans Füsli, Beschribung der götlichen müly, so durch die gnad gottes angelassen […] (Description of the Godly Mill which Operates by God's Grace), Zürich 1521, frontispiece woodcut

Fig. 2 The first Zurich disputation held in the city hall in the year 1523. Hand colored pen and ink drawing in Heinrich Thomann's copy of Heinrich Bullinger's History of the Reformation, 1605

in Zurich; here "the first church founding of the Reformation" took place.[4] The political community received an elevation in the church congregation. Zurich did justice to this configuration through many individual measures. The introduction of the Reformation into the city and in rural areas was based on surveys of the guilds and congregations; in the end, they needed to decide which doctrine was correct. The council issued mandates from that point on with the intention of orienting secular order to divine law. In the 1520s, the council issued an impressive number of mandates—fifty—with exactly this intention. The episcopal court was decentralized to follow parish designations and continued as a marriage court; judgments were reached by laypeople.

But it wasn't just the organization of the Zurich church that was marked by the institutional form of day-to-day political life. Theology itself, indeed the most central aspect of it—the doctrine of the Mass or Holy Communion—was also shaped by it. Zwingli contested the sacrificial character of Mass and the real presence of Christ in the bread and wine. This was in sharp contrast to Luther and a divergence between them that was never overcome. For Zwingli, Holy Communion transformed the congregation of believers into the body of Christ. According to him, this "sacrament" is "a signal of commitment, like sewing a white cross on one's clothing to show that one wants to be Swiss." Similar to how the Swiss (*Eidgenossen*, literally "oath brothers") publicly testified to their shared identity through periodically reiterated oaths, "one publically connects oneself to all believers [through this sacrament]." Oath and sacrament were mirror images. In Zurich, both acts took place in the Grossmuenster. According to an expert on the Reformed movement, the "Holy Communion is the Christian community's 'oath day,' which is analogous to the 'oath day' (coniuratio) in the civil community."[5]

With his municipally based concept of church and understanding of the sacraments, Zwingli was not only the reformer for Zurich but also for the entire Upper German area (i.e High German speaking regions of Southern Germany, Alsace and Switzerland).[6] Hundreds of priests from Switzerland and Southern Germany sat at his feet during his disputations; about one thousand were present for the Second Zurich Disputation. Zwingli's teachings were being preached from Berne to Strasbourg and from Augsburg to Nuremberg; however, his influence was temporally limited. As early as 1525, Zwingli's followers were expelled from Nuremberg, and in 1530, his statement of faith (*Fidei ratio*) wasn't even the subject of negotiations at the Diet of Augsburg. Zwingli's followers were considered to be agitators; Luther supported this opinion in 1525 and later energetically and successfully enforced it. With Zwingli's death in 1531 in the course of Europe's first religious war, his influence in Germany was further reduced.

Christoph Schappeler:
A Theology of Freedom for the Serfs

Memmingen was one of the Southern German imperial cities that implemented the Reformation according to Zwingli. Christoph Schappeler was the preacher here, starting in 1513. He maintained contact to his home, Saint Gallen. Erasmus of Rotterdam had been one of his academic teachers; Joachim von Watt (Vadian), St. Gallen's reformer, was one of his friends; and Zwingli was one of his theological mentors. Schappeler presided in part over the Second Zurich Disputation and returned to Saint Gallen after narrowly escaping execution in Memmingen in June 1525. In December 1524, events escalated in Memmingen;[7] four months later, riots occurred from Thuringia in Central Germany to Trento in Northern Italy and Austrian Salzburg to Alsace.

On the feast of Saint Nicholas 1524, Schappeler offered the congregation of St. Martin bread and wine, Holy Communion in both forms, for the first time. Like the reformers in Zurich, he understood Holy Communion to be a memorial celebration; bread and wine were therefore not the body and blood of Christ. The council's comments about the massive break with tradition were relaxed. It did not want to prescribe rules for the clergy; the clergy should preach whatever they thought they could answer for before God and the public. These events had an immediate effect on the second parish in the city, the Marienkirche (Our Lady's Church). Women from this congregation loudly demanded the same liturgical reforms from the council. It hoped to de-escalate the situation by recommending that women take part in the church services at St. Martin. This was for naught, because a few days later an unprecedented event occurred on Christmas in Our Lady's. Pastor Megerich claimed he was "chased into the sacristy with much aggressiveness by Lutheran women and men … punched with fists, pushed" and pelted with stones. In addition, the altarpieces and liturgical vessels were ravaged. The riot lasted two hours before the mayor and several council members stepped in and took the pastor into protective custody; otherwise, he would "have been killed in the sacristy."[8]

Naturally, this was not a sustainable solution, but the mayor hoped a disputation would yield one. A disputation had been long demanded by Schappeler's followers but was refused each time by the traditional (Catholic) believers . In the first week of January 1525, a disputation finally took place in the presence of the entire clergy, all council members, and one representative selected from each guild. It was, without a doubt, a copy of the Zurich Disputations, even if the audience was not as large. Schappeler had worked out seven theses that one could describe as conforming to Zwingli's doctrine, but the work was for naught. The orthodox clergy did not comment, the council decided euphemistically and not in accordance with the facts, and everyone was apparently "in agreement about the matter." It was probably due to a bad conscience that the council commissioned external expert opinions from two lawyers and two theologians. But their concerns did not have any effect; the Reformation was implemented in Memmingen anyway.[9]

In the city's hinterland—about twenty-five villages and hamlets belonged to the Memmingen territory—these events had an electri-

3 Egli/Finsler, *Werke*, vol. 2, p. 323 [The quotes that follow are located on pp. 323 f., 339 f., 344 f.]. **4** Moeller, *Disputationen*, p. 321. **5** Schmidt, *Häretisierung*, p. 235 [there you can also find the prior citations]. **6** Locher, *Zwinglische Reformation*. **7** Kroemer, *Einführung*. **8** The source is edited by Miedel, *Memminger Reformationsgeschichte*, p. 173. **9** Pfundner (ed.), *Religionsgespräch*, pp. 23–65.

fying effect. There, the peasants now demanded that pastors in the rural churches preach like Schappeler in St. Martin in Memmingen. Even before these demands, the crowds coming to hear Schappeler's interpretation of the Scriptures from rural areas every Sunday had reached such a level that the council established its own security guards in the church and guarded the city gates with additionally mustered citizens. Schappeler must have had a charismatic character. His followers repeatedly and forcefully demanded that the city stop the old rites. They even formed an informal police squad that kept watch in front of his house when death threats against him were heard. The peasants not only listened to Schappeler's preaching but also took advice from him. And this advice was about more than just theological and liturgical questions.

In January and February 1525, the first peasant mobs formed in Upper Swabia. Only the Memminger villages remained quiet. In a petition at the end of February 1525, they did, however, demand that their grievances, which were "contrary to the word of God," be rectified. Among the grievances they named were excesses regarding serfdom, increases in bonded labor, limitations in the use of common ground, including hunting and fishing rights, and the wrongful use of the tithe. In addition, they demanded from council members that "we want to follow the designation and content of the divine word, and limit it to that. And we will happily accept what the divine word gives and takes away, and the limits that it sets."[10] The standard for assessing the complaints was thus established: the divine word. The Memmingen Council answered in a surprisingly friendly way. It "also wanted to follow God's word" and promised to abolish serfdom in its territory and to remove limitations on hunting and fishing. It wanted to wait to assess the other complaints after the necessary legal clarifications. That was in early March.

The effect this had in the villages of Upper Swabia is not documented. Memmingen had the reputation of being progressive; it was the first imperial city in Upper Swabia to subscribe to the Reformation. Yet it soon also had the reputation for being the site of conspiratorial activities of the peasantry. On March 6, fifty representatives of the Upper Swabian *Haufen* (militia)—from Baltring, the Allgau, and Lake Constance—seized the Kramer guild room, developed a form of new charter, and discussed their common complaints. They also sent a message to Ulm, to the representative of their feudal lords, the captains, and council members of the Swabian League, that they had incorporated themselves into a "Christian Association" which represented approximately fifty thousand peasants.

The *Memminger Bundesordnung* ("Memmingen Federal Order") was the charter of this "Christian Association." In addition, the region's grievances were summarized in written form and taken to Augsburg, where they were printed. They were soon called the *Twelve Articles of the Swabian Peasantry*. Both programs began an impressive victory march. The twelve articles had twenty-eight printing runs, and the federal order had eleven. Together, they made up the central manifesto of the Peasants' War, which had an effect in Alsace and Thuringia, Franconia and Switzerland. To make Thomas Müntzer into a theoretician of the Peasants' War is thus incorrect. This interpretation was the work of Luther and has been reinforced through constant repetition. In reality, Müntzer's influence was limited to Thuringia, and his apocalyptic agenda for the peasants was of limited value.

What exactly Schappeler preached in Memmingen can be only vaguely construed from council protocols. They were socially engaged sermons that defended poor people against the rich, criticized nepotism among guild members, denounced the tithe as unscriptural, and reprehended church donations as the exploitation of the common man. Schappeler was a valiant defender of the new doctrine. The Augsburg bishop banned him in 1524. In the Swabian League, he was regarded as the mastermind of the rioting peasants. In Wittenberg, he was immediately made responsible for the *Twelve Articles*. Was Schappeler on the side of the peasants? Did he sit with them in the Kramer guild room (the hall of the merchants' guild where the peasants formulated their demands) and work on drafts of the programs? And if so, did it have an effect?

Schappeler left no estate, and his correspondence was not preserved. Whether he wrote pamphlets, following the custom of the times, is unclear. Nevertheless, indications show that Memmingen's development into one of the great centers of the Reformation wouldn't have been possible without Schappeler. It was the intellectual and theoretical center of the revolution of the common man of 1525—not only because of Schappeler, but also due to him.

The *Memmingen Federal Order* can be described as a constitutional concept for Upper Swabia intended to guarantee that a functioning administration and legal system would continue under the leadership of selected representatives of the *Haufen* (the militia's captains, colonels).[11] It was accompanied by all sorts of anti-clerical and antifeudal measures. Priests who weren't open to the Reformation should be "suspended" by their congregations; military in the service of the authorities should leave the nobles' castles. Some versions of the Federal Order were accompanied by a so-called judge list. It named people who should assess whether or not the peasants' demands were in line with divine law. The list was made up exclusively of reformers: Luther and Melanchthon, followed by reformers from Strasbourg and Zurich under Zwingli's leadership, and many preachers from smaller imperial cities. This is a tremendously revealing document from the peasants' camp, because it says nothing less than that the peasants, in modern terms, saw the theologians as constitutional judges. Following this logic, Holy Scripture was the constitutional text of Christian society and needed only to be properly interpreted. The rebelling peasants, however, did not entrust themselves with the task and therefore requested it of the theologians. Christoph Schappeler was missing from the list, though. Had he advised the peasants? Had he provided them with the names?

The *Twelve Articles of the Swabian Peasants*[12] was the product of a long development. The articles emerged in the first weeks of 1525 in peasant camps, and from mid-March on, they could be purchased at markets (fig. 3). They demanded that the priest be chosen by the congregation and the tithe be used for church purposes; that serfdom be abolished and limitations on hunting and fishing be removed; that common forests, fields, and pastures be returned to the people; that bonded labor be reduced; that the contractual obligations be set out in the fief letters be observed; that a new assessment of farm productivity be set; that punishments have legal norms; and that the custom

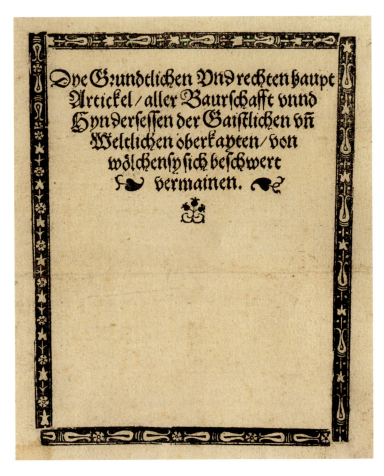

Fig. 3 Dye grundtlichen vnd rechten haupt artickel, aller baurschafft […]
(The Fundamental and Correct Chief Articles of All the Peasants […]),
Augsburg 1525, frontispiece

called heriot (*Todfall*) be totally abolished. All organizational changes
—from the choice of priest to the administration and use of the tithe
to the use of the commons and forests—should occur for the good
of the community. The articles were penned in the hope that they
would be accepted as being in line with the word of God; they would,
however, cede demands "if explained based on Scripture." The logical
inversion of this argument is that the peasants would have made further demands if these were justified by Scripture. Essentially, three
demands gave the *Twelve Articles* their effectiveness: the ability to
choose priests, laws based on the criteria of God's word, and—above
all—"freedom" through the abolition of serfdom. From written complaints from the villages and dominions, we know serfdom was in
first or second place. The *Twelve Articles* stated: "Thirdly, the custom
to date has been that the lords have bound us as their own, which is
miserable, considering that Christ redeemed and saved us all with his
precious bloodshed, the shepherd and the lord alike with no exception. Therefore, how is demonstrated by Scripture, we state that we
are free and want to be free […], We have no doubt that you, as true
and just Christians, will gladly release us from serfdom or, you can
refer to the gospel, in which this is stated."

In the end, all the reformers were against the abolition of serfdom. Luther was the most vehement about it, but Melanchthon
and Zwingli also shared the opinion, always referencing the New
Testament in their arguments. The authority is given by God, and

therefore even "serfdom is in accordance with God,"[13] according to
Zwingli. Basing freedom on the Gospel would mean making the
Christian freedom "fleshly," Luther stated, citing the Apostle Paul.
Schappeler was of a different opinion. At the request of the Council
of Memmingen, he assessed peasants' demands, writing an expert
opinion about it titled *Christian Freedom*. It read: "The gospel does not
say anything about serfdom …, even though many Christians think
that Paul gives an indication that serfdom should be maintained."[14]
He was not alone in this opinion. It was already included in old legal
texts such as the *Schwabenspiegel*, and Erasmus of Rotterdam also supported this stance in his *Fürstenspiegel* for Charles V. In both cases,
freedom was justified based on theological arguments.

In Wittenberg, Schappeler's position was considered scandalous. Melanchthon immediately made Schappeler and his definition
of freedom responsible for the Peasants' War. That conflict had experienced first a violent acceleration through the *Twelve Articles* and
then an unforeseen radicalization after the lords took military
countermeasures. After battles in the summer, Emperor Charles V
had praised the general of the lords, Georg Truchsess of Waldburg,
who, "against several hundred thousand men," beat the peasants
into obedience; it was "an act, whose equal had not been seen in the
empire in the course of human memory." Pope Clemens VII also
thanked, crediting the Swabian League with preserving the Western
world. The Pope viewed the peasants as violent criminals who had
been stirred up by the reformers and who would have not only destroyed every form of constitution in the empire but could have also
let Italy, Spain, and Gaul (France) go up in flames as well.[15]

These presumed associations make it clear that the Reformation, as it had been characterized by the Swiss, had lost its chance in
the empire after 1525—at all events on its margins. This area included
today's Western Switzerland, Vaud, Valais, and the most prominent
city in the region, Geneva (fig. 4).

Jean Calvin:
Theology in the Laboratory of the Modern Age

The implementation of the Reformation was linked to unrest in
the cities and countryside. Congregations pushed the Reformation
forward. The Reformation's implementation was accompanied by
revolts in about two hundred cities. In regions where the Peasants'
War took place it was based on the hope for a renewal of church
and religion. This was also the case in Geneva—and therefore also
for Jean Calvin, under whose influence the city became the global
center of Reformed churches. Around the year 1500, the city still

10 Baumann (ed.), *Akten*, pp. 113–126. **11** Most recent edition by Seebaß,
Artikelbrief, pp. 77–87. **12** The version printed in Augsburg (Version M), from
Alfred Götze, is widely considered to be the oldest version: Götze, *Artikel*,
pp. 8–15. **13** Egli/Finsler, *Werke*, vol. 4, p. 355. **14** The questionable assessment is included in a transcript from the eighteenth century. Printed [also the
other works attributed to Schappeler] by Braun, *Aktenstücke*, vol. 9, pp. 241–
270; ibid., vol. 10, pp. 1–28. The quote is located in issue 10, p. 14. **15** Fürstlich
Waldburg-Wolfegg'sches Gesamtarchiv, Schloss Wolfegg, Archivkörper Senio-
ratsarchiv [presently at Schloss Zeil], Urkunde 81.—Stadtarchiv Augsburg,
Schwäbischer Bund, Fasz. 7.

Fig. 4 a Hans Asper, Portrait of Huldrych Zwingli, 1549

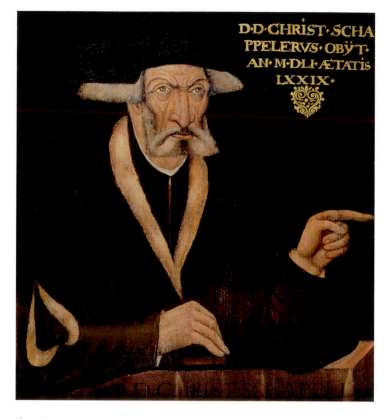

Fig. 4 b Hans Asper, Portrait of Christoph Schappeler, c. 1551

had a bishop who was under the protection of the Duke of Savoy. In 1534, citizens cast out the bishop, and with the help of Berne, the Duke of Savoy was militarily defeated. Both instances were a craftsmen's revolution, as was the case in many bishop cities in the late Middle Ages.

Now structurally organized like Zurich or Memmingen, the emerging city of Geneva could develop its autonomy. The arrangement of the church was part and parcel of this process. In 1535, Mass was done away with, and church property was seized by the council. This was the situation in 1536, as Calvin arrived in Geneva. The city had about ten thousand residents, with flourishing trade of international dimensions and open political conditions. Geneva had become a republic in the sense of the free towns and cities in the empire and it remained the only city in Europe with this political form intact until well into the nineteenth century. It's no coincidence that one of the most fascinating state theories of the modern era, the *Contrat Social* (the "Social Contract"), was written by Geneva native Jean-Jacques Rousseau. The Geneva-Berne axis guaranteed close communication with the leading Swiss theologians Huldrych Zwingli and his successor, Heinrich Bullinger. Their first communication took place in 1549 (*Consensus Tigurinus*); it was updated in 1566 to *Confessio Helvetica Posterior*. This became a profession of faith for reformed churches in France, Hungary, Poland, Scotland, and the Palatinate. Its success was based on Calvin's theology and the ethical maxims that emerged from it.

Calvin, a Frenchman, wasn't successful in Geneva at first. The citizens even forced him to leave the city in 1538. It was only with Calvin's second call to duty in 1541 that his Reformation work could begin. The Geneva church took its determinant form through its *Ordonnances Ecclésiastiques* ("Ecclesiastical Ordinances") a church ordinance that Calvin had drafted. It was effected in November 1541 by the Council of Two Hundred, the *Conseil général*, and was published as a *police écclésiastique*.[16] The political community, not the ecclesiastical community (parish), took this decisive step. This form of ratification proves that theoretically, every citizen willingly and voluntarily approved the decision. From then on, the Geneva church was characterized by four offices. Pastors were responsible for proclaiming the Gospels and administering the sacraments. Academic doctors supervised the correct interpretation of Scripture. Elders monitored the moral life of the citizens. Finally, deacons managed the communalized donations and supported the poor and infirm from these funds. The church maintained its civil character through its appointments to office. In Geneva, the appointment to office was never a religious matter; it was much more in the hands of council members. The council was responsible for appointing the elders; in the case that they were not entirely responsible, they at least had to give consent, as they did with the appointment of pastors. The College of Pastors ensured that theologically homogenous announcements were made in the city and in the rural parishes that belonged to it, and the Consistory monitored the maintenance of a strict moral code. But even the church punishments of the Consistory maintained their character as the judgments of a secular court; indeed, one of the four *syndics* in the city acted as chairman. In theological history, the Geneva church constitution is termed "presbyterial-synodal," but it wouldn't be out of place to replace "presbyterial" with "communal."

Fig. 4c Flemish painter, Portrait of Jean Calvin, c. 1530

Calvin created a thriving community beyond Geneva, ensuring that his ideas would travel widely. This occurred through his academy (soon to have fifteen hundred students), thirty printing shops, the many Calvinist refugees who created a European communication network, his international correspondence, and his memorable, simply written treatises. Calvin's ideas also spread because he—unlike Luther—supported congregations in the underground, thereby freeing them from the tutelage of the state. In France, 1,240 congregations were created that invoked Calvin. Only through the Saint Bartholomew's Day Massacre, which took place in August 1572, did the so-called Huguenots (French Calvinists) suffer a marked setback. In England, Scotland, and the Netherlands, a rich congregational life in the spirit of Calvin developed—naturally, however, also accompanied by challenges there as well.

On September 16, 1620, the Puritans departed from England on the Mayflower. They crossed the Atlantic, landing at last in Massachusetts. There they began a new chapter in Reformation history: the trans-Atlantic Reformation. The political systems the Puritans developed in New England were shaped by the same spirit that had been taught in the republics of the reformers.

16 Rivoire/van Berchem (eds.), *Sources*, no. 794. **17** Wandel, *Eucharist*. **18** Schmidt, *Religions- und Konfessionsräume*.

As with the church regulations in Zurich and Memmingen, the *Ordonnances Ecclésiastiques* reached well into the political and social spheres. One could better say it shaped the mentality to a high degree. This was also the case for the *Institutio*, Calvin's main theological work, which he reworked constantly from the first version from 1536 in Basel until the final version from 1560 in Geneva. With his understanding of Holy Communion and later his theory of double predestination, Calvin left his mark on the Reformation movement in the form of a new Christian denomination.

The understanding of Holy Communion led to the fiercest and most serious controversies among the Christian denominations and they have not been overcome to this day.[17] For Calvin, much like for Zwingli, Holy Communion was defined by its character as a legacy. Redemption was a historical event completed on Golgotha. For Calvin, during Holy Communion, Christ resides within the believer, with the act of communion strengthening and deepening the belief. The celebration verged on a mystical event. For this reason, Holy Communion must be kept pure. That is why Calvin placed so much emphasis on discipline.

His predestination doctrine interprets the vindication or damnation of a person as a decision that God has already made. To be damned was unbearable for a person in the sixteenth century. Pastors alleviated this problem through a psychology of "feeling that one is chosen." "The ability to contribute to the glorification [of God] actively and freely [is], for the Calvinist Christians, a reliable sign that they are chosen, since God endows all his Chosen with *fides efficax*, effective belief."[18] Max Weber later drew on this in his work on the spirit of capitalism.

BIBLIOGRAPHY

Baumann, Franz Ludwig (ed.) (1877), *Akten zur Geschichte des deutschen Bauernkrieges aus Oberschwaben*. Freiburg im Breisgau. **Blickle**, Peter (2015), *Die Reformation im Reich*. 4th ed. Stuttgart. **Braun**, Friedrich (1903/04), Drei Aktenstücke zur Geschichte des Bauernkrieges. In: *Blätter für bayerische Kirchengeschichte*, vol. 9 (1903), pp. 241–270; ibid., vol. 10 (1904), pp. 1–28. **Egli**, Emil/**Finsler**, Georg (eds.) (1908), Huldreich Zwingli: Sämtliche Werke. Vol. 2, Leipzig. **Egli**, Emil/**Finsler**, Georg (eds.) (1927), Huldreich Zwingli: Sämtliche Werke. Vol. 4, Leipzig. **Götze**, Alfred (1902), Die zwölf Artikel der Bauern. Kritisch herausgegeben. In: *Historische Vierteljahrschrift*, vol. 5, pp. 8–15; digital version available from: http://daten.digitale-sammlungen.de/~db/003/bsb00039675/images/indes.html [04/19/2016]. **Kroemer**, Barbara (1981), *Die Einführung der Reformation in Memmingen* (= Memminger Geschichtsblätter. Jahresheft 1980). Memmingen. **Locher**, Gottfried (1979), *Die Zwinglische Reformation im Rahmen der europäischen Kirchengeschichte*. Göttingen/Zürich. **Miedel**, Julius (1895), Zur Memminger Reformationsgeschichte. In: *Beiträge zur bayerischen Kirchengeschichte*, vol. 1, pp. 171–179. **Moeller**, Bernd (1970), Zwinglis Disputationen. Studien zu den Anfängen der Kirchenbildung und des Synodalwesens im Protestantismus. In: *Zeitschrift der Savigny-Stiftung für Rechtsgeschichte, Kanonistische Abteilung*, vol. 56, pp. 275–324; ibid., vol. 60 (1974), pp. 213–364. **Pfundner**, Thomas (ed.) (1993), *Das Memminger und Kaufbeurer Religionsgespräch von 1525. Eine Quellenveröffentlichung mit einem Überblick* (= Memminger Geschichtsblätter. Jahresheft 1991/92). Memmingen, pp. 23–65. **Rivoire**, Émile/**Van Berchem**, Victor (eds.) (1930), *Les sources du droit du Canton de Genève*. Vol. 1. Aarau. **Schmidt**, Heinrich R. (1987), Die Häretisierung des Zwinglianismus im Reich seit 1525. In: Blickle, Peter (ed.): *Zugänge zur bäuerlichen Reformation* (= Bauer und Reformation. 1). Zürich, pp. 219–236. **Schmidt**, Heinrich Richard (2013), *Religions- und Konfessionsräume*. Available from: Europäische Geschichte online, http://ieg-ego.eu/search?SearchableText=Religions-+und+ Konfessionsräume&submit=+&po [10/15/2015]. **Schnyder**, Caroline (2008), *Reformation*. Stuttgart. **Seebaß**, Gottfried (1988), *Artikelbrief, Bundesordnung und Verfassungsentwurf. Studien zu drei zentralen Dokumenten des südwestdeutschen Bauernkrieges*. Heidelberg. **Wandel**, Lee Palmer (2006), *The Eucharist in the Reformation, Incarnation and Liturgy*. New York.

CAUGHT UP IN THE SWIRL OF CONFLICTS

The confrontation with the French King and the Ottoman campaigns of conquest occupied Emperor Charles V more than the Reformation. On the level of imperial politics the issue of religion was therefore shelved. The Reformation was political dynamite and occasioned several wars. Some territories were committed to Protestantism, others were not. Princes who had turned Protestant joined forces with Catholic princes to crush the peasant uprising in 1525 and the 1535 Münster Rebellion.

The fragility of peace became obvious in 1542, when war broke out between Protestants and Catholics. In 1546, Emperor Charles confederated himself with the Protestant Maurice of Saxony, who had deserted to him, to wage war against the Protestant princes. The Protestants lost the war. The tide turned in 1552. The emperor was defeated after Maurice changed sides once again and allied himself with the French king. Charles V abdicated; the Lutheran confession was granted official recognition in the Peace of Augsburg.

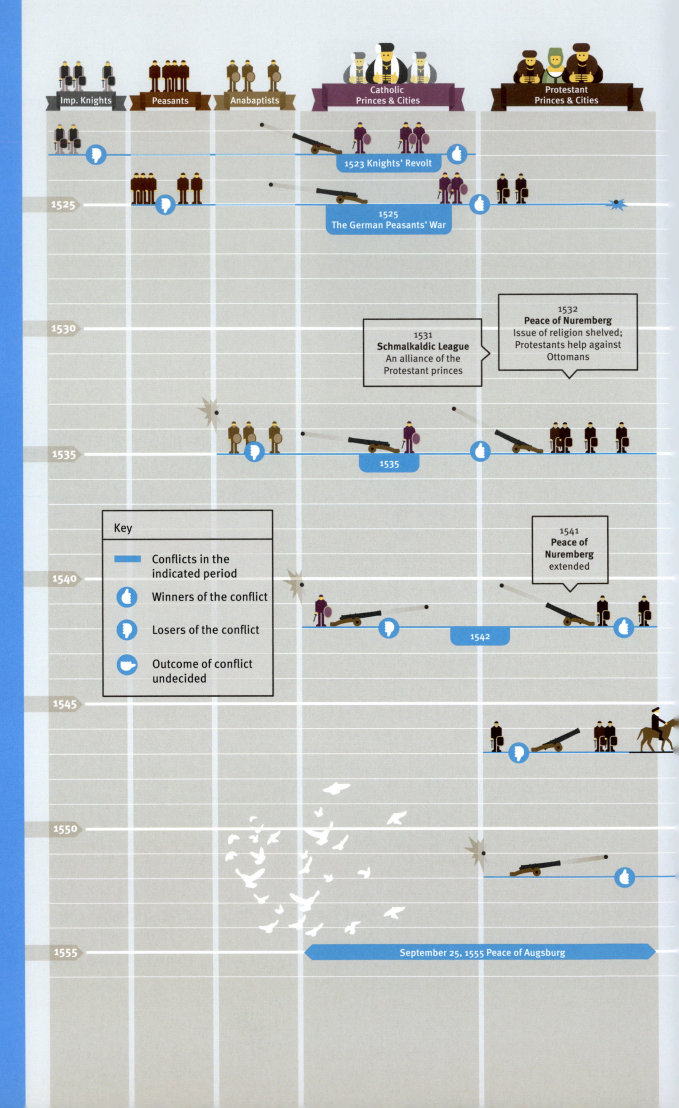

Imp. Knights   Peasants   Anabaptists   Catholic Princes & Cities   Protestant Princes & Cities

1523 Knights' Revolt

1525

1525 The German Peasants' War

1530

1531 **Schmalkaldic League** An alliance of the Protestant princes

1532 **Peace of Nuremberg** Issue of religion shelved; Protestants help against Ottomans

1535

1535

Key

▬ Conflicts in the indicated period

👍 Winners of the conflict

👎 Losers of the conflict

✊ Outcome of conflict undecided

1540

1541 **Peace of Nuremberg** extended

1542

1545

1550

1555   September 25, 1555 Peace of Augsburg

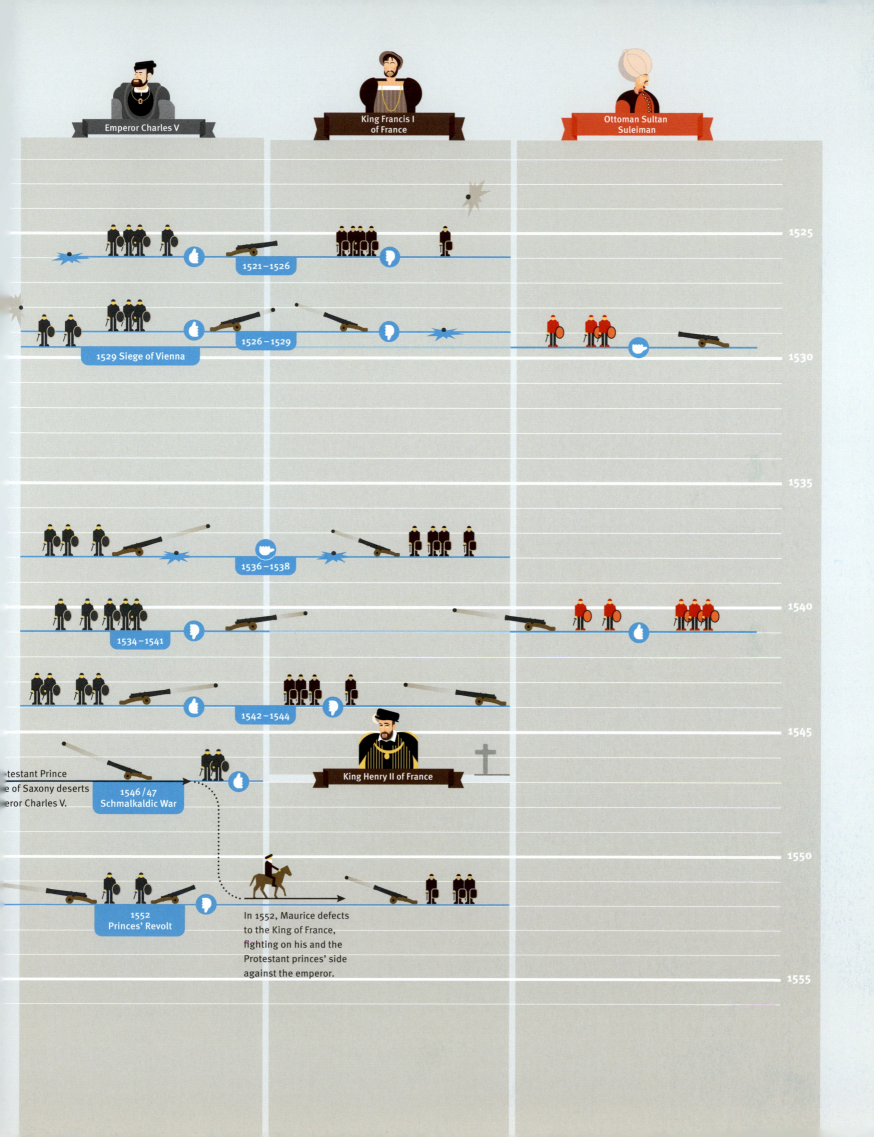

Emperor Charles V

King Francis I
of France

Ottoman Sultan
Suleiman

1525

1521–1526

1529 Siege of Vienna

1526–1529

1530

1535

1536–1538

1540

1534–1541

1542–1544

1545

King Henry II of France

Protestant Prince
...e of Saxony deserts
...eror Charles V.

1546/47
Schmalkaldic War

1550

1552
Princes' Revolt

In 1552, Maurice defects
to the King of France,
fighting on his and the
Protestant princes' side
against the emperor.

1555

IV

The Cultural Impact of the Reformation

KATRIN HERBST

Lutherana Tragoedia Artis?
The Impact of the Reformation on Art History

There is an illustrated Reformation broadsheet that reveals the impact Lutheran doctrine had on craftsmen and makes a subject of the artists who belonged to this group (fig. 1). It displays a three-column text by Hans Sachs entitled *The Clergy and Quite a Number of Craftsmen Complaining about Luther*. The situation is portrayed in the accompanying woodcut by painter and graphic artist Hans Sebald Beham. On the left, it shows the complaining craftsmen and artists gathered behind their leader, a Catholic dignitary. Immediately behind him, a painter with paintbrush and maulstick in his hands is clearly recognizable. The accompanying text, which elaborates on "The Complaint of the Godless," specifies a number of other professions which, like the painters, directly depended on church commissions for their living: bell founders, organists, gilders, illuminators, goldsmiths, and sculptors; glass painters, stonemasons, carpenters; singers and scriveners, as well as chandlers and parament makers. Martin Luther, to them, was a "dangerous man," because he "very much holds in contempt church buildings, ornaments, and embellishments; he is not wise."[1]

Martin Luther, against whom this complaint is made, confronts the representative of Catholicism from the right-hand side of the woodcut. He, too, has a number of followers gathered behind him: in his retinue, a farmer carrying a flail and a group of citizens in plain dress are depicted. In spite of robe and mortarboard, which he wears as attributes of his superior status, Luther is quite clearly depicted as the spokesman of the common people. In his reply, he invokes Scripture, holding an open Bible out to his accusers. The text confirms his objection by proclaiming, "The Judgment of Christ," and is visually personified by a representation of Christ as Judge of the world, watching the secular controversy as a higher authority from an opening in the clouds.

Introducing the painting profession, which had been immediately affected by the Reformation and to which Beham himself belonged, the broadsheet adds a social element to the theological dispute between the Old and the New Church. Behind the excessively polemical topos of the artist's complaint, there lurks a hint at the existential conflict faced by the artists of the time; for, regardless of their own religious convictions—Beham was quite sympathetic to the ideas of the Reformation, as were a number of other artists—the break with the practices of the Catholic faith spelled a drastic decline in the demand for sacred art. On top of this, the fierce criticism of images, especially on the part of the more radical reformers, had put the existence of art in the churches under the general suspicion of idolatry. As a consequence, massive acts of destruction against ecclesial sculptures and images occurred, in which the artistic heritage of the Middle Ages was destroyed with axes, picks, and hammers, or burned on pyres.[2]

Lutherana tragoedia is the succinct formula coined in this context by the great humanist Erasmus of Rotterdam who witnessed, and reported on, the events at close range during the unrest of the Reformation, particularly in Basel.[3] Especially in view of the iconoclastic riots he repeatedly described in dismay, this formula seemed accurate concerning the fate suffered by late-medieval art in his time.[4] In fact, the Reformation, with the political, social, and cultural developments it initiated, can probably be said to have had a more far-reaching impact on European art history than any previous historical movement. Admittedly, the destruction of works of art in the name of religion was not a new phenomenon. What was unprecedented, however, was the spread of vandalism across ever larger parts of Europe, and the theology underpinning it. More works of art were destroyed in Europe during the Reformation than in any other period before.[5]

Why was it that images that had for centuries been a natural part of people's devotional practice in churches were suddenly seen as instruments of a misguided faith? What, precisely, was the point of the reformers' criticism of images? And why was the theological rejection of images vented in acts of destruction in which even former donors of images would every so often turn into iconoclasts?[6]

---

1 "All Kirchen Pew/zir/und geschmuck/Veracht er gar/er ist nit cluck." 2 See, for instance, Blickle et al., *Macht*; Dupeux/Jezler/Wirth, *Bildersturm*; Schnitzler, *Ikonoklasmus*; Scribner, *Bilder*; Aston, *Iconoclasts*. 3 There is an early mention of this in Erasmus' letter to Beatus Rhenanus, dated May 27, 1521, see Allen/ Allen, *Opus Epistolarum*, vol. 4, p. 499. 4 For a connection between the Erasmus-coined concept and art, see Rüstow, *Lutherana tragoedia artis*. 5 See Aston, *Iconoclasts*, p. 5. 6 For examples, see Christin, *Frankreich*, pp. 62–64.

Ein neuryer Spruch/ wie die Geystlicheit vnd etlich Handtwercker vber den Luther clagen.

Der geitzig clagt auß falschem müt/
Seit im abgat an Eer vnd Güt.
Er zürnet/dobet/vnde wüt/
Jn dürstet nach des grechten plůt.

H. B. 26

Die warheit ist Got vnd sein wort/
Das pleibt ewiglich vnzerstort.
Wie ser der Gotloß auch rumort/
Gott bschützt sein diener hie vnd dort.

Der Grecht sagt die Gotlich warheit/
Wie hart man jn veruolgt/verleit.
hofft er in Gott doch alle zeit/
Pleibt bstendig in der grechtigkeit.

Die clag der Gotlosen.

Hör vnser clag du strenger Richter/
Vnd sey vnser zwitracht ein schlichter.
Eh wir die hend selb legen an/
Martin Luther den schedlich man.
Der hat geschriben vnd gelert/
Vnd schir das gãz Teütsch land verkert.
Mit schmehen/lestern/nach vnd weit/
Die Erwirdige Gaistlichait.
Von jren pfrůnden/Rent vnd zinst/
Vnd verwürfft auch jren Gozdinst.
Der Vätter gepot/vnd auffsetz/
Haißt er vnnütz/vnd menschen gschwetz
Helt nichts von Aplaß vnd Fegfewr/
Die Meß kům auch kainr Sel zu stewr.
All Kirchen Pew/Zir/vnd geschmuck/
Veracht er gar/er ist nie cluck.
Des clagen die Prelaten ser/
Pfaffen/Münch/Stationirer.
Glockengiesser vnd Organisten/
Goltschlager vnd Illuministen.
Hadtmaler/Goltschmit vñ bildschnitzer
Ratschmit/Glaßmaler/seydensitzer.
Stainmetzen/Zimerleüt Schreiner/
Paternoster/Kerzen macher.
Die Permenter/Singer vnd Schreyber/
Fischer/Zopffnun vnd pfaffen Weyber.
Den allen ist Luther ein bschwert/
Von dir wirt ein Vrteil begert.
Sunst werdt wir weiter Appellirn/
Vnd dem Luther die Pfrend recht schirn/
Müß Prümen/oder Reuocirn.

Antvort D. Martini.

Actuum .1.

O da erkenner aller hertzen/
Hör mein antwort des ist kein schertzen.
Die schreyen fast ich thůn mich fren/
Vnd wöllen doch nit Disputirn.
Sonder mich mit worten schrecken/
Jn thut we das ich thu auffdeckn.
Jr grossen geytz vnd Simoney/
Jr falsch Gozdinst vnd Gleissnerey.
Jr Bannen/Auffsetz vnd gepot/
Vor aller welt zu schand vnd spott.
Mit deinem wort/das ich denn ler/
Nun jn abgeet an gut vnd Eer.
So kunden sy dein wort nit leiden/
Dunt mich schelten/hassen vnd neiden.
Wenn ich hett gschwigen vnd gelert/
Das sich jr Reich vmb het gemert.
So wer kein besser auff gestandn/
Jn langer zeit in Teutschen Landn.
Dis ist auch die vrsach ich sag/
Das gegen mir auch stent in clag.
Der Hantwercks leut ein grosse zal/
Den auch abgeet in disem val.
Seyt diß Apgötterey entnimpt/
Also seynd vber mich ergrimt.
Von erst des Baals Tempel knecht/
Den jr jarmarck thut nimmer recht.
Vnd Demetrius der werckman/
Dem sein handwerck zu ruck wil gan.
Her durch dein wort das ich thů schreibn/
Jr disen soll mich nitt abtreibn/
Bey deinem vrteil will ich pleiben.

3. Regů.18.

Actuů.19.

Das Vrteil Christi.

Joãnis. 5.

Das mein gericht das ist gerecht/
Nů merck vermaints gaistlichs geschlecht.
Was ich euch selb beuolhen han/
Das jr in die ganz welt solt gan.
Predigen aller Creatur/
Das Euangeli rain vnd pur.
Dasselbig hant jr gar veracht/
Vnd vil newer Gozdinst auff pracht/
Der ich doch kein geheissen hab/
Vnd verkaufft sie vmb gelt vnd gab.
Mit Vigil/Jartäg vnd Selmessen/
Den witwen jr die heüser fressen/
Vnd vespert auch das Himelreich/
Jr seyt den Doten grebern gleich.
Vñ schlacht zu dot auch mein propheten/
Der gleich die Phariseer thetten.
Also veruolgt jr die warhait/
Die euch teglichen wirt geseit.
Vnd so jr euch nit pessern wert/
Jr vnkumen.Darumb so kert.
Von euwerm falschen widerstreit/
Dergleichen jr handtwercks leyt.
Die jr mein wort veracht mit dutz/
Von wegen ewerß aygen nutz.
Vnd hört doch in den worten mein/
Das jr nit sollt sorgfeltig sein/
Vmb zeitlich gůt/gleich den Haydn/
Sõder sucht das Reich gots mit freudn.
Das zeitlich wirt euch wol zufalln/
Sunst wert jr in der hellen qualln/
Das ist mein vrteil zu euch alln.

Mar. vltio.

Mathei.15.

Math.23.

Luce.13.

Mathei.6.

Hans Sachs Schuster.

Fig. 1 Sebald Beham/Hieronymus Höltzel (printer), Ein neuwer Spruch wie die Geystlichkeit und etlich Handwerker über den Luther clagen (The Clergy and Quite a Number of Craftsmen Complaining about Luther), c. 1524, with text by Hans Sachs

Reformation Criticism of Images

The iconoclastic controversy of the sixteenth century was triggered by Luther's theological colleague Andreas Bodenstein, also called Karlstadt, and his Augustinian brother Gabriel Zwilling. In sermons they delivered in Wittenberg during Luther's stay at Wartburg Castle, the two called for radical repentance. Their central point was the concentration on the pure Word of God, and renunciation of pomp and worldly ornaments, wealth, and the materialization of grace through indulgences and donations. The pioneers of this movement were the Augustinians themselves: on January 10, 1522, they removed paintings, sculptures, and crucifixes from their church and burned them in the courtyard of their Wittenberg monastery.[7] The act was intended as a strong signal of the irreversibility of the Reformation process and the radical nature of its ideas. Taking up this signal, in his sermons Andreas Bodenstein von Karlstadt drew the attention of his listeners to the apparent contradiction between the teaching of the pure faith and the ecclesial practices manifested in the adoration of holy images. The feeling of unease among the population and the heated atmosphere that had been caused by the radical sermons were a dangerous combination. Sporadic acts of violence against sculptures and images occurred in the Parish Church. Contrary to older research on Wittenberg, however, there can be no question of a well-targeted iconoclasm.[8] Significantly, the collection of relics in the Castle Church, which had made Wittenberg a place of saint veneration, was at first spared and was only dissolved three years later.

The heated atmosphere had been fueled by Karlstadt and Zwilling, and there was urgent need for action. Responding to the pressure exerted by Karlstadt, the city council on January 24, 1522, resolved to have the pictures from the Parish Church removed under supervision of the authorities. Article 13 of the Wittenberg church order stated the following: "Likewise, images and altars in the churches shall be removed to avoid idolatry, three altars without images being enough."[9] Three days later, Karlstadt's treatise *On the Removal of Images, and That There Should Be No Beggars Among Christians* was published, in which the council order was theologically substantiated. Karlstadt, whose treatise denounced images as false gods, objected to any pictorial representation of saints, which, he argued, would lead to false worship and idolatry. He strongly condemned idol worship and concluded that this misguided form of piety could be terminated only by removing all images from the churches. His work served as the theological foundation to publicly justify the council's decision. What is interesting in Karlstadt's argument is the social concern addressed in tandem with his image criticism. It would be better, he wrote, for the money spent on the production of precious imagery and the associated endowments to be given to fellow human beings in their capacity as the true images of God—that is to say, to the poor and needy. He thus combined his image criticism with social demands, anticipating what was to become a frequent aspect in the church constitutions of other cities.[10]

When Luther returned from Wartburg Castle in 1522, he initially tried to calm the atmosphere of unrest in his *Invocavit Sermons* by preaching restraint and prudence. He neutralized Karlstadt's criticism of images by taking a moderate stand in his sermons and treatises.[11] In his opinion, there could be no question that the worship of images and statues representing saints was wrong in principle. He argued, however, that the faithful could not be deprived of this practice unless their true faith had been strengthened by sermons in such a way that images were no longer needed. Luther called this argument a "spiritual and orderly putting away of images."[12] He modified Karlstadt's criticism in counting images in churches among the *adiaphora*, that is, matters neither necessary for the service of God nor opposed to it.[13]

As a preacher and a theologian, Luther had only marginally touched upon the question of images in the time before his return to Wittenberg. Obviously, he did not consider it a matter of great importance theologically. What is interesting in this context is his approach to the Decalogue's prohibition of images, again and again invoked by the reformers in their criticism. In his Bible translation, Luther had still rendered the First Commandment in full length, that is, with the inclusion of the ban on images. In his catechisms, on the other hand, he invariably quoted the First Commandment in its abridged version, omitting any mention of the prohibition of images.[14] Only when taking a stand on works righteousness did Luther make reference to the Decalogue. In his sermon *On Good Works*, printed in 1520, he criticized religious donations as an attempt to buy God's grace, again basing his rejection on the First Commandment.

In his 1525 treatise *Against the Heavenly Prophets, Concerning Images and the Sacrament*, in the chapter "On the Destruction of Images," Luther turned directly against Karlstadt.[15] The conflict, which had been sparked by the dispute about images, forced him to refine his theological position on this matter. And although he disapproved of some of the image-related practices of faith, Luther vehemently declared himself against the destruction of images in churches, which he condemned as a relapse into Old Testament ways of thinking and rejected on theological grounds: "In novo testamento non curat Christus imagines."[16]

Luther's public position against the protagonists of the Wittenberg movement had far-reaching consequences: "Those weeks of March saw the beginning of a differentiation process of world-historical significance in the ranks of the first reformers. It is character-

7 Norbert Schnitzler considers this aspect as the germ of the symbolism of Reformation iconoclasm, a viewpoint convincingly disproved by Natalie Krentz. See Schnitzler, *Wittenberg*, p. 73; Krentz, *Ritualwandel*, p. 153, and the essay by Natalie Krentz in this volume. **8** Krentz, *Ritualwandel*; for the events in Wittenberg, see also Koerner, *Reformation*; Schnitzler, *Wittenberg*; Schnitzler, *Ikonoklasmus*; Michalski, *Aspekte*. **9** According to Schnitzler, *Wittenberg*, p. 74,

note 14. Original: "Item, die bild und altarien in den kirchen söllen auch abgethon werden, damit abgoetterey zu vermeyden, dann d(r)ey altaria on bild genug seind." **10** Schnitzler invokes Zurich (1524) and Soest (1531) as examples. See Schnitzler, *Wittenberg*, p. 72; Egli, *Aktensammlung*, no. 1899; Jezler, *Bildersturm*, p. 77. **11** For Luther's stand on images, see Scribner, *Bilder*; Stirm, *Bilderfrage*; Schwebel, *Kunst*, pp. 55–58. **12** *LW* 40, 85 (*WA* 18, 68, 21: "ein geyst-

Fig. 2 Anonymous, Illustration of an iconoclastic attack from: Eyn Warhafftig erschröcklich Histori
von der Bewrischen uffrur/ so sich durch Martin Luthers leer inn Teutscher nation/ Anno M.D.XXV. erhebt [...]
(A True Shocking History of the Peasant Turmoils), c. 1527–30

istic of the situation back then and the demonstrative function of the image question that this inevitable process was sparked by a problem which, from a fundamentally theological point of view, was of secondary importance."[17] The image question did indeed become the focal point of Reformation doctrine. Thanks to Luther's intervention and his moderate attitude, attacks on sacred images and sculptures were largely prevented in Ernestine Saxony. Karlstadt's writings and criticism of images, by contrast, became the starting point of a reform movement in Southern Germany, Alsace, and Switzerland, which shortly afterward abandoned the old truths of faith in a much more radical way. In particular, the preaching and writings of Swiss reformer Huldrych Zwingli in Zurich and, a little later, Jean Calvin in Geneva played a major part in radicalizing the image question.[18] It should be noted that none of the reformers, not even Zwingli or

Calvin, explicitly called on the public to take the law into their own hands and mete out justice against images, or even incited them to iconoclastic riots. Sacred works of art were protected by church law; their destruction was considered a sacrilege and was severely punished—usually by death—according to the laws then in existence.[19] In his 1523–24 *Lectures on Deuteronomy*, Luther, who had himself coined the term "Bildersturm" (literally, "image storm"),[20] was also one of the first to warn against its consequences: "No one who sees the iconoclasts raging thus against wood and stone should doubt that there is a spirit hidden in them which is death-dealing, not life-giving, and at the first opportunity will also kill men."[21] Here it becomes clear that Luther was afraid of the destructive power of a movement that, having around this time come under the influence of Zwingli, in particular, was at the risk of going out of control.

lich bild abthun"). **13** For Luther's theological position on images, see Stirm, *Bilderfrage*, p. 30. Stirm points out that Luther had already voiced this attitude in his 1516 lecture on Romans. **14** Margarete Stirm is the first to have pointed out this special peculiarity. See Stirm, *Bilderfrage*, pp. 17, 22 f. In what follows I am referring to Stirm's theological analysis of Luther's attitude in the iconoclastic controversy. **15** WA 18, 67–84. **16** "In the New Testament, Christ does not

worry about images." *WA* 28, 716, 13 f. See Stirm, *Bilderfrage*, p. 59. **17** Michalski, *Ausbreitung*, p. 47; see also Scribner, *Bilder*, pp. 9–20, 51–68. **18** For the positions of Zwingli and Calvin in the image question, see, for instance, Altendorf/Jezler, *Bilderstreit*; Christin, *Frankreich*; Stirm, *Bilderfrage*; Schwebel, *Kunst*. **19** Jezler, *Von den Guten Werken*, p. 27. **20** Hodler, *Bildersturm*, pp. 52 f. **21** *WA* 14, 620, translation according to Aston, *Iconoclasts*, p. 6.

Reformation Iconoclasms

Starting in 1524 and lasting well over a decade, iconoclastic riots occurred in Switzerland, Alsace, and Southern Germany (see infographic following this essay).[22] Their epicenter was Zwingli's place of activity, the city of Zurich. At Zwingli's instigation, the municipal council, in 1524, for the first time rescinded the protection that church law granted to sacred imagery and ordered its destruction. The decision was implemented by builders, members of the guilds, and the three urban lay priests, among them Zwingli himself. To avoid a riot, the council ordered that the city's churches be closed from June 20 to July 2, 1524.[23] By order of the authorities, the churches were cleared behind closed doors; at the same time it was decreed that statues and images that had been given to the church, for example, by ecclesiastical institutions or citizens be repossessed and picked up by their donors.

Zurich was to become the role model for the removal of pictures from churches, prompting many other cities and municipalities to follow suit. Sometimes, however, things would get out of hand; on several occasions, as in the looting of Ittingen Monastery on July 18, 1524,[24] the people perpetrated acts of uncontrolled image destruction and got ahead of council decisions by taking unauthorized action and putting councils and municipalities under political pressure (fig. 2). In Bern, for instance, the public order was threatened by a riot in the cathedral. The council responded by issuing decrees but still could not prevent repeated acts of violence and sacrilege against images. In 1534, it was the council itself that further aggravated the situation by adopting a resolution prohibiting the private possession of sacred art. Those citizens who, only six years before, had exercised their statutory right of taking back church donations were now requested to destroy their sacred images with their own hands. The resolution, which was to put a stop to the private adoration of images, was implemented by conducting house searches and confiscating works of art, which again resulted in new waves of destruction.[25]

In Strasbourg—which, due to the activities of Martin Bucer, Wolfgang Capito, and Caspar Hedio, had become one of the centers of the early Reformation—iconoclastic riots broke out in the same year as in Zurich.[26] Here, it was particularly the city's population that repeatedly requested the destruction of images and even readily lent a hand in these actions. In these events, the city council could at best only channel the violence. Bucer, who first took a rigorous stand against images himself, clearly rejected their arbitrary destruction later on. His treatise *That Images Will No Longer Be Tolerated by the God-Fearing* eventually provided the theological basis for a decision of the council, which on February 14, 1530, ordered the remaining images, statues, and altars to be removed from Strasbourg's churches.[27]

The situation in the Empire calmed down temporarily toward the end of the 1530s, only to flare up again with renewed vigor in the 1550s, when under the influence of Calvin a second iconoclastic wave broke out across Europe that particularly hit the German territories, France, the Netherlands, and Scotland. In England, Calvin's teachings fueled the Puritans' hostility toward images. Churches all over the country were "purified" of their copious late-medieval decorations.[28] Frescoes were completely covered with whitewash; all across the country, wooden sculptures and crosses were burned on huge pyres. In all of this, the specific development of the Reformation in England had something of the effect of a fire accelerant. In 1534, King Henry VIII had split with the Church of Rome, simultaneously declaring himself head of the Church of England. Thus, other than in the piecemeal territories on the continent, the English monarch's support of the Reformation was, in the years to follow, tantamount to the nationwide execution of his decisions. Not surprisingly, then, no other European country carried out the destruction of late-medieval statues and images as consistently as England.[29]

But also on the continent, especially in territories that had adopted Calvinism as their new creed, the late-medieval colorfulness of the churches disappeared under the uniform whitewash of the reformed faith. The extent of iconoclastic activities can be gleaned from surviving primary sources: "For France, Fr. Samerius in 1569 arrives at a total of more than 10,000 churches [that had been "purified"]. Three years later, Jean de Monluc counts 20,000 churches, adding 2,000 monasteries."[30] And even though these numbers should be taken with a grain of salt, they nevertheless provide some idea of how radical the consequences of this break with the Catholic practices of faith were in terms of aesthetics and art history.

It is clear from these brief examples that the general concept of "iconoclasm" comprises a whole variety of different actors, motifs, and practices. There are other examples, which cannot be described in detail here, such as the rigorously iconoclastic course of action pursued by the Anabaptists in Münster in 1534, or the early iconoclastic riots in the Baltic region, which started simultaneously with the first image-removing actions in Zurich.[31]

The example of Nuremberg shows that clear commitment to the Reformation does not necessarily lead to the comprehensive removal or even destruction of works of art. Here, unlike in other Southern German imperial cities, no iconoclasm occurred.[32] For instance, the larger-than-life *Angelic Salutation* by Veit Stoss, finished in the same year Luther published his Ninety-Five Theses, was hidden from the eyes of the faithful by a cover, but remained at its prominent position in the choir of St. Lawrence's.[33] At the council's behest, the liturgical implements and other objects of value (which in other places had been melted down) were stored away, and a prohibition to sell them was imposed.

The restraint exercised in Nuremberg was mainly due to a happy mixture of thoughtful council decisions and a rather moderate stance of the theologians there who did not seem to share the views of the radical reformers. Another important factor in this context is that Nuremberg had evolved into a flourishing center of the arts and of

---

22 For a geographical and chronological overview, see Michalski, *Ausbreitung*; Michalski, *Bilderstürme*. **23** Jezler, *Von den Guten Werken*, p. 75. **24** Ibid., p. 78. **25** Sladeczek, *Bern 1528*. **26** Frank Muller associates the beginning of the iconoclasm with the arrival of Karlstadt in Strasbourg, see Muller, *Bildersturm*, p. 205.

27 Ibid., p. 88. **28** The name "Puritans" has its origin in this call for purification. **29** For the Reformation in England, see, for instance, Aston, *Iconoclasts*; Howard, *Art*. **30** Christin, *Frankreich*, p. 61. **31** See, primarily, Michalski, *Ostseeraum*. **32** For the Reformation in Nuremberg, see especially Litz, *Nürnberg*; Seebaß,

The Ship of the Romish Church.
Burning of Images.
Ship over your trinkets & be pac king you papists.
The Temple well purged.
The Papists packing away their Paltry.

Fig. 3 Anonymous, King Edward the Iconoclast (detail), from: John Foxe, Ecclesiastical History conteyning the Acts and Monuments of Martyrs, 1641 (reprint of the original edition London 1563): The picture detail shows the removal of sacred works of art from a church, the images being destroyed and shipped off.

humanism. It is a likely conclusion that the deep-rooted appreciation of artistic quality on the part of the prosperous and politically influential citizens did much to protect the imagery in the city's churches.

In fact, cases are known, even from the centers of iconoclasm, where sacred imagery was spared from destruction due to its inherent value. Examples of this include Hans Multscher's *Man of Sorrows* on the central pillar of the main portal of Ulm Cathedral, which was preserved thanks to a special decree of the city council, and the *Ghent Altarpiece* by the brothers van Eyck, "spared only because it was surrounded by the aura of a great work of art."[34] Aesthetic appreciation is also expressed by Bern chronicler Valerius Anshelm in his lament over the mindless destruction of sacred statues, sculptures, and images in the city church: "The Church of St. Vincent should have been spared for the sake of its decorations and art but the brisk alacrity would not permit any prudence, or else many a useful thing would have been saved that has now been lost for the sake of mockery."[35]

Images as Works of Art

The image criticism of the reformers and the resulting controversy in public discourse helped to reassess the significance of works of art. Yet, even in the furor of the iconoclasts, there is an echo of the religious perception of images that they so vehemently rejected. Images of saints that had not fallen prey to the first unchecked destructive impulses were officially and publicly put on trial in many places. They were indicted, convicted, publicly humiliated, mutilated as during torture, beheaded, or burned at the stake by the hands of an executioner.[36] However, once the close, mutual identification of images and saints had been suspended, the original purpose of the image as the symbol of a now obsolete faith no longer mattered. Of course, this also changed the perception of art itself. The representations of saints once elevated through devotion were "disenchanted" in the course of the Reformation. What remained were works of art that, in their capacity as art, gained autonomy, now being perceived predominantly under the aspect of their intrinsic aesthetic value.[37]

This transformation was also stimulated by a far more material side to the "cleansing" of church interiors during the Reformation. The riches of late-medieval churches and monasteries that had been spared from destruction quite often were simply sold as objects of value. This is especially true for the sacred art in England. Having been removed from the churches since the reign of Edward VI, statues, sculptures, and images were ferried across the English Channel by whole shiploads in the second-half of the sixteenth century (fig. 3). At the same time as the second massive wave of iconoclasm, a new market for works of sacred art evolved on the continent. These works passed into private ownership after being sold at the ever more frequent auctions in France and the Netherlands.[38]

Artists' Fates

However, it was the artists themselves who were most directly affected by the Reformation. As becomes manifest in the broadsheet by Hans Sachs and Hans Sebald Beham, many of the less well-known artists became unemployed as a result of the severe criticism that the

Mittelalterliche Kunstwerke. **33** See the essay by Susanne Kimmig-Völkner in this volume. **34** Michalski, *Aspekte*, p. 72. **35** Quoted after Sladeczek, *Bern 1528*, p. 101. Original: "St. Vincentz söllte umb der zierd und kunst willen sin bliben, aber der zů gäch ifer mocht nitt verdanck nemmen, sunst wer wol vil nutzlichs behalten, das umb ein spott spöttlich ist verloren." **36** Warnke, *Geschichte*, pp. 91–98; Christin, *Frankreich*, p. 64; Schnitzler, *Ikonoklasmus*, pp. 214–217; Koerner, *Reformation*, pp. 104–136. **37** See Koerner, *Reformation*; Hofmann, *Luther*. **38** Christin, *Frankreich*, p. 66; Howard, *Art*, p. 233.

Veyt Pildhawer.

Vil schöner Pild hab ich geschnitten	Die weren weyt in Marck vn Stetten
Künstlich auff welsch vnd deutschen sitten	So aber ich das selb nit kan
Wiewol die Kunst yetz nimer gilt	Muß ich ein anders fahen an
Ich kündt dan schnitzen schöne pilt	Vnd wil mit meiner Hellenparten
Tacket vnd die doch leben thetten	Eyns großmöchtigen Fürsten wartten

Fig. 4 Peter Flötner, *Veyt Pildhawer*, c. 1530/40.

reformers leveled at work-based piety. In fact, with the theological attacks against their sculptures and images, their profession as a whole was caught in a crossfire of criticism. As early as 1522, Karlstadt had complained about the theological ignorance of artists whose images, he thought, were hardly suitable for spiritual edification: "Who has a right to say that images are useful, if their makers are useless?—Nobody has."[39]

The religious implications of their works usually brought with them personal, professional, material, and ideological conflicts. Even though art-historical scholarship now clearly differentiates between the individual beliefs of an artist and those of his customers,[40] both spelled potential danger for the artists' activities. Cases

are known from the time of the Calvinist iconoclasms where artists and artisans, in demonstration of their conversion to the reformed faith, were themselves engaged in the destruction of images—even going so far as to destroy their own works.[41] In other cases, the radical commitment of their customers to their faith had calamitous effects for the artists. For instance, Hans Sebald Beham himself, together with his brother Barthel and Georg Pencz, was evicted from Lutheran Nuremberg as an "ungodly painter." All three were accused of consenting to illustrate the anti-Lutheran *Protection Speech* by radical reformer Thomas Müntzer.[42]

Although, as is evidenced by Cranach's workshop in Wittenberg, there were artists who quite successfully worked for customers of either confession, it hardly comes as a surprise that particularly the less well-known painters, graphic artists, and sculptors, were forced to find new sources of income because of their precarious job situation as a result of the Reformation. Only a few of them benefited from the opportunity to compensate for lost earnings with secular commissions. Many artists gave up their profession altogether. In a petition filed on February 3, 1525, Strasbourg artists, while taking a generally positive view of the Reformation, expressed their concern that the resulting decline in commissions would push them into financial ruin. Due to a lack of professional alternatives, they asked the council to consider as many of them for political office as possible—a request they were eventually granted. Similar petitions by artists from Nuremberg, Augsburg, and Basel have also been preserved.[43]

Nuremberg artist Peter Flötner provides an even more drastic example of the professional reorientation of his fellow artists. In one of his woodcuts from around 1530–40, he portrays a mercenary foot soldier whom an inscription identifies as a former sculptor. It also contains the following lament: "Many a fair image did I cut/With expert art in the Latin and the German manner/Alas, Art's without honor now/Or else I'd be cutting many a fair image still."[44] To illustrate his fate, the orphaned tools, exchanged for sword and halberd, are shown at his feet (fig. 4).

Another way out of their dilemma was for artists to move to territories less affected by the consequences of the Reformation. Hans Holbein the Younger, for instance, upon his mentor Erasmus of Rotterdam recommending him to the English humanist Thomas More, moved from Basel to London in 1526. In his professionally induced exile to England, where the Reformation had not yet been introduced, he reached the apex of his career when he was appointed court painter to Henry VIII.

The direct and indirect impact of the Reformation on art production was very severe. Contemporary artists were also greatly concerned about this development. The humanistically-minded painter, graphic artist, and writer Heinrich Vogtherr the Elder, with

39 Karlstadt, *Von der Abthuung der Bilder*, f. B 3; see Warnke, *Geschichte*, p. 69. Original: "Wer darff sagen, das Bilder nutz sind, wan yre Bildmacher unnutz seind? Nyemand." **40** See Tacke, *Kunst und Konfession*; see also the essay by Andreas Tacke in this volume. **41** Christin, *Frankreich*, p. 65. **42** Heard/Whitaker, *Northern Renaissance*, p. 126. **43** Christensen, *Art*, p. 167. The Strasbourg

petition is published in Dupeux/Jezler/Wirth, *Bildersturm*, p. 60, cat. no. 184. **44** Original: "Vil schöner Pild hab ich geschnitten/Künstlich auff welsch vnd deutschen sitten/Wiewol die Kunst yetz nimmer gilt/Ich künde dan schnitzen schöner pilt."

Fig. 5 Lucas Cranach the Younger, Christ Crucified, 1571

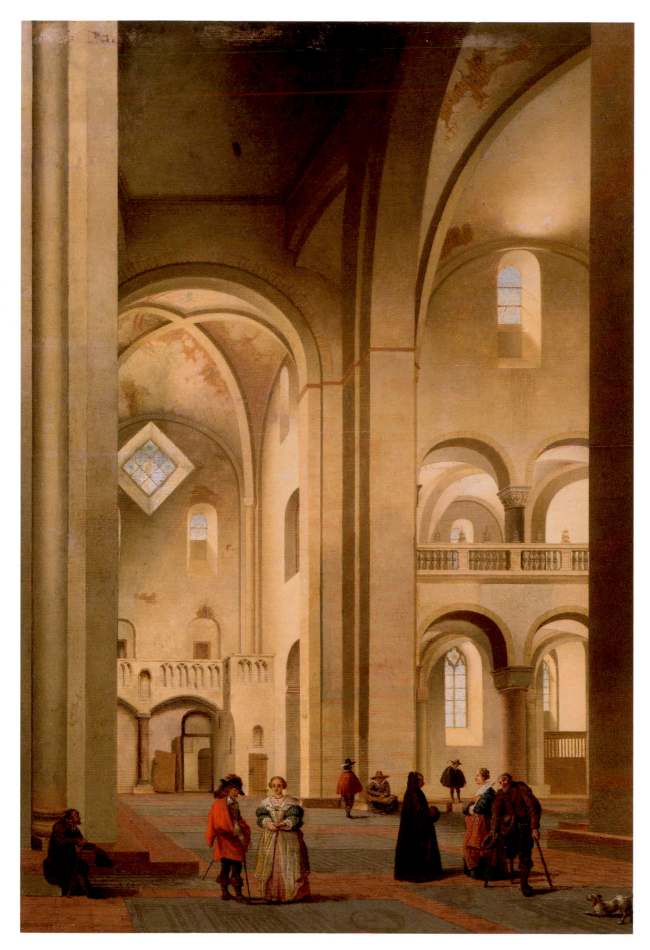

Fig. 6 Pieter Jansz. Saenredam, Interior of St. Mary's Church in Utrecht (Holland), 1637.
   "Cleansing" the interior of churches became a symbol of confessional change.

regard to the state of things in his time, complained, "Now in the whole German nation of our time, a noticeable diminishing and derogation has been inflicted on all subtle and liberal arts, causing many to refrain from such arts and busy themselves otherwise, wherefore it can be foreseen that in a few years it will be hard to find a painter or woodcarver in the German lands."[45] In an attempt to rescue the arts in Germany, he published a textbook intended to raise the artistic quality of the painters and sculptors working there.

New Pictorial Topics and Strategies

The negative view of the situation of the arts as a result of the Reformation was transmitted to, and has long been preserved by, art history. A change of perspective occurred only recently in this field. The works of a distinctly Protestant type of art and the artists' search for new forms of expression are now acknowledged as a genuine quality of this art.[46] Notwithstanding the general decline in commissions of artworks, there were, in fact, genres that came into their own during the Reformation. An example of this is the epitaph, a type of memorial portrait that reached its heyday following the changes brought about by Lutheran funeral and burial practices. Also, the Reformation boosted printmaking, another field in which many well-known artists were active. This included illustrations for the emerging production of books as well as countless pamphlets and broadsheets, for which there was a growing market.

A genre directly affected by the changing theological conditions was panel painting. From the viewpoint of painting, the Word, which was at the center of the new faith, was an abstract entity. At the same time, the criticism of old religious practices had questioned the visual suggestiveness of art in its very essence. Artists were forced to come up with new pictorial strategies in order to take this circumstance into account. This was especially true for altarpieces and devotional pictures. Here, the Word literally came to the fore since commentary was increasingly incorporated into the pictures in the form of text passages and Bible quotations. One prominent example of this trend is the crucified Christ from Cranach's workshop in Wittenberg (fig. 5). Through the text panel mounted on the cross, the painting addresses the viewer in direct speech, as it were, gaining a whole new immediacy. At the same time, Lucas Cranach the Younger reduces his representation to a few elements which, as detailed pieces of scenery, are lined up in front of a deep sky.

This simplification of image motifs and the tendency toward abstraction in the pictorial representation are frequent stylistic features of the new Protestant-oriented art, which also spread to other pictorial genres. The naturalistic representation is replaced with a rather symbolic representation that negates the impression of spatial depth, thus almost dissolving the illusionist pictorial space. With respect to English art, this phenomenon has been described as a deep-rooted distrust against any form of realism: "The portrait of a sitter that looked too lifelike might be mistaken for something idolatrous. To take one obvious example, the adoption of perspective in a two-dimensional painting, or in inlaid furniture or paneling, might suggest a reality that was not to be believed, not to be trusted. It opens up a different view from the conventional one that contemporaries simply did not understand the clever tricks of some of the greatest artists of Continental Europe and needed some trained, well-travelled master to explain it to them. It suggests rather that the British knew the tricks of perspective but chose to ignore them, or use them very sparingly and thoughtfully as occasion demanded."[47] This thesis also explains why the almost microscopically precise detail in the portraits of such a successful painter as Hans Holbein the Younger in England remained without artistic successors. Instead, the second-half of the sixteenth century saw the flowering of the highly stylized art of the Elizabethan court whose emblematic, mask-like portraits developed in a completely different direction. England, in the course of this development, moved further and further away from the continent in terms of art.

If one compares the characteristics of the national art developments in Europe, the impact of the Reformation on art is as clearly discernible as the demarcation lines between the different denominational spheres of influence. This is particularly obvious in the territories that came under the influence of Calvinism. After the huge market for sacred art had disappeared, the artists were forced to discover new pictorial topics. In England, these topics were mainly found in portraits, which in the seventeenth century accounted for the majority of the total art production there. In the Netherlands, the century after iconoclasm became the "Golden Age," with artists successfully specializing in other pictorial genres such as still lifes, genre scenes, landscapes, and seascapes. Additionally, the purist aesthetics of the whitewashed church interiors, which, following the change of confession had been deprived of their late-medieval adornments, still bear witness to the introduction of Calvinism in these territories (fig. 6).

In the territories that remained under Catholic influence, on the other hand, a different phenomenon can be observed. The Church of Rome responded to the Reformation criticism of images in the decree *De invocatione, veneratione reliquiis sanctorum et sacris et imaginibus*, adopted at the last session of the Council of Trent in December 1563. In it, images were rehabilitated in a sacred context. The subsequent Counter-Reformation increasingly relied on the suggestive power of painting, architecture, and sculpture, seeking to implement a new emotional relationship between God and the faithful by overwhelm-

---

45 Hofmann, *Luther*, p. 130. Original: "jetz zu vnsern zeiten in gantzer Teutscher Nation/allen subtilen vnnd freyen Kuensten/ein merckliche verkleynerung vnd abbruch mit gebracht hat/Dardurch viel verursacht/sich von solchen Kuensten ab zu ziehen/vnd zu andern handtierunge greiffen/Der halben es sich wol

ansehen lasset/als ob in kurtzen Jaren wenig deren handtwerck/als Mahler/ vnd Bildschnitzer/in Teutschem land gefunden werden sollten." **46** See Koerner, *Reformation*; Jonckheere, *Antwerp Art*; Howard, *Art*. **47** Howard, *Art*, p. 234.

ing the latter with sensory stimuli. In the seventeenth century, the art in these territories is characterized by its opulent splendor; entire church interiors were completely redesigned and underpinned with the pictorial programs of the Baroque era.

In most cases, however, such "baroquizations" were carried out to the detriment of the existing medieval art. In the course of the Counter-Reformation, the imagery and interior decoration of those Catholic churches that had survived the iconoclasms all too often fell prey to the process of Catholic renewal. A prominent example is the Gothic choir screen of Strasbourg Cathedral: it had been spared during the Reformation and was only demolished in 1682 in the course of the Catholic renewal under Louis XIV.

Conversely, in the territories under Lutheran influence, there is a large number of churches in which the late-medieval plethora of images has been almost completely preserved, and whose interior decoration has survived the Reformation and the subsequent centuries unharmed. This was due not only to Luther's moderate attitude toward images but also to the fact that church interiors were not subjected to the Baroque renovations associated with the Counter-Reformation. About twenty years ago, art history research turned its attention to the paradoxical phenomenon of the "preserving power of Lutheranism."[48]

In more recent research, the general assessment of the Reformation as a tragedy for the arts has been replaced by a much more nuanced view. It has been shown that the reformers' hostility to images, far from being a uniform phenomenon, included significant theological discrepancies in the matter of images, with correspondingly different consequences for art history. Quite rightly, the question has been put forth of whether, as far as this aspect is concerned, "Lutheran and Catholic views are more closely related to each other than is Luther's, on the one hand, to Zwingli's and Calvin's, on the other."[49]

Looking once more at the broadsheet quoted at the beginning of this essay, it becomes clear that its polemics have been refuted by history. For after all, it was the very same Martin Luther, into whose mouth the broadsheet had put the condemnation of the ungodly artists and artisans of the Catholic Church, who, with his position on iconoclasm, rendered a great service to the arts. Indeed, while the broadsheet holds the Wittenberg Reformer liable for the consequences his teachings had on the lives of painters and artisans, it has become evident that in many places Luther, directly or indirectly, became the savior of precisely this art in the wake of the Catholic Church.

48 Fritz, *Kraft*. **49** Schwebel, *Kunst*, p. 59.

BIBLIOGRAPHY

Allen, Percy S./**Allen**, H. M. (eds.) (1922), *Opus Epistolarum Des. Erasmi Roterodami*. Vol. 4. Oxford. **Altendorf**, Hans-Dietrich/**Jezler**, Peter (eds.) (1984), *Bilderstreit. Kulturwandel in Zwinglis Reformation*. Zürich. **Aston**, Margaret (1988), *England's Iconoclasts. Laws Against Images*. Oxford. **Blickle**, Peter et al. (eds.) (2002), *Macht und Ohnmacht der Bilder. Reformatorischer Bildersturm im Kontext der europäischen Geschichte* (= Historische Zeitschrift, Beihefte NF. 33), München. **Christensen**, Carl C. (2000), *Art and the Reformation in Germany*. Athens/OH. **Christin**, Olivier (2000), Frankreich und die Niederlande—der zweite Bildersturm. In: Dupeux, Cécile/Jezler, Peter/Wirth, Jean (eds.) (2000), *Bildersturm. Wahnsinn oder Gottes Wille?* Straßburg/Zürich, pp. 57–66. **Dupeux**, Cécile/**Jezler**, Peter/**Wirth**, Jean (eds.) (2000), *Bildersturm. Wahnsinn oder Gottes Wille?* Straßburg/Zürich. **Egli**, Emil (ed.) (1879), *Aktensammlung zur Geschichte der Zürcher Reformation in den Jahren 1519–1533*. Zürich. Reprinted in 1973. **Fritz**, Johann Michael (ed.) (1997), *Die bewahrende Kraft des Luthertums. Mittelalterliche Kunstwerke in evangelischen Kirchen*. Regensburg. **Heard**, Kate/**Whitaker**, Lucy (2011), *The Northern Renaissance. Dürer to Holbein*. London. **Hodler**, Beat (2000), Bildersturm auf dem Land. Der "Gemeine Mann" und das Bild. In: Dupeux, Cécile/Jezler, Peter/Wirth, Jean (eds.) (2000), *Bildersturm. Wahnsinn oder Gottes Wille?* Straßburg/Zürich, pp. 52–56. **Hofmann**, Werner (ed.) (1983), *Luther und die Folgen für die Kunst*. München. **Howard**, Maurice (2008), Art and the Reformation. In: Tim Ayers (ed.), *The History of British Art 600–1600* (= The History of British Art series. 1), London, pp. 231–241. **Jezler**, Peter (2000), Von den Guten Werken zum reformatorischen Bildersturm—Eine Einführung. In: Dupeux, Cécile/Jezler, Peter/Wirth, Jean (eds.) (2000), *Bildersturm. Wahnsinn oder Gottes Wille?* Straßburg/Zürich, pp. 20–27. **Jezler**, Peter (2000), Der Bildersturm in Zürich 1523–1530. In: Dupeux, Cécile/Jezler, Peter/Wirth, Jean (eds.) (2000), *Bildersturm. Wahnsinn oder Gottes Wille?* Straßburg/Zürich, pp. 75–83. **Jonckheere**, Koenraad (2012), *Antwerp Art after Iconoclasm. Experiments in Decorum 1566–1585*. New Haven/London. **Koerner**, Joseph Leo (2004), *The Reformation of the Image*. Chicago. **Krentz**, Natalie (2014), *Ritualwandel und Deutungshoheit. Die frühe Reformation in der Residenzstadt Wittenberg (1500–1533)* (= Spätmittelalter, Humanismus, Reformation. Studies in the Late Middle Ages, Humanism and the Reformation. 74). Tübingen. **Litz**, Gudrun (2000), Nürnberg und das Ausbleiben des "Bildersturms." In: Dupeux, Cécile/Jezler, Peter/Wirth, Jean (eds.) (2000), *Bildersturm. Wahnsinn oder Gottes Wille?* Straßburg/Zürich, pp. 90–96. **Michalski**, Sergiusz (1984), Aspekte der protestantischen Bilderfrage. In: *Idea. Jahrbuch der Hamburger Kunsthalle*, vol. 3, pp. 65–85. **Michalski**, Sergiusz (1990), Die protestantischen Bilderstürme. Versuch einer Übersicht. In: Scribner, Robert W. (ed.) (1990), *Bilder und Bildersturm im Spätmittelalter und in der frühen Neuzeit* (= Wolfenbütteler Forschungen. 46). Wiesbaden, pp. 69–124. **Michalski**, Sergiusz (2000), Die Ausbreitung des reformatorischen Bildersturms 1521–1537. In: Dupeux, Cécile/Jezler, Peter/Wirth, Jean (eds.) (2000), *Bildersturm. Wahnsinn oder Gottes Wille?* Straßburg/Zürich, pp. 46–51. **Michalski**, Sergiusz (2002), Bilderstürme im Ostseeraum. In: Blickle, Peter et al. (eds.), *Macht und Ohnmacht der Bilder. Reformatorischer Bildersturm im Kontext der europäischen Geschichte* (= Historische Zeitschrift, Beihefte NF. 33), München, pp. 223–237. **Muller**, Frank (2000), Der Bildersturm in Strassburg 1524–1530. In: Dupeux, Cécile/Jezler, Peter/Wirth, Jean (eds.) (2000), *Bildersturm. Wahnsinn oder Gottes Wille?* Straßburg/Zürich, pp. 84–89. **Rüstow**, Alexander (1959/60), Lutherana tragoedia artis. Zur geistesgeschichtlichen Einordnung von Hans Baldung Grien angesichts der erstmaligen Ausstellung seines Gesamtwerkes in Karlsruhe. In: *Schweizer Monatshefte*, vol. 39, no. 9, pp. 891–906. **Schnitzler**, Norbert (1996), *Ikonoklasmus—Bildersturm. Theologischer Bilderstreit und ikonoklastisches Handeln während des 15. und 16. Jahrhunderts*. München. **Schnitzler**, Norbert (2000), Wittenberg 1522—Reformation am Scheideweg? In: Dupeux, Cécile/Jezler, Peter/Wirth, Jean (eds.) (2000), *Bildersturm. Wahnsinn oder Gottes Wille?* Straßburg/Zürich, pp. 68–74. **Schwebel**, Horst (2002), *Die Kunst und das Christentum. Geschichte eines Konflikts*. München. **Scribner**, Robert W. (ed.) (1990), *Bilder und Bildersturm im Spätmittelalter und in der frühen Neuzeit* (= Wolfenbütteler Forschungen. 46). Wiesbaden. **Seebass**, Gottfried (1997), Mittelalterliche Kunstwerke in evangelisch gewordenen Kirchen Nürnbergs. In: Fritz, Johann Michael (ed.), *Die bewahrende Kraft des Luthertums. Mittelalterliche Kunstwerke in evangelischen Kirchen*. Regensburg, pp. 34–53. **Sladeczek**, Franz-Josef (2000), Bern 1528—Zwischen Zerstörung und Erhaltung. In: Dupeux, Cécile/Jezler, Peter/Wirth, Jean (eds.) (2000), *Bildersturm. Wahnsinn oder Gottes Wille?* Straßburg/Zürich, pp. 97–103. **Stirm**, Margarete (1977), *Die Bilderfrage in der Reformation* (= Quellen und Forschungen zur Reformationsgeschichte. 45). Gütersloh. **Tacke**, Andreas (ed.) (2008), *Kunst und Konfession. Katholische Auftragswerke im Zeitalter der Glaubensspaltung 1517–1563*. Regensburg. **Warnke**, Martin (1973), Durchbrochene Geschichte? Die Bilderstürme der Wiedertäufer in Münster 1534/35. In: id. (ed.), *Bildersturm. Die Zerstörung des Kunstwerks*. München, pp. 65–98.

Iconoclasm

The Reformation period is also marked by the controversy about dealing with religious images. Reformation theology was marked by the abolition of images.

Catholics
Catholic theology distinguished between the image as an object and the image content. Believers addressed their prayers not to the image as an object but only to its content. The image was venerated because it represents the divine.

Lutherans
Luther thought images were useful for educational purposes. To his mind, they were convenient for teaching Christians their own faith. Lutherans directly address their prayer to Christ.

Reformed Protestants
Believers address their prayers immediately to the invisible Father. There can be no image of Him. Images are rejected because they can easily be turned into idols. They were therefore removed.

◀ Mass of Saint Gregory from Münster (Westphalia), 1491 (detail)

The eyes of the clerics on the painting were scratched out. In so doing, the iconoclasts probably sought to assail church officials.

Reformation iconoclasm

The Reformation iconoclasm meant that visual art works representing Christ and the saints were removed from the churches. Citizens believed to serve God more sincerely with their works and prayers than with magnificent church interiors.

- ● 1521–1529
- ● 1530–1622

STOCKHOLM

TALLINN

TARTU

RIGA

COPENHAGEN

KÖNIGSBERG (KALININGRAD)

STETTIN

BRUNSWICK · BERLIN

AMSTERDAM
MÜNSTER
BREDA
ANTWERP
GÖTTINGEN
MAASTRICHT
ZWICKAU
GHENT

IMPERIAL CITY OF ROTHENBURG

PRAGUE

CAEN
ROUEN
STRASBOURG
LE MANS
AUGSBURG

TOURS
ZURICH
GENEVA
LYON
LAUSANNE
GRENOBLE

Destroyed relief from Wageningen, Netherlands (detail), Arnt van Tricht, 1548 ▶

The heads of Jesus and God as the Father were removed during the Reformation iconoclasm in 1578.

ANDREAS TACKE

Here I Rest:
A New Perspective on Fine Art
during the Reformation Era

Martin Luther had barely breathed his last when images of him lying on his deathbed were already being produced. These depicted the great Reformer in quiet repose, as a direct and intentional response to those who expressed hopes that Luther might have been taken in his death throes by the devil for having renounced the true and Catholic faith. This view was advanced in the late nineteenth century by Paul Majunke, a priest who was active as a politician and publicist on the Catholic side during the so-called *Kulturkampf*, the clash of cultures that divided Catholic and Protestant Germany. According to his interpretation, these paintings were a piece of spin by the reformers, designed to "silence the lying mouths of the devil and his associates" who would inevitably claim that Luther had died a "sudden, unexpected and, above all, undignified death."[1]

When we turn to the bare facts, we find that contemporary sources do indeed mention the presence of two painters at the time and place of Luther's demise. One of these was an anonymous artist from Eisleben, and the other was Lucas Furtenagel from Halle (Saale) (fig. 1). In fact their sketches were used as the template for paintings that were in turn to become the foundation for a specific iconographic tradition of deathbed portraits of Luther.[2] Such portraits were subsequently churned out by the Cranach workshop in astonishing numbers (fig. 2).[3] They did in fact proclaim a uniform message: in death as in life ("Here I stand"), Martin Luther had remained true to the new evangelical creed. Had he indeed been possessed by the devil, he surely would have died with a twisted grimace on his face. But, as Luther's quiet and composed mien in the paintings demonstrates, this had definitely not been the case.

But back in the nineteenth century, Majunke was intent on revealing these deathbed portraits as historical fakes. As an experienced protagonist of the *Kulturkampf*, he even revived the outdated claim that Luther had died by his own hand.[4] He did so with all the outward signs of an earnest scholar, even claiming in his foreword that his study was "not intended for popular consumption, but only for an academic audience."

In the course of the *Kulturkampf*, which had been stirred up by Chancellor Otto von Bismarck after the successful founding of the German Empire in 1870/71, quite a number of such absurdities began to resurface from where they had been buried in the refuse of history. In this light, it is slightly ironic that there was also a debate over the official deathbed portrait of Bismarck himself, which eventually grew into a full-fledged media scandal. Two "paparazzi" had gained access to his dying room and made unauthorized photographs that showed the deceased in a realistic manner, with his chin bound up. This was in stark contrast to the "official" and popular image, which depicted the revered founder of the German Empire serenely lying in state, as painted by Emanuel Grosser or Franz von Lenbach.

Interpretation, Exploitation, and Polemics

As with many other academic subjects, a proper understanding of the age of the Reformation is not really possible unless the story of its perception by scholars of history is taken into account. In Germany, more than anywhere else, interpretations proliferated as a direct result of political circumstances.[5] Perhaps because it was so obvious, one particular question related to our topic has largely been ignored in art history, or was only addressed in passing: how exactly was artistic production, especially the famous works created by Lucas Cranach the Elder, harnessed by the respective ideologies? Another constant in these interpretations is the supposed friendship between Luther and Cranach—a construct whose evolution into a given certainty can be traced by research over many generations and in various media.[6]

Much of what is currently being published on the occasion of the five hundredth anniversary of the Reformation fits seamlessly into this tradition of ideologically biased and schematic interpretation. One example is the way that the term "German" is still being interpreted as referring primarily to a political nation, much as the nineteenth century would have seen it. In the light of recent insights provided by the discipline of cultural-historic geography,[7] which defines space and time as dynamic historic entities, this interpretation is certainly obsolete.

When 2017 has passed, we may need to ask ourselves if this so-called Luther Decade (the designation under which the preparations for the Reformation Jubilee took place in Germany) has squandered a host of opportunities for real academic research. This includes above all the fact that an earlier approach, summarized under the term "transitional period", was not always kept in mind.

Fig. 1 Lucas Furtenagel, Martin Luther on his Death Bed,
February 18 or 19, 1546

Fig. 2 Lucas Cranach the Elder – Workshop,
Martin Luther on his Death Bed, 1546

This perception understands the year 1517 as one component of a lengthy and ongoing process *(longue durée)*[8] instead of the nineteenth-century tradition of emphasizing this year as an epochal watershed. When we turn to the artistic production of this particular year, we can clearly observe that there were no sudden changes from one day to the next, as traditional religious subjects were still being produced alongside the new images. A near-ideal example of this continuity is provided by the famous workshop of Cranach the Elder in the town of Wittenberg.[9] Surely the time is ripe for art history as a discipline to finally shift its perspective and focus research on these hitherto neglected aspects.

Considering the long-term structures of European history, the controversies surrounding the deathbed images of both Luther and Bismarck may be taken as prime examples of how defamatory mechanisms can make appearances throughout history recurrent simply because of their inherent suitability as ideological weapons. Obviously, it has been accepted practice throughout history to denounce and vilify opponents in any serious debate—and this holds true for theological disputes as well!

Luther himself was an eloquent proponent of this method of denunciation, which he employed in both spoken and written statements, but also in the imagery that was inspired by him or his fellow reformers. He would readily pour out all manners of insults over his theological and political opponents.[10] Chief among these was Cardinal Albert of Brandenburg: as this "bishop of shit was a false and lying man," Luther exhorted his audience to abstain from "publicly praising or exalting this pernicious, shitty priest," lest one make a saint out of the very "devil".[11]

1 Majunke, *Lebensende*, p. 10. 2 See Dieck, *Totenbilder*. 3 For a listing of these portraits, visit the research data compiled by Dr. Michael Hofbauer (Heidelberg), which is hosted as a research Wiki "CranachNet" by the Library of the University of Heidelberg. This site is certainly set to benefit the international research on Cranach. Available: http://corpus-cranach.de [11/02/2015]. 4 Majunke, *Lebensende*, p. 28. 5 For this reason, the contributions on the art of the Reformation period made by Anglo-American scholars in the last few decades cannot be overestimated. A few are named in the notes below, but the following are recommended in general, for example: Wood, *Altdorfer*; Koerner, *Reformation*; Silver, *Maximilian*. 6 For further information, see also a doctoral thesis (supervised by the author) currently being written in the Department of Art History of the University of Trier: Anja Ottilie Ilg, *Cranach der Ältere in Bildern, Literatur und Wissenschaft*. 7 Kaufmann, *Geography*. 8 As reported in: Winterhager, *Ablaßkritik*. 9 Tacke, *Stamm*. 10 The use of the term "devil" in Luther's diatribes differs from the one assumed by Lyndal Roper in her studies: Roper, *Body*; id., *Körper*. 11 WA 50, 348–351; see Tacke, *Rollenporträts*.

The Reformation was marked by massive polemics from its very first years, good examples being Luther's *Passion of Christ and Antichrist* (1521) and the illustrations made for his so-called *September Testament* (1522). Cranach's woodcut images for the later publication were so explicit in their agitation against the Pope that those pictures showing the Beast and the Whore of Babylon wearing a papal tiara had to be toned down for the second edition, the *December Testament* (1522). This was probably done at the insistence of Elector Frederick the Wise, who was still hoping to somehow contain the confrontation over religious policy between the Emperor and the Pope. In this case, we observe Lucas Cranach the Elder firmly by Luther's side as a creative inventor of imagery that unambiguously expressed the Reformer's anti-Roman stance.[12] His attitude had been clearly stated as early as *Passion of Christ and Antichrist* in May 1521, and now culminated in the equation of the Pope with the devil. Consequently, the last pair of woodcut images depicts Christ ascending to heaven as the disciples and Mary look on, while the Pope, again identified by his tiara, descends to hell surrounded by infernal creatures.

These two pictures are representative of the tone of the entire book, in which thirteen antithetical images on paired pages draw comparisons between the life of Christ and the doings of the Pope. Each picture is accompanied by a description (lat. *subscriptio*) which, like the image itself, proclaims a clear message. In *The Descent of the Pope into Hell*, for instance, the caption identifies him as the "beast" and a "false prophet." As Cardinal Albert of Brandenburg was the highest-ranking representative of the Papal Church in the empire, he was definitely in line to receive his share of anti-Roman polemic. Considering this, it is quite astonishing that the cardinal himself did not stoop to reply to Luther's rough style in kind. While those theologians who were allied to him (such as Hieronymus Emser, who was in the employ of Duke George of Saxony) did try to react in a similar manner, none of them came close to matching the wit and compelling strength of expression given to the Reformer.

Yet although this has long been ignored by scholars of the period, Albert of Brandenburg did react to Luther's attacks, as the cardinal attempted to refute him through the medium of fine art. In marked contrast to the Reformer, Albert did not put his trust in the emerging mass medium of printed images, especially pamphlets, but preferred paintings as his vehicle. The Cranach the Elder workshop alone was to produce some 180 paintings commissioned by Albert, with which he intended to influence a smaller and more elite audience. Consequently, Cranach's paintings were designed to be displayed in the enclosed spaces of either churches or princely palaces.

Cardinal Albert was one of those contemporary opponents of Luther whose fate it was to be belittled and villainized in the Prussian-dominated German national historiography of the nineteenth century. The overpowering desire to elevate the importance of Luther and the significance of the Reformation to the status of a nationwide movement by sidelining contesting historical personages was a phenomenon that persisted far into the twentieth century. In the case of Cardinal Albert of Brandenburg, this aspect has fortunately become the subject of recent in-depth studies.[13] In the course of these analyses, it has also been recognized that a whole bundle of related subjects had been left unexplored by past genera-

tions of scholars. In the German Empire, in order to stay within our nineteenth-century academic context, universities had little inclination to study the Catholic side of the process of confessional formation. Since then much progress has been made. In 1990, on the occasion of Cardinal Albert's five hundredth birthday anniversary, an international conference[14] and an exhibition[15] in his honor took place in Mainz. Another exhibition was hosted in Halle in 2006,[16] preceded and accompanied by no less than three separate symposia in 2003, 2004, and 2006,[17] all of them dedicated to the subject of Albert of Brandenburg. If we add to this the exhibition "Cranach im Exil" ("Cranach in Exile"), which took place in Aschaffenburg in 2007,[18] we can confidently state that from the point of view of cultural and art history, Cardinal Albert is now finally and firmly established as a historical protagonist. His example allows us to assert that representatives of the Catholic Church during the first years of the Reformation did not merely stare dumbly at Luther as if they had somehow been hypnotized,[19] as many scholars of cultural history and art history have assumed until recently. They actually seem to have retained some degree of initiative, and eventually acted on it—even in the very heartland of the Reformation movement.

It would be wrong to judge these Catholic patrons only from the ultimate outcome—the loss of large parts of Germany to the new faith—without taking the entire dynamic process into account. Only by this latter approach can we hope to reach a balanced evaluation. Yet the Catholic protagonists did "lose," and were therefore judged by the winners in the history books. In our case, Cardinal Albert eventually capitulated before the ascendancy of the Reformation in Halle and retreated to his remaining Catholic archbishopric of Mainz in 1540/41, to spend most of the rest of his life in his castle at Aschaffenburg. Prior to this, his main ally in Central Germany had already passed away: Duke George the Bearded of Saxony had been a man whom the Prussian historians would later brand as a "hater of Luther." The Reformer himself had mocked George without mercy,[20] and it must have given him great satisfaction when George's successor, Duke Henry the Pious, joined the cause of the Reformation. Both Albert and George are suitable examples of how Catholic patrons in the heartland of the Reformation reacted to the spread of the new creed[21] by commissioning works of art as a direct countermeasure.

Some Research Questions on the History of Art in the Age of the Reformation

Even though the subject of works of art with a Counter-Reformation bias in the period "preceding" the Council of Trent has been neglected by scholars in the past,[22] recent research now enables us to make two basic assertions: first, were we to employ only the traditional methods of analysis, a dilemma would immediately ensue where those works of art chosen for examination did not clearly and completely differ from older, preceding works. Surely, a mere retention of some traditional ways and methods of depicting subjects in art or architecture should not be taken as immediate proof of an opposition to Luther. If we wish to ascertain an intentional reaction to the Reformer or a rejection of the Reformation itself, we need to carry out a comprehensive analysis of the respective context of each particular work of art. Consequently, any new approach to the research dilemma defined above would have to target specific case studies, which in turn would need to employ methods of context analysis.

Such an approach allows us to discern that the adherents of the established church in Germany did indeed react during the first years of the Reformation. Lavishly endowing churches with paintings was one way of influencing the faithful. In this endeavor, the Catholic protagonists basically stuck to conservative and often retrospective subjects and styles. Certain subjects only became Catholic causes when their rejection by the Protestants made them controversial. There were even some positive reactions to the criticism of the reformers, such as an increased striving for simplicity and austerity. But Catholic reactions also included a marked increase in the range of expression and the sumptuous execution of paintings. This direction can clearly be discerned in works such as the cycle of saints and passions painted by the so-called Meßkirch Master in 1536–40. These few remarks should suffice to show that the actual position of apparently Catholic-commissioned works of art can only be judged after a comprehensive appraisal of their context.

Our second basic problem, from an academic point of view, is directly connected to the question of the religious position of works of art discussed above. It concerns the position of artists who created them. This problem stems from the traditional preoccupation of art history with the persona of the artist. In nineteenth- and twentieth-century Germany, this inevitably led to attempts at defining the religious identity of Reformation-era artists. Today, we can calmly assert that past scholars were rather too keen on reducing the subject of confessional strife and art to a matter of religious affiliation of the individual artist.[23]

It is a fascinating aspect no doubt, but today's history of art needs to concentrate more on structural and less on personal matters. It is not the artists who should be the primary focus of research but the works they created. For a discipline that has traditionally concentrated on writing the "history of artists," this is new terrain indeed; this approach practically amounts to an act of liberation, as we are no longer forced to pursue controversial and often unsubstantiated theories on how the artist was positioned in his time. Instead, we can now analyze which specific theological positions are contained in a particular work of art. From this, we can then make deductions concerning its impact.[24]

It should be obvious that the religious attitude of an artist and the religious message proclaimed by a work of art pose two entirely different sets of problems. Nevertheless, they have been lumped together, without comment or justification, in research studies until recently. As a result, a lopsided perception of the religious attitudes

of the era, the artists, and their works of art persists to this day.[25] In terms of the question we are pursuing here, it is actually irrelevant whether, for example, Lucas Cranach the Elder, Albrecht Dürer, or Matthias Grünewald served two different masters or whether they would have been willing and able to work for adherents of the two different creeds simultaneously. Dominated as it was by Prussian views, German national historiography in the nineteenth century (whose basic currents persisted well into the twentieth century), would certainly have given this particular aspect precedence. Only recently has art history as a discipline begun to free itself from this kind of moralizing and judgment so typical of the nineteenth and twentieth centuries. This has allowed it to reconstruct the phenomenon of the liberty of the artist in this time of religious schism through individual case studies such as Sebald Beham,[26] Hans Baldung Grien,[27] or Heinrich Vogtherr the Elder.[28]

The Cranach Workshop: Open to All Sides

This assertion certainly holds true for Cranach the Elder. On the one hand, his Wittenberg workshop continued to produce commissioned works of art for Catholic customers, while on the other it had no qualms about working for Luther and his allies. This was probably inevitable given that the two branches of the Wettin dynasty, the Ernestine and Albertine lineages, for which Cranach worked as an official court painter of the Saxon electors, represented the full range of potential subjects, representative techniques, and customer personalities that were to be found in both camps in the religious conflict (and all of this to be served by a single workshop).

The Ernestine branch of the Wettin dynasty, which resided in Wittenberg and Torgau, joined the cause of the Reformation, first in the person of Frederick the Wise, and then of John the Steadfast and John Frederick the Magnanimous. The Albertine lineage in Dresden, on the other hand, remained militant protagonists of the Catholic Church until the death of Duke George of Saxony in 1539. In a similar way, neither of the Saxon lineages and their respective courts presents a homogenous picture of religious adherence. Hieronymus Rudelauf, a councillor of the Saxon elector mostly active in Torgau, is a good example. He is known to have commissioned a painting on a subject that was decidedly Catholic from Cranach the Elder in the 1520s (fig. 3). He was also generally mistrusted by Luther and Georg Spalatin for his faithful adherence to Rome.[29]

But the workshop of Cranach the Elder went even further than this by accepting commissions from Catholic customers outside the circle of their Wettin patrons. One of these was Cardinal Albert of Brandenburg, who kept the workshop busy for a number of years with his decidedly Catholic commissions. These included a cycle of

12 Russell, *Understanding*. **13** Jendorff, *Verhältnis*. **14** Jürgensmeier, *Erzbischof*. **15** Reber, *Albrecht*. **16** Schauerte/Tacke, *Kardinal*. **17** Tacke, *Kontinuität*; id., *Zeitenwende*; id., *Liebe*. **18** Ermischer/Tacke, *Exil*. **19** Tacke, *Bildpropaganda*. **20** Id., *Konfessionalisierung*. **21** For the sake of convenience, I use this simplistic designation here. For a differentiated approach, see Jörgensen, *Terminologie*. **22** For a comparison including examples from other countries, see Tacke, *Auftragswerke*. The research question for counter-reformatory art was

first outlined by the author in: Tacke, *Stift*. **23** Packeiser, *Austausch*. **24** The futility of any such discussion was brought home to me by some of the reactions I received when I presented my doctoral thesis in art history on the "Catholic Cranach" in 1989: Tacke, *Großaufträge*. **25** This is discussed in detail by Münch, *Leid*, pp. 11–23. **26** See Wiemers, *Weibermacht*; id., *Meßgebetbuch*. **27** Weber am Bach, *Baldung Grien*. **28** Muller, *Vogtherr*. **29** Brinkmann/Kemperdick, *Städel*, pp. 235–242.

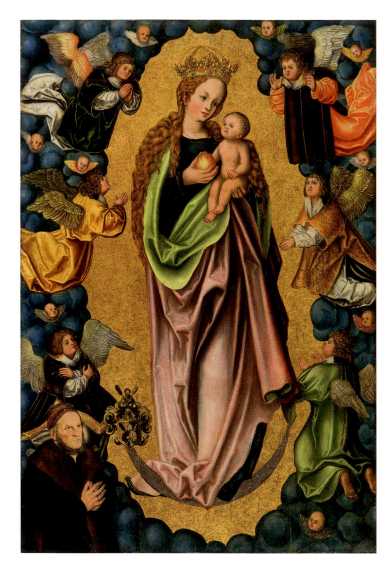

Fig. 3 Lucas Cranach the Elder – Workshop, Virgin on the Crescent Moon worshipped by the Donor Hieronymus Rudelauf, c. 1522–25

paintings for the cathedral (or *Stiftskirche*) in Halle (Saale), which comprised 142 depictions of saints and scenes of the Passion, most of them intended for the sixteen altars that had been newly raised in this edifice.[30] While this cycle of paintings has largely been destroyed, one altar dedicated to Mary Magdalene has survived (in Aschaffenburg), along with some individual panels[31] and fragments. A magnificent painting of Saint Maurice, now in New York (fig. 4),[32] can also be included in the context of the works that Cardinal Albert of Brandenburg commissioned from Cranach for Halle Cathedral.

Completed between 1519/20 and 1525, the Cardinal's paintings received the full disapproval of the Wittenberg reformers, as they were clearly intended to be used for prayer, ritual, and the adoration of relics according to the traditional ways.[33] Their inclusion in a cult of saints along late-medieval lines[34] was reason enough from a Wittenberg point of view to oppose Albert's cathedral as a citadel of the old creed.

Although the veneration of martyrs was reevaluated in the age of the religious schism, it was continued in the form in which it was practiced in Halle an der Saale[35] (Halle on the Saale) and this was understood in Wittenberg. Yet further commissions of paintings

from the Cranach workshop for Halle Cathedral show that Cardinal Albert was not about to simply give in to the growing Reformation movement in Central Germany.[36] The Reformer himself or Philipp Melanchthon needed only to step out of their houses in Wittenberg and walk a few paces in order to see for themselves the numerous Catholic paintings ordered by the cardinal that were under preparation in the spacious Cranach workshop. These paintings included not only the 142 pieces mentioned above (some of them of extreme size), but also a group of four pictures, signed and dated, of Cardinal Albert in the guise of Saint Jerome. Two of these (now in Darmstadt and Ringling) show the church father (actually Albert) in his study, while the other two (now in Berlin and Zollikon) place him in a countryside setting.

The latter two do not show Saint Jerome in the traditional role of a penitent, but, again, as a scholar engaged in writing (fig. 5).[37] This would have seemed fitting, as Cardinal Albert had himself adopted the role of an official translator of the Bible in 1525, 1526, and twice in 1527. This was a direct consequence of the condemnation of Luther's German translation as false and void by representatives of the Catholic Church. The message borne by these paintings of Saint Jerome was therefore clear: if the Latin *Vulgate* was to be translated at all, this could only happen under the authority of the official church, whose highest-ranking representative in the Holy Roman Empire was none other than Cardinal Albert of Brandenburg. And, as it happened, an official Catholic Bible translation from Latin into German was indeed compiled under the patronage of the cardinal in the very years when he had himself portrayed in the guise of the venerable translator. Hieronymus Emser's edition of the New Testament was published as early as 1527, while Johannes Dietenberger's complete Bible was available by 1534.

The reformers may also have wondered at two other paintings, both of which depicted the patron, Albert of Brandenburg, in the company of another church father, Saint Gregory. Once again, these two works are an unambiguous testimony of the patron's Catholic position during the great religious struggle of this period. In this case, Cardinal Albert had asked Cranach the Elder to emphasize the sacrificial aspect of Holy Mass.[38] Albert was obviously commenting on an ongoing debate with these magnificent large-formatted depictions of Saint Gregory celebrating Mass, and his urgent appeal was to adhere to the divinely ordained and exemplary theology and practice of the church fathers. Albert's portrait for the pulpit of Halle Cathedral, which depicts him in the guise of the saintly Pope Gregory, may well be yet another expression of this concern. The list of Catholic works of art commissioned and influenced by Cardinal Albert could easily be expanded. The above examples should suffice, however, to assert a prominent place for Albert of Brandenburg in any future history of "Counter-Reformatory Art of the Reformation Era."[39]

Another essential candidate for such a study would be George the Bearded, Duke of Saxony, Albert's closest ally in Central Germany. Like the cardinal, he was an opponent of Luther who was not only versed in theology himself, but ably advised by Hieronymus Emser and later by Johannes Cochlaeus. The latter was to become well known for his "commentaries on Luther," as he was the first to discuss the life and doctrine of the Reformer and the history of the religious schism from a distinctly Catholic point of view. Just like Albert of Brandenburg, Duke George saw art as a weapon in the struggle with the new creed. This can easily be discerned in the case of the newly-established cult of Saint Benno in Meissen Cathedral, which was lavishly endowed and celebrated. Luther himself condemned this adoration, a mere eight days before the ritual enshrinement, in his treatise *"Widder den newen Abgott und alten Teuffel, der zu Meyssen sol erhaben werden* (Against the new idol and the old devil about to be canonized in Meissen)."[40] Another example is the decoration of Duke George's personal funerary chapel in Meissen Cathedral, for which Lucas Cranach the Elder produced an image of the Schmerzensmann (Man of Sorrows).[41]

Clearly, these two examples need to be seen in the context of the ongoing battle with Luther's theological position. This holds true as well for the contemporaneous decoration of the façade of the ducal palace in Dresden. Here, the George Gate of the George Palace, both named after their princely builder, was used by George the Bearded as a canvas for the visualization of a complex theological agenda. This was intended as a direct Catholic answer to the provocation of the Reformation, especially to the new Lutheran creed, and the subject executed by Cranach the Elder, "Law and Mercy," could well be understood as a correction of deviations from the Catholic point of view.

Any attempt at a comparative study of "Counter-Reformatory Art Preceding the Council of Trent" needs to pay particular attention to those regions of the empire in which the territorial rulers remained Catholic. In Central Germany, these comprised, among others, the members of the so-called Dessau League, who had earlier convened in Mühlhausen, and who were later to form the League of Halle. This circle consisted of Catholic princes and church dignitaries who did not confine themselves to taking political and clerical action against the Reformation, but also pressed the fine arts into service for their defensive ideological struggle against the expanding new creed that was threatening their territories.

Their number should by rights include some of the princes who were later to be labeled as supporters of Luther by the Prussian-dominated historiography of nineteenth-century Germany, such as the Elector of Brandenburg, Joachim II. He is actually an ideal example for this "period of transition," a prince who was open to religious changes for mostly political reasons, even receiving the communion under both kinds in 1539, while "personally" remaining attached to traditions in ritual matters. His collection of relics was comparable in importance and size to the one that his uncle, Cardinal Albert of Brandenburg, had amassed.[42] And, like his uncle, he commissioned the workshop of Cranach the Elder with the creation of a large number of paintings of saints and scenes of the Passion. These were meant to adorn the altars of the cathedral in Berlin (the *Stifts-*

Fig. 4
Lucas Cranach the Elder –
Workshop, Saint Maurice,
c. 1520 – 23

30 Tacke, *Großaufträge*, pp. 16–169. **31** The recent attribution to this cycle of a painting by Dr. Bettina Seyderhelm (Regional Church Office of the Evangelical Church in Central Germany) received a lot of media attention but does not stand when formal and stylistic criteria are taken into account: Seyderhelm, *Kreuztragungstafel*. **32** Ainsworth/Waterman, *Paintings*, pp. 73–77; Ainsworth et al., *Maurice*. **33** Hamann, *Liber*. **34** See the contributions in Tacke, *Reliquienkult*. **35** Following the Council of Trent the Catholic Church rearranged the veneration of saints and retained only those saints that were "historically" documented. This was a reaction to the "ridicule" by Luther's followers, who mocked the veneration of saints, such as Luther did himself in the case of Albert of Brandenburg's *Hallesches Heiltum* (a collection of relics in Halle). **36** An overview of this process is given in: Chipps Smith, *Scheitern*. **37** Tacke, *Hieronymus*. **38** Hecht, *Gregorsmessen*. **39** Tacke, *Hilfe*; id., *Help*. **40** Volkmar, *Heiligenerhebung*. **41** Koeppe, *Discovery*. **42** See Tacke, *Reliquienschatz*.

Fig. 5 Lucas Cranach the Elder – Workshop, (Archbishop)
Albert of Brandenburg as St. Jerome in His Study, 1526

kirche),[43] for which he also established a specific liturgy, again following the lead of his uncle in Halle. Surprisingly, this endowment of the Berlin *Stiftskirche*, which Joachim had accomplished in the space of but a few years, survived his death in 1571 (at least partially) by many years. This is just one striking example that Catholic works of art were still to be found in the heartland of Brandenburg-Prussia even after the conclusion of the Council of Trent. It can be surmised that they formed an integral part of a liturgy that continued to follow the old creed.

The Effect of the Reformation on the Artists

We can now attempt to outline the conditions that would confront those artists who were determined to keep up their creative production in these changing times. We should probably start with the collective and individual lament of artists, an inevitable reaction to the Reformation's huge impact on the "art market," which could influence individual biographies in a massive way.[44] To this day, the

negative repercussions of the Reformation have hardly been touched upon by scholars, apart from indicating the preferences or dislikes of individual artists, such as Jörg Breu in Augsburg.[45]

Another aspect that would deserve scholarly attention is the high level of adaptability that an artist would have needed in order to stay in business. One facet of this was the increased mobility demanded by the "job market."[46] Only by frequently shifting his workshop (and setting his personal religious beliefs aside) could an artist stay in touch with those prospective patrons who alone provided the basis for his creative existence. Consequently, Hans Holbein the Younger gave up Basel for London to attend upon King Henry VIII of England, the sculptor Daniel Mauch followed Prince-Bishop Érard de la Marck from Ulm to Liège, while the brothers Hans Sebald and Barthel Beham, who had been evicted from the imperial city of Nuremberg for their radical support (!) of Luther's cause, were forced to seek employment respectively from Cardinal Albert of Brandenburg and the Catholic Duke of Bavaria, William IV, in Munich.

Yet many an artist would also embrace the opportunity to try out new subjects as a way of cornering new segments of the "art market." The workshop of Cranach the Elder, for instance, increased its production of profane subjects from the mid-1520s on, for instance, with its images of ill-matched lovers.[47] In general, it seems that German Renaissance art tended to become more erotic or even pornographic during this period, likely following the ancient economic adage that "sex sells".

Along with these new subjects, artists were also trying out an array of new techniques. Friedrich Hagenauer, for example, specialized in both carved wood and small-format cast-metal medallions. He had originally learned the art of sculpting from his father, who had created the wooden statuary for Matthias Grünewald's *Isenheim Altarpiece*. But when his hometown turned Protestant, the demand for religious sculptures dried up and he had to leave Strasbourg in order to try his luck as an itinerant craftsman. With his very specific niche art, the point of saturation would inevitably come after a few years' stay in any city. Thus, he had to adapt to a life of mobility in order to make his living.

Cranach the Elder was spared these hard choices. He managed to retain his extremely productive base in Wittenberg throughout the years following 1517. For him, the Reformation developed into a win-win situation as his sales actually increased.[48] His documented real estate and housing property as well as his tax revenue all suggest that his economic fortunes were constantly on the rise.[49] This favorable creative situation is echoed by his hasty reply to a letter he received in December 1537, some twenty years after Luther had posted his theses: "There is a lot indeed that I should write, but I simply have too much work on my hands."[50]

43 Id., *Großaufträge*, pp. 170–267. **44** Id., *Querela*. See also the contribution by Katrin Herbst in this volume. **45** Morall, *Breu*. **46** Tacke, *Auswirkungen*; id., *Impact*. **47** See Stewart, *Unequal*. **48** Statistical material documenting this aspect is given in: Tacke, *Auswirkungen*. **49** See contributions in Lück et al., *Spuren*. **50** Tacke, *Auftragslage*.

BIBLIOGRAPHY

Ainsworth, Maryan W./**Waterman**, Joshua P. (2013), *German Paintings in the Metropolitan Museum of Art, 1350–1600*. New Haven/London. **Ainsworth**, Maryan W./**Hindriks**, Sandra/**Terjanian**, Pierre (2015), Lucas Cranach's Saint Maurice. In: *The Metropolitan Museum of Art Bulletin*, vol. 72, no. 4. **Brinkmann**, Bodo/**Kemperdick**, Stephan (2005), *Deutsche Gemälde im Städel, 1500–1550*. Mainz. **Chipps Smith**, Jeffrey (2006), Die Kunst des Scheiterns. Albrecht von Brandenburg und das Neue Stift in Halle. In: Schauerte, Thomas/Tacke, Andreas (eds.), *Der Kardinal. Albrecht von Brandenburg, Renaissancefürst und Mäzen*. Regensburg. Vol. 1, pp. 17–51. **Dieck**, Alfred (1962), Cranachs Gemälde des toten Luther in Hannover und das Problem der Luther-Totenbilder. In: *Niederdeutsche Beiträge zur Kunstgeschichte*, vol. 2, pp. 191–218. **Ermischer**, Gerhard/**Tacke**, Andreas (eds.) (2007), *Cranach im Exil. Zuflucht—Schatzkammer—Residenz*. Regensburg. **Hamann**, Matthias (2014), *Der Liber Ordinarius Hallensis 1532. Liturgische Reformen am Neuen Stift in Halle an der Saale unter Albrecht Kardinal von Brandenburg*. Münster. **Hecht**, Christian (2006), Die Aschaffenburger Gregorsmessen: Kardinal Albrecht von Brandenburg als Verteidiger des Meßopfers gegen Luther und Zwingli. In: Schauerte, Thomas/Tacke, Andreas (eds.), *Der Kardinal. Albrecht von Brandenburg, Renaissancefürst und Mäzen*. Regensburg. Vol. 2, pp. 81–115. **Jendorff**, Alexander (2006), Ein problematisches Verhältnis. Kardinal Albrecht von Brandenburg und die preußisch-deutsche Historiographie. In: Tacke, Andreas (ed.), *"… wir wollen der Liebe Raum geben." Konkubinate geistlicher und weltlicher Fürsten um 1500*. Göttingen, pp. 187–251. **Jörgensen**, Bernt (2014), *Konfessionelle Selbst- und Fremdbezeichnungen. Zur Terminologie der Religionsparteien im 16. Jahrhundert*. Berlin. **Jürgensmeier**, Friedhelm (ed.) (1991), *Erzbischof Albrecht von Brandenburg (1490–1545). Ein Kirchen- und Reichsfürst der Frühen Neuzeit*. Frankfurt am Main. **Kaufmann**, Thomas DaCosta (2004), *Toward a Geography of Art*. Chicago. **Koeppe**, Wolfram (2002), An Early Meissen Discovery: A Shield Bearer Designed by Hans Daucher for the Ducal Chapel in the Cathedral of Meissen. In: *Metropolitan Museum Journal*, vol. 37, pp. 41–62. **Koerner**, Joseph Leo (2004), *The Reformation of the Image*. London/Chicago. **Lück**, Heiner/**Bünz**, Enno/**Helten**, Leonhard et. al. (eds.) (2015), *Das ernestinische Wittenberg. Spuren Cranachs in Schloss und Stadt*. Petersberg. **Majunke**, Paul (1891), *Luthers Lebensende. Eine historische Untersuchung*. 5th ed. Mainz. **Morrall**, Andrew (2001), *Jörg Breu the Elder: Art, Culture and Belief in Reformation Augsburg*. Aldershot. **Münch**, Birgit Ulrike (2009), *Geteiltes Leid. Die Passion Christi in Bildern und Texten der Konfessionalisierung, Nordalpine Druckgraphik von der Reformation bis zu den jesuitischen Großprojekten um 1600*. Regensburg. **Muller**, Frank (1997), *Heinrich Vogtherr l'Ancien. Un artiste entre Renaissance et Réforme*. Wiesbaden. **Packeiser**, Thomas (2002), Zum Austausch von Konfessionalisierungsforschung und Kunstgeschichte. In: *Archiv für Reformationsgeschichte*, vol. 93, pp. 317–338. **Reber**, Horst (1990), *Albrecht von Brandenburg. Kurfürst, Erzkanzler, Kardinal, 1490–1545*. Mainz. **Roper**, Lyndal (2010), Martin Luther's Body: The "Stout Doctor" and His Biographers. In: *The American Historical Review*, vol. 114, no. 2, pp. 351–384. **Roper**, Lyndal (2012), *Der feiste Doktor. Luther, sein Körper und seine Biographie*. Göttingen. **Russell**, William R. (1994), Martin Luther's Understanding of the Pope as the Antichrist. In: *Archiv für Reformationsgeschichte*, vol. 85, pp. 32–44. **Schauerte**, Thomas/**Tacke**, Andreas (eds.) (2006), *Der Kardinal. Albrecht von Brandenburg, Renaissancefürst und Mäzen*. Vol. 1 (catalogue). Vol. 2 (essays). Regensburg. **Seyderhelm**, Bettina (2015), Zur Kreuztragungstafel aus der Kirche Pratau bei Wittenberg. In: Seyderhelm, Bettina (ed.), *Cranach-Werke am Ort ihrer Bestimmung. Tafelbilder der Malerfamilie Cranach und ihres Umkreises in den Kirchen der Evangelischen Kirche in Mitteldeutschland, [...]*. Regensburg, pp. 208–221. **Silver**, Larry (2008), *Marketing Maximilian: The Visual Ideology of a Holy Roman Emperor*. Princeton/Oxford. **Stewart**, Alison G. (1979), *Unequal Lovers: A Study of Unequal Couples in Northern Art*. New York. **Tacke**, Andreas (1989), Der Reliquienschatz der Berlin-Cöllner Stiftskirche des Kurfürsten Joachim II. von Brandenburg. Ein Beitrag zur Reformationsgeschichte. In: *Jahrbuch für Berlin-Brandenburgische Kirchengeschichte*, vol. 57, pp. 125–236. **Tacke**, Andreas (1991), Das Hallenser Stift Albrechts von Brandenburg. Überlegungen zu gegen-reformatorischen Kunstwerken vor dem Tridentinum. In: Jürgensmeier, Friedhelm (ed.), *Erzbischof Albrecht von Brandenburg (1490–1545). Ein Kirchen- und Reichsfürst der Frühen Neuzeit*. Frankfurt am Main, pp. 357–380. **Tacke**, Andreas (1992), *Der katholische Cranach. Zu zwei Großaufträgen von Lucas Cranach d. Ä., Simon Franck und der Cranach-Werkstatt 1520–1540*. Mainz. **Tacke**, Andreas (2004), "hab den hertzog Georgen zcu tode gepett." Die Wettiner, Cranach und die Konfessionalisierung der Kunst in den Anfangsjahrzehnten der Reformation. In: Marx, Harald/Hollberg, Cecilie (eds.), *Glaube und Macht. Sachsen im Europa der Reformationszeit, Essays for the 2nd Saxon State Exhibition*, Dresden, pp. 236–245. **Tacke**, Andreas (ed.) (2005), *Kontinuität und Zäsur. Ernst von Wettin und Albrecht von Brandenburg*. Göttingen. **Tacke**, Andreas (ed.) (2006), *"Ich armer sundiger mensch." Heiligen- und Reliquienkult in der Zeitenwende Mitteldeutschlands*. Göttingen. **Tacke**, Andreas (ed.) (2006), *"… wir wollen der Liebe Raum geben." Konkubinate geistlicher und weltlicher Fürsten um 1500*. Göttingen. **Tacke**, Andreas (2006), Albrecht als Heiliger Hieronymus. Damit der "Barbar überall dem Gelehrten weiche!" In: Schauerte, Thomas/Tacke, Andreas (eds.), *Der Kardinal. Albrecht von Brandenburg, Renaissancefürst und Mäzen*. Regensburg. Vol. 2, pp. 117–129. **Tacke**, Andreas (2007), Mit Cranachs Hilfe. Antireformatorische Kunstwerke vor dem Tridentinum. In: Brinkmann, Bodo (ed.), *Cranach der Ältere*. Ostfildern, pp. 81–89. **Tacke**, Andreas (2007), With Cranach's Help: Counter-Reformation Art before the Council of Trent. In: Brinkmann, Bodo (ed.), *Cranach the Elder*. London, pp. 81–89. **Tacke**, Andreas (ed.) (2008), *Kunst und Konfession. Katholische Auftragswerke im Zeitalter der Glaubensspaltung, 1517–1563*. Regensburg. **Tacke**, Andreas (2011), "ich het euch vil zuschreiben, hab aber vil zuschaffen." Cranach der Ältere als "Parallel Entrepreneur," Auftragslage und Marktstrategien im Kontext des Schneeberger Altares von 1539. In: Pöpper, Thomas/Wegmann, Susanne (eds.), *Das Bild des neuen Glaubens. Das Cranach-Retabel in der Schneeberger St. Wolfgangskirche*. Regensburg, pp. 71–84. **Tacke**, Andreas (2014), Aus einem Stamm. Zum Ende einer Kontroverse über die konfessionelle Ausrichtung der Cranach-Werkstatt nach 1517. In: Greiling, Werner/Schirmer, Uwe/Schwalbe, Ronny (eds.), *Der Altar von Lucas Cranach d. Ä. in Neustadt an der Orla und die Kirchenverhältnisse im Zeitalter der Reformation*. Wien/Köln/Weimar, pp. 417–425. **Tacke**, Andreas (2015), Verlierer und Gewinner. Zu den Auswirkungen der Reformation auf den Kunstmarkt. In: Greiling, Werner/Kohnle, Armin/Schirmer, Uwe (eds.), *Negative Implikationen der Reformation. Gesellschaftliche Transformationsprozesse 1470–1620*. Wien/Köln/Weimar, pp. 283–316. **Tacke**, Andreas (2015), Luther und der "Scheißbischof" Albrecht von Brandenburg. Zu Rollenporträts eines geistlichen Fürsten. In: Syndram, Dirk/Wirth, Yvonne/Zerbe, Doreen (eds.), *Luther und die Fürsten, Selbstdarstellung und Selbstverständnis des Herrschers im Zeitalter der Reformation*. Dresden, pp. 114–125. **Tacke**, Andreas (2015), Querela Artificis. Formen der Künstlerklage in der Reformationszeit. In: Münch, Birgit Ulrike/Tacke, Andreas/Herzog, Markwart/Heudecker, Sylvia (eds.), *Die Klage des Künstlers. Krise und Umbruch von der Reformation bis um 1800*. Petersberg, pp. 60–69. **Tacke**, Andreas (2015), Gleich dem Kaninchen vor der Schlange? Altgläubige und die Wittenberger Bildpropaganda. In: Stiftung Schloss Friedenstein Gotha/Museumslandschaft Hessen-Kassel (ed.), *Bild und Botschaft. Cranach im Dienst von Hof und Reformation*. Heidelberg, pp. 82–87. **Tacke**, Andreas (2016), Winners and Losers: The Impact of the Reformation on the Art Market. In: Nakamaru, Toshiharu/Hirakawa, Kayo (eds.), *Sacred and Profane in Early Modern Art*. Kyoto, pp. 37–58. **Volkmar**, Christoph (2002), *Die Heiligenerhebung Bennos von Meißen (1523/24). Spätmittelalterliche Frömmigkeit, landesherrliche Kirchenpolitik und reformatorische Kritik im albertinischen Sachsen in der frühen Reformationszeit*. Münster. **Weber am Bach**, Sibylle (2006), *Hans Baldung Grien (1484/85–1545). Marienbilder in der Reformation*. Regensburg. **Wiemers**, Michael (2002), Der Kardinal und die Weibermacht. Sebald Beham bemalt eine Tischplatte für Albrecht von Brandenburg. In: *Wallraf-Richartz-Jahrbuch*, vol. 63, pp. 217–236. **Wiemers**, Michael (2005), Sebald Behams Beicht- und Meßgebetbuch für Albrecht von Brandenburg. In: Tacke, Andreas (ed.), *Kontinuität und Zäsur. Ernst von Wettin und Albrecht von Brandenburg*. Göttingen, pp. 380–398. **Winterhager**, Wilhelm Ernst (1999), Ablaßkritik als Indikator historischen Wandels vor 1517. Ein Beitrag zu Voraussetzungen und Einordnung der Reformation. In: *Archiv für Reformationsgeschichte*, vol. 90, pp. 6–71. **Wood**, Christopher (1993), *Albrecht Altdorfer and the Origins of Landscape*. London/Chicago.

SUSANNE KIMMIG-VÖLKNER

The Saints in the Late Middle Ages and after the Wittenberg Reformation

Luther's childhood and youth were marked by intensive worship of saints as was typical for the time. This is most often mentioned in relation to his imploring Saint Anne for help during his "lightning experience" close to Stotternheim near Erfurt. Before the Reformation, the cosmos of saints in the Western Church consisted of thousands upon thousands of persons, real or imaginary, to whom the faithful could pray. From a theological standpoint, the saints were meant to act as advocates for God and set an example for a devout and saintly lifestyle. In the early days, a person could become a saint solely on the basis of a veneration by the people. It was only since the twelfth century, that this happens exclusively through canonization by the Pope.

In the late Middle Ages, worship of the saints intensified. It became customary, as in Martin Luther's case, for a child to be given the name of the saint on whose feast day he or she was baptized. The saints functioned not only as personal patrons, however, but were responsible for every aspect of life. Countries, cities, guilds, and brotherhoods stood under their protection, and for every situation in life there was a "responsible" saint. In the region north of the Alps, especially the fourteen Holy Helpers but also Saint Anne, the mother of Mary, enjoyed special popularity. Cults of relics proliferated, as did pilgrimages, during which not only the mortal remains of saints but also miraculous objects and artworks were revered.

As a result, the actual function of saints receded decidedly into the background; they were viewed much more as helpers than intermediaries between humans and God. During the course of the Reformation, gradually Luther distanced himself from the idea that saints were essential in the life of a believer. After a time, he completely refrained from the invocation of saints. Only Christ (*solus Christus*) and faith (*sola fide*) led to the grace of God, which led him to the conclusion that the saints could not possibly act as mediators between the faithful and God. With some local exceptions, the celebration of saints' feast days as holidays was discontinued, as was appealing or praying to them. However the saints did not disappear from Lutheran faith altogether, instead, they lived on as paragons of faith, as *exempla fidei*. Remembering them ought to inspire the faithful to follow Christ and to proclaim the Gospel.

TIMO TRÜMPER

Art in the Service of Politics: Cranach and the Reformation

The art of Lucas Cranach the Elder and his sons was specifically put in the service of the Ernestine court's politics and the Reformation. The electors of Saxony—namely, Frederick the Wise, John the Steadfast, and John Frederick the Magnanimous—employed the court artist and his workshop not merely for the purpose of courtly representation but also to bolster their claim to power, their diplomatic purposes, and, not least, to establish the new Lutheran faith. This essay looks into the new pictorial concepts and strategies Cranach and his sons created in this context, highlighting the innovation and productivity of a workshop that served the Ernestine dukes over several decades.

The Appointment of Lucas Cranach the Elder

When he was appointed court painter by Elector Frederick III of Saxony, also known as Frederick the Wise, Lucas Cranach the Elder was no stranger to the prince, for he had already worked for the Ernestine court in Coburg around 1500/01.[1] From 1499 on, the fortress city and residential seat of Coburg—not far from the painter's birthplace at Kronach—was mainly used by the elector's brother, Duke John the Steadfast. Another potential point of contact is Vienna, where Cranach is known to have stayed in 1502/03 and where he made the acquaintance of the humanist circle around Conrad Celtis, who was also attached to Frederick the Wise. The Saxon elector might even have played a role in bringing Cranach and Celtis together.[2] In 1504, Cranach was appointed to the Saxon court; in the subsequent year, he relocated to Wittenberg, where he received his first salary payment in the amount of forty guilders on April 14, 1505.[3] Right from the start of his appointment, he was paid a considerable salary in the amount of one hundred guilders per year; he also received meals in

the court's kitchen, clothes, a horse and fodder, and, in addition, fees for individual works. This was about equal to the salary that the Emperor paid to Jacopo de' Barbari, who had been employed as court painter in Wittenberg between 1503 and 1505,[4] as well as to the one hundred guilders Emperors Maximilian I and Charles V were paying to Albrecht Dürer.[5] Although there is little reliable information regarding Cranach's biography before he settled in Wittenberg, his high salary suggests both an existing reputation and the Saxon elector's wish to permanently keep the painter in Wittenberg. But what objectives, precisely, did the elector pursue by enlisting Cranach? Did they justify his raiding of the state budget? And what artistic qualities could Cranach offer the elector?

Political and Cultural Consolidation

When Cranach arrived in Wittenberg, the city was experiencing a major upswing following the 1485 Treaty of Leipzig. The partition of the Wettin lands into the Ernestine electorate and the Albertine duchy, which entailed a significant weakening of their foreign policies, had become a heavy burden for Frederick the Wise.[6] The considerable competition between the two lines was further reinforced by the fact that the Albertine duchy had received the better part of the territories,[7] which created an urgent need for strengthening the Ernestine portion. With the aim of externally legitimizing themselves as true successors to the Ascanian electors, the Ernestine princes also sought to revive Wittenberg's tradition as their residential city.[8] Together with the Duchy of Saxony and the residence city of Wittenberg, the electorship had been transferred to the Wettin line only when the Ascanian dynasty became extinct in 1423. With Frederick's accession to power, Wittenberg regained some of its old

---

1 See Koepplin, *Cranach*, p. 114. Johann Müller's claim that Cranach participated in the pilgrimage of Frederick the Wise in 1493 is not corroborated elsewhere, and must thus be considered unlikely. See Schuchardt, *Lucas Cranach*, vol. 1, pp. 37–46; see also Hansmann, *Hofmaler*, pp. 45–56. 2 See Schade, *Malerfamilie*, p. 15; also Bierende, *Humanismus*; Heiser, *Frühwerk*. 3 See Schade,

Malerfamilie, p. 23. 4 See ibid., p. 378, note 109. 5 See Ludolphy, *Friedrich der Weise*, p. 107. 6 See Blaschke, *Leipziger Teilung*. 7 Compensation payments were agreed for this reason. See Ludolphy, *Friedrich der Weise*, p. 68; Rogge, *Herrschaftsweitergabe*, pp. 216–226. 8 See Cárdenas, *Friedrich der Weise*, pp. 16 f.

significance. At the same time, the new center of his reign was to fulfill the function of a spiritual and political heart to Frederick's territory, too, which entailed a major revitalization in terms of culture and urban planning.[9]

Next to rebuilding the castle, a key element of this strategy was the foundation of Wittenberg University, which in 1502 received the approval of Emperor Maximilian I. In 1506, the new Castle Church of All Saints was completed. Among the altars Frederick the Wise donated to it[10] was the St. Catherine Altarpiece (fig. 1). It was the first prestigious commission, to be followed by many others of its kind that the elector awarded to the newly appointed Cranach.[11] The likely connection between the subject matter of the altar—Saint Catherine as the patron saint of scholars—and the foundation of the university is evidence of the close relationship between art, religion, and politics.[12] There are other examples that show the deployment of Cranach's art during his first years at Wittenberg. The 1509 Wittenberg reliquary book (*Heiltumsbuch*) contains 117 woodcuts by Cranach with representations of the elector's relic collection, the third largest at that time.[13] Collections of this kind did not only serve the purposes of piety and indulgence; as the object of pilgrimages, they also were an important economic factor and provided a considerable boost to the elector's image. It seems only logical, then, that Cranach's illustrations came without the usual accompaniment of saints or prayers and were instead preceded by portraits of Frederick the Wise and his brother John the Steadfast.[14] The double portrait refers to their joint government and emblematizes the idea of princely representation and the fraternal concord, as well as the territorial lords' concern for the salvation of their subjects.[15]

Frederick had made the personal acquaintance of the imperial court at Vienna between 1494 and 1498, which provided an important model for his own cultural politics in Wittenberg. Intensely promoting and enlisting the arts, Emperor Maximilian I had added a whole new dimension to the ruler cult.[16] Prints, especially, could be reproduced in high volume, and their widespread distribution made it possible to influence public opinion. It was a medium that the Emperor used a lot and that also became of great importance to Frederick, not least because Cranach was the appropriate artist for it.[17] To be sure, the enlistment of art for the specific cultivation of a ruler's image was nothing new; under Frederick and his successors, however, it probably played a more important role than ever before.[18] Wittenberg became an important center of image propaganda, supplying significant stimuli for Reformation art in particular.

Art in the Service of Courtly Diplomacy

Crypto-portraits of the two brothers, Frederick and John, are embedded into the religious subject matter[19] on the outer wings of a *Holy Kinship* altar of 1509 (fig. 2).[20] The portraits of Emperor Maximilian I and one of his privy councilors in the central panel of this altar place it in the context of imperial politics. In conjunction with the Ernestine court's political allegiance to the imperial dynasty, as expressed by the Holy Kinship's familial ties, the altar implies the Emperor's unequivocal commitment to the Saxon electorate.[21] In 1508, relations between the imperial estates, which were led by the electors, and the Emperor had become rather tense.[22] It would therefore seem logical to assume that the picture fulfilled a political agenda. In addition, the altar might even have been used for diplomatic purposes, for example, as a gift to the imperial court. Other political statements can be found on later images, such as the various hunting scenes made by Cranach the Elder and Cranach the Younger from 1529 on. The apparent harmony of the hunting parties in these images suggests a close relationship between the Emperor in Vienna and the Saxon electors.[23]

The Deer Hunting of 1544 (today at the Kunsthistorisches Museum in Vienna) shows Elector John Frederick out hunting with Emperor Charles V near Hartenfels Castle in Torgau (fig. 3). As a diplomatic gift to the imperial court, the painting might have served to improve relations between the two parties. Cranach the Younger, for this purpose, depicts an event that never actually took place—there was no common hunting party in Torgau. The clearly identifiable castle architecture in the background is used in a highly specific manner: it illustrates the elector's self-confidence and claim to power.[24] The two escutcheons of the electoral Saxon coat of arms in the painting's upper corners emphasize the representative ambitions and the reference to the commissioner. Cranach the Younger's hunting picture presents a fictitious idyll that had nothing to do with the political realities on the eve of the Schmalkaldic War. Against the background of the denominational conflicts in the empire, the gift of the painting was to ease the tensions between the Saxon electors and the Habsburg court.[25]

The exchange of works of art that also served representative purposes was an element of early modern court culture and strengthened mutual relations.[26] The many courtly portraits that resulted from the enormous productivity of the Cranach workshop were particularly suited for this purpose.[27] A commission frequently

9 See Neugebauer, *Am Anfang*, p. 82. **10** See Stievermann, *Lucas Cranach*, p. 66. **11** Lucas Cranach the Elder, *St. Catherine's Altar*, 1506, Dresden State Art Collections. **12** See Kolb, *Bestandskatalog*, particularly p. 380. **13** For the reliquary book, see Cárdenas, *Friedrich der Weise*. **14** Lucas Cranach the Elder, *Elector Frederick the Wise and Duke John the Steadfast*, 1510, mixed technique on wood, Schloss Friedenstein Gotha. **15** See Merkel, *Bruderbilder*. **16** For a comprehensive account, see Michel/Holleger, *Kaiser Maximilian I.* **17** See Adriani, *Maximilian I.*, p. 217. **18** See Christensen, *Princes and Propaganda*; Trümper, *Inszenierungsstrategien*. **19** Crypto-portraits are representations of saints or their assistants bearing the facial features of living persons. **20** Lucas Cranach the Elder, *Triptych of the Holy Kinship*, 1509, Städel Museum, Frankfurt

am Main. **21** See Brinkmann/Kemperdick, *Deutsche Gemälde*, p. 224. **22** See Ludolphy, *Friedrich der Weise*, p. 195 f. **23** Lucas Cranach the Elder, *The Deer Hunting*, 1544, Prado, Madrid. Lucas Cranach the Younger, *Stag Hunt of Elector John Frederick*, 1544, oil on wood, 116 × 176.5 cm, Kunsthistorisches Museum, Wien. Contrary to both a widely held view and the picture's misleading title, the 1529 *Stag Hunt* from Vienna does in my opinion not present any clearly identifiable protagonists: Lucas Cranach the Younger, *The Stag Hunt of Elector Frederick the Wise*, 1529, Kunsthistorisches Museum, Wien. **24** See Müller, *Schloß*. **25** This can be ascertained via the painting's provenance. See Marx/Kluth, *Glaube und Macht*, p. 159. **26** With regard to Cranach, see Dohe, *Aemulatio*. **27** See ibid., p. 45.

Fig. 1 Lucas Cranach the Elder, Saint Catherine's Altar, 1506. Triptych showing the martyrdoms of
Saint Catherine of Alexandria (central panel), Saint Dorothy, Saint Agnes and Saint Cunegund
(left wing) as well as Saint Barbara, Saint Ursula and Saint Margaret (right wing)

Fig. 2 Lucas Cranach the Elder, Triptych of the Holy Kinship (so-called Torgau Princes Altar), 1509.
Central Panel: crypto-portraits of Emperor Maximilian und Sixtus Oelhafen (?) (behind the balustrade);
left wing: Prince Elector Frederick the Wise as Alphaeus (Father of Apostle James);
right wing: Prince Elector John the Steadfast as Zebedee (Father of Apostle John)

Fig. 3 Lucas Cranach the Younger, *Stag Hunt of Prince Elector John Frederick I with Emperor Charles V with the Hartenfels Palace in Torgau as a backdrop*, 1544

referred to in this context are the sixty double portraits John Frederick the Magnanimous had Cranach paint in 1533 in memory of his predecessors.[28] Supplemented by text fields with panegyrics praising the imperial fidelity of those portrayed, these paintings are a memorial offensive and, at the same time, a strategy aiming to strengthen relations with the Emperor and, thus, the Saxon electorate itself. The fact that Luther can be identified as the author of at least one of these texts is further evidence of how closely prince, artist, and reformer cooperated at the Wittenberg court.[29]

Art in the Service of the Reformation

At the beginning of the Reformation, Cranach entered a new field of activity that was to play an important role over the following years. While the graphic works of his early Wittenberg years were dominated by subject matters typical of the sacred and courtly context, Cranach now created propagandistic broadsheets and mocking caricatures as book illustrations, which were widely disseminated.[30] One of these was the woodcut *Heaven and Hell Wagon of Andreas Bodenstein* (1519), the first Protestant pamphlet made by Cranach.[31] Its commissioner, Wittenberg theologian Andreas Bodenstein, reported to Georg Spalatin, the elector's closest confidant,

about the artist's difficulties in realizing this work,[32] which provoked violent reactions when it was published. One who complained about the illustration to Frederick the Wise, for example, was the theologian Johannes Eck.[33] In 1521, Cranach illustrated Martin Luther's powerful diatribe against the Pope, *Passion of Christ and Anti-Christ*, whose success was due not least to the easily understandable woodcuts (fig. 4).[34] Cranach's illustrations to Luther's first translation of the New Testament, the so-called *September Testament* of 1522 (numbering about three thousand copies), also included extreme provocations against the Pope which were deleted in the second edition following Duke George of Saxony's appeal to Frederick the Wise.[35]

The genesis of these first anti-papal works in the immediate vicinity of the Wittenberg court demonstrates once more the close cooperation between reformers, privy councillors, and court artist Lucas Cranach. Cranach's art was now increasingly used to influence public opinion and to lend visual expression to the criticism of the Roman Church, and its utilization on behalf of the Reformation and the political objectives of the Saxon electors increased in the following years. This is manifest most clearly in the numerous Luther portraits that were produced in Cranach's workshop from 1520 on—and which to this day shape our image of the central figure of the Reformation. It is obvious that these portraits also served propagandistic

Fig. 4
Lucas Cranach the Elder, Höllensturz des Papstes (The Pope Goes to Hell). From: Martin Luther, *Passional Christi und Antichristi* (The Passion of Christ and Anti-Christ), Wittenberg 1521.
This pamphlet shows woodcuts with scenes from the life of Christ mounted antithetically with contrasting images of the Pope.

28 See Schuchardt, *Lucas Cranach*, vol. 1, pp. 89 f.; Schade, *Malerfamilie*, p. 435. **29** See Ludolphy, *Friedrich der Weise*, pp. 18 f. **30** See Kunz, *Anmerkungen*, pp. 88 f. **31** Lucas Cranach the Elder, *Heaven and Hell Wagon of Andreas Bodenstein, called Karlstadt*, 1519, Hamburger Kunsthalle. **32** See Münch, *Zeitgenossen*, p. 75. **33** See Stiftung Schloss Friedenstein Gotha/Museumsland-schaft Hessen Kassel, *Bild und Botschaft*, p. 112. **34** Martin Luther, *Passional Christi und Antichristi*, Erfurt 1521. **35** See Brinkmann, *Cranach der Ältere*, p. 200; Stiftung Schloss Friedenstein Gotha/Museumslandschaft Hessen Kassel, *Bild und Botschaft*, p. 118.

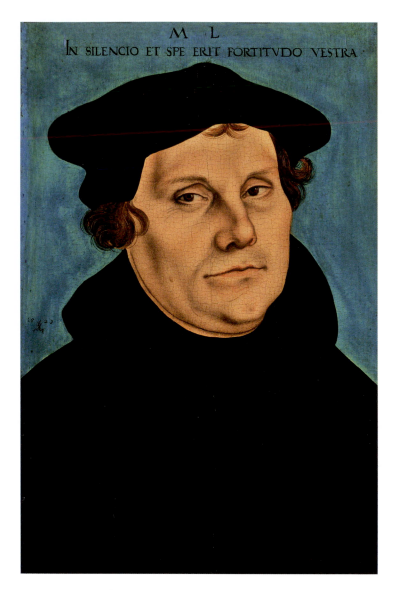

Fig. 5 Lucas Cranach the Elder, Martin Luther, 1529

Fig. 6 Lucas Cranach the Elder, Katharina von Bora, 1529

purposes, as did the many easily reproducible marriage portraits of Luther and Katharina von Bora made between 1525 and 1529. On the one hand, these portraits are evidence of the great popularity enjoyed by this couple; on the other, the traditional form of the couple portrait suggests an artistic sanction of the marriage between former monk and former nun, which the Catholic Church had so sharply condemned (figs. 5 and 6).[36]

Illustrating Lutheran Doctrine

The most important pictorial subject matter conceived to illustrate Lutheran doctrine was without any doubt the Allegory of "Law and Grace" (see the illustration following this essay). It brings home the central idea of the doctrine of justification, namely that man finds salvation through faith and God's grace alone. Existing art historical research does not entirely agree on the extent to which the two stylistically seminal paintings of the topic in Gotha and Prague were informed by printed archetypes.[37] In any case, the topic was given a

whole new prominence by these two representative versions.[38] The crucial questions in this context are what motivated these paintings and what political conditions played a role in their making. With the exception of their date of origin, 1529, little is known about their genesis. It can be assumed, however, that they were manufactured, in cooperation with Luther, in the immediate context of the court. This is confirmed by the provenance of the Gotha painting. Listed in the inventory since 1659, it very probably entered the Gotha ducal collection as dynastic inheritance from the Saxon electors.

The decisions taken at the 1526 Diet of Speyer provided the Lutheran-minded princes with a legal basis for the Reformation of the church within their territories.[39] The Reformation had continued to spread, especially in the Electorate of Saxony, and the church and school visitations carried out between 1526 and 1530 were the precondition for replacing preachers, dissolving monasteries, and the secularization of property. Hence the entire school and church system was placed in the hands of the territorial lord, whom Luther, due to the complicated situation of the church, had appointed as "emergency bishop" (*Notbischof*).[40] This was the beginning of the constitutional restructuring of the church "from above," and it paved the way for the foundation of a territorial church. In connection with the visitations in the Saxon electorate, it was noted that both the ecclesiastical doctrine itself and its teaching by pastors were in need of restructuring. In 1529, Luther therefore composed the *Small Catechism* as an introduction to the Christian faith. Published in the same year, the *Large Catechism* was primarily intended as an instruction for the pastors themselves; illustrations by Cranach were added from the second edition onward. The consolidation and teaching of the Lutheran doctrine in electoral Saxony was pursued with vigor by the territorial lord and Luther himself. Strikingly, the attempts at formulating the new faith and the creation of the new pictorial subject of "Law and Grace" in painting occurred in the same year.

Luther had realized early on that images are capable of conveying abstract didactic content, and in a 1529 sermon he aptly referred to such works as "mnemonic images" (*Merkbilder*).[41] This combination of text and image works well with the Protestant theological principle of *sola scriptura*, that is, the idea that scripture alone infallibly conveys the message of salvation. Next to the subject matter of "Law and Grace," other favorite topics of Lutheran didactic pictures are the New Testament stories of the adulteress and of Jesus blessing the children, which Cranach disseminated in a large variety of formats and versions from the 1530s onward.[42] As with "Law and Grace," these representations include Bible quotations in German to support the didactic function for all who could read.

The Self-Promotion of the Saxon Electors as Guardians of Lutheranism

The government of Elector John the Steadfast, who in 1525 followed his brother Frederick, reinforced efforts to strengthen the new Lutheran faith in terms of content and institutions—and in the context of these efforts, Cranach's "Law and Grace" panels played a substantial role. The version preserved today in Gotha was followed by numerous copies and variants, the Saxon duchy being the heartland of their distribution.[43] The most prominent work of art in this succession is the 1555 monumental altar at St. Peter and Paul's Church in Weimar by Lucas Cranach the Younger (fig. 3 in Ingrid Dettmann's essay in this volume).[44] After the loss of the electorship following the capitulation of Wittenberg and the choice of Weimar as new residential town, the altar served not merely as an epitaph for Duke John Frederick, who had died in 1554; it also expressed the claim to power

of the Ernestine dynasty, which after its tremendous defeat needed to develop a new self-image. The key message of Lutheranism is conveyed by the subject matter of "Law and Grace" on the central panel of the altar. What is exceptional is that the altar also shows representations of Martin Luther and Lucas Cranach the Elder, thus honoring both men. In addition, the expanded personnel in the picture illustrates the achievements of the Ernestine court, whose patronage and protection laid the foundation not only for the flowering of arts and sciences (e.g., Luther's professorship at Wittenberg University) but also for the spread of Lutheranism. As becomes particularly clear in the dedication inscription on the predella, the altar is a clearly formulated confession of the Lutheran faith.[45] The Ernestine princes saw themselves as defenders of the "true" Protestant faith, and this attitude was to have repercussions well into the seventeenth century.[46]

It was not the first time that the defense of the Reformation was used for the self-promotion of the Ernestine court. By about 1538, Elector John Frederick the Magnanimous had styled himself as a protector of Lutheranism: a portrait panel by Lucas Cranach the Younger at the Toledo Museum of Art in Ohio shows the elector in the company of Reformation pioneers Luther and Melanchthon, shielding them with his broad shoulders and ready to use violence if it should become necessary to defend them, as may be concluded from his tight grip on the hilts of his two swords (fig. 7).[47] The painting, which could be the fragment of an altar, is an important example of how visual art is capable of responding to current political trends and making effective public statements. Against the background of the denominational conflicts intensifying all over the empire around the end of the 1530s, the elector's self-aggrandizement as a military protector of Lutheranism marks a major new strategy, which can also be found in a number of prints.

Conveying Topical Messages

Cranach's major artistic innovation was the ability to flexibly respond to current events, and, depending on functional context and target, he and his workshop used different pictorial solutions for this purpose. He enhanced traditional topics with crypto-portraits, for instance, to convey topical messages and respond to a specific political context. Sometimes, to suggest a harmonious situation in troubled times, incidents were invented and supplemented by elements that clearly refer to the respective commissioners. Both strategies served the practice of courtly exchanges in accordance with diplomatic custom. Anti-papal propaganda in pamphlets and Refor-

36 See Brinkmann, *Cranach der Ältere*, p. 194. **37** Erichsen and Spira, for example, have evaluated the dating of the Erlangen woodcut completely differently. See Erichsen, *Gesetz und Gnade*, p. 100; Stiftung Schloss Friedenstein Gotha/Museumslandschaft Hessen Kassel, *Bild und Botschaft*, p. 172. **38** Lucas Cranach the Elder, *Law and Grace*, 1529, Stiftung Schloss Friedenstein Gotha and Prague National Gallery. **39** See Wallmann, *Kirchengeschichte Deutschlands*, p. 61. **40** Ibid., p. 62; Tullner, *Geschichte*, p. 57. **41** Spira, *Lucas Cranach, der Maler Luthers*, p. 57. **42** Stiftung Schloss Friedenstein Gotha/Museums-

landschaft Hessen Kassel, *Bild und Botschaft*, pp. 189–205. **43** See Fleck, *Glaubensallegorie*, p. 94. **44** Lucas Cranach the Younger, *Altarpiece*, 1555, St. Peter and St. Paul, Weimar. **45** "…Ihren im flammenden Krieg standhaft dem Bekenntnis getreuen Eltern …" (*… to their parents who remained steadfast to their faith in the blaze of war…*) **46** See on this topic Westphal, *Nach dem Verlust der Kurwürde*; Klinger, *Großmütig und standhaft*. **47** Lucas Cranach the Younger, *Elector John Frederick the Magnanimous and the Wittenberg Reformers*, c. 1538, Toledo Museum of Art.

Fig. 7
Lucas Cranach the Younger,
Prince Elector John Frederick
the Magnanimous and the
Wittenberg Reformers, c. 1538

mation writings was expressed in particularly drastic and striking illustrations that condensed the message to its essence to make it easily understandable for a broad audience. Didactic pictures with Reformation content, along with the establishment of a new territorial church, served the consolidation of the Lutheran faith, leading to the complete reinvention of the topic of "Law and Grace."

The electors of Saxony knew very well how to use Cranach's art for their purposes. Starting with Frederick the Wise's self-promotion, the great artistic potential was, from early on, placed in the service of the court and the Reformation and used as propaganda for the new faith. For this purpose, Cranach in his capacity as court artist developed a number of concepts that made him an indispensable and highly effective instrument for both the Ernestine electors and Martin Luther.

BIBLIOGRAPHY

Adriani, Götz (2014), Kaiser Maximilian I. und die Bildmedien. In: Adriani, Götz/Schmauder, Andreas (eds.), *1514: Macht—Gewalt—Freiheit. Der Vertrag zu Tübingen in Zeiten des Umbruchs*. Tübingen, pp. 217–278. **Bierende**, Edgar (2002), *Lucas Cranach d. Ä. und der deutsche Humanismus. Tafelmalerei im Kontext von Rhetorik, Chroniken und Fürstenspiegel*. München/Berlin. **Blaschke**, Karlheinz (2002), Die Leipziger Teilung der wettinischen Länder von 1485. In: Schirmer, Uwe/Thieme, André (eds.), *Beiträge zur Verfassungs- und Verwaltungsgeschichte Sachsens. Ausgewählte Aufsätze von Karlheinz Blaschke, aus Anlaß seines 75. Geburtstages* (= Schriften zur Sächsischen Geschichte und Volkskunde. 5). Leipzig, pp. 323–335. **Brinkmann**, Bodo (ed.) (2007), *Cranach der Ältere*, exhibition catalogue, 23 November 2007 – 17 February 2008, Städelsches Kunstinstitut Frankfurt and Royal Academy London. Ostfildern-Ruit. **Brinkmann**, Bodo/**Kemperdick**, Stephan (2005), *Deutsche Gemälde im Städel, 1500–1550* (= Kataloge der Gemälde im Städelschen Kunstinstitut Frankfurt am Main. 5). Mainz. **Cárdenas**, Livia (2002), *Friedrich der Weise und das Wittenberger Heiltumsbuch. Mediale Repräsentation zwischen Mittelalter und Neuzeit*. Berlin. **Christensen**, Carl (1992), *Princes and Propaganda. Electoral Saxon Art of the Reformation* (= Sixteenth Century Essays & Studies. 20). Kirksville. **Dohe**, Sebastian (2015), *Aemulatio, Anspruch und Austausch. Cranachs Kunst im höfischen Dienst*. In: Stiftung Schloss Friedenstein Gotha/Museumslandschaft Hessen Kassel (eds.), *Bild und Botschaft. Cranach im Dienst von Hof und Reformation*. Heidelberg, pp. 43–50. **Erichsen**, Johannes (2015), Gesetz und Gnade. Versuch einer Bilanz. In: Syndram, Dirk (ed.), *Luther und die Fürsten. Selbstdarstellung und Selbstverständnis des Herrschers im Zeitalter der Reformation*. Dresden, pp. 97–114. **Fleck**, Miriam Verena (2010), *Ein tröstlich gemelde. Die Glaubensallegorie "Gesetz und Gnade" in Europa zwischen Spätmittelalter und Früher Neuzeit* (= Studien zur Kunstgeschichte des Mittelalters und der Frühen Neuzeit. 5). Korb. **Hansmann**, Ruth (2010), "Als haben wir angesehen unsers dieners und lieben getreuen Lucas von Cranach Ehrbarkeit, Kunst und Redlichkeit"—Lucas Cranach als neu bestallter Hofmaler in kursächsischen Diensten. In: Weschenfelder, Klaus/Müller, Mathias/Böckern, Beate/Hansmann, Ruth (eds.), *Apelles am Fürstenhof. Facetten der Hofkunst um 1500 im Alten Reich*. Berlin, pp. 45–56. **Heiser**, Sabine (2002), *Das Frühwerk Lucas Cranachs des Älteren. Wien um 1500—Dresden um 1900* (= Neue Forschungen zur deutschen Kunst. 4). Berlin. **Klinger**, Andreas (2003), Großmütig und standhaft. Zum ernestinischen Bild Johann Friedrichs im 17. Jahrhundert. In: Bauer, Joachim/Hellmann, Birgitt (eds.), *Verlust und Gewinn. Johann Friedrich I., Kurfürst von Sachsen* (= Bausteine zur Jenaer Stadtgeschichte. 8). Weimar, pp. 41–59. **Koepplin**, Dieter (1974), Cranach bis zum 32. Lebensjahr. In: Falk, Tilman/Koepplin, Dieter (eds.), *Lukas Cranach. Gemälde—Zeichnungen—Druckgraphik*. Vol. 1. Basel/Stuttgart, pp. 105–184. **Kolb**, Karin (2005), Bestandskatalog der Staatlichen Kunstsammlungen Dresden—Cranach-Werke in der Gemäldegalerie Alte Meister und der Rüstkammer. In: Marx, Harald/Mössinger, Ingrid (eds.), *Cranach. Gemälde aus Dresden. Mit einem Bestandskatalog der Gemälde in den Staatlichen Kunstsammlungen Dresden*. Köln, pp. 199–524. **Kunz**, Armin (2010),

Anmerkungen zu Cranach als Graphiker. In: Messling, Guido (ed.), *Die Welt des Lucas Cranach. Ein Künstler im Zeitalter von Dürer, Tizian und Metsys*. Brüssel, pp. 80–93. **Ludolphy**, Ingetraut (2006), *Friedrich der Weise. Kurfürst von Sachsen 1463–1525*. Leipzig. **Marx**, Harald/**Kluth**, Eckhard (eds.) (2004), *Glaube und Macht. Sachsen im Europa der Reformationszeit*. Dresden. **Merkel**, Kerstin (2011), Bruderbilder—Herrscherbilder. Inszenierte Bruderliebe als Garant für politische Qualität der Frühen Neuzeit. In: Tacke, Andreas/Heinz, Stefan (eds.), *Menschenbilder. Beiträge zur Altdeutschen Kunst*. Petersberg, pp. 231–144. **Michel**, Eva/**Hollegger**, Manfred (eds.) (2012), *Kaiser Maximilian I. und die Kunst der Dürerzeit*. München. **Müller**, Matthias (2004), *Das Schloß als Bild des Fürsten. Herrschaftliche Metaphorik in der Residenzarchitektur des Alten Reichs*. Göttingen. **Münch**, Birgit Ulrike (2015), "Viel scharpffe Gemelde" und "lesterliche Figuren." Cranach und seine Zeitgenossen auf dem Schlachtfeld druckgrafischer Fehden. In: Stiftung Schloss Friedenstein Gotha/Museumslandschaft Hessen Kassel (eds.), *Bild und Botschaft. Cranach im Dienst von Hof und Reformation*. Heidelberg, pp. 72–81. **Neugebauer**, Anke (2011), Am Anfang war die Residenz—Forschungen und Perspektiven. In: Lück, Heiner (ed.), *Das ernestinische Wittenberg: Universität und Stadt (1486–1547)* (= Wittenberg-Forschungen. 1). Petersberg, pp. 82–92. **Rogge**, Jörg (2002), *Herrschaftsweitergabe, Konfliktregelung und Familienorganisation im fürstlichen Hochadel. Das Beispiel der Wettiner von der Mitte des 13. bis zum Beginn des 16. Jahrhunderts* (= Monographien zur Geschichte des Mittelalters. 49). Stuttgart. **Schade**, Werner (1974), *Die Malerfamilie Cranach*. Dresden. **Schuchardt**, Christian (1851–71), *Lucas Cranach des Aeltern Leben und Werke*. 3 vols. Leipzig. **Spira**, Benjamin (2015): Lucas Cranach, der Maler Luthers. In: Stiftung Schloss Friedenstein Gotha/Museumslandschaft Hessen Kassel (eds.), *Bild und Botschaft. Cranach im Dienst von Hof und Reformation*. Heidelberg, pp. 51–62. **Stievermann**, Dieter (1994), Lucas Cranach und der kursächsische Hof. In: Grimm, Claus (ed.), *Lucas Cranach. Ein Malerunternehmer aus Franken*. Regensburg, pp. 66–77. **Stiftung Schloss Friedenstein Gotha/Museumslandschaft Hessen Kassel** (ed.) (2015), *Bild und Botschaft. Cranach im Dienst von Hof und Reformation, Ausstellung Stiftung Schloss Friedenstein Gotha und Museumslandschaft Hessen Kassel*. Heidelberg. **Trümper**, Timo (2015), Inszenierungsstrategien der Ernestiner. Die Cranachs als Diener des Hofes. In: Stiftung Schloss Friedenstein Gotha/Museumslandschaft Hessen Kassel (eds.), *Bild und Botschaft. Cranach im Dienst von Hof und Reformation*. Heidelberg, pp. 17–28. **Tullner**, Mathias (1996), *Geschichte des Landes Sachsen-Anhalt*. 2nd ed. Opladen. **Wallmann**, Johannes (2012), *Kirchengeschichte Deutschlands seit der Reformation*. 7th ed. Tübingen. **Westphal**, Sigrid (2007), Nach dem Verlust der Kurwürde. Die Ausbildung konfessioneller Identität anstelle politischer Macht bei den Ernestinern. In: Wrede, Martin/Carl, Horst (eds.), *Zwischen Schande und Ehre. Erinnerungsbrüche und die Kontinuität des Hauses. Legitimationsmuster und Traditionsverständnis des frühneuzeitlichen Adels in Umbruch und Krise* (= Veröffentlichungen des Instituts für Europäische Geschichte Mainz. Abteilung für Universalgeschichte. Beiheft 73). Mainz, pp. 173–192.

The Side of Law   # The Side of Grace

THE LEFT HALF OF THE PAINTING
shows scenes from the Old Testament. They illustrate human life
under divine law and show a judging Christ.

THE RIGHT HALF OF THE PAINTING
shows scenes from the New Testament. They illustrate God's grace.
It cannot be earned, but is bestowed on humankind.

The painting
"Law and Grace"

was painted in 1529 by Lucas Cranach the Elder (1472 – 1553).
By analyzing the picture we can decipher Luther's motives for
juxtaposing Law and Grace. It was important to him that humans
cannot earn God's grace through acts of their own, but that the
sinner experiences God's grace only through the faith in Jesus
Christ.

The person on the left hand is shown as a condemned sinner, on
the right hand he is redeemed. According to Luther, humans are
justified through faith alone.

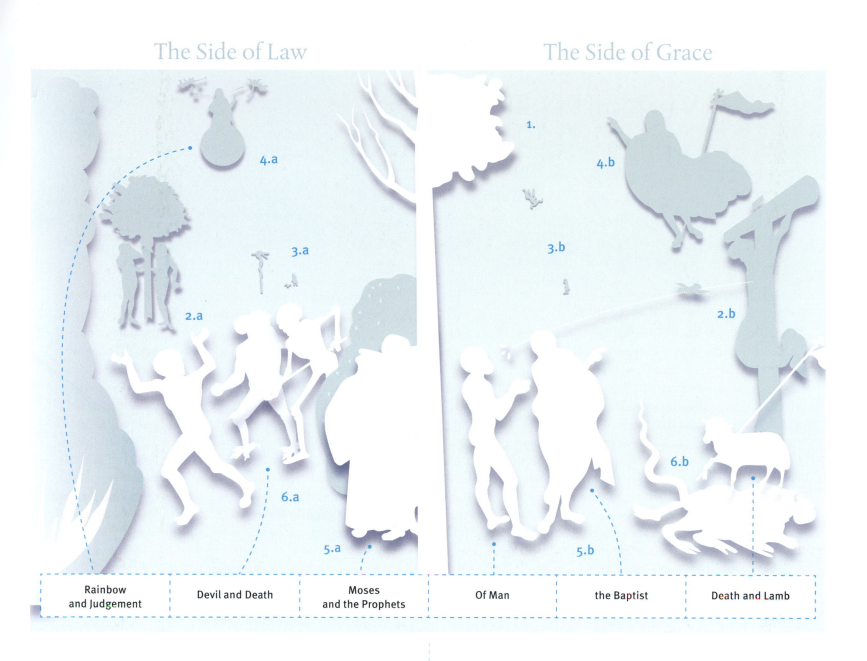

4.a

3.a

2.a

6.a

5.a

Rainbow and Judgement	Devil and Death	Moses and the Prophets

1.

4.b

3.b

2.b

6.b

5.b

Of Man	the Baptist	Death and Lamb

1 The Tree

A tree at the center, one side dried up, the other green, divides the picture into two parts.

2.a The Fall of Man

Adam and Eve in Paradise eat the forbidden fruit from the tree of the knowledge of good and evil. By violating God's prohibition, they become mortal and are expelled from Paradise.

3.a Nehushtan, the Bronze Serpent

As a punishment for sins the Israelites had committed, God sent venomous snakes. But those who looked at Nehushtan, the bronze serpent Moses had erected, survived the bite.

2.b Crucifixion

For the believers, salvation and eternal life come from Christ's sacrificial death, his crucifixion, and resurrection. Through the saving blood flowing from the wound in Christ's side God acts on man, who depends on His grace.

3.b Annunciation to the Shepherds

An angel announces to the shepherds the birth of Jesus which brings about the time of grace.

4.a The Last Judgement

Heralded by two angels playing the trombone, Christ is enthroned on the globe. The sword of justice and the lily of grace identify him as the judge.

5.a Group of Prophets

Encircled by other prophets Moses points at the tablets of the law. Violating this law will result in man's damnation.

6.a Hell

Humans cannot observe the law by themselves. Therefore, Death and the Devil drive the sinner into Hell.

4.b Resurrection

The risen Christ is floating above the empty rock tomb; he has overcome Death.

5.b John the Baptist

He refers the naked person to Christ on the cross. The sinner turns towards Christ in prayer.

6.b The Lamb of God

The Lamb of God, a symbol of Christ, crushes Death and the Devil, whom Christ has overcome.

JOHANNES SCHILLING

Martin Luther and Music

Martin Luther's Love of Music

"Musicam semper amavi"—I have always loved music.[1] This is Martin Luther's credo. Music—forever—a lifelong love. Luther grew up with music, perhaps songs sung by his mother or heard on the street. According to his own testimony, Luther also grew up with a number of sacred hymns. These included Christmas carols such as *Ein Kindelein so Löbelich* ("A Child So Praiseworthy") and *Sei Willkommen, Herre Christ*, ("Be Welcome Lord Christ") as well as the Easter hymn *Christ Is Risen*, which was sung at the feast of the Resurrection during his youth (fig. 1). The Latin and German hymn traditions that Luther adopted and transformed were incorporated into the Protestant church and musical life, and they still exist today. The tradition has remained alive in the church and cultural spheres, through German texts and translations into other languages.

"Sing to the Lord a new song, sing to the Lord, all the earth!" begins the foreword to the *Bapstsches Gesangbuch* (1545), the last hymnal published during Luther's lifetime. "For God has strengthened our heart and given us courage through his dear Son, whom he has given to us for the salvation from sins, death, and the devil. All those who earnestly believe in this cannot resist singing and telling of this with joy and passion so that others can also hear the good news and join in."[2] The text epitomizes the core of Luther's love of music: that the Gospel, the good news of Jesus Christ, is disseminated among all people. This was the objective of Luther's hymns and music, as well as the basis for his statement: "Next to theology, I give music the highest place."[3]

The Role of Music in Luther's Education

We don't know exactly what Luther learned about music theory and practice at his various schools, but more information is available about his university education in Erfurt. *Musica* was one of the *artes liberales* (the seven liberal arts) and a fundamental academic subject that all students were obliged to learn before proceeding to a higher level. The term *ars* combined a variety of subjects that were later separately categorized under arts and sciences. Luther praised music as being both *optima ars*[4] and *optima scientia*.[5]

The seven subjects were subdivided into the categories *trivium* (three ways) and *quadrivium* (four ways). The first group consisted of grammar, rhetoric, and dialectic or logic, in which students learned the correct use of language, how to form it in speech, and how to employ it well in intellectual debate. The *quadrivium* included subjects connected with numbers and proportions: arithmetic, geometry, astronomy, and music. Grammar, the first and foremost of the *artes*, is frequently represented by the rod as an inherently strict subject to master (fig. 2). According to the statutes of Erfurt University from 1412, Music was taught on the basis of Johannes de Muris' music theory.[6] Luther probably also read and studied music from this treatise. Yet around the year 1500, a change was taking place: *musica* was no longer conceived as *ars* in the sense of *scientia* but as *ars musica* in the sense of *musica practica*. Music's previous status as a quadrivial discipline took a back seat as music moved closer to grammar and rhetoric. The humanist Crotus Rubeanus later described Luther as a "*musicus et philosophus eruditus*" in 1520; that is, he was highly educated in music and philosophy.[7] Luther could also play the lute and tabulate, i.e. was versed in the notation of music tabulature.[8] He perhaps had become familiar with the works of contemporary composers of his time, such as Josquin des Prez (fig. 3), Ludwig Senfl, and Heinrich Finck,[9] whom Luther subsequently termed as the fixed stars of music.[10]

Luther heard music performed in churches and at the university within the context of church services, ecclesiastical high feast days, holy days, and festive university events. Celebrations marking the election of the rector, the beginning of the semester, and examination periods also involved music in both instrumental and vocal forms. As a monk, however, Luther was primarily exposed to music in the monastery, where it was ever present as an element of the liturgy. The rules of Luther's order, i.e. *The Rule of Saint Augustine*, define the practice of choral prayer this way: "When you pray to God in psalms and hymns, what is spoken by the mouth should also dwell in the heart. And only sing what is to be sung according to the rules."[11] One of the tasks allotted to the master of novices was instructing the monks in liturgical singing. Luther's monastery apparently did not have an organ.[12]

Fig. 1 "Christ has Risen" from: Martin Luther, Geistliche Lieder aufs Neue gebessert zu Wittenberg, sog. Klug'sches Gesangbuch (Newly Improved Sacred Songs from Wittenberg; so-called Klug Hymnal), Wittenberg 1533

Luther and the Origin of Reformation Hymnals

Luther's opinions on music and its place in life can best be gleaned from his fundamental statements on the subject. These are spread throughout several decades of the Reformer's life, providing an authentic impression of his deep love for music.[13] The earliest relevant text from Luther relating to music is a letter to Georg Spalatin from the end of 1523. The correspondence is also devoted to the birth of the *Evangelisches Gesangbuch* (Protestant hymnal). Luther invites Spalatin to participate in a joint undertaking; although it never came to fruition in the envisioned form, its intentions and plans can be inferred from Luther's letter.

"Grace and peace! I have a plan inspired by the prophets and fathers of the church to create German psalms for the people […] sacred hymns, to ensure that the word of God remains disseminated among the people through the medium of song. We are therefore searching for suitable poets. As you are gifted and have a supreme command of the German language that you have perfected through much practice, I request you to work with us on our plan and attempt to transform a psalm into a hymn according to the example I have included here. My specific intention is to avoid all modern expressions and language customary at court; the people should sing texts that are simply written in everyday expressions in pure and appropriate language. The sense should be completely clear and as close to the psalm texts as possible.

1 WA. TR 5, 557, 18 (no. 6248); essential to this topic: Schilling, *Musik*. 2 WA 35, 477, 6 – 9. 3 "Proximum locum do Musicae post Theologiam," in: WA 30/II, 696, 12; see WA. TR 1, 490 f.; WA. TR 3, 636, 3 – 7; WA. TR 6, 348, 17 – 26. 4 WA. TR 2, 434, 8 – 11. 5 WA. TR 2, 518, 6 – 14. 6 Kleineidam, *Universitas*. 7 WA. B 2, 91, 142. 8 WA. TR 5, 657, 10 – 12. 9 Orth, *Geschichte*, p. 127. 10 WA. TR 4, 215, 21 – 216, 13; WA. TR 2, 11, 24 – 12, 2. 11 *Rule of St. Augustine* ch. 2, sect. 3 f., See Zumkeller, *Augustiner-Eremiten*, col. 1033 – 1039, here col. 1034. 12 Körndle, *Orgelspiel*, pp. 29 f. 13 In addition to the texts quoted below, it is particularly in the prefaces to the hymnals that Luther expounds his concepts of music, see WA 35, 474 – 484.

Fig. 2 Philosophy and the Seven Liberal Arts, hand-colored woodcut, from:
Gregor Reisch, Margarita philosopica. Straßburg 1504

For this reason, it is important to adopt a free style, retaining the sense of the text while not literally adhering to the exact wording, and substituting other more suitable expressions where necessary. I myself do not possess the ability to formulate these texts according to my concept and therefore wish to establish whether you are a Heman, Asaph, or Idithun [singers of the Old Testament]. I am also sending my request to Johann Dolzig, who is equally eloquent and articulate, but only if you both have time for this undertaking; you probably do not have very much free time.

Nevertheless, I request you to take my seven Penitential Psalms and their interpretations from which you can extract the sense of each psalm. Or if you would like to take on a particular psalm, you could choose the first Penitential Psalm 'O Lord, do not rebuke me in your anger' (Psalm 6) or the seventh, 'Hear my prayer, O Lord' (Psalm 143). I have allocated the second Penitential Psalm, 'Blessed is he whose transgression is forgiven' (Psalm 32) to Johann Dolzig, as I have already translated 'Out of the depths' (Psalm 130), and 'Have mercy upon me, O God' (Psalm 51) has already been allocated. Should these perhaps be too difficult, you could choose both 'I will bless the Lord at all times' and 'Rejoice in the Lord, O ye righteous,' Psalms 34 and 33, or Psalm 104, 'Bless the Lord O my soul.' Please write back in any case so that we know which texts to expect from you. Farewell in God."[14]

Luther's relationship with and love of music found greatest expression in his hymns. This is demonstrated in the letter addressed to Spalatin, which provided an initial impetus for Luther's blossoming gift for hymnal poetry and its subsequent development. Luther had compiled a number of principles for this project: 1. The Gospel should become familiar to all people through song. 2. The Psalms provide a good example and model for Protestant hymns. 3. The words of the text should be simply expressed in everyday language and be appropriate and comprehensible in meaning. 4. Freedom of expression is permitted "as long as the sense is retained." Luther provides no information about the melodies, but we can surely add the following instruction: The melodies should correspond to the texts, be accessible and singable, and permit the congregation to join in enthusiastically and "sing with heart and soul."

This was the initial impulse for the first reformatory hymn settings and collected volumes of hymns. Reformation hymn books became the virtual hallmark of the newly flourishing Protestant churches, as *nota ecclesiae*. The very first hymn sheets were single-printed pages with one or two hymns, and from there the path led to the first Lutheran hymnal (German: "*Achtliederbuch*," literally eight-hymn book). It was issued around the turn of the year 1523/24 and contained four hymns by Luther, including *Dear Christians One and All Rejoice*. It also contained three hymns by Paul Speratus, including *The Grace of God Has Come to Man*, plus an anonymous text. The path then continued to the first Erfurt hymn books and, subse-

IOSQVINVS PRATENSIS.

Fig. 3 Josquin Desprez, Woodcut after a painting in St. Gudule, from: Pieter van Opmeer, Opus chronographicum orbis universi a mundi exordio usque ad annum M.DC.XI, Antwerpen 1611

quently, to the Wittenberg choral hymn book. This first hymnal for choir with sacred songs, the *Geystliche gesangk Buchleyn* ("A Sacred Song Booklet"), was Johann Walter's creation.[15] The volume's first edition contained 38 hymns in German and five Latin chants.[16] Further landmarks include the publication of the *Wittenberger Gemeindegesangbuch* ("The Wittenberg Congregation Hymnal") in 1529, the year of the *Catechisms*, which has survived only in a 1533 edition (fig. 4), and the last hymnal published during Luther's lifetime, the 1545 *Bapstsche Gesangbuch*, ("Bapst's Hymnal") named after Leipzig printer Valentin Bapst.[17]

Martin Luther and Polyphonic Song

Luther's second fundamental text on the subject of music is a letter written seven years after the first. It was sent not from Wittenberg but from the Veste Coburg, where Luther spent the summer of 1530 as an outcast. Impatient and distrustful, awaiting judgment on the confession by the Diet of Augsburg, Luther was nevertheless industrious. The letter was addressed to composer Ludwig Senfl, one of the most significant master musicians of his time. Senfl was not a theologian or an inhabitant of electoral Saxony. Since 1523, he had

14 Schilling, *Martin Luther*, p. 66 f., no. 34; original Latin text: *WA*.B 3, 220 f. (no. 698). **15** Johann Walter, the "original cantor of the Reformation," was born in Kahla in 1496 and was employed as a bass singer in the court ensemble of Frederick the Wise from 1520 or 1521 onward. He was appointed cantor of St. Mary's Church in Torgau in 1527, municipal cantor in Torgau in 1529 and, in

1548, director of the court ensemble in Dresden. He returned to Torgau during the final years of his life, where he died in 1579. Standard reference works: Blankenburg, *Johann Walter*; Gurlitt, *Johann Walter*; Brusniak, *Johann-Walter-Studien*. **16** Summary in: Blankenburg, *Johann Walter*, pp. 137–142. **17** For further historical details, see Beutel, *Lied*.

Fig. 4
Martin Luther, Geistliche Lieder aufs Neue gebessert zu Wittenberg, Klug'sches Gesangbuch (Newly improved sacred songs from Wittenberg, so-called Klug hymnal), Wittenberg 1533. Next to the frontispiece an inscription by the Lutheran theologian Ernst Salomon Cyprian, librarian at the princely library at Friedenstein Palace in Gotha: "Libellus rarissimus" – an extremely rare book

been in the services of the Bavarian Dukes, who remained true to the old faith. Luther admired and revered Senfl,[18] who was also highly respected by other contemporaries (fig. 5).

"Grace and peace in Christ! Although my name is so intensely abhorred that I must fear that you, dear Ludwig, may not receive and be able to read the letter I am sending you, this fear has been assuaged by the love of music wherein I see your precious talent and endowment given by God. This love has also raised my hopes that my letter will not bring any harm to you, as who would wish to reprimand even a Turk if he loves art and heaps praise on artists? I however would go as far as to praise your Dukes of Bavaria, even though they are not inclined to share my opinions, and place them above others because they nurture and value music so highly. There is indeed no doubt that many seeds of positive qualities are present in the disposition of those who are captivated by music, whereas those who are not captivated are in my opinion no better than stumps and stones. For we know that music is also abhorrent and intolerable to the demons. And I am free in my judgment and do not hesitate to assert that there is no art after theology that could be equal to music, as it alone apart from theology is able to provide what theology can provide on its own: a calm and joyful heart. We have clear evidence that the devil, the son of miserable sorrows and restless activity, flees from both the voice of music and the word of theology. This explains why the prophets employed no other art [ars] as frequently as music; they formulated their theology not in geometry, arithmetic, nor astronomy but in music, enabling them to bring theology and music into closest juxtaposition when proclaiming the truth in psalms and hymns.

But why am I praising music and attempting to depict or rather disfigure such thoughts on such a small sheet of paper? Yet my heart floweth over and my love of that which has so often refreshed me and freed me from deepest troubles simply gushes out of me. Now I return to my request to you: if you have a copy of the hymn 'In pace in id ipsum,' please have a copy made and send it to me. This melody [tenor] has delighted me from my earliest youth, and now even more that I understand these words. I have never seen this antiphon in a version composed for several voices but do not wish to burden you with the effort of composing the piece and hope that you already have a multi-voice setting among your previous compositions.

I very much hope that the end of my life is imminent; the world hates and abhors me, and I, in turn, am weary of the world and am sick of it. For this reason, may the good shepherd and guardian (1 Peter 2:25) take away my soul (1 Kings 19:4). This is why I have begun to sing the antiphon and wish to hear it composed (in multiphonic form). In case you do not have it or know of it, I am sending it to you with the notation of the melody so you can perhaps compose it after my death if you wish. Let the Lord Jesus be with you in eternity, Amen. Please forgive my presumptuousness and loquacity. With respectful greetings to the entire chorus of your music. From Coburg, October 4, 1530. Martin Luther."[19]

While confined in the Veste Coburg, Luther compiled interpretations of numerous psalms, and the intention and execution of psalter studies represented a central focus of his work during this period.[20] Luther was particularly taken with Psalm 118:17: "I shall not die, but live and declare the works of the Lord—*Non moriar sed vivam et narrabo opera domini*".[21] He made his own setting of the verse in his only surviving multiphonic composition, a brief motet providing evidence of his compositional talent (fig. 6).[22]

According to reports by Luther's physician, Matthäus Ratzeberger, and the composer Sixtus Dietrich, Luther regularly sang multiphonic vocal music at home in Wittenberg with his sons and students. This is also a sign of Luther's extraordinarily high regard for music, particularly vocal works including choral settings. He considered music one of the best methods of communicating the Gospel; music was the *viva vox evangelii* (the living voice of the Gospel).[23] At the consecration of the Castle Church in Torgau on October 5, 1544, Luther called prayer and songs of praise the response to the word communicated by God to the people.[24]

The Quintessence of Luther's View on Music

Luther's 1538 foreword for a collected edition issued by music publisher Georg Rhau displays the essence of his thoughts on music.[25] Johann Walter, whose musical career was closely entwined with Luther's hymn compositions and attempts at the liturgical renewal of the church service since the 1520s, later compiled a free translation of this text in his didactic poem *Lob und Preis der himmlischen Kunst Musica* ("Praise and Glory of the Noble Art of Music") (fig. 7).[26] The slim volume was also published by Georg Rhau in Wittenberg in 1538, probably within the context of his *Symphoniae iucundae*, collected editions of choral music. Luther provided a "foreword for all good hymn books" for Walter's didactic poem in rhyming couplets. The personified "Lady Musica" speaks in the foreword, praising music as the greatest joy on earth that is not only pure of sin but pleases God better than all other pleasures of the world. Music makes the heart stand still, willing to receive divine truth. The foreword closes with the words "The best time of the year is mine," which has taken on independent life as a hymn.[27]

In the Latin foreword to the *Symphoniae iucundae* ("sweet symphonies"), Luther describes music as a gift for all creation. Nothing is completely devoid of sound or tonal order, and this divine wonder

Fig. 5 Hans Schwarz, Medal showing the portrait of the composer Ludwig Senfl, 1519

18 *WA.TR* 5, 557, 11 f. **19** Text according to Schilling, *Martin Luther*, pp. 133–135, no. 83; original Latin text: *WA.B* 5, 635–640 (no. 1727). Senfl's response has not survived. Related in content is a record dating from the year 1530 Peri tes musikes. In: *WA* 30/II, 695 f. **20** See Luther's letter to Melanchthon dated [April 24] 1530. In: Scheible, *Melanchthons Briefwechsel*, pp. 124–128 (no. 891); *WA.B* 5, 285–288 (no. 1552). Translation in: Schilling, *Martin Luther*, pp. 114 f. (no. 68). **21** Psalm 118:17. **22** Edition: Rüppel/Zimmer, *Martin-Luther-Chorheft*, p. 23. **23** See also below and note 27. **24** Text of the consecration sermon: *WA* 49

(XL–LXV [recte: XLV] 588–614; also in: Martin Luther, Deutsch-deutsche Studienausgabe. Vol. 2, Leipzig 2015, pp. 851–891. In translation: Schilling/Lohrengel, *Predigt*. **25** See *WA* 50, 364–374; Text and translation into the German language: Schilling, *Exemplare*. A juxtaposition of Luther's text and Walter's adaptation also in: Blankenburg, *Johann Walter*, Appendix VIII, pp. 439–445. **26** Johann Walter: Sämtliche Werke VI, Kassel et al. 1970; Gurlitt, *Facsimile*. **27** Thus in *Evangelisches Gesangbuch* (Protestant Hymnal), no. 319.

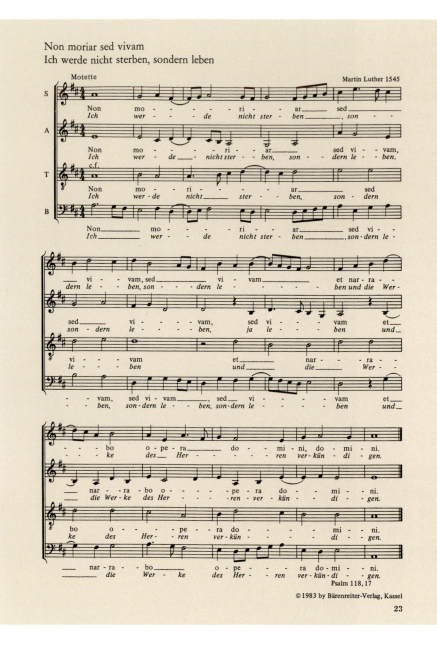

Fig. 6
Martin Luther, Motet Non moriar, sed vivam
(I shall not die but live), from: Johann Rüppel/
Ulrich Zimmer (eds.), Martin-Luther-Chorheft
1983, Kassel 1983, p. 23

is especially manifested in living creatures. In comparison to the human voice, however, this has little value, as the richness and variety of the human voice is second to none. The essential issue is that music, according to the word of God, is the mistress and controller of human emotion ("domina et gubernatrix affectuum humanorum").[28] It is capable of brightening up the sorrowful, startling the joyful, giving hope to the despairing, belittling the arrogant, and comforting lovers. No other medium can exert more influence on emotions.[29] For this reason, a special affinity between the word of God and music has always been recognized through the ages. Humans alone above all creatures are given the word linked to the voice

so that they are able to praise God through words and music. Luther sees the miracle of this art best displayed in multiphonic music.

That is why Luther is keen to introduce music as a school subject. The development was, of course, also associated with the concept of music within the *artes* canon. But it additionally corresponded to the newly recognized significance of these *ars* and *disciplina*. Luther was convinced that students who had mastered music were "well disposed to all skills."[30] To this end, he believed it was crucial to teach music in schools. Luther highly prized the educational value of music: "Youth should always become acquainted with this art as it produces fine and skilled individuals."[31] Music is essential not

28 *WA* 50, 371, 2. **29** Luther particularly underlines the consolatory character of music in a letter to Matthias Weller *WA.*B 7, 104–106 (no. 2139). **30** *WA.*TR 1, 490, 31 f. (no. 968). **31** Ibid., 42 f. (no. 968). **32** Michael Praetorius: Syntagma musicum 1, Wittenberg 1614/15 (reprint: Kassel et al 1959), p. 451; illus-

trations in: Blankenburg, *Johann Walter*, p. 423. **33** See Rautenstrauch, *Luther*. **34** See Martin Luther: An die Ratherren aller Städte deutsches Lands, dass sie christliche Schulen aufrichten und halten sollen. In: *WA* 15, 9, 27–53.

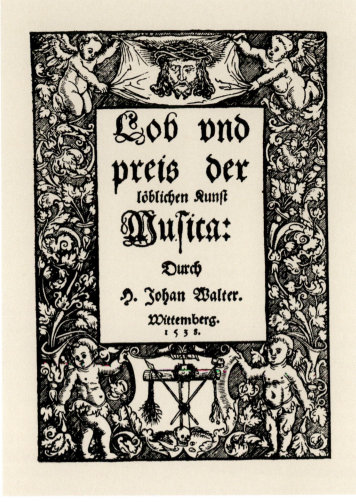

Fig. 7 Johann Walter, Lob und Preis der löblichen Kunst Musica
(Praise and Glory of the Noble Art of Music), Wittenberg 1538

merely for its social benefits, however. It is also vital for consolation and edification, as well as for providing access to a different, quasi-redeemed world. Individuals devoted to music outgrow the world and their own personal limitations and rediscover themselves on a higher plane. This is why theology and music are so closely related: just as mankind has received the gift of life from Jesus Christ, it has received back its existence from music in an external manner: *ab extra. Nos extra nos*. This is valid not only for music but also for music-making. Moreover, "being beside oneself" is therefore a reason for joy and for jettisoning all hardships that burden humanity and prevent people from achieving happiness.

Johann Walter, also a vital figure in both the Reformation and music history, reports that "Lutherus, the holy man of God […] took great pleasure in music as choral or figural hymns"—that is, monodic or multiphonic vocal music—"and I passed many pleasant hours singing with him and frequently observed that the good man became so merry and cheerful from singing that he could never become tired of music or be satiated by it and was able to speak about music with such great joy."[32]

Cultural Consequences of the Protestant Music Culture

A rich Protestant musical culture developed out of its reformatory origins in Wittenberg and Torgau, beginning in schools in Saxony and flourishing during the century of Reformation particularly in Central Germany.[33] Its influence was observed throughout Protestant Germany and beyond. North German organ culture could not have been conceived without this impulse from the Reformation. Dietrich Buxtehude established his *Abendmusiken* (evening concerts) in St. Mary's Church in Lübeck, laying the foundation stone for a bourgeois musical culture in the proud Hanseatic city. The effects of this Protestant music were disseminated beyond the confines of the church into the culture of society and continue to make an impact today. Ultimately, the development of Germany as a musical nation was in part shaped by the reformatory impulse, which exerts its influence still today. The Torgau Kantorei (church choir) became the prototype and model for all Protestant choral ensembles, transforming into reality Luther's objective of making music a constitutive element in schools.[34] Music should sound in praise of God and for the pleasure of humanity, whom God has graciously granted with an ability to sing—alone or together, for themselves or for others, and for the whole world.

BIBLIOGRAPHY

Beutel, Albrecht Beutel (2001), Lied. V. Kirchenlied. In: Ueding, Gert (ed.), *Historisches Wörterbuch der Rhetorik*. Vol. 5. Tübingen, pp. 270–275. **Blankenburg**, Walter (1991), *Johann Walter: Leben und Werk*. Tutzing. **Brusniak**, Friedhelm (ed.) (1998), *Johann-Walter-Studien. Tagungsbericht Torgau 1996*. Tutzing. **Gurlitt**, Wilibald (1933), Johann Walter und die Musik der Reformationszeit. In: *Luther-Jahrbuch*, vol. 15, pp. 1–112. **Gurlitt**, Wilibald (ed.) (1938), *Facsimile edition: Johannes Walter: Lob und Preis der löblichen Kunst Musica 1538*. Kassel. **Kleineidam**, Erich (1964/69), *Universitas Studii Erffordensis. Vols. 1 and 2* (= Erfurter theologische Studien. 14, 22). Leipizig. **Körndle**, Franz (2003), Orgelspiel in Erfurter Kirchen des späten Mittelalters. In: *Mitteilungen des Vereins für die Geschichte und Altertumskunde von Erfurt*, vol. 64, N. F. 11, p. 29–39. **Orth**, Siegfried (1967), Zur Geschichte der Musikpflege an der ehemaligen Universität Erfurt. In: *Beiträge zur Geschichte der Universität Erfurt (1392–1816)*, vol. 13, p. 91–147. **Rautenstrauch**, Johannes (1907), *Luther und die Pflege der kirchlichen Musik in Sachsen (14.–19. Jahrhundert). Ein Beitrag zur Geschichte der katholischen Brüderschaften, der vor- und nachreformatorischen Kurrenden, Schulchöre und Kantoreien Sachsens*. Leipzig. Reprint: Hildesheim 1970. **Rüppel**, Johann/**Zimmer**, Ulrich (eds.) (1983), *Martin-Luther-Chorheft 1983*. Kassel/Basel. **Scheible**, Heinz (ed.) (2007), *Melanchthons Briefwechsel*. Texts vol. 4, 1. Stuttgart/Bad Cannstatt. **Schilling**, Johannes (1983), *Martin Luther, Ausgewählte Schriften*. Vol. 6: *Briefe*. 2nd ed. Frankfurt am Main. **Schilling**, Johannes (2008), Die erhaltenen Exemplare von Georg Rhaus Symphoniae iucundae (1538) und Martin Luthers Vorrede. In: Weiss, Ulman (ed.), *Buchwesen in Spätmittelalter und Früher Neuzeit. Festschrift für Helmut Claus zum 75. Geburtstag*. Epfendorf, pp. 251–265. **Schilling**, Johannes (2010), Musik. In: Beutel, Albrecht (ed.), *Luther Handbuch*, 2nd ed. Tübingen, p. 236–244. **Schilling**, Johannes/**Lohrengel**, Jan (ed.) (2015), Martin Luther, Predigt zur Einweihung der Schlosskirche in Torgau. In: Claussen, Johann Hinrich/Rössler, Martin (eds.), *Große Predigten. 2000 Jahre Gottes Wort und christlicher Protest*. Darmstadt 2015, pp. 63–86. **Walter**, Johann (1970), *Sämtliche Werke VI*. Kassel et al. **Zumkeller**, Adolar (1994), Augustiner-Eremiten. In: Finscher, Ludwig (ed.), *Die Musik in Geschichte und Gegenwart*. Vol. 1: Sachteil. Kassel et al.

ANDREW SPICER

Martin Luther and the Material Culture of Worship

English merchants and travelers to the German states in the late seventeenth and eighteenth centuries were surprised by the interiors of the Lutheran churches they visited. They commented on the ornaments and ceremonies that had survived from the Roman Catholic past, particularly pointing out the altar paintings or retables, organs, statues, and vestments that remained in the churches. For these visitors, the visual contrast between Lutheran places of worship and the more austere continental Reformed churches as well as the whitewashed English parish churches, purged of their religious imagery, could not have been more marked. Some of these visitors highlighted the closer resemblance between these Lutheran places of worship and Catholic churches. It was a parallel that was treated with a degree of suspicion by some travelers, one of whom remarked after visiting Wittenberg: "[T]he people here, as in most places, where the Lutheran religion prevails, have a strong tincture of Romish superstition."[1] These church interiors echoed, to a degree, the pre-Reformation liturgy and religious practices, which had actually been lost in many Catholic churches as they were modified in accordance with the reforms that emanated from the Council of Trent. The continuity of some of these church interiors with their medieval predecessors has been described as the "preserving power" of Lutheranism.[2] Nonetheless, alongside the surviving imagery and liturgical items, these churches were also filled with new Lutheran ecclesiastical furnishings, the subtleties of which may have been lost on English travelers. To what extent could they distinguish between a Catholic and a Lutheran altarpiece, for example, or did they just see an altarpiece that represented a visual continuity with the pre-Reformation past?

Furthermore, over the course of the Reformation Lutherans had taken possession of the existing parish churches, which had originally been designed for the celebration of the Mass, and reorganized them to meet their own liturgical needs. It was not until the mid-sixteenth century that the first purpose-built churches were erected for Lutheran worship. The earliest of these was the chapel at Hartenfels Castle in Torgau; in 1544, Luther preached at the building's inauguration. This was the first of a series of princely chapels to be constructed, a number of which were influenced by Torgau's design. However, with one or two exceptions, it was not until the early seventeenth century that the first major churches were built to accommodate sizeable local com-

munities rather than smaller princely households. While some of these churches experimented with novel architectural arrangements, others adopted more conservative forms. The appearance and design of these new churches as well as those inherited by the confession were shaped as much by the liturgical needs of Lutheran worship as by the princes and city councils that controlled and influenced the implementation of the religious changes.

Martin Luther did not provide a clear confessional statement about what he regarded as the appropriate layout and appearance of a place of worship. In the course of his writings, though, he did make occasional references to aspects of the ceremonies and setting for services, particularly the administration of the sacraments. He was also responsible for composing the liturgies that were used in the Wittenberg churches. This essay will therefore focus on both the Reformer's concerns and forbearance on issues relating to places of worship as well as the evolution of the material culture of Lutheran worship into the seventeenth century.

For Martin Luther, the appearance and arrangement of church interiors were a matter of conscience and and not to be determined by imposed regulations that were legalistically enforced.[3] In 1516, he had criticized the Catholic Church's requirement "to build this and that church or that we ornament them in such and such a way, or that singing be of a certain kind or the organ or the altar decorations, the chalices, the statues and all of the other paraphernalia which are contained in our temples. Finally it is not necessary that the priests and other religious wear the tonsure or go about in distinctive garb […] For all of these things are shadows and signs of the real thing and thus are childish."[4]

These rites and practices had not been prescribed by scripture but had been instituted by the Church over subsequent centuries. The celebration of the Mass was very different from the Last Supper, which had taken place "without any display of vestments, gestures, chants, or other ceremonies."[5] For Luther, "all things that Christ did not institute are optional, voluntary, and unnecessary, and therefore also harmless"; they were regarded as *adiaphora*, matters of indifference.[6] He commented in 1528: "[I]mages, bells, Eucharistic vestments, church ornaments, altar lights, and the like I regard as things indifferent. Anyone who wishes may omit them."[7] Christians had the freedom to choose whether to retain these aspects of worship.

Luther argued: "... let the old practice continue. Let the Mass be celebrated with consecrated vessels, with chants and all the usual ceremonies in Latin, recognizing the fact that these are merely external matters which do not endanger the consciences of men. But besides that, through the sermon keep the consciences free, so the common man may learn that these things are done not because they have to be done in that way or because it would be heresy to do them differently, as the nonsensical laws of the Pope insist. For one must attack rigorously and roughly those tyrants who would ensnare and coerce by means of laws, in order that Christian freedom may remain intact."[8]

Furthermore, Luther regarded the focus of some individuals on these elements of worship as a distraction that did not bring them to a knowledge of Christ: "[T]his emphasis on externals is an enticement of the devil, which he uses to mislead his people, so that they leave the Pope and yet do not come to Christ. They are neither papist nor Christian but continue to hang on to external things as much as the papists do."[9] In his *Against the Heavenly Prophets in the Matter of Images and Sacraments* (1525), he attacked "these honor-seeking prophets who do nothing but break images, destroy churches, manhandle the sacrament [...] they have not set aright the conscience which is nonetheless most important and most necessary in the Christian teaching."[10]

Luther considered religious imagery in similar terms to other external matters of worship, but following the iconoclasm that took place at Wittenberg during his absence at Wartburg, he was forced to explain his position following accusations from Andreas Karlstadt that he was a defender of images. In March 1522, Luther preached in his third Lenten sermon that images were "unnecessary, and we are free to have them or not, although it would be much better if we did not have them at all. I am not partial to them."[11] This statement has been regarded as a rhetorical ploy, for in the following sermon, Luther commented "that images are neither here nor there, neither evil nor good; we may have them or not, as we please."[12] In *Against the Heavenly Prophets*, Luther argued that he was not a defender of images—"the matter of images is a minor, external thing"—but attacked the greater evil of iconoclasm:[13] "[...] no one is obligated to break violently images even of God, but everything is free, and one does not sin if he does not break them with violence. One is obligated to destroy them [images] with the Word of God, that is not with the law in a Karlstadtian manner, but with the Gospel. This means to instruct and enlighten the conscience that it is idolatry to worship them, or trust in them, since one is to trust alone in Christ. Beyond this let the external matters take their course. God grant that they may be destroyed, become dilapidated, or that they remain. It is all the same and makes no difference, just as the poison has been removed from the snake."[14]

Luther reiterated his opposition to iconoclasm in 1530 but also expressed his view that religious imagery could play a devotional role: "Images or pictures taken from scripture and from good histories [...] I consider very useful yet indifferent and optional."[15] While he condemned the images at shrines that received the adoration of pilgrims: "Images for memorial and witness, such as crucifixes and images of saints, are to be tolerated."[16] Luther also posed the question as to why it was a sin to have an image of the crucified Christ before his eyes, when it was acceptable to have a mental image in his heart when he heard the Passion preached.[17] Besides this contemplative purpose, Luther had long accepted the didactic value of images and stated that they should be tolerated "for the sake of the sucklings."[18] He even proposed that the pictures from his German Bible should be painted on walls "for the sake of remembrance and better understanding."[19] So while Luther did not regard images as necessary, he increasingly recognized that they could serve as an aid to devotion or assist the young and uneducated in their faith.[20]

In spite of Luther's reluctance to prescribe the appropriate setting for worship, he did acknowledge in 1520 that "we would not disallow the building of suitable churches and their adornment; we cannot do without them. And public worship ought rightly to be conducted in the finest way. But there should be a limit to this, and we should take care that the appurtenances of worship be pure, rather than costly."[21] This was an issue that Luther returned to in 1544, when he preached at the inauguration of the castle chapel in Torgau. The German Reformer rejected the notion that the building was "a special church" or "better than other houses where the Word of God is preached. If the occasion should arise that the people did not want to or could not assemble, one could just as well preach outside by the fountain [in the courtyard of the castle at Torgau] or somewhere else."[22] While dismissing the medieval rite of consecration and sanctity of a particular site, Luther acknowledged that the community nonetheless needed somewhere for "the holy sacrament to be administered" and "a place where we can come together, pray and give thanks to God."[23] This emphasis on preaching and the sacraments reflected the *Confession of Augsburg* (1530), which had stated that the Church is "the assembly of all believers among whom the Gospel is preached in its purity and the holy sacraments are administered according to the Gospel."[24]

Luther was initially hesitant about introducing liturgical changes at Wittenberg because of "the weak in faith, who cannot suddenly exchange an old and accustomed order of worship for a new and unusual one."[25] His reforms reflected his conviction that the "preaching and teaching of God's Word is the most important part of divine service" but also his indifference to other aspects of religious practice.[26] When it came to the setting for Communion, Luther questioned in his *Concerning the Order of Public Worship* (1523) "the external additions of vestments, vessels, candles and palls, of organs and all the music, and of images," but concluded that "they can be tolerated

I am grateful to Dr. Margit Thøfner for her insightful comments on an earlier version of this essay. **1** Spicer, *Churches*, pp. 3 f.; Hanway, *Account*, vol. 2, p. 215. **2** See Fritz, *Kraft*. **3** Michalski, *Reformation*, pp. 13, 40 f. **4** LW 25, 487. **5** LW 36, 52. **6** LW 36, 168. **7** LW 37, 371. **8** LW 36, 254. **9** LW 36, 262. **10** LW 40, 81. **11** WA 10/III, 26, 5 f. **12** LW 51, 81, 86; Michalski, *Reformation*, pp. 14 f. **13** LW 40, 90 f. **14** LW 40, 91. See also LW 36, 259 f. **15** LW 37, 371. **16** LW 40, 91 f. **17** LW 40, 99–100. **18** WA 1, 271, 9 f. **19** LW 40, 99; 51, 41. **20** Michalski, *Reformation*, pp. 28 f.; Dillenberger, *Images*, pp. 92 f. See also Heal, *Christ*, pp. 43–59. **21** LW 45, 285 f. **22** WA 49, 592, 32–35. **23** LW 51, 333 f., 337. **24** Noll, *Confessions*, p. 89. **25** LW 53, 19. **26** LW 53, 68. See Karant-Nunn, *Reformation*, pp. 114–119.

Fig. 1 Simon Schröter, Pulpit on the gallery of the Torgau Palace Church
        decorated with scenes from the New Testament, 1544

Fig. 2 Wolfenbüttel, Main Church dedicated to the Blessed Virgin Mary, 1608–23.
    Choir with high altar, pulpit and princes' gallery

until they can be completely removed."[27] Regarding vestments, "we think about these as we do about the other forms. We permit them to be used in freedom, as long as the people refrain from ostentation and pomp."[28] Three years later in his *German Mass*, he commented: "[On Sundays] we retain the vestments, altar, and candles until they are used up or we are pleased to make a change. But we do not oppose anyone who would do otherwise. In the true Mass, however, of real Christians, the altar should not remain where it is, and the priest should always face the people as Christ doubtless did in the Last Supper. But let that await its own time."[29]

This implied that ultimately there would not be an altarpiece or retable, so that the priest could face the congregation from behind the altar. Although Luther's liturgical changes did not significantly alter the setting for the Eucharist, there was an expectation that some tolerated aspects of the service would change over time, although in practice this did not happen. Furthermore, Luther did not want to impose this service on his followers. As the opening statement to the preface of the German Mass made clear, those who adopted this

liturgy should not "make it a rigid law to bind or entangle anyone's conscience, but use it in Christian liberty."[30]

The Reformer's unwillingness to specify the requirements for ceremonies and services, and his categorization of them as *adiaphora*, led to different interpretations of the setting of Lutheran worship. While there was some continuity with the Catholic past, new religious images and liturgical furnishings embellished church interiors during the course of the sixteenth and seventeenth centuries. These new furnishings heightened the importance of the ritual spaces within the church, where the sermon was preached and the sacraments administered.

Although there had been preaching in German churches before the Reformation, principally in urban areas, according to Luther it had been "perverted by spiritual tyrants," resulting in the Word of

27 *WA* 12, 214, 34 f. **28** *LW* 53, 22, 31. **29** *LW* 53, 69. **30** *LW* 53, 61.

Fig. 3 Freudenstadt, Protestant Town Church, c. 1608.
Altar, baptismal font and pulpit at the intersection
of the L-shaped town church. Photo before 1945

Fig. 4 Schmalkalden, Wilhelmsburg Palace,
Palace Chapel

God being silenced or subverted.[31] The Reformer believed Christian congregations should "never gather together without the preaching of God's Word and prayer, no matter how briefly." This was so important, that "when God's Word is not preached, one had better neither sing nor read, or even come together."[32] Initially, existing medieval pulpits were used by the Lutherans, although they were sometimes relocated within the nave to a place where they were most effective for preaching to the congregation. New pulpits were also commissioned, one of the earliest being for the Marienkirche (St. Mary's Church) in Lübeck, which was erected in 1533 with an iconographic scheme of five panels with accompanying texts: Moses with the Ten Commandments; John the Baptist Preaching with the Lamb of God; Christ as the Good Shepherd; Christ Instructing His Apostles to Spread His Teachings throughout the World; Christ Warning against False Prophets. These scenes were either devised or approved by Johannes Bugenhagen, who had overseen the city's Lutheran Reformation, and linked the Law of the Old Testament with the Gospel message of Christ.[33]

Just over a decade later, the new gallery pulpit was erected in the castle chapel at Torgau, placed halfway along the south wall of the building (fig. 1). It had elaborately carved polychrome reliefs of scenes from the New Testament, which also connected the Law and

the Gospel: Christ Jesus in the Temple; Christ and the Woman Taken in Adultery; and Christ Driving the Money Changers from the Temple.[34] The importance of preaching can be seen in the number of pulpits that were commissioned, often by wealthy townsmen, for Lutheran churches during the later sixteenth century. There were over two hundred pulpits constructed just in the period between 1595 and 1615. These new pulpits were made from wood or stone, and included carved panels depicting Christocentric themes, the four evangelists, or biblical scenes evoking the preaching of the Word. The pulpit installed in the new church at Wolfenbüttel had a particularly elaborate iconography (fig. 2). The structure was supported by a figural column of Moses with the tablets of the Law; statuettes of prophets Moses and Saint John the Baptist, representing the Old and New Law, appear over the door, while the staircase and body of the pulpit were adorned with sculptures of the twelve disciples. These figures flanked scenes from the life of Christ, with reliefs of the Resurrection and Ascension above the door, and the Last Judgment, the Heavenly Jerusalem, and Ezekiel's vision of the Resurrection around the pulpit. At Ratzeburg, the significance of the pulpit is further emphasized by a full-size portrait of the city's first Lutheran minister on the back wall, so that even outside services there was a constant reminder of the Word being preached from this location.[35]

Fig. 5 Freudenstadt, Protestant Town Church, c. 1608.
  View from the pulpit into both wings of the church. Photo before 1945

It was important for congregations to be able to see not only the pulpit but also the altar during the course of the service. For this reason, some parishes moved the pulpit nearer to the chancel so that the congregation was facing in the same direction for both the sermon and the Eucharist. Different approaches to the placement of the pulpit can be seen in three urban churches built in the early seventeenth century. At Bückeburg, the elevated pulpit is sited halfway along the nave, whereas at Wolfenbüttel, it was installed at the chancel entrance. The innovative design of the Freudenstadt church brought the pulpit and altar together at the intersection of the arms of the L-shaped building (fig. 3).[36] An alternative arrangement saw the pulpit being placed above the altar to form a single vertical axis at the east end of the church. In the princely chapel erected at Schmalkalden between 1585 and 1590, the gallery pulpit was situated behind and overlooking the altar (fig. 4).[37] A similar arrangement—with a *Kanzelaltar* or pulpit-altar—was proposed by Joseph Furttenbach the Younger in his treatise *KirchenGebäw* (1649), which was intended to provide the best conditions and place for the minister to preach to his congregation. This was also considered to be an optimal location for the organ, which surmounted the pulpit.[38] Although a few churches adopted this *Prinzipalstück* arrangement, it remained relatively rare before the eighteenth and nineteenth centuries.[39]

In addition to the pulpit, the provision of seating was also important for establishing order within the church during the sermon; Luther himself had stated that sermons should not be longer than half an hour and the entire service completed within an hour, "for one must not overload souls or weary them."[40] Seating was intended to encourage a more attentive congregation by restricting movement around the church interior, although complaints still appear in visitation returns about people wandering about the building during the sermon.[41] In existing churches, the erection of galleries increased the capacity of the building to accommodate the entire parish for the Sunday services.[42] The use of galleries was slightly

31 *WA* 12, 35, 5 f. **32** *LW* 53, 11. **33** Chipps Smith, *Sculpture*, pp. 59–61; Lee, *Transformations*, pp. 160–162. **34** Chipps Smith, *Sculpture*, pp. 87–90; Koerner, *Reformation*, pp. 408–410; Dillenberger, *Images*, pp. 108 f. **35** Chipps Smith, *Sculpture*, pp. 105–108; Chipps Smith, *Architecture*, p. 170; Königsfeld/ Grote, *Altar*; Karant-Nunn, *Reformation*, p. 136. See also Thøfner, *Framing*, pp. 119–122. **36** Chipps Smith, *Architecture*, pp. 167–173. **37** Johannsen, *Palace Chapel*, pp. 39–41; Großmann, *L'église*, pp. 259, 265; Badstübner, *Rezeption*, pp. 260–263. **38** Fisher Gray, *Body*, pp. 113–117. **39** Koerner, *Reformation*, pp. 427 f. **40** *LW* 53, 12. **41** Christman, *Pulpit*, p. 272. See also Strauss, *Success*, pp. 49 f. **42** Karant-Nunn, *Reformation*, p. 196; Fisher Gray, *Churches*, pp. 47 f.

Fig. 6 Torgau, Hartenfels Palace, Palace Chapel, Reconstruction of the original altar

different in princely chapels. At Torgau, for example, there was a private entrance to the gallery from the castle; the prince and his entourage could follow the service from this raised vantage point, while his household gathered for the service below. The ducal pew in Wolfenbüttel is above the family mausoleum and overlooks the pulpit in front of it.[43] In churches across the empire, the elites were assigned privileged positions within the building, but seating was also organized according to gender so as to ensure order and decorum during services. At Freudenstadt men and women were accommodated in the different arms of the L-shaped building, yet they could both see the altar and pulpit (fig. 5).[44]

Furttenbach recommended seating at the front of the church for the municipal officials facing the congregation; the women were to be seated beneath the pulpit, while men were to sit at the back and in the surrounding galleries. His treatise even took account of the different shape and sizes of the sexes when it came to specifying the provision of seating.[45] The arrangement of fixed seating was more problematic where there was more than one liturgical focal point, which often meant that some members of the congregation were unable to see simultaneously both the altar and the pulpit. This was the situation at St. Anna's Church in Augsburg, where the altar and pulpit were not in close proximity to each other. This difficulty was resolved by having benches with backrests that were designed to flip over (Drehgestühl), so that the seating, as appropriate, faced either the altar or the pulpit. It illustrates how far Lutherans were able to overcome the liturgical and logistical difficulties posed by their use of existing buildings to ensure that the congregation's attention was focused in the appropriate direction.[46]

43 Koerner, *Reformation*, p. 414; Chipps Smith, *Architecture*, p. 170. **44** Chipps Smith, *Architecture*, p. 172. **45** Fisher Gray, *Body*, pp. 111–113. **46** Ibid., p. 113; Fisher Gray, *Churches*, p. 58; Drummond, *Church Architecture*, p. 20.

Fig. 7 Hans Walther, Design for the communion altar of the Frauenkirche (St. Mary's Church) Dresden

Alongside preaching, the sacraments of baptism and Communion also had their own ritual spaces within the building. In spite of Luther's expectation that medieval altars would be replaced in due course, many remained and continued to be used for the celebration of Communion. Side altars had been rendered superfluous with the rejection of private and requiem Masses; in parts of the empire, such as East Frisia, Mecklenburg, and Weimar, there were official orders for their removal, but elsewhere the decision was left to individual parishes. However, in some German states new smaller altars were erected in the mid-sixteenth century between the nave and the chancel, which were used for weekday and Sunday services, while the medieval high altar at the east end was reserved for feast days. These small altars were more like Communion tables, which meant that the pastor could face the congregation during the service.[47] At Wolfenbüttel, a secondary altar was installed at the conjunction of the nave and chancel, while the principal altar with a retable remained at the east end (fig. 2).[48] Freestanding principal altars were also commissioned for new churches, such as the one created for the chapel at Torgau in the early 1540s (fig. 6). This is in the form of a table, with four carved angels supporting the top. There are similarities with Schmalkalden Chapel, where the four evangelists bear the altar table (fig. 4). By the early seventeenth century, however, an altarpiece had been erected behind the Torgau altar. It was only in Württemberg and parts of Thuringia that freestanding altars became the norm.[49]

The continuity with late-medieval settings for the Eucharist could be seen in the monumental altar constructed in Dresden's Frauenkirche between 1572 and 1579 (fig. 7). The carved stone altarpiece depicts the Last Supper, flanked by pairs of Corinthian pillars; on the front of the altar itself, there is a predella of the Passover Meal; above the altarpiece is a crucifix framed by the tablets of the Ten Commandments. The structure was surmounted by a statue of the resurrected Christ, with statues of the evangelists and other figures, together with scriptural texts, evoking the sanctity of the Word. The Dresden altar influenced the design of the monumental altarpiece erected in the new church at Wolfenbüttel in 1623.[50] Although the altars at Torgau and Dresden illustrate alternative settings for the Eucharist, the freestanding altar that Luther mooted did not replace the more traditional forms, although these were tempered with a more evangelical iconography.

There was also a significant degree of continuity surrounding baptism, which is perhaps not surprising as Luther made only limited changes to the rite. Although his baptismal liturgy refers to the font, he makes no comment about its appearance or placement within the church building. Medieval fonts continued to be used and still survive in significant numbers across Germany, including at Wittenberg (fig. 8). Fonts were usually located at the west end of the church, near the entrance to the building, and remained in this position after the Reformation in a number of Lutheran states. The ritual significance of the baptismal setting did lead to the erection of enclosures around the font demarcating its importance within the church, although few of these have survived. Baptism was intrinsically tied to preaching; according to Luther, baptism only occurred when "water and the Word of God are conjoined."[51] Some communities therefore sought to link preaching and the sacraments spa-

Fig. 8 Wittenberg, St. Mary's Town Church. Choir with the baptismal font by Hermann Vischer the Elder (1457) and the "Reformation Altar" by Lucas Cranach the Elder (1547)

tially by moving the font to the front of the church so that it was in close proximity to the altar and pulpit, such as at Freudenstadt and, initially, Bückeburg.[52] This had been taken a step further at the castle chapel at Schmalkalden, where the baptismal basin was incorporated into the altar (fig. 4).[53] Moving the font established a single ritual focal point at the front of the church.

Although Luther came to reject confession as a sacrament, he recognized the importance of reflective penitence and the consolation that came from absolution. The *Confession of Augsburg* also advocated the retention of confession but specified that it was unnecessary for this to include the enumeration of an individual's sins. Confession and examination on the tenets of faith came to be part of the preparation, and a prerequisite, for receiving Communion. Lucas Cranach the Elder's Wittenberg altarpiece in the Town Church of St. Mary's depicts Johannes Bugenhagen, symbolically holding the keys of Saint Peter, seated in a confessional chair listening to the penitent kneeling beside him; the furnishings resemble those of the late-medieval Catholic rite. Confessional chairs and benches continued to have their place, but in some churches these gave way to specially erected compartments or small rooms where the minister examined individuals and heard their profession of faith in private.[54]

Besides these ritual spaces, religious imagery was another element that distinguished Lutheran places of worship from those of other Protestant confessions. In some churches medieval altarpieces remained in situ after the Reformation, such as the high altar in the Frauenkirche in Nuremberg with its Marian iconography and scenes from the life of Christ and the Virgin. At Zwickau, the Wolgemut altar in the Marienkirche, incorporating a statue of the Virgin and Child with eight female saints, was retained through pressure from the Lutheran congregation. However, the survival of medieval religious art should not be over emphasized as it varied across the empire; in some states much of it had been removed or replaced by the late sixteenth century.[55] New altarpieces or retables were commissioned for these places of worship. Although Luther had accepted the retention of altarpieces in the preface to his *German Mass*, he ultimately aspired for their removal. By 1530, he had changed his position and proposed that "whoever has a wish to place panels on the altar" should depict the Last Supper on them with two accompanying verses that allowed the faithful to reflect, and praise God. He therefore sought to combine image and word in the altarpiece.[56]

It is a theme that is seen in a number of new Lutheran altarpieces, together with other Christocentric iconography such as the Crucifixion and Resurrection.[57] The Passover/Last Supper is portrayed in the central panel of the altarpiece painted by Lucas Cranach for the principal church at Wittenberg in 1547, which is flanked by representations of baptism and confession; the predella shows Luther preaching to the congregation.[58] The depiction of the sacraments was also included in the background of altarpieces that focused on the *Confession of Augsburg*.[59] In the late sixteenth and seventeenth centuries, traditional winged altarpieces gave way to more monumental structures—with similar Christological iconography— particularly in parts of Saxony (such as those erected at Dresden and Wolfenbüttel) and Northern Germany, Schleswig-Holstein, and Prussia.[60] Lutheran altarpieces did not always include visual imagery; in some parts of the empire where there was a strong Reformed influence, biblical texts were painted in the central panel. The influence of Emden in northwest Germany, for example, led to altarpieces being inscribed with biblical quotations or key texts such as the Ten Commandments.[61] These alternative types illustrate how Lutheran material culture could be adapted to particular local circumstances rather than having a single confessional approach.

Although there were regional variations, some pre-Reformation statues including Marian imagery survived the confessional changes across the empire, but concerns were expressed about those that were considered to have become the focus of idolatry. Luther had rejected the cult of saints but recognized their significance as exemplars for their adherence to the faith.[62] He accepted the allegorical portrayal of Saint Christopher as the bearer of Christ but dismissed what he regarded as the idolatrous depiction of some other saints. New statues of Saint Christopher and local saints were produced after the Reformation, but these increasingly came to be replaced by biblical or Christological images. From the 1530s and 1540s, Lutheran images assumed a more didactic purpose, emphasizing the importance of the Word of God. Biblical themes took precedence—such as the crucified or resurrected Christ, the evangelists, apostles, or prophets—together with Christian virtues. The elaborate decoration and statuary on the Wolfenbüttel pulpit illustrates how far this iconography had developed by the early seventeenth century.[63] Religious images were, however, an emotive issue in the Reformation, and their survival varied across the empire, due to iconoclastic outbursts or Reformed pressure for their removal from places of worship. For some communities, the use of images and other *adiaphora* became a confessional statement to distance themselves from the adherents of the Reformed faith.[64]

Conclusion

Luther's principal concern when it came to worship was both the preaching of the Word of God and the appropriate administration of the sacraments. As existing churches were reconfigured for Lutheran worship, the significance of the altar, baptismal font, and pulpit sometimes led to them being enclosed—emphasizing the importance of these ritual spaces—or moved to provide a single liturgical focal point for the worshippers. However, these changes were not prescribed by Martin Luther himself, who did not wish to dictate to congregations the arrangement and appearance of places of worship. It was a matter of Christian freedom to decide whether to retain and use medieval ecclesiastical furnishings and liturgical items. These were not fundamental matters for Luther, although he did in some instances express an expectation that things might change over time. The Lutheran Reformation was implemented across the empire and beyond by princes, city governments, and other religious reformers and clergy whose personal interests, political concerns, and theological convictions had an influence in shaping the setting for worship.

The construction of princely chapels and the new churches of the early seventeenth century allowed for some experimentation with the arrangements for Lutheran worship, such as the development of the *Prinzipalstück* at Schmalkalden or the segregation of the congregation at Freudenstadt. Along with the exceptional retention of some medieval ecclesiastical art and furnishings, new altarpieces

47 Karant-Nunn, *Reformation*, pp. 120 f.; Nischan, *Protestants*, pp. 96 f.; Yates, *Liturgical Space*, p. 12; Fisher Gray, *Body*, p. 115; Deiters, *Epitaphs*, pp. 64–67. **48** Hamberg, *Temples*, p. 75; Chipps Smith, *Architecture*, p. 170. **49** Chipps Smith, *Sculpture*, pp. 90 f., 439; Koerner, *Reformation*, pp. 362, 407 f.; Nischan, *Protestants*, p. 96. **50** Chipps Smith, *Sculpture*, pp. 90–92, 100–104; Königsfeld/Grote, *Altar*. **51** *LW* 51, 185. **52** Chipps Smith, *Architecture*, pp. 169, 172 f.; Thøfner, *Framing*, pp. 110–118. **53** Koerner, *Reformation*, pp. 425 f. **54** Karant-Nunn, *Reformation*, pp. 94–99; Rittgers, *Reformation*; Christman, *Pulpit*, pp. 282–284; Koerner, *Reformation*, pp. 258, 329–331; Range, *Sacrament*. **55** Heal, *Cult*, pp. 64–76, 116–128; Heal, *Papist*; Karant-Nunn, *Reformation*, pp. 123 f., 254 f. **56** *LW* 13, 375. **57** Michalski, *Reformation*, pp. 31–34; Heal, *Cult*, pp. 298–300; Münch, *Art*, pp. 408–415; Noble, *Lucas Cranach*, p. 110. **58** Dillenberger, *Images*, pp. 102–105; Koerner, *Reformation*, pp. 69–80, 321–339; Noble, *Lucas Cranach*, pp. 97–137. **59** Brückner, *Bekenntnisgemälde*. **60** Nischan, *Protestants*, pp. 97 f.; Chipps Smith, *Sculpture*, pp. 101–104; Königsfeld/Grote, *Altar*. **61** See Diederichs-Gottschalk, *Schriftaltäre*; Münch, *Art*, pp. 415–417. **62** See the contribution by Susanne Kimmig-Völkner in this volume. **63** Michalski, *Reformation*, pp. 31–36; Chipps Smith, *Sculpture*, p. 108. See also Heal, *Cult*, p. 147. **64** Heal, *Papist*.

and pulpits were erected that employed religious imagery and iconography that established a new Lutheran aesthetic. The use of religious imagery varied across the empire; in some regions it was tempered by Reformed influences or was defiantly retained as a demonstration of the Christian freedom of Lutheran congregations. The Lutheran church interior and the material culture of worship could therefore vary remarkably; it could preserve aspects of the medieval past, experiment with new liturgical arrangements, respond to other theological beliefs, or represent the interests of its patron. This was possible because the material culture and setting of Lutheran worship was not fundamental to the actual preaching of the Word of God and the celebration of the sacraments.

BIBLIOGRAPHY

Badstübner, Ernst (2015), Die Rezeption von Schlosskapellen der Renaissance im protestantischen Landkirchenbau, Schmalkalden und die hessische Herrschaft. In: Harasimowicz, Jan (ed.), *Protestantischer Kirchenbau der Frühen Neuzeit in Europa. Grundlagen und neue Forschungskonzepte*. Berlin, pp. 257–270. **Brückner**, Wolfgang (2007), *Lutherische Bekenntnisgemälde des 16. bis 18. Jahrhunderts. Die illustrierte Confessio Augustana*. Regensburg. **Chipps Smith**, Jeffrey (1994), *German Sculpture of the Later Renaissance, c. 1520–1580. Art in an Age of Uncertainty*. Princeton. **Chipps Smith**, Jeffrey (2015), The Architecture of Faith: Lutheran and Jesuit Churches in Germany in the Early Seventeenth Century. In: Harasomowicz, Jan (ed.), *Protestantischer Kirchenbau der Frühen Neuzeit in Europa. Grundlagen und neue Forschungskonzepte*. Berlin, pp. 161–174. **Christman**, Robert (2008), The Pulpit and the Pew. Shaping Popular Piety in the Late Reformation. In: Kolb, Robert (ed.), *Lutheran Ecclesiastical Culture, 1550–1675*. Leiden, p. 259–303. **Deiters**, Maria (2012), Epitaphs in Dialogue with Sacred Space: Post-Reformation Furnishings in the Parish Churches of St Nikolai and St Marien in Berlin. In: Spicer, Andrew (ed.), *Lutheran Churches in Early Modern Europe*. Farnham, pp. 63–96. **Diederichs-Gottschalk**, Dietrich (2005), *Die protestantischen Schriftaltäre des 16. und 17. Jahrhunderts in Nordwestdeutschland: Eine kirchen- und kunstgeschichtliche Untersuchung zu einer Sonderform liturgischer Ausstattung in der Epoche der Konfessionalisierung*. Regensburg. **Dillenberger**, John (1999), *Images and Relics. Theological Perceptions and Visual Images in Sixteenth-Century Europe*. New York. **Drummond**, Andrew L. (1934), *The Church Architecture of Protestantism. An Historical and Constructive Study*. Edinburgh. **Fisher Gray**, Emily (2012), Lutheran Churches and Confessional Competition in Augsburg. In: Spicer, Andrew (ed.), *Lutheran Churches in Early Modern Europe*. Farnham, pp. 39–62. **Fisher Gray**, Emily (2016), The Body of the Faithful: Joseph Furttenbach's 1649 Lutheran Church Plans. In: Spicer, Andrew (ed.), *Parish Churches in Early Modern World*. Farnham, pp. 103–118. **Fritz**, Johann Michael (1997), Die bewahrende Kraft des Luthertums. Mittelalterliche Kunstwerke in evangelischen Kirchen. Regensburg. **Großmann**, Dieter (1995), L'église à tribunes et les tribunes des églises en Allemagne au XVIᶜ siècle. In: Guillaume, Jean (ed.), *L'église dans l'architecture de la Renaissance*. Paris, pp. 257–266. **Hamberg**, Per Gustaf (2002), *Temples for Protestants. Studies in the Architectural Milieu of the Early Reformed Church and Lutheran Church*. Gothenburg. **Hanway**, Jonas (1753), *An Historical Account of British Trade over the Caspian Sea*, 2 vols. London. **Heal**, Bridget (2007), *The Cult of the Virgin Mary in Early Modern Germany. Protestant and Catholic Piety, 1500–1648*. Cambridge. **Heal**, Bridget (2011), "Better Papist than Calvinist": Art and Identity in Later Lutheran Germany. In: *German History*, vol. 29, pp. 584–609. **Heal**, Bridget (2014), Seeing Christ: Visual Piety in Saxony's Erzgebirge. In: Chipps Smith, Jeffrey (ed.), *Visual Acuity and the Arts of Communication in Early Modern Germany*. Farnham, pp. 43–59. **Johannsen**, Hugo, The Protestant Palace Chapel. Monument to Evangelical Religion and Sacred Rulership. In: Andersen, Michael/Nyborg, Ebbe/Vedsø, Mogens (eds.) (2010), *Masters, Meanings & Models. Studies in the Art and Architecture of the Renaissance in Denmark*. Copenhagen, pp. 33–53. **Karant-Nunn**, Susan C. (1997), *The Reformation of Ritual. An Interpretation of Early Modern Germany*. London. **Koerner**, Joseph Leo (2004), *The Reformation of the Image*. London. **Königsfeld**, Peter/**Grote**, Rolf-Jürgen (1987), Altar, Raum und Ausstattung der Hauptkirche Beatae Mariae Virginis. Restaurierung und Geschichte. In: Möller, Hans-Herbert (ed.), *Die Hauptkirche Beatae Mariae Virginis in Wolfenbüttel*. Hannover, pp. 117–168. **Lee**, Bonnie B. (2008), Communal Transformations of Church Space in Lutheran Lübeck. In: *German History*, vol. 26, pp. 149–167. **Michalski**, Sergiusz (1993), *The Reformation and the Visual Arts. The Protestant image question in Western and Eastern Europe*. London. **Münch**, Birgit Ulrike (2014), The Art of the Liturgy: The Lutheran Tradition. In: Palmer Wandel, Lee (ed.), *A Companion to the Eucharist in the Reformation*. Leiden, pp. 399–422. **Nischan**, Bodo (2004), Becoming Protestants. Lutheran Altars or Reformed Communion Tables? In: Maag, Karin/Witvliet, John D. (eds.), *Worship in Medieval and Early Modern Europe. Change and Continuity in Religious Practice*. Notre Dame, pp. 84–111. **Noble**, Bonnie (2009), *Lucas Cranach the Elder. Art and Devotion of the German Reformation*. Lanham, Md. **Noll**, Mark A. (ed.) (1991), *Confessions and Catechisms of the Reformation*. Leicester. **Range**, Matthias (2011), The "Third Sacrament": Lutheran Confessionals in Schleswig (North Germany). In: King, Chris/Sayer, Duncan (eds.), *The Archaeology of Post-Medieval Religion*. Woodbridge, pp. 53–66. **Rittgers**, Ronald K. (2004), *The Reformation of the Keys. Confession, Conscience and Authority in Sixteenth-Century Germany*. Cambridge. **Spicer**, Andrew (2012), Lutheran Churches and Confessional Identity. In: Spicer, Andrew (ed.), *Lutheran Churches in Early Modern Europe*. Farnham, pp. 1–15. **Strauss**, Gerald (1975), Success and Failure in the German Reformation. In: *Past & Present*, vol. 67, pp. 30–63. **Thøfner**, Margit (2012), Framing the Sacred. Lutheran Church Furnishings in the Holy Roman Empire. In: Spicer, Andrew (ed.), *Lutheran Churches in Early Modern Europe*. Farnham, pp. 97–131. **Yates**, Nigel (2008), *Liturgical Space. Christian Worship and Church Buildings in Western Europe, 1500–2000*. Aldershot.

SUSANNE KIMMIG-VÖLKNER

Luther, the Virgin Mary, and the Saints. Catholic Images as a Key to Understanding the Lutheran Concept of Salvation

As is well known, Luther preached his last sermons at St. Andrew's Church in Eisleben. The pulpit from which he proclaimed the Gospel for the last time has been preserved in situ.[1] Behind the preacher stands, to this day, a late fifteenth-century painting of a crowned Madonna on a crescent moon in a sunburst (fig. 1).[2] Studies of Lutheran iconography usually focus on that epitome of Lutheran doctrine, "Law and Grace." But where do the numerous religious images preserved from before the Reformation fit into this iconography, including images that portray supposed "idols"? For artworks similar to the painting on the pillar in Eisleben are to be found in many other Lutheran churches. Research on them has usually been limited to their period of origin, largely ignoring a contextualization within Lutheran iconic practice. The above question is the starting point of the following contribution, which focuses on a small selection of image types and themes frequently found in Lutheran churches.

Crescent Moon Madonnas

In his exegesis on the *Magnificat*, Luther refers to the exaggerated representation of the Virgin Mary in art, arguing that the plethora of attributes that artists heap upon Mary hides her true, exemplary character.[3] From its beginnings, Lutheranism ascribed to the Virgin Mary, as well as to the saints, the function of *exemplum fidei*, paragon of faith, replacing the Catholic notion of Mary as mediator and advocate before God. This perspective changed the way in which Mary was venerated: the Lutheran reformers stressed that the way to God lay not through Mary's intercession but through Christ's work alone.[4] The reformers, therefore, rejected representations of Mary as Queen of Heaven or Madonna of Mercy since these distracted from her proper place in the scheme of salvation and assigned to her a role properly belonging to Christ.[5]

Although Luther, as early as 1521, criticized the excessive veneration of Mary and, by implication, representations of her in art—criticism echoed by other reformers of the Wittenberg school—it is remarkable how many crescent moon Madonnas are preserved in Lutheran churches to this day. For example, in 1594 the Annaberg city council presented a winged retable with such an image, attributed to Hans Hesse,[6] to the church in nearby Buchholz.[7] In the process of being installed, the panels were, for the most part, painted

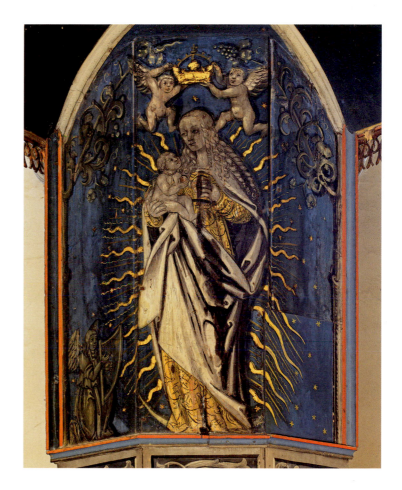

Fig. 1 Virgin on the Crescent Moon on the Luther pulpit of Saint Andrew's Church in Eisleben, 1518 with later enhancements (detail). The pulpit is preserved in situ.

1 With the exception of the staircase, which was rebuilt in the nineteenth century. **2** The panels served the secondary purpose of pillar coverings, but restoration work has revealed that they were placed there during the construction of the pulpit in 1518. See Schöne, *Bestands- und Schadenserfassung*, pp. 17 f. **3** *WA* 7, 569, 12−17. **4** See Düfel, *Stellung*, pp. 239−242; Kreitzer, *Reforming Mary*, p. 135; Münkler, *Sündhaftigkeit*, pp. 41 f.; Schimmelpfennig, *Geschichte*, pp. 10 f.; Stirm, *Bilderfrage*, p. 79; Tappolet, *Marienlob*, pp. 38, 46. **5** See Düfel, *Stellung*, p. 239; Kreitzer, *Reforming Mary*, p. 136; Michalski, *Reformation*, pp. 34 f.; Schimmelpfennig, *Geschichte*, p. 9; Tappolet, *Marienlob*, pp. 149−152; Weimer, *Luther*, pp. 31, 33. **6** Sandner, *Hesse*, pp. 60, 64. **7** See Eisbein, *Altar*, in particular p. 51; Magirius, *Franziskanerkloster*, in particular pp. 25−27; Melzer, *Historia*, p. 107.

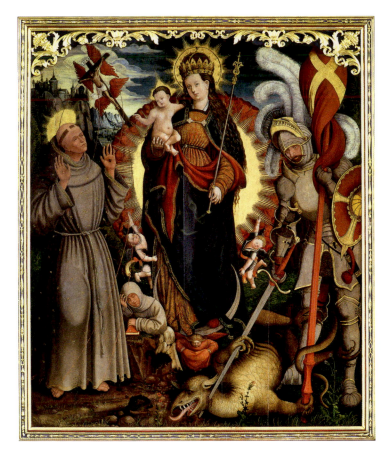

Fig. 2 (Attributed to) Hans Hesse, Virgin Mary retable, probably c. 1521, Annaberg-Buchholz, St. Catherine's Church.
Traces of the sixteenth century retouching have disappeared.

over and the images of saints replaced by events from the Gospels.[8] However, the central panel showing a crescent moon Madonna remained almost untouched (fig. 2). Only the supporting figure of Saint Francis was completely transformed into an angel of the Last Judgment. The painter gave him a sword in one hand and a pair of scales in the other. In the right-hand pan sat a poor, contrite sinner, and in the left-hand one a priest, a cardinal, and the devil with a millstone. Only the crucifix from the vision of Saint Francis remained untouched, but the blood streaming from Christ's side now poured into the contrite sinner's scale-pan, causing it to weigh more than the two clergymen plus the devil and the millstone together.[9]

The painting's apocalyptic theme, already suggested in its original plan with its allusion to the promise of salvation, is now vigorously foregrounded through the changes made to the figure of Saint Francis. The painter transformed the saint's vision into a monumental scene from the Apocalypse, in which Saint George the Dragon Slayer now functions as the Archangel Michael (Rev. 12:7 – 9). A comparison with other representations of the Last Judgment from the late sixteenth century shows that this is a fairly standard example of paintings on this theme (fig. 3). The stream of blood, which literally adds weight to the believer's penance, is visual proof of Christ's mercy. It is a motif widely represented in Reformation art, not least through Lucas Cranach's "Blood of Grace" in his "Law and Grace" series. Salvation through the blood of Christ is proclaimed in the Book of Revelation (Rev. 1:5), whereby the weighing of souls is ele-

vated to the status of a biblical event. In the Book of Revelation, the fight with the dragon follows directly after the appearance of the Woman of the Apocalypse (Rev. 12:1 – 6). John describes how a pregnant woman clothed with the sun, with the moon beneath her feet and a crown of twelve stars on her head, will appear in the heavens. The crescent moon Madonna is certainly modeled on this biblical figure. The figure was gradually associated with the Virgin Mary, and by the fifteenth century at the latest, it was overwhelmingly interpreted as representing the Queen of Heaven.

Although two-thirds of the central panel appears not to have been painted over, replacing Saint Francis with the Angel of the Apocalypse effected a reinterpretation of the whole painting. When the panels were opened, the promise of salvation on the Day of Judgment was revealed as fulfilled. In interpreting the crescent moon Madonna as the Woman of the Apocalypse, Lutheranism reverted to what was probably the original meaning of this iconographic motif. In the case of the Buchholz retable, what is striking is how much of the original painting was retained. Above all, elaborate, sumptuously painted sections of the picture were spared from the later painter's brush, thus preserving the aura of a masterpiece from an older tradition.

This reading of the Buchholz painting as the Woman of the Apocalypse may also be applied to other crescent moon Madonnas that survived the sixteenth and seventeenth centuries in Lutheran churches, including the *Goldene Maria* in the Church of the Trinity in Görlitz—a winged retable with a crescent moon Madonna in the shrine, that stood on the main altar of this Lutheran church until the beginning of the eighteenth century (fig. 4).[10] When the wings are opened, the heavily gilded feast day side of the retable presents scenes in relief from the life of the Virgin Mary. Scenes from the Passion of Christ are set against the gilded background of the second transformation, while the third is decorated with four paintings of scenes representing the fulfillment of salvation, from the Crucifixion to the Last Judgment. With the exception of the Madonna in the shrine, all the images are based on themes from the Gospels. The crescent moon Madonna belongs to the iconography of the Book of Revelation. In this example, the figure links to the second transformation of the retable with its representation of the Last Judgment stretching over two panels. This creates a starkly eschatological series of images in which the biblical Mary gestures toward the fulfillment of salvation at the end of time.

Evidently the Lutherans of the Church of Our Lady in Zittau deliberately chose to retain a Gothic crescent moon Madonna in the church's retable (fig. 5), for the compilation of the retable coincided with the installation of a whole new set of church furnishings in 1619. These included both a new pulpit and new religious paintings,[11] suggesting that the older image of the Virgin Mary was not added to the retable for reasons of economy but was intentionally put to further use. Over the sculpture is written in splendid gold letters: "Maria honoranda non adoranda." The pastor of the congregation at that time, Kaspar Tralles, quoted these words in his sermon to mark the reconsecration of the church:[12] "Ye shall honor Mary but not worship her," he admonished his flock. Besides instructions for the use of images in Lutheran churches, the sermon included explanations of the Virgin Mary's place in Lutheranism.[13]

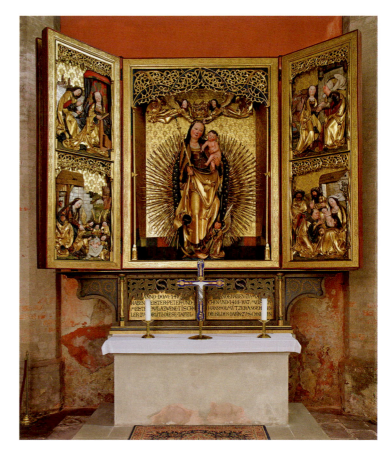

Fig. 3 Archangel Michael weighing souls. Detail from the left wing
of the so-called Bose Retable that was donated by the Bose family
for the Merseburg Cathedral, 1516

Fig. 4 A Late Gothic winged altar known as the "Golden Mary,"
c. 1510–15, Görlitz, Church of the Holy Trinity

The *Angelic Salutation*

The open altar wings showing the Annunciation complete the series of images in Zittau. The announcing angel on the inner side of the right-hand panel, God's representative bearing his message to Mary, inclines toward her. She stands on the left at a reading desk, her right hand raised in greeting, her left hand to her breast, symbolizing her desire to take the divine message to heart.

Over the reliefs in the wings, in golden letters on a black background, stand the initial words of the *Magnificat*, creating a link to Mary's hymn of praise. The events of the Virgin Mary's visit to Elizabeth (Luke 1:39–56) support the Lutheran interpretation of the Annunciation:[14] Mary treasures and glories in the grace God has imparted to her. She herself stresses her role as the humble handmaid of the Lord that Luther saw in her, making her the "prototype

and role model of the faith and church."[15] In Lutheran sermons of the sixteenth century, Mary was celebrated as the first person to compose a hymn of praise to the Christian God.[16]

One of the most renowned examples of pre-Reformation Madonna images surviving in Lutheranism is without doubt the *Angelic Salutation* by Veit Stoß in the Church of St. Lawrence, Nuremberg (fig. 6). The three-dimensional sculpture shows the Annunciation: Mary is framed by a rosary with medallions showing scenes from her life. Donated by the Nuremberg patrician Anton Tucher, the sculpture has remained in its place in the chancel arch to this day. The tradition of hiding the sculpture behind a curtain began when it was installed; it was probably revealed to the faithful only on high holy days and other special occasions.[17] The story that the Nuremberg reformer Andreas Osiander ordered the *Angelic Salutation* to be veiled lest he be dazzled by its rich gold paint while he was preaching

8 In the nineteenth century, under the direction of Clausen Dahl in Dresden, the original paintings of the retable were uncovered. Only the records of the *Sächsischer Altertumsverein (Saxon Antiquaries Society)* and the chronicles of Christian Melzer bear witness to this retouching today. See Melzer, *Historia*, pp. 107–112; Sächsisches Hauptstaatsarchiv Dresden—Staatsarchiv Dresden (SächsHStAD), Königlich Sächsischer Verein für Erforschung und Erhaltung vaterländischer Altertümer, no. 274: Buchholz Kirche, Die Restauration der Altarbilder. **9** See SächsHStAD, no. 274 (note 8 above), fol. 204; Melzer, *Historia*, pp. 108 f. **10** See SächsHStAD, no. 274 (note 8 above), fol. 41; Speer, *Fröm-*

migkeit, pp. 146 f., 165; Winzeler, *Dreifaltigkeitskirche*, p. 55. **11** See Hrachovec, *Slavnostní.* **12** See ibid., p. 26, note 40. **13** Tralles' elucidations served to define Lutheranism against the idolatry of Catholicism on the one hand and the iconoclasm of Calvinism on the other. He saw the use of images in Lutheran churches positively, understanding them as a public avowal of Lutheran faith and a sign of the orthodoxy of Lutheran belief. ibid., p. 38. **14** See Düfel, *Stellung*, p. 240; Kreitzer, *Reforming Mary*, p. 138; Wenz, *Maria*, pp. 69 f. **15** See Wenz, *Maria*, p. 69. **16** See Kreitzer, *Reforming Mary*, p. 139. **17** See Ganz, *Gruß*; Taubert, *Gruß*.

Fig. 5 Composite retable with a late Gothic Virgin on the Crescent Moon, c. 1500 – 1619, Zittau St. Mary's Church. The retable is composed of older and newer panels.

of which come from Luke's Gospel (1:26 – 38), as a glorification of the Mother of Jesus, in which the phrase "blessed be the fruit of thy womb" transforms the angel's salutation into a hymn of praise to Christ. Instead of being an invocation to Mary, the *Ave Maria* now functioned as a tribute to Mary's firmness of faith, which God rewarded with proof of his grace in the form of the immaculate conception and Mary's divine motherhood.[20] Following Luther, the standard German translation of the Latin *gratia plena* became "Holdselige"—sweetly blessed. Lutheranism thus distinguished its understanding of Mary's role from that of the Catholic Church by emphasizing her humanity.[21] She functioned no longer as mediator but as God's instrument, humbly and modestly receiving God's gift of grace.[22]

In the fifteenth century, representations of the Annunciation emphasizing Mary's humility were already becoming widespread; one of the most common variants portrays Mary receiving the news from Gabriel in her chamber (fig. 7).[23] The Virgin Mary is studying the Bible; her indoor surroundings allude to her commitment to house and home and, by extension, to the family. She is the embodiment of a modest, home-loving, family-oriented girl. Her devout reading points to a life lived in faith.[24] Mary thus represents Lutheranism's ideal of a young woman,[25] perhaps too because the indoor Annunciation scenes are stocked with elements from the Apocrypha and from Christian mysticism symbolizing Mary's qualities. Their combination of biblical images and allegorical content virtually predestine these historical paintings to be ideal Lutheran teaching material.

Coronation of the Virgin

There is, of course, a palpable discrepancy between visualizing the Virgin Mary as a humble young woman and as the Queen of Heaven. Jutta Desel has established that in Thuringia, one of the most frequent themes in pre-Reformation iconography is the Coronation of the Virgin.[26] As is well known, even before the Reformation the Virgin Mary was considered the embodiment of the church, the *ecclesia*. The ecclesiological dimension of Mary's significance for Lutheranism is based both on its interpretation of the *Magnificat* and on John's Gospel, in which Christ entrusts his mother Mary to John's care (John 19:25 – 27). In Lutheran sermons of the sixteenth century, this act is interpreted as the church's being given into the care of the faithful: the church cares for the faithful as a mother for her children, and *vice versa*.[27]

The retable of the main altar of St. Mary's Church in Mühlhausen, Thuringia, presents Mary in her role as paragon of the church. The composite retable, probably assembled between 1608 and 1612[28] (fig. 8), features a late Renaissance canopy, supported by Corinthian columns, spanning the altar table, above which is a winged retable, originally from 1525, centered on a Crowning of the Virgin with Trinity and flanked by images of various saints. The canopy is capped by a stepped top piece with a painting of the Ascension and angels bearing instruments of the Passion. Above that is a crescent moon Madonna, probably late Gothic. The inscriptions both on the predella

is one of the myths of the Reformation. The *Angelic Salutation* was doubtlessly preserved, firstly because the sculpture was greatly valued by the family who had donated it,[18] and secondly, because the motif did not offend Lutheran sensibilities in ways that might have prompted its removal.

Representations of the Annunciation are to be found, for the most part, together with other images on the outside of the retables' wings, whereby the Virgin Mary and Gabriel are typically assigned to separate panels. Mary is portrayed as the first person to learn of the impending arrival of the Savior in this world and of her divine motherhood. Lutheranism preserved the Feast of the Annunciation in its calendar, as well as other holy days associated with the Virgin Mary, while resolutely shifting the focus to the figure of Jesus, thus emphasizing a purely Christological interpretation of the Gospel.[19] Luther interpreted the *Ave Maria*, the words

Fig. 6 Veit Stoss, Angelic Salutation or "Angel's Greeting" (Annunciation), Nuremberg, Saint Lawrence's Church, 1518

Fig. 7 Albrecht Dürer, The Annunciation, from The Small Passion, 1510

and in the shrine directly beneath the Crowning of the Virgin date from the early seventeenth century. The latter runs: "The sweetly blessed and sanctified Virgin Mary is a paragon of the Christian church, who through the power of the Holy Ghost shall be crowned in Heaven with eternal glory by God the Father for His beloved Son's sake. Rev. 12. V. I."

This inscription expounds the correct interpretation of the central image: Mary's being crowned does not raise her to the status of Queen of Heaven; rather, she receives the Crown of Virtue, together with symbols of ecclesiastical authority. The allusion to the Woman of the Apocalypse, both through the reference to the Book of Revelation and through the crescent moon Madonna capping the entire structure, emphasizes the status of the Virgin Mary in her traditional role as *Ecclesia*.[29]

Exempla Fidei and Allegories of Faith

Besides representations of the Virgin Mary and depictions of other events from the Gospels, many images of non-biblical saints can be found in Lutheran churches. For the most part, they depict individual figures recognizable by their traditional attributes, though the observant visitor might discover the occasional scenic representation. The most popular saints are from the category of Holy Helpers. In the late Middle Ages, Saint Christopher was firmly established as one of the most popular saints and is thus frequently depicted in a range of contexts. His significance for Luther is apparent from two of his sermons, which he preached in Lochau and Wittenberg in 1528 and 1529 respectively.[30] Luther saw Saint Christopher as epitomizing Christian faith (fig. 9). The faithful should bear his image in mind at

18 As may be seen in a painting created for the Tucher family around 1646. See Taubert, *Gruß*, p. 67. 19 See Harasimowicz, *Kunst*, p. 41; Kreitzer, *Reforming Mary*, p. 27. 20 See Kreitzer, *Reforming Mary*, p. 30; Tappolet, *Marienlob*, p. 124. 21 See Kreitzer, *Reforming Mary*, pp. 27, 31 f.; Schimmelpfennig, *Geschichte*, p. 10; Tappolet, *Marienlob*, pp. 44–46, 125 f.; Wenz, *Maria*, p. 69. 22 See Düfel, *Stellung*, p. 246; Kreitzer, *Reforming Mary*, pp. 32, 44, 140 f. 23 See Lüken, *Verkündigung*, pp. 41–64; Schiller, *Ikonographie*, p. 57. 24 See

Kreitzer, *Reforming Mary*, pp. 31, 140. 25 See the contributions of Susan Karant-Nunn and Franziska Kuschel to this volume. 26 See Desel, *Leiden*, p. 11. 27 See Kreitzer, *Reforming Mary*, p. 119. 28 See Otte/Sommer, *Darstellung*, pp. 68, 80; Dehio/Gall/Eißing, *Handbuch*, pp. 838, 850. 29 See Koch, *Glauben*, pp. 49–51, 54–57; Kreitzer, *Mary*, pp. 118 f. 30 *WA* 27, 384, 15–390, 9 (no. 77); *WA* 29, 498, 15–505, 40 (no. 58).

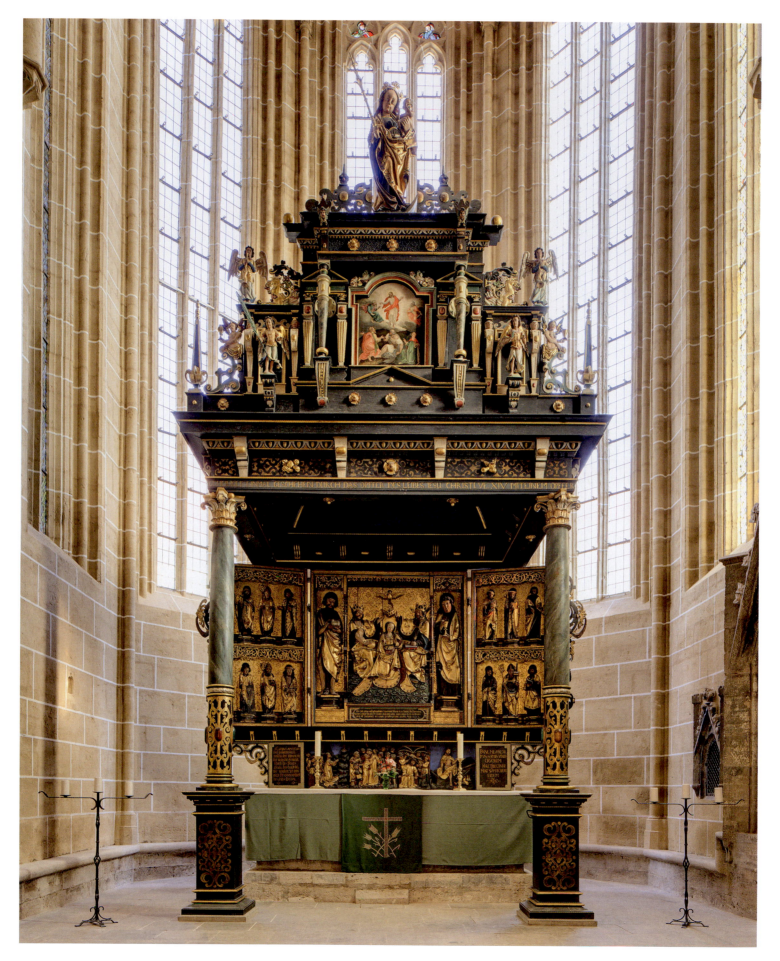

Fig. 8 Altar architecture with a late Gothic retable showing the Crowning of the Virgin Mary,
c. 1525/1610, Mühlhausen (Thuringia), St. Mary's Church

all times, Luther said, and went so far as to declare that those who have not yet set eyes on it should go and see it while they could.[31]

Using the example of Saint Christopher, Luther expounded on the principles of faith that should inspire Christians and preachers of the Gospel. He stressed that "Christopher is not a person but a model for all Christians to emulate,"[32] thus emphasizing the saint's fictional nature. The depiction of Christopher, said Luther, contains the following qualities: His gigantic size stands for piety; whoever strives to be pious has to be big, strong, and courageous, as only such a person can bear the weight of faith, symbolized by the child Christopher carries. The saint's staff stands for Holy Scripture; whenever the burdens of life became too heavy to bear, a Christian should seek the support of the Bible.[33] The satchel on the saint's belt, containing fish and bread, represents God's providence; through his strong faith, Christopher overcomes the dangerous shallows and sea monsters of life. Luther interpreted the motif as representing the sacrament of baptism: the child baptizes the saint in the raging waters of the river. In sum, Luther ascribed an allegorical function to Christopher, glossing his representation thus: "So you see how well Christian teaching is embodied in a physical image, in which we may see faith, love, good works and the holy cross."[34]

Luther incorporated references to other saints into his sermons on Saint Christopher, through minor allusions designed to increase his listeners' understanding. Besides Saints Catharine, Barbara, and Michael, he made reference to Saint George.[35] According to legend, George was able to defeat the dragon because he drew his strength from his faith in Christ. As with Saint Christopher, Saint George's profound piety enabled him to undergo much suffering: "And so the artist has depicted Saint George for us with the dragon. But in later years, when God's word was taken away from the faithful, beautiful paintings such as this were misused in the service of idolatry."[36]

In this sentiment, which is also expressed in Luther's sermon of October 26, 1528, in Lochau, Luther approves of using the iconographic motif of Saint George the Dragon Slayer to represent the prototype of the sincere believer. Invoking the aid of Saints George and Christopher in times of need, however, was for Luther a form of idolatry. But like the Virgin Mary, they could legitimately serve as *exempla fidei*, which is why many writers made use of their legends in a variety of Lutheran religious texts.

Devotional Pictures

Published sermons and devotional books, instructions on writing sermons and composing pictures,[37] calendars of saints, lives of martyrs, and other exemplary histories—all these play a role in Lutheran religious *memoria* (memorial piety). Such writings went through numerous editions and attracted much interest.[38] Besides a few sixteenth-century tracts on images and their place in Lutheranism, the

Fig. 9 Sebald Beham, Saint Christopher with the Moon in an Aureole. Woodcut, first half of the sixteenth century

above-mentioned genres provide sometimes very precise instructions on various types of images. Some texts contain detailed descriptions of the portrayal of Saint Christopher.[39] It is clear that very early on, Lutheranism established basic iconographic guidelines derived from Luther himself. Images were to serve as instructional material and *aide-mémoires*,[40] that is, reminders of Christ. The Reformation postulated that people thought in images, and that through the power of the emotions they imagined what was portrayed as vividly present.[41] A number of authors, therefore, recommended that the legends of the saints be memorized with the help of pictures so that the faithful could follow in Christ's footsteps according to their example. The images thus functioned similarly to late-medieval devotional pictures.

Melanchthon or his disciple Paul Eber composed a detailed set of instructions on how to use religious calendars, according to which all Christians should possess a calendar for private study and to meditate on historical events, the Gospels, and the lives of the saints,[42] with whom the authors wished their readers to identify.[43]

31 In a sermon preached on July 25, 1529, Luther made direct reference to the depiction of Saint Christopher in the *Barfüßerkirche*. See *WA* 29, 498, 20. **32** *WA* 29, 500, 18 f. **33** *WA* 27, 389, 34 f. **34** *WA* 27, 390, 7–9. **35** *WA* 27, 386, 13 f., 24 f.; *WA* 29, 501, 5 f., 17 f.; *WA* 34/II, 226, 3, 11, 21 f. **36** *WA* 27, 386, 24–27. **37** See Wimzböck, *Augen*, p. 438. **38** See Brückner, *Zeugen*; Fuchs, *Heiligen-*

memoria, p. 595. **39** See Goldwurm, *Kirchen Calender*, p. 51r; Hondorf, *Calendarium*, p. 412. **40** *WA* 18, 80, 6–8. **41** See Wimböck, *Augen*, p. 438. **42** See Fuchs, *Heiligenmemoria*, pp. 602–613; Pohlig, *Gelehrsamkeit*, pp. 418–421. **43** See Vinzenz Sturm, Vorrede zum Calendarium Sanctorum Andreas Hondorfs. In: Hondorf, *Calendarium*, p. A ii r – A iiii v.

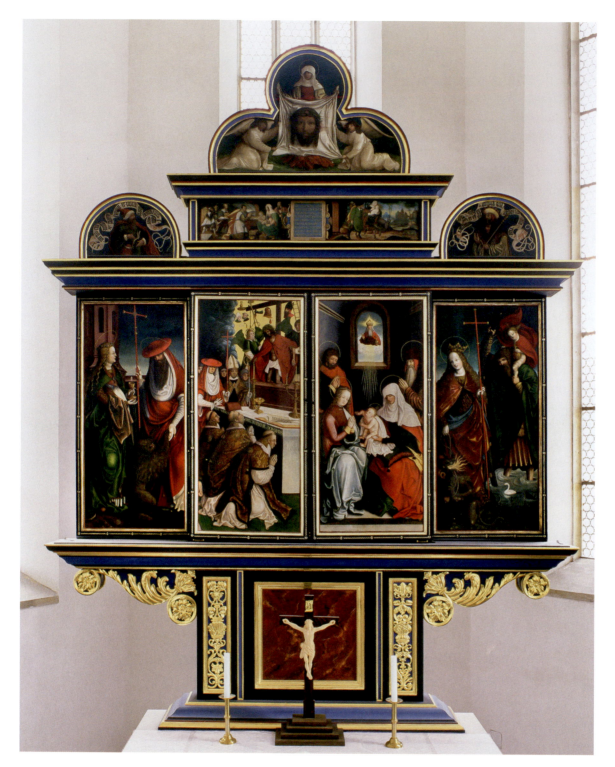

Fig. 10
(Attributed to) Hans Hesse,
Retable of St. Mary's, c. 1521,
Annaberg-Buchholz,
St. Catherine's Church.
Saint Veronica with her veil is
shown on the top of the retable.

Christ's Passion, replicated in saintly legends, comforted the faithful and engendered pity (*compassio*) in them. It seems likely that Lutheranism was thus connecting with the late-medieval practice of *devotio moderna*, a spiritual movement whose members strove to create within themselves a personal sense of piety.

The legend of Saint Veronica's Veil is an illustration of such inner spirituality (fig. 10). Fifteenth-century depictions of this motif are characterized by a marked striving for naturalism: in the spirit of *devotio moderna*, the depictions urge the faithful to internalize what they are seeing. Thus, in their calendars of the saints, Gold-

wurm and Hondorff refer to the many images of Saint Veronica in churches. However, they see Christ's countenance as being replicated not on her veil but in her heart.[44] The motif of the Man of Sorrows, frequently encountered in Lutheran iconography, also echoes this attitude. In the tradition of mysticism, the image of the risen Christ, marked by suffering, reminds the faithful of their sins, the consequences of which Christ bears on their behalf.[45] In Lutheranism, in accordance with the doctrine of justification, the image embodies the grace imparted to the believer through Christ's sacrifice.

In the Tradition of *Devotio Moderna*

The foregoing essay shows that in the early days of Lutheranism, word and image went hand in hand. Easier access to the printed word and higher rates of literacy in the early modern era favored the development of polymedial spiritual practices. Text-supported iconography fostered an orthodox interpretation of religious images, avoiding ambiguities. Images were present not simply "to contemplate, to bear witness, to recall, to serve as a sign."[46] Rather, they were intended to evoke an emotional response, causing the observer to identify with the passion of Christ and follow him. Pre-Reformation images or image motifs were ideally suited for evoking this *compassio* since they had been conceived to this end within the context of *devotio moderna*. They simplified meditative contemplation and reinforced the believer's experience of Christ's Passion promoted by sixteenth-century Lutheranism. Luther himself very early on ascribed an exemplary function to the saints, illustrating their roles in this respect through allegories elaborated with graphic symbolism. The next generation of Wittenberg theologians utilized similar conventions in their sermons, as well as exploring the meditative qualities of traditional iconography and thus endowing the latter with additional functions in Lutheran praxis.

---

44 See Goldwurm, *Kirchen Calender*, 55v–56r; Gedik, *Bildern*, 125v. **45** See Muth/Schneiders, *Riemenschneider*, p. 131; Schmidt-Hannisa, *Passion*, p. 71. **46** *WA* 18, 80, 6 f.

BIBLIOGRAPHY

Brückner, Wolfgang (1974), Zeugen des Glaubens und ihre Literatur. In: id. (ed.), *Volkserzählung und Reformation. Ein Handbuch zur Tradierung und Funktion von Erzählstoffen und Erzählliteratur im Protestantismus*. Berlin, pp. 520–578. **Dehio**, Georg/**Gall**, Ernst/**Eißing**, Stephanie (2003), *Handbuch der deutschen Kunstdenkmäler*, Thüringen. 2nd ed. München. **Desel**, Jutta (1994), *"Vom Leiden Christi oder von dem schmertzlichen Mitleyden Marie": die vielfigurige Beweinung Christi im Kontext thüringischer Schnitzretabel der Spätgotik*. Weimar. **Düfel**, Hans (1968), *Luthers Stellung zur Marienverehrung* (= Kirche und Konfession. 13). Göttingen. **Eisbein**, Manfried (2005), Der Buchholzer Altar und seine wechselvolle Geschichte. In: Dülberg, Angelica (ed.), *Ästhetik und Wissenschaft. Beiträge zur Restaurierung und Denkmalpflege* (= Arbeitshefte des Landesamtes für Denkmalpflege Sachsen. 8). Altenburg, pp. 48–64. **Fuchs**, Thomas (1998), Protestantische Heiligenmemoria im 16. Jahrhundert. In: *Historische Zeitschrift*, vol. 267, pp. 587–615. **Ganz**, David (2003), Ein 'Krentzlein' aus Bildern. Der Englische Gruß des Veit Stoss und die Entstehung spätmittelalterlicher Bild-Rosarien. In: Frei, Urs-Beat/Bühler, Fredy (eds.), *Der Rosenkranz: Andacht, Geschichte, Kunst*. Bern, pp. 152–169. **Gedik**, Simon (1597), *Von Bildern und Altarn, In den Euangelischen Kirchen Augspurgischer Confession/Wolgegründter Bericht, sampt kurtzer Widerlegung des newlich aussgegangenen Zerbestischen Buchs, menniglich in diesen letzten gefehrlichen leufften, wieder die Caluinische Newrung der Bilder und Altarstürmer, zu wissen sehr nützlich und nötig*. Magdeburg. **Goldwurm**, Kaspar (1559), *Kirchen Calender. Ein Christlich vnd nützlich Buch in welchem nach Ordnung gemeiner Calender die Monat Tag vnd die fürnembsten Fest des gantzen jars mit irem gebrauh Auh der Heiligen Apostel und Christlichen Bischoff Leerer vnd Martyrer Glaub Leben vnd bestendige bekantnuss [...]*. Frankfurt am Main. **Harasimowicz**, Jan (1996), *Kunst als Glaubensbekenntnis* (= Beiträge zur Kunst- und Kulturgeschichte der Reformationszeit. 359). Baden-Baden. **Hondorf**, Andreas (1575), *Calendarium historicum oder der Heiligen Marterer Historien*. Frankfurt am Main. **Hrachovec**, Petr (2010), Slavnostní vysvěcení interiéru kostela Panny Marie v Žitavě 8. září 1619. Příspěvek k poznání raně novověkého luteránského sakrálního prostoru v zemích Koruny české. In: *Fontes Nissae*, vol. 11, pp. 11–46. **Koch**, Ernst (2011), "von Glauben eine Jungfrau, von Liebe eine Mutter." Marienverehrung im Bereich der Wittenberger Reformation. In: Seidel, Thomas A./Schacht, Ulrich (eds.), *Maria. Evangelisch*. Leipzig, pp. 43–57. **Kreitzer**, Beth (2004), *Reforming Mary. Changing Images of the Virgin Mary in Lutheran Sermons of the Sixteenth Century*. New York. **Lüken**, Sven (2000), *Die Verkündigung an Maria im 15. und frühen 16. Jahrhundert: historische und kunsthistorische Untersuchungen*. Göttingen. **Magirius**, Heinrich (2003), Das Franziskanerkloster zu Annaberg 2003. In: Magirius, Heinrich/Burkhardt, Hans (eds.), *Die "Schöne Tür" in der Sankt Annenkirche zu Annaberg*. Dresden, pp. 19–27. **Melzer**, Christian (1924), *Historia Schneebergensis renovata. D. i. Erneuerte Stadt- und Berg-Chronica der im Ober-Ertz-Gebürge Meissens geleg. St. Schneeberg*, ed. Heinrich Harms zum Spreckel. Vol. 1. Schneeberg. **Michalski**, Sergiusz (1993), *The Reformation and the Visual Arts. The Protestant image question in Western and Eastern Europe*. London. **Münkler**, Marina (2009), Sündhaftigkeit als Generator von Individualität. Zu den Transformationen legendarischen Erzählens in der Historia von D. Johann Fausten und den Faustbüchern des 16. und 17. Jahrhunderts. In: Strohschneider, Peter (ed.), *Literarische und religiöse Kommunikation in Mittelalter und Früher Neuzeit*. Berlin, pp. 25–61. **Muth**, Hanswernfried/**Schneiders**, Toni (2004), *Tilman Riemenschneider. Bildschnitzer zu Würzburg*. Würzburg. **Otte**, Heinrich/**Sommer**, Gustav (1881), *Beschreibende Darstellung der älteren Bau- und Kunstdenkmäler des Kreises Mühlhausen* (= Beschreibende Darstellung der älteren Bau- und Kunstdenkmäler der Provinz Sachsen. 4). Halle (Saale). **Pohlig**, Matthias (2007), *Zwischen Gelehrsamkeit und konfessioneller Identitätsstiftung*. Tübingen. **Schimmelpfennig**, Reintraud (1952), *Die Geschichte der Marienverehrung im deutschen Protestantismus*. Paderborn. **Sandner**, Ingo (1983), *Hans Hesse. Ein Maler der Spätgotik in Sachsen*. Dresden. **Schiller**, Gertrud (1966), *Ikonographie der christlichen Kunst*. Vol. 1. Gütersloh. **Schmidt-Hanissa**, Hans-Walter (2005), Eingefleischte Passion. Zur Logik der Stigmatisierung. In: Borgards, Roland (ed.), *Schmerz und Erinnerung*. München, pp. 69–82. **Schöne**, Peter (2014), *Restauratorische Bestands- und Schadenserfassung durch Atelier für Konservierung und Restaurierung Peter Schöne*. **Speer**, Christian, *Frömmigkeit und Politik: Städtische Eliten in Görlitz zwischen 1300 und 1550* (= Hallische Beiträge zur Geschichte des Mittelalters und der Frühen Neuzeit. 8). Berlin. **Stirm**, Margarete (1977), *Die Bilderfrage in der Reformation*. Gütersloh. **Tappolet**, Walter (ed.) (1962), *Das Marienlob der Reformatoren*. Tübingen. **Taubert**, Johannes (1978), Der Englische Gruß des Veit Stoß in Nürnberg. In: id. (ed.), *Farbige Skulpturen. Bedeutung, Fassung, Restaurierung*. München, pp. 60–72. **Weimer**, Christoph (1999), *Luther, Cranach und die Bilder. Gesetz und Evangelium—Schlüssel zum Reformatorischen Bildgebrauch*. Stuttgart. **Wenz**, Gunter (2003), Maria in der protestantischen Frömmigkeitspraxis. In: Sebastian Anneser (ed.) (2003), *Madonna. Das Bild der Muttergottes*. Lindenberg im Allgäu, pp. 69 f. **Wimböck**, Gabriele (2007), Durch die Augen in das Gemüt kommen: Sehen und Glauben—Grenzen und Reservate. In: Wimböck, Gabriele/Leonhard, Karin/Friedrich, Markus (eds.), *Evidentia: Reichweiten visueller Wahrnehmung in der Frühen Neuzeit*. Münster, pp. 427–450. **Winzeler**, Marius (2011), *Dreifaltigkeitskirche Görlitz*. Dößel.

INGRID DETTMANN

Martin Luther as a Saint? The Portrait of the Reformer between Holy Icon and Denominational Identity in the Sixteenth Century

Martin Luther was one of the most frequently portrayed figures of the early modern period. His image appeared in a broad variety of media and genres in both sacred and secular contexts. Particularly during the initial phase of the Reformation, people were avid to see the monk who had opposed both the Pope and the church. Albrecht Dürer, for example, expressed the wish "to come to Doctor Martinus and make a meticulous sketch of him for a copperplate etching to commemorate the memory of this Christian man who helped me overcome my greatest fears" in a letter addressed to Georg Spalatin in 1520.[1] Dürer's wish to meet Luther in person to prepare his portrait never actually materialized, but shortly afterward Lucas Cranach the Elder, court painter of Elector Frederick the Wise, produced the first copper engravings of the Augustinian monk (1520). Other artists also oriented themselves to this image, disseminating the Luther model in variant forms.[2] One of these images is Hans Baldung's woodcut made in 1521 that styles Luther as a saint (see fig. 1 in the essay of Christiane Andersson in this volume). The monk is gazing into the distance in contemplation, almost lost in reverie, in front of an open Bible. He has received enlightenment, prominently represented by the radiant halo, through the Holy Ghost, who is hovering over him in the form of a dove.

The open book of the Holy Script in his hand suggests that Luther's holiness originated from the revelations bestowed through his Bible studies. The Holy Script would subsequently become a characteristic attribute of the Reformer. The reference to traditional holy iconography was intended to verify the legitimacy of the Reformation doctrine, which the Augustinian monk had taken from the Bible as the fundamental source of Christian truth.[3] Baldung's woodcut served as propaganda. The effect of this print and many other similar images can be gleaned from a report sent by the papal nuncio Aleander, who wrote the following in disbelief to Cardinal Giulio de' Medici, the vice-chancellor of the church, on December 18, 1521, in Worms: "Recently, he has been portrayed with the dove above his head and the Lord's Cross, or in a different image with a radiant crown; and people buy this, kiss it, and even carry it into the palace."[4] No comments by Luther himself on this phenomenon have survived; this, however, does not necessarily indicate that the Reformer was indifferent to the use and mass distribution of his image, which had even subsequently become an object of veneration. Luther fundamentally rejected the concept of saints as intercessors and bringers of salvation and the ritual veneration associated with them, but he considered the keeping of these figures as role models and witnesses of faith compatible with Christian life.[5] The Reformer himself was also perceived as being a role model in his staunch defense of his doctrine before powerful opponents. He was thus raised to the status of a martyr in Melchior Ramminger's thesis, also published in 1521, and his appearance before the Diet of Worms was compared with the Passion of Christ.[6] The canonization and heroizing of Luther was therefore not restricted to visual images but to other media, in particular numerous writings.[7]

Martin Luther's translation of the New Testament was a fundamental step for the Reformation. His consummate achievement of making the Gospel universally accessible suggests a particularly close association with one of the Evangelists. A woodcut illustration by Cranach the Elder in the *New Testament* printed by Hans Lufft in Wittenberg in 1529 depicts Saint Matthew with the features of Martin Luther (fig. 1).[8] The mirror held by the angel focuses the light of the

1 Cited in Heidrich, *Nachlass*, pp. 180 f. 2 Warnke, *Cranachs Luther*, pp. 23–31. 3 "If there is goodness in me, it is not my own, but that of my dear God and my Savior Jesus Christ whose gifts I should not deny, namely that I understand the Holy Scripture much (or at least slightly) better than before." *WA* 53, 256, 16–19. 4 Cited in Kalkoff, *Depeschen*, pp. 58 f. 5 See Pinoma, *Heiligen*. See also the contribution by Susanne Kimmig-Völkner to this volume. 6 Melchior Ramminger, Doctor Mar. Luthers Passio durch Marcellum beschrieben [1521]; id., Ain schöner newer Passion [1521]. 7 See Preuß, *Martin Luther*, pp. 28–72; Kolb, *For all the Saints*, pp. 103–138; Kolb, *Umgestaltung*; Scribner, *Sake*, p. 14–36; Kolb, *Prophet, Teacher, Hero*; Kaufmann, *Anfang*, pp. 266–333. 8 Here Cranach is possibly referencing Sebald Behams's woodcut depicting Luther with a mortarboard spiritually inspired during his translation of the New Testament. The image appears on the title page of Luther's New Testament published by Hans Hergot in 1524 in Nuremberg. Zschelletzschky, *Maler*, pp. 245–249. 9 "Ich hab mein theologiam nit auff ein mal gelernt, sonder hab immer tieffer und tieffer grubeln mussen." *WA*.TR 1, 146, 12, 352. 10 The *Physiologus* is a work dating from the

Holy Spirit on the Reformer, who is writing—an unorthodox motif that Cranach never repeated. Nevertheless, the image conveys the fact that Luther's translation was regarded as divine inspiration. Cranach does not depict Luther solely as an Evangelist but also as a scholar. He presents him as a learned man working in the privacy of his study, receiving enlightenment through conscientious study. At the same time, the woodcut highlights the significance of the theologian's intellectual achievements.[9] Here both aspects are irrevocably intertwined.

A further detail makes a reference to Luther's theological conflict with the church. Cranach places two partridges in the foreground, which the *Physiologus* interprets as a sign for the Imitation of Christ.[10] These creatures are said to steal and hatch eggs from other birds. When the fledglings turn into adults, however, they recognize their true mother and follow her, turning their backs on the false parents. Within the context of this role portrayal, the traditional source assumes a new significance in relation to the Reformation. Mature Christians accordingly follow the true doctrine of Martin Luther, turning away from the false doctrine of the early church. This is because Luther is the first to enable believers to comprehend the Gospel and follow Christ on the strength of his New Testament translation. The statement of the woodcut is addressed to a chosen circle: the readers of the New Testament in Martin Luther's translation. These readers will also find the truth of Christianity according to the principle *sola scriptura*, purely through serious Bible study. Unlike Hans Baldung's provocative one-page print, which sold quickly and in large quantities to the general public, Cranach's woodcut had more to offer to educated readers who will comprehend the allusions not only as a hagiographic classification of Luther's achievements, but also the instruction to become active, that is, undertake Bible study. The use of old viewing habits to convey a new message, however, presupposes a differentiated interpretation of what is displayed, which is highly dependent on the prior knowledge of the viewers and the context of the picture. The sacred role portrait used in this case to acknowledge Luther's achievement in the genuine proclamation of the Gospel was a common type of image and was also employed by Luther's adversary Cardinal Albert of Brandenburg. The cardinal had previously been portrayed twice by Cranach as Saint Jerome in his study (in 1525 and 1526) (see fig. 5 in the essay of Andreas Tacke in this volume), the church father who had compiled the *Vulgate*. There had therefore been no break in iconographical tradition. This kind of identification image could have varied foundations, making reference to analogies of virtue, status, name, or events.[11]

A visual parallel between Martin Luther and his name patron had been undertaken as early as 1519. Johannes Eck and Martin Luther confronted one another at the Leipzig Debate; it is presum-

Fig. 1 Lucas Cranach the Elder,
Luther as Apostle Matthew, 1529

ably no coincidence that one was portrayed below a picture of George the Dragon Slayer and the other below a representation of Saint Martin.[12] Luther himself saw his vocation and actions as an emulation of biblical saints, placing himself in the series of the Evangelists, apostles, and prophets.[13]

This is illustrated by a broadsheet produced by Jacob Lucius the Elder (fig. 2).[14] The woodcut manufactured between 1550 and 1560 transposes the historical event of salvation, the Baptism of Christ, to the flood plains of the River Elbe close to Wittenberg. The event is experienced by John Frederick the Magnanimous with his wife, Sibylle of Cleves, and their three sons, kneeling before the town of their residence, which had been lost after the Schmalkaldic War in 1547.

Early Christian period that provided a symbolic interpretation of the behavior and characteristics of animals, bringing them into connection with the Christian history of salvation; Lauchert, *Geschichte*, p. 20, no. 18. **11** Polleross, *Identifikationsporträt*; id., *Anfänge*. **12** Warnke, *Cranachs Luther*, p. 8. **13** "So say I, Doctor Martinus Luther, Evangelist of our Lord Jesus Christ…" *WA* 30, 3, 366, 8; "Wen ich mich rhümen wolte, mochte ich mich in gott noch woll der Aposteln und Evangelisten inn Deutschen lande einen rhümen, wens gleich dem teuffel und allen seinen bischoffen und Tyrannen leide were: denn ich weis, das ich den glawben und die wahrheit gelertt habe und noch lere von gots gnaden." *WA* 19, 261, 24; "Aber weil ich der Deutschen Prophet bin (Denn solchen hoffertigen namen mus ich mir hinfort selbs zu messen meinen Papisten und Eseln zur lust und Gefallen)" *WA* 30, 3, 290, 28. On Luther's self-perception, see Holl, *Luther*; Preuß, *Martin Luther*, pp. 96–130. **14** For more information on this woodcut, see Hofmann, *Luther*, pp. 228 f., cat. no. 101; Schade, *Kunst*, pp. 422–424, no. F 43; Bott, *Martin Luther*, p. 362, cat. no. 482; Koerner, *Reformation*, p. 76; Töpfer, *Vorbildwirkung*, pp. 43–45; Leps, *Taufe*, pp. 300 f., no. 227.

Fig. 2 Jacob Lucius the Elder, Broadsheet showing the Baptism of Christ in the Elbe near Wittenberg, witnessed by Luther and the Family of Prince Elector John Frederick the Magnanimous, 1556–58

Adhering to the example of traditional altarpieces, which feature depictions of their benefactors accompanied by saints, Martin Luther appears in this image as the patron saint, as it were, of the princely family. Standing behind the ruling couple, he has placed his hand on John Frederick's shoulder. Whereas the use of old church imagery leads observers to associate Luther's habitus with that of an interceding saint who is commending the princely couple to Jesus Christ, the text below the representation clarifies that the intercession is not the task of the Reformer, but a sign of the revealed grace of God. As in the predella of the *Wittenberg Altarpiece,* Luther is pointing to Christ as the sole redeemer. Within this context, the text of the broadsheet compares Luther to John the Baptist.[15] Therefore, Luther can here be seen as representing the Christocentric doctrine of justification adhered to by the princely dynasty. In this manner, the woodcut acts as a Protestant commemorative and denominational image, implying an exemplary affiliation of sacred and secular power and presenting the Ernestines as the protectors of the Wittenberg Reformation.[16] The representation of Luther as a type of patron saint is the expression of a tendency to elevate the Reformer as the highest authority in questions of faith. He thereby becomes the "symbol for the theological, political, and social movement that he represented."[17]

Lucas Cranach the Younger's Altar in St. Peter and Paul's Church in Weimar presents a genuine Protestant visual program (fig. 3). The central panel is a monumental depiction of Cranach's "Law and Grace" motif, illustrating Martin Luther's doctrine of justification. The typological juxtaposition of the motifs is executed here in the tonal depths of the painting, in which the scenes from the Old Testament in the background are prophetic of or contrast with the concepts of redemption depicted in the foreground. The Reformer himself is represented directly at the front as the antitype of Moses. He points to an open Bible, displaying it to observers and thereby again referencing the gestures of the prophets who direct sinners, tormented by death and the devil, to the tablets of commandments. Here Luther is setting the righteousness of works and the human fear of hell against the grace of God in the Sacrifice of the Cross. His gesture is primarily intended for the congregation gathered before the princely burial place which is thereby integrated into the events of salvation. His mediating role is, however, limited to the procla-

15 "As Saint John shows, the dear man was followed by Martin Luther in the land of Saxony." 16 Hofmann, *Luther*, p. 228; Töpfer, *Vorbildwirkung*, p. 45. 17 Kolb, *Umgestaltung*, p. 203.

Fig. 3 Lucas Cranach the Younger, Weimar Altar, 1555, Weimar, Town Church of St. Peter and St. Paul's (Herder Church)

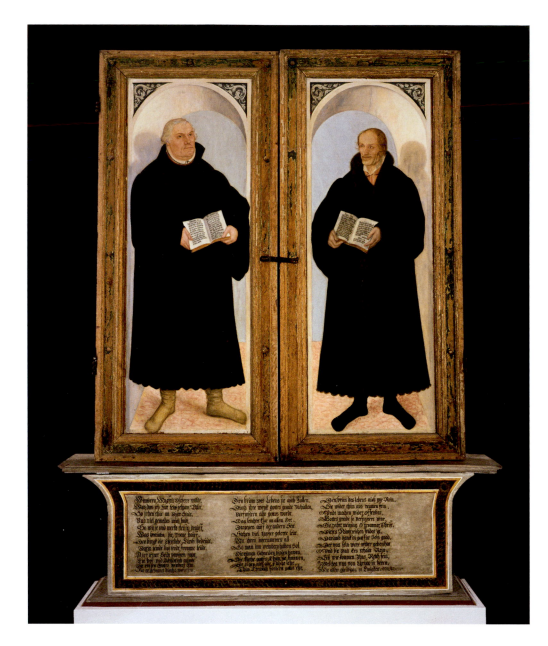

Fig. 4
Lucas Cranach the Younger,
The Vineyard Retable, closed with full length
portraits of Luther and Melanchthon, 1582,
Salzwedel, Johann-Friedrich-Danneil-Museum

mation of the Good News and does not extend to intercession with God. The disconcertingly prominent representation of Luther on the altar retable does not signify that the figure of the Reformer is granted saintliness in the old church sense of the term. Nevertheless, his implementation in the biblical scene transforms Luther into a witness, as well as makes him an integrative element of the events of salvation, which continue up to the present day. He is actively engaged in the events depicted on the central panel. Whereas John the Baptist points toward the crucified Christ and the Lamb of God, Luther interprets the bloody sacrifice within the context of the Holy Scripture, which he has thus given new validity.[18] The Ernestine family are acknowledging Luther's theological

authority through this altarpiece. As the political situation was unstable after the death of the Reformer, and the compromises achieved in the Interim of Augsburg in 1548 provoked intense intra-Protestant controversies, the prominent representation of Luther is also a declaration of belief in orthodox Lutheran doctrine on the part of the ruler and his family.[19]

Lucas Cranach the Younger's so-called Vineyard Retable from the Abbey Church in Salzwedel represents a further expression of denominational identity: a work unfurling not merely a pro-Reformatory but also an anti-Catholic concept (fig. 4).[20] The formal proximity of holy figures on altar retables and the depiction of the Reformer are particularly prominent in the life-size full-length portraits of Martin Luther

---

18 In the open book, the following text is legible: "The blood of Jesus Christ cleanses us of all our sins. Let us therefore come to the throne of grace that we might obtain mercy and find grace to help in times of need. And as Moses lifted up the serpent in the wilderness, so must the Son of man be lifted up, that all who believe in him should not perish, but have eternal life." 1 John 1:7; Hebrews 4:16; John 3:14 f. **19** Boettcher, *Cranach*, pp. 108 f.; Poscharsky, *Wittenberg*, pp. 279 f. **20** Currently housed in the Johann Friedrich Danneil Museum, Salzwedel; on the Vineyard Retable, see Kambach/Pietsch, *Weinberg-Altar.* **21** See Roberts, *Protestantische Kunst*, pp. 332. **22** On the theme of the vineyard in works of Cranach the Younger, see Schulze, *Lucas Cranach d. J.*, pp. 191–

Fig. 5 Veit Thiem, Luther Triptych, 1572, Weimar, St. Peter und Paul's Church (Herder Church)

and Philipp Melanchthon on the exterior panel of the side wings.[21] Prior to this period, only saints had been portrayed as individual figures on the exterior panels of altar wings. In this altarpiece, the saints are replaced with the Wittenberg reformers, not for the purpose of ritual veneration, but as the representatives of their doctrine.

Demonstratively and almost in a preaching manner, the pair present open books with legible texts to observers of the altar: in Luther's case, verses from the New Testament and, in Melanchthon's case, an interpretation of the Letter to the Romans. The images clearly illustrate the reformatory focus on the written word that they are conveying. The script on the predella provides an appropriate comment on the task of the reformers who are working in the vineyard of the Lord on the central panel: "They are eradicating all false doctrines […] and once more reveal the grace of God which had been so eclipsed. The righteous opinion, O you devout Christian, is the subject of this work of art."[22] The didactic value of the altar retable generally representing a pro-Reformatory visual program stands clearly in the foreground.

The full-length portraits of the reformers on the exterior altar wings are rooted in an iconographic tradition that was established after Luther's death in 1546. Since that time, independent life-size portraits of the Reformer have been found in almost all churches.

These depictions are all based on Luther's epitaph which was designed by Lucas Cranach the Younger and was to be set up in the Wittenberg Castle Curch. They all served both as a commemoration of the deceased and a recognition of the Reformation.[23] Their connection with the altar retable is, however, unique.

A further exception is Veit Thiem's so-called Luther Triptych (fig. 5).[24] The work is an iconic representation of the Reformer at three different stages of his life: on the left wing, he is portrayed as an Augustinian monk, on the right wing as Junker Jörg, and on the central panel as a Protestant cleric.[25] In the latter image, he is, however, not holding the Holy Script, but a book containing his personal prayer for his death.[26] The Christocentrism inconspicuously expressed in Luther's prayer appears at first glance to have been transformed into a form of Luther-centrism. Below the half-length portraits, the Reformer's biography is presented in verse form. The earliest reference to the triptych, which is currently housed in the City Church of Weimar, can be found in a list of Duke Ernest the Pious's Gotha Collection dating from 1644, indicating that the triptych was only used within private circles and not publicly displayed in a church. The triptych is most probably a work commissioned by John William, Duke of Saxe-Weimar, or his wife, Dorothy Susanna, illustrating the duke's strict Lutheran convictions.[27] The resemblance

202. **23** Slenczka, *Lebensgroß*; id., *Konfessionskultur*; id., *Cranach der Jüngere*, pp. 125 f. **24** On the Luther triptych, see Schulze, *Lucas Cranach*, pp. 118 f.; Koerner, *Reformation*, pp. 389 f.; Hoffmann, *Luthertriptychon*. **25** The frame and the hinges appear to originate from the nineteenth century. ibid., p. 16. **26** "My heavenly Father, one God and the Father of our Lord Jesus Christ, a God

of Grace, praise and thank you for revealing to me your Son Jesus Christ whom I affirm, whom I have loved and praised, whom the Pope in Rome and his horde of unbelievers have pursued and reviled. I therefore ask you, my dear Jesus Christ, to take my soul to you. O, my heavenly Father ..." **27** Hoffmann, *Luthertriptychon*, p. 35.

of the memorial work to a winged altarpiece was most probably intentional and suggests a personal rather than ritual veneration of Luther. The focus is on the remembrance of the deceased Reformer, which was to be kept alive through the representation of different stages of his life and his exemplary deeds.

The illustrated examples demonstrate a paradox of Protestant art that made use of conventional iconographic models to convey its own inherent message. This is equally true of representations of the Reformer. On the one hand, Luther rejected the veneration of saints, but, on the other, he himself was presented as one in words and images at a relatively early stage. Literature and art during the Reformation stylized Martin Luther as the chosen preacher of the Gospel, confessor and witness of the truth, evangelist, apostle, and prophet and the guarantor of true belief. This explains why Luther was even portrayed in individual portraits with a halo during the euphoric early phase of the Reformation as the divinely inspired monk and doctor of theology. The focus of Luther's personal and monastic piety was, however, his proximity to God. The recognizability of old church imagery suggests to observers that there was no break with the church. The continuity with tradition was upheld and renewal was sought merely through reference to biblical transmission. Here the reference to Luther's holiness is interconnected with the knowledge he obtained from his study of the Holy Script. The fact that Luther and other reformers had become increasingly integrated in biblical scenes since the 1540s reflects Luther's aspiration to concretize the Holy Script as the only valid source of truth whose witnesses and proclaimers are the followers of his doctrine. A further intention was the presentation and consequent legitimization of the Reformation in harmony with biblical history.[28]

Luther's primary task as reformer was to proclaim his doctrine of Grace based on the Gospel. An attempt was certainly made to emphasize this aspect in representations of his image by providing him with Holy Scripture as his attribute. As the message of salvation was, however, closely linked with the figure of the Reformer, the form and intention of these representations occasionally appeared to diverge in different directions. After Luther's death, the commemoration of the Reformer remained in the foreground, linked with the commitment to Luther's doctrine. The identification of Luther and other reformers with saints, which in modern times appears slightly disconcerting, has its foundations and justification in the transformation regarding the significance of the saints who were then merely conceived as models of faith. It is therefore no surprise that the papal nuncio Aleander was scandalized by the representation of Luther as a saint, whereas Luther's followers had no problems with this concept.

28 Boettcher, *Trägheit*, pp. 56 f.; Boettcher, *Luther*, pp. 94 f.

BIBLIOGRAPHY

Boettcher, Susan R. (2004), Are the Cranach Luther Altarpieces Philippist? Memory of Luther and Knowledge of the Past in the Late Reformation. In: Lindemann, Mary (ed.), *Ways of Knowing. Ten Interdisciplinary Essays*. Boston/Leiden, pp. 85–112. **Boettcher**, Susan R. (2003), Von der Trägheit der Memoria. Cranachs Lutheraltarbilder im Zusammenhang der evangelischen Luther-Memoria im späten 16. Jahrhundert. In: Eibach, Joachim/Sandl, Marcus (eds.), *Protestantische Identität und Erinnerung. Von der Reformation bis zur Bürgerrechtsbewegung der DDR*. Göttingen, pp. 47–70. **Bott**, Gerhard (ed.) (1983), *Martin Luther und die Reformation in Deutschland*. Frankfurt am Main. **Heidrich**, Ernst (ed.) (1908), *Albrecht Dürers schriftlicher Nachlass. Familienchronik, Gedenkbuch, Tagebuch der niederländischen Reise, Briefe, Reime, Auswahl aus den theoretischen Schriften: mit neun Zeichnungen und drei Holzschnitten Dürers*. Berlin. **Hoffmann**, Helga (2015), *Das Weimarer Luthertriptychon von 1572. Sein konfessionspolitischer Kontext und sein Maler Veit Thiem* (= Beiträge zur Thüringischen Kirchengeschichte. NF 5). Langenweißbach/Erfurt. **Hofmann**, Werner (ed.) (1983), *Luther und die Folgen für die Kunst*. München. **Holl**, Karl (1932), *Luther* (= Gesammelte Aufsätze zur Kirchengeschichte. 1), 6th ed. Tübingen. **Kalkoff**, Paul (1897), *Die Depeschen des Nuntius Aleander vom Wormser Reichstage 1521*. Halle (Saale). **Kambach**, Ulrich/**Pietsch**, Jürgen M. (eds.) (1996), *Der Weinberg-Altar von Lucas Cranach dem Jüngeren aus der Mönchskirche in Salzwedel*. Spröda. **Kaufmann**, Thomas (2012), *Der Anfang der Reformation. Studien zur Kontextualität der Theologie, Publizistik und Inszenierung Luthers und der reformatorischen Bewegung*. Tübingen. **Koerner**, Joseph Leo (2008), *The Reformation of the Image*. Chicago. **Kolb**, Robert (1987), *For all the Saints. Changing Perceptions of Martydom and Sainthood in the Lutheran Reformation*. Macon/GA. **Kolb**, Robert (1988), Die Umgestaltung und theologische Bedeutung des Lutherbildes im späten 16. Jahrhundert. In: Rublack, Hans-Christoph (ed.) (1992), *Die lutherische Konfessionalisierung in Deutschland: Wissenschaftliches Symposion des Vereins für Reformationsgeschichte 1988*. Gütersloh, pp. 202–231. **Kolb**, Robert (1999), *Martin Luther as a Prophet, Teacher, Hero. Images of the Reformer, 1520–1620*. Grand Rapids/MI. **Lauchert**, Friedrich (1889), *Geschichte des Physiologus von Dr. Friedrich Lauchert*. Straßburg. **Leps**, Sabrina (2015), Taufe Christi in der Elbe im Beisein Martin Luthers und Johann Friedrichs des Großmütigen mit seiner Familie. In: Syndram, Dirk (ed.): *Luther und die Fürsten. Selbstdarstellung und Selbstverständnis des Herrschers im Zeitalter der Reformation*. Dresden, pp. 300 f. **Pinoma**, Lennart (1977), *Die Heiligen bei Luther*. Helsinki. **Polleross**, Friedrich (1993), *Das sakrale Identifikationsporträt. Ein höfischer Bildtypus vom 13. bis zum 20. Jahrhundert* (= Manuskripte zur Kunstwissenschaft. 18). 2 vols. Worms. **Polleross**, Friedrich (1993), Die Anfänge des Identifikationsporträts im höfischen und städtischen Bereich. In: *Frühneuzeit-Info*, vol. 4, pp. 17–36. **Poscharsky**, Peter (2015), Von Wittenberg nach Weimar. In: Seyderhelm, Bettina (ed.), *Cranach-Werke am Ort ihrer Bestimmung*. Regensburg, pp. 274–295. **Preuss**, Hans (1933), *Martin Luther. Der Prophet*. Gütersloh. **Roberts**, Daniela (2007), Protestantische Kunst im Zeitalter der Konfessionalisierung. Die Bildnisse der Superintendenten im Chorraum der Thomaskirche zu Leipzig. In: Wegmann, Susanne/Wimböck, Gabriele (eds.), *Konfessionen im Kirchenraum*. Leipzig, pp. 325–344. **Schade**, Günter (ed.) (1983), *Kunst der Reformationszeit*. Berlin. **Schulze**, Ingrid (2004), *Lucas Cranach d. J. und die protestantische Bildkunst in Sachsen und Thüringen*. Bucha. **Scribner**, Robert W. (1994), *For the Sake of Simple Folk*. Cambridge. **Slenczka**, Ruth (2001), Lebensgroß und unverwechselbar. Lutherbildnisse in Kirchen 1546–1617. In: *Luther. Zeitschrift der Luther-Gesellschaft*, vol. 82, pp. 99–116. **Slenczka**, Ruth (2011), Städtische Konfessionskultur im Spiegel der Kirchenausstattung. Die Mönchskirche von Salzwedel und das Weinbergretabel von Lucas Cranach d. J. (1582). In: Fajt, Jiří/Franzen, Wilfried/Knüvener, Peter (eds.), *Die Altmark von 1300 bis 1600. Eine Kulturregion im Spannungsfeld von Magdeburg/Lübeck/Berlin*. Berlin, pp. 421–493. **Slenczka**, Ruth (2015), Cranach der Jüngere im Dienst der Reformation. In: Enke, Roland/Schneider, Katja/Strehle, Jutta (eds.), *Lucas Cranach der Jüngere. Entdeckung eines Meisters*. München, pp. 125–137. **Töpfer**, Thomas (2012), Zwischen bildungskultureller Vorbildwirkung und politischer Legitimitätsstiftung. Die Universität Wittenberg in der lutherischen Bildungslandschaft der zweiten Hälfte des 16. Jahrhunderts. In: Tanner, Klaus (ed.), *Konstruktionen von Geschichte. Jubelrede—Predigt—protestantische Historiographie* (= Leucorea-Studien zur Geschichte der Reformation und der Lutherischen Orthodoxie. 18). Leipzig, pp. 43–45. **Warnke**, Martin (1984), *Cranachs Luther. Entwürfe für ein Image*. Frankfurt am Main. **Zschelletzschky**, Herbert (1975), *Die "drei gottlosen Maler" von Nürnberg. Sebald Beham, Barthel Beham und Georg Pencz. Historische Grundlagen und ikonologische Probleme ihrer Graphik zu Reformations- und Bauernkriegszeit*. Leipzig 1975.

ANJA TIETZ

Martin Luther and the Changes in German Burial Practice in the Sixteenth Century

Apart from special arrangements during times of plague in the late Middle Ages, the first large burial sites situated outside settlements (sometimes called "God's acres," or *Gottesäcker*) were established in Germany after 1500. These replaced the burial plots that had characterized churchyards inside villages and towns throughout the Middle Ages. Emperor Maximilian I (fig. 1) played an important role in the burial reforms of the early modern era. So did Pope Julius II and Pope Leo X, who wanted to move the burial sites outside of the areas where people lived and worked partially because the churchyards there were too small but, above all, for reasons of hygiene.[1] From 1506 onward, Emperor Maximilian pursued the establishment of a burial site outside the residential city of Innsbruck. It was consecrated in 1510. After the creation of this cemetery, the Emperor determined to attain further papal privileges of this kind for the lands under his reign, including Freiburg, Constance, Vienna, Graz, and Nuremberg.

The measures taken corresponded to both the growth in population since the late Middle Ages and new knowledge about medicine and hygiene gained during the late Middle Ages and the early modern era. This knowledge was influenced by Greek physicians of antiquity such as Hippocrates and Galen, as well as the Persian physician Avicenna. The Twelve Tables, from around 450 B.C.E., only allowed burial outside of settlements: "A dead person should never be buried or cremated within the city."[2] Notions about medicine and hygiene were limited in the late Middle Ages and early modern era, compared with later times. But they strongly influenced burial practice for a long time. We can recognize the tendency to move burial sites in various kinds of sources: in the recommendations from physicians, the decrees of rulers, essays in political science, and writings on the theory of architecture (whose principles have their foundations in antiquity and remain valid in the modern era). In addition, the closing of churchyards within the boundaries of towns was pursued because they had become too small in the late Middle Ages. We find this phenomenon particularly in German residential and imperial cities.[3]

Beyond this, one can observe first signs of the secularization and communalization of burials in the early modern era. The city administration was heavily involved in the creation of new burial sites outside city walls. Repeatedly, burial sites next to communal hospitals outside the city became new cemeteries for the citizens. Sources report that the moving of burial plots out of the areas where people lived was somewhat problematic from the outset. In many places, such attempts involved prolonged debates between city rulers, the church, and the population, and opposition arose for various reasons. In order to make extramural cemeteries attractive for the population, in many cases they were furnished with witnesses to the adoration of the Passion of Christ (Holy Soil, Holy Sepulcher, Via Dolorosa). Additionally, new burial sites were frequently made more attractive by employing special architecture.[4]

Around twenty years after the first attempts by Emperor Maximilian I to alter burial practices, Martin Luther gave his opinion on the matter in his publication, *Whether One May Flee from the Deadly Plague* (1527). Luther wrote this piece in the context of the outbreak of plague in Breslau and in response to the request of the Breslau pastors for a relocation of burial plots (fig. 2).[5] Luther's approval led to his recommendation being taken up in the Protestant Church orders and the movement of burial sites, advocated under the banner of Reformation. Luther's arguments for a burial site outside of town were, alongside reasons of health, both biblical arguments and ones based on the pastoral concern of fostering rest and devotion. As Barbara Happe recognizes, in the sixteenth century, when many of these cemeteries were established, "there began a wave of relocation of general cemeteries which took on a scope hitherto unknown in the history of Christian burial sites."[6]

Because of Luther's stance, the location of burial sites became a confessional statement in the early modern era. What was originally a hygienic measure thus became an indicator of support for Luther,

1 For more background and an extensive bibliography, see Tietz, *Gottesacker*. On burials in the sixteenth century, see also: Grün, *Friedhof*; Melchert, *Entwicklung*; Derwein, *Geschichte*; Schweizer, *Kirchhof und Friedhof*; Hüppi, *Kunst und Kult*; Peiter, *Friedhof*; Happe, *Entwicklung*; Illi, *Toten*; Koslofsky, *Trennung*; id., *Konkurrierende Konzepte*; id., *Reformation*. **2** From Table 10. Cited according to: Flach, *Zwölftafelgesetz*, p. 146. **3** See in greater detail Tietz, *Gottesacker*. **4** See in greater detail ibid. **5** Whether One May Flee from a Deadly Plague. In: *LW* 43, 115–139; Ob man vor dem sterben fliehen möge [1527]. In: *WA* 23, 323–386. **6** Happe, *Entwicklung*, p. 186.

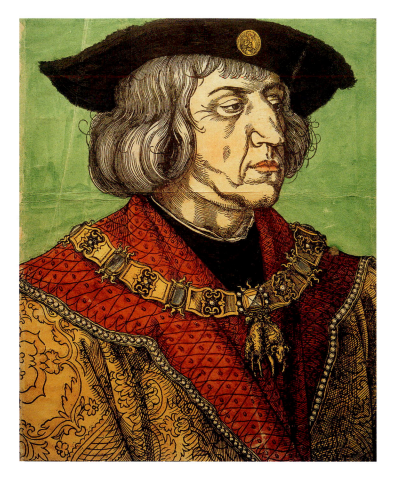

Fig. 1 Hans Burgkmair the Elder (after Albrecht Dürer),
Portrait of Emperor Maximilian I, 1519

the cemetery had been established, and fifteen years after the introduction of the Reformation in Halle in 1542, the cemetery was enclosed by its unique arcades built between 1557 and 1590.[8]

Its antithesis in terms of foundation story is the cemetery in the residential and mining town of Eisleben, in the county of Mansfeld (fig. 4). It was established in 1533 on unconsecrated farmland to the northeast of the town, most likely on Luther's recommendations. The counts of Mansfeld, the city fathers, and, not least, the Lutheran pastor Caspar Güttel would have all played an important role. Although Catholic priest Georg Witzel had been at St. Andrew's Church in Eisleben since the summer of 1533 (the city of Eisleben still had dual confessions at that time), he was not mentioned at all in connection with the new cemetery. He railed against cemeteries outside cities and against the followers of Martin Luther in his essay *Von den Todten und yhrem Begrebnus* ("On the Dead and Their Burial"), which was printed repeatedly in Catholic Leipzig from 1535 on. Soon after the cemetery in Eisleben had been established, the city fathers had a surrounding portico built in 1538–39, with more added to it in 1560. The portico may have been inspired by the Leipzig cemetery. Like the later architecture at the city cemetery in Halle, it served as a place of rest for the upper class.[9]

The arrangement and styling of these new cemeteries outside cities after 1500 proved a particular challenge for the initiators of burial reforms. Alongside the holy earth procured from the Vatican Teutonic Cemetery and the creation of burial sites at holy graves and crossroads, the architectural design used for the new burial places played a significant role in improving the population's acceptance and appreciation of them. The new type of architecture used *Schwibbögen* (German for diaphragm arches) of various forms, and became prevalent both in Catholic areas and in those influenced by Luther's teachings, as demonstrated by written recommendations concerning the burial sites' design. As far as we know, this type of construction first emerged in 1513–14 at the aforementioned Innsbruck cemetery of the Hospital of the Holy Spirit. In the sixteenth and seventeenth centuries, cemeteries with diaphragm arches were established in numerous cities. This architectural term refers to highly decorated arcades, as in Innsbruck, but also to column installations reminiscent of protective roofs. The early and frequent occurrence of these designs in Central Germany could be explained by Martin Luther's recommendation to move burial sites and attend to their special upkeep.[10]

The confessional status of the burial sites and their users could be recognized by the way in which the sites were arranged. The difference between a Protestant and a Catholic cemetery became visible by the fact that besides the usual chapel Protestants placed a pulpit in the center of their cemeteries. Regarding the form of burial, the individual burial plot, and the burial ceremony, in Lutheran areas a change of emphasis was seen from the afterlife to this earthly life, from the dead to the living. The new faith was manifest, for instance, in inscriptions and sculptures, but also in the increasingly common use of funeral sermons.[11]

Since original decorations are extant in only a few cases, the works of art from the Eisleben cemetery are especially remarkable

as the writings of Georg Witzel and his son suggest. Thus, if Catholic towns also joined the Lutheran movement, this might well have been due to a joint desire for better conditions in town churchyards. The most recent studies clarify the conditions under which the cemeteries were created and designed in Central Germany during the sixteenth century.[7] In spite of sometimes scant source material, we can work out important basic characteristics of their construction. With respect to the background of their creation, there are strong differences which correspond to the various motivations for establishing a burial site at the beginning of the sixteenth century.

The cemetery at the Episcopal see and trading city of Halle was founded outside the city in 1529 in the wake of Emperor Maximilian's reform of burial practices, and was inspired by the example of St. John's and St. Roch's cemeteries in Nuremberg, consecrated in 1519 (fig. 3). The initiator of the Halle cemetery, apart from the town council, was above all Hohenzollern Cardinal and Archbishop of Magdeburg, Albert of Brandenburg. In the first half of the sixteenth century, he developed the city into an archbishop's residence and a bulwark against the Reformation in Wittenberg. However, the improvement of hygiene in the city also played an important role for him, as it did for other rulers. After three years of deliberations with the council, an extended cemetery was established at St. Martin's Chapel (to the east of Halle, and outside the city). This site had already been used in the Middle Ages when plagues broke out. Around thirty years after

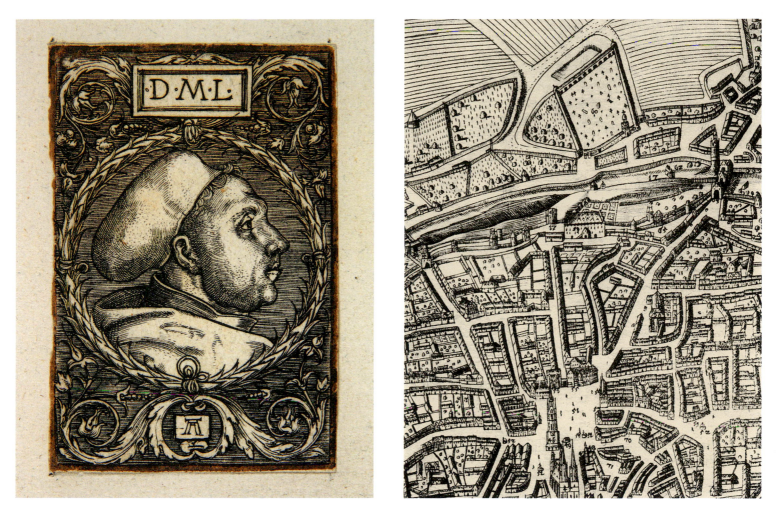

Fig. 2 Albrecht Altdorfer, Martin Luther with Doctoral Cap, before 1530

Fig. 3 City map of Halle, conceived by Councilor Johann Kost and Librarian Nicolaus Keyser. Drawn by Friedrich Daniel Bretschneider
and engraved by Johann Wüsthoff (copper plate engraving), appendix to: Gottfried Olearius, Halygraphia Topo-Chronologica […], Leipzig 1667.
The Town Cemetery lies outside the walls and can be seen in the upper third of the picture as a slightly oblique rectangle

(fig. 5). As investigations have shown, they were clearly created by leading artists of the region of Saxony. In terms of their content and design, they point in most cases to the Cranach workshop, whose iconographic repertoire was often imitated.[12] Repeated motifs on the epitaphs at the Eisleben Cemetery are the suffering, crucifixion, and resurrection of Christ; resurrection scenes; and the confession of orthodox faith. In several cases there are complex theological statements. Inscriptions often refer to an exact Bible verse. In terms of content, these epitaphs are closely connected with Martin Luther and his teachings, as is shown for example by the early epitaph for the family of the mining proprietor Wolf Buchner from 1557–58 as well as the epitaph for the Heidelberg family from 1561. Large epitaphs in churches often take the form of a triptych and thus continue the tradition of personal altarpieces, but only in the case of Eisleben do we have an example of an epitaph with multiple panels from a cemetery. The format of the epitaphs in the cemetery at Eisleben was generally simpler—quadrangular or, in conformity with the rearward wall-niche, half-round. The Halle Cemetery, named a *coemiterium* (resting place) in Lutheran fashion, is in various ways a vehicle of

Reformation thought. Alongside the inscriptions and unparalleled reliefs of the arcades, which teach the faith in a special way, the memorial rooms were lavishly embellished with paintings since the seventeenth century at the latest. The emphasis of the images and inscriptions was placed on biblical scenes that featured Christ (mostly in his death and resurrection).

The new type of architecture brought with it the preconditions for an elaborate grave design. In comparison with other burial sites with a similar kind of architecture, the Halle Cemetery arcades were adorned with unparalleled artistic decoration (fig. 6). Although a large number of the original arches are no longer preserved, early photographs and drawings demonstrate their erstwhile design. Both the spandrel areas and the pillars were decorated with typical Renaissance motifs: tendrils and strapwork, cornucopias, fruit, hybrid

---

7 See Tietz, *Gottesacker*. **8** Ibid. **9** See ibid. **10** See in greater detail ibid. **11** On funeral sermons, see below and in more detail Tietz, *Gottesacker*. **12** See Wipfler, *Greber*; Schulze, *Epitaphgemälde*.

Fig. 4 Historical town view of Eisleben seen from the North.
The cemetery is shown in the foreground to the right.

Fig. 5 Epitaph of the family of the mining entrepreneur Wolf Buchner from Eisleben Town Cemetery
(formerly diaphragm arch no. 23), 1557/58. Presently at the museum Martin Luther's Birth House, Lutherstadt Eisleben

and mythical creatures, birds, masks, heads, and cherubs. In addition, in some cases family crests were incorporated directly into the design or attached to the middle of the arch as an individually worked piece. We can assume on account of the very individual design of the arches that the motifs were largely chosen by those paying for the work.

The unique characteristic of the Halle Cemetery reliefs is surely the playfulness of the motifs. They remind us of the representations of the heavenly garden with its plants and fruit, or of prayer book illustrations with tendril and flower motifs that can also be interpreted christologically. We can assume that the effect of the design was intended, since for Martin Luther, death appears in a new light than previously taught. It is not punishment, but sleep that leads to new life. In his Easter sermon of 1532, Luther says: "If you see a Christian die and see nothing more than a dead corpse lying there, and before your eyes and ears there is only the grave, songs for the dead, words for the dead, vain death, then you should remove such a deathly picture from your sight and in faith see another picture in its place. Not as if you saw a grave and a dead body, but vain life and a beautiful, airy garden and paradise, and in it no dead person, but only new, living, joyful people."[13] In one of his table talks of the same year, Luther said of the afterlife, in accordance with the book of Revelation, "in Christ we all possess eternal life; there will be a new heaven and a new earth, where grass and flowers will be as beautiful as emeralds and all creatures in their splendor."[14] The playfully arranged tendrils with various motifs seem to be a symbol for the lightness of heart with which Luther was able to face human death.

Alongside pictorial representations, inscriptions are part of graves, especially in Lutheran Protestantism. In connection with his theological teachings, Luther thought long and hard about appropriate Bible verses for burial sites and made numerous recommendations.[15] Since the Word of God and right exegesis of scripture are central to Luther's theology, Bible verses are constitutive elements of the burial site. But Luther also thought the combination of text and illustration was good—for Bibles, wall-paintings, and altars. After he had recommended "death, the final judgment, and resurrection" as fitting pictorial representations in 1527, he wrote in 1542 in the preface to his book of funeral hymns: "If the graves should be honored in other ways, it would be fine to paint or write good epitaphs or verses from scripture on the walls above (where there are such) so that they may be seen by those who go to a funeral or to the cemetery."[16] Additionally, he wrote: "Such verses and inscriptions would more fittingly adorn a cemetery than other secular emblems, such as shields and helmets."[17]

Luther also suggested twenty-six inscriptions, of which four were rendered in rhyme to aid memory: Gen. 49:29 (free paraphrase); Job 19:25 f.; Ps. 3:6; Ps. 4:9a; Ps. 17:15; Ps. 49:16; Ps. 116:15; Isa. 25:7 f.; Isa. 26:19; Isa. 26:20; Isa. 57:1 f. (free paraphrase); Ezek. 37:12; Dan. 12:2; Hos. 13:14; Exod. 3:6a and Matt. 22:32b; John 6:39; Rom. 14:7–9; 1 Cor. 15:19; 1 Cor. 15:22; 1 Cor. 15:54b-57; Phil. 1:21; 1 Thess. 4:14; Luke 2:29 f. (free rhyme); Luke 2:29–32 (free rhyme); John 11:25 f. (free rhyme); Job 19:25–27 (free rhyme).[18] The content of the Bible verses reflect Luther's view of death and burial. The texts make reference

above all to the resurrection of the dead. Like John 11:25 f. ("Christ is the truth, he is the life / And resurrection he will give / Who trust in him will life obtain / Though he may in the grave have lain / Who lives and trusts will never die / But praise him in eternity") they make it clear that assurance of salvation is the central point of the doctrine. This would later be discussed intensively at the Council of Trent (1545–63). A comparison between those inscriptions recommended by Martin Luther and those present in the Halle Cemetery reveals that the majority overlap: of the twenty-six recommended sayings in the foreword to the funeral hymns, most can be found in the arcades of the city cemetery.[19]

The elements of the funeral ceremony were also intended to bear witness to and demonstrate eschatological optimism. This optimism can be seen, for example, in the funeral music and sermons that begin in Central Germany, the most important area of the Reformation. Thus, the cemetery became one of "the most important places for the proclamation of the divine word,"[20] not only iconographically, but on all other levels. Therefore, alongside the church building, the cemetery belongs to the "genuine places of the creation of confessional identity."[21] In the end, the consequence of both the new design of cemeteries and a new type of funeral ceremony was a proclamation by various means, as Martin Luther would have desired: "Indeed, one cannot bring God's words and deeds too often to the attention of the common man. Even if God's word is sung and said, preached and proclaimed, written and read, illustrated and pictured, Satan and his cohorts are always strong and alert for hindering and suppressing God's word. Hence our project and concern is not only useful, but necessary—in fact, very badly needed."[22]

It is important here to recognize that the Wittenberg Reformation both continued with the tradition and innovatively developed it. The funeral ceremony had to give comfort as well as proclaim and strengthen the faith of those present. The burial site was designed appropriately as a place of rest and devotion. Contrary to the objections of Luther's opponent Georg Witzel that those who followed the Reformer neglected graves, we can observe a special aesthetic care in the sixteenth and seventeenth centuries.

Other reformers also worked to change burial practices. Huldrych Zwingli and his successors spoke out in favor of moving burial sites outside of Zurich for reasons of hygiene and to hinder grave-cults.[23] What greater comfort can be offered for the grieving than prayer for the deceased, the announcement of his or her name from the pulpit after death, the accompaniment of the dead to the grave, and subsequent prayer in the church? However, great difficulties arose in carrying through with the new approach to the dead and their graves.

13 WA 36, 161 (Sermon of March 31, 1532). This sermon is not included in LW. This citation is based on the German rendering according to Steinwede, Martin Luther, p. 132. 14 Quoted according to: Steinwede, Martin Luther, p. 128. 15 See also Tietz, Stadtgottesacker, pp. 32–34. 16 On the following, see LW 53, 328; WA 35, 480. 17 LW 53, 330; WA 35, 481. 18 LW 53, 328–331; WA 35, 480–483. 19 See Tietz, Gottesacker. 20 Harasimowicz, Heilsgewissheit, p. 129. 21 Wimböck, Kirchenraum, Bilderraum, Handlungsraum, p. 34. 22 WA 10/II, 458 f.; LW 43, 43. 23 See Rohner-Baumberger, Begräbniswesen, pp. 11 f., 101–103.

Fig. 6 Halle, City Cemetery, arch no. 23 (originally 13) with reliefs and banderol in the region of the architrave

The reformers in Geneva before and after Jean Calvin were of the opinion that the church's role in the case of death should be restricted to a pastoral conversation with the grieving family because the church is for the living.[24]

In 1536, an extramural plague-cemetery outside the city (*Plainpalais*) was declared a general burial ground without gravestones and was divided into areas according to social status. The dead were laid in the ground naked, without ceremony, and without the accompaniment of the pastor. There was merely a prayer said for their rest until the resurrection. Private notes reveal that even convinced supporters had problems with these radical ideas.[25]

Later Developments

Although burial sites outside town boundaries were established in numerous German cities in the sixteenth century, other towns held on to tradition and only moved their cemeteries during the second wave of relocation in the eighteenth and nineteenth centuries.[26] This later reform of burial practices was again advocated by the Emperor—this time, Joseph II. The reasons given for removing the graves from the city were the lack of space in churchyards and warnings from physicians.[27]

In connection with renewed burial reforms, the type of construction popularized in the Holy Roman Empire of the German Nation during the sixteenth century developed further. As described in a study from 1825: "If a large sum is on offer for the creation of a cemetery, the surrounding wall can be either wholly or partly furnished with porticos and arcades. In such halls, monuments of value and significance find their places and this arrangement is not only the most beautiful, but also the most appropriate. If on account of the costs it is not possible to surround the churchyard completely in this way with arcades, then perhaps the upper end wall can be thus decorated. If there is space, this end can form a semicircle, or at the end of the site a mortuary can be built, with arcades to the left and the right."[28] The form which once emerged in the design of burial sites outside towns has found repeated application right up to the present day. One example is the city cemetery of Brixen (South Tyrol), which was last extended in 1990 and surrounded with arcades.

24 See ibid., pp. 17–31. **25** See Kammeier-Nebel, *Wandel*, p. 107. **26** See Happe, *Entwicklung*, p. 15 (map); id., *Ordnung und Hygiene*. **27** See Steckner, *Luftangst*; Happe, *Gottesäcker*. **28** Voit, *Anlegung und Umwandlung*, p. 12.

BIBLIOGRAPHY

Derwein, Herbert (1931), *Geschichte des christlichen Friedhofs in Deutschland.* Frankfurt am Main. **Flach**, Dieter (ed.) (2004), *Das Zwölftafelgesetz* (= Texte zur Forschung. 83). Darmstadt. **Grün**, Hugo (1925), Der deutsche Friedhof im 16. Jahrhundert. In: *Hessische Blätter für Volkskunde*, vol. 24, pp. 64–97. **Happe**, Barbara (1981), *Die Entwicklung der deutschen Friedhöfe von der Reformation bis 1870* (= Untersuchungen des Ludwig-Uhland-Instituts der Universität Tübingen im Auftrag der Tübinger Vereinigung für Volkskunde. 77). Tübingen. **Happe**, Barbara (1988), Gottesäcker gegen Mitnacht und freyer Durchzug der Winde. Hygiene auf dem Friedhof des 18. und 19. Jahrhunderts. In: *Jahrbuch des Instituts für Geschichte der Medizin der Robert Bosch Stiftung*, vol. 7, pp. 205–231. **Happe**, Barbara (2003), Ordnung und Hygiene. Friedhöfe in der Aufklärung und die Kommunalisierung des Friedhofswesens. In: Arbeitsgemeinschaft Friedhof und Denkmal. Zentralinstitut und Museum für Sepulkralkultur Kassel (eds.), *Raum für Tote. Die Geschichte der Friedhöfe von den Gräberstraßen der Römerzeit bis zur anonymen Bestattung.* Braunschweig, pp. 83–110. **Harasimwicz**, Jan (1996), Die "Heilsgewissheit" in der nordeuropäischen Sepulkralkunst des 16. Jahrhunderts. In: id. (ed.), *Kunst als Glaubensbekenntnis. Beiträge zur Kunst- und Kulturgeschichte der Reformationszeit* (= Studien zur deutschen Kunstgeschichte. 359). Baden-Baden, pp. 127–143. **Hüppi**, Adolf (1968), *Kunst und Kult der Grabstätten.* Olten. **Illi**, Martin (1992), *Wohin die Toten gingen. Begräbnis und Kirchhof in der vorindustriellen Stadt.* Zürich. **Kammeier-Nebel**, Andrea (1999), Der Wandel des Totengedächtnisses in privaten Aufzeichnungen unter dem Einfluß der Reformation. In: Arnold, Klaus/Schmolinsky, Sabine/Zahnd, Urs Martin (eds.), *Das dargestellte Ich. Studien zu Selbstzeugnissen des späteren Mittelalters und der frühen Neuzeit* (= Selbstzeugnisse des Mittelalters und der beginnenden Neuzeit. 1). Bochum, pp. 93–116. **Koslofsky**, Craig (1995), Die Trennung der Lebenden von den Toten: Friedhofsverlegungen und die Reformation in Leipzig, 1536. In: Oexle, Otto Gerhard (ed.), *Memoria als Kultur* (= Veröffentlichungen des Max-Planck-Instituts für Geschichte. 121). Göttingen, pp. 335–385. **Koslofsky**, Craig (1999), Konkurrierende Konzepte von Gemeinschaft und die Verlegung der Friedhöfe, Leipzig (1536). In: id./Jussen, Bernhard (eds.), *Kulturelle Reformation. Sinnformationen im Umbruch. 1400–1600* (= Veröffentlichungen des Max-Planck-Instituts für Geschichte. 145). Göttingen, pp. 193–208. **Koslofsky**, Craig (2000), *The Reformation of the Dead. Death and Ritual in Early Modern Germany, 1450–1700.* New York et al. **Melchert**, Herbert (1929), *Die Entwicklung der deutschen Friedhofsordnungen.* Dessau. **Peiter**, Katharina (1968), *Der evangelische Friedhof—von der Reformation bis zur Romantik.* 2 vols. PhD thesis, Humboldt-Universität Berlin. **Rohner-Baumberger**, Ursula (1975), *Das Begräbniswesen im calvinistischen Genf,* PhD thesis, Universität Basel. **Schulze**, Ingrid (2000), Protestantische Epitaphgemälde aus der Zeit um 1560/70 in Eisleben. In: Jendryschik, Roswitha (ed.), *Mitteldeutschland, das Mansfelder Land und die Stadt Halle. Neuere Forschungen zur Landes- und Regionalgeschichte. Protokoll des Kolloquiums zum einhundertsten Geburtstag von Erich Neuß am 28./29. Mai 1999 in Halle* (= Beiträge zur Regional- und Landeskultur Sachsen-Anhalts. 15). Halle (Saale), pp. 131–155. **Schweizer**, Johannes (1956), *Kirchhof und Friedhof. Eine Darstellung der beiden Haupttypen europäischer Begräbnisstätten.* Linz. **Steckner**, Cornelius (1979), Über die Luftangst. Chemische Anmerkungen zum Tod. In: Boehlke, Hans-Kurt (ed.), *Wie die Alten den Tod gebildet. Wandlungen der Sepulkralkultur 1750–1850* (= Kasseler Studien zur Sepulkralkultur. 1). Mainz, pp. 147–150. **Steinwede**, Dietrich (2006), *Martin Luther. Leben und Wirken des Reformators.* Düsseldorf. **Tietz**, Anja (2012), *Der frühneuzeitliche Gottesacker. Entstehung und Entwicklung unter besonderer Berücksichtigung des Architekturtypus Camposanto in Mitteldeutschland* (= Beiträge zur Denkmalkunde. 8), Halle (Saale). **Tietz**, Anja A. (2004), *Der Stadtgottesacker in Halle (Saale),* Halle (Saale). **Voit**, Michael (1825), *Ueber die Anlegung und Umwandlung der Gottesäcker in heitere Ruhegärten der Abgeschiedenen. Ein Wort zu seiner Zeit an alle christlichen Gemeinden Teutschlands.* Augsburg. **Wimböck**, Gabriele (2007), Kirchenraum, Bilderraum, Handlungsraum: Die Räume der Konfessionen. In: Wegmann, Susanne/Wimböck, Gabriele (eds.), *Konfessionen im Kirchenraum. Dimensionen des Sakralraums in der Frühen Neuzeit* (= Studien zur Kunstgeschichte des Mittelalters und der Frühen Neuzeit. 3). Korb, pp. 31–54. **Wipfler**, Esther Pia (2000), "Wenn man auch sonst die Greber wolt ehren…" Zu den gemalten Epitaphien des Eisleber Kronenfriedhofes. In: Knape, Rosemarie (ed.), *Aufsätze zur Ausstellung "… von daher bin ich." Martin Luther und der Bergbau im Mansfelder Land, vom 25. März bis 12. November 2000 in Martin Luthers Sterbehaus Eisleben,* Eisleben, pp. 281–305.

AUSTRA REINIS

Martin Luther and the Art of Dying

In the Middle Ages, people usually died in their homes, cared for by their families, in contrast to the modern era, in which many people leave home to die in a hospital or nursing home. Death and dying were not hidden away but took place in plain sight not only of adults, but also of teenagers and children. Much more often than is the case today, death came to people early and unexpectedly. Repeated waves of the plague and other infectious diseases killed adults and children too; women often died in childbirth; the infection of a small wound could have deadly consequences.

In a Christian society in which religion played a much larger role than it does today, most dying persons sought the assistance of a priest to prepare them for a "good death" and a peaceful transition from this life into the next. In what follows, I will characterize the spiritual care that dying persons received from medieval clergy, in other words, the type of care that Martin Luther would have witnessed as a child and a young man. I will proceed to describe how his principal theological insights led Luther to reform the spiritual care offered to the dying, and how Luther's approach to pastoral care was appropriated by his colleagues and followers. In conclusion, I will comment on how the Lutheran understanding of the good death led to a new, Lutheran funerary culture.

The Late-Medieval Art of Dying

Medieval priests taught dying persons to call for both medical and spiritual assistance. They considered the latter more important than the former, because they believed the eternal fate of the soul to be at stake at the moment of death. Surviving liturgical manuals, such as the Rituale of Bishop Henry I of Breslau from the fourteenth century, show that sick persons were expected to confess their sins to their priest, who would then absolve them. Thereupon they received the sacraments of the Eucharist, or Communion, and the anointing of the sick. Psalms and prayers were spoken, and the rituals were performed in Latin, the liturgical language of the medieval church.[1] Confession was the most important aspect of medieval preparation for death, because only persons who had been reconciled with God by having confessed all of their mortal, that is, very serious, sins could hope to escape eternal damnation. Moreover, the church taught that dying persons could not be certain of their eternal salvation. Even if they had remembered and confessed all their mortal

sins, they could not know whether God had elevated them to a state of grace. And even if they had attained a state of grace, they could not be certain that they would succeed in remaining in this state until the moment they died.[2]

Because eternal salvation was at stake at the moment of death, it was considered necessary for people to prepare to die while they were still in good health. Clergy thought it wise to teach Christian laypersons to minister to the dying, given that, especially at times of plague, priests were either already dead, or so busy they were unable to attend every deathbed. To assist with this, theologians and clergy devised a variety of self-help books or handbooks known by the Latin term *ars moriendi*, or "Art of Dying."

One of the most widely-disseminated of these books was the anonymous *Art of Dying Well* (*Speculum artis bene moriendi*) (c. 1414–18). Originally written in Latin, it circulated in manuscript before the invention of the printing press and was translated into several languages, including English.[3] This book consisted of a variety of sections: instructions to caregivers in the form of exhortations to dying persons to confess their sins, questions to ask of dying persons to elicit a confession of faith, prayers to be said with and by the dying, instructions on how dying persons were to face the demonic temptations (*Anfechtungen*) they could expect on their deathbed, and a series of concluding prayers.[4] A condensed version of the *Art of Dying Well*, consisting of the exhortations, the demonic temptations illustrated with vivid woodcuts, and a series of concluding admonitions to prayer along with prayer texts, was also published in a variety of languages, including German, but not English. The five demonic temptations it taught dying Christians to resist were these: to doubt their faith, to despair of their salvation, to fail to be patient in suffering, to believe they deserved salvation on account of all their good works, and to regret leaving behind their material possessions.[5] Thus, in tempting the dying to despair of their salvation, the devil suggests that he has sinned so much that it is impossible for God to forgive him. He even quotes scripture (Eccles 9:1): "Because no one knows whether he is worthy of God's hate or love" (fig. 1).[6] Against the devil's temptation to despair, an angel admonishes the dying person not to give in to despair but rather to keep on hoping. It was important to learn to expect and resist these temptations, because the person who gave in to any one of them would face eternity in hell.

Fig. 1 The devil tempts a dying man who is despairing of his sins, in:
Eyn loblich unnd nutzbarlich buchlein von dem sterben / [...]
(A well-ordered and useful little book about dying), Leipzig 1507

Martin Luther's *Sermon on Preparing to Die* (*Eyn Sermon von der Bereytung zum Sterben*) (1519)

Commenting on these books on preparing to die, Luther once wrote: "Many books have been written … on how we are to prepare for death: nothing but error, and people have become more downcast."[7] His own *Sermon on Preparing to Die* (1519) became a best seller, probably because Luther accurately diagnosed and addressed the overriding spiritual concern of devout persons of his day: despair of eternal salvation and fear of hell.

Martin Luther rejected the traditional teaching that Christians could not be certain of their eternal salvation. On the contrary, he taught

that Christians could rest assured of their salvation, and that this assurance could be attained through faith in God's gracious promise to forgive sins. This teaching, which came to be known as justification by faith, became the basis for Lutheran teaching on preparing for death.

The title of Luther's *Sermon on Preparing to Die* (1519) is a bit misleading, because Luther did not preach it from a pulpit. He initially wrote it in response to a request from a certain Markus Schart, a counselor and servant of Elector Frederick the Wise of Saxony (1463–1525). Very soon, however, he had it published for devotional reading by all Christians, and especially those close to death. The booklet became tremendously popular—by 1525 it had already been reprinted twenty-four times in German. Latin, Danish, and Dutch translations followed (fig. 2).[8]

In line with tradition, Luther taught that dying persons were to draw up a will, to seek reconciliation with loved ones and neighbors, and to receive the traditional deathbed sacraments. In his exhortation to confession, however, Luther broke with tradition; he instructed dying persons to confess not all of their sins, but only the serious sins that lay most heavily on their consciences.[9] This was a radical break with tradition, because the church had taught for hundreds of years that even one unconfessed mortal, or serious, sin would send a person to hell for eternity. The remainder of the sermon consisted of instruction on the meaning of the deathbed sacraments. These are best understood, Luther writes, when one recognizes that they help one overcome the demonic temptations. Luther speaks of these temptations as images of death, sin, and hell; they correspond to the late-medieval demonic temptation of despair of salvation. Luther teaches that the images or temptations can be overcome by meditating on Christ's passion. When Christians are tempted to despair of salvation on account of the certainty of impending death, the gravity of their sins, or the fear of damnation, they are to contemplate the death of Christ on the cross, through which their own death and sin are defeated and eternal life is obtained for them. Thus, when the dying Christian contemplates the image of sin, the devil holds up to him all those who have sinned and who have been damned on account of fewer sins than his. This the Christian is not to do; instead, he is to contemplate the image of grace.

Christ, Luther writes, "takes your sins upon himself and overcomes them for you with his righteousness out of sheer mercy, and if you believe that, your sins will never do you harm."[10] In conclusion, Luther encourages dying persons to receive the deathbed sacraments joyfully, and to trust in the certainty of salvation that is Christ's gift. Luther concludes his sermon as follows: "Thus we read in Psalm 110 [111:2], 'Great are the works of the Lord, selected according to his pleasure.' Therefore, we ought to thank him with a joyful heart for showing us such wonderful, rich, and immeasurable grace and mercy against death, hell, and sin, and to laud and love his grace

1 Franz, *Rituale*, pp. 32–39. **2** Grosse, *Heilsungewißheit*, pp. 35–39. **3** The boke of the craft of dying. In: Horstman, *Yorkshire Writers*, pp. 406–420. **4** O'Connor, *Dying*, pp. 7–10. **5** Ibid., p. 9. **6** *Eyn loblich vnnd//nutzbarlich buchlein vo(n) dem ster//ben* [1507], fol. [Avj]v. Orignal: Wan keiner weysz ob er gotes hasz oder liebe wirdig sey. **7** *WA* 41, 699. Original: Multi libri … scripti,

quomodo ad mortem praeparare debeamus: merus error et homines bedrubter worden. **8** Reinis, *Reforming*, p. 48. **9** Ibid., pp. 50–52. **10** *LW* 42, 105; *WA* 2, 697. Original: Nympt er … deyn sund auff sich und yn seyner gerechtickeit auß lauter gnaden dir ubir windt: ßo du das glaubist, ßo thun sie dyr nymmer schaden.

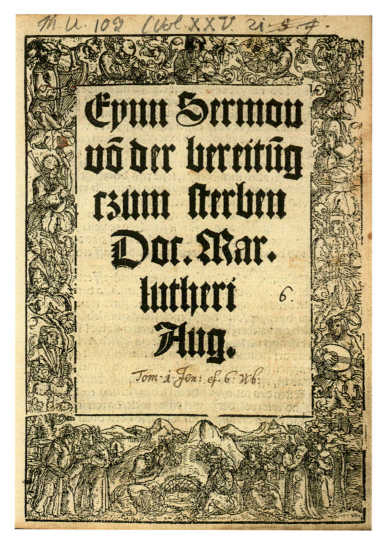

Fig. 2 Martin Luther, *Eyn Sermon von der Bereytung czum sterben* (A sermon on preparing to die), Leipzig 1519

Troestung an Hertzog Friderich Churfuersten zu Sachssen (1525) upon hearing the deathbed confession of the dying elector. The following morning, the elector's son, Sebastian of Jessen, read the letter to his dying father, and the elector received Communion. Later the same day, the elector made his will and died.[14] The principal theme of the letter is justification by faith. When a Christian believes that Christ has made full satisfaction for his sins, then he becomes a child and heir of God.[15] "Neither sin, death, hell, or the devil can harm such a person. Nor can he be damned, but rather he will eternally be saved through faith and heartfelt trust in God's true Word and bottomless grace, goodness and mercy," the author concludes (fig. 3).[16]

The occasion for the writing of Steffan Castenbaur's *Ain koestlicher/guotter notwendiger Sermon/vom Sterben* (1523) could not have been more different from that of Spalatin's *Troestung*. While Spalatin sought to comfort one of the most powerful men of the Holy Roman Empire, the author of this pamphlet, Steffan Castenbaur, an imprisoned Augustinian monk, may likely have been consoling himself while waiting for his trial on heresy charges and the death sentence that would inevitably follow. Having studied theology at the University of Vienna, Castenbaur was transferred in 1520 to the Augustinian monastery in Rattenburg am Inn, a small but well-to-do mining town. As the new prior of the monastery, he became known for his preaching, in which he propagated Luther's ideas. On November 17, 1522, Archduke Ferdinand of Austria ordered the city council of Rattenburg to arrest Castenbaur. Castenbaur was charged with spreading Luther's teachings and inciting insurrection. For a year and a half, from November 1522 until the summer of 1524, Castenbaur languished in prison, first in Rattenburg, and then, from March 1523, in Mühldorf.[17] It was during his time in Mühldorf that Castenbaur wrote his sermon on dying. Fortunately for him, a variety of circumstances, including unrest among the populace, eventually led to his release from prison. Castenbaur continued his career as reformer, first in Augsburg, then in Nuremberg, Hof, Sulzbach, and finally, in Eisleben.[18]

In his sermon, Castenbaur views his reader—and very likely, himself—as being afraid and unwilling to die. He argues that instead, Christians should love, desire, and joyfully accept death. Rather than primarily viewing death negatively as punishment for sin, Christians should view it positively: "[T]hrough Christ it has become a precious good for Christians because through it all our suffering and sin ceases."[19] And rather than fearing divine judgment, "we" are to remember that "the almighty God himself has placed it in our power to escape this same verdict and sentence, that it cannot harm us, through faith in Jesus Christ and utter trust in his fatherly goodness. [Gott der allma(e)chtig hatt das vns selbst in gewalt geben Das wir künnden dem selbigen vrtayl vnnd Sentzenntz [sic!] entgeen vnnd das er vns nitt schaden kan oder mag durch den glaube(n) in Jhesum Christum vnd gantz vertrawen in sein va(e)terlich gu(e)t …]"[20] Luther's doctrine of justification by faith informs this statement.

Other Lutheran writings on dying took the form of handbooks for laypersons for accompanying the dying on their last journey. One of the most popular of these was Johannes Odenbach's *Ein Trost Büchlin fur die Sterbenden* (1528) (fig. 4). Odenbach appears to have served as pastor in two parishes in the territory of Palatinate-Zwei-

rather than fearing death so greatly. Love and praise make dying very much easier, as God tells us through Isaiah, 'I shall curb your mouth in its praise of me, so that you will not perish' [Isa. 48:9]. To that end may God help us, etc. Amen."[11] Thus Luther draws on motifs found in traditional *ars moriendi* works, like the temptation to despair, but rejects their central teaching that dying Christians cannot be certain of their salvation.[12]

The Art of Dying after Luther

Luther's teaching that salvation is certain, and that Christians may joyfully and confidently approach death and divine judgment, found its way into numerous works on dying written by his contemporaries and by later Lutheran pastors.[13] These works were written by adherents of the Reformation in various German territories and addressed a wide variety of situations. Some, like Luther's *Sermon on Preparing to Die*, were sermons written to comfort particular prominent individuals. Thus Georg Spalatin , who served as private secretary and court preacher to Elector Frederick the Wise, wrote his *Eine*

brücken, in Obermoschel from 1528 until 1548, and then in Lauterecken until his death in 1554 or 1555. His handbook became a considerable publishing success, with over eighteen editions printed between 1528 and 1561.[21] The booklet, as the author explains in his foreword, consists of three parts: first, sayings meant to lead the sick person to desire death; second, consolation out of the New Testament; and third, formulas of confession and prayer to be said out loud to the sick person to console him.[22] Of these materials, the reader or caregiver may select those that seem most helpful in any given situation. The New Testament passages, which extend over twelve pages, aim to assure the dying person that he can be confident of his salvation. For example, in the words of Jesus: "I am the resurrection and the life. Those who believe in me, even though they die, will live, and everyone who lives and believes in me will never die" (John 11:25–26).[23] Such a collection of scripture passages would have been particularly useful and comforting in a situation where the caregiver or the dying person was too poor to be able to afford an entire New Testament.[24] Two things indicate that the booklet was meant to be used primarily by laypersons: although four formulas of confession are provided, the customary pastoral words of absolution are missing. No provision is made for administering the Lord's Supper, which would have required the presence of a pastor.[25]

Perhaps the most creative of the early Lutheran books on dying is the anonymous *Euangelisch lere vnd vermanung / eines sterbenden menschen* published in Leipzig in 1522 or 1523. The territorial ruler, Duke George the Bearded of Saxony (1471–1539), a determined opponent of the Reformation, sought to hinder the spread of Lutheran ideas with measures such as prohibiting the printing and sale of Luther's writings. These efforts notwithstanding, Lutheran sentiment in Leipzig remained strong.[26] The booklet *Euangelisch lere* addresses the situation of the dying Lutheran in a city without Lutheran clergy. It proposes that a Lutheran may call for a priest and receive the traditional last rites of confession, communion, and unction, providing that in his heart he interprets these rites in a Lutheran way. It also teaches the dying person how to evade the questions of a priest who seeks to determine whether he is a "Lutheran heretic" or a "good Christian." For example, to the priest's question, "Do you believe

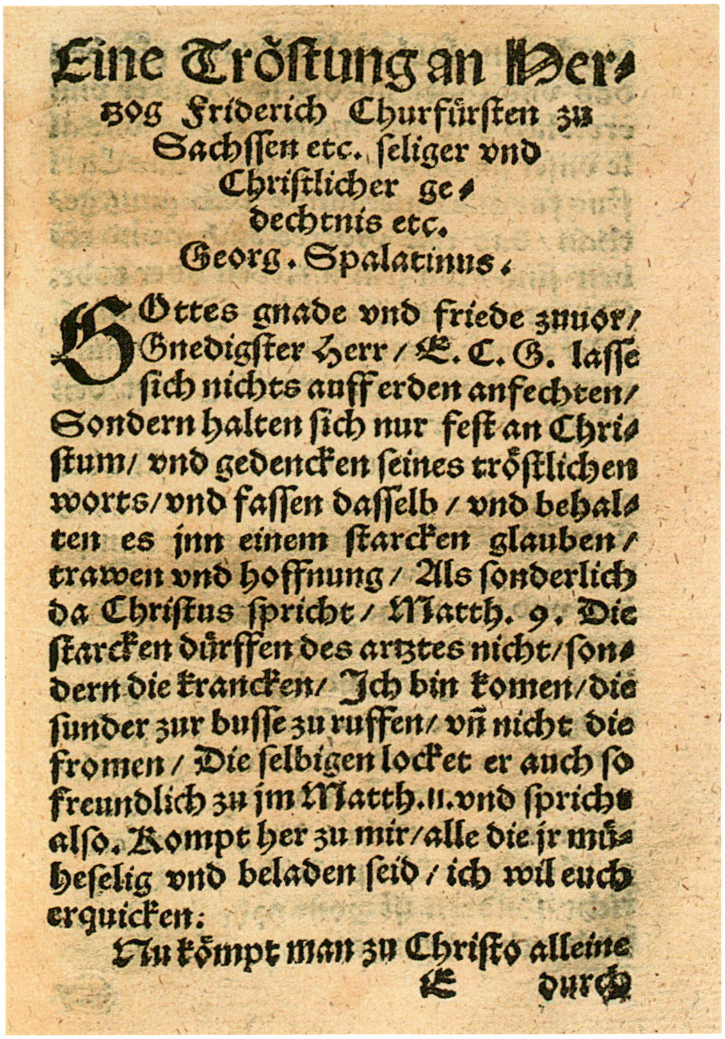
Eine Tröstung an Her=
zog Friderich Churfürsten zu
Sachssen etc. seliger vnd
Christlicher ge=
dechtnis etc.
Georg. Spalatinus.

GOttes gnade vnd friede zuuor/
Gnedigster Herr / E. C. G. lasse
sich nichts auff erden anfechten/
Sondern halten sich nur fest an Chri=
stum/ vnd gedencken seines tröstlichen
worts/ vnd fassen dasselb / vnd behal=
ten es jnn einem starcken glauben /
trawen vnd hoffnung / Als sonderlich
da Christus spricht / Matth. 9. Die
starcken dürffen des artztes nicht/son=
dern die krancken/ Jch bin komen/die
sunder zur busse zu ruffen/ vñ nicht die
fromen / Die selbigen locket er auch so
freundlich zu jm Matth. 11. vnd spricht
also. Kompt her zu mir/alle die jr mü=
heselig vnd beladen seid / ich wil euch
erquicken.
Nu kompt man zu Christo alleine
E durch

Fig. 3 Georg Spalatin, Eine Troestung an Hertzog Friderich Churfürsten zu Sachssen [...] (A letter of consolation to Duke Frederick Elector of Saxony). In: Johannes Odenbach, Ein Trost=Büchlin fur die sterbenden (A comforting book for the dying,) Wittenberg 1535

11 *LW*, 42, 115; *WA* 2, 697. Original: [W]ie geschrieben steet ps. 110 [111:2]. Die werck gottis seyn groß und außerwelet nach allem seynenn wolgefallenn. Derhalben muß man tzu sehen, das man yhe mit grossen freuden des hertzen danck seynem gotlichen willen, das er mit unß widder den tod, sund und hell ßo wunderlich, reichlich und unmeßlich gnad und barmhertzickeyt ubet, und nit ßo sere fur dem tod furchten, allein sein gnad preyssen und lieben, dann die liebe und das lob das sterben gar sere leichteret, wie er sagt durch Jsaiam: Jch wil zeumen deynen mund mit meynem lob, das du nit untergehest. Des helff unß Gott etc. Amen. **12** Reinis, *Reforming*, p. 47. **13** Schottroff, *Bereitung*, pp. 107–134. **14** Höss, *Spalatin*, pp. 277–279; Spalatin, *Friedrichs*, pp. 64–68. **15** Reinis, *Reforming*, pp. 124–127. **16** Eine Tro(e)stung an Her=/tzog Friderich Churfu(e)rsten zu//Sachssen etc. In: Johannes Odenbach, *Ein Trost//Büchlin fur die//Sterbenden* [1535], fol. Ev. Original: Einem solchen menschen/schadet auch weder su(e)nde/tod/helle/noch Teuffel./Er kan auch nicht verdampt werden/sondern wird durch den glauben vnd hertzliche zuuersicht auff Gottes warhafftigs Wort vnd abgru(e)ndliche gnade/gu(e)te vnd barmhertzigkeit/ewig selig. **17** Moeller, *Sterbekunst*, pp. 744–748. **18** Ibid., pp. 764–675, 747, 751. **19** S. Castenbaur [Agricola], *Ain ko(e)stlicher/gu(o)tter//notwendiger Sermon/vo(m) Sterbe(n) [1523]*, fol. Aiijr. Original: [D]urch Christum ist es ain kostbarliche gu(o)thait worden/den Christen menschen dann dardurch ho(e)rte all vnser layd vnnd sünd auff. **20** Ibid., Gott der allma(e)chtig hatt das vns selbst in gewalt geben Das wir künnden dem selbigen vrtayl vnnd Sentzenntz [sic!] entgeen vnnd das er vns nitt schaden kan oder mag durch den glaube(n) in Jhesum Christum vnd gantz vertrawen in sein va(e)terlich gu(e)t ... **21** Reinis, *Reforming*, p. 179. **22** Odenbach, *Ein Trost Büchlin fur die Sterbenden [1535]*, fol. Aiijv. **23** Ibid., fol. Br. Original: Ich bin die Aufferstehung vnd das leben/wer an mich gleubt/der wird leben/ob er schon stu(e)rbe/Vn(d) wer da lebt vnd gleubt an mich/der wird nicht sterben ewiglich. **24** Reinis, *Reforming*, p. 184. **25** Ibid., p. 181. **26** Hoyer/Schwarz, *Bürgerschaft*, pp. 109 f.; Koslofsky, *Dead*, pp. 58 f.

Fig. 4 Johannes Odenbach, Ein Trost=Büchlin für die sterbenden (A comforting book for the dying), Wittenberg 1535

there are seven sacraments?" the dying person is to answer: "I believe what a Christian is to believe and therefore I have requested the sacraments, which I do not wish to hold in contempt. And even if there were a hundred sacraments, I would consider them sacraments. And I ask that you would not dispute with me concerning such matters; I am too simple, etc."[27] The dying person presents himself as a simple Christian who is unaware of Luther's teaching that there are only two genuine sacraments, baptism and Communion. By answering as instructed, he can remain true to his convictions, while still receiving last rites and an honorable burial in his family's burial plot in consecrated ground (fig. 5).[28]

Lutheran Funerary Culture

Besides encouraging a more theologically confident and joyful approach to dying as reflected in the Lutheran handbooks on dying, Luther's teaching of justification by faith also led to significant changes in funerary culture. Since Lutheran Christians trusted God to forgive their sins, they expected that at the moment of death, their souls would proceed directly to God in heaven. Belief in purgatory thus became obsolete. Funeral masses, and masses for the dead, by means of which the living had helped shorten their own or their loved ones' time in purgatory, were abolished. The preaching of a funeral sermon and the singing of funeral hymns soon became the most prominent parts of Lutheran funeral ritual.[29] In 1542, Luther published a collection of funeral hymns entitled *Christliche Geseng Lateinisch vnd Deudsch, zum Begrebnis*. These were meant to be sung by the local schoolteacher and schoolboys as they accompanied the funeral procession to the cemetery.[30] With respect to the funeral sermon, Luther taught that its purpose was to console the bereaved and to hold up hope of the resurrection.[31] The first published Lutheran funeral sermons are those Luther himself preached for the Saxon Electors Frederick the Wise[32] and John the Steadfast,[33] in 1525 and 1532 respectively.

Toward the end of the sixteenth century, upper-class families and members of the nobility not only asked pastors to preach funeral sermons but also arranged for the sermons to be printed for distribution among family, neighbors, and friends. The printed sermons took on a life of their own as a popular form of devotional literature.[34] The biographical sections of these printed sermons commonly devoted considerable space to the manner in which the deceased had died—in other words, to assuring family and friends that their loved one had died a peaceful and blessed death in confident hope of the resurrection.[35] Many printed funeral sermons included poems (*epicedia*) written in honor of the deceased.[36] Some even included the musical scores of funeral compositions wealthy families commissioned to be performed at the funerals of their loved ones.[37] These poems and musical scores give evidence of the emergence of Lutheran poetic and musical traditions linked to the Lutheran art of dying.

Lutheran burial customs also led to the development of new traditions in painting and sculpture. With respect to places of burial, Luther wrote: "A cemetery rightfully ought to be a fine quiet place, removed from all other localities, to which one can reverently go and stand and meditate upon death, the last Judgment, and the resurrection …"[38] In the Middle Ages, the more prominent dead were commonly buried under the floors of their parish churches, preferably near the altar where the Eucharist was celebrated, while the less well-to-do were laid to rest in the churchyard. By the fifteenth century, however, across Europe, churchyards had become excessively crowded, and new cemeteries were founded outside city walls.[39] The practice of burying the most prominent individuals inside churches, however, continued, as with Luther himself, who was not buried in a cemetery, but rather in the Castle Church in Wittenberg.[40]

Some well-heeled Lutherans commissioned elaborate epitaphs for their dead. Thus an elaborately carved marble epitaph in the City Church in Wittenberg commemorates the life and death of the young nobleman and student Matthias von Schulenburg, who died in 1569. It consists of a statue of the deceased in prayer, and three images of Jesus—Jesus praying at Gethsemane, Jesus on the cross, and Jesus as the resurrected and triumphant Lord.[41]

Fig. 5 Anonymous, Euangelisch lere vnd vermanung eines sterbenden menschen zu den sacramenten vnd letzter hinfart [...] (Evangelical teaching and instruction to a dying person about the sacraments and the last journey), Leipzig 1522 or 1523

Epitaphs in the form of paintings, often with explanatory captions in writing, also became common. Especially well known is the epitaph for the theologian and pastor Paul Eber by Lucas Cranach the Younger, also located in the City Church in Wittenberg. It is a polemical work, portraying, on the left side, the destruction of the vineyard of the Lord by Catholic clergy, and on the right, its careful cultivation by the reformers, among them Martin Luther, Philipp Melanchthon, and Paul Eber himself (see fig. 1 in the essay of Stefan Rhein in this volume).[42]

In conclusion, Luther's joyful and confident approach to death and dying was disseminated by his followers in the form of dozens of writings on how to prepare to die and how to give help to dying persons. With the funeral sermons he preached for Saxon Electors Frederick the Wise in 1525 and John the Steadfast in 1532, and the collection of funeral hymns he published in 1542, Luther also set the stage for a new funeral ritual, which in turn led to the development of distinctively Lutheran funerary traditions in poetry, music, sculpture, and painting.

27 *Euangelisch lere*, fol. [Aiv]v. Original: [I]ch glaub was ein cristen me(n)sch glauben soll/vn(d) darumb so hab ich begert der sacrament d[aß] ich s[i]e nit verachten will/vn(d) wan ir hundert wern/ich wolt sie fur sacrame(n)t halte(n)/vn(d) b[eg]er ir wolt von solicher matery nit wider mit mir disputirn ich bin jn zu einfeltig, etc. **28** Reinis, *Reforming*, pp. 144 f. **29** Kolb, *Orders*. **30** Luther, *Geseng*; Arbeitsgemeinschaft Friedhof und Denkmal, *Fried*, pp. 7, 13, 30. **31** *LW* 53, 326–327; *WA* 35, 479. **32** *WA* 17, I, 196–227. **33** *LW* 51, 231–255; *WA* 36, 237–270. **34** Niekus-Moore, *Patterned Lives*. **35** Niekus-Moore, *Praeparatio*. **36** Linton, *Poetry*. **37** Bolin, *Sterben*. **38** *LW* 43, 136–137; *WA* 23, 375. See also Anja Tietz' contribution to this volume. Original: [E]in begrebnis solt ja billich ein feiner stiller ort sein, der abgesondert were von allen o(e)rten, darauff man mit andacht gehn und stehen ku(e)ndte, den tod, das Ju(e)ngst gericht und afferstehung zu betrachten ... **39** Koslofsky, *Dead*, pp. 40 f. **40** Bellmann/Harksen/Werner, *Denkmale*, pp. 46 f.; Junghans, *Luther*, pp. 182–184. **41** Zitzlaff, *Begräbnißstätten*, pp. 109–112; Bellmann/Harksen/Werner, Denkmale, p. 184. **42** Junghans, *Luther*, p. 129, 133 f.; Bellmann/Harksen/Werner, *Denkmale*, p. 183.

BIBLIOGRAPHY

Arbeitsgemeinschaft Friedhof und Denkmal (ed.) (2010), *Mit Fried und Freud ich fahr dahin. Protestantische Begräbniskultur der Frühen Neuzeit. Eine Ausstellung des Museums für Sepulkralkultur Kassel und des Stadtmuseums Gera.* Kassel. **Bellmann**, Fritz/**Harksen**, Marie-Luise/**Werner**, Roland (eds.) (1979), *Die Denkmale der Lutherstadt Wittenberg.* Weimar. **Bolin**, Norbert (1989), *Sterben ist mein Gewinn (Phil. 1,21): Ein Beitrag zur evangelischen Funeralkomposition der deutschen Sepulkralkultur des Barock, 1550–1750 (= Arbeitsgemeinschaft Friedhof und Denkmal e.V.).* Kassel. **Castenbaur** [Agricola], Steffan (1523), *Ain ko(e)stlicher gu(o)tter notwendiger Sermon vo(m) Sterbe(n).* Augsburg. **Euangelisch lere** *vnd vermanung eines ster bende(n) menschen zu(o) den sacramenten vn(d) letzte(r) hinfart* (1522). Leipzig. **Eyn loblich** *vnnd nutzbarlich buchlein vo(n) dem sterben* (1507). Leipzig. **Franz**, Adolf (ed.) (1912), *Das Rituale des Bischofs Heinrich I. von Breslau.* Freiburg im Breisgau. **Grosse**, Sven (1994), *Heilsungewißheit und Scrupulositas im späten Mittelalter: Studien zu Johannes Gerson und Gattungen der Frömmigkeitstheologie seiner Zeit.* Tübingen. **Höss**, Irmgard (1989), *Georg Spalatin, 1484–1545. Ein Leben in der Zeit des Humanismus und der Reformation.* Weimar. **Horstman**, Carl (ed.) (1896), *Yorkshire Writers. Richard Rolle of Hampole and his Followers.* Vol. 2. London. **Hoyer**, Siegfried/**Schwarz**, Uta (1983), Die Leipziger Bürgerschaft und die frühe Reformation. In: Sohl, Klaus (ed.), *Leipzig: Aus Vergangenheit und Gegenwart. Beiträge zur Stadtgeschichte.* Vol. 2. Leipzig, pp. 99–117. **Junghans**, Helmar (1996), *Martin Luther und Wittenberg.* München. **Kolb**, Robert (2014), Orders for Burial in the Sixteenth Century Wittenberg Circle. In: Dingel, Irene/Kohnle, Armin (eds.), *Gute Ordnung. Ordnungsmodelle und Ordnungsvorstellungen in der Reformationszeit.* Leipzig, pp. 257–279. **Koslofsky**, Craig (2000), *The Reformation of the Dead. Death and Ritual in Early Modern Germany 1450–1700.* New York. **Linton**, Anna (2008), *Poetry and Parental Bereavement in Early Modern Germany.* Oxford. **Luther**, Martin (1542), *Christliche Geseng Lateinisch vnd Deudsch, zum Begrebnis.* Wittenberg. **Moeller**, Bernd (1999), Sterbekunst in der Reformation: Der "köstliche, gute, notwendige Sermon vom Sterben" des Augustiner-Eremiten Stefan Kastenbauer. In: Felten, Franz/Jaspert, Nicholas (eds.), *Vita Religiosa im Mittelalter. Festschrift für Kaspar Elm zum 70. Geburtstag.* Berlin, pp. 739–765. **Niekus-Moore**, Cornelia (1993), Praeparatio ad Mortem: Das Buch bei Vorbereitung und Begleitung des Sterbens im protestantischen Deutschland des 16. und 17. Jahrhunderts. In: *Pietismus und Neuzeit: Ein Jahrbuch zur Geschichte des neueren Protestantismus,* vol. 19, pp. 9–18. **Niekus-Moore**, Cornelia (2006), *Patterned Lives: The Lutheran Funeral Biography in Early Modern Germany.* Wiesbaden. **O'Connor**, Mary Catherine (1966), *The Art of Dying Well: The Development of the Ars moriendi.* New York. **Reinis**, Austra (2007), *Reforming the Art of Dying: The ars moriendi in the German Reformation (1519–1528).* Aldershot, U.K. **Schottroff**, Luise (2012), *Die Bereitung zum Sterben: Studien zu den frühen reformatorischen Sterbebüchern.* Göttingen. **Spalatin**, Georg (1851), *Friedrichs des Weisen Leben und Zeitgeschichte.* Neudecker, Christian Gotthold/Preller, Ludwig (eds.). Jena. **Spalatin**, Georg (1535), Eine Tro(e)stung an Hertzog Friderich Churfu(e)rsten zu Sachssen etc. In: Odenbach, Johannes (ed.), *Ein Trost Büchlin fur die Sterbenden.* Wittenberg. **Zitzlaff**, Ernst (1896), *Die Begräbnißstätten Wittenbergs und ihre Denkmäler.* Wittenberg.

LOUIS D. NEBELSICK

"es sey hieuor etwo ein sepulcrum gewesen": Martin Luther and the Sixteenth-Century Beginnings of Archaeological Research in Central Europe and Scandinavia

Martin Luther's first exposure to archaeology is recorded in remarks he made two decades after his visit to Rome in 1511. Sadly, much of what the older Luther said he remembered about the young monk Martin's itinerary is interlaced with embittered anti-papal rhetoric, and only isolated flashes of what must have been genuine memories crop up amid the rancor. He remembers running through endless churches and catacombs like "a mad saint [...] believing all the lies and nonsense" he was told about them.[1] This ironic quip deliberately derides the majestic monuments which must have awed the young provincial monk from small-town Saxony.

Typically, Luther uses the derogatory word "Klufften," (dank crevices) in order to describe the catacombs of St. Sebastian he had visited. This formulation clearly reflects his later rejection of the saving power of the thousands of martyrs' bodies that were said to lie there. But it also mirrors his rebuke of sixteenth-century humanist antiquarians' narratives that saw Rome's early Christian remains as haptic proof of the legitimacy of St. Peter's pontifical legacy. This discourse would gain embittered urgency after the Council of Trent, when the archaeology of early Christianity was added to the ammunition of the Counter-Reformation.[2]

Strangely for us, Luther's description of Rome ignores the remains of Rome's antique grandeur altogether.[3] However, while the appreciation of the auratic quality of ruins was, of course, alien to his late-medieval mindset,[4] Luther was clearly aware of the memorial qualities architectural relics could have. This awareness lies behind his heinous recommendations made in 1543 that Jewish homes, yeshivas, and synagogues be "set on fire and what will not burn be covered with soil, so that no stone or slag would be seen for all times."[5] Moreover, despite his feigned indifference to his ancient Roman surroundings, the Reformer later remembers an observation

that he made as a young monk on the high banks of the Tiber. The exposed layer of rubble, which was as high as "two Landsknecht's pikes,"[6] was so thick that the foundations of present day houses stood where the roofs of the ancient buildings would have been.[7] Obviously, angry polemic also lurks just under the surface of this statement, i.e., vainglorious Rome sits on an enormous rubbish tip, but not many sixteenth-century provincial tourists of that day would have been able to discern anthropogenic layers and understand their stratigraphic consequences.

His observations about indigenous archaeological findings were equally astute. During a pastoral visit to the prosperous residential town of Torgau on the Elbe in 1529, Luther had his first recorded dealings with local archaeological finds. He had taken part in a princely commission which addressed a report that nine or ten pots which were said to have contained the skulls and bones of small children (i.e., shattered cremated bones). They had been found by peasants in the domain of the former Cistercian nunnery Marienpforte near Sitzenroda just south of Torgau which had been recently secularized and purloined by the prince elector. Witnesses were heard on the matter and, after careful deliberation, the commission, obviously under Luther's lead, determined that the vessels which contained human remains had a form which had not been in use in the past fifty to one hundred years. The commission logically concluded that remains of an ancient pagan cemetery had been found.[8] With this verdict, Martin Luther and his confederates broke with the long-standing and almost universally held conviction that excavated vessels were *ollas natura formatas* (pots formed by nature) which grew in the fertile soil spontaneously like tubers or were fashioned by subterranean dwarfs.[9] In the spirit of humanist rationality, they firmly anchored the urns from Sitzenroda and those like it in Saxony's prehistoric heathen past.

Fundort	Zahna.	Wie Nr.31 : 13 a.	Alter Katalog		Haupt-Katalog 31 : 13 e.
Kreis	Wittenberg.	Grab 10.	Zettel-Katalog		
Reg.-Bez.	Merseburg. Halle	Wie Nr.31 : 13 a.			

E.K.Nr.321.   Negativ-Nr. 5174

Geschenk : wie Nr.31 : 13 a.

Derkschale Offentar nicht Zugehörig

Topf, abgesetzter Hals, in seinem Unterteil wagerechte Cannelüren, Schulter mit Fazetten und darüber Kanne= lüren. 2 kl.br.Henkel (mit senkr.Kannelüren) gegenstän= dig am Halsansatz.
Farbe: gelbbraun mit ge= schwärzten Partien.

H. = 14 cm; o.Dm.= 18 1/2cm gr.Dm 22 cm; Bd.Dm.= 5 1/2cm.

1:5

Lit. Jahresschrift: 14/1926 - S.89 ff.

Fig. 1
Late Bronze Age pottery from the barrow cemetery near Zahna. Record Card from the Finds Archive of the State Office for Heritage Management and Archaeology Saxony-Anhalt, Halle, 1928

Wittenberg, the Hub of Reformation-Period Archaeological Research

Although this is the only recorded archaeological foray of the Reformer into local prehistory, it would set a pattern for further antiquarian ventures of his associates in the heartland of the Lutheran Reformation. Crucially, Luther and his committee had opened the door for an autonomous inquiry into the past of Germany beyond the limits of the Roman Empire and outside the scope of written sources. In his *De natura fossilium* written in 1546, for instance, Saxony's pioneering geologist Georg Agricola expanded on Luther's findings by debunking fairy tales of self-generated or dwarf-thrown pots. After considering the evidence, he came to the conclusion that they were "urns in which the ancient Germans who had not turned to Christianity stored the ashes of their dead."[10]

This first recorded explicit ethnic attribution of excavated prehistoric artefacts in Central Germany seems to have inspired other Saxon scholars to test Agricola's theory by excavating prehistoric sites. Luther's closest confederate, Philipp Melanchthon, whose wide-ranging scholarly interests included antiquarian studies, made meticulous descriptions of excavations in a barrow at Landsberg near Halle (Saale) in a lecture held in 1560, clearly seeing it as

a monument anchored in Saxony's pre-Christian past.[11] Moreover, Agricola's pupil and dean of the University of Wittenberg, Petrus Albinus, was animated by the scholarly debate about the origin of "wild urns" to excavate in the autumn of 1587 a series of Bronze Age barrows from an extensive cemetery in the forest between the villages Zahna and Marzahna which lie a few miles northeast of Wittenberg (fig. 1). He found pottery, remains of human bones, ash, and charcoal protected by stone packings. Albinus' coherent account of his findings published in his *Meißenische Chronica* of 1590 is thought to be the earliest excavation report of a prehistoric site in Germany.[12] Moreover, Albinus seems to have been aware of a series of further excavations in Central Germany as he stated, quite rightly, that stone structures protecting the urns were a ubiquitous feature of prehistoric cremations in Saxony as well as in Thuringia. All these scholars enquired into the archaeological past in the spirit of rational humanist observation, but they are also characterized by an intense interest in exploring an unwritten record of a distant past, something that had no precedent either in Medieval Central European Scholarship or among contemporary Catholic scholarly communities.

1 *WA* 31/I, 226b 9f. **2** Erenstoft, *Sacred Past*; Frend, *Early Christianity*. **3** Böhmer, *Romfahrt*, pp. 139–151. **4** Schnapp, *Discovery*, pp. 97–100. **5** Martin Luther, *Von den Jüden und iren Lügen* (On the Jews and Their Lies) [1543], in: *WA* 53, 417–552. **6** *WA.TR* 3 (no. 3700). **7** Schneider, *Rom*, p. 132. **8** "es sey hieuor etwo ein sepulcrum gewesen." Gummel, *Forschungsgeschichte*, p. 13; Kühn, *Geschichte*, pp. 16 f.; Mennung, *Vorstufen*, p. 39; Müller, *Urnenfund*; Schmidt, *100 Jahre*, p. 17. The original verdict of the commission is quoted at

the head of this article. The exact find spot of the urns is typical for cemeteries of the Bronze Age Lusatian Culture. This cemetery site was rediscovered in the 1930s and is a hilltop site about a mile north-east of Sitzenroda, used now and probably then as a sand pit (Orts-Akte Landesamt für Archäologie Sachsen). **9** Stemmermann, *Anfänge*, pp. 67–71. **10** Bierbaum, *Sachsen*, p. 15. **11** Stock, *Sachsen-Anhalt*, p. 138; Schmidt, *100 Jahre*, p. 17. **12** Walter/Göricke, *Petrus*.

Interestingly, the rapid spread of Luther's Reformation to Northern Germany and Scandinavia was also accompanied by the advent of archaeological enquiry. Nicolaus Marschalk, a congenial Greek philologist and publisher, first brought archaeology to the north.[13] After studies in Erfurt, he came to the freshly founded University of Wittenberg in 1502, taught Greek, obtained his doctorate and founded his own publishing house. Ugly spats with his academic colleagues made him accept a call to the court of Henry V Duke of Mecklenburg in the winter of 1505 under whose patronage this multitalented humanist, who had adopted the Latinized nom de plume Thurius (the Thuringian) was involved in diplomatic, academic, and publishing ventures.

At that time Duke Henry, in tandem with his co-ruling brother, was in the process of carefully introducing Luther's Reformation to Mecklenburg and thus gradually freeing themselves from both papal and imperial authority. It was in this context that the Duke asked Marschalk to conduct wide-ranging genealogical research into his lineage. In 1520/21 Marschalk published his *Chronicon der Mecklenburgischen Regenten*, a lengthy genealogical poem chronicling the ancestry of Mecklenburg's ruling house. Like many court humanists he crafted this panegyric narrative enmeshing carefully researched historical personalities with freely fantasized fictional ancestors which not only justified the legitimacy of the regent but also served as a metaphoric exposé of his ideals and aspirations and entangled his heritage with regional history and geography. In a significant departure from tradition, which would mandate threading the duke's ancestral ties back to Western European Royalty and ultimately Brutus, Aeneas, or other Roman protagonists,[14] he forged ancestral bonds to Slavic royal families. Moreover, Marschalk/Thurius traced the Duke's lineage back to the court of Alexander the Great, Rome's rival in the memory of ancient imperial glory, where Greek was spoken. This was not only the language of the Gospels but, according to Luther and his acolytes, intimately connected to German.[15]

Clearly, this aberrant narrative's agenda was to legitimize his duke's goal of achieving autonomy in the Holy Roman Empire and independence from the Roman Curia. A second volume published by Marschalk in 1521, *Annalium Herulorum ac Vandalorum Libri Septem*, has a broader ethno-historical agenda. It integrates ancient monuments into a panegyric account of Mecklenburg's distant pagan past. This included not only surprisingly exact descriptions of archaeological finds and features but also an attempt to place characteristic ancient monuments in sequence and assign them to historically known ethnic groups. Thus, he suggested that Megalithic Neolithic tombs were built by the Germanic Heruli and Bronze Age barrows by their successors, the Slavic Abodrites. Simple Iron Age and Imperial Roman Period flat cemeteries with Spartan cremations, which he could only have known about through excavations, were seen as the burials of their servants.

The beginnings of Scandinavian prehistoric research can be linked to Heinrich von Rantzau, a leading Germanophone nobleman from Danish Holstein who came to Wittenberg as a 12-year-old student, studied with Melanchthon, and was welcomed at Luther's table.[16] He then made a meteoric career at the Danish court, where he was advisor to the king from 1554 until his death. Besides being instrumental in furthering humanist scholarship in Denmark by amassing a huge library, he introduced archaeology to Scandinavia. Mirroring the activities of Italian and Southern German Humanists, who were avidly collecting and editing Roman inscriptions, von Rantzau initiated an ambitious project to record and publish Denmark's rune stones, and in the process conducted excavations in the ancient Danish royal tumuli in Jellinge.[17] He was quite consciously treating the remains of aboriginal Danes as equals of what were thought were their Mediterranean contemporaries and thus obviously bolstering the claims of the Scandinavian kingdoms to legitimacy and longevity on a par with the south.

While the results of this survey of sixteenth century central and Northern European archaeology may, at first glance, seem meagre, it is worth noting that, at a time when antiquarians within the bounds of the ancient Roman empire were eagerly excavating Roman remains, the systematic excavation, recording, and interpretation of prehistoric finds was all but exclusively initiated in Wittenberg and carried out by disciples of the Lutheran reform.

Excavation, Elevation and Desecration: the Reformation and the Archaeology of Holy Bodies

In order to further contextualize this sixteenth-century flurry of archaeological enquiry in the Lutheran lands, it is worth considering the changes affecting traditional excavation activity at that time. Since Antiquity and particularly in the Middle Ages, wilfully digging into the past was almost always an act of piety entangled in strategies of religious and temporal legitimization.[18] No church could be consecrated without a fragment of a saint's body or something it had touched enclosed in its altar, and tombs containing hallowed corpses were considered to be powerful purveyors of grace. Thus holy bodies were fated to an unruly and in many cases unseemly death. Countless tombs were plundered, corpses exhumed and dismembered, artefacts mauled and clothing shredded. Once found, the scraps of bodies and rags were squirreled away and subsequently dispersed by their pious plunderers. They would then be encased in gorgeous receptacles, elevated on altars, and become foci of ritual devotion.

The impact of the Reformation on this archaeology of the holy was drastic, particularly as Luther's key concept *sola gratia* (salvation by God's grace alone) excluded any intervention by the saints. Early Protestants not only made mockery of both the retrieval and empowerment of relics but also saw the veneration of the saints as an evil impediment actively preventing sinners from attaining God's grace.[19] In most cases, the devaluation of the importance of holy relics, though fundamental, was undramatic. The tombs and chapels of the saints went derelict and were gradually reused or demolished, the valuable reliquaries were recycled and their contents thrown away or sold to believers in the south. With the hope for salvation focused on the pulpit, the clutter of reliquaries and shrines which encrusted late-medieval churches was simply in the way.

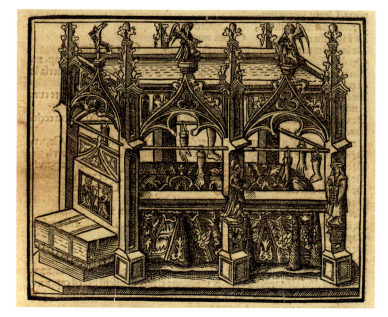

Fig. 2 Hieronymus Emser, Vita Bennonis (Life of [Saint] Benno), frontispiece. Woodcut showing the sepulcher of Saint Benno in the Meissen Cathedral before its renovation in the Renaissance style after 1524. Votives in the shape of body parts can be seen dangling from the canopy.

Yet there were more dramatic turns of event as the fate of St. Benno of Meissen shows.[20] In the late fifteenth century, both the episcopal see in Meissen and the Prince Electors of Saxony began petitioning Rome to canonize Benno, an obscure eleventh-century bishop of Meissen who had become the focus of rustic local veneration (fig. 2). His claims to beatitude included a highly unlikely vita replete with a fantastic tale involving a miraculous fish from the Elbe, which was to be his attribute. Despite appropriate financial enticements, the curia was slow to respond and it was only in 1523, six years after Luther's posting his theses, that Pope Hadrian canonized Bishop Benno. Clearly, he was sensing a chance to reassert papal and episcopal authority in Saxony and strengthen the hand of Catholic George Duke of Saxony, who controlled Meissen, against Luther's patron, the Saxon Prince Elector Frederick the Wise who ruled Wittenberg. The ceremony that followed in Meissen in 1524 had St. Benno's bones excavated with golden shovels, swathed in cloth of gold and elevated onto the high altar. After elaborate celebrations, they were then re-interred in the saint's newly renovated eternal home, trimmed with costly imported marble.

Martin Luther saw all this as a wanton provocation. He responded with a furious pamphlet called *Against the new idol and old devil which is to be exhalted in Meissen*.[21] The impact that this controversy had on the popular imagination was reported by the reformer Friedrich Myconius. He records that in the same summer an eerie scatological pantomime was staged in Buchholz in Saxony's Erzgebirge (Ore Mountains) Ore Mountains.[22] A mob of miners and loutish lads impersonating book-bearing clerics with sieves on their heads and gaming boards tucked under their arms barged into an abandoned mine. Under the direction of a "bishop" lording under a filthy canopy, with a basket for a mitre and flanked by guards of honour brandishing dung forks, they began an excavation. Soon Benno's "relics" were found, a horse skull, ass bones and a cow's jaw which were then tossed onto a manure cart and paraded to the town square. There, the "bishop" praised Benno's holy ass bones and proclaimed an indulgence. The bones and a papal effigy were finally cast into the market fountain.

Interestingly, life would follow art half a century later. In 1539, an iconoclastic mob attacked the Meissen Cathedral, which had become a Catholic atoll in a Protestant ocean, and demolished Benno's ostentatious Renaisance tomb. According to Protestant sources, they then dug up his remains, paraded them down the cathedral hill and threw them into the Elbe which churned through the arches of the town's bridge.[23] While this was a fate usually reserved for heretics' ashes, in this case it was particularly apt as St. Benno's attribute was, after all, an Elbe fish. Catholics, however, relate that the prescient faithful had managed to exhume his remains and secret them away well before the attack. After a long anabasis, St. Benno's bones were finally re-interred in Munich's St. Mary's Church in 1580, where he is venerated to this day as the Bavarian capital's patron saint.

Ironically, Martin Luther himself is said to have barely escaped Benno's intended fate. While Wittenberg was occupied by imperial forces in 1547, after the rout of the Protestants at Mühlberg, legend has it that Emperor Charles V personally had to prevent the fanatical Duke of Alba and his Spanish troops from excavating Luther's bones, burning them in public, and, of course, strewing his ashes into the Elbe.[24] With the renaissance of the relic cult after the Council of Trent, masses of corpses were once again on the move. Rome's catacombs, thought wrongly to be martyr's cemeteries, were systematically mined in order to replenish the barren churches of re-conquered Protestant bishoprics with holy bodies. The carefully assembled skeletons were fitted out with inspiring hagiographies, encrusted with gaudy jewels, and swathed in gorgeous vestments. They were then donated or sold to the barren churches of the north, festively translated and paraded to and enshrined in their new destinations: glass show cases set in splendid baroque altars.[25] This process would not only lead to an unprecedented upsurge in sacred pageantry, but also mark the beginnings of Christian archaeology, as late-sixteenth-century scholars scrambled to record the intricate ground plans and vivid but fragile frescoes of the plundered catacombs.[26]

To conclude this review on the archaeology of sacred corporality in Central Germany, it is worth considering the mirrored paratheatrical formulae of saintly elevation and mocking degradation

13 Schimpff, *Norddeutschland*; Brather, *Interpretationen*, pp. 12 f.; Sasse-Kunst, *Marschalk*. 14 For fictional incorporation of Roman heroes in Royal and imperial lineages, Tanner, *Aeneas*. Emperor Maximilian's ancestors included not only ancient rulers but also Greek and Roman gods and heroes, Christ's apostles and Israelite kings. Wierschin, *Heldenbuch*, pp. 112–115. 15 Knape, *Deutsche Sprache*, pp. 103–108. 16 Hansen, *Rantzau*. 17 Klindt-Jensen, *His-*

tory, p. 15; Schnapp, *Discovery*, pp. 167–169. 18 Brown, *Cult*. 19 Luscher, *Symbolsystem*. 20 Finucane, *Canonizations*, pp. 207–241. 21 Volkmar, *Benno*, pp. 157–180. 22 Now Annaberg-Buchholz, Scribner, *Popular Culture*, pp. 71–103. 23 Raguin, *Art*, p. 35, Cover. 24 Junghans, *Kaiser Karl V.* 25 Koudounaris, *Bodies*. 26 Erenstoft, *Sacred Past*.

in which this "archaeology" was imbedded. These carnavalistic performances, which were so firmly anchored in medieval concepts of sacred bodies, remained resilient despite all the dogmatic and ideological paradigm shifts in which they were contextualized. Martin Luther, who was acutely sensitive to implications of ritual action, recognized the essentially sustaining quality of the looking glass world of carnival and its associated conventions of ritualized mocking which accompanied the early Protenstant ritual violence against images and relics. While he initially regarded carnivalistic anticlerical outbursts with benign toleration[27] he would later reject them entirely.[28]

From Memorial Piety to Constructed Memories: the Archaeology of Ancestors

The sale of indulgences, the fuse that ignited Luther's rebellion, was just one facet of elaborate medieval memorial culture. The concept that prayers and offerings of the living could alter the fate of the deceased subtly entangled filial and religious piety with the salvation of ancestors and became a powerful agent both for the lavish furnishings of churches and graveyards but also as a solid basis of eclesiastical funding. Graves surmounted by ostentatious memorial architecture and art which encrusted the walls and floors of town and monastery churches became the focus of rituals and prayer facilitating the salvation of the forebears' sin-ridden souls. Martin Luther's insistence that a sinner can only partake of God's gift of grace in her or his lifetime, however, made memorial ritual superfluous.[29]

In most cases, however, the impact of these changes was softened by continuities in familial piety. While the chants and masses for the dead fell silent and the unpaid orants drifted away, funerary chapels, family vaults, and elaborate grave monuments in town churches continued to memorialize the deceased.[30] Remarkably, it was particularly the graves of the high nobility, which were located in monasteries or chantry chapels built expressly to insure an eternal chain of prayers, which were at greatest risk of destruction. The all-but-universal abandonment of Central Germany's religious houses at the beginning of the Reformation, and their subsequent dereliction and demolition, led to the wholesale loss of countless graves of once-powerful nobles, sinners all, who had relied on monastic prayer to guarantee their felicitous afterlife.

At the same time, however, the growth of literacy and historical consciousness among commoners forced noble lineages to stress their legitimacy with courtly panegyric and other open displays stressing their claims to power based on long-scale genealogical continuities. This animated ruling families to celebrate the memories of their forebears just as their physical remains and memorials were in the process of disappearing. An excavation strategy realized by Margaretha von Watzdorf (fig. 3) in West Saxon Weißenfels shows the impact of this development.[31] Margaretha, a noble woman from an influential Thuringian lineage, who had joined the town's Poor Clares convent in 1515, witnessed its enforced secularization during the town's visitation (i.e a police action enforcing Protestant doctrine and practice) in 1540. When the abbess and five of her faithful sisters were expelled from their convent, Margaretha took the lead and together twelve others converted. Although they were allowed to remain in their convent as lay sisters running a girls' school, they were unable to prevent Prince-Elector Maurice of Saxony, who had made a fortune liquidating church property, from authorizing the quarrying of the convent's imposing church. Only the nuns' choir was to remain as the school's chapel.

Margaretha, however, had bonded with Anne of Denmark (fig. 4), the resolute Danish wife of Maurice's retiring brother Augustus. Both had stayed in the convent during their honeymoon. When Augustus succeeded to electoral dignity in 1556, "Mother Anne," as she was called, began playing an important role in Saxon politics. Margaretha convinced Anne, and she in turn her henpecked husband, to restore her half-ruined church by claiming that it had been the ancestral burial ground of an obscure branch of Augustus's Wettin lineage. In order to underline her story, Margaretha accompanied the rebuilding of the church with large-scale excavations sponsored by the princess. After a year's diggings, she discovered a waterlogged wooden coffin with robust "manly bones" on November 25, 1561. Margaretha was sure they belonged to Margrave Frederick Tuta, a thirteenth-century ancestor of the prince. This grave conveniently lay outside the church proper in the ambulatory of the former cloister, which obviously necessitated upsizing the new building. It was to be one of the most ambitious examples of sacred architecture realized in sixteenth-century Saxony.[32] While most of the excavated bones were carefully reburied in the new church, the bizarre fact is recorded that Margaretha sent the princess "moss" from a skull as well as a few bones from her excavations. Anne, an enthusiastic amateur pharmacist, needed them for her "medicines"—in this case the ground-up human bones and "moss" probably formed the basis of a blood clotting salve.[33]

Margaretha's dig, of course, stands in the tradition of the iconic female archaeologist, St. Helena, the mother of Constantine the Great, whose legendary excavations for the fragments of the true cross in Jerusalem were long seen as a seminal and indeed wildly successful attempt to verify the identification of a site, in this case Golgotha, through spadework.[34] Yet Margaretha's specific mission to unearth noble ancestors' bodies also reflected fifteenth and sixteenth-century trends in the legitimization strategies of Central

---

27 WA.B 2 (no. 265 f.). **28** Mack, *Fastnacht*. **29** For medieval memorial culture, see Oexle, *Memoria*. **30** Brinkmann, *Grablegen*; Meys, *Memoria*. **31** Meier, *Evidenz*, p. 162. **32** Sadly her impressive Renaissance church was demolished in the mid-nineteenth century as it was seen as obstructing traffic: Fick, *Klar-* en-*Kloster*. Only the medieval apse which had survived the initial demolition of the church was taken down and rebuilt on the Weißenfels cemetery where it still serves as its funerary chapel. **33** Porterfield, *Healing*, pp. 69 f. **34** Baert, *Heilig hout*.

Fig. 3 Grave slab of Margaretha von Watzdorf, 1570,
after Carl Peter Lepsius, Historische Nachricht von dem
St. Clarenkloster zu Weißenfels (Historical accounts
on the Poor Clares convent in Weißenfels), Nordhausen 1837

Fig. 4 Lucas Cranach the Younger,
Anne of Denmark, Electress of Saxony, 1565

Fig. 5 Embossed vessel of the Lusatian Culture, c. 1300 BC. Mounted with tin by Haug von Maxen around 1560

Fig. 6 Ambrosius Holbein, upper edge of the frontispiece of Erasmus of Rotterdam's commentary of the New Testament, Basel 1522. Arminius and his army attack Varus and his Roman troops who are already fleeing from the left. In the lower right corner a German cuts out a Roman tax collector's tongue.

European noble houses. They were delving into their ancestries in a fierce competition to shore up their claims to titles and territory in an increasingly literate and critical political forum.[35] Sixteenth-century genealogical *panegyrics* and *epithalamia* (at times excessively flattering eulogies and nuptual lyrics and genealogical poetry) typically grafted surprisingly accurate family histories to brazen invention, thrusting noble lineages back into mythological prehistory and filling the coffers of humanist courtiers who fabricated them.

The disruption of organized memorial piety during the Reformation led to a spate of further excavation activity. A prime example is recorded in Saxony. By the beginning of the seventeenth century the prince elector's Wettin lineage was faced with the loss of their medieval princely tombs which were being buried under the collapsing masonry of the dynasty's secularized chantry chapel in the church of the Altzella monastery near Meissen. Prince Elector John George I, whose credibility had been shaken by his vacillating alliances and military defeats during the Thirty Years' War, launched the country's first mandated rescue excavation to retrieve and protect his ancestors' graves in 1638. Remarkably, after a tortuous sequence of repeated excavation, neglect, and even desecration, the princely tombs' grave markers were finally collected in a newly built memorial chapel closely modelled on a Greek temple at the end of the eighteenth century. The ornately sculptured slabs of Christian sinners in desperate need of perpetual intercession

and prayer had finally morphed into monuments to ancestral heroes hollowed by a setting whose architecture was modeled on a pagan Greek shrine.[36]

The genealogical archaeology of these times was, however, not exhausted by rooting out the graves of known historical ancestors. Archaeological attempts to extend a regent's genealogical taproots into primeval layers of prehistory can be traced back to the fifteenth century. In 1488, for instance, Emperor Frederick III ordered an excavation to recover the Burgundian hero Seyfried/Siegfried from his alleged barrow in Worms with unsatisfactory results. Had the exhumation been successful, then the adoption of this legendary hero into his ancestral line would have bolstered the legality of Frederick's dubious annexation of large swaths of Burgundian territory after Charles the Bold's demise.[37]

Analogous efforts by Thurius in Mecklenburg to use spadework to connect with distant ancestors were discussed above. A close confederate of Luther, the Wittenberg-educated scholar Joachim Ernest Prince of Anhalt, was engaged in a similar mission. In 1569 he commissioned excavations on the northern rim of the Harz Mountains searching in vain for the bones of his eleventh century ancestor Esico under the floor of the castle church at the family seat of Ballenstedt. He was more successful in his diggings in a barrow near Bernburg where he found "ancient German" urns containing cremated bones "of highbred bodies."[38]

35 Heck/Jahn, *Genealogie*. **36** Lippert, *Altzelle*; Magirius, *Altzella*. **37** Conflicting reports make it difficult to be sure whether it was Frederick or his son Maximilian who dug for Siegfried but evidence favors the father: Diekamp, *Niebelungen*; Wood, *Maximilian*. **38** Brunn, *Anhalt*, p. 31; Schmidt-Theilbier, *Köthener Land*.

From Miraculous Relics to Chambers of Miracles: the Birth of Archeological Collections

Yet there were also more subtle methods by which a region's pre-historic past could be woven into the self-narration of noble lineages. In the sixteenth century, courtly patterns of collecting and display in Lutheran Saxony were undergoing a radical change in focus from amassing miraculous relics (*Heiltum*) to collecting and displaying miracles of nature and the ancient past (*Wunderkammer*).[39] Such collections, which had their roots in the scholarly collections of Italian patricians and educated transalpine burghers, were playing an increasingly crucial role in the ostentation of ruling houses during the sixteenth century. Emperor Rudolf II, whose impressive collections of art and *naturalia* played a crucial role in the rituals of imperial self-representation, was the first regent to put his collections on display, in this case at his court in Prague's Hradčany palace.[40] Besides purchasing Mediterranean antiquities, like most of his contemporary regents, he began collecting pottery for this collection from Bronze Age Lusatian Culture cemeteries in Lower Silesia, commissioning excavations in 1577 and 1595.[41] This unusual northern focus of his archaeological collecting must be seen in the context of his attempts to secure the loyalty of his Protestant Silesian subjects.[42] His collection did not survive the sack of Prague in the Thirty Years' War, but a fifteenth century BC-embossed urn which was decorated with elaborate Renaissance tin fittings in 1560 (fig. 5) does survive from the collection of Haug von Maxen. He was Rudolf's imperial commissioner in Upper Lusatia, which was at the time hotly contested between Protestants and Catholics, and seems to have been imitating his master by collecting local antiquities and having them fitted for ostentatious display.

In Saxony, collecting relics looked back on a proud tradition. In the Pre-Reformation period, it had hosted the two largest collections of miraculous relics, Cardinal Albert of Brandenburg's *Heiltum* in Halle (Saale) and Prince Frederick the Wise's relic collection in Wittenberg said to have been Europe's largest.[43] In the later sixteenth century, the Albertine prince electors in Dresden continued this tradition by amassing vast secular collections of marvellous and precious objects which became the precursors of the magnificent *Grüne Gewölbe*.[44] Not surprisingly it was Queen Anne, the sponsor of Margaretha von Watzdorfs' excavation, who began purchasing and integrating vessels from the ubiquitous "Lusatian" cemeteries into the princely collections in the 1560s. While Anne may have initially thought she was buying natural earth-grown wonders, at least her husband Prince Augustus, who authorized a pricy purchase in 1578, realized that these vessels came from cremation burials of prehistoric peoples living as "heathens."[45]

The exact role these vessels played in court ceremony is unclear. The fact that Haug von Maxen's urn is decorated like contemporary drinking mugs makes it highly likely that prehistoric vessels were being presented on elaborately furnished banqueting tables or sideboards. This would clearly signalize not only the pride that their owners took in the aboriginal Germanic past but also their celebration of their ancestral links to it. There is a remarkable irony to the fact that, in early Reformation Saxony, devout Protestants who had fervently damned, dispersed, and destroyed the collections of relics and reliquaries of Christian saints, because they inspired pagan devotion,[46] would champion collecting and displaying relics from the country's pagan past as a patriotic virtue.

Luther, Arminius, and the Rise of German Protestant Patriotism

Although Martin Luther himself was only marginally involved with the discipline of prehistoric archaeology in Central and Northern Europe, its emergence is inescapably entangled with Martin Luther's reform and the ensuing attempts to find diachronic paths to legitimacy and ancestry outside of the all-encompassing embrace of Rome. This interest in the material culture of the distant past is, of course, just one facet of an all-encompassing enquiry into the nature and history of the ancient Germans which is intimately linked to the discovery of the manuscript of Publius Cornelius Tacitus' *Germania* in 1452. Written in 98 AD, this was the only comprehensive account of the ancient Germans which had survived from Antiquity and, pertinently, gave detailed information about their successful revolt against the Romans under the Cheruscan leader Arminius. It was finally published by Germany's leading humanist, and the Empire's first poet laureate Conrad Celtis in 1490.[47] Celtis propagated what he felt were Tacitus' crucial messages: despite their poverty and barbarity, the Germanic tribes were the aboriginal inhabitants of Europe whose artless lifestyle and rustic virtues and manners set them so clearly and virtuously apart from decadent Rome. Moreover, the positive view of Germanic simplicity and austere moral and martial values contrasted well with what popular prejudice saw as the luxuriating, corrupt, and sly Italians in general and papal Rome in particular. The majority of German humanists, who depended on noble and imperial patronage, while welcoming upgrading their Germanic ancestors still saw Arminius, who had betrayed his oath to the Roman Empire, as an ambiguous figure, and based on ancient sources such as Lucius Annaeus Florus, his struggle for Germanic freedom as backsliding to barbarism (fig. 6). This was clearly not the case in early Reformation Saxony. The humanist knight Ulrich von Hutten, a disciple of Luther and firebrand opponent of papacy and empire, wrote an elegy glorifying Arminius and in 1520 exhorted Prince Elec-

39 Laube, *Reliquie*, pp. 139–194. **40** Kaufmann, *Maximilian II*; Walther, *Adel*. **41** Seger, *Maslographia*. **42** Bahlcke, *Späthumanismus*. **43** Fey, *Reliquienschätze*, pp. 11–36. The *Wittenberg Heiltum* was being shown as late as 1525, see Krentz, *Ritualwandel*, pp. 378–381. **44** Syndram, *Kunstkammer*. **45** Gummel, *Forschung*, p. 13, pl. 1; Kühn, *Geschichte*, p. 17; Bierbaum, *Sachsen*. **46** See Kühne, *hyn und her*. **47** Stadtwald, *Vienna Circle*.

Fig. 7 Alfonso Pelzer, Statue of Arminius ("Herman the German"), 1888–97, New Ulm, Minnesota

tor Frederick the Wise to defend Saxony against Rome as did his ancestor Arminius, so that he "should not be ashamed of his descendants." In stressing ancestral bonds between the ancient German rebel and the prince elector, Hutten was alluding to the learned equation between the Cherusci, Arminius' tribe, and Central Germany's Saxons—something which would be a prime mover in the political instrumentation of Tacitus' legacy in Central Germany.[48]

While Hutten's poem was couched in learned Latin, charismatic Swabian humanist Johannes Carion would make the Germanic rebellion and its leader known to a wider public. His *Chronicon Carionis*, published in Wittenberg in 1532, was edited, and perhaps largely written, by his friend and mentor Philipp Melanchthon, and traced world history from the creation of Adam to the ascension of Emperor Charles V. Couched in breezy, highly readable German and presented in a clear layout and handy format, it became a standard reference work among Protestant German school children and educated burghers alike during the course of the sixteenth century including Martin Luther himself.[49] Arminius' crushing defeat of Varus' Roman Legions in 9 AD is featured as the crucial event in the reign of Tiberius next to Christ's death. It is interesting that he used the fully spurious equation of Arminius, who is only known to us by this Roman nickname, and German "Hermann." This fabrication is thought to have originated among Melanchthon's circle of Wittenberg humanists; perhaps even Luther himself was the perpetrator, as he is recorded as mulling the name's meaning in the early 1530s.[50]

While Luther initially seems only to have had a marginal interest in ancient Germans, his attitude changes in the later 1530s when Arminius and his rebellion are mentioned more often in Luther's recorded statements and *table talks*. This clearly reflects the anxieties of the times. Protestant rebellion against the Holy Roman Empire was imminent and Luther's confrontation with the Pope and his humanist supporters, such as Erasmus, had reached a fever pitch.[51] In a table talk recorded by Georg Rörer, Luther is quoted as saying: "As to Arminius, if I were a poet I would celebrate him. I love him whole heartedly, He was called duke Herman and ruled over the Harz country. The Harz's natives are the Cheruscans […] If I now had an Arminius and he a Doctor Martin, we would then look for (i.e., attack and destroy) the Turks."[52] It is telling that Luther is locating the homeland of Arminius' Cheruscans tribe around the Central German Harz massif, a further fallacy that was propagated by Wittenberg's humanists. They continued to do so even after eminent scholars, including Melanchthon himself, made it clear that a close reading of the sources saw Arminius and his Cheruscans living and fighting on the Northwest German plain.[53] Moreover, Luther saw the contemporary "Harzers," among which he proudly counted himself, as their direct descendants.[54] The Reformer's remarkable statement that he would seek a showdown with the Turks, were Arminius at his side, underscores what he clearly saw as their close, almost fraternal relationship. Moreover, there is a subtle subtext here, involving Arminius, the ancient German freedom fighter and contemporary of

Christ, prefiguring Luther's quest for Christian freedom, which is woven into early Lutheran panegyrics.

The Franconian reformer and desciple of Luther, Andreas Althammer, wrote an enormously influential commentary to Tacitus' *Germania* in 1536 which would enshrine this connection in the minds of the Lutheran faithful. He claimed that "the liberator of Germany Hermann [which he read as 'man of the army'; annotation of the author] had been reborn in Luther the Cheruscan." Moreover, in a wild digression from historical feasibility, Althammer would claim that the first Holy Roman Emperor Charlemagne had been coerced by the Pope to force the Cheruscans (in fact it was the Saxons) to convert to the false tenets of superstitious Catholicism, and it was the Saxon Martin Luther, a Cheruscan, who would reinstall pure Christianity in Saxony.[55] This remarkable attempt to interweave the fate of what was seen as ancient Germany's emancipator from the Roman yoke and modern Germany's liberator from the Roman Pope would pave the way for nationalistic mythologies which would eventually lead to both Luther's and Arminius' canonization as German national heroes in the nineteenth century (fig. 7).

48 Junghans, *Hütten*. **49** Seifert, *Schulwesen*, p. 335; *WA* 53, 10, 53. **50** *WA* 31/I, 205–206/Concordia XIII, 59. For Luther's wildly speculative etymologies of Herman/Arminius, see *WA* 1, 419; *WA* 6, 7043. For the complex humanist and early Lutheran reactions to Arminius, see Mertens, *Instrumentalisierung*. **51** Spitz, *Humanism*. **52** *WA*.TR 5, 415 (no. 5982). **53** Kösters, *Varusschlacht*, p. 72. **54** *WA* 3 (no. 3464c). **55** Kaiser, *Kanonisierung*; Kaufmann, *Luther als Held*. For the perception of Arminius' rising as a cornerstone of German Protestant Nationalism, see Hirschi, *Origins*.

BIBLIOGRAPHY

Baert, Barbara (2001), *Een erfenis van heilig hout: de neerslag van het teruggevonden kruis in tekst en beeld tijdens de Middeleeuwen*. Leuven. **Bahlcke**, Joachim (2005), Religion, Politik und Späthumanismus. Zum Wandel der schlesisch-böhmischen Beziehungen im konfessionellen Zeitalter. In: Gabler, Klaus (ed.) *Kulturgeschichte Schlesiens in der Frühen Neuzeit*. Berlin, pp. 69–92. **Bierbaum**, Georg (1927), Zur Geschichte der Altertumsforschung in Sachsen. In: *Bautzener Geschichtshefte*, vol. 5, no. 1, pp. 15–38. **Böhmer**, Heinrich (1914), *Luthers Romfahrt*, Leipzig. **Brather**, Sebastian (2004), *Ethnische Interpretationen in der frühgeschichtlichen Archäologie: Geschichte, Grundlagen und Alternativen*. Berlin. **Brown**, Peter (1982), *The Cult of the Saints: Its Rise and Function in Latin Christianity* (= The Haskell Lectures on History of Religions. 2). Chicago. **Brinkmann**, Inga (2010), *Grabdenkmäler, Grablegen und Begräbniswesen des lutherischen Adels*. München. **Brunn**, Wilhelm Albert von (1958), Kenntnis und Pflege der Bodendenkmäler in Anhalt. In: *Jahresschrift für mitteldeutsche Vorgeschichte*, vol. 41/42, pp. 28–71. **Diekamp**, Busso (2004), "Nibelungenstadt:" Die Rezeption der Nibelungen in Worms. In: Hinkel, Helmut (ed.), *Nibelungen-Schnipsel. Neues vom Alten Epos zwischen Mainz und Worms*. Mainz, pp. 146–147. **Erenstoft**, Jamie Beth (2008), *Controlling the Sacred Past: Rome, Pius IX, and Christian Archaeology*. Ann Arbour. **Fey**, Carola (2006), Beobachtungen zu Reliquienschätzen deutscher Fürsten im Spätmittelalter. In: Tacke, Andreas (ed.), *"Ich armer sundiger mensch." Heiligen- und Reliquienkult am Übergang zum konfessionellen Zeitalter*. Göttingen, pp. 11–36. **Fick**, Astrid (2001), *Das Weißenfelser St. Klaren-Kloster. Zum 700-jährigen Bestehen*, Weißenfels. **Finucane**, Ronald C. (2011), *Contested Canonizations: The Last Medi-*

eval Saints, 1482–1523. Washington, D.C., pp. 207–241. **Frend**, William H. (1996), *The Archaeology of Early Christianity. A History.* Minneapolis. **Gummel**, Hans (1938), *Forschungsgeschichte in Deutschland. Die Urgeschichtsforschung und ihre historische Entwicklung in den Kulturstaaten der Erde.* Berlin. **Hansen**, Reimer (2005), Heinrich Rantzau. Ein Humanist und Politiker aus der Schule Philipp Melanchthons. In: Hansen, Reimer (ed.), *Aus einem Jahrtausend historischer Nachbarschaft. Studien zur Geschichte Schleswigs, Holsteins und Dithmarschens.* Malente, pp. 151–176. **Heck**, Kilian/**Jahn**, Bernhard (eds.) (2000), *Genealogie als Denkform in Mittelalter und Früher Neuzeit.* Berlin. **Hirschi**, Caspar (2012), *The Origins of Nationalism: An Alternative History from Ancient Rome to Early Modern Germany.* Cambridge. **Junghans**, Heimar (1987), Kaiser Karl V. am Grabe Martin Luthers in der Schlosskirche zu Wittenberg. In: *Lutherjahrbuch*, vol. 54, pp. 100–113. **Junghans**, Heimar (1988), Der nationale Humanismus bei Ulrich von Hutten und Martin Luther. In: *Ehrenburg Hefte*, vol. 22, pp. 147–170. **Kaiser**, Ronny (2014), Kanonisierung und neue Deutungsräume. Die Grenzen der Antike in Andreas Althammers Comentaria zur Germania des Tacitus (1536). In: Heinze, Anna et al. (eds.), *Grenzen der Antike: Die Produktivität von Grenzen in Transformationsprozessen.* Berlin, pp. 353–372. **Kaufmann**, Thomas DaCosta (1978), *Variations on the Imperial Theme in the Age of Maximilian II. and Rudolph II: Studies in Ceremonial, Art and Collecting.* New York. **Kaufmann**, Thomas DaCosta (2013), Luther als Held. Einige Bemerkungen zur frühreformatorischen Text- und Bildpublizistik. In: Aurnhammer, Achim/Pfister, Manfred (eds.), *Heroen und Heroisierungen in der Renaissance* (= Wolfenbütteler Abhandlungen zur Renaissanceforschung. 28). Wiesbaden, pp. 85–144. **Klindt-Jensen**, Ole (1975), *A History of Scandinavian Archaeology.* London. **Knape**, Joachim (2000), Humanismus, Reformation, deutsche Sprache und Nation. In: Gardt, Andreas, *Nation und Sprache, Die Diskussion ihres Verhältnisses in Geschichte und Gegenwart.* Berlin, pp. 103–138. **Kösters**, Klaus (2009), *Mythos Arminius: Die Varusschlacht und ihre Folgen.* Münster. **Koudounaris**, Paul (2013), *Heavenly Bodies: Cult treasures and spectacular saints from the Catacombs.* London. **Krentz**, Nathalie (2014), *Ritualwandel und Deutungshoheit. Die frühe Reformation in der Residenzstadt Wittenberg (1500–1533).* Tübingen. **Kühn**, Herbert (1976), *Geschichte der Vorgeschichtsforschung.* Berlin/New York. **Kühne**, Hartmut (2006), "die do lauffen hyn und her, zum heiligen Creutz zu Dorgaw und tzu Dresen …:" Luthers Kritik an Heiligenkult und Wallfahrten im historischen Kontext Mitteldeutschlands. In: Tacke, Andreas (ed.), *"Ich armer sundiger mensch." Heiligen- und Reliquienkult am Übergang zum konfessionellen Zeitalter.* Göttingen. **Laube**, Stefan (2011), *Von der Reliquie zum Ding: Heiliger Ort—Wunderkammer—Museum.* Berlin. **Lippert**, Woldemar (1896), Die Fürsten- oder Andreaskapelle im Kloster Altzelle und die neue Begräbniskapelle von 1786. In: *Neues Archiv für Sächsische Geschichte und Altertumskunde*, vol. 17, pp. 33–74. **Luscher**, Birgit (2008), *Reliquienverehrung als Symbolsystem: volkskirchliche Praxis und reformatorischer Umbruch: zum Wittenberger Reliquienschatz und zur Transformation des symbolischen Denkens bei Luther.* Münster. **Mack**, Fritz (1967), Evangelische Stimmen zur Fastnacht. In: Bausinger, Hermann (ed.), *Masken zwischen Spiel und Ernst* (= Volksleben. 18), pp. 35–49. **Magirius**, Heinrich (1962), *Die Baugeschichte des Klosters Altzella.* Berlin. **Meier**, Hans-Rudolf (2010), Die Evidenz der Dinge. Frühneuzeitliche "Archäologie" in Klöstern. In: Hakelberg, Dietrich/Wiwjorra, Ingo (eds.), *Vorwelten und Vorzeiten. Archäologie als Spiegel historischen Bewußtseins in der Frühen Neuzeit* (= Wolfenbütteler Forschungen. 124), Wiesbaden, pp. 153–172. **Mennung**, Albert (1925), *Über die Vorstufen der prähistorischen Wissenschaft im Altertum und Mittelalter, Veröffentlichungen der Gesellschaft für Vorgeschichte und Heimatkunde des Kreises Calbe I.* Calbe. **Mertens**, Dieter (2004), Die Instrumentalisierung der "Germania" des Tacitus durch die deutschen Humanisten. In: Beck, Heinrich et al. (eds.), *Zur Geschichte der Gleichung "germanisch-deutsch." Sprache und Namen, Geschichte und Institutionen* (= Ergänzungsbände zum Reallexikon der germanischen Altertumskunde. 34). Berlin/New York. **Meys**, Oliver (2009), *Memoria und Bekenntnis. Die Grabmäler evangelischer Landesherren im Heiligen Römischen Reich Deutscher Nation im Zeitalter der Konfessionalisierung.* Regensburg. **Müller**, Georg (1890), Ein Urnenfund im 16. Jahrhundert. In: *Neues Archiv für sächsische*

*Gesch*ichte, vol. 11, p. 156. **Oexle**, Otto Gerhard (1994), Memoria in der Gesellschaft und in der Kultur des Mittelalters. In: Heinzle, Joachim (ed.): *Modernes Mittelalter. Neue Bilder einer populären Epoche.* Frankfurt am Main, pp. 297–323. **Porterfield**, Amanda (2005), *Healing in the History of Christianity.* New York. **Raguin**, Virginia Chieffo (2010), *Art, Piety and Destruction in the Christian West, 1500–1700.* Farnham. **Sasse-Kunst**, Barbara (2010), Die Gräber der Obotriten und Heruler des Nikolaus Marschalk (um 1470–1525)—eine Korrektur der Forschungsgeschichte zu den Megalithgräbern und zur ethnischen Deutung. In: Armbruester, Tanya/Hegewisch, Morten (eds.), *Beiträge zur Vor- und Frühgeschichte der Iberischen Halbinsel und Mitteleuropas. Studien in honorem Philine Kalb* (= Studien zur Archäologie Europas. 11). Bonn, pp. 247–265. **Schimpff**, Volker (1990), Der Beginn der archäologischen Forschung in Norddeutschland: Zum Wirken von Nikolaus Marschalk Thurius in Mecklenburg. In: *Rostocker Wissenschaftshistorische Manuskripte*, vol. 18, pp. 70–73. **Schmidt**, Berthold (1986), 100 Jahre Bodendenkmalpflege im Arbeitsbereich des Landesmuseums für Vorgeschichte Halle (Saale). In: *Jahresschrift für Mitteldeutsche Vorgeschichte*, vol. 69, pp. 15–60. **Schmidt-Theilbier**, Erika (1986), Bodendenkmalpflege im Köthener Land. In: *Jahresschrift für Mitteldeutsche Vorgeschichte*, vol. 69, pp. 133–149. **Schnapp**, Alain (1997), *The Discovery of the Past.* New York. **Schneider**, Hans (2011*), Martin Luthers Reise nach Rom—neu datiert und neu gedeutet* (= Studien zur Wissenschafts- und Religionsgeschichte. 10). Berlin. **Scribner**, Robert W. (1987), *Popular Culture and Popular Movements in Reformation Germany.* London/Ronceverte. **Seger**, Hans (1911), Maslographia 1711–1911. In: *Schlesiens Vorzeit in Bild und Schrift*, vol. 6, pp. 1–16. **Seifert**, Arno (1996), Das höhere Schulwesen. Universitäten und Gymnasien. In: Hammerstein, Notker (ed.), *Handbuch der deutschen Bildungsgeschichte. Vol. I: 15. bis 17. Jahrhundert. Von der Renaissance und der Reformation bis zum Ende der Glaubenskämpfe.* München, pp. 197–374. **Spitz**, Lewis William (1996), *Luther and German Humanism.* Aldershot. **Stadtwald**, Kurt (1993), Patriotism and Antipapalism in the Politics of Conrad Celtis's "Vienna Circle." In: *Archiv für Reformationsgeschichte*, vol. 84, pp. 83–102. **Stemmermann**, Paul Hans (1934), *Die Anfänge der deutschen Vorgeschichtsforschung: Deutschlands Bodenaltertümer in der Anschauung des 16. und 17. Jahrhunderts.* Leipzig. **Stock**, Michael (2011), Ur- und frühgeschichtliche Archäologie und Landeskunde—Beispiele aus Sachsen-Anhalt. In: *Denkströme, Journal der Sächsischen Akademie der Wissenschaften*, vol. 6, pp. 137–167. **Syndram**, Dirk (2004), Über den Ursprung der kursächsischen Kunstkammer. In: *Dresdner Hefte. Beiträge zur Kulturgeschichte.* Sonderausgabe, pp. 3–14. **Tanner**, Marie (1993), *The Last Descendant of Aeneas: The Hapsburgs and the Mystic Image of the Emperor.* Philidelphia. **Volkmar**, Christoph (2002), *Die Heiligenerhebung Bennos von Meißen (1523/24): Spätmittelalterliche Frömmigkeit, landesherrliche Kirchenpolitik und reformatorische Kritik im albertinischen Sachsen in der frühen Reformationszeit.* Münster. **Walter**, Hans/**Göricke**, Günter (2001), Frühe wissenschaftliche Ausgrabung des Petrus Albinus (1543–1598) und ihre Bedeutung für die Geschichte der Paläontologie. In: *Geoprofil*, vol. 10, pp. 76–90. **Walther**, Gerrit (1998), Adel und Antike. Zur politischen Bedeutung gelehrter Kultur für die Führungselite der Frühen Neuzeit. In: *Historische Zeitschrift*, vol. 266, pp. 359–385. **Wierschin**, Hans (1976), *Das Ambraser Heldenbuch Maximilians.* Bozen. **Wood**, Christopher S. (2005), Maximilian als Archäologe. In: Mülle, Jan-Dirk/Ziegeler, Hans-Joachim (eds.), *Maximilians Ruhmeswerk: Künste und Wissenschaften im Umkreis Kaiser Maximilians I.* Berlin, pp. 131–184.

V

Polemics and Conflicts

ANNE-SIMONE ROUS

Crisis Management in Denominational Conflicts Resulting from the Reformation

Luther's posting of his Ninety-Five Theses in 1517 exacerbated the conflict already existing within the church, creating ongoing crisis situations[1] that the authorities dealt with in different ways. As always, the problems involved had to do with control, sanction, or distribution, giving rise to cooperation conflicts with far-reaching implications.[2] All three aspects may be found in (ecclesiastical) politics during the Reformation era. Both church and Emperor saw themselves exposed to a threat they judged to be existential—the division of the church. The decision makers (secular and ecclesiastical princes and their advisers) were forced to function as crisis managers—with varying degrees of success.

The Crisis of the Church

The question of how Emperor and Pope should deal with the problem of Martin Luther after 1517 began as an acute decision-making quandary that soon reached a crisis stage. For both sides—for Luther as well as the Catholic Church—the *point of no return* had been reached. The standard procedure in dealing with the situation, which had been effective in the case of two earlier critics of the church, John Wyclif and Jan Hus, no longer functioned. For since 1311 there had been repeated calls for a "head and limbs" reform of the church.[3] Wyclif, who in the 1370s had questioned the Pope's claim to absolute power and understanding of the church's role, had not been officially arraigned because he enjoyed a high level of popular support; it was feared that arresting him would provoke a popular uprising. Only after the Council of Constance in 1415 was he officially condemned for heresy. His bones and writings were burned, as was his "disciple" Jan Hus, who, in order to deter further criticism, was condemned to death. While Rome's early-warning system functioned, at this time the Pope did not try to de-escalate the situation by offering to carry out reforms. His failure to do so lead to increased pressure on the church establishment. The humanists, who championed an ethical ideal of humanity, could not ignore the church's crisis of credibility. Erasmus of Rotterdam's response was ambivalent, and the papacy was not particularly disturbed by his largely ironic criticism.[4] Luther later criticized the humanist, saying that he lacked courage.[5] In 1517, the consequences of Luther's posting his Ninety-Five Theses were not immediately predictable, since their author was apparently a mere monk from the insignificant little town of Wittenberg.

The entire organization of the church must, however, have felt threatened by Luther's teaching. If the Pope had agreed to the reformers' demands, the consequences would have been a thoroughgoing restructuring of the church. Pope and bishops recognized the Reformation as a major threat to their power positions; they thus had to deal with a crisis that threatened their very survival. The reformers criticized inter alia the Vatican's lifestyle and its false interpretation of the Bible, and consequently the Roman Catholic clergy was the reformers' direct adversary. This reduced the conflict to a bipolar confrontation. Since the issue was not only one of personal consequences but, primarily, of basic differences in interpretations of religion, the debate centered on who had the right to make such interpretations, leading to a crisis of authority within the church. The invention of the printing press allowed the debate to be carried out using high-profile, insulting polemics disseminated via pamphlets, thus exacerbating the crisis further. A sober handling of the crisis thereby became impossible. Moderates' attempts at mediation between the parties had only limited success as religious faith was such an integral part of the life and thinking of those living in the early modern era. At issue for each individual believer was nothing less than the choice between heaven or hell, paradise or purgatory, and nobody could ignore these issues. On January 3, 1521, the Pope issued the bull of excommunication, *Decet Romanum Pontificem*, against the Reformer Martin Luther. This was the first climax of the crisis.

Emperor Charles V as Crisis Manager

The attacks on the church affected not only Pope, cardinals, and bishops but the secular powers as well. During the time that the reform of the empire—bringing its administration in line with the structural changes of the dawning modern age—was still in full swing, the acceptance of the Reformation by entire estates and influential princes of the empire shook the principle of rule "by the grace of God" to its foundations. Action had to be taken. Crisis management as such consists of several phases, each with its appropriate techniques.[6] Before the crisis breaks loose it can at most be anticipated, that is, recognized at an early stage, allowing information to be gathered and preparations made in good time for possible scenarios, and thus perhaps averting a worsening of the situation. If the crisis becomes acute, rational decision making, flexible thinking, the resolute application of authority, and clear communication are essential if it is to be contained. Ideally, the conflict parties' opposing interests can be resolved through conciliation and mediation and their divergent aims reconciled by realigning interests and preferences.

What options were open to the Emperor? It was impossible to anticipate the developments after the posting of the Ninety-Five Theses and the accordingly for Charles V to prepare to confront the movement Luther had triggered. He could only react by rapidly working to collect information on which to base a reasonably flexible set of options. He had reports sent to him from all the territories of the empire, and when he saw that Luther enjoyed widespread support, he knew how difficult the task was that he was facing. Charles V pursued the clear goal of remaining true to his orthodox beliefs and of making no concessions to the new faith.[7] Thus no misunderstandings could arise. Many princes did not follow the Emperor's line, first and foremost the rulers of Hesse and Saxony. In Saxony itself, the Reformation divided the ruling family.[8] While Duke George of the House of Wettin's Albertine line, whose capital was Dresden, remained a devout Roman Catholic (fig. 1), his cousin Elector Frederick of the Ernestine line in Torgau joined the new faith. Recognizing the weak points in his position, the Emperor concluded that he had no choice but to appeal to these apostate princes, which he did with great urgency. In so doing, he could rely on the princes' disciplining each other to remain loyal to their Emperor.

Parallel to the situation among the princes, a conflict had emerged between Luther and the House of Wettin's Albertine line. Luther took issue with the Catholic Duke George of Saxony's opposition to a renewal of the church and called him a "water blister."[9] Polemics and invectives flowed from both sides. By 1525, the differences between the orthodox Duke George and Martin Luther were clearly irreconcilable, for George resolutely rejected Luther's request to stop attacking him and his teaching. Elector Frederick the Wise tried in vain from his seat in Torgau to mediate between the two, but conflicts between the two Saxon lines that preceeded the Reformation prevented him from being an ideal mediator. Thus the exchange of polemics spread unabated and with it the mutual demonizing of the opposing parties. The abysmal level of debate resulted in a loss of prestige for both sides, and the absence of any de-escalation strategy led to further exacerbation. When Luther refused to withdraw his theses at the Imperial Diet of Worms, the situation intensified. The Emperor did not react at once. Only after a delay of nearly four weeks did he place Luther under the imperial ban, on May 26, 1521. In doing this, he had committed the procedural blunder of sending the decree to the princes after the Imperial Diet had ended, which later allowed the ban's legality to be widely questioned. But at that juncture its legality was not at issue. Having to wait for the Emperor's decision gave Luther a head start and had a de-escalating effect.[10]

Fig. 1 Hans Brosamer, Duke George of Saxony, the Bearded, after 1534

The Wartburg Sojourn: The Result of Successful Risk Management

Although the Emperor had promised him safe conduct for his return from the Imperial Diet, Luther's physical safety nevertheless was in fact at risk after his performance in Worms. The Elector of Saxony, Frederick, considered him to be in great danger on his journey home—after all, in 1415 the church critic Jan Hus had, despite similar assurances, been arrested in his lodgings in Constance and executed.

1 See Hutzschenreuther/Griess-Negra, *Krisenmanagement.* **2** See Urbanski, *Funktionsweise,* p. 41. **3** In the original: "in capite quam in membris." See Council of Vienne, 1311/12, and also the Inaugural Decree of the Second Sitting of the Council of Basel in 1432. See Frech, *Reform.* **4** See Desiderius Erasmus, Dialogus, Iulius excluso e coelis [1513]. In: Welzig, *Schriften.* **5** "...we see that the Lord has granted you neither the courage nor the disposition, openly and confidently together with us to attack those monsters [the Popes] [...]." See Letter from Martin Luther to Erasmus of Rotterdam, April 15, 1524. In: *WA* 18, 601 f. **6** See Pearson/Mittroff, *Crisis.* **7** See the essay by Heinz Schilling in this volume. **8** See the text by Martin Eberle in this volume. **9** *WA* 10/II, 55, 19 f., 22 f. **10** See the essay by Heinz Schilling in this volume.

So the elector secretly arranged for Luther to be kidnapped and held in protective custody in the Wartburg, thus allowing him to escape the clutches of the Emperor's henchmen. There is no doubt that Luther was indeed pursued, for Charles V later admitted that he regretted his promise of safe conduct. Though the *Edict of Worms*, which placed Luther under the imperial ban, was backdated and thus irregular, the Catholic Duke George of Saxony could now act against Luther and his teachings in accordance with imperial law. Luther was an outlaw and could thus be killed without fear of punishment. His compulsory sojourn in the Wartburg deflated the crisis to some extent as he had, so to speak, been taken out of the line of fire. This clever move allowed tempers to cool and minds to focus on the impending confrontation and social tumult. Luther himself functioned as crisis manager at this time. When the Wittenberg city fathers appealed to him for help in a situation of escalating radicalization he argued for moderate reforms.

Religious Colloquies

On a theological level, conflict management in the sixteenth century took the form of religious colloquies. No less than seventeen of these took place between orthodox and Protestant theologians, in addition to fourteen between members of Protestant denominations.[11] Even if no agreement could be reached, boundaries were drawn that clarified issues further. A war of religion arising from misunderstandings or uncertainties could thus, for the time being, be averted.

The *Pack Affair*:
A Case of Successful Disaster Management

In the meantime, the princes of the empire were becoming increasingly uneasy since it was unclear how far the Reformation was going to progress. Each side claimed sole legitimacy as God's representative on earth, and thus tensions were bound to increase. In 1528, an intrigue further exacerbated the conflict which is known as the the so-called *Pack Affair*. Otto von Pack, a privy counselor of the Catholic Duke George of Saxony, invented an alliance between a number of Catholic estates of the empire, allegedly founded the previous year, which was preparing a military offensive against the Landgrave of Hesse and the Elector of Saxony on account of their pro-Lutheran policies. The two princes, thus threatened, immediately prepared for a counter-offensive, developing a plan of operation that would have involved first an attack on the bishoprics of Bamberg and Würzburg followed by the occupation of the Bishop of Mainz's territories.[12] When Landgrave Philip of Hesse, the leader of the Protestant princes, was shown a copy of the "treaty of alliance," he was convinced of the existence of a Catholic plot. In addition, the letter in which Pack revealed the "Catholic alliance" to the Landgrave was composed in the handwriting of Philip's sister, Elizabeth, Duchess of Saxony, virtually vouching for the authenticity of Pack's assertions.[13] Pack's intrigue thus appeared to be successful; for both the Landgrave of Hesse and the Duke of Saxony, the scenario seemed perfectly plausible.

But Elector John of Saxony desisted from following Philip of Hesse's rash impetuosity. He first asked Martin Luther for his opinion on the situation. Acting as a good mediator,[14] Luther urged caution, rejected the plan for a preemptive attack, and suggested first establishing whether the alleged pact had imperial authority. Only with great difficulty could the Elector of Saxony persuade the Landgrave of Hesse to delay taking action. A second opinion, obtained from Philipp Melanchthon and Johannes Bugenhagen, also urged seeking a peaceful solution. During this crisis the Wittenberg theologians repeatedly admonished the two princes not to endanger the peace in the empire. And, indeed, as it turned out the apparently authentic document was a forgery: both Duke George of Saxony and King Ferdinand of Bohemia, the brother of the Emperor, swore that they had nothing to do with the matter and declared that they had been the victims of calumny (fig. 2). Under interrogation in Kassel, Pack thereupon admitted the forgery. Duchess Elizabeth also revealed that Pack had dictated the letter to her, saying she had believed him because she had heard rumors that the peasants were planning an uprising and that Philip had ambitions to be Roman king.[15] Had these rumors been true, it would have been perfectly logical to form a Catholic alliance. Landgrave Philip continued to believe in the existence of such an alliance, refusing for some time to surrender Pack to the authorities. After a year Philip released him, and Pack lived the life of a hunted fugitive until finally, eight years later in the Netherlands, he was apprehended and executed.

This episode is an impressive example of how easily prejudicial assumptions can be manipulated to start a major crisis. At the same time, it shows clearly how important it is to obtain reliable information and examine the situation from all angles, which should always take precedence over taking action.

The *Augsburg Confession* as Compromise Formula?

At the Augsburg Imperial Diet of 1530, Emperor Charles V rejected the *Augsburg Confession*. Philipp Melanchthon had specifically worded this written defense of the Reformation to highlight the many points of agreement with the Catholic Church. In addition, sending Melanchthon the conciliator to Augsburg while keeping Luther in Coburg was designed to facilitate reaching a compromise. Nevertheless, on the Emperor's instructions the Catholic theologians Johannes Eck, Johann Faber, and Johannes Cochlaeus refuted the *Augsburg Confession*. The *Augsburg Confutation*, a written indictment of the Reformation, allowed Charles V to confirm the *Edict of Worms* and deny Melanchthon's request for recognition of the new faith. The three Catholic theologians had nevertheless agreed to fifteen articles of the *Augsburg Confession*, which was the reason why the Protestants did not receive a written copy of the *Confutation*. The Emperor also refused to see Melanchthon's answer to the Catholic side's criticisms, the *Apology of the Augsburg Confession*, thus preventing a continuation of the theological debate, which might have paved the way for a viable compromise. The Emperor rightly saw the unity of empire and church in danger and opted for to break off the negotiations completely so as not to give the new faith further opportunity to spread its ideas. Taking a defensive stance, he used his imperial authority to abandon the process of compromise and confirmed the proscription of the faith of the Protestant estates of the empire.

Fig. 2 Sandro Botticelli, The Calumny of Apelles, around 1496–97. The painting mirrors the early modern understanding of calumny: The king, depicted with donkey ears, listens to Presumption and Ignorance. Before him stand Hate bearing a torch, and Slander, who is attended by Fraud and Villainy. Behind the accused, who has been dragged forward, stand Repentance dressed in black and the naked Truth, who calls upon heaven as her witness.

When in 1539 Duke George of Saxony died, his brother Henry immediately introduced the Reformation into the dukedom and celebrated the first Lutheran church service in Albertine Saxony in the Dresden Kreuzkirche (fig. 3). This change of government, however, contributed only indirectly to an easing of tensions.

Formation of Strategic Alliances

Those Protestant estates of the empire who refused to bow down to the Emperor saw the ruling that concluded the Diet of Augsburg as exposing them to the danger of attack by an imperial army bearing a warrant for breach of the peace. For their own protection, they founded the Schmalkaldic League in 1531 in the town of Schmalkalden, Thuringia, further cementing the split.[16] Since alliances against the Emperor were forbidden, this gave Charles V an additional argument to proceed against supporters of the new faith. The leaders of the Schmalkaldic League were the two most powerful Protestant princes: Landgrave Philip of Hesse and Elector John Frederick of Saxony (fig. 4). These "Captains of the League" were little inclined to function as mediators. Landgrave Philip was an out-and-out cham-

11 See Dingel, *Religionsgespräche*. **12** See Jadatz, *Religionspolitik*, p. 62. **13** See Rous, *Geheimdiplomatie*, p. 316. **14** His action fulfilled all the criteria of mediation: "In international mediation, a third party, not itself a party to the conflict, intervenes from without in the negotiation process between two or more conflict parties with the intention of effecting a reconciliation of interests through appropriate strategies and thus resolving the conflict in part or in whole. The mediator does not apply force, though he may introduce his own resources into the negotiation process to directly or indirectly exert pressure on one or more of the conflict parties." Urbanski, *Funktionsweise*, p. 19. **15** See Duchess Elizabeth to Philip of Hesse, July 9, 1528. In: Thieme, *Korrespondenz*, no. 137, pp. 244 f. **16** See Haug-Moritz, *Schmalkaldische Bund*.

Fig. 3 Heinrich Epler, Bronze relief on the altar of the Kreuzkirche in Dresden with a depiction
of the first Protestant church service in Saxony in 1539, 1900

pion of the new faith and advocated an aggressive foreign policy for the league. Elector John Frederick pursued a policy of restraint—he was, after all, also a friend of Martin Luther. He remained a staunch supporter of the Protestant credo and strengthened the reformers' resolve not to make too many concessions to the Emperor. Martin Luther was very grateful for this: "At Augsburg he (Elector John) was inspired by the Holy Ghost, for he ignored the command of the Emperor not to have a sermon preached. Instead he had the Gospel itself preached again and again, despite the imperial mandate. [...] He did not yield to threats and did not deviate so much as a finger's breadth from the true religion and God's word, although he thereby placed himself in great danger."[17]

The Schmalkaldic League suffered from a shortage of funds, lukewarm support from its towns and princes, and differences of opinion among its members.[18] But strategic mismanagement by the league leaders was only one reason for its unfavorable position at the start of the Schmalkaldic War of 1546–47. The war started after the Emperor had concluded a truce with France and could thus devote his attention to his main problem within the Holy Roman Em-

pire—how to destroy the Schmalkaldic League. His biggest coup was persuading the ambitious Maurice of Saxony to join his side, thus depriving the Protestants of their brightest leader. None of the league members had imagined such a worst-case scenario: their militarily most talented prince turning his back on the Protestant alliance and, out of pure self-interest, joining the enemy. The league leaders had allowed themselves to be misled and fed with false promises by Maurice for far too long, and he himself successfully avoided a personal debate on the matter. Not only did the league leaders fail to integrate him into the alliance but they also did not hear of his changing sides until it was too late. Thus their preparations for the impending campaign were based on false premises and could not be adapted at short notice. Based on past experience, Maurice's conduct was indeed unimaginable for them. In addition to its inability to see beyond the immediate situation, the league was lulled into false

17 Johannes Aurifaber/Johannes Adler, *Colloquia, oder Tischreden Dr. Martin Luthers [1566]*. Eisleben, p. 173. **18** See Rous, *Geheimdiplomatie*, pp. 327–331.

Von Gotts Gnaden Johanns Friderich Hertzogk zu Sachssen des Heiligen Römischen
Reichs Ertzmarsschalck/ vnd Churfürst/ Landtgraff in Düringen Marggraffe zu
Weissen/ vnd Burggraff zu Magdeburgk etc

Fig. 4 Unknown German artist, Prince Elector John Frederick I on horseback, c. 1548

optimism by protracted negotiations with numerous potential supporters. The league leaders received a series of evasive answers to requests for support sent to towns, dukedoms, and individual princes. At best they could only hope that, if the war took a favorable turn, the town mayors and princes who were now standing on the sidelines would rally to their cause. Although they had failed to analyze the task facing them properly, and despite woefully inadequate financial resources, the league leaders decided to risk war.

The Schmalkaldic War

The increasingly heated atmosphere between 1530 and 1545 demanded a definitive settlement of the deadlocked situation in the empire. But the Emperor, who was frequently absent due to the problems of his vast empire, could only attend to the problem after making peace with France and concluding an armistice with the Ottoman Empire. The Emperor's aim was to destroy the Schmalkaldic League, whereas that of the Protestants was victory over the Emperor. Many estates of the empire had striven in vain to persuade the league's members to relent and stand down. Their continued refusal to do so made war inevitable if the Emperor was not to lose his authority. In the Schmalkaldic League crisis, Duchess Elizabeth of Rochlitz played a central role as mediator. Though she acted professionally, she was unsuccessful. She wrote dozens of letters to those in authority in an attempt to avert war. She begged her former protégé Duke Maurice not to go over to the side of the devil's followers, that "generation of vipers."[19] Espionage on both sides increased (fig. 5). When war nevertheless broke out, Elizabeth supported the Schmalkaldic League by establishing an intelligence headquarters in Rochlitz, from where she sent coded messages to the league leaders.[20] In this way she warned them of Maurice's intentions and supplied intelligence on the enemy's army. Shortly after the war forced her to leave her headquarters, the Schmalkaldic League suffered its decisive defeat at Mühlberg (fig. 6).

Charles V owed his success in this battle not least to the military prowess of his army commander Maurice of Saxony, whom the Protestants henceforth named "Judas of Meissen."[21] He also owed this sobriquet to his taking over the electorship of Saxony from his defeated cousin John Frederick of Saxony. Yet in 1552 he turned in disillusionment against the Emperor and led the rebellion of the princes, bringing Charles V to the brink of defeat and forcing him to release the imprisoned leaders of the Schmalkaldic League. On the political stage, the lines were now clearly drawn. In the Religious Peace of Augsburg, which Charles's brother Ferdinand signed in 1555, a formula was found that brought peace to the empire: *cuius regio, eius religio*. The sovereign henceforth decided the religion of his realm. However, the rift between the denominations could not thereby be healed. The French Wars of Religion (1562–98) and the Thirty Years' War (1618–48) were bloody conflicts which are generally held to be wars of religion.[22] Only the Peace of Westphalia of 1648 was finally able to create a lasting religious peace.

Religious Policy and Interdenominational Conflicts in the seventeenth and eighteenth Centuries

It was not only the Emperor who contributed to the escalation or de-escalation of tension in international politics. The denominational loyalty of individual princes also had an effect on alliances and matrimonial policy. Changes of denominational allegiance by various princes in the seventeenth century in particular were a constant source of uncertainty in the empire.[23] In many cases there were rumors that the second-most important sovereign of the empire, the Elector of Saxony, was considering converting to Roman Catholicism.[24] When Frederick Augustus I of Saxony actually embraced Catholicism in 1697, ultimately in order to become King of Poland, his pragmatism allowed a constructive solution to the problem in the *Corpus Evangelicorum* and averted a crisis.

The conversion of the Elector of Saxony created a curious situation in his capital city of Dresden: the mostly Protestant population had to come to terms with a predominantly Roman Catholic court that attracted many Italian and French musicians, actors, and merchants. Numerous disputes are recorded. In Dresden, two centuries after the Reformation, its long-term effects can be observed as if it were under a magnifying glass, including smoldering conflicts, disputes over precedence, and the creation of rival factions. Rumors of a re-Catholicization of Dresden by force were rife.[25] When in 1726 the deacon of the aforementioned Protestant Kreuzkirche in Dresden was murdered by a fanatical Roman Catholic, who was perhaps mentally ill, a riot broke out in the city in which several people were injured. The city governor, August Christoph von Wackerbarth, was forced to place the Catholics in protective custody. The more than one thousand Protestant insurgents were subdued only with the aid of several hundred soldiers. The mob, that "raging and raving, […] was resolved to exterminate the Catholics entirely," laid waste to Catholics' homes and conducted a "ritual desecration of religious symbols."[26] Only after the murderer Franz Laubler was publically executed and five thousand soldiers quartered in the city for several months did peace return to Dresden.[27] For some time, conspiracy theories persisted that further attacks on Protestants had been thwarted only because Laubner had struck too early.[28] The escalation of events in Dresden underscored the danger of civil unrest a ruler's conversion and attendant ideological radicalization could lead to. This uprising must also be seen as an emerging crisis: since his conversion, the Elector of Saxony had been faced with the dilemma either of forcing his people to convert to Catholicism or of allowing a fatal dichotomy to continue to exist within the city.

Summary

For the most part, crises develop slowly although they may also be provoked by sudden irruptions. The crisis in the church came to a head at the turn of the sixteenth century through a failure to de-escalate the situation. This offers a textbook example of the differ-

Fig. 5 Unknown artist, The Preparation and Onset of the Schmalkaldic War. From the cycle:
Scenes from the life of John Frederick I, the Magnanimous, of Saxony, 1600–30.
At the bottom left corner a spy is observing the recruitment of troops for the Schmalkaldic War.

ent phases of a crisis.[29] First the triggering of an early-warning system (1311), followed by an awareness that goals may be endangered (1415), and judging an acute crisis to be controllable (up until 1517), and then finally the development of an uncontrollable crisis (after 1517) with outbursts of violence (1546–47).[30] This typical developmental acceleration is also reflected in the unfolding political crisis. The Emperor still considered himself to be in charge of the situation at the Imperial Diet of Worms in 1521. Yet he finally recognized the danger to imperial peace in the ideologically highly charged situation created by the *Pack Affair* of 1527. His incapacity to achieve unity among the princes and his rejection of the *Augsburg Confession* in 1530 led to the creation of rival factions and finally to the Schmalkaldic *War* of 1546–47. Later the political upheavals attendant to the conversion of princes in the seventeenth century bear witness to the capacity of denominational loyalties to spark crises among the ruling houses. Last but not least, the denominational crisis once more flared up in the Dresden uprising of 1726. Thus the explosive force latent in the reforming of religious confessions was being felt over a period of two centuries, though its effect was felt most intensely in the disputes and conflicts of the sixteenth century.

19 Duchess Elizabeth to Duke Maurice, October 8–11, 1564, quoted in *Sächsisches Hauptstaatsarchiv—Staatsarchiv Dresden* (SächsHStAD), 12803 PN Werl, no. 4, fol. 379. **20** See Rous, *Geheimschrift*. **21** See Haug-Moritz, *Judas*. **22** Characteristics of wars of religion: division or exacerbation of existing conflicts within a territory by superimposition of a denominational dimension, transformation of social groups into denominational parties, activation of external allies and spreading of the conflict, Europeanization and international complexity of the conflicts. See Brendle, *Religionskriege*. **23** See Lotz-Heumann, *Konversion*. **24** SächsHStAD, 10024 Geheimer Rat (Geheimes Archiv), Projekt an Kursachsen wegen Annehmung der katholischen Religion (Correspondence of Emperor Ferdinand II with Elector John George I of Saxony), 1620, Loc. 10331/6; Geheimes Staatsarchiv Preußischer Kulturbesitz (GStA PK Berlin), I. HA Geheimer Rat, Rep. 41, Beziehungen zu Kursachsen, Schreiben des Kurfürsten Friedrich Wilhelm von Brandenburg an den Feldmarschall-Leutnant Lorenz von Hofkirch vom 6. Augustus 1652 wegen des beabsichtigten Übertritts des sächsischen Kurprinzen zum Katholizismus, no. 1612. **25** See Leibetseder, *Mord*, p. 62. **26** Anonymous, Ausführliche und wahrhaffte Relation von dem den 21. Maji dieses 1726. Jahres in Dreßden von einem Gottvergessenen Bösewicht an dem wohlseligen Herrn M. Hahnen grausam verübten Priester-//Mord. Nebst unterschiedenen gewissen Particularien, so denen bißherigen unwahren Erzehlungen entgegen gesetzet warden [1726], p. 8; Leibetseder, *Hostie*, p. 105. **27** See ibid. **28** See ibid., p. 72. **29** See Hutzschenreuter/Griess-Negra, *Krisenmanagement*, pp. 48–50. **30** See ibid., pp. 47–51.

Fig. 6 Virgil Solis, Defeat and Capture of Prince Elector John Frederick I of Saxony
at the Battle of Mühlberg, Nürnberg, c. 1547

BIBLIOGRAPHY

Brendle, Franz (ed.) (2006), *Religionskriege im Alten Reich und in Alteuropa*. Münster. **Dingel**, Irene (1997), Religionsgespräche. In: *Theologische Realenzyklopädie*. Vol. 28, pp. 631–681. **Frech**, Karl Augustin (1992), *Reform an Haupt und Gliedern. Untersuchung zur Entwicklung und Verwendung der Formulierung im Hoch- und Spätmittelalter*. Frankfurt am Main. **Haug-Moritz**, Gabriele (2002), *Der Schmalkaldische Bund 1530–1541/42. Eine Studie zu den genossenschaftlichen Strukturelementen der politischen Ordnung des Heiligen Römischen Reiches Deutscher Nation* (= Schriften zur südwestdeutschen Landeskunde. 44). Leinfelden-Echterdingen. **Haug-Moritz**, Gabriele (2007), Judas und Gotteskrieger. Kurfürst Moritz, die Kriege im Reich der Reformationszeit und die 'neuen'

Medien. In: Blaschke, Karlheinz (ed.), *Moritz von Sachsen—ein Fürst der Reformationszeit zwischen Territorium und Reich* (= Quellen und Forschungen zur sächsischen Geschichte. 29). Leipzig, pp. 235–259. **Hutzschenreuther**, Thomas/ **Griess-Negra**, Torsten (eds.) (2006), *Krisenmanagement*. Wiesbaden. **Jadatz**, Heiko (2008), Religionspolitik und Fürstenpolemik. Der Streit zwischen Herzog Georg von Sachsen und Martin Luther über dessen Brief an Wenzeslaus Linck vom 14. Juni 1528. In: Beyer, Michael/Flöter, Jonas/Hein, Markus (eds.), *Christlicher Glaube und weltliche Herrschaft. Zum Gedenken an Günther Wartenberg* (= Arbeiten zur Kirchen- und Theologiegeschichte. 24). Leipzig, pp. 59–72. **Leibetseder**, Mathis (2009), *Die Hostie im Hals. Eine "schröckliche Bluttat" und*

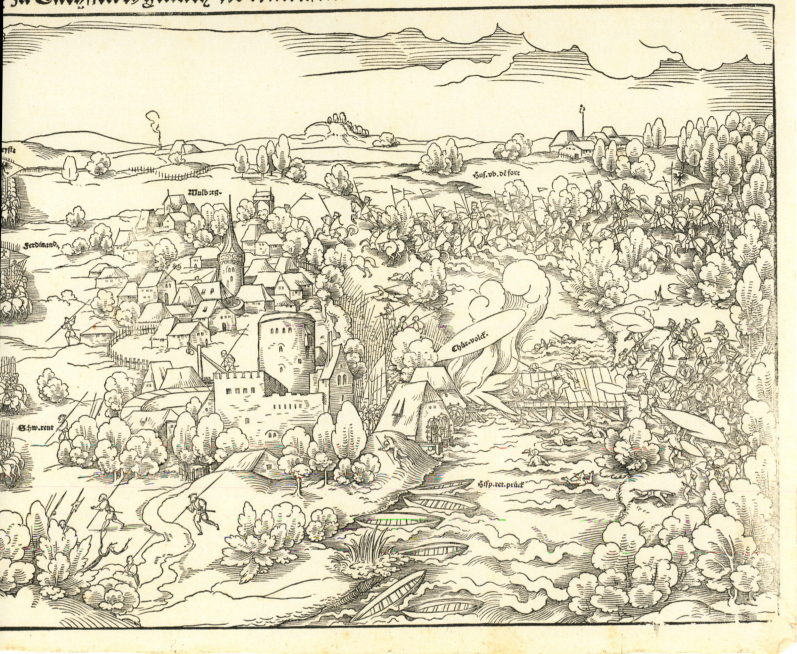

der Dresdner Tumult des Jahres 1726. Konstanz. **Leibetseder**, Mathis (2011), Mord zum Mittag. Die Tötung des Kreuzkirchendiakons Hermann Joachim Hahn (1726). In: *Dresdner Hefte*, vol. 107, pp. 60–68. **Lotz-Heumann**, Ute (2007), *Konversion und Konfession in der Frühen Neuzeit* (= Schriften zur Reformationsgeschichte. 205). Gütersloh. **Pearson**, Christine M./**Mittoff**, Ian I. (1983), From Crisis Prone to Crisis Prepared: A Framework for Crisis Management. In: *The Executive*, vol. 7, no. 1, pp. 48–59. **Rous**, Anne-Simone (2016), *Geheimdiplomatie in Sachsen. Spione—Chiffren—Interzepte*, unpublished postdoctoral thesis, University of Erfurt. **Rous**, Anne-Simone (2014), Die Geheimschrift der Herzogin Elisabeth von Rochlitz im Schmalkaldischen Krieg 1546/47. In: Schellenberger,

Simona (ed.), *Eine starke Frauengeschichte. 500 Jahre Reformation*. Markkleeberg, pp. 47–52. **Thieme**, André (ed.) (2010), *Die Korrespondenz der Herzogin Elisabeth von Sachsen und ergänzende Quellen* (= Quellen und Materialien zur sächsischen Geschichte und Volkskunde. 3,1). Vol. 1: 1505 to 1532. Leipzig. **Urbanski**, Kevin (2012), *Zur Funktionsweise von Mediationsverfahren in den internationalen Beziehungen* (= Schriften zu theoretischen und empirischen Problemen der Politikwissenschaft. 17). Marburg. **Welzig**, Werner (ed.) (1968), *Ausgewählte Schriften*. Darmstadt.

INGRID DETTMANN

Luther's Adversaries

Albert of Brandenburg, a descendent of the Hohenzollern dynasty and the Archbishop of Magdeburg, became one of the most powerful princes of the Holy Roman Empire by acquiring the ancillary office of Archbishop of Mainz in 1514. In doing so, he also purchased the rank of a prince-elector. For a five-figure sum, Pope Leo X granted him a special permit for the accumulation of offices, something that was not actually permitted under canon law. The debts Albert ran up to the Fugger banking house was paid off through the sale of indulgences in his territories. Luther sharply criticized the sale of indulgences and initially hoped that his employer would concur. Because of his financial needs, however, Cardinal Albert remained an adversary of Luther and the Reformation—despite his support for church reform by council.

Johann Eck, the eloquent theologian from Ingolstadt, was the best known among opponents of the Reformer and also the most assailed from the Protestant side. At first he was actually open-minded about Luther. The publication of his critical comments (*Adnotationes*) about Luther's Ninety-Five Theses led to a complete break between them. In the 1519 Leipzig debate against Luther and Karlstadt, Eck defended his positions on indulgences, the doctrine of justification, human freedom, and also the roles of the Pope and the church—all with theological proficiency and rhetorical brilliance. He obtained the papal bull *Exsurge Domine* threatening Martin Luther's excommunication in 1520, and worked to have it distributed throughout Germany. In response, Luther then referred to him in further polemics as "Doctor Pig" or "Dr[.]eck" (a German play on words, "Dreck" meaning filth).

Thomas Murner, a Franciscan monk from Alsace, fought Luther and his teachings with barbed commentaries and satirical pamphlets. Much like Luther, however, he criticized the abuses of the church and demanded comprehensive reforms in his texts from the 1520s. The main contribution to his anti-Lutheran polemic was the extensive 4,800-verse poem *About Luther, the Great Fool* (1522), which is illustrated with numerous woodcuts. Thoroughly tongue-in-cheek, one print portrays a cat in monk's habit who is strangling a Lutheran fool. Murner's name had previously been altered by his antagonists into "Murnarr" (a German play on words meaning "Murner the "Narr," i.e "fool"). When the Reformation was implemented in Strasbourg in 1524, the printing of Murner's texts was promptly forbidden.

Luther found yet another sharp critic in Johannes Cochlaeus. The theologian, who had been educated in the humanities, tried to have Luther retract his writings at the Diet of Worms in 1521. He also proposed a public debate, which Luther harshly rejected. A lifelong personal enmity grew out of this theological conflict. In 1530, Cochlaeus helped write the *Confutatio Augustana* (Papal Confutation), the Catholic refutation of the *Augsburg Confession*.

BENJAMIN HASSELHORN

Luther and Politics

Introduction

"But it was only the reforming activity of Luther that transformed the religious ferment, which had been seething throughout Christendom for centuries, into a political power, and the reason was that he fused the numerous religious issues into one church issue. It was only in this way that a decisive step toward freedom could be taken. Luther is above all a *political* hero; we must recognize this in order to judge him fairly and to understand his preeminent position in the history of Europe. [...] The weak point in Luther was his theology; if it had been his strong point, neither he nor his church would have been of any use for the political work which he accomplished."[1]

This appraisal of Luther is unusual. In theological as well as in historical research of the Reformation, it has been common practice for about a hundred years to see Luther's theological discovery, his "Tower Experience,"[2] which revealed to him the "merciful God" who made man righteous through faith alone and not through works, as his essential achievement.[3] It goes without saying that scholarship categorizes Luther's life and work according to the historical—and also the social and political—contexts of his time. But understanding Luther as a strong politician and a weak theologian is, to say the least, a rather deviant position. Normally, Luther is not considered a gifted politician. The opinion given by Johannes Haller, a Baltic historian who worked in Tübingen, may serve as an example. In his book *Epochen der deutschen Geschichte* from 1923, which was extra-

ordinarily successful, Haller quoted Luther's conduct at the Diet of Worms as a crucial political mistake because he did not take what Haller considered a unique chance: all he had to do in Worms was, according to Haller, signal a willingness to have his criticism of indulgences and the church be examined by a general council (fig. 1). By doing so, Haller was sure, he would have gotten the estates of the empire on his side, and nothing would have stood in the way of the root and branch reform Luther strived for: "One might be angry with Luther because he neither saw nor used this. But he was no politician; all he was concerned about was his right to his own conviction, and it cannot be expected of anybody to act against his personality."[4] Luther, to put it even more pointedly, was no politician but an apocalypticist, a person seeing himself in the way a prophet does, one who took little interest in trivial matters such as the actual realization of his ideas on earth.

Whoever tries to get a general idea of the political Luther is confronted with a confusing abundance of different and contradictory interpretations and judgments. This is mainly due to the fact that a clear distinction between politics and theology in Luther's thinking and acting can hardly be drawn. This is true in a principal sense as well: historically and systematically, religion and politics have always correlated with each other, if only because all religions seek their fulfilment within the basic social conditions given and that there is hardly any kind of political organization to be found that would renounce some, at least in a wider sense, religious foundations. Never-

---

1 Chamberlain, *Grundlagen*, pp. 840, 845 [emphasis in the original]: "Doch erst die Reformationstätigkeit Luther's hat jene religiöse Gärung, die schon Jahrhunderte die Christenheit durchdrang, zu einer politischen Macht umgestaltet, und zwar dadurch, dass sie die vielen religiösen Fragen zu einer kirchlichen Frage umwandelte. Hierdurch erst ward es möglich, einen entscheidenden Schritt zur Befreiung zu tun. Luther ist vor Allem ein *politischer* Held; um ihn gerecht zu beurteilen, um seine überragende Stellung in der Geschichte Europa's zu begreifen, muss man das wissen. [...] Der schwache Punkt war bei Luther seine Theologie; wäre sie seine Stärke gewesen, er hätte zu seinem politischen Werke nicht getaugt, seine Kirche auch nicht." 2 The classic source for the so-called Tower Experience is Martin Luther, Vorrede zum ersten Band der Gesamtausgabe seiner lateinischen Werke [1545]. In: *WA* 120, 54, 179–187. See also Peters, *Turmerlebnis*. In the early twentieth century, research in history of theology focusing on the theological approach was initiated by the Berlin church historian Karl Holl, who thereby started the "Luther-Renaissance": Assel, *Aufbruch*. 3 The quote could be dismissed as

a verdict given by a nationalist at the turning of the nineteenth to the twentieth century, the German Christian author Houston Stewart Chamberlain. But this would make things too easy because in those days—and nowadays, at least partly, again—it was quite common to have a negative view of Luther's theological doctrine, especially among liberal Protestant theologians. Not without good reason did Chamberlain himself refer to the great liberal theologian Adolf Harnack, in whose view it was true Luther had rediscovered the Gospel, but in his theology peculiarly stuck fast in the inconsistencies of the old dogma; in the following period, a whole branch of theological history adopting this opinion could be named, starting from Ernst Troeltsch up to the latest efforts in reviving liberal theology. See Harnack, *Dogmengeschichte*, pp. 466–474; Ernst Troeltsch, Luther und die moderne Welt [1908]. In: id., *Gesamtausgabe*, vol. 8, pp. 59–97. In this context, it has to be mentioned that liberal Protestantism does have an "uncovered flank" turned toward the nationalist movement. See Kinzig, *Harnack*, p. 24. See also: Graf, *Rad*, pp. 174–178. 4 Haller, *Epochs*, p. 123.

Fig. 1 Luther at the Diet of Worms, from: Ludwig Rabus, Historien der Heyligen Außerwölten Gottes Zeügen, Bekenern vnd Martyrern, Straßburg 1557

theless, the two spheres remain distinguishable, and Luther is usually perceived as a person whose interests are most of all to be positioned within the religious sphere—that is, the sphere that concerns humans in the scope of eternity. But political thinking in terms of reflecting on the conditions of social existence was by no ways far from the Reformer's mind. In spite of the preeminence of theology in Luther's thought—explicitly to be granted in this context—the following essay shall cast a closer view on Luther as a politician. Some specific aspects of Luther's action will therefore be highlighted from the perspective of political history. Thereafter Luther's own thoughts and actions will be examined with regard to their political implications. In this case, the focus will be on the question whether or when Luther actually had a clear notion of the political consequences of his work. The following argument will try to show that Luther's politics arose from his theology—they were political theology, meaning that Luther's political decisions derived from his belief.[5] Thereby, politics also became an essential matter in Luther's life—so, when viewing Luther from the perspective of political history, it is exactly this aspect that still exerts a lasting fascination.

Political Dimensions of Luther's Early Reform Activities

In the early phase of the Reformation, though, there was remarkably little awareness of contemporary social and political conditions reflected in Luther's behavior. In the years between 1517 and 1521 it seems that Luther did not have any feeling for the broader political contexts of his time—he was definitely and exclusively interested in his theological discovery. The tenor of his arguments was at first polite, later on becoming more polemical, but, as far as the matter in question was concerned, he was clearly opposed to all spiritual and secular authorities who stood in his way. Luther's posting of his theses on October 31, 1517, might have passed as authorized by his position as a professor of theology—but his refusal to succumb to the disciplinary measures the Roman Curia had been taking against him from 1518 on was already an act of resistance.

Essentially, however, the topic of his theses was theologically marginal. Indulgences as a part of the late-medieval sacrament of penance were not yet specified in a dogma, so that theologians were having detailed discussions on this subject. While some of them stressed, on the one hand, that indulgences only worked if the believer felt "repentance from the heart" (*contritio*), others assumed that contrition based on fear of hell (*attritio*) was sufficient.[6] But Luther, siding with the former on the whole, went one critical step further and thus touched upon the key question. For him, repentance from the heart was not only indispensable but also totally sufficient as a precondition for forgiveness—making all that was left of indulgency then, especially buying a letter of indulgence, superfluous.

Seen in the light of church policy and of imperial politics, no better starting point for unhinging the church of the early sixteenth century could have been found than the sale of indulgences, for the practice of indulgences bundled all the relevant problems in church and in social life together, something that many had seen as an issue before Luther. The church reform movements which became increasingly perceptible in the course of the fifteenth century, took offense at the way of life practiced by the minor and the high clergy, at the quantification and fiscalization of faith, at theological uncertainties and quarrels, and finally at the love of luxury and splendor the Popes cherished. All these evils accumulated in the practice of indulgences. In the case of the lifestyle of the clergy, the so-called St. Peter's indulgence for Archbishop Albrecht of Brandenburg serves as an example. It had in fact become necessary because he had accumulated offices, a practice which was actually illegal, and therefore had to make payments to the Pope; the quantification of faith was seen in the trade with letters of indulgence, which tended to make forgiveness of sins a matter solely depending on the payment of a sum of money; the theological uncertainties arose because indulgence was not yet fixed in dogma; the Pope's pomposity was targeted because indulgencies were used to increase the curial budget.[7] Against the background of higher demands on the church combined with a critical position with regard to it, and against the backdrop of a political Europe in process of "radical change"[8] which included the freshly made reforms in the empire, the so-called Turkish threat, the French-Habsburg conflict, and the virulent social problems—it was simply politically brilliant to make the criticism of indulgence the starting point of a fundamental church criticism.

Whether Luther actually realized these facts or not is, however, a highly controversial issue.[9] His theses were very moderate in their tone, showing clearly that he made efforts to appear as a faithful son of the papal church and not expose himself as a target of criticism in this respect. Some of Luther's comments made even before October 31, 1517, however, suggest that he was fully aware of the possible consequences of his criticism, and there was indeed enough explosive force in the Ninety-Five Theses, at least as far as their implications were concerned, which were aimed at the institutional foundations of the late-medieval church.[10] Thus, on the one hand, it is disputed whether Luther already argued—though not openly—against the sacrament of penance as such, with the topic of indulgence in his theses, but there can be no doubt that he had laid the foundations for this discussion.[11]

When Luther made his appearance in public, it is unlikely that any considerations in terms of political wisdom should have been relevant to him, neither on October 31, 1517, nor in the years that followed. In this period, Luther was only interested in the religious truth, and he was absolutely not willing to make any politically motivated concessions. This is shown in the case of the aforementioned politically "wrong decision" at the Diet of Worms in 1521. At a time when his publications found wide acceptance, and calls for a comprehensive church reform were almost universal, Luther refused to submit his cause to a general council. For he had found a long time before that not only the Pope but also the councils could fail, that they had failed in the past, and that it was the Holy Scripture and its correct exegesis alone that could claim to be true. This was logically consequent and plausible, but highly dangerous on the political level because he thus took a position totally apart from those accepted as normal and worth discussing by the church, and thus risked excommunication and imperial ban.

In Worms in 1521, Luther thought and acted in this "un-political" sense—that is, as a person, who did not care about the political consequences of his actions. At this point, however, it also becomes obvious that very often it is the "apolitical" in particular that may have an enormous political effect. For Luther's public refusal to retract his writings with reference to his personal conscience produced reactions ranging from admiration to enthusiasm all over the empire. So, whether intentional or not, what Luther did in Worms really was politics. With his famous saying, "Here I stand, I can do no other"[12] —proclaimed by Luther though not literally but de facto before Emperor and empire in Worms—this scenario became the foundation myth of Protestantism. Political calculation, however, should not be presumed to have been behind it. Luther's exclamation "I am through, I am through!"[13] after his appearance in Worms rather indicates that he did not see the Worms episode in a wider political context, but from his individual point of view—in this instance, as a personal trial.

---

5 On this context, see Hasselhorn, *Politische Theologie*, pp. 9–15, with further references. **6** See Slenczka, *Schrecken*. **7** On criticism of indulgence in the decades preceding the Reformation, see Winterhager, *Ablasskritik*. **8** Schilling, *Rebell*, pp. 13–55. **9** See ibid., pp. 157–167; and Aland, *Thesen*. **10** This mainly refers to Luther's Lectures on Romans 1515/16. In: *WA* 56. See Kantzenbach, *Martin Luther*, p. 74. **11** See Lohse, *Luthers Theologie*, pp. 117–119. See also Slenczka, *Antwort*, pp. 299 f. **12** In the Weimar Edition of *Luther's Works*, the famous quote from the talk in Worms—"here I stand, I can do no other"—is still included, but it is missing in the earliest references: "As your Majesty and Worship wishes to get a simple answer, I will give a harmless one without any hairsplitting. Unless I am convinced by the testimony of the scriptures or by clear reason (for I do not trust either in the Pope or in councils alone, since it is well known that they have often erred and contradicted themselves), I am bound by the scriptures I have quoted and my conscience is captive to the Word of God. I cannot and will not recant anything, since it is neither safe nor right to go against conscience. May God help me. Amen." *WA* 7, 838, 2–9. **13** Wrede, *Deutsche Reichstagsakten*, p. 853.

Fig. 2 Handlung Artickel vnnd Jnstruction so fürgenömen worden sein vonn allen Rottenn vnnd hauffen der Pauren, Zwickau 1525

Luther's Doctrine on Authorities and the Peasants' War

This political perspective loomed larger in the following years when the reform plans Luther had developed were put into action. Two fundamental situations of political decision making stand out from among the numbers of decisions he had to make: the year 1525 when Luther had to opt for one side in the conflict between peasants and princes, (fig. 2), and the year 1530, when the Schmalkaldic League was founded and one authority confronted the other. Luther's position on the Peasants' War has been widely criticized. Not only have Marxists reproached him for being a "princes' servant,"[14] but also from a certain Catholic point of view he was seen as partly being responsible for the outbreak of the Peasants' War. Moreover, in Protestant research on church history Luther's partisanship against the peasants has led to a highly controversial discussion.[15]

The central document of the Peasants' War, the Twelve Articles adopted by the Swabian Peasants of 1525, did not only refer to traditional law, as they had done before, but also to divine law. They were fundamentally inspired by what was largely a misconstrued interpretation of Luther's essay *On the Freedom of a Christian*.[16] It was obvious that the peasants took up reform ideas and applied them to their own social and political situation. As a result Luther initially took an open view of the peasants' demands. But he disapproved of their taking up arms from June 1524 on in order to enforce their demands. In the first days of May 1525, when 300,000 peasants were already in revolt and had pillaged monasteries and castles, Luther published his *Exhortation to Peace*, or admonition, to both sides.[17] Yet, in the course of this very month he would change his opinion and harshly called for the authorities to operate against the peasants by force of arms.[18]

This call to arms indeed may have been unnecessary. The peasants' riots were bloodily suppressed, and Luther's partisanship for the authorities had damaged his popularity so much so that he was obliged to explain his stand point. But he did not retract anything; on the contrary, he even added fuel to the fire: "I do know that my little book severely hurts the peasants and all those who are on their side. I am glad about that from all my heart, and if it did not hurt them, it would hurt me."[19]

Luther had two good reasons to side with the princes: a theological one and a political-pragmatic one—and at this point, a certain careful political reasoning on his part came into play. His theological reason was the opinion he had gained from the Pauline Epistles that authority was divinely ordained. According to Romans 13—"Let every soul be subject unto the higher powers. For there is no power but of God: the powers that be are ordained of God"—and to an adoption of Augustine's *The City of God*, Luther supported, on the one hand, a separation of ecclesiastical and state spheres in principle and, on the other hand, was of the opinion that a functioning state was a gift from God, a "miracle."[20] Consequently, an uprising against the authorities, in his eyes, was an uprising against God himself, and in any case forbidden. This was the reason, so he argued, why the peasants, in rising up against the divinely ordained authorities in violent revolt, had put themselves in the wrong. The fact that he saw his Reformation threatened by the "rebel spirits" reveals his political-pragmatic reasoning. He had always railed against the authorities' depravity, but he understood very well that the only way to carry through the Reformation was to do it with them and not against them. Obviously he could not count on any support by the clergy, so the princes were the only remaining group powerful enough to get the implementation of his reform work going. It can be assumed, however, that the theological reason was much more relevant to Luther than the political-pragmatic one, which is backed up by the fact that Luther gave his princes a great deal of trouble with his second fundamental political decision. Founding the Schmalkaldic League, the most important Protestant alliance in the Reformation era, in 1530/31 met with considerable difficulties. One of reasons for this was based on the theological doubts Luther had. The Schmalkaldic League was constituted after the adherents of the Lutheran denomination had struggled in vain for acknowledgment by the Roman Catholic party, and above all by the Emperor, at the Diet of Augsburg in 1530 (fig. 3). Luther was reluctant to do anything in opposition to the Emperor as the divinely ordained authority. In his opinion, any resistance was permitted only in cases where the

ALLE·MENSCHEN·VND·ALLER·MENSCHLICHE·GERECHTIGKEIT·IST·WIE·EIN·BLVM·DAS·
GRAS·VORDORRET·DIE·BLVM·FELLT·AB·ABER·DAS·WORTT·DES·HERRN·BLEIBT·IN·EWIGKEIT

ALLE·FVRSTEN·3V·SACHSSEN·M·H·3·BRANDENBERG·D·H·V·LEVNEBVRG·H·P·V·BRAVNSCHWIG

WIRTTENBERG POMMEREN ANNHALD'T

MANSFELT   P·G·V·NASSAW   SCHWARCSBERG   TECKELENBVRG

STRASBVRG AVSPVRG FRANCKFVRT COSTANC3 VLM ESLINGEN

REVDLINGE MEMMINGEN LINDAW HALL HEILBRAVN BIBRVCH KEMPTEN YSNI

BREMEN HAPVRG MAGDEBVRG MAGDEBVRG EIMBICK GOTTINGEN

GOBLAR   BRAVNSCHWIG   HANNVBER   MINDEN

1542

Fig. 3
Michel Müller, Design
for a common flag for the
Schmalkaldic League, 1542

authorities interfered with questions of faith, and in such cases by passive disobedience at most, by no means by open revolt. The Schmalkaldic League, however, was like a military alliance and therefore—at least in Luther's eyes—had a whiff of rebellion about it, something he absolutely wanted to avoid. Moreover, it was not only the Lutheran denomination that joined politically in the Schmalkaldic League; reformed Protestants, vehemently rejected by Luther, were within its ranks as well. Luther eventually gave in and approved the foundation of the league after he had been informed that the imperial constitution was by no means absolutist but aristocratic, so that, in reality, it was not the Protestant subjects who rebelled against a Roman Catholic Emperor, but one authority in favor of Reformation who offered legitimate resistance to the other authority who suppressed the Reformation (fig. 4).[21]

In these two cases—the Peasants' War and the founding of the Schmalkaldic League—but also in other contexts, Luther acted on the basis of his political convictions, which had a theological foundation and were later called the doctrine of the two kingdoms or the doctrine of the two regiments (fig. 5).[22] They are theologically founded on his understanding, drawn from the Pauline Epistles, of authority being divinely ordained. Luther was anything but a systematic political thinker. His political statements, given at various times and in various situations, are quite chaotic: on the one hand, authorities come from God; one is not allowed to resist them. On the other hand, God must be obeyed rather than man, consequently, authorities must not be obeyed if they pervert justice or interfere with matters of faith. And finally Luther had granted the prince the right to be an emergency bishop.[23]

Conclusion

Luther's intellectual world is sometimes bewildering and therefore not always easy to reconstruct. This might be the main reason for the confusingly contradictory assessments of Luther as a politician mentioned at the beginning. But it is also the main reason why the reiterated assertions about the one-dimensional political consequences of his work miss the mark: Luther was neither the ancestor of the authoritarian state or a subservient spirit nor was he an early democrat.

14 Typical in: Engels, *Der deutsche Bauernkrieg*, p. 55. **15** Fundamentally contributing to research in Peasants' War: Buszello/Blickle/Endres, *Der deutsche Bauernkrieg*. **16** Martin Luther: Von der Freiheit eines Christenmenschen [1520]. In: *WA* 7, 20–38. **17** Martin Luther: Ermahnung zum Frieden auf die zwölf Artikel der Bauernschaft in Schwaben. In: *WA* 18, 291–334. **18** Martin Luther: Wider die räuberischen und mörderischen Rotten der Bauern. In: *WA* 18, 357–361. **19** Martin Luther to Wenzeslaus Linck, June 20, 1525. In: *WA*.B 3, 536. See also: Martin Luther, Ein Sendbrief von dem harten Büchlein wider die Bauern. In: *WA* 18, 384–401. **20** Martin Luther: Vorlesungen über Jesaja und Hoheslied.

In: *WA* 31/II, 590. **21** See Schilling, *Rebell*, pp. 481–487. **22** Fundamental on this topic: Mantey, *Zwei-Reiche-Lehre*. **23** The idea that the sovereign should take over the task of an "emergency bishop" is from: Martin Luther: An den christlichen Adel deutscher Nation von des christlichen Standes Besserung [1520]. In: *WA* 6, 404–469. The limits of the duty to obey are stressed in: Martin Luther, Epistel S. Petri gepredigt und ausgelegt [1523]. In: *WA* 12, esp. 334, 32–335,4. Fundamental to Luther's understanding of authorities: Martin Luther: Von der Obrigkeit, wie weit man ihr Gehorsam schuldig ist [1523]. In: *WA* 11, 245–281. On this, see also Zschoch, *Glauben*.

Fig. 4 Martin Luther, *An den Christlichenn Adel deutscher Nation* (To the Christian Nobility of the German Nation), Wittenberg 1520

There is no one-way trajectory leading "from Luther to Hitler"[24] nor for that matter from Luther to the social theorist Jürgen Habermas.

Political consequences of the Reformation can of course be discussed all the same. Luther himself was anything but a democrat. In his opinion, all authority—the secular one included—derives directly from God and not from the people. Luther certainly would not have advocated any form of secularization embracing all spheres of life. Still, his emphasis on granting the state its own right with regard to the church and his upgrading the secular sphere set off a development that did include the option of secularization.[25]

What makes Luther important to the politics of his time and for the further history of Europe is, however, not really based on these kinds of unintended consequences. It rather goes back to the fact that Luther relegated politics to a secondary rank in relation to the last things, the essential values which really mattered to him. In the political sphere, then, he made these last things—to him this was the newfound Gospel with the doctrine of justification at its center—the main guideline of political decisions. There was no place for compromises on this matter. In this way, Luther, who had always furtively made fun of the wise diplomats in his circle, like Spalatin or Melanchthon, introduced a dimension of unconditionality into the sphere of politics that when working for the good could be inspiring, but if harnessed for the bad could end in disaster.

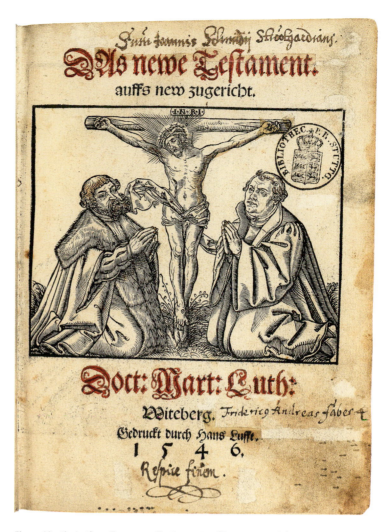

Fig. 5 Martin Luther, Das newe Testament auffs new zugericht (The New Testament), Wittenberg 1546

24 McGovern, *From Luther to Hitler*; Wiener, *Martin Luther*. **25** See Schilling, *Rebell*, p. 629.

BIBLIOGRAPHY

Aland, Kurt (1983), *Die 95 Thesen Martin Luthers und die Anfänge der Reformation*. Gütersloh. **Assel**, Heinrich (1993), *Der andere Aufbruch. Die Lutherrenaissance—Ursprünge, Aporien und Wege. Karl Holl, Emanuel Hirsch, Rudolf Hermann*. Göttingen. **Buszello**, Horst/**Blickle**, Peter/**Endres**, Rudolf (eds.) (1995), *Der deutsche Bauernkrieg*. 3rd ed. Paderborn et al. **Chamberlain**, Houston Stewart (1899), *Die Grundlagen des neunzehnten Jahrhunderts, Zweite Hälfte*. München, pp. 840, 845 (English: Chamberlain, Houston Stewart (1912), *Foundations of the Nineteenth Century. A Translation from the German by John Lees, M. A., D. Lit. (Edin.) with an Introduction by Lord Redesdale,* 2nd ed. New York. Available from: www.hschamberlain.net/grundlagen). **Engels**, Friedrich (1970), *Der deutsche Bauernkrieg [1850]*. Frankfurt am Main. **Graf**, Friedrich Wilhelm (1988), *Wir konnten dem Rad nicht in die Speichen fallen. Liberaler Protestantismus und "Judenfrage" nach 1933*. In: Kaiser, Jochen-Christoph/Greschat, Martin (ed.), *Der Holocaust und die Protestanten. Analysen einer Verstrickung*. Frankfurt am Main, pp. 151–185. **Haller**, Johannes (1930), *Epochs of German history*, London. **Harnack**, Adolf (1931), *Dogmengeschichte*. 7th ed. Tübingen. **Hasselhorn**, Benjamin (2012), *Politische Theologie Wilhelms II*. Berlin. **Kantzenbach**, Friedrich Wilhelm (1965), *Martin Luther und die Anfänge der Reformation*. Gütersloh. **Kinzig**, Wolfram (2004), *Harnack, Marcion und das Judentum. Nebst einer kommentierten Edition des Briefwechsels Adolf von Harnacks mit Houston Stewart Chamberlain*. Leipzig. **Lohse**, Bernd (1995), *Luthers Theologie in ihrer historischen Entwicklung und in ihrem systematischen Zusammenhang*. Göttingen. **Mantey**, Volker (2005), *Zwei Schwerter—zwei Reiche. Martin Luthers Zwei-Reiche-Lehre vor ihrem spätmittelalterlichen Hintergrund*. Tübingen. **McGovern**, William Montgomery (1941), *From Luther to Hitler. The history of Fascist-Nazi political philosophy*. Boston. **Peters**, Albrecht (1961), *Luthers Turmerlebnis*. In: *Neue Zeitschrift für Systematische Theologie und Religionsphilosophie*, no. 3, pp. 203–236. **Schilling**, Heinz (2012), *Martin Luther. Rebell in einer Zeit des Umbruchs*. München. **Slenczka**, Notger (2007), "Allein durch den Glauben": Antwort auf die Frage eines mittelalterlichen Mönchs oder Angebot zum Umgang mit einem Problem jedes Menschen? In: Bultmann, Christoph/Leppin, Volker/Lindner, Andreas (eds.), *Luther und das monastische Erbe* (= Spätmittelalter, Humanismus, Reformation. 39). Tübingen, pp. 291–315. **Slenczka**, Notger (2007), Der endgültige Schrecken. Das Jüngste Gericht und die Angst in der Religion des Mittelalters. In: *Das Mittelalter*, vol. 12, no. 1, pp. 97–112. **Troeltsch**, Ernst (2001), *Kritische Gesamtausgabe*. Vol. 8. Berlin. **Wiener**, Peter F. (1945), *Martin Luther—Hitler's spiritual ancestor*. London et al. **Winterhager**, Wilhelm Ernst (1999), Ablasskritik als Indikator historischen Wandels vor 1517. Ein Beitrag zu Voraussetzungen und Einordnung der Reformation. In: *Archiv für Reformationsgeschichte*, vol. 90, pp. 6–71. **Wrede**, Adolf (ed.) (1896), *Deutsche Reichstagsakten unter Kaiser Karl V. Jüngere Reihe*. Vol. 2: Der Reichstag zu Worms 1521. Göttingen. **Zschoch**, Hellmut (2015), Der im Glauben freie Untertan. Luthers Wahrnehmung und Deutung von Obrigkeit. In: *Luther*, vol. 86, pp. 70–84.

ROBERT KLUTH

Luther's Two Kingdoms Doctrine

Luther's "two kingdoms" or "two regimes doctrine" is an expression which was coined in the period after 1918. At this time the German Lutherans stood in opposition to the regulatory political power for the first time in their history following the abdication of the Kaiser as head of the church. Two Protestant theologians, Karl Barth and Emanuel Hirsch, formulated the term "the two kingdom doctrine" apart from another in 1922. Hirsch became spokesperson for the German Christians, the Protestants supporting the Nazi Government after 1933, and later a supportive member of the S.S. (Nazi Elite troops). Karl Barth held after 1945 the "two kingdoms doctrine" responsible for loyalty to authority and thus for the insufficient resistance to the Hitler dictatorship. After 1945, an extensive controversy in Germany about the two kingdoms doctrine ensued which was simultaneously a debate about the Protestant position regarding the legitimacy of resistance. It was focused on how Christians should behave in response to a totalitarian state.

According to Luther the two kingdoms are a secular and a religious one. Humankind lives continuously and simultaneously in both spheres. He is subject to secular authority over his body and is bound to obedience. Luther strove to define several passages from Romans 13 in order to show that a Christian may not exercise resistance to authority. According to Luther, those tyrants must be patiently tolerated. He felt that Christians in the secular kingdom were held captive and subjugated. Furthermore, Luther thought this was necessary, because people are naturally sinful and only few people lead a truly Christian life. To prevent the world from sinking into anarchy, the secular sword must give direction and maintain order.

On the other hand, in the spiritual kingdom, a Christian is freed by God's grace. Here he can recognize himself as a sinner and thus see his neighbor as a cherished being. This Christian freedom helps mankind to treat his neighbor ethically.

Luther never dealt with the relationship between theology and politics in a systematic fashion but rather in the context of concrete problems. The distinction between the two kingdoms, therefore, is a posthumous reconstruction of how Luther saw the relationship between religion and politics.

PETER VON DER OSTEN-SACKEN

Martin Luther's Position on Jews and Judaism[1]

Sola scriptura: Scripture Alone

Martin Luther was a scholar of the Sacred Scriptures with all his heart. For more than three decades he held the position of professor of biblical exegesis at Wittenberg. During this period he was mainly concerned with the Old Testament, starting with more than two years of interpreting Psalms. With some interruptions, he spent the last ten years of his calling mainly devoted to the study of the first book of Moses. He repeatedly voiced his opinions on the Jews during this time, in lectures, in his writings (especially in 1523, 1538, and 1543), and in a memorable text that may be taken as a testament of sorts, the *Exhortation against the Jews*—completed only days before his death. What Luther had to say for, about, and against the Jews was generally derived from his Bible-based theology. His views were rooted in a long tradition and they eventually took on a characteristic form that was deeply intertwined with his personality. Thus, his position on Judaism can only be properly described, explained, and appreciated when seen within the context of the Reformer's Bible-oriented theology. His battle cry, *Sola scriptura* (Scripture Alone), is also in this case the center around which his thoughts revolve.

Luther's Perception of the Jews in the First Years of the Reformation

As his interpretation of Psalms in 1513–15 reveals, Luther's perception of the Jews during the early years of his tenure in Wittenberg fully embraced the anti-Jewish traditions of the church. He not only took over, but in part also greatly intensified its anti-Jewish statements. He regularly employed the language of the gutter for his defamation of the Jews,[2] and roundly denied that there was any hope of salvation for the Jewish people in the Last Judgment.[3] This was in fact clearly

contrary to the Augustine tradition that his order followed. It is only in 1515/16 with his lectures on the Epistle to the Romans that this picture begins to change. His discovery of the Gospel of redemption by the love of God (which was not conditional on any human action) led him to hope that the dismissive stance of Jews toward the Gospel might now change. He began to massively criticize the established behavior of the church toward the Jews not only in his lectures on the Epistle to the Romans[4] but also in other statements.[5] He also became open to the concept that Israel would convert to the Christian faith in its entirety and thus be saved in the end (Romans 2:26).[6] Although he hesitated to consider this a Pauline certainty, he nevertheless accepted it as the way the church fathers understood the Apostle.[7] For Luther, acknowledging the enduring love of God for the people of Israel at this point had recognizable consequences for the behavior toward the Jews that he now demanded.[8]

In 1523, it looked as if the time had come for Luther to pull together all the strands of his changed attitude toward the Jews. When he was confronted with the accusation that he had denied that Jesus was not born to the Virgin as the Son of God but solely as a son of Abraham, he wrote the treatise *That Jesus Christ Was Born a Jew*[9] in response. Therein, he set out that the Nazarene was both—a Jew and the son of a virgin as promised in Isaiah 7:14. This treatise was not only meant to refute the accusations leveled at him but to open the Gospel of Christ to the Jews at the same time. By publishing this evidence that Jesus was the Messiah promised in the Old Testament, Luther hoped to attract a number of Jews to the Christian faith.[10] The treatise had a clear missionary goal, therefore, despite unfounded claims to the contrary that have persisted to this day. Its impact did actually extend into some Jewish circles, less for its train of argument (which largely follows the beaten track of traditional Christology) but for its biting criticism of the attitude and behavior of leading

1 This essay refers to the following publications, which have been partially expanded upon: Von der Osten-Sacken, *Margaritha*; id., *Feindschaft*; id., *Orientierung*. The last of these forms the foundation for the following deliberations, with several additions and occasional short passages taken from the other two. While the monography *Margaritha* contains a comprehensive bibliography and an exhaustive history of research, additional sources can be found in *Feindschaft*. Recent monographical works include: Kaufmann, *Judenschriften*; id.,

Juden; Bering, *Antisemit*. In this essay quotes will be largely restricted to references to the Weimarer Ausgabe (*WA*). **2** *WA* 55/II, 582, 1427–584, 1467. **3** *WA* 55, 106, 14 f.; 438, Rgl. 21. **4** *WA* 56, 436, 13–23. **5** *WA* 55/I, 428, 29–429, 18 (Operationes in Psalmos). **6** *WA* 56, 435,6–9; 436,25–437,18; 438,12–26; 439,7–440,5; 7, 599,35–600,1; 600,27–34 (Magnificat). **7** *WA* 56, 438, 23 f. **8** *WA* 5, 429, 13–18; 7, 601, 1–5; see 56, 433, 24–435, 2; 436, 13–23. **9** *WA* 11, 307–336. **10** *WA* 11, 314, 27 f.; 315, 23 f.; 325, 19 f.; 336, 22–24.

figures of the church. Luther accused them of a defamatory and humiliating treatment of the Jews living in their midst. His argument was that "Jews had been mistreated to this day in such a way that any good Christian should have considered joining them, while I myself, if I had been a Jew, would rather have become a swine than a Christian after observing the oafs and thugs who teach and administer the Christian faith. Surely they have treated the Jews as if they were dogs, and not men."[11] Luther was confident that "if you are friendly with the Jews and instruct them clearly in the Holy Scriptures, quite a few will become devoted Christians and return to the faith of their fathers, the prophets and patriarchs," from which they have severed themselves by denying Jesus as the Messiah.[12] He gave substance to his plea for a truly Christian treatment of Jews in his closing comments. Here, he demanded that Christians should "let them live and work amongst us, so that they may find reason and space to be amongst us, to listen to our Christian message and observe our Christian lives."[13] The aim of the economic and social integration postulated in these brief words was the hoped-for religious incorporation.

The Demonization of Jews and the Call for Violence against Them

Twenty years later, when Luther published his three polemic treatises against the Jews in 1543, much had obviously changed in his attitude, certainly enough to warrant the impression that a complete about-face had taken place.

A few years earlier it had already become clear that the Reformer had changed his previous views. Luther's liege lord, Elector John Frederick I of Saxony, had expelled the Jews from his territory in 1536. When Josel of Rosheim, the spokesman and advocate of the Jews in the Holy Roman Empire of the German Nation, wrote the Reformer a letter from the Saxon boarder asking him to forward his petition to the elector in view of Luther's favorable statements from 1523, Luther harshly rejected the petitioner. His reply was that his lobbying for better conditions for Jews then had been motivated by missionary considerations, but as they had continued to remain inimical to Christianity, he was not to be counted on.[14] Only a year later, Luther railed against alleged attempts by Jews in Moravia to convert Christians to Judaism in his treatise *Against the Sabbathans* (1538).[15] When he was subjected to direct[16] and indirect[17] attacks from the Jewish side in consequence of this writing, he retorted by publishing the aforementioned three polemic treatises against Jews and Judaism in quick succession. The longest and best known of these is *On the Jews and their Lies*,[18] whose title repeats his main accusation formulated in the *Sabbathans* treatise. Despite this first anti-Jewish tract of 1543 contains long passages in its first and larger part in which Luther treats Judaism almost objectively, in spite of his polemics.[19] Yet later, particularly in the final parts of the treatise, he displays a depressing enmity toward Jews. The Reformer paints Jews in the blackest hues,[20] declaring them children of Satan who insult Jesus, Mary, and Christians in their holy services, and who are bent on causing damage to Christians in whichever way they can.[21]

Fig. 1 Relief of the so-called Judensau (Jews' sow) on the Town and Parish Church Wittenberg, fourteenth century. Inscription from the eighteenth century based on Martin Luther

Fig. 2 Wieland Schmiedel, Contusion, 1988. Bronze plaque with a stone border with writing recessed into the ground beneath the relief of the so-called Jews' sow. Text by Jürgen Rennert following Ps 130,1 (hebr.)

In 1523 Luther had still roundly denounced the traditional accusations against Jews (murdering Christian children for their blood, poisoning wells, piercing the body of Christ in the shape of the host) as being mere "foolishness."[22] Now, in contrast, he was advancing slanderous hints that there might be some truth lying behind those allegations.[23] He cleverly insinuated: Even if they do not actually do this, they are definitely willing to.[24] But the culmination of these treatises is the repeated demand for forceful measures against the Jews by the authorities, in order to make them compliant to the Gospel.[25] These demands included a comprehensive social, economic, and religious impoverishment of the Jews and did not shrink at recommending pillaging, destroying, robbery, forced labor, and, in the end, even expulsion. The central charge that pervades the first and longest catalogue of such measures was that the Jews blasphemed against the Christian religion at every opportunity. Christian tolerance of this blasphemy would surely count as complicity and evoke the wrath of God.[26]

Luther's polemic in defense of a perceived Christian truth against Jewish lies is augmented by the two other treatises published in the same year. In *On the Shem Hamphoras and the Lineage of Christ*, he poured forth his scatological scorn and ridicule over the anti-Jesuanic medieval Jewish diatribe *Toledot Yeshu* (*The Origin of Jesus*) and the rabbis as interpreters of the Scriptures.[27] In reply he proved Jesus' descent from King David and the tribe of Judah.[28] This is also the treatise in which Luther exploits to excess the defamatory relief of the so-called Jews' sow which was mounted on his own Town and Parish Church of St. Mary's in Wittenberg, with the aim of denigrating the Jewish interpretation of the Scriptures (figs. 1 and 2). In his third pamphlet, *On the Last Words of David*, he defended the interpretation of the Old Testament in accordance with the Christian belief in the Trinity by expounding on 2 Samuel 23.[29]

Three years after these writings, Luther repeated the essence of his accusations against the adherents of Judaism in the aforementioned *Exhortation against the Jews* (1546), only a few days before his death.[30] He indented that the declamation of the pamphlet would put pressure on the counts of Mansfeld, who had granted sanctuary to Jews recently expelled from Magdeburg, and force them to expel the refugees in turn. Here, too, the gist of his argument was: chose baptism or leave. And once again, Luther went far beyond a mere religious debate with his prejudiced accusations, which included treason, murderous abuse of their medical skills, and other "foolery."

Explanations for the Change in Luther's Attitude toward the Jews

There is, as yet, no consent among Luther scholars on how the differences between the treatise of 1523 and his later statements on the Jews (particularly in the writings of 1543) can be explained, or how serious they actually were. According to an oft-repeated interpretation, Luther had been deeply disappointed that his empathic courtship with Judaism embodied in his treatise of 1523 had not led to the fulfillment of his missionary ambitions. Thus, his initial openness had eventually turned to hate. A different interpretation, which has dominated research in the past decades, has Luther's theological stance on Judaism essentially remain unchanged throughout his life.

For Luther, they had always been subject to the wrath of God, from which only the acceptance of Jesus as the Messiah could save them. In this, Luther was in accord with the established doctrine of the old church. It was only his actions that changed over time, prompted by external factors. These are said to include the (obviously irritating) tidings that Moravian Jews were converting Christians to Judaism, or the alleged blasphemies of the Christian religion that he claimed to have registered only recently.

Further explanations could be added, but for an initial understanding, considering the two previously mentioned ones should suffice at this point. Others may be referred to below.[31] Therefore the explanation that the Reformer had been disappointed as a missionary nor the one claiming that only his conduct, not his theology, had changed are sufficient to describe and explain his about-face or encompass the entire problem. Certainly as his reply to Josel of Rosheim's request shows, he was disappointed that his treatise of 1523 had not led to any conversions of Jews. Nevertheless, he himself, though he had hoped for many converts had always reckoned with only a few.[32] Many of his theological thoughts about the Jews remained a constant for decades in his theological opinions—Luther always perceived them like all humans without Christ as "cursed in their sins and dead under the devil."[33] The assertion that there was no change at all in his theology of the Jews is however scuppered by a number of hard facts. In the years preceding his first treatise on the subject in 1523, Luther had gradually adopted the ancient certainty of Saint Paul that God would continue to be faithful to his Chosen People, even after they had failed to accept Jesus as the Messiah (Romans 2). From this theological insight, he deducted the positive consequences that he expected from Christians in their dealings with Jews, which were expounded in his treatise of 1523 and other statements of this period. Only later did he come to see the Jews as a people without a future. During the years leading up to his 1523 treatise, he would only go as far as calling them "stubborn," but later this would change to "cast out" (of their role as God's chosen people).[34] In 1523, and even before, his statements on the Jewish community were combined with a severe criticism of the church. By 1543, he was praising Christians as exemplary servants of God from the beginning up to the end of the world—in clear contrast to what he thought of the Jews.[35] In 1523 he preach human solidarity with Jews. Yet in 1543 he taught people to fear them,[36] even denying their basic humanity.[37] When he began his career as a professor of theology, he even justified Jewish "blasphemies" as grounded in Scripture, and therefore unproblematic.[38] Yet by 1543 Luther, an expert on invectives himself,

11 *WA* 11, 314, 29–315, 4. **12** *WA* 11, 315, 14–17; see 325, 18 f. **13** *WA* 11, 336, 31–33, see also: 336, 27–29. **14** *WA.B* 8, no. 3157, 89–91. **15** *WA* 50, 309–337. **16** *WA* 53, 473, 11 f. **17** *WA* 53, 417, 14–20; 552, 29–31. **18** *WA* 53, 411–552. **19** *WA* 53, 417–511. **20** See the anti-Jewish listings of vices in: *WA* 53, 502, 1–14; 514, 30–515, 8. **21** *WA* 53, 522, 29–531, 7. See earlier: 513, 1–522, 19. The entire treatise is otherwise steeped in allegations of blasphemy. **22** *WA* 11, 336, 24–26. **23** *WA* 53, 530, 18–28; 538, 25–29; 613, 22–24 and (indirectly) 522, 3 f. **24** *WA* 53, 482, 12–18. **25** *WA* 53, 522, 29–531, 7; 536, 19–537, 17; 541, 25–542, 4. **26** *WA* 53, 541, 25–542, 4, and more. **27** See as

a *pars pro toto*: *WA* 53, 587, 1–25. **28** *WA* 53, 573–648. **29** *WA* 54, 16–100. For more on these three treatises, see the following section. **30** *WA* 51, 195 f. **31** For more on the subject and its scholarly research, see the overview by Brosseder, *Stellung*, and its continuation in: Von der Osten-Sacken, *Margaritha*, pp. 15–46. **32** See *WA* 11, 315, 15 f. (many); 314, 27 f.; 315, 23 f.; 325, 19 f.; 336, 22–24 (few). **33** *WA* 11, 318, 2. **34** *WA* 53, 418, 19–22. **35** *WA* 53, 547, 20–548, 3. **36** *WA* 53, 446, 12–15. **37** *WA* 53, 479, 24–27. **38** *WA.B* 1, 23 f. (Letter to Georg Spalatin from January 31, 1514). **39** *WA* 53, 538, 8–10; 541, 35–542, 2 and more.

would classify these insults as satanic in repeated theological statements.[39] Theological reasons lay behind both his rejection of violence in matters of faith in 1523[40] and his call for violence against Jews in later years, when he saw it as a catalyst for their conversion or expulsion. This was justified as "honoring both our Lord and Christendom, and proving our Christian dedication to God."[41] As so often in such cases Luther's change in his attitude to the Jews is best seen as the result of a combination of multiple factors which play a more or less crucial role. It is primarily one aspect which is of special importance. Without recognition of it, it would prove difficult to adequately explain the hate that permeates Luther's final writings.

At the Center of the Conflict

One event that turned out to be pivotal is the encounter Luther had with two or three traveling Jews in Wittenberg. These men requested one or more letters of recommendation from him with which to apply for safe conduct in the Electorate of Saxony. Luther could not pass up the opportunity and tried to convince them that the correct interpretation of the Old Testament leads on to Jesus Christ. His words fell on deaf ears, however. In the end, he did write the letters of recommendation, but added a phrase asking the recipient to help the bearers in the name of Christ. Luther was told later on that the supplicants had commented on these letters as being well-written but marred by the mention of the "thola," a word meaning "he who was hanging" (on the cross), and a known derogatory term for the Nazarene. They had then returned the letters, as consistently as Luther wrote these letters in the name of Jesus Christ.

Luther would often mention this scene, quite possibly because he had had no other significant encounters with Jews.[42] The first time he did so was some three years after his 1523 treatise in an interpretation of Psalm 109, which already had a long history of anti-Jewish exegesis.[43] Here we find his first disparaging attack against the Jews in the context of allusions to the disappointing and mutually provocative encounter in Wittenberg. Luther demonized and branded Jews as Children of the Devil, in a way familiar from his anti-Jewish treatises of 1543. These kinds of attacks appear in Luther's later writings whenever the question of the correct exegesis of the Old Testament surfaces, as it did during the Wittenberg encounter. This point was correctly identified a hundred years ago, in the award-winning doctoral thesis of Reinhold Lewin, a rabbinical student, who saw the issue of exegesis as the epicenter of all conflicts between Luther and Judaism.[44]

The rejection of the Gospel by the Jews, and their denial of the Christian interpretation of Scripture in particular, weighed heavily on Luther. This can clearly be demonstrated by two hard facts: the publishing of no less than three extensive anti-Jewish treatises in 1543, and the basic tenures common to all three of them. If he had clamored for an expulsion of the Jews only for the reason of creating Protestant church territories with a religiously homogenous population (as is often claimed), the first treatise alone would have been enough to accomplish this. Yet Luther wrote three, and in all three the concern is with the claim to truth and the implantation of the Christian—Trinitarian and Christological—interpretation of the

Old Testament. On the one hand, Luther tried to justify this claim with detailed arguments expounding the Christological meaning of the messianic prophesies—a point that had repeatedly been disputed between Jews and Christians over the ages. This was his primary argument in *On the Jews and Their Lies*. On the other hand, he presented incontrovertible proof taken from Scripture of the descent of Jesus and his mother from the lineage of David in his second treatise. And finally, Luther explained the Trinitarian meaning behind the concept of God as contained in the Old and the New Testaments in his third treatise. Whatever we may think of the factuality of Luther's evidence from a modern perspective, we can at least concede that he did truly attempt to provide what he must have considered to be factual arguments under the given circumstances of the time. But he was not satisfied with presenting factual arguments and chose particularly in the first two treatises to mix them with an increasingly excessive demonization of the Jews. They were the original recipients and custodians of the Hebrew Bible, they understood its language perfectly, but they insisted on a literal reading of the texts, thus deviating from Christian interpretation. The Reformer formulated his approach to discrediting Jewish scriptural scholarship concisely in the first and second treatises, practiced it on many pages, and made use of it in the third tractate as well, saying: "We Christians are forbidden to believe the reasoning and explanations of the rabbis on scripture or to judge them as righteous, on pain of the loss of God's grace and life eternal. We may only read them to perceive what damned devilry they are hatching, so that we may better protect ourselves against it."[45] This repeatedly asserted devilish character of Jewish exegesis gave Luther the pretext and justification for pouring out all manner of abuse over the Jews, and particularly their rabbis. In attacking them, he felt he was actually contesting the devil himself, who was using them to mock God and Christendom.[46]

Through this demonization of the Jews, Luther was obviously trying to erect a final theological bulwark against a danger that had been looming ever larger during his final years, i.e. the fact that the Jewish method of Bible exegesis, with its strictly literal interpretation of Scripture, had been finding increasing favor in Christian circles.[47] Then what he felt was under threat was nothing less than the interpretation of the Old Testament, which had always struggled to find confirmation for the basic tenets of Christian tradition, in particular the article of faith of the birth of the Son of God by the Virgin Mary. Luther attempted to overcome the Jews' "No" to the Christian exegesis of Scripture at the level of theological consciousness and theological argumentation by differentiation between Christian knowledge of the content and Jewish knowledge of the words. In countless passages, he thus emphasized that the Jews have the language, the word, but that the Christians possessed "the meaning and the reason of the Bible"[48] in the shape of the New Testament. Or, as stated in many passages in his Genesis lectures: They have the word and we the substance, they have the husk and we the fruit.[49] In essence, this meant: We possess the truth, while they hold the lie. Way back in Worms, he had insisted on being "disproved through scriptural evidence or pure reasoning."[50] Now, a good twenty years later, he seems to have felt that this kind of refutation was ill-suited for his theological counterattack on the nagging rejection of the Jews. He resorted to the time-proven clerical tradition of demonization, a step that could hardly have been more drastic. This immoderate reaction is clear proof of how big a threat to his church Luther perceived the Jews, their scriptural exegesis with its insistence on literal interpretation of Scripture, and the support this was finding in Christian circles. Moreover the excessive vehemence of his attacks also implies that he was combating his very own doubts on the stringency of his Trinitarian-Christological (and ultimately allegorical) interpretation of the Hebrew Bible in making the Jews his target.[51]

Luther had given in to the temptation not only of distancing himself from Jewish opinions, which he fought and refuted verbally, but of ridding himself of the Jews themselves—be it through conversion or expulsion. He felt justified in demanding this course (which left no future prospect for Judaism) as he saw a clear danger that the church itself would incur the wrath of God if it continued to tolerate the enemies of the Gospel, who blasphemed against Mary, Jesus, and Christianity.[52]

Contemporaries[53]

Among the Jewish contemporaries of Luther, Josel of Rosheim, the spokesman of the Jewish community in Germany, is certainly the most eminent. Except for the rebuttal he had received in Saxony in 1537, he often was succesful in representing the communities that had been entrusted to him and enjoyed the support of Emperor Charles V for Jewish interests. His relations with Luther, however, were marked by disappointment. When rumors spread in the Alsace, based on the Reformer's first anti-Jewish treatise of 1543, that Luther had sanctioned the killing of Jews, Josel convinced the city council of Strasbourg to ban any reprints of it. Josel, an Alsatian, summed up Luther in his memoirs with a Hebrew play on words saying Luther—*isch lo tahor*—an unclean man, as a reaction to Luther's having urged that "every Jew, young or old, be destroyed and killed."[54] Jewish reactions to Martin Luther are otherwise dominated by the question of what the Reformation and the Reformer could do to improve the situation of the Jewish community. Just as Luther had expressed the expectation that some Jews would now convert to Christianity, a significant number of Jews saw the Reformation as a sign that Christianity would open up to Judaism—a misapprehen-

sion that Luther's conversational partners in Wittenberg in 1525/26 obviously shared.[55] Yet others, such as the Italian Rabbi Jechiel ben Rabbi Shmuel, were quick to identify the specific core of the Reformer's theology and realize the stark contrast between Luther's justification by faith alone and the Jewish doctrine of free will.[56] Another Jewish statement from the 1540s, while hardly able to conceal its disappointment with Luther's development, nevertheless applauds him for proclaiming the descent of Jesus "from a Jewish family." It would be interesting to find out whether specific Jewish reactions of the Reformation period (such as the few cited above) subsequently became common attitudes.

Turning to the evangelical contemporaries of Luther, we find that their attitudes toward the Jews mirror the full range of what we have observed in Luther's personal development, including all the negative and positive aspects. The following examples clearly illustrate this: Martin Bucer, a Strasbourg reformer, wrote a letter of recommendation for the Jews of Saxony at the request of Josel of Rosheim as late as 1537. Yet only a few years later, he enforced a new ordinance for Jews in Hesse that mirrored Martin Luther's propositions in the 1543 treatises. An anonymously published assessment that defended Jews accused of ritual murder was probably authored by the Nuremberg reformer Andreas Osiander in 1529. Its clear insights on theology, law, and politics as well as its analytical strength make it a gem of Reformation publishing. Justus Jonas the Elder, a lawyer and close supporter of Luther in Wittenberg, used the familiar disparaging tone when he spoke of his Jewish contemporaries in an epistle accompanying his Latin translation of Luther's treatise *Against the Sabbathans*. But this did not keep him from emphasizing the eternal debt of gratitude that Christians owed the Jews for what they had received from the wealth of their tradition, including the Messiah himself, the Son of God and Savior. In the case of Philipp Melanchthon, we find him exposing the conviction and burning of thirty-eight Jews who had been accused of desecrating the host in Berlin in 1510 as an act of judicial murder on the occasion of the Frankfurt princes' convention of 1539. This led to a rehabilitation of the Jewish community in the Electorate of Brandenburg, which in turn paved the way for a renewed immigration of Jews. Yet in 1543 he also sent a copy of Luther's pamphlet *On the Jews and Their Lies* to Philip, the Landgrave of Hesse, along with words of recommendation. Urbanus Rhegius, who led the Reformation in the Duchy of Braunschweig, was resolutely rebuffed when he attempted to pros-

40 Martin Luther: Von weltlicher Obrigkeit, wie weit man ihr Gehorsam schuldig sei (On Secular Authority) [1523]. In: WA 51, 585–625. **41** WA 53, 523, 3–5, referring to the destruction of synagogues as abodes of blasphemy. **42** WA 20, 569, 31–570, 12; WA.TR 3, 370 (no. 3512); 4, 619 f. (no. 5026); 4, 517 (no. 4795); WA 53, 461, 28–462, 5. For further references, see WA 31/II, 162, 28 f.; 50, 313, 1–6; 53, 589, 12–19. The descriptions vary somewhat but to no significant extent. **43** WA 20, 569, 31–570, 12. **44** Lewin, *Stellung*, pp. 51–61. **45** WA 53, 644, 24, 30–33 ("On the Shem …"); see WA 53, 479, 22–35 ("On the Jews …"). **46** WA 53, 590, 23–31. **47** For a criticism of this group, see WA 53, 587, 1–6; 54, 30, 13–25; 55, 15–17; 92, 25–33 and more, plus many additional passages in Luther's lecture on Genesis of 1535–1545. **48** WA 54, 29, 3–6. **49** WA 42, 596, 11–37; 597, 21–31; 599, 4–19; 600, 20–37, and

more. **50** WA 7, 838, 4–9. **51** This impression is confirmed by the many examples where he accuses the Jews of the very methods he himself employs. See (with more detail): Von der Osten-Sacken, *Margaritha*, pp. 224–230, 291–293. For the interpretation of projections by innuendo, see Reik, *Psychoanalyse*, pp. 213–248. **52** For a more detailed discussion of the allegations of blasphemy, which tries to do justice to both Luther and the Jews he attacked, see Von der Osten-Sacken, *Margaritha*, pp. 178–230. **53** For reasons of space, references are only given in the following enumeration of names where they cannot be found in the respective sections of the author's monography: Von der Osten-Sacken, *Margaritha*. **54** Fraenkel-Goldschmidt, *Iosephi de Rosheim*, p. 74. **55** WA 53, 461, 28–31. **56** See Ben-Sasson, *Reformation*, pp. 239–326, especially 255 f.

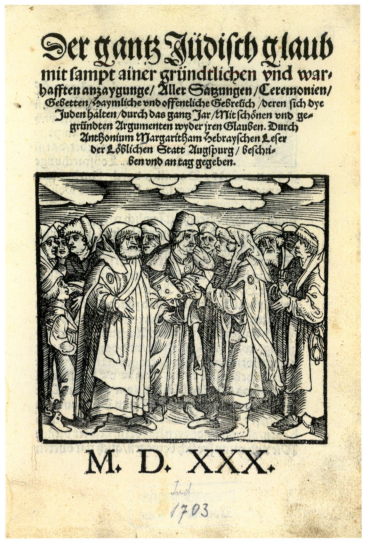

Fig. 3 Anton Margaritha, Der gantz jüdisch Glaub: mit sampt einer gründtlichen vnd warhafften anzaygunge / Aller Satzungen / Ceremonien /
Gebetten […] (The Whole Jewish Belief), Augsburg 1530

elytize in the synagogues of Hannover and Braunschweig. But in spite of these negative experiences, he continued to champion the cause of Braunschweig's Jews when the religious authorities of the city tried to evict them, in the unshakable belief that God was keeping his covenant with the original Chosen People.

Johann Eck, the Reformer's main opponent in the early years, published his treatise *A Refutation of a Small Book on the Jews* in 1541. In this volume, he attempted to disprove the anonymous assessment of the Nuremberg ritual murders mentioned above by citing an array of related fanciful atrocity stories. He actually concurred with Luther in demanding the complete marginalization and degradation of all Jews as a means of encouraging them to convert. But in contrast to the Reformer, he adhered to the Augustine tradition in refusing to consider their expulsion.

While he was writing his anti-Jewish treatises, Luther listened to Anton Margaritha's exposition of Judaism as it was read aloud on table (fig. 3). Born as the son of a rabbi, Margaritha was baptized in

1522 and joined the Catholic camp. During the Imperial Diet of Augsburg of 1530, he was summoned to justify his work *The Whole Jewish Belief*, which had recently appeared in two editions in only two months. This work combined a translation of the Jewish book of prayers from Hebrew into German with additional information on Jewish rites and customs, and was garnished with accusations against the creed he had rejected. In a disputation with Josel of Rosheim, Margaritha was soundly defeated and evicted from the city of Augsburg. He went on to become a lector of Hebrew in Leipzig and later in Vienna. Luther in 1543 found an ideal pretext in Margaritha's book for his claim that he had only now heard that the Jews were mocking Jesus Christ and the Christians in their religious services (an assertion that was manifestly untrue). Thus, the writings of the convert contributed to the defamatory attacks Luther made against the Jews and Judaism and helped to justify the Reformer's call for their comprehensive impoverishment and eventual removal.

In order to round out the broad spectrum of contemporary attitudes and statements on Jews outlined above, we close with an anonymous letter written to the First Councel Secretary of the city of Nuremberg, Lazarus Spengler. The unknown author pleaded that each religious community ("Christians, Jews, and Anabaptists") should be allowed to attend to their respective religious affairs, as long as they kept the common peace. Luther knew of such pleas for tolerance, but he thought nothing of them. In his view, they were the beginning of the degradation of the Gospel.

Summary

When Martin Luther held his first lecture in 1513–15, he based it on the following thesis: "If the Old Testament could be interpreted through human reasoning, without recourse to the New Testament, then I should consider the New Testament to have been given in vain."[57] This particular perspective on the Bible was not an original thought on the part of Luther but had been around as far back as the beginnings of Christianity—Luther himself referred to Galatians 2:21 in this respect. But the obvious and growing sensitivity with which he reacted to the threat of futility that loomed before him in the shape of the Jews, their established exegesis, and their Christian supporters truly sets the Reformer apart. For how long would he be able to keep up the assertion that Isaac had taught the basic tenets of Christianity to his family all throughout his life?[58] Or that Jacob had died uttering, "I depart in the name of Christ"?[59] These are extreme examples, to be sure, and there are other instances where the correlation between the Old Testament and the New is more transparent.

But in general, modern scholarly theology, following a historical-critical approach, has laid the interpretation of the Hebrew Bible along dogmatic Trinitarian and Christological lines to rest. What has persisted to this day is the perception of a pronounced contrast between Law and Gospel that was favored by Luther. The Reformer himself, to be sure, found it in both the Old and the New Testaments. Yet what prevailed is the notion promoted by Luther that the law as judging mankind represents the old Testament, while the Gospel which literates mankind represents the New Testament.

Ro. .1. Es wird offenbart gottes zorn von hymel vber aller menschen gotelos wesen vnd vnrecht

Isaia .7. Der Herr wird euch selbs ein zeichen geben/Sihe/eine Jungfraw wird schwanger sein vnd einen son geperen/

Sie sind alle zumal sundere/ vnd mangeln/das sie sich gottes nicht rhümen mugen Ro. .3.

Die sunde ist des todes spies/ Aber das gesetz ist der sunden krafft 1.Co .15. Das gesetz richtet zorn an Ro .4.

Durchs gesetz kompt erkentnus der sunden. Ro. .3. Das gesetz vnd die propheten gehen bis auff Johannes zeit. Math. 11.

Der gerecht lebt seines glaubens Ro.1. Wir halten das ein mensch gerecht werde durch den glauben/on werg des gesetzs. Ro. .3.

Sihe/das ist Gottes lamb/das der welt sunde tregt S. Joh.bap. Jo.1. In der heyligunge des geystes/zum gehorsam/ vnd besprengung des bluts Jhesu Christi 1. Pet. .1.

Der tod ist verschlungen ym sieg/ Tod/wo ist dein spies? Helle/wo ist dein sieg? Danck habe Gott/ der vns den sieg gibt durch Jhesum christu vnsern herrn 1. Cor.

Fig. 4 Lucas Cranach the Elder, Law and Grace, woodcut, c. 1529–32

A good example of this stance is provided by the depictions of "Law and Gospel" painted by both Lucas Cranach the Elder and the Younger and their workshop (fig. 4). In principle, this perception of the Old Testament as the embodiment of law is on the same level with the interpretation of the Hebrew Bible according to traditional Christian dogma. There is no allowance in it for the insight that Torah might mean something different from Luther's concept of law or that religion according to law in the Jewish sense might be something different than its Christian interpretation. The Torah, the law doubtlessly stands at the center of Jewish religion. Yet as the written Torah—together with the oral Torah—as a gift of God is based upon his love, so it has supported the Jewish community through the ages by generating remembrance and trust, responsibility, prayer, and hope.

Sadly, Luther's writings against the Jews have poisoned the hearts of many Christians. In the sixteenth and seventeenth centuries, they were used as justification for the banishment of the Jewish population from certain towns in the empire. In the late nineteenth and twentieth centuries, his treatises were used by Christians and non-Christians alike to pour oil into the fire of a lethal anti-Judaism. Interestingly, it was Luther himself who formulated a wise maxim (incidentally ignoring the iniquity of his own anti-Jewish utterances), which could serve for orientation in this historical context: "That is a great danger indeed: if we forget the things that have gone

57 WA 55/II, 6, 26–28. **58** WA 43, 483, 16–26. **59** WA 44, 814, 17f.

before, we may have to endure them again."[60] This sounds very much as if he had anticipated the well-known expression of the Spanish-American philosopher George Santayana: "Those who cannot remember the past are condemned to repeat it."[61]

If we take this remembering to include the question of what constitutes right action in the stream of time, we will inevitably arrive at the conclusion that this demands a rejection of Luther's absolutism. It stands in a tradition, which goes back to the church's beginnings:[62] We possess the truth, while you hold the lie. The problem is not about the either-or-controversy about biblical exegesis This should and must be particularly if the respective Jewish and Christian approaches are mutually respected. This discussion may even become stormy at times, as long as fairness is maintained. However the necessary step in superseding Luther is only made when the debate is done on an equal footing, with each party retaining its certainty of faith, but not even entertaining the quiet or whispered attitude: The nutritious kernel belongs to one side, while the other has the useless shell. If the debate is held from the standpoint of equality then the opportunity arises for a chance of mutual understanding in an atmosphere of increasing mutual trust, and indeed in some cases learning from and for each other. Some encouraging initial steps toward such a new quality relationship between Jews and Christians have indeed been made in the last few decades. Yet these are beginnings which should be confirmed in an unlimited scope.

BIBLIOGRAPHY

Bering, Dietz (2014), *War Luther Antisemit? Das deutsch-jüdische Verhältnis als Tragödie der Nähe*. Berlin. **Ben-Sasson**, Haim Hillel (1969–70), *The Reformation in Contemporary Jewish Eyes* (= Proceedings of the Israel Academy of Sciences and Humanities. 4, 12). **Brosseder**, Johannes (1972), *Luthers Stellung zu den Juden im Spiegel seiner Interpreten* (= Beiträge zur ökumenischen Theologie. 8). München. **Fraenkel-Goldschmidt**, Hava (1970), *Iosephi de Rosheim Sefer Hammiknah. Ex autographo auctoris descripsit prolegominis et annotationibus instruxit*. Jerusalem. **Kaufmann**, Thomas (2013), *Luthers "Judenschriften:" Ein Beitrag zu ihrer historischen Kontextualisierung*. 2nd ed. Tübingen. **Kaufmann**, Thomas (2014), *Luthers Juden*. Stuttgart. **Lewin**, Reinhold (1911), *Luthers Stellung zu den Juden: Ein Beitrag zur Geschichte der Juden in Deutschland während des Reformationszeitalters* (= Neue Studien zur Geschichte der Theologie und der Kirche. 10). Reprinted ed., 1973. Berlin. **Reik**, Theodor (1975), *Der eigene und der fremde Gott. Zur Psychoanalyse der religiösen Entwicklung* (= suhrkamp taschenbuch. 221). Frankfurt am Main. **Santayana**, George (1906), *The Life of Reason or the Phases of Human Progress: Introduction and Reason in Common Sense*. 1920 ed. New York. **Von der Osten-Sacken**, Peter (2002), *Martin Luther und die Juden. Neu untersucht anhand von Anton Margarithas "Der gantz Jüdisch glaub" (1530/31)*. Stuttgart. **Von der Osten-Sacken**, Peter (2008), Martin Luther und die Juden. Ende einer Feindschaft? In: de Vos, J. Cornelis/Siegert, Folker (eds.): *Interesse am Judentum. Die Franz-Delitzsch-Vorlesungen 1889–2008* (= Münsteraner Judaistische Studien. Wissenschaftliche Beiträge zur christlich-jüdischen Begegnung. 23). Berlin, pp. 262–281. **Von der Osten-Sacken**, Peter (2014), Martin Luther und die Juden. Eine Orientierung. In: Arbeitsgemeinschaft Christen und Juden im Evangelischen Kirchenkreis Spandau (eds.): *... unser Erinnern steht gegen das Vergessen. 25 Jahre Arbeitsgemeinschaft Christen und Juden im Evangelischen Kirchenkreis Spandau*. Berlin, pp. 45–48.

---

60 *WA* 42, 168, 14 f. **61** Santayana, *Reason*, p. 284. **62** See the example of the Gospel of John, especially John 5:31–47; 8:37–45; 14:1–7.

DEAN PHILLIP BELL

Martin Luther, the Jews, and Judaism: Theology and Politics in Context

Introduction

The subject of Martin Luther and his relationship with Judaism and the Jews is extremely complex. This complexity is due to the fact that Luther wrote in a tumultuous age, that he wrote frequently and often in highly charged ways about these and other subjects, and that his theology and its political ramifications have frequently been discussed since his own day.[1]

Luther's position regarding the Jews was shaped by a variety of factors. Luther may have encountered some individual Jews in person, though the evidence for such encounters is scant. It is true that Jews resided in or close to places that Luther lived at various times during his life and that Luther referred to contemporary and historical Jews regularly, especially in his last writings. During his final days in his hometown of Eisleben, which was home to several dozen Jews, a brief encounter with local Jews may have further provoked a sermon in which Luther railed against the Jews: "Now, the way things stand with the Jews is this: that they daily blaspheme and slander our Lord Jesus Christ. Since they do this, and we know about it, we should not tolerate it. For if I tolerate in my midst someone who slanders, blasphemes, and curses my Lord Jesus Christ, then I make myself a participant in the sins of another [1 Tim. 5:22]. But if I already have enough sins of my own, then you lords should not tolerate them but drive them away. If, however, they convert, give up usury, and receive Christ, then we will gladly regard them as our brothers."[2]

There is evidence that Luther had close ties with at least one convert from Judaism, Bernardus Hebraeus (formerly Rabbi Jacob Gipher). Direct contact with contemporary Jews was very limited and of little consequence to Luther, however. Although he called for, and is often credited with fueling, exclusionary territorial policies in parts of Germany (particularly in the 1530s and 1540s) and although his later writings are infused with recommendations for anti-Jewish actions, Jews themselves were generally not a practical concern for Luther. Rather, "Jews" and "Judaism" formed part of a larger theological perspective and problem for Luther. Luther engaged and utilized them as a conceptual category of oppositional "strawmen," against which he crafted his own Christology. As with other aspects of his theology, when it came to Jews and Judaism Luther was simul-taneously a traditionalist, drawing from long-standing and typically negative attitudes toward the Jewish people and their religion, and a pioneer, addressing many different biblical texts and concepts and theological concerns to define and advance his religious platform.

Past studies of Luther's writings about Jews and Judaism have frequently pointed to changes in Luther's views over time. The early Luther, as reflected in *That Jesus Christ was Born a Jew* (1523) (fig. 1), has appeared to many historians (as well as many of Luther's contemporaries) to be friendly to Jews, in that he hoped for Jewish conversions to what he considered a purer and more pristine faith. Old, battered, and disgruntled, including by the lack of Jewish conversions, Luther's later writings about the Jews in the late 1530s and 1540s took on increasingly anti-Jewish and violent tones.[3] More recently, however, scholars have noted a continuity of views in Luther's works—from his earliest commentaries on Psalms to his last sermons.[4] The truth may be somewhere in between. In Luther's writings about Jews and Judaism one can find both change and continuity.[5] Many of Luther's fundamental theological teachings and positions remained consistent throughout his career, even if some of his rhetoric and his practical-legal advice shifted over time.

Reception and Impact of Luther's Writings about the Jews and Judaism

Despite myriad modern interpretations of and reactions to Luther's writings about Jews, even in his own time Luther received a very mixed response to his comments—to his language if not generally to his theological or even practical comments regarding the Jews. Reinhold Lewin at the beginning of the twentieth century argued that one of Luther's last and perhaps most infamous works against the Jews, *On the Jews and Their Lies* (1543), "had no appreciable influence among Luther's contemporaries, for it failed completely to at-

---

1 See, for example, the broad discussion of Luther in the articles in Helmer, *Luther*. 2 "An Admonition against the Jews" (1546) in Pelikan/Lehmann, *Luther's Works*, here at *LW* 58, 458 f., presented in Schramm/Stjerna, *Bible*, pp. 200–202. 3 See Oberman, *Roots*, p. 45. 4 See Edwards, *Battles*, pp. 137 f.; see also Brosseder, *Stellung*, pp. 270–275. 5 See Brosseder, *Stellung*, pp. 35 f.

tain the spectacular literary success which Luther's early work *That Jesus Christ Was Born a Jew* had enjoyed."[6] What is more, as the Reformation historian Heiko Oberman pointed out, it was not only in the seventeenth century that we are able to find a more "positive" view of Jews among Lutherans, one that deemphasized anti-Jewish sensibilities by focusing on Christian guilt.[7]

Even among other reformers of his day, Luther's vigorous and hostile anti-Jewish rhetoric of his later years was occasionally rebuffed and ignored. Andreas Osiander, the Lutheran minister from Nuremberg famous for his arguments against blood libel accusations,[8] sent a written apology for Luther's tirades to the Venetian Jewish scholar Elias Levita, who worked closely with many Christian scholars interested in the Hebrew language.[9] Luther's close colleague Philipp Melanchthon also sought to downplay Luther's rhetoric,[10] and even the translator of Luther's anti-Jewish works, Justas Jonas, possessed a different view of the Jews than Luther. Jonas saw the possibility of the fusion of Jews and Christians into one body in a way that Luther found unacceptable.[11] The Lutheran reformer Urbanus Rhegius argued strongly for toleration of Jews, with hopes of eventual conversion, in response to the 1539/1540 attempts by the Lutheran clergy of Braunschweig to expel the Jews from that city.[12]

The Zwinglian Heinrich Bullinger of Zurich complained to another reformer, Martin Bucer of Strasbourg, of Luther's "lewd and houndish eloquence" and his "scurrility which is appropriate for no one and still less for an old theologian."[13] Bucer himself noted that Luther's work *Of the Unknowable Name and the Generations of Christ* was "piggish" and "murky" and could not be defended even if written by a swineherd.[14] Indeed, Luther's language could be quite scatological. As he did with other groups that he saw as in opposition to "true Christianity," Luther derided Jews with a range of negative words and associations. Such invectives against the Jews were far-ranging, though some words seem to have been particularly frequent and especially associated with the Jews—including "lies," "blasphemy," and "cursing."[15]

Of course such criticism needs to be taken in context. Rhegius's position, for example, is not couched in the inflamed rhetoric of the later Luther; but it is still primarily aimed at missionizing and then converting Jews. And even those scholars who supported the preservation of Jewish writings, such as Johannes Reuchlin, were not particularly or necessarily philo-Semitic. Erasmus, to take one famous example, who many have thought to be the forerunner of enlightened and tolerant thought, was himself very "intolerant" when it came to the subject of the Jews.[16] Luther's Catholic archenemy John Eck also published very hostile pamphlets against the Jews. Reapplying the negative view of Jews and Judaism that was both rampant and cultivated by his theological forerunners and contemporaries, Eck went so far as to label Luther and his Wittenberg colleagues themselves as "Judaizers."

Aside from the realm of theology, Luther's writings about Jews and Judaism could and did have significant political impact, at times leading to anti-Jewish legislation, such as the expulsion of the Jews from Saxony in 1536 and 1543 and the restrictions against the Jews of Hesse in 1539.[17] In Braunschweig, the publication of Luther's *On the*

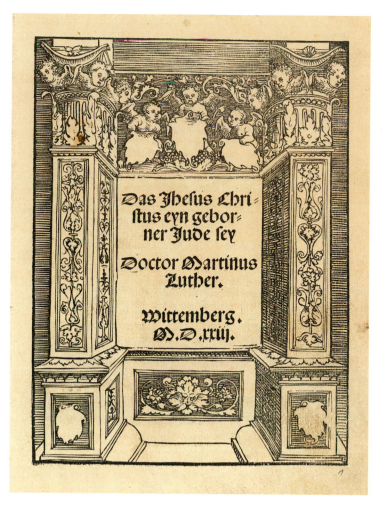

Fig. 1 Martin Luther, *Das Jhesus Christus eyn geborner Jude sey* (That Jesus Christ was Born a Jew), Wittenberg 1523. With woodcuts by Lucas Cranach the Elder

Jews and Their Lies sparked mounting measures against the Jews, until 1546 when the Jews were finally ordered expelled from the city.[18] The case of Braunschweig, however, also betrays the reality that anti-Judaism was nothing new to Reformation Germany and that Luther's writings were coopted as a means to justify what clearly was a trend of increasing marginalization of the Jews for several years previously. While specific practical political and legal consequences and connections can be found between Luther's writings—particularly in the sermons and political negotiations at the end of his life[19]—and harsh legal measures against the Jews, it is not entirely appropriate to connect them all to Luther. Indeed, the large majority of Jewish expulsions throughout the German cities and even a number of large territories predated Luther by up to one hundred years.

Luther's Views on Jews and Judaism

What exactly was Luther's attitude toward Jews and Judaism, then? Luther was deeply concerned with both of these subjects, which played a central role in his theology and writings throughout his career. A large majority of Luther's works, from exegesis to daily conversation, revolves around the Hebrew Bible/Old Testament and so naturally addresses issues related to Jews and Judaism. Luther's writings about Jews and Judaism stretch from his earliest works on the Psalms in 1513/1514 to just three days before his death in 1546.[20] "The Jews interested and irritated Luther," the historian Thomas Kaufmann notes, "because for him their simple existence in their dispersion, persecution, and marginalization through Christian society was a witness of divine judgment, as he saw in the Bible."[21] Like the papacy, the devil, Enthusiasts (Luther's early opponents among his own circle), and even the Turks, the Jews were a constant enemy fundamentally opposed to Christians:[22] "The Jews were the opposite of what Luther considered to be fundamental to being a Christian."[23] As such, Jews and Judaism provided an oppositional Other that helped Luther to define what, in his mind, were true Christianity and legitimate Christian belief and behavior.

Luther regularly returned to a number of core issues related to the Jews. While the language in his later writings is increasingly scatological and violent, his earliest writings are also infused with negative and anti-Jewish stereotypes and arguments. In his first Psalms lectures from the middle of the second decade of the sixteenth century, for example, Luther castigated the Jews both for crucifying Jesus and denying that it was a sin to have done so. He also lambasted them for a love of gold, honor, and flesh—that is, greed, arrogance, and carnality—and what he termed their meditations "on vanities and false frenzies according to their own ideas about scripture."[24] In his glosses to Psalm 78, Luther asserted that "... God rejected them [the Jews] altogether according to the flesh and killed the standing of the synagogue and put the Law to death, in which they nevertheless think they are living, but they are not alive before God. The fact that their sacrifices and ceremonies and works are dead, this God did with the word alone, for He removed them and determined that they should come to an end. But since they were unwilling, the wrath of indignation was sent upon them."[25]

But Luther did not simply criticize the Jews and assert the end of the Old in the New Dispensation. Throughout his writings, Luther reviewed biblical history to criticize the papacy and to recast the biblical Israelites as true Christians. He drew a parallel, for example, between the Babylonian Exile of Israel and the Babylonian Captivity of the church in his own day. Put another way, in Luther's theology the "true Israel," that is, the "church," has been exiled in much the same way that the ancient Israelites had been.[26] Luther distinguished historical Jews—the Jews of the past—from the Jews of his own day.[27] But for Luther, as for other Christian theologians, the most conspicuous Jews of the day were "we miserable Christians." Here the replacement of the Chosen People of the Hebrew Bible was assumed as it had been in traditional Christian thought. As a category[28] "the Jews" were linked by Luther to other groups and leveraged in his criticism of fellow Christians and the state of the church in its final stages of Reformation. Accordingly, Luther wrote, "Moreover, through the worship of Baal there was depicted a monstrous form of righteousness and superstitious piety which prevails widely to this day. By means of this the Jews, heretics, and monks, that is arrogant individualists, worship the true God according to their own

idea with most ridiculous zeal; with their excessive piety they are worse than the most ungodly, that is, for the sake of God they are the enemies of God ..."[29]

The end of the Babylonian Captivity, the freeing of the church at the end of days, was not, for Luther, contingent upon the Jews themselves, but rather upon internal Christian transformation. Oberman concludes that, "Jewish obstinacy retards the coming end as little as Jewish conversion hastens it. For Luther a "Jew-free" Germany will never lead to the "Millennial Kingdom."[30] Therefore, Oberman asserts, Luther's writings, even the later ones, should not be read as an appeal to the rabble to harm the Jews, but rather as an attack on the authorities, demanding that they relinquish their self-serving and avaricious policies, as reflected in their relations with the Jews.[31] Other scholars have also noted that indeed the later writings of Luther (and probably the earlier ones as well) were never really directed at or against the Jews—they were written for a Christian audience.[32] Of course, that fact alone does not change the anti-Jewish nature of the texts or the practical consequences to which they could give rise when co-opted by civic and territorial rulers.

Luther's Early Works

In his 1523 *That Jesus Christ was Born a Jew* many scholars have seen a "tolerant" Luther, who argued that the Jews should be dealt with gently and instructed with proper scriptural passages.[33] Yet that text is really directed at heretics and written in response to allegations against several of Luther's theological positions (most especially his position related to Mary), that is, not against or to the Jews themselves. The main themes of the text revolve around biblical interpretation,[34] the Messiah,[35] and criticism of the contemporary church. And while the text has often been read quite "positively" as repre-

6 Wallmann, *Reception*, p. 75. **7** Oberman, *Roots*, p. 124. **8** See Hsia, *Myth*, pp. 138–140. **9** Oberman, *Roots*, p. 47. **10** Ibid., p. 47. **11** Ibid., p. 49; see also Oberman, *Impact*, pp. 114 f. **12** Hendrix, *Toleration*, p. 191; Of course even from the 1536 Saxony expulsion we cannot be entirely certain to what extent Luther had a hand in practical political maneuvers—see Brosseder, *Stellung*, p. 355. **13** Baron, *History*, vol. XIII, p. 228. **14** Gutteridge, *Mouth*, p. 320. **15** Bering, *Antisemit*, p. 134. **16** Oberman, *Impact*, p. 102; regarding Erasmus and the Jews, for example, see Markish, *Erasmus*. **17** See Ries, *Zusammenhang*, pp. 630 f. **18** Ibid., pp. 638 f. **19** Kaufmann, *Juden*, pp. 7–9. In addition, for a more in-depth examination of the broader theme of Luther's Jewish writings, see Kaufmann, *Judenschriften*. **20** Ehrlich, *Juden*, p. 72; Kaufmann, *Jews*, p. 71. **21** Ibid., pp. 71 f. **22** Ibid., p. 73. **23** Ibid., p. 72. **24** *LW* 10, presented in: Schramm/Stjerna, *Bible*, p. 45. **25** *LW* 11. In: Schramm/Stjerna, *Bible*, p. 47. **26** *LW* 25, Lectures on Romans, 1515/16, p. 421. **27** Oberman, *Roots*, p. 106. **28** Brosseder, *Stellung*, pp. 346 f. **29** *LW* 25, 422. **30** Oberman, *Roots*, p. 117. **31** Ibid., p. 121; Brosseder notes Luther's distinction between Kaiser's Jews and Moses's Jews; see Brosseder, *Stellung*, p. 373. **32** Edwards, *Battles*, p. 132; Brosseder, *Stellung*, p. 359. **33** *LW* 45, 229. **34** *LW* 45, 208, regarding his use of Old Testament evidence that the Jews will accept; p. 209, where he notes that the Jews are extreme literalists. **35** *LW* 45, 213–215 in particular, where he discusses the Jews mistaken waiting for the Messiah.

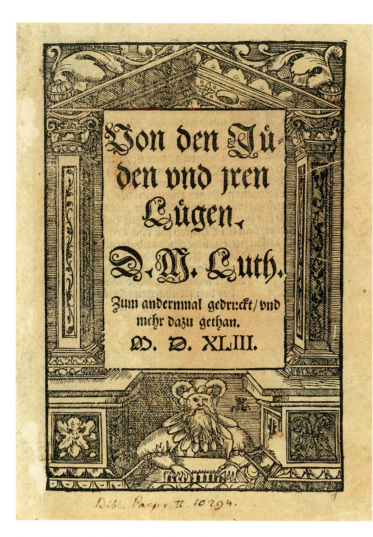

Fig. 2 Martin Luther, Von den Jueden vnd jren Luegen
(On the Jews and Their Lies), Wittenberg 1543

church, medieval, and contemporary writers that shaped his opinions more than the presence of any real-life conversation partners. What is more, Luther used his early works as a convenient foil against the papacy specifically and Catholicism more generally. It was earlier Christians who had failed to provide Jews an adequate proclamation of the Gospel.[39] As Kaufmann notes, Luther's concern with the Jews was never really a mission to the Jews but a theological struggle for truth of Gospel and purity of an embattled church.[40] The tone and focus of his discussion of Jews in this work was already evident in earlier writings, such as his lectures on Romans from 1515–16. In those glosses he noted: Contra quod multi mira stultitia superbiunt et Judeos nunc canes, nunc maledictos, nunc, ut libet, appellant, cum ipsi etiam | eque | nesciunt, qui aut quales sint coram Deo. Audacter prorumpunt in blasphemas agnominationes, ubi debuerant compati illis et sibi similia timere. Ipsi econtra quasi certi de se et illis temere pronunciant se velut benedictos et illos maledictos. Quales nunc sunt Colonienses theologi, qui non pudent zelo suo stultissimo in suis articulis, immo inerticulis et ineptiis Judeos dicere maledictos.[41]

Luther's Later Works

It has been noted that Luther's attitude toward the Jews seemed to become more radical after 1538, and particularly so in his last works. It is worth pointing out, however, that Luther's later writings are highly polemical and directed against all his enemies, not just the Jews, and that his later writings, for all their harsh and bitter vindictive, continue his earlier theological and exegetical work very logically. If not for the concluding sections of his *On the Jews and Their Lies* (1543), his later, most hated work would hardly differ from his earlier writings (fig. 2). What is more, already in the middle years of the 1530s, especially in his wide-ranging commentary to Genesis, Luther increasingly engaged and criticized rabbinic commentaries to the Bible, stoking his negative attitudes toward the Jews (fig. 3). In commenting on Genesis 25:21, for example, he asserted, "We acknowledge, of course, that it is a great benefit that we have received the language [Hebrew] from them [the Jews]; but we must beware of the dung of the rabbis, who have made of Holy Scripture a sort of privy in which they deposited their foulness and their exceedingly foolish opinions. I am advising this because even among our own theologians many give too much credit to the rabbis in explaining the meaning of scripture."[42] His career-long and overriding interest in the Hebrew Bible and his engagement with what he considered to be the proper translation and exegesis of Hebrew texts contributed substantially to Luther's views of Jews and Judaism and was closely related to his theology.[43]

senting the expressions of a Luther more open and friendly to Jews, at least in the context of missionizing, it is clear that Luther was less concerned about converting Jews en masse than that any such conversions be what he considered deep and true conversions.[36] While Luther clearly hoped for some Jewish conversions, he never seemed to hold out hopes that massive conversions were even possible. In his 1521 *Magnificat*, he had already written, "Although the vast majority of them [the Jews] are hardened, yet there are always some, however few, that are converted to Christ and believe in Him … We ought, therefore, not to treat the Jews in so unkindly a spirit, for there are future Christians among them, and they are turning every day."[37] Luther would continue this theme in *That Jesus Christ was Born a Jew*. Unfortunately, he observed, "[i]nstead of this we are trying only to drive them by force, slandering them, accusing them of having Christian blood if they don't stink, and I know not what other foolishness. So long as we thus treat them like dogs, how can we expect to work any good among them?"[38]

It bears repeating that Luther spoke about, but not with Jews. Outside two or three converts from Judaism, it was what Luther read and heard about Jews and Judaism in the Bible and from early

36 Kaufmann, *Jews*, p. 84. **37** *LW* 21. In: Schramm/Stjerna, *Bible*, p. 74. **38** *LW* 45. In: Schramm/Stjerna, *Bible*, p. 83. **39** Kaufmann, *Jews*, p. 78. **40** Ibid., p. 75. **41** Ficker, *Vorlesung*, p. 261. **42** *LW* 4, cited in Schramm/Stjerna, *Bible*, p. 130. See Kaufmann, *Jews*, p. 88. **43** Helmer, *Hermeneutic*.

Hie hebt sich an. Genesis das erst buch der
fünff bucher moysi. Das erst Capitel ist võ
der schöppfung der werlt vnd aller creaturen.
vnd von den wercken der sechs tag.

N dem anfang
hat got beschaf
fen hymel vnd
erden. aber dye erde was
eytel vnd lere. vnd die vin/
sternus warn auff dē ant/
litz des abgrunds. vnd der
geist gots swebet oder ward getragen auff dē
wassern. Vñ got der sprach. Es werde dz liecht
Vñ das liecht ist worden. vñ got sahe dz liecht
das es gutt was. vnd er teylet das liecht võ der
vinsternus. vnd das liecht hyeß er den tag. vnd
die vinsternus die nacht. Vñ es ward abent vñ

morgen eyn tag. Vnd got der sprach. Es wer/
de das firmament in dem mittel der wasser. vñ
tayle die wasser võ dē wassern. Vñ got machet
das firmament. vnd teylet die wasser. dy do wa
ren vnder dem firmament. von dē dy do waren
ob dem firmament. vnd es ist also geschehen
vnd got hieß das firmament den hymel vnd es
ist der abent vñ der morge der ander tag wordē
vñ got sprach aber. Es sulle gesamelt werde dy
wasser. die vnder dem hymel seynd. an eyn statt.
vñ erscheyne die durre. vnd es ist also geschehē
Vñ got hieß die durre dz ertreich. Vñ dy sam
nungen der wasser. hieß er die mere. vnd got sa
he das es was gut. vnd sprach. Die erde gepere
grunend kraut. das do bringe den samen. vnd
dy opfelbawm. dz holtz. dz do bringe dy frucht
nach seym geschlecht. des same sey in ym selbs
auff der erde. vnd es ist also geschehen. vnd die
erd bracht grunend kraut. vnd bringenden sa/

Fig. 3　Depiction of the Creation showing the creation of Eve, from: Biblia, Nürnberg 1483.
　　　　Printed in the printing workshop of Anton Koberger

Although Luther had initially rejected accusations that Jews committed ritual murder and host desecration, he later considered that such accusations could in fact contain a kernel of truth (fig. 4).[44] Outside his own theological development and efforts to defend himself from attackers or to stake out his own theological positions and his increasing criticism of rabbinic exegesis, the appearance of "expert" testimony from the writings of the Jewish apostate Anton Margaritha and the Christian Hebraist Sebastian Münster further encouraged Luther to adopt more negative positions about Jews.[45]

In his last major writings that mention the Jews, Luther's theological concerns and positions had changed little from his earliest works. His *Treatise on the Last Words of David* (1543),[46] for example, focuses upon questions of exegesis, the Trinity, and the Messiah, while criticizing the Jews and his perception of their arrogant notion of descent along the way. Like other anti-Jewish polemicists in the Middle Ages, Luther noted that the fact that Jews had been in dispersion and persecuted for 1,500 years was itself testimony that they had been rejected by God, that the Messiah had already come, and that the Jews blindly refused to see such truth: "… these false and unknown Jews or Israelites who have wrought no miracle these 1,500 years, who have interpreted no writings of the prophets, who have perverted everything, who have done nothing in the open but underhandedly and clandestinely, like children of darkness, that is, of the devil, have practiced nothing but blasphemy, cursing, murder, and lies against the true Jews and Israel, that is, against the apostles and prophets."[47] What is more, he continued, "… they continue this daily and thus prove that they are not Israel or Abraham's children and in addition [are] despoilers, robbers, and perverters of Holy Scripture …"[48]

Luther's *Against the Sabbatarians (Letter to a Good Friend)* (1538) also rehearses a number of his ongoing concerns, particularly discussions of the Messiah, the Babylonian Exile, and circumcision. Again, Luther concludes with a play on the concept of "Jew": "So you must tell them that they themselves should take the initiative in keeping Moses' Law and becoming Jews. For they are no longer Jews, since they do not observe their Law. When they have done this, we shall promptly emulate them and also become Jews."[49]

Among Luther's later writings that address the Jews is the infamous *On the Jews and Their Lies*. This work is perhaps the most significant one written by Luther because of its frequent appropriation since the sixteenth century. There are four major parts to this work. In the first part Luther spends a great deal of ink discussing questions of Jewish boasting regarding lineage, circumcision, and homeland. In the second part Luther attacks Jewish exegesis at length. In part three Luther relates reputed calumnies of Jews against Jesus and Mary, and in part four Luther offers his infamous advice to secular and ecclesiastical authorities on what should be done with the Jews, who cannot be truly converted to Christianity.[50]

Part one echoes the bulk of Luther's previous writings about Jews, though here Luther is very pointedly not concerned with converting any Jews, an act that he assumes to be impossible.[51] Luther goes through a litany of accusations he has raised previously, including that Jews revile Christianity and that they boast of their nobility

with "devilish arrogance."[52] In a very apocalyptic vein, Luther notes that "Jews, Turks, papists, radicals abound everywhere," claiming to be the Church and God's people.[53] Luther's discourse proceeds from his standard barrage and turns perceptibly against the Jews in a radical way, however. He urges a seven-point program for dealing with the Jews: their synagogues should be burned or buried; their houses razed and destroyed; their idolatrous prayer books and Talmudic writings should be confiscated; their rabbis should be forbidden from teaching; all privileges of safe-conduct should be abolished; they should be prohibited from exacting usury and their monetary possessions should be confiscated; they should be forced to earn their keep by the sweat of their brow, or, if good Christians fear them, they should be driven away completely.[54] It is in these final "recommendations" that much of Luther's anti-Jewish reputation was forged. As noted earlier, one cannot discount the practical advice forwarded by Luther in these painful passages. Luther had indeed come to the conclusion that the Jews writ large could never be converted and so needed to be removed from Christian society. But this position was in most respects no different from his earliest position, in which he assumed a place for Jews in Christian society only upon true conversion to Christianity. In a certain sense, the "advice" proffered at the end of this treatise represents the practical culmination of Luther's theological position. The application of this advice in his own day and at other times in German history has made Luther's disturbing rhetorical flourishes extend far beyond theological musings.

Conclusions

The subject of Luther and his relationship to the Jews has not always been clearly defined nor free of partisan commentary. Before briefly surveying the complex use and misuse of Luther and his theology in modernity, I should note that nineteenth- and early twentieth-century Jews themselves often had positive opinions of Luther, despite his negative writings about Jews and Judaism. Heinrich Heine, for example, attributed "Geistfreiheit" to Luther; Hermann Cohen compared Luther with Moses; and Franz Rosenzweig showed a great deal of respect for Luther the Bible translator.[55] On the other hand, even in his own time and within his own camp many opposed either Luther's message or his method and language of conveying it.

The discussion of Luther and the Jews cannot be limited to Luther's writings about Jews and Judaism or the sixteenth-century and early modern responses to them. Well into modernity, Luther's writings could, in fact, be leveraged in support of a wide range of religious and political causes, in the case of the Jews, from Jewish emancipation and assimilation to racial anti-Semitism. But to what extent can a straight line be drawn between Luther and his theology and the subsequent appropriation of both since Luther's death?

44 Kaufmann, *Jews*, p. 76. **45** Ibid., p. 94. **46** See *LW* 15. **47** *LW* 15, 344. **48** *LW* 15, 344. **49** Against the Sabbatarians (1538). In: *LW* 47, 79. **50** See *LW* 47, introduction, pp. 133 f. **51** *LW* 47, 137. **52** *LW* 47, 143. **53** *LW* 47, 175. **54** *LW* 47, 268 f. **55** Ginzel, *Kronzeuge*, p. 189.

Fig. 4 The host desecration by the Jews in Passau. Broadsheet, c. 1495

Some scholars have asserted that Luther's Jewish writings have had an enduring, and largely negative, influence, making Luther one of the "fathers of modern anti-Semitism," and they find a direct historical link connecting Luther's works to the anti-Semitic and genocidal actions of Hitler and the Nazis against the Jews.[56] Other scholars have argued that Luther's anti-Jewish works had little real influence on the treatment of the Jews in subsequent history.[57] This argument is based on several assertions: that Luther's most infamous work against the Jews, On the Jews and Their Lies, had no great impact on Luther's contemporaries and it never succeeded in achieving the success of his early work That Jesus Christ Was Born a Jew,[58] and that Luther's three late anti-Jewish works were not published again until the seventeenth century and were not again popular until the twentieth century. On the Jews and Their Lies, however, was referenced in several mid-sixteenth-century expulsions of the Jews from German cities or territories.[59] Regardless of whether Luther's writings were read directly, the lack of publication does not negate the possibility of discussion or dissemination of ideas, some of which, of course, drew from broader Christian anti-Semitism. Once we reach the nineteenth century there were powerful Protestant spokesmen, including Adolf Stöcker and Heinrich von Treitschke, who were active in stirring up anti-Semitism along nationalistic lines. Stöcker, labeled by some as a forerunner of Hitler, was referred to in certain circles as the "Second Luther."[60] His rabid anti-Jewish speeches encouraged the removal of Jews from positions of power and influence, while his "religious-national terminology served as a fruitful ideological source and as a political incentive in fomenting racial and even anti-Christian anti-Semitism."[61]

In the twentieth century, we are not hard-pressed to find Luther enlisted in the Nazi propaganda against the Jews—witness the closing of Veit Harlan's Jud Süss from 1941, material made available in Der Stürmer,[62] or any number of actions and statements by Nazis. The terrible pogrom and destruction of Kristallnacht occurred on the eve of Luther's 455th birthday and was frequently connected with Luther's writings.[63] In November of 1938, one German official leaving ranks noted that, "it should be realized that the wicked Nazis have simply carried out the instruction of Luther. The synagogues have been burnt, just as the father of Protestantism required."[64] Once Hitler did come to power, individual Lutheran, and for that matter Protestant, pastors' positions often depended very much upon individual personality and environment. Some pastors supported pan-German associations with their virulent anti-Semitism and anti-Christian volkish tendencies.[65] On the other hand, others spoke out against such volkish policies, especially as they pertained to non-Aryan legislation that affected participation in the church. In May of 1936, members of the Confessing Church took the bold step of speaking out in a lengthy memorandum to Hitler; yet in the end they did not disavow anti-Semitism, only the militant Nazi version of it.[66] Ironically, during the 1920s and 1930s many within the Confessing Church "compared and even equated Judaism with the völkisch movement, including National Socialism."[67] Hans Hofer, for example, a staunch Lutheran and spokesman for the Conservatives warned that members of the volkish movement turn "'… the nation and national-

ity … into a religious value … There are Germans who simply deify our peoplehood' yet 'peoplehood should not be exalted as if it were divine.'"[68] For Hofer, worship of the nation is a degradation to the levels of Judaism; witness the terrible consequences when a people idolizes nationalism as when the Old Testament is shorn of the New Covenant, he argued.[69] For Hofer, volkish and Nazi racism also prevented evangelical preaching and conversion. Other Conservatives, such as Heinrich Frick, grouped volkish, Nazi, and Zionist nationalism together.[70] With the establishment of the "Third Reich" in the early 1930s, some connected the Nazis and the Jews in their rejection of the true Messiah: The Nazis made a political messiah of the Führer, and the Jews remained bogged down in their crude materialism of the Old Testament.[71] Uriel Tal has suggested that Conservatives may have deliberately drawn such connections between Jews and Nazis in an effort to garner support from the groups for whose attention they competed with the Nazis.[72]

The topic of Luther and the Jews has been particularly significant since the Shoah for at least two reasons. First, since the Nazis frequently appropriated and misappropriated medieval and Lutheran anti-Jewish discourse and imagery in their media and propaganda campaigns against the Jews, both Jews and Christians have felt compelled to reconsider the extent to which the Nazis twisted such discourse and imagery and the extent to which such latent and blatant anti-Jewish depictions festered and eventually helped to usher in the calamities and horrors of the twentieth century. Second, the interest in the subject of Luther, the Jews, and Judaism has also been related to Jewish and Christian dialogue over the past several decades, to Christian expressions of sympathy for the Jews who suffered, and even concession of Christian guilt in the Holocaust. In particular, many Lutherans have lately condemned the harsh anti-Jewish message and language of their theological founder.[73]

Now that we have contextualized Luther and examined some of his writings about the Jews and Judaism, as well as the later impact of his works, a few concluding observations are in order. First, Luther has been interpreted in a variety of often opposing ways since the sixteenth century. Even by the end of the sixteenth century it might not be too outrageous to suggest that Luther was not really a "Lutheran" in some ways; put another way Lutheran orthodoxy developed alongside and even at times away from Luther's own ideas. Second, Luther's vision of the Jews was largely theological and rhetorical in nature. Jews formed part of a devilish group subverting the true church (or true Judaism), which also helped indicate the end of days. For Luther, Jews of ancient Israel were markedly different from contemporary Jews, who Luther argued were not really Jews at all. In fact, for Luther it was more appropriate to view early Christians as the true Jews, heirs to the ancient Israelites. What is more, the concept of the "Jew" was largely a prop for Luther's attacks on his own society. Even in his later blandishments against contemporary Jews, Luther used the "Jews" to strike out against those who he believed misused their authority. His later and violent polemics were certainly not restricted to the Jews; at the same time, his view of the Jews and the primary issues associated with the concept of "Jews" remained remarkably salient and consistent throughout his career.

Third, Jews and Judaism were important to Luther's core religious concerns, especially key issues such as: biblical exegesis, faith and works, lineage and descent, and apocalypticism. There is no doubting that Luther was vehement against, even dismissive of, contemporary Jewry and vastly anti-Jewish in many of his theological discussions. One also cannot disregard Luther's later inflammatory rhetoric. He intended his writings to have, and they certainly did have, social and political tones and implications. Luther wanted to impact contemporary politics and he lobbied viciously for the expulsion of the Jews in areas where he had some personal influence. Nonetheless, seen within the broader scope of his thought, we cannot hold Luther accountable for later, modern misappropriations of his writings. Even sixteenth-century appropriation of his later works seems difficult to defend given the lack of his direct political influence in most places, the often negative reaction to his harsh words, and the history of anti-Jewish action that preceded his verbal tirades—though of course he was at times cited in support of such action. In fact, Luther was not the only Protestant theologian used in such a way. The famous sixteenth-century Jewish *Shtadlan* (or advocate) Josel of Rosheim protested that the works of the south German reformer Martin Bucer were used to the same end.[74] Luther must, however, be seen within a very anti-Jewish tradition that has been appropriated, knowingly and unknowingly, throughout the ages; he must also be read within the broader context of his own works. In the end, Luther's relationship to the Jews and Judaism provides a central lens through which to understand many of Luther's core theological concerns, even as it sheds light on the negative attitudes he and others shared about the Jews and Judaism throughout history.

---

56 Wallmann, *Reception*, p. 72. 57 Ibid., pp. 72 f. 58 Ibid., p. 75. 59 See, for example, Bell, *Settlement*. 60 Gutteridge, *Mouth*, pp. 6 and 10. 61 Tal, *Lutheranism*, pp. 203. 62 See Brosseder, *Stellung*, pp. 182–192. 63 See Gritsch, *Luther*, p. 56. 64 Gutteridge, *Mouth*, p. 177. 65 Ibid., p. 37. 66 Ibid., pp. 158 f. 67 Tal, *Lutheranism*, p. 203. 68 Ibid., p. 204. 69 Ibid., p. 204. 70 Ibid., p. 205. 71 Ibid., p. 207. 72 According to Tal, "the people, youth, the masses, and also from the liberal professions and the intellectuals" (ibid., p. 210). 73 Rau, *Geleitwort*, p. xv. 74 Josel notes that Bucer's writings have had the effect of stirring up the common people [*gemain Volck*] and inciting them against the Jews, pointing to the events on the streets of Friedburg where "a poor Jew was struck and his life taken, while the perpetrators jeered: 'see, Jew, the writings of Bucer say that your goods should be taken and distributed among the poor.'" See *Trostschrift*, in Fraenkel-Goldschmidt, *Joseph*, p. 331 [in the German text].

BIBLIOGRAPHY

Baron, Salo (1969), *A Social and Religious History of the Jews*. New York. **Bell**, Dean Phillip (2006), Jewish Settlement, Politics, and the Reformation. In: Bell, Dean Phillip/Burnett, Stephen G. (eds.), *Jews, Judaism, and the Reformation in Sixteenth-Century Germany*, Leiden, pp. 421–450. **Bering**, Dietz (2014), *War Luther Antisemit? Das deutsch-jüdische Verhältnis als Tragödie der Nähe*. Berlin. **Brosseder**, Johannes (1972), *Luthers Stellung zu den Juden im Spiegel seiner Interpreten; Interpretation und Rezeption von Luthers Schriften und Äußerungen zum Judentum im 19. und 20. Jahrhundert vor allem im deutschsprachigen Raum*. München. **Edwards**, Mark U. (1983), *Luther's Last Battles. Politics and Polemics, 1531–1546*. Ithaca. **Ehrlich**, Ernst L. (1985), Luther und die Juden. In: Kremers, Heinz (ed.), *Die Juden und Martin Luther: Geschichte, Wirkungsgeschichte, Herausforderung*. Neukirchen-Vluyn, pp. 72–88. **Ficker**, Johannes (ed.) (1908), *Anfänge reformatorischer Bibelauslegung. Vol. 1: Luthers Vorlesung über den Römerbrief 1515/16*. Leipzig. **Fraenkel-Goldschmidt**, Hava (ed.), *Joseph of Rosheim: Historical Writings*, Jerusalem, pp. 328–349. **Ginzel**, Günther B. (1985), Martin Luther: Kronzeuge des Antisemitismus. In: Kremers, Heinz (ed.), *Die Juden und Martin Luther: Geschichte, Wirkungsgeschichte, Herausforderung*. Neukirchen-Vluyn, pp. 189–210. **Gritsch**, Eric W. (1996), Luther and the State: Post Reformation Ramifications. In: Tracy, James D. (ed.), *Luther and the Modern State in Germany*. Kirksville, Mo., pp. 45–60. **Gutteridge**, Richard (1976), *Open Thy Mouth for the Dumb: The German Evangelical Church and the Jews 1879–1950*. Oxford. **Helmer**, Christine (2002), Luther's Trinitarian Hermeneutic and the Old Testament. In: *Modern Theology* vol. 18, no. 1 (January, 2002), pp. 49–73. **Helmer**, Christine (ed.) (2009), *The Global Luther: A Theologian for Modern Times*. Minneapolis. **Hendrix**, Scott H. (1990), Toleration of the Jews in the German Reformation: Urbanus Rhegius and Braunschweig (1535–1540). In: *Archiv für Reformationsgeschichte*, vol. 81, pp. 189–215. **Hsia**, R. Po-Chia (1988), *The Myth of Ritual Murder: Jews and Magic in Reformation Germany*. New Haven. **Kaufmann**, Thomas (2006), Luther and the Jews. In: Bell, Dean Phillip/Burnett, Stephen G. (eds.), *Jews, Judaism, and the Reformation in Sixteenth-Century Germany*. Leiden, pp. 69–104. **Kaufmann**, Thomas (2011), *Luthers "Judenschriften": Ein Beitrag zu ihrer historischen Kontextualisierung*. Tübingen. **Kaufmann**, Thomas (2014), *Luthers Juden*. Stuttgart. **Markish**, Shimon (1986), *Erasmus and the Jews*, trans. Anthoy Olcott. Chicago. **Oberman**, Heiko A. (1994), *The Impact of the Reformation*. Grand Rapids. **Oberman**, Heiko A. (1984), *The Roots of Antisemitism in the Age of Renaissance and Reformation*, trans. James I. Porter. Philadelphia. **Pelikan**, Jaroslav/**Lehmann**, Hartmut T. (eds.) (1955), *Luther's Works* (LW, hereafter), vols. 1–55. St. Louis. **Rau**, Johannes (1985), Geleitwort. In: Kremers, Heinz, *Die Juden und Martin Luther—Martin Luther und die Juden: Geschichte, Wirkungsgeschichte, Herausforderung*. Neukirchen-Vluyn, pp. v–xx. **Ries**, Rotraud (1984), Zum Zusammenhang von Reformation und Judenvertreibung: Das Beispiel Braunschweig. In: Häger, Helmut/Peri, Franz/Quirin, Heinz (eds.), *Civitatium Communitas: Studien zum europäischen Städtewesen. Festschrift Heinz Stoob zum 65. Geburtstag*. Köln, pp. 630–654. **Schramm**, Brooks/**Stjerna**, Kirsi I. (eds.) (2012), *Martin Luther, the Bible, and the Jewish People: A Reader*. Minneapolis. **Tal**, Uriel (1985), On Modern Lutheranism and the Jews. In: *Leo Baeck Institute Yearbook*, vol. 30, pp. 203–211. **Wallmann**, Johannes (1987), The Reception of Luther's Writings on the Jews from the Reformation to the End of the nineteenth Century. In: *Lutheran Quarterly* vol. 1, pp. 72–97.

THOMAS KAUFMANN

Luther and the Turks

From the last days of May 1453 on, when the troops of the Ottoman Empire under Sultan Mehmed II had taken Constantinople, Latin (i.e. Roman Catholic) Europe sensed an increasing threat from this adversary from the East, the "antichrist" or "archenemy" of Christianity as it was called. Enea Silvio Piccolomini, the humanist scholar holding the *Cathedra Petri*, the Pope's throne, under the papal name of Pius II, sought support for a crusade against the Turks from the Emperor, the Holy Roman Empire, and the other European powers. With the formerly Christian continents Africa and Asia being completely conquered by Islam, Europe, so Pius II reasoned, was the last bulwark left for Christianity. "Europe, this is the homeland" of the Christians ("Europa id est patria"),[1] he exclaimed. His efforts, however, did not bear any considerable fruit. A common military and political phalanx formed by the "Christian" states of Europe against the "Islamic" enemy never came into being—in spite of the substantial promises of indulgence made by the Curia and the medial impact they had using the brand-new printing system with movable type[2] for distribution. The vested interests of some European Catholic countries that sometimes even formed alliances with the Turks against other Christian states were stronger than the notion of the Christian West the Pope kept evoking. The feverish quest for a sea route to India, which eventually resulted in the globally momentous discovery of America, was due to Turkish dominance and trade control in the Levant.

"No Reformation without Turks"

In 1456, an army of Christian crusaders under the command of Giovanni da Capistrano, a charismatic preacher and member of a mendicant order, successfully defended Belgrade.[3] Toward the end of the fifteenth and in the early sixteenth centuries, however, most military encounters ended in favor of the Ottomans. From 1460 on, the Peloponnese was under Turkish administration; in 1461, the town of Trebizond on the Black Sea, then the last Christian outpost in this region, was taken; in 1516/17, under the reign of Selim I, Egypt and Syria were conquered and the Mameluke rule defeated.

Then, under the leadership of Suleiman I, called the Magnificent, more and more advances into Europe succeeded: In 1521, Belgrade was conquered; in 1522, the Knights of Saint John of Jerusalem gave up on the island of Rhodes (fig. 1). Now, Venetian and Genoese trade routes were under Turkish control. In the battle of Mohacs, a place in Southern Hungary (August 29–30, 1526), the Ottomans won a victory over the army commanded by King Louis II of Hungary and Bohemia. From this time on, Hungary was ruled by a vassal regime established by Suleiman's grace. Finally, during September and October 1529, the Turks laid siege to Vienna.

The military and political Ottoman danger influenced the internal dynamism as well as the actual course of the Reformation in a way that is hardly to be overestimated, so that even the phrase was coined, "No Reformation without Turks!"[4] The importance of the "Turkish danger" for the Reformation is complex and to be considered on several levels. On the one hand, in the late fifteenth century, it had caused an expansion of propaganda for indulgences; more and more campaigns were launched above all within Central Europe promising plenary indulgence, particularly for supporting the fight against the Turks. All these activities, however, indirectly contributed to the crisis of the system of indulgences itself, questioning its credibility because a crusade, either headed or initiated by the Pope, never came about.

On the other hand, reports about assaults made by dangerous, barbarous warriors from the East (fig. 2) impacted the formation and intensification of an apocalyptic mentality within Roman Catholic Christianity. The "Reconquista" of Spain, accompanied by "ethnic cleansings" and the expulsion of Jews and Muslims, reached its peak in 1492 with the removal of all traces of Muslim rule from Granada, events that were no less guided by an apocalyptic rage than were some campaigns by Italian preachers of repentance from mendicant orders, or the eruptions of penitential piety that manifested in German pilgrimages. There seemed to be no clearer proof of God's wrath on his Christianity than the fact that he used the Turkish scourge to punish them. Then, the "Turkish question" influenced the political situation of the Reformation movement. From the middle of the 1520s on, some princes of the empire intensified their support for the reform ideas propagated by Luther and others but were not yet able to achieve lasting toleration of the new faith. So they had

---

1 On written records and context of this quotation, see Mertens, *Europa*. **2** Döring, *Türkenkrieg*. **3** On details, see Matschke, *Kreuz*, pp. 155–189. **4** Kaufmann, *Türckenbüchlein*, p. 62.

SVLIMAN · OTOMAN · REX · TVRC · X ·

Fig. 1 Agotino Veneziano, Suleiman I, the Magnificent, 1535.
Suleiman I is depicted with a crown that was produced in Venice and which symbolizes
the Ottoman Sultan's claim to power, which exceeded that of the Emperor and the Pope.

themselves compensated for their military support of the Habsburgs in the war against the Ottomans by means of concessions granted in the way of reformational reorganization of church policy in their respective territories.[5]

Luther, the "Friend of Turks"?

Martin Luther's earliest and particularly momentous comments on the Turks were made in the context of the quarrels about indulgences. In his explanations of his Ninety-Five Theses,[6] which actually were meant to substitute the disputation that had been cancelled, the Augustinian monk from Wittenberg set the contemporary Ottoman crisis against a historical-theological backdrop. In his eyes, it was for this reason that the Turks were the heavenly Lord's instrument with which to punish Christianity. While lots of people dreamed of going to a "holy war" against the Turks, Luther said that it was only necessary to fight their own sins but not the scourge God used for punishment. This remark was taken up in the bull that threatened Luther with excommunication[7] and was condemned; from this time on, the insinuation that Luther declined war with the Turks, and in this respect was guilty of complicity with the archenemy of Christianity, was a regular element of Roman Catholic polemics against the man from Wittenberg. It should be evident that the close relationship between the phenomenal expansion of the system of indulgences and the Turkish question[8] contributed to the young Luther's reserve concerning any appeals to war against the Turks, which more often than not were combined with plenary indulgence.

It seems that information about Luther, the "Friend of Turks," even reached the Sultan's court. In 1532, Suleiman is said to have asked an envoy from the empire about Luther's age; when hearing, supposedly to his regret, that the Reformer was already forty-nine years old, he still reassured him that he remained Luther's "gracious master."[9]

Publications in 1528/29

Luther's extensive reformational publishing in the 1520s was of crucial importance for the forming of a reform movement and for establishing the Reformation.[10] Now and again he managed to mention the Turks in passing,[11] but it was not before 1528/29 that a thorough debate on them started in Wittenberg, which means from a historical point of view it was closely connected with the Ottomans' military advances into Central Europe.

The paper *Instructions for the Visitors* (Commissioners of the Visitation) from 1528, which was drafted jointly by the Wittenberg reformers, is a key document with a set of rules and standards con-

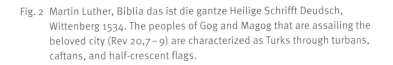

Fig. 2 Martin Luther, *Biblia das ist die gantze Heilige Schrifft Deudsch*, Wittenberg 1534. The peoples of Gog and Magog that are assailing the beloved city (Rev 20,7–9) are characterized as Turks through turbans, caftans, and half-crescent flags.

cerning doctrine and discipline. This manual was frequently used in the course of visitations that took place during the introduction of the territorial reforms. It includes, for the first time, a basic outline of Luther's characteristic attitude toward the Turks in his later years. While some Protestant preachers, adherents of Anabaptism,[12] for instance, shared Luther's early reformational opinion that defense against the Turks[13] was out of question, because God used them to

5 See Fischer-Gelati, *Ottoman Imperialism*. **6** Martin Luther: Resolutiones disputationum de indulgentiarum virtute [1518]. In: *WA* 535, 35–39. **7** Paragraph 34 of the bull *Exsurge Domine* is: "Proeliari adversus Turcas est repugnare Deo visitanti iniquitates nostras per illos." Denzinger, *Enchiridion*, no. 1484, p. 492; see also *WA* 7, 140 f.; 443. **8** See notes in: Kaufmann, *Türckenbüchlein*, pp. 61 f., 219–224. **9** "Ad hunc (sc. to the Turkish sultan) legatus missus vir egregius nomine Schmaltz, Hagenensis civis, hunc interrogavit, quot annorum esset Lutherus; respondit 49 annorum. Ad quod Turca: Utinam

iunior esset; er sol einen gnedigen herrn an mir wissen (he shall know me to be a merciful master).—Hoc audiens (sc. Luther) levata manu et signo crucis facto dixi (sc. that is: Luther said): Behut mich Gott fur diesem gnedigen herrn! (May God save me from this merciful master!)" *WA*.TR 2, 508, 3–8 (no. 2537a). The episode from the records of Luther's table talks by Konrad Cordatus is dated March 1532. **10** See Kaufmann, *Geschichte*, pp. 266–278; 303–307; id., *Anfang*, pp. 356–434. **11** References are meticulously compiled and analysed in: Ehmann, *Luther, Türken und Islam*, pp. 227–268. **12** See references

punish the sinful, the Wittenberg reformers for their part now taught that the secular authorities did have a right, even a duty, to defend their subjects against the Turks. For Luther and his fellow campaigners, the question of the Turkish war represented a specific case for applying their political ethics. They felt that the Turks not only were striving to "ruin" the Christian countries, "to violate and murder women and children, but also trying to take away territorial justice, God's service, and all good order."[14] Therefore, war against the Turks under the leadership of the secular authorities was no "crusade," which had become an impossible thing to do for Protestant theologians, but a "right service to God."[15] This was seen in the sense of Christian service within the order of the three estates established by God in his creation, i.e. he *status politicus* (secular authorities), the *status ecclesiasticus* (clergy), and the *status oeconomicus* (peasantry). In denying any "respectability" (*honor*),[16] despising marriage, selling children, and breaching rights of ownership, the Turks violated, according to the *Instructions for the Visitors* the order of the three estates established by God. Resistance against them, even by military means, was thus imperative.

Luther's "knowledge" about the Turks was mainly based on the report given by a certain Georgius, a man from Transylvania, in a book that had frequently been printed from the end of the fifteenth century on. When he was young, this man had been kidnapped from his home and repeatedly sold as a slave in the Ottoman Empire. After decades in slavery under the crescent, Georgius managed to escape to Rome where he joined the Order of St. Dominic. It is true that the extremely extensive description of Turkish customs and religion[17] conveyed a highly unfavorable view of the enemies of Christianity. Nonetheless Georgius did not refrain from also depicting the cultural achievements of the Ottomans in detail including the extraordinary works of architecture, the earnestness in practicing their religious discipline, the authority of their military and political order, the clear hierarchy in gender relations, hygiene, care for the poor, and much more. All the same, Georgius interpreted all that was beautiful and impressive in Turkish culture in accordance with the apostle Paul's warning of Satan's camouflage, who used to disguise himself as an angel of light (2 Cor. 11:14). When Luther published Georgius' book in 1530 in a Latin version,[18] he maintained the same line; this edition gave the impetus to a very successful German edition circulated by the spiritualist Sebastian Franck.[19]

Important aspects of Georgius' book also influenced Luther's first substantial comments on this topic, his strongly apocalyptic *An Army Sermon against the Turks*.[20] This paper was written in fall 1529, in the days when the European public was in a turmoil because of the Turks at the gates of Vienna (fig. 3). Unlike in earlier texts, here Luther

Fig. 3 Erhard Schön, Türkische Grausamkeiten, c. 1530.
This sheet appeared in the context of a cycle of illustrated broadsheets on the issue of the Turks published by Hans Guldenmund in Nürnberg.

worked with an exegetical concept also adopted by other Wittenberg theologians: in their opinion, Ezekiel 38 and 39 and Daniel 7 (fig. 4), which he applied to the Turks, showed that the conflict with the Ottomans was part of an eschatological scenario. To Luther, the Turk was the "ultimate and worst rage of the devil against Christ, by which he […] pours out all his wrath against glorious Christ, also God's heaviest punishment on earth for the ungrateful and godless ones who contempt and persecute Christ and his word."[21] The ultimate

in Kaufmann, *Türckenbüchlein*, pp. 47–54, 191–207. **13** "Es schreyen auch etliche Prediger frevelich vom Türcken, man sol dem Türcken nicht widderstehen, Darumb das Rache den Christen verboten sey." (Even some priests speak up sinfully about the Turks, that one should not resist the Turk, on the reason that vengeance was forbidden for Christians.) *WA* 26, 228, 33 f. **14** *WA* 26, 229, 26–27. **15** *WA* 26, 229, 45–46: "ein rechter Gottes dienst." **16** *WA* 26, 229, 32. On the doctrine of the three estates in the context of Luther's debate about the Turks, see Francisco, *Martin Luther*, pp. 131–141. **17** Best availability for

study: the bilingual edition by Klockow, *Georgius de Hungaria*. **18** Luther's preface is edited in: *WA* 30/II, 205–208. **19** For more details and the necessary references, see Kaufmann, *Türckenbüchlein*, pp. 171–177, 207–210. **20** *WA* 30/II, 160–197. **21** *WA* 30/II, 162, 20–24: "(der) letzte und ergeste zorn des teuffels widder Christum, damit er […] seinen grym gantz ausschüttet widder Christus reich, Dazu auch die grösseste straffe Gottes auff erden uber die undanckbarn und gotlosen verechter und verfolger Christi und seines worts."

key to interpreting the Turkish problem was to be found, according to Luther, in Daniel 7:8, where Daniel foretells a small horn growing on a huge animal and ousting three powers. Luther applied this image to the Ottoman sultan who had taken Egypt, Greece, and Asia Minor. The human eyes on the horn (Dan. 7:8) symbolized the Koran, a law containing nothing divine but only "vain human reason without God's word and spirit."[22] The horn's mouth (Dan. 7:8), so Luther prophesied, was Mohammed, who placed himself above Christ and denied his divinity. The Turkish rage foretold the closeness of the Last Judgment; it was necessary to fight them violently. He who slew a Turk "slays [...] an enemy of God and blasphemer against Christ."[23] In view of the irrefutable risk of Christians being taken prisoners by Turks and being caused to deny their faith, Luther put an extra emphasis on teaching them the catechetic basics of Christian faith he had just explained in his *Small Catechism* and his *Large Catechism*: "So now learn [...] the Ten Commandments, the Lord's Prayer, the creed [i.e., the Apostles' Creed], and learn them well, especially this article where we say: And in Jesus Christ His only son [...]." For all depends on this article; it is because of this article that we are called Christians [...]. [...] And by this article our faith is different from all other professions of faith on earth, because the Jews do not have it, the Turks and Saracens do not have it either, furthermore no papist nor false Christian nor any other infidel, but the true Christians alone."[24] Knowledge about the catechism should enable Christians in Turkish captivity to reassure themselves in any situation of the foundations of their being Christian. Most of all, they should perceptibly concentrate on the article on Christ: "[...] and when you get to this article, press your thumb on a finger or give yourself some other kind of sign with your hand or your foot, so that you can imagine it well and make it memorable [...]."[25] Accordingly, Luther perceived the Turkish challenge as a cause for intensifying the efforts to lay the foundation for a religious awareness in Christians and to prepare Christianity for the approaching of the Last Judgment.

According to Luther's pointedly anti-Catholic view, the Turks represented a human religion of orthopraxic lawfulness marked by fulfilling religious commandments of the kind adherents of the papal church also supported. It was just that Mohammed's followers implemented this devout religious meritocracy in a much more convincing fashion than the "Romans" did.[26] Thus, in contrast to Turks, Jews and "papists," it became evident for Luther that the "Christian essence and religion are something very different and much more sublime/than nice and courtly church splendor/gestures/pretense/

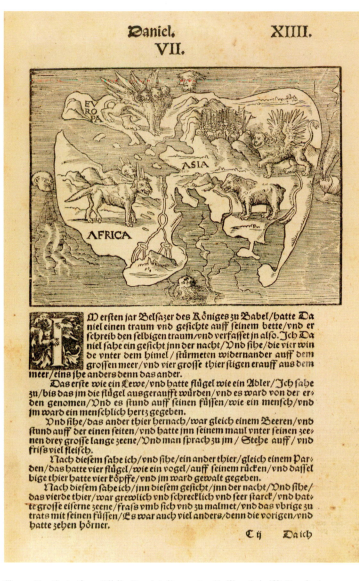

Fig. 4 Martin Luther, Biblia Das ist die gantze Heilige Schrifft Deudsch, Wittenberg 1534. World map with the vision of Daniel (Dan 7:2–8), which was repeatedly used in Wittenberg prints

tonsures/ monks' habits/ fasts/ holiday/ praying the Hours/ pale face,"[27] namely to become righteous before God only by believing in Christ, the Son of God.[28] While the Pope and the Jews refused to acknowledge Christ as the only way to salvation, Luther said, the Turks accepted him as a great prophet, but took offense at his being the Son of God. According to Luther, the avowal of Christ deter-

---

22 *WA* 30/II, 168, 17: "eitel menschliche vernunfft on Gottes wort und geist." **23** *WA* 30/II, 173, 7–8: "erwürget [...] einen feind Gottes und lesterer Christi." **24** *WA* 30/II, 186, 1–18: "So lerne nu [...] die zehen gebot, dein vater unser, den glauben [d. i. das Apostolische Glaubensbekenntnis] und lerne sie wol, sonderlich diesen artickel da wir sagen 'Und an Jesum Christ seinen einigen Son [...].' Denn an diesem artickel ligts, von diesem artickel heissen wir Christen [...]. [...] Und durch diesen artickel wird unser glaube gesondert von allen andern glauben auff erden, Denn die Jüden haben des nicht, Die Türcken und Sarracener auch nicht, dazu kein Papist noch falscher Christ noch kein ander ungleubiger, sondern allein die rechten Christen." **25** *WA* 30/II, 186, 21–25: "[...] und wenn du auff diesen artickel kömpst, so drucke mit dem daumen auff einen finger odder

gib dir sonst etwa ein zeichen mit der hand odder fuss, auff das du diesen artickel dir wol einbildest und mercklich machest [...]." **26** *WA* 30/II, 206, 3–22; see Kaufmann, *Sicht*, pp. 58–60. **27** *WA* 30/II, 207, 35–39. Vorrede Luthers zu Georgius de Hungarias Tractatus, zit. nach der Übersetzung Sebastian Francks. In: Sebastian Franck, Sämtliche Werke. Kritische Ausgabe mit Kommentar, Bd. 1: Frühe Schriften, hrsg. von Peter Klaus Knauer, Bern 1983, p. 240, 35–37: "Christenlich wesen und religion etwas vil anders unnd höchers sein/ dann ein schön höflich Kirchengebreng/ gebären [sc. Gebärden]/ schein/ platten/ kappen/ fasten/ feyertag/ siebenzeyt/ bleichs angesicht." **28** *WA* 30/II, 207, 35–39. **29** *WA* 47, 62, 18–24 (Exegesis 3 and 4 John, 1539). Similarly in: *Großer Galaterkommentar* [1535]: "Was ist ein Papatus, Turcatus et totus mundus erga

mines which attitude to take with regard to any religious manifestation—how emphatic it ever may be: "Even if the Pope and the Turk raised people from the dead and flagellated themselves so that blood was shed, and even if you fasted for weeks on water and bread, I still know that you are not the resurrection nor the life or ascension and way to heaven, but that you deceive me and seduce me with all of this."[29] Starting out from the justifying belief in Christ, Luther decided on the worthlessness in principle of "the belief of Jews and Turks … and of those (who insist) on their deeds."[30] Luther sometimes also used the term "Turk" as an ambiguous insult against anyone opposing the doctrine of justification.

Luther's Later Texts on Turks and their Religion

In his later statements on the Turks, Luther kept to the tendencies outlined here. One publication, prompted by new military advances made by Suleiman, that is particularly outstanding is *"The Admonition to Pray against the Turks"*[31] (1541). It states that faith is the deciding armor, and repentance and prayer are the most important means of battling the Turks. With the Turks, God's wrath came upon a Christianity that despised the Gospel; military action, judged with increasing skepticism by the aging Reformer, should only be taken on orders from the secular authorities. True prayer,[32] central to the *Admonition,* emphasized that it was the guilt with regard to God that actually had motivated the punishment from heaven manifest in the Turkish danger. Going back to the fundamentals in a similar form, the Wittenberg Reformer summed up the plea for protection against Christ's foes, the Pope and the Turks, in the children's song "Lord, keep us in thy Word and work" (1541/42; fig. 5): "Restrain the murderous Pope and Turk, Who fain would tear from off thy throne Christ Jesus, thy beloved Son."[33] Of all hymns, this song became the most popular identity marker for Lutheran Protestantism during the early modern period.

Both previously mentioned writings, Luther's *An Army Sermon against the Turks* and his *Admonition,* are to be seen in close historical relationship with his most important literary debates about the Muslims' holiest scripture, the Koran: There was, on the one hand, a rather loose and quite unconventional translation of a refutation of the Koran (*Confutatio Alcorani*),[34] written in Latin in the time about 1300 by the Dominican Ricoldus de Montecrucis. There, long passages from the incriminated scripture were cited, and it was considered one of the most important sources for Christian knowledge about the Koran in the Middle Ages. On the other hand, there were the expertise and the prefaces by Luther and Melanchthon, who together made it possible that a first printing of the twelfth-century Latin translation of the Koran by Robert of Ketton could be done in Johannes Oporinus's printing shop in Basel.[35] This enormous task was headed by the Zurich theologian and philologist Theodor Bibliander who, besides the translation of the Koran, also published other notable writings concerning Christian discussion on Islam and its Holy Book. It is thanks to him and the intervention by the Wittenberg reformers that the Basel council then gave up its former policy of censoring any printing of the Koran.

But what caused Luther, who, at the same time, led a literary campaign against Judaism and the distribution of Jewish scriptures, to make the Koran available to the Christian West? According to a hint given by Luther himself, he had been skeptical with regard to Ricoldus's *Confutatio;*[36] he could not imagine that the Turks' religion might be as pathetic as it appeared in the mirror held up by its Christian critic Ricoldus. This had also been an argument in favor of reprinting Georgius of Hungary's treatise, because Luther wanted to make it clear that the "Turkish religion" did have its attractive sides, which might be tempting, and that it had to be taken seriously. On "Shrove Tuesday"[37] in 1542, however, he had come upon a copy of the Latin translation of the Koran, "but translated very badly, so that I should wish to see a clearer one."[38] This may have been the manuscript that was to be printed in Basel shortly after. In any case, Luther concluded from his studies on the Koran, which certainly were not really intensive, that the unfavorable judgment given by Ricoldus—Luther called him "Brother Richard"—was correct. In this respect—and in a similar way by his dissemination of Georgius of Hungary's treatise—Luther substantially contributed to the fact that under his authority tendentious medieval sources on Islam were also spread in the course of the Reformation.

In Luther's eyes, distributing the Koran was an important journalistic means to the end of combating Islam. So, in contrast to the censoring practiced by the Roman Catholic Church, he was confident, as far as the "Turkish religion" was concerned, that nothing would do it more harm than widely spreading its "abstruse" ideas, a solution he sometimes also recommended against Christian rivals. Luther was sure that religious and erudite persons who came to reading the Koran would devote themselves to disproving its errors.[39] Just as the nothingness of the Jews, in his opinion, could by no way become more obvious than by dragging their secrets out into the

unum Christum?" *WA* 40/II, 21, 10 (manuscript). **30** Martin Luther, Epistel S. Petri gepredigt [1523]. In: *WA* 12, 285, 4 f.: "der Juden und Turcken glawb […], und dere[r], die auff yhren wercken (sc.: insist)." According to Luther, the "other religions" stand for human works and efforts with regard to God. "[…] non media via inter cognitionem Christi et operationem humanam. Postea nihil refert, sive sit Papista, Turca, Iudeus, una fides ut altera." Martin Luther: Großer Galaterkommentar [1535]. In: *WA* 40/I, 603, 10–604, 2 (manuscript). Neither Jewish nor Turkish ethos does Luther treat with respect, see *WA* 46, 459, 13 f. "Iam Mohamet, sub quo will Turca uns alle haben, hat Christum lang hinweg geworffen. Bapst ist ein wenig kluger, non abiecit scripturam ut Turca, sed ist nicht weit a Turcis et Iudeis, quia depravavit, imo prorsus abolevit veram intelligentiam scripturae et suos Canones." (Already Mohamet (sic), under whose reign Turkey wants us all to be, has rejected Christum for a long time, the Pope is somewhat more prudent, he did not reject the Scripture as the Turk did, but is not far from Turks and Jews …) *WA* 49, 16, 19–23. **31** *WA* 51, 585–625. **32** *WA* 51, 608, 24–611, 26. **33** Jenny, *Lieder,* pp. 118 f; 304 f. **34** *WA* 53, 261–396; very helpful because of a parallel printing of Luther's Latin model text and a translation made by him: Ehmann, *Ricoldus de Montecrucis.* **35** *WA* 53, 561–572; for more references, see Kaufmann, *Judenschrifften,* pp. 108 f; Bobzien, *Koran,* pp. 159–275. **36** *WA* 30/II, 205, 3–10. **37** *WA* 53, 272, 16. For more details on the context, see Bobzien, *Gedanken.* **38** *WA* 53, 272, 16–17: "doch seer ubel verdolmetscht, das ich noch wünschet einen klerern zusehen." **39** See *WA* 53, 570, 28–29.

Ein Liedt/Erhalt vns Herr bey deinem Wort/etc. Sampt Ein schön andechtich Gebet/Der heiligen Christlichen Kirchen Zu der hohen Ehrwirdigen vnd heiligen Drey Faltikeit/Got dem Vater/ Gott dem Son/vnd Gott dem heiligen Geist/vmb erhaltung bey dem wort der warheit vnd der Seligkeit/vnd vmb schutz widder die feinde des Worts/ als Türcken vnd Bbst gestellet etc.

Erhalt vns HERr bey deinem Wort/vnd steur des Bapsts vñ Türcken mort/die Jhesum Christum deinen Son/wöllen stürzen von deinem Thron.

Beweiß deine macht Herr Jhesu Christ/der du Herr aller herren bist/ Beschirm dein Arme Christenheit/ das sie dich lobe in ewigkeit.

Gott Heiliger Geist du Tröster werd/gib deinem Volck einerley syn auff Erd/stehe bey vns yn der letzten not/gleyd vns ins leben aus dem tod.

Jhr anschleg HERr zu nichten mach/las sie treffen die böse sach/vñ stürtze sie jnn die gruben ein/Die sie machen den Christen dein.

So werden sie erkennen doch/ das du vnser Got lebest noch/vnnd hilffts gewaltig deiner schar/Die sich auff dich Verlesset gar.

Zu Gott dem Vater.

ACh lieber Vater/du Got alles trostes/ Aller gnaden vnd barmherzikeit/der du bist im himel/ vñ siehest/Wie die gewaltigen auff erden/als der türck vnnd der Bapst/sich vnter stehen/Deinen lieben Son Jhesum Christum vnsern Herrn/wilchen du vns/O gütiger Vater/aus grundloser barmherzikeit geschencket vnd gegeben hast/den bittern tod am Stam des Creutz für vns zu leiden/sein heiliges teures blut vmb vnser sünde willen zuuergiessen/Vnd vom Teufel vnd ewigem verdamnis zuerlösen/Von deiner rechten wilchen sein ewiger thron ist/zustürzen/Deine liebe Kirchen zu dempfen/Vñ dein heiliges Wort aus zu rotten/wir bitten dich du starcker Got/Der du zu nicht machest/allen rath/allen gewalt der gotlosen vndmechtigen auff erden/Du wollest jrent vnchristlichen greulichen fürnemen steuren/vnd wehren/Deine liebe Christenheit/vnter dem schatten deiner flügel beschützen vñ beschirmen vñ bey deinem heiligen vñ allein seligmachende Wort gnediglich erhalten/Durch Christum Jhesum deinen lieben Son vnsern HERR/AMEN.

Zu Gott dem Son.

O HERr Jhesu Christe/du Son des alleroghesten/vñ Hailand der ganzen welt/du Got der herscharen/Der du für vns durch dein heiliges leiden vñ sterben/den ewigen Todtüberwunden/den teufel gefangen/ die hell gestürmet/Die sünde ausgeleschet/Vñ durch deine heilige aufferstehung vnd himelfart Die ewige selikeit vnd das ewige leben erworben vñ vns geschenckt hast/Wir bitten dich von ganzem herzen/Dieweil du siehest/Wie sich deine abgesagete feinde/Der Türcke vnd der Bapst/so mutwillig widder dich auff lehnē/Vñ deine liebe Kirchen/Die du durch dein blut erworben hast/so greulich verfolgen/Du wollest dich nachmals/wie du den zuuor vñ allezeit gethan hast bewer ysen/jrem Blutdürstigen tyrannischem mutwillen wehren/vñ furkomen sie stürzen/vnd deine werde Christenheit befrieden/auff das sie dich lobe/vnd dir dancken/der du lebest vnd regierest mit Got dem Vater in einikeit des heiligen geists in ewigkeit/AMEN.

Zu Gott dem Heiligen Geist.

O Heiliger Geist/du werder Tröster/du ewiger glanz erleucht vnser herzen/vnd zünde sie an/ mit deiner gnade/Das liebe Euangelium/Das ewige Wort/wilchs vns allein selig macht/zubekennen/vñ hilff vns/Das wir dabei mögen bestedig bleibē/welche jo nicht von vns du einiger tröster jn allerlei not vñ anfechtung/sondern stercke vns mit deiner Almechtigen inwendigen krafft/Das wir vns für keinerlei Tyrannei Des Türcken vnd des Bapsts fürchten noch entsetzen mögen/Verleihe vns eine ritterlichen Kampff des Glaubens widder alle/vnsere feinde zu kempffen/stehe vns bey Vnnd hilff vns durch CHRistum Jhesum Vnsern lieben HERRN/Wilchem sey Lob EHR Vnd Preiss in ewigkeit/ AMEN.

Durch Pancratius Kempff Brieffmaler.

Fig. 5   Pancratius Kempff, Erhalt uns Herr bei deinem Wort (Lord, keep us in thy Word and Work),
Magdeburg between 1547 and 1549. Among the damned a Turk can be recognized,
along with members of the Roman church. The Luther hymn is placed directly under the image.
The prayer text in the lower portion of the page was written by Leonhard Jacobi.

open, publication of the Koran would prove what untenable kind of religion the impostor Mohammed had established.[40] Furthermore, the untruthfulness of Mohammed's religion ensued from the claim of the Koran as a "new book" surpassing the Bible.[41] For Luther, in light of the supposed lies of the foreign religion, such as Islamic denial of Roman Catholic dogmas concerning Trinity and Christology, and ignorance of the original sin being the cause of human failings[42], the truth of Christianity could be proved quite clearly. In this way, revealing the false doctrines of the foreign religions to the public would mean, according to Luther, that people would turn away from Turks, Jews, and heathens, and turn toward the Father of the crucified God instead.[43] Luther also perceived the doctrines taught by the Anabaptists and by Michael Servetus, who denied the Trinity, as contemporary actualizations of those diabolic doctrines the Koran contained. In this way, for the Wittenberg Reformer the discussion of the Holy Scripture of the Turks took place within a hermeneutical horizon reflecting his present concerns.

Summary

To sum up, it can be said that Luther's perception of the Turks was closely connected with experiences of contemporary history, which he interpreted within the horizon of biblical texts. Luther regarded the Turks as God's scourge to inflict punishment for the sins of the papal church and the disobedience of Christianity to the Gospel. In 1529, Luther heard about a prophecy made by Johannes Hilten, a Franciscan monk from Eisenach, who had died more than two decades previously. He had foretold the capture of Europe and devastation of "Germania" by the Turks.[44] It was also on the basis of this prophecy that Luther was convinced that the end of history was imminent. Reception of "ethnographic" knowledge[45] as provided, for instance, by Georgius of Hungary was, for Luther, aimed at warning Christianity of the temptations coming from the diabolical "Turkish religion." With the Turks drawing nearer and nearer, military confrontation had to be faced by taking defensive measures under the command of the secular authorities. The "Turkish danger" also prompted the Reformer to sum up the central ideas of the Christian faith in the form of catechism; this was imperative to provide Christianity with the inner strength needed for spiritual survival under the crescent. Luther's reception and distribution of medieval anti-Islamic Christian literature makes it clear that he saw himself in agreement with the traditions of the Latin Church as far as the essential differentiating doctrines were concerned: that of original sin, Mohammed's claim to be a prophet, the doctrine of Trinity, and that of the two natures of Christ. Luther's polemic strategy of excessive "Turkisization" of his inner-Christian adversaries—the papal church and the Protestant "heretics"—had as its goal a fundamental attack on an exegesis of Christian faith that valued human reason and works of piety in accordance with his understanding of the doctrine of justification.

BIBLIOGRAPHY

Bobzien, Hartmut (1995), *Der Koran im Zeitalter der Reformation* (= Beiruter Texte und Studien. 42). Stuttgart. **Bobzin**, Hartmut (2004), "Aber itzt … hab ich den Alcoran gesehen Latinisch …" Gedanken Martin Luthers zum Islam. In: Medick, Hans/Schmidt, Peer (ed.), *Luther zwischen den Kulturen. Zeitgenossenschaft—Weltwirkung*. Göttingen, pp. 260–276. **Denzinger**, Heinrich (1999), *Enchiridion symbolorum definitionum et declarationum de rebus fidei et morum*, verbessert, erweitert und ins Deutsche übertragen … von Peter Hünermann. 38th ed. Freiburg im Breisgau et al. **Döring**, Karoline Dominika (2013), *Türkenkrieg und Medienwandel im 15. Jahrhundert* (= Historische Studien. 503). Husum. **Ehmann**, Johannes (1999), *Ricoldus de Montecrucis, Confutatio Alcorani (1300) Martin Luther, Verlegung des Alcoran (1542). Kommentierte lateinisch-deutsche Textausgabe* (= Corpus Islamo-Christianum, Series Latina. 6). Würzburg/Altenberge. **Ehmann**, Johannes (2008), *Luther, Türken und Islam. Eine Untersuchung zum Türken- und Islambild Martin Luthers (1515–1546)* (= Quellen und Forschungen zur Reformationsgeschichte. 80). Gütersloh. **Fischer-Gelati**, Stephen A. (1959), *Ottoman Imperialism and German Protestantism 1521–1555*, Cambridge, MA; Reprint 1972. New York. **Francisco**, Adam S. (2007), *Martin Luther and Islam. A Study in Sixteenth-Century Polemics and Apologetics* (= History of Christian-Muslim Relations. 8). Leiden/Boston. **Höfert**, Almut (2003), *Den Feind beschreiben. "Türkengefahr" und europäisches Wissen über das Osmanische Reich 1450–1600* (= Campus Historische Studien. 35). Frankfurt am Main/New York. **Jenny**, Markus (1985), *Luthers geistliche Lieder und Kirchengesänge* (= Archiv zur Weimarer Ausgabe der Werke Martin Luthers. 4). Köln/Wien. **Kaufmann**, Thomas (2006), *Konfession und Kultur. Lutherischer Protestantismus in der zweiten Hälfte des Reformationsjahrhunderts* (= Spätmittelalter und Reformation. Neue Reihe 29). Tübingen. **Kaufmann**, Thomas (2008): *"Türckenbüchlein." Zur christlichen Wahrnehmung "türkischer Religion" in Spätmittelalter und Reformation* (= Forschungen zur Kirchen- und Dogmengeschichte. 97). Göttingen. **Kaufmann**, Thomas (2010), *Geschichte der Reformation*, 2nd ed. Berlin. **Kaufmann**, Thomas (2012), *Der Anfang der Reformation. Studien zur Kontextualität der Theologie, Publizistik und Inszenierung Luthers und der reformatorischen Bewegung* (= Spätmittelalter, Humanismus, Reformation. 67). Tübingen. **Kaufmann**, Thomas (2013), *Luthers "Judenschriften." Ein Beitrag zu ihrer historischen Kontextualisierung*. 2nd ed. Tübingen. **Kaufmann**, Thomas (2017), Luthers Sicht auf Judentum und Islam. In: Schilling, Heinz (ed.), *Der Reformator Martin Luther. Eine wissenschaftliche und gedenkpolitische Bestandsaufnahme* (= Schriften des Historischen Kollegs Kolloquien. 92). Berlin/München/Boston, pp. 53–84. **Klockow**, Reinhard (1992), *Georgius de Hungaria, Tractatus de Moribus, Condicionibus et Nequitia Turcorum* (= Schriften zur Landeskunde Siebenbürgens. 15). 2nd ed. Köln/Weimar/Wien. **Matschke**, Klaus-Peter (2004), *Das Kreuz und der Halbmond. Die Geschichte der Türkenkriege*. Düsseldorf/Zürich. **Mertens**, Dieter (1997), Europa id est patria, domus propria, sedes nostra … Zu Funktionen und Überlieferung lateinischer Türkenreden im 15. Jahrhundert. In: Erkens, Franz Rainer (ed.), *Europa und die osmanische Expansion im ausgehenden Mittelalter* (= Zeitschrift für Historische Forschung. Beiheft 20). Berlin, pp. 39–57.

---

40 *WA* 53, 570, 30–33; 34–571, 3. **41** "At hoc figmentum Mohameti esse novum hic liber testatur." *WA* 53, 571, 40–41. **42** *WA* 53, 572, 4–7. **43** *WA* 53, 571, 30–34. **44** See references in Kaufmann, *Konfession und Kultur*, pp. 435–441. **45** Höfert, *Feind*.

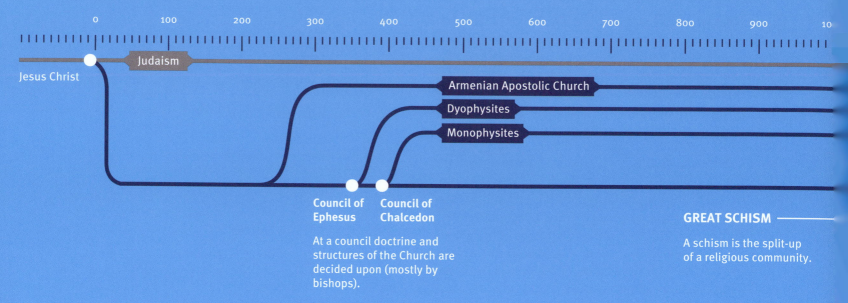

Jesus Christ

Judaism

Armenian Apostolic Church

Dyophysites

Monophysites

Council of Ephesus

Council of Chalcedon

At a council doctrine and structures of the Church are decided upon (mostly by bishops).

GREAT SCHISM ——

A schism is the split-up of a religious community.

Protestantism is diverse. In contrast to the Roman Catholic Church, there is no Pope. The Bible is the decisive authority.

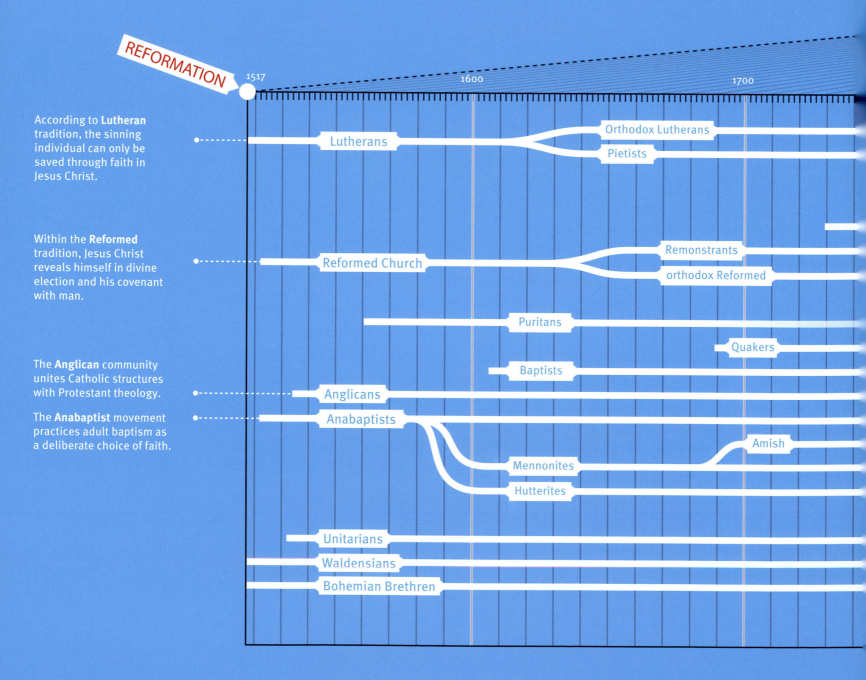

REFORMATION

According to **Lutheran** tradition, the sinning individual can only be saved through faith in Jesus Christ.

Lutherans

Orthodox Lutherans

Pietists

Within the **Reformed** tradition, Jesus Christ reveals himself in divine election and his covenant with man.

Reformed Church

Remonstrants

orthodox Reformed

Puritans

Quakers

Baptists

The **Anglican** community unites Catholic structures with Protestant theology.

Anglicans

The **Anabaptist** movement practices adult baptism as a deliberate choice of faith.

Anabaptists

Amish

Mennonites

Hutterites

Unitarians

Waldensians

Bohemian Brethren

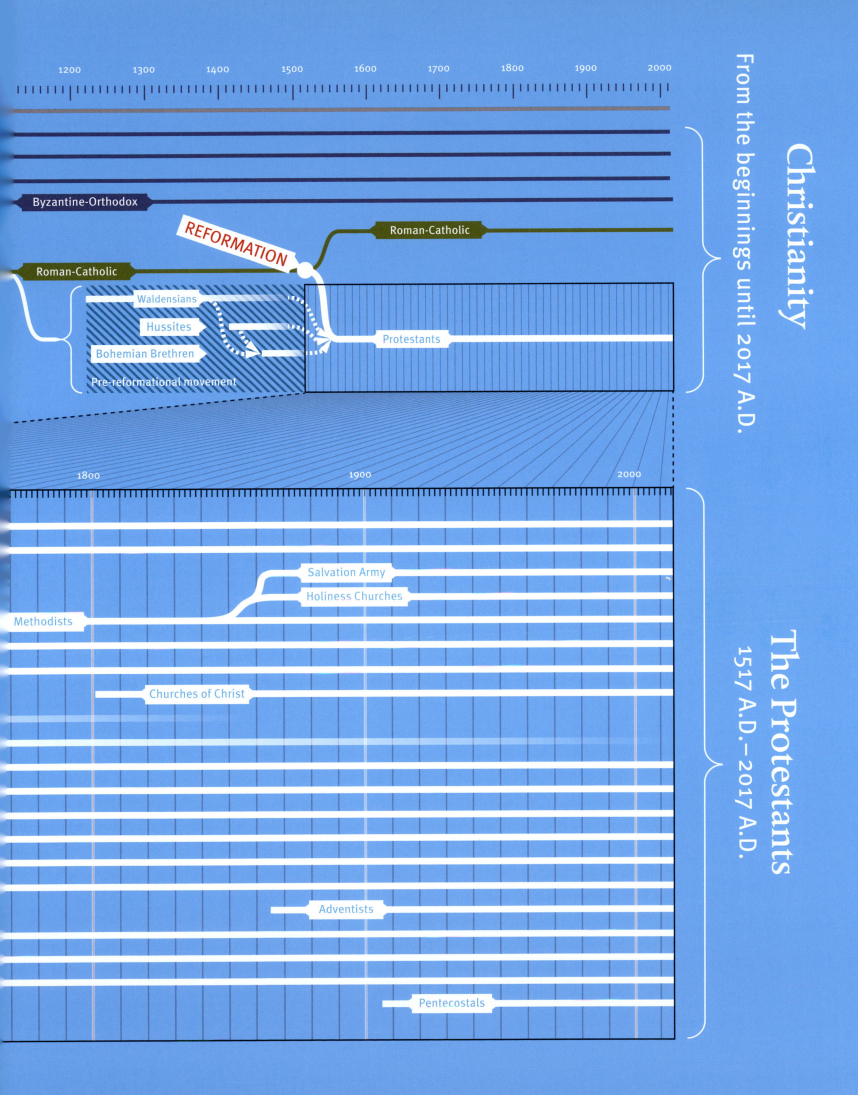

Christianity
From the beginnings until 2017 A.D.

1200 1300 1400 1500 1600 1700 1800 1900 2000

Byzantine-Orthodox

REFORMATION

Roman-Catholic

Roman-Catholic

Waldensians

Hussites

Bohemian Brethren

Pre-reformational movement

Protestants

1800 1900 2000

The Protestants
1517 A.D. – 2017 A.D.

Salvation Army

Holiness Churches

Methodists

Churches of Christ

Adventists

Pentecostals

ROBERT KOLB

The Lutheran Confessions:
A Genre to Define the Church

In Martin Luther's youth, most Western European Christians believed that being Christian centered on human beings' carrying out sacred rituals and other good works in order to gain God's gifts and favor. Some understood that God's grace initiates or aids that process, but the weight of maintaining the relationship with God fell on human efforts. Luther found this definition of being Christian to be a crushing burden. His own struggles with his inability to please God sufficiently were compounded by presuppositions regarding God's almighty power that he had learned from so-called "Ockhamist" instructors as he began to follow the career path imposed upon him by monastic superiors. He was destined for the classroom, assigned to doctoral studies, so that he might become a professor of Bible.

In his first lectures—on the Psalms (1513–15), Romans (1515–16), and Galatians (1516)—Luther came to define being Christian differently: as a relationship initiated by God the Creator, who creates through speaking (Gen. 1). Through his conversation with human creatures he creates community with them. God's Word became the center of the Christian life. The sermon as God's side of the conversation with his people replaced the sacred ritual of the Mass as the heart of worship. Scripture became the place of God's presence, from which his power to save sinners from their alienation from God (Rom. 1:16) proceeded on the basis of his promise of deliverance and new life through the death and resurrection of Jesus, the second person of the Trinity in human flesh (John 1:1–14).

This emphasis on God's Word informed not only Luther's teaching and preaching but also the thinking of his colleagues at the University of Wittenberg, above all, Philipp Melanchthon. After both church and imperial government had condemned Luther in 1521, Melanchthon became the public, diplomatic representative of those adhering to the Wittenberg Reformation, in the service of the Electors of Saxony. He naturally became the author of the speech to be delivered to Emperor Charles V at the Diet of Augsburg in 1530 to explain to Charles why the Elector of Saxony and other adherents of the Wittenberg Reformation were introducing Luther-style reforms in their lands. As he formulated this speech that the Saxon vice-chancellor Christian Beyer was to deliver to the imperial diet, Melanchthon first entitled his explanation a "defense" (Latin: apologia). He changed its title to "confession" (confession). This reflects a change in tactic. Originally, the evangelical representatives to the diet had planned only to explain their reforms. The challenge published by Johann Eck, professor at the University of Ingolstadt and chief engineer of Luther's excommunication, had denied that Luther's followers were part of the church, adherents of its catholic tradition.[1] Therefore, Melanchthon expanded his explanation to demonstrate that in twenty-one key points of Christian teaching, the Wittenberg reformers were absolutely faithful to biblical teaching and the catholic tradition. These "articles of faith" preceded the explanation of seven points of reform in Beyer's speech.[2]

For over a decade the Wittenberg reformers had been exploiting Johannes Gutenberg's invention of movable type. Luther quickly recognized the potential of the printed word for spreading his appeal for reform after the printers had recognized the potential market for his Ninety-Five Theses on Indulgences in 1517/1518. Thus, it was inevitable that Beyer's speech would land in print, as it did in 1531. As a document with official status as a statement of the evangelical princes and cities and with semilegal status as a formal presentation in the imperial diet, the *Augsburg Confession*[3] quickly became for those seeking reform along Luther's lines a symbol, a kind of creed, an extension of the creeds of the ancient church.

In the Middle Ages the term "confession" had been used for "telling the truth" about one's own sins, especially in the sacrament of penance, and about God, in praise of him and his works. "Confess" had occasionally been used as a synonym for "teach" in the sense of a formal statement by a council or bishop. Melanchthon built upon Luther's use of the word in his 1528 *Confession on the Lord's Supper* to devise a new designation for the definition of being Christian, to express one's faith on the basis of scripture. Luther's treatise had presented an extended analysis of the presence of Christ's body and blood in the Lord's Supper but concluded with a kind of doctrinal last will and testament, following the outline of the Apostles' Creed, stating Luther's teaching on God as Father, Son, and Holy Spirit, Creator, Redeemer, and Sanctifier.

In formulating his expression of biblical, catholic teaching, Melanchthon also used the *Schwabach Articles*, a brief statement of the theology of the churches in the lands that sought an alliance to defend the evangelical reform, composed chiefly by the Wittenberg theologians in 1529,[4] and the *Marburg Articles*, summaries of the church's teaching prepared as the basis for agreement between

Luther with his followers and Hulrych Zwingli with his, also in 1529, at the colloquy of Marburg.[5] The articles of the *Augsburg Confession* defending the reforms introduced by Evangelical churches stem from a series of memoranda labeled, since the eighteenth century, the *Torgau Articles*, because the process formulating an explanation of these reforms took place in Torgau. Melanchthon prepared drafts in German for reading before the representatives of the rulers of the German lands—and later for the German reading public—and in Latin for the learned, especially the theologians. At a few points it is clear that he differentiated somewhat his two audiences. On June 25, 1530, Christian Beyer read the German version to the diet on behalf of his elector, Johann, and six other princes of the empire, as well as the cities of Nuremberg and Reutlingen.

Emperor Charles rejected the *Augsburg Confession* and organized a commission to draft a confutation. He disapproved of the first draft by a group headed by Johann Eck because its harshness precluded any hope of rapprochement between the two sides. Eck led a second commission in drafting what the evangelicals labeled the "Papal Confutation" (*Confutatio*), presented to the imperial diet on August 3, 1530.[6] Luther's followers refused to accept the condition laid down by Charles for their receiving a copy of the confutation— that they not reply to it. However, notes supplied to Melanchthon by colleagues put at his disposal an accurate text. He began his response almost immediately. Entitled the *Apology of the Augsburg Confession*, this much more extensive commentary on the *Augsburg Confession* met the critique of the confutation.[7]

Melanchthon's defense concentrated on what he clearly believed to be the most critical issue for Wittenberg reform: the restoration of human righteousness in God's sight through the sacrificial death and life-restoring resurrection of Jesus Christ and through the trust in the promise of life and salvation wrought by Christ's work, created in human hearts by the Holy Spirit. Melanchthon's presentation of the doctrine of justification from scripture, reinforced with references to the ancient church fathers, taught that sinners receive forgiveness of sins and new life by God's grace, without condition, through the trust that restores the human side of the relationship with God by placing full confidence for all of life in the promise of Jesus Christ. The Holy Spirit creates that faith through the re-creating Word of God as it comes in oral, written, and sacramental forms. The person justified by faith produces good works, living in new obedience and bearing the fruits of faith in praise of God and love for others.

The *Augsburg Confession* and the *Apology* also affirmed that God gathers the faithful around the proclaimed Word and the sacraments of baptism, the Lord's Supper, and absolution into his church. The documents convey Luther's understanding of the power of that Word and also God's presence in the Word, particularly in the special, unique form of his body and blood under the bread and wine of the Lord's Supper. They made clear that God had created the structures of human life, including family and societal institutions, as good and that in a sinful world Christians must participate in the often untidy work of fostering public order and societal harmony. The *Apology* particularly focused on points of difference with the *Confutatio*.

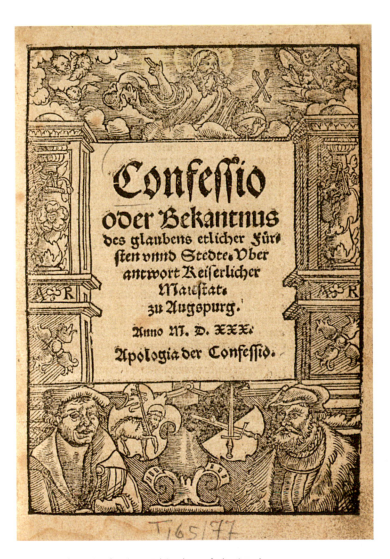

Fig. 1 Augsburg Confession and Apology oft the Augsburg Confession, written by Philipp Melanchthon, Title page

1 Kolb/Nestingen, *Sources*, pp. 33–82. **2** Dingel, *Bekenntnisschriften*, pp. 85–225; Kolb/Wengert, *Book of Concord*, pp. 30–105. **3** Maurer, *Historical Commentary*; Grane, *Augsburg Confession*. **4** Dingel, *Bekenntnisschriften, Quellen und Materialien*, pp. 38–42; Kolb/Nestingen, *Sources*, pp. 83–87. **5** Dingel, *Bekenntnisschriften, Quellen und Materialien*, pp. 44–46; Kolb/Nestingen, *Sources*, pp. 89–92. **6** Immenkötter, *Confutatio*; Kolb/Nestingen, *Sources*, pp. 106–139. **7** Dingel, *Bekenntnisschriften*, pp. 236–709; Kolb/Wengert, *Book of Concord*, pp. 109–294; Peters, *Apologia*.

Fig. 2 Andreas Herneisen, Confessio paininting from Windsheim, 1601, Bad Windsheim. Delivery of the Confessio Augustana
to Emperor Charles V. on June 25, 1530 and depiction of the liturgical practices of the Protestant church

Fig. 3 Johann Dürr, The reading of the confessional document by the Saxon chancellor Dr. Christian Beyer, 1630

The *Augsburg Confession* only slowly emerged as an authority, an adjudicator to aid interpretation of scripture on the basis of its biblical argument. In the 1530s its later role as an ecclesiastical norm had not yet taken shape. Therefore, as Charles V pursued a plan to bring adherents of the old faith together with Evangelical reformers in a colloquy, the Evangelical princes asked Melanchthon to expand the confession's formulation of the doctrine of justification. This *Confessio Augustana Variata* of 1540, with revisions in 1542,[8] did that, but it also incorporated language on the Lord's Supper reflecting the *Wittenberg Concord* of 1536. It had reconciled the Wittenberg theologians with Martin Bucer, the reformer of Strasbourg, and other Southern German church leaders, who had tried to form a bridge between Zwingli's rejection of the actual presence of Christ in the Lord's Supper and Luther's position. Melanchthon used terminology that in 1540 adequately expressed Luther's belief that Christ's body and blood are present in the sacrament but that later was interpreted by adherents of Jean Calvin as permitting their view of a spiritual presence of Christ. This finally led to the rejection of this *Variata* by the Lutheran churches.

The *Smalcald Articles*, an agenda for the German Evangelicals to use at the papally called council that finally met in Trent in 1545, also began to take its place as an authoritative summary of Wittenberg theology.[9] When Pope Paul III summoned the council in 1536, he launched a diplomatic initiative to bring representatives from Evangelical lands to it. Elector John Frederick of Saxony wanted Luther to write another personal confession of faith, explicitly addressing critical ideas in his program for reform of teaching and ecclesiastical life. This wish combined with the need for a summary statement of Wittenberg theology for use at the council. Although seriously ill, Luther undertook the task of composing this kind of statement in December 1536 and early January 1537, aided by a committee of his Wittenberg colleagues with three others from the wider Wittenberg circle and with the assistance of an amanuensis.

This agenda for the council, later dubbed the *Smalcald Articles*, contains three sections. In the first, Luther stated the basis of Christian teaching, on which both sides agreed, the doctrines of the Trinity and of the person of Christ, in which divine and human natures are united in the one person. In the second section, Luther laid down the "chief article" of the faith, regarding the "office and work of Jesus Christ, or our redemption." He wrote, "Nothing in this article can be conceded or given up, even if heaven and earth should pass away." The Reformer summarized this fundamental axiom regarding deliverance from sin and alienation from God with a few Bible passages, including Romans 4:25, confessing that Christ "died for our sins and was raised for our justification" as well as passages, quoting John the Baptist's words pointing to Jesus, "Behold, the Lamb of God, who takes away the sins of the world" (John 1:29), and affirming that God restores human justice through trust in Christ on the basis of his unconditional favor or grace. Luther clarified the meaning of salvation by grace through faith in Christ alone by sketching three areas of medieval church life that undermined and opposed this teaching: the teaching and practice of the Mass with associated pious practices designed to win God's approval, monastic life that aimed at earning

heaven more easily than life in the secular world, and the papacy with its control of the church. The third section treats fifteen other topics, from "the law" and "sin" to matters of church practice, that Luther believed reasonable people could discuss and in which they could perhaps find agreement.[10]

The alliance formed to defend the adherents of the *Augsburg Confession* in 1531, the Smalcald League, met in the town of Schmalkalden in early 1537. Kidney stones afflicted Luther, and he played a minimal role in the discussions there. The league's leaders decided to use the *Augsburg Confession* as its agenda for the council, but they recognized that the office of the papacy would also command attention. They commissioned Melanchthon to compose a *Treatise on the Power and Primacy of the Pope (Tractatus de Potestate et Primatu Papae)*.[11] In it he criticized the claims of the papacy to divinely appointed power over all other bishops in the church, to divinely appointed power over all secular rulers, and to the allegiance of all Christians on pain of their losing salvation. Melanchthon's argument rested on extensive biblical citation and a detailed survey of the development of papal claims and power in the church's history, with examples of respected theologians who had rejected papal supremacy in the church. When the *Smalcald Articles* were published in 1538, with some expansion by Luther, the treatise was printed with it in a German translation of the original Latin, and its independent nature was lost to subsequent generations. At the end the *Smalcald Articles* were never submitted to the council. The council began 1545 in Trento. First it was planned for Mantua but later the Pope compounded with the emporer for Trento as meeting place.

As followers of Luther and Melanchthon sought to replace the doctrinal authority of bishops and councils in the 1540s and 1550s, they turned frequently also to Luther's *Large* and *Small Catechisms*.[12] They had quickly become standard texts for Christian instruction after their appearance in 1529. Though not the only catechetical textbook used in Lutheran churches—Johannes Brenz's also enjoyed widespread use—the *Small Catechism* has determined the elemental language and thought structures of generations of children. In the Middle Ages, "catechism" referred to the groundwork of Christian instruction, built around the core of the Apostles' Creed (faith), the Lord's Prayer (hope), and the Decalogue or lists of virtues and vices (love), along with the *Ave Maria* as a text for prayer to the Virgin Mother. Medieval catechesis had been conducted not through handbooks or classrooms but through preaching. As a monk and as a substitute preacher in Wittenberg, Luther had frequently preached on parts of the catechism. His *Large Catechism* presents edited sermons from 1528 and 1529 on the Ten Commandments (the law that

8 Dingel *Bekenntnisschriften, Quellen und Materialien*, pp. 120–167; pp. 169–218. **9** Dingel, *Bekenntnisschriften*, pp. 718–785; Kolb/Wengert, *Book of Concord*, pp. 297–328. **10** Führer, *Artickel*; Russell, *Articles*. **11** Dingel, *Bekenntnisschriften*, pp. 796–837; Kolb/Wengert, *Book of Concord*, pp. 330–344. **12** Ibid., *Bekenntnisschriften*, pp. 852–910 [*Small Catechism*], 912–1162 [*Large Catechism*]; Kolb/Wengert, *Book of Concord*, pp. 347–375 [*Small Catechism*], pp. 379–480 [*Large Catechism*]; Peters, *Commentary*; Arand, *That I may Be His Own*.

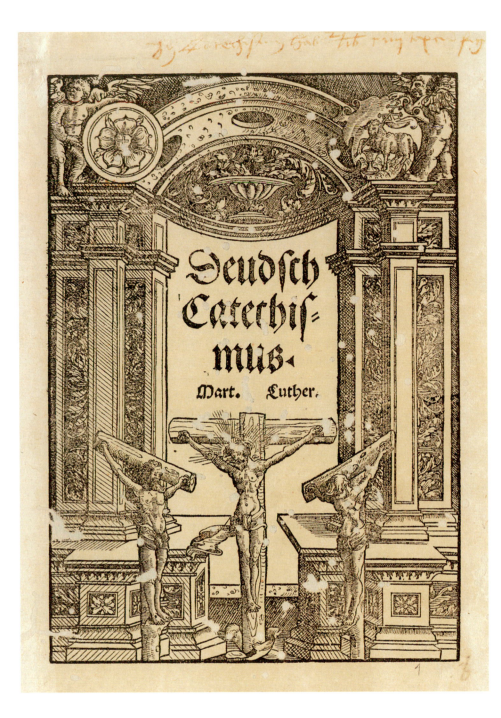

Fig. 4
Title page of Martin Luther's
Large Catechism,
Wittenberg 1529

diagnoses the sinner's problem), the Creed (the gospel that provides deliverance from sin and death), and the Lord's Prayer (the believer's turning to God and seeking to do his will in daily life). Sermons on sacramental forms of the Word of God, baptism, and the Lord's Supper complete the *Large Catechism*; an *Admonition to Confession and Absolution* found its way into the work's second edition.

The *Small Catechism* took form as an *enchiridion*, or handbook, the name catechetical textbooks had borne in the Middle Ages. Soon it altered the meaning of "catechism" to refer primarily to such a handbook. It included the five topics of the *Large Catechism* plus a form for confessing sin and receiving absolution. It then completed its task as a handbook for Christian living with sections on the daily devotional life of believers in prayer and turning to God's Word, and on the practice of the callings that God gives to his people in their homes and occupations, in society, and in the congregation of believers.

These documents became a basis for the governing of ecclesiastical life in various ways in the Lutheran territorial and municipal churches. They slowly began serving as an expression of what the early church labeled a "rule of faith" (*regula fidei*), sometimes a specific summary of biblical teaching, such as in creeds, sometimes more informally a generally understood body of teaching drawn from scripture. In the early 1530s the Wittenberg theologians began speaking of their *corpus doctrinae* (body of doctrine), centered on the ancient creedal statements and the doctrine of justification by faith in Christ. By the 1550s they labeled the *Augsburg Confession*, usually along with one or more of these other documents by Luther or Melanchthon, as their *corpus doctrinae*. Shortly before his death, in 1560, Melanchthon published a collection of his most important writings, which he entitled his *Corpus Doctrinae*; the term thereby became a designation for a published collection of key writings defining the faith and setting the standard for the church's public teaching. With the appearance of several of these across the German landscape in the 1560s and early 1570s, the desire to have a single "body of doctrine" for the churches of the Wittenberg Reformation grew. However, any such collection with the title *Corpus Doctrinae* was viewed as a rival to Melanchthon's collection, something to which many objected. As theologians moved to reconcile the disputing factions within the Wittenberg circle, the designation "Formula of Concord," following Evangelical usage more than thirty years old, emerged.[13]

The final document to be added to the secondary authorities of the Wittenberg Reformation bore that title. It emerged from attempts to solve the conflicts that erupted after Luther's death as his followers went through the process of sorting out the legacy that he and his colleagues, particularly Melanchthon, had left behind. Every movement goes through a similar adjustment as disciples of founders struggle to determine how best to sort out what they have received from their mentor(s). Within the Wittenberg circle this period of adjustment was marked by rancor that arose out of feelings of betrayal that materialized in the wake of the defeat of the Smalcald League by Emperor Charles V in the Smalcald War of 1546–47. Charles made it clear that he intended to enforce the *Edict of Worms* of 1521 and eliminate Luther-style reform.

After his victory over Saxon Elector Johann Friedrich the Elder and Hessian Landgrave Philipp, Charles organized a committee to forge an interim settlement to govern German church life until the Council of Trent would determine official forms of teaching and practice for the Western church. The so-called *Augsburg Interim* conceded Communion and clerical marriage to the Evangelicals. However, it also imposed medieval views of salvation through faith on the basis of the works it produces, continued use of the Mass as a sacrifice for sin, and other elements of the medieval understanding of Christian existence.[14]

A storm of protest erupted, led by Melanchthon. However, the University of Wittenberg had fallen to Johann Friedrich's cousin, Maurice, an Evangelical who had placed himself at the Emperor's disposal in the war, and who had received Johann Friedrich's electoral title and much of his lands as prize for his military aid. Charles applied pressure on Maurice to accept the *Augsburg Interim*. The nobility and towns in the Saxon diet adamantly opposed this. Melanchthon and his colleagues in Wittenberg were drafted by their new elector to aid in formulating a Saxon religious policy that would appear to be conforming to the *Augsburg Interim* but would preserve the proclamation of justification by faith in Christ.[15] The proposal, dubbed the *Leipzig Interim* by its critics, fostered a sense of betrayal among many of Luther's and Melanchthon's students and followers, who believed that Melanchthon and his colleagues had abandoned the Reformation. Melanchthon felt betrayed by these friends and students turned critics, attributing to bad faith on their part their inability to understand that he was trying to save evangelical pulpits for Evangelical preaching. The distrust and animosity fostered in this atmosphere of threat and menace to Wittenberg teaching and reform lasted a quarter century and nursed a number of the disputes over precise elements of that teaching.[16]

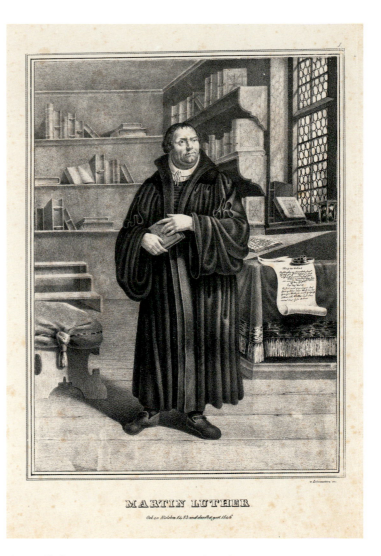

Fig. 5 Wilhelm Baron von Löwenstern, Martin Luther, c. 1840

These disputes began soon after the presentation of the Leipzig proposal to the Saxon diet in late December 1548. By 1552, both evangelical princes who were striving to gain legal status for their faith in the empire, and theologians, who were seeking the unity for which Christ prayed for his church, were attempting to find solutions to the disputes. Two broad strategies coalesced without becoming fixed programs. One group, later labeled by scholars the "Gnesio-Lutherans," favored placing the solution in the hands of theologians, formulating explicit, detailed expressions of teaching faithful to the Bible, and condemning by name false teachers as well as false teaching. In general, the opposing "Philippist" party thought a synod of theologians would only find more to dispute and so favored a solution negotiated by princes and municipal representatives; this group found more general statements of proper teaching sufficient and opposed condemnations, counseling instead *amnistia*, simply forgetting the sources of conflict. Throughout the 1550s and 1560s, variations of these approaches emerged and failed.

13 Dingel, *Melanchthon.* **14** Kolb/Nestingen, *Sources*, pp. 146–182. **15** Ibid., pp. 184–196. **16** Dingel, *Culture of Conflict.*

Fig. 6
Albrecht Dürer, Portrait of Philipp
Melanchthon, 1526.
The inscription shows Dürer's high regard
for the humanist: "Philipps Züge konnte
Dürer mit geschickter Hand nach dem
Leben zeichnen, den Geist jedoch nicht"
("Dürer was able to capture the likeness
of Philipp, but not his spirit")

The issues dividing the members of the Wittenberg circle fall into three categories. First, the willingness of Melanchthon and his colleagues to compromise in areas of church practice that were neutral, or *adiaphora*, neither forbidden nor commanded by scripture, raised questions of the proper stance of the church toward secular government and society, especially in times of persecution. This debate also made clear the importance of ritual as a vehicle for conveying the content of God's Word.

Second, the Wittenberg instructors had held in tension the Bible's presentation of the Creator as almighty and responsible for everything with its insistence that the Creator holds his human creatures responsible for all that he calls them to do. Most Christian

theologians have tried to find some recipe for combining obedience to God with his pure grace. Luther and Melanchthon resisted the temptation; they held in tension God's demand for unconditional, complete obedience to his commands with his unconditional mercy, their distinction of law from gospel. In working with this tension, the reformers' disciples fell into disagreements over whether good works are necessary for salvation, what role the human will plays in the Holy Spirit's conversion of the sinner into God's child, what role God's law plays in the Christian life, and how to understand God's unconditional choosing of his people to be his own. Similarly, the deviant views of the justification of sinners by grace through faith in Christ's work advanced by Andreas Osiander were decisively rejected by almost all other adherents of the Wittenberg Reformation. The answers to these questions account for more than half of the *Formula of Concord*. It largely brought an end to these disputes.

Third, the Reformation took place alongside a revival of Platonic thought and a rethinking of the medieval Aristotelian worldview. Both militated against what Luther held to be the biblical appreciation of God's ability to use selected elements of the created order to effect his will in this world. On the basis of a presupposition adapted from his "Ockhamist" instructors, Luther presumed that the flesh and blood of Jesus, the written words of scripture, the spoken words that deliver its content, and the water of baptism and the bread and wine of the Lord's Supper could be instruments through which God conveys his forgiving and life-restoring power. The implications of this presupposition shaped three articles of the Formula of Concord—on the Lord's Supper, the relationship of the two natures of Christ, and his descent into hell.

One attempt after another to reconcile the disagreeing points of view within the Wittenberg circle had failed between 1552 and 1568. In 1568 Duke Christoph of Württemberg, a leading force in the search for unity among the German evangelicals, sent his leading theologian and ecclesiastical diplomat, Jakob Andreae, to his cousin, Duke Julius of Braunschweig-Wolfenbüttel, to aid in the introduction of the Reformation to Julius's newly inherited dukedom. Christoph asked Andreae to attempt while in Northern Germany to solicit support for a new plan for reconciling doctrinal differences. Andreae did that with five articles on key issues dividing the Wittenberg circle. These articles of doctrine were simply stated, without any attention to contrary teaching.[17] Andreae's efforts were met with indifference when not with outright rejection. He returned to his home in Tübingen, and in 1573 produced a detailed document in the form of *Six Sermons on the Divisions among the Adherents of the Augsburg Confession*, which appealed specifically to theologians, apart from princely support, and contained condemnations of false teachings and false teachers.[18] Other leaders in the Wittenberg circle encouraged his efforts and urged him to recast his proposal in the name of the Tübingen faculty in a more academic form. He issued his own *Swabian Concord*, as it was later labeled, in 1574;[19] Martin Chemnitz and David Chytraeus led Northern German revisions of the document, completed in 1575.[20] In the meantime the governments of Saxony, Baden, and Henneberg had commissioned another attempt to formulate harmony, resulting in the *Maulbronn Formula* of 1576.[21]

Political developments in electoral Saxony had brought about the fall of leading Philippist theologians who had moved in the direction of a spiritualizing view of the Lord's Supper. Elector August, brother and successor of Elector Maurice, requested Andreae's help in reestablishing a more Luther-like theological position in the electorate. The two decided to use this as an opportunity to try once more to establish general unity among those adhering to Luther's way of thinking. August constituted a committee with Andreae, Chemnitz, Chytraeus, his own faithful theologian, Nikolaus Selnecker, and two representatives of the Elector of Brandenburg, Andreas Musculus and Christoph Körner. During 1576 and 1577 they hammered out the final text of the Formula of Concord.[22]

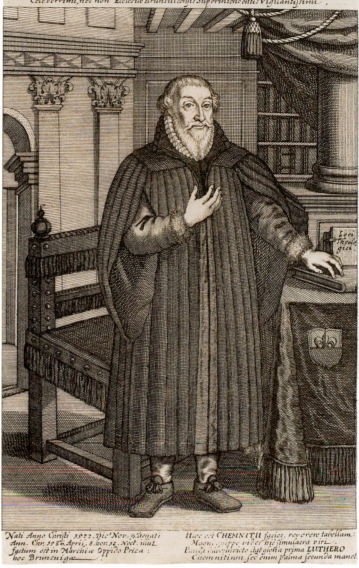

Fig. 7 Unknown artist, Martin Chemnitz the Elder, 1586

Andreae then set out to assemble support from as many evangelical churches within the German lands as possible. Through intense and determined negotiations he attracted the support of the new Elector of the Palatinate, Louis VI, as well as Brandenburg and about two-thirds of the German-speaking evangelical churches. Despite intense criticism, particularly from Calvinist circles,[23] the *Book of Concord*, the collection of confessions that Andreae assembled in 1578–80, became the standard definition of what the Wittenberg Reformation had meant for Lutherans in many parts of the world to this day.[24]

17 Dingel, *Bekenntnisschriften, Quellen und Materialien*, pp. 14–20. **18** Ibid., pp. 26–82. **19** Ibid., pp. 85–136. **20** Ibid., pp. 141–275. **21** Ibid., pp. 279–340. **22** Dingel, *Bekenntnisschriften*, pp. 1184–1652; Kolb/Wengert, *Book of Concord*, pp. 486–660. **23** Dingel, *Concordia controversa*. **24** For overviews, see Arand/Kolb/Nestingen, *The Lutheran Confessions*; Wenz, *Theologie*; Schlink, *Theology*.

Fig. 8
Jakob Lederlein,
Iakob Andreae, 1581

BIBLIOGRAPHY

Arand, Charles P./**Kolb**, Robert/**Nestingen**, James Arne (2012), *The Lutheran Confessions, History and Theology of the Book of Concord*. Minneapolis. **Arand**, Charles P. (2000), *That I may Be His Own. An Overview of Luther's Catechisms.* Saint Louis. **Dingel**, Irene (1996), *Concordia controversa, Die öffentlichen Diskussionen um das lutherische Konkordienwerk am Ende des 16. Jahrhunderts.* Gütersloh. **Dingel**, Irene (2008), The Culture of Conflict in the Controversies Leading to the Formula of Concord (1548–1580). In: Robert Kolb (ed.), *Lutheran Ecclesiastical Culture, 1550–1675.* Leiden, pp. 15–64. **Dingel**, Irene (2012), Melanchthon and the Establishment of Confessional Norms. In: id. et al. (eds.), *Philip Melanchthon. Theologian in Classroom, Confession, and Controversy.* Göttingen, pp. 161–179. **Dingel**, Irene (ed.) (2014), *Die Bekenntnisschriften der Evangelisch-Lutherischen Kirche.* Göttingen. **Dingel**, Irene (ed.) (2014), *Die Bekenntnisschriften der Evangelisch-Lutherischen Kirche, Quellen und Materialien*, vols. 1 and 2. Göttingen. **Führer**, Werner (2009), *Die Schmalkaldischen Artickel.* Tübingen.

Grane, Leif (1987), *The Augsburg Confession, a Commentary*. Trans. John H. Rasmussen. Minneapolis. **Immenkötter**, Herbert (ed.) (1979), *Die Confutatio der Confessio Augustana vom 3. August 1530.* **Kolb**, Robert/**Nestingen**, James Arne (eds.) (2001), *Sources and Contexts of the Book of Concord*. Minneapolis. **Kolb**, Robert/**Wengert**, Timothy J. (eds.) (2000), *The Book of Concord*. Minneapolis. **Maurer**, Wilhelm (1986), *Historical Commentary on the Augsburg Confession*. Trans. H. George Anderson. Philadelphia. **Peters**, Albrecht (2009–12), *Commentary on Luther's Catechisms*, ed. Gottfried Seebaß. Trans. Charles P. Schaum, Holger Sonntag, Thomas H. Trapp. 5 vols. Saint Louis. **Peters**, Christian (1997), *Apologia Confessionis Augustanae. Untersuchungen zur Textgeschichte einer lutherischen Bekenntnisschrift (1530–1584)*. Stuttgart. **Russell**, William R. (1994), *The Schmalkald Articles: Luther's Theological Testament*. Minneapolis. **Schlink**, Edmund (1961), *Theology of the Lutheran Confessions*. Trans. Paul F. Koehneke and Herbert, J. A. Boumann. Philadelphia. **Wenz**, Gunther (1996–97), *Theologie der Bekenntnisschriften der evangelisch-lutherischen Kirche*. 2 vols. Berlin.

CHRISTIANE ANDERSSON

Polemical Prints and the Censorship of Images in Reformation Germany

Martin Luther's attack on the dogma and practices of the Catholic Church beginning in 1517 led not only to religious upheaval but also to profound political and social conflicts in Germany. The German population, especially in larger cities such as Nuremberg, Augsburg, Strasbourg, and Wittenberg, were intensely interested in these issues, resulting in a sudden, enormous demand for information and in a momentous increase in religious writing and polemical diatribes articulating different viewpoints. The output of printers and publishers[1] grew exponentially. In 1523–24 approximately one thousand times as many books and pamphlets were published as in 1517, now mostly in German rather than Latin, according to Rolf Engelsing's statistics.[2] But the new forms of mass communication were not exclusively printed; it was the combination of oral, written, and visual means of expression that spread Luther's new evangelical doctrine. Woodcut illustrations provided visual representations of the ideas expressed in printed texts. People accustomed to "reading" pictures, a habit trained through long exposure to Catholic religious images, applied this skill to polemical images disseminated by Lutheran printers. The Catholic hierarchy quickly recognized the dangers of visual and text-based polemics and subjected them to censorship.

As a means of political control, some form of censorship has always existed in Western culture. Prior to the Enlightenment in the eighteenth century, censorship was customary, a right taken for granted by those in power. Religious heresy and criticism of political authorities were considered intolerable, especially in the printed media. Even the early defenders of free speech in the sixteenth century limited the realms in which they considered it should be applied. For example, in his *Utopia* of 1516, Sir Thomas More demanded freedom of thought but within certain limits. He did not tolerate a diversity of opinion concerning divine providence or the immortality of the soul.[3] The Protestant reformers also did not grant freedom of thought in matters of religious belief. Martin Luther employed censorship against his former allies in 1525 and Huldrych Zwingli instituted it in 1523 in reformed Zurich.[4]

Censorship had been an important concern of the Catholic Church earlier but acquired a new urgency in reaction to the popularity of Martin Luther's new theology and the danger of its spread through the print media. Censorship became the critical component

of the imperial response to Luther's appearance before the Diet of Worms, the imperial assembly attended by Emperor Charles V and the Catholic princes in April 1521. Following Luther's refusal to disavow what were considered his heretical beliefs and his reaffirmation of the basis for his doctrine at Worms, Emperor Charles V on May 25, 1521, promulgated the *Edict of Worms*.[5] In this document he condemned Luther and his followers and decreed the censorship of all of their writings past and future, and of all printed material deemed contrary to Catholic belief or directed against the papacy, Catholic prelates, princes, or Catholic theological faculties at universities. Nothing injurious to them could be printed, bought, sold, or owned, openly or secretly. Any libelous books already in circulation were to be confiscated and publicly burned. It was also forbidden to "have someone write, print or have printed, or affirm or defend the writings or opinions of Martin Luther, or anything contained in these writings, in any language." The edict demanded preventive censorship, requiring that all texts with any religious content should be approved prior to publication by city magistrates or by a university theological faculty. The edict also stipulated the way in which its regulations were to be publicized: it should be read aloud to townspeople "word for word and with a loud voice" in all locations where edicts and mandates were customarily posted. They were often read aloud from the pulpits as well.

The *Edict of Worms* delegated the responsibility of enforcing its regulations to Catholic professors of theology at local universities for theological texts and to city councils for all other printed matter, such as the multitude of polemical broadsheets (see fig. 2 in the essay of Ingrid Dettmann in this volume). City councils issued local censorship ordinances, which generally followed closely the wording of the edict, and, as stipulated in that document, appointed themselves as the censoring body, as was the case in Nuremberg. The local ordinances required printers to swear an oath of compliance with the rules and to hand over for advance inspection every text intended for publication, so that permission to print could be granted or denied.

1 Edwards, *Printing*. 2 Engelsing, *Analphabetentum*, p. 32. 3 Surtz/Hexter, *Thomas More*, vol. IV, pp. 10–20. 4 Erler/Kaufmann, *Handwörterbuch*, vol. III, col. 1910. 5 Kalkoff, *Entstehung*; id., *Wormser Edikt*.

Fig. 1 Hans Baldung Grien, *Martin Luther with the dove*, 1521,
from: *Acta et res gestae D. Martini Lutheri in comitiis principum
Wormaciae*, Straßburg 1521

The polemical writings of this period which were targeted by
the edict were primarily single-sheet broadsheets, in which the text
and a woodcut were printed together on a large, folio-sized sheet; if
the text extended to more than a single page, the pages were bound
together as a pamphlet. Pamphlets were short and flimsy booklets
usually bound only in thick paper—a cheap, lightweight form of
binding that kept costs low and made transporting pamphlets easier.
Mobility was essential for polemical writing, both to make a profit
and to evade the censors. Pamphlets were offered for sale at fairs and
markets in many distant towns to expand their audience. And to
avoid being destroyed, offensive material had to be moved quickly
beyond the jurisdiction of a local censor.[6]

The edict stated in particular that both texts and images were
equally subject to censorship, and included artists along with authors and printers among those who were to be punished for violating the edict's regulations. Evidence of the importance of censoring
woodcut illustrations in books or broadsheets is seen for example
in Nuremberg, where the town council, when banning offensive
tracts, was particularly careful to confiscate the woodblocks from
which the offending woodcut illustrations had been printed, in ad-

dition to the texts themselves. The need to censor images as well as
texts reflects the low rate of literacy in Germany during the early
sixteenth century.[7] Luther perfectly understood the potential per-
suasiveness of printed pictures for the illiterate and the value of visual polemics for the evangelical cause. This is evident in the special
care he devoted to the woodcuts that illustrated his tracts published
in Wittenberg under his close supervision, images designed in the
workshop of his friend, Lucas Cranach the Elder.

Among the numerous polemical projects on which Luther and
the Cranach workshop collaborated, the *Passional Christi et Antichristi*
of 1521 was one of the earliest and most famous antipapal publications, an initial salvo in the polemical campaign that Luther and his
associates in Wittenberg lobbed against the Catholics (fig. 2).[8] This
established an effective tactic that Lutherans used countless times in
future attacks on the papists by directing the word of God itself
against their opponents. The *Passional* contrasted the self-indulgence
and total neglect of priestly functions by the papal curia and the
Pope, who was characterized as the Antichrist, with the exemplary
life of Christ. In a series of thirteen antithetical pairs of woodcuts,
each page opening juxtaposes an episode from Christ's ministry on
the left with a papal practice on the right that both text and image
suggest is diametrically opposed to Christ's teachings. The polemical message is expressed in each instance by the text under the
woodcuts, which was cleverly chosen to emphasize Christ's devotion to his mission and to his followers on the one hand, versus
the institutionalized neglect of parishioners by the Pope and the
Catholic hierarchy on the other. For example, the seventh pair of
images shows Christ on the left preaching to the multitude. The biblical passage below tells of Christ's profound commitment to preaching about his father's kingdom (Luke 4:43–44). The contrasting
image on the right shows the Pope neglecting to preach but rather
presiding over a lavish meal accompanied by a bishop, a canon, and
a monk. The text below sarcastically describes the overworked bishops as gluttonous "animals" devoted only to living well, quoting
Isaiah 56:12, and as being far too busy with their political intrigues
to preach God's word. The Pope and his entourage, seated in splendor under a canopy while gorging themselves, waited upon by servants who deliver at the table not one but three dishes at a time, and
serenaded by musicians, are all accusatory motifs that recur in later
polemical images. Another double page contrasts Christ's humility
with papal pride: Christ is shown on his knees, humbly washing and
kissing the feet of his apostles, while the power-hungry Pope, regally
enthroned under a canopy, accompanied by a cardinal, an archbishop, and a monk, allows an Emperor, a king, and German princes
to kiss his feet.

The *Passional Christi et Antichristi* was the first full-blown polemical pamphlet issued by the Lutherans in Wittenberg. The low rates
of literacy in Germany in 1521 suggest that the woodcuts probably
carried far more polemical weight than the brief texts printed below
them. Philipp Melanchthon and Johann Schwertfeger, who chose
the texts from the Bible and from papal decretals, added these ironic
commentaries that underscore the satirical message of the images,
but the woodcuts express powerful and unambiguously critical

Fig. 2 Martin Luther/Lucas Cranach the Elder (woodcuts), so-called "Völlerei des Papstes" (The Gluttony of the Pope), from: Martin Luther,
   Passional Christi und Antichristi, Wittenberg 1521. While Christ preaches the realm of God in nature, the Pope is succumbing to gluttony.
   At the same time the bishops are neglecting their offices, as they are adapting to the degenerate lifestyle of the Pope.

messages, even to those who were unable to read the texts. The ten-line epilogue that appears instead of a colophon at the end of the pamphlet is believed by some to have been written by Luther himself.[9] The originators of this publishing project must have been keenly aware of the inflammatory nature of the *Passional*, because neither the compilers of the texts, nor the printer (Johann Rhau-Grunenberg), nor the place of publication (Wittenberg) is named. Anonymity was advisable, since the first edition of the *Passional* was issued shortly after the Diet of Worms, whose strict censorship regulations were surely the reason why no one was inclined to claim credit for the pamphlet. The epilogue preemptively addresses the anticipated objections by censors and offers its own rationale, explaining why the pamphlet should not be considered libelous: everything the text mentions was not only accepted Catholic practice but even set forth in canon law. In the *Passional* the Wittenberg reformers astutely used the effective polemical tactic of turning their opponents' own words against them. The pamphlet's enormous popularity is demonstrated by the demand it created: several new editions

were published in German and one in Latin during the second half of the year 1521 alone.[10]

Another polemical tract disseminated from Wittenberg in 1526 that was also published anonymously to evade the censors is *Das Babstum mit seynen Gliedern: gemalet und beschryben*. This illustrated catalogue of the Catholic hierarchy criticizes the proliferation of Catholic monastic orders and their godless habits.[11] As in the *Passional*, Luther was directly involved in its publication and in this case wrote the preface and the epilogue in Wittenberg. Printed both as a pamphlet comprising several pages and on a single, double-folio sheet as a large illustrated broadsheet, it shows in the first edition fifty-seven woodcuts of members of the monastic orders and other representatives of the Catholic Church, while the second edition in-

6 Gawthrop/Strauss, *Protestantism*, pp. 32 ff. **7** Engelsing, *Analphabetentum*, pp. 32–34. **8** Cranach, *Passional Christi*; Kawerau, *Passional Christi*, vol. III. **9** Hofmann, *Luther*, p. 178, no. 50A. **10** Koepplin/Falk, *Cranach*, I, p. 330, no. 218. **11** Andersson/Talbot, *Mighty Fortress*, cat. no. 205.

cluded seventy-three woodcuts on several sheets. Again the woodcuts were created in the Cranach workshop in Wittenberg but copied the same year by Hans Sebald Beham in Nuremberg.[12]

To fully understand Luther's diatribe against monasticism one must bear in mind contemporary events: the tract was published the year after Luther had preached against the Catholic practice of monastic life and had married the former nun Katharina von Bora, a union demonstrably intended as Luther's answer to monasticism. Writing in the preface to the tract, Luther describes the utter failure of Catholic attempts to impose sexual abstinence on monks, nuns, and clerics, and repeats his view that they should marry, since the Bible nowhere prescribes a life of celibacy. Again new editions of the tract were published in short order: in the same year (1526), Hans Guldenmund in Nuremberg published *Das Babstum mit seynen gliedern gemalet und beschryben, gebessert und gemehrt* in an expanded edition, as the new title indicates, with woodcuts by the local artist Hans Sebald Beham.[13] The illustrations, based on the Cranach woodcuts but somewhat simplified, were increased to seventy-four individual images of clerics. Their great number effectively emphasizes the enormous proliferation of Catholic monastic orders that are ridiculed in this publication. Unlike the *Passional*, here the texts rather than the images most effectively convey the polemical message. In the epilogue Luther again takes up the issue of the likely censorship of his tract, asserting that it is not libelous but merely calls attention to widely known offenses committed by the Catholics—and that in doing so, it fulfills God's will.

Nuremberg had long been an important center of the publishing industry, and once the imperial free city officially became Protestant in 1525, local publishers became ever more active in issuing large editions of anti-Catholic works. Contemporary documents reveal that this heightened activity occurred both out of religious conviction and for profit. Published in Nuremberg in 1527, *A Wondrous Prophecy of the Papacy* (fig. 3) is one of the best documented examples of the censorship of anti-papal polemics in Reformation-era Germany.[14] This pamphlet depicts the history and ultimate defeat of the papacy. It consists of thirty allegorical woodcuts by Erhard Schön with explanatory texts that appear alongside each of the woodcuts, and are primarily intended to explain the allegorical symbolism of the images. They were written by Andreas Osiander, the Lutheran preacher at the Church of St. Lawrence in Nuremberg. Two rhyming couplets that appear below each image and the epilogue (*Beschlusredt*) were composed by the famous poet of Nuremberg, Hans Sachs. The *Wondrous Prophecy* is based on much older prophetic sources castigating the Catholic Church and its worldly ways, tracts that were attributed to the Calabrian abbot Joachim of Fiore and to a certain Bishop Anselmus of Marsico. Over time two prophetic texts by these authors had been brought together; the result became known in a number of manuscript and printed versions.[15] The first of these critical manuscripts to be printed, *Joachimi Abbatis Vaticinia circa Apostolicos Viros et Ecclesiam Romanam*, appeared in Bologna in 1515. In his introduction to the *Wondrous Prophecy*, Osiander describes two books containing these prophecies, which he had discovered in the libraries of the Carthusian monastery and

Fig. 3 Erhard Schön (woodcuts)/Hans Sachs/Andreas Osiander, Eyn wunderliche Weyssagung von dem Bapstumb (A Wondrous Prophesy of the Papacy), Nürnberg, 1527

of the city council in Nuremberg. The older volume, dated 1278, contained only pictures, he noted, while the more recent one—already about one hundred years old in 1527—contained texts with images that did not correspond to each other.

These texts served his polemical needs perfectly, as evidence that the increasing sinfulness and impending demise of the papacy had already been foretold in medieval times, predating Luther by several centuries. But since Osiander had little trust in what he considered a heavily edited text in the Bolognese edition, and because he suspected that it therefore obscured the full extent of the original author's criticism of the medieval church, he simply ignored the Bolognese text and composed his own to explain the meaning of the woodcuts. He evidently trusted the authenticity of the Bolognese woodcuts, which Erhard Schön copied faithfully with minimal changes, far more than the text. He stated that the images seemed to him to speak powerfully and directly, and he assumed that intelligent people would understand them. But for the benefit of simple folk, he provided his own explanation of the images: *Doch ist eyn ausslegung dartzu gesetzt umb der eynfeltigen willen; denn vernuenftig leut sehen on alle ausslegung was es ist.*

Adapting a common strategy of Reformation polemicists, Osiander employed a medieval prophecy as a means to reveal how the sinfulness of the papacy had endured over centuries and was not a recent problem revealed by Luther alone. He evaluated the development of the papacy from the times of Emperor Constantine to his own period, dwelling on the Pope's worldly habits, on his misuse of his religious authority as a temporal lord and warmonger, and on his total neglect of his spiritual duties. Osiander interpreted these perversions as signs that the Pope is the Antichrist, a common accusation among polemicists. He demonstrated that the Pope's sins prophesied in the thirteenth-century text came to be fulfilled in later times. Osiander judged the Pope's conduct by the standard of God's Word but maintained that the Pope heeded only the counsel of Satan. Osiander in 1527 still held out hope for the reform of the papacy and the triumph of the Word, which he defined as Lutheran preaching and service to God's people.

To achieve the desired contemporary relevance, Osiander and Schön made certain adjustments to the Bolognese model. For example, the city of Rome illustrated in the Bolognese pamphlet was changed in the *Wondrous Prophecy* to a view of Nuremberg, easily recognizable by the double city walls, the well-known churches of St. Lawrence and St. Sebald, the castle on the hill, and the Frauentor city gate in the foreground. Another means of giving topical relevance to his work was the change in the figure of an unidentified monk holding a flower and sickle in the Bolognese woodcut; this became a portrait of Martin Luther in the habit of an Augustinian monk holding a giant rose, his heraldic emblem (fig. 3). The sickle became a symbolic instrument used to "mow down" the sinful flesh, a reference to Isaiah 40:6–8.

As was customary for Reformation polemical writing, Osiander's pamphlet was published in reaction to a particular political situation. The Catholic princes' victory in the Peasants' War of 1525 led them to believe they had defeated not only the peasants but also the Protestants, whose inflammatory preaching they held responsible for the peasants' uprising. A feeling of defeat on the part of Lutherans led to Luther's call to arms in 1526. In the *Wondrous Prophecy* Osiander exhorted his followers to vigorously resume their anti-Catholic diatribes, rhymes, songs, and satirical pictures to "show the papists what they're worth."[16]

When Nuremberg's city councillors saw Osiander's pictorial prophecy, they considered it to be too incendiary so soon after the city had adopted the Lutheran faith in March 1525, when every effort was being made to avoid further antagonizing Emperor Charles V and the Catholic princes. Osiander had ignored the city's regulation of preventive censorship. Although once Nuremberg became a Protestant city, the *Edict of Worms'* censure of Lutheran writings was no longer being carried out, but the requirement for preventive censorship of all texts intended for publication had been maintained. At this time it was being directed primarily against the radical reformers and Anabaptists. The councillors reprimanded Osiander for circumventing the preventive rule that required showing manuscripts to the local censor, Lazarus Spengler, prior to publication.

They felt Osiander's tract had no redeeming value but would only offend and embitter the local population and would bring the councillors trouble.[17]

The censorship of the *Wondrous Prophecy* proved to be ineffective, however, since at least three known editions were issued during the same year, 1527, by Hans Weiss in Wittenberg, by Kaspar Kantz in Zwickau, and by Jakob Köbel in Oppenheim on the Rhein, and numerous others followed. The councillors later stated that they did not consider Erhard Schön's woodcuts to be particularly offensive, since they were merely copies after older illustrations that Osiander had discovered in the medieval books he cited. Following Hans Guldenmund's second request for restitution of the woodblocks from which the woodcut illustrations had been printed, about three months later the council reversed its earlier decision to impound the woodblocks and returned them to him. Its members justified their decision with the argument that similar woodcuts in the Bolognese tract of 1515 had existed earlier and had not given offense in the period prior to the Reformation. The publisher Guldenmund was even granted permission to reprint his retrieved woodblocks, provided that they were accompanied only by the original medieval text, not by Osiander's and Sachs's offensive verses.[18] One of the woodblocks from among the thirty used for the Wittenberg edition of 1527 of the *Wondrous Prophecy* is preserved in Nuremberg.[19]

Luther was one of the first recipients of Osiander's first edition from Nuremberg and was the driving force behind the decision to reprint it in Wittenberg, as he wrote in a letter of April 29, 1527, to Georg Spalatin.[20] It must have been a high priority as it took less than a month for the Wittenberg edition to appear, as Luther reported in a letter to Wenzeslaus Linck.[21] Luther wrote that he approved of the pamphlet's portrait of him holding the rose and sickle, and of the text. Predictably enough the pamphlet elicited not only reprints and imitations but also critical reactions, most importantly the tract published around 1530 by Theophrastus of Hohenheim, who was known as Paracelsus, *Ein Ausslegung der Figuren, so zu Nuernberg gefunden seind worden, gefuert in grundt der Magischen Weissagung*. To him the thirty woodcuts were magic images with which a troubled institution like the papacy

12 Hollstein, *German Engravings*, vol. III, p. 56. 13 Ibid., pp. 236 f. 14 *Eyn wunderliche Weyssagung von dem Babstumb wie es yhm biss an das endt der welt gehen sol, in figuren oder gemäl begriffen, gefunden zu Nürnberg ym Cartheuser Closter vnd ist seher alt.* Andersson, *Censorship*, pp. 170–178 and figs. 8.5–8.9. All thirty woodcuts are illustrated in Schreyl/Freitag-Stadler, *Welt des Hans Sachs*, p. 17–31, cat. no. 25. 15 On the *Wondrous Prophecy*, see Hofmann in Müller/Seebass, *Andreas Osiander*, vol. II, pp. 403–407. Roland Bainton assumed the Bologna edition of 1515 was the direct model, as did Warburg, *Weissagung*. 16 *Last uns auch auffs new widder anfahen, schreiben, tichten, reymen, singen, malen und zeygen das edle goetezen geschlecht, wie sie verdinet und wert sind.* WA 19, 42, 23 f. and 43,7 f. 17 *dises buechlein mehr eyn anzundung und verbitterung des gemeynen mans dann etwas anders verursach, darzue eynem erbern rath allerley nachteils und gremschafft bey vilen erfolgen mog.* Hampe, *Nürnberger Ratsverlässe*, p. 238, no. 1580. 18 Ibid., p.274, no. 1921. 19 Germanisches Museum, *Katalog, Erster Theil*, pp. 27–28 with illustration 104–118. 20 WA.B 4, 196, 4–6 (no. 1098). 21 Dated May 19, 1527, ibid., p. 203, lines 10–14, no. 1106.

Fig. 4
Hans Selbald Beham, Luther as an Evangelist,
title woodcut from: Martin Luther,
Das new Testament Deütsch, Nürnberg 1524

could be diagnosed and cured. He harshly attacked the moral decay and pride of the curia but defended the institution itself.

Osiander's *Wondrous Prophecy* is one of the most fascinating instances of the ineffectiveness of censorship. The Nuremberg councillors' attempts to suppress the pamphlet arose from their real fear of repercussions from the recently victorious Catholic princes in territories nearby. They were especially vigilant in their efforts to prevent the circulation of the pamphlet beyond the city gates. Pointing out that it had been printed without their knowledge, the councillors wrote to the city councils in Frankfurt and Coburg and requested that all copies be bought up at Nuremberg's expense and destroyed. At the same time at home they sought to offset the printer Guldenmund's considerable financial loss, demonstrating their ha-

bitual social concern for the preservation of his livelihood and for the well-being of his family, not least in order that they would not become costly wards of the state.

Erhard Schön's woodcut portraying Luther with his heraldic emblem, the rose, and the symbolic sickle was only one of many censored portraits of the Reformer. Even his likeness had a polemical effect and, like his writings, was subject to censorship after the *Edict of Worms* was decreed in 1521. In Nuremberg certain images of him were not tolerated after the edict, but several years later all images of him were censored, reflecting the changing political climate.

In 1520, prior to the edict, the Nuremberg, printmaker Hans Sebald Beham had produced a small woodcut portrait showing Luther in profile wearing his doctor's cap and gown, seated at his desk, looking reverently at a small sculpture of the crucified Christ, with the dove symbolizing the Holy Spirit hovering above him (fig. 4).[22] The rays of a halo emanating from his head characterize Luther as a saint or an evangelist. Such an image would have been contrary to Luther's own teaching on the veneration of saints, but the Reformer had no control over portraits of himself made in distant parts of Germany. The saintly visage presumably suited the expectations of potential buyers who were accustomed to the image traditions of late-medieval piety. Beham's image of Luther is based on traditional medieval author portraits of the evangelists shown writing the Gospels, a type of image that often precedes the beginning of each Gospel in illuminated or printed Bibles. Beham gave Luther all the trappings of a divinely inspired evangelist, and thereby characterized Luther's writings as divine revelation comparable to the Gospels. Indeed the woodcut served as the title-page illustration for Luther's New Testament, printed in Nuremberg by Hans Hergot in editions between 1524 and 1526.

On May 3, 1521, shortly before the proclamation of the edict, but after Luther's appearance at Worms, the Nuremberg city council forbade the sale of all portraits of "Luther with the Holy Spirit"[23] for fear they would enrage Catholics. In fact, the papal nuncio, Girolamo Aleandro, angrily reported in 1521 that he had observed common folk in Worms buying such prints and kissing Luther's visage. Aleandro denounced all images of the "holy" Luther and demanded they be destroyed.[24]

The council's ban against Luther's image "with the Holy Spirit" must have been directed specifically against Beham's small woodcut, which was surely well known in Nuremberg. But it would have applied equally to similar portraits by other printmakers that were disseminated throughout Germany, such as a woodcut of the Reformer with a halo and the dove by Hans Baldung Grien (fig. 1) created in Strasbourg,[25] and an etching made after 1520 by Hieronymus Hopfer in Augsburg.[26] Both were reverse copies of an engraved portrait by Cranach the Elder.[27] A similar etching of Luther by Daniel Hopfer of Augsburg bears an inscription contrasting the ephemeral nature of Luther's physical appearance with the immortality of his soul: *Des lutters gestalt mag wol verderbenn, Sein cristlich gemiet wirt nymer sterben M.D.X.X.III.*[28]

A slightly later woodcut of 1530 by Lucas Cranach the Elder also shows Luther writing at his desk with the dove of the Holy Spirit hovering above.[29] Cranach made the hagiographic reference more specific than Beham: Cranach's Luther appears in the guise of Saint Matthew, identified by the evangelist's symbol, the angel, who stands next to Luther's writing table providing divine inspiration. Cranach's woodcut author portrait illustrated many of the later editions of Luther's translation of the New Testament published in Wittenberg by Hans Lufft beginning in 1530.

In 1524, three years after the censorship of images of Luther with the dove, the Nuremberg council banned all portraits of Luther.[30] This may initially seem surprising in so Lutheran an environment, since at that time Nuremberg was well on its way to officially declaring itself to be a Protestant city, as occurred the following year in 1525. But censoring Luther's portrait served as an urgent attempt to mend diplo-

matic relations with the Catholic Emperor Charles V, who was outraged by the free imperial city becoming Protestant. Locally, however, it appears unlikely that the ban was consistently carried out, since Beham's censored woodcut portrait of 1521 was reused in Nuremberg in 1524 by the Protestant publisher Hans Hergot as the title-page illustration for a vernacular edition of the New Testament, *Das new Testament Deütsch.* Nuremberg's archives have produced no evidence that this edition attracted any attention from the local censors.

A related image of Luther shown in the guise of a saint is Jacob Lucius the Elder's illustrated broadsheet, *The Baptism of Christ in the Elbe River before Wittenberg,*[31] dated 1556–58, of which a version with Latin text was also printed (see fig. 2 in the essay of Ingrid Dettmann in this volume). Saint John the Baptist is shown baptizing Christ in the Elbe River at Wittenberg rather than in the Jordan, with John Frederick I, the Elector of Saxony, his spouse, Sibylle von Cleve, and their three sons kneeling in reverence on the opposite bank. Luther appears in the customary manner of a patron saint, laying his hand on the shoulder of the elector in the traditional gesture of intercession, and pointing with the other toward the baptism being performed.

Catholic images of Luther often relied on the popular fascination with monsters and misbirths, which had played an important role in popular visual culture before the Reformation and soon became one of the most common forms of visual propaganda, both in support of theological arguments and character assassination of the opponent. In 1529 the Catholic publicist Johannes Cochlaeus published his anti-Lutheran tract *The Seven-Headed Martin Luther (Martinus Lutherus Septiceps)* in simultaneous German and Latin editions, illustrated with a satirical title-page portrait of Luther by Hans Brosamer (fig. 5). Much like Protestant polemics, Cochlaeus's strategy was to attack Luther with his own words, quoting from his writings to demonstrate that his theology was full of contradictions. Cochlaeus intended to obviate the need for Catholic priests to read the Reformer's own "poisonous" texts themselves. Brosamer's title-page woodcut presents Luther as a multiheaded charlatan in obvious analogy to the seven-headed dragon described in Revelations, chapter 13, which signified the devil. The seven-headed portrait of Luther was certainly intended as a rebuttal to Luther's identification of the Pope as Antichrist, a major polemical message contained in the *Passional Christi et Antichristi* of 1521. To show that Luther speaks with "seven tongues" rather than presenting a single, coherent theology, Brosamer's woodcut ironically subverts the traditional Protestant manner of portraying Luther as a monk piously clutching his Bible, transforming him into a monster whose seven heads represented his sevenfold contradictory and diabolical nature.[32] The heads offer a

22 Hollstein, *German Engravings*, vol. III, no. 56. Hofmann, *Luther*, p. 154. **23** Hampe, *Nürnberger Ratsverlässe*, p. 205, no. 1339. **24** Brieger, *Aleander*, p. 24. **25** Hollstein, *German Engravings*, vol. II, p. 154, no. 270. **26** Ibid., vol. XV, p. 119, no. 96. **27** Ibid., vol. VI, no. 96. **28** Ibid., no. 121. **29** Jahn, *Cranach*, pp. 776 f. **30** Hampe, *Nürnberger Ratsverlässe*, p. 221, no. 1455. **31** Strauss, *German Single-Leaf Woodcut*, vol. III, p. 850, no. 899; Röttinger, *Beiträge*, no. 85. **32** Newman Brooks, *Seven-Headed Luther*, p. 233.

Fig. 5 Hans Brosamer, Seven-Headed Martin Luther, title-page woodcut to Johannes Cochlaeus,
Sieben Köpfe Martin Luthers (Seven-Headed Martin Luther), Leipzig 1529

spoof of his academic credentials with the oversized doctor's hat; as Saint Martin, one of the saints whose veneration Luther had forbidden; as an infidel wearing a turban; as a renegade priest defrocked since his excommunication in 1520 and thus only masquerading as a clergyman; as *Suermerus* (*Schwärmer*), or radical sectarian, whose folly is shown by the hovering bees in his bonnet; as *Visitator*, referring to his leading role during the first visit to congregations in Saxony completed a year earlier; and as Barabbas, the thief who was set free in Christ's stead by Pontius Pilate.

The Reformation pamphlets and broadsheets discussed here are representative of an early form of mass communication that played such a critical role in the rapid dissemination and propagandistic reinforcement of evangelical theology. Similar tactics were soon employed by the Catholic camp as well, although in far smaller numbers. Protestant polemics sought to construct and solidify an ideological relationship between Luther and his followers by providing powerful arguments to justify Luther's break with the church and to convince potential converts to do likewise. Reformation publicists aimed at discrediting their adversaries or destroying them in effigy. Polemical attacks often required the simplification and vulgarization of issues. Not infrequently the first casualty in this process was truth itself, especially in later years as the polemical exchange grew more heated and the stakes ever greater. Effectiveness was paramount, and successful polemics engendered imitations, adaptations, parodies, or reverse parodies on all sides of the political spectrum. Reformation propagandists communicated by means of the culture they shared with their audience, relying heavily on prior familiarity with image traditions, popular belief, and local customs. Protestant publicists adapted old images to new purposes, benefitting from the recognition factor of familiar ideas in different contexts with new meanings. Generally the Protestants were more inventive and more productive in their polemical output than the Catholics.

Ultimately neither the imperial court nor the Catholic princes nor even local councils were capable of enforcing the regulations of preventive censorship. The rules set forth in the *Edict of Worms* in 1521 were inconsistently carried out, as is obvious from the frequent, ever more emphatic reissuing of the regulations, sometimes with identical texts. In an edict of 1524, Charles V stated his intention of reinforcing what he had decreed in the *Edict of Worms* only three years earlier. In 1527 Ferdinand, Charles's brother, once again issued censorship regulations in a document.[33] In 1548 Charles V complained outright that previous decrees had been ineffective. The Edict of Speyer (1570) outlawed the operation of printing presses in more remote places that were hard for the authorities to control, and allowed presses to operate only in free imperial cities, or in towns where a princely court or a university was located. Evidently the Emperor felt he could only rely on representatives of these institutions.

Despite official disapproval, pamphleteers flourished. They benefitted from the general leniency of local censors, from cheap paper, convenient trade routes, and the ease with which censored broadsheets and pamphlets could be smuggled quickly from one town to the next. The authorities, in contrast, had to deal with numerous impediments to effective censorship, such as overburdened, easily

bribed, or outright sympathetic censors, a multitude of political jurisdictions, lax magistrates, conflicts between ecclesiastical and lay authorities, pressure from Protestant populations, and mutual aid among Protestant publishers. Many of them exercised their own form of "reverse" censorship by refusing to print any pro-Catholic material.

An assessment of the censorship of illustrated broadsheets and pamphlets during the German Reformation must be based on the local political circumstances. These changed radically, sometimes in only a few weeks, and they varied from one city to the next. Fervent believers on both sides of the religious conflict continued to test the limits of tolerance.

---

33 Thüringisches Hauptstaatsarchiv Weimar (ThHStAW), Ernestinisches Gesamtarchiv (EGA), Reg. H4.

BIBLIOGRAPHY

Andersson, Christiane/**Talbot**, Charles (1983), *From A Mighty Fortress: Prints, Drawings and Books in the Age of Luther, 1483–1546*. Detroit. **Andersson**, Christiane, The Censorship of Images in Nuremberg 1521–1527: Art and Politics in the Reformation. In: Zika, Charles/Eichberger, Dagmar (eds.) (1998), *Dürer and His Culture*. Cambridge, U.K., pp. 164–178, 230 f. **Brieger**, Theodor (1884), *Aleander und Luther 1521: Die vervollständigten Aleander-Depeschen nebst Untersuchung über den Wormser Reichstag. Quellen und Forschungen zur Geschichte der Reformation*, Gotha. **Cranach** the Elder, Lucas (1972), *Passional Christi und Antichristi, mit einem Nachwort von Hildegard Schnabel*. Berlin. **Edwards**, Mark U. (1994), *Printing, Propaganda and Martin Luther*. Berkeley/Los Angeles/Oxford. **Engelsing**, Rolf (1973), *Analphabetentum und Lektüre: Zur Sozialgeschichte des Lesens in Deutschland zwischen feudaler und industrieller Gesellschaft*. Stuttgart. **Erler**, Adalbert/**Kaufmann**, Ekkehard (eds.) (1984), *Handwörterbuch zur deutschen Rechtsgeschichte*. Berlin. **Gawthrop**, Richard/**Strauss**, Gerald (1984), Protestantism and Literacy in Early Modern Germany. In: *Past and Present*, vol. 104, pp. 31–55. **Germanisches Museum** (ed.) (1892), *Katalog der im germanischen Museum vorhandenen zum Abdrucke bestimmten geschnittenen Holzstücke vom XV.–XVIII. Jahrhundert, Erster Theil*. Nürnberg. **Hampe**, Theodor (1904), *Nürnberger Ratsverlässe über Kunst und Künstler im Zeitalter der Spätgotik und Renaissance*. Wien/Leipzig. **Hofmann**, Werner (ed.) (1983), *Luther und die Folgen für die Kunst*. München. **Hollstein**, Friedrich W. H. (1954 ff.), *German Engravings, Etchings and Woodcuts 1400–1700*. Amsterdam. **Jahn**, Johannes (ed.) (1972), *Lucas Cranach der Aeltere, 1472–1553, Das gesamte graphische Werk*. München. **Kalkoff**, Paul (1913), *Die Entstehung des Wormser Ediktes*. Leipzig. **Kalkoff**, Paul (1917), *Das Wormser Edikt und die Erlasse des Reichsregiment und der einzelnen Reichsfürsten*. München/Berlin. **Kawerau**, Gustav (1885), *Passional Christi und Antichristi, Lucas Cranachs Holzschnitte mit dem Texte von Melanchthon. Deutsche Drucke älterer Zeit*. 3rd ed. Berlin. **Koepplin**, Dieter/**Falk**, Tilman Falk, (1974), *Lukas Cranach: Gemälde, Zeichnungen, Graphik*. Basel. **Müller**, Gerhard/**Seebass**, Gottfried (eds.), *Andreas Osiander der Aeltere: Gesamtausgabe*. Gütersloh. **Newman Brooks**, Peter (ed.) (1983), *Seven-Headed Luther: Essays in Commemoration of a Quincentenary, 1483–1983*. Oxford, U.K. **Röttinger**, Heinrich (1921), *Beiträge zur Geschichte des sächsischen Holzschnitts*. Straßburg. **Schreyl**, Karl-Heinz/**Freitag-Stadler**, Renate, (eds.) (1976), *Die Welt des Hans Sachs: 400 Holzschnitte des 16. Jahrhunderts*. Nürnberg. **Strauss**, Walter L. (ed.) (1974), *The German Single-Leaf Woodcut 1500–1550*. New York. **Surtz**, Edward/**Hexter**, Jack H. (eds.) (1965), *Thomas More: Complete Works*. New Haven. **Warburg**, Aby (1980), Heidnisch-antike Weissagung in Wort und Bild zu Luthers Zeiten. In: Wuttke, Dieter (ed.), *Aby Warburg: Ausgewählte Schriften und Würdigungen*, 2nd ed. Baden Baden, pp. 244–246.

Luther in
the United States
of America

HARTMUT LEHMANN

Martin Luther's Eventful Career in the New World

The Discovery of Martin Luther in America in the Course of the Nineteenth Century[1]

In 1783, the year that England officially and legally recognized the independence of its thirteen rebellious colonies in North America, the three hundredth birthday of Martin Luther went uncelebrated in America. Not even the small Lutheran congregations in Pennsylvania and South Carolina hosted any special Luther celebrations. One searches in vain in the founding fathers' works for references to Martin Luther. George Washington, Thomas Jefferson, Benjamin Franklin, and their comrades in arms looked to archetypes from ancient Rome and ancient Greece, not sixteenth-century Germany. And when the founding fathers proclaimed the separation of church and state, or stood up for the freedom of religion and belief, they did not make reference to the German Reformer but rather to the English and French Enlightenment thinkers of the eighteenth century.

However, the interest in Martin Luther in the United States was awakened not much later, at the beginning of the nineteenth century. It was initially Unitarians, such as Scottish-born Robert Aitken or English-born Joseph Priestley, who commemorated Luther in their publications in the first decade of the nineteenth century. The *Essay on the Spirit and Influence of the Reformation by Luther* by Charles François Dominique de Villers was published in 1804 in French, was translated into English in 1807, and was much read in America. For all of three aforementioned authors, Luther's achievement was that he overcame the superstition of the Middle Ages and brought freedom to Europe. They further stressed that, in doing so, Luther established the fundamental prerequisites for the Enlightenment.

One generation later, in the 1830s, American Unitarians began to publish their own works about Luther. Thomas Bayley Fox wrote in 1836 that the Reformation had achieved the first effective blow against both the fallacies and the despotism of the old church. In 1839, Hannah Farnham Sawyer Lee published a work entitled *The Life and Times of Martin Luther*, in which she attacked the Catholic Church even more than had Fox. For Fox and Lee, admittedly, a glaring contradiction existed between the ideas propagated by Luther and the concepts promulgated by the supporters of the "Second Great Awakening" and Pietism, which latter was particularly widespread in Pennsylvania. In the view of the Unitarians, therefore, Luther's achievements were not really of a religious or theological nature. Rather, the fight that he had led was much more about moral, political, and ecclesiastical freedoms, even if they had to concede that these freedoms had still not been entirely attained even in their own time.

The Unitarians were one of the smallest American denominations at that time. They enjoyed influence only in the area around Boston, in particular among the intellectuals around Harvard University. A much wider audience was reached by the Evangelicals, who in the course of the "Second Great Awakening" gained members in all the colonies, not least through the many organizations that were founded then to support internal and external missions. The fact that, within only a few decades, Luther became ever more popular in the New World can primarily be credited to the Evangelicals who had discovered Luther at almost the same time as the Unitarians. Already in 1827, a glowingly positive biography of Luther was published in a series put out by the American Sunday School Union. The tenor of this publication, and numerous further treatises about Luther and the Reformation, was fiercely anti-Catholic. Luther was great, they said, because he had led the fight against the Pope. Luther was important because he had exposed the mismanagement and intrigues of the Popes and the Catholic Church. In short, the German Reformer Martin Luther served as a principal witness for those looking for arguments to prevent the immigration of Irish and Italian Catholics into the United States. Luther's contribution as a reformer was, however, reduced to a single point in these arguments—his fight against the Catholic Church. In this matter, the Evangelicals and Unitarians, who otherwise relentlessly opposed each other, agreed.

Starting in the 1830s, a third group spoke out regarding Luther in the United States: the Transcendentalists. The Transcendentalists were followers of a form of Romanticist idealism characterized by religious and humanist tendencies. Ralph Waldo Emerson, who had revered Luther since his childhood, had by far the largest influence. In 1835, Emerson held a lecture about Luther that was printed and widely disseminated shortly thereafter. The gist: Emerson spoke of Luther the prophet, comparable to the prophets of the Old Testament; Luther the universally gifted genius; and Luther, one of the greatest heroes of human history. According to Emerson, Luther was to sixteenth-century Germans what Homer had been to the Greeks,

Moses to the Jews, Alfred to the Anglo-Saxons, and Washington to the Americans. According to Emerson, Luther's unique historical role was that, as a scholar, he had initiated a great spiritual, ecclesiastical, and political revolution based solely on the word (i.e., Scripture). Further, as per Emerson, Luther's legacy belongs to all of humankind. In later years, Emerson compared Luther to Pericles, Caesar, Mirabeau, Daniel Webster, and Goethe. Nearly all followers of Transcendentalism agreed with Emerson's opinion. Theodore Parker did not want to miss a detour to Wittenberg during his trip to Europe, because he hoped to catch a glimpse of Luther's spirit. From the garden of the Augustinian monastery he broke several twigs from a linden tree and some leaves from a rose bush as souvenirs.

Emerson distanced himself from Luther some years later, for example, in a letter to Margaret Fuller in 1843. Another advocate of Transcendentalism, Orestes Augustus Brownson, even converted to Catholicism in 1844 and became one of the fiercest critics of Luther in American Catholicism. However, the influence of the Romanticist school of thought (i.e., the Transcendentalists) cannot be stressed enough. Highly educated authors such as Emerson and Brownson released Luther from his connection to the Protestant denominations and placed him among the great thinkers and leaders of human history. An abridged and translated edition of Luther's *Table Talks* became a best seller in the middle of the nineteenth century. American readers from Charleston and Savannah to New York and Boston enjoyed Luther's extreme mode of expression and his stories, which seemed to offer the readers a glimpse of a decisive phase of the transition from the Dark Ages to modernity.

Since the early nineteenth century, it became commonplace for young Americans to study at a European university for a while; France and Great Britain were strongly preferred, but some also studied in Germany. In 1818, George Bancroft was the first to choose a German university. Bancroft stayed in Göttingen until 1820, and then spent a further year in Berlin. Numerous others followed him, such as Frederic Henry Hedge, a close friend of Emerson's who, years later (in 1852), translated Luther's *Ein feste Burg* into English ("A Mighty Fortress"). Only three of the numerous American theologians who studied in Germany will be named here: Charles Hodge was a Presbyterian who became one of the formative figures of the Princeton Theological Seminary; Henry Boynton Smith studied in Halle and Berlin and became the leading church historian at the Union Theological Seminary in New York; and George Park Fisher studied in Halle and became a church historian at the Yale Divinity School. For the rest of their lives, these scholars remained closely connected to their German teachers and the German historiography of the Reformation. They were in touch with August Tholuck in Halle. They knew Leopold von Ranke's *History of the Reformation in Germany*, which had been translated into English in the mid-1840s. For all American theologians who had studied in Germany in the nineteenth century, for all their lives, Luther remained an idol.

Of the scholars who emigrated to the United States over the course of the nineteenth century, Philip Schaff had the most impressive career. As a young Swiss man he had been awarded a (post-doctoral) habilitation degree in Berlin at the beginning of the 1840s.

Fig. 1 Thomas Circle (after Ernst Rietschel),
Martin Luther Monument, Washington, D. C., 1884

1 For more detailed information, see Lehmann, *American Imagination*, pp. 23–193; id., *Entdeckung Luthers*; id., *Pilgrimage*; id., *Lutherjubiläen*; id., *Luther Statues*.

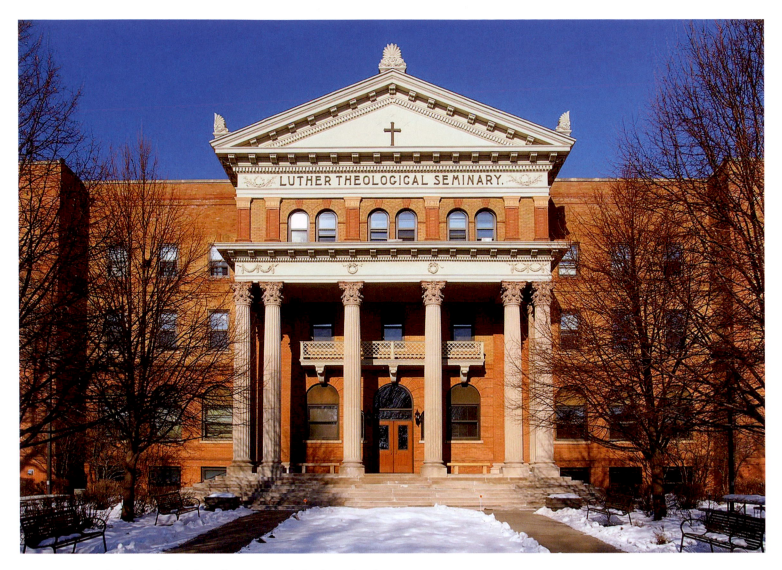

Fig. 2 Bockman Hall at the Luther Seminary (formerly United Church Seminary),
St. Paul, Minnesota, built 1902

After several years at a small college in Pennsylvania, he was appointed to the Union Theological Seminary in New York, where he played a unique role as an intermediary between the German and American intellectual worlds for several decades. Schaff explained the qualities of the American universities to his German friends, and the achievements of German scholarship to his American colleagues. It was always clear to Schaff that Martin Luther was one of those prominent personalities of German history who were worth touting in the New World. According to Schaff in 1847, the Wittenberg reform movement had become a worldwide movement that inflamed the hearts of millions within only a few years. For Schaff, no one person had accomplished more to foster the reign of God on earth than Martin Luther. He believed that Luther's work should be completed in the New World. The last great work that Schaff published in 1888 was a consideration of the Reformation in Germany.

Back to George Bancroft. It was Bancroft, in his monumental history of the United States, who established a direct connection be-

tween the Reformation in Germany and the political developments in the New World. In the first volume of his work, which was published in 1834, Bancroft asserted that the settlement of New England was a direct consequence of the Reformation. Luther was one of the four fathers of the modern world—next to Columbus, Gutenberg, and Calvin. In 1874, in the tenth and final volume of his work, Bancroft, who had served seven years as the American ambassador in Berlin, returned to the topic of Luther. According to Bancroft, the son of a simple miner from Eisleben who had concentrated his studies on St. Paul and St. Augustine, had changed the world. In revealing the fallibility of the Pope, Luther had killed superstition at its very source. Bancroft asserted that Luther stood for the same principles that Thomas Jefferson later championed. John Lothrop Motley, Bancroft's younger and equally famous colleague, who had studied in Göttingen and Berlin between 1831 and 1833, supported the same theses in his books. According to Motley, without Luther, the Reformation never would have been a success, and Protestantism never would have be-

Fig. 3 Tom Torrens, bust of Martin Luther on the campus
of the Pacific Lutheran University, Tacoma, Washington, 1984

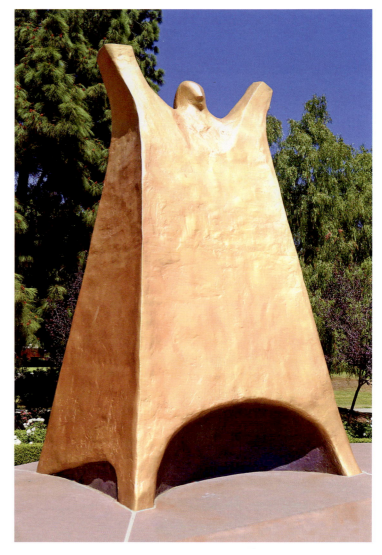

Fig. 4 Sir Bernardus Weber/Jim Gulbranson, so-called Enormous Luther,
a modern sculpture of Martin Luther on the campus of the California
Lutheran University, Thousand Oaks, Ventura County, California, 1964

come a world power. The educated middle class of nineteenth-century America eagerly read Bancroft's and Motley's works.

In 1883, when the four hundredth birthday of Martin Luther came around, it was a matter of course that all American universities and the large Protestant denominations would organize special celebrations. Perhaps the most impressive of these was organized in Boston by the venerable Massachusetts Historical Society on November 10, 1883. Everyone who was anyone was there. The ceremonial address was given by Frederic Henry Hedge, professor of German literature at Harvard, who was then seventy-eight years old. According to Hedge, the "Saxon" Reformer was responsible for the most precious attributes of the commonwealth: civil liberties and national independence. Anglo-Americans owed him a great debt. After Columbus discovered the New World, it was Luther who established the spiritual and political principles with which the New World was developed, Hedge continued. Philip Schaff gave the ceremonial address at the Evangelical Alliance's celebration in New York on

November 13, 1883. Congregationalists, Presbyterians, Methodists, and Episcopalians joined in Schaff's hymn of praise. If Luther had lived in 1776, he certainly would have shed his blood for the American Revolution, a Congregationalist senator from Iowa said. Without Luther in Germany, Washington never would have been possible in America. The Americans owed Luther thanks for the invaluable blessing of civil liberties in a free commonwealth, said a Lutheran pastor from Pennsylvania. Even though American Catholics continued to persist in their criticism of the German Reformer in 1883, two decades after the American Civil War, Luther had reached the height of his renown in the New World.

The Consecutive Dissociation from Martin Luther in America since the End of the Nineteenth Century[2]

For various reasons educated Americans who did not belong to Lutheran synods distanced themselves bit by bit from Luther in the late nineteenth and early twentieth centuries. For one thing, the scholarly performance of the large American universities improved steadily after the Civil War, and ambitious young Americans no longer needed to travel to Europe to get a good education. They could receive an equivalent, in some disciplines even better, education if they went to Harvard, Yale, Princeton, Columbia, the University of Chicago, or the University of Wisconsin. In addition, many of the young Americans who did study in Leipzig, Halle, or Berlin in the decades before the First World War were put off by the growing German nationalism and the nationalist portrayals of Luther that were widespread in Germany after 1883.[3] The Germans claimed Luther's heritage for themselves to such a degree that the Americans asked themselves what they or their history had to do with him anymore.

The founding of the American Society of Church History in 1888 was an expression of the increased self-confidence of American church historians. Just two years later, in 1890, the young society took on an ambitious task: a thirteen-volume characterization of the American denominations, written by leading church historians from the leading divinity schools. The project, which was completed in 1893 after an astonishingly short period of three years, had serious consequences for Luther's position in the New World.

The second volume, for example, which was written by Albert Henry Newman about Baptist churches, included an unfavorable characterization of Luther's historical importance that highlighted his oppression of the Baptists' predecessors. The image of Luther conjured up by Williston Walker in the third volume, which outlined the history of the Congregationalists, was equally critical. Luther was obviously cast in a good light in the fourth volume, written by Henry Eyster Jacobs about the Lutheran churches, and, with some reservations, in the fifth volume, written by J. M. Buckley about the Methodists. In contrast, criticism dominated in the sixth volume, written by Robert Ellis Thompson about the Presbyterians. In the volume about the Reformed churches, penned by E. T. Corwin and Joseph Henry Smith, Geneva and Heidelberg took center stage, not Wittenberg and Eisenach. In his volume about the Catholic Church in America, Thomas O'Gorman ignored Luther completely. The authors of the volumes dedicated to the further, smaller denominations did not think to sing Luther's praises. The bottom line: Luther's special position, which the speakers of 1883 had vaunted, was significantly relativized in the rapidly and widely disseminated multivolume American church history. In the volumes about the individual denominations, their own heroes took center stage, not Luther. Aside from the volume about Catholicism, Luther was still credited only with certain achievements in the early years of the Reformation, but nothing more. At the same time, in this collection of essays Luther seemed to be the sole property of the Lutherans. There was no longer any mention of Luther having positively changed the whole course of human history, or having

Fig. 5 Hans Schuler, Statue of Martin Luther in Baltimore, Maryland, 1936

made a special contribution to the success of the United States, as numerous keynote speakers had stated in 1883.

Shortly thereafter, the American Society of Church History initiated a collection of essays entitled *Heroes of the Reformation*, which took a similar tack. Of course, Henry Eyster Jacobs from the Lutheran Theological Seminary in Philadelphia wrote an extremely positive characterization of Luther for this series. However, in addition to Luther's biography, and to a certain extent on par with him as other heroes of the Reformation, there were equally positive biographies of Melanchthon, Erasmus, Zwingli, Balthasar Hubmaier, Theodor Beza, Thomas Cranmer, and John Knox. Luther seemed to be just one of many reformers, no longer the great and sole pioneer of a new epoch in world history. Ephraim Emerson was especially critical of Luther's achievements in his volume about Erasmus, as was Henry Clay Vedder in his volume about the Baptist and farmer-theologian Hubmaier. All of the volumes sold well. Many advanced to become the standard texts for college and university courses. In the decade before 1914, a multivolume work with the title *Heroes of the Nations* was published in New York and London. For Germany, the editors chose only Bismarck and Frederick the Great, as well as Blücher, but not Luther.

Furthermore, a range of monographs was published before 1914, and the authors of these studies dealt with single episodes of Luther's life extremely critically. For example, James Harvey Robinson, who had studied in Freiburg and Strasbourg and taught modern history at Columbia from 1895 to 1919, acknowledged in his work not only the merits of Leopold von Ranke, who was revered in Protestant circles, but also those of Catholic historian Johannes Janssen. Preserved Smith, a pupil of Robinson's who taught for some years at Cornell, subjected Luther's *Table Talks* to a critical analysis with the help of psychoanalysis. William Walker Rockwell, who had completed his doctorate in Marburg in 1904, produced an intensely documented study of Landgrave Philip of Hesse's bigamy, in which Luther played a less than glorious role.[4] Writing around the same time, John Alfred Faulkner, a Methodist who had studied in Bonn and Leipzig, dealt critically with Luther's relationship with tolerance and his position on the Peasants' War. Other examples could also be named. It is interesting that the historians of the Reformation in Germany at the time never took note of any of these American works that were critical of Luther. In Germany after 1883, it was believed that only Germans were truly able to understand Luther properly. What we see in the period before 1914 can be described as the "re-confessionalization" of Luther, because only the Lutherans still revered him as a church father, and the "re-nationalisation" of Luther, because they more and more considered his legacy to be exclusively theirs. Within a few decades, Luther, for whom a great monument had been erected in Washington, D.C., in 1884, had returned from the New World, back to his home in Wittenberg.

As the American Presbyterian, and Congregationalist, and Reformed churches celebrated Calvin's four hundredth birthday in 1909, the American Lutherans began to prepare the celebration of the four hundredth anniversary of the beginning of the Reformation in 1917. In spring of 1917, however, half a year before the celebration, the United States joined the Allies in the war against imperial Germany. The German navy had ruthlessly ignored the interests of neutral countries and sunk their ships, for example, in 1915, the *Lusitania*, which was sailing under the American flag. At the beginning of 1917, when the German navy command went a step further and proclaimed unrestricted submarine warfare, Washington declared war on the government in Berlin. American Lutherans, who wanted to celebrate Luther in October of 1917, found themselves in a dilemma. How could they stage a big celebration in the United States for their church father Luther, when Germany was simultaneously using Luther's legacy in propaganda against the Allies? Many Lutherans, who had emigrated to America only shortly before 1914 and had not been naturalized, were interned. All Lutherans were suspected of not being loyal citizens. After the United States entered the war, all of them were exposed to widespread xenophobia and forced Anglici-

zation. German-language publications, even German-language church bulletins, were prohibited. The situation was particularly difficult for the Norwegian, Danish, Swedish, and Finnish Lutheran communities in the United States. On the one hand, they did not want to betray their Lutheran faith; on the other, what mattered for them was to emphasize their political allegiance to the United States.

In a common meeting on October 31, 1917, the American Historical Association and the American Society of Church History commemorated the beginning of the Reformation in 1517. The speaker was the most renowned American scholar of the Reformation, Preserved Smith from Cornell University, who made an attempt to explain the Reformation from a historical perspective. Today one would describe his method as an attempt at a thorough historical contextualization. There was no trace of hero worship in his statements, and he avoided the then political situation in equal measure. The famous Congregationalist pastor Frank Wakeley Gunsaulus from the University of Chicago chose a different route. He used Luther to polemicize against Germany's war propaganda. According to Gunsaulus, together with Kant, Lessing, Goethe, Schiller, Bach, Mendelssohn, Beethoven, and Steuben, Luther belonged to the "good" Germany, which was in a relentless war against the Prussian autocracy, Prussian militarism, Prussian despotism, and the Prussian imperial cult. The more the German side in 1917 evoked Luther's spirit of struggle in order to overcome the increasing war weariness, the more Luther came under the suspicion that German militarism might in fact be a legacy of the Reformation.

The American church historians naturally also spoke up in 1917. As in 1883, their journals produced special editions. In contrast to 1883, they did not organize any celebrations. The manner in which they commemorated Luther's life and work is very interesting. There was no mention any more of what Luther had achieved for the progress of humankind. Luther was thereby stripped of all the cultural and political achievements that American scholars had praised so highly in 1883. Only his religious position remained: the person who had feared desperately for his salvation and sought divine grace. What remained, was Luther as *homo religiosus*. In defiance of anti-German propaganda, the representatives of all the Protestant denominations could agree with this notion. After 1918, it was hoped that this notion could build a bridge to those German Reformation historians who had also seen a *homo religiosus* in Luther in the course of the Luther renaissance. It should be mentioned, for the sake of comprehensiveness, that the American Catholics used the opportunity of the Reformation anniversary to declare emphatically they had known all along that Luther's legacy would have a malignant effect on German history. In this they agreed with Catholic German Luther critics such as Heinrich Denifle and Hartmann Grisar.

In the course of the National Socialist seizure of power, the so-called German Christians took over the leadership in many German

2 For more in-depth information, see Lehmann, *American Imagination*, pp. 195–301; id., *Lutherjubiläen*; id., *Welthistorische Wirkungen*. **3** See the contributions by Dorothea Wendebourg, Stefan Laube and Jan Scheunemann to this volume. **4** See also the contribution by Franziska Kuschel to this volume.

Fig. 6
Stain glass window showing Martin
Luther, St. Matthew's Lutheran Church,
Charleston, South Carolina

territorial church administrations in 1933 and 1934. For them, Luther was the congenial predecessor of Adolf Hitler. They never tired of emphasizing that modern German history had led from the Reformation in the sixteenth century via the rise of Prussia in the seventeenth and eighteenth centuries to German unification in 1870/71, and, finally, to the Third Reich. Hitler and many of his followers also emphatically referenced Luther, in particular the heinous anti-Semitic works that he wrote later in life. Shortly after *Kristallnacht* in November 1938, the German Christians did not miss the chance to publish a large edition of the central passages of Luther's defamatory publication *On the Jews and Their Lies.* In light of the increasing discrimination and rabble-rousing, as well as the frequent threat of physical violence, the only choice remaining for German Jews if they had the chance, was to emigrate. Those who could do so, made their way to the United States. Emigrants such as Paul Tillich and Thomas Mann were responsible for making the violent excesses of the National Socialists known to a wider public in the United States. Naturally, Luther, who had been understood as a *homo religiosus* since 1917, was once again pulled into the swirl of political propaganda. Two publications caused a furor in Germany already during the Second World War, but in particular after 1945. The first, from 1941, was *From Luther to Hitler: The History of Fascist-Nazi Political Philosophy,* by the political scientist William Montgomery McGovern of Northwestern University. The other, *Martin Luther: Hitler's Spiritual Ancestor,* was published in 1945 by Peter F. Wiener, a German emigrant. Both authors proposed the same thesis. Whereas Frank Wakeley Gunsaulus had argued in 1917 that it was important to differentiate between a "good" and a "bad" Germany—and that Luther belonged to the "good Germans"—McGovern and Wiener presented a diametrically opposed thesis. For them, the disastrous development of German politics—characterized by expansionism, militarism, and enthusiasm for war—ran from Luther directly to Hitler, in particular from Luther's anti-Semitism to Hitler's extermination of the Jews.

The full extent of the National Socialists' extermination of the Jews only became known in the United States after 1945. As a result, Christians and Jews alike pondered the question, how and how much Luther's works were connected to the Holocaust. American Lutherans were particularly challenged to find an answer to this question. In 1983, for example, church historian Mark U. Edwards, who taught at Harvard, critically inquired about the connection between Martin Luther and National Socialism. The Evangelical Lutheran Church in America (ELCA) appealed to the Jewish community in 1994 with a declaration in which they decidedly distanced themselves from Luther's hate-filled anti-Semitic writings. They painfully acknowledged that modern anti-Semites had exploited Luther's works to sow more hate. They themselves were committed to treating the Jewish community with love and respect. They therefore prayed for increased cooperation and understanding between Jews and Christians. A few years later, in 1998, the ELCA released guidelines for Lutheran-Jewish talks, in which they again expressed the same thoughts. Just a few years ago, a professorship for Holocaust Studies was established at one of the leading Lutheran universities, the Pacific Lutheran University in Tacoma, arguing that young Lutherans should know what happened in the Holocaust.

At the end of the twentieth and the beginning of the twenty-first century, Lutherans belong to the traditional denominations in America, along with Presbyterians, Congregationalists, and Episcopalians. They do not play a dominant role in the religious life of the country. This is not because American Lutherans have been divided over central theological questions since the nineteenth century and have time and again carried out these disputes in public. A much more decisive factor is that in the last century other religious movements grew significantly while the traditional denominations stagnated. Baptists and Pentecostals, i.e., religious movements that Luther had opposed with all his might, have been particularly dynamic in the twentieth century. Due to immigration from Central and South America, also the Catholic Church has grown considerably in the United States. Therefore, it is the descendants of Luther's adversaries that are shaping the religious life of the New World at the beginning of the twenty-first century. In 1883, the members of the various Protestant denominations sang Luther's praises. Today, maintaining Luther's legacy is the task of only the Lutherans, much as it was in the eighteenth and early nineteenth centuries. Thus, it would seem that Luther's career in the New World is right back where it started.

BIBLIOGRAPHY

Lehmann, Hartmut (1983), Die Entdeckung Luthers im Amerika des frühen 19. Jahrhunderts. In: Bernd Moeller (ed.), *Luther in der Neuzeit.* Gütersloh, pp. 151–159. **Lehmann,** Hartmut (1988), *Martin Luther in the American Imagination.* München. **Lehmann,** Hartmut (2012), "A Pilgrimage to Wittenberg, the So-Called Protestant Mecca." Anmerkungen zum amerikanischen Deutschland-Tourismus im 19. Jahrhundert. In: id., *Luthergedächtnis 1817 bis 2017.* Göttingen, pp. 44–58. **Lehmann,** Hartmut (2012), Die Lutherjubiläen 1883 und 1917 in Amerika. In: id., *Luthergedächtnis 1817 bis 2017.* Göttingen, pp. 78–93. **Lehmann,** Hartmut (2012), The Luther Statues in Washington, D.C., and Baltimore. In: id., *Luthergedächtnis 1817 bis 2017.* Göttingen, pp. 94–109. **Lehmann,** Hartmut (2012), Luthers welthistorische Wirkung gezeigt am Beispiel der USA und Australiens im ausgehenden 19. und frühen 20. Jahrhundert. In: id., *Luthergedächtnis 1817 bis 2017.* Göttingen, pp. 110–125.

MARY JANE HAEMIG

Luther and the Reformation in America. Minnesota, 1917 as Case Study

American Protestants are, whether they know it or not, heirs of the Wittenberg Reformation led by Martin Luther. The first Europeans to arrive in North America considered Luther among their spiritual forefathers. The Pilgrims of Massachusetts were strict Calvinists who counted Luther and his Reformation in their lineage, though they saw other reformers as more important. Jamestown settlers were adherents of the Church of England, another entity influenced by Luther's reforming ideas. Lutherans began arriving in North America in the 1620s and 1630s.

Luther's Reformation, born and spread in sixteenth-century Germany, has had global consequences. Though known for many things—its rejection of papal claims to authority and power, its claim that every Christian could understand and interpret the Bible, its elevation of ordinary pursuits as sacred and not inferior to "clerical" callings—the Reformation had, at its heart, an insight that drove all else: the belief that God is merciful and grants salvation to humans, not because of anything a human does, intends, says, or thinks, but because God wants to be merciful, God wants to reconcile humans to himself in Jesus Christ, and God deeply desires a relationship with humans. The death and resurrection of Jesus Christ accomplish all that is necessary for human salvation and reconciliation to God. Faith is not primarily about human intentions or acts—ritualistic or otherwise—designed to gain God's favor but rather about trust in God's promise of mercy grounded on God's work in Christ for us. Faith (itself a gift of God) in that promise brings forgiveness of sin, life, and salvation. Luther's insight resulted, by the end of the sixteenth century, in the development of churches independent of the Roman papal hierarchy. Lutheran churches arose in Germany and Scandinavia and were scattered in other parts of Europe. Other reformers, inspired at least in part by Luther yet understanding his insights in different ways and taking them in different directions, formed other churches independent of Rome, such as the Church of England, the Reformed churches of the Netherlands, France, Switzerland, and Germany, and the Presbyterian churches of England and Scotland. Even some of the re-

forms in the Roman Catholic Church in that era (for example the Council of Trent) can be attributed to the challenges posed by Luther and the Reformation.

The five-hundredth anniversary of the Protestant Reformation offers an opportunity to consider the reforming ideas of Luther and the Wittenberg Reformation and their manifold impacts. The anniversary also leads us to consider how this occasion was observed and celebrated in the past. This essay will consider briefly the history of Lutherans in North America and then focus on the four-hundredth anniversary of the Reformation in 1917.

Lutherans in the United States[1]

Lutherans first entered North America in the seventeenth century. Swedes and Finns came to the colony of New Sweden (later Delaware) and Lutherans were present in the Dutch colony of New Amsterdam (later New York) in the 1620s. In the 1730s refugees from Salzburg came to Georgia. Lutherans came to what are now the U.S. Virgin Islands, then a Danish colony in the Caribbean, in the 1660s. The most significant Lutheran presence in the colonial period was that of Germans in Pennsylvania. Thousands immigrated, beginning in the 1630s and 1640s; some stayed in Pennsylvania while others followed the mountain valleys into Virginia and North Carolina. Though the Swedish and Dutch churches sent some pastors to North America, pastors were few and congregations scattered. The "father" of the Lutheran church on American soil was Heinrich Melchior Mühlenberg.[2] Educated at Göttingen and Halle, Germany, Mühlenberg accepted a call to serve the Lutherans of Pennsylvania. Arriving in 1742, he never returned to Europe. Mühlenberg traveled and preached throughout colonial America, gathered Lutheran congregations, and organized the first Lutheran synod in North America, the "Pennsylvania Ministerium" (1748). German Lutheran immigrants began arriving in Halifax, Nova Scotia, in 1750. Lutherans loyal to the English crown entered Canada from New York at the time of the American War of Independence.

After the War of Independence (1775–87), Lutheran immigration virtually ceased and a distinct Lutheran theological identity was almost lost. Increasingly, Lutherans adopted practices employed by Reformed and Methodist groups, notably practices associated with revivals. Lutherans sought to make common cause with other Christians to fight the perceived dangers of rationalism. In 1820 the General Synod was formed, bringing together most Lutheran synods. The Synod founded Gettysburg Seminary in 1825. Samuel Simon Schmucker, professor at Gettysburg Seminary, was the leader of the "American Lutherans" who advocated giving up distinctive Lutheran beliefs and adopting different practices for the sake of becoming more like other American Protestant Christians. Schmucker published an *American Recension of the Augsburg Confession* (1855) in which he asserted the *Augsburg Confession* of 1530, a key defining document for Lutherans, had five errors. Schmucker's efforts caused a reaction and, fueled also by a new focus on the Lutheran Confessional writings in Europe, many Lutherans sought to recover what was distinctly Lutheran. By the 1850s the General Synod contained two parties, the "American Lutheran" party and the "Confessional" party. Southern synods left the General Synod at the time of the Civil War (1861–65). Northern synods of a confessional bent formed the General Council in 1866 and founded a seminary at Philadelphia. In 1918 these three bodies merged to form the United Lutheran Church in America (ULCA).

A second wave of immigration, from about 1830 to World War I, brought Lutherans from Scandinavia and Germany primarily to the Upper Mississippi River valley, the Northern Great Plains, and the Pacific Northwest. Some European institutions (e.g., the mission seminaries in Germany and Norway), sent pastors to tend the immigrants; some groups relied at least in part on lay preachers. These immigrants founded congregations and formed synods generally along language lines. These synods founded colleges (e.g., St. Olaf College, Wartburg College, Gustavus Adolphus College) and seminaries (e.g., Luther Seminary and Wartburg Seminary). By the end of the nineteenth century, Swedes, Germans, Norwegians, Danes, Finns, and Slovaks all had formed at least one language-specific synod. Generally on friendly terms with one another yet differing in structure and theological emphases, these synods began to merge in the early twentieth century. The *National Lutheran Commission for Soldiers' and Sailors' Welfare*, formed in 1917, became an important means for inter-synodical cooperation. The *National Lutheran Council* (1918) continued such cooperation in foreign relief efforts and domestic missions. A second surge of synodical mergers took place in the 1960s when synods historically associated with Germans, Norwegians, and Danes merged to form the *American Lutheran Church* (ALC); the ULCA merged with synods historically associated with Swedes, Finns, Slovaks, Icelanders, and Danes to form the *Lutheran Church in America* (LCA). Women were first ordained in the ALC and LCA in 1970. The ALC and the LCA merged with the *Association of Evangelical Lutheran Churches* (AELC) in 1988 to form the *Evangelical Lutheran Church in America* (ELCA). Disputes within the ELCA over ecumenism (1999) and sexuality (2009) resulted in the formation of two centrist

Lutheran denominations, the *Lutheran Congregations in Mission for Christ* (LCMC) in 2001 and the *North American Lutheran Church* (2010).

The *Lutheran Church–Missouri Synod* (LCMS) was founded by Saxons who, beginning in 1835, fled the forced union of Lutheran and Reformed churches in Saxony. Led most influentially by Carl Ferdinand Wilhelm Walther, the LCMS has been marked by congregational autonomy and strict loyalty to the Lutheran Confessional writings. Disputes with other Lutheran synods kept the LCMS from merging with those synods. In the 1970s, it split over the use of historical-critical methods for understanding the Bible; congregations leaving the LCMS formed the *Association of Evangelical Lutheran Churches* (AELC) in 1976. Over twenty other small Lutheran bodies (e.g., the *Wisconsin Evangelical Lutheran Synod*), also exist in North America.

Lutheran religious practice has traditionally been marked by sermon, sacraments (baptism and the Lord's Supper), catechism, Bible study, and hymn singing. Confirmation instruction, a basic catechesis in the Lutheran understanding of the Christian faith, has been an important part of Lutheran lives.

The first sixty years of the twentieth century were marked by a growth in numbers of members and congregations and by steady growth in church-related institutions. Publishing houses produced hymnals, devotional texts, popular and theological works, as well as music for congregational use. More recently Lutheran numbers have stagnated or fallen. Exact figures are difficult to determine as not all who claim to be Lutheran maintain formal membership ties to a Lutheran church. Although the official statistics of the churches list about seven million Lutherans in America, surveys and estimates show that thirteen to fourteen million Americans consider themselves Lutheran. Prior to World War I, the Lutheran population was primarily rural. Since the 1920s, urbanization has accelerated; many heavily Lutheran rural areas in the Great Plains and Midwest have suffered severe population declines.

Lutheran strength in and influence on American culture varies by region. Lutherans are virtually absent from the New England states. Lutherans are stronger in the Mid-Atlantic states (particularly Pennsylvania and New York), founding a number of colleges and seminaries there. Lutherans in the South are scattered, located mainly in the Appalachian valleys of Western Virginia, North Carolina, and South Carolina, and in the Texas hill country. Lutherans have been strongest in the upper Midwest. Culturally their influence was nearly pervasive there during the twentieth century. Lutheran colleges educated large numbers of students; Lutheran contributions to the arts, particularly music, were significant. Though Montana and Nebraska have notable Lutheran populations, the Great Plains and intermountain West are dominated by other groups. Lutherans have been present on the West Coast—particularly in Washington State and in Southern California—since the late nineteenth century. Post–World War II population movements aided

---

1 The most recent history of Lutherans on the North American continent is Granquist, *Lutherans*. **2** See the essay of Hermann Wellenreuther in this volume.

Fig. 1 Statue of Martin Luther on the campus of the Wartburg Theological Seminary,
Dubuque, Iowa, dedicated on August 1, 1921 (copy after Ernst Rietschel)

modest Lutheran growth on the West Coast. Lutherans in Canada are located in the major cities, in southwestern Ontario, in the prairie provinces, and in pockets elsewhere.

Lutherans founded numerous hospitals, schools, colleges, and other institutions in both the United States and Canada (fig. 1). Many of these continue to be church related, while others have cut church ties. The *Lutheran Service Association* represents over three hundred Lutheran health and human services organizations. Together these organizations serve over six million people annually and compose one of the largest service providers in the United States. The impact of Lutheran colleges and universities is ongoing. Lutheran organizations own more than thirty-five colleges and universities. As highly educated clergy continue to be important for Lutherans, more than twelve Lutheran seminaries exist, run by various Lutheran bodies. Congregations and church-related entities own many child-care facilities and schools. Though no Lutheran has been President of the United States, Lutherans have served as senators, representatives, state governors, and in many other positions. Lutheran pastor Frederick Augustus Muhlenberg of Pennsylvania was the first Speaker of the United States House of Representatives.

Lutherans, immigrating primarily from northern continental Europe, differed in both theology and culture from the Calvinists and Anglo-Saxons who set the cultural and religious tone of much of North America. Key questions for North American Lutherans have concerned how they can function in this religious-cultural setting, that is, how they can be both Lutheran and American. In addition, Lutherans faced the issue of how Lutherans speaking different languages and coming from different varieties of Lutheranism could work together. Living in North America with its variety of Christian groups, Lutherans have seen their relationships with other Christians as both threat and opportunity—threat because such relationships could dilute distinctive Lutheran beliefs, and opportunity because they provide occasion to witness to unity in Christ. In the twentieth century, Lutheran participation in ecumenical and interfaith initiatives has varied. Some joined the *World Council of Churches* (WCC) when it was organized in 1948 and the *National Council of Churches* (NCC) in 1950, and some like the LCMS have avoided ecumenical involvement.

Celebrations of the Reformation Quadricentennial in 1917

Lutherans arrived in North America beginning in the 1600s but consciousness of Luther and the reformations he inspired arose in North America primarily after 1800. In the first half of the 1800s, Luther was admired by diverse religious groups for a variety of reasons. While Unitarians saw in Luther a forerunner of the Enlightenment and the champion of personal liberty and other values dear to Americans, American-style evangelicals saw a reformer who sought to return to the truths of the early church and a champion of the Bible, and all saw in him their anti–Roman Catholic sentiments affirmed.[3] The four-hundredth anniversary of Luther's birth in 1883 was occasion for considerable celebration. A great number of speeches and

publications—as well as the placement of a statue of Martin Luther in Washington, D. C.—attest to the high esteem in which Luther was held. Luther was seen as a heroic man, attacking papal corruption and medieval superstition, defending liberty, and fighting for religious freedom, a true forerunner of the modern world. His German heritage was viewed positively, as embodying qualities of truthfulness, loyalty, simplicity, and fearless faith.[4]

Some nineteenth-century emphases were reaffirmed in 1917. The four-hundredth anniversary of the Reformation came at a time when the United States was at war with Germany. Compared to 1883, much less was written about Luther and fewer celebrations were held. Still, a variety of American Christians honored Luther. Union Theological Seminary, New York City, sponsored a Luther celebration in fall 1917 at which the church historian William Walker Rockwell praised Luther's teaching of the priesthood of all believers as a democratic concept. Arthur Cushman McGiffert, president of Union Seminary, praised Luther's conduct in the fight against Rome. A Congregationalist, F. W. Gunsaulus, at the University of Chicago praised Luther's translation of the Bible as his defining moment. Even Baptists praised Luther as a theologian of the Bible. A number of scholarly and popular articles and books about Luther were published in 1917. American Roman Catholic publications claimed they had always known that nothing good could be expected from Luther and Germany.[5]

At the congregational level, many Christian traditions honored Luther and the Reformation anniversary. In Duluth, Minnesota, for example, many congregations—not only Lutheran—touched on Reformation themes: The Minister of the First Baptist Church of Duluth, Edward Sayles, preached on Martin Luther on Sunday evening. At Glen Avon Presbyterian Church, the topics for the morning and evening services were "The Reformation Anniversary" and "Luther's Window into Heaven."[6] Even at First Unitarian Church, the minister's subject was "Martin Luther and His Message to Us."[6] In Minneapolis, the morning sermon at Plymouth Congregational Church on October 28, 1917, was "Luther the Liberator," at St. Mark's Episcopal Church "Luther the Great Reformer" was the subject and at Westminster Presbyterian Church, "Martin Luther: the Man and his work."[7]

Lutherans had begun in 1909 to plan Reformation anniversary celebrations.[8] Lutherans sought to lift up the particular theological insights of the Reformation. The New York Committee for the Reformation Quadricentennial used the slogan, "Education, Information, and Transformation."[9] Numerous efforts were made to educate Lutherans about Luther and the Reformation and to connect Reformation insights to contemporary challenges. Against the tide of much of Social Gospel Protestantism, which saw benevolent good works as the core of the faith, Lutherans emphasized individual salvation by grace through faith alone.

---

3 Lehmann, *Entdeckung*. 4 Id., *Impact*. 5 Id., *Lutherjubiläen*. 6 *Duluth Herald*, October 27, 1917, p. 5. 7 *Minneapolis Tribune*, Saturday, October 27, 1917. p. 20. 8 Lehmann, *Lutherjubiläen*, p. 86. 9 Nytroe, *Reformation*, p. 63.

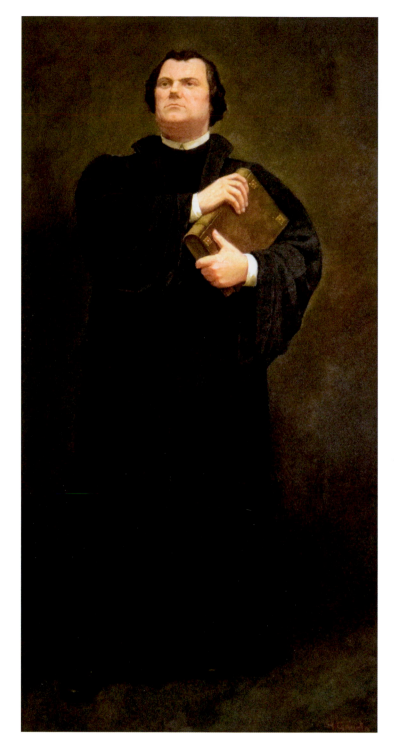

Fig. 2 Herbjørn Nilson Gaustå, Martin Luther, 1912.
The Norwegian-American artist reflects the way
of thinking of Lutheran immigrants.

In April 1917 the United States entered World War I and was at war with Germany. German Americans were subject to intimidation and harassment; institutions associated with German culture were forced to close or change their names; the teaching and speaking of German was discouraged. For many Americans, Scandinavians were indistinguishable from Germans and so were subject to similar treatment.[10] Lutherans did not have the luxury of focusing solely on theological insights or on claims concerning the beneficial results of the Reformation for society and culture. In response to the new situation, they de-emphasized the Reformation's geographic location and, while continuing to emphasize theological insights, also emphasized the Reformation's link to the development of democracy and to the civil liberties embodied in the United States' constitution. The Reformation was seen as a source of the American Revolution, of American liberties, and of American values.[11] Commenting on Reformation celebrations on the East Coast, DeSales University's Sarah Nytroe has noted: "celebrating the past became an opportunity to remind not only Lutherans but all Americans that the very democratic ideals they fought for in World War I were firmly rooted in the person of Martin Luther and the spirit of the Reformation. In their addresses and sermons to congregants during the Quadricentennial year, Lutheran pastors also crafted an historical link between the work of Luther in the Reformation and the civil and political liberties nourished in the twentieth century."[12]

The same emphases were seen in Minnesota. In 1917 Lutherans, though a large part of Minnesota's population, were still regarded as immigrants. Many lived and worshipped in the languages of Northern Europe—German, Norwegian, Swedish, Danish, and Finnish. A large number were German Americans, immigrants from or descendants of immigrants from the country with which America was at war. Reformation anniversary celebrations used the Reformation and Luther to support American values generally and American purposes in World War I.

Though the Reformation has often been celebrated on or around October 31 (the date on which Luther's Ninety-Five Theses were posted in Wittenberg), Reformation anniversary celebrations took place at various times during 1917. The Norwegian Lutheran Church held a Reformation Festival at the Minnesota State Fairgrounds on September 30, 1917, with about three thousand present (fig. 2).[13] Sunday services, particularly those on October 28, 1917, the closest Sunday to Reformation Day, honored the Reformation. Community celebrations were held in many places. In St. Paul, two "Joint Jubilee Services"—one in English and one in German—were held on Sunday October 28, 1917. More than fifteen thousand attended.[14] Another "Joint Lutheran Celebration" was held on Sunday, November 11, 1917.[15] This celebration, in English, began with the singing of *Onward, Christian Soldiers* and featured anthems by Mozart, Haydn, and Handel sung by a jubilee chorus, as well as two addresses by prominent Lutheran figures. Luther's hymn *A Mighty Fortress Is Our God* was sung. A "Reformation Festival" under the auspices of the Minneapolis Lutheran Young People was held at the Minneapolis Auditorium on Monday evening, October 29, 1917. A new cantata, *The City of God*, was sung by a chorus of five hundred.[16] The program included two addresses and several hymns.

Smaller communities too had celebrations. A program from a Reformation celebration in Waseca County, Minnesota, gives some insight into celebrations in small towns and rural areas. Dated September 16, 1917, it is headed in German, "Program for the celebration of the four hundredth anniversary of the Lutheran Church Reformation. Sponsored by the congregations in Waseca and neighboring counties."[17] A morning program in German was followed by an afternoon program in English. Both featured a brass band, four hymns, recitation of the Apostles' Creed, prayers, a massed choir and a children's choir, a sermon, and a thank offering. The only hymn used in both celebrations was Luther's *A Mighty Fortress*.

Sermon titles and newspaper reports show that theological themes were very important in these celebrations. Positive descriptions of how Luther and the Reformation had influenced culture were also common. At the festival service in Minneapolis, the two addresses were titled "Luther and the Reformation" and "Justification by Faith." A celebration at Gustavus Adolphus College[18] included an address on the "Influence of the Reformation on the Educational and Social Life of the World." These illustrate typical theological and historical emphases of Reformation celebrations.

The 1917 celebrations also sought to show that Luther and his Reformation initiated, upheld, or inspired values dear to Americans. A report from Red Wing, Minnesota, illustrates the juxtaposition of these contextual concerns and more traditional theological emphases. Under the headline "Jubilee Services at St. John's: German Lutheran Church to Observe Anniversary of Reformation Next Sunday," the Red Wing Daily Republican[19] reported the subject of the morning sermon, "That the Reformation has brought to the world real democracy and that all democratic governments owe their existence to Martin Luther and that the Church of the Reformation is the real church of every democratic government" (delivered in German), and the evening sermon (in English), "What the Bible has done for Luther and what Luther has done for the Bible."

It was quite common for Lutherans to portray Martin Luther as the champion of liberty and democracy. In "Lutheran Churches of City Pay Honor to Luther's Memory" on October 30, 1916 (before the United States entered World War I), the Minneapolis Morning Tribune[20] reported that many Lutheran churches observed Reformation Sunday and described Luther's work under the subheading "Began Personal Liberty." It related that Dr. A. F. Elmquist told his congregation at St. John's English Lutheran Church that "Luther's declaration marked the beginning not only of personal religious liberty but of political liberty," and, "If it had not been for the Reformation we would not be enjoying many of our present political liberties." Such sentiments were magnified after the United States entered World War I. Dr. Frank Nelson, speaking at the large celebration of the Reformation anniversary at the Minneapolis Auditorium, called Luther "an advocate of liberty and freedom within the realm of gov-

ernment. He believed that all authority is vested in the people having the right to say under what form of government they are to live. […] It is the doctrine of individual liberty that made Plymouth Rock historic on American soil."[21]

Today scholars understand that Luther's concept of Christian liberty was not primarily individualistic or political, but rather was a different sort of freedom in the sight of God and humans, a freedom from fear of God's condemnation and a freedom for service to others. Nor was Luther an advocate of political democracy. Democracy, as Americans know it, was unknown in Luther's time. Scholars would agree, however, that some emphases of the Reformation were among the developments in the Western world that led to democracy and an emphasis on individual freedoms.

Reformation celebrations in late October/early November 1917 took place at a time when civil authorities particularly encouraged patriotic aspects of religion. President Wilson declared Sunday, October 28, 1917, as a "day of supplication and prayer […] to the end that the cause for which we give our lives and treasure may triumph and our efforts be blessed with high achievement."[22] In this context, it is hardly surprising that Luther was not only identified with the causes of personal and political liberty, but was also directly identified with the cause for which Americans believed they were fighting—to make the world safe for democracy. For many who celebrated, Luther was removed from Germany and stood on the American side.

The Red Wing Daily Republican reported on special services to celebrate the four hundredth anniversary: "In a most inspiring and patriotic Reformation address at Trinity Lutheran Church last evening […] Dr. D. G. Ristad declared that Lutherans who had pro-German sentiments, were opposing the teachings of Dr. Martin Luther, the great reformer. […] In his remarks, the Ladies' Seminary president called attention to the great world war of the present day and said that the fight to make "The World Safe for Democracy" was the basic principle on which Martin Luther waged his battles against the Roman government just four hundred years ago."[23]

Professor William Stearns Davis of the University of Minnesota, speaking at a Reformation festival at Hope Lutheran Church, Minneapolis, declared "Martin Luther never would have tolerated the war Germany now is waging." His remarks removed Luther from Ger-

10 Granquist, *Lutherans*, p. 225. **11** Nytroe, *Reformation*. **12** Nytroe, *Reformation*, p. 74. **13** *Lutheran Church Herald*, vol. 1/17, October 26, 1917, p. 236. **14** *St. Paul Pioneer Press*, October 29, 1917, p. 3. **15** Program in Luther Seminary archives, O. M. Norlie Collection. **16** *Minneapolis Morning Tribune*, October 14, 1917, p. B11. **17** Programm der Feier des Vierhundert Jaehrigen Jubilaeums der luth. Kirchenreformation. Veranstaltet von den Gemeinden in Waseca County und den angrenzenden Counties. September 16, 1917. Minnesota History Museum, BR 327. P76 1917. **18** *St. Paul Pioneer Press*, Sunday, November 4, 1917, p. 11. **19** *Red Wing Daily Republican*, October 26, 1917, p. 4. **20** *Minneapolis Morning Tribune*, October 30, 1916, p. 6. **21** *Minneapolis Morning Tribune*, Tuesday, October 30, 1917, p. 4. **22** Benedict, *History*, p. 386. **23** *Red Wing Daily Republican*, Monday, October 29, 1917, p. 2.

many, calling Luther "one of the greatest men in the world's history" and claiming "Luther was too great a man to belong only to one nation. He belongs to the whole world and it is as an international personality that we now commemorate his memory."[24]

Lutherans used these celebrations to emphasize their own loyalty to America. The Minneapolis Morning Tribune,[25] reporting on the large celebration of the Reformation anniversary at the Minneapolis Auditorium attended by more than eight thousand, spent the first four of its six paragraphs on the patriotic sentiments expressed by a main speaker. Under the headline: "Lutherans' loyalty is Reaffirmed at Quadri-Centennial: Minnesota College President Declares Church Stands United Back of Wilson," the newspaper reported that Dr. Frank Nelson said, "The Lutheran church is an American church, standing unitedly and loyally back of our President—Woodrow Wilson—in the present world conflict." Nelson boldly claimed: "Lutheranism is synonymous with patriotism. [...] The history of this church is one of loyalty to government and devotion to the principles of freedom and justice. It believes in education, liberty and freedom of conscience."

He continued, asserting that Lutherans were "by the side of George Washington in the Revolutionary war" and "supported Lincoln during the Civil War," and, "Today thousands of young Lutherans from every section of our country are following the flag of the republic, ready and willing to die for the principles of democracy and freedom of thought, the very principles upon which Martin Luther began to build his great work 400 years ago." Other programmatic elements affirmed the same emphases. The program concluded with the hymn *God Bless Our Native Land!*

Lutherans (and Protestants generally) used the 1917 Reformation celebrations to talk about key theological themes. They also used these themes to connect with their American context and to declare and prove their loyalty to America. Martin Luther became not only the great reformer of the church but also the great champion of individual liberty and political democracy, and Lutherans the loyal citizens fighting for American values. While efforts to reshape Luther into a supporter of American democracy and war aims seem questionable today, those efforts do raise questions about attempts to make Luther and the Reformation into eager supporters of anything current in our culture as well as questions about how our culture today shapes our view of Luther and the Reformation.

Lutherans and other heirs of Luther today face many of the same challenges that their ancestors faced. What continued relevance do Luther's insights have? How can traditions formed in sixteenth-century Europe find continuity and creativity in North America? How will the five hundredth anniversary of the Reformation reflect and shape our images of Luther and the Reformation?

BIBLIOGRAPHY

Benedict, Bertram (1919), *A History of the Great War*. Vol. 1. New York. **Granquist**, Mark (2015), *Lutherans in America: A New History*. Minneapolis. **Lehmann**, Hartmut (2012), Die Entdeckung Luthers im Amerika des frühen 19. Jahrhunderts. In: id. (ed.), *Luthergedächtnis 1817 bis 2017*. Göttingen, pp. 35–43. **Lehmann**, Hartmut (2012), Die Lutherjubiläen 1883 und 1917 in Amerika. In: id. (ed.), *Luthergedächtnis 1817 bis 2017*. Göttingen, pp. 78–93. **Lehmann**, Hartmut (2014), Luther's Impact on the United States and Australia at the Turn of the Twentieth Century. In: *Lutheran Quarterly*, vol. 28 (Spring 2014), pp. 49–69. **Nytroe**, Sarah (2012), The American Reformation Quadricentennial, 1917. In: *Lutheran Quarterly*, vol. 16 (Spring 2012), pp. 57–82.

---

24 *Minneapolis Morning Tribune*, Monday, November 5, 1917. **25** *Minneapolis Morning Tribune*, Tuesday, October 30, 1917, p. 4.

PROTESTANTS OVERSEAS

In the 17th and 18th centuries, many Protestants emigrated to America. New Protestant groups emerged in the wake of revivalist movements succeeding each other. Not all Protestants in the United States are organized in Church associations. The large groups of non-denominational Christians are organized locally and independently of one another, similar to the Churches of Christ and Disciples of Christ.

The Southern Baptist Convention in the United States is the largest Protestant group. In contrast to the smaller American Baptist Churches USA (ABCUSA), they do not allow the ordination of women. The United Methodist Church has a strong Church hierarchy. The Evangelical Lutheran Church in America is organized similarly. Its more conservative counterpart is the Lutheran Church–Missouri Synod.

THE LARGEST PROTESTANT GROUPS, DISTRIBUTION IN THE UNITED STATES ACCORDING TO COUNTIES, IN 2010

- Southern Baptist Church in the United States
- United Methodist Church
- Evangelical Lutheran Church in America
- Non-denominational Christians
- Lutheran Church–Missouri Synod
- Christian Churches and Churches of Christ
- American Baptist Churches USA
- Others

Alaska

310 miles

Hawaii

155 miles

310 miles

Seattle · Portland · Minneapolis · Buffalo · Detroit · Chicago · New York · Salt Lake City · Cleveland · Denver · Cincinnati · San Francisco · Washington, D.C. · Las Vegas · Oklahoma City · Memphis · Los Angeles · Phoenix · Atlanta · Houston · Orlando · New Orleans · Miami

PROTESTANT MIGRATION TO THE UNITED STATES
from 1620 to the middle of the 18th century

1638 Lutherans
1656 Quakers
1683 Mennonites
1607 Anglicans
1735 Moravian Brethren
1727 Amish
1633 Reformists
1734 Lutherans
1620 Puritans (Pilgrim Fathers)
1683 Presbyterians
1731 Schwenkfelders

SHARE OF PROTESTANTS IN THE TOTAL POPULATION
Religion in percent

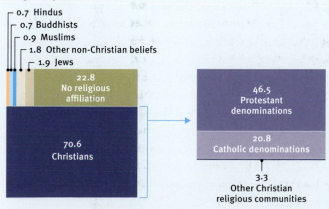

- 0.7 Hindus
- 0.7 Buddhists
- 0.9 Muslims
- 1.8 Other non-Christian beliefs
- 1.9 Jews

22.8 No religious affiliation

70.6 Christians

46.5 Protestant denominations

20.8 Catholic denominations

3.3 Other Christian religious communities

U.S. population: 318.9 million (in 2014)

MARTIN LUTHER IN US-AMERICAN NEWSPAPERS

Martin Luther has always been an issue in US-American newspapers. He received the greatest attention during the 20th century, particularly in the 1930s and 1960s. The 1980s are marked by, among other things, the Luther quincentenary in 1983. Since the turn of the millennium, however, the Reformer has become less and less an issue in U.S. newspapers.

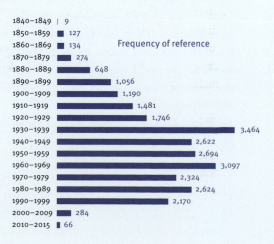

Frequency of reference

Period	Frequency
1840–1849	9
1850–1859	127
1860–1869	134
1870–1879	274
1880–1889	648
1890–1899	1,056
1900–1909	1,190
1910–1919	1,481
1920–1929	1,746
1930–1939	3,464
1940–1949	2,622
1950–1959	2,694
1960–1969	3,097
1970–1979	2,324
1980–1989	2,624
1990–1999	2,170
2000–2009	284
2010–2015	66

MICHAEL HOCHGESCHWENDER

Protestantism
in the United States

In discussions about the connection between religion and national identity, the United States is often spoken of as a Protestant nation. This description may be indisputably correct both historically and in the present day, but it also exhibits three major deficits. Firstly, it completely omits not only the historical but still current spiritual heritage of the Native Americans (i.e., the religions of the native peoples of the North American continent), but also the Catholic traditions of the Spanish, French, Irish, Germans, and Poles, which reaches back to the colonial era. Catholics were not even considered in the seemingly tolerant discourse of the Christian nation until 1950.[1]

Secondly, the assumption of a Protestant nation obscures the numerous upheavals and conflicts within American Protestantism. No distinction is made between the Anglicans, (i.e., members of the Church of England, who operate under the name "Episcopalian" since American independence), and the supporters of Puritan-Calvinist traditions. Lutheranism did not belong to the core components of Protestantism, which were critical for American national identity until well into the twentieth century. This problem was exacerbated by a further, theological distinction, namely between ritual churches and antiritualists. The Lutherans, like the Anglicans/Episcopalians, Orthodox churches, and the Catholics, belonged to the hierarchical, tradition-oriented religious communities, which relied on sacramental, ritual traditions, and which were regarded skeptically by the majority of Americans. The Calvinist and Baptist churches and sects, however, which were consciously organized in a bottom-up fashion, felt themselves decidedly antiritualist. In line with this belief, they asserted that they and they alone were the true, egalitarian, anti-institutional and liberal America. Following this point of view, Protestants were those who based their belief exclusively on the immediate, individual experience or encounter with the Lord and Savior Jesus Christ in the Word of the scripture or, in the Pentecostal tradition, with the Holy Ghost, and who, other than this experience, ultimately did not recognize any specific ecclesiasticism, not to mention sacramentalism.

The exceptional emphasis that Calvinism had gained since the seventeenth century shaped Americans' relationship to the Bible in particular. The Anglican *King James Version* of the Holy Scriptures also served as a schoolbook until the end of the nineteenth century, when it was used to teach reading and writing. Even the Baptists and many radical Anabaptist communities accepted the authenticity of this translation, whose value for the English language was almost as high as the value of Luther's translation for the development of High German. Debates about the Bible between Catholics and Protestants in the nineteenth century, or between fundamentalists and liberals in the twentieth century, were therefore consistently also debates about the United States' national self-perception.

The third limitation is particularly relevant. Until 1920, the United States and, more precisely, the British colonies in North America pre-independence, were not particularly ecclesiastical, at least not from a formal perspective. Recent research about religious statistics has shown that, excluding puritanical New England, in the eighteenth century the church membership rate (i.e., the rate of active church participation), was well under 20 percent in most colonies and individual states. That means that more than 80 percent of Americans did not participate in institutional church activities.[2] In New England, the proportion was about 25 percent. Only around 1920 were more than 50 percent of Americans members of a church; by the 1950s, the proportion had risen to 90 percent. In this respect, one could speak of a reverse secularization. The proportion of active church members during this whole period dropped continually in Europe, with the exception of the so-called Second Religious Age between 1850 and 1950, in which there was an unusually high proportion of active church members; in contrast, in the United States it rose sharply in the midst of dynamic industrialization processes.

The United States was not a Christian-Protestant nation from the outset; it was gradually transformed into one. However, even this statement requires a double modification. On the one hand, in addition to the Protestant revivalist movements, which will be discussed later in this essay, the growing ecclesiasticism was the result of an influx of Catholic immigrants, who had a very different idea of piety than the Lutherans and the Calvinists. On the other hand, the Americans in the 1920s who were not affiliated with churches were not atheists, agnostics, or members of a different religion. They considered themselves to be Christians; they read the Bible and prayed alone or together with their immediate family. It's possible that they even considered themselves to be members of an invisible church of God, as they had learned from the Protestant churches. Nonetheless, they were definitely not pious churchgoers in the European sense.

Fig. 1 Benjamin West, Penn's Treaty with the Indians, 1771/72

Irrespective of these restrictions and modifications, the statement that the United States is a Protestant nation does indeed make sense.[3] Despite the fact that the proportion of confessing Christians (including Catholics) in the United States sank from 78 percent to around 70 percent between 2007 and 2014, around 50 percent of Americans are still Protestant Christians of various denominations. At the same time, contrary to statements that would suggest otherwise, the United States became neither more religiously pluralistic nor more atheistic. The proportion of non-Christians remained relatively constant at around 5 percent, and agnostics and atheists around 4 percent.[4] It was primarily the proportion of persons who are not connected to a church, but are not by any means necessarily unbelievers, that rose in the last decade to a current level of nearly 20 percent of the population. Irrespective of the drop in institutional Christianity, it would be incorrect to assert that Christianity in general and Protestantism in particular have suffered a statistically meaningful loss of significance. A stable majority of Americans actively belongs to Protestant denominations. From a historical perspective, Protestantism's importance is even higher. Wherever religion played a role in public life in the nineteenth and early twentieth centuries, the connotation was that it was exclusively Protestant, ideally Calvinist.[5] Without Protestantism and its diverse varieties, discussions about national identity—in particular American exceptionalism, the belief of being chosen, that the nation had a special role—would be unthinkable.[6] Even when new research proves that piety and religious knowledge don't always go hand in hand, and that the most pious Christians in the United States often know alarmingly little about their own and other religions,[7] there can be no doubt of the emotional, social, and cultural significance of Christian traditions.[8] In the following, the historical roots of this finding will be examined.

From a Protestant Christian perspective, the religious founding history of the United States goes back to the early seventeenth century, as the first English, Swedish, German, and Dutch settlers ar-

1 See Jenkins, *Anti-Catholicism*, pp. 1–46. **2** Finke/Stark, *Churching*, pp. 22–109. **3** See however objections by Eck, *America*. **4** These numbers come from a survey by the Pew Research Institute, URL: www.pewresearch.org [09/21/2015]. **5** See Weiß, *Zivilreligion*, pp. 27–92. **6** Fluck, *Exceptionalism*. **7** Prothero, *Literacy*. **8** Putnam/Campbell, *American Grace*; Wolfe, *Transformation*.

A s.w. View of the BAPTIST MEETING HOUSE, Providence, *R.I.*

Fig. 2   Samuel Hill, View of the Baptist Meeting House, Providence, R.I., engraving from the August 1789 issue of the Massachusetts Magazine

rived on the East Coast; there, beyond the Atlantic and far from their European homelands, they founded settlements.[9] In contrast to the Spaniards and Portuguese, who were primarily motivated by a mix of religious and economic reasons, and the Catholic Church, which acted as an independent entity, the majority of the Protestant settlers were driven by economic motives. Despite the fact that many of the colonies, in particular in the southern part of the present-day United States (Virginia and the Carolinas) but also New York, New Jersey, and later Maryland, simply adopted the state-church system of the English motherland, the Anglican Church was not involved as an independent actor. The colonists may have been obligated to pay tithe to the Church of England and take part in church services even after 1776, even when they themselves were not Anglicans, but at least they could "buy" their way out of their Sunday duties. The Anglican colonies were less tolerant of those with other beliefs—Baptists, Jews, and Catholics suffered active discrimination—but they

had a certain pragmatic indifference about the piety of their subjects, which is why the proportion of believers was not even 10 percent in the South in 1770. And even these believers were primarily Scots-Irish Presbyterians or Baptists and not Anglicans. The colonies never had their own Anglican bishop; their administration was handled simply and rather poorly by the bishop of London. The Anglican Church in North America was marked by a lack of priests, disorganization, nepotism, corruption, and wretched administration. It was also elitist, despite the fact that the colonial elites of the eighteenth century were turning more and more to the various types of Deism, that is, the enlightened and rationalist belief in an inactive Creator without a dogmatic reference to the Trinity or Christology, and were abandoning the church of their fathers.

The situation in puritan New England was completely different. There, above all in the Massachusetts and Connecticut colonies, a de facto Calvinist-Puritanical theocracy ruled, which finally separated institutionally from Anglicanism in 1662. The mistrustful Puritans, who were intent on their own orthodoxy, at times persecuted those of other faiths violently. Quakers and Baptists, who were particular targets, went on to found their own colony, Rhode Island, under the leadership of Roger Williams; as a result of their persecution, their colony was consciously based on the principles of religious tolerance. As a result of their rigid doctrine, the Puritans had difficulties with their Native American neighbors, in some cases insisting on their eradication; they thus also lacked Native American converts. At the end of the seventeenth century, in 1692, there were even the North American witch hunts, in which twenty-one people were killed. The Puritans, however, were the only ones who apologized to their victims after the fact. Only one community, Salem, actually carried out the witch hunt; they were strongly censured for it by the Puritans in Boston. All in all, as a result of their strict beliefs about being chosen, the Puritans remained a minority even in New England, which made both religious and political dominance extremely difficult. Even their own children had difficulties becoming part of the congregation of the chosen. This structural crisis, the inability to effect a transition from persecuted, exclusive minority religion to state religion, led therefore to a serious crisis at the beginning of the eighteenth century, whose end was the Puritans' collapse. Influenced by the enlightenment, one part of the Puritan elites turned to Deism, much like the slave owners of the southern states; the rest joined Congregationalist communities. Nevertheless, the tradition of Puritanism remained alive and well in the New England colonies through the American Revolution and well into the nineteenth century, not least of which in the literary tradition.

The religious situation in the mid-Atlantic colonies was particularly varied. In Pennsylvania, a religiously tolerant but politically highly elite minority of Quakers set the tone. The Quakers got into disputes with the Anglicans, Presbyterians, and, in the eighteenth century, the enlightened Deists over the question of armed defense against the neighboring native peoples. Similar to the Baptists of Rhode Island, the pacifist Quakers sought a settlement with the tribes. In this respect, the Quakers refused to let the other settlers access the native peoples' land; they also, however, refused to militarily defend the same settlers against attacks. This led to the violent overthrow of the Quaker elite in 1777, during the American Revolution; they had depended on the protection of the royal court in London up until that point. The same is true for the Catholic minority in Maryland, which set up a political system based on religious tolerance in the seventeenth century; they were attacked by Jesuits and Protestants in equal measure. When the landowning Calvert family converted from Catholicism to Anglicism in the 1670s, the experiment of a policy of genuine Catholic tolerance in the time of Catholic reform and Counter-Reformation came abruptly to an end. Maryland became an Anglican colony with a state church. Much like in Pennsylvania, settlers from Anabaptist communities and historic peace churches (i.e., Quakers, Mennonites, Hutterites, Pietists, and other minorities that were persecuted in Europe) settled in New Jersey and New York. Yet these often tiny minorities mostly isolated themselves spiritually and spatially from the society around them; for this reason, their influence remained marginal. The small minority of Scandinavian Lutherans was quantitatively no less inconsiderable; they had originally settled the Swedish colony, which was located in the border area between Delaware, New Jersey, and Pennsylvania, along the Delaware River.

Against the backdrop of this complex religious situation, to which the African slaves of the southern states also contributed—they typically were either Protestants or followed syncretic cults like Voodoo or Santería; only a very small minority in the French colonies or Maryland were baptized Catholics - a movement began that would change the religious map of the United States forever: the evangelical revivalist movement of the 1740s.[10] Like all revivalist movements of the eighteenth and nineteenth centuries, the evangelical revivalist movement of the 1740s was embedded in a transatlantic, even global, context. This new form of piety was very well received in North America, above all due to the ambiguous religious situation and a high number of unaffiliated potential believers. In several respects, the revival of evangelicalism was related to European Pietism. Pietism emphasized a direct, personal, and highly emotional relationship to Jesus Christ as savior and redeemer. Evangelicalism gave expression to two of the colonists' socio-cultural tendencies, which remained important for the later period as well. On the one hand, it challenged people to an individual decision. Even more than during the Reformation, religion became separated from tradition and instead became a question of individual conscience. This step did not directly democratize Protestant Christianity, but it did individualize it. In this rather indirect way, the revivalist movement contributed to bringing about the American Revolution (1774–83).[11] On the other hand, the revivalist movement adapted itself to the anti-academic anti-intellectualism of the rural majority, who felt themselves neglected by the academically educated preachers; among the revivalists, anyone who felt called to do so could preach and form their own congregation. This led to the creation of countless small, local church congregations and sects, all of which did not recognize a larger ecclesiastical unit above them and all of whom were extremely critical of state churches. This local focus and the small scale (i.e., the primacy of the single congregation above the church) has shaped the understanding of many Americans to this day.

Fig. 3 (Attributed to) Joseph Badger,
Jonathan Edwards at age 48, 1751

In the end, the separation of church and state, as it was sought by the enlightened Deists, could only be so easily implemented after the Revolution because the revivalist religious groups (including the Methodists and the Baptists) and the revivalists within established churches, above all Presbyterians, strongly rejected the idea of a state church.[12] Moreover, without the sheer number of revivalist Protestants, the success of the revolution itself would not have been guaranteed. Many Methodists may have remained loyal to the crown, but the majority of the soldiers in the revolutionary Continental Army had ties to evangelicalism, and therefore differed greatly in their beliefs from the enlightened rationalism of the elitist revolutionary leaders (George Washington, Thomas Jefferson, Thomas Paine, and Alexander Hamilton). It was thus no coincidence that the Continental Congress set up a separate military chaplaincy for the troops and supplied them with twenty thousand bibles. Today, there is no doubting the Protestant character of the revolutionary masses of that era. And in that moment, the idea of a Protestant nation—the Christian Sparta, as some in that era had dubbed it—began to take form.

9 Williams, *America's Religions*, pp. 103–174. **10** Kidd, *Great Awakening*. **11** Kidd, *God of Liberty*. **12** Dreisbach/Hall, *Faith*. On the further development, see Green, *Second Disestablishment*.

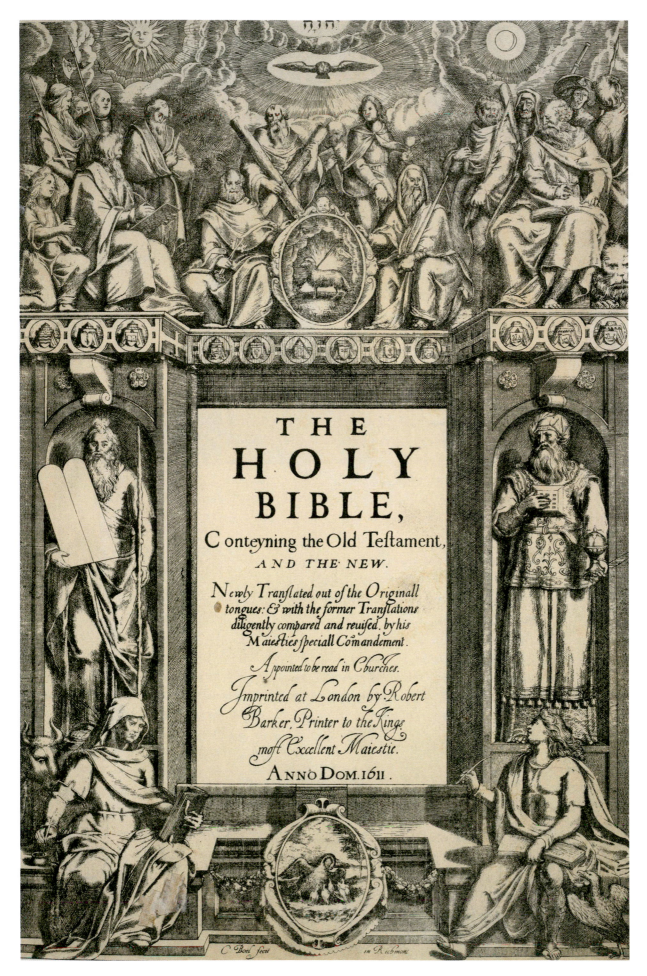

Fig. 4 Frontispiece to the first edition of the so-called King James Bible, London 1611

In the period of crisis after the revolution (in the decades between 1790 and 1860, but particularly in the 1820s and 1830s), further revivalist movements took hold.[13] This time, the urban middle classes of the Northeast were the primary supporters. From a religious point of view, the second revivalist movement was characterized by a renunciation of the central dogmas of Calvinism. Whereas the movement around 1740 had been based on the orthodoxy of double predestination, the absolute priority of the concepts of mercy, poverty, and suffering, and the idea of the *massa damnata* (the idea that the majority of people have already been condemned to eternal damnation by God), in the second revival the picture changed. Between 1810 and 1840, the revivalist movement was characterized by unconditional acceptance of the capitalist market economy and individual profit seeking,[14] the primacy of good deeds over mercy, and a missionary holy universalism that was connected with an optimistic, if also apocalyptic, anthropology. The end of the world seemed to be at hand, and it was the duty of the American Christians to prepare for the returning of the Lord by creating the perfect society in the United States.

For this reason, the New England revivalists took up radical social reform; the observance of the Sabbath, judicial reform, the temperance movement, the women's movement, and abolitionism (the fight against slavery) all became part of their passionately proclaimed agenda. Evangelicals and liberals banded together to form a reform coalition, which fell apart only at the turn of the twentieth century. Moreover, both groups were united in their fanatic hatred of the Catholicism of the Irish and German immigrants who arrived in droves from 1845 onward. Neither the evangelicals nor the liberals could imagine the United States as a nation without a Protestant leader and a Protestant identity, despite the fact that the majority of the population still did not belong to a religious community. In the course of the formation of the United States' national identity, a specific notion of American Protestantism was formed; it was local, anti-intellectual, revivalist, antihierarchical, antiritualistic, apocalyptic, emotional, patriotic, and capitalist. Non-American religions were hereafter measured against this standard. In addition, liberals and evangelicals loaded the idea of the nation with (civil-) religious concepts. The idea of exceptionalism became more aggressive and missionary. But while the nationalistic liberals defined the nation primarily militarily, the majority of evangelicals held on to their pacifist ideals, even during the Civil War (1861–65). The *crusader nation* was therefore only to a limited extent a purely religious construct.[15]

At the same time, in the course of the second revival movement, religious offerings continued to become more diverse. The Mormons and Spiritualists were founded. While the Spiritualists arose as an explicitly modern, individualistic religion without clergy or dogma, and with the claim of scientific proof of the Beyond, the Mormons developed a nationalist profile with highly hierarchical characteristics, a nonbiblical revelation, and a polytheistic theology and anthropology. Despite their holy nationalism, these characteristics, combined with their bent toward polygamy, led to violent civic persecution. This led the founding of the temporarily independent Mormon state in Utah in the 1850s, which didn't join the Union until 1890.[16]

Fig. 5 Unknown illustrator, Witchcraft at Salem Village, from:
William A. Crafts, Pioneers in the Settlement of America.
Vol. I: From Florida in 1510 to California in 1849.
Boston: Samuel Walker & Company, 1876

After the Civil War, in the 1880s, a further revivalist movement returned to the theological roots of Calvinist orthodoxy.[17] The social impulse of the second revivalist movement was continued by so-called Post-millennials within social Protestantism through the *social gospel*. These Post-millennials believed that God demanded that they create a perfect society so that Christ could come again, and the thousand years of peace following the apocalypse would be justified; this explains their radical social activism. The majority of evangelicals ascribed however to premillennialism, which was based more on mercy and a doctrine of predestination. It was the era of the *hell and damnation preachers*, who all declared nationalism and capitalism to be the central values of the American-Protestant identity.

Two further events between 1880 and 1925 were critical for future developments. Firstly, congregations emerged on the margins of Protestant revivalist Christianity that were primarily concerned with the spiritual and material well-being of their members. In their eyes, Christianity was not about Christ suffering for us on the cross but rather about prosperity and well-being. Accordingly, they required positive thinking, optimism, and consumerism and promised all who believed in God a rosy future. This movement repeatedly linked up with the Pentecostals, who were founded in 1905, and the Pentecostal revival, which continued through the entire twentieth century. Pentecostalism and the *gospel of prosperity* developed into the most dynamic religious groups of the new century. Secondly, there was a break between liberals and evangelicals. The national ban on alcohol, Prohibition (1920–33), was their last social reform project together.[18] The trigger for the break was the evangelicals' defensive position toward German liberal theology, cultural Protestantism,

13 Hochgeschwender, *Amerikanische Religion*, pp. 77–116. **14** Noll, *God and Mammon*. **15** See, by contrast, Morone, *Hellfire Nation*; Jewett/Wangerin, *Mission und Verführung*, and, in particular, Preston, *Sword of the Spirit* with his highly balanced representation. **16** Bushman, *Mormonism*. **17** Hochgeschwender, *Amerikanische Religion*. **18** Welskopp, *Prohibition*, pp. 11–50.

CLASSROOM IN PROPOSED BRYAN UNIVERSITY OF TENNESSEE

Fig. 6 Poster satirizing the so-called Monkey Trial (Scopes Trial) held in the Dayton, Tennessee Court House. At the end of the trial a law was enacted which forbade theories that contradicted the message of the Bible about the origins of humankind to be taught in state financed schools and universities.

and the historical-critical exegesis, and Darwinism in the natural sciences. This was an untenable position for both secular liberals and liberal Protestants, the latter of whom now defined themselves as mainstream or mainline Protestants, and strongly differentiated themselves from evangelicalism.

Around 1910, Fundamentalism, which was by far more radical, arose from the ranks of the evangelicals. Fundamentalism found its origins as a movement made purely from professors and intellectuals, who held to the literal interpretation of the Holy Scripture, in contrast to the historic-critical method. Contrary to modern prejudices, the Fundamentalists were not backward and violent ideologues. Many of them taught at well-known American universities. Almost all of them were pacifists and therefore against the United States' participation in the First World War, which led to the prompt accusation from the liberals that they lacked patriotism. Since they, in the Calvinist tradition of biblical interpretation, did not recognize a central interpretation principle in the Bible (a *theologia crucis* as defined by Luther) but rather allowed both the Old and New Testament equal validity, they couldn't find a solution to the fact that Darwinism overthrew their understanding of Genesis. The media reaction to the Scopes trial in Dayton, Ohio, in 1925 thus sealed the fate of the first generation of Fundamentalists.[19]

From 1925 onward, Fundamentalism was considered to be provincial and out-of-touch. But even liberal, optimistic cultural Protestantism, which greeted modernity so euphorically, found itself in a serious crisis after the harrowing events of the First and Second World Wars. The decades between 1930 and 1970 became an era of neo-orthodoxy determined above all by Reinhold Niebuhr and his followers. Mainstream Protestantism became neo-orthodox; evangelicalism, Pentecostalism, and fundamentalism lost ground. The latter groups were able to secure influence in the South, where Protestantism was growing among the African American communities, and in the Midwest. The neo-orthodoxy was responsible for ushering in a new heyday of American Protestantism in the 1950s and 1960s. At the same time, with the end of the Americanism debates under Pope Leo XIII in the 1890s, American Catholicism was able to reach its high point of unity and power.

Whereas ultimate optimism dominated everywhere in 1965, the following two decades nearly brought the complete downfall of the mainstream churches.[20] Catholicism was affected by this decline with some delay in the 1980s and 1990s; the sexual abuse scandals around 2000, however, increased the number of secessions from the church. Nevertheless, the immigration of Hispanics has helped to keep the number of Catholics constant; the Pentecostals and the evangelicals have also profited from this influx. The reasons for the collapse of mainline Protestantism are unclear. One possible reason could be the politicization of the Episcopalians, Lutherans, Presbyterians, and other denominations in the course of the African American civil rights movement. General modernization and secularization processes (e.g., the suburbanization of the United States) certainly also played a role.

All of this did not, however, lead to a decline of religiosity among Americans but rather to a new revivalist movement, which was shaped by Billy Graham in the 1950s but really gained ground after 1970, after the "revolts" of 1968. In the context of the "culture wars," the vast majority of evangelicals and Pentecostals turned to conservatives with regard to questions about national identity, and not to liberals. One major reason for this was the activist policy of the Supreme Court, which banned school prayer in 1962, allowed abortion in the first trimester in 1973, and legalized homosexuality in 2003, thus paving the way for homosexual marriage. As a result, right-wing evangelicalism became more and more fundamentalist, choosing the fights over abortion and school curricula for biology (Darwinism and evolution) as the arenas for intensely fought political power battles.

In contrast, left-wing evangelicalism saw itself obligated by problems of social policy and the equality of blacks and whites and men and women.[21] There was bitter infighting among the Baptists, Methodists, and other denominations, above all in the South; in the course of these fights, the right-wing evangelicals began to identify more and more with the Republican Party. They became more nationalist, pro-capitalist, and militarist than ever before. The claims that they controlled foreign policy under presidents Ronald Reagan

(1981–89) and George W. Bush (2001–09) can, however, be justifiably called into doubt.[22] In fact, there are many indicators that these neo-fundamentalist revivalist movements have lost steam since the end of the 1990s and reached their high point in 2005.[23] It was in fact the Pentecostals who profited from the decline of the evangelicals, while the decline of the liberal mainstream proceeded with seemingly unstoppable speed.

Lutheranism had to dovetail itself into this religious landscape over the course of those 350 years.[24] Like Catholicism, Lutheranism did not belong to the religions that were important for American national identity. It had the reputation of being a ritualist church, and a church of migrants, despite the fact that the first Lutheran pastor was already active in New Sweden in 1640. In the eighteenth century, Pennsylvania was a stronghold of German Lutheran Christians; this group remained marginal, however, and was regarded suspiciously by patriotic politicians such as Benjamin Franklin, as its members were not of British heritage. Many of them were influenced by the German Pietist movement from Halle on the Saale and were close to the first revivalist movement, without directly being affected by it. The nineteenth century became a phase of ecclesiastical, religious and ethno-cultural divisions. At one point, no less than seventy independent Lutheran synods existed in the United States. One part of the tensions resulted from the Prussian forced union in 1817, which forced the Prussian Lutherans into a single ecclesiastical organization together with the Calvinists. This in turn led to a mass exodus of anti-union Lutherans in the 1820s who were subject to harsh persecution measures by the Prussian authorities. These "old" Lutherans today make up the Missouri Synod, which definitely exhibits characteristics of evangelical theology.

The great majority of the American Lutherans were, however, German and Scandinavian immigrants from the period after the American Civil War. Most of them settled in a triangle in the Midwest between Cincinnati, St. Louis, and Milwaukee, or in Wisconsin and Minnesota. In the time before the First World War, it was common to hear German spoken on the streets in Cincinnati's Over-the-Rhine neighborhood, for example. Since the Germans and the Scandinavians did not get along with each other very well, both due to the language difference and to divergent practices of piety, they created separate synodic organizations. They both had difficulty, however, establishing themselves in their new environment. Scandinavians and Germans had the reputation of being slow and not very lively, either mentally or economically. To boot, they drank beer in public, even on Sundays, which found heavy opposition among the abstinent evangelicals and liberals starting back in the 1850s.

The German Lutherans had additional difficulties. Between 1871 and 1914 they openly expressed the ethos of their fatherland and celebrated the successes of the Prussian German Empire, which led to doubt about their national loyalty toward the United States. In the environment of the First World War, this led to violent persecutions; there were lynchings, churches were burned, and libraries were destroyed. The process of Americanization of the church services had begun before 1913; after 1917 there was hardly a single German-speaking Lutheran church in the United States. The situation stabilized after the two World Wars. The majority of the Lutherans had grown together with the neo-orthodox mainstream; in the 1950s, they were considered to be full members of this movement. Soon they were sharing the Eucharist with Episcopalians, the Church of Christ, the Methodists, and other mainstream churches. But the Lutherans were then also drawn into the downward trend of the mainstream churches. Between 1990 and 2009, they lost nearly 20 percent of their members. Today there are only about 4.5 million Lutherans in the United States, less than 10 percent of the Lutherans worldwide.

BIBLIOGRAPHY

Alitt, Patrick (2003), *Religion in America since 1945: A History*. New York. **Amstutz**, Mark R. (2014), *Evangelicals and American Foreign Policy*. New York. **Bushman**, Richard Lyman (2008), *Mormonism: A Very Short Introduction*. New York. **Douthat**, Robert (2012), *Bad Religion: How We Became a Nation of Heretics*. New York. **Dreisbach**, Daniel L./**Hall**, Mark David (eds.) (2014), *Faith and the Founders of the American Republic*. New York. **Eck**, Diana (2001), *A New Religious America: How a "Christian Country" Has Become the World's Most Religiously Diverse Nation*. New York. **Finke**, Roger/**Stark**, Rodney (1992), *The Churching of America, 1776–1990: Winners and Loser in Our Religious Economy*, New Brunswick. **Fluck**, Winfried (2016), American Exceptionalism: Ein Schlüssel zum amerikanischen Selbstverständnis. In: Lammert, Christian et. al. (eds.), *Handbuch Politik USA*. Wiesbaden, pp. 15–28. **Gasawa**, Brantley W. (2014), *Progressive Evangelicals and the Pursuit of Social Justice*. Chapel Hill. **Green**, Steven K. (2010), *The Second Disestablishment: Church and State in Nineteenth-Century America*. New York. **Hochgeschwender**, Michael (2007), *Amerikanische Religion: Evangelikalismus, Pfingstlertum und Fundamentalismus*. Frankfurt am Main. **Jenkins**, Philip (2003), *The New Anti-Catholicism: The Last Acceptable Prejudice*. Oxford. **Jewett**, Robert/**Wangerin**, Ole (2008), *Mission und Verführung: Amerikas religiöser Weg in vier Jahrhunderten*. Göttingen. **Kidd**, Thomas S. (2007), *The Great Awakening: The Roots of Evangelical Christianity in Colonial America*. New Haven. **Kidd**, Thomas S. (2010), *God of Liberty: A Religious History of the American Revolution*. New York. **Miller**, Steven P. (2014), *The Age of Evangelicalism: America's Born-Again Years*. New York. **Moran**, Jeffrey P. (2002), *The Scopes Trial: A Brief History with Documents*. Boston. **Morone**, James A. (2003), *Hellfire Nation: The Politics of Sin in American History*. New Haven. **Noll**, Mark A. (2000), *Das Christentum in Nordamerika*. Leipzig. **Noll**, Mark A. (ed.) (2002), *God and Mammon: Protestants, Money and the Market, 1790–1860*. New York. **Preston**, Andrew (2012), *Sword of the Spirit, Shield of Faith: Religion in American War and Diplomacy*. New York. **Prothero**, Stephen (2007), *Religious Literacy: What Every American Needs to Know—and Doesn't*. San Francisco. **Putnam**, Robert D./**Campbell**, David E. (2010), *American Grace: How Religion Divides and Unites Us*. New York. **Weiss**, Jana (2015), *Fly the Flag and Give Thanks to God: Zivilreligion an US-amerikanischen patriotischen Feiertagen, 1945–1992*. Trier. **Welskopp**, Thomas (2010), *Amerikas große Ernüchterung: Eine Kulturgeschichte der Prohibition*. Paderborn. **Williams**, Peter W. (2002), *America's Religions: From Their Origins to the Twenty-First Century*, 3rd ed. Urbana. **Wolfe**, Alan (2003), *The Transformation of American Religion: How We Actually Live Our Faith*. Chicago. **Wuthnow**, Robert (1988), *The Restructuring of American Religion*. Princeton.

19 Moran, *Scopes Trial*. **20** Wuthnow, *Restructuring*; Allitt, *Religion*; Douthat, *Bad Religion*, pp. 19–148. **21** Gasaway, *Progressive Evangelicals*. **22** Amstutz, *Evangelicals*. **23** Miller, *Age of Evangelicalism*. **24** Noll, *Christentum*, pp. 221–226.

HERRMANN WELLENREUTHER

Martin Luther, Heinrich Melchior Mühlenberg and the Lutheran Church in North America

The history of Lutheranism in North America is a two-faceted subject. The one facet is the formation, spreading, and significance of the Lutheran Church in North America; the other, and more comprehensive, facet is the significance, role, and impact of Martin Luther. Luther was of fundamental importance both for the Lutheran Church in Europe and North America and for a number of other Protestant churches and sects, whose foundation was based on Luther as an essential aspect of their Protestant self-understanding. In the course of its North American history, the Lutheran Church has had changing perceptions of Martin Luther as "its" founding father. This has to do not only with the importance of Pietism in the eighteenth-century history of the Lutheran Church, but also with the Church's splitting into various synods. Each of these synods had a different relationship to Luther, who was either seen as the representative of, and witness to, a more conservative theology or as the founder of a theology open to the currents of the day.

In the Protestant churches of North America, the relationship to Martin Luther encompasses a broad spectrum of positions, which are often divided within one church. Some in the Baptist Church and its many subgroups, for instance, emphasize its "Protestant roots" and, hence, Luther as the founder, while others trace the establishment of the Church to English Congregationalism and its rejection of the Anglican Church community model.[1] In addition, some congregations consider Jean Calvin, others Martin Luther, as the founder of their theology.[2] Even more complex is the relationship to Luther in the American Methodist Church. The essential differences can be summarized in the words of writer Shannon Leigh O'Neil: "Whereas Lutherans place emphasis on faith alone, Methodists believe in faith-based actions."[3]

For the movement which, today, is broadly referred to as "Protestantism," Lutheran theology plays a greater role than its founder, Martin Luther. It is not surprising, then, that while the concept of "Lutheranism" receives a separate entry in the renowned *Encyclopedia of American Religious History*,[4] Martin Luther as the founder of the Lutheran Church does not. On the other hand, there are separate entries both on Heinrich Melchior Mühlenberg (fig. 1), who is referred to as the "patriarch of the Lutheran Church in North America,"[5] and on the "Evangelical Lutheran Church in America."[6] Is "Patriarch of the American Lutheran Church" an apt sobriquet for Heinrich Melchior Mühlenberg?[7] This is a question with many facets, and in order to answer it we need to take a closer look at Mühlenberg's life and his activities.

Heinrich Melchior Mühlenberg was born on September 11, 1711, in Einbeck, in what is today Lower Saxony in Northern Germany, the fourth son and the seventh of nine children. His father was a master of Einbeck's influential cobblers' guild; his mother, née Anna Marie Kleinschmied, may have been the daughter of a garrison officer from the small beer-brewing town. His parents owned three houses. Mühlenberg received a good education, and he was one of the first theology students to attend the Georg August University in Göttingen, which had been recently founded. He studied there with Joachim Oporin, who, after having held a position at Kiel University, had just been appointed professor of theology in Göttingen, and who had a reputation as a moderate Pietist. In Göttingen, Mühlenberg met other Pietists and joined a group of revivalists. He objected, however, to Lutheran separatists, some of whom he had come across in the Harz Mountains town of Zellerfeld and in Einbeck. It was therefore only natural for him to leave Göttingen for Halle, the most important center of Pietism in Germany. After a sojourn that lasted a little more than a year, Gotthilf August Francke, director of the Glaucha Institutes in Halle, helped him find a position as Lutheran deacon in the domain of the Pietist noblewoman Henrietta Sophie Freifrau von Gersdorff in Großhennersdorf in Upper Lusatia, where he was trained to become a parish priest. A year later, he followed a call from Halle to a pastorate in Philadelphia—a city with which Mühlenberg was probably unfamiliar.

During the months before his departure on April 16, 1742, Mühlenberg did not familiarize himself with Philadelphia and greater Pennsylvania (fig. 2), but instead made an extensive round trip taking leave of the circle of converts he had gotten to know. He then traveled to London, where he spent almost two months with

---

1 "The origins of Baptist thought and practice can be seen in the late sixteenth century in English Congregationalism, which rejected the prevalent 'parish' structure of church life (Church of England) where everyone in a given community was a member of a neighborhood parish and where children were baptized," American Baptist Churches, *Our History*. Asplund, *Register*, p. 5 note * doesn't count the "Dunkards or German Baptists" as real Baptists as they do not immerse the baptized once, but three times. 2 See "Baptist Theology," in: Espín/Nickoloff, *Dictionary*, p. 118. 3 Cited according to O'Neil, *Difference*. 4 Queen/Prothero/Shattuck, *Encyclopedia*, vol. 1, pp. 404–407. 5 "He is generally considered to be the patriarch of Lutheranism in the United States," Queen/Prothero/Shattuck, *Encyclopedia*, vol. 2, pp. 460 f. 6 Ibid., vol. 1, pp. 233–236. 7 The following account is largely based on Wellenreuther, *Mühlenberg*; Wellenreuther/Müller-Bahlke/Roeber, *Transatlantic World*.

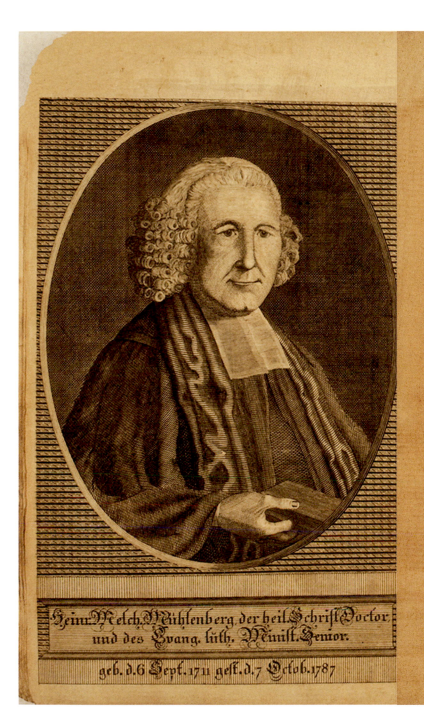

Heinr. Melch. Mühlenberg der heil. Schrift Doctor
und des Evang. luth. Minist. Senior.

geb. d. 6 Sept. 1711 gest. d. 7 Octob. 1787

Henry A. Muhlenberg

Denkmal

der

Liebe und Achtung

welches

Seiner Hochwürden dem Herrn

D. Heinrich Melchior Mühlenberg,

verdienstvollesten Senior des Evangelisch-Lutherischen Ministeriums in Nord-America,

und

treueifrigsten ersten Lehrers an der St. Michaelis-
und Zions-Gemeinde in Philadelphia,

ist gesetzet worden.

Samt

desselben Lebenslaufe.

Philadelphia:

Gedruckt bey Melchior Steiner, in der Rees-strasse,
zwischen der Zweyten- und Dritten-strasse, 1788.

Fig. 1 Portrait of Heinrich Melchior Mühlenberg in the commemorative volume: Henry A. Mühlenberg, Denkmal der Liebe
und Achtung welches seiner Hochwürden dem Herrn D. Heinrich Melchior Mühlenberg […] ist gesetzet worden.
Samt desselben Lebenslaufe (Monument of Love and Respect, dedicated to Reverend Dr. Heinrich Melchior Mühlenberg […]. Published along with his curriculum vitae.) Philadelphia, 1788

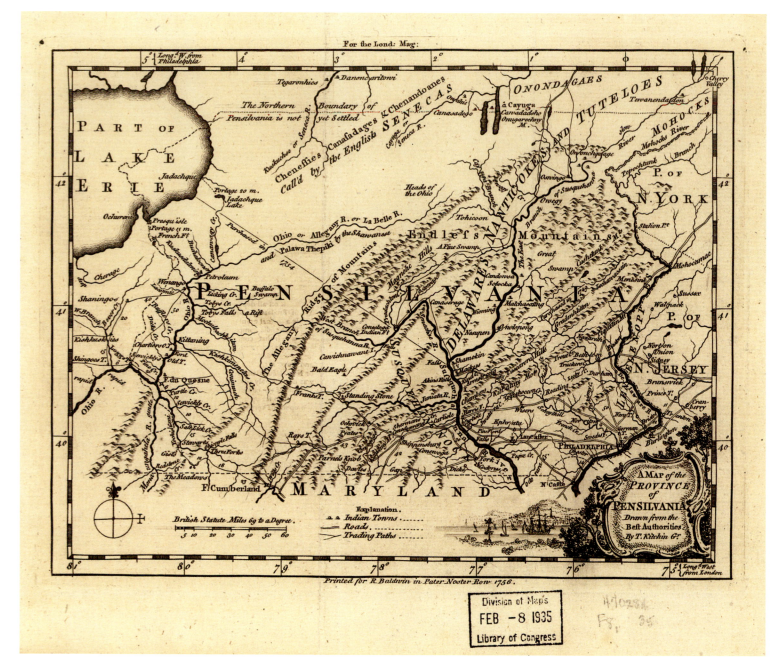

Fig. 2 Thomas Kitchin, A Map of the Province of Pennsylvania, printed by R. Baldwin for the The London Magazine, or, Gentleman's Monthly Intelligencer, Dec. 1756

Lutheran court chaplain Friedrich Michael Ziegenhagen, under whose guidance he deepened his knowledge of theology.

After a voyage of average length, the young theologian reached Charleston, South Carolina, on September 22. From there, he went on to Ebenezer, Georgia, where in the course of a few weeks' sojourn he got to know the congregation of Salzburg exiles and their difficulties. He then traveled back to Charleston, and on November 12, 1742, in a tiny boat, he continued on to Philadelphia (fig. 3), which he reached, after two stormy weeks of sailing along the coast, on November 25, "at eight in the morning."[8]

What did the young minister bring with him? Of immediate importance were letters from Court Chaplain Ziegenhagen and Gotthilf August Francke to the congregation in Philadelphia as well as to smaller rural congregations in New Hanover and New Providence, both not too distant from Philadelphia—letters that gave witness to his vocation, his qualifications, and his theological credibility. This presented no problems but in the long run other characteristics turned out to be more important. Unlike the other thirteen ministers sent from Halle, who hailed from ministers' families, Mühlenberg came from a large family of craftsmen, whose sturdy manners lacked affectation, and from whom he had learned to assert himself among his siblings at an early age. He had a robust nature, he was strong and healthy, and he was used to physical exertion. In addition, he had received a reasonable, mostly homiletics-based theological education, supplemented by pedagogy, in Halle (where he had taught at the Glaucha Institutes) and, in Großhennersdorf, where he became acquainted with the usual expectations and problems of a Lutheran congregation. In addition, he had learned to divide society into two distinct groups: an "in-group," consisting of members who had experienced a true conversion in the sense of Halle Pietism; and an "out-group," whose members had not. Last but not least, he had brought with him two experiences from Halle and Großhennersdorf that would strongly shape his first years in America: the carefully cultivated enemy image of the Moravian Pietists, whose original congregation, the self-described "Pilgrim Congregation" from Herrnhut, lived only a few kilometers away from Großhennersdorf; and the strong and firm belief in guaranteed theological qualifications—"guaranteed" in the sense that said qualifications required authentication by prominent Pietist theologians.

But a few shortcomings began to appear as well. Mühlenberg spoke English—during the crossing he had even preached in English—but there was still significant room for improvement; and the future minister had virtually no knowledge about the country and its people (a lack shared, by the way, by Ziegenhagen and Francke, which was to prove particularly detrimental when it came to selecting other ministers).

In what respects did Heinrich Melchior Mühlenberg differ from the other ministers who followed him from Halle in the next twenty-five years? Why is it that his picture has become engraved in the memory of the Lutheran Church in North America—and not those of minister Justus Heinrich Christian Helmuth, who worked much longer in Philadelphia, or Johann Friedrich Handschuch, who wanted to make the Philadelphia congregation a particularly sacred one, thereby plunging it into its most serious crisis? These questions are not easily answered. To start with the obvious: Mühlenberg worked purposefully, but without visible effort, to become recognized in Pennsylvania society. One important step in this direction was his marriage to Anna Maria, the daughter of Conrad Weiser, on April 22, 1745—Weiser being the most prominent and most influential German settler of the day, one of the first German justices of the peace, as well as the colony's agent for Indian affairs. In the 1750s, Mühlenberg made the acquaintance, and won the friendship, of the two most important and prominent Anglican ministers, Reverends Richard Peters and William Smith. They were the first ministers to preside over the Anglican Church in Philadelphia, and they had considerable influence with the owner of the colony and its governor. Unlike the majority of German settlers in Pennsylvania, Mühlenberg, by the beginning of the French and Indian War, had established an excellent network of connections within the political elite. Perhaps even more important were the epistolary and personal relationships he built among the members of the Lutheran congregations in the mid-Atlantic colonies. To this end, he traveled extensively to the centers of German settlers, such as Lancaster, Tulpehocken, and Reading in Pennsylvania, and to the congregations in the Raritan Valley in New Jersey, where he tried to settle the fierce dispute between minister Johann Augustus Wolf and his congregation,[9] and finally to the Lutheran congregation in New York. There was hardly any Lutheran congregation, and few Lutheran ministers in North America with whom Mühlenberg did not at some point exchange letters.

Exceptions, however, prove the rule, and these entailed the greatest problems the young minister from Einbeck had to face. Before 1742, there had only been a single Lutheran congregation in North America that had been guided in the principles of Halle's Pietism: Ebenezer in the Georgia colony. It was presided over by ministers Johann Martin Boltzius and Israel Christian Gronau, who had been sent from Halle; Mühlenberg had visited it immediately after his arrival in Charleston. The members of all other Lutheran congregations were from the two traditional German emigration areas, Baden and Württemberg. Theirs was a Lutheranism unaffected by Pietist ideas, and whose moral standards corresponded more to village life than to the high ambitions characteristic of the sharp church discipline of Pietism. That is to say, that the ninety-five Lutheran congregations that made up the ecclesiastical landscape Mühlenberg entered around 1740 were, from his theological perspective, all living in the unholy status of non-converts. Those converted were usually not members of the Lutheran congregations but Baptists (Brethren, Dunkers, etc.) or Mennonites—all of whom invoked Martin Luther as the founder of Protestantism.[10]

8 Mühlenberg, *Autobiographie*, p. 22. **9** Wolf had been sent to New Jersey by the Hamburg Ministerium; it quickly became clear that his conception of his office as minister could not be brought into line with that of the members of his congregation. The conciliation procedure, in which Mühlenberg played a leading role, ended with a ruling against Wolf. **10** In my article, "The World according to the Christian People in North America," in: Wellenreuther/Müller-Bahlke/Roeber, *Transatlantic World*, pp. 99–124, I have tried to give an outline of the religious landscape of North America; for the number of Lutheran congregations there, see ibid., p. 104.

Fig. 3 A Plan of the City and Environs of Philadelphia. Engraved and published by Matthew Albert Lotter, 1777

Mühlenberg and the other thirteen ministers from Halle came to congregations where, at least during the first decades, they met with outright skepticism. They were seen as "penetists" [Pietists]—a disparaging term used in Baden and Württemberg for those associated with the prohibition of dancing, fiddling, and merrymaking at festivities or in pubs.

At the time of Mühlenberg's arrival, the ninety-five Lutheran congregations were pastored by seven ministers; after 1742, these were joined by forty-three ministers from all parts of Germany, of whom, albeit with some reservations, only Georg Samuel Klug, Caspar Stoever, Tobias Wagner, Johann Albert Weygand, Johann Georg Bager, Johann Siegfried Gerock, and Paul Daniel Bryzelius met Mühlenberg's high expectations. Of course, this is not to say that the ministers marginalized by Mühlenberg administered their office poorly—even though some of them, such as Johann Valentin Krafft and Johann Conrad Andreae, were made a model for the negative stereotype of Lutheran pastors in the colonial public in general and in Christoph Saur's newspaper in particular due to their immoral lifestyle.

All of this explains the highly problematic situation Mühlenberg was faced with—and that neither Gotthilf August Francke nor Court Chaplain Ziegenhagen had prepared him for. At the same time, this context not only qualifies the significance of some of Mühlenberg's achievements, it also makes his impressive success stand out more clearly. Even though he never explicitly said so, Mühlenberg had a number of ambitious plans. Next to developing and strengthening the cohesion between, on the one hand, the Lutheran congregations and, on the other, the institutes in Halle and their Pietism, he also strove to design a general church constitution for the Lutheran congregations in America. These projects failed institutionally because of the legal obstacles opposing a stronger cohesion, and because Gotthilf August Francke, who lacked an understanding of the Lutheran congregations in North America and their situation, turned down the church constitution submitted to him by Mühlenberg and his colleagues from Halle (the other ministers had not been involved in the discussions).[11] Therefore, other solutions had to be found. After 1760 Mühlenberg reconvened the so-called United Ministry as a body that brought together both Lutheran pastors as well as lay members. The first assembly of ministers met from August 15 to 20, 1748. According to the minutes, its purpose and objective was "the closer union of the preachers and of the United Congregations, and for mutual consultation and agreement in matters concerning all the congregations." The expected participants were "the preachers, elders, and deacons of all the frequently mentioned congregations."[12] From the sixteen Lutheran ministers in the mid-Atlantic colonies, preachers Peter Brunnholz, Handschuch, John Christopher Hartwick, Mühlenberg, Swedish provost John Sandin, as well as delegates from eight congregations attended this first meeting. With the exception of Reverend Hartwick, pastor of the Lutheran congregation in New York, all of them had been selected according to the criteria of Halle Pietism; ministers who held different theological views had not been invited. In other words, when it was founded, and even after 1760, the assembly was a meeting of Halle-dependent ministers. This restriction, however—and this was the novelty of this institution—did not apply to the congregations: they had been expressly invited to send delegates (usually parish council members) to the meetings. The composition of this assembly remained the same even after the end of the French and Indian War in 1763. But now a new era began. Seven Lutheran pastors attended the assembly in 1761; ten in 1762; and fifteen in 1763—not counting the guests from the Swedish Lutheran and Anglican Churches.[13] Even more important was the fact that, according to the minutes, the number of congregation delegates had increased dramatically. The minutes taken at the 1763 assembly record the following delegates:

1. From the Philadelphia congregation, the trustees, elders and deacons present.
2. From Germantown, John Groothaus, John Nebal, Adolf Gillman and John Engel.
3. From White Marsh or Barren Hill, Christoph. Robin, Valentine Muller, Matth. Sommer.
4. From Lancaster, Esquire Kuhn and Caspar Singer.
5. From Yorktown, across the Susquehanna, Jacob Billmeyer.
6. From Frederickstown, in Maryland, no one was present on account of the lateness of the season, but instead there was a written report.
7. From Providence, no one had come, partly because the elders are offended since they had expected me to return.
8. From New Hanover, Mr. Michael Walter.
9. From Reading, on the Schuylkill, Jacob Rabolt.
10. From Tulpehocken, Andreas Kreuzer and Jacob Fischer.
11. From New Germantown, Bedminster, etc., in Jersey, none were present, because the invitation had not been correctly delivered.
12. From New York, a letter of excuse [by Rev. Weygand] from the Low German Congregation, but from the High German a delegate, Peter Grim.
13. The Low and High German Congregations in Hackensack, Remmersbach, Wahlkiel, etc., had sufficiently excused themselves, having paid us a visit several weeks before and reported the condition of the church.
14. From Rhinebeck, Camp, Staatsburg, Claverack in the Province of New York, two hundred miles from here, an adequate excuse was received. They stand in friendly relations towards us.
15. From Earltown, Conestoga and Muddy Creek, in Pennsylvania, Conrad Schreuber and John Schultz.
16. From Easton, on the Delaware, Greenwich, etc., two delegates.
17. From Macunschy, Heidelberg, Jordan, etc., nobody came on account of the danger from Indians [for a sufficient excuse, because a short time before the Indians had killed several of our members].

11 Francke, Letter to Mühlenberg, June 24, 1756, in: Mühlenberg, *Korrespondenz*, pp. 293 f. 12 General Council of the Evangelical Lutheran Church in North America, *Documentary History*, p. 7. 13 Ibid., pp. 57, 68, 63.

18. From Indianfield, Saccum, and Upper Dublin Frederick Wambold, Melchior Knceple, Valentin Pough and Jacob Timanus.
19. From Upper Milford, Allentown, etc., a letter of excuse, on account of fear of attacks by the Indians.
20. From Cohenzy, in Jersey, no one, because I had been there and noted the circumstances.
21. From Conewaga, Manchester and Paradise in Pennsylvania a written application and delegate, Nicolaus Biedinger.
22. From Oley, Whitendahl, etc., an excuse on account of fear of the Indians, and
23. from Winchester, in Virginia, written communications [because they also are in danger of Indian troubles].[14]

The increase from eight to twenty-three congregations that sent their elders or delegates to the assembly demonstrates its double function and significance. It was not just a committee where ministers met, exchanged ideas, and adopted resolutions, but also, and above all, a place where more and more of the well over one hundred Lutheran congregations met whose delegates made a decisive contribution to transforming the individual congregations into the joint body of a church. And there is yet something else that the increase shows: the Lutheran Church was not only created on the basis of a common religious attitude. Rather, what emerged from the regular exchange among Lutheran congregation members at the annual meeting was the mutual interest in one another. This development was boosted by another important innovation in the congregations themselves, namely by the introduction of the confirmation.[15] The confirmation songs that were widely circulated as broadsides emphasized the special importance of this act, that is, as confirming the baptismal vows of parents and godparents and as a *rite de passage* into the Eucharist assembly.

Of course, Heinrich Melchior Mühlenberg was not the only one to deserve credit for the rise and growing importance of this assembly. It was he, however, who repeatedly took the initiative and shouldered the bulk of the tasks connected with presiding over the assembly such as, among other things, writing and copying individual invitation letters, editing the minutes and dispatching them to colleagues, as well as to Court Chaplain Ziegenhagen and Gotthilf August Francke, corresponding with ministers and congregations, and setting the agenda(s). The tasks of the assembly increased, and so did the workload connected with the office of its president (for instance, young theologians who had been trained in Pennsylvania or neighboring colonies were ordained deacons and ministers; also, a growing number of disciplinary infractions had to be dealt with). Having held the office as president since 1748, Mühlenberg therefore decided to resign in 1771; he remained, however, an active member of the assembly.

A start had thus been made in 1763. It should be remembered, however, that what is today the third-largest Church in North America was still a small and tender plant in a year when the colonies were contending both with Pontiac's Rebellion (a bloody Indian uprising) and the so-called Paxton Boys Riots (a vigilante retaliation in the aftermath of that rebellion), in which German settlers also played a nefarious role. But this Church also suffered from a serious crisis that had occurred in the Philadelphia congregation. On March 15, 1759, the preacher Handschuch wrote to Ziegenhagen and Francke, what had taken place. According to this letter, the Church council, on December 18, "with a zealousness, which had presumably been brought about by God Himself, had unanimously" decided "to encourage a whole Christian congregation, all and sundry, old and young, male and female, to take on a new righteous being in Christ Jesus, and to bear witness to that congregation in the name of God that, from now on, no piper, no drunkard, no fornicator and adulterer, no quarreler, no blasphemer, no dancer, no thief, nor any other unrighteous person or the likes of him, living in direct opposition to the healing grace and teaching of our Lord Jesus Christ, will be allowed to take the Holy Supper with us, baptize children in the congregation, or be buried in our already tiny cemetery."[16]

Handschuch's zealous endeavor "to encourage a whole Christian congregation, all and sundry ... to take on a new righteous being in Christ Jesus" had, a couple of years before, already failed in Lancaster, Handschuch's first station as a preacher, and then in Germantown. According to the report Mühlenberg sent to London and Halle on October 9, 1760, this endeavor was met with fierce resistance, in particular, from the Württemberg members of the congregation. In order to prevent a schism, Mühlenberg went back to Philadelphia, resumed his office as head preacher (which he angrily gave up a little later, only to be scathingly rebuked by Francke and Ziegenhagen) and set about his perhaps most ambitious undertaking in an attempt to remedy the basic evil that had enabled Handschuch's attempt: he drafted a church constitution with the assistance of leading members of the congregation which put the whole structure of the congregation upon an entirely new basis. The key element of this constitution was the transformation of the Church council from self-appointed and essentially corrupt into an annually elected body. Against this background, the relationship between Church council and minister was redefined so that the latter was given independent status as well as new and more extensive obligations. Laymen henceforth played a decisive role. The document was signed on October 19, 1762, "at the very moment when God's merciful eyes shone through the bleak clouds," as Mühlenberg wrote to Francke and Ziegenhagen on December 1, 1762. With the signatures of the preachers and all congregation members, "a long-desired peace, as well as a complete Church order, had been concluded."[17]

The worst crisis—the one that had pushed Mühlenberg to the end of his tether—had thus been overcome. At the same time, it seems to me that Mühlenberg managed to bring about the decisive breakthrough in creating the foundation of a viable and cohesive Church body, inasmuch as the majority of congregations rather quickly adopted the major part of this new Church order (the first to do so, in 1767, being Lancaster, the most important, most influential and largest congregation after Philadelphia).

In January of the same year, the until then fatherly relationship between Mühlenberg and Gotthilf August Francke slipped into its worst crisis—a crisis from which it had not recovered when Francke died two years later. As Mühlenberg's son lacked the talent necessary to become a pharmacist, Francke had introduced him to a Lübeck merchant, who took him on as an apprentice. This merchant was the brother of Francke's closest collaborator, and he treated Friedrich August Konrad (i.e. Frederick Augustus Conrad) Mühlenberg so poorly that the young man, at the first opportunity, got himself recruited to return to North America with a British regiment destined there. Francke wrote to Mühlenberg about his son's "rash resolution," hoping that "prayer and the tears of his beloved parents will also bring back this misguided son."[18] Meanwhile, reliable sources had informed Mühlenberg about his son's desolate situation, who himself confirmed these reports upon his return. Mühlenberg obviously felt so badly cheated that he stopped writing to Ziegenhagen and Francke between 1766 and 1768, which meant that the cornerstone of the relationship between Philadelphia and Halle had been shattered for good. The "fraternal" exchange of letters degenerated into a business correspondence.

It was during these years that Mühlenberg's major health problems were beginning to show. The most irritable organs were his bronchi and lungs, but he also suffered from rheumatism and, later on, from deafness. This notwithstanding, he set out on a long journey to Ebenezer, Georgia, with his wife and his youngest daughter in 1774/75. On behalf of Friedrich Michael Ziegenhagen, he there endeavored in vain to settle the dispute between Christian Rabenhorst and Christian Friedrich Triebner, the two ministers of the congregation. Upon Mühlenberg's return to Philadelphia, the city was in full revolt, and after careful reflection, he came to the decision that, with everything focused on war and politics, as minister he would no longer be of importance in Philadelphia. He therefore bought a house in New Providence, renovated it, and in early 1776 moved with his unmarried daughter to the country. Also, he thought hard about what a Lutheran (and a Lutheran minister, at that) should do and not do in a period of revolutionary change. The starting point for his reflections was the commandment in chapter thirteen of Paul's Letter to the Romans: "Let every soul be subject unto the higher powers." It was a belief that he would not, and could not, doubt.

The only question was what would happen when it was unclear who these "higher powers" were: in 1776, they could have been the Continental Congress, the Committee of Inspection and Observation (nearer to his home), the far-sighted eye of the revolutionary powers, or, on the other side of the Atlantic, the King of England, to whom Mühlenberg, when still in the Electorate of Hannover, had pledged fidelity and obedience. In August 1776, he drafted his first reflections: "If God's governance ordains or suffers that a king or a parliament or a congress should have power over me, then I must be subject to and serve two discordant masters at the same time." Of course, this would not work, simply because the Bible explicitly forbade the serving of two masters at a time. Mühlenberg was to discover the theological answer a year later, in November 1777. It deserves to be quoted in detail, especially in light of the continuing controversy over his political attitude: "If it is objected that we ceased to pray publicly for His Britannic Majesty George III ever since the declaration of *independence* and accordingly committed sin,

it may be said in reply that we were not allowed to engage in politics and had to observe the express command of God's Word in Romans 13: Let every soul be subject unto the higher powers which have authority over you and protect you *pro t[empore]*, or for the time being. Daniel 2: God, who rules over all things, changeth the times and the seasons. He removeth kings and setteth up kings according to His most holy will and without asking any of His creatures. Whosoever therefore resisteth the government that has overwhelming power, resisteth God and His ordinance, for no government exists without God's will and permission."[19]

The solution lay in the Latin words "pro tempore," which answered the question as to the authority to whom Lutherans owed obedience, namely to the authority exerting actual power in the relevant locality. This way, the Lutheran settlers, whose political convictions denied them a spontaneous political response, had been given a biblically grounded answer as to what authority Paul had had in mind. They now could rely on Daniel's phrase that God rules over all things and that nothing happens that is not according to his will.

Mühlenberg spent the last years of his life, withdrawn from the world, in New Providence. As a final contribution to the development of the Lutheran Church, he corrected and revised the completed manuscript of the first Lutheran hymnbook of the Pennsylvanian Church, which the United Ministerium, a little while earlier, had decided to publish (and for which Mühlenberg's successor in Philadelphia, his friend and colleague Justus Heinrich Christian Helmuth, was responsible). Heinrich Melchior Mühlenberg died on October 7, 1787, only three weeks after the new constitution for what was to become the United States of America had been adopted.

Do Mühlenberg's undisputed achievements justify the honorary title of "Patriarch of the American Lutheran Church"? The answer is difficult, not least because the emergence and development of this Church and its ninety-five separate congregations cannot be limited to the accomplishments of a single person. Mühlenberg, albeit undisputed *primus*, was one of fourteen ministers from Halle who all saw themselves as Halle Pietism's standard-bearers in Pennsylvania. To draw a first conclusion, it was a vision that failed—because the settlers from Baden and Württemberg quite simply refused to follow the men from Halle. This is not to say that these people lived a wicked and sinful life. On the contrary, a detailed analysis of German hymns between 1730 and 1830 clearly shows that the religious mood of the settlers is best described by the terms "pious" and "pietist."[20] The question as to whether eighteenth-century Lutherans were

14 Ibid., p. 65. **15** Confirmation was introduced in Württemberg in 1723; emigrants from this part of the country brought it with them to Pennsylvania, see Wellenreuther, *Citizens*, pp. 99–104. **16** Handschuch to Ziegenhagen and Francke, March 15, 1759, Franckesche Stiftungen zu Halle (Saale) (AFSt), M4 C10, no. 2. **17** Mühlenberg to Francke and Ziegenhagen, December 1, 1762, in: Mühlenberg, *Korrespondenz*, pp. 578–583. **18** Gotthilf August Francke to Mühlenberg, August 28, 1766, in: Mühlenberg, *Korrespondenz*, vol. 3: 1763–1768, pp. 438f. **19** Tappert/Doberstein, *Journals*, vol. 3, p. 101. **20** See Wellenreuther, *Citizens*, chapter 3.

pietistically minded, is still a subject of controversy and debate. As for Mühlenberg and the other men from Halle, this question must be answered in the affirmative; where the majority of Lutheran settlers in the mid-Atlantic states are concerned, however, it must be in the negative. Neither can this question be answered unambiguously from the point of view of the institutional development of the Lutheran Church in Pennsylvania. For the key factor for the development of the United Ministerium was not its foundation but the significantly increased willingness of the Baden and Württemberg Lutherans as well as their ministers—and not one was a real Pietist—to contribute to the formation of the Lutheran Church of America. On the other hand, it is undisputed that Mühlenberg, in drafting the Church constitution that was to be adopted by the congregation in Philadelphia in October 1762, played the crucial role and made his perhaps most important contribution by providing a common basis for the long-term consolidation of the congregations.

And Martin Luther? Has the reference to him, or to his work, any relevance for the consolidation of the ninety-five or more congregations into one Church? The question must be answered in the negative. In the writings of both Mühlenberg and his colleagues from Halle, there are only few references to Martin Luther. Luther's *Small Catechism* was, of course, a liturgical cornerstone—and thus a mainstay in the education of the young. But beyond this, and next to the sixteen songs by Luther in the Lutheran hymnal, to which Mühlenberg had put the finishing touches, there is hardly any evidence to support Luther's significance. Also, these sixteen songs were a significantly smaller number than the almost thirty church songs by Luther to be found in the *Halle* and *Marburg hymnals*. In other words, Luther, though always present in the religious world of Lutherans and Protestants, was certainly not omnipresent or even prominent.

The myths about Mühlenberg that adorn his memory arose immediately after his death. The direction in which they were to go is adumbrated by the poem that Mühlenbergh's friend and successor, Justus Heinrich Christian Helmuth, published as a broadside elegy entitled *On the Death of the Departed Father Mühlenberg*:

"A funeral song strike up today,
Weep for the pious man;
Let the lament resound aloud;
He is no more, the pious man!
Weep for him, young and old,
Our father's dying for us all too soon!
He's dying, and yet he cannot die;
Has left the battlefield, true peace to find,
And risen high above destruction,
To hasten to the place where he arose;
That he now reaps what he has sown,
Eternal glory's crown does wear."[21]

---

21 The German original is published in Helmuth, *Denkmal*, pp. 45, 49.

BIBLIOGRAPHY

Aland, Kurt et al. (eds.) (1968–2002), *Die Korrespondenz Heinrich Melchior Mühlenbergs aus der Anfangszeit des deutschen Luthertums in Nordamerika* (= Texte zur Geschichte des Pietismus, Abt. 3, Handschriftlicher Nachlaß, August Hermann Francke. 3). 5 vols. Berlin/New York. **American Baptist Churches**, *Our History*. Available: www.abc-usa.org/what_we_believe/our-history [07/15/2015]. **Asplund**, John (1794), *Universal Register of the Baptist Denomination in North America for the years 1790, 1791, 1792, 1793, and part of 1794*. Boston/MA. **Espín**, Orlando O./**Nickoloff**, James B. (eds.) (2007), *An Introductory Dictionary of Theology and Religious Studies*. Collegeville/MN. **General Council** of the Evangelical Lutheran Church in North America (1898), *Documentary History Evangelical Lutheran Ministerium Pennsylvania and Adjacent States. Proceedings of the Annual Conventions from 1748 to 1821*. Compiled and translated from Records IX the Archives and from the Written Protocols. Vol. 7. Philadelphia. **Helmuth**, Justus Heinrich Christian (1787), *Denkmal der Liebe und Achtung*. Philadelphia. **Mühlenberg**, Heinrich Melchior (1881), *Autobiographie*, ed. by Wilhelm Germann. Allentown/PA. **Mühlenberg**, Heinrich Melchior (1987), *Die Korrespondenz Heinrich Melchior Mühlenbergs aus der Anfangszeit des deutschen Luthertums in Nordamerika. Vol. 2: 1753–1762* (= Texte zur Geschichte des Pietismus, Abt. 3, Handschriftlicher Nachlaß, August Hermann Francke. 3), ed. by Kurt Aland et al. Berlin/New York. **Mühlenberg**, Heinrich Melchior (1987), *Die Korrespondenz Heinrich Melchior Mühlenbergs aus der Anfangszeit des deutschen Luthertums in Nordamerika. Vol. 3: 1763–1768* (= Texte zur Geschichte des Pietismus, Abt. 3, Handschriftlicher Nachlaß, August Hermann Francke. 4), ed. by Kurt Aland et al. Berlin/New York. **O'Neil**, Shannon Leigh, *Difference between Lutheran and Methodist Churches*. Available: http://classroom.synonym.com/difference-between-lutheran-methodist-churches-7827.html [11/25/2015]. **Queen II**, Edward L./**Prothero**, Stephen R./**Shattuck**, Gardiner H. Jr. (eds.) (2001), Encyclopedia of American Religious History. Revised Edition. 2 vols. New York. **Tappert**, Theodore G./**Doberstein**, John W. (eds.) (1942–58), *The Journals of Henry Melchior Muhlenberg*. 3 vols. Philadelphia. **Wellenreuther**, Hermann (2013), *Citizens in a Strange Land. A Study of German-American Broadsides and their Meaning for Germans in North America, 1730–1830*. University Park/PA. **Wellenreuther**, Hermann (2013), *Heinrich Melchior Mühlenberg und die deutschen Lutheraner in Nordamerika 1742–1787. Wissenstransfer und Wandel eines atlantischen zu einem amerikanischen Netzwerk*. Berlin. **Wellenreuther**, Hermann/**Müller-Bahlke**, Thomas/**Roeber**, A. Gregg (eds.) (2013), *The Transatlantic World of Heinrich Melchior Mühlenberg in the Eighteenth Century* (= Hallesche Forschungen. 35). Halle (Saale).

ROBERT KLUTH

Church Organization in the United States

Luther's thesis of the "priesthood of all believers" had put traditional church's principles of ecclesiastical organization fundamentally into question. Tradition alone was thus no longer enough to legitimize church hierarchy. In Protestantism, three church constitutions—ideal-typically separate one from another—were developed, each one laying out the fundamental principles of the organizational structure of the church as an institution.

The Episcopalians (from the Greek episcopos, meaning "bishop") organize their church with a bishop-oriented constitution. The church is led by bishops, upon whom other parts of the church are hierarchically dependent. The constitutions of the Anglican Church, the Methodists, some Lutheran churches, and some smaller denominations correspond to this structure. The Presbyterian constitution (from the Greek presbyteros, meaning "the elder") is derived from the reformed tradition. In this case, a council of elders presides over the congregation. Several of these councils come together to form presbyteries, which can subsequently meet in synods, or parliaments, of ecclesiastical self-administration. The synod makes decisions that affect the denomination and discusses current developments. The Congregationalists (from the Latin congregare, meaning "gather together") are autonomous church congregations. Each congregation acts under its own responsibility with no central leadership, but rather a loose network of different groups of the faithful. Although general assemblies of the congregations are held, the resulting decisions have no binding authority over individual congregations. The Anabaptists, Pentecostals, and the Baptists are organized in this way.

ROBERT KLUTH

Wandering Symbols.
The Perception of Martin Luther in the United States
and Martin Luther King in East Germany (1983–89)

There is no reason to hold that confusion is less fundamental
than is order.[1]—*Alfred North Whitehead*

The expressions of visitors in art galleries display a poorly concealed
disappointment that only paintings can be seen there.[2]—*Walter Benjamin*

Had anyone at the time of the Reformation claimed that an apple with a bite taken out of it represented the most profitable business in the world and not the Fall of Man, he would have provoked storms of laughter. Our world is full of symbols on which we depend to provide orientation in a complex existence. These symbols also form the communicative building blocks of our culture of memory.

In ancient times, it was a custom among friends to break an object into two pieces, each friend keeping one part. When these friends reencountered one another, the two fragments were placed next to each other and the friends recognized each other by means of the missing part. This is also the context of one of Plato's dialogues: ever since Zeus split androgynous human beings into two parts, they have been searching for their missing half. "Each of us is therefore one piece (σύμβολον, or *symbol*) of a single human being."[3] Symbols are counterparts and form the basis in the search for unity and identity. Symbols mean "something" when projected on societies.[4] The members of these societies recognize similarities and differences based in symbols. In the words of Niklas Luhmann, they guarantee "that two separate persons can relate to the same thing in their communication."[5] If symbols stand for historical events, they should be able to tell a contemporary society something about "its" past. The objective is the recognition of one's own historical issues.

At the same time, historical symbols are always confronted with a paradox. The symbolic presence[6] should outshine the actual intangible history, intangible because past can never really be recalled.[7] History can never be re-experienced. It is this paradox that transforms historical symbols into transcendent objects that mediate between the visible and the invisible. The observer must comprehend something that no longer exists and yet still retains significance. Historical symbols transcend arbitrary, contingent everyday life and provide structure in the great disorder prevailing in past and present. Each commemoration symbolically drops an anchor into the endless stream of history. Historical symbols always entail a social search for meaning within a historical context, as a historically relevant counterpart is conjured up and envisaged for each individual symbol, meaning that historical symbols are simultaneously question and answer.

The reformer Martin Luther and the Reverend Dr. Martin Luther King Jr. have both been transformed into historical symbols. Interestingly enough, both personalities have evoked lively interest in the country of the other, Martin Luther in the United States and Martin Luther King in Germany: Martin Luther still inspires a significant response in the United States as a reformer, and Martin Luther King is revered in Germany for his untiring fight for justice. And yet what perceptions of identity are concealed behind the responses to these international symbols?

1 Whitehead, *Modes*, p. 50. **2** Benjamin, *Einbahnstraße*, p. 138. **3** Platon, Symposium, 191d. In: Eigler, *Platon Werke*, vol. 3. **4** This is Clifford Geertz's definition of symbolic action: Geertz, *Description*, p. 10. **5** Berndt/Drügh, *Kultur*, p. 349; see Luhmann, *Gesellschaft*. **6** See Soeffner, *Überlegungen*, p. 42. **7** Fayet, *Vokabular*, pp. 7 f. **8** Martin Luther King was invited to East Berlin by Provost Heinrich Grüber, who saw a connection between King's struggle against racial segregation and his own suffering in a concentration camp. Geheimes Staatsarchiv Preußischer Kulturbesitz (GStA PK), VI. HA, Nl Grüber, H., no. 992, Proposal for an epilogue by Heinrich Grüber for a book on Martin Luther King; Geheimes Staatsarchiv Preußischer Kulturbesitz (GStA PK), VI. HA, Nl Grüber,

H., no. 485, letter from Heinrich Grüber to Martin Luther King, July 15, 1963; Geheimes Staatsarchiv Preußischer Kulturbesitz (GStA PK), VI. HA, Nl Grüber, H., no. 485, invitation of Heinrich Grüber to Martin Luther King, December 12, 1963; For more details on this visit, see Höhn/Klimke, *Breath*, pp. 89–105. **9** Bundesarchiv, BArch DY 30/J IV 2/3/4337, Protocol no. 135/88 of the secretariat of the East German Communist Party's central committee, December 5, 1988. **10** Bundesarchiv, BArch DZ 9/2652, Manuscript of a speech by Werner Rümpel, first Vice President and General Secretary of the East German Peace Council in the sixteenth Polytechnic Secondary School Berlin-Marzahn on the occasion of the renaming of the school as "Martin-Luther-King School," January

Martin Luther King in the East Germany Memorial Culture

Martin Luther King visited Berlin on September 13, 1964 (fig. 1). Following the official reception in West Berlin, he also preached twice in East Berlin as a result of substantial public demand (fig. 2).[8] This visit left its mark on East Germany. During the years following the visit, Martin Luther King would be multiply "deployed" in East German memorial culture despite the fact that the visit in 1964 had initially not been a success for the country. Not one East German official had formally greeted the civil rights leader while he was in East Berlin, and Martin Luther King had compared the divided city to American segregation in his sermon. This was all forgotten in the official commemorations of Martin Luther King in East Germany. In 1989, the secretariat of the East German Communist Party's central committee launched a memorial event[9] for Martin Luther King including the renaming of a school in East Berlin as the "Martin Luther King School."

At the official ceremony, the general secretary of the East German Peace Council, Werner Rümpel, declared that Marin Luther King's dreams, had become "reality" during his visit in the "humanist socialist society of the East Germany."[10] A similar sentiment had been expressed a year previously by the East German Christian Democratic Union's leader Gerald Götting during an official celebration commemorating the twentieth anniversary of Marin Luther King's death. According to Götting, negotiations for disarmament between the USSR and the United States represented the implementation of Martin Luther King's legacy, but only because of pressure exerted by the socialist states: "When the socialist states proclaim in their military doctrine that they do not declare a state or a population as their enemy, [...] they can simultaneously declare that they have fulfilled the legacy of Martin Luther King under our terms."[11] The actual minimal effects that Martin Luther King's concepts had on East German foreign policy are illustrated by East Germany's failure to acknowledge the invitation to the festive event marking the Martin Luther King holiday in the United States in 1989.[12]

The "Drum Major of Justice"[13] (Götting) was not a central figure in the official East German view of history; Angela Davis had far greater significance. At the beginning of the 1970s, the civil rights activist accused of an incident involving firearms became "a fixed element of the political-ideological iconography of the East German Communist Party's regime"[14] and a heroine of the "other America." A postcard campaign under the motto "One million roses for Angela Davis" fueled demands for Davis's release from a US prison. After

Fig. 1 Advertisement for the Protestant Church's congress in West Berlin's Waldbühne amphitheatre announcing a speech by Martin Luher King on September 13, 1964

her acquittal, she visited East Germany in 1972. The party officials greeted her with a bouquet of red roses and were completely unprepared for the reaction of the young East German population, which went far beyond "the framework of 'decreed solidarity.'" Instead of the two to three thousand supporters anticipated, almost fifty thousand turned out to welcome her.[15]

A comparison between this image and the disregard demonstrated by officials during Martin Luther King's previous visit in 1964 revealed the contradictory impression the civil rights activist made in East Germany. Marin Luther King's nonviolent approach did not harmonize with the official doctrine of "armed combat for peace." Moreover his technique of nonviolent opposition also had opposite results. A radio interview with the civil rights leader was broadcast in East Germany in the 1960s in which Martin Luther King urged his followers to bring their toothbrushes with them to the demonstration as they would most probably be arrested and interned. Fritz Müller, a youth pastor from Brandenburg, was deeply impressed by the interview and wrote the song *Der kleine Jonny* ("Little Jonny").[16] The chorus contains the lines "One day we will be free./King has said so." This song of resistance gained popularity within church circles. The current German president Joachim Gauck wrote in his biography that this song became one of the most poignant symbols of comfort for one of his catechists: she always took a toothbrush with

9, 1989. **11** Bundesarchiv, BArch DZ 9/2652, Manuscript of a speech by Gerald Götting, Chairman of the Christian Democratic Union of East Germany on the occasion of a memorial event commemorating the twentieth anniversary of Martin Luther King's assassination on April 4, 1988. The President of the Peace Council of East Germany, Günther Drefahl, made a similar comment in 1989. According to him, King was the herald of Gorbachev's new policies. He had recognized the consequences of the arms race at an early stage and had demanded "the permanent elimination of all forms of violence in international relationships." Bundesarchiv, BArch DZ 9/2652, speech manuscript of Prof. Dr. Dr. h. c. Günther Drefahl, President of the Peace Council of East Germany, Janu-

ary 10, 1989. **12** Bundesarchiv, BArch DZ 9/2652, letter from Willi Stoph, the chairman of the cabinet of East Germany to Coretta Scott King about an invitation to the celebration of Martin Luther King Day in 1987, January 14, 1988. **13** Stadtarchiv Halle, S15 Gött, N 126 no. 10, vol. 3, proposal for a speech on the occasion of the "International Salute to the Life and Legacy of Dr. Martin Luther King Jr." **14** Lorenz, *Heldin*, p. 2. **15** Quotation in: ibid., p. 12. **16** Archive of the Deutsches Historisches Museum, Interview with Fritz Müller by Agnes Fuchsloch, on November 26, 2014.

Fig. 2 Martin Luther King preaching in St. Mary's Church in the center of East Berlin on September 13, 1964

commemoration of Martin Luther King in East Germany did, however, have a certain trigger function: Martin Luther King's tactic of nonviolent civil disobedience, which spread from the United States via the West German peace movement to the East Germany, ultimately found expression in the Monday demonstrations.

When Martin Luther King preached in St. Mary's Church in Berlin in 1964, he was following in a great tradition of remembrance in his commemoration of Martin Luther, the "great reformer" as Martin Luther King called him. Apart from the common name, Martin Luther King had no connection whatsoever with Lutheran theology.[20] Martin Luther King's name was nevertheless a powerful symbol for German society. If a victim of racist persecution shared a name with the great Reformer, this permitted the resurrection and positive revaluation of historical narratives dating back to the nineteenth century, transforming a figure of German national identity temporarily invalidated during the Nazi period into a positive figure of Christian resistance. High officials in East Germany had also made this connection, even though they were ultimately unable to enforce their interpretation of Martin Luther King as representing "the other America." In November 1989, the nonviolent protests that had originated in churches gained such momentum that they ultimately achieved the fall of the wall. In this case, the symbol of "Martin Luther King" had also become a catalyst of social processes.

Martin Luther in the US Memorial Culture

On November 6, 1983, in the Basilica of the National Shrine of the Immaculate Conception in Washington, D. C., 2,500 people gathered to celebrate the five-hundredth anniversary of Martin Luther's birth. This event was broadcast live on television, and marked the start of the Luther anniversary year. Its highlight was a play based on the words of Luther, his contemporaries such as Jean Calvin and those he influenced including Marin Luther King Junior.[21] The fact that the largest Catholic church in America was the location for this event was a sign of reconciliation on the part of American Lutherans. The *New York Times* made the connection between the festive ceremony and the acknowledgement of Luther's piety by Pope John Paul II.[22] The remembrance was simultaneously a symbol and a wish: it was intended not only to represent Luther's influence on American history but to help bridge contemporary differences.

Martin Luther only made reference to the New World on two occasions.[23] The nineteenth century, however, saw him as a hero whose Protestant struggle for freedom could at last be implemented in the United States.[24] At that same time, he was a symbol of American anti-Catholicism [25] years before being interpreted as the spiritual predecessor of German Hitlerism in the twentieth century.[26] Ultimately, the

her to school, which helped her to hold her ground as a Christian in the face of official East German Communist Party doctrine.[17]

A survey of 350 members of East Germany's opposition, who had played a role in the 1980s provided confirmation of Martin Luther King's central "orientation and role model function." In fact, Marin Luther King came in second place after Mahatma Gandhi.[18] In the same survey, this civil rights leader was even more popular than Jesus Christ (third place) and Dietrich Bonhoeffer (fourth place). It has yet to be established whether a direct line can be traced between the initial impact of Martin Luther King and the peaceful revolution in the East Germany.[19] The atmosphere associated with the

17 Gauck, *Winter*, pp. 284–286. **18** Geisel, *Suche*, pp. 353–357. Nearly 48 percent voted in favor of the statement "was very important," and only 5.1 percent selected "of no consequence." **19** Höhn/Klimke, *Breath*, pp. 102–104. **20** Deutsches Rundfunkarchiv Babelsberg, DRA K2001005, Martin Luther King greets the citizens of East-Berlin and brings greetings from West-Berlin, September 13, 1964; for a summary of the research into the choice of the name "Martin Luther": Branch, *Waters*, p. 47. **21** Briggs, *Luther's Role*, p. A22.

22 Ibid. **23** Schilling, *Rebell*, p. 26. **24** Lehmann, *Imagination*; Wipfler, *Pictures*, p. 188; Baglyos, *American Lutherans*, p. 56. **25** Lehmann, *Imagination*, p. 48. **26** McGovern, *Luther*. **27** Chandler, *Roman Catholics*. **28** The basis for the text appears to have been a conference at the Concordia Theological Seminary: an article along the same line of argument had already appeared in the *New York Times*: Briggs, *Scholars*. **29** Pelikan, *Relevance*. **30** Chapman, *500 years*. **31** Will, *Luther's Quest*. **32** It was unfortunately not possible for me to

commemoration of Martin Luther in the America of 1983 took on a completely new dimension: the *Lutheran Council of America* was now in favor of reconciliation between denominations and religions.

Luther was represented during the festivities as an extraordinary historical figure whose achievements also had an influence on the United States. The *Los Angeles Times* headline read, "At the Age of 500, Martin Luther Is Becoming 'a Man for all Christians.'"[27] The Reformer could now be viewed as a man of common understanding on the strength of the fact that "Roman Catholic bishops, East German Communist leaders, Jewish scholars, and local councils of churches" were now all discussing Luther's legacy. The writer concluded that "if the Jews can forgive Luther for his verbal excesses," the Catholic Church could perhaps rescind his excommunication and possibly even make him a saint.[28]

An extended essay appearing in the *New York Times*, written by the church historian and editor of the English translation of Luther's works, Jaroslav Pelikan, met with a wide reaction. Pelikan viewed Luther as the founder of the modern concept of families and therefore the founder of modern statehood.[29] Along the same line of argument, the *Chicago Tribune* identified Luther as the source of modernity: "[I]t is impossible to imagine the modern world without him. More than anyone else, Luther was responsible for unleashing the forces that have shaped the world as we know it."[30] George Will, writing in the *Washington Post*, even saw Luther as a founding father of the United States: he was in favor of the responsibility of freedom, the state, modernism, the family, and individuality. Will argued that Luther's theology had had far-reaching consequences: "You, reader, are living in a country that is, in no small measure, a consequence." He concluded: "So this Republic, 207 years old, should honor a Founding Father born 500 years ago."[31]

The anniversary week held by the *Lutheran Council of America* ran along similar lines.[32] A musical entitled *Martin Luther, Rebel, Priest* displayed Luther's "human qualities"[33] in its representation of a singing Reformer who drank beer and outdid himself in a song about his spouse, Katharina von Bora: "Katie, Katie, Funny Lady, Will You Be My Wife." Luther's "less humanitarian characteristics"[34] such as his anti-Semitism, which was also a theme of the musical, did not prevent the musical composer from presenting Luther in a "heroic light" at the end of the work with the words "Here I stand."

Generally speaking, the focus in the United States in 1983 was on a divided Germany in which such different conceptions of Luther could exist alongside each other. The *New York Times*, in its headline "Each Germany Has Found Its Own Martin Luther,"[35] highlighted the paradoxical situation of two parallel historical interpretations in the separate German states. The *Christian Science Monitor*[36] commented extensively on Luther's hateful views on Jews and farmers,

ultimately assigning him responsibility for ending the medieval unity of the church.

It is conspicuous that the East German peace movement within church circles was a recurring theme. The American press frequently interpreted the anniversary as a struggle between the East German establishment and the church based opposition for the symbol of Luther.[37] In contrast, the *Chicago Tribune* commented on the Luther anniversary as follows: "Two artificial nations [that] are becoming increasingly aware how much they want to be one."[38] Here Luther is deemed a German symbol rather than a conciliator as was the case during the anniversary week. He is the symbol of reawakening nationalism after Hitler and for a divided German nation that could play a geopolitical role within the framework of the Cold War. He is seldom assigned direct connections with the United States today. These articles are similar to reports of field research carried out in a distant and somewhat strange land.

The only active measure undertaken by the American government to mark Luther's anniversary was a commemorative postage stamp with a portrait of the Reformer (fig. 3). This was the only symbol of the anniversary for which a state agency was responsible and did not originate in church circles. A statement by the postal service made it clear that the sate by no means intended to make a religious declaration. Luther had significance because he "eventually" initiated compulsory education: "The approach taken by the US Postal Service, however, has been acknowledged by all concerned: The US government does not want to be accused of giving the 'stamp of approval' to religious groups commemorating their spiritual milestones."[39] It was the Republican William E. Dannemeyer, a US congressman and a member of the *Lutheran Church–Missouri Synod*, who was behind the issuing of the stamp. As the Methodist church had only just received a rejection for a similar request, the decision in favor of the Luther commemorative stamp was controversial.[40]

Jewish Americans also found this commemoration disagreeable and reacted to the commemorative stamp with protests. Partly as a result of the imbroglio surrounding the Luther stamp, the German theologian Johannes Wallmann was invited to attend a discussion on the legacy of Luther's anti-Semitic writings at the *American Jewish Committee*.[41] The *New York Times* described this conference as a fruitful discussion that did not, however, achieve any consensus. Rabbi Manfred Vogel contradicted Wallmann's viewpoint as follows: "With his ethnic-national anti-Semitism, Luther's figure invades the modern era."[42] Here Luther is portrayed as a symbol of Nazi Germany, of which American Jews still had vivid recollections.[43]

A 1983 text by the German American rabbi Albert Friedlander illustrates how painful the commemoration of Luther was for the Jewish population. In it he conjures up an image of a Luther fortress

consult the archives of the Lutheran Council of America. The correspondence "between U.S. government officials and officials of the German Democratic Republic, Sweden, Denmark, Norway and Finland embassies" would have provided interesting material for this enquiry: Archives of the Evangelical Lutheran Church in America, LCU 24/1, LCU 24/2, LUTHERAN COUNCIL IN THE U.S.A. Martin Luther Jubilee, 1974, 1977, 1979–84, 1967. **33** Ames, *Musical*. **34** Ibid. **35** Markham, *Germany*. **36** Pond, *Martin Luther*. **37** Tomforde,

Luther Celebration; Drozdiak, *German Party*; Benetazzo, *East Germany*; Markham, *East Germany*. **38** Kilian, *Nationalism*. **39** Dart, *Religion Notes*. **40** Csongos, *Martin Luther*. **41** Wallmann, *Judenschriften*. **42** Austin, *Scholars*. **43** Appropriately, the only article appearing in The American Israelite in 1983 was a brief report on the official rejection of the Lutheran theses on the Jews by the Lutheran World Federation: Tanenbaum, *Lutherans*.

Fig. 3 US Postage commemorative stamp for Martin Luther, 1483–1983, with a portrait based on Lucas Cranach the Elder, issued November 11, 1983

with a torture chamber in the basement. He imagines a confrontation with Luther: "We are sitting opposite each other in the dark basement and Brother Martin cannot see me. What he does see is a distorted figure, a hellish mask. And this hurts me […] Oh Martin, I cannot do it like this and I do not wish to do it. I do not wish to make my farewell here in the darkness. We must go up to where you can recognize me again as one of the people of God."[44]

The latent tension in this description is relativized by Friedlander when he relates an episode that took place in Atlanta at Martin Luther King's grave: "Not long ago, I visited a grave in Atlanta. Someone standing beside me leaned on my arm. 'Free at last!' is inscribed on the gravestone and the father wept. 'Here I stand, Martin Luther King,' he said to me. 'Do you know who I am? I am Abraham, and Isaac is lying there.' And I thought of the script 'that Jesus Christ was born a Jew' and of the firm foundation of the Hebrew Bible on which Christianity is based. Brother Martin from Eisleben, you have saved this territory for Christianity, even if I have to fight with you to retain my own place."[45] Friedlander, who had personally participated in the march from Selma to Montgomery,[46] assigns symbols to Martin Luther King originating from Protestant and biblical traditions. The quotation "Here I stand" and the figures of Abraham and Isaac are meant to help lead the troubled relationship between Jews and Christians back to its common origin: the Hebrew Bible.

Martin Luther's standing in the United States has oscillated between the concrete (the American conception of Germany) and the symbolic (a reconciliatory figure in America's marketplace of religions). His universal interpretation as the "Father of Protestantism" and his use as a particular emblem of a divided Germany has also had a politicial connotation.

Plural Identities or Blinkered Identity?

As our everyday language is insufficient to capture the cornucopia of facts and the complexity of history, we invent symbols for past events. Particularly in cases of personalities within Christian contexts there has been a revival of iconic traditions. Dorothea Wendebourg paints a similar picture: "Why would we continue celebrating anniversaries if we did not believe that that which is remembered and that which is celebrated still have a connection with our own lives?"[47] In other words, we are unable to catch up with the perspective of the symbol from its own perspective.[48] This systematic non-availability within historical symbolism is rooted in the non-availability of past events. This non-availability is, however, necessary to enable the symbol to at least tell us "something."[49] We do not have the symbols at our disposal; they have us at their disposal, just as a sickness takes possession of us.[50] We adhere to the images and signs from the past that point back to our own identity. Our own identity therefore legitimates these symbols, even though these memories do not find any correspondence in terms or logic.

Commemorative anniversaries create identity stability and enclose their non-availability. At the same time, the event that is being celebrated becomes unhistorical, as history by definition cannot be repeated. Esthetic perception replaces the actual events and becomes the precondition for both the memory of the past and expectations of the future. Thomas Macho expresses this concept in a nutshell: commemorations are a "symbolic construction." They stand for the "political dominance over time which from a qualitative perspective corresponds to dominance over territories."[51] The symbol sets of today maintain a dominance of the present over the past. As this dominance is however only apparently natural, a large portion of self-delusion is embedded in every anniversary. As demonstrated by the historical symbols of Martin Luther and Martin Luther King, anniversaries always possess their own internal dynamics, refusing to be confined to a single meaning. In pluralistic societies, such commemorations are far removed from the politics of history and necessarily disputed. Their association with individual and social identity always conceals an element of emotional turmoil.

Consequently, commemorations approach like thunderstorms: we cannot control the unavoidable symbolic downpour, but we can critique it. When the historical view beyond national borders blurs the apparent certainties of contemporary symbolism, the current identitarian movement that attempts to line history up blurs as well.

44 Friedlander, *Juden*, p. 263. **45** Ibid. **46** Der Anfang einer Reise auf der Suche nach Versöhnung oder: Auf der Suche nach Menschen der Versöhnung. Momente der Begegnung mit Albert H. Friedlander, in: www.imdialog.de; Arbeitskreis Kirche und Israel in der Evangelischen Kirche Hessen und Nassau (06.2004). Available from: www.imdialog.org/md2004/06/01.html [06/23/2015]. **47** Wendebourg, *Vergangene Reformationsjubiläen*, p. 279 f. **48** Mersch, *Paradoxien*, p. 46. **49** Eco, *Symbol*, p. 331. **50** This concept was formulated by the Belgian philosopher Rudi Visker. See Visker, *Filosofie*, pp. 25–29, 101–136. **51** Schmitt, *2015?*

BIBLIOGRAPHY

Ames, Lynne (1983), *Play Offers Different Luther: New Musical Offers a Different Luther*. New York Times, November 6, 1983. **Austin**, Charles (1983), *Scholars Debate the Influence of Luther on Anti-Semitism*. New York Times, October 16, 1983. **Baglyos**, Paul A. (1999), *Americans Lutherans at the Dawn of the Republic*. Lutheran Quarterly, vol. 13, pp. 51–74. **Benetazzo**, Piero (1983), *East Germany rehabilitates old heroes: Churches see old symbols as new myth*; The state preaches peace, arms for war East Germany rehabilitating Luther, Wagner, Frederick II. Christian Science Monitor, March 14, 1983, p. 1. **Benjamin**, Walter (1980), Einbahnstraße. In: Tiedemann, Rolf/Schweppenhäuser, Hermann (eds.) (1980), *Walter Benjamin. Gesammelte Schriften*, vol. 10. Frankfurt am Main, pp. 83–148. **Berndt**, Frauke/**Drügh**, Heinz J. (2009), Kultur. Einleitung. In: id. (ed.), *Symbol: Grundlagentexte aus Ästhetik, Poetik und Kulturwissenschaft*, Frankfurt am Main, pp. 339–356. **Branch**, Taylor (1988), *Parting the Waters: America in the King Years, 1954–1963*. New York. **Briggs**, Kenneth A. (1983), *Luther's Role in Christianity Evaluated on His 500th Birthday*. New York Times, November 8, 1983, p. A22. **Briggs**, Kenneth A. (1983), *Scholars Call Luther a Man for All Christians*. New York Times, June 5, 1983, p. 1. **Chandler**, Russell (1983), *Roman Catholics Participate in Quincentennial of His Birth: At Age of 500, Martin Luther Is Becoming a Man for All Christians*. Los Angeles Times, November 10, 1983, p. d1. **Chapman**, Stephen (1983), *Martin Luther, 500 years later*. Chicago Tribune, November 6, 1983, p. d2. **Csongos**, Frank T. (1982), *Martin Luther stamp approved*. United Press International, October 29, 1982. **Dart**, John (1983), *Religion Notes: Postal Service to Issue Stamp Honoring 'Secular' Luther*. Los Angeles Times, October 8, 1983, p. b7. **Drozdiak**, William (1983), *A German Party Finds New Hero in Martin Luther: Luther Is Extolled as 'Bourgeois Revolutionary' East German Party, Church in Tug-of-War Over Luther*. Washington Post, November 10, 1983. **Eco**, Umberto (2009), Symbol. In: Berndt, Frauke/Drügh, Heinz J. (eds.), *Symbol: Grundlagentexte aus Ästhetik, Poetik und Kulturwissenschaft*. Frankfurt am Main, pp. 325–335. **Eigler**, Gunther (ed.) (1990), *Platon Werke*, vol. 3, 2nd ed. Darmstadt. **Fayet**, Roger (2007), *Das Vokabular der Dinge*. In: Österreichische Zeitschrift für Geschichtswissenschaften, vol. 18, pp. 7–31. **Friedlander**, Albert H. (1983), Aus der Sicht eines Juden. In: Schultz, Hans Jürgen (ed.), *Luther kontrovers*. Stuttgart/Berlin, pp. 252–264. **Gauck**, Joachim (2010), *Winter im Sommer—Frühling im Herbst: Erinnerungen*. München. **Geertz**, Clifford (1973), Thick Description: Toward to an Interpretive Theory of Culture. In: id., *The Interpretation of Cultures. Selected Essays*. New York, pp. 3–30. **Geisel**, Christof (2005), *Auf der Suche nach einem dritten Weg: das politische Selbstverständnis der DDR-Opposition in den achtziger Jahren*. Berlin. **Höhn**, Maria/**Klimke**, Martin (2010), *A Breath of Freedom: The Civil Rights Struggle, African American GIs, and Germany*. New York. **Kilian**, Michael (1983), *German nationalism growing*. Chicago Tribune, September 10, 1983, p. 9. **Lehmann**, Hartmut (1988), *Martin Luther in the American Imagination*. München. **Lorenz**, Sophie (2013), *'Heldin des anderen Amerikas.' Die DDR-Solidaritätsbewegung für Angela Davis, 1970–1973*. In: Zeithistorische Forschungen/Studies in Contemporary History, 10, H. 1, p. 2. Available from: www.zeithistorische-forschungen.de/1-2013/id=4590 [04/07/2016]. **Luhmann**, Niklas (2009), Die Gesellschaft der Gesellschaft. In: Erndt, Frauke/Drügh, Heinz J., *Symbol: Grundlagentexte aus Ästhetik, Poetik und Kulturwissenschaft*, Frankfurt am Main, pp. 395–409. **Markham**, James M. (1983), *Each Germany Has Found Its Own Martin Luther*. New York Times, July 1, 1983, p. A2. **Markham**, James M. (1983), *East Germany Finally Embraces Luther: East German y Is Embracing Luther*. New York Times, May 8, 1983. **McGovern**, William Montgomery (1941), *From Luther to Hitler. History of Fascist-Nazi Political Philosophy*. Boston. **Mersch**, Dieter (2005), *Paradoxien der Verkörperung. Zu einer negativen Semiotik des Symbolischen*. In: Berndt, Frauke/Brecht, Christoph (eds.), *Aktualität des Symbols*. Freiburg im Breisgau, pp. 33–52. **Pelikan**, Jaroslav (1983), *The Enduring Relevance of Martin Luther 500*. New York Times, September 18, 1983. **Pond**, Elizabeth (1983), *Martin Luther: Two Germanys give accolades on his 500th anniversary*. Christian Science Monitor, April 20, 1983, p. 12. **Schilling**, Heinz (2012), *Martin Luther: Rebell in einer Zeit des Umbruchs*. München. **Schmitt**, Oliver Maria, *2015? Können Sie vergessen!* Frankfurter Allgemeine Zeitung, December 31, 2014, p. 9. **Soeffner**, Hans-Georg (2004), Protosoziologische Überlegungen zur Soziologie des Symbols und des Rituals. In: Schlögl, Rudolf/Giesen, Bernhard/Osterhammel, Jürgen (eds.), *Die Wirklichkeit der Symbole: Grundlagen der Kommunikation in historischen und gegenwärtigen Gesellschaften*. Konstanz, pp. 41–72. **Tanenbaum**, Rabbi Marc H. (1983), *Lutherans Reject Anti-Semitic Teachings*. American Israelite, August 25, 1983. **Tomforde**, Anna, *Luther celebration with political tone*. Boston Globe, November 9, 1983. **Visker**, Rudi (2005), *Vreemd gaan en vreemd blijven: filosofie van de multiculturaliteit*. Amsterdam. **Wallmann**, Johannes (2014), Die Evangelische Kirche verleugnet ihre Geschichte. Zum Umgang mit Martin Luthers Judenschriften Teil II. In: *Deutsches Pfarrerblatt*, vol. 7. **Wendebourg**, Dorothea (2014), Vergangene Reformationsjubiläen. Ein Rückblick im Vorfeld von 2017. In: Schilling, Heinz (ed.): *Der Reformator Martin Luther 2017: Eine wissenschaftliche und gedenkpolitische Bestandsaufnahme*. Berlin, pp. 261–281. **Whitehead**, Alfred North (1938), *Modes of Thought*. New York. **Will**, George F. (1983), *Luther's Quest*. Washington Post, November 6, 1983. **Wipfler**, Esther Pia (2011), *Martin Luther in Motion Pictures: History of a Metamorphosis*. Göttingen.

MARTIN LUTHER ✝ King

Civil rights leader Martin Luther King and Martin Luther share the same name. But how similar are these two great figures of world history? Here's a juxtaposition of the most important stages in the lives of the two men.

King claims to have had an experience of God in Montgomery in 1957, which encouraged him in his fight against racism.

King was a Baptist minister. In his theology, he did not make any reference to Martin Luther. Important impulses came from the philosophy of Mahatma Gandhi and theologian Walter Rauschenbusch.

The young Mike King Jr. was renamed Martin Luther King Jr. by his own father. When visiting East Berlin in 1964, he declared: "I come to you not altogether as a stranger, for the name that I happen to have is a name so familiar to you, so familiar to Germany, and so familiar to the world, and I am happy that my parents decided to name me after the great Reformer."

AWAKENING

THEOLOGY

THE NAME MARTIN LUTHER

Luther tells of an awakening experience when reading Romans, which goes down in history as the "Tower Experience."

Luther's theology was based on his findings in the Bible. Faith in Christ is sufficient for attaining salvation; good works are not necessary for this purpose. Luther rejected believers' baptism, as practiced by Anabaptists.

In 1517, the Reformer changed his name from Luder to Luther. He called himself "Eleutherius", the free one, adopting the "th" for his name.

Martin Luther

The day before his death, King said that he had seen the promised land.

I have a dream

"I have a Dream"
1963, Washington, D.C.

King was shot by a white racist in 1968.

In Germany, 71 institutions are named after Martin Luther King.

MOST FAMOUS QUOTE

DEATH

AFTERLIFE

"Here I stand, I can do no other."
1521 Worms

Luther died in his hometown of Eisleben in 1546, probably from a stroke.

In 1883, the 400th anniversary of Luther was celebrated. A copy of the Luther statue in Worms was made, shipped to the US and erected in Washington, D.C.

Here I stand ...

The quote was put into Luther's mouth after his interrogation at the Diet of Worms in 1521.

JOANNA REILING LINDELL

Early Printed Protestant Reformation Material in United States Collections: A Preliminary Guide for Researchers

Scholars of any historical field understand the enriching and intimate realm of original artifacts. For all the convenience and importance of modern printings and the Internet, they cannot replace the study of original sources. This is not only because of the sensory experience, which is so rich and satisfying—the feel and smell of the paper, the look of dense inks, variations in printing, and the solidity of the object in hand—but also for the tangible connection to the object itself that was created, used, and distributed by those whom we study. These are among the reasons why historians and scholars in general so deeply value library and museum collections. They are what makes the important collections of early printed Reformation material in the United States compelling to explore.

The sixteenth century was unquestionably one of the most expansive times of change in the history of the modern world, many aspects of which are examined in this volume. The rapid replication and dissemination of information through the implementation of the printing press across Europe starting in the mid-fifteenth century, and a dynamic, robust climate of intellectual exploration, formed the beginnings of modern culture.

Medieval book production in Europe, while yielding glorious results, created relatively minimal numbers of books annually in a given locale because of the labor-intensive process and the expense of parchment and vellum. After the 1454 invention of the printing press by Johannes Gutenberg, printing began to spread rapidly across Europe, and by the end of the fifteenth century presses were present in over two hundred European cities, and an estimated six million books had been printed, more than had been produced by hand throughout the entire medieval period.[1] This new reality represented an original landscape of potential knowledge and education through literary and visual means. The shift from a manuscript culture of the medieval period to a print culture of the sixteenth century is not only significant historically, but it is also pertinent to the collections highlighted here. A culture of collecting printed material began as early as the sixteenth century, in part because the material was accessible. It was not merely the press itself that aided the movement, but rather the reformers' astute understanding of how to use its output as a new kind of active media.[2]

Why do strong collections of early printed Reformation material exist across the United States? The answer is perhaps simple, and also too complex to fully address here. Significant numbers of Prot-

estants have historically lived in America, with concentrations in certain geographic regions. With specific consideration to Lutherans in America from the seventeenth century on, the development of increasing numbers and organization of Lutheran synods was in part linked to the need for and subsequent establishment of seminaries and colleges to educate Lutheran clergy.[3] One of the first Lutheran seminaries to be established in the United States was the Lutheran Theological Seminary at Gettysburg in 1826,[4] a seminary whose library collection is mentioned below. It is an obvious, but vital, point to make: many of the highlighted collections reside in seminary and college libraries that exist as educational resources for scholars, clergy, and laity.

Some collections began from the passionate dedication of private collectors. Many of these private collections have now entered into public institutions. Others function as an educational and cultural resource open to scholars, including the *Thrivent Financial Collection of Religious Art* in Minneapolis, Minnesota. While the scope and historic range of the Thrivent Financial Collection encompasses the wider Western Christian tradition with objects from the thirteenth to the twenty-first centuries, within the collection are some important Reformation prints, pamphlets, and historic letters such as portraits of Reformation figures by Albrecht Dürer, Lucas Cranach the Elder, Hans Brosamer (fig. 1), and Sebald and Barthel Beham. Also included is a woodcut portrait of Luther by Hans Baldung Grien, which, some years ago, inspired the start of a search for connections to additional Reformation collections rich in early books and pamphlets. Baldung's popular and controversial portrait *Martin Luther as an Augustinian Friar* (see fig. 1 in the contribution of Christiane Andersson to this volume) was created in 1521 to initially illustrate the title page of the first edition of *Acts and Deeds of Dr. Martin Luther* (*Acta Et Res Gestae, Dr. Martini Lutheri*) published in Strasbourg in 1521 by Johann Schott, who subsequently used the portrait in multiple additional texts.

Luther's influence on the modern world extends well beyond his role as a sixteenth-century religious and cultural revolutionary. For many American Protestants, their cultural link to the notion of religious freedom is strongly related to the force started by the bold Reformers from the early modern period. For collections and institutions, gathering and preserving Reformation history seems intensely pertinent to the historical Protestant American experience.

In silentio et spe erit fortitudo vestra.
Martinus Luther abconterfect.

Hanns Guldenmundt zu Nürmberg.

Fig. 1 Hans Brosamer (after Lucas Cranach the Elder),
Martin Luther, 1530

Observations and Parameters

Due to space considerations, this essay will avoid in-depth reflection on key Reformation books and pamphlets and instead focus on U.S. public and private library collections primarily comprising books strong in early to mid-sixteenth-century material. Some general observations are helpful to note in listing the collections. The particular background or history of an institution, and, for private collections, personal beliefs and heritage of a collector, often inform the guiding vision of the initial creation. Private collectors of this material tend to have been Protestant, for example. Strong holdings are also found in places where this material is of contextual significance, further emphasizing the immense impact of the Reformation, as with the *Folger Shakespeare Library's* Reformation collections, which enrich their understanding of the early modern world as it relates to Shakespeare.

While some libraries and institutions have a specific understanding of the number of objects among their Reformation material, many do not. This is not typically for lack of interest. Rather, the extensive scope or specific focus of some collections may have pre-

vented a devoted cataloguing of Reformation holdings. Dedicated funding and time necessary for specific cataloguing is not always readily available. Some institutions catalogue individual Reformation works in a subcollection within their overall holdings. Meticulous systems in place often empower the individual scholar to find the information he or she seeks, but befriending librarians and colleague scholars and enlisting their expertise and guidance is also certainly an invaluable part of the research process.

While this essay intends to serve as a guide to scholars, it is by no means exhaustive. There are undoubtedly a great number of places in the United States where original sources and early editions can be consulted. This essay seeks to highlight collections with volumes considered exceptional in number, scope, or rarity, and that feature first editions and early printings. Websites for the highlighted collections will be referenced and included in footnotes and bibliography to offer quick direction; in our highly digital age, these typically offer the most current updates. Some collections have a more detailed web presence than others. To be sure, the exploration of collections set forth here must be considered a starting point.

With access to collection catalogues, ability to search databases, and scanned material increasingly available online, scholars have access to more information than ever before, a situation akin to the explosion of knowledge from the invention of the printing press. Preliminary research nearly always begins online today. In the initial creation of lists of collections, some of the most wide-ranging stand out because they highlight their Reformation holdings and programming. But, also, in searching WorldCat for important works across the United States, it became increasingly clear where a great deal of material is to be found. In exploring this topic, two superb collections—and exemplars of this topic— were visited: the *Folger Shakespeare Library* and the *Richard C. Kessler Reformation Collection*. Additional history and background on these collections will be provided.

Collections

The Lutheran Theological Seminary at Gettysburg maintains the *A. R. Wentz Library*, with extensive holdings of rare and significant Reformation books and imprints.[5] This seminary is one of the oldest Lutheran seminaries in the Unites States, with a robust history of religious education. The University of Illinois at Urbana–Champaign keeps a large number of Reformation-period materials in its *Rare Book and Manuscript Library*, along with strong holdings of incunabula (books printed with movable type before 1500).[6]

J. S. Bridwell Library in the Perkins School of Theology at Southern Methodist University in Dallas, Texas, has in-depth special collections devoted to the Reformation and Counter-Reformation, of some

1 Sharp, *Germany*, p. 35. **2** For a comprehensive exploration of printing during this time, see Edwards, *Printing*. **3** Granquist, *Lutherans*, p. 151. **4** Ibid. **5** Gettysburg Seminary, *A. R. Wentz Library*. Because of the close contextual relationship with books printed prior to 1500, called incunabula, they will be mentioned as pertaining to highlighted collections. Such material is historically collected not only for its content but also for the books' place in the history of printing. **6** University of Illinois at Urbana–Champaign, *Book Collections*.

five thousand objects.[7] Concordia Seminary in St. Louis, Missouri, has extensive holdings related to the Protestant Reformation and early modern period, a Center for Reformation Research, and a rare-book collection of approximately 5,700 volumes composed of several specific groupings that can be browsed by call number or series search.[8]

Some collections, while small in size, are nevertheless notable. The *Gruber Rare Books Collection*, housed at the JKM Library[9] serving the Lutheran School of Theology at Chicago, contains some three hundred books from the early modern period. Among the holdings are a copy of Luther's Ninety-Five Theses, the *Theologia Deutsch* (Luther's first publication of 1516), copies of the *September* and *December Testaments* of 1522, Erasmus's second edition of the Greek New Testament, the 1534 Bible translation by Luther, and original editions of the 1529 *Large Catechism*, Augsburg Confession (1530), and *Achtliederbuch*, the first Lutheran hymnal (1524).[10] It comes as no surprise that the collection, amassed by L. Franklin Gruber in the early twentieth century, focuses on Reformation material—Gruber was formerly the president of a Lutheran seminary, Maywood Seminary.

Preservation of institutional heritage is sometimes wonderfully expressed through rare-book collections: Augustana University in Sioux Falls, South Dakota, holds a number of examples by Luther and Melanchthon in its special collections. Among them are four sixteenth-century editions of the Augsburg Confession (*Confessio Augustana*), the source from which the college's name derives.[11]

Columbia University's Burke Library at Union Theological Seminary, in New York City, houses a special collection in its rare books and manuscripts department known as the *Reformation Tracts Collection*. The Burke is one of the largest theological libraries in North America, and much of its large collection's creation dates to 1838 with the seminary's acquisition of a large portion of the library of Benedictine monk and German biblical scholar Leander van Ess, containing manuscripts, thousands of early printed books and pamphlets, and incunabula.[12]

A great number of early printed Reformation sources are found in Princeton, New Jersey, among Princeton University's impressive and immense collections. In the Princeton Theological Seminary *Rare Book and Pamphlet Collections* are numerous early examples including bibles, and objects related to the German and Swiss reformations. Princeton's holdings comprise several distinct collections as well as miscellaneous objects. The *Trendelenburg Collection*, acquired around the 1870s, contains some one hundred Reformation tracts, featuring sermons and controversial pamphlets.[13] Of special note is the *Scheide Library*,[14] which has resided on the grounds at Princeton for many decades but was bequeathed after the recent passing of William H. Scheide in 2015. Between the Rare Books and Scheide Library collections, Princeton's historical and rare Bible and incunabula holdings are comprehensive and astounding.

Early twentieth-century alumnus Bernhard K. Schaefer made a gift of some two hundred pamphlets and books by Luther around 1956.[15] The *Schaefer collection* was enriched in 1967 with 170 additional objects, a gift that was illuminated in an exhibition commemorating the 450th anniversary of Luther's nailing of the theses.[16] A rarity of the second gift of the Schaefer collection was a first edition of the

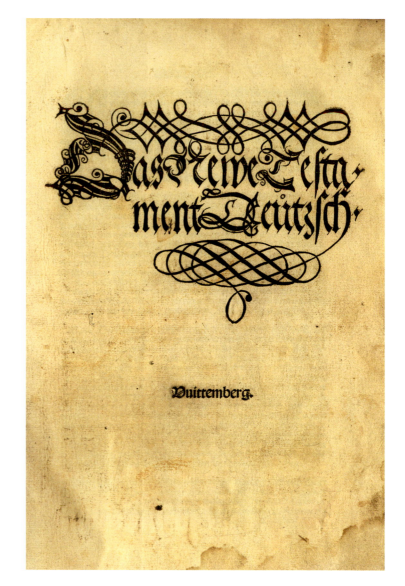

Fig. 2 Martin Luther, *Das Newe Testament Deutzsch* (The New Testament [in] German), Wittenberg 1522 (so-called September Testament)

Ninety-Five Theses, the *Disputatio* (Basel: Adam Petri, 1517). The exhibition contained objects from the Schaefer and Scheide collections, as well as the special collections.[17] A coherent distillation of the collection's significance, first used in 1967 and still found today on the special-collections website, emphasizes Luther's "force as a fomentor, disputant, tractarian, and theologian; his importance as a translator of the Bible; and his influence beyond central Europe, and especially in America."[18]

The history of printing as much as the textual information contained within has long informed the acquisitions of early books and manuscripts in the *Beinecke Rare Book and Manuscript Library* at Yale University in New Haven, Connecticut.[19] The superb scope of the collections has been enhanced for decades by significant gifts and active acquisitions. Beginning at the end of the nineteenth century, surging in the 1970s, and continuing today, the Beinecke library has maintained a strong commitment to acquiring original editions of Luther's works as well as Reformation pamphlets.[20]

Passionate scholar-collectors have certainly been a crucial source of many fine Reformation collections in the United States. One such collector was Harold J. Grimm, an educator, writer, and historian in Ohio and Indiana, who slowly collected Reformation-era books and pamphlets during his lifetime. These form the core of the *Harold J. Grimm Reformation Collection* at Ohio State University Libraries' Rare Book and Manuscript Library, which now numbers over 550 rare books by Reformation figures.[21]

The *Newberry Library* in Chicago has extensive holdings on religion and theology in general, ranging from church history and canon law to sacred music and manuscripts. Rare books relating to religious reform are the highlights, with examples of Protestant and Catholic political and religious tracts, pamphlets, and pedagogy.[22]

The *Harry Ransom Center* at the University of Texas at Austin has particularly strong religious holdings covering a range of historical sources related to Judaism and Christianity. Among the Ransom Center's collections is a rare copy of the Gutenberg Bible,[23] one of only forty-eight surviving copies, and an invaluable contextual resource for studying the history of the printing press as related to the Reformation. Sixteenth-century editions of the *Book of Common* Prayer for the service of the Church of England and an autographed manuscript of Martin Luther's *De Elevatione* are additional objects of note.[24]

Special collections of the *Sheridan Libraries* at Johns Hopkins University in Baltimore, Maryland, contain substantial material and emphasis related to the Reformation and Counter-Reformation in their libraries' philosophy and religion departments. Vernacular biblical translations, along with numerous pamphlets and works by first- and second-generation Reformers, are to be found.[25]

In Washington, D.C., at the Library of Congress, within the Rare Book and Special Collections Division, are groupings referred to as the *Reformation Collection* and the *Luther Collection*. Many imprints by Luther at the library, along with an outstanding array of contextual material from an enormous collection of incunabula, vast sixteenth-century material, early vernacular bibles, and the *Medieval and Renaissance Manuscript Collection* all make for a rich resource for Reformation scholars.[26]

Harvard University's *Early Books and Manuscripts Collection* at the Houghton Library in Cambridge, Massachusetts, holds extremely abundant early material. Their copious Reformation holdings are among a vast collection with early examples dating from 3000 B.C.E. to 1600 C.E. (and continuing to the present day in other collections).[27] Harvard has extensive collections of medieval manuscripts as well as incunabula, additionally enriching the research experience for visiting scholars. Complementary to the material in the Houghton Library are additional significant holdings in the Andover-Harvard Theological Library for Harvard Divinity School.[28] The Harvard collections constitute one of the largest resources for Reformation scholars in the country.

Another comprehensive collection in the United States is the *Richard C. Kessler Reformation Collection*, housed at Emory University's Pitts Theology Library in Atlanta, Georgia, which was established in 1987. With nearly 3,700 books, pamphlets, prints, and manuscripts dating from 1500 to 1570, and over 1,040 items by Luther alone, this collection of rare and valuable documents is an outstanding example

Fig. 3 Lucas Cranach the Elder, Illustration of the Book of Revelation (Satan bound), from: Martin Luther, Das Newe Testament Deutzsch (The New Testament [in] German), Wittenberg 1522 (so-called September Testament)

7 Southern Methodist University, *Reformation and Counter-Reformation*. **8** Concordia Seminary, *Reformation Resources*. **9** The official name of the library "JKM" combines initials from three previously separated institutions, and refers historically to Jesuit-Krauss-McCormick. **10** Klein, *Rare Books Collections*. **11** Augustana University, *Books in Special Collections*. **12** Columbia University Libraries, *The Burke Library Collection*. **13** Bishop, *German Reformation Pamphlets*, p. 183. **14** Princeton University Library, *Scheide Library*. **15** Harbison, *Luther Pamphlets*, p. 266. **16** Wagner, *Luther Exhibition*, p. 103. **17** Ibid. **18** Ibid.; Princeton University Library, *Scheide Library*. **19** Babcock, *Early Books*. **20** Ibid. **21** Ohio State University Libraries, *The Harold J. Grimm Reformation Collection*. **22** The Newberry, *Religion*. The rare-book collections at the Newberry are composed of acquisitions from numerous religious institutions in the Chicago area. **23** The Ransom Center copy of the Gutenberg Bible is one of only five complete copies in the United States. Formerly known as the "Pforzheimer copy," it was acquired by the Ransom Center in 1978. **24** Harry Ransom Center, *Religion*. **25** Johns Hopkins Sheridan Libraries & University Museums, *Reformation*. **26** Library of Congress, *Europe*. **27** Houghton Library, *Early Books & Manuscripts Collection*. **28** Andover-Harvard Theological Library, *Historical Collections*.

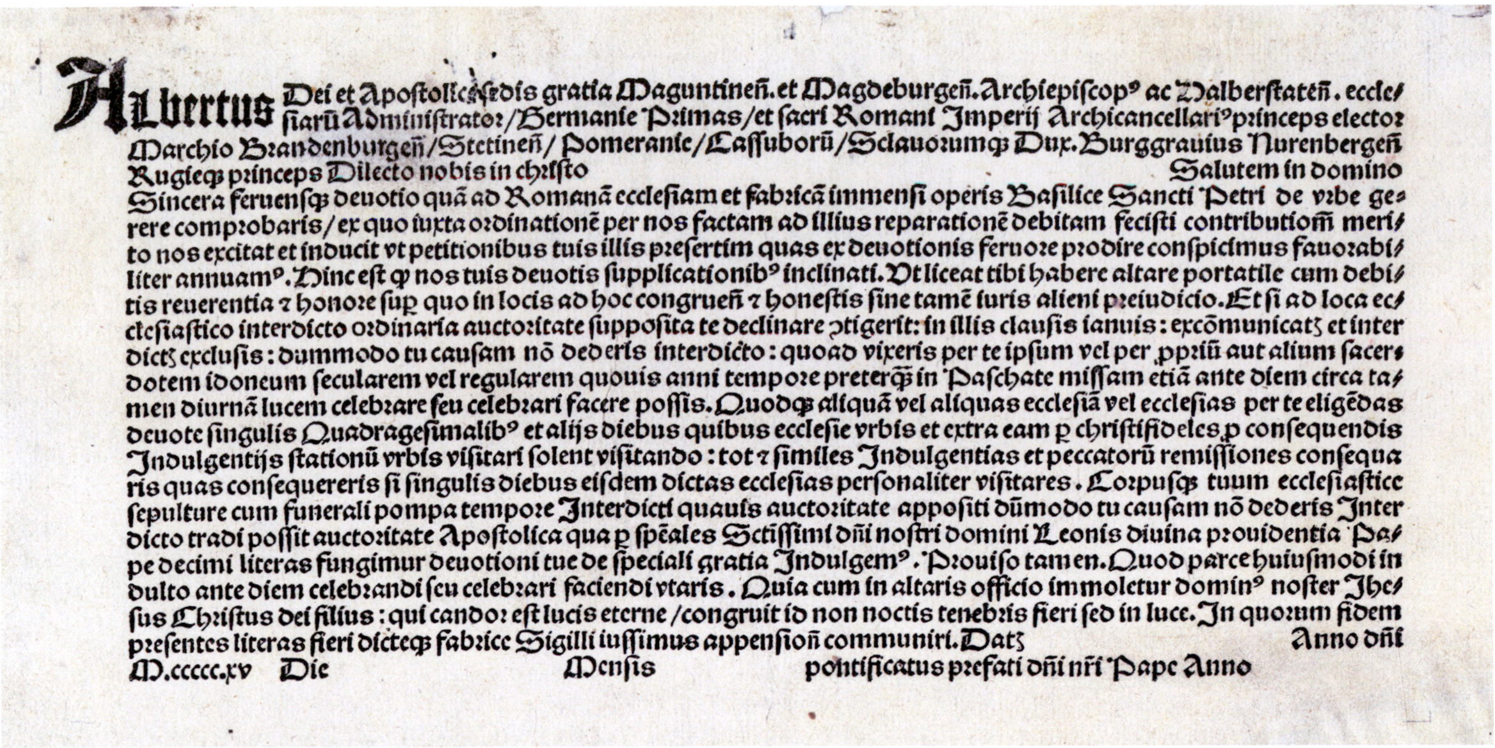

Albertus Dei et Apostolice sedis gratia Maguntineñ. et Magdeburgeñ. Archiepiscop⁹ ac Halberstateñ. eccle/siarũ Administrator/Germanie Primas/et sacri Romani Imperij Archicancellari⁹ princeps elector Marchio Brandenburgeñ/Stetineñ/Pomeranie/Cassuborũ/Sclauorumq₃ Dux. Burggrauius Nurenbergeñ Rugieq₃ princeps Dilecto nobis in christo Salutem in domino
Sincera feruensq₃ deuotio quã ad Romanã ecclesiam et fabricã immensi operis Basilice Sancti Petri de vrbe ge/rere comprobaris/ex quo iuxta ordinationẽ per nos factam ad illius reparationẽ debitam fecisti contributioñ meri/to nos excitat et inducit vt petitionibus tuis illis presertim quas ex deuotionis feruore prodire conspicimus fauorabi/liter annuam⁹. Hinc est q̃ nos tuis deuotis supplicationib⁹ inclinati. Vt liceat tibi habere altare portatile cum debi/tis reuerentia ⁊ honore sup quo in locis ad hoc congrueñ ⁊ honestis sine tamẽ iuris alieni preiudicio. Et si ad loca ec/clesiastico interdicto ordinaria auctoritate supposita te declinare ꝯtigerit: in illis clausis ianuis: excõmunicat₃ et inter/dict₃ exclusis: dummodo tu causam nõ dederis interdicto: quoad vixeris per te ipsum vel per ꝓpriũ aut alium sacer/dotem idoneum secularem vel regularem quouis anni tempore preterq₃ in Paschate missam etiã ante diem circa ta/men diurnã lucem celebrare seu celebrari facere possis. Quodq₃ aliquã vel aliquas ecclesiã vel ecclesias per te eligẽdas deuote singulis Quadragesimalib⁹ et alijs diebus quibus ecclesie vrbis et extra eam p christifideles ꝓ consequendis Indulgentijs stationũ vrbis visitari solent visitando: tot ⁊ similes Indulgentias et peccatorũ remissiones consequa/ris quas consequereris si singulis diebus eisdem dictas ecclesias personaliter visitares. Corpusq₃ tuum ecclesiastice sepulture cum funerali pompa tempore Interdicti quauis auctoritate appositi dũmodo tu causam nõ dederis Inter/dicto tradi possit auctoritate Apostolica qua p spẽales Sctissimi dñi nostri domini Leonis diuina prouidentia Pa/pe decimi literas fungimur deuotioni tue de speciali gratia Indulgem⁹. Prouiso tamen. Quod parce huiusmodi in/dulto ante diem celebrandi seu celebrari faciendi vtaris. Quia cum in altaris officio immoletur domin⁹ noster Jhe/sus Christus dei filius: qui candor est lucis eterne/congruit id non noctis tenebris fieri sed in luce. In quorum fidem presentes literas fieri dicteq₃ fabrice Sigilli iussimus appensioñ communiri. Dat₃ Anno dñi M.ccccc.xv Die Mensis pontificatus prefati dñi nri Pape Anno

Fig. 4 A letter of indulgence with unfilled empty spaces published by the Archbishopric of Mainz under the auspices of Archbishop Albert of Brandenburg 1515

of a dedicated assemblage of Protestant Reformation material. The fact that Martin Luther published more during his lifetime than all of his colleagues informs the collecting principles of the *Kessler collection*, which strives to continuously acquire all examples included in Josef Benzing's thorough listing, *Lutherbibliographie*.[29] Such objects constitute only part of the acquisitions scope of the *Kessler collection*, which already includes examples by many of Luther's contemporaries on numerous topics. This collection and its digital-image archive are invaluable resources for scholars and students.

Scholarship drives all the programming content and acquisitions for the *Kessler collection*, and its formation arose from the passionate commitment of several individuals. The dynamic name behind the collection is collector Richard C. Kessler, who, along with his wife, Martha, is primary supporter and benefactor. A significant number of Reformation objects at the Pitts Library came originally from the immense acquisition of 220,000 objects from the library of the Hartford Seminary Foundation around 1975, containing some one thousand Reformation objects. Under the direction of Dr. Channing Renwick Jeschke, this acquisition helped establish the Candler School of Theology among the nation's top theological libraries. Jeschke, also a church historian, became acquainted with Kessler in the 1980s through board work at a theological seminary. Kessler, a Lutheran layperson, asked Jeschke for guidance in creating a collection emphasizing key Reformation works with the intent that the collection reside at the Pitts. With Kessler's involvement, and under the direction of the current Margaret A. Pitts Professor of Theological Bibliography and director of the library, Dr. M. Patrick Graham, the collection continues to expand.

Special highlights include a 1522 first edition of Luther's translation of the New Testament, *The September Testament* (figs. 2 and 3), with its bold woodcut illustrations by Lucas Cranach the Elder, including twenty-one illustrations of the book of Revelation after Albrecht Dürer's seminal *The Revelations of John the Divine* or *Apocalypse* series of 1498; an indulgence, 1515, issued by the Catholic Church, archdiocese of Mainz (fig. 4); twenty-eight papal bulls; a first edition of Philipp Melanchthon's *Loci communes*; numerous catechisms and hymnals; and the five first editions of Erasmus's Greek New Testament.

With a welcoming rare-book study room for scholars, the Pitts regularly receives researchers. *Emory University* is notable too for its annual Reformation Day celebration and programming. In scope and size, the *Kessler collection* is undoubtedly one of, if not the, most comprehensive Reformation collections in the country (fig. 5).

One of the other major European Reformation collections is found within the vast collections of early modern material in the esteemed *Folger Shakespeare Library* in Washington, D.C. Works by Luther as well as many other important Reformers such as Martin Bucer, Jean Calvin, Erasmus of Rotterdam, Philipp Melanchthon, and Huldrych Zwingli are found there. As is true for the *Kessler collection*, woodcut illustrations by Hans Holbein and Lucas Cranach the Elder are abundant in many books and pamphlets. Throughout the history of the Folger, various library directors and librarians have recognized the vitality and importance of the Reformation within the history of the early modern period, a fact that has inspired continual acquisitions; Benzing's *Lutherbibliographie* is consulted annually for new accessions.[30]

The *Folger's* holdings on the continental Reformation are made up of two collections, and of various individual objects. The first grouping came as a part of a larger collection from English collector Sir Thomas Phillips; in 1958 a sizeable number of Reformation pamphlets was acquired for the library within the Phillips collection acquisition. This added 250 Reformation pamphlets to the Folger collections. In the annual report of 1978, in which details of the Stickelberger collection's acquisition are noted, the then director O. B. Hardison, Jr., reflects that the 1950s had been "a particularly active time at the Folger for the study of sixteenth- and seventeenth-century religious thought in England, with particular emphasis on the Nonconformists."[31] He goes on to write that scholars then connected to the library recommended specifically the further acquisition of continental Reformation material.[32] Cultivation of collaborative relationships among Folger staff and European colleagues at the Erasmushaus in Basel[33] was apparently encouraged and recognized as having led to the Folger's initially being offered the Stickelberger collection in 1976, followed by the successful acquisition of the second-largest collection of Reformation material for the library in 1977, with the acquisition of the Dr. Emanuel Stickelberger collection en bloc at auction in Basel.[34] Stickelberger was a Swiss collector and scholar whose amassed material on the Reformation numbered 870 objects at the time of the Folger acquisition, 180 of which were titles by Luther, with a number of additional examples by Erasmus, Melanchthon, Zwingli, and Calvin.[35] The catalogue written on the occasion of the Stickelberger acquisition reflects that its inclusion at the Folger, "one of the world's greatest and most beautiful libraries," is wonderfully consistent as "a pleasure and a help to many more bibliophiles and scholars," Stickelberger, having been a bibliophile as well as a serious scholar, profoundly studied these works with an eye toward the creation of novels, plays, and other writings.[36] Many examples in the Stickelberger collection were re-bound by the collector; their contents or bindings were actually covered with sheets from incunabula.

Since the earlier acquisitions, many hundreds of additional relevant objects have been acquired. While the Folger enjoys a stellar reputation, and heartily welcomes researchers from all over the world, its impressive Reformation holdings are little known to scholars. Highlights of the Folger holdings include a Basel edition of the *December Testament*, Luther's translation of the New Testament; numerous works by Luther (including Luther Bibles), Zwingli, and Melanchthon, with numerous polemical pamphlets and biblical translations; and a small, rare, unrecorded prayer book, *Ein Betbüchlin*. Various important incunabula further enrich study. Understandably, their holdings include impressive material related to the English and Swiss reformations.

In 1983 an exhibition was organized at the Folger to mark the quincentenary of the birth of Martin Luther, in collaboration with the Lutheran Council of the United States of America, the University of Maryland, and the Lutheran Church of the Reformation in Washington, D. C.; a small catalogue was produced, with support from Lutheran Brotherhood.[37] Any serious study of the printed material of the Reformation makes clear not only how influential and profoundly brilliant a thinker and theologian Luther was, but

Fig. 5 Books from the Richard C. Kessler Reformation Collection, Pitts Theology Library, Candler School of Theology, Emory University Atlanta

also how many gifted scholars, writers, and other Reformers were active contemporarily. This preliminary survey of collections illuminates the vibrant time in which Luther lived as much as it does his contributions to Western history. The Reformation was a defining time for the development and expansion of the modern world, challenging core ideas and inspiring freedoms that we continue to wrest with today.

Taken as a whole, these collections reflect a shared commitment to history, individual collectors' passionate approaches to preservation and study, and, often, the laudable desire to make these resources available. For some of the institutions and collectors, recognition of heritage is additionally related. All scholars of this remarkable time period will wish to participate in the humanistic tradition of returning *ad fontes*, "to the sources." After all, this is foundational to Luther's scholarship and writing and, ultimately, the Reformation as a whole. Happily, in the United States, a rich abundance of locations exist in which to make this possible.

29 Personal Interview with library director, Dr. M. Patrick Graham, October 29, 2015. Details regarding the history of the creation and growth of the Kessler collection came out of this in-person interview. **30** In-person interviews with Folger staff: Dr. Michael Witmore, director; Daniel De Simone, Eric Weinmann librarian; and Dr. Georgianna Ziegler, Louis B. Thalheimer Associate Librarian and Head of Reference, October 24, 2015. Many historical details about the collection formation resulted from in-person research and interviews. **31** Hardison, *Folger Shakespeare Library*. **32** Ibid. **33** Erasmushaus is an antiquarian book dealer in Switzerland, since 1800. **34** Hardison, *Folger Shakespeare Library*. **35** Ibid. **36** Sebass/Sebass/Tammann, *Reformation*, p. 5. **37** Folger Shakespeare Library, *Martin Luther*.

BIBLIOGRAPHY

Adover-Harvard Theological Library (2016), *Historical Collections (including Rare Books)*. Harvard Divinity School. Available: http://library.hds.harvard.edu/collections/rare-books [02/10/2016]. **Andersson**, Christiane/**Talbot**, Charles (1983), *From a Mighty Fortress: Prints, Drawings, and Books in the Age of Luther, 1483–1546*. Detroit. **Augustana College**. *Books in Special Collections*. Available: https://augustana.edu/x34666.xml [10/12/2015]. **Babcock**, Robert G. (2013), *Early Books and Manuscripts*, Yale University Library, Beinecke Rare Book & Manuscript Library. Available: http://beinecke.library.yale.edu/collections/curatorial-areas/early-books-and-manuscripts [02/08/2016]. **Bishop**, William W. (1904), German Reformation Pamphlets in the Princeton University Library. In: *The Princeton University Bulletin*, vol. 15, no. 3, pp. 183–208. **Columbia University Libraries** (2015), *The Burke Library Collection Development Policy*. Available: http://library.columbia.edu/locations/burke/the-burke-library-collection-development-policy.html [01/10/2016]. **Concordia Seminary** (2016), *Reformation Resources/Center for Reformation Research*. Available: www.csl.edu/library/the-center-for-reformation-resources-collection [02/23/2016]. **Edwards**, Mark U. Jr. (2004), *Printing, Propaganda, and Martin Luther*. Minneapolis. **Folger Shakespeare Library** (1983), *Martin Luther (1483–1546): A Jubilee Exhibition at the Folger Shakespeare Library*, Washington, D.C. **Gettysburg Seminary** (2016), *A. R. Wentz Library*. Available: www.ltsg.edu/resources-services/library [02/26/2016]. **Granquist**, Mark A. (2015), *Lutherans in America: A New History*. Minneapolis. **Harbison**, E. Harris (1956), Luther Pamphlets. *The Princeton University Library Chronicle*, vol. 17, no. 4, pp. 265–267. **Hardison Jr.**, O. B. (1977), *The Folger Shakespeare Library: Annual Report of the Director. The Folger Shakespeare Library*. Washington, D.C. **Harry Ransom Center**, *Religion*, the University of Texas at Austin. Available: https://www.hrc.utexas.edu/collections/guide/religion/ [04/06/2016]. **Houghton Library** (2016), *Early Books & Manuscripts Collection*. Harvard College Library. Available: http://hcl.harvard.edu/libraries/houghton/collections/early.html [02/10/2016]. **Johns Hopkins Sheridan Libraries** & University Museums (2015), *Reformation*. Special Collections. Available: http://guides.library.jhu.edu/c.php?g=202543&p=1335415 [02/26/2016]. **Klein**, Ralph W. (2012), *Rare Books Collections*. Lutheran School of Theology at Chicago. Available: http://collections.lstc.edu/ [02/23/2016]. **Library of Congress** (2010), *Europe*. Rare Books and Special Collections. Available: www.loc.gov/rr/rarebook/guide/europe.html [02/26/2016]. **Nauert**, Charles G. (2006), *Humanism and the Culture of Renaissance Europe*. New Approaches to European History. 2nd ed. Cambridge. **Ohio State University Libraries** (2000), *The Harold J. Grimm Reformation Collection: Guide and Inventory.to Rare Books and Manuscripts*. Available: https://library.osu.edu/finding-aids/rarebooks/reformhome.php [02/23/2016]. **Pitts Theology Library** (2016), *Richard C. Kessler Reformation Collection*. Emory University. Available: http://pitts.emory.edu/collections/selectholdings/kessler.cfm [01/30/2016]. **Princeton University Library** (2015), *Scheide Library*. Department of Rare Books and Special Collections 2015. Available: http://rbsc.princeton.edu/divisions/scheide-library [02/02/2016]. **Seebass**, Adolf/**Seebass**, Tilman/**Tammann**, Verena (1977), *Reformation: Catalogue of the Emanuel Stickelberger Collection purchased by the Folger Shakespeare Library*. Washington, D.C./Basel. **Sharp**, Ellen (1983), Germany in the Age of Luther. In: Andersson, Christiane/Talbot, Charles (1983), *From a Mighty Fortress: Prints, Drawings, and Books in the Age of Luther, 1483–1546*. Detroit. pp. 28–39. **Southern Methodist University**, Bridwell Library Perkins School of Theology (no date), *Reformation and Counter-Reformation*. Available: www.smu.edu/Bridwell/SpecialCollectionsandArchives/Overview/ReformationandCounterReformation [10/02/2015]. **The Folger Shakespeare Library**, *Printed Books*. Available: www.folger.edu/printed-books [10/02/2015]. **The Newberry**, *Religion*. Available: www.newberry.org/religion [10/10/2015]. **University of Illinois** at Urbana-Champaign (2012), *Book collections. Rare Book and Manuscript Library*. Available: www.library.illinois.edu/rbx/collections_book_collections.html [01/10/2016]. **Wagner**, Paul (1967), A Luther Exhibition. Selections from the Gift of Bernhard K. Schaefer. *The Princeton University Library Chronicle*, vol. 29, no. 1, pp. 103–106. **Whitford**, David M. (ed.) (2008), *Reformation and Early Modern Europe: A Guide to Research*. Kirksville, Missouri.

ANNE-SIMONE ROUS

Travel Reports and Letters from Emigrants

Many people turned their backs on Europe in the eighteenth and nineteenth centuries. From Germany alone, 5.4 million moved to the United States. Selling quickly to a mass audience, printed travel reports painted a romantic image of America, which further encouraged the migration. With America as their goal, many hoped for a better life. Bundles of letters and journals from many families have survived, constituting a separate field of research in travel literature. It is estimated that 280 million letters were sent to Germany from the US in the period from 1818 to 1914, among which 100 million were private correspondence. Only very few of these have been preserved. To date, the largest collection contains 13,000 pieces, some of which, through the course of scholarly work, are now digitally accessible online (www.auswandererbriefe.de).

Most emigrants were craftspeople, workers, farmers, or small business owners who were hit especially hard by poor harvests and rising costs. Some began to keep journals during the long, adventurous Atlantic crossing, which were then handed down to their families and, in some cases, are still in existence today. Those who left could maintain contact with those left behind through the mails. In their letters, they emphasized the openness, freedom, and technological possibilities in the New World. They continually try to convince friends and relatives of the advantages of emigrating. Disappointed expectations are mentioned only rarely. Shared experiences are remembered wistfully. Both sides had a strong need for information and wished to share in the joys and sorrows on the other side of the ocean. The tensions surrounding both setbacks and progress were regularly discussed. While encountering differences between their homeland and America, the authors would experience asynchrony in every-day aspects. Tradition provided orientation and stability in a strange place. At the same time, it was possible to develop close relationships among émigré families through the celebration of (religious) holidays and the establishment of associations. The cohesion among German Lutheran congregations seems to have been very strong. Reports back to the homeland often mirrored intercultural conflicts when it came to topics such as slavery, railroad construction, handling money, or methods of child-rearing—in short, aspects of civilization. Patterns of political thought were disputed regarding democracy and freedom of speech. Contingent upon the necessary critical source review of authenticity and trustworthiness, the letters are also invaluable to mentality research. Beyond the individual history, they can also be gleaned for social-historical interrelationships.

THOMAS E. RASSIEUR

Lutheran Paintings
in America

There is no great, theologically grounded collection of Lutheran paintings in America. Even Protestant institutions such as the Museum and Gallery at Bob Jones University have no significant concentration of Reformation-oriented pictures made in the sixteenth century. Though collectors and museum officials who acquired the objects sometimes had a strong interest in the Reformation, most Lutheran paintings in American collections appear to have been acquired for their connection to Lucas Cranach the Elder and his son Lucas Cranach the Younger. Collectors and curators seem to have sought them primarily for their mastery, their artistic style, and their signatures and secondarily for their religious slant and historical interest. The same collections usually have many more pictures that one would associate with Catholicism or no particular religion at all. Unsurprisingly, the largest concentration of Lutheran paintings is in the Metropolitan Museum of Art, New York, but many others are scattered in museums along the East Coast and throughout the Midwest.

While an exhaustive inventory is beyond the scope of this essay, it is possible to present an ample sampling of Lutheran portraits and religious subjects in American collections. This is the first attempt to make a such a survey and it should serve as the basis for an enquiry into confessional aspects of the pictures' iconography. The *Cranach Digital Archive*[1] makes it possible to assess in which collections Cranach paintings are being curated on a global scale. This essay will focus on their religious iconography. Some studies on the provenance of artworks will be included in order to ascertain the interests of the collectors. This will make it possible to verify if paintings like the collections of printed material Joanne Reiling Lindell has discussed in this volume were collected more because of their spectacular art historical importance than because of religious motifs. Taken together, the American holdings offer a rich array. The portraits represent Luther, his wife and close associates, his protectors, and his followers. The religious pictures treat the central themes of Christ's sacrifice and teachings as seen from the reformers' perspective.

Portraits

The most obvious examples of Lutheran art are portraits of Luther and his associates. When Luther married Katharina von Bora in 1525, Cranach's studio churned out numerous versions of their portraits in various formats. We do not know whether these were distributed as gifts or whether they were purchased as mementoes, but their original owners certainly used them to mark their support of the reform movement.[2] The Morgan Library & Museum, New York, possesses a pair of small tondos—circular pictures. They are very closely related to other examples. Luther tondos are in the Luther House, Wittenberg[3] and the Stadtmuseum (Town Museum) Nördlingen.[4] One of Katharina is in the Gemäldegalerie (Picture Gallery), Berlin.[5] The Öffentliche Kunstsammlung (Public Art Collections) Basel[6] has a similar pair, though a bit more of the sitters' bodies are shown. Pierpont Morgan, the founder of the Library and Museum that bears its name, bought his pair from the collection of the earls de Grey in 1909, the year in which George Robinson, the father of the last Earl de Grey, Frederick Robinson, died.

Portraits of Luther and Katharina continued to be produced over the course of their lives. Sometimes the images reprised earlier moments in their lives. A pair of portraits in the *Muskegon Museum of Art*, Muskegon, Michigan, show Luther as Junker Jörg from his 1521 sojourn at the Wartburg along with a young Katharina; yet, the Luther portrait is dated 1537 (fig. 1).[7] The likeness of Luther is based on Cranach prototypes from the early 1520s in Leipzig and Weimar. Its reprisal may have been prompted by the submission of Luther's *Schmalkald Articles* in 1537. During recent conservation and research, conservator Barry Bauman was able to reconstruct effaced inscriptions, traces of which could still be found at the top and bottom of the pictures.[8] Using photographs of a similar pair of pictures, belonging to a small church, Unserer Lieben Frauen Auf Dem Berge in Penig, Saxony, and published nineteenth-century inventory notes of a pair then in the collection of Maximilian von Schreibershofen but now missing, Bauman discovered that Luther's read: DOCTOR MARTINUS LUTHER, PROPHETA GERMANUS ANNO 1521 IN PATHMO AETATIS SUAE 38. DEPINGEBATUR [Doctor Martin Luther, German prophet, depicted in 1521 in Patmos at the age of 38.]

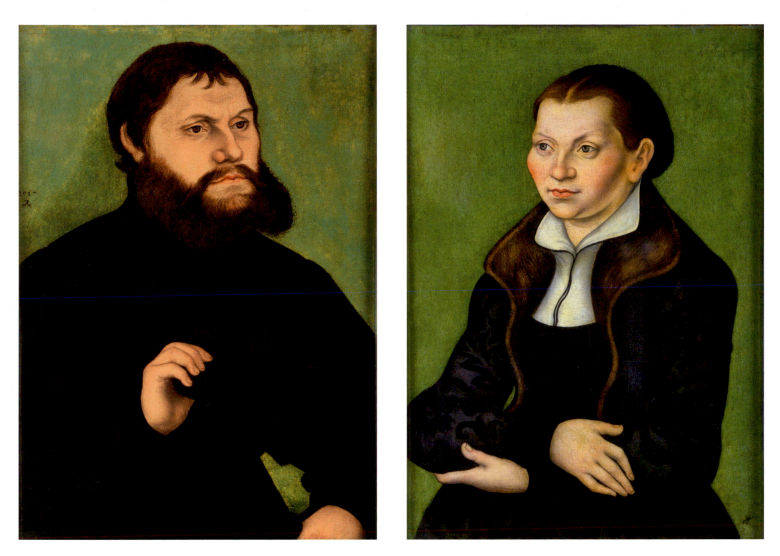

Fig. 1 Lucas Cranach the Elder (workshop), Martin Luther as Junker Jörg and Katharina von Bora, 1537

PESTIS. ERAM. VIVENS. MORIĒS. PRO MORS. TUA. PAPA. [I was a pestilence for you while living; when I die, I will be your death, Pope.] The mention of Patmos refers to the Greek island where the apostle John received and recorded the vision that he chronicled in the book of Revelations. Luther likened his isolation and inspired writing in the Wartburg to John's experience.

Katharina's inscription read: KATHARINA A BOR VXOR ACERRIMI CHRISTI JESV SALVATORIS NOSTRI PER GERMANIÃ APOSTOLI DNI DOCTORIS MARTINI LVTHERI [Katharina von Bora, wife of the most ardent apostle of Germany of the Lord our Savior Jesus Christ, Doctor Martin Luther.]

The museum, then known as the Hackley Art Gallery, acquired the pictures from the E. and A. Silberman Galleries, New York, in 1939. Wilhelm Valentiner, director of the Detroit Institute of Arts and former curator of paintings at the Metropolitan Museum of Art vouched for their authenticity as works by Lucas Cranach the Elder. They are now regarded as workshop productions, and Bauman strongly suspects that the Muskegon pictures are actually the "missing" pictures described in the Schreibershofen inventories.

1 Citations of paintings by Lucas Cranach the Elder, his workshop, and his followers usually refer to the Cranach Digital Archive (Cranach Digital Archive 2016, Stiftung Museum Kunstpalast Düsseldorf/Technische Hochschule Köln. URL: http://lucascranach.org/ [04/07/2016] [CDA], which has partially superseded the standard printed catalogue raisonné, Friedländer/Rosenberg, *Paintings*. For objects not in the CDA, Friedländer and Rosenberg citations are given where possible. CDA: US_MLMNY_B3-114-Fa,b. 2 Schuchardt, *Privileg und Monopol*. 3 CDA: DE_LHW_G11. 4 CDA: DE_SMN_25. 5 CDA: DE_smbGG_637. 6 CDA: CH_KMB_177; CDA: CH_KMB_177a. 7 CDA: US_MMA_39-5. 8 See Barry Bauman Conservation (n. d.). Available: www.baumanconservation.com/SolvingTheCranachMystery.html [04/07/2016].

Fig. 2 Lucas Cranach the Younger, Martin Luther and Philipp Melanchthon, 1558

Fig. 3 Triptych with an image of Christ as Salvator Mundi (The Savior of the World) in the midst of a Hamburg family, 1573–82

The Metropolitan Museum of Art has a portrait of Luther from about 1532.[9] The mechanical stiffness of the image suggests that this is a product of a copyist in Cranach's workshop. Several related variants are known, as are pendants showing Philipp Melanchthon. Half-length versions of the composition, showing Luther's torso and hands, were also available. This group of portraits appears to have gone into production about 1532 as a means of catering to rising Protestant self-awareness following the Diet of Augsburg. Luther is shown in the black robes of a Protestant preacher. The Metropolitan's version shows especially close affinity to a fine Cranach drawing in the collection of the dukes of Buccleuch,[10] but their relationship is unclear. The drawing could be the prototype for the whole series of portraits, or it could record a prime version of the painting.

A portrait dated 1546, apparently produced on the occasion of Luther's death, is in the Harvard Art Museums.[11] The likeness relies on those produced by the workshop about 1540, such as one from Wittenberg.[12] Lucas Cranach the Younger carried on his father's trade in Lutheran imagery. A half-length portrait of Luther in the Philadelphia Museum of Art was produced by the son's workshop in 1555 and goes back to the same sources as the earlier, larger picture at Harvard.[13] Cranach the Younger often showed Luther together with his colleagues as figures in narrative altarpieces, but the North Carolina Museum of Art has a unique work that presents Luther together with Philipp Melanchthon as a double portrait of academicians (fig. 2).[14] The painting was made in 1558, but the date has been altered to read 1550 in an attempt to make it appear to be the work of Lucas Cranach the Elder, who died in 1553. The posthumous likeness of Luther again relies on productions of the elder Cranach's workshop from about 1540.[15] Though now grizzled, Melanchthon was still alive and would live on for another two years. Unlike Luther, he remained gaunt throughout his life. His shirt, similar to that seen in Albrecht Dürer's engraved portrait of him from 1526, was now long out of fashion. Also unchanged from four decades earlier was Melanchthon's dishevelment.

The Crocker Art Museum in Sacramento has a portrait of Melanchthon produced in the younger Cranach's studio in 1580.[16] The painting is recorded as having entered the Dresden collection of John George I, Elector of Saxony, in 1621. John George was a Protestant, but he often sided with the Habsburgs and other Roman Catholic powers, for he belonged to the Albertine line of the House of Wettin, longtime competitors of the Ernestine line that included Luther's protectors Frederick the Wise, John the Steadfast, and John Frederick the Magnanimous. In 1532, shortly after John Frederick the Magnanimous inherited the Electorate of Saxony, he commissioned Cranach the Elder to produce sixty pairs of posthumous portraits, each showing John Frederick's uncle Frederick the Wise and his father, John the Steadfast. Two slips of paper bearing printed texts were glued to the surface of each picture: a small one attached near the top identifies the sitter, and a larger one at the bottom bears a poem in which the sitter recites his own achievements. The ghost writer of the unsigned verses may have been Luther himself.

Fig. 4 Lucas Cranach the Elder,
Portrait thought to be of Lukas Spielhausen, 1532

Coming on the heels of the establishment of the *Schmalkaldic League* of Protestant princes in 1531, the portrait commission was politically charged. Frederick's poem proclaims his establishment of the University of Wittenberg, saying that from there God's word came forth. It also states that the imperial electors had chosen Frederick as Emperor and that due to his advanced age he had honorably stepped side, choosing Charles V instead. John states that he helped put down the peasant revolt, bravely took a stand for his faith, and overcame his opposition to the election of Emperor Ferdinand I to reconcile with Charles V. By distributing such testimonies, John Frederick staked his claim as the rightful heir of the electorate, scion

9 CDA: US_MMANY_55-220-2; Ainsworth/Waterman, *German Paintings*, pp. 85–87, no. 18. **10** Watercolor on parchment, 21.9 × 19.1 cm. The Buccleuch Living Heritage Trust, Boughton House, Kettering, Northamptonshire, England. **11** Not in CDA. **12** CDA: DE_LHW_G72. **13** Not in CDA. **14** CDA: US_NCMAR_GL-60-17-65. **15** CDA: DE_LHW_G70. **16** CDA: US_CAMS_1872-59.

Fig. 5 Lucas Cranach the Elder, Crucifixion of Christ, 1532

Fig. 6 Lucas Cranach the Elder, The Crucifixion Witnessed by the Converted Centurion, 1536

of an old, distinguished, powerful family whose religious views did not preclude loyalty to the empire. This propaganda campaign had some urgency, for the Saxons had outraged Charles by supporting Luther, signing the *Augsburg Confession*, voting against his brother Ferdinand, and forming the *Schmalkaldic League*. Charles had refused to validate John Frederick's legitimacy as an elector.[17]

Extant records show that the workshop completed the job in 1533. Many of the 120 paintings survive, and they display varying degrees of quality. The Metropolitan Museum of Art owns a fine pair of the Frederick and John portraits, plus an additional example of John.[18] Though removed from their original frames, the pair seems to have been together from the time they emerged from the workshop. They are of particularly good quality; correspondingly, the faces are thought to have been painted by Cranach himself. The verso of the Frederick panel bears the Saxon coat of arms, which suggests that the two pictures were hinged as a diptych and that the arms would have been displayed when the diptych was closed. The extra portrait of John appears to be more of a run-of-the-mill product of the workshop, but its appearance is also diminished by its condition. The design used for the series of Frederick portraits is sometimes thought to derive from Albrecht Dürer's engraving of the elector produced in 1524. Certainly Cranach would have been familiar with Dürer's print, but his reversal, simplification, and stylization of the composition gives his work a wholly different effect.

A small-scale full-length group portrait in the Toledo Museum of Art embodies the intertwined relationships of Luther, his fellow reformers, the Saxon electors, and the Cranach family.[19] Painted around 1543 by Lucas Cranach the Younger while he was still working in his father's studio, it shows John Frederick in the foreground with ten men crammed in behind him (see fig. 7 in the essay of Timo Trümper in this volume). We easily recognize Luther and Melanchthon. The youthful-looking man next to Luther appears to be Georg Spalatin, who was John Frederick's tutor and one of Luther's closest associates. To John Frederick's left is probably Saxon chancellor Gregor Brück, who was deeply involved in negotiating the interaction between the reformers and governmental bodies. Brück's son Christian married Cranach the Younger's sister Barbara; Cranach the Younger married Brück's daughter Barbara; and, after her death, he married Melanchthon's niece. Since some of the faces are partly obscured, it is difficult to say if they were identifiable to their contemporaries. At the right is a partial face that appears to be a portrait, but the panel is cut down. This may be a slightly trimmed wing of an altarpiece or perhaps a fragment of a much larger composition.

A group portrait in the Metropolitan Museum of Art is one of the rare Lutheran paintings in America that originated outside the Cranach circle.[20] The triptych shows an unidentified family: a male on the left wing and a woman on the right flank a central panel showing five family members gathered close to a figure of Christ as *Salvator Mundi*, Savior of the World (fig. 3). Gold chains, thick fur, jewels, and fine clothing mark this as a wealthy family. We appear to be dealing with three generations, for inscriptions give the ages of the sitters, ranging from six to fifty-four. The family probably resided in Hamburg, for the orb grasped by Christ reflects an image of the city's skyline, punctuated by six church spires. The woman on the right wing wears traditional Hamburg costume. The inscription above Christ is John 14:19, "Because I live, ye shall live also." Passages from Psalms are inscribed close to each of the four oldest members of the family. All the passages are quoted directly from Johannes Bugenhagen's Low German edition of Luther's Bible, first published in 1534 shortly after completion of the High German version. The unusual conceit of placing the donor family in direct proximity to Christ—with no prayerful gesture to distance them—may show their allegiance to the Gnesio-Lutherans ("Genuine Lutherans"), who believed that Christ's body and blood were physically present in the Eucharist. Though the triptych is sometimes interpreted as commemorating a marriage between the man and woman on the outer panels, it is more likely an epitaph, as Joshua Waterman suggests, perhaps originally sited in proximity to a family tomb.

In some cases we cannot be certain of a portrait sitter's stance on the reform movement. The Metropolitan Museum of Art owns a portrait whose richly attired sitter is tentatively identified as Lukas Spielhausen (fig. 4).[21] He wears a signet ring bearing the initials *LS*, and the verso of the panel is stamped with the Spielhausen family coat of arms. Spielhausen earned a doctorate in law in 1524 and by 1531 was *Hofprokurator*—court lawyer—at John the Steadfast's residence in Torgau. This was his post when Lucas Cranach the Elder painted this portrait, which is dated 1532. Spielhausen later moved on to Weimar, a reform-oriented city, where he held various offices, including mayor. The Reformation took hold there in 1525, and Luther visited several times. When John Frederick I emerged from captivity in 1552 after having been captured at the Battle of Mühlberg in 1547, he made Weimar the new seat of the Ernestine branch of the Saxon household. If Spielhausen is indeed the sitter, the portrait depicts a man near the center of the secular power structure behind the Reformation.

Though not painted as Lutheran works of art, the portraits of Moritz Buchner and his wife, Anna Lindacker, present a couple who were probably in the upper-middle-class circle supporting Luther.[22] Like Luther, Buchner's boyhood roots were in Eisleben, and his family had mining interests in Mansfeld. The family was extremely successful. Moritz moved to Leipzig where he became a city official. These marriage portraits, dated 1518 and belonging to the Minneapolis Institute of Art, show him wearing a rich fur mantle and his wife draped in gold. After the Leipzig debate of 1519, the city—especially its wealthier inhabitants—embraced the reform movement. This tendency of Leipzig's affluent denizens to support Luther is borne out by the preponderance of rich signatories to a petition to Duke George of Saxony requesting the reassignment of an abandoned Catholic church for the use of Andreas Bodenstein in 1524.[23]

A portrait of an unidentified sitter in the Nelson-Atkins Museum of Art, Kansas City, presents a figure in sober attire appropriate for a reformer.[24] Though one cannot say much about the sitter, there is a Lutheran connection that arises from scientific investigation. The beech panel on which it was painted comes from the same tree that produced panels on which Cranach and his workshop painted portraits of Luther, Melanchthon, Frederick the Wise, John Frederick, and John the Steadfast's son John Ernest. Hence, we are here almost certainly confronted with a Lutheran painting, but understanding of its full meaning awaits identification of the sitter.

Fig. 7 (Attributed to) Lucas Cranach the Elder, The Baptism of Christ in the Jordan, c. 1546

Religious Subjects

The sacrifice of Christ is central to the Lutheran theology, and American collections contain at least three pictures, two Crucifixions and a Lamentation, that treat the subject directly. In a Crucifixion scene in the Indianapolis Museum of Art, Christ gazes down at the faithful, those who will receive the salvation of his sacrifice, who are to his right (fig. 5). The Virgin Mary swoons into the arms of John the Evangelist. Mary Magdalene embraces the cross. Despite their transgressions, the thief and the soldier Longinus, who with his spear inflicted the wound in Christ's side, will be saved, for in the end they had faith. The soldiers who prefer to gamble for Christ's clothes rather than accept the assurance of his promise, and the bad thief, whose eyes turn away from Christ, will not be saved. Cranach has placed a cardinal, a monk, and a Turk behind the cross; in a sense Christ has turned his back on them completely.

In the later 1530s, Cranach developed a larger, denser, more chaotic version of the Calvary scene, an example of which is in the Art Institute of Chicago.[25] The Magdalene now attends to the Virgin, and a soldier, perhaps Longinus, now embraces the cross. Comparison of the Chicago panel to one of similar size and composition, in Dessau, Germany, demonstrates the workshop's ability to produce variations on a theme.[26] Moreover, it serves as a warning that we may want to be wary of making overly specific interpretations of details. For example, in the Dessau version, the Magdalene kneels in prayer to Christ rather than embracing the cross or attending to the Virgin.

17 Ainsworth/Waterman, *German Paintings*, pp. 78–84. 18 Ibid., pp. 78–84, nos. 17a–c; CDA: US_MMANY_46-179-1, US_MMANY_46-179-2, US_MMANY_71-128. 19 CDA: US_TMA_1926-55. 20 Ainsworth/Waterman, *German Paintings*, pp. 235–242, no. 55. 21 CDA: US_MMANY_1981-57-1; Ainsworth/Waterman, *German Paintings*, pp. 66–69, no. 14. 22 CDA: US_MIA_57-10, US_MIA_57-11. 23 Scribner, *Popular Culture*, pp. 160–162. 24 CDA: US_NAMAKC_31-112. 25 Not in CDA. Friedländer/Rosenberg, *Paintings* pp. 144 f., no. 377. 26 CDA: DE_AGGD_16.

Fig. 8 Lucas Cranach the Elder, Feast of Herod, 1531

The demand for Crucifixion scenes continued for decades. A small panel in the Minneapolis Institute of Art offers a simplified version of the family workshop formula as it continued late in the life of Cranach the Younger.[27] The players have been reduced to Christ, the two thieves, the swooning Virgin group, a cross-embracing Magdalene, Longinus on foot, plus a few of the unfaithful. An unusual and clearly didactic Lutheran take on the Crucifixion is in the National Gallery, Washington, D.C. (fig. 6).[28] The only figure present apart from Christ and the two thieves is the mounted centurion. Though unnamed in the Bible, he is often identified as Longinus. Two inscriptions give voice to Christ and the soldier. As Christ is about to expire, he addresses God: VATER IN DEIN HET BEFIL ICH MEIN GAIST [Father, into thy hand I commend my spirit]. The passage comes from Luther's translation of the Bible, Luke 23:46. Upon witnessing this act of self-sacrifice, the centurion proclaims: WARLICH DISER MENSCH IST GOTES SVN GEWEST [Truly, this man was the Son of God], Mark 15:39. Under Luther's theology, the centurion is saved solely due to his faith, and with his conversion he

becomes a Christian knight, a soldier of God. A larger variant, produced two years later, is in the Yale University Art Gallery.

The Cranach workshop turned out many diminutive didactic paintings illustrating passages from the Bible. Sometimes the inscriptions are in Latin, but more often they appear in German. A Baptism of Christ in the Cleveland Museum of Art bears a Latin inscription, in which God in heaven entreats the viewer: HIC EST FILIVS MEVS DILECTVS IN QVO MICHI BEN COMPLACITVM EST [This is my Beloved Son in whom I am well pleased, hear Him] (Matt. 17:5).[29] The dove of the Holy Spirit descends to Jesus as John the Baptist uses a large jug to draw water from the Jordan River (fig. 7). This charming panel appears to be somewhat unusual among those emanating from the Cranach workshop in that the wood has been identified as oak rather than the usual beech.

Around 1520, Cranach's workshop began to produce paintings of Christ and the Adulteress, and a decade later he added Christ Blessing the Children as a regular theme. The Metropolitan Museum of Art has two small paintings of these subjects very similar to the pair from the

Herzogliches Museum Gotha. These pictures act as illustrative examples of the lessons offered by the didactic formula of Cranach's *Law and Grace*. In both, Christ contradicts the impulse of those who would impose traditional standards to deny access to Christ's grace. *Christ Blessing the Children* bears the verse Mark 10:14: LASSET DIE KINDLIN ZV MIR KOMEN.VND WERET INEN NICHT.DENN SOLCHER IST DAS REICH GOTTES. ~ MARCVS.X. [Suffer the little children to come unto me, and forbid them not: for of such is the kingdom of God. ~Mark 10].

The Apostles thought the children unworthy of Christ's attention, but he corrects them. Similarly, *Christ and the Adulteress* is inscribed with John 8:7: WER VNTER EVCH ON SVNDE IST. DER WERFFE DEN ERSTEN STEIN AVFF SIE. ~IOH~VIII~ [He that is without sin among you, let him first cast a stone at her. ~Joh ~8].

Jesus rejects the Pharisees' reliance of the Law of Moses, protects the woman, and uses the moment to teach all involved. Luther used King Herod as an archetype of bad governance. Borrowing from a fifteenth- century poem by Caelius Sedulius, he wrote a hymn contrasting Herod and Christ:

> Was fürcht'st du, Feind Herodes, sehr,
> Daß uns gebor'n kommt Christ der Herr?
> Er sucht kein sterblich Königreich,
> Der zu uns bringt sein Himmelreich.
> [Herod, why dreadest thou a foe
> Because the Christ comes born below?
> He seeks no mortal kingdom thus,
> But brings his kingdom down to us.][30]

The Wadsworth Atheneum, Hartford, Connecticut, owns a relatively large panel of the Feast of Herod, attributed to Lucas Cranach the Elder and dated 1531, a decade prior to the first publication of Luther's hymn (fig. 8).[31] Salome holds the platter bearing the decapitated head of John the Baptist, which echoes and contrasts with the plate of fruit brought in by another figure to the right. When Cranach repeated the composition in a version painted two years later and now in the Städel Museum, Frankfurt am Main, the figure bearing the fruit looks outward to engage the viewer.[32] In a third version in the Staatliche Kunstsammlungen Dresden, painted in 1537, and attributed to Lucas Cranach the Younger, further changes appear.[33] The figure carrying the plate of fruit is different, and a new figure appears who points to the fruit. This pointing figure has the same hairstyle and facial features as the fruit bearer had in the Hartford version. This invites the question as to whether the Cranachs had a certain historical figure in mind as the one to persuade Herod to change his ways. Interestingly enough, all three versions present an unidentifiable background figure wearing the wide-brimmed red hat of a cardinal. The Dresden version belongs to a group of paintings on the theme of "The Power of Women," one which bore negative connotations, and the Hartford version may have come from such a series.

Conclusion

Although artistic images provoked complex, often negative responses during the Reformation, it is clear that the Cranachs and other artists catered to a desire for tangible manifestations of faith, whether likenesses of religious leaders and their supporters or didactic images laying out tenets of belief and moral lessons. Three centuries later a stream of paintings fulfilling such needs began to flow toward America. Some of the pictures that came have returned to Europe, but a substantial number have remained. They are so scattered that they seem mostly absent, but the above parade of pictures demonstrates that American collections contain an ample representation of portraits depicting Luther and the key figures of the Reformation as well as a range of pictures that illustrate the central messages of his teachings.

I hope this survey is a step toward raising awareness of the treasures that are available to those who take an interest in this topic; yet, it just scratches the surface, for it is confined to paintings. All the major encyclopedic museums of America have print collections containing significant examples of Reformation art. To a much lesser extent, drawings may be found as well. Joanna Reiling Lindell's introduction to Lutheran library collections will lead one to untold numbers of illustrated books. As for medals, they are waiting to be found at the Metropolitan Museum and the American Numismatic Society in New York and the Walters Art Museum in Baltimore. Most of the sixteenth-century Lutheran art in America is in places that are not predominantly Lutheran, and it is not noted for its bling; so, it rarely takes center stage, but with patience and persistence one can find a strong representation of this art, which was shaped by and helped to shape new ways of thinking that affected European and American culture well beyond the role of Luther's followers.

BIBLIOGRAPHY

Ainsworth, Maryan W./**Waterman**, Joshua P. (2013), *German Paintings in the Metropolitan Museum of Art, 1350–1600*. New York. **Friedländer**, Max J./**Rosenberg**, Jakob (1978), *The Paintings of Lucas Cranach*. Ithaca. **Schuchardt**, Günter (2015), Privileg und Monopol—Die Lutherportraits der Cranach-Werkstatt. In: ibid. (ed.), Cranach, Luther und die Bildnisse. Regensburg 2015, pp. 24–53. **Scribner**, Robert W. (1988), *Popular Culture and Popular Movements in Reformation Germany*. London.

27 CDA: US_MIA_2007-62a-b. 28 CDA: US_NGA_1961-9-69. 29 Not in CDA. 30 Translation by George MacDonald. 31 CDA: US_WAMA_1936-339. 32 CDA: DE_SMF_1193. 33 CDA: DE_SKD_GG1923.

VII

Luther's
Legacy

DOROTHEA WENDEBOURG

Reformation Anniversaries and Images of Luther

For citizens of the Western world, it seems perfectly natural to commemorate significant events and important figures in history through anniversaries—collective celebrations marking historical milestones such as centenaries, half-centenaries, even occasionally quarter-centenaries. The culture industry of the West is constantly generating celebrations to commemorate discoveries and inventions, battles and revolutions, composers, poets, scientists, clerics, politicians and the like, thus fixing them in the collective cultural consciousness as key events and figures of a shared history—while at the same time keeping itself in business. But it would be misleading to assume that this way of engaging with the significant past is somehow natural, almost preordained. For the tradition of commemorating historical events and figures at regular intervals is itself a product of history and is no more than five centuries old. It owes its origin to the Reformation.

The historical anniversary was invented by Protestant universities, which in the sixteenth century began to commemorate the milestone dates of their own foundations. In 1617, what had hitherto been merely a local, academic practice spread to a wider social, indeed international, context with the first centenary of Martin Luther's posting of his Ninety-Five Theses in 1517, thereby establishing it as a key event of the Reformation, and beyond that of all historical events it has shaped.[1] As a result of the rivalry of two Protestant princes, the electors of Saxony and the Palatinate—the one a Lutheran and the other a member of a Reformed church, each striving to establish himself as leader of the Protestant faction within the Holy Roman Empire by sponsoring such festivities—October 31, 1617, became the hundredth anniversary of the start of the Reformation. This 1617 anniversary was observed in almost all Protestant estates of the empire, as well as in the Lutheran kingdoms of Denmark and Sweden. So impressive were the celebrations of that year that in many places Luther's posting of the Ninety-Five Theses was henceforth commemorated every hundred, every fifty, even every twenty-five years. A similar tradition was founded for other events of Reformation history, including in 1630 for the presentation of the *Augsburg Confession* and in 1655 for the conclusion of the Peace of Augsburg. The success of this new form of commemorative celebration did not escape the attention of Protestantism's denominational opponents, as well as of groups wishing to observe nonecclesiastical anniversaries. Thus the anniversary became the ubiquitous component of cultural life that it is today. Especially since the Age

of Historicism in the nineteenth century, during which anniversaries enjoyed a popularity as great as that of historical monuments, everywhere in the Western world new occasions were constantly being found for commemorative historical celebrations, whereby the preference now seemed to be for biographical commemoration—anniversaries of the births and deaths of famous men, occasionally of famous women too. Admittedly, this enriching and strengthening of cultural memory was no mere preoccupation with the past. Rather, each age celebrated in the mirror of the past those great and momentous aspects of its own life whose origins were traceable to the past it was celebrating—in other words, what the age itself considered great and momentous. Thus anniversaries became social mega-events in which each age celebrated itself, continually restaging past events from its own perspective. And if the Reformation had become one such event, it was because those celebrating it considered it a pivotal event in their own history, which in commemorating they continually reaffirmed fundamental aspects of their own present.

A society's cultural memory, like human memory in general, is most emphatically linked to individual people and their deeds. Such was also the case regarding the anniversary celebrations commemorating the Reformation. From the beginning, a significant component of these was the commemoration of reformers active at that time—though with differences: specific Protestant denominations associated themselves with different reformers, in addition to which individual countries and regions commemorated those men who had brought the Reformation to their lands as their own particular reformers. Yet none of these was celebrated so often and in so many different denominations and countries as was Martin Luther. With him, the Reformation had begun; with him the celebrated posting of the Ninety-Five Theses, symbolic of the whole Reformation, was associated. His life story offered especially rich material for commemoration, and thus from the very start Luther played a prominent role in Reformation anniversaries. With the growing emphasis in anniversary culture as a whole on biographical data and the attendant personalization of anniversaries—a nineteenth-century development mentioned above—it became widespread practice within Lutheranism and beyond to make Martin Luther the central focus of the Reformation. Not just anniversaries associated with Luther's biography but all Reformation anniversaries became large-scale "Luther events." As those celebrating the anniversaries commemo-

Fig. 1 Wunderwerck D. Martin Luthers: Der Päpstliche Stuel will sincken. Das ist: Eine kurtze Abbildung
auß der Weissagung deß heiligen Propheten Danielis, Freiberg 1618

rated the Wittenberg Reformer, they constantly redefined, leaping back over the centuries, their own self-image. Luther became a mirror in which each age celebrated and invoked its most cherished goals and values. In short, a figure from history was transformed into a historical image—or rather a series of such images.

At its beginning stood Luther the doctor and redeemer of the church. The anniversaries of the seventeenth and eighteenth centuries were social mega-events in which the symbiosis of church, culture, and political community, characteristic of the post-Reformation Confessional Age, was displayed in an exuberant abundance of church services, academic speeches, commemorative publications, social activities, concerts, theater performances, fireworks displays, gun salutes, the decorating of churches and houses, and other activities. In these ways, people celebrated the Protestant renewal of the church and its liberation from papal yoke and error. Martin Luther was the church's new Moses, who by restoring the true Gospel had paved the way for its renewal and liberation: "All people,

great and small, who have come to know the Gospel, Luther's teaching, praise and honor God from their hearts that they have lived to see this jubilee year. A century ago, all was gloom; all were forced to do hard labor for the infernal Pharaoh".[2] Indeed, through his teaching, Luther was the angel who according to the prophet Daniel (Dan. 12) was to appear at the end of time, or according to the Revelation of Saint John the Divine (Rev. 14, 6 f.) was to announce the Eternal Gospel to the world. Through his preaching, which shook the papacy to its foundations, he fulfilled the prophet Daniel's vision of another angel who would liberate his people from all their godless enemies (fig. 1).[3] In this spirit, people celebrated the year 1617. And likewise Luther, the doctor of the church, was eulogized at the centenary of the *Augsburg Confession* in 1630, as well as in the following century, when the Reformation was celebrated "in the year 1717 after the birth of Christ, the year 200 after the revealing of the Antichrist,"[4] not only in Germany but in Denmark and Norway to an even greater extent (fig. 2).

1 On the origins and history of Reformation anniversaries, see Wendebourg, *Vergangene Reformationsjubiläen*. **2** "All Menschen Kinder groß und klein/Die zum Erkendnüß kommen seyn/Deß Evangeli Luthers Lehr/die sagn Gott hertzlich Lob und Ehr/Daß sie erlebt deß Jubel Jahr/Vor hundert Jahrn es elend war/Da man dem

Höllischen Pharao/In schwere Dienst must ziehen da." Illustrated pamphlet: "Wunderwerck D. Martin Luthers" (1618) quoted in Kaufmann, *Reformationsgedenken*, p. 309. **3** Ibid., pp. 307 f. **4** "Anno a Christo nato MDCCXVII. Antichristo manifestato CC." See Wendebourg, *Vergangene Reformationsjubiläen*, pp. 268 f.

Fig. 2
Medallion struck for the Luther bicentennial 1717, with depiction of Frederick IV (1699–1730), Denmark, 1717

At the 1817 anniversary, which was celebrated with an equal abundance of ecclesiastical, academic, and musical events and public festivals, it was no longer Luther the doctor of the church who was commemorated. The Enlightenment had given rise to a different image of the Reformation, one that determined that the most significant aspect of this event lay not in its religious or ecclesiastical nature but in its wider influence. This influence, initially felt within the Protestant churches, had long since spread and developed outside the churches to embrace all of humanity,[5] helping it to break free from superstition and intolerance and to embrace freedom of conscience, maturity, and self-determined moral values. Thus the Luther who was celebrated that year was no longer simply the representative of a religious denomination but a key figure in world history: "Your light shone out, and from the dust downtrodden humanity rose up,"[6] were the words of a song composed for the first Reformation anniversary of the nineteenth century, which Lutherans and members of the Reformed churches celebrated together as a pan-Protestant festival—and in which, indeed, Roman Catholics and Jews also participated. With his theses on indulgences which constituted the first public criticism of the church's oppressive doctrines, Luther had kindled the flame of the Enlightenment. By not recognizing the hierarchy of the church, he had championed the right to self-determination of all humanity; through his translation of the Bible, he had promoted general education; and by appealing to his conscience before the Emperor at Worms, he had opened the door to freedom of conscience and tolerance. In short, with Luther came "the dawn of religious freedom." This commentary on the Reformation anniversary of 1817 comes from the pen of the Jewish publisher Saul Asher.[7] Asher's sentiment, which was echoed by other Jewish voices throughout the century up to the anniversary of 1917,[8] demonstrates that the image of "Luther the proponent of the Enlightenment" had become firmly anchored in the secular consciousness. But there were also dissenting voices. Lutheran circles rejected this image as a distortion and demanded a resolute orientation toward Luther the theologian and man of the church.

Thus, 1817 was the first anniversary to witness a certain pluralisation in images of Luther and the Reformation.

Yet on the whole, in Europe and particularly in Germany, the dominant image was that of the reformer who had courageously stood his ground against Pope and Emperor, paving the way for the Enlightenment, universal education, tolerance, freedom of conscience, and maturity. Throughout the land, this heroic figure was displayed to the public in the form of statues of metal and stone. The posting of the Ninety-Five Theses on October 31, 1517, in itself nothing more than the traditional method of publishing theses for debate on Wittenberg University's bulletin board—whose purpose was served by the door of the Castle Church—was recast as the dramatic gesture of a hammer-swinging revolutionary (fig. 3). On the four-hundredth anniversary of Luther's birth in 1883, the first major anniversary explicitly dedicated to the person of Luther, this revolutionary was celebrated in churches and lecture halls, in streets and squares, in speeches and writing, and with much music. But a new image was added to that of Luther the much-praised forerunner of the Enlightenment, one that hitherto had played at most a peripheral role—that of the "German Luther," a figure with whom a people only recently united in national statehood could identify. "None other of the new nations has ever seen a man […], who so absolutely embodies, for good or ill, the innermost being of his people. […] We Germans do not find this at all puzzling; we simply say: he is flesh of our flesh and blood of our blood," intoned the renowned Berlin historian Heinrich von Treitschke in his anniversary lecture *Luther and the German Nation*.[9] In 1883 this image was not yet dominant. But in the following decades the "German Luther" was increasingly in the foreground. It became ubiquitous during the First World War, when the four-hundredth anniversary of the Reformation fell in the decisive war year of 1917. There was no lack of critical voices insisting on the Reformer's primarily religious role— "The most important thing about Luther was not that he was German but that he preached the Gospel"[10]—as well as on the supranational significance of his message—"Luther belongs not just to

Fig. 3 Ferdinand Pauwels, Luther hammers the Ninety-Five Theses on the door of the Wittenberg Castle Church, 1872

us but to all humanity."[11] Nevertheless, in 1917 the message that drowned out all others and was disseminated in countless writings proclaimed the "German Luther," the "Man of Ore" who was to strengthen the national resolve and stiffen the morale of both soldiers at the front and citizens back home.

In the United States, images of Luther underwent a different development. Here the Lutherans' first major celebration of a Reformation anniversary took place in 1817, making them the first religious group in the still-young republic to make the history of their own denomination "an object of commemorative culture."[12] Looking back to the Reformation helped Lutherans determine their own position in a country in which they had but recently arrived. Thus the rediscovery of the Gospel by Martin Luther, the doctor of the church, was seen as a prelude to Lutheranism's spreading the Gospel, under very different circumstances, on the new continent: "The light that Luther set ablaze shines over this land too […]. Here where the blackest darkness once covered the land like night, where the deadly snakebite of savages brought a terrible awakening, the Temples of God now stand […]," sang the Lutherans of 1817.[13] It was the "doctor of the church" according to the seventeenth- and eighteenth-century anniversary tradition who was extolled in such tones, overwhelmingly in German and by congregations who maintained links with Germany. But at the 1817 celebrations, "Luther the proponent of the Enlightenment" also had his advocates, who championed him in a manner likewise suited to the American context. To the Reformation, eulogized as a "glorious revolution," the world owed the "happy

5 See Bornkamm, *Geistesgeschichte*, pp. 18 f. 6 Quoted in: Wendebourg, *Reformationsjubiläen*, p. 292. 7 Ibid., p. 327. 8 See Wendebourg, *Jews*; German version: id., *Gesegnet*. 9 Quoted in: Wendebourg, *Vergangene Reformationsjubiläen*, p. 304. 10 Ernst Troeltsch, Ernste Gedanken zum Reformations-Jubiläum, quoted in: Wendebourg, *Vergangene Reformationsjubiläen*, p. 306.

11 Karl Holl in his pioneering anniversary speech "Was verstand Luther unter Religion?" at Berlin University's official celebrations, quoted in: Wendebourg, *Vergangene Reformationsjubiläen*, p. 306. 12 Flügel, *Deutsche Lutheraner*, p. 81. 13 Quoted in: ibid., note 64.

Fig. 4 Curt Mücke, postcard commemorating "Luther Day in 1000-year-old Nordhausen," inscribed with a text from the first mayor Heinz Sting (NSDAP)

the Bible and revealed our inheritance, by the force of religious conviction we have gained our civil and religious liberty," wrote a Presbyterian theologian.[16] At the same time as the Germans were beginning to foreground "Luther the German," an American historian declared: "To Martin Luther, above all men, we Anglo-Americans are indebted for national independence and mental freedom."[17] And a Methodist theologian, explicitly alluding to events in American history, wrote: "Find the birthplace of liberty—Wittenberg. There was the world's 'Declaration of Independence' written, and Martin Luther's Reform is the apostle and prophet of human freedom."[18]

Despite emphasis on the international significance of Luther, indeed his special significance for America, his German origins had always been included in his praise. This made it difficult to speak of him with enthusiasm at the 1917 anniversary—because, for the past six months, Germany and the United States had been at war. The anniversary was indeed celebrated, but the exuberance of 1883 had disappeared. Frequently the emphasis was on the religious and theological aspects of Luther's influence rather than on its societal "happy effects." It was still possible to highlight these but as effects that had taken root in America and not in Germany, thus implying that Americans, not Germans, were Luther's true heirs. The American Lutherans of Scandinavian origin were especially concerned to emphasize this line of reasoning, for they did not wish to see their church vilified as a specifically German denomination and themselves open to the charge of political disloyalty. They thus abjured their coreligionists not to allow the supranational figure of Luther to be sequestered by "intellectual burglary," maintaining that Luther and Thomas Jefferson were "kinsmen"—indeed, that "the religious liberty, which was won by the heroism of Martin Luther, was a precursor of the civil liberty which [...] 1776 has become our heritage."[19] As far as Germany was concerned, this perspective allowed a distinction to be made between a good Germany that upheld Luther's values and the bad Germany now waging war on America. A Methodist compatriot could thus exhort Americans to follow "this nobler German" and not "the modern skeptical and superstitious Germany which would germanize mankind with the help of Krupp guns, poison gases, and liquid fire." True to the memory of "Luther, Kant, Lessing, Goethe, Schiller, Bach, Mendelssohn and Beethoven, Steuben, Herkimer, De Calb, Carl Schurz and Franz Sigel," they should protest "against Kaiserism and despotism," just as Luther had in Worms with his "Here I stand, I can do no other, so help me God."[20]

Meanwhile in Germany the "German Luther" was making further inroads. At the anniversary celebrations after the First World War, especially in 1921, when the four-hundredth anniversary of Luther's appearance before the Imperial Diet of Worms was widely celebrated, the "Hero of Worms" was co-opted to rebuild the confidence of a nation defeated in war and humiliated by the Treaty of Versailles, whose economy lay in ruins.[21] In 1933, the year in which not only the National Socialists seized power but also, ten months later, the 450th anniversary of Martin Luther's birth was celebrated, for many Germans better times seemed to have arrived. Luther was hailed as the "Prophet of the Germans" who had augured this change.[22] The henchmen of the new regime in the Protestant church, the German Christians, planned to transform the "great Luther cel-

effects" of freedom of religion, free speech, and universal education. And since freedom of religion was the "parent of civil freedom," it was to the Reformation that it indirectly owed political freedom, which was most completely realized in the United States.[14] The pastors and their congregations who celebrated the anniversary in this spirit did so in English. Like the German Lutherans, they celebrated together with other Protestant churches—which in America were much more diverse in nature than those back home. Yet in contrast to celebrations in Germany, making the posting of the Ninety-Five Theses a key event for all Protestants resulted in Luther's being numbered among all reformers rather than being elevated above them.

Things were very different in 1883 (see fig. 1 in the contribution of Hartmut Lehmann). The reason was not only that the occasion was the four-hundredth anniversary of Luther's birth but also that American Lutherans had grown in both numbers and national importance. As a result, the Wittenberg Reformer was now eulogized in endless writings and speeches, by Lutherans as well as by Protestants from other churches—indeed, though not without demur, by American Jews, too.[15] Now Luther in particular, not the Reformation as a whole, was seen as the source of social change: "Luther opened

Fig. 5 The Martin Luther Monument destroyed
by the Allied bombing of Dresden in front
of the equally destroyed Church of St. Mary's, 1945

could be reduced to the simple formula: "Luther and Germany!"[24] Indeed, many an anniversary speaker condensed the formula even further to "Luther and Hitler" (fig. 4).[25]

The so-called Jewish question played but a marginal role at the anniversary celebrations, a fact much deplored by the malicious anti-Semitic newspaper *Der Stürmer*, which repeatedly the charged the Protestant church that, as always, it was "hushing up" Luther's anti-Jewish writings instead of broadcasting them to the people. In contrast one anniversary speaker at a mass rally of the German Christians in Berlin eulogized "Luther's nationalistic message" for aiming at making Christianity "racially appropriate," which included enforcing the "Aryan paragraph" in the church and emancipating it from the Old Testament.[26] Admittedly, these sentiments appealed only to a hard core and contravened the hopes pinned on the celebrations, for after this speech German Christians left the organization in droves. And so those voices that rejected the nationalistic image of a "German Luther" and that even regarded the entire tendency to reduce Luther to his political and cultural influence as erroneous, did not go unheard. Dietrich Bonhoeffer and others declared that Luther was "a true witness of the grace of Jesus Christ," and his ministration was "not limited to the German people." And the famous Swiss theologian Karl Barth wrote that Luther was no more and no less than a "doctor of the Christian church" who interpreted Holy Scripture.[27] It was voices such as these that opened the way for a return to the essential Luther image that had characterized the anniversaries of the seventeenth and eighteenth centuries.

It is no wonder that the first Luther anniversary after the fall of the *Third Reich*, the four-hundredth anniversary of his death in 1946, which was celebrated with remarkable festivity, was completely dominated by this ecclesiastical, theological image of Luther. The "German Luther" had been definitively cast onto the ash heap of history (fig. 5); now people expected the interpreter of Holy Scripture to provide moral support in a time of universal breakdown. Yet in the same year, with the republication of Friedrich Engels's *The Peasant War in Germany* in the embryonic GDR (German Democratic Republic, East Germany), a new development was taking place: the creation and dissemination of socialist images of Luther. At first Engels's line of denouncing Luther as a cowardly "prince's lackey," in contrast to Thomas Müntzer the plebian revolutionary, was preached. But as the socialist German state felt the need for positive historical antecedents, it began to evaluate the Wittenberg Reformer anew. The 450th anniversary of the Reformation in 1967, and even more so the five-hundredth anniversary of Luther's birth in 1983,

ebration" of that year into a missionary event for their newly founded National *Reich* Church: "On this day of remembrance, that merely looks backwards in time, a new house of Martin Luther's German church will be consecrated. [...] The hour has come to missionize the people," declared the new *Reich* Church government.[23] For if all Protestants united in the service of this *Reich*, the masses who had become alienated from the church but who enthusiastically supported Hitler's regime would, conversely, return to what had become a truly German Protestant church. This anniversary program

14 The Praeses of the Evangelical Lutheran Synod of the State of New York, Frederick Henry Quitman, in his anniversary sermon, quoted in: ibid., p. 96. **15** Wendebourg, *Jews*, pp. 257 f. **16** Quoted in: Lehmann, *Imagination*, p. 182. **17** Frederic Henry Hedge in his speech at the official anniversary celebrations of the Massachusetts Historical Society, quoted in: ibid., p. 179. **18** Quoted in: ibid., p. 183. **19** Quoted in: ibid., p. 284. **20** The popular theologian Frank Wakeley Gunsaulus in his anniversary speech, "Martin Luther and the Reformation", at the University of Chicago, quoted in: ibid., p. 276. Of interest is the choice of the last five men in this list of names—all Germans who emigrated to America and who fought in the War of Independence or distinguished themselves in the later political life of the United States. **21** See Wendebourg, *1921*.

22 See, for instance, Preuß, *Prophet*; id., *Hitler*. **23** Appeal of the *Reich* Church government on the occasion of the anniversary, in *Gesetzesblatt der Deutschen Evangelischen Kirche* 1933. **24** According to the Göttingen professor of theology Hermann Dörries in his official anniversary speech at the university, printed in Dörries, *Deutschland*, p. 19. **25** The title of a publication by an Erlangen professor of theology. See Preuß, *Luther und Hitler*. **26** Reinhold Krause, the *Gau* Chairman of Berlin at the so-called Sports Palace Rally (Sportpalastkundgebung). See Wendebourg, *Vergangene Reformationsjubiläen*, p. 274. See also Jan Scheunemann's contribution to this publication. **27** Both quotes with sources in Wendebourg, *Vergangene Reformationsjubiläen*, p. 275.

Fig. 6
Postage stamps with the portrait
of the Reformer from France and Bulgaria
on the occasion of Martin Luther's 500th
birthday, 1983

were celebrated not only by the church but also, with much pomp, by the government. On both occasions a Luther stamp was issued—and, incidentally, in 1983 in other Eastern Bloc countries too. Luther was now considered "one of the greatest Germans," according to the chairman of the state council of the GDR. As an actor in the "early bourgeois revolution," a necessary stage on the road to the proletarian revolution, the Reformer now played a positive role in the socialist republic's view of history.[28] "Luther the proponent of the Enlightenment" and the "German Luther" had thus fused into a new constellation. The church celebrations, on the other hand, which ran parallel to those of the government, insisted that the real significance of the Reformer's life lay in his ecclesiastical and theological achievements—the church had learned from a long series of anniversaries that had gone awry by sticking to theology.

The celebrations being held at the same time in the West, on both sides of the Atlantic, cannot be summarized so simply. The anniversary of 1983[29] was celebrated at all levels with a wide range of events: church services, official ceremonies, exhibitions, and much more. In many Western countries, Luther stamps were issued as well, not only in Germany but in other European countries, including some with no tradition of Lutheranism (fig. 6), as well as in many countries of the Americas. This phenomenon illustrated once more that the Wittenberg Reformer was being honored as a figure of worldwide significance beyond the Protestant churches. What image of Luther motivated the commemoration in each case remained an open question. At the same time, critical voices were raised: in Germany, Protestant pastors and the Protestant media denounced especially Luther's anti-Jewish writings—in the United States, these writings were made known to a wider public for the first time. Significantly, Roman Catholics celebrated this anniversary in large numbers, creating yet another new image of Luther: the supradenominational "Father in Faith," common to all Christians.[30] It was the latest in a long series of Luther images, but one that in the intervening decades has faded into the background. It appears that the anniversary of 2017 will not create its own special image of Luther; neither will it highlight one from the past. But after all, it is the Reformation that should be celebrated and not a particular reformer.

BIBLIOGRAPHY

Bornkamm, Heinrich (1970), *Luther im Spiegel der deutschen Geistesgeschichte*. 2nd ed. Göttingen. **Dörries**, Hermann (1934), *Luther und Deutschland* (= Sammlung gemeinverständlicher Vorträge. 169). Tübingen. **Flügel**, Wolfgang (2012), Deutsche Lutheraner? Amerikanische Protestanten? Die Selbstdarstellung deutscher Einwanderer im Reformationsjubiläum 1817. In: Thanner, Klaus/Ulrich, Jörg (eds.), *Spurenlese. Reformationsvergegenwärtigung als Standortbestimmung (1717–1983)* (= Leucorea-Studien. 17). Leipzig, pp. 71–99. **Kaufmann**, Thomas (2010), Reformationsgedenken in der Frühen Neuzeit. In: *Zeitschrift für Theologie und Kirche*, vol. 107, pp. 285–324. **Lehmann**, Hartmut (1988), *Martin Luther in the American Imagination*. München. **Maron**, Gottfried (1993), 1883–1917–1933–1983: Jubiläen eines Jahrhunderts. In: id., *Die ganze Christenheit auf Erden. Martin Luther und seine ökumenische Bedeutung*. Göttingen, pp. 188–208. **Preuß**, Hans (1933), *Martin Luther. Der Prophet*. Gütersloh. **Preuß**, Hans (1933), Luther und Hitler. In: *Allgemeine Evangelisch-Lutherische Kirchenzeitung*, vol. 66, cols. 970–979, 994–999. **Preuß**, Hans (1933), *Luther und Hitler*. Erlangen. **Wendebourg**, Dorothea (2011), Die Reformationsjubiläen des 19. Jahrhunderts. In: *Zeitschrift für Theologie und Kirche*, vol. 108, pp. 270–335. **Wendebourg**, Dorothea (2012), Jews Commemorating Luther in the Nineteenth Century. In: *Lutheran Quarterly New Series*, vol. 26, pp. 249–270. **Wendebourg**, Dorothea (2013), 'Gesegnet sei das Andenken Luthers!' Die Juden und Martin Luther im 19. Jahrhundert. In: *Zeitschrift für Religion und Geistesgeschichte*, vol. 65, pp. 235–251. **Wendebourg**, Dorothea (2013), Das Reformationsjubiläum des Jahres 1921. In: *Zeitschrift für Theologie und Kirche*, vol. 110, pp. 316–361. **Wendebourg**, Dorothea (2014), Vergangene Reformationsjubiläen. Ein Rückblick im Vorfeld von 2017. In: Schilling, Heinz (ed.), *Der Reformator Martin Luther 2017* (= Schriften des Historischen Kollegs. 92). Berlin, pp. 261–281.

28 References and sources in: ibid., pp. 276 f. See also Jan Scheunemann's contribution to this publication. **29** See Wendebourg, *Vergangene Reformationsjubiläen*, pp. 278 f. **30** See Maron, *1883*, p. 198.

Ninety-Five Theses

In his Ninety-Five Theses of 1517, Luther criticized the practice of indulgences. He was bothered by the fact that the faithful could reduce the amount of punishment they had to undergo for their sins by making money payments. The Ninety-Five Theses are considered the starting point of the Reformation. For a long time, it was doubtful whether Luther had really nailed his theses to the door of the Wittenberg Castle Church on October 31, 1517. This is now disputed, no single eye-witness report of the event has ever been found. Philipp Melanchthon was the first to mention the story a few decades later. For centuries, Luther's "posting of the theses" was an important event for commemoration among Protestants. 100 years after the alleged hammer blows, a plethora of fanciful images began to develop. The portal of the Wittenberg Castle Church became a place of historical projections. If one compares some of these representations, the rich variety of portals and prints becomes obvious.

1617 Martin Luther uses an oversized goose quill to write on the entrance door.

1717 On the 200th anniversary of the Reformation, a lonely Luther is shown nailing a print of his theses to a door featuring

1840 Luther does not himself pick up the hammer but has the theses nailed to a Gothic church portal.

1917 While World War I is in full force, Luther vigorously nails a three-column print of his theses to the portal, thus clearly distinguishing between war

2014 A Playmobil Luther wields a hammer, posting his theses with a seal.

STEFAN LAUBE

Homely Audacity: Memories of Luther between Hero Worship and Enchanted Idyll

Postcards of "Wonderful Opposites"

Two different trees on picture postcards dating from World War I provide polarizing images of Martin Luther: One shows the Reformer standing under an oak tree with Otto von Bismarck, one of the most prominent German politicians of the nineteenth century, and the other shows Martin Luther surrounded by his family at home next to a Christmas tree. Postcards enjoyed great popularity at the beginning of the twentieth century, and postmen would deliver whole sacks of cards with selected images and inscribed with brief messages. These postcards included images of Luther shown in a variety of contexts ranging from mythical and heroic to idyllic and homely and reached a huge audience.[1] Luther himself is a figure of contrast par excellence, equally in his element whether depicted in world-historical or political contexts or in the comfort and coziness of the domestic sphere. Other defining personalities from German history such as Frederick the Great, Goethe, and Bismarck are far less convincing when placed on these two sides of a coin.

A postcard sent from the front in World War I with a handwritten notation marking the anniversary of the Reformation in 1917 shows Luther and Bismarck standing together under a "German oak;" the tree trunk is decorated with the Luther rose and an element of von Bismarck's family coat of arms—a clover leaf festooned with oak leaves. The illustration is encircled by bands bearing well-known quotations: Luther's "A mighty fortress is our God" and Bismarck's "We Germans fear God, but nothing else in the world" (fig. 1). Presented in an ahistorical context, the Reformation and German politics are presented within the framework of natural history. Both Luther and Bismarck, who steadfastly, courageously, and vigorously defied the resistance of their eras, appear to have grown naturally out of the ground. In the late Enlightenment period, Johann Gottfried Herder had already described Luther as the "oak tree of the German people!" who had braved the storm and still sprouted green leaves. On this postcard this metaphor was now extended, typically for the times by incorporating military components.[2] Bismarck is depicted wearing a cuirass, but Martin Luther is also shown with a breastplate and both are carrying swords. Anyone thinking that this image could only have been created in times of war—to mark the anniversary of the Reformation in 1917, for example—is mistaken. The headquarters of the *Evangelischer Bund* (Protestant Federation), which sold reproduc-

tions on commission, introduced the *German Oaks* woodcut to the market in 1909, available either in an inexpensive "simple, smooth" frame or in a high-quality "finely ornamented oak frame."[3]

This postcard compresses history to a teleological concept. Luther and Bismarck were both well-known Protestant role models. One marked the beginning and the other the end of a political development charged with elements of redemption. "The holy Protestant realm of the German nation completes itself […] within this process we can recognize the path of God between 1517 and 1871" were the words of Adolf Stoecker, the anti-Semitic founder of the Christian Social Party, who would subsequently be named court chaplain, directly after the 1871 Proclamation of the German Empire in Versailles.[4] With a little editing, and the uniting of noncontemporaneous figures, the anonymous artist who created the postcard has created an easily recognizable trademark, translating the words of historians, journalists, and pastors into an image. Luther and Bismarck have been placed in the limelight as exemplary representatives of "Germanness;" both introspection and active piety have now become virtually entwined in the tree trunk.

Thomas Nipperdey's dictum for Luther's anniversary year 1983 —"Luther is completely different from us"—would not have been understood by a large fraction of the population.[5] Their main focus was to transform Luther into a contemporary witness and an advocate of their political objectives. This "modern Luther rhetoric"[6] was adopted most intensively by the nationalist-minded bourgeoisie: the appropriation of Luther and the Reformation had little significance for rural and urban workers.[7] In the period of historicism, it seemed as though everything that could be gleaned from the distant past was legitimate, suitable for upholding continuity and providing orientation. In the nineteenth century, history had become the most prominent interpretive guideline, and historical consciousness was raised by regular perusal of easily memorized images and figures. The contents of text books for history published in the days of the German Empire were intended to cement historical interpretations in pupils' minds. In fact, the nation did not possess anything resembling a collective identity originating from the depths of a "popular soul," as our postcard suggests. On the contrary, it had largely been constructed and invented by an influential elite, who had designed a historical framework in order to suit themselves—from Hermann's victory over the Romans in the Teutoburg Forest and Henry IV's Walk to

Fig. 1 Post card, Three German Oaks, 1917.
Kunstverlagsanstalt (Art Printing House) Gerhard Stelling

ing the lute on which he may have played a hymn of praise or a Christmas carol; perhaps it was his unforgettable *From Heaven Above to Earth I Come*. Two friends have joined the joyous family celebrations of the great man who is not at all depicted as such. Luther's wife's aunt Muhme Lehne, shivering slightly, warms herself at the stove, which like the entire room is faithfully recreated from Luther's original sitting room in the greatest detail, and a kitten licking itself is also enjoying the stove's friendly heat."[8]

Thus an icon of Protestant family life emerges. A number of features catch the eye on closer perusal; the objects even possess a concrete, tactile quality. The textures of clothing, the musical instrument, the table setting, and the tiled stove have been recognizably created in minute detail. This form of representation is intended to turn Luther into a friend, someone perhaps close enough to reach out and touch.[9] Schwerdgeburth's engraving enjoyed enormous popularity. Fine-art publishers such as the *Kunstverlagshandlung Hanfstaengls Nachfolger* in Berlin sold images of Luther's private life in enormous quantities. The Christmas picture was offered in three different printed forms: as a photogravure or a photograph on cardboard or glass in different sizes. Luther in this way gained entrance into German family homes. The Luther family Christmas motif was also reproduced in illustrated magazines, calendars, and postils. The engraving seems both authentic and apolitical in equal measure. In fact, Luther never actually sat under a Christmas tree on Christmas Eve.[10] The earliest established sources for Christmas celebrations with a decorated Christmas tree date from around the end of the sixteenth century. Decorated trees most probably only became fashionable around 1800, when Protestants started using Christmas trees to decorate their sitting rooms.[11]

Both postcards display Martin Luther in highly contrasting contexts; even the very earliest representations of Luther attracted and integrated divergent settings. During the age of religious conflict in the sixteenth century, depictions of Luther ranged from saint to devil and from ascetic religious hero to monster. This all changed during the nineteenth century, when Luther increasingly became a figure of national consensus whose charisma could no longer be completely ignored even by Catholics. Memories of Luther, however, continued to draw their strength from contrasts—in our examples, from the patriotic veneration of a hero to a romantic and magical idyll. Heinrich von Treitschke expressed these two extremes in a nutshell in his anniversary speech in 1883, which would canonize Luther's image for the next few decades in a national conservative sense: "A foreigner

Canossa barefoot in the snow, to Luther who had proclaimed his clear conscience before the Emperor Charles V at the Diet of Worms.

In a radical change of scene, the second postcard shows a living room in the former Augustinian monastery in Wittenberg, where Luther is sitting with his family around a large table bearing a decorated Christmas tree lit with candles (fig. 2). This colored postcard is also from the World War I era. The outbreak of war was accompanied by an outburst of national pride throughout most parts of society. Countless German soldiers visualized this very image at the beginning of August 1914 when they were told they would be returning home by Christmas as triumphant victors. The postcard depicts the Christmas motif from the steel-engraving cycle devoted to Luther's life created in 1843 by Carl August Schwerdgeburth, an engraver at the Weimar court. The viewer sees a "cozy home" with which many Protestants could identify. The following commentary appeared in the art periodical *Deutsches Kunstblatt* in 1858: "This is definitely the most beautiful of all the illustrations, radiating a very human beauty: *Luther surrounded by his family on Christmas Eve 1536*. Here we have pure domestic bliss with no hate, discord, dispute, or work, but a holiday instead: a festive Christmas Eve. The candles on the Christmas tree are burning brightly, the grateful children are joyous, the youngest sitting on his mother's lap. Luther is still hold-

1 Rentzsch, *Postkartenalbum*. **2** See Demandt, *Baum*, p. 234. **3** Grote, *Bund*, p. 60. **4** See Kupisch, *Idealismus*, p. 85. **5** Nipperdey, *Luther*, p. 31. **6** Burkhardt, *Lutherfeiern*, p. 228 (original: "Luther-Heute-Rhetorik"). **7** The lack of knowledge of Luther is demonstrated by a survey among Silesian recruits who believed that Luther was an inventor of gunpowder, warlord and imperial chancellor. See Scharfe, *Nach-Luther*, pp. 11 f. **8** Carl August Schwerdgeburth's Lutherbilder-Cyklus. In: Eggers, *Kunstblatt*, p. 260. **9** Kruse, *Lutherlebenbilder*, p. 52. **10** Nagy, *Paradies*. **11** Even though Luther must therefore not have known of this custom, he succeeded in increasing the significance of Christmas Eve compared to the feast of St. Nicholas. The Christ Child as a gift for humanity was what prompted him to relocate the custom of exchanging presents from a Roman Catholic saint's day to December 25.

Fig. 2 Post card (after Carl August Schwerdgeburth),
Luther surrounded by his family in Wittenberg on Christmas Eve 1536

would probably be at a loss and ask himself how such wonderful opposites could be united in a single soul: his potent crushing rage and the ardency of his pious belief, so much wisdom and so much childlike innocence, such great profound mysticism and so much zest for life, such monstrous roughness and so much tender kindheartedness [...]. We Germans see no enigma in all of this; we simply say that this is blood from our blood."[12] The foundations for this conception of Luther had been laid back in the eighteenth century.

Personality Models in the Eighteenth Century

Pietism and Enlightenment had added a number of new, forwardlooking facets to Luther's image. On the one hand, he was viewed as a credible pastor striving for justification, and on the other hand, a moral citizen, scholar, and respectable family man.[13] Whereas orthodox Protestants had at best seen the authoritative expression of a divine doctrine in Luther, representatives of Pietism and the Enlightenment were certain that the Reformation must continue to be developed. Luther's work alone had the potential to change the status quo on both personal and social levels. In the mirror of the sub-

jective beliefs of Pietism, Luther was primarily seen as a human being. This model was taken up by followers of the somewhat religiously critical Enlightenment. They valued Luther as an individual who had freed himself from the shackles of authority. An engraving illustrating an ode composed by the Lutheran pastor and poet Johann Andreas Cramer shows an image of Luther without pangs of guilt or signs of his struggle of faith and without any allegorical transfiguration We see a virtuous citizen who is more closely connected to earthly realms than to the concept of salvation (fig. 3).

This shift of emphasis from prophet and church father to a fighter for the freedom of conscience and tolerance in the Enlightenment can be clearly comprehended in a work by Gotthold Ephraim Lessing. In 1774, Lessing published the religiously critical volume *Fragmente eines Unbekannten* (Fragments from an Unnamed Author) —a text by Hermann Samuel Reimarus, a high school professor and classical scholar from Hamburg who had died in 1768—and undertook a critical review of these fragments. This brought him into conflict with the orthodox pastor Johann Melchior Goeze. In his first response to Goeze, which was followed by the eleven *Anti-Goeze* texts, Lessing repeatedly makes reference to Luther's radical spirit:

"Luther! You great misjudged man! And from no others more misjudged than by the shortsighted, pigheaded boors, who step into your shoes and follow the path you blazed, screeching but at the same time indifferently strolling along! You have liberated us from the yoke of tradition. Who will liberate us from the unbearable yoke of the written word! Who will finally succeed in bringing us a form of Christianity that you would teach us in our time, as Christ himself would teach us? Who indeed—."[14]

During the late Enlightenment, the memory of Luther was expanded in a significant way. It was not without a prophetic impulse; Luther had in his time propagated the concept of national identity. Herder postulated that the German people possessed a single "mindset"[15] that had also been shaped by Luther. As was customary during the nineteenth century, he venerated Luther for his German virility and courage. Nevertheless, the budding cosmopolitanism in education that Herder observed was transformed within the context of the Napoleonic foreign occupation into a culture that attempted to define specific national traits. Johann Gottlieb Fichte, Ernst Moritz Arndt, and Friedrich Ludwig Jahn declared Luther to be a national icon and the epitome of the German soul to resounding public acclaim. Luther's courage and determination "is natural and definitely no miracle. This is indeed evidence for German gravity and sentiment."[16]

This initial elevation of Luther to national hero was, however, not only propagated by public speeches, such as the *Reden an die deutsche Nation* (Addresses to the German Nation) quoted above, presented in the form of lectures by Fichte in Berlin, but also in the fields of visual arts and theater. Since the beginning of the nineteenth century, German citizens had been collecting donations for a monument to Luther to be erected in Wittenberg. Additionally, Zacharias Werner's drama *Martin Luther oder die Weihe der Kraft* (Martin Luther, or the Consecration of Strength) was premiered in Berlin on June 11, 1806. In times of socio-political instability across Europe, bracketed by the devastating defeats suffered by Napoleon's opponents at the battles of Austerlitz as well as those of Jena and Auerstedt, Werner's drama was a resounding success.[17] One scene best represents its content. During the Diet of Worms, the Emperor drops his scepter upon seeing Luther. The scepter is subsequently taken up by his imperial chamberlain, the Elector of Brandenburg. This "transfer" of imperial power from the Habsburgs to the Hohenzollern anticipates historical reality sixty-five years later with the establishment of the German Empire.

Popular Media in the Nineteenth Century: Image, Scene, Object

In the modern age, myths can only evolve when they are anchored in collective memory—through songs, poems, and commemorative ceremonies or through striking images and familiar places and objects. These media used in commemorating Luther are characterized by the fact that they deliberately reduce complexity, permitting them to be permanently stored and recalled. In the case of Luther this mechanism is particularly well reflected in historical images, dramas, and places of remembrance.

Historical images, the most static of these media, project pathos and monumentality onto a two-dimensional screen, whether it is an

Fig. 3 Johann Martin Preisler, Martin Luther, c. 1770

imposing panorama painted in oil or a mass-produced print. Despite the necessity of systematically simplifying complex strands of the plot in a painting, these representations from the nineteenth century with its faith in history were aimed at historical accuracy. The detailed manner of painting concealed their fictitiousness, thereby increasing the belief in the reality which these works of art represent. In an age in which photographic images did not yet compete with paintings, these pictures appeared to be directly recording the events they aimed to portray. In the popular imagination, the historical events became identical with their depiction, thereby transmogrifying the image into a historical document.

In the nineteenth century, the world of theater altered the perceptions and habits of a substantial proportion of the population much as television did in the twentieth century. The young and old, rich and poor, and male and female were all keen to see persons acting on stage with whom they could personally identify. Theater, which combines reality and illusion as well as identity and appearances, was a kind of laboratory in which experiments were undertaken on the human condition with all its entanglements. As a visual, auditory, and emotional stimulus, theater as an art form exploited human beings with all their senses, creating total submission to the plot.

12 Treitschke, *Nation*, pp. 138, 155. **13** Bornkamm, *Geistesgeschichte*, pp. 11–16. **14** Lessing, *Absagungsschreiben*, pp. 125 f. **15** Herder, *Urkunden*, pp. 15 f. (original: "Denkart"). **16** Fichte, *Reden*, p. 184 (sixth speech). **17** Karnick, *Bühnenfigur*, pp. 260 f.

Fig. 4 Hermann Freihold Plüddemann, Luther at the Diet of Worms, 1864

The break with tradition that accompanied the Reformation entailed the construction of new origin stories that required authentic locations and objects for their confirmation. "Luther locations" have therefore continued to stimulate the collective imagination right up to the present day. Luther's pilgrims have congregated in the "sanctuaries" of Luther's residencies down through the centuries to admire the Protestant "relics." Be it in Wittenberg or the Wartburg Castle, these physical places of commemoration have always conveyed an element of alienation between the past and the present, but this could be diminished with the aid of remembrance. Luther's private living quarters, however, offer particularly poignant possibilities of identification; everyone has been at home in some way and at some time.

Hero on Paintings

The monk stands opposite the Emperor, who reigns over half of the western hemisphere, and refuses to utter the required recantation. There is no other event in the life of Luther that has invited such copious mythologizing. This explains why artists were so attracted to this scene. At least sixteen nineteenth-century representations of the confrontation at the Diet of Worms in 1521 are still in existence.[18] Hermann Freihold Plüddemann painted *Luther vor dem Reichstag zu*

Worms (Luther at the Diet of Worms) in 1864 at a time when liberal and national tendencies were still mutually reinforcing each other just before their programs were beginning to diverge (fig. 4). Plüddemann, a graduate of the Art Academy in Düsseldorf who was taught by Carl Joseph Begas in Berlin, was captivated not only by the character of Luther but also of Columbus. He considered these two individuals to be the symbols of progress in the early modern period. Both had ventured to new shores by the means they had at their disposal: Columbus with his ship and Luther with the Bible.

Plüddemann aimed at historical reconstruction in his painting, but at the same time he clearly wanted viewers to know which figure should be the most prominent. Numerous individuals are sitting and standing in an almost overcrowded room. The Emperor is enthroned under a canopy on a raised platform. A lone monk is standing at the center of the painting. Luther is illuminated by a light source emanating from beyond the left margin of the picture. His pose suggests a stage actor. His eyes are turned upward and his right hand is raised, pointing simultaneously toward the heavens and to a crucifix, while his left hand rests on the Bible. The steadfast Reformer is placed in the limelight, courageously defending his faith and the Gospel. Here Plüddemann is surely depicting the moment when Luther uttered his unconfirmed sentence, "Here I stand and cannot do otherwise." These words characterize Luther as an individual fighter challenging

Fig. 5 Photographic Reproduction of the Luther Festival from 1907. Scene from Otto Devrient's Luther Pageant in Weimar.
Churchgoer in front of the Palatial Church discuss Luther's thesis posting, 1883

authority. In the painting his expression displays his clear conscience and trust in God. Interestingly Luther does not look seventeen years older than his adversary, Emperor Charles V. While the Emperor, who was young at the time, appears to have aged conspicuously under the burden of his imperial office, Luther is shown bursting with vitality. Luther's pose gives the impression that he is departing from the earthly sphere as he seems to be following orders from heaven. Whereas this historically renowned figure is vertically composed as an individual and is shown connected to God, the assembly of individuals is reduced to a passive theater audience. More or less fascinated, they observe the unfolding drama celebrating the intimate communication between a human being and the invisible God. Luther's thirst for action and his individuality are therefore only one side of the coin; on the other, Luther simultaneously appears as the executor of a divine will.

Plüddemann's painting must have been familiar to many school-children in Prussia. On the initiative of the Emperor Kaiser Wilhelm, the image was reproduced as an oleograph and displayed in every Prussian school during the 1880s. At this time, national stereotypes were increasingly being projected onto the figure of Luther, which were barely compatible with his character. Observers were forced to develop a new concept of the Reformer originating from an interpretation of Luther that was above all propagated by Heinrich Treit-

schke in his 1883 Luther anniversary speech: Luther had stood in Worms "as the leader of the nation, heroic as the people's patron saint" before the Emperor who wore the crown as a "stranger" and neglected "the call of the nation." Luther's Christianity of conscience could also have been interpreted anthropologically, but Treitschke narrowed it down to the "German soul." Numerous teachers and pastors would follow his interpretation over the next few decades.[19]

Luther on Stage

It was in the theater that Luther was brought to life.[20] Otto Devrient would create the most successful Luther pageant:[21] his work was performed 440 times in thirty-six cities between 1883 and 1914.[22] Plays about Luther were modeled on sacred dramas from the sixteenth century, which had involved numerous amateur performers recruited from the local population.[23] Moreover, like the modern festival concept, it was heavily influenced by the Oberammergau passion plays, which had seventeenth-century origins. Inspired by

18 Holsing, *Luther*, pp. 479f. **19** Kohnle, *Luther*, pp. 53f. **20** Reichelt, *Erlebnisraum*, pp. 97–103. **21** Devrient, *Luther*. **22** Letter from Klara Devrient to the Bavarian Ministry of Cultural Affairs, October 13, 1933. See Laube, *Fest*, p. 369, note 193. **23** Metz, *Drama*.

the intensity of performances in this small Bavarian village, Otto Devrient's father, Eduard, campaigned for the establishment of theater festivals across the whole of the fatherland in order to promote national awareness.[24] In addition to his son, Hans Herrig and Friedrich Lienhard also created popular plays about Luther.

Otto Devrient's drama has its premier in Jena in 1883. A local society had been organized by high school principal Gustav Richter to guarantee the work's annual performance. Participation in this project was considered a great honor and distinction but also required intense personal commitment. Devrient, who had been employed by the court theater in Weimar since 1873, first as an actor and subsequently as its director, was more predestined for this task than any other. He had celebrated his greatest success in Weimar with the production of both parts of Goethe's Faust in the form of a medieval mystery play trilogy. The four-hundredth anniversary of Luther's birth provided a suitable occasion for the establishment of the festival. The roles of Martin Luther and Katharina von Bora were played by professional actors; Devrient was not only author and director of the drama, but simultaneously undertook the principal role of Luther. Almost all of the one hundred additional actors were amateurs. The magazine *Gartenlaube* reviewed the drama as follows: "It must be said that an ensemble of professional actors would possibly have performed Devrient's festival work on a higher artistic level, but hardly with the same enthusiastic conviction and to such folkloristic effect."[25] According to the review, the amateur actors had transported themselves into the era of Luther with the aid of historical costumes, "thereby intensifying Protestant awareness."[26] Most of the amateurs served as purely decorative onstage extras, although those with small speaking roles presumably found their tasks more exciting. We can assume that participation in this theatrical event would be vividly engraved in each individual's memory (fig. 5). The large numbers of spectators were also readily able to identify with the Reformer as an individual personality. The festival drama made it feasible to appropriate the mythical past while participating in a contemporary event. Devrient's play was published in thirty-eight editions between 1884 and 1905 and performed to great acclaim sixteen times at the Krolloper music hall in Berlin between October 31 and December 1, 1901.[27] An association for the promotion of popular German-Protestant folk dramas had been founded shortly before these performances, and by 1901 it numbered one thousand members. Devrient saw it as his personal social mission to familiarize all groups of the population with Protestantism.

Devrient's work perfectly recreated the ambivalence of Luther's persona. Luther was shown both as a heroic man of action and a loving family man. Luther's life was related in a seven separate parts: (1) Luther struggles to attain the true faith as a monk in the Augustinian monastery in Erfurt; (2) Luther nails his Ninety-Five Theses on the door of the Wittenberg Castle Church; (3) Luther stands before the Emperor Charles V at the Diet of Worms; (4) Luther translates the New Testament disguised as Junker Jörg at Wartburg Castle; (5) Katharina von Bora is a nun in Nimbschen nunnery and escapes with Luther's help; (6) Luther's has feelings for Katharina and they marry in 1525; and (7) Luther, a few months before his death, is surrounded by his family. What is immediately striking is that the homely Luther stands equivalent to the heroic Luther. The final two scenes are set in Luther's sitting room in Wittenberg—which is, however, only described in the stage directions as "reflecting great homeliness"—in the year 1545, after two decades of family life.[28] In the drama, Katharina von Bora's life takes on a far more prominent role than described in history books or in Luther's biographies. Events that could project a negative impression of Luther—such as the Peasants' Revolt—are, as so often in those times, swept under the rug. There is an extensive focus on the topics of indulgences and the posting of the Ninety-Five Theses to the door. Devrient employs a healthy portion of pathos in his depiction of the so-called posting of the theses: Luther employs forceful blows of the hammer when personally nailing his theses to the door of the Castle Church. At the first blow of the hammer, he cries, "Christ crucified! My dispute is in thy name." On the second blow, "Christ crucified! I am preparing your work of salvation." On the third, "Christ crucified! I am hammering the print of the nails." And on the fourth blow, "Christ crucified! Permit it! I am bearing your suffering!"[29] No one disputed the historical accuracy of the posting of the theses in the nineteenth century, an event whose authenticity was not called into question until Erwin Iserloh doubted it 1961.[30]

Devrient's historical drama unfolds over an impressive six hours, including intermissions. "Despite the beauty of his poetry, this was without doubt a hard challenge for the enthusiasm and resilience of the audience."[31]

Aura in Authentic Locations

Relics from Luther's lifetime, which were presented with a great emphasis on their authenticity, appear to have surpassed the theatrical experience by a long shot. In particular, Luther's sitting room in Wittenberg seems to have evoked strong emotions (fig. 6). Just prior to the beginning of World War I, the then director of the Luther Hall commented as follows: "Oh what immeasurable wealth of the most authentic and solemn atmosphere is conjured up here that cannot be recreated in any theater."[32] The Berlin sculptor Johann Gottfried Schadow had previously emphasized that there was probably no other location more suitable to recall "the spirit of Luther in his personal image than in this room, provided that we have familiarized ourselves with Luther's way of life and living conditions. Then we can feel his presence here much more immediately than when we stand before his portrait."[33] The sensual experience of authentic space was particularly fascinating to the sightseers in the sitting room, because the Reformation was becoming increasingly alien to a society which stood under the impact of urbanization and industrialization. Visitors to Luther's sitting room and the neighboring chambers frequently spoke of "hallowed halls" in their comments in the visitors' book and conjured up a far bigger size of this room, which is by extension rather small. This genuine fascination with Luther's sitting room was based on the compelling ambiguity that its mundane reality reflected the world-historical significance of Luther. A visitor's book entry from

Fig. 6 Wittenberg, Luther House, View into the Lutherstube (Luther's living room)

Luther's house dating from 1833 reads as follows: "The simple and unpretentious nature of these venerated men provides the most convincing proof of our immortality."[34] The juxtaposition of sensual proximity and spiritual distance creates an aura that almost anyone would find hard to resist.

By the second half of the sixteenth century, the interest in the veneration of Luther had focused on the sitting room of the family man and celebrated professor as the site of his famous table talks. Today, visitors to the museum can still walk directly through this room. Architectural research has established that the chamber must have been created sometime between 1535 and 1538 with the placing of wooden partitions within a larger room. With the exception of the cubature of the room, and perhaps the benches fixed to the wall and the wooden paneling, nothing else can be dated back to Luther's era. The five-story stove with twenty-seven figurative tiles—which show images of the Evangelists, personifications of the Liberal Arts, and christological illustrations—dating from 1602 and the painted walls dating from 1629, which were reexposed as part of the anniversary celebrations of the Reformation in 1967, are still visible today. The room's other moveable pieces of furniture are spartan. The most

noticeable objects are the robust table and the double window seats. The table, at least, is thought to be from Luther's lifetime.[35]

It was not important if the furnishings in Luther's sitting room were genuine, but rather that visitors considered it genuine. Luther's famous ink stain is another of these spurious relics.[36] The stain itself is a naïve illustration of Luther's so-called claim (i.e., words most likely put into his mouth) that he had fought the devil with ink. Ink stains were splashed onto the wall at Wartburg Castle as well as the Coburg Fortress, and they were repeatedly renewed during subsequent centuries. The intention was to provide a tangible representation of one of Luther's metaphors, but it remained a paradox that an event that had never taken place in this way was meant to authenticate the location.

24 François, *Oberammergau*, p. 283. **25** Ziel, *Otto Devrient*, p. 691. **26** Erfurth, *Geschichte*, p. 151. **27** Devrient, *Luther*. **28** Devrient, *Festspiel*, p. 110. **29** Id., *Luther*, p. 28. **30** Leppin, *Monumentalisierung*. **31** Erdmann, *Lutherfestspiele*, p. 4. **32** Dunkmann, *Lutherhaus*. **33** Schadow, *Denkmäler*, p. 93. **34** Adolph und Moritz Kemy, May 31, 1833, quoted from: Stiftung Luthergedenkstätten, *Einschreibe Buch*. **35** Laube, *Lutherhaus*, pp. 93–99. **36** Joestel, *Wurf*.

The variant of the seemingly apolitical Luther, the trope of the Reformer as a dedicated family man, was free to unfold in his sitting room. The idyllic family life attributed to Luther was intended to repair the fractures of the traditional domestic world resulting from industrial development. There is sufficient evidence to prove that Luther's sitting room was actually the location of his table talks (Tischgespräche), although the opinion is still upheld that Luther gave many of these talks in the *refectorium* (dining room). Luther's marriage in 1525 is said to have transformed the monastery, which was deserted by then, into a family home. He is said to have strummed the strings of the lute and sung his own hymn compositions together with his family in his sitting room. In the nineteenth century it was the metamorphosis of a monastery into a Protestant manse that made Luther's sitting room a mythic memorial: "The same rooms that had once nurtured the most genuine spirit of Catholicism and had been a place of austere self-righteousness, offering sanctuary from the world, are now pervaded with the purest Protestant spirit of a free and joyful life of faith, Moreover the place where monks dedicated to chastity spent their days has been transformed into a hearth of conjugal happiness and a cozy home for genuine German family life. It is the same building yet a different one through and through."[37]

Accelerator of Familiarity

Historical schoolhouse paintings, theatrical plays involving masses of amateur performers, and tourist pilgrimages to significant places in Martin Luther's life all served the same objective. That is, they all attempted to popularize the figure of the Reformer, who was steadily becoming a more and more distant figure during the nineteenth century, and to familiarize him to individuals who had ever-diminishing connections with his achievements.

The nineteenth century reception of Luther's life and works seems strangely heterogeneous. Remarkably, his dramatic theological conflicts played a largely invisible role. The questions "How do I attain a merciful God?" or "How can I become righteous before God?" were concrete realities for Luther. This theological-existential approach to the world must have disconcerted an increasingly secularized society. Many saw Luther merely as an outsider per se without involving themselves with his complex relations with God. The doctrine of justification as the core of Protestant faith is a construct that is difficult to understand and almost impossible to visualize. This explains why it rarely plays a role in public memory. The initiators of popular memory benefitted from the fact that there was more to him than the "theological Luther," but that alongside this aspect there was also the "political Luther" and the "folksy Luther;" he was both a hero and a man of flesh and blood who flourished particularly well in visual and material cultures. While his theological agenda remained inaccessible, his attractiveness as a human being increased. The Luther depicted in the visual arts imprinted himself in the collective memory as did his representation in the performing arts and the relics prominently displayed in authentic

settings. These media enactments lent Luther a spiritual and essential aura while largely concealing the fact that this Luther was not the genuine embodiment of his history. Rather, he was just a construct of the minds and imaginations of professors, historians, philologists, lawyers, journalists, artists, and composers.

Whether homely or heroic, the memory of Luther is shaped by images oscillating between historical reality and myth. History as memory tends to use well-devised images, which in this case are all the more convincing the earlier they molded Luther's veneration. Even in cases where modern source criticism has exposed them as false, such images were never lost, replaced, or corrected. Of course the following scenes were bound to create tensions between history as memory and history as scholarship: Luther defiantly announcing to the Emperor, "Here I stand and cannot do otherwise;" Luther posting his theses hammer in hand; Luther sitting next to the Christmas tree surrounded by his loved ones; and, of course, the ink stain on the wall of his study.

Humans would not be human if they did not possess the tendency to suppress complex, highly differentiated interconnected strands of tradition that run counter to their own projections. This is expressed more positively in the words of the Dresden architect and art historian Cornelius Gurlitt: "I believe in the sagas of Wittenberg as I do in the truth of fairy tales and poetry, namely in the strength of their spiritual prowess […]."[38]

---

37 Stein, *Geschichte*, p. 20, on the subject of the reflections of the private biography of Luther in the Luther House, see Rietschel, *Luther*, p. 11. **38** Gurlitt, *Lutherstadt*, p. 261.

BIBLIOGRAPHY

Bornkamm, Heinrich (1955), *Luther im Spiegel der deutschen Geistesgeschichte*. Heidelberg, pp. 11–16. **Burkhardt**, Johannes (1988), Reformations- und Lutherfeiern. Die Verbürgerlichung der reformatorischen Jubiläumskultur. In: Düding, Dieter/Friedemann, Peter/Münch, Paul (eds.), *Öffentliche Festkultur. Politische Feste in Deutschland von der Aufklärung bis zum Ersten Weltkrieg* (= Rowohlts Enzyklopädie. 462, Kulturen & Ideen), Reinbeck bei Hamburg, pp. 212–237. **Demandt**, Alexander (2005), *Über allen Wipfeln. Der Baum in der Kulturgeschichte*. Düsseldorf. **Devrient**, Otto (1883), *Luther. Historisches Charakterbild in sieben Abteilungen. Ein Festspiel zur vierhundertjährigen Geburtstagsfeier Luthers, dargestellt von den Bewehren Janas*. Jena. **Devrient**, Otto (1901), *Luther. Historisches Charakterbild in 7 Abteilungen. Unter dem Protektorat Sr. Kgl. Hoheit des Prinzen Friedrich Heinrich von Preußen, aufgeführt und dargestellt von Mitgliedern evangelischer Gemeinden vom Verein zur Förderung deutsch-evangelischer Volksschauspiele im Neuem Kgl. Operntheater (Kroll)*. Berlin. **Dunkmann**, Karl (1911), Das Lutherhaus in Wittenberg. Zum Reformationsfest am 31. Oktober 1911. In: *Daheim. Ein deutsches Familienblatt*, vol. 48/4 (October 28, 1911). **Eggers**, Friedrich (ed.), *Deutsches Kunstblatt. Zeitschrift für bildende Kunst, Baukunst und Kunsthandwerk*, vol. 9, pp. 259–261. **Erdmann**, Gustav Adolf (1888), *Die Lutherfestspiele. Geschichtliche Bedeutung, Zweck und Bedeutung derselben für die Bühne*. Wittenberg. **Erfurth**, Richard (1910), *Geschichte der Stadt Wittenberg*, Part 1. Wittenberg. **Fichte**, Johann Gottlieb (1808), *Reden an die deutsche Nation*. Berlin. **Francois**, Etienne (2001), Oberammergau. In: id./Schulze, Hagen (eds.), *Deutsche Erinnerungsorte*. Vol. 3. München, pp. 274–291. **Grote**, Heiner (1986), Der Evangelische Bund zur Wahrung der deutsch-protestantischen Interessen (1886–1914). In: id./Fleischmann-Bisten, Walter (eds.), *Protestanten auf dem Wege. Geschichte des Evangelischen Bundes* (= Bensheimer Hefte. 65). Göttingen, pp. 9–85. **Gurlitt**, Cornelius (1931), *Lutherstadt Wittenberg. Mit acht Abbildungen nach Originalen* (= Westermanns Monatshefte. 903), pp. 257–264. **Herder**, Johann Gottfried (1993), Über die ersten Urkunden des menschlichen Geschlechts, 1769. In: id., *Sämtliche Werke*. Vol. 5. Hildesheim. **Holsing**, Henrike (2004), *Luther—Gottesmann und Nationalheld. Sein Image in der Historienmalerei des 19. Jahrhunderts*. online publication URL: http://kups.ub.uni-koeln.de/2132/ [11/30/2015], thesis, Universität zu Köln. **Joestel**, Volkmar (1992), Der Wurf mit dem Tintenfaß. In: id., *Legenden um Martin Luther und andere Geschichten aus Wittenberg*. Berlin, pp. 52–57. **Karnick**, Michael (1991), Martin Luther als Bühnenfigur. Historische Wertung und Dramaturgie. In: Schnitzler, Günter (ed.), *Bild und Gedanke. Festschrift für Gerhard Baumann zum 60. Geburtstag*. München, pp. 258–270. **Kohnle**, Armin (2002), Luther vor Karl V. Die Wormser Szene in Text und Bild des 19. Jahrhunderts. In: Laube, Stefan/Fix, Karl-Heinz (eds.), *Lutherinszenierung und Reformationserinnerung*. Leipzig, pp. 35–62. **Kruse**, Joachim, Drei graphische Folgen von Lutherlebenbildern des 19. Jahrhunderts, In: Eidam, Hardy/Seib, Gerhard (eds.), *"Er fühlt der Zeiten ungeheuren Bruch und fest umklammert er sein Bibelbuch…" Zum Lutherkult im 19. Jahrhundert*. Berlin, pp. 40–54. **Kupisch**, Karl (1955), *Zwischen Idealismus und Massendemokratie. Eine Geschichte der evangelischen Kirche in Deutschland 1815–1945*. Berlin. **Laube**, Stefan (1999), *Fest, Religion und Erinnerung. Konfessionelles Gedächtnis im Königreich Bayern*. München. **Laube**, Stefan (2003), *Das Lutherhaus Wittenberg. Eine Museumsgeschichte*. Leipzig. **Leppin**, Volker (2008), Die Monumentalisierung Luthers. Warum vom Thesenanschlag erzählt wurde—und was davon zu erzählen ist. In: Ott, Joachim/Treu, Martin (eds.), *Luthers Thesenanschlag—Faktum oder Fiktion*. Leipzig, pp. 69–93. **Lessing**, Gotthold Ephraim (1973), Absagungsschreiben an Goeze, Anhang der *Parabel*, 1778. In: id., *Werke*. Vol. 8: Theologiekritische Schriften III, ed. by Herbert G. Göpfert, München. **Metz**, Detlev (2013), *Das protestantische Drama. Evangelisches geistliches Theater in der Reformationszeit und im konfessionellen Zeitalter*. Köln/Weimar/Wien. **Nagy**, Sigrid (2003), *Es wuchs ein Baum im Paradies. Wie Luther im 19. Jahrhundert zum Weihnachtsbaum kam*. Weimar. **Nipperdey**, Thomas (1986), Luther und die moderne Welt. In: id., *Nachdenken über Deutsche Geschichte*. Essays. München, pp. 31–44. **Schadow**, Johann Gottfried (ed.) (1825), *Wittenbergs Denkmäler der Bildnerei, Baukunst und Malerei mit historischen und artistischen Erläuterungen*. Wittenberg. **Scharfe**, Martin (1996), Nach-Luther. Zu Form und Bedeutung der Luther-Verehrung im 19. Jahrhundert. In: Eidam, Hardy/Seib, Gerhard (eds.), *"Er fühlt der Zeiten ungeheuren Bruch und fest umklammert er sein Bibelbuch…" Zum Lutherkult im 19. Jahrhundert*. Berlin, pp. 11–23. **Reichelt**, Silvio (2013), *Der Erlebnisraum Lutherstadt Wittenberg. Genese, Entwicklung und Bestand eines protestantischen Erinnerungsortes*. Göttingen, pp. 97–103. **Rentzsch**, Siegfried (ed.) (1983), *Martin Luther. Ein Postkartenalbum*, Leipzig. **Rietschel**, Georg (1888), *Luther und sein Haus*. Halle (Saale). **Stein**, Hermann (1888), *Geschichte des Lutherhauses*. Wittenberg. **Treitschke**, Heinrich von (1908), Luther und die deutsche Nation. Vortrag, gehalten in Darmstadt am 7. November 1883. In: id., *Ausgewählte Schriften*. Vol. 1. 4th ed. Leipzig, pp. 136–158. **Ziel**, Ernst (ed.) (1883), *Otto Devrient und sein Luther-Festspiel* (= Gartenlaube. 42).

A Living Monument

Wittenberg Luther Memorial

𝔏 8 Luther trails with a total length of almost 1,250 miles

560 miles in Thuringia, 342 miles in Saxony, 255 miles in Saxony-Anhalt, 60 miles Bavaria

57 Luther memorials worldwide

Since the end of the 19th century, a remarkable number of memorials have been erected. In Central Europe, there are 40 Luther memorials today.

197 Luther churches worldwide

179 Luther churches exist in Germany, another 18 abroad.

Luther Trees

On the occasion of Reformation anniversaries, trees would often be planted in memory of Martin Luther, the most widespread being the Luther oak, in many cases, a common oak tree. In some places, also Luther beeches and Luther lindens can be found. A very famous specimen is the Luther oak in Wittenberg. At its location, Luther in 1520 burnt his copy of the papal bull threatening him with excommunication.

97 LUTHER OAKS Most of these trees can be found in Saxony (20) and Lower Saxony (17).

6 LUTHER BEECHES **8 LUTHER LINDENS** **1 LUTHER ELM**

Luther as a movie star

Luther's life is the subject of many movies which commemorate the great Reformer. Luther is the hero of movies and documentaries produced in such diverse locations as Australia and Hollywood, but most often in Germany.

1911 **D** Doktor Martinus Luther	1913 **D** Die Wittenberger Nachtigall	1923 **D** Martin Luther: His Life and time	1927 **D** Luther – Ein Film der deutschen Reformation	
1939 **D** Das unsterbliche Herz	1952 **BRD** Der gehorsame Rebell	1953 **USA/BRD** Martin Luther	1964 **AUS** Luther	**BRD** Der arme Mann Luther
1965 **GB** Luther	1967 **DDR** Credo: Martin Luther – Wittenberg 1517	1968 **BRD** Der Reformator	**USA** Luther	1974 **USA/UK/Kanada** Luther
1976 **YUG** Disput u noći	1981 **F** Frère Martin	1983 **GB** The Meaning of Life: The Adventures of Martin Luther	**BRD** Martin Luther	**DDR** Martin Luther
GB/USA Martin Luther, Heretic	**DDR** Ein Schüler aus Mansfeld – Die Jugendjahre Martin Luthers	**DDR** Bürger Luther – Wittenberg 1508-46		
DDR Der die Zeit beim Worte nahm – Martin Luther auf der Wartburg	1984 **DDR** Martin Luther & Thomas Müntzer oder Die Einführung der Buchhaltung			
1990 **D** Mitten in Europa – Deutsche Geschichte	1992 **D** Wir Deutschen	1996 **D/F** Lutherbilder	1999 **D** 2000 Jahre Christentum	2000 Luther (Opera)
2003 **D/USA** Luther	**D** Martin Luther – Ein Leben zwischen Gott und Teufel	**D** Filmstar Martin Luther	2004 **F** Luther gegen den Papst	
2005 **D** Luther –Sein Leben, Werk und Erbe	2007 **D** Martin Luther – Kampf mit dem Teufel	2008 **D** Luther und die Nation	**D** Die Deutschen	

JAN SCHEUNEMANN

Luther in the German Dictatorships of the Twentieth Century

"In this way Hitler completes the work Martin Luther started …" (1933)[1]

In April 2014, the German political magazine Cicero caused a stir. Its cover showed a portrait of Martin Luther in front of burning synagogues. The cover story, "Anti-Semite Luther," visually connected the Wittenberg Reformer to the millionfold murder of European Jews by Nazi Germany. There is no doubt: In his late polemic work *On the Jews and Their Lies* (1543) Luther had demanded exercising "harsh mercy" against the Jews, removing them, destroying their houses and burning their synagogues and schools. Therefore, the author of the *Cicero* article concluded, "Actually, Luther had demanded what was realized in the Kristallnacht nearly four hundred years later"[2]

This opinion continued a way of thinking that had developed in World War II. It considered Martin Luther a forerunner of Nationalist Socialism and an approver of racist anti-Semitism, evidently expressed by the formula "From Luther to Hitler." This argument was supported by Julius Streicher, publisher of the Nazi magazine *Der Stürmer*, who defended his anti-Semitic agitation during the Nuremberg Trials on April 29, 1946, as follows: "There has been anti-Semitic printed material for centuries. So, a book, written by Dr. Martin Luther, was confiscated at my house. He would stand in the dock in my place today if the prosecution considered this book. In his book *The Jews and Their Lies*, Dr. Martin Luther refers to the Jews as a breed of snake that must be exterminated and whose synagogues are supposed to be burned down …"[3] (In view of such statements, it is not surprising that the search for a logical explanation of the German failure of civilization led to a conclusion that the roots of German National Socialism lay in the period of Reformation and referred to Martin Luther as an "early precursor of Fascism" and "Hitlers Spiritual Ancestor" (fig. 1).[4]

Such interpretations can be explained by the ill-fated reception of the Reformer in the "Third Reich." No small number of Germans regarded National Socialism as a completion of the Reformation and Hitler as a new Luther: "Hitler is the greatest German, who can only be compared to Luther."[5] The NSDAP (Nazi Party) and Hitler himself had contributed to this analogy. The Nazi propaganda retrospectively put Hitler's announcement of the NSDAP program on February 24, 1920, in the Munich Hofbräuhaus on a level with Luther's posting of his theses on October 31, 1517.[6] In an NSDAP meeting in October 1923 in Nuremberg, Hitler called Martin Luther, Frederick the Great, and Richard Wagner "three of our greatest German men" who had become "heroes of their people" through their will, determination, and absolute readiness to fight. They were his role models whom he wanted to follow according to his conception of a true statesman and a national führer.[7] In his book *Mein Kampf*, published in 1925/26, Hitler referred to the three "great fighters" as rare historical personalities who were politicians as well as thought leaders—and above all, he was referring to himself.[8] There is no doubt that Hitler was noticed as a preternatural phenomenon by the populace. He was seen as a wonder man and a savior at the same time. Kurt Lüdecke, for example, who initially belonged to Hitler's closest followers and financiers but eventually fell into disgrace, literally described his first encounter with Hitler as an awakening. "I do not know how to describe the emotions that swept over me as I heard to this man. His words were like scourge. When he spoke of the disgrace of Germany, I felt ready to spring at any enemy. His appeal to German manhood was like a call to arms, the gospel he preached a sacred truth. He seemed another Luther. […] I experienced an exaltation that could be linked only to religious conversion."[9]

Germany's devastating defeat in the First World War, the German Revolution of 1918/19, and the foundation of the Weimar Re-

---

1 Coch, *Luther*, p. 2. Original: "So vollendet Hitler das Werk, das Luther begonnen hat …" 2 Pfeiffer, *Seite*, p. 18. Original: "Judenfeind Luther … scharfe Barmherzigkeit … Im Grunde hatte Luther damit das gefordert, was knapp 400 Jahre später in der Reichspogromnacht realisiert wurde." 3 International Military Tribunal, *Prozess*, p. 346. Original: "Antisemitische Presseerzeugnisse gab es in Deutschland durch Jahrhunderte. Es wurde bei mir zum Beispiel ein Buch beschlagnahmt von Dr. Martin Luther. Dr. Martin Luther säße heute sicher an meiner Stelle auf der Anklagebank, wenn dieses Buch von der Anklagevertretung in Betracht gezogen würde. In dem Buch 'Die Juden und ihre Lügen' schreibt Dr. Martin Luther, die Juden seien ein Schlangengezücht, man soll ihre Synagogen niederbrennen, man soll sie vernichten …" 4 See McGovern, *From Luther to Hitler*; Wiener, *Martin Luther*; Eberan, *Luther?*, pp. 110–115. 5 Werdermann, *Martin Luther und Adolf Hitler*, p. 3. 6 See Griesmayr, *Ideal*, p. 77. 7 See Jäckl/Kuhn, *Aufzeichnungen*, p. 103. Original: "drei unserer größten deutschen Männer … Helden ihres Volkes." 8 Hitler, *Kampf*, pp. 231f.; see Longerich, *Hitler*, pp. 127, 140. Original: "große Kämpfer." 9 Luedecke, *Story*, pp. 13f.

Fig. 1 "Hitlers Kampf und Luthers Lehr/Des deutschen Volkes gute Wehr" ("Hitler's struggle and Luther's teaching/The German people's good defense"). Post card honoring Martin Luther's 450th birthday, November 1933

Weimar Republic, conformed with National Socialism and National Protestantism. Above all, the National Socialist religious movement, the *Deutsche Christen* (German Christians), celebrated Hitler as "an organ and instrument of God," as "the führer, empowered by God, determined to rescue the German people from decline and to reestablish its existence," as written by the Protestant theologian and publisher Johannes Müller.[11]

Because the takeover by the Nazi Party in 1933 coincided with Martin Luther's 450th birthday, the Protestant Church seized the occasion to celebrate the Reformer as a *völkisch* (national) hero and thus to emphasize their compatibility with National Socialism and their will to actively cooperate in establishing a "Volksgemeinschaft" (people's community).[12] The incoming *Reich* bishop, Ludwig Müller, declared, "It is a gift of God to celebrate this 450th birthday of Martin Luther at the time when the German people is rising and building up a new *Reich*. [...] God gave our country a rare führer. [...] We want to spread Luther's fighting spirit, that is determined to succeed, to our people; the new German, awakened and aroused by the German revolutions, is supposed to be deeply grabbed and moved by the freeing message of Christ, as resurrected for the German soul by Martin Luther, the 'most German of all Germans'."[13]

As an essential role model for all Germans, Luther provided a perfect projection surface (fig. 2). His fight against Rome could be revived and defended against an alleged threat to the German nation by internal and external enemies. This secular view as the "deutscher Luther" (German Luther) had certainly been pre-formed in the nineteenth century. On occasion of his four-hundredth birthday in 1883, the Reformer and theologian, herald and interpreter of the Gospel Martin Luther had resigned and given way to the secular, political Luther. For the prominent Berlin historian Heinrich von Treitschke, Luther represented no less than the "innermost nature of his people"[14]—an interpretation that became the defining image of Luther in the following decades and had a prolonged effect.[15]

The "Deutsche Luthertag" (German Luther Day) planned throughout the German *Reich* for November 1933 aimed to represent a unique and strong German Protestantism and honor Luther as "standard bearer of German *Volkstum*, or folkdom."[16] Academic Luther festivities took place at a total of ten German Universities, such as in Jena, where church historian Karl Heussi, under the motto "Heil Luther" (Hail Luther), spoke about "Luthers deutsche Sendung" (Luther's German mission). The titles of the vast number of celebratory speeches and publications given and published by historians and theologians in 1933 on the occasion of the Luther jubilee leave no doubt about their contents: *Volk und Rasse bei Martin Luther* (Folk and

public were traumatic experiences for the majority of the nationally oriented Protestants. Hence, they enthusiastically appreciated the takeover by the Nazi Party in January 1933, definitely encouraged by Hitler's self-dramatization as a God-fearing man whose doings were based on Christianity and Christian values. Again and again, the new *Reich* chancellor initially emphasized the key role of the two great Christian confessions in building up a National Socialist Germany.[10] The *Reich* government enacted ordinances that forbade criticizing religious communities which, in view of rampant atheism, was gratefully appreciated by the churches. Moreover, antiliberalism, anticommunism, as well as a hatred for the democratic order of the

10 See Becker, *Euphorien*, pp. 37 f. **11** Müller, *Gegner*, p. 152. Original: "Organ und Werkzeug Gottes ... von Gott bevollmächtigte[n] Führer, der das deutsche Volk vor dem Untergang rettet und seinen Bestand neu begründen soll." **12** See Küllmer, *Inszenierung*, p. 10. **13** Luther-Tag 1933. Flugblatt zur 450jährigen Wiederkehr des Geburtstages Martin Luthers 10. November 1933 (Luther Day 1933. Pamphlet on the 450th recurrence of Martin Luther's Birthday on November 10, 1933) [privately owned by Jan Scheunemann]. Original: "Es ist ein Gottesgeschenk, dass dieser 450. Geburtstag Martin Luthers in einer Zeit gefeiert wird, da das deutsche Volk aufsteht und ein neues Reich baut. [...] Gott

hat unserem Land einen Führer geschenkt, wie ihn ein Volk nur selten hat. [...] Wir wollen den Lutherischen Kampfgeist, der zur Entscheidung drängt und bis zur Entscheidung durchdringt, hinaustragen in unser Volk; der durch die deutsche Revolution aufgeweckte und aufgerüttelte deutsche Mensch soll tief innerlich gepackt und ergriffen werden von der befreienden Botschaft Christi, wie Luther der Deutscheste aller Deutschen sie für die deutsche Seele neu hat erstehen lassen." **14** Treitschke, *Nation*, p. 25. Original: "innerste Wesen seines Volkes." **15** See Lehmann, *Deutsche*, pp. 126–137. **16** See Bräuer, *Luthertag*; Buss, *Luthertag*; Willenberg, *Luthertag*, pp. 195–237. Original: "Ban-

Bildbericht
für das deutsche
Christenvolk
Jahrgang 1 / Nummer 12
1. November-Woche 1933
Zum 450. Geburtstag
Dr. Martin
Luthers

S. A. wacht am Denkmal Martin Luthers zu Berlin   Phot. Hirtz

Fig. 2 On the occasion of Martin Luther's 450th birthday in 1933
members of the NSDAP storm troopers stand guard in front
of the Luther monument in Berlin.

Race in Luther's Works) (Heinrich Bornkamm), *Luther und Hitler* (Luther and Hitler) (Hans Preuß), *Luther als Deutscher* (Luther as a German) (Hanns Rückert). Ceremonies took place in the "Luther towns" of Wittenberg, Eisleben, and Coburg, and people gathered in churches for festive worship services.

A violent contradiction became apparent, however: the new rulers had little interest in the Luther jubilee. The central ceremony of "Luther Day," planned for November 10, 1933, even had to be postponed because a national referendum on the withdrawal of Germany from the League of Nations, which the government of the *Reich* had scheduled for November 12, and the precursory propaganda event, made the Luther festivities impossible. On November 13, 1933, Reinhold Krause, *Gau* (district) chairman of the *Deutsche Christen* (German Christians), spoke about "Luther's *völkisch*—or, national—mission" at a demonstration in the Berlin Sports Palace.[17]

He had a "deutsche Volkskirche" (a German people's church) in mind, ruled by the new state's claim to totality. Though his demand for a "artgemäßen Christentum" (species-appropriate Christianity) and the enforcement of the Aryan paragraph in the Protestant Church was hailed by the twenty thousand listeners, Krause's speech marked the beginning of the end of the German Christians religious movement, which lost thousands of members after that.

The "völkisch" Luther, however, was not the only perception of the Reformer at that time. The Swiss theologian and professor of theology in Bonn, Karl Barth, opposed the political usurpation of Luther as the "great German" and purely regarded him as a "teacher of the Christian church."[18]

As a cofounder of the *Bekennende Kirche* ("Confessing Church"), Barth belonged to that minority in the Protestant Church that opposed the persecution of the Jews. Anti-Semitism was wide-spread among Protestantism during the Nazi period, and Luther was referred to regarding the "Jewish question." Historian Theo Sommerlad from Halle, Saxony-Anhalt, regarded Luther's Reformation as a "national revolution," as a "struggle for existence of the German people against the domination of Germanic mentality and sensibility by the Roman Church, which is contaminated by Semitism."[19] On occasion of the Luther jubilee in 1933, the Nazi press did not only emphasize the anti-Semitism of the Reformer but also accused the Protestant Church and Luther historians of concealing Luther's "downright fanatic fight against the Jews."[20] Actually, this accusation was groundless as several editions of Luther's anti-Semitic works—in particular the critical *Weimar Edition*, vol. 53 (1920)—were publicly accessible.[21] Moreover, since the nineteenth century, when the racist, anti-Semitic interpretations of Luther's works had multiplied, and particularly since the 1920s, there had been publications of *florilegia*: compilations of excerpts from Luther's anti-Jewish works that underscored his harshest statements by comments and annotations as well as typographical emphases.[22] Here Martin Sasse, regional bishop of Thuringia, undoubtedly reached a nadir with his pamphlet *Martin Luther über die Juden. Weg mit ihnen!* (Martin Luther about the Jews. Get rid of them!) It was published some weeks after Kristallnacht with a circulation of one hundred thousand (fig. 3). Its foreword read: "On November 10, 1938—Luther's birthday—the synagogues are burning in Germany. [...] ... In this hour, the voice of the sixteenth-century prophet of the Germans must be heard. He—initially out of ignorance—had been a friend of the Jews, and he ultimately became—driven by his conscience as well as experience and reality—the greatest anti-Semite of his time and admonisher of his people against the Jews."[23]

nerträger des deutschen Volkstums." **17** Rede des Gauobmannes der Glaubensbewegung Deutsche Christen in Groß-Berlin Dr. Krause, gehalten im Sportpalast am 13. November 1933 (nach doppeltem stenografischem Bericht), Berlin 1933. Original: "Die völkische Sendung Luthers." **18** Barth, *Luther*, p. 11. Original: "große[n] Deutschen ... Lehrer der christlichen Kirche." **19** Sommerlad, *Sozialismus*, pp. 1 f. Original: "nationale Revolution ... Daseinskampf des deutschen Menschen gegen die Überfremdung germanischer Denk- und Empfindungsart durch die vom Semitismus angesteckte römische Kirche." **20** *Der Stürmer*, November 1933, cited from Brosseder, *Stellung*, pp. 184 f. Original:

"geradezu fanatischen Kampf gegen das Judentum." **21** See Leppin, *Judenschriften*. **22** See Kaufmann, *Juden*, pp. 154–170; Kaufmann, *Lutherflorilegien*. **23** Sasse, *Martin Luther*, p. 2. Original: "Am 10. November 1938, an Luthers Geburtstag brennen in Deutschland die Synagogen. [...] In dieser Stunde muss die Stimme des Mannes gehört werden, der als der Deutschen Prophet im 16. Jahrhundert aus Unkenntnis einst als Freund der Juden begann, der, getrieben von seinem Gewissen, getrieben von den Erfahrungen und der Wirklichkeit, der größte Antisemit seiner Zeit geworden ist, der Warner seines Volkes wider die Juden."

Fig. 3 Frontispiece of the pamphlet "Martin Luther about the Jews. Get rid of them!," written by the state bishop of the Thuringian Protestant Church Martin Sasse, 1938

"Germany and the Germans," given at the *Library of Congress* in Washington, D.C. In this speech, Mann referred to Luther as "a gigantic incarnation of the German nature" and admitted, "I do not love him …" Luther's "anti-European thinking" appeared particularly strange to Thomas Mann, who on the one hand actually regarded the Reformation as an act of liberation, but on the other hand saw the disastrous results of the schism it had caused. Luther's understanding of authority had founded German obedience and thus paved the way for Nazi barbarism. Four years later, Mann called the Reformer a "bull-necked barbarian of God," who had been willing to shed blood and called for the murder of the rebellious peasants. For Mann, Luther was "bastion and fate of a man," "furiously nationalist and ant-Semitic" at the same time.[26]

Luther's anti-Semitism, mentioned here in passing by Thomas Mann, did not play a role in the postwar perception. Instead, his works against the rebellious peasants, published in 1525, became an indicator of Luther's status in German history. In particular, the Communists who were seeking power in East Germany were convinced that Luther had betrayed the peasants. The Reformation era played a key role in the self-image of the Communist Party of Germany and later the Socialist Unity Party of (East) Germany. They primarily deduced their tradition of class struggle from the Peasants' revolts, whereas Luther was considered reactionary. But this view was not unique. The simultaneous existence of different aspects of Luther in the Marxist press corresponded with the "Janus-faced character of the beginning," diagnosed by historical research. Thus, the *Volkszeitung*, the local newspaper of the Communist Party in Saxony-Anhalt, described Luther as a "man of strong belief" and an "archetype of power and strength" on occasion of the four-hundredth anniversary of his death in 1946. The newspaper *Tägliche Rundschau*, published by the Soviet Military Administration, agreed. Here, Luther was characterized as "a vivid fighter and archetype of German character and mind" as well as "a lifeguard, indefatigable fighter of his great time for Germany and its unity."[27]

In 1946, Eisleben, the town where Luther was born in 1483 and died in 1546, received the name "Lutherstadt Eisleben" (Luther town Eisleben) in honor of the Reformer. The Communist part of Germany, however, was henceforth dominated by a negative image of Luther. The withering assessment of Luther was contrasted with the glorification of the revolutionary leader of the German peasant uprising, Thomas Müntzer, who had been executed in 1525. The difference between the two of them could not have been more obvious: "Luther is the enlightener and Reformer, Müntzer the believer and revolutionary. While Luther is bright, Müntzer is enlightened. […] One—a loyal subject and obedient servant of his prince—lives in comfort and honorably dies at an old age in his soft

"Martin Luther, the Gravedigger of German Freedom" (1946)[24]

In May 1946, Germany lay in ruins (fig. 4). In view of the complete defeat, reliance on the "German Luther" was no longer conceivable. On the contrary, after World War II, Germany faced a radical reckoning with the Reformer from Wittenberg, mostly stated by those who had left Nazi Germany. Thomas Mann surely was the most prominent of the expatriate voices. Although he initially had been an admirer of Luther—he had kept a bust of Luther in his study!—his reservations regarding this "rough person with a strong mind and a powerful imagination" were growing in the early 1930s due to the comparisons between Luther and Hitler. Mann started to consider German history as a history of evil that culminated in Adolf Hitler.[25] At the end of May in 1945, the expatriate author, who had lived in America since 1939, completely broke with Luther in his speech

24 Abusch, *Irrweg*, p. 20. Original: "Martin Luther, der Totengräber der deutschen Freiheit". **25** See Hamacher, *Werkplan*, pp. 28, 44, 47. Original: "gemütsstarke[n] und bildgewaltige[n] Grobian zu Wittenberg." **26** Mann, *Deutschland*, p. 1133; Mann, *Gewaltigen*, p. 376. Original: "eine riesenhafte Inkarnation deutschen Wesens… Ich liebe ihn nicht … Anti-Europäisch … stiernackige Gottesbarbar[en] … ein Fels und ein Schicksal von einem Menschen … furios nationalistisch und antisemitisch." **27** *Volks-Zeitung*, Febru-

ary 18, 1946; *Tägliche Rundschau*, February 19, 1946. Original: "Janusköpfigkeit des Anfangs … glaubensstarken Mann … Urbild von Kraft und Stärke" and "glaubensstarker Kämpfer und Typus deutscher Charakter- und Geisteshaltung … dem Leben zugewandter und in seiner großen Zeit nie erlahmender Kämpfer für Deutschland und seine Einheit." **28** *Neues Deutschland*, May 14, 1946. Original: "Luther ist der Aufklärer und Reformist, Münzer der Gläubige und Revolutionär. Luther ist 'helle,' Münzer ist erleuchtet.[…] Der eine führt

Fig. 4 Ernst Rietschel's Luther monument from 1885, which stands in front of the Frauenkirche (Church of St. Mary's) in Dresden, was damaged and torn from its plinth during the Allied bombing of Dresden on February 13, 1945. After restoration it was re-erected on its former position on February 12, 1955.

helm—headed for Hitler and ended up with the breakdown of the "Third Reich." According to Abusch, Luther fatally set the course of history that eventually led to reaction and stagnation: "Luther became the greatest intellectual power of the German counterrevolution for centuries."[29] Abusch primarily based himself on Friedrich Engels, who more than one hundred years earlier had laid the foundations for the materialist theory of history with his work *Der deutsche Bauernkrieg* (The Peasant War in Germany) (1850), written under the impact of the failed revolution of 1848.

"Martin Luther, one of the German people's greatest sons" (1983)[30]

In fact Abusch's negative perception of Luther determined the 1960s. Yet the Socialist Unity Party of East Germany planned to establish socialism in the German Democratic Republic (East Germany), founded in 1949, and therefore demanded to redefine its relationship to German history. Presenting itself as a socialist nation, the new state needed positive contact points in history. This reorientation consequently meant refusing those who considered German history a misery. In May 1953, the central organ of the Socialist Unity Party, *Neues Deutschland* (New Germany), clearly declared: "Denying progress and interpreting history as a perpetual misery is a reactionary and anti-national concept that obviously serves to destroy the national dignity and consciousness of the German people."[31] From this time on, the "progressive" moments of German history were brought into focus. Regarding Luther and the Reformation at such moments had rather practical reasons: Eisleben, Mansfeld, Wittenberg, Eisenach, and Erfurt—the most important towns connected with the life of the Reformer—were situated on East German territory. As large regions of the "workers' and farmers' state" had been affected by the Reformation, East Germany was literally "Lutherland."

Moreover, Reformation history was a highly explosive political subject for the atheist socialist state, as it always implicated a theological, church-related dimension. Unlike during National Socialism, the East German churches preponderantly opposed the leaders of the social and political elite. The part Luther played in the Socialist Unity Party's concept of history represented nothing but the continuation of state policy toward the church by other means. The research on the Reformation, carried out by East German non-Marxist church historians, as well as the anniversary celebrations, independently organized by the Protestant Church of the GDR, can be seen as a denial of the Socialist Unity Party's claim to power.[32]

The change of the Marxist image of Luther, started in 1960, is closely linked to the name Max Steinmetz, historian and professor at Leipzig University. With the "Early Bourgeois Revolution," he es-

bed; the other—a hungry and freezing rebel—is chased from place to place, tortured and ignominiously put to death."[28]

Alexander Abusch probably had the most long-term influence on the negative perception of Martin Luther. His work *Der Irrweg einer Nation*, written in his Mexican exile and published in 1946, had a large readership and deeply influenced the young East German nation's conception of history. Abusch, who later was appointed as minister of culture of the German Democratic Republic (GDR, East Germany), considered German history as a series of failed revolutionary attempts and hence a misery. The national disaster had started with Luther, then—via Prussian militarism, Bismarck, and Kaiser Wil-

als staatstreuer Untertan und gefügiger Unteroffizier seines Fürsten ein behäbiges Leben und stirbt hochbetagt und hochbewürdet im weichen Bett, der andere heizt hungrig und frierend als Meuterer von Ort zu Ort und fällt zerschunden und verhöhnt unterm Beil." **29** Abusch, *Irrweg*, p. 23. Original: "Luther wurde zur größten geistigen Kraft der deutschen Gegenrevolution für Jahrhunderte." **30** Honecker, *Parteinahme*, p. 11. Original: "Martin Luther, einer der größten Söhne des deutschen Volkes." **31** *Neues Deutschland*, May

14, 1953. Original: "Die Leugnung des Fortschritts und die Darstellung der deutschen Geschichte als einer ununterbrochenen Misere ist eine reaktionäre und antinationale Konzeption, die objektiv dazu dient, die nationale Würde und das Nationalbewusstsein des deutschen Volkes zu zerstören." **32** See Stengel, *SED*, p. 356.

Fig. 5 A historical festive parade on October 29, 1967 in Wittenberg. It included reenactments of a series of events from Germany's history, including Luther posting his theses in 1517.

—competing with the church's concept of the event—was supposed to preserve the "primacy of the state" and to present the festivities as a "secular event." After debates on the interpretation of the Reformation, the religious members of the state commission resigned to emphasize their protest against political monopolization and East Germany's entry restrictions against West German visitors. In the end, state and church celebrated the event separately.

Things had changed completely when planning began for Martin Luther's five-hundredth birthday celebration in 1983.[36] In its pursuit of international attention, and bearing Wittenberg's touristic potential in mind, the government was interested in a more harmonious relationship with the churches. A summit talk between governmental and church representatives to coordinate the preparations of the jubilee had already taken place in March 1978. Remarkably enough, the leader of the Socialist Unity Party of Germany and head of state, Erich Honecker, assumed the chair of the GDR's Martin Luther Committee in 1980. He invited the bishops of the Evangelical Churches of Thuringia and Saxony to take part in the conferences of the state committee (fig. 6). A preparatory church commission had already met in December 1978 under the direction of Werner Leich, regional bishop of the Evangelical Lutheran Church in Thuringia. Under the slogan "Fearing, Loving, and Trusting God," the church focused on the theological message of the Reformation, whereas the government used the Luther jubilee as a way to mobilize all of society.[37] While the church organized central events and seven regional church congresses, the government had Luther sites redeveloped at great cost, exhibitions organized, artworks commissioned, documentaries and television films made, and stamps printed. In fifteen *Thesen über Martin Luther* (Theses on Martin Luther), the GDR presented its generally binding view of a heroic reformer and finally stated, "Luther's heritage is preserved in the socialist German national culture."[38] Gerhard Bendler, one of the best-known Marxist Luther specialists, published a Luther biography that for the first time took Luther's theology into account.[39]

West Germany was surprised at the "big fuss" over Luther that broke out in its neighboring country. The Socialist Party leaders' plan to boost the German Democratic Republic's reputation with the help of the Luther jubilee, however, was not successful. High-ranking politicians and state officials from Western countries did not visit the GDR unless they were invited by the churches, as for instance Richard von Weizsäcker, who took part in the Evangelical Church Assembly in Wittenberg in 1983. The church-friendly policy displayed by the leadership of the Socialist Unity Party on the occasion of the jubilee was refused by no small number of its members, who welcomed the "normalization" of the relationship with the churches after the jubilee (fig. 7). The hype about Martin Luther was over.

tablished an explanatory model that connected the Reformation and the German Peasants' War to a unique national revolutionary movement. Henceforth, this concept paradigmatically determined the entire East German body of research on the early modern period of history and thus provided the necessary conditions for a Marxism-based, nontheological and nonreligious research on the Reformation and Luther. While Luther initially was condemned as "a servant of the aristocracy," the approach of the "German Early Bourgeois Revolution" made the Reformer part of the socialist heritage.[33]

For the first time, Luther's increased importance became obvious to the public on the occasion of the 450th anniversary of the Reformation in 1967; in East Germany it was celebrated as "one of the most tremendous mass movements of our older national history" (fig. 5).[34] The Reformation was regarded as an "expression of the revolutionary readiness of the suppressed and exploited masses, particularly of the peasants, to get rid of economic, social, and spiritual ties," read a paper of the State Secretary for Church Affairs, which regarded these "positive traditions" as "a legitimate claim" of the government to host the festivities.[35] The Central Committee of the Socialist Unity Party appointed a preparatory commission that

33 See Bräuer, *Martin Luther*; Roy, *Luther*. Original: "Fürstenknecht." **34** Steinmetz, *Bedeutung*, p. 48. Original: "eine der gewaltigsten Massenbewegungen unserer älteren Nationalgeschichte." **35** Begründung des Beschlusses des Ministerrates über den 450. Jahrestag der Reformation vom 18.1.1966 (Explanation of the cabinet's resolution on the 450th anniversary of the Reformation, January 1, 1966). Bundesarchiv Berlin, DO 4/2417. Original: "Ausdruck der revolutionären Bereitschaft der unterdrückten und ausgebeuteten Massen und vor

allem der Bauern, sich aus den ökonomischen, sozialen und geistigen Fesseln zu befreien ... progressive Traditionen ... legitimen Anspruch ..." **36** See Maser, *Butter*. Original: "Primat des Staates ... säkulares Ereignis." **37** Original: "Gott über alle Dinge fürchten, lieben und vertrauen." **38** See Lehmann, *15 Thesen*; id., *Entstehung*. Original: "Luthers progressives Erbe ist aufgehoben in der sozialistischen deutschen Nationalkultur." **39** See Brendler, *Revolution*.

Fig. 6 During the constitutive meeting of the Martin-Luther-Comittee of the GDR: General Secretary of the Central Comittee of the SED (Communist Party) and Chairman of the State Council of the GDR Erich Honnecker (3rd from the left) and the State Bishops of the Protestant Churches in Thuringia and the Church Province of Saxony Werner Leich (3rd from the right) and Werner Krusche (1st on the right)

Fig. 7 The (East German) State and (Communist) Party leader Erich Honnecker lays a wreath at the Luther Monument in Wittenberg on the occasion of his 500th birthday.

BIBLIOGRAPHY

Abusch, Alexander (1946), *Der Irrweg einer Nation. Ein Beitrag zum Verständnis deutscher Geschichte*. Berlin. **Barth**, Karl (1933), Luther. In: id., *Lutherfeier 1933*, likewise *Theologische Existenz heute*, vol. 4, pp. 8–12. **Becker**, Frank (2005), Protestantische Euphorien. 1870/71, 1914 und 1933. In: Gailus, Manfred/Lehmann, Hartmut (eds.), *Nationalprotestantische Mentalitäten. Konturen, Entwicklungslinien und Umbrüche eines Weltbildes* (= Veröffentlichungen des Max-Planck-Institutes für Geschichte. 214). Göttingen, pp. 19–44. **Bräuer**, Siegfried (1983), *Martin Luther in marxistischer Sicht von 1945 bis zum Beginn der achtziger Jahre*. Berlin (Ost). **Bräuer**, Siegfried (1986), Der Deutsche Luthertag 1933 und sein Schicksal. In: Bartel, Horst et al. (eds.), *Martin Luther. Leistung und Erbe*. Berlin (Ost), pp. 423–434. **Brendler**, Gerhard (1983), *Martin Luther. Theologie und Revolution*. Berlin (Ost). **Brosseder**, Johannes (1972), *Luthers Stellung zu den Juden im Spiegel seine Interpreten. Interpretation und Rezeption von Luthers Schriften und Äußerungen zum Judentum im 19. und 20. Jahrhundert vor allem im deutschsprachigen Raum* (= Beiträge zur Ökumenischen Theologie. 8). München. **Buss**, Hansjörg (2013), Der Deutsche Luthertag 1933 und die Deutschen Christen. In: *Kirchliche Zeitgeschichte*, vol. 26, no. 2, pp. 272–288. **Coch**, Friedrich (1933), *Luther und Hitler. Christenkreuz und Hakenkreuz*. Vol. 4 (October), p. 2. **Eberan**, Barbro (1985), *Luther? Friedrich "der Große"? Wagner? Nietzsche? …? …? Wer war an Hitler schuld? Die Debatte um die Schuldfrage 1945–1949*. München. **Fest**, Joachim (1973), *Hitler. Eine Biografie*. Frankfurt am Main/Berlin. **Griesmayr**, Gottfried (1944), *Das völkische Ideal*. Berlin. **Hamacher**, Bernd (1996), *Thomas Manns letzter Werkplan "Luthers Hochzeit." Edition, Vorgeschichte und Kontexte* (= Thomas-Mann-Studien. 15). Frankfurt am Main. **Hitler**, Adolf (1938), *Mein Kampf*. München. **Honecker**, Erich (1980), Unsere Zeit verlangt Parteinahme für Fortschritt, Vernunft und Menschlichkeit. In: *Martin Luther und unsere Zeit. Konstituierung des Martin-Luther-Komitees der DDR am 13. Juni 1980 in Berlin*. Berlin (Ost), pp. 9–18. **International Military Tribunal** (ed.) (1947), *Der Prozess gegen die Hauptkriegsverbrecher vor dem Internationalen Militärgerichtshof. Nürnberg 14. November 1945–Oktober 1946. Vol. 12: Verhandlungsniederschriften 18. April 1946–2. Mai 1946*, Nürnberg. **Jäckl**, Eberhard/**Kuhn**, Axel (eds.) (1980), *Hitler. Sämtliche Aufzeichnungen 1905–1924* (= Quellen und Darstellungen zur Zeitgeschichte. 21). Stuttgart. **Kaufmann**, Thomas (2014), *Luthers Juden*. Stuttgart. **Kaufmann**, Thomas (2015), Antisemitische Lutherflorilegien. Hinweise und Materialien zu einer fatalen Rezeptionsgeschichte. In: *Zeitschrift für Theologie und Kirche*, vol. 112, pp. 192–228. **Küllmer**, Björn (2012), *Die Inszenierung der Protestantischen Volksgemeinschaft. Lutherbilder im Lutherjahr 1933*. **Lehmann**, Hartmut (1983), Die 15 Thesen der SED über Martin Luther. In: Geschichte in Wissenschaft und Unterricht, vol. 34, pp. 722–738. **Lehmann**, Hartmut (2012), Zur Entstehung der 15 Thesen über Martin Luther für die Luther-Ehrung der DDR im Jahre 1983. In: id., *Luthergedächtnis 1817–2017*. Göttingen, pp. 213–256. **Lehmann**, Hartmut (2012), "Er ist wir selber: der ewige Deutsche." Zur langanhaltenden Wirkung der Lutherdeutung von Heinrich von Treitschke. In: id., *Luthergedächtnis 1817 bis 2017*. Göttingen, pp. 126–137. **Leppin**, Volker (2016), Luthers "Judenschriften" im Spiegel der Editionen bis 1933. In: Oelke, Harry et al. (eds.): *Martin Luthers "Judenschriften." Die Rezeption im 19. und 20. Jahrhundert*. Göttingen, pp. 19–43. **Longerich**, Peter (2015), *Hitler. Biografie*. München. **Luedecke**, Kurt G. W. (1937), *I knew Hitler. The Story of a Nazi Who Escaped the Blood Purge*. New York. **Mann**, Thomas (1990), Deutschland und die Deutschen. In: id., *Gesammelte Werke in dreizehn Bänden*. Vol. 11. Frankfurt am Main, pp. 1126–1148. **Mann**, Thomas (1990), Die drei Gewaltigen. In: id., *Gesammelte Werke in dreizehn Bänden*. Vol. 10. Frankfurt am Main, pp. 374–383. **Maser**, Peter (2013), *"Mit Luther alles in Butter?" Das Lutherjahr 1983 im Spiegel ausgewählter Akten*. Berlin. **McGovern**, William Montgomery (1941), *From Luther to Hitler: The History of Fascist Nazi Political Philosophy*. Boston. **Müller**, Johannes (1933), Adolf Hitler und seine Gegner. In: *Grüne Blätter. Zeitschrift für persönliche und allgemeine Lebensfragen*, vol. 35, pp. 148–157. **Pfeiffer**, Christian (2014), Die dunkle Seite des Reformators. In: *Cicero. Magazin für politische Kultur*, vol. 4 (April), pp. 16–23. **Roy**, Martin (2000), *Luther in der DDR. Zum Wandel des Lutherbildes in der DDR-Geschichtswissenschaft*. Bochum. **Sasse**, Martin (1938), *Martin Luther über die Juden. Weg mit ihnen!* Freiburg im Breisgau. **Sommerlad**, Theo (1933), Martin Luther und der deutsche Sozialismus. In: *Thüringisch-Sächsische Zeitschrift für Geschichte und Kunst*, vol. 12, pp. 1–38. **Steinmetz**, Max (1967), Die nationale Bedeutung der Reformation. In: id./Stern, Leo (eds.), *450 Jahre Reformation*. Berlin (Ost), pp. 44–57. **Stengel**, Friedemann (2013), Die SED und das christliche nationale Erbe. In: *Händel-Jahrbuch*, vol. 59, pp. 351–359. **Treitschke**, Heinrich von (1883), *Luther und die deutsche Nation. Vortrag, gehalten in Darmstadt am 7. November 1883* (Lecture, delivered in Darmstadt, November 7, 1883). **Werdermann**, Hermann (1936), *Martin Luther und Adolf Hitler. Ein geschichtlicher Vergleich*. Gnadenfrei. **Wiener**, Peter F. (1985), *Martin Luther. Hitler's Spiritual Ancestor*. London. **Willenberg**, Nicola (2012), Mit Luther und Hitler für Glauben und Volkstum. Der Luthertag 1933 in Dresden. In: Tanner, Klaus/Ulrich, Jörg (eds.), *Spurenlese. Reformationsvergegenwärtigung als Standortbestimmung (1717–1983)* (= Leucorea-Studien zur Geschichte der Reformation und der Lutherischen Orthodoxie. 17). Leipzig, pp. 195–237.

BRAD S. GREGORY

Where to Stand?
Luther and the Unintended Reformation

"Hier stehe ich": there is perhaps no better-known three-word sentence in the German language than this one attributed to Martin Luther. Despite its apocryphal character, the sentence captures well the sense of the endlessly quoted, culminating words he reportedly said when pressured to recant his views at the Diet of Worms in the presence of the recently elected Charles V in April 1521: "I have been subdued ("überwunden") through the scriptures I have brought forth and my conscience is held captive to the Word of God, as a result of which I cannot and will not recant anything, because to act against conscience is burdensome, injurious ("unheilsam"), and dangerous. God help me! Amen."[1] Luther knew where he stood and why.

The quincentenary of Luther's Ninety-Five Theses is a fitting occasion to reflect on the long-term influences of the Protestant Reformation, which have been many. This essay will address just one (very widespread) consequence of the Reformation: the fact of unintended Protestant pluralism as the historical product of a foundational commitment to the self-sufficient authority of scripture. This phenomenon accompanied the Reformation from its beginnings in the early 1520s and has persisted throughout the history of Protestantism to the present. In order to grasp it one must read not only Luther but also authors that, like him, rejected Rome and papal authority, but who disagreed with him about how the Bible was to be interpreted and applied. This essay seeks to counterbalance a scholarly tendency to concentrate on Luther's theology to the neglect of its unintended consequences, a tendency still notable even in the early twenty-first century in regions where Lutheranism became the state-supported form of Christianity as a result of the Reformation. Some of Luther's ideas affected much more than Germany or Scandinavia, in ways he did not intend and indeed which he vehemently denounced. He started something he could not control, as was already apparent in the early 1520s. It is certainly legitimate to begin consideration of the

Reformation proper with Luther's foundational claims, iconically expressed at the Diet of Worms. Yet following where they led historically should curb temptations to conflate those claims with the Reformation as such, perhaps especially as we reflect on the quincentenary of its beginnings.

Standing before the young Holy Roman Emperor, Luther refused to acquiesce because of his commitment to God's Word and the hold it had on him: "I have been subdued through the scriptures I have brought forth and my conscience is held captive to the Word of God."[2] His dedication was rooted in biblically immersive years of prayer and reflection, study and struggle, preaching and lecturing (on the Psalms, Romans, and Galatians) as a professor of sacred theology and an Observant Augustinian friar in Erfurt and Wittenberg. Luther's objections to certain aspects of indulgences were followed by a series of escalating interactions with fellow theologians that deepened his resolve; beginning in 1518, this process expanded into fundamental questions about the character and locus of authority in the church.[3] In part through the direct confrontation with his most prolific and determined early opponent, Johann Eck, at the Leipzig Debate in July 1519, Luther came to believe that the Bible was not merely the primary but, in principle, the only authority for Christian faith and life—because the acceptance of the specific assertions of any patristic, conciliar, papal, or other ostensible authority was contingent on whether they were congruent with scripture.[4] Luther's principal treatises in his "Wunderjahr" of 1520 all presuppose the same foundational emphasis on God's Word, known by its Latin catchphrase *sola scriptura*: his attacks on a wide range of ecclesiastical institutions and practices in his blockbuster address to the German nobility *An den christlichen Adel deutscher Nation*, his criticism of the traditional sacramental system in *The Babylonian Captivity of the Church*, and his articulation

1 Kurzer Bericht über die Verhandlungen mit Luther in Worms mit Einschiebung einer Übersetzung der Rede und Gegenrede Luthers vom 18. April [1521]. In: *Historische Kommission, Reichstagsakten*, VII.80, pp. 569–586 at 581,27–582,2. **2** Ibid. **3** See Hendrix, *Luther*; Bagchi, *Opponents*. **4** Martin Luther, Disputatio excellentium … Ioannis Eccii et D. Martini Lutheri Augustiniani [1519]. In: *WA* 279, 23–28: "Nec potest fidelis Christianus cogi ultra sacram scripturam, que est proprie ius divinum, nisi accesserit nova et probate revelatio; immo ex iure divino prohibemur credere nisi quod sit probatum vel per scripturam divinam vel per manifestam revelationem, ut Gerson etiam etsi recentior in multis locis asserit et divus Augustinus antiquior pro singulari canone observant …"

of the relationship between faith and works in *The Freedom of a Christian*. "One thing and one thing alone is required [*opus est*] for Christian life, righteousness, and freedom. That one thing is the most holy Word of God, the Gospel of Christ."[5]

A conviction about God's Word in the Bible as Christianity's bedrock authority, in principle separate from conciliar decrees, papal pronouncements, canon-legal principles, and patristic opinions, was what legitimated the movement later known as the Protestant Reformation and made Luther's refusal to recant at Worms an imperative he felt he had no choice but to obey. Most of Luther's contemporaries who in the 1520s also rejected the authority of the Roman Catholic Church shared this commitment to *sola scriptura*. Scripture as an alternative standard to criticize tradition and reject papal authority liberated them from inherited religious institutions, practices, and demands they now regarded as unjustified and burdensome impositions that imperiled rather than served souls in Christians' quest for salvation. *Sola scriptura* exploded the impasse that had stymied any efforts at systemic ecclesiastical reform in the Holy Roman Empire and elsewhere in Latin Christendom, notwithstanding the multiple reforms and renewals that had been under way for decades prior to 1520 (in the Observant religious orders, new confraternities, the *devotio moderna*, Erasmian humanism, and so forth).[6] In his address to the lay estate to assume emergency measures for the reform of Christendom in 1520, Luther attacked theologians' claims that only the Pope could interpret scripture as "an outrageous invented fable" (*frevel ertichte fabel*), self-servingly usurped and based on willfully distorted interpretations of biblical passages invoked to support the claim (such as readings of Jesus and the keys given to Peter in Matt. 16:18–19).[7] Having rejected the traditionally understood distinction between clergy and laity in asserting that the laity were also members of the spiritual estate, Luther asked, "Why should we not also have the power to taste [*zuschmecken*] and judge what is correct or incorrect concerning faith?" Adducing passages from Paul's letters to the Corinthians, he asserted, "Regarding all these and many other passages [*spruchen*] we should become courageous and free [...] and compel [defenders of the Pope] to follow the better interpretation and not their own."[8]

In contrasting his understanding of God's Word with that of contemporaries who defended Rome, Luther was obviously aware that rival interpretations of scripture existed. He seems also to have understood that *prima facie*, at least for Christians in general, neither the interpretation of God's Word nor the clarity of scripture was

self-evident. In *The Freedom of a Christian*, for example, he wrote, "Yet you might ask, 'What then is this Word, and in what manner is it to be used, since there are so many words of God?'"[9] No question was more fundamental than this to the Reformation if scripture was to serve as the basis for Christian faith and life that justified the rejection of Rome, critique of tradition, and condemnation of papal authority. If *sola scriptura* was to function as intended, the Bible had to be *clear* about everything that mattered. If scripture was in any significant ways unclear and therefore prompted disagreement and controversy, questions about its correct interpretation would return, reintroducing the issue of authoritative interpreters that *sola scriptura* was supposed to render superfluous. This would play directly into the hands of Luther's Roman critics, as he well understood in attacking the papal monopoly on biblical interpretation near the outset of his *Address to the Christian Nobility*.[10] In 1525 he broached the issue explicitly in his vehement response to Erasmus on the (non-)place of free will in salvation. Erasmus's claim that the Bible was obscure on many points wrongly repeated, according to Luther, an especially objectionable, obscurantist tactic of papal theologians—"that pestilent maxim of the sophists" that was "sent into the world by the unbelievably malicious prince of all the demons himself"—who wanted to retain their wrongful stranglehold on the (mis)interpretation of the Gospel rather than to have it proclaimed accurately to one and all for the good news it was.[11] Nothing less than the radical difference between saving liberation and skeptical desolation was at stake in the clarity of the Bible for the proponents of *sola scriptura*: "Those who deny that the scriptures are supremely clear and plain [*lucidissimas et evidentissimas*] leave us with nothing except darkness."[12]

Fortunately, according to Luther, scripture was clear; and therefore, because of God's scriptural promises, salvation was assured and where to stand was evident. In *The Bondage of the Will* Luther insisted more than once on the clarity of the Bible as a whole, distinguishing between the difficulties of certain biblical passages and the clarity of scripture's essential content.[13] In addition, he contended that whatever words might be obscure in some places are elsewhere clarified in the Bible and serve to reinforce its core message.[14] "For what of great importance can remain hidden in the scriptures after the seals have been broken, the stone rolled away from the sepulcher, and that greatest mystery proclaimed: Christ, the Son of God, became man, God is three and one, Christ suffered for us and will reign eternally? [...] Therefore the fact of the matter is that the contents of

5 Martin Luther, Tractatus de libertate christiana [1520]. In: *WA* 7, 50,33–35. Luther's version in his own German translation differs somewhat from the Latin, but the point is the same: "Hatt die seele keyn ander dinck, wider yn hymel noch auff erden, darynnen sie lebe, frum, frey und Christen sey, den das heylig Evangely, das wort gottis von Christo geprediget."; Martin Luther, Von der Freiheit eines Christenmenschen [1520], in: *WA* 7, 22,3–5. **6** For the way in which Luther broke this late-medieval impasse, see Brady, Jr., *German Histories*, pp. 146–156; on the reforms and renewals that antedated the Protestant Reformation, see Gregory, *Unintended Reformation*, pp. 84f., and the literature cited ibid. p. 422 (notes 25f.). **7** Martin Luther, An den christlichen Adel deutscher Nation

von des christlichen Standes Besserung [1520]. In: *WA* 6, 411,33–412,10, quotation at 411,33. **8** *WA* 6, 407, 412,20–31, quotations at 412,21–23. **9** Martin Luther, De libertate christiana [1520]. In: *WA* 7, 51,12 f.: "Quaeres autem, 'Quod nam est verbum hoc, aut qua arte utendum est eo, cum tam multa sint verba dei?'" Luther offered a significantly different vernacular version for a wider audience, avoiding reference to "so many words of God": "Fragistu aber 'wilchs ist denn das wort, das solch grosse gnad gibt, Und wie sol ichs gebrauchen?;'" Martin Luther, Von der Freiheit eines Christenmenschen [1520], in: *WA* 7, 22,23 f. **10** Luther, Adel, in: *WA* 6, 411 f. **11** Martin Luther, De servo arbitrio [1525], in: *WA* 18, 653,32; 653,11 f. In the preceding passage that concludes with the

all the scriptures have been made evident [*sunt proditae*], although there are certain passages with unknown words that are still obscure."[15] Luther seems to have believed that the Bible's clarity would preempt any legitimate controversy about its interpretation: "For all the articles maintained by Christians ought to be not only most certain as such [*ipsis certissimi*], but also confirmed against adversaries by such obvious and clear passages so as to shut them all up [*tam manifestis et claris scripturis firmati, ut omnibus os obstruent*], such that they cannot contradict them with anything."[16] Relatedly, in the same treatise Luther distinguished—in a dichotomizing, scholastic fashion—between what he called the "internal clarity" and "external clarity" of scripture. The latter was especially important for the Bible's shared, intersubjective meaning among Christians yearning for the certainty of God's saving Word. Otherwise, how could a common understanding of Christian truth and a coherent community of faith be sustained? Again, skepticism was the alternative as far as Luther was concerned.

Fortunately the Bible's external clarity meant, according to Luther, that "absolutely nothing [*nihil prorsus*] remains that is obscure or ambiguous, but everything in scripture is through the Word brought forth into the clearest light and declared to the entire world."[17] Scripture's external clarity was the basis for judgments that were "of the greatest relevance to teachers and preachers of the Word; it is used when we strengthen the weak in faith and confute adversaries [...] For among Christians it ought to be imprinted most steadfastly that the holy scriptures are a spiritual light far brighter than the sun itself, especially in those things pertaining to salvation or what is necessary [*vel necessitate*]."[18] For everything that counted and was important, the proper interpretation of the Bible provided a standard according to which its foundational clarity for Christians might be reinforced, and rival interpretive claims refuted.

Essential for the discernment implied in this process of teaching, preaching, correcting, and refuting, and both experientially and logically prior to it, is what Luther called the internal clarity of scripture. By means of it, "through the Holy Spirit or rather the singular gift of God, one judges and discerns with the greatest certainty any and all dogmas and opinions as they pertain to oneself and one's individual salvation."[19] Scripture's internal clarity was made manifest through divinely guided (and therefore guaranteed) interior spiritual experience.

Knowledge of scripture per se did not provide it. Luther was adamant that even extensive familiarity with the Bible need not imply any genuine comprehension of it: "No person sees one *iota* of what is in the scriptures unless he has the Spirit of God; everyone's heart is darkened such that even if they can discuss and quote everything in scripture, they nevertheless grasp or truly understand nothing of it."[20] The devastating damage to all human faculties as a result of original sin meant that neither reading per se, nor linguistic training, nor grammatical acuity, nor their combination was sufficient to understand God's Word aright. Without the inspiration of the Holy Spirit in interpreting scripture, one could not discern its clear meaning and thus its saving truth: the dynamic between the accusatory law of the Old Testament that made one aware of one's sinful impotence before God, and therefore one's desperate need for the joyful promises of his saving Gospel in the New Testament. Luther was clear: "The Spirit is necessary [*requiritur*] for understanding all scripture and every part of it."[21]

So we begin with Luther and where he stood, beholden to God's Word and insistent on the clarity of scripture. What happens when we set aside his writings and look further afield, recognizing that the Protestant Reformation was bigger than Luther's theology or experience? One of the most striking facts about the early Reformation, Protestantism through the end of Thirty Years' War and English Revolution, and indeed the entire history of Protestantism down to the present is the overwhelming lack of evidence to support claims about the perspicuity of scripture. The actual, unintended Reformation suggests something nearly the opposite to Luther's adamant proclamations about the Bible. Five centuries of exegetical controversies among those who rejected Rome testify to the lack of Luther's "external clarity," while his "internal clarity" was claimed in one form or another by those party to such controversies, and thus proved unworkable in practical terms in a manner that has never been resolved. The remainder of this essay will consider each of these points in turn.

Anyone at all familiar with the Reformation as a whole knows that it proved much easier to repudiate papal authority and reject Rome than it did to agree about the meaning and application of the Bible as a foundational, alternative authority for Christian doctrine and life. Acquiring this familiarity, however, requires more than reading volumes of the *Weimarer Ausgabe*. Karlstadt, Zwingli, Hubmaier, Grebel, Sattler, and others among Luther's contemporaries made incontestably clear how abundant were disagreements about scripture's interpretation even if we limit ourselves to the 1520s in the Holy Roman Empire and Switzerland. Casting a wider geograph-

second quoted phrase, Luther elaborates on the two-front threat to the proper understanding of scripture by "fanatics" and papists who respectively claimed the authority of the Spirit and ambiguity of the scriptures (which thus needed an authoritative interpreter): "Neque illos probo, qui refugium suum ponunt in iactantia spiritus. Nam satis acre mihi bellum isto anno fuit et adhuc est cum istis Phanaticis, qui scripturas suo spiritui subiiciunt interpretandas, quo nomine et Papam hactenus insectatus sum, in cuius regno hac voce nihil vulgatius aut receptius est, Scripturas esse obscuras et ambiguas, oportere spiritum interpretem ex sede Apostolica Romae petere, cum nihil perniciosius dici possit, quod hinc homines impii sese supra Scripturas extulerint et ex ipsa fecerint, quicquid collibitum fuit, donec prorsus scripturis conculcatis nihil nisi hominum furiosorum somnia et crederemus et doceremus. Breviter non est humanum inventum illa vox, sed incredibili malicia ipsiusmet principis omnium daemonum in orbem missum virus." *WA* 18, 653,2–12. **12** *WA* 18, 656,10 f. **13** *WA* 18, 606–609, 653–656, and most explicitly at 606,22–24, 30–31. **14** "Si uno loco obscura sunt verba, at alio sunt clara. Eadem vero res, manifestissime toti mundo declarata, dicitur in scripturis tum verbis claris, tum adhuc latet verbis obscuris." *WA* 18, 606,33–35. **15** *WA* 18, 606,24–31. **16** *WA* 18, 656,25–28. **17** *WA* 18, 609,12–14. **18** *WA* 18, 653,28–31. **19** *WA* 18, 653,14–16. **20** *WA* 18, 609,6–9. **21** *WA* 18, 609,11 f.

ical and chronological net among those who embraced *sola scriptura*—including the history of Protestantism in Britain and later the United States, for example—reinforces the point with much more evidence.[22] What seems less commonly recognized is the important corollary that follows: this abundant evidence undermines the foundational claim about the clarity of scripture that was intended and needed for the Bible to function as Luther and others had sought. Put another way, Luther's "Here I stand" led immediately and historically to a skeptical question he wanted to avoid: *Where* to stand?

Protagonists stood all over the place and thus became antagonists. From the beginning of the Reformation they stood on opposite sides of numerous issues, many of which proved bitterly divisive. It is unnecessary to rehearse the disagreements about the sacraments of the Eucharist and baptism, the permissibility or not of religious images, the applicability or not of the Gospel to questions of socio-economic and political reform, the reality or not of free will, the character of ministry and the church, which marked the 1520s in Germany and Switzerland.[23] To be sure, in order to see some of these disagreements we must historically reintegrate the magisterial reformers such as Luther, Zwingli, Melanchthon, and Bucer with the so-called radical reformers such as Karlstadt, Hubmaier, Grebel, and Müntzer. But they *should* be reintegrated, since all these protagonists and many more rejected the (alleged) authority of the Roman Church and adhered to what Luther called the external and internal clarity of scripture. They agreed about the clarity of God's Word but disagreed about its meaning—and therefore, taken together, undermined the plausibility of its perspicuity on which they insisted. The result was what the history of Protestantism has empirically and historically exhibited ever since: an open-ended range of rival and incompatible claims about what God's Word means and how it is to be understood, with the social correlate of divergent groups of Protestant Christians believing and worshipping in the ecclesial correlate of institutionally discrete Protestant churches.

The claim is sometimes made in this context that those who affirmed *sola scriptura* in the Reformation (and since) agreed on "central Reformation principles" but differed on "secondary issues," the point being to defend Luther's contention that what was essential to salvation was (and is) clear even if some matters have unfortunately proven contentious.[24] Yet such a hierarchical categorization is untenable. There is no plausible way to relegate the tradition- and church-dividing disagreements on the Eucharist, for example, to a second-tier concern if we consider Luther's own condemnations of Zwingli and his colleagues before, during, and after the Marburg Colloquy in 1529. If either Luther or Zwingli (or others) had regarded this issue as less centrally important, they presumably would have compromised on it for the sake of concord (as

they did on multiple other issues). Similarly, there is no persuasive way to regard the matter of infant versus believer baptism as anything less than fundamentally important for the Swiss Brethren, Mennonites, Hutterites, or any other among the Anabaptist groups of the sixteenth century, doubly so when we consider the willingness of so many Anabaptists to endure death for their commitment to this principle.[25]

According to them, it marked the essential ecclesiological difference between the "true church" and "false churches," among which they identified the Lutheran and Reformed no less than the Roman Catholic. And in their view, scripture was clear in its *opposition* to infant baptism; in Balthasar Hubmaier's opinion, for example, nothing was more evident in the Bible than that believers and not infants were to be baptized.[26] A virtually inexhaustible number of additional examples could be adduced, from the Reformation era or since, that undermine the assertions of Luther and other anti-Roman reformers about the "external clarity" of scripture on the sacraments and much else that Protestants disputed. Ironically, those who insisted that the Bible was clear show clearly that it was not. Many of their disagreements also make clear that the respective hermeneutical antagonists regarded the issues in dispute, however others might retrospectively assess them, as being of fundamental rather than secondary importance.

Nor does the early German Reformation, the Reformation era, or the history of Protestantism as a whole offer evidence for what Luther called the internal clarity of scripture. Instead all three show an open-ended plethora of rival claimants interiorly and individually convinced that they had been experientially gifted with God's necessary guidance even as they disagreed among themselves and condemned one another, thereby collectively subverting the viability of the shared principle they proclaimed. The early German Reformation offers numerous examples of those who agreed with Luther that one had to be enlightened and led by God in order to understand scripture properly. As Zwingli put it, "God reveals himself through his own Spirit, and we cannot learn from him without his Spirit," for "after God has taught us with his anointing, that is, with his Spirit, we need no one to instruct us because there is no more falsehood but rather the plain truth in which we should remain."[27] Müntzer pushed the issue further, but his insistence on the necessary role of the Spirit in understanding God's living Word lay on the same spectrum as that of Zwingli and Luther (which is partly why he so infuriated the latter): "whoever does not feel the spirit of Christ within him, indeed who is not certain he possesses it [*nit gwyszlich haet*], is not a member of Christ, he is of the devil."[28] Luther, as is well known, was also generous in attributing the devil's influence to those who disagreed with him.[29] These and other reformers who insisted on the

22 For both the early German Reformation and subsequent Protestantism, see Gregory, *Unintended Reformation*, pp. 86–96, 109–112. For a few examples attesting to Protestant social and exegetical heterogeneity in the United States beginning the period of its status as a British colony to the present, see Hall, *Worlds*; Valeri, *Merchandize*; Butler, *Awash*; Seeman, *Persuasions*; Noll, *Beginning*; Hatch, *Democratization*; Thuesen, *Discordance*; Noll, *Work*. **23** For just a

few examples in a massive scholarly literature, see Edwards, *Luther*; Wandel, *Eucharist*; Burnett, *Karlstadt*; Koerner, *Reformation*; Roth/Stayer, *Companion*. **24** For two such examples (from which these quoted phrases are also drawn), see Edwards, *Luther*, p. 197; McKee, *Katharina*, pp. 265 (second quotation), 273. **25** On Anabaptists and martyrdom in the Reformation era, see Gregory, *Salvation*, pp. 114–116, 197–249; Gregory, *Anabaptist*. **26** See Balthasar Hubmaier,

necessity of Luther's internal clarity of scripture disagreed vehemently among themselves in the 1520s, with doctrinally, socially, and politically divisive consequences.

Of course, insistence on the testimony and guidance of the Spirit did provide a ready explanation when one was confronted by opponents with different claims about baptism, the Lord's Supper, unjust feudal relations, or any other matter of contention: despite their insistence to the contrary, they were mistaken in claiming to be guided by God. Unfortunately, one's opponents could (and did) turn this right around. So the shared commitment to the internal clarity of scripture simply produced opponents respectively convinced that they were Spirit-led interpreters of God's Word, but their rivals were not. A necessary principle engendered irresolvable disputes. In his *On the Freedom of the Will*, Erasmus discerned the practical problem: "What am I to do when many persons allege different interpretations, each one of whom swears to have the Spirit?"[30] Or in other words: *Where* to stand? Of course, it is not the case that none of the respective antagonists *could* have been correct and in fact really have been guided by God. But there was no way impartially or convincingly to adjudicate among their rival claims. Luther's assertion about the internal clarity of scripture was stillborn in practical terms, just as his proclamation about its external perspicuity was subverted by the incompatible assertions of the controversialists who affirmed it.

The central, unintended problem internal to the Protestant Reformation derived from its own foundational first principle, the very basis that Luther invoked to justify his repudiation of the Roman Church and to defy Charles V to his face. Despite protestations to the contrary, there is no evidence that scripture was clear in the sense alleged by Luther and his contemporaries or by those who, since the sixteenth century, have asserted that it was (or is). "The Bible, I say, the Bible only, is the religion of Protestants!" thundered William Chillingworth in England in 1638, as though this somehow stated a viable platform for doctrinal agreement rather than concisely summarized the source of the problem, evident by then for more than a century.[31] The American Presbyterian theologian Charles Hodge was less animated in echoing Chillingworth more than two centuries later, in a culture by then enamored of scientific progress and the cult of "facts": "The duty of the Christian theologian is to ascertain, combine, and collect all the facts which God has revealed concerning himself and our relation to Him. These facts are all in the Bible. This is true because everything revealed in nature, and in the constitution of man concerning God and our relation to Him, is contained and authenticated in Scripture. It is in this sense that 'the Bible, and the Bible alone, is the religion of Protestants.'"[32] In fact, the collective cultural impact of disagreements about biblical

interpretation undermined claims about scripture's clarity and inspired skepticism about its authority. The issue persists today among self-proclaimed evangelicals who seem not to see that among the plethoric assertions about what the Bible means in the early twenty-first century, nothing makes their choice to stand where they do any more compelling than other Protestants' choices to stand somewhere else.

Today, however, aside from its undoubted importance to the personal lives of those who make their respective choices, the content of what is chosen hardly matters for any wider social or cultural influence. What Luther started in 1517 has unquestionably shaped the subsequent course of Western history—indeed, through European colonialism and imperialism, the Protestant Reformation and a divided Western European Christianity affected world history in transformative ways. But the manner in which Western modernity eventually coped in political terms with the problem of unsought, contentious Christian pluralism—a problem that not only characterized relations among Protestants but also, of course, relations between Protestants and Roman Catholics—marks a major difference in comparison to early modern Europe. The unsought effects of Luther's "Hier stehe ich" were addressed very differently in the sixteenth and seventeenth centuries than they are now.

In early modern Europe, Lutheran or Reformed Protestant confessional regimes provided coercive incentives about where to stand in ways analogous to those of Catholic confessional regimes, with penalties and prosecution for nonconformists. Dissidents were punished. By contrast, in modern, liberal regimes, where politically protected individual religious freedom has become the institutional means of addressing the outcomes of unintended Christian pluralism inherited from the Reformation era, that pressure has been lifted. In contrast to scripture's demonstrated contentiousness, the Reformation's long-term effects are clear now that they are unimpeded by confessional constraints. You can believe anything so long as you obey the state's laws (including the ways in which those laws control religion). You can stand wherever you want: you can be as adamantly opposed or utterly indifferent to religion as arbitrarily supportive of some form of it. And so the consequences of Luther's unintended Reformation ironically can be felt more expansively in the midst of advanced secularization. Modern philosophy's failed foundational ambitions, widely recognized in recent decades following a run that started in the seventeenth century, have augmented the arbitrariness of a culture no longer constrained by intra-Christian doctrinal disputes as it was five centuries ago. Luther's stand created the skepticism he wanted to avoid. Where to stand now? Wherever.

Uber Doctor Balthazars Touffbüchlin, waarhaffte, gründte antwurt, durch Huldrychen Zuiglin [1526]. Repr. in: Westin/Bergsten, *Schriften*, p. 173. See, more broadly, Chatfield, *Hubmaier*. **27** Huldrych Zwingli, Von Klarheit und Gewissheit des Wortes Gottes [1522], pp. 369,25–27; 370,12–15. **28** Thomas Müntzer, Das Prager Manifest [Kürzere deutsche Fassung; 1. November 1521]. In: Franz, *Schriften*, p. 492,15–17. Müntzer refers here to Rom 8:9: "Anyone who does not

have the Spirit of Christ does not belong to him" (NRSV). **29** Edwards, *Luther*. **30** Desiderius Erasmus, De libero arbitrio diatribe, sive collation [1542]. Basel, sig. b1. **31** Chillingworth, *Religion*, p. 375. **32** Hodge, *Theology*, p. 11.

BIBLIOGRAPHY

Bagchi, David V. N. (1991), *Luther's Earliest Opponents: Catholic Controversial-ists, 1518–1525*. Minneapolis. **Brady**, Thomas A. Jr. (2009), *German Histories in the Age of Reformations, 1400–1650*. Cambridge. **Burnett**, Amy Nelson (2011), *Karlstadt and the Origins of the Eucharistic Controversy: A Study in the Circulation of Ideas*. Oxford/New York. **Butler**, Jon (1990), *Awash in a Sea of Faith: Christianizing the American People*. Cambridge, Mass./London. **Chatfield**, Graeme (2013), *Balthasar Hubmaier and the Clarity of Scripture: A Critical Reformation Issue*. Eugene, Ore. **Chillingworth**, William (1638), *The Religion of Protestants a Safe Way to Salvation*. Oxford. **Edwards**, Mark U. Jr. (1975), *Luther and the False Brethren*. Stanford. **Egli**, Emil/**Finsler**, Georg (eds.) (1905), *Huldreich Zwinglis Sämtliche Werke*. Vol. 1. Berlin, pp. 328–384. **Franz**, Günther (ed.) (1968), *Schriften und Briefe* (= Quellen und Forschungen zur Reformationsgeschichte. 33). Gütersloh, pp. 491–512. **Gregory**, Brad S. (1999), *Salvation at Stake: Christian Martyrdom in Early Modern Europe*. Cambridge, Mass./London. **Gregory**, Brad S. (2007), Anabaptist Martyrdom: Imperatives, Experience, and Memorialization. In: Roth, John D./Stayer, James M. (eds.), *A Companion to Anabaptism and Spiritualism, 1521–1700*. Leiden, pp. 467–506. **Gregory**, Brad S. (2012), *The Unintended Reformation: How a Religious Revolution Secularized Society*. Cambridge, Mass./London. **Hall**, David D. (1989), *Worlds of Wonder, Days of Judgment: Popular Religious Belief in Early New England*. New York. **Hatch**, Nathan O. (1989), *The Democratization of American Christianity*. New Haven/London. **Hendrix**, Scott H. (1981), *Luther and the Papacy: Stages in a Reformation Conflict*. Philadelphia. **Historische Kommission** bei der Bayerischen Akademie der Wissenschaften (ed.) (1896), *Deutsche Reichstagsakten unter Kaiser Karl V.* Vol. 2. Gotha. **Hodge**, Charles (1873), *Systematic Theology*. Vol. 1. New York. **Koerner**, Joseph Leo (2004), *The Reformation of the Image*. Chicago/London. **McKee**, Elsie Anne (1999), *Katharina Schütz Zell*. Vol. 1. Leiden. **Noll**, Mark A. (2000), *The Work We Have to Do: A History of Protestants in America*. Oxford. **Noll**, Mark A. (2015), *In the Beginning Was the Word: The Bible in American Public Life, 1492–1783*. Oxford/New York. **Roth**, John D./ **Stayer**, James M. (eds.) (2007), *A Companion to Anabaptism and Spiritualism, 1521–1700*. Leiden. **Seeman**, Erik R. (1999), *Pious Persuasions: Laity and Clergy in Eighteenth-Century New England*. Baltimore. **Thuesen**, Peter J. (1999), *In Discordance with the Scriptures: American Protestant Battles Over Translating the Bible*. Oxford/New York. **Valeri**, Mark (2010), *Heavenly Merchandize: How Religion Shaped Commerce in Puritan America*. Princeton. **Wandel**, Lee Palmer (2005), *The Eucharist in the Reformation*. Cambridge. **Westin**, Gunnar/**Bergsten**, Torsten (eds.) (1962), *Schriften* (= Quellen zur Geschichte der Täufer. 9). Gütersloh.

Appendix

Glossary

Absolution
A part of the sacrament of penance; the forgiving of sins

Albertines
One of the lineages of the Saxon House of Wettin, established in consequence of the dynastic split in 1485; obtained the electoral title in 1547

Altar benefice
Assets donated to establish and maintain an altar and the cleric servicing it

Anabaptists
A Christian movement which demanded adult Baptism, in the case of those baptized as infants, a renewal was deemed necessary (hence: Ana-baptists, re-baptizers)

Antichrist
New-Testament concept that only appears in the Epistles of John and 2 Thessalonians; the adversary of Christ who was expected to rule over the end of time; identified with the Papacy by Luther in 1520

Anti-Clericalism
Widespread criticism of the clergy that arose during the Middle Ages; usually targeting the lax ethical standards of priests and monks

Anti-Judaism/Anti-Semitism
A perception, based on the Gospel of John, that the Jewish people were the murderers of Christ; this view became one of the foundations of racist enmity against Jews in the nineteenth century

Antinomian Controversy
A theological controversy between "real" Lutherans (Gnesio-Lutherans) and the followers of Melanchthon concerning the role of Law in the life of the faithful

Apocalypticism
An interpretation of events as presaging the approaching catastrophic end of the world

Apostolic See
The designation for the seat of the bishopric of Rome and a synonym for the Pope's position of authority

Augsburg Interim
A law proclaimed at the Imperial Diet of Augsburg in June 1548; providing interim regulations for the Protestant estates until a council could be convened to resolve the religious dispute; its only concessions were the lay chalice and the marriage of clerics

Augsburg Confession
A document of confession presented by the Protestant imperial estates in 1530; the 28 articles explained their faith in the context of Scripture; still valid in Lutheran churches to this day

Augustinian Hermits/Mendicants, Friars
An order of mendicant friars that Martin Luther joined in Erfurt in 1505

Baptism
The sacrament of acceptance into the Christian community

Battle of Mühlberg
A battle fought on April 24, 1547 between the imperial and Saxon armies; Elector John Frederick was captured and forced to resign in the Capitulation of Wittenberg

Bishopric, Diocese
The area over which a bishop had religious (and sometimes political) authority

Body of Christ
A term used in the controversy over the Eucharist in which the definite relation between the physical body of Christ and the Host was hotly debated

Bohemian Brethren, Unity of the Brethren
An association of various religious groups (Waldensian, Taborite and Utraquist) in late fifteenth-century Bohemia that established a distinct fraternal church

Bowl, Cup
The upper part of a chalice

Broadsheet
A single-page print, often illustrated, often containing the latest news; an effective way of influencing public opinion in the Early Modern era

Brotherhood, Fraternity
An association whose male members performed pious works (common prayer, services, assistance for the sick, the helpless and travelers)

Calvinism
An appellation for the teachings of Jean Calvin, coined by his enemies but rejected by him

Canon
A standard or collection of normative rules

Canon
A cleric belonging to a collegiate or cathedral chapter who lives according to ecclesiastical rules

Canonist
A teacher of Roman-Catholic church law

Cardinal
The highest rank in the Roman Church below the Pope; often combined with a bishopric

Catechism
A manual for teaching the fundamentals of Christian belief; the Reformed churches use the Heidelberg Catechism of 1563

Catholicism
The self-conception of the Catholic Church as being universal and exclusive; an arrogant presumption in the eyes of the Lutherans

Celibacy
The obligation of the holders of church offices to remain unmarried; practiced predominantly in the Catholic Church

Chapter, Confraternity
A clerical community without the strict regulations of monkhood, but an obligation of common prayer

Chasuble
liturgical vestment

Christian Freedom
Luther's conviction derived from his reading of Galatians that the use of coercion in matters of faith was wrong; not applicable to strictly political affairs in his view

Church of England, Anglican Church
The official church that was established in England in 1529, encompassing Protestant theology and Catholic liturgy

Church Order
Regulations governing church matters for congregations

Colloquy of Worms
An attempt to return to religious unity made in Worms in 1557; it failed due largely to the conflicting positions among the attending Protestant theologians

Common Chest
The common budget of a church congregation from which all expenses were paid; an important tool for funding the communal care of the poor

Commoner
A contemporary term for the non-noble and non-clerical majority of the population, encompassing both peasants and townsfolk

Confessing Church
A movement of German Protestants under Nazi rule that opposed the officially sanctioned "German Christians"

Confessio Augustana
see Augsburg Confession

Confession
A term which came into use when Christianity split into three different churches (Catholics, Lutherans, Reformed)

Confessionalization/Confessional Age
A development in the sixteenth century that saw the widespread interference of religion in political, cultural and intellectual affairs

Confirmation
A Christian ritual that completes the grace bestowed by Baptism; a sacrament in the Catholic Church

Consecration
The consecration and transubstantiation of the Host in Catholic practice

Corporal
A textile for covering the altar

Council
A gathering of church prelates and the Pope to decide important church affairs

Council of Trent
A council, held in three sittings between 1545 and 1563 in the Italian city of Trent, which laid the foundations for the modern Roman Church

Councilors
The leading administrative officials of a territorial state; a professional group which increased its influence during the sixteenth century

Creed
A comprehensive summary of the fundamental tenets of Christian faith; the Augsburg Confession is based on early Christian creeds of the third and fourth centuries AD

Crossing, Intersection
The area where the nave and the transept of a church building intersect

Cuius Regio, Ejus Religio
"The religion of a territory is determined by that of its ruler" – the legal principle established by the Peace of Augsburg to determine the respective confessions of the Empire's many territories

Devotion
A meditative prayer

Devotional Image
A picture intended to focus devotion; in the pre-reformatory church, miracles would often be ascribed to such images

Diet
The irregularly convened assemblies of the estates of the Holy Roman Empire

Dispensation
A permission to deviate from general regulations of canonical law on an individual basis; often the privilege of papal authority

Disputation
A dispute conducted according to scientific principles and strict rules

Doctrine of the Two Realms, Two Kingdoms Doctrine
The distinction between the spiritual sphere of pure Christianity and the worldly sphere which is ruled by law and force; adapted by Luther from Augustine

Doctrine of the Three Orders
The hierarchy of the social orders in the early modern age; a division into the clergy, the nobility and the commoners (burghers and peasants) according to their respective functions

Doctrine of Justification
The insight, which Luther first derived from reading the epistles of Paul, that only faith in the promised grace of God ensures justification

Dogma, Dogmata
A binding doctrine on church matters set up by the Pope

Ecclesiology
The theological study of the Church

Ecumenical Christianity
A Greek word originally describing the entirety of populated earth; from the twentieth century on a collective term for all Christian denominations

Edict
A law proclaimed by the Emperor after approval by the imperial estates

Edict of Worms
An edict issued by Emperor Charles V at the close of the Diet of 1521 that placed Luther under an imperial ban; completely ignored by the Elector of Saxony

Eleutherius
Greek for the free or freed one, an academic appellation which Luther used in reference to his family name from 1517/18

Emperor
Head of the Empire, chosen by the Electors and crowned by the Pope

Enlightenment
An intellectual movement originating in eighteenth-century France that questioned the rationality of existing structures and perceptions

Enthusiasts
see left or radical wing of the Reformation

Epitaph
A memorial plaque for a deceased person, usually consisting of an inscription and an image

Ernestines
One of the lineages of the Saxon House of Wettin established in consequence of the dynastic split in 1485; held the electoral title until 1547

Eucharist
see Holy Communion, Eucharist, Host

Eucharistic Controversy
The controversy between Lutherans and Reformed Protestants on the question of the symbolic or real presence of Christ in the Eucharist

Evangelical
Self-appellation of the supporters of Luther and Calvin, denoting their adherence to a doctrine which closely followed the Gospel

Excommunication
The legal expulsion from the Church, pronounced by the Pope as a punishment that included the withdrawal of all rights and promises of salvation

Extreme Unction
The sacrament of compassion, administered to the dying in remembrance of the Passion of Christ; rejected by the Reformation as unfounded in Scripture

Famulus
A student, apprentice or assistant

Fiscal Officer
An executive officer of a medieval ruler or bishop

Floral Initial
The floral ornamentation of an enlarged initial letter in Gothic book illumination

Free Churches
Unlike official, state-controlled churches, these denominations evolved independently in the wake of the Reformation

German Christians
An association of German Protestants during the Third Reich that cooperated with the regime's official religious policy; opposed by the "Bekennende Kirche" or Confessing Church

German Peasants' War
A widespread and violent revolt of the German lower classes in 1525 that was crushed by the nobility; strongest in southern Germany and Thuringia

Gnesio-Lutherans
A derisive term for the opponents of Melanchthon's followers, who saw themselves as "true" Lutherans

Gospel
From Old English "godspel": good news; In Luther's view, this promise of God's grace and salvation contrasted with the Law of the Old Testament

Grace, Mercy
The unconditional love that God bears mankind in spite of its sins

Gravamina
Official complaints that the Empire lodged with the Curia during the fifteenth and sixteenth centuries; summarized by Luther in his treatise on the German nobility of 1520

Habit
The specific attire of religious orders

Hebrew Bible
A term for the first part of the Bible, the Old Testament

Heresy
A doctrine or belief contrary to the teachings of the church and the positions of authorities

Heretic
A teacher of heresies who deviates from the established order and doctrine

Hermeneutics
The theory and method of interpreting texts; in theology: the interpretation of Scripture by Luther

Holy Communion
see Holy Communion, Eucharist, Host

Holy Communion, Eucharist, Housel
A sacrament and the liturgical reenactment of the Last Supper of Jesus Christ; a frequent part of religious services; the Reformation emphasized its role in strengthening the bond of the congregation

Holy Mass, Mass
A term for the rite of the Eucharist used in Catholicism; derived from Latin *Ite, missa est*, the concluding words of the service

Holy Relics
A collection of relics; the sacred treasures of a church

Host, Bread
The wafer or bread consecrated during Mass; transformed into the body of Christ according to Catholic belief

Huguenots
A term used for French Protestants; subjected to persecution in France

Humanism
An educational movement originating in late-medieval Italy that attempted to revive the learning of antiquity; Erasmus of Rotterdam was one of its most important proponents

Hussites
Supporters of Jan Hus

Iconoclasm
The (spontaneous or organized) removal of devotional images and other ornaments from churches; a frequent occurrence in reformed areas

Idol
A man-made object of veneration; the term was often applied by Luther in criticism of excessive wealth

Imperial Ban
A proscription issued by the king or emperor in conjunction with the imperial courts of law and the electors which stripped the condemned of all rights and protection throughout the Holy Roman Empire

Imperial Chamber Court
The supreme court of law of the Holy Roman Empire

Imperial City, Free Imperial City
A city or town that was a direct subject of the Emperor; its representatives had the right to participate in imperial diets

Imperial Estates
The constituting political bodies of the Empire, made up of more than 300 church and lay princes, prelates, knightly orders, counts and lesser lords as well as the free imperial cities; all entitled to sit and vote in imperial diets

Indulgence
The remission of sins for the living and the deceased in exchange for pious works, prayer, or payment

Instruments of the Passion
The instruments with which Christ was tormented according to the story of the Passion

Interdict
The withholding of spiritual services and benefits as a punishment

Interim
A compromise between confessional parties on matters pending clarification by a council

Invocavit Sermons
Sermons held by Luther after his return from Wartburg Castle to quiet the situation in Wittenberg in March 1522

justification by Works
Part of the Doctrine of Justification; the assertion that pious works will secure God's justification; rejected by Luther

Lay Chalice
The partaking of the wine by the lay members of the congregation; denied to them by the Roman Church since 1215; demanded by Hussites and the Reformation

Leaders/Captains of the League
The founders and official leaders of the Schmalkaldic League (Landgrave Philip of Hesse and Elector John Frederick I of Saxony)

League of Gotha/League of Torgau
An alliance which was formed in 1526 to protect the Reformation in reaction to a compact made by Catholic princes in Dessau; the foremost members were Elector John of Saxony and Landgrave Philip of Hesse

Left or Radical Wing of the Reformation
A modern appellation for tendencies in the Reformation that were more radical than Luther and Calvin; mostly used to designate the Anabaptists

Leipzig Disputation
A theological dispute between Johannes Eck, Martin Luther and Andreas Karlstadt in 1519

Letter of Indulgence
A certificate confirming the acquisition of an indulgence

Liberal Arts
The seven Liberal Arts (Arithmetic, Geometry, Astronomy, Music, Grammar, Rhetoric, and Dialectic) have been viewed as the basis of intellectual education since antiquity

Liturgical Vestment
The attire worn by the clergy for services or Mass

Liturgy
Regulations governing the conduct of religious services

Luther's Rose
The signet used by Luther: A rose and cross enclosed by a golden ring; used from 1523 to mark his official printed publications

Luther's Eschatology
The doctrine and study of the final events occurring at the end of time; in Luther's view the return of Christ and the end of the world were imminent

Luther's Large/Small Catechism
A manual for children and preachers consisting of five principal sections (the Ten Commandments, the Creed, the Lord's Prayer, Baptism and Holy Communion)

Lutheran
Originally a derisive name given by the opponents of the Reformation to the followers of Luther, the term was adopted in a positive sense from 1530

Lutheran Protestantism
Churches which accept the Augsburg Confession as the basis of their teachings

Marburg Colloquy
An unsuccessful dispute on the question of the Eucharist held in 1529 between the Lutherans (Luther and Melanchthon) and the Swiss reformer Huldrych Zwingli

Mercenary Soldiers
A type of German paid soldier in the fifteenth and sixteenth centuries

Mining Rights, Regalia
The right to exploit mineral resources which formed a part of traditional royal or princely prerogatives

Modern Devotion
A religious movement of the fourteeth and fifteenth centuries that called for a renewal of Christian life through inward devotion and pious practices (such as caring for the sick and poor or teaching in schools)

Monk, Friar
A member of a spiritual fraternity dedicated by eternal vows to a life of poverty, austerity, chastity and obedience to the will of God

Monstrance
A precious ornamental vessel for displaying the Host; its use was abolished by the Reformation

Mysticism
The experience of the immediate presence of God; literature pertaining to this phenomenon

New Testament
The second part of the Bible which consists of the Four Gospels, the Acts of the Apostles, the Epistles and the Book of Revelation

Nodus, Knob
A knob ornamenting the stem of a chalice

Novitiate
A one-year period of preparation for new members of an order preceding the taking of vows

Nun
A female member of a religious order

Old Testament
see Hebrew Bible

Order
The subdivisions of monasticism which are mainly named after their founders and have different historical developments

Ordination
The appointment of a cleric to preach in a specified congregation; it replaced the ordination to priesthood

Ordination to Priesthood
A sacrament that, according to Roman tradition, can only be bestowed by a bishop to confer a new quality on a cleric; rejected by the Reformation and replaced by the ordination

Ottoman Empire
The territory controlled by the Ottoman dynasty (in Asia Minor, the Balkans, North Africa and the Crimea) from its capital in Constantinople

Pall
A linen cloth stiffened with cardboard for covering the Eucharist chalice

Pamphlet
A slim publication of between two and 16 pages, cheap and easy to publish, which dealt with current subjects; often sold by hawkers; a popular medium during the early Reformation era

Papal Brief
A papal edict less formal than a Bull

Papal Bull of Excommunication
The papal document that excommunicated Martin Luther in 1521

Papal Bull Threatening Excommunication
A formal document, issued by Pope Leo X in 1520, threatening Martin Luther with excommunication, publicly burned by him in response

Papal Church
A term used for the medieval Roman Church; employed by Luther to denounce his opponents

Pastor, Preacher
A church office introduced in the fifteenth century to increase the emphasis on preaching

Paten
The plate or bowl containing the Host during the Eucharist

Patriarch
The highest rank of bishop

Patrimonium Petri
The patrimony of Saint Peter; the possessions of the medieval Roman Church in central Italy, an alleged gift by Emperor Constantine

Peace of Augsburg
A law passed by the Imperial Diet of Augsburg in 1555 which conceded the free exercise of religion and the territorial integrity of the Lutheran estates

Penance and Reconciliation
A sacrament in the Roman Church that encompassed confession, absolution and reconciliation; rejected by Luther, who asked believers to change their way of living instead

Pericope
A selected Biblical text, intended for reading during sermons at a specific date in the liturgical year; a collection of such texts in a book

Philippists
Followers of Philipp Melanchthon; opponents of the Gnesio-Lutherans

Pietism
A movement striving for a renewal of Christianity, especially in the Lutheran Church of the seventeenth century, which was viewed as paralyzed by formal orthodoxy

Pilgrimage
The religious custom of visiting a site where relics or saints' burials are displayed; rejected by the Reformation

Pinnacle, Finial
Miniature spires in gothic architecture

"Posting of the Theses"
Martin Luther's public posting of ninety-five theses against the sale of indulgences on October 31, 1517; it remains a matter of debate whether the nailing on the door of the Wittenberg Castle Church actually occurred

Predestination
The doctrine that the fate of every human has been determined by God; in contrast to Calvin, Luther did not accept a predestination to damnation

Prelate
A cleric holding a leading position in the church (bishop, abbot, cardinal)

Priesthood of All Believers
A concept based on the principle of congregational churches which states that the faithful can perform the services of pastor and preacher on a reciprocal basis

(Prince) Elector
Noble rank entitling the holder to participate in the election of a new Emperor

Promise of Salvation
According to Luther's perception, God's promise of salvation in Christ is the foundation of Christian faith

Prophet
In the Old Testament, a bearer of God's revelations; in Christian tradition the last prophet is John the Baptist; Luther's adherents saw him as a prophet

Protestants
An appellation for the supporters of the Reformation used since the Imperial Diet of Speyer in 1529

Protestation at Speyer, Protest at Speyer
In 1529, a reformed minority group of the imperial estates protested against the majority, contesting the legitimacy of majority votes in matters of belief

Purgatory
An intermediate state between Paradise and Hell where the deceased undergo purification; rejected by Luther as unfounded in Scripture

Real Presence
Luther's doctrine of the actual presence of the body and blood of Christ in, with and under the elements of the Eucharist

Reformatio
Latin: a renewal or improvement; in the Middle Ages, this pertained mostly to institutions of the Church

Reformed Protestantism
The self-appellation of the followers of Zwingli and Calvin

Relics
Material remains associated with saints or objects which had somehow become the focus of religious devotion

Religious Dispute
see disputation

Retable, Reredos
A framing structure raised behind and above an altar; versions with two or more opening wings are called a "winged retable"

Revelation
The manifestation of God in Jesus Christ; for Luther, this was indissolubly connected to Scripture

Right to Resist
Luther originally held that any resistance to authority was forbidden according to Romans 13, but in 1530, he was convinced by Saxon jurists that the Protestant princes' military opposition to the Emperor was permissible

Roman Curia
The governing and administrative offices of the Holy See

Sacrament
A Christian rite for realizing the actual presence of God; in Luther's view, these had to be a combination of divine institution and a physical component; as penance did not fit this definition, it was rejected; eventually, the Reformation retained only two sacraments, the Eucharist and Baptism

Saiger Process
The separation of elements in a molten mass; part of the process of producing metals

Schism
The separation of a group from a church for non-doctrinal reasons

Schmalkaldic War
The war which erupted in 1546/47 between the Schmalkaldic League and the Emperor; it resulted in the strengthening of the imperial position against the Protestant princes and cities

Schmalkaldic Articles
A confessional treatise penned by Luther to serve as the theological basis of the Schmalkaldic League

Schmalkaldic League
The defensive association of the Protestant princes and cities which was concluded in 1531 in the town of Schmalkalden; defeated by the Emperor in 1546/47

Scholar
A student at a medieval college or university

Scholasticism
The strictly regulated medieval educational framework which placed great emphasis on the authority of texts and teachers

Scroll
A length of paper or parchment rolled up for storage

Seat of Mercy, Mercy Seat
A particular motif in sculpture and painting depicting the Trinity; God the Father holding a crucifix above which the dove of the Holy Spirit soars

Sede Vacante, Vacancy
The vacancy of the position (or seat) of a bishop, Pope or ruler

Sermon
A public lecture (in the vernacular) expounding a topic from the Bible; the principal part of any Protestant service

Social Orders
see Doctrine of the Three Orders

Sola Fide/Sola Gratia/Sola Scriptura/Solus Christus
The basic principles of the Protestant faith summarized in Latin phrases: by faith alone/ by grace alone/by Scripture alone/through Christ alone

Staple Right
The obligation of merchants in transit to offer their goods for sale at specified locations

Superintendent
A Lutheran church office that replaced the former functions of bishops; as Lutheran rulers were also the head of the church in their domains, superintendents would be subordinate to them

Table Talks
Luther's companions had made notes of the table talks of the Reformer after his death; these were published in 1566 by Anton Lauterbach

Taborites
A group of radical Hussites named after the Bohemian town of Tabor

Territorial Lord
The ruler of a defined territory

Third Reich
The period of National Socialist rule in Germany (1933–45)

Transubstantiation
A Roman Catholic doctrine – the transformation of the substance of the Eucharist into the body and blood of Christ while retaining its outward properties, adopted by the Fourth Lateran Council in 1215; this view was rejected by the Reformers

Treaty of Prague
This treaty was concluded on October 14, 1546 between Emperor Charles V and Duke Maurice of Saxony; the latter promising the Emperor military support in return for the electoral dignity of Saxony and substantial parts of the Ernestine lands

Trefoil/Quatrefoil
An architectural ornament composed of intersecting circles; used in late Romanesque and Gothic windows and arches

Tridentine
Another name for the Council of Trent; often used to designate the resolutions which were passed by this assembly

Trinity
The consubstantial nature of God consisting of the Father, the Son and the Holy Spirit

Truce
A temporary agreement to maintain peace and settle conflicts

Turk Tax
A special tax raised in the Empire to finance defensive measures against the Turkish threat

Universal Monarch
A term used in Habsburg propaganda to describe the position of Charles V as the supreme ruler of the world, defender of Christianity and fount of law and justice

Universal Priesthood
see Priesthood of All Believers

Utraquists
A moderate faction of the Hussites who bore the lay chalice as their emblem; in the eyes of the Roman Church they were merely schismatic, not heretic

Vatican
The possessions of the Pope in Rome, to which were attached diverse territories in Italy (the Patrimonium Petri)

Vicar
A cleric who substitutes for a priest in diverse functions

Visitation
Latin: a visit; the formalized inspection of the conditions in a congregation; the practice was intensified by the Reformers after 1528

Vulgate Bible
Latin: widespread, common; the Latin version of the Bible which was derived from the Hebrew and Greek originals; the foundation of Roman Catholic doctrine

Waldensians
A heretical movement founded by the merchant Peter Waldo in the twelfth century that allied itself with the Hussites and strove to join the Reformation

Wettins, House of Wettin
The ruling dynasty of Saxony

Zwickau Prophets
During Luther's absence from Wittenberg in 1521, three craftsmen from Zwickau appeared and claimed to be the bearers of a special revelation

Index of Persons

Brief Biographies

Albert [Albrecht] of Brandenburg (1490–1545)
1514: Archbishop of Mainz and Magdeburg, 1518: Cardinal, as a promoter of the sale of indulgences and the highest-ranking clerical office holder of the Holy Roman Empire, one of Martin Luther's leading opponents.

Bora, Katharina von (1499–1552)
Came from Saxon rural nobility, nun. Following her escape from the Marienthron Cistercian abbey in Nimbschen (1523), she married Martin Luther (1525) and lived with him in the former Augustinian monastery in Wittenberg. She bore Luther six children: Johannes (1526–1575), Elisabeth (1527–1528), Magdalena (1529–1542), Martin (1531–1565), Paul (1533–1593) and Margarethe (1534–1570). Her successful management of the household played a major role in securing the family's livelihood. Katharina von Bora died from injuries she suffered in a road accident near Torgau while fleeing the plague. Her grave is located in the Marienkirche (St. Mary's Church) in Torgau.

Bugenhagen, Johannes (1485–1558)
(also called Pomeranus)
Reformer, pastor of the Town and Parish Church of St. Mary's in Wittenberg (starting 1523), superintendent of the Saxon electoral district, founder of the Lutheran Church in Northern Germany and Denmark, Martin Luther's companion, friend and confessor. Bugenhagen officiated at his marriage to Katharina von Bora, baptized their children and gave Luther's funeral sermon.

Calvin, Jean (1509–1564)
Swiss reformer of French descent, theologically influenced by Luther, Melanchthon, Zwingli and Bucer. Calvin advocated a doctrine of predestination under which God bestows His grace upon some chosen people, while others are predestined to damnation. Calvin accepted only two sacraments as valid: baptism and the Eucharist, which he saw as a powerful symbol of Christ's presence through the Holy Spirit (spiritual presence). Calvin drafted a strict ecclesiastical ordinance for the city of Geneva.

Charles V (1500–1558)
of the House of Habsburg, was King Charles I of Spain from 1516 on. He was elected King of the Romans in 1519 as Charles V and was crowned Emperor in 1530 by Pope Clement VII in Bologna. In 1556, he abdicated the Spanish crown in favor of his son Philip II and the imperial crown in favor of his brother Ferdinand I. He considered himself to be the protector of the Christian West from the Ottoman Turks and as defender of the Roman Catholic faith. On May 8, 1521, Charles issued the *Edict of Worms*, which imposed the imperial ban on Luther and prohibited his writings. In the Battle of Mühlberg (1547), his army defeated the Schmalkaldic League. Charles V decreed the Augsburg Interim in 1548 in order to achieve his religious policy objectives, but it fell through. Despite his concerns, the Peace of Augsburg was concluded on September 25, 1555, which recognized the Lutheran confession.

Cranach, Lucas the Elder (1472–1553)
German painter and graphic artist, as of 1505: court painter to the Elector of Saxony, council member (1519–1549) and mayor of Wittenberg (elected 1537, 1540, 1543). There, he managed a large painting workshop and owned several properties, a pharmacy and a printing shop. Cranach was a witness at Martin Luther's wedding to Katharina von Bora. Luther was the godfather of Cranach's youngest daughter, Anna. Cranach's numerous portraits of reformers and of his employers shape our perception of key Reformation figures to this day.

Cranach, Lucas the Younger (1515–1586)
Painter, second son of Lucas Cranach the Elder. After the death of his older brother Hans (1537), he took on a leading role in his father's workshop, which he managed starting in 1550.

Frederick III of Saxony, the Wise (1463–1525)
Elector of Saxony (as of 1486), Arch-Marshal and Governor of the Holy Roman Empire, patron of Martin Luther. Frederick the Wise ruled together with his younger brother, John the Steadfast. He founded the University of Wittenberg in 1502. After the death of Emperor Maximilian I in 1519, he waived his candidacy for the throne and instead supported Charles I of Spain, who received the imperial crown as Emperor Charles V; afforded Luther safe conduct to the Diet of Worms in 1521 and allowed him to stay under his protection at Wartburg Castle after the ban imposed by the *Edict of Worms*.

John I, the Steadfast (1468–1532)

Elector of Saxony (as of 1525). He consolidated the Reformation in the Electorate of Saxony and, in 1529, was among the princes representing the Protestant minority at the Diet of Speyer (the Protestation), calling upon the Wittenberg theologians Martin Luther, Johannes Bugenhagen, Justus Jonas and Philipp Melanchthon to draft the *Torgau Articles*, which in turn served as the basis for the *Augsburg Confession*. Together with Landgrave Philip of Hesse, he was the leader of the Schmalkaldic League, which was formed in 1531.

John Frederick I, the Magnanimous (1503–1554)

Last Ernestine Elector of Saxony (1532–1547). A decisive supporter of the Reformation; in 1547, John Frederick I and Landgrave Philip of Hesse led the army of the Schmalkaldic League against the Emperor's forces at the Battle of Mühlberg. The military defeat in this battle resulted in his being taken prisoner, the loss of large sections of his territory and his removal as Elector. When he was released from captivity in 1552, as a Duke, he moved his residence to Weimar.

John Frederick II, the Middle One (1529–1595)

was a prince from the Ernestine line of the House of Wettin. He held the title of Duke of Saxony.

Leo X (1475–1521)

Pope (1513–1521). Born Giovanni de Medici, son of Lorenzo "the Magnificent" and Clarice Orsini. 1483: appointed protonotary apostolic; 1489: became a Cardinal. Promoted the sale of indulgences to finance the reconstruction of St. Peter's Basilica, inducing Martin Luther to publish his Ninety-Five Theses against this practice, which sparked the Reformation. On June 15, 1520, he issued the Papal Bull *Exsurge Domine* threatening Luther with excommunication, and he proceeded to excommunicate Luther on January 3, 1521, in the Bull *Decet Romanum Pontificem*.

Maurice of Saxony (1521–1553)

as of 1541: Duke of Albertine Saxony; 1541–1549: Duke of Sagan and starting 1547, Elector of Saxony. In December 1532, at the age of eleven, he came to the court of his godfather, Cardinal Albert of Brandenburg. He took part in the campaigns of Charles V against the Turks and the French. Although a Lutheran, he fought on the Emperor's side in the Battle of Mühlberg in 1547, against his father-in-law, Philip of Hesse, and his Ernestine cousin, John Frederick I of Saxony, whose Electoral office was transferred to him in return. Because of his betrayal, he received the name "Judas of Meissen."

Melanchthon (actually Schwartzerdt), Philipp (1497–1560)

Reformer, humanist, philologist, theologian, textbook author and neo-Latin poet; alongside Martin Luther, he was the driving force behind the Reformation and the principal author of the *Augsburg Confession*. Born in Bretten as the son of the Elector's armorer, his intellectual talent was evident early on. After studying at the Universities of Heidelberg and Tübingen, he was appointed to the newly created chair in Greek language at the University of Wittenberg in 1518, on the recommendation of Johannes Reuchlin. Called *Praeceptor Germaniae* (Germany's teacher) by his contemporaries, Melanchthon reformed the educational system according to humanist principles and introduced the three-tiered school system. He composed the first work of Evangelical dogma in 1521, with his *Loci communes*.

Spalatin, Georg (1484–1545)

German humanist, theologian, reformer and historian. After his ordination as a priest, Spalatin became the tutor to future Elector John Frederick I in 1508. In 1512, Elector Frederick the Wise appointed him to manage the university library in Wittenberg Castle. In 1514, he became court chaplain and secretary of the university; in 1515, he became canon of St. George's convent in Altenburg and, in 1528, Superintendent of Altenburg. Spalatin composed a *Chronicle of Saxony and Thuringia* (1510), as well as biographies of Frederick the Wise and John the Steadfast.

Tetzel, Johannes (1465–1519)

Indulgence preacher. Studied theology in Leipzig and entered the Dominican monastery there in 1489. In 1504, Tetzel began his work selling indulgences, at first for the Teutonic Knights. In 1516, he was named sub-commissioner by the bishopric of Meissen for the sale of indulgences for the reconstruction of St. Peter's Basilica in Rome. Starting in 1517, Tetzel was engaged in the sale of indulgences in the bishoprics of Halberstadt and Magdeburg at the behest of the Archbishop of Mainz, Albert of Brandenburg. His unscrupulous methods induced Luther to publish his Ninety-Five Theses against the sale of indulgences. Tetzel died of the plague in 1519 in Leipzig.

Zwingli, Huldrych (1484–1531)

Zurich reformer. Ordained a priest in 1506, Zwingli became pastor of the Grossmünster (Great Minster Church) in Zurich in 1519. In 1522, he published the first of his Reformation writings, attacking the custom of fasting. At Zwingli's behest, the Zurich City Council revised school, church, and marriage regulations and enacted laws to uphold public morals. Church icons were abolished, along with masses and priestly celibacy. In 1525, Zwingli published his confessional statement, *Commentary on True and False Religion*. Working together with Leo Jud, he translated the Bible into Swiss German between 1524 and 1529 (*the Zürich Bible*). On October 1–4, 1529, the Marburg Colloquy was held at the invitation of Landgrave Philip of Hesse, in which Zwingli and Luther took part. However, no agreement was reached as to the biblical foundations of the Eucharist. In 1531, Zwingli was taken prisoner and killed in the Second Kappel War.

Authors

Prof. Dr. Christiane Andersson
Professor of Art History
Department of Art and Art History
301, Art Building
Bucknell University of Pennsylvania
Lewisburg, PA 17837
USA
cander@bucknell.edu

Dean Phillip Bell, PhD
Provost and Vice President
Spertus Institute for Jewish Learning
and Leadership
610 S. Michigan Avenue
Chicago, IL 60605
USA
dbell@spertus.edu

Prof. Dr. Peter Blickle
Scheidter Str. 48
D-66123 Saarbrücken
blickle.peter@t-online.de

Dr. Michael Fessner
Girondelle 90
D-44799 Bochum
michaelfessner@hotmail.com

Prof. Dr. Brad S. Gregory
Professor of History and Dorothy G.
Griffin Collegiate Chair; Director,
Notre Dame Institute for Advanced Study
Department of History
219 O'Shaughnessy Hall
University of Notre Dame
Notre Dame, IN 46556
USA
bgregor3@nd.edu

Prof. Dr. Mary Jane Haemig
Luther Seminary
2481 Como Ave
St. Paul, MN 55108
USA
mhaemig@luthersem.edu

Prof. Dr. Michael Hochgeschwender
Lehrstuhl für Nordamerikanische
Kulturgeschichte, Kulturanthropologie
und Empirische Kulturforschung
Amerika-Institut der Ludwig-Maximilians-
Universität München
Schellingstr. 3
D-80799 München
michael.hochgeschwender@
lrz.uni-muenchen.de

Prof. Dr. Susan C. Karant-Nunn
Director, Division for Late Medieval
and Reformation Studies
Regents' Professor of History
The University of Arizona
Tucson, AZ 85721
USA
karantnu@email.arizona.edu

Prof. Dr. Thomas Kaufmann
Lehrstuhl für Kirchengeschichte
Georg-August-Universität Göttingen
Theologische Fakultät
Rohnsweg 13
D-37085 Göttingen

Prof. Dr. Robert Kolb
Concordia Seminary
St. Louis, MO 63105
USA
kolbr@csl.edu

Dr. Natalie Krentz
Friedrich-Alexander-Universität Erlangen-
Nürnberg
Lehrstuhl für Geschichte der Frühen Neuzeit
Kochstr. 4
D-91054 Erlangen
natalie.krentz@fau.de

Prof. Dr. Hansjörg Küster
Lehrstuhl für Pflanzenökologie am
Institut für Geobotanik der Leibniz Universität
Hannover
Leibniz Universität Hannover
Institut für Geobotanik
Nienburger Straße 17
D-30167 Hannover
kuester@geobotanik.uni-hannover.de

PD Dr. Stefan Laube
Institut für Kulturwissenschaft
Humboldt-Universität zu Berlin
Unter den Linden 6
D-10099 Berlin
stefan.laube@culture.hu-berlin.de

Prof. Dr. Dr. h.c. Hartmut Lehmann
Honorarprofessor im Fach Kirchengeschichte
Theologische Fakultät
Christian-Albrechts-Universität Kiel
Caprivistrasse 6
D-24105 Kiel
hrw.lehmann@t-online.de

Prof. Dr. Volker Leppin
Evangelisch-Theologische Fakultät
Institut für Spätmittelalter und Reformation
Liebermeisterstr. 12
D-72076 Tübingen
volker.leppin@uni-tuebingen.de

Joanna Reiling Lindell
Director and Curator
Collection of Religious Art
Thrivent Financial
625 Fourth Ave. S.
Minneapolis, MN 55415
USA
joanna.lindell@thrivent.com

John T. McQuillen, Ph.D.
Assistant Curator of Printed Books & Bindings
The Morgan Library & Museum
225 Madison Avenue
New York, NY 10016
USA
jmcquillen@themorgan.org

PD Dr. Stefan Michel
Arbeitsstellenleiter des Akademie-Vorhabens
»Briefe und Akten zur Kirchenpolitik Friedrichs
des Weisen und Johanns des Beständigen 1513
bis 1532. Reformation im Kontext frühneuzeitli-
cher Staatswerdung«
Sächsische Akademie der Wissenschaften
Karl-Tauchnitz-Str. 1
D-04107 Leipzig
michel@saw-leipzig.de

Prof. Dr. Dres. h.c.
Peter von der Osten-Sacken
Kiesstr. 5
D-12209 Berlin
p.vdos@t-online.de

Professor Andrew Pettegree
School of History
University of St Andrews
71 South Street
St Andrews
Fife
KY16 9QW
Scotland, UK
admp@st-andrews.ac.uk

Thomas E. Rassieur
John E. Andrus III Curator of
Prints and Drawings
Minneapolis Institute of Art
2400 Third Avenue South
Minneapolis, MN 55404
USA
trassieur@artsmia.org

Johanna Reetz, M.A.
Weickelsdorfer Hauptstr. 29
D-06721 Osterfeld
jreetz@archlsa.de

Dr. Austra Reinis
Missouri State University
Department of Religious Studies
901 S. National Ave.
Springfield, MO 65897
USA
Austra.Reinis@MissouriState.edu

Holger Rode, M.A.
Weickelsdorfer Hauptstr. 29
D-06721 Osterfeld
hrode@archlsa.de

PD Dr. Philipp Robinson Rössner
Heisenbergstipendiat der DFG
Lecturer in Early Modern History
University of Manchester
Oxford Road
Manchester
M13 9PL
England, UK
philipp.roessner@manchester.ac.uk

Dr. phil. habil. Anne-Simone Rous
Ostrauer Str. 4
D-01277 Dresden
asrous@gmail.com

Prof. Dr. Dr. h. c. mult. Heinz Schilling
Berlin

Prof. Dr. Dr. Johannes Schilling
Esmarchstr. 64
D-24105 Kiel
jschilling@kg.uni-kiel.de

Prof. Dr. Luise Schorn-Schütte
Lehrstuhl für Neuere Allgemeine Geschichte unter
besonderer Berücksichtigung der Frühen Neuzeit
Johann Wolfgang Goethe-Universität Frankfurt
am Main
Historisches Seminar
Norbert-Wollheim-Platz 1
D-60323 Frankfurt am Main
schorn-schuette@em.uni-frankfurt.de

Günter Schuchardt
Burghauptmann
Wartburg-Stiftung
Auf der Wartburg 1
D-99817 Eisenach

Prof. Dr. Dr. h.c. Hans-Joachim Solms
Lehrstuhl für Altgermanistik
Germanistisches Institut
Martin-Luther-Universität Halle-Wittenberg
Ludwig-Wucherer-Straße 2
D-06108 Halle (Saale)
solms@germanistik.uni-halle.de

Prof. Dr. Christopher Spehr
Lehrstuhl für Kirchengeschichte
Theologische Fakultät der
Friedrich-Schiller-Universität Jena
Fürstengraben 6
D-07743 Jena
christopher.spehr@uni-jena.de

Professor Andrew Spicer
Professor of Early Modern European History
Department of History, Philosophy
and Religion
Faculty of Humanities and Social Sciences
Tonge Building
Gipsy Lane Campus
Oxford
OX3 0BP
England, UK
p0073869@brookes.ac.uk

Prof. Dr. Dr. Andreas Tacke
Lehrstuhl für Kunstgeschichte
Universität Trier, FB III
D-54296 Trier

Dr. Martin Treu
Kupferstr. 10
D-06886 Lutherstadt Wittenberg
karl.thust@arcor.de

Prof. Dr. Hermann Wellenreuther
Em. Professor für deutsche, britische,
amerikanische und atlantische Geschichte
der Frühen Neuzeit
Merkelstr. 33
D-37085 Göttingen
hwellen@gwdg.de

Prof. Dr. Dorothea Wendebourg
Humboldt-Universität zu Berlin
Lehrstuhl für Kirchengeschichte
Burgstr. 26
D-10178 Berlin
dorothea.wendebourg@
theologie.hu-berlin.de

State Office for Heritage Management
and Archaeology Saxony-Anhalt –
State Museum of Prehistory
Landesmuseum für Vorgeschichte
Richard-Wagner-Str. 9
D-06114 Halle (Saale)

Dr. Ingrid Dettmann
Dr. Tomoko Elisabeth Emmerling
Dr. Katrin Herbst
Susanne Kimmig-Völkner M. A.
Robert Kluth M. A.
Franziska Kuschel M. A.
Prof. Dr. Harald Meller
Prof. Dr. Louis D. Nebelsick
Dr. Jan Scheunemann
Dr. Björn Schlenker
Dipl.-Hist. Andreas Stahl
Dr. Anja Tietz

Luther Memorials Foundation
of Saxony-Anhalt
Collegienstr. 54
D-06886 Lutherstadt Wittenberg

Mirko Gutjahr M. A.
Dr. Dr. Benjamin Hasselhorn
Dr. Stefan Rhein

Foundation Schloss Friedenstein Gotha
Schloss Friedenstein
D-99867 Gotha

Prof. Dr. Martin Eberle
Dr. Timo Trümper

Abbreviations

LW	Luther's Works, American Edition, ed. Jaroslav Pelikan et al., 59 vols. Philadelphia, PA 1955–2009
WA	Martin Luther: D. Martin Luthers Werke. Kritische Gesamtausgabe (Weimarer Ausgabe), 120 vols. Weimar, 1883–2009
WA.B	Weimarer Ausgabe, Abteilung Briefwechsel
WA.TR	Weimarer Ausgabe, Abteilung Tischreden
WA.DB	Weimarer Ausgabe, Abteilung Deutsche Bibel

Illustration Credits

akg-images
Andersson fig. 4
Kaufmann fig. 1

Amsterdam, Rijksmuseum
Herbst fig. 6, Liszt Collection
© akg-images/Quint & Lox

Andersson, Prof. Dr. Christiane
Andersson fig. 3

**Arnsberg, Westfälische Auktionsgesellschaft
für Münzen und Medaillen**
Wendebourg fig. 2, Lot 2716

**Atlanta, GA, Pitts Theology Library,
Emory University**
Lindell Fig. 4, Ms. 85
Lindell Fig.5, (photo: Joanna Reiling Lindell)

Augsburg, Staats- und Stadtbibliothek
Kolb fig. 3, Graph 22/4b

Bad Windsheim, Stadt
Kolb fig. 2, (photo: Photo & Studio Heckel)

Baltimore, MD, Luther Monument
Lehmann fig. 5, © Edwin Remsberg/Alamy
Stock Photo

Basel, Universitätsbibliothek
Schorn-Schütte fig. 1, Ew 494 Folio, XLI
Krentz fig. 3, © akg-images
Nebelsick fig. 6, FG V 42-42a
Schorn-Schütte fig. 2, Ew 494 Folio, XLI

Berlin, Catawiki BV
Wendebourg fig. 6
http://www.catawiki.de/catalog/briefmarken/
lander-gebiete/bulgarien-bgr/5756285-martin-
luther-1483-1546
http://www.catawiki.de/catalog/briefmarken/
lander-gebiete/frankreich-fra/5346581-martin-
luther?area=8d3d3dc217afd5e751560fce56f07
b6651d22035

**Berlin, Stiftung Deutsches Historisches
Museum**
(photos: Sebastian Ahlers, Indra Desnica,
Arne Psille)
Andersson fig. 6, R 98/1813
Kluth fig. 1, Do2 2015/228,
(photo: Berlin/I. Desnica)
Kluth fig. 3, Do2 2015/687
Kuschel fig. 3, 1989/1547.1
Kuschel fig. 4, 1989/1547.2
Michel fig. 5, 1988/705
Michel fig. 7, Gm 95/56
Michel fig. 10, KG 2005/43
Rous fig. 5, Kg 58/16

**Berlin, Geheimes Staatsarchiv – Preußischer
Kulturbesitz**
Treu fig. 3, Geheimes Staatsarchiv Preußischer
Kulturbesitz (abgekürzt GStA PK), I. HA
Geheimer Rat, Rep. 13 Religionsstreitigkeiten
im Reich zwischen Katholiken, Lutheranern und
Reformierten; Religionsgespräche, Kalender-
sachen, Unionsverhandlungen, Restitutions-
edikt, Nr. 4-5a, Fasz. 1

Berlin, Landesarchiv, Fotosammlung
Kluth fig. 2, F Rep. 290 Nr. 0100183/
photographer: J. Jung

**Berlin, Sammlung Archiv für Kunst
und Geschichte**
Krentz fig. 3, ©akg-images
Laube fig. 5, Luther Festival from 1907. (...)
Leipzig 1907, Leipzig-Stötteritz (Dr. Trenkler & Co.)
1907, © akg-images
Neblsick fig. 6, FG V 42-42a
Schorn-Schütte fig. 2, Ew 494 Folio, XLI

**Berlin, Staatliche Museen zu Berlin,
Preußischer Kulturbesitz – Kupferstichkabinett**
Andersson fig. 1, © bpk/Kupferstichkabinett,
Staatliche Museen zu Berlin
Kuschel fig. 5, KdZ 4794
(photo: Volker H. Schneider)
Tacke fig. 1, KdZ 4545
© bpk/Kupferstichkabinett, SMB
Tietz fig. 1, Inv. Nr. 500 – 1965,
© photo: akg-images

**Braunschweig, Herzog Anton Ulrich-Museum,
Kunstmuseum des Landes Niedersachsen**
Karant-Nunn fig. 1, 3329 (photo: Museum's
own photographer)

Stadt Braunschweig, Städtisches Museum
Rössner fig. 1, B 31

**Brussels, Cathedral of St. Michael and
St. Gudula**
H. Schilling fig. 4, Von Mylius – Own Work,
GFDL, https://commons.wikimedia.org/w/
index.php?curid=7734624

Charleston, SC, St. Matthew's Lutheran Church
Lehmann fig. 7, By Cadetgray – Own work, CC
BY-SA 3.0, https://commons.wikimedia.org/w/
index.php?curid=13334659

Cleveland, OH, The Cleveland Museum of Art
Rassieur fig. 7, Gift of Mrs. Charles E. Roseman
in memory of Charles E. Roseman, Jr. 1953.143

Dresden, Ev.-Luth. Kreuzkirchgemeinde
Rous fig. 3, (photo: Denise Kühne, 2012)

**Dresden, Sächsische Landesbibliothek –
Staats- und Universitätsbibliothek Dresden
(SLUB)**
Hasselhorn fig. 2, Hist. Germ. B 178, 48
(photo: Bernd Walther)
Nebelsick fig. 3, Sammlung Saxonica,
Hist.Sax.A.429.m-3.1836/37,1/3
Schorn-Schütte fig. 3, Lit.Germ.rec.B.2039
Wendebourg fig. 5, © SLUB Dresden/Deutsche
Fotothek/Peter, Richard sen.

Dresden, Staatliche Kunstsammlungen
Dresden – Kupferstich-Kabinett
Kimmig-Völkner fig. 9, A 1015 in A 140 e, 1 [D
XVI, Beham, H. S., Pauli (886-1237 V). Pauli 12]
Bartsch 1 © Deutsche Fotothek/Richter, Regine

Dubuque, IA, Wartburg Theological Seminary
Haemig fig. 1, By Dirk Hansen – Own Work,
CC BY-SA 3.0, https://commons.wikimedia.org/
w/index.php?curid=23910689

Düsseldorf, Hetjensmuseum Düsseldorf,
Deutsches Keramikmuseum
Gutjahr fig. 4b

Eisenach, Wartburg-Stiftung
Krentz fig. 2, © akg-images
Spehr fig. 3, Wartburg-Stiftung Th 837 a
(Scan: ThULB Jena)
Wendebourg fig. 3, © akg-images

Lutherstadt Eisleben, Evangelische Kirchen-
gemeinde St. Andreas-Nicolai-Petri, St. Andreas
Kimmig-Völkner fig. 1, © Bildarchiv Photo
Marburg (photo: Uwe Gaasch)

Lutherstadt Eisleben, Luther Memorials Foun-
dation of Saxony-Anhalt, Luther's Birthplace
Museum
Tietz fig. 5, © Luther Memorials Foundation of
Saxony-Anhalt

Florenz, Galleria degli Uffizi
Rous fig. 2, 146, © bpk/Alfredo Dagli Orti

Frankfurt a. M., Museum Angewandte Kunst
Nebelsick fig. 5, Inv. Nr. 6184

Frankfurt a. M., Städelmuseum
Tacke fig. 3, Bildnummer: 46038 , © Städel
Museum – ARTOTHEK
Trümper fig. 2, © akg-images

Frankfurt a. M., Universitätsbibliothek
Osten-Sacken fig. 3, Digitale Sammlungen
Judaica (2008)/PPN: 20362937X

Freiburg i. B., Präsentation Link
Stahl/Schlenker fig. 6, 2007

Freiburg i. B., Universitätsbibliothek
J. Schilling fig. 2, Ink. A 7315, d

Freudenstadt, Evangelische Stadtkirche
Spicer fig. 3, © Bildarchiv Photo Marburg
Spicer fig. 4, © Bildarchiv Photo Marburg

Genf, Bibliothèque publique et universitaire
Blickle fig. 4c, © akg-images/Erich Lessing

Gotha, Foundation Schloss Friedenstein
Kimmig-Völkner fig. 7, 48,18
Kolb fig. 6, 8,29
Rous fig. 1, 38,78
Rous fig. 4, G 15,56
Rous fig. 6, G35,30a/b
Trümper fig. 5, SG 18
Trümper fig. 6, SG 17

Görlitz, Dreifaltigkeitskirche
Kimmig-Völkner fig. 4, © Verlag Janos Stekovics

Halberstadt, Gleimhaus – Museum der
deutschen Aufklärung
Kolb fig. 5, Inventar-Nr. P2 Luther 2

Halle (Saale), Franckesche Stiftungen zu Halle
Fessner fig. 1–3, BFSt: S/KEF: Vol 064
Wellenreuther fig. 3, BFSt: S/Kt 0242

Halle (Saale), Institut für Diagnostik und Konser-
vierung an Denkmalen in Sachsen-Anhalt e.V.
Leppin fig. 1, (photo: J. Meinhardt-Degen)
Gutjahr fig. 2, (photo: J. Meinhardt-Degen)

Halle (Saale), State Office for Heritage Manage-
ment and Archaeology Saxony-Anhalt – State
Museum of Prehistory
Gutjahr fig. 1, (photo: M. Ritchie)
Gutjahr fig. 4a, HK 667:106:63k (photo: J. Lipták)
Gutjahr fig. 5, HK 667:106:63f (photo: J. Lipták)
Gutjahr fig. 6, HK 667:207:197p (photo: J. Lipták)
Gutjahr fig. 7, HK 667:106:57a (photo: J. Lipták)
Gutjahr fig. 8, HK 667:130:1 (photo: J. Lipták)
Gutjahr fig. 9, HK 207/206 (photo: J. Lipták)
Küster fig. 1 (photo: M. Ritchie)
Küster fig. 2 (photo: J. Lipták)
Küster fig. 3 und 4 (photos: V. Dresely, J. Dietzsch)
Nebelsick fig. 1
Rode/Reetz fig. 1, HK 3500:133:3 n,
HK 3500:294:115 d, HK 9408:28:10 r, p, q,
HK 4100:2751:13 j, HK 738:64:116
(photos: J. Reetz, R. Kluttig-Altmann)
Rode/Reetz fig. 2 (J. Reetz)
Rode/Reetz fig. 3, J. Reetz
Rode/Reetz fig. 4, HK 4100:1971:728 m,
4100:2799:1020 q (photo: J. Reetz)
Rode/Reetz fig. 5, HK 3500:339:134 d
(photo: J. Reetz)
Rode/Reetz fig. 6, HK 738:22:19
(photo: A. Hörentrup)
Rode/Reetz fig. 7, HK 4100:2799:1020 h,
4100:2016:30 au, 4100:1618:588 g
(photo: J. Lipták)
Rode/Reetz fig. 8, HK 4100:2751:1044 a
(photo: J. Reetz)
Rode/Reetz fig. 9, HK 4100:2751:1044 b,
802:23:748, 667:106, 60 a;b (photos: J. Reetz,
J. Lipták, R. Kluttig-Altmann)
Rössner fig. 5, HK 2006:12311 (jug) und 12312
(coins), (photo: J. Lipták)
Stahl/Schlenker fig. 4, © Luther Memorials
Foundation of Saxony-Anhalt
Stahl/Schlenker fig. 7, HK 2004:9232 r
(photo: J. Lipták)
Stahl/Schlenker fig. 8, HK 2004:9232 i
(photo: J. Lipták)
Stahl/Schlenker fig. 9, HK 2004:9232 g
(photo: J. Lipták)
Stahl/Schlenker fig. 10, HK 2004:9232 g
(photo: J. Lipták)
Stahl/Schlenker fig. 11, HK 2004:9232 l/300
(photo: J. Lipták)
Stahl/Schlenker fig. 12, HK 2004:9232 s
(photo: J. Lipták)
Tietz fig. 6, (photo: LDASA Archiv)

Halle (Saale), Stiftung Dome und Schlösser
in Sachsen-Anhalt, Stiftung Moritzburg –
Kunstmuseum des Landes Sachsen-Anhalt
Schorn-Schütte fig. 1, Mo. KHW.M. 366/2u
Rössner Fig. 4, Münzkabinett: MOMK 25806

Halle (Saale), Universitätsarchiv der Martin-
Luther-Universität Halle-Wittenberg
Michel fig. 2, Rep. 1, U 95

Halle (Saale), Universitäts- und Landes-
bibliothek Sachsen-Anhalt
Pettegree fig. 1, VD16 B 2127, Digitalisat der
Universitäts- und Landesbibliothek Halle
Tietz fig. 3, AB 38 9/h, 11 (3)

Hannover, Niedersächsisches Landesmuseum
Tacke fig. 2, Bildnummer: 35292, © Landesmuseum Hannover – ARTOTHEK

Hartford, CT, Wadsworth Atheneum
Museum of Art
Rassieur fig. 8, The Ella Gallup Sumner and
Mary Catlin Sumner Collection Fund, 1936.339
(Foto: Allen Phillips \ Wadsworth Atheneum)

Heidelberg, Universitätsbibliothek
Bell fig. 3, Biblia, Sign.: Q 325-8 Folio INC,
Seite: Vr

Indianapolis, IN, Indianapolis Museum of Art
Rassieur fig. 5, Public Domain

Jena, Friedrich-Schiller-Universität, Thüringer
Landes- und Universitätsbibliothek
Treu fig. 1–2, Ms.App.25
Spehr fig. 4, Sign. 4 Op.theol. V,7(1) 1r
Spehr fig. 5 and 6, 4 Bud Var. 635 (8)

Kassel, Bärenreiter-Verlag
J. Schilling fig. 6, © Im Bärenreiter-Verlag
zu Kassel 1938
J. Schilling fig. 7, (BA 6346), S. 23,
© Im Bärenreiter-Verlag zu Kassel 1983

Kimmig-Völkner, Susanne
Kimmig-Völkner fig. 2 and 10

Koblenz, Bundesarchiv
Scheunemann fig. 4, picture 183-28752-0002,
© Bundesarchiv (photo: Braun)
Scheunemann fig. 5, picture 183-F1031-0209-
003, © Bundesarchiv (photo: Helmut Scharr)
Scheunemann fig. 6, picture 183-W0613-040,
© Bundesarchiv (photo: Schneider)
Scheunemann fig. 7, picture 183-1983-1110-
026, © Bundesarchiv (photo: Heinz Himdorf)

Leipzig, Kustodie der Universität Leipzig
Kuschel fig. 6, Inv. Nr. 0037/90
(photo: M. Wenzel)

Leipzig, Museum der bildenden Künste
Michel fig. 6, © bpk, photo: Bertram Kober
(Punctum Leipzig)
Spicer fig. 7, © bpk/Museum der bildenden
Künste, Leipzig (photo: Michael Ehritt)

Leipzig, Stadtarchiv
Fessner fig. 4, RRA (F) 85

Leipzig, Universitätsbibliothek
Tietz fig. 5, Off.Lips.:Stö.146

London, British Museum London,
Department of Prints and Drawings
Osten-Sacken fig. 4, 1895-1-22-285

Madrid, Museo del Prado
H. Schilling fig. 3, © Museo Nacional del Prado

Marburg, Hessisches Staatsarchiv Marburg
Hasselhorn fig. 3, StA MR, Best. 3, Nr. 616, Bl. 73r

Memmingen, Wissenschaftliche Stadtbibliothek
Blickle fig. 3, Sign. 8°13.252 k

Merseburg, Vereinigte Domstifter zu Merse-
burg und Naumburg und des Kollegiatstifts
Zeitz, Dom Merseburg
Kimmig-Völkner fig. 3, © State Office for Heritage
Management and Archaeology Saxony-Anhalt,
State Museum of Prehistory (photo: J. Lipták)

Minneapolis, MN, Thrivent Financial Collection
of Religious Art
Andersson fig. 1, 90-03
Lindell fig. 1, 01-02

Mühlhausen, Marienkirche
Kimmig-Völkner fig. 8, (photo: Tino Sieland
© Mühlhäuser Museen)

München, Bayerische Staatsbibliothek
Hasselhorn fig. 4, Rar. 1544, title page
J. Schilling fig. 3, 11804452 Res/2 Chron. 57-1
11804452 Res/2 Chron. 57-1
Karant-Nunn fig. 4, Res/2 P. lat. 848#Beibd.1
Kolb Fig. 1, H.ref. 729 p, title page
Kuschel fig. 2, Sign. 4 H.mon.23m
Pettegree fig. 2, Res/4 Polem. 3340,17, title page
Pettegree fig. 4b, Res/4 Th.u. 103,IV,23, title page
Reinis fig. 1, 4 Inc.c.a. 1082, fol. A5v
Reinis fig. 2, Res/4 Th.u. 103,XXV,21, title page
Reinis fig. 3, Res/Asc. 2455#Beibd.2, fol. E1r
Reinis fig. 4, Res/Asc. 2455#Beibd.2
Spehr fig. 2, Rar. 1646#Beibd.4, title page

München, Staatliche Graphische Sammlung
München
Bell fig. 4, 118307

Muskegon, MI, Muskegon Museum of Art
Rassieur fig. 1, Hackley Picture Fund Purchase,
1939.5
Rassieur fig. 2, Hackley Picture Fund Purchase,
1939.6

New Ulm, MN
Nebelsick fig. 7, wikipedia: Author jonathun-
der; Link: https://commons.wikimedia.org/
wiki/File:HermannHeightsMonument.jpg?
uselang=de
Stahl/Schlenker fig. 2, Spangenberg 1925, 503
numb. l. 32 cm.

New York, NY, Granger – Historical Picture
Archive
Hochgeschwender fig. 6, © Granger, NYC./Alamy

New York, NY, Metropolitan Museum of Art
Tacke fig. 4, © bpk/The Metropolitan Museum
of Art

New York, NY, The Morgan Library & Museum
McQuillen fig. 2, PML 49060, f. a2r.
(photo: Graham Haber)
McQuillen fig. 3, ARC 1157.042
(photo: Graham Haber)
McQuillen fig. 4, ARC 558
(photo: Graham Haber)

Nordhausen, Stadtarchiv
Wendebourg fig. 4, StadtA NDH, Best. 9.1.1./
C 05-0, postcard

Nürnberg, Germanisches Nationalmuseum
Dettmann fig. 2, H 7499
Herbst fig. 1, HB 26
Herbst fig. 4, H 7495
Kolb fig. 8, MP 635a, Kapsel-Nr. 9

Nürnberg, Scheurl-Bibliothek
Herbst fig. 2, pamphlet Nr. 160c
(photo: Harald Fischer Verlag GmbH)

Nürnberg, Staatsarchiv
Fessner fig. 5, Karten und Pläne 230, Seite 45

Nürnberg, St. Lorenz
Kimmig-Völkner fig. 6, © Wolfgang Gülcker

Paris, Musée du Louvre
Karant-Nunn fig. 3, © akg-images

Paul, Maurizio
Stahl/Schlenker figs. 3 and 5, 2007

Philadelphia, PA, Library Company
of Philadelphia
Herbst fig. 3, *Wing F2035 [1053.F (Vol. 2 only)]
p. 651

Philadelphia, PA, Museum of American Art
Hochgeschwender fig. 1, © bpk/Lutz Braun

Philadelphia, PA, University of Pennsylvania
Hochgeschwender fig. 4, By Church of England
– Public Domain, https://commons.wikimedia.
org/w/index.php?curid=1528052

Princeton, NJ, Princeton University
Stahl/Schlenker fig. 2, Spangenberg 1925, 503
numb. l. 32 cm.

Providence, RI, John Carter Brown Library,
Brown University
Hochgeschwender fig. 2, © Box 1894, Provi-
dence, R.I. 02912, Courtesy of the John Carter
Brown Library at Brown University

Raleigh, NC, North Carolina Museum of Art
Rassieur Fig.. 3, Gift of the Samuel H. Kress
Foundation, GL.60.17.65

Regensburg, Fürst Thurn und Taxis, Zentral-
archiv – Hofbibliothek – Museen
Tietz fig. 2, DeS KF 3509, Fürst Thurn und Taxis
Zentralarchiv, Portraitsammlung

Roch-Lemmer, Irene
Tietz fig. 4, I. Roch-Lemmer

Rotterdam, Museum Boijmans Van Beuningen
Kaufmann fig. 3, MB 2010/2 H (PK),
(photo: Tom Haartsen, Ouderkerk a/d Amstel)

Salzburg, Kunstsammlungen der Erzabtei
St. Peter
Leppin fig. 2

Salzwedel, Johann-Friedrich-Danneil-Museum
Dettmann fig. 4, © Jürgen M. Pietsch, Spröda

Sarasota, FL, Bequest of John Ringling,
Collection of the John and Mable Ringling
Museum of Art, State Art Museum of Florida
Tacke fig. 5, SN308

Scheunemann, Jan (private property)
Scheunemann fig. 2, aus: Bildbericht für das
deutsche Christenvolk, Jahrgang 1/Nummer 12,
1. November-Woche 1933
Scheunemann fig. 3

Schmalkalden, Schloss Wilhelmsburg,
Schlosskapelle
Spicer fig. 4, © Constantin Beyer

Stahl, Andreas
Stahl/Schlenker fig. 1

St. Gallen, Kantonsbibliothek Vadiana
Blickle fig. 4b

Stiftung Dome und Schlösser in Sachsen-
Anhalt, Dom zu Halberstadt
Rössner fig. 3, 006, © State Office for Heritage
Management and Archaeology Saxony-Anhalt,
State Museum of Prehistory (photo: J. Lipták)

Stockholm, Kungl. Myntkabinettet
J. Schilling, fig. 5

St. Paul, MN, Bockman Hall, Luther Seminary
Haemig fig. 2
Lehmann fig. 2, © wikimedia by McGhiever

Stuttgart, Württembergische Landesbibliothek
Hasselhorn fig. 5, Ba deutsch 1546 01
Solms fig. 3, Bb deutsch 1523 05

Tacoma, WA, Pacific Lutheran University
in Tacoma
Lehmann fig. 3, (photo: John Froschauer)

Thousand Oaks, CA, California Lutheran
University
Lehmann fig. 4, (photo: Brian Stethem)

Toledo, OH, Toledo Museum of Art, Gift of
Edward Drummond Libbey
Trümper fig. 7, 1926.55. (photo: Photography
Incorporated, Toledo)

Torgau, Evangelische Schlosskirche
Spicer fig. 1, Wikipedia, © Andreas Praefcke
Spicer fig. 6, © www.architektur-blicklicht.de

Washington, D.C., Library of Congress
Hochgeschwender fig. 5, By Baker, Joseph E.,
ca. 1837–1914, artist. [Public domain],
via Wikimedia Commons
https://commons.wikimedia.org/wiki/File
%3ASalem_witch2.jpg
Schorn-Schütte fig. 4, Washington D.C., Library
of Congress; http://hdl.loc.gov/loc.gmd/
g3200.ct000725C, Gemeinfrei, https://commons.
wikimedia.org/w/index.php?curid=5079907
Wellenreuther fig. 2, (photo: Library of Congress),
Public domain

Washington, D.C., Luther Monument
Lehmann fig. 1, © wikimedia by Slowking4

Washingthon, D.C., National Gallery of Art
Rassieur fig. 6, Samuel H. Kress Collection,
1961.9.69, Public Domain

Weimar, Klassik Stiftung Weimar
Kaufmann fig. 2, Signatur: Cl I: 58 (b) und (c)

**Weimar, Stadtkirche St. Peter und Paul
(Herderkirche)**
Trümper fig. 1 and Dettmann fig. 3,
© Evang.-Luth. Kirchengemeinde Weimar,
(photo: Constantin Beyer)
Dettmann fig. 5, © photo: akg-images

**Weimar, Thüringisches Hauptstaatsarchiv
Weimar, Ernestinisches Gesamtarchiv**
H. Schilling fig. 1, Nr. ThHStAW, EGA, Reg. E 82

Wien, Kunsthistorisches Museum
Nebelsick fig. 4, Inv. Nr. 3141,
© photo: akg-imagesprivate coll
Trümper fig. 3, Inv. Nr. 856,
© photo: akg-images/Erich Lessing

Wien, Österreichische Nationalbibliothek
H. Schilling fig. 2, Cod. Vind. 1859

Wikimedia
Hochgeschwender fig. 3, https://commons.
wikimedia.org/w/index.php?curid=11778523
By Church of England – http://dewey.library.
upenn.edu/sceti/printedbooksNew/index.
cfm?TextID=kjbible&PagePosition=1 Color level
(pick white point), cropped, and converted to
JPEG (quality level 88) with the GIMP 2.6.6.,
Public Domain, https://commons.wikimedia.
org/w/index.php?curid=1528052

Wellenreuther, Herrmann (private property)
Wellenreuther fig. 1, (photo: Herrmann Wellenreuther)

**Lutherstadt Wittenberg, Evangelische
Stadtkirchengemeinde, Stadt- und Pfarrkirche
St. Marien**
Küster Fig. 5, © Fokus GmbH Leipzig
Osten-Sacken fig. 1, © onnola, CC BY-SA 2.1

Osten-Sacken fig. 2, © Jürgen M. Pietsch, Spröda
Rhein fig. 1, © Fokus GmbH Leipzig
Spicer fig. 8, © Jürgen M. Pietsch, Spröda

Lutherstadt Wittenberg, Wittenberg Seminary
Herbst fig. 5, 5
Rössner fig. 2, A VII.33, © State Office for Heri-
tage Management and Archaeology
Saxony-Anhalt, State Museum of Prehistory
(photo: J. Lipták)

**Lutherstadt Wittenberg, Luther Memorials
Foundation of Saxony-Anhalt**
Andersson fig. 2, ss 40
Andersson fig. 5, grfl. XI 1127
Bell fig. 1, CGH 89
Bell fig. 2, Ag 4° 227c
Gutjahr fig. 3, P1
Hasselhorn fig. 1, Ag 4° XIIa 1581e
J. Schilling fig. 1 und 4, ss 1009, © State Office
for Heritage Management and Archaeology
Saxony-Anhalt, State Museum of Prehistory
(photo: J. Lipták)
Kaufmann fig. 4, Signatur: 10997
Kolb fig. 4, Ag 4° 210 b, Title page
Kuschel fig. 1, Sign. Ag 4° 242 d
Laube fig. 1, 4 C 11321
Laube fig. 2
Laube fig. 3, 4 IV 9270
Laube fig. 4, G 58
Laube fig. 6, © State Office for Heritage Man-
agement and Archaeology Saxony-Anhalt, State
Museum of Prehistory (photo: J. Lipták)
Leppin fig. 3, fl IIIa 208
Leppin fig. 6, Sign. Ag 4° 1850
Leppin fig. 7, Ag 4° 189f, Kn D 69 und Ag 4°
191f, © State Office for Heritage Management
and Archaeology Saxony-Anhalt, State Museum
of Prehistory (photo: J. Lipták)
McQuillen fig. 1, I5/1387, © State Office for
Heritage Management and Archaeology
Saxony-Anhalt, State Museum of Prehistory
(photo: J. Lipták)
Michel fig. 1, CGH 497
Michel fig. 3, SG 10
Michel fig. 4, K 17
Pettegree fig. 2, Ag 4 197p
Pettegree fig. 4a, Ag 4 202 m
Rössner fig. 2, ss 3579, © State Office for
Heritage Management and Archaeology
Saxony-Anhalt, State Museum of Prehistory
(photo: J. Lipták)
Solms fig. 1, Kn K 1, © State Office for Heritage
Management and Archaeology Saxony-Anhalt,
State Museum of Prehistory (photo: J. Lipták)
Solms fig. 2, Ag 4 212 h
Solms fig. 4, ss 1009, © State Office for Heritage
Management and Archaeology Saxony-Anhalt,
State Museum of Prehistory (photo: J. Lipták)
Spehr fig. 1, Ag 4° 191 u
Trümper fig. 4, ss 40

Wolfenbüttel, Marienkirche (Hauptkirche)
Spicer fig. 2, Wikipedia: © Misburg 3014

Wolfenbüttel, Herzog August Bibliothek
Dettmann fig. 1, Inv.Nr. Bibel-S. 792
Karant-Nunn, fig. 2, I 8257
Kolb fig. 7, A 25670
Kaufmann fig. 5, Blatt ist fol. 32 der Hand-
schrift: Cod. Guelf. 31.8 Aug. 2°
Wendebourg fig. 1, Signatur: 38.25 Aug. 2°,
fol. 310

World History Archive
Scheunemann fig. 1, © World History Archive/
Alamy Stock Photo)
Wörlitz, Evangelische Kirchengemeinde
St. Petri Wörlitz der Evangelischen Landes-
kirche Anhalts in Deutschland
Leppin fig. 4, © KsDW, Bildarchiv, Heinz
Fräßdorf

Würzburg, Universitätsbibliothek
Krentz fig. 1, Delin.VI,8,14

Zürich, Zentralbibliothek Zürich
Blickle fig. 1, Zwingli 106: a.1
Blickle fig. 2, Zürich MS B 316
Küster fig. 5, Ms. A 2, S. 150

**Zentralbibliothek Zürich, Graphische
Sammlung und Photoarchiv**
Blickle fig. 4a, Inv. 500 000 051, Sys. 005 203
666

Zittau, Frauenkirche
Kimmig-Völkner fig. 5, © Jürgen Matschie

Zwickau, Ratsschulbibliothek
Nebelsick fig. 2, Sign. 24.3.13 (12)

Sources of Infographics

The infographics shown in this publication and further infographics can be downloaded as posters free of charge at the website www.here-i-stand.com.
Content management: Robert Kluth, Anne-Simone Rous
Creative management: Jakub Chrobok (Golden Section Graphics GmbH)
Maps and geovisualization: Jonas Parnow
Project management: Annemarie Kurz
Copy editing (German): Anni Peller
Translations into English: Christoph Nöthlings (Leipzig), Gloria Kraft-Sullivan (Burgdorf)
Academic consultant: Dr. Martin Treu

Endpaper
Timeline
Research: Anne-Simone Rous
Graphics: Jakub Chrobok, Daniela Scharffenberg
Sources and literature:
Geiss, Immanuel (1989), Geschichte im Überblick. Daten und Zusammenhänge der Weltgeschichte. Reinbek bei Hamburg.
Schilling, Heinz (2012), Martin Luther. Rebell in einer Zeit des Umbruchs. Eine Biographie. München.
Kohler, Alfred (2008), Expansion und Hegemonie 1450–1558. Paderborn.

Page 28/29
The World around 1500
Research: Anne-Simone Rous, Robert Kluth
Graphics: Barbara Mayer
Sources and literature:
Haywood, John (2002), Der neue Atlas der Weltgeschichte. Von der Antike bis zur Gegenwart. 2nd ed. Gütersloh/München, map 3.04.
Kennedy, Paul (1989), Aufstieg und Fall der großen Mächte. Ökonomischer Wandel und militärischer Konflikt von 1500 bis 2000. Frankfurt am Main.
Oliphant, Margaret (1993), Atlas der Alten Welt. Eine atemberaubende Reise zu den Hochkulturen der Menschheit. München.

Page 38
Money Stories
Research: Anne-Simone Rous, Robert Kluth
Graphics: Jaroslaw Kaschtalinski, Christophorus Halsch
Sources and literature:
Clemens, Joos (2016), "Beichtbrief aus der Ablasskampagne des Erzbischofs Albrecht von Mainz, ausgestellt auf den Fritzlarer Schöffen Cyriak Iring und seine Ehefrau Eila." In: Digitales Archiv der Reformation. Available: www.reformationsportal.de/visitationsakten/detailviews-und-pdf-export/detail/stat_showcase_00000053.html [06/21/2016].

Häberlein, Mark (2006), Die Fugger. Geschichte einer Augsburger Familie (1367–1650). Stuttgart.
Gilbert, Felix (1996), Venedig, der Papst und sein Bankier. Frankfurt am Main/New York.
Benrath, Gustav Adolf (1977), Ablaß. In: Theologische Realenzyklopädie (TRE). Vol. 1. Berlin/New York, pp. 347–364.
Hamm, Berndt (2016), Ablass und Reformation – erstaunliche Kohärenzen. Tübingen.

Page 46/47
Luther Places, Famous and Unknown
Research: Anne-Simone Rous, Jan Scheunemann
Graphics: Anton Delchmann
Sources and literature:
Scheunemann, Jan/König, Judith (2016), Luther war hier. Available: www.luther-erleben.de/luther-war-hier/start [06/22/2016].

Page 84/85
Marriage Politics during the Reformation
Research: Anne-Simone Rous
Graphics: Jakub Chrobok, Verena Muckel
Sources and literature:
Rous, Anne-Simone (2009), Dynastie und Prestige. Die Heiratspolitik der Wettiner. Köln/Weimar.
Schwennicke, Detlev (1998), Europäische Stammtafeln, new series. 1,1 and 1,2. Frankfurt am Main.

Page 106/107
Monk against Emperor
Research: Robert Kluth
Graphics: Barbara Mayer, Jaroslaw Kaschtalinski, Verena Muckel
Sources and literature:
The text of the speech follows Georg Spalatin: Kurzer Bericht über die Verhandlung mit Luther in Worms mit Einschiebung einer Übersetzung der Rede und Gegenrede Luthers vom 18. April. In: Wrede, Adolf (ed.) (1883), Deutsche Reichstagsakten. jüngere Reihe. Vol. 2. Gotha, pp. 581 f. The rebuttal of Emperor Charles V follows: Reuter, Fritz (ed.) (1971), Der Reichstag zu Worms von 1521. Reichspolitik und Luthersache. Worms, pp. 225–235.
Marsch, Angelika (1980), Bilder zur Augsburger Konfession und ihren Jubiläen. Weißenhorn.
Oberman, Heiko A. (1986), Luther. Mensch zwischen Gott und Teufel. München.
Schilling, Heinz (2012), Martin Luther. Rebell in einer Zeit des Umbruchs. München.

Page 123
Translation of the Bible
Research: Anne-Simone Rous, Robert Kluth
Graphics: Barbara Mayer
Sources and literature:
Reinitzer, Heimo (1983), Biblia deutsch.
Luthers Bibelübersetzung und ihre Tradition.
Wolfenbüttel.
Rautenberg, Ursula (1999), Buchhändlerische
Organisationsformen in der Inkunabel- und
Frühdruckzeit. In: Tiemann, Barbara (ed.),
Die Buchkultur im 15. und 16. Jahrhundert.
Vol. 2. Hamburg, pp. 339–376.
Volz, Hans (1972), Einleitung. In: id. (ed.),
Martin Luther, Die gantze Heilige Schrifft
deudsch. Wittenberg 1545. Letzte zu Luthers
Lebzeiten erschiene Ausgabe. Herrsching,
pp. 33*–144*.
Volz, Hans (1978), Martin Luthers deutsche
Bibel. Entstehung und Geschichte der Luther-
bibel. Hamburg.

Page 142/143
Wittenberg
Research: Robert Noack
Graphics: Jakub Chrobok, Nick Oelschlägel
Sources and literature:
Lück, Heiner/Bünz, Enno/Helten, Leonhard
et al. (ed.) (2015), Das ernestinische Wittenberg (= Wittenberg-Forschungen). Vol. 1. Petersberg 2015, pp. 30–48, 82–92, 93–116, 117–
120, 121–134, 135–145, 164–169; vol. 2.1 and
2.2: pp. 9–24, 33–76, 127–150, 239–254,
265–292, 315–334, 335–344; vol. 3: pp. 313–
422

Page 154
The Reformation Movement
Research: Robert Kluth, Niels Reidel
Graphics: Barbara Mayer, Fabian Dinklage
Sources and literature:
The data basis for the introduction of the Refor-
mation is: Schindling, Anton (ed.) (1990), Die
Territorien des Reichs im Zeitalter der Reforma-
tion und Konfessionalisierung. Land und Kon-
fession 1500–1650. Vol. 1–7. Münster; Achter-
berg, Herbert (1928), Luthers Reformation.
Länder und Städte. In: Luedtke, Gerhard/
Mackensen, Lutz (eds.),
Deutscher Kulturatlas. Vol. 3: Vom Humanis-
mus zum Rokoko. Berlin, p. 215.
Moeller, Bernd (1987), Reichsstadt und Refor-
mation. Berlin.
Isaiasz, Vera/Lotz-Heumann, Ute/Mommertz,
Monika (2007), Stadt und Religion in der
frühen Neuzeit. Soziale Ordnungen und ihre
Repräsentationen. Frankfurt am Main/New
York.

Page 190/191
Reformation Networks
Research: Anne-Simone Rous, Mareile Alferi,
Ingrid Dettmann, Johanna Furgber, Annemarie
Knöfel, Mike Leske, Monika und Dietrich Lücke
(Cranach), Christine Mundhenk (Melanchthon),
Brigitte Parsche, Niels Reidel, Julius Roch,
Stefanie Wachsmann
The data basis on the correspondence of
Melanchthon was graciously provided by the
Melachthon-Forschungstelle at the Heidel-
berger Akademie der Wissenschaften under the
direction of Dr. Christine Mundhenk and the
data basis for the correspondence of Cranach
by Dr. Monika Lücke and Dietrich Lücke (further
information at www.haw.uni-heidelberg.de and
http://lucascranach.org/archival-documents).
Graphics: Fabian Dinklage
Sources and literature:
The data basis is provided by the following
editions of letters:
Vogt, Otto (ed.) (1888), Dr. Johannes Bugenhagens Briefwechsel. Stettin.
Böcking, Eduard (ed.) (1859), Ulrich von
Hutten, Vlrichi Hvtteni Eqvitis Germani Opera
Qvæ Reperiri Potvervnt Omnia: Briefe von 1521
bis 1525. Vol. 1,2/2, e. Leipzig.
D. Martin Luthers Werke, Weimar 1883–2009
(Weimarer Ausgabe). Vols. WA.BR 1–18.
Scheible, Heinz (ed.), as of vol. T 11 Mundhenk,
Christine (ed.) (1977ff.), Melanchthons Brief-
wechsel. Kritische und kommentierte Gesamt-
ausgabe, im Auftrag der Heidelberger Akade-
mie der Wissenschaften. Stuttgart-Bad Cann-
statt.
Böhmer, Heinrich (ed.) (1931), Thomas
Müntzers Briefwechsel. Leipzig.
Lanz, Karl (ed.) (1844–46), Korrespondenz des
Kaisers Karl V. Aus dem königlichen Archiv und
der Bibliothèque de Bourgogne zu Brüssel.
3 Vols. Leipzig.
Brandenburg, Erich, as of vol. 3 Hermann,
Johannes/Wartenberg, Günther/Winter,
Christian (eds.) (1900–1904/1992–2006),
Politische Korrespondenz des Herzogs und
Kurfürsten Moritz von Sachsen. 5 vols. Berlin.
Stiftung Museum Kunstpalast Düsseldorf/Tech-
nische Hochschule Köln (eds.), Cranach Digital
Archive. Available: http://lucascranach.org/
archival-documents [06/22/2016].
Ullmann, Ernst (ed.) (1993), Albrecht Dürer.
Schriften und Briefe. Leipzig.
Thausing, Moritz (ed.) (1872), Dürers Briefe,
Tagebücher und Reime. Nebst einem Anhange
von Zuschriften an und für Dürer. Wien.

Page 206/207
Caught up in the Swirl of Conflicts
Research: Robert Kluth
Graphics: Katharina Schwochow
Literature:
Blickle, Peter (2004), Die Revolution von 1525.
4th ed. München.
Emich, Birgit (2010), Frühe Neuzeit (1500–
1800). Internationale Beziehungen. In: Der
grosse Ploetz. Die Chronik zur Weltgeschichte.
Göttingen, pp. 212–213.
Emich, Birgit (2010), Deutschland 1493–
1790/92. Heiliges Römisches Reich. In: Der
grosse Ploetz. Die Chronik zur Weltgeschichte.
Göttingen, pp. 265–274.
Kohler, Alfred (1999), Karl V. 1500–1558. Eine
Biographie. München.

Page 221
Iconoclasm
Research: Robert Kluth, Stefanie Wachsmann
Graphics: Anton Delchmann, Katharina
Schwochow
Sources and literature:
The pictures are as following:
Seewald, Mass of St. Gregory, 1491, oil on
wood, 101 cm × 76 cm, Stadtmuseum Münster,
shelfmark: GE-0181-2, photo: Tomasz Samek.
Arnt van Tricht, Holy Trinity Relief, 1548, sand-
stone, polychromy, 88,5 × 84,5 × 9,5 cm,
Rijksmuseum Amsterdam, shelfmark: BK-NM-
3099-A. Available: http://hdl.handle.
net/10934/RM0001.COLLECT. 486432.
[06/22/2016].
Scholten, Frits/De Werd, Guido (eds.) (2004),
Een hogere werkelijkheid: Duitse en Franse
beeldhouwkunst 1200–1600 uit het Rijksmuseum Amsterdam. Amsterdam, p. 54.
The data basis for the map can be found in:
Michalski, Sergiusz (2000), Die Ausbreitung
des reformatorischen Bildersturms 1521–1537.
In: Dupeux, Cécile/Jetzler, Peter/Wirth, Jean
(eds.), Bildersturm: Wahnsinn oder Gottes
Wille? Zürich, pp. 46–51.
Christin, Olivier (2000), Frankreich und die Niederlande – Der zweite Bildersturm. In: Dupeux,
Cécile/Jetzler, Peter/Wirth, Jean (eds.), Bildersturm: Wahnsinn oder Gottes Wille? Zürich,
pp. 57–66.
For the theological background of image wor-
ship see: Wirth, Jean (2000), Soll man Bilder
anbeten? Theorien zum Bilderkult bis zum
Konzil von Trient. In: Dupeux, Cécile/Jetzler,
Peter/Wirth, Jean (eds.), Bildersturm: Wahnsinn oder Gottes Wille? Zürich, pp. 28–37.

Page 240/241
The Painting "Law and Grace"
Research: Ingrid Dettmann
Graphics: Verena Muckel
Sources and literature:
Stiftung Schloss Friedenstein Gotha/Museums-landschaft Hessen Kassel (eds.) (2015), Bild und Botschaft: Cranach im Dienst von Hof und Reformation. Heidelberg, pp. 170–171, cat.-no. 42.
Reinitzer, Heimo (2006), Gesetz und Evangelium. Über ein reformatorisches Bildthema, seine Tradition, Funktion und Wirkungsgeschichte. Hamburg: Vol. 1, pp. 46–51, 244, cat.-no. 260. Vol. 2, p. 250.
Stiftung Schloss Friedenstein Gotha (ed.) (1994), Gotteswort und Menschenbild. Werke von Cranach und seinen Zeitgenossen. Vol. 1: Malerei, Plastik, Graphik, Buchgraphik, Dokumente. Gotha, pp. 20–21, cat.-no. 1.3.

Page 348/349
Christianity and Protestants
Research: Robert Kluth
Graphics: Jakub Chrobok
Sources and literature:
Kunter, Katharina (2012), 500 Jahre Protestantismus. Eine Reise von den Anfängen bis in die Gegenwart. Bonn.
Hochgeschwender, Michael (2007), Amerikanische Religion. Evangelikalismus, Pfingstlertum und Fundamentalismus. Frankfurt am Main.
The English Wikipedia article on "Protestantism" has been consulted for the distinction of the various denominations, see: https://en.wikipedia.org/w/index.php?title=Protestantism&oldid=725607265 [06/22/2016], as well as the website of the World Council of Churches, World Council of Churches—member churches, https://www.oikoumene.org/en/member-churches/list?set_language=en. [06/22/2016].

Page 385
Protestants Overseas
Research: Robert Kluth
Graphics: Katharina Schwochow
Sources and literature:
Origin of the data on the denomination majority:
Grammich, Clifford/Hadaway, Kirk/Houseal, Richard et. al. (2012), 2010 U.S. Religion Census: Religious Congregations & Membership Study. Association of Statisticians of American Religious Bodies, Association of Religion Data Archives. Available: www.TheARDA.com, 2012, www.rcms2010.org [04/01/2016].

The data concerning the frequency of Luther being cited in newspapers were gathered with ProQuest Historical NewspapersTM, ProQuest (Ann Arbor, Michigan). Available: www.proquest.com/products-services/pq-hist-news.html [06/22/2016].
Origin of the data concerning religious affiliations is the Religious Landscape Study, Pew Research Center's Religion & Public Life Project (Washington, D. C.), February 25, 2008. Available: www.pewforum.org/religious-landscape-study [06/22/2016].
For the history of immigration see MORRIS, Richard Brandon/Brandon, Jeffrey (1996), Encyclopedia of American History. 7th ed. New York.

Page 410/411
Martin Luther and Martin Luther King
Research: Robert Kluth
Graphics: Anton Delchmann
Sources and literature:
The King-quote is from the speech given by Martin Luther King Jr. in East Berlin: Martin Luther King begrüßt die Ost-Berliner und überbringt Grüße aus West-Berlin, Berlin September 13, 1964, Deutsches Rundfunkarchiv Babelsberg, shelfmark: DRA K2001005.
Concerning the naming of Martin Luther King Jr. see: Branch, Taylor (1988), America in the King years. Parting the Waters. Vol. 1. New York, pp. 44–49.
Carson, Clayborne (ed.) (1989), A guide to research on Martin Luther King, Jr., and the modern black freedom struggle. Stanford /CA.
Carson, Clayborne et al. (eds.) (2008), The Martin Luther King, Jr. Encyclopedia. Westport/CT.

Page 439
Ninety-Five Theses
Research: Robert Kluth
Graphics: Jaroslaw Kaschtalinski, Christophorus Halsch
Sources and literature:
The images from left to right:
Unknown artist, Dream of Frederick the Wise (broadsheet), after 1617, copper plate engraving, 56,7 × 35,4 cm, Deutsches Historisches Museum Berlin, shelfmark: Gr 55/824
Medaille auf die 200 Jahrfeier der Reformation, 1717, silver, Stiftung Schloss Friedenstein Gotha, shelfmark: 4.1/3998.
Georg Emanuel Opiz, The Beginning of the Reformation—Luther, Nailing His Ninety-Five Theses Onto the Portal of Wittenberg Castle Church, Oktober 31, 1517. c. 1840, chalk and pen lithograph, 57,5 × 67,5 cm, Deutsches Historisches Museum Berlin, shelfmark: Gr 90/73.

Osmar Schindler, War—Luther, Posting His Theses—Peace, confirmation deed, 1917, Farbdruck, 33,5 × 24,7 cm, Stiftung Luthergedenkstätten Wittenberg, shelfmark: fl V 8104.
Tobias Schneider, Playmobil figure of Luther Posting His Theses, 2015, digital photograph. Available: www.theglade.com, www.theglade.com/toleblog/wp-content/uploads/2015/05/Luther-Thesenanschlag.jpg [03/17/2016].
Holsing, Henrike (2004), Luther-Gottesmann und Nationalheld. Sein Image in der deutschen Historienmalerei des 19. Jahrhunderts. Köln. Available: http://kups.ub.uni-koeln.de/volltexte/2007/2132/ [05/28/2013].
Ott, Joachim/Treu, Martin (eds.) (2008), Luthers Thesenanschlag—Faktum oder Fiktion. Leipzig.

Page 450
A Living Monument
Research: Anne-Simone Rous, Robert Kluth
Graphics: Jaroslaw Kaschtalinski
Sources and literature:
Johann Gottfried Schadow's Luther Monument in Lutherstadt Wittenberg can be seen in the foreground (picture available at: http://reiseland.sachsen-anhaltbilder.de), while the background shows representations of Ernst Rietschel's 1868 Luther Monument from Worms.
Eidam, Hardy/Seib, Gerhard (eds.) (1996), "Er fühlt der Zeiten ungeheuren Bruch und fest umklammert er sein Bibelbuch …". Zum Lutherkult im 19. Jahrhundert. Berlin.
Kammer, Otto (2004), Reformationsdenkmäler des 19. und 20. Jahrhunderts. Eine Bestandsaufnahme. Berlin.
Wipfler, Esther Pia (2011), Martin Luther in motion pictures. History of a metamorphosis. Göttingen.
Cornelissen, Barbara (2003), Luther-Eiche, Lutherin-Baum, Luther-Rose—Die Umweltgruppe der Lünerner Kirche hält Traditionen wach. In: Naturreport. Jahrbuch der Naturförderungsgesellschaft für den Kreis Unna e.V. Vol. 7, pp. 89–93.

Trailer
The Greatest Religions of the World
Research and Graphics: Jakub Chrobok
Source:
Maoz, Zeev/Henderson, Errol A. Henderson (2013), The World Religion Dataset, 1945–2010. Logic, Estimates, and Trends. In: International Interactions. Available: www.thearda.com/Archive/Files/Descriptions/WRDNATL.asp [06/22/2016].

Translations

Martin Baumeister (Nürnberg)

Andreas Tacke, Here I Rest: A New Perspective on Fine Art during the Reformation Era (pp. 222–229); Peter von der Osten-Sacken, Martin Luther's Position on Jews and Judaism (pp. 323–330).

Lindsay Chalmers-Gerbracht (Gau-Odernheim)

Luise Schorn-Schütte, Europe and the World around 1500 (pp. 20–27); Philipp Robinson Rössner, Economics and Religion in the Late Middle Ages and Reformation Period (pp. 30–37); Johanna Reetz / Holger Rode, Early Modern Domestic and Dining Culture in Wittenberg Reflected by Prestigious Archaeological Finds (pp. 144–153); Mirko Gutjahr, The First Protestant Parsonage? Luther's House and Household According to Archaeological Evidence (pp. 165–172); Johannes Schilling, Martin Luther and Music (pp. 242–249); Ingrid Dettmann, Martin Luther as a Saint? The Portrait of the Reformer between Holy Icon and Denominational Identity in the Sixteenth Century (pp. 270–276); Stefan Laube, Homely Audacity: Memories of Luther between Hero Worship and Enchanted Idyll (pp. 440–449).

Mary Dellenbaugh (Berlin)

Franziska Kuschel, Marriage: A Constant Work in Progress. An Examination of the Lutheran Understanding of Marriage and Family (pp. 183–189); Peter Blickle, The Republic of Reformers: Hulrych Zwingli, Christoph Schappeler, and Jean Calvin (pp. 199–205); Michael Hochgeschwender, Protestantism in the United States (pp. 386–393); Hartmut Lehmann, Martin Luther's Eventful Career in the New World (pp. 370–377).

Gloria Kraft-Sullivan (Burgdorf)

Benjamin Hasselhorn, Luther and Politics (pp. 315–321); Thomas Kaufmann, Luther and the Turks (pp. 340–347).

Alan McDonnell (Meißen)

Hansjörg Küster, Landscape Usage in Mansfeld Land (pp. 39–45); Andreas Stahl / Björn Schlenker, Luther in Mansfeld: Excavations and Accompanying Architectural Research on Martin Luther's Parents' Home (pp. 57–71).

Benjamin Marschke (Oldenburg)

Hartmut Lehmann, Martin Luther's Eventful Career in the New World.

Louis D. Nebelsick (Landesamt für Denkmalpflege und Archäologie Sachsen-Anhalt – Landesmuseum für Vorgeschichte)

Andreas Stahl / Björn Schlenker, Luther in Mansfeld: Excavations and Accompanying Architectural Research on Martin Luther's Parents' Home (pp. 57–71); Volker Leppin, Becoming a Reformer (pp. 86–91); Mirko Gutjahr, The First Protestant Parsonage? Luther's House and Household According to Archaeological Evidence (pp. 165–172); Stefan Laube, Homely Audacity: Memories of Luther between Hero Worship and Enchanted Idyll (pp. 440–449).

Christoph Nöthlings (Leipzig)

Michael Fessner, Mining and Metallurgy in Mansfeld Land in the Time of Martin Luther (pp. 48–55); Heinz Schilling, The Tied Majesty. The Emperor's (version of) "Here I stand, I can do no other..." (pp. 99–105); Hans-Joachim Solms, Luther and the German Language (pp. 124–130); Stefan Rhein, Friends and Colleagues: Martin Luther and His Fellow Reformers in Wittenberg (pp. 192–197); Katrin Herbst, Lutherana Tragoedia Artis? The Impact of the Reformation on Art History (pp. 210–220); Timo Trümper, Art in the Service of Politics: Cranach and the Reformation (pp. 231–239); Hermann Wellenreuther, Martin Luther, Heinrich Melchior Mühlenberg and the Lutheran Church in North America (pp. 394–402).

Bill Ray (Berlin)

Harald Meller, Why Luther Archaeology? (p. 56); Martin Eberle, The Saxon Dynasty and Ernestine Wittenberg (p. 83); Martin Treu, Disputations and the Main Writings of the Reformation (p. 98); Günter Schuchardt, Luther at Wartburg Castle (p. 122); Susanne Kimmig-Völker, Fleeing Nuns and Declining Pastoral Care: The Reformation and Monasteries (p. 164); Tomoko Emmerling, Luther Archaeology. Results and Promise (p. 173); Ingrid Dettmann, Luther's Adversaries (p. 314); Robert Kluth, Luther's Two Kingdoms Doctrine (p. 322); Church Organization in the United States (p. 403); Anne-Simone Rous, Travel Reports and Letters from Emigrants (p. 419).

Stephen Richards (Frankfurt am Main)

Natalie Krentz, The Wide-Ranging Impact of the Reformation (pp. 74–82); Stefan Michel, Why Wittenberg? How a Small Electoral City in Saxony Was Transformed into the Hub of the Reformation (pp. 134–141); Susanne Kimmig-Völkner, Luther, the Virgin Mary, and the Saints. Catholic Images as a Key to Understanding the Lutheran Concept of Salvation (pp. 261–269); Anne-Simone Rous, Crisis Management in Denominational Conflicts Resulting from the Reformation (pp. 304–313); Dorothea Wendebourg, Reformation Anniversaries and Images of Luther (pp. 432–437).

Christiane Rietz (Leipzig)

Jan Scheunemann, Luther in the German Dictatorships of the Twentieth Century (pp. 451–458).

Samuel Shearn (Oxford)

Christopher Spehr, Martin Luther and the Protestant Church Service (pp. 155–163); Anja Tietz, Martin Luther and the Changes in German Burial Practice in the Sixteenth Century (pp. 277–283).

Mirko Wittwar (Morsbach)

Volker Leppin, Becoming a Reformer (pp. 86–91); Martin Treu, Luther's Posting of His Theses: Much Ado about Nothing? (pp. 92–97).

Lenders to the Luther Exhibitions USA 2016

Germany

Stiftung Deutsches Historisches Museum, Berlin

Stadt Braunschweig, Städtisches Museum Braunschweig

Kunstsammlungen der Veste Coburg

Wartburg-Stiftung Eisenach

Evangelische Andreasgemeinde Erfurt

Forschungsbibliothek Gotha der Universität Erfurt

Foundation Schloss Friedenstein Gotha

Thüringisches Staatsarchiv Gotha

Evangelische Marktkirchengemeinde Halle (Saale), Marienbibliothek

State Office for Heritage Management and Archaeology Saxony-Anhalt – State Museum of Prehistory, Halle (Saale)

Stadtarchiv Halle (Saale)

Universitäts- und Landesbibliothek Sachsen-Anhalt, Halle (Saale)

Zentrale Kustodie der Martin-Luther-Universität Halle-Wittenberg

Universitätsarchiv der Martin-Luther-Universität Halle-Wittenberg

Evangelische Kirchengemeinde St. Andreas-Nicolai-Petri, Lutherstadt Eisleben

Lutherstadt Eisleben

Luther Memorials Foundation of Saxony-Anhalt

Wittenberg Seminary, Lutherstadt Wittenberg

Städtische Sammlungen, Lutherstadt Wittenberg

Kulturhistorisches Museum Magdeburg

Landesarchiv Sachsen-Anhalt

Mühlhausen Town Archive

Bayerisches Nationalmuseum, München

Stiftung Dome und Schlösser in Sachsen-Anhalt, Domschatz Halberstadt

Stiftung Dome und Schlösser in Sachsen-Anhalt, Kunstmuseum Moritzburg Halle (Saale)

Thüringisches Hauptstaatsarchiv Weimar

Vereinigte Domstifter zu Merseburg und Naumburg und des Kollegiatstifts Zeitz

Klassik Stiftung Weimar

Evangelische Kirchengemeinde St. Petri Wörlitz der Evangelischen Landeskirche Anhalts in Deutschland

Evangelische Kirchengemeinde Zeitz

City of Zerbst/Anhalt

Switzerland

HMB – Historisches Museum Basel

United States of America

Thrivent Financial Collection of Religious Art, Minneapolis

The Metropolitan Museum of Art, New York

Scheide Library, Princeton University Library

Luther Seminary Library, St. Paul

The Exhibition Project "Here I Stand"

Luther Exhibitions USA 2016

A cooperation of the State Museum of Prehistory, Halle (leading institution), the Luther Memorials Foundation of Saxony-Anhalt, the Deutsches Historisches Museum and the Foundation Schloss Friedenstein Gotha

With the Minneapolis Institute of Art, The Morgan Library & Museum, New York, and the Pitts Theology Library of the Candler School of Theology at Emory University, Atlanta

with the support of the Foreign Office of the Federal Republic of Germany

 Federal Foreign Office

 Landesamt für Denkmalpflege und Archäologie Sachsen-Anhalt LANDESMUSEUM FÜR VORGESCHICHTE

 STIFTUNG Luthergedenkstätten IN SACHSEN-ANHALT

 DEUTSCHES HISTORISCHES MUSEUM

 Stiftung Schloss Friedenstein Gotha

Mia Minneapolis Institute of Art

The Morgan Library & Museum

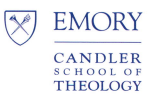 EMORY CANDLER SCHOOL OF THEOLOGY

General Director
Harald Meller
(State Office for Heritage Management and Archaeology Saxony-Anhalt – State Museum of Prehistory)

Project Steering Committee
Martin Eberle
(Foundation Schloss Friedenstein Gotha), Ulrike Kretzschmar
(Stiftung Deutsches Historisches Museum), Stefan Rhein
(Luther Memorials Foundation of Saxony-Anhalt)

Project Management
Tomoko Elisabeth Emmerling
(State Office for Heritage Management and Archaeology Saxony-Anhalt – State Museum of Prehistory)

Project Team
Ingrid Dettmann, Johanna Furgber, Konstanze Geppert, Katrin Herbst, Susanne Kimmig-Völkner, Robert Kluth, Ralf Kluttig-Altmann, Franziska Kuschel, Lea McLaughlin, Louis D. Nebelsick, Robert Noack, Anne-Simone Rous, Julius Roch, Stefanie Wachsmann
(State Office for Heritage Management and Archaeology Saxony-Anhalt – State Museum of Prehistory)

Academic Advisory Board
Mirko Gutjahr
(Luther Memorials Foundation of Saxony-Anhalt)
Louis D. Nebelsick
(State Office for Heritage Management and Archaeology Saxony-Anhalt – State Museum of Prehistory),
Martin Treu
(Lutherstadt Wittenberg),
Timo Trümper
(Foundation Schloss Friedenstein Gotha)

Public Relations
Tomoko Elisabeth Emmerling, Julia Kruse, Norma Literski-Henkel, Alfred Reichenberger
(State Office for Heritage Management and Archaeology Saxony-Anhalt – State Museum of Prehistory),
Marco Karthe, Carola Schüren
(Foundation Schloss Friedenstein Gotha),
Florian Trott
(Luther Memorials Foundation of Saxony-Anhalt),
Boris Nitzsche, Barbara Wolf
(Stiftung Deutsches Historisches Museum)

Design of Promotional Media
Klaus Pockrandt (Halle [Saale]), Brigitte Parsche
(State Office for Heritage Management and Archaeology Saxony-Anhalt – State Museum of Prehistory)

Exhibitions

"Martin Luther: Art and the Reformation",
Minneapolis Institute of Art,
October 30, 2016 through January 15, 2017

**"Word and Image:
Martin Luther's Reformation",**
The Morgan Library & Museum,
New York,
October 7, 2016 through January 22, 2017

**"Law and Grace: Martin Luther,
Lucas Cranach, and the Promise of Salvation",**
Pitts Theology Library of the Candler School
of Theology at Emory University, Atlanta,
October 11, 2016 through January 16, 2017

Exhibition Team Minneapolis
Kaywin Feldman, Duncan and
Nivin MacMillan Director and President

Matthew Welch,
Deputy Director and Chief Curator

Thomas E. Rassieur, John E. Andrus III
Curator of Prints and Drawings and Curator
of the exhibition *Martin Luther: Art and
the Reformation*

Jennifer Starbright,
Associate Registrar for Exhibitions

Rayna Fox, Executive Assistant to
the Deputy Director and Chief Curator

Jennifer Komar Olivarez,
Head of Exhibition Planning and Strategy,
Interim Department Head, Decorative Arts,
Textiles, and Sculpture

Michael Lapthorn, Exhibition Designer

Karleen Gardner, Director of Learning
Innovation

Kristin Prestegaard, Chief Engagement Officer

Alex Bortolot, Content Strategist

Aubrey Mozer, Corporate Relations Manager

Eric Bruce, Head of Visitor Experience

Juline Chevalier, Head of Interpretation and
Participatory Experiences

Michael Dust, Head of Interactive Media
and Senior Producer

Mary Mortensen, Senior Advancement
Executive

Eric Helmin, Graphic Designer/Digital Brand
Integration

Tammy Pleshek, Press & Public Relations
Specialist

Exhibition Team New York
Colin B. Bailey, Director;
the project was initiated in 2013 under
director William Griswold and continued
under Peggy Fogelman, Acting Director

John Bidwell, Astor Curator of Printed Books
and Bindings and Curatorial Chair

John T. McQuillen, Assistant Curator of Printed
Books and Bindings and curator of *Word and
Image: Martin Luther's Reformation*

John D. Alexander, Senior Manager of
Exhibition and Collection Administration,
and his colleagues, including Alex Confer,
Paula Pineda, Lindsey Stavros, and
Sophie Worley

Frank Trujillo, Associate Book Conservator,
Lindsay Tyne, Assistant Paper Conservator,
and James Donchez, Art Preparator

Marilyn Palmeri, Imaging and Rights Manager,
with Eva Soos and Graham Haber, Photographer

Patricia Emerson, Senior Editor

John Marciari, Charles W. Engelhard
Curator of Drawings and Prints, and
Jennifer Tonkovich, Eugene and Claire Thaw
Curator of Drawings and Prints

Patrick Milliman, Director of Communications
and Marketing, with Michelle Perlin und
Moriah Shtull

Linden Chubin, Director of Education, and
his colleagues, including
Anthony Del Aversano, Mary Hogan Camp,
Alicia Ryan, Jacqueline Smith, and Paula
Zadigian

Susan Eddy, former Director of Institutional
Advancement, and Anita Masi, Associate
Director of Development

Tom Shannon, Director of Facilities, and Jack
Quigley, Chief of Security

The exhibition was designed by Stephen
Saitas and lighting by Anita Jorgensen

Miko McGinty and her team,
including Paula Welling and Anjali Pala,
designed the exhibition graphics

Concept
Louis D. Nebelsick in collaboration with
Ingrid Dettmann, Susanne Kimmig-Völkner,
Franziska Kuschel
(State Office for Heritage Management and
Archaeology Saxony-Anhalt –
State Museum of Prehistory)

Adviser
Eike Jordan

Exhibition Team Atlanta
Richard Adams,
Head of Public Services

Rebekah Bedard, Reference Librarian
and Outreach Coordinator

Patrick Graham, Director

Armin Siedlecki, Head of Cataloging

Organization and Conceptualization
Ingrid Dettmann, Tomoko Emmerling,
Susanne Kimmig-Völkner, Robert Kluth,
Franziska Kuschel, Louis D. Nebelsick
(State Office for Heritage Management
and Archaeology Saxony-Anhalt –
State Museum of Prehistory)

Project Assistance
Susanne Kimmig-Völkner, Franziska Kuschel
(State Office for Heritage Management
and Archaeology Saxony-Anhalt –
State Museum of Prehistory)

Consultants
Kerstin Bullerjahn, Andreas Hille, Ralf Kluttig-
Altmann, Jan Scheunemann, Björn Schlenker,
(State Office for Heritage Management
and Archaeology Saxony-Anhalt –
State Museum of Prehistory);
Mirko Gutjahr (Luther Memorials Foundation
of Saxony-Anhalt);
Ute Däberitz, Bernd Schäfer, Timo Trümper,
Jekaterina Vogel, Uta Wallenstein
(Foundation Schloss Friedenstein Gotha);
Rosmarie Beier-de Haan, Sabine Beneke,
Leonore Koschnick, Sven Lüken, Matthias
Miller, Brigitte Reineke
(Stiftung Deutsches Historisches Museum);
Christian Philipsen (Stiftung Dome und
Schlösser in Sachsen-Anhalt);
Johanna Reetz, Holger Rode (Osterfeld)

Provision and Management of Exhibits
Andrea Lange, Roman Mischker, Irina Widany
(State Office for Heritage Management
and Archaeology Saxony-Anhalt –
State Museum of Prehistory);
Christine Doleschal, Petra Gröschl, Karin
Lubitzsch, Jutta Strehle (Luther Memorials
Foundation of Saxony-Anhalt);
Thomas Huck, Jürgen Weis
(Foundation Schloss Friedenstein Gotha)

**Conservation and Restoration,
Supervision and Advice**
Karsten Böhm, Heiko Breuer, Karoline Danz,
Friederike Hertel, Vera Keil, Katrin Steller,
Christian-Heinrich Wunderlich
(State Office for Heritage Management
and Archaeology Saxony-Anhalt –
State Museum of Prehistory);
Karin Lubitzsch, Andreas Schwabe
(Luther Memorials Foundation of
Saxony-Anhalt);
Michaela Brand, Kay Draber, Sophie Hoffmann,
Martina Homolka, Ulrike Hügle, Matthias Lang,
Elke Kiffe, Barbara Korbel, Antje Liebers,
Jutta Peschke
(Stiftung Deutsches Historisches Museum);
Helmut Biebler, Marie-Luise Gothe, Brigitte
Pohl, Gunter Rothe
(Foundation Schloss Friedenstein Gotha);
Sebastian Anastasow (Hundisburg);
Katrin Brinz (Halle [Saale]);
Eva Düllo (Berlin);
Thomas Groll (Magdeburg);
Angela Günther (Dessau-Roßlau);
Kerstin Klein (Halle [Saale]);
Andrea Knüpfer (Halle [Saale]);
Albrecht Körber (Dresden);
Andreas Mieth (Berlin);
Sybille Reschke (Leipzig);
Johannes Schaefer (Altenburg);
Peter Schöne (Halle [Saale]);
Ulrich Sieblist (Questenberg);
Christine Supianek-Chassay (Erfurt);
Hartmut von Wieckowski (Petersberg);
Beatrix Kästner (Meusebach)

Loan and Transport Management
Urte Dally, Susanne Kimmig-Völkner,
Franziska Kuschel
(State Office for Heritage Management
and Archaeology Saxony-Anhalt –
State Museum of Prehistory)

Transportation
hasenkamp Internationale Transporte GmbH,
Masterpiece International

The exhibition team would like to thank the
many colleagues—also those not mentioned
here—who have helped to make the exhibitions
in New York, Minneapolis, and Atlanta come
about.

Accompanying Publications

Editors
Harald Meller
(State Office for Heritage Management
and Archaeology Saxony-Anhalt –
State Museum of Prehistory),
Colin B. Bailey
(The Morgan Library & Museum),
Martin Eberle
(Foundation Schloss Friedenstein Gotha),
Kaywin Feldman
(Minneapolis Institute of Art),
Ulrike Kretzschmar
(Stiftung Deutsches Historisches Museum),
Stefan Rhein
(Luther Memorials Foundation of
Saxony-Anhalt)

Conceptualization
Ingrid Dettmann, Tomoko Emmerling,
Katrin Herbst, Susanne Kimmig-Völkner,
Robert Kluth, Franziska Kuschel, Louis D.
Nebelsick, Robert Noack, Anne-Simone Rous
(State Office for Heritage Management
and Archaeology Saxony-Anhalt –
State Museum of Prehistory)

Image Copyright Search, Image Editing
Robert Noack
(State Office for Heritage Management
and Archaeology Saxony-Anhalt –
State Museum of Prehistory)

Project Supervision at Sandstein Verlag
Christine Jäger-Ulbricht, Sina Volk,
Norbert du Vinage (Sandstein Verlag)

Design Concept
Norbert du Vinage (Sandstein Verlag)

Production
Sandstein Verlag

Printing and Finishing
Westermann Druck Zwickau GmbH

Accompanying Volume
"Martin Luther and the Reformation"

Coordination
Anne-Simone Rous, Katrin Herbst,
Susanne Kimmig-Völkner, Robert Kluth,
Louis D. Nebelsick
(State Office for Heritage Management
and Archaeology Saxony-Anhalt –
State Museum of Prehistory)

Volume Editor
Anne-Simone Rous
(State Office for Heritage Management
and Archaeology Saxony-Anhalt –
State Museum of Prehistory)

Expert Editing
Martin Treu (Lutherstadt Wittenberg),
Eva Bambach-Horst (Bensheim),
Susanne Baudisch (Dresden),
Kathleen Dittrich (Hinterhermsdorf),
Mareike Greb (Leipzig),
Barbara Fitton Hauß (Lörrach),
Carola Hoécker (Heidelberg),
James Matarazzo (Oxford, Großbritannien),
Katrin Ott (Jena),
Marion Page (Cirencester, Großbritannien),
Emanuel Priebst (Dresden),
Georg D. Schaaf (Münster),
Ulrich Schmiedel (Munich),
Karen Schmitt (Stuttgart),
Lutz Stirl (Berlin),
Timo Trümper (Foundation
Schloss Friedenstein Gotha),
Susann Wendt (Leipzig),
Kerstin Bullerjahn, Ingrid Dettmann,
Katrin Herbst, Susanne Kimmig-Völkner,
Robert Kluth, Ralf Kluttig-Altmann,
Franziska Kuschel, Anne-Simone Rous,
Jan Scheunemann
(State Office for Heritage Management
and Archaeology Saxony-Anhalt –
State Museum of Prehistory)

Proofreading

German
Anne-Simone Rous, Tomoko Emmerling,
Ingrid Dettmann, Katrin Herbst, Susanne
Kimmig-Völkner (State Office for Heritage
Management and Archaeology Saxony-Anhalt
– State Museum of Prehistory)

English
Jim Bindas and his colleagues Laura Silver,
Stephanie Martin, Heidi Mann (Books &
Projects, Minneapolis);
Louis D. Nebelsick, Tomoko Emmerling, Ingrid
Dettmann, Susanne Kimmig-Völkner, Lea
McLaughlin, Robert Noack, Anne-Simone Rous
(State Office for Heritage Management and
Archaeology Saxony-Anhalt – State Museum
of Prehistory)

Infographics: Research and Concept
Ingrid Dettmann, Susanne Kimmig-Völkner,
Robert Kluth, Franziska Kuschel, Robert Noack,
Anne-Simone Rous (State Office for Heritage
Management and Archaeology Saxony-Anhalt
– State Museum of Prehistory);
Jakub Chrobok, Barbara Mayer, Jan Schwochow
(Golden Section Graphics)

Infographics: Realization
Golden Section Graphics:
Jan Schwochow (managing director),
Jakub Chrobok, Barbara Mayer,
Anton Delchmann, Verena Muckel,
Jaroslaw Kaschtalinski, Katharina Schwochow,
Nick Oelschlägel, Daniela Scharffenberg,
Fabian Dinklage, Christophorus Halsch,
Annemarie Kurz (project management),
Anni Peller (proofreading)

Design
Simone Antonia Deutsch (Sandstein Verlag)

Image Processing
Jana Neumann (Sandstein Verlag)

Type
Gudrun Diesel (Sandstein Verlag)

Catalogue
"Martin Luther:
Treasures of the Reformation"

Volume Editors

German

Ralf Kluttig-Altmann (State Office for Heritage
Management and Archaeology Saxony-Anhalt
– State Museum of Prehistory)

English

Katrin Herbst (State Office for Heritage
Management and Archaeology Saxony-Anhalt
– State Museum of Prehistory)

Proofreading

German

Ralf Kluttig-Altmann, Ingrid Dettmann,
Tomoko Emmerling, Johanna Furgber,
Dirk Höhne, Susanne Kimmig-Völkner,
Lea McLaughlin, Anne-Simone Rous
(State Office for Heritage Management and
Archaeology Saxony-Anhalt – State Museum
of Prehistory); Saskia Gresse (Nuremberg)

English

Katrin Herbst (State Office for Heritage
Management and Archaeology Saxony-Anhalt
– State Museum of Prehistory),
John McQuillen (The Morgan Library & Museum),
Schneiders-Sprach-Service (Berlin)

Translations

English – German

Martin Baumeister (Nuremberg);
Michael Ebmeyer (Berlin);
Lea McLaughlin, Louis D. Nebelsick
(State Office for Heritage Management
and Archaeology Saxony-Anhalt –
State Museum of Prehistory);
Christiane Rietz (Leipzig);
Sigrid Weber-Krafft (Siegen)

German – English

Martin Baumeister (Nuremberg),
Krister Johnson (Magdeburg),
Schneiders-Sprach-Service (Berlin),
Samuel Shearn (Oxford, Großbritannien),
George Wolter (Halle [Saale])

Design
Norbert du Vinage (Sandstein Verlag)

Image Processing
Jana Neumann (Sandstein Verlag)

Type
Katharina Stark, Christian Werner,
(Sandstein Verlag); Kathrin Jäger

Maps
Birte Janzen (State Office for Heritage
Management and Archaeology Saxony-Anhalt
– State Museum of Prehistory)

Source Map:
Golden Section Graphics GmbH, Berlin

Cover Images

Catalogue
Lucas Cranach the Elder, workshop
"Martin Luther", 1528
Luther Memorials Foundation
of Saxony-Anhalt, G 16

Accompanying Volume
Lucas Cranach the Elder
"Martin Luther as an Augustinian Monk", 1520
Luther Memorials Foundation
of Saxony-Anhalt, fl IIIa 208

Frontispiece Images

Catalogue and Accompanying Volume
Lucas Cranach the Elder
"Law and Grace", 1529 (detail)
Foundation Schloss Friedenstein Gotha, SG 676

Foreword Images

© Thomas Köhler/photothek

Bibliographical
Information
Catalogue and accompanying volume

The Deutsche Nationalbibliothek holds a record
of this publication in the Deutsche National-
bibliografie; detailed bibliographical data can
be found under: http://dnb.ddb.de

This work, including its parts, is protected by
copyright. Any use beyond the limits of copyright law without the consent of the publisher
is prohibited and punishable. This applies,
in particular, to reproduction, translation,
microfilming and storage and processing in
electronic systems.

Catalogue
ISBN 978-3-95498-221-9 (German)
ISBN 978-3-95498-224-0 (English)

Accompanying volume
ISBN 978-3-95498-222-6 (German)
ISBN 978-3-95498-223-3 (English)

Both volumes in slipcase
ISBN 978-3-95498-231-8 (German)
ISBN 978-3-95498-232-5 (English)

© 2016
Landesamt für Denkmalpflege
und Archäologie Sachsen-Anhalt,
Sandstein Verlag

Made in Germany

Website and online/
Poster exhibition

#HereIstand. Martin Luther,
the Reformation and its Results

General Director
Harald Meller (State Office for Heritage
Management and Archaeology Saxony-Anhalt
– State Museum of Prehistory)

Project Steering Committee
Martin Eberle (Foundation Schloss Friedenstein
Gotha), Ulrike Kretzschmar (Stiftung Deutsches
Historisches Museum), Stefan Rhein (Luther
Memorials Foundation of Saxony-Anhalt)

Project Management
Tomoko Emmerling (State Office for Heritage
Management and Archaeology Saxony-Anhalt
– State Museum of Prehistory)

Academic Advisory Board
Mirko Gutjahr (Luther Memorials Foundation
of Saxony-Anhalt), Martin Treu (Lutherstadt
Wittenberg), Timo Trümper (Foundation Schloss
Friedenstein Gotha)

Coordination
Robert Kluth (State Office for Heritage
Management and Archaeology Saxony-Anhalt
– State Museum of Prehistory)

Concept
Robert Kluth, Katrin Herbst (State Office
for Heritage Management and Archaeology
Saxony-Anhalt – State Museum of Prehistory)

Curators
Robert Kluth, Anne-Simone Rous (State Office
for Heritage Management and Archaeology
Saxony-Anhalt – State Museum of Prehistory)

In Collaboration with
Ingrid Dettmann, Katrin Herbst, Susanne
Kimmig-Völkner, Franziska Kuschel, Robert
Noack (State Office for Heritage Management
and Archaeology Saxony-Anhalt – State
Museum of Prehistory)

and
Mareile Alferi, Johanna Furgber, Annemarie
Knöfel, Mike Leske, Lea McLaughlin, Brigitte
Parsche, Julius Roch, Stefanie Wachsmann
(State Office for Heritage Management and
Archaeology Saxony-Anhalt – State Museum
of Prehistory), Niels Reidel (Foundation Schloss
Friedenstein Gotha)

Concept and Realization
Website and Infographics
Golden Section Graphics: Jan Schwochow
(managing director), Jakub Chrobok, Barbara
Mayer, Anton Delchmann, Verena Muckel,
Jaroslaw Kaschtalinski, Katharina Schwochow,
Nick Oelschlägel, Daniela Scharffenberg,
Fabian Dinklage, Christophorus Halsch,
Annemarie Kurz (project management),
Anni Peller (proofreading)

3D Scans
Lukas Fischer in collaboration with:
Robert Noack (State Office for Heritage
Management and Archaeology Saxony-Anhalt
– State Museum of Prehistory)

Poster Printing
Druck+Verlag Ernst Vögel GmbH, Stamsried

Design of Promotional Media
Alexander Schmidt (Halle [Saale]),
Birte Janzen (State Office for Heritage
Management and Archaeology Saxony-Anhalt
– State Museum of Prehistory)

Translations
Christoph Nöthlings (Leipzig),
Gloria Kraft-Sullivan (Burgdorf)

Thanks to

Markus Lahr, Vinn:Lab, Forschungsgruppe
Innovations- und Regionalforschung,
Technische Hochschule Wildau

Paul Daniels, Head of Arts and Archives,
Luther Seminary, St. Paul

Google Docs

Stefan Hagemann

Henning Kiene, EKD

Martin Klimke

Paul Klimpel

Monika Lücke und Dietrich Lücke

Konrad Kühne (Archiv für Christlich-
Demokratische Politik, Konrad Adenauer
Stiftung)

Ulrich Mählert (Bundesstiftung zur
Aufarbeitung der SED Diktatur)

Christine Mundhenk (Melanchthon-
Forschungsstelle der Heidelberger Akademie
der Wissenschaften)

Stefan Rohde-Enslin (museum-digital)

Christian Staffa, Evangelische Akademie
zu Berlin

Michael Weyer-Menkhoff, Archiv der Berliner
Stadtmission

Agnes Fuchsloch, Andrea Fußstetter, Ann-Kathrin
Heinzelmann, Angelika Kaminska, Jan-Dirk
Kluge, Ilka Linz, Wolfgang Röhrig, Nicola
Schnell, Werner Schulte, Magnus Wagner
(Stiftung Deutsches Historisches Museum)

Birte Janzen, Julia Kruse, Katrin Legler, Janine
Näthe, Brigitte Parsche, Alfred Reichenberger,
Anne Reinholdt, Monika Schlenker, Manuela
Schwarz, Andreas Stahl, Bettina Stoll-Tucker,
Anna Swieder (State Office for Heritage
Management and Archaeology Saxony-Anhalt
– State Museum of Prehistory)

BR 327 .M37 2016b

Martin Luther and the
Reformation

Catholics worldwide

not specified

0   100 %
Catholics in relation to other denominations

Religious demographics
Figures in million, as of 2010

Christianity	Islam	Hinduism	Buddhism	Judaism	Other	Non-religious
					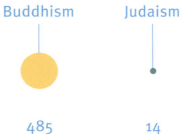	
2,112	1,555	1,017	485	14	949	788